THE

WAR OF THE REBELLION:

A COMPILATION OF THE

OFFICIAL RECORDS

OF THE

UNION AND CONFEDERATE ARMIES.

PREPARED, UNDER THE DIRECTION OF THE SECRETARY OF WAR, BY

The late Lieut. Col. ROBERT N. SCOTT, Third U. S. Artillery.

PUBLISHED UNDER THE SUPERVISION OF

Lieut. Col. HENRY M. LAZELLE, Twenty-third U. S. Infantry

PURSUANT TO ACTS OF CONGRESS.

SERIES I—VOLUME XX—IN TWO PARTS.

PART I—REPORTS.

WASHINGTON:
GOVERNMENT PRINTING OFFICE.
1887.

PREFACE.

By an act approved June 23, 1874, Congress made an appropriation "to enable the Secretary of War to begin the publication of the Official Records of the War of the Rebellion, both of the Union and Confederate Armies," and directed him "to have copied for the Public Printer all reports, letters, telegrams, and general orders not heretofore copied or printed, and properly arranged in chronological order."

Appropriations for continuing such preparation have been made from time to time, and the act approved June 16, 1880, has provided "for the printing and binding, under direction of the Secretary of War, of 10,000 copies of a compilation of the Official Records (Union and Confederate) of the War of the Rebellion, so far as the same may be ready for publication, during the fiscal year"; and that "of said number, 7,000 copies shall be for the use of the House of Representatives, 2,000 copies for the use of the Senate, and 1,000 copies for the use of the Executive Departments."*

This compilation will be the first general publication of the military records of the war, and will embrace all official documents that can be obtained by the compiler, and that appear to be of any historical value.

---

*Volume I to V distributed under act approved June 16, 1880. The act approved August 7, 1882, provides that—

"The volumes of the official records of the war of the rebellion shall be distributed as follows: One thousand copies to the executive departments, as now provided by law. One thousand copies for distribution by the Secretary of War among officers of the Army and contributors to the work. Eight thousand three hundred copies shall be sent by the Secretary of War to such libraries, organizations, and individuals as may be designated by the Senators, Representatives, and Delegates of the Forty-seventh Congress. Each Senator shall designate not exceeding twenty-six, and each Representative and Delegate not exceeding twenty-one of such addresses, and the volumes shall be sent thereto from time to time as they are published, until the publication is completed. Senators, Representatives, and Delegates shall inform the Secretary of War in each case how many volumes of those heretofore published they have forwarded to such addresses. The remaining copies of the eleven thousand to be published, and all sets that may not be ordered to be distributed as provided herein, shall be sold by the Secretary of War for cost of publication with ten per cent. added thereto, and the proceeds of such sale shall be covered into the Treasury. If two or more sets of said volumes are ordered to the same address the Secretary of War shall inform the Senators, Representatives or Delegates, who have designated the same, who thereupon may designate other libraries, organizations, or individuals. The Secretary of War shall report to the first session of the Forty-eighth Congress what volumes of the series heretofore published have not been furnished to such libraries, organizations, and individuals. He shall also inform distributees at whose instance the volumes are sent."

The publication will present the records in the following order of arrangement:

The **1st Series** will embrace the formal reports, both Union and Confederate, of the first seizures of United States property in the Southern States, and of all military operations in the field, with the correspondence, orders, and returns relating specially thereto, and, as proposed, is to be accompanied by an Atlas.

In this series the reports will be arranged according to the campaigns and several theaters of operations (in the chronological order of the events), and the Union reports of any event will, as a rule, be immediately followed by the Confederate accounts. The correspondence, &c., not embraced in the "reports" proper will follow (first Union and next Confederate) in chronological order.

The **2d Series** will contain the correspondence, orders, reports, and returns, Union and Confederate, relating to prisoners of war, and (so far as the military authorities were concerned) to State or political prisoners.

The **3d Series** will contain the correspondence, orders, reports, and returns of the Union authorities (embracing their correspondence with the Confederate officials) not relating specially to the subjects of the *first* and *second* series. It will set forth the annual and special reports of the Secretary of War, of the General-in-Chief, and of the chiefs of the several staff corps and departments; the calls for troops, and the correspondence between the National and the several State authorities.

The **4th Series** will exhibit the correspondence, orders, reports, and returns of the Confederate authorities, similar to that indicated for the Union officials, as of the *third* series, but excluding the correspondence between the Union and confederate authorities given in that series.

ROBERT N. SCOTT,
Major, Third Art., and Bvt. Lieut. Col.

WAR DEPARTMENT, *August* 23, 1880.

Approved:

ALEX. RAMSEY,
Secretary of War.

CONTENTS.

CHAPTER XXXII.

(v)

CONTENTS OF PRECEDING VOLUMES.

VOLUME I.

VOLUME II.

VOLUME III.

VOLUME IV.

VOLUME V.

VOLUME VI.

VOLUME VII.

VOLUME VIII.

CHAPTER XVIII.

VOLUME IX.

VOLUME X—IN TWO PARTS.

CHAPTER XXII.

Operations in Kentucky, Tennessee, North Mississippi, North Alabama, and Southwest Virginia. March 4–June 10, 1862.

VOLUME XI—IN THREE PARTS.

CHAPTER XXIII.

The Peninsular Campaign, Virginia. March 17–September 2, 1862.

VOLUME XII—IN THREE PARTS.

CHAPTER XXIV.

Operations in Northern Virginia, West Virginia, and Maryland. March 17–September 2, 1862.

VOLUME XIII.

CHAPTER XXV.

VOLUME XIV.

CHAPTER XXVI.

VOLUME XV.

CHAPTER XXVII.

CHAPTER XXXII.

OPERATIONS IN KENTUCKY, MIDDLE AND EAST TENNESSEE, NORTH ALABAMA, AND SOUTHWEST VIRGINIA.

November 1, 1862–January 20, 1863.

SUMMARY OF THE PRINCIPAL EVENTS.*

Nov.   1, 1862.—The command of General Braxton Bragg, C. S. Army, extended over troops in Department of East Tennessee.

Skirmish in Henderson County, Ky.

3, 1862.—General Bragg resumes command of Department No. 2.†

5, 1862.—Action at Nashville, Tenn.

Affair near Piketon, Ky.

6, 1862.—Skirmish at Garrettsburg, Ky.

7, 1862.—General Bragg resumes immediate command of the Army of the Mississippi, which is divided into two army corps, the First under Lieut. Gen. Leonidas Polk, and the Second under Lieut. Gen. William J. Hardee.

Skirmish at Gallatin, Tenn.

Skirmish at Tyree Springs, Tenn.

Skirmish at White Range, Tenn.

8, 1862.—Skirmish at Burkesville, Ky.

Skirmish on the Cumberland River, near Gallatin, Tenn.

9, 1862.—Skirmish at Silver Springs, Tenn.

Skirmish at Lebanon, Tenn.

12, 1862.—Capture of courier station on Stone's River, Tenn.

13, 1862.—Lieutenant-General Hardee assumes command of the Second Corps, Army of the Mississippi.

Skirmish near Nashville, Tenn.

15–20, 1862.—Reconnaissance from Edgefield Junction toward Clarksville, Tenn.

17–29, 1862.—Expedition from Sparta, Tenn., into Kentucky.

18, 1862.—Skirmish at Rural Hill, Tenn.

19, 1862.—Skirmish at Tunnel Hill, Ky.

Reconnaissance toward La Vergne, Tenn.

Skirmish near Tompkinsville, Ky.

20, 1862.—The Confederate Army of Tennessee constituted, to consist of E. Kirby Smith's, Polk's, and Hardee's army corps.

24, 1862.—General Joseph E. Johnston, C. S. Army, assigned to a command embracing Western North Carolina, Tennessee, Northern Georgia, Alabama, Mississippi, and Eastern Louisiana.

Skirmish near Tompkinsville, Ky.

25, 1862.—Skirmish at Calhoun, Ky.

---

* Of some of the minor conflicts noted in this "Summary," no circumstantial reports are on file.

† On October 24, 1862, the command had been temporarily transferred to Lieutenant-General Polk.

Nov. 25, 1862.—Skirmish at Clarksville, Tenn.

26, 1862.—Lieutenant-General Polk assumes command of "Polk's Corps," Army of Tennessee.

26–27, 1862.—Reconnaissance to La Vergne, Tenn., and skirmish.

26–30, 1862.—Operations about Springfield, Tenn.

26–Dec. 1, 1862.—Expedition from Edgefield to Harpeth Shoals, Clarksville, &c., Tenn.

27, 1862.—Skirmish at Mill Creek, Tenn.

28, 1862.—Skirmishes on the Carthage road, near Hartsville and Rome, Tenn.

29–Dec. 1, 1862.—Reconnaissance from Stewart's Ferry, Stone's River, to Baird's Mills, Tenn., and skirmishes *en route.*

Dec. 1, 1862.—Skirmish near Nolensville, Tenn.

3, 1862.—Attack on Union forage train on the Hardin pike, near Nashville, Tenn.

4, 1862.—General Joseph E. Johnston, C. S. Army, assumes the command to which he was assigned November 24.

Skirmish in Floyd County, Ky.

Skirmish on the Franklin pike, near Holly Tree Gap, Tenn.

Capture of outpost near Stewart's Ferry (or Ford), Stone's River, Tenn.

4– 5, 1862.—Capture of transports, and skirmishes near Prestonburg, Ky.

6, 1862.—Skirmish near Kimbrough's Mill, Mill Creek, Tenn.

7, 1862.—Action at Hartsville, Tenn.

9, 1862.—Skirmish at Dobbins' Ferry, near La Vergne, Tenn.

Reconnaissance toward Franklin, and skirmish near Brentwood, Tenn.

11, 1862.—Skirmish at La Vergne, Tenn.

Skirmish near Nashville, Tenn.

11–12, 1862.—Reconnaissance from Nashville to Franklin, Tenn., and skirmishes on the Wilson Creek pike and at Franklin.

12, 1862.—Skirmishes at Cherokee Station and Little Bear Creek, Ala.*

14, 1862.—Attack on forage train and skirmish on the Franklin pike, near Nashville, Tenn.

15–16, 1862.—Violation of flag of truce.

20, 1862–Jan. 5, 1863.—Carter's raid into East Tennessee and Southwest Virginia.

21, 1862.—Skirmish on the Wilson Creek pike, Tenn.

22, 1862–Jan. 2, 1863.—Morgan's second Kentucky raid.

23, 1862.—Lieut. Gen. E. Kirby Smith, C. S. Army, resumes command of the Department of East Tennessee.

Skirmish near Nashville, Tenn.

24, 1862.—Skirmish near Nashville, Tenn.

24, 1862–Jan. 1, 1863.—Expedition into East Tennessee, and skirmish at Perkins' Mill, on Elk Fork, December 28.

25, 1862.—Skirmish on the Wilson Creek pike, between Brentwood and Petersburg, Tenn.

Skirmish at Prim's blacksmith shop, Edmondson pike, Tenn.

26, 1862.—Capture of guerrilla camp in Powell County, Ky.

Mutiny of the Anderson Cavalry.†

26, 1862–Jan. 5, 1863.—The Stone's River, or Murfreesborough, Tenn., Campaign.

---

* See reconnaissance from Corinth, Miss., toward Tuscumbia, Ala., &c., December 9–14, Series I, Vol. XVII, Part I, p. 541.

† See report of Maj. Nelson H. Davis, February 4, 1863, in "Correspondence, etc.," Part II, of this volume.

Jan. 8–14, 1863.—Wheeler's raid, including affairs at Mill Creek, Harpeth Shoals, and Ashland, Tenn.

9, 1863.—The Army of the Cumberland divided into three army corps, the Fourteenth, Twentieth, and Twenty-first, under Maj. Gens. George H. Thomas, Alexander McD. McCook, and Thomas L. Crittenden.

10, 1863.—Skirmish at Clifton, Tenn.

13–15, 1863.—Reconnaissance from Murfreesborough to Nolensville and Versailles, Tenn.

13–19, 1863.—Reconnaissance from Nashville to Harpeth River and Cumberland River Shoals, Tenn.

17, 1863.—Brig. Gen. D. S. Donelson, C. S. Army, assigned to command of the Department of East Tennessee, vice Brigadier-General Heth, ordered to Virginia.

19, 1863.—Skirmish near Woodbury, Tenn.

NOVEMBER 5, 1862.—Action at Nashville, Tenn.

REPORTS.

No. 1.—Brig. Gen. James S. Negley, U. S. Army.
No. 2.—Col. Robert F. Smith, Sixteenth Illinois Infantry.
No. 3.—General Braxton Bragg, C. S. Army, commanding Army of Tennessee.
No. 4.—Brig. Gen. Nathan B. Forrest, C. S. Army, commanding cavalry.

No. 1.

Report of Brig. Gen. James S. Negley, U. S. Army.

HEADQUARTERS UNITED STATES FORCES,
Nashville, Tenn., November 5, 1862.

SIR: I have the honor to inclose you an official report of a small affair with the enemy to-day. I do not apprehend an attack upon Nashville in force before the arrival of re-enforcements. The enemy continue to concentrate troops at Murfreesborough and toward Nashville. Their force positively exceeds 25,000, of which at least 5,000 are cavalry. They have about forty pieces of artillery, and it is now certain that a portion of Bragg's army is at Murfreesborough; but whether they will maintain a position at Murfreesborough or this side is not plainly indicated by their present operations. Their cavalry approach our lines daily, and are engaged in driving off stock and negroes. My command is in fine spirits and the transportation in excellent condition.

With assurances of high personal esteem, I am, yours, very truly,

JAS. S. NEGLEY,
Brigadier-General, Commanding.

Lieutenant-Colonel DUCAT,
Chief of Staff.

[Inclosure.]

HEADQUARTERS UNITED STATES FORCES,
Nashville, Tenn., November 5, 1862.

SIR: This morning at 2 o'clock Forrest's (rebel) cavalry, numbering about 3,000, with four pieces of artillery, opened a sharp fire on our picket line, on the south, between the Franklin and Lebanon pikes. The picket line on the Murfreesborough road gradually withdrew, for the purpose of bringing the enemy under the guns of Fort Negley, two of which were opened upon the enemy and drove him speedily beyond the range.

Almost simultaneously with the attack on the south, John Morgan's forces (2,500 strong, with one piece of artillery) made a dash on Colonel Smith's command, on the north side of the river, with the evident intention of destroying the railroad and pontoon bridges. After a sharp contest, in which several companies of Illinois troops behaved with great gallantry, Morgan was repulsed, leaving a stand of regimental colors in our hands, 5 killed, and 19 wounded. He then burned an old railroad building in Edgefield and retreated to Gallatin.

Finding the enemy on the south taking a position beyond our picket lines, Colonel Roberts, with two regiments of infantry and one section of artillery, was ordered to advance on the Murfreesborough road, while I took the Sixty-ninth Ohio Infantry, with a portion of the Seventy-eighth Pennsylvania, Fourteenth Michigan, and Colonels Stokes' and Wynkoop's cavalry, with two sections of artillery, numbering, in all, about 1,400 men, and pursued that portion of the enemy on the Franklin pike. They were speedily driven from every position by our artillery until we reached a distance of 7 miles from the city. Colonel Stokes' cavalry was here directed to charge upon the enemy's rear and then retreat, with a view of bringing him to a stand; but the main body of the enemy, with their artillery, had suddenly turned into a lane to the left, while our cavalry, in the excitement of the chase, pursued a small portion of the enemy within 5 miles of Franklin, capturing some prisoners, killing several, and taking a drove of cattle. Previous to the return of Stokes' cavalry, the enemy appeared in considerable force upon our left, front, and rear, with the evident intention of cutting off the cavalry and our retreat. The infantry and artillery were immediately moved forward a mile, to the support of our cavalry, which was ordered to rejoin the column immediately.

Upon receiving intelligence from my vedettes that the enemy was in force a mile to our rear, masking a battery close to the road, the head of the column was immediately placed to the rear and hastened forward to the position occupied by the enemy, fortunately getting our artillery into position and action, forcing the enemy to retire, which he did in great confusion and with considerable loss, after which he succeeded in getting his artillery into position, and a brisk firing ensued for about half an hour, during which time our forces had to be frequently shifted, to avoid their range.

Ascertaining that the enemy greatly outnumbered our force, and were aiming to make a charge on both of our flanks, the troops were slowly retired, upon favorable ground, toward the city. At the same time the cavalry was so disposed as to divert the coming charge of the enemy on our rear, and lead them upon the Fourteenth Michigan Infantry. The object succeeded admirably, an entire regiment of cavalry making the charge receiving a fire so destructive as to drive them back in great disorder. The enemy then planted several guns on the turnpike, which were driven off before they could charge their pieces. Our forces then retired in good order toward the city, the enemy making one more attempt to get in our rear, nearer the city, but were immediately driven off by a regiment of infantry and a section of artillery, which had been ordered forward as a reserve. The concerted plans of the enemy, who had Hanson's brigade of four Kentucky regiments and two Tennessee regiments of infantry, with five batteries of artillery, were defeated, and enabled our troops to give an additional proof of their efficiency and valor.

As we did not reoccupy the field of action, the enemy's total loss is unknown, but is represented by prisoners to have been large. Twenty-three prisoners were captured, including 2 captains of Morgan's artillery. Our casualties of the day were 26 wounded and 19 missing.

I have the honor to remain, very respectfully, your obedient servant,

JAS. S. NEGLEY,
Brigadier-General, Commanding.

Lieutenant-Colonel Ducat,
Chief of Staff.

No. 2.

Report of Col. Robert F. Smith, Sixteenth Illinois Infantry.

HEADQUARTERS SIXTEENTH ILLINOIS VOLUNTEERS,
Edgefield, Tenn., November 5, 1862.

SIR : In compliance with orders received from brigade headquarters, I have the honor to report, for the information of the general commanding, that this morning, about daylight, the rebel force, under General Morgan, numbering not less than 2,000, attacked my pickets at the railroad station, and succeeded in surrounding the company stationed there (Company E, Sixteenth Illinois, Captain Wilson). The outposts were immediately called in by Captain Wilson, and, after a severe skirmish, the company succeeded in cutting its way through the enemy and reaching camp. Company K, Sixteenth Illinois, under command of First Lieutenant Woodall, with 10 men of Company D, under Lieutenant Sommerville, who were stationed on the White's Creek pike, were now completely cut off from camp, but all succeeded in returning safely by reaching the river and marching under the shelter of its bank to the intrenchments.

Company C, Captain Rowe, which was stationed on the Gallatin pike, had by this time attacked and driven back the enemy's left, when the right also fell back, leaving 5 of their wounded in our hands.

We took from the enemy, besides the wounded, 2 prisoners, 2 horses, bridles, saddles, &c., and one regimental flag.

The officers and men engaged all behaved with unusual coolness and bravery, especially Companies E and C.

I cannot close my report without mentioning the excellent conduct of the mounted scouts belonging to Captain Twyman's independent command. I have rarely seen their equal for bravery and efficiency.

The casualties in my command are as follows : Wounded, 5 ; missing, and probably taken prisoners, 6.

I am, with much respect, your obedient servant,

R. F. SMITH,
Colonel, Commanding Sixteenth Illinois Volunteers and Post.

ACTING ASSISTANT ADJUTANT-GENERAL,
Second Brigade, First Division, Army of the Mississippi.

No. 3.

Report of General Braxton Bragg, C. S. Army, commanding Army of Tennessee.

KNOXVILLE, TENN., *November* 9, 1862.

We had a brisk skirmish with the enemy near Nashville on the 5th, killing and wounding about 100. Our loss very slight. Destroyed a large number of cars, engines, water-tanks, and bridges on Nashville and Louisville road. Brigadier-General Forrest was in command. Enemy is re-enforcing. Our forces are moving up. I leave to-morrow for the front.

BRAXTON BRAGG.

General S. COOPER,
Adjutant and Inspector General.

No. 4.

Report of Brig. Gen. Nathan B. Forrest, C. S. Army, commanding cavalry.

BRIGADE HEADQUARTERS,
La Vergne, Tenn., November 6, 1862.

GENERAL: Agreeably to orders received, I moved my commands on the night of the 4th instant in the direction of Nashville, distributing them as follows: Col. John T. Morgan's regiment [Fifty-first Alabama], of Partisan Rangers, and Capt. W. C. Bacot's battalion, Forrest's regiment, to the right of the Murfreesborough pike, with instructions to move forward on the Lebanon, Stone's River, and Chicken pikes, and to drive in the Abolitionists' pickets at daylight, which was done agreeably to orders and in gallant style, killing and wounding several, with the loss of 1 man killed and 2 horses wounded. Lieutenant-Colonel [A. A.] Russell, Partisan Rangers, on Murfreesborough pike, followed by Colonels [J. B.] Palmer's and [R. W.] Hanson's brigades, with four batteries of artillery, commanded by Major [R. E.] Graves, after proceeding to Dogtown, 3½ miles from Nashville, encountered the Abolitionists' pickets, at which place he (Colonel Russell) was ordered to dismount his command, press forward, and drive in the pickets. He succeeded in driving them to their first line of fortifications with considerable firing for 1½ miles. I here found them in some force behind a brush and log fortification around a high hill on right of pike. Here they made a stand, but after a short resistance [I] drove them from their position and gained the hill, at which place I planted my rifle battery of four pieces and opened fire on Jones' Hill, 1½ miles distant. At this time the firing was heard from Colonel [John T.] Morgan, at Edgefield. About the same time Colonel [James W.] Starnes opened fire on the Nolensville pike, he having been ordered, with Colonel [G. G.] Dibrell's regiment, Major [D. C.] Douglass' battalion, Captains [S. L.] Freeman's and [Franklin] Roberts' batteries, to the left of Murfreesborough pike, down the Nolensville, Mill Creek, and Franklin pikes. The engagement now became general, Captains Freeman's and Roberts' batteries having opened from Nolensville pike a vigorous fire on Saint Cloud's Hill. The firing was kept up until 10 o'clock, when I withdrew my forces.

Our loss in this action was 3 killed, 10 wounded, and 5 missing. Loss of Abolitionists, 15 killed, 20 prisoners, and supposed 20 wounded, one shell from Nolensville pike killing 5 in fortifications.

I then moved Colonels Starnes' and Dibrell's regiments and Captain

Freeman's and Roberts' batteries out on the Franklin pike 5 miles. The Abolitionists were in ambush with four regiments of infantry, twelve pieces of artillery, and a battalion of [William B.] Stokes' cavalry, commanded by Brigadier-General [James S.] Negley. They opened fire upon us from their position. I placed Freeman's and Roberts' batteries (four pieces each) on left of Franklin pike, between the Nolensville and Franklin pike, and returned their fire. After a spirited contest of an hour, they gave way, falling back down the Franklin pike toward Nashville. At this time I ordered my cavalry to charge, which order was quickly obeyed, their infantry and cavalry retreating down the pike toward Nashville. From this position my guns commanded the pike and played upon the Abolitionists with good effect, killing and wounding some 20 at one fire, which caused them to break and flee in disorder. I followed them up for a mile, when my artillery ammunition gave out and I withdrew my forces.

My loss in this action was 1 killed and 3 wounded. Loss of Abolitionists, 40 killed, 20 prisoners, and reported 60 wounded.

After this engagement I moved back to La Vergne.

Great credit is due Captain Freeman, of Freeman's battery, and Lieutenant [J. H.] Wiggins, commanding Roberts' battery, and their officers and men, for their coolness and discretion during this engagement. My officers and men acted well during the day, obeying with promptness each command.

All of which is respectfully submitted.

N. B. FORREST,
Brigadier-General.

Lieut. Col. J. A. BUCKNER,
   Assistant Adjutant-General.

NOVEMBER 5, 1862.—Affair near Piketon, Ky.

Reports of Col. John Dils, jr., Thirty-ninth Kentucky Infantry, with congratulatory letter from Maj. Gen. H. G. Wright.

HEADQUARTERS CAMP FINNELL,
November 10, 1862.

SIR : I took possession of this post on the 5th instant. The Confederates were camped 8 miles below this place, at Coal Grove (force 500 or 600, cavalry and infantry), but got notice of my approach in the night, when I was within 4 miles of them. The panic, I learn, was great. My little force entered their camp not more than one hour after the train left, but we pursued them, and in their camp and flight we captured about 75 prisoners, 150 guns, 3 wagons, a lot of tents, horses, and mules. I pursued within 20 miles of the Pound Gap, but my men were marched down, marching 30 miles the last day, and eating nothing but a little beef at night. This post is 100 miles from Catlettsburg, on the Ohio River, and the nearest force (Federal) is Ashland, 100 miles from here. The nearest Confederate force is 50 miles, Logan Court-House, Va. That force is 1,500 or 2,000, under Floyd and Witcher. My force that is armed, about 400. I will do the best I can, but there ought to be more force in this valley.

Your obedient servant,

JOHN DILS, JR.,
Colonel Thirty-ninth Kentucky Regiment.

General HORATIO G. WRIGHT.

HEADQUARTERS CAMP FINNELL,
November 17, 1862.

GENERAL: I sent you a dispatch a few days ago of my wnereabouts and success, so far as then able to report. The number of prisoners I have taken so far is 95, most of them rebel soldiers; paroled 60; some refused parole; preferred taking the oath or joining the Union Army. Some few bad rebel citizens I will have to send to Camp Chase. Captured 4 of Marshall's wagons, about 40 head of cattle, driving out of the State about 50 mules and horses, a large lot of tents, but the most of them worthless; about 200 guns of various make, but the most of them, as the rebels say, were captured of General Cox, at Princeton, in Mercer County, Virginia. Among the prisoners are 1 captain and 4 lieutenants. I have visited in the vicinity of Pound Gap, on the Virginia line. The enemy have nearly all left for Abingdon, Va. Marshall's entire force, I learn, has been ordered to Richmond, Va.; also all the available force they can spare are ordered that way, as I can learn from reliable source. I think I can hold this point at present, if I am only supplied with the right sort of arms. I must have Springfield or Enfield rifles. The guns at the mouth of Sandy for my men I cannot use in this service. I think I am a judge of this matter, and I cannot see any good reason why my wants in this particular are not supplied. I have some of the best men in the service, and best marksmen the Government can boast of; think nothing of marching 30 or 40 miles over the roads in these rough mountains, if necessity requires it, in twenty-four hours. Such men ought to be sustained. They have already routed and captured more men and property than all the forces ever sent up the Sandy Valley. We challenge investigation.

Very respectfully, your obedient servant,

JOHN DILS, JR.,
Colonel Thirty-ninth Kentucky Regiment.

General HORATIO G. WRIGHT.

P. S.—The Pound Gap of Cumberland is within 45 miles of Abingdon, Va.

HEADQUARTERS DEPARTMENT OF THE OHIO,
Cincinnati, Ohio, November 19, 1862.

Col. J. DILS, Jr.,
Comdg. 39th Regt. Kentucky Vols., Piketon, Pike County, Ky.:

COLONEL: Your report, dated Camp Finnell, November 10, 1862, of your pursuit of the enemy, in which your command captured 75 of the enemy, 150 guns, 3 wagons, &c., has been received.

The commanding general [H. G. Wright] directs me to express to you his lively satisfaction with the gallantry and endurance exhibited by yourself and your command; also with the general result of your operation, which, though accomplished without loss on your part, does you no less credit.

I am also instructed by the general commanding the department to inform you that Colonel Cranor, with a considerable force, is on the way up the Big Sandy Valley. You should, at once, put yourself in communication with Colonel Cranor and co-operate with him.

I am, colonel, very respectfully, your obedient servant,

C. W. FOSTER,
Assistant Adjutant-General.

NOVEMBER 6, 1862.—Skirmish at Garrettsburg, Ky.

Report of Brig. Gen. Thomas A. Davies, U. S. Army, commanding District of Columbus, Ky.

LA GRANGE, TENN., *November* 11, 1862—9.20 p. m.

Maj. Gen. H. W. HALLECK, *General-in-Chief:*

The following dispatch just received from General Davies, at Columbus:

The expedition commanded by Brigadier-General Ransom has proved a great success. It came up with Colonel Woodward's rebel force, 800 strong, near Garrettsburg; had a short engagement; killed 16 of his men, among them 1 captain and a lieutenant; wounded 40, including 1 captain and 2 lieutenants; took 25 prisoners, all their horses and 50 mules, and a large number of arms and equipments, half the camps of Colonel Woodward's men, including his own, routing the whole concern, and driving them out of the State of Kentucky. Our loss, 3 killed and 7 wounded.

U. S. GRANT,
Major-General.

NOVEMBER 12, 1862.—Capture of courier station, on Stone's River, Tenn.

Report of Maj. Gen. Thomas L. Crittenden, U. S. Army.

STONE'S RIVER,
November 12, 1862—2 p. m.

Twenty of the courier line were captured at this place at daylight this morning. The country between here and Nashville is reported infested by gangs of guerrillas. Two companies of cavalry are all I can spare for this service, and they are insufficient. Unless protected, they will all be captured. I respectfully suggest that a line of couriers be established from here to Nashville, and I can then withdraw my couriers from that line and place them on the line to Silver Springs, and I would also suggest that the brigade under command of Morgan be left here until some arrangement can be made for the safety of the line.

By order of Major-General Crittenden:

G. C. KNIFFIN,
Captain and Commissary of Subsistence.

Lieut. Col. ARTHUR C. DUCAT, *Chief of Staff.*

NOVEMBER 15–20, 1862.—Reconnaissance from Edgefield Junction toward Clarksville, Tenn.

REPORTS.

No. 1.—Col. William P. Carlin, Thirty-eighth Illinois Infantry, commanding brigade.
No. 2.—Lieut. Col. David McKee, Fifteenth Wisconsin Infantry.

No. 1.

Reports of Col. William P. Carlin, Thirty-eighth Illinois Infantry, commanding brigade.

HEADQUARTERS THIRTY-FIRST BRIGADE,
November 20, 1862.

CAPTAIN: As the long delay in obeying the telegraphic instructions of Major-General McCook to march to Nashville may occasion surprise,

I must inform him that on the night of the 14th I received orders by telegraph from Major-General Rosecrans to send two regiments toward Clarksville, and then south to Cumberland River, to co-operate with General Negley in capturing or dispersing guerrillas. The command started at 3 o'clock a. m. on the 15th, and has not yet returned. When last heard from, it was about 2 miles from Cumberland River and 40 miles from this point. During the whole time they have been without tents or baggage and in the rain day and night, but in good spirits. Lieutenant-Colonel McKee, Fifteenth Wisconsin, commanding, had captured a considerable number of prisoners and provisions collected for the rebel army. I hope the command will be here to-day, and I shall march for Nashville to-morrow.

Hoping that the delay has occasioned no detriment to the public service,

Your obedient servant,

W. P. CARLIN,
Colonel Thirty-eighth Illinois Volunteers, Commanding.

Capt. JOHN A. CAMPBELL,
Assistant Adjutant-General.

EDGEFIELD JUNCTION,
November 20, 1862.

COLONEL: The expedition ordered out to co-operate with General Negley has just returned, having been out five days. Lieutenant-Colonel McKee, commanding, captured 46 guerrillas, about 100 small-arms, 18 horses, 20 mules. Nothing was seen or heard of General Negley's expedition. The expedition has marched 100 miles without tents, in the rain every day and night but one.

W. P. CARLIN,
Colonel, Commanding.

Lieut. Col. J. P. GARESCHÉ.

No. 2.

Report of Lieut. Col. David McKee, Fifteenth Wisconsin Infantry.

CAMP OF THE FIFTEENTH WISCONSIN VOLUNTEERS,
Edgefield Junction, Tenn., November 21, 1862.

COLONEL: In obedience to your order of November [14], I left the camp of your brigade, at Edgefield Junction, on Sunday morning at 3.30 o'clock, with the command assigned to me, to wit: Thirty-eighth Illinois Volunteers, Major Gilmer commanding; Fifteenth Wisconsin Volunteers, Major Johnson commanding, and Lieutenant Reynolds, of Company B (cavalry), of the Thirty-sixth Illinois Volunteers, with 10 men, and proceeded to reconnoiter the country in the direction of Clarksville.

I proceeded from Edgefield Junction, by way of Goodlettsville, to the junction of the Louisville and Springfield turnpikes, and thence up Manser's Creek, by way of Johnson's Mill and —— pikes, on the ridge leading to the old Nashville and Clarksville road, at a point near the junction of the roads leading to Clarksville and Springfield, from

Nashville, by way of White's Creek; thence, on the old Clarksville road, down —— Creek, past the residence of Dr. Bainbridge, to the Fountain settlement, and encamped the first night out at the Wells' Creek Meeting-house, within 2 miles of Coopertown.

At daylight on the following morning I resumed the march, by way of Coopertown, and thence, turning to the left, I proceeded, on the Springfield and Charlotte road, a distance of about 12 miles, to the crossing of the Nashville and Turnersville road with that road, when the command was encamped for the night near the residence of Mr. James Bradley.

The next morning, at 6.30 o'clock, the march was resumed on the Springfield and Charlotte road, crossing the Nashville and Clarksville turnpike (it is not macadamized at this point) at the house of Mr. Williamson Gatewood, and thence to the crossing of the Cumberland River at Harpeth Shoals, a distance of about 13 miles by the route traveled. The road traveled on this route for a greater portion of the way is extremely bad, and, in some places, almost impassable, and entirely impracticable for the passage of artillery, except in cases of great emergency. The country through which we passed is tolerably well supplied with forage of all kinds.

The command returned from Harpeth Shoals, by way of the Charlotte and Springfield road, to Mr. Gatewood's, and thence, on the Nashville and Clarksville turnpike, to within sight of Nashville. The latter is a good road, and passable for all kinds of transportation and artillery.

On this expedition the command captured 47 prisoners, 18 horses, 20 mules, 3 wagons, and about 100 small-arms. The arms captured were principally of a worthless character, and, for want of transportation, were mostly broken up and destroyed, the best of them only being retained and brought into camp. I caused to be destroyed by fire one distillery and two dwelling-houses, and the outbuildings connected therewith, which were notoriously used as refuges for guerrilla parties. I also destroyed at and in the neighborhood of Harpeth Shoals several barrels of spirituous liquors and about 50 barrels of salt.

I cannot speak too highly of the conduct of the officers and men of my command. They marched and encamped under almost incessant rains and in deep mud without murmur or complaint, and were always ready and anxious for effective service. Special notice is due to Major Gilmer, Thirty-eighth Illinois Volunteers; Major Johnson, Fifteenth Wisconsin Volunteers, and Lieutenant Reynolds, of Company B (cavalry), Thirty-sixth Illinois Volunteers, for the splendid manner in which their separate commands were managed and cared for. To Lieutenant Reynolds and the cavalrymen under his command I am particularly indebted for their untiring activity in scouting the country, and for the capture of the greater number of prisoners. Lieutenant Ferriman, Thirty-eighth Illinois Volunteers, acting quartermaster for the command, and Adjutant Hauff, Fifteenth Wisconsin Volunteers, performed their respective duties excellently, and deserve credit.

I attach hereto a list of prisoners taken, together with a statement of charges against them.

I am, colonel, very respectfully, your obedient servant,

DAVID McKEE,
Lieutenant-Colonel, Commanding Expedition.

Col. W. P. CARLIN,
Commanding Thirty-first Brigade.

SPECIAL ORDERS, } HDQRS. DEPARTMENT OF THE CUMBERLAND,
    No. 22.   }   *Nashville, Tenn., November* 21, 1862.
          *   *   *   *   *   *   *

XXII. The commanding general notices with much pleasure the successful expedition sent out by Col. W. P. Carlin, commanding Thirty-first Brigade, in the direction of Clarksville, two infantry regiments, under Lieutenant-Colonel McKee, having marched 100 miles, over muddy roads, in five days, through constant rains, without tents, having returned with 46 prisoners, 100 small-arms, 18 horses, and 20 mules, taken from the guerrillas, who infest the country. This handsome little success, which shows what good infantry can do under an enterprising leader, reflects much credit on all who were engaged in it.

          *   *   *   *   *   *   *

By command of Major-General Rosecrans:
                              W. H. SIDELL,
        Major Fifteenth U. S. Infantry, Assistant Adjutant-General.

NOVEMBER 19, 1862.—Reconnaissance toward La Vergne, Tenn.

REPORTS.

No. 1.—Brig. Gen. Joshua W. Sill, U. S. Army, commanding division.
No. 2.—Col. Edward N. Kirk, Thirty-fourth Illinois Infantry, commanding brigade.

No. 1.

Report of Brig. Gen. Joshua W. Sill, U. S. Army, commanding division.

                    HEADQUARTERS SECOND DIVISION,
                                   November 19, 1862.

GENERAL: I inclose herewith the report of Colonel Kirk, Thirty-fourth Illinois, commanding Fifth Brigade. He went considerably farther than I had intended and directed, but the provocation probably justified it. The movements of this officer can never be reproached with lack of activity or daring. The First Tennessee Cavalry has been reporting in small squads all day long. The total present may have amounted to 200, of which 120 are still out, making a scout around my camp.

I would prefer that the whole regiment should encamp here, so as to be ready for an emergency. As it is, they come irregularly, and usually without rations or blankets.

Your obedient servant,

                                   J. W. SILL,
                      Brigadier-General, Commanding.
Maj. Gen. A. McD. McCook,
    Commanding Right Wing, Fourteenth Army Corps.

No. 2.

Report of Col. Edward N. Kirk, Thirty-fourth Illinois Infantry, commanding brigade.

                    HEADQUARTERS FIFTH BRIGADE,
                                   November 19, 1862.

SIR: I have the honor to report that I have made a reconnaissance to the front and left, as you ordered last night One of my regiments, Thirtieth Indiana, being out on picket duty, I took the other four, *i. e.*, Thirty-fourth Illinois, Seventy-ninth Illinois, Seventy-seventh Pennsylvania, and Twenty-ninth Indiana, and Edgarton's battery, which were, as you ordered, disposed of as follows:

The Seventy-ninth Illinois and one section of artillery were left as a general reserve, at a point about 1½ miles to the front, where the picket line crosses the Murfreesborough pike. The Twenty-ninth Indiana and one section of artillery were placed in position at a point on the Stone's River pike, concealed from view about the same distance to the front. With the other two regiments and section of artillery I moved out the dirt road, which diverges from the Murfreesborough pike, where the Seventy-ninth Illinois was left in reserve.

We marched with the most perfect silence, hoping to surprise some of the rebel parties which have been annoying your camp. Having gone about 3½ miles on the dirt road, and finding no enemy, I sent five companies of the Thirty-fourth Illinois, with a citizen guide that I pressed in, to a point on the Stone's River pike directly opposite, with orders to move down the pike quietly until they formed a junction with the Twenty-ninth Indiana, with a view of picking up any of the rebels that might be prowling around that neighborhood. With the remaining forces, now reduced to about 700 infantry and one section of artillery, I moved across to the Murfreesborough pike at a point about 4 miles from our picket line. All along this part of our march I noticed evidences of the recent presence of the enemy—picket fires still burning, &c., but saw no enemy. I had reached the pike, and was about to return to camp, when three shots were fired from a rebel picket near my left flank. I then started down the pike toward La Vergne. My advance soon came up with a small squad of some 20 cavalry, who fell back upon a reserve of two or three companies, who took position at a toll-gate about 4 miles from La Vergne; several of them dismounted and went into the toll-gate house. I dropped a few shells among them, two shells passing through the house, when the whole party hastily fled. About this point we also found infantry pickets, but they also fell back without firing a gun.

The rebel force seemed to be disposed as follows: First, small vedettes of cavalry; second, cavalry reserves; third, main body of cavalry and infantry, say, in all, a regiment or two of each ; but they seemed frightened, and so I pursued them until I reached the top of the hill which overlooks the town of La Vergne. My position was a beautiful one. The road is nearly straight for about 1½ miles down to and beyond the town. Here the rebels had rallied, and we had a fine view of their column of cavalry in front and infantry in their rear. After firing a dozen shells among them, they seemed to scatter, but rallied twice and started toward us, but the well-directed fire of the artillery was too much for them. They finally retreated through the town and over the hill beyond. I pursued them no farther; your orders required me to return by 10 a. m.; it was now 8, and I was 8 miles from camp. I captured a few suspicious characters, which I will send up to you under guard.

I did not go down to La Vergne to ascertain the effect of our shells; many of them burst in the street close to the troops, and must have done considerable execution. Here, as at Claysville, the rebels must have overestimated our force as we dashed down upon them; otherwise I am sure they would have stood their ground and given us fight.

I am entirely satisfied with the conduct of every officer and man I had with me.   This report is so hastily written that I fear it will be unintelligible.

Very respectfully, your obedient servant,

E. N. KIRK,
Commanding Fifth Brigade.

Capt J. E. STEARNS,
Assistant Adjutant-General, Second Division.

NOVEMBER 19, 1862.—Skirmish near Tompkinsville, Ky.

Report of Col. James R. Howard, Alabama cavalry.

CAMP KIRBY, *November* 20, 1862.

GENERAL: I have the honor to submit to you a report of a scout made by me into Kentucky.

On the 17th instant a portion of my command took up their line of march from camp near Sparta for the Kentucky line.   When about 75 miles over the Kentucky and Tennessee line, we encountered a large force of the enemy's cavalry, gave them fight, and, after a brisk engagement of about half an hour, with the assistance of Divine Providence, we completely routed them, killing 27, and wounding a large number. Our loss, 4 men killed and 3 wounded.   My command behaved gallantly, especially the officers, and too much praise cannot be given to my adjutant, Noah D. Rothrock, for his valuable assistance and gallantry on the occasion.   We followed up the enemy and had a short hand-to-hand engagement, and again cut them up badly, bringing out from them nearly 5,000 head of hogs.   While accomplishing this, the enemy rallied twice, and on both occasions we repulsed them, bringing the hogs safely through, and turning them over to Major [John J.] Murphy, commissary of subsistence.

Another portion of my command made a scout with a train of wagons, and succeeded in bringing them out safely, loaded with flour and bacon. They encountered no regular forces, but were much annoyed by bushwhackers.   None of our men were hurt, but we gave them a Southern lesson.

I have the honor, general, to be, very respectfully, your obedient servant,

JAMES R. HOWARD,
Colonel, Commanding Cavalry.

Lieut. Gen. E. KIRBY SMITH,
Commanding Department of East Tennessee.

NOVEMBER 24, 1862.—Skirmish near Tompkinsville, Ky.

Report of Col. Joseph R. Scott, Nineteenth Illinois Infantry.

HDQRS. 39TH BRIG., 12TH DIV. (CENTER),
14TH CORPS D'ARMÉE,
Hartsville, Tenn., November 28, 1862.

SIR: I respectfully report the arrival of my command at this point at 2 p. m. to-day; also the arrival of my train from Cave City, via Gallatin, with five days' rations and ammunition.

On the afternoon of the 24th instant the enemy made a slight demonstration upon Tompkinsville with cavalry and artillery. My pickets, aided by cavalry, repulsed them, capturing one, a private of Hamilton's company, who reports the attacking party to have been a detachment of Scott's cavalry, 700 strong, with three mountain howitzers. They came from Sparta, by way of Bennett's Ferry, crossing the Cumberland at Celina. Hamilton's company has been enforcing the conscript law and guarding stock between Celina and Gainsborough.

Being induced to believe that the enemy was crossing the Scottsville road, preparatory to attacking me from that quarter in the morning, I, in obedience to marching orders, received the night previous, left Tompkinsville by that road at 9 p. m. on the evening of the 24th instant. I failed to meet the enemy; took the branch road to La Fayette, and from thence to Hartsville. It is reported that the enemy occupied Tompkinsville on my departure. I met with no interruption in my march until within 3 miles of Hartsville, when I came upon a body of rebel cavalry, of whom I took 2 prisoners. They report themselves as belonging to Bennett's cavalry, 200 of whom, under the command of Colonel Bennett himself, left their camp at Stone's River, 6 miles from Murfreesborough, on a scout this side of the Cumberland yesterday evening, having ridden all night. They report Morgan and Duke encamped in similar positions around Murfreesborough, where there is also a large force of infantry. The rebel cavalry fled, at my approach, in the direction of Dickinson's Springs, 8 miles from here. Upon nearing the town, I met a detachment of the Second Indiana Cavalry, attached to the troops at this point, who reported the capture, by this party of rebels, of a forage train and one company of cavalry. I immediately sent one regiment of infantry after them, directing the cavalry to make a detour, in order to intercept them on the road. The infantry has returned, and report the cavalry as having missed the enemy, and gone forward in pursuit.

I received dispatches by courier to-night, and will immediately follow your instructions in regard to scouts. I relieve the troops of the Second Brigade, First Division, who march from here to-morrow morning.

I am, sir, very respectfully, your obedient servant,

JOS. R. SCOTT,
Colonel, Commanding Thirty-ninth Brigade.

Capt. D. BRADEN, *Assistant Adjutant-General.*

NOVEMBER 26–27, 1862.—Reconnaissance to La Vergne, Tenn., and skirmish.

REPORTS, ETC.

No. 1.—Brig. Gen. Joshua W. Sill, U. S. Army, commanding division.
No. 2.—Lieut. Col. Peter B. Housum, Seventy-seventh Pennsylvania Infantry.
No. 3.—Capt. Thomas E. Rose, Seventy-seventh Pennsylvania Infantry.
No. 4.—Congratulatory letter from General Braxton Bragg to Brig. Gen. Joseph Wheeler, C. S. Army, commanding cavalry.

No. 1.

Report of Brig. Gen. Joshua W. Sill, U. S. Army, commanding division.

HEADQUARTERS SECOND DIVISION,
November 27, 1862.

GENERAL: Hearing some vague rumors yesterday concerning a heavy force of the enemy, reported to be at La Vergne, I dispatched Col. E. N. Kirk, Thirty-fourth Illinois, commanding Fifth Brigade, to make a reconnaissance in that direction. His report is herewith inclosed.* Quite a heavy firing was kept up on both sides. There was also heavy firing on the Nolensville road, which occurred during a reconnaissance, made by a portion of Sheridan's command. Being averse to unnecessary expenditure of ammunition, and feeling sure that it might create alarm in the city, I particularly enjoined on Colonel Kirk not to fire at all if he could avoid it. I think there was entirely too great a waste of ammunition. The reconnaissance developed the presence of cavalry at La Vergne, probably the same which has occupied that place for some time under Wheeler. One of the prisoners states that on Stewart's Creek, some 5 miles beyond La Vergne, there has been an encampment of infantry; what force he does not know; thinks a brigade. Another prisoner states that, while the skirmish was going on, he saw a cavalryman of his company, who had just come from Stewart's Creek, and reported that their infantry was moving, and was within 2 miles of La Vergne. This is all I know of the approach of the enemy rumored in the city. The 3 prisoners will be sent you early in the morning. One of the prisoners states that Wheeler commands six regiments, viz, the First and Third Alabama, Robertson's battalion, Faulkner's battalion, Douglass' battalion, Hagan's battalion.

In my letter of yesterday I referred to the great length of my picket line. It requires the best part of a day to make the circuit. My left is picketed quite close to camp; the front line extends to join Sheridan's line. Behind me, 1½ miles, I understand that Crittenden's three divisions are posted, on Mill Creek, with another picket line. The total length of it does not, I suppose, equal that of my single division. I respectfully urge the location of this division to the right of the present position, nearer to Sheridan's; unless it be expected that we should meet the enemy on this road, when I would advise the selection of other ground farther to the front. I am not sufficiently conversant with the ground in front to venture an opinion as to where we could go with more advantage. It seems to me, however, that, in view of a certain contingency, some change ought to be made.

Before closing, I desire to be acquainted with the construction which I should place on that part of General Orders, No. 21, Headquarters Fourteenth Corps, limiting the supply train of a division to 50 wagons. My quartermaster seems to think that the 50 wagons include the ammunition train. Now, as my ammunition train numbers 35 wagons, I should have 15 wagons left for supply train. Is there not a mistake on his part?

In case a change of location is to be made, I would like to know it early, so that the movement can be commenced by sunrise.

Very respectfully, your obedient servant,

J. W. SILL,
Brigadier-General, Commanding.

Maj. Gen. A. McD. McCook,
Commanding Right Wing.

---

* Not found.

No. 2.

Report of Lieut. Col. Peter B. Housum, Seventy-seventh Pennsylvania Infantry.

HDQRS. SEVENTY-SEVENTH REGT. PENNSYLVANIA VOLS.,
In Camp, November 27, 1862.

CAPTAIN: In reply to Special Orders, No. —, of this date, asking why the detachments sent out on the left of La Vergne did not move up rapidly and charge the rebel battery, as ordered, I give you a statement of the operations of the Twenty-ninth Indiana Regiment, Major Collins, and Seventy-seventh Regiment, both under my command, until the detachment under Colonel Dodge, Thirtieth Indiana, joined me.

After receiving orders to join the Seventy-seventh to the Twenty-ninth and assume command, I proceeded, as ordered, to take and hold the grove on the left of the Murfreesborough road, and keep the right a specified distance from the road. When in the grove, and in line of battle, the skirmishers thrown in advance from the Twenty-ninth Indiana Regiment became engaged in front and on the left. I at once ordered Company B, of Seventy-seventh, Captain Rose, forward on the left of the line already deployed, with orders to advance as rapidly as circumstances would permit. As soon as deployed, he became engaged with the enemy, when I ordered the whole line forward to the bed of the stream, and immediately crossed, when it became necessary to march the line by the left flank to get under cover of the woods, and also to cross a ravine which was in front. As soon as a sufficient distance had been taken to the left to cover the troops, I ordered an advance, with the injunction from Captain Wagner not to advance too rapidly on the woods, or too close on the line of skirmishers. After advancing some distance, I was ordered to again move by the left flank to what I thought would be a point opposite the battery, and advance on it. After marching by the flank what I supposed a sufficient distance, I again resumed the march by the front, and advanced steadily, under a severe fire, when I observed the enemy moving to our left, and supposing the object might be to outflank us on our left, their line in front already exceeding our line in length or front, I ordered a halt, and sent Lieutenant Walker, of the staff, to the left, to notify the cavalry to keep a strict watch to prevent any attempt to flank us on the left, at the same time notifying Colonel Kirk that probably an attempt would be made to outflank us. Lieutenant Walker returning, I immediately ordered the men forward, when, from the maneuvering of the enemy in front, I ordered two additional companies forward on the line of skirmishers. At this moment Colonel Dodge joined me on the right, when he also threw one company forward on the line of skirmishers; thus re-enforced, and the skirmish line strengthened, I ordered a rapid advance, clearing the woods of the enemy. Colonel Dodge now came to me, and, as my superior officer, he assumed command and ordered me to change front forward on the left company. When the whole line was thrown forward in the new direction, he ordered an advance to the edge of the woods. At this point he ordered the Twenty-ninth Regiment forward, supported by the Seventy-seventh and Thirtieth, to charge the battery, while moving forward as rapidly as the ground would admit of, and obstructed, as it was, by a number of fences, which had to be torn down as they advanced, and also under a severe fire from the rebel battery on the hill in front. About the time the advance was tearing down a heavy fence, the firing of the battery ceased.* We advanced to the top of a hill in the rear of La Vergne, when Colonel Dodge received orders to return to town.

I thought at the time, and think so still, that our advance through the woods was as rapid as circumstances would admit of. The only time lost was when I directed the cavalry to reconnoiter on our left. Halting at that time was thought to be a necessity.

Hoping the above will fully explain the matter referred to in Orders, No. —, I remain, respectfully, yours,

P. B. HOUSUM.

Capt. D. C. WAGNER,
    Assistant Adjutant-General.

No. 3.

Report of Capt. Thomas E. Rose, Seventy-seventh Pennsylvania Infantry.

CAMP NEAR INSANE ASYLUM,
            November 29, 1862.

SIR: In compliance with the request of Lieutenant-Colonel Housum, commanding Seventy-seventh Regiment, I have the honor to make the following report of the part that I took in the skirmish near La Vergne, Tenn.:

When the Seventy-seventh had formed on the left of the Twenty-ninth Indiana, I was ordered to take one company and deploy it forward as skirmishers, and join on the left of the skirmishers of the Twenty-ninth, which I did, and which post I had the honor to hold throughout the skirmish. After I had got my company into position, we were ordered to advance across the woods, and over a ditch, which was the bed of a small creek; thence across an open space to the edge of the grove on the left of the town. From the time I first deployed the company, the enemy had kept firing on us, and in a short time after we entered the latter grove the firing became quite heavy upon my position of the line. At this time the whole line of skirmishers was ordered to halt, and my little band sustained the concentrated fire of the rebels for a considerable length of time, when the rebels advanced toward us with a loud cheering, which cheering we as lustily returned. My portion of the command being at this time re-enforced, we charged upon them, and drove them back through the woods into and across an open space to the next grove beyond, their officers using their utmost endeavors to rally them, which they partially succeeded in doing behind a fence on the opposite edge of the grove. They did not stay our progress, however, and one portion of the rebels returned pell-mell down the road toward the Lebanon pike, and the other in tolerable order toward the railroad. We were here ordered to move by the right flank, which we did for about 150 or 200 yards, and then advanced directly across the railroad at an angle of about 20 degrees, our right thrown forward, striking the railroad first, and, when the left of my line had passed over the railroad about 100 yards, I discovered a section of artillery belonging to the enemy a little to the front, but almost upon my right flank. I immedi-

---

* NOTE ON ORIGINAL.—The line of skirmishers passed through a field on our left, and advanced through the woods in the direction of the hill on which the rebel battery was placed.

ately signaled my skirmishers to change direction to the right, to gain the rear of the battery, which they did until we had wheeled about 30 degrees, when we encountered about 300 dismounted cavalry, which at first I took to be a regiment of infantry. We attacked them with a loud cheer, and they immediately began to give way, but disputed the ground for probably 100 yards, when they fled precipitately to their horses, which were posted in the rear of the battery. We pushed at double-quick toward the battery, but, as soon as the cavalry reached their horses, both cavalry and artillery commenced a thundering retreat, and we continued in full pursuit, although we were a quarter of a mile in advance of our main reserve, until an orderly came up, stating that he was the bearer of an order from the brigade commander directing us to fall back, which we did until we neared the town, where I assembled my skirmishers and returned to the regiment.

Your obedient servant,

THOS. E. ROSE,
Captain, Comdg. Seventy-seventh Pennsylvania Volunteers.

S. T. DAVIS,
Adjutant Seventy-seventh Regt. Pennsylvania Volunteers.

No. 4.

Congratulatory letter from General Braxton Bragg to Brig. Gen. Joseph Wheeler, C. S. Army, commanding cavalry.

HEADQUARTERS ARMY OF TENNESSEE,
Murfreesborough, November 27, 1862.

General WHEELER, *Chief of Cavalry :*

GENERAL : The general commanding directs me to thank you for your successful engagement with the enemy to-day. He also desires you will express to the First Alabama Regiment (one of his old corps) his appreciation of their gallant conduct, not unexpected, which you refer to in your report.* He further directs me to state that you expose yourself too recklessly in affairs of this character.

I am, general, your obedient servant,

GEORGE WM. BRENT,
Assistant Adjutant-General.

NOVEMBER 26–30, 1862.—Operations about Springfield, Tenn.

Report of Lieut. Col. Daniel F. Griffin, Thirty-eighth Indiana Infantry.

HEADQUARTERS THIRTY-EIGHTH INDIANA VOLUNTEERS,
Edgefield Junction, Tenn., December 2, 1862.

SIR : In pursuance of your orders, of date November 25, I proceeded with my command and 22 wagons, leaving camp at 7.30 o'clock on

---

* Not found.

the morning of the 26th ultimo, arriving at Springfield, Robertson County, Tennessee, at 3.30 p. m. of the same date. Immediately on arrival, pickets were thrown out on all avenues of approach to the town, and Company E, Capt. William L. Carter commanding, placed on duty as provost guards. Immediate search was made for subsistence stores, as contemplated by your orders, and flour, to the number of 1,143 barrels, found stored. Of this I immediately had loaded 249 barrels on the wagons then at hand, and parked them for the night close to my com mand, sending at the same time a courier forward for further supply of wagons.

Examinations made on the 27th resulted in the finding of one lot of 106 barrels of flour, another of 40 barrels, and three lots of bacon—say something more than 3 tons—for correct statement of which I would refer to reports of Lieutenant Hollister, acting brigade commissary.

On the evening of November 27, Lieutenant-Colonel Kell, commanding Second Ohio Volunteers, arrived with his regiment and wagon-train, and assumed command of the post. From that date two companies of my command were doing provost guard duty, two on picket duty, and the others escorting trains, or such other duties as were required by the demands of the expedition.

On Saturday, November 29, I proceeded, with four companies of my command, under Lieutenant-Colonel Kell, Second Ohio Volunteers, to the Logan Mills, situated on Red River, Kentucky, 13 miles north of Springfield, on the old Russellville road, returning from there after dark, and, when about one-half mile from Springfield, the rear, or rather the straggling portion of the command (the march having been a very severe one), was fired upon by bushwhackers, wounding in the leg severely Joseph Candiere, Company B, of my regiment. Three shots were fired, and the wound inflicted with buckshot, evidently fired from a shot-gun. These facts coming to my knowledge, I immediately sent out a detachment of two companies, under Maj. John B. Glover, with orders to arrest all men found in the immediate vicinity of the firing, and to bring them and all arms found in their possession to camp. This duty was promptly performed, and 10 of the citizens living in the immediate neighborhood brought to camp and turned over to the provost-marshal, together with 3 shot-guns and 5 rifles. The citizens were held in custody until the next evening, when a court of inquiry, consisting of Maj. J. B. Glover, Capt. William L. Carter, Lieut. James V. Kelso, and myself, after a thorough investigation, being satisfied of their innocence, discharged them, retaining, however, their guns, which were brought to this camp, and now await your order as to what disposition shall be made of them.

Monday, December 1, a. m., my command was relieved by the Thirty-third Ohio Volunteers, and, as soon as the companies then on picket could be called in, started for this camp, arriving here at 6 p. m., bringing with us 3 prisoners, who were turned over to us by the citizens of Springfield, together with 1 horse and 3 guns, which I have brought with me to this camp. Prisoners are members of Morgan's and Woodward's guerrilla bands.

Very respectfully, your obedient servant,

D. F. GRIFFIN,
Lieut. Col., Comdg. Thirty-eighth Regiment Indiana Volunteers.

GEORGE H. VANDEGRIFT,
Acting Assistant Adjutant-General, Ninth Brigade.

NOVEMBER 26–DECEMBER 1, 1862.—Expedition from Edgefield to Harpeth Shoals, Clarksville, &c., Tenn.

Report of Lieut. Col. James S. McClelland, Twenty-fifth Illinois Infantry.

HEADQUARTERS TWENTY-FIFTH ILLINOIS VOLUNTEERS,
Camp near Edgefield, Tenn., December 2, 1862.

GENERAL : In pursuance of your order, received the night of November 26, I left camp at 11 o'clock with the Twenty-fifth Illinois, Major Nodine ; Thirty-fifth Illinois, Lieutenant-Colonel Chandler, and one company of the Thirty-sixth Illinois Cavalry, Captain Sherer. My instructions from General Davis were to march to Harpeth Shoals, to intercept 1,200 cavalry (said to have crossed there), and, if possible, cut them up.

I moved my command 16 miles, and halted for breakfast; rested two hours, and moved on near to Harpeth Shoals; encamped and sent out scouts.

Having received such information as convinced me that no enemy in any force was near, I moved at 8 o'clock next morning, 28th, to a camp 1 mile east of Coopertown, on the Nashville and Clarksville road. At 12 o'clock at night I received orders to march to Harpeth Shoals or Clarksville, to intercept a force said to be at Trenton, Todd County.

In obedience to this order, I separated my teams, and sent those already loaded, with the prisoners, under a strong escort, to a camp at Edgefield, and, with the balance of my command, left camp at 3 a. m., 29th, and arrived at Port Royal at 11 a. m., where I learned that no force was then near Trenton, but that Woodward's command had crossed the Cumberland below and at Clarksville some time during the 28th. I therefore went into camp with my infantry force, and sent the cavalry on to Clarksville. They reported to me before daylight on the morning of the 30th that, on their arrival at Clarksville, they found the advance of Colonel Bruce's command occupying the town, and that the enemy, 700 strong, was in camp 10 miles south of Clarksville, and they expected to make an attack on the camp at daybreak of the 30th. On hearing this, I left my camp at 8.30 a. m., and marched to Sycamore Creek and encamped.

December 1, marched at 8.30 o'clock and arrived in camp, near Edgefield, at 4.30 p. m. My march in a direct line was 97 miles in some less than five days, besides the scouting done by parties sent out for the purpose of obtaining information. The cavalry command labored faithfully, and I cannot speak in too high terms of their promptness and efficiency, as well as good conduct, on the march. Great credit is due Capt. S. B. Sherer for the discipline he enforced.

During the march I captured on the road going south 3 wagons, loaded with 20 barrels of whisky, with the owner and his teamsters, and found on his person $3,080 of Confederate bills, in sheets. I brought in near 500 bushels of wheat, 150 bushels of corn, 16 barrels of flour, and 5 barrels of salt. I captured over 20 prisoners, 11 of whom I had turned over ; 2 I paroled (they being sick and wounded), and the balance I released unconditionally for want of sufficient evidence against them. I also brought in 20 head of horses, 10 head of mules, and 6 guns. All of the above property was taken from persons known to be disloyal, and receipts were given by my quartermaster and approved by a commissioned officer in all cases where any owner could be found, or family of owner to give them to. Most of the property taken belongs to men serving in the rebel army. I found the roads leading from

Robertson County across the Cumberland south bore evidence of being much used, and, from information received from citizens, large supplies of provisions and other supplies have been sent south through these routes. I found abundance of almost all kinds of supplies through the southern portion of Robertson and northwest part of Cheatham Counties, while the mass of the citizens are avowedly disloyal. Great care was taken by myself, in which I was aided effectually by the commanding officers under my command, to prevent any pillaging. A few mules and horses were taken by unauthorized parties. All such were promptly sent back to their owners, and the parties taking them punished.

I have to report the loss of Capt. Charles A. Clark, Company A, Twenty-fifth Illinois. He was division officer of the day, and while in discharge of his duty was shot by a private of Company E, Twenty-fifth Illinois, said private having been placed under guard for disorderly conduct. The shooting occurred while on the march and in the rear of the command, and was not brought to my notice for several hours afterward, or I should have had the criminal shot on the spot. I reported him, with two others implicated, under a strong guard. They are now in prison in Nashville. Captain Clark was my most efficient line officer, and his death has created a vacuum that cannot be filled. The shot entered the brain, and death was instantaneous. He fell as he had ever lived during his term of service, promptly discharging his duties as an officer.

I took provisions for three days of all except meat, and for the supplies needed and used by the command I gave receipts.

Respectfully, your obedient servant,

J. S. McCLELLAND,
Lieutenant-Colonel Twenty-fifth Illinois Volunteers.

Brigadier-General WOODRUFF,
Commanding Thirty-second Brigade, Ninth Division.

NOVEMBER 27, 1862.—Skirmish at Mill Creek, Tenn.

Report of Brig. Gen. Philip H. Sheridan, U. S. Army.

HDQRS. ELEVENTH DIV., FOURTEENTH ARMY CORPS,
Camp on Mill Creek, November 27, 1862.

MAJOR: This morning I directed a reconnaissance in force in the direction of Nolensville, under the direction of Colonel Schaefer, supported by two regiments and a section of artillery, under Colonel Greusel. I inclose herewith their instructions. Colonel Schaefer found the enemy's pickets 2 miles in my front; drove them in until they were supported, a short distance beyond Mill Creek, by a section of artillery, and about 2,000 cavalry. These he drove without difficulty to Nolensville, and then turned to the right to the Edmondson pike, leaving Colonel Greusel to cover his rear.

These commands have returned to camp. Colonel Schaefer reports having killed several of the enemy; the body of only one was recovered. There were no indications of infantry, nor any determined resistance of cavalry. The colonel captured some rebel flour at Mill Creek. I know of no engagement at La Vergne. I learn by a note from General Sill that he sent a party there, and Colonel Schaefer reports about twelve artillery shots in that direction.

The crossing of Mill Creek, on the Nolensville road, is not bad; the bridges have been burned; 3 prisoners were captured. The cavalry was Texas Rangers, commanded by Wharton.

I have the honor to be, major, your obedient servant,

P. H. SHERIDAN,
Brigadier-General, Commanding.

[Inclosure.]

HDQRS. ELEVENTH DIV., FOURTEENTH ARMY CORPS,
Camp on Mill Creek, November 26, 1862.

Col. NICHOLAS GREUSEL,
Commanding Third Brigade:

COLONEL: The general commanding directs that you take the Thirty-sixth and Eighty-eighth Illinois Infantry, and follow in the rear of the command of Colonel Schaefer, on the Nolensville pike, to-morrow morning at 4 o'clock. On arriving at Concord Church, or at the crossing of Mill Creek, you will take up a position to assist and cover the movements of Colonel Schaefer. One section of Barnett's battery without caissons will be directed to accompany you. You will take your position on Mill Creek, if possible, watching the La Vergne road; also the Nolensville road and the valley on the opposite side of the creek till 12 o'clock m., and threaten the enemy who are encamped at or near Nolensville, so as to prevent them from attacking with their full force the command of Colonel Schaefer. You must maintain your position, if possible, at that point until the hour indicated, when you will slowly return toward camp. The general does not consider it prudent to cross Mill Creek, unless it would be as a feint to relieve Colonel Schaefer from any attack which might be made in force against him; then it would be best to cross over a portion of your infantry only, as the crossing is very bad. In case Colonel Schaefer should meet with a large force of the enemy, he is directed to fall back; in which case you will fall back also.

The general commanding trusts to your good judgment in the execution of the foregoing instructions.

I have the honor to be, colonel, your obedient servant,

GEORGE LEE,
First Lieutenant and Acting Assistant Adjutant-General.

NOVEMBER 28, 1862.—Skirmishes on the Carthage road, near Hartsville and Rome, Tenn.

Reports of Col. John M. Harlan, Tenth Kentucky Infantry, commanding brigade, with congratulatory orders.

HEADQUARTERS SECOND BRIGADE, FIRST DIVISION,
Camp at Castalian Springs, Tenn., November 29, 1862—4.30 a. m.

GENERAL: Major [Samuel] Hill has returned to Hartsville, and reports that he followed the rebel cavalry beyond Rome, and recaptured 7 of the wagons. The wagons were recaptured on the south side of the river, near Rome. He also reports that he took several prisoners; had some 3 or 4 men killed; drove them some 18 miles, and killed 15 or 20 of them. Major Hill reports also that there are no rebels on this side of the river. The party which attacked and captured the train yesterday morning numbered 200. I inclose report of adjutant of the cavalry detachment, from which you will see the casualties of the cavalry. I have written to Major Hill for all the facts connected with the pursuit, which I will receive at Gallatin, and will then, if desired, make a formal report. It was rather a bold act in the cavalry to go as far as they did, and the result creditable to it. Supposing that the report of Major Hill to Colonel Hays, herein embodied, contains all the facts which you expected Colonel Hays to ascertain, I have ordered him to move down this morning. The order will not reach him, so that he can get here before 1 o'clock. If you have no objection, I will wait here until to-morrow morning, as the march from Hartsville to our camp, beyond Gallatin, will be 18½ miles, which is quite a severe one, unless necessary to be made. As to this, please answer immediately, telling the courier to bring it in haste.

Respectfully,

JOHN M. HARLAN,
Colonel, Commanding Brigade.

—

CAMP AT CASTALIAN SPRINGS,
December 4, 1862.

CAPTAIN : On the night of the 28th November, I transmitted to the division commander, in a brief note, all the facts of which I was then in possession in reference to the capture, on that day, near Hartsville, by Morgan's rebel cavalry, of a part of the train of the Second Indiana Cavalry, together with an officer and some of the soldiers of that regiment. I also advised the division commander of the recapture, on the same day, by Major Hill, commanding the Second Indiana Cavalry, of the larger portion of his train. Being uninformed at that time of all the circumstances connected with the capture and recapture of the train, I requested Lieut. Col. W. H. Hays, of the Tenth Kentucky Infantry, he being in command of the detachment from this brigade then on duty at Hartsville, composed of the Tenth Indiana Volunteers, Lieutenant-Colonel Carroll, Tenth Kentucky Volunteers, and Southwick's battery, as well as of the Second Indiana Cavalry, then temporarily attached to my command, to obtain from Major Hill a detailed report of all the facts. Major Hill made that report to me promptly, and forwarded it to my headquarters at this place, but by some accident it was not handed to me until this morning.

Although several days have elapsed, I deem it due to Major Hill and his command that I shall make known in an official form and to the proper authorities all the facts connected with the affair of November 28, as detailed by him. I do this the more readily as I learn that some one—I do not know whom—has made a report, which has reached department headquarters, in reference to this matter. But as I am unadvised as to whether that report does full justice to Major Hill and his command, I owe it to them to submit the following, based upon Major Hill's report to me.

On the morning of the 28th, a forage train, consisting of 10 wagons, was sent from the Second Indiana Cavalry, under an armed escort of 40 men, in charge of Lieutenant Brush, Company H, an escort which would seem sufficient, and which, if properly handled, would have proven itself sufficient. When the train reached a point about 2 miles east of Hartsville, on the Carthage road, it was attacked both in front and rear by rebel cavalry. The train was surrendered without any resistance whatever on the part of the escort, nearly the whole of whom fell into the hands of the enemy. The few who then escaped returned to camp and advised Major Hill of what had occurred.

Major Hill immediately ordered out his command, and proceeded with all dispatch to the point designated, where he found, as he states, infantry and cavalry drawn up in line of battle. Major Hill states that, although he knew of the vicinity of Colonel Scott's brigade, Dumont's division, which was *en route* to relieve the detachment from my brigade at Hartsville, he could not reconcile Colonel Scott's presence with the capture of his train, and, hence, he was delayed for an hour in ascertaining who he was. As soon as he ascertained that the force which he saw was Colonel Scott's command, he resumed the pursuit of the rebel cavalry, and carried it on with vigor, taking several prisoners. He met with no resistance until he reached the Cumberland River, in the vicinity of Rome. At that point his passage was disputed with considerable resoluteness. As soon, however, as he reached the opposite bank, the enemy who composed the rear guard fled in dismay, and were not rallied until they came to the camp of the rebel Colonel Bennett, where, in conjunction with his command, they were disposed to make a stand. Major Hill halted his advance, and awaited the coming up of more of his men; but, perceiving that the enemy were becoming bolder, and the fire too warm to be comfortable, he ordered a charge, having at that time only 90 men, the remainder not being able to keep up in the rapid pursuit which he had given the rebels. On sounding the charge, Bennett's men became confused, and as his (Hill's) men opened fire upon them with pistols, broke ranks, totally disorganizing those who had come to their camp for protection. In crossing a bridge in rear of Bennett's camp, the enemy crowded together so as to blockade it. Hill's skirmishers, dismounting, opened fire with capital execution. Immediately on passing the bridge the force which was in camp dispersed, when Hill, pushing those who remained in the road, succeeded in recapturing 7 of his wagons and 8 of his men, who had been taken with the teams. Major Hill followed on for 12 miles south of the ford at Rome, where, the enemy having been re-enforced, he discontinued the pursuit, bringing off the recaptured property. He also captured a wagon belonging to Colonel Bennett.

Major Hill reports the following casualties, viz: Three men of Company H, names unknown, killed while prisoners; 1 lieutenant and 36 men missing at the date of the report.

Major Hill reports that the capture of the train, in his opinion, is attributable to the gross carelessness of Lieutenant Brush, commanding the train guard.

The loss of the enemy was heavy when it is considered that they had a great advantage over Major Hill, both in numbers and position, and were enabled to increase the distance between him and them by reason of the delay already referred to. As the statements are so conflicting as to the number of rebels killed, Major Hill makes no report upon that point beyond what his own personal observation authorizes him to state. He saw 12 dead rebels in the road.

Major Hill concludes:

I have to return my thanks to you for the very valuable services rendered me by a lieutenant of your command; I have unfortunately forgotten his name. Capt. D. A. Briggs conducted the extreme advance with great credit to himself; but, in mentioning him, I will add that all the 138 men who followed beyond the Cumberland River deserve honorable mention for their alacrity in the pursuit.

I take great pleasure in stating that the name of the officer in my brigade to whom Major Hill refers is Lieut. D. F. Allen, Company C, Tenth Indiana Volunteers. I learn from several sources that his conduct was most commendable.

The daring exhibited by Major Hill and his gallant little band in pursuing a superior enemy beyond the Cumberland for several miles, nearly 18 or 20 miles from their camp at Hartsville, and the desperate fierceness with which they charged the enemy, recapturing and bringing back to camp nearly their entire train during the night of the same day on which they were taken, reflect the highest credit upon them, and deserves, as it will no doubt receive, the favorable notice of the commanding general of the department. Their conduct in these respects is worthy of general emulation.

Respectfully,

JOHN M. HARLAN,
Colonel, Commanding Second Brigade.

Capt. ED. C. DENIG,
Acting Assistant Adjutant-General.

—

SPECIAL FIELD ORDERS, ⎱ HDQRS. FOURTEENTH ARMY CORPS,
⎰ DEPARTMENT OF THE CUMBERLAND,
No. 5. ⎰ *Nashville, November 30, 1862.*

* * * * * * *

VII. The general commanding has learned with much satisfaction of the good conduct and energy displayed by a detachment of the Second Indiana Cavalry, under Major Hill, in pursuing a party of 200 of the enemy's cavalry, killing some 15 or 20 of them, and retaking the greater part of a Government train just captured by them through the carelessness of one of our foraging parties. This little affair is very creditable to the cavalry, and the general commanding takes pleasure in noticing it.

By command of Major-General Rosecrans:

C. GODDARD,
Major and Acting Assistant Adjutant-General.

———

NOVEMBER 29–DECEMBER 1, 1862.—Reconnaissance from Stewart's Ferry, Stone's River, to Baird's Mills, Tenn., and skirmishes en route.

REPORTS.

No. 1.—Brig. Gen. James D. Morgan, U. S. Army.
No. 2.—Col. Silas C. Toler, Sixtieth Illinois Infantry.

No. 1.

Reports of Brig. Gen. James D. Morgan, U. S. Army.

HDQRS. SECOND BRIG., SEVENTH DIV., 14TH ARMY CORPS,
Stone's River, Tenn., December 2, 1862.

CAPTAIN: The two regiments from my command ordered forward Saturday returned last evening. They went to Baird's Mills, about 17 miles to the front; had some skirmishing with the enemy's pickets, but met with no large force. Twelve prisoners were taken, 5 horses and 1 mule, 5 revolvers, 2 double-barreled shot-guns, 1 rifle, buggy, and harness. The prisoners were sent to Nashville this morning.

Very respectfully, your obedient servant,

JAMES D. MORGAN,
Brigadier-General, Commanding.

Captain CONNER,
Assistant Adjutant-General, Seventh Division.

—

HDQRS. SECOND BRIG., FIRST DIV., ARMY OF THE MISS.,
Stone's River, Tenn., November 30, 1862.

MAJOR: In compliance with instructions from the general commanding Fourteenth Army Corps, two regiments from my brigade, the Sixtieth Illinois and Tenth Michigan, Colonel Toler, of the Sixtieth Illinois, commanding, left camp at 2 o'clock p. m., on the new pike, with orders to proceed to Baird's Mills and Rural Hill, and examine the roads and country, and, if they met the enemy, to whip them.

At 4 p. m. three regiments of cavalry, under the command of Colonel Milliken, passed through my lines on the Lebanon road. I advised the colonel to send a battalion of his command out on the Statesville road, and by so doing the whole of the country to the left of the Murfreesborough pike would be covered. The colonel's instructions prevented his doing so. I inclose a rough draft of the roads named.

A scouting party of 25 mounted infantry, under the command of Captain Powell, was sent out on the Statesville road yesterday. They met a party of guerrillas about 7 miles out, drove in their advance, taking 2 rifles and 1 horse. The main body was found strongly posted on the opposite side of a creek, and in number three or four to one. The captain thought it advisable not to attack them, his command being poorly armed.

The work on the bridges progressing slowly; will be ready in a few days for planking.

Very respectfully,

JAMES D. MORGAN,
Brigadier-General, Commanding.

Major GARESCHÉ, *Chief of Staff.*

———

No. 2.

Report of Col. Silas C. Toler, Sixtieth Illinois Infantry.

HDQRS. SIXTIETH REGT. ILLINOIS VOL. INFANTRY,
Camp on Stone's River, December 2, 1862.

LIEUTENANT: In accordance with orders of November 29, we moved on Central or Rock River pike, and bivouacked for the night at Widow Hays' spring, 5 miles from Rock River. At daylight next morning marched on the same road to Gallatin and La Vergne road; changed direction to the right on that road to Chicken road or old Central pike, on which we moved to Baird's Mills, reaching there about 1.30 p. m., and bivouacked for the night. The Central pike is macadamized, but very rough country, broken and hilly, but no serious obstructions which would serve to impede or delay the march of any considerable number of troops. The Gallatin and La Vergne road is narrow and rough, and crossed frequently by neighborhood roads. We struck the Chicken road about 1 mile east of Rural Hill and 8 miles from Baird's Mills, and changed direction to the left on Chicken road, passing through Glades-ville, 3 miles on. The Statesville road strikes off to the right from the Chicken road 3 miles from Baird's Mills. The Chicken road is a good dirt road, with but few neighborhood crossings.

Small squads of rebel cavalry are continually crossing through the country between Rural Hill and Baird's Mills. At Baird's Mills we were joined by Colonel Milliken's command of cavalry. We were menaced by small squads of rebel cavalry at different points, and at Baird's Mills they appeared in some considerable force on the Murfreesborough and Lebanon pike. After a sharp skirmish, they retired in the direction of Murfreesborough. They were Morgan's men. He is encamped at Black's Shop, 9 miles from Baird's Mills, toward Murfreesborough. His force is said to be 3,000 men, mostly mounted, and three pieces of artil-lery. We captured some of the enemy's pickets. We captured 12 pris-oners, 1 mule, 5 horses, 1 buggy, 4 saddles and bridles, 3 double and 1 single barrel shot-guns, 1 Yager rifle, and 5 revolvers.

We left Baird's Mills at 7 o'clock a. m. of December 1, and returned to camp, passing over the same route we went out. Nothing of interest occurred on our way back. Officers and men under my command be-haved well, and deserve credit for good discipline and order during the march.

Very respectfully,

S. C. TOLER,
Colonel, Commanding Expedition.

Lieut. THEO. WISEMAN,
Acting Assistant Adjutant-General.

DECEMBER 1, 1862.—Skirmish near Nolensville, Tenn.

Report of Brig. Gen. John A. Wharton, C. S. Army, commanding Cavalry Brigade.

HEADQUARTERS CAVALRY BRIGADE,
Nolensville, Tenn., December 1, 1862—5 p. m.

GENERAL: * * * I had a skirmish with the enemy to-day, and my battery drove them from their position very quickly.

*   *   *   *   *   *   *

Very respectfully, your obedient servant,

JNO. A. WHARTON,
Brigadier-General, Commanding.

Lieutenant-General [L.] POLK, &c.

DECEMBER 3, 1862.—Attack on Union forage train on the Hardin pike, near Nashville, Tenn.

Report of Col. George W. Roberts, Forty-second Illinois Infantry.

HDQRS. ROBERTS' BRIG., 11TH DIV., 14TH ARMY CORPS,
Camp Sheridan, December 21, 1862.

MAJOR: I have the honor to report in the cases of Brigade Quarter-master D. B. Sears, Regimental Quartermaster S. B. Hood, and Lieut. O. A. Clark, formerly of my command, but now prisoners of war, that on the 3d day of December, 1862, they were on duty in attendance with a forage train from my brigade, under command of Lieutenant-Colonel

Walworth, which proceeded 10 miles on the Hardin pike, then turned to the left and loaded, about 3 miles from said pike.   Before starting, I placed General Orders, No. 17, in the hands of Quartermaster Sears, and enjoined strict obedience in regard to all points, and specified particularly the receipting for property.   I learn from direct testimony that Quartermaster Sears was very active to see that all the wagons were well loaded; that the exact number was ascertained, and that he then insisted that Quartermaster Hood, of the Twenty-second Illinois, Forage-master Bruce, of General Palmer's division train, and Lieut. O. A. Clark should go with him to the house of the proprietor and receipt. They went.   The house was distant (as I am informed) from the guard of the rear of the train about 300 yards.

Quartermaster Sears did not ask for a personal guard; in fact, as he says, did not think of it.   While Quartermaster Sears was receipting, the others were invited to take dinner, which they did.   Before Quartermaster Sears had completed his receipts, a force of Texan Rangers, of about 200, began firing on the train and escort.   Bruce, who was first out of the house, mounted his horse, and escaped with a ball through his coat and another in the hip of his horse.   The other officers, seeing the Rangers between them and the train, remained at the house, and were taken.

The Rangers charged on Sergeant Huerson, of Company E, Forty-second Regiment Illinois Volunteers, and 17 men, of same regiment, who were posted as a lookout or vedette.   But the sergeant formed his men, and fired into them by volley, advanced on them, still firing, dared them to come on, and completely drove them back.   The Rangers wounded 8 mules, and Quartermaster Sears states that they declared that if it had not been for the "little major," as they called the sergeant, they would have captured part of the train.

I think that Herson deserves notice.   He has been with me in several close matters, and is brave beyond question.   I sent forward a recommendation for his promotion, but it is returned, refused.

Respectfully, your obedient servant,
G. W. ROBERTS,
Colonel, Commanding.

Major SIDELL,
Acting Assistant Adjutant-General.

DECEMBER 4, 1862.—Skirmish on the Franklin pike, near Holly Tree Gap, Tenn.

Report of Col. Robert H. G. Minty, Fourth Michigan Cavalry.

HEADQUARTERS FOURTH MICHIGAN CAVALRY,
Camp Rosecrans, Tenn., December 4, 1862.

SIR: I have the honor to hand you the following report of my scout on the Franklin pike this day:

At 7.30 a. m. I marched, with 302 officers and men.   When 8 miles from Nashville, I met the enemy's pickets, which were driven, by Companies I and L, as far as the junction of the Wilson Creek and Franklin pikes (9 miles from Nashville), and then some 2 miles down the Wilson Creek pike.   Here I recalled the two companies, and, leaving D company at the junction, moved forward on the Franklin pike.   About 2 miles out, we again met the enemy's pickets (about 70 men), and drove them before us through Holly Tree Gap (6 miles from the junction), and to within about 1 mile from Franklin. No obstruction of any kind has been placed in the gap, which is naturally one of the strongest positions I have ever seen.

Two bridges have been destroyed on the road, one about 3 miles north of the gap, the other about $2\frac{1}{2}$ miles south. Wagons can pass both by taking the fields east.

One of the rebels was wounded by a carbine ball in left shoulder. We met with no loss. I returned to camp at 8 o'clock p. m., having ridden about 45 miles.

I am, respectfully, your obedient servant,
ROBT. H. G. MINTY,
Colonel, Commanding.

Lieutenant CHAMBERLAIN,
Acting Assistant Adjutant-General, First Cavalry Division.

DECEMBER 4, 1862.—Capture of outpost near Stewart's Ferry (or Ford), Stone's River, Tenn.

REPORTS.

No. 1.—Brig. Gen. James D. Morgan, U. S. Army.
No. 2.—Maj. D. W. Holman, C. S. Army.

No. 1.

Report of Brig. Gen. James D. Morgan, U. S. Army.

HDQRS. SECOND BRIG., FIRST DIV., ARMY OF THE MISS.,
Stone's River, Tenn., December 4, 1862.

COLONEL : This morning about 3 o'clock a sergeant and 9 men of Captain Powell's company mounted scouts, stationed at Stewart's Ford, $2\frac{1}{2}$ miles on our right, were attacked by a mounted force of the enemy of about 60 men. All of our men succeeded in making their escape, with their arms and accouterments, but with the loss of their horses. Two were wounded, 1 severely. The enemy made their approach upon our right from the direction of the Murfreesborough pike. I have no cavalry to cover my flank in that direction. I had supposed that vedettes were stationed from the Murfreesborough pike toward my right.

I sent out yesterday a foraging party about 4 miles to the front, on the Lebanon pike; 2 men were taken, 1 a mounted scout of Captain Powell's company, and a teamster; they were paroled and returned to camp almost as soon as the train. I returned them to duty, ignoring the paroles, and with orders that they be charged with the arms lost.

Very respectfully, your obedient servant,
JAMES D. MORGAN,
Brigadier-General, Commanding.

Col. J. P. GARESCHÉ.

No. 2.

Report of Maj. D. W. Holman, C. S. Army.

CAMP NEAR LA VERGNE, TENN.,
December 4, 1862.

CAPTAIN : I have the honor to report that, with the approval of the brigadier-general commanding, I left my encampment near Stone's River about 12 o'clock last night with 50 men, a part of Captain [J. T.] Martin's company, of my battalion, and proceeded in the direction of Stewart's Ferry, on Stone's River, 12 miles distant, for the purpose of capturing some of the enemy's pickets. By traveling obscure roads and recrossing Stone's River about 1½ miles above Stewart's Ferry, we came in between the enemy's main force at McWhirtersville [Donelson] and Stewart's Ferry. When within a quarter of a mile of the pickets, I dismounted 20 men, and sent them 300 yards ahead, and ordered them to proceed noiselessly to the place, first ordering them to surrender, and, if they refused, to fire. A part of the mounted men under Captain Martin, and the balance under Lieutenants [T.] Banks and [A. S.] Chapman, were so disposed on either side of the road as to catch any who might attempt to make their way to the main force. Sergeant [J. M.] Critz, who commanded the squad of dismounted men, when within 15 steps of the reserve, ordered them to surrender. They refused, and one of them fired. Immediately my 20 men fired; 1 lieutenant and 2 privates were left dead upon the spot. I think the whole reserve (9 men) were either killed or wounded; but the cedar undergrowth was so very thick that we did not see them, nor could not, without carefully searching, which we did not have time to do. Three horses were killed, and we captured 6, with bridles, saddles, &c., 2 excellent Belgian guns, 1 pistol, several India-rubber coats, &c. The two vedettes, who were some distance from the reserve, made their escape through the bushes, and we did not have time to pursue them. Being within 1 mile or less of a large force, I thought it but prudent to move away at once, and with as much rapidity as practicable. At sunrise this morning I got back to my camp without the loss of a man, horse, or anything else.

I must be permitted to commend the coolness and gallantry of Captain Martin, Lieutenants Banks and Chapman, and Sergeant Critz. I cannot mention the names of privates, but they all did their duty, and nobly.

I am, captain, very respectfully, your obedient servant,

D. W. HOLMAN,
Major, Commanding.

Capt. D. G. REED, *Assistant Adjutant-General.*

DECEMBER 4-5, 1862.—Capture of transports, and skirmishes near Prestonburg, Ky.

REPORTS.*

No. 1.--Col. Jonathan Cranor, Fortieth Ohio Infantry.
No. 2.--Col. John N. Clarkson, Virginia State Line Cavalry.

No. 1.

Report of Col. Jonathan Cranor, Fortieth Ohio Infantry.

HDQRS. DIST. E. KY., *Louisa, December 8, 1862.*

MAJOR: I have the honor to submit to you the following report:

On the morning of the 3d [4th] instant, an engagement took place between about 200 of the Thirty-ninth Kentucky, who were guarding some push-boats which were loaded with commissary and quartermaster stores for the Thirty-ninth, and were *en route* for Piketon, and about

---

* See also Floyd to Letcher, Series I, Vol. XXI, p. 1065.

800 rebels, mostly mounted, under command of Colonel Clarkson. The engagement took place about 4 miles below Prestonburg.

The enemy succeeded in capturing the boats, not, however, until after 14 or 15 of them had been killed, and they had killed 2 of the Thirty-ninth. They took away and destroyed from 50 to 100 stand of arms, about 300 suits of fatigue uniforms, 7,000 rounds of ammunition, a small lot of commissaries, 1 tent, and 2 push-boats. A considerable portion of the articles with which the boats were loaded have since been recovered, the enemy in his hurry not taking time to destroy them. The boats were loaded at Catlettsburg by the assistant quartermaster of the Thirty-ninth, by orders of Colonel Dils, without my knowledge or consent. I was not aware that they contained either arms or clothing until since their capture. Learning after they had started that there was a possibility that they might be captured, after they reached this point (which took seven days), I sent a guard with them from here to Peach Orchard, at which point they said Colonel Dils was to send a guard to meet them. I sent a company of cavalry, with instruction to scout the surrounding country, especially toward Logan, Va., to ascertain if there was any danger. I ordered them to guard the boats beyond Peach Orchard, or until they should meet the guards sent by Colonel Dils, which they did, when they returned, and reported no enemy in striking distance.

Information was afterward received that an effort would be made to capture them, which was communicated to the adjutant and quartermaster who were in charge, and they advised to drop back to Peach Orchard, and there await Colonel Dils' arrival; after which they received an order from Colonel Dils, stating to them that he was in daily communication with the country through which they would have to pass; that there was no danger, and for them to press ahead as fast as possible. Owing to the low stage of water, they were unable to make more than 4 or 5 miles per day.

Colonel Dils' regiment, as you are aware, is as yet unorganized. He claims that he is independent, and not subject to any authority, except the military powers of Kentucky.

As soon as I heard of the capture, I started out 350 cavalry to pursue them, if possible to form a junction with the forces of Colonel Dils, and drive them out or give them battle. I have not yet heard from the cavalry, but learn that Colonel Dils, with most of his command, is at Paintsville, and will fall back to Peach Orchard.

Owing to the scarcity of forage and the difficulty of getting supplies, I have yet brought only a part of my force to this point. I have not cavalry sufficient to do that amount of scouting which seems to be necessary in this district.

I have the honor to be, very respectfully, your obedient servant,

J. CRANOR,
Colonel, Commanding District of Eastern Kentucky.

Maj. N. H. McLEAN,
Assistant Adjutant-General, Department of the Ohio.

No. 2.

Report of Col. John N. Clarkson, Virginia State Line Cavalry.

HDQRS. FIRST BRIGADE, VIRGINIA STATE LINE,
Camp at Mouth of Pond Creek, Pike Co., Ky., December 7, 1862.

SIR: In obedience to your instructions, I proceeded with my command, composed of detachments of the First, Second, and Third Regiments, on the 3d ultimo, in the direction of Pike County, Kentucky, and early on the following morning reached Prestonburg. At that place I was informed that several boats were on their route up the Sandy River, loaded with large supplies of ammunition and clothing intended for the troops stationed at Piketon, and that on the previous night they had stopped a short distance below the town. Without delay, I moved the column down the banks of the river, and discovered nine boats, attended by a strong guard, in readiness to receive my attack. The information of our approach had been carried before us by a Union man in that vicinity. After a spirited contest of an hour's duration, we succeeded in dislodging the enemy, numbering about 300 men, and utterly routed them.

In the fight we lost 2 men killed and 7 wounded. The loss of the enemy was at least 25 killed and about the same number wounded, besides 25 prisoners, which we have with us.

Our capture proved exceedingly valuable, consisting of a large number of Enfield rifles (500) and ammunition, with all the accouterments necessary for 800 or 1,000 men. It gave us sufficient clothing of every description to thoroughly equip the greater portion of the force under my command. The supply of sugar, coffee, and salt was large, and was nearly all brought off by the men. The men having appropriated all they desired or needed of the plunder, the boats were destroyed. The value of the captured property can safely be estimated at $250,000.

I am grieved to state that Captains Kessler and Findlay were painfully, though not dangerously, wounded. They are able, however, to be conveyed with us, and shall not be left to fall into the hands of the enemy. Lieutenant Levi Hampton was killed on the side of the enemy. Hearing that a regiment was stationed at Piketon, I directed my course on the evening of the same day toward that place, with the purpose of disbanding this force.

Colonel Dils, the commandant of the post, had received intelligence of our presence in the country, and we encountered him during the night on the road between Prestonburg and Piketon with a heavy force. A sharp skirmish ensued, in which the enemy were completely dispersed, with the reported loss of Colonel Dils. This report, though coming through his own officers, is not entirely credited. Here one of our men was killed instantly and two others wounded. At Piketon we met with no resistance, and captured there and in that vicinity about 25 prisoners. We used and destroyed the stores left at that point, and proceeded directly to this place, the mouth of Pond Creek, which we reached yesterday afternoon.

In the space of three days we have made a tour of not less than 140 miles through the enemy's country, over rugged pathways and roads; and, besides the captures above stated, we have brought off about 100 cattle, more than 150 horses, and many negroes. The population loyal to the South have been reassured of our capacity to protect them, and many have joined our standard. A feeling of uneasiness and unsafety has been diffused among our enemies and those friendly to their cause. The organization of the enemy has been for the time destroyed, and the route for our friends to come to us is left open and unimpeded by the foe. I am gratified to be able to state that the men, in spite of long and tedious marches, in spite of privation and chilling weather, have displayed a spirit and determination worthy of high commendation.

The officers in battle and on the march have conducted themselves in a praiseworthy manner.

By order of Col. John N. Clarkson, commanding First Brigade, Virginia State Line.

I am, very respectfully, your obedient servant,

M. WOODS,
Acting Assistant Adjutant-General.

Maj. Gen. J. B. FLOYD.

DECEMBER 6, 1862.—Skirmish near Kimbrough's Mill, Mill Creek, Tenn.

REPORTS.

No. 1.—Brig. Gen. Joshua W. Sill, U. S. Army.
No. 2.—Col. Harvey M. Buckley, Fifth Kentucky Infantry, commanding brigade.
No. 3.—Col. Charles Anderson, Ninety-third Ohio Infantry.
No. 4.—Lieut. Col. Milton Barnes, Ninety-seventh Ohio Infantry.
No. 5.—Capt. T. R. Palmer, inspector First Division, Twenty-first Army Corps.

No. 1.

Report of Brig. Gen. Joshua W. Sill, U. S. Army.

CAMP MILL CREEK, *December* 6, 1862—7 p. m.

GENERAL: Our forage train was attacked by cavalry and artillery to-day. I presume it was Wheeler's command. We had 1 man killed and 2 wounded. The enemy captured 8 of the wagons of Hascall's division, which were out on the same road. Will send you written report to-morrow morning.

J. W. SILL,
Brigadier-General.

General McCOOK.

No. 2.

Report of Col. Harvey M. Buckley, Fifth Kentucky Infantry, commanding brigade.

HEADQUARTERS FOURTH BRIGADE,
December 7, 1862.

CAPTAIN: The following is a brief statement of the skirmish on yesterday, between the enemy and the guard of forage train:

I left camp in command of the First Ohio, Ninety-third Ohio, and Fifth Kentucky, and two sections of Battery H. Arrived at the point indicated by forage-master to fill the train about noon of yesterday, which place is about 7 miles from this camp. We discovered the enemy about one-half mile in front of us, numbering about 15 or 20 mounted men. Lieutenant Ludlow, of battery, brought his gun to bear upon them, and fired two shots, after which they disappeared. I then ordered the First Ohio to the front and right to protect the wagons, which were gathering forage near Kimbrough's Mill. The Fifth Kentucky was thrown to the front, and left to protect the wagons foraging near Ham's house. The Third Indiana Cavalry, of two companies, under Captain Vanosdol, were ordered to the front, and here I would say that no men could have behaved better than those two companies, nor could any one have maneuvered them to better advantage than the captain in command. We had arrived upon the ground but a very short time before we were attacked to the front and left, for particulars of which I refer you to Colonel Barnes' report, forwarded herewith. Having filled as many wagons as we could without bringing the train into camp after night, I ordered the two sections of artillery in advance of the train, and the First Ohio immediately in advance of the artillery. Hearing at this time pretty heavy firing of cannon in front, the Fifth Kentucky was ordered forward in rear of the First Ohio and the artillery, the Ninety-third Ohio having been left in the rear to protect the train, as well as the Ninety-seventh Ohio and Captain Vanosdol's cavalry. We had proceeded but a short distance toward camp before we discovered the enemy drawn up in pretty strong force before us. I ordered up one piece of artillery, and opened fire upon them. We were answered by artillery, but they soon gave way, upon which we proceeded on to camp, arriving there near sundown.

As to what happened in our rear about the time of our leaving for camp, I refer you to Colonel Anderson's report, who had command of the rear guard. As to the part taken by the First Ohio, I would refer you to report of Major Stafford, filed herewith.* One of my escort is missing; another had his horse wounded.

The conduct of the men and officers engaged would have satisfied the most exacting. I am indebted to my aide, Lieutenant Harman, of the Ninety-third Ohio, for his energy and promptness in carrying all orders. The only loss from the train of this division is one wagon of the battery, which was destroyed by ourselves, the mules having become unruly and broken the tongue.

H. M. BUCKLEY,
Colonel, Commanding Fourth Brigade.

Captain STEARNS.

No. 3.

Report of Col. Charles Anderson, Ninety-third Ohio Infantry.

CAMP NEAR NASHVILLE, *December* 6, 1862.

SIR: In obedience to your order to take charge of the defense of the rear of the forage train, I halted my command this evening at about 3 o'clock parallel with, and close to, its rear. Whilst waiting in this position for the trains to move on, upon the top of the hill, a little west of the Franklin and Lebanon road, and southwest from the house of Mr. Ham, and above that of ———, I saw a number of the enemy, on foot, and led by three horsemen, rushing down the valley which lies to the north of my position, in a westerly direction. They made great clamor by shouting, and their purpose evidently was to intercept the train in its march homeward upon the slope of the hill, and at the bend of the road as it enters into the valley. I immediately ordered my regiment to

---

* Not found.

march in double-quick time through certain gaps and gates upon the eastern side of, and close to, the road, which was then filled with our wagons. My purpose was, having slight advantage in distance as well as in the declivities of the hill, to make the same point before them, and to cut them off from any attack on my charge. In this effort I succeeded, but not in sufficient time to prevent them spreading themselves in most favorable ground and shelter before my regiment could ensconse itself behind the fence which I desired as a cover. After a volley from Company F, Company A having been detached in support of a battery in advance, a rapid and irregular fire now ensued throughout both bodies of combatants. This lasted until, apparently, being satisfied that the Ninety-third Regiment could not be moved from its position, and, consequently, that they could not succeed in the purpose of their ambuscade and assault, they fled precipitately and universally as far up the valley as we could see.

Our loss in this action was but 1 killed and 3 wounded. Considering the closeness of the range, the deliberateness and duration of the enemy's fire, and the almost rash exposure of several of my companies, these casualties are strangely small in number. What injury was inflicted upon the enemy I cannot undertake to say, and will not guess. Neither will I, in my inexperience in such matters, profess to estimate his numbers. They certainly seemed to be largely in excess of our own, and the whole command of the expedition was, in my opinion, surrounded on all sides by large numbers of our foes. It greatly delights me to speak in high and earnest praise of the gallantry and firmness of this new regiment in this its first fight. Every officer and man seemed resolved to do his best, and where all have so well succeeded in that noble effort it might be invidious to distinguish by name particular persons. Notwithstanding my disposition to regard that restraint upon special praises, I feel myself compelled to specify two instances of marked courage and pertinacious bravery. The one was that of William Gosshorn, fourth corporal in Company F, and the other that of William C. Stewart, private Company C, acting color-bearer. The former, after being painfully wounded in the thigh by one of the first rounds of the engagement, deliberately went into line and loaded and fired at the enemy seven or eight times. The latter, in this his first battle, stood out in front of his company, and of the regiment, with his tall figure and ever-glorious banner elevated to their highest reach, nor could he be persuaded to bend his person, nor to lower his colors.

In conclusion, perhaps overrating the merits of my regiment and the importance of its conduct, I feel free to say, in justice to its men and officers, that I think any less merit than that shown in this fight would have probably lost us our entire train, and it seems to me, now, that this attack, at this time and place, was preconcerted, together with various feints elsewhere, to accomplish that special object. Vanity or undue partiality to my own men may mislead me in this opinion; if so, I can only offer the apology that the error is as natural as it is frank.

All of which is respectfully submitted.

CHARLES ANDERSON,
Colonel Ninety-third Regiment Ohio Volunteer Infantry.

Capt. WILLIAM MANGAN,
Acting Assistant Adjutant-General.

No. 4.

Report of Lieut. Col. Milton Barnes, Ninety-seventh Ohio Infantry.

HDQRS. NINETY-SEVENTH REGT. OHIO VOL. INFANTRY,
December 6, 1862.

COLONEL: In compliance with your order to report the part taken by the Ninety-seventh Regiment as escort for the forage train in our encounter with the enemy this day, and the result, I have the honor to report the following, viz:

Under your instructions, I proceeded with the regiment, in charge of the Twenty-first Brigade train, to the outposts of General Sill's division, where I found a train on the route from that division with an escort of three regiments, commanded by Colonel Buckley. He informed me that it would not be safe to venture out beyond with one regiment only, and suggested that I should accompany him, and unite our forces, which I did, and reported to him for orders. I proceeded, following in the rear of his train to a point about 2 miles beyond a brick church, on the railroad. Here the whole train had halted. I had previously thrown three companies to the rear of our own brigade train, and the quartermaster in charge had reported the train all right. I then went forward, after heavy firing in the advance, and met Colonel Buckley, who immediately ordered me forward, with five companies of my command, to support the Louisville Legion, which I did, taking with me the remaining two also. I formed in order of battle in the rear of that regiment, and deployed one company (Company E, Captain Egan) to the left. This company advanced as skirmishers until they reached the brow of the hill on the left, bearing to the front through a piece of woods into an open field, where they discovered the enemy in force, mounted. Several rounds were fired by them and several from the enemy, which, overreaching them, took effect in the battle-line of the regiment, resulting in the death of 1 man and the slight wounding of another. I then moved across the ravine through the woods to the support of my skirmishers, and gained a position under the brow of the hill, and discovered there a large body of rebel cavalry, retreating and bearing around to the right, at a distance beyond the range of musketry. Considerable firing was now heard on our right and in our rear, and I saw the Louisville Legion retreating back the road toward the train. I awaited orders, but receiving none, I moved slowly back to where I had first left the train, which still remained there, but Colonel Buckley had gone back some distance toward the railroad, with a portion of his forces and battery, and I suppose was engaging a rebel battery which I learned had been planted in our rear, and was attempting to cut off our retreat. By this time it became evident that we were almost, if not quite, surrounded, and would have to cut our way through. The train I found was moving rapidly to the rear. In the mean time I had received no orders what to do. I agreed with Colonel Anderson, of the Ninety-third Ohio Volunteers, to take the left and he the right of the road and between us preserve the train. Here was a curve in road to the left, around a hill. I proceeded across the curve to intersect the road again. While doing so, a furious charge was made upon the train from the right by a regiment of rebel infantry and of cavalry from the woods on the opposite side of the hill, but Colonel Anderson coming up promptly, they gave way. I was moving rapidly in that direction, when I received an order from Colonel Buckley to form in order of battle on the right of the road, and move to the front to support the battery, which I did, the train still moving on in that direction.

When I came in sight of the enemy, they were retreating in all directions, and we passed safely through. My loss in men was 1 killed and 1 wounded. The Twenty-first Brigade train, the only one I was authorized to guard, came safely into camp. Several teams belonging to the Sixth Division, variously estimated at 6, 12, and 14, were reported as having been captured while out foraging on their own account without a guard, but I know nothing of this officially. The loss to the train was only 2 mules shot.

I have the honor to remain, colonel, your obedient servant,

M. BARNES,
Lieut. Col. Ninety-seventh Regt. Ohio Volunteer Infantry.

Colonel WAGNER,
Commanding Twenty-first Brigad

No. 5.

Report of Capt. T. R. Palmer, Inspector First Division, Twenty-first Army Corps.

HDQRS. FIRST DIVISION, TWENTY-FIRST ARMY CORPS,
February 2, 1863.

CAPTAIN: In compliance with your order, I have investigated the facts connected with the loss of certain wagons from a forage train of this division, December 6, 1862, and respectfully present the following report:

At the time when the capture took place, General Orders, No. 30, had not been received, and foraging was done by brigades. This was not the result of any order, general or special, but simply a custom for the time being. It was not customary, however, for these brigade trains to be composed exclusively of wagons from a single brigade. With each brigade train were sent out foraging wagons from division headquarters, from the ammunition train, and from the general supply train. Besides this, if, as frequently occurred, especially with the batteries, either of the other brigades had not forage enough to last until its regular time for foraging should arrive, teams enough were sent from them to obtain a supply. It was not customary in such cases to send additional escort with such surplus wagons, but only sufficient men to load them, and all the wagons were regarded as one train under the same escort, equally entitled to the protection of the escort. So completely did all constitute one train, that the brigade quartermaster in charge of the train would generally receipt for the forage obtained by these extra wagons, and arrange accounts with the other quartermasters on his return.

On December 2, four days previous to the capture, the Fifteenth Brigade forage train had taken with it several wagons of the Twenty-first Brigade without any additional escort, and Lieutenant Sterne, quartermaster, Fifteenth Brigade, had receipted for the forage obtained by those wagons. That train had also obtained part of its forage in the same fields where the wagons were captured December 6. What wagons, and how many, should be allowed to any brigade train was regulated by the division quartermaster, Capt. L. D. Myers.

Lieutenant-Colonel Barnes, Ninety-seventh Ohio, who commanded the escort, evidently regarded himself as in charge only of the wagons of the Twenty-first Brigade. He is a man whose veracity and honor as a gentleman are above suspicion, but after careful examination I am satisfied that, according to custom and general understanding, all the wagons were equally under his protection.

Neither did the size of the train make any unusual escort necessary. There were at that time five regiments in the Fifteenth and Twentieth Brigades of this division, and their forage trains usually numbered from 70 to 90 wagons. The Twenty-first Brigade had then but four regiments, and on that day had only about 60 wagons in the forage train, including those of the Fifteenth Brigade.

During the advance of the train no distinction was made by Lieutenant-Colonel Barnes between the wagons properly belonging to the Twenty-first Brigade and others. His regiment marched in a body in front of the entire train. Six wagons from division headquarters led the train; several ammunition wagons (not considered as belonging to any brigade) were in the train. The wagons of the Fifteenth Brigade were in the rear simply because it was the most convenient place for them to file in with the train as it started. After passing the camp of General Sill's division, two pieces of artillery followed the train, showing that the wagons of the Fifteenth Brigade were considered part of the train and under the escort. Up to this time, December 6, it was not known that any train had been attacked, nor had the enemy indicated his presence. As Lieutenant-Colonel Barnes came to General Sill's division, he was told that a reconnaissance had discovered the enemy in front, and he was advised to unite his train with General Sill's, just starting. This was done, General Sill's train taking the advance.

Upon arriving where forage could be obtained, according to custom, the forage-master estimated how many wagons could be filled, and detached them from the rear. These 15 wagons filed to the right and left into corn-fields; that on the left adjoining the road, that on the right only separated from the road by Mill Creek, easily forded. Four wagons were loaded, started back, and arrived in camp safely. The other wagons, while loading, no one of them more than 300 yards from the road, were attacked and captured. The other 7 wagons, belonging to the Fifteenth Brigade, had passed on with the rest of the train. The train had advanced but a short distance when firing was heard at the front, perhaps 1½ miles from where these wagons were loading. Lieutenant-Colonel Barnes ordered three companies to halt, wait for the train to pass, and cover the rear, while he moved to the front with the other seven companies, in obedience to Colonel Buckley's order. Not more than 100 rods in advance of where these wagons were loading, the road turns to the right and ascends a hill among cedars. At the foot of this hill were the three companies, while the wagons were parked on the top of the hill or scattered to the right and left for forage. The two pieces of artillery also moved to the front, leaving the rear unprotected, except by three companies. While a brisk skirmish was going on in front, a body of rebel cavalry, perhaps 300 in number, came along Mill Creek, on our right, under cover of the hill, around the point of hill that here separates the road from the creek, crossed the road, captured the wagons, and took them behind a hill, on our left, and still farther to our rear. Upon this last hill the rebels had planted artillery, which commanded the corn-fields where the wagons had been loading and the road itself, completely cutting off retreat. Shortly after this our troops came back from the front, engaged their artillery, and drove them back, thus securing a safe passage homeward for the train.

From the best information I can obtain, these wagons were not an unusual distance from the road nor from the rest of the train. The whole affair was a repetition of a plan frequently adopted by the rebels, viz, to attack briskly in front while their cavalry make a dash upon an unprotected rear. The ground was admirably selected by the rebels, and I do not doubt that they would have captured the entire train had not the union of the two trains rendered the escort unusually large.

I am, sir, very respectfully, your obedient servant,

T. R. PALMER,
Inspector First Division.

Capt. R. LODER,
Inspector Twenty-first Army Corps.

DECEMBER 7, 1862.—Action at Hartsville, Tenn.

REPORTS, ETC.

No. 1.—Maj. Gen. William S. Rosecrans, U. S. Army, commanding Department of the Cumberland, and resulting correspondence.

No. 2.—Return of casualties in the Union forces.

No. 3.—Maj. William McMichael, assistant adjutant-general, U. S. Army.

No. 4.—Col. John M. Harlan, Tenth Kentucky Infantry, commanding Second Brigade, First Division.

No. 5.—Col. Edward M. McCook, Second Indiana Cavalry, commanding First Cavalry Brigade.

No. 6.—Maj. Samuel Hill, Second Indiana Cavalry.

No. 7.—Col. Absalom B. Moore, One hundred and fourth Illinois Infantry, commanding Thirty-ninth Brigade.

No. 8.—Capt. John Wadleigh, One hundred and fourth Illinois Infantry.

No. 9.—Lieut. Robert V. Simpson, One hundred and fourth Illinois Infantry.

No. 10.—Lieut. Col. Gustavus Tafel, One hundred and sixth Ohio Infantry.

No. 11.—Capt. Carlo Piepho, One hundred and eighth Ohio Infantry.

No. 12.—Capt. Joseph Good, One hundred and eighth Ohio Infantry.

No. 13.—General Braxton Bragg, C. S. Army, commanding Army of Tennessee, with instructions to Brigadier-General Morgan, and congratulatory orders.

No. 14.—Return of casualties in the Confederate forces.

No. 15.—Brig. Gen. John H. Morgan, C. S. Army, commanding expedition.

No. 16.—Col. Roger W. Hanson, Second Kentucky Infantry, commanding First Brigade, Breckinridge's division.

No. 17.—Col. Thomas H. Hunt, Ninth Kentucky Infantry, commanding detachment First Brigade.

No. 18.—Maj. James W. Hewitt, Second Kentucky Infantry.

No. 19.—Capt. James T. Morehead, Ninth Kentucky Infantry.

No. 1.

Reports of Maj. Gen. William S. Rosecrans, U. S. Army, commanding Department of the Cumberland, and resulting correspondence.

NASHVILLE, TENN.,
December 7, 1862—11 p. m.

General Thomas dispatches me that one of his brigades, Dumont's, posted at Hartsville, was probably surprised by two regiments of infantry and three of cavalry, and captured. I await news from the front to dispose for an attack of the enemy at Stewart's Creek, 9 miles this side of Murfreesborough. The movement toward Hartsville is also to be ascertained, as Polk is reported to have left Murfreesborough by the Lebanon [pike] on Friday. Thomas is yet at Gallatin with two divisions, minus the captured brigade, to cover that region until our railroad brings necessaries of clothing and cavalry arms. If the rebels fight us in force, it will be a great gain. If not, we can continue our forward movement. Our great difficulties will come from their numerous cavalry harassing us and cutting off our forage parties and trains. I am arming our cavalry, who are not more than one-fourth of their effective force, and much cowed from that fact and want of arms. Before bringing them in conflict with the rebel cavalry, cannot you send me those from Indianapolis?

W. S. ROSECRANS,
Major-General, Commanding.

Maj. Gen. H. W. HALLECK,
General-in-Chief.

GALLATIN, *December* 7, 1862.

Major-General ROSECRANS:

Lieutenant-Colonel Carroll, commanding Tenth Indiana, reports that the enemy attacked the forces under Colonel Scott at Hartsville this morning, and captured them, burning the wagons, &c. They are said to be 5,000 strong in infantry, besides their cavalry. Colonel Miller went out with his brigade from Castalian Springs; found the enemy drawn up in line of battle this side of Hartsville. Colonel Harlan has gone to the assistance of Colonel Miller, taking all of his brigade except a section of artillery. In addition, I have sent out General Fry to take command and report to me the actual state of affairs. The troops seen at Scottsville may be our own on their way to Carthage. They should be there about this time.

GEO. H. THOMAS,
Major-General, U. S. Volunteers.

NASHVILLE, *December* 7, 1862.

Major-General THOMAS, *Gallatin:*

Do I understand that they have captured an entire brigade of our troops without our knowing it, or a good fight?

W. S. ROSECRANS,
Major-General.

P. S.—Answer quick.

GALLATIN, *December* 7, 1862.

General ROSECRANS:

Colonel Harlan reports that Major Hill, Second Indiana Cavalry, informed him that the whole force which stood was captured; about half gave way. The fight lasted about an hour and a quarter. I will send particulars to-morrow. The enemy can be intercepted before reaching Murfreesborough. Colonel Harlan reports three regiments of cavalry and two of infantry on this side of the river, and two regiments of infantry on the other side, with five pieces of artillery.

GEO. H. THOMAS,
Major-General.

NASHVILLE, *December* 7, 1862—11 p. m.
(Received December 8, 1862.)

Maj. Gen. GEORGE H. THOMAS:

Get the arms our fugitive troops have thrown away at Hartsville.   It seems to me impossible that the entire brigade could have surrendered. Are there none left?

W. S. ROSECRANS,
Major-General.

—

GALLATIN, *December* 8, 1862.

General ROSECRANS:

Colonel Harlan has not yet sent me a detailed report of the affair at Hartsville, but I learn from some of his officers that they buried upward of 80 of the One hundred and fourth Illinois and only a few of the other two regiments.   This fact indicates that the other two regiments behaved badly.   They were the One hundred and sixth and One hundred and eighth Ohio Volunteers.   Scouts from the other side report that the enemy's cavalry is still hovering about the river.

GEO. H. THOMAS,
Major-General.

—

GALLATIN, *December* 8, 1862.

General ROSECRANS:

Colonel Harlan has gathered up all the arms and property left at Hartsville.   He will send in a detailed report to-day, which I will forward by mail if received in time.   The entire force, except one company and about 100 cavalry, so far as I can learn, were captured.

GEO. H. THOMAS,
Major-General.

—

WAR DEPARTMENT,
Washington, December 9, 1862.

Major-General ROSECRANS,
Nashville, Tenn.:

The President directs that you immediately report why an isolated brigade was at Hartsville, and by whose command; and also by whose fault it was surprised and captured.

H. W. HALLECK,
General-in-Chief.

—

NASHVILLE, TENN.,
December 9, 1862—1.30 p. m.

Maj. Gen. GEORGE H. THOMAS,
U. S. Volunteers, Commanding Center, Gallatin, Tenn.:

President demands explanation of Hartsville affair.   Report in detail exact position, strength, and relative distances of your troops between Gallatin and Hartsville at that time, and causes of the disaster as far as known to you.

By command of General Rosecrans:

J. P. GARESCHÉ,
Assistant Adjutant-General and Chief of Staff.

NASHVILLE, TENN., *December* 9, 1862—11 p. m.

Maj. Gen. H. W. HALLECK, *General-in-Chief:*

In reply to your telegram, inquiring why the brigade was stationed at Hartsville, I respectfully state that it was necessary to cover the crossing of the Cumberland River against rebel cavalry, who would essay to attack our road and capture our trains. We have, for all our immense line of front communications, picket, and couriers, less than 4,000 cavalry, and the enemy not less than 10,000, who are much relieved by guerrilla scouts, and can concentrate for mischief with almost perfect secrecy and impunity. The subjoined copy of General Thomas' report shows that it was a pretty full brigade, posted strongly, with a cavalry regiment for picket duty on the north side of the river, in a commanding position; that it was strongly supported within 9 miles, and, but for being surprised and making feeble resistance, it would have been succored, and the enemy badly whipped. That outpost was stronger and better supported than our outpost at Rienzi, 7 miles below Corinth, last summer. The difference was in the superiority and number of rebel cavalry:

Hartsville was garrisoned by the Thirty-ninth Brigade, Twelfth Division (Dumont's), for duty, and was commanded by Col. A. B. Moore, One hundred and fourth Illinois. There was also a regiment of cavalry posted there, the Second Indiana, sent there by your order. The effective force not known. The troops were posted so as to guard the ford and the approaches from the direction of Lebanon, and the cavalry for picket duty and scouting. Col. J. M. Harlan, Second Brigade, First Division, was posted at Castalian Springs. This brigade reports 2,725 men present for duty. Colonel Miller, commanding the Fortieth Brigade, was also posted at Castalian Springs, sent there to relieve Colonel Harlan. This brigade reports 2,274 men present for duty. The last two brigades mentioned were 9 miles distant from Hartsville when the attack was made. As soon as cannonading was heard, Colonel Harlan ordered Colonel Miller to march with his command in the direction of Hartsville, and, with a portion of his brigade, followed Colonel Miller, and orders were given to the cavalry from these headquarters to be vigilant and scour the country, so that no enemy could approach without giving timely notice to the garrison. Colonel Harlan, upon being relieved by Colonel Scott at Hartsville, informed me that the position was strong and defensible; added to the information received from my officers, led to the belief that the officer in command allowed himself to be surprised, which resulted in the capture of nearly his whole force. The attack was sudden, and so quickly decided that it was impossible for re-enforcements to reach Hartsville in time to take part in the action, and the enemy have been defeated and probably cut off before crossing the river.

GEO. H. THOMAS,
Major-General.

W. S. ROSECRANS,
Major-General, Commanding.

———

WAR DEPARTMENT,
Washington, December 10, 1862.

Major-General ROSECRANS, *Nashville, Tenn.:*

The most important of the President's inquiries has not been answered. What officer or officers are chargeable with the surprise at Hartsville and deserve punishment?

H. W. HALLECK,
General-in-Chief.

———

NASHVILLE, TENN., *December* 10, 1862—midnight.

Maj. Gen. H. W. HALLECK, *General-in-Chief:*

Additional information from Colonel Limberg and Captain Good, One hundred and eighth Ohio Volunteer Infantry, who were present in the affair at Hartsville, but escaped capture, shows that there were no cavalry vedettes out in that direction, no picket guard, and apparently no camp guard; that the first notice in camp of the presence of the enemy was given by an orderly, or servant, that the enemy's cavalry was coming up and wheeling, by fours, into line on the opposite side of a ravine, about 400 yards distant from our camp; that they were quietly formed without a shot being fired at them; that the artillery did nothing to disturb them; that only two companies of skirmishers turned out; that the infantry stood in line of battle at "ordered arms," and allowed the enemy to dismount and advance, as skirmishers, within 100 yards before they commenced firing. The artillery allowed the enemy's mountain howitzers, and probably two other pieces, to move up into position without disturbing them. It was finally brought out of the woods, and fired a few shots, with little effect, as the enemy advanced in line of skirmishers. Closing in, our troops soon fell into confusion, ran to their camp in a crowd, where the enemy's artillery played on them, and they soon hoisted a white flag and surrendered. The behavior of the Second Indiana Cavalry seems to have been as spiritless as their picketing. The enemy hastily exchanged their Austrian for our Springfield rifles, leaving many arms on the field; drove their prisoners across the river, waist-deep, and retreated so hastily that, when our succor arrived, a light battalion of cavalry pursued them across the river and retook three wagon-loads of our arms. Probably 30 wagons lost. These facts indicate pretty clearly where the blame lies. It is pretty certain that the enemy's force did not exceed 2,500 men—two regiments of mounted, and, possibly, two dismounted cavalry. No official reports yet in.

W. S. ROSECRANS,
Major-General, Commanding.

—

HDQRS. 14TH ARMY CORPS, DEPT. OF THE CUMBERLAND,
Nashville, Tenn., December 22, 1862.

Brig. Gen. LORENZO THOMAS,
Adjutant-General, U. S. Army, Washington, D. C.:

GENERAL: I have the honor herewith to transmit all the official reports that have been received at these headquarters of the battle at Hartsville, Tenn., on the 7th instant.

I am, general, very respectfully, your obedient servant,

W. S. ROSECRANS,
Major-General, Commanding Department.

[Indorsements.]

HEADQUARTERS OF THE ARMY,
January 13, 1863.

Respectfully returned to Major-General Rosecrans, to ascertain and report who are the guilty officers concerned in the surrender of Hartsville, Tenn.

By order of Major-General Halleck:

J. C. KELTON,
Assistant Adjutant-General.

The within reports and statements show that the United States forces captured at the above place December 7, 1862, were either surprised or that great negligence was displayed in failing to prepare for the enemy's attack. The rebels were in sight before any disposition for action was made of the infantry, a part of which was assaulted before being fairly in line. The fight lasted less than one hour and a half. The loss was about 150 in killed and wounded. Two brigades of our troops, under Colonel Harlan, were at Castalian Springs, only 9 miles distant from the scene, but their commander had no intimation of an anticipated attack from Colonel Moore, who commanded at Hartsville, or he could have moved forward, so as to be able to co-operate immediately upon the morning of the fight. Colonel Moore, One hundred and fourth Illinois, the brigade commander, was a prisoner at the time the within documents were submitted, and his own report does not, therefore, appear; but, from the evidence given, the disaster seems to be attributable mainly to his ignorance or negligence.

W. S. ROSECRANS,
Major-General, Commanding Department.

FEBRUARY 13, 1863.

I respectfully recommend that Colonel Moore, One hundred and fourth Illinois Volunteers, be dismissed the service for neglect of duty, in not properly preparing for the enemy's attack on Hartsville, Tenn.*

H. W. HALLECK,
General-in-Chief.

Approved:

EDWIN M. STANTON,
Secretary of War.

No. 2.

Return of casualties in the Union forces engaged at Hartsville, Tenn., December 7, 1862.

[Compiled from nominal list of casualties, returns, &c.]

Command.	Killed.		Wounded.		Captured or missing.		
	Officers.	Enlisted men.	Officers.	Enlisted men.	Officers.	Enlisted men.	Aggregate.
104th Illinois Infantry		25	5	126	23	545	724
2d Indiana Cavalry					11	346	357
13th Indiana Battery (section)		1		2	1	22	26
11th Kentucky Cavalry, Company E					2	42	44
106th Ohio Infantry	2	20	3	38	16	413	492
108th Ohio Infantry		10		30	20	393	453
Total	2	56	8	196	73	1,761	2,096

OFFICERS KILLED.—Capts. William Y. Gholson and Hermann Reintanz, One hundred and sixth Ohio. OFFICERS MORTALLY WOUNDED.—Lieuts. Moses M. Randolph and Milton Strawn, One hundred and fourth Illinois.

* Colonel Moore was not dismissed the service; his resignation was accepted on account of disability, to take effect September 9, 1863, by Special Field Orders, No. 244, Paragraph 1, from Headquarters Department of the Cumberland, of that date.

No. 3.

Report of Maj. William McMichael, Assistant Adjutant-General, U. S. Army.

HEADQUARTERS OF THE ARMY.

The battle at Hartsville, Tenn., which resulted in the defeat and surrender of the United States troops at that place, occurred December 7.

Our forces consisted of the Thirty-ninth Brigade, Army of the Cumberland (One hundred and sixth and One hundred and eighth Ohio Infantry, and the One hundred and fourth Illinois Infantry), with the Second Indiana Cavalry and a section of Nicklin's (Thirteenth Indiana) battery. The Eleventh Kentucky Cavalry is mentioned in one of the reports as having a small force in action.

No official report of this fight is furnished from the officer who commanded. The accounts are from officers of the several commands engaged. Their substance is as follows :

Major Hill, Second Indiana Cavalry, relates that, on the 6th, scouts were out, and no signs of the enemy appeared. Early on the morning of the 7th, the enemy appeared, and immediately advanced upon and attacked our force. Major Hill represents the cavalry as having behaved with gallantry.

Col. E. M. McCook, commanding cavalry brigade, in submitting this account, says the Second Indiana Cavalry and One hundred and fourth Illinois Infantry "fought gallantly; the other regiments of the brigade fled disgracefully, leaving their comrades to make a hopeless fight against superior numbers." Colonel McCook was not in the action, but derived his opinion from the testimony of individuals who had participated in it.

Captain Wadleigh, One hundred and fourth Illinois Infantry ; Captain Good, One hundred and eighth Ohio Infantry, and Lieut. Col. Gustavus Tafel, commanding One hundred and sixth Ohio Infantry, each present an account of the part taken by his own regiment, and all agree in stating that the commands with which they served behaved unexceptionably. All accounts agree that the enemy were in sight before any disposition to receive their attack was made. The troops assembled hurriedly. It seems to have been a surprise, but sufficient time elapsed to form our men in line.

The fight lasted one hour and a quarter, having commenced between 6.30 and 7 a. m. Colonel Moore, One hundred and fourth Illinois Infantry, commanded our forces in the action.

At Castalian Springs, 9 miles from Hartsville, two brigades of our troops were encamped. The first intelligence they had of this action was the sound of firing. They moved forward to the assistance of the Hartsville force. The firing having ceased, and, anticipating an attack, they formed in line of battle 1½ miles before Hartsville ; but their commander, Colonel Harlan, having observed a column of smoke in the direction of the Hartsville camp, again moved rapidly forward ; found our troops had surrendered and the enemy in retreat, but succeeded in recapturing a part of our force and property.

Colonel Harlan is of opinion that the enemy crossed the Cumberland on the night of the 6th, and encamped. He received no intimation of an attack from Colonel Moore, or he could have co-operated to resist it. The enemy's force is said to have consisted of three regiments of infantry, Gano's and Bennett's cavalry, a battalion of Texan Rangers, and eight pieces of artillery. Two regiments of infantry, one regiment of cavalry, and a battery were seen on the opposite side of the river. They did not participate in the action, the artillery being alone engaged in throwing shell into our camp.

Our loss in killed and wounded was about 150, the majority of whom belonged to the One hundred and fourth Illinois Infantry.

From the reports submitted, it is impossible to form a reliable estimate of the conduct of the respective regiments, each officer reporting being disposed to give a favorable account of the action of the command to which he was attached; but the following facts are apparent: First, the attack was unexpected, and no intelligence had been sent to, or effort made to co-operate with, the two brigades of the United States forces, stationed only 9 miles distant from the scene of action; secondly, the fight lasted only one hour and a quarter. If the troops had either retreated or made a longer resistance, they could have fallen back to or been joined by the troops above alluded to, when our forces would have outnumbered the enemy.

W. McMICHAEL,
Assistant Adjutant-General.

No. 4.

Report of Col. John M. Harlan, Tenth Kentucky Infantry, commanding Second Brigade, First Division.

HEADQUARTERS SECOND BRIGADE, FIRST DIVISION,
Camp near Gallatin, Tenn., December 12, 1862.

CAPTAIN: On the morning of the 7th instant, about 7.30 o'clock, I heard cannonading very distinctly in the direction of Hartsville, at which place was stationed the Thirty-ninth Brigade, of General Dumont's division, the Second Indiana Cavalry, and two pieces of Nicklin's battery, all under the command of Colonel Moore, One hundred and fourth Illinois. You will remember that at that time four regiments of my brigade (the Tenth Indiana, Fourth Kentucky, Tenth Kentucky, and Seventy-fourth Indiana) and my battery (Southwick's), and also Colonel Miller's brigade, of Dumont's division, were encamped at Castalian Springs, 9 miles from Hartsville, and 7½ miles from Gallatin.

As soon as the cannonading commenced, I dispatched a courier to Hartsville, to ascertain the cause of the firing. At the same time I dispatched another courier in the same direction, with orders to proceed rapidly up the road, and if he heard musketry, or could learn any facts which indicated that a fight was probably going on at Hartsville, to return with all possible speed to my camp and report. Simultaneously with this, I directed each regiment of my brigade to be in readiness to march at a moment's notice. Within a very short while after the last courier was started, I received information from Captain Hudnall (Fourth Kentucky), commanding the picket company on the Hartsville road (nearly a mile distant from camp), to the effect that he thought he could hear heavy musketry in the direction of Hartsville. I communicated at once the fact to Colonel Miller, whose brigade belonged to the same division as Colonel Moore's, and suggested the propriety of his marching his brigade to Hartsville as rapidly as the men could go, preceded by the small detachment of the Seventh Kentucky Cavalry (Major Faulkner), then at Castalian Springs, and under his immediate command. This suggestion Colonel Miller promptly adopted, and in a few minutes was on the march. I followed immediately and rapidly after him with the Tenth Kentucky (Lieutenant-Colonel Hays) and the Seventy-fourth Indiana (Colonel Chapman), and four pieces of Southwick's battery, leaving the Fourth Kentucky (Colonel Croxton) and the Tenth Indiana (Lieutenant-Colonel Carroll), with two pieces of artillery, in camp at Castalian Springs, to guard my own as well as Colonel Miller's camp, and to resist any attack upon that point. My intention was to go within 3 or 4 miles of Hartsville, and thus keep within supporting distance both of my own men, at the springs, and of Colonel Miller in his advance to Hartsville. I left orders for the Fourth Kentucky and Tenth Indiana to be in constant readiness to obey any summons which I might send back to them.

When I arrived within about 3 miles of Hartsville, word was sent to me from the front that some of the enemy were seen ahead, and a request from Colonel Miller that I would come forward rapidly with my men and assume command, as there were some indications of a fight. This summons was obeyed. I went in person to the front and assumed command. My regiments, already moving rapidly, increased their pace, and marched as fast as men ever marched. Believing, from the information received, that the enemy would resist us, I sent, before going to the front, an order back for the Fourth Kentucky to join me as soon as possible, which order was obeyed with the utmost alacrity.

Upon arriving at the front, I found that Colonel Miller's brigade had formed in line of battle about 1½ miles this side of Hartsville. His battery was in position, and had, previous to my arrival, fired one or two shells into the wood beyond, where some of the enemy were seen. Up to that time we had not met a single straggler on the entire route. No one could be seen to give any information as to what had happened. The firing had ceased some little while before this. Whether the enemy had been repulsed and had retired, or whether our entire force had been captured, we could not tell. Just then, however, from an eminence near by, I observed a dense smoke rising from the direction of Colonel Moore's camp. I then became satisfied that all had been lost, and that my only chance was to push forward, and, if possible, catch the enemy before he crossed the river, and thereby also save some of our captured men. A rapid advance was ordered; we moved across the country directly toward Colonel Moore's camp, which was also the shortest route to the ford, near Hartsville, where the rebels would necessarily recross the river.

Upon the arrival of Faulkner's cavalry at Colonel Moore's camp, which was about 400 yards from the ford, and in full view of it, some of the rebel cavalry were seen crossing the river, and had some of our teams with them. They were fired upon by Faulkner's men, when they abandoned the wagons and fled precipitately across the river. In addition to the rebel cavalry who were seen crossing the river, I observed myself several hundred rebel cavalry on the hill on the south side of the river, moving off on the Lebanon road. Each of them appeared to have a man behind him on his horse. I ordered Nicklin's battery, of Miller's brigade, to fire across at the retiring rebels, which order was promptly obeyed, and resulted in the killing of a few of the rebels, as I was afterward informed. Pursuit was utterly impracticable; it would have required at least an hour and a half to cross the river at that point and ascend the high bank on the south side. The enemy, as I learned, recrossed their infantry, as well as their prisoners, with the horses of their cavalry. In addition to all this, I did not deem it prudent to cross the river with the force then at my disposal, being entirely unadvised as to what strength the enemy had on the south side in reserve.

Some of our wounded officers expressed to me the opinion (which I think is sustained by subsequent developments) that the rebels had on the south side a reserve force, which had not crossed, but were near enough in an emergency to have assisted those who made the attack upon Moore. This was the opinion of Major Hill, of the Second Indiana Cavalry. These facts, in connection with the time which would necessarily be occupied in crossing, induced me, upon consultation with my brother officers, to abandon all further pursuit.

I found that the enemy had succeeded before our arrival in running across the river all the wagons and mules of Colonel Moore's brigade and the Second Indiana Cavalry, except 11 wagons and 13 mules, which were recaptured. A large number of the tents had been burned and a large number of the guns of our men had been taken off by the rebels.

Deeming it my duty to save as much of the public property of Colonel Moore's brigade as I could, I sent back to Castalian Springs, and ordered up 25 wagons from Colonel Miller's and my brigades, with which to carry off the recaptured property. The wagons arrived about dark, and were immediately loaded, when Colonel Miller and I returned with them to our camp, at Castalian Springs.

The Tenth Kentucky Regiment, of my brigade, having arms which were, in many respects, very defective, and in some respects entirely useless to them, they were allowed to take out of the lot of recaptured guns 309, as well as 36,000 rounds of cartridges to suit them. That regiment turned over its old guns to the ordnance officer of the division, and will account to him for the guns retained, as above stated. This step was absolutely necessary, because there was no supply of ammunition on hand in the ammunition train of the division to suit the caliber of their guns (.71½), and because my brigade at the time was ordered to Hartsville, at which point there were reasons to apprehend that we would be attacked by the rebels. The exchange will add, in my judgment, one-third to the efficiency of that regiment in battle. If this step is not approved, the regiment will return to the proper officer, if ordered, all the guns thus received, and take such others as will be given them. The balance of the ordnance stores recaptured have been turned over to the ordnance officer of the division.

As to the killed and wounded, I found upon the field 55 dead Union soldiers, a large majority of whom were identified by papers upon their persons as belonging to the One hundred and fourth Illinois. These were buried by details from Colonel Miller's and my commands. Among those killed was Captain Gholson, acting assistant adjutant-general (as I learn) of Colonel Moore's brigade. He was the only Union officer killed and left on the field.

We found on the field 15 dead rebels, who were also buried, among whom were 3 officers. One of them was identified as Lieutenant Rogers, of Bullitt County, Kentucky, and another, Lieutenant Thomas, of Hardin County, Kentucky.

The total wounded on our side amounted to nearly 100, a majority of whom belonged to the One hundred and fourth Illinois. I have already inclosed to you a list of their names. They are all at Hartsville, except such as have been moved away. Those there now, with a few exceptions, as I learned from the surgeon in charge, could not be moved. I left them as comfortably provided for as could be expected under the circumstances.

Quite a lot of provisions was saved, all of which I left for the use of the wounded, except 1,236 pounds of bacon, 470 pounds of rice, and a small quantity of salt, beans, and hard bread, which were turned over to my brigade commissary, who will account for them. One of the captured wagons, with 4 mules, was left with the surgeon in charge of the wounded, to be used to haul wood for them.

I found in a house near the battle-field wounded rebels, whom I paroled, and a roll of which I have forwarded to the Adjutant-General of the United States Army. I forward also to you a list of said rebels, to be forwarded, if necessary, to department headquarters. This list includes some wounded rebels, found upon my return to Hartsville on the 10th instant.

I had no means of ascertaining the exact number of rebels killed and wounded, but I did ascertain that they removed most of their wounded and some of their killed; and from all I could gather it is quite probable that the number of rebels killed and wounded, if it did not exceed, at least equaled the number of killed and wounded on our side.

The rebel force engaged amounted to not less than five regiments and one battery. Two of the regiments were the Second and Ninth Kentucky (rebel) Infantry, of General Hanson's brigade, and three were from Morgan's cavalry brigade, and I am inclined to the opinion that there were other rebel regiments on the south side of the river, in close supporting distance. Some of our wounded officers assure me that they saw this force. If such a force was there, it was, no doubt, for the purpose of holding the ford, while the rebel troops retired across the river after the fight had concluded. The entire rebel force on the field was under the immediate command of Morgan.

The average number of cartridges found to be missing out of the three hundred and odd cartridge-boxes saved was about six, and in a very large number there did not appear to be any cartridges missing. Fully three-fourths of the guns recaptured were loaded, and many of them capped.

The rebels crossed the river during the night of the 6th, at two places, a few miles below Hartsville. The infantry crossed at a ferry. They were most of the night, as I learned, in crossing. They united a short distance from Hartsville, and formed in line of battle between the camp of Colonel Moore and the Gallatin and Hartsville pike. The fight lasted about an hour—probably an hour and a quarter, not longer. The enemy captured and took with them two pieces of Nicklin's battery, which had been sent to Hartsville but a few days previous to the fight. These two pieces had evidently been well served, since I found upon the field two caissons of the rebel battery entirely disabled. From Hartsville a plain, direct road leads to the two points where the rebels crossed the river.

I did not receive at any time during the night of the 6th any intimation from the commandant at Hartsville that the enemy was crossing near his camp. Had I known, or even suspected, that such was the case; or had I been advised even at daylight on the morning of the 7th, of the approach of the rebels; or had the force at Hartsville held out but a little longer, the result in either case might have been very different. In marching to Hartsville I did so without any specific orders; but I felt it to be my duty to march to the assistance of the force stationed there, if attacked by the enemy; and I am very sure that both Colonel Miller and myself, as well as our respective commands, did all that men could do to reach Hartsville in time to aid our brethren.

I do not deem it my duty to express in this official report any opinion which I may have in regard to the causes which led to the unfortunate disaster at Hartsville. That opinion might do injustice to the officers and men, whose conduct may be the subject of inquiry before a proper tribunal.   My sole purpose has been, in compliance with the order of the division commander, to give such facts as my visit to Hartsville elicited.

Very respectfully, your obedient servant,

JOHN M. HARLAN,
Colonel, Commanding Second Brigade.

Capt. EDWARD C. DENIG,
Acting Assistant Adjutant-General.

No. 5.

Report of Col. Edward M. McCook, Second Indiana Cavalry, commanding First Cavalry Brigade.

HEADQUARTERS FIRST CAVALRY BRIGADE,
December 14, 1862.

LIEUTENANT : In compliance with the request of the colonel com manding the division, asking for all the information I have gained concerning the late affair at Hartsville, I have the honor to inclose a copy of the official report of Maj. Samuel Hill, Second Indiana Cavalry.   He embodies only a history of the part taken by his regiment in the engagement.   From unofficial statements, made by various officers and men, I am satisfied that, while the One hundred and fourth Illinois and Second Indiana Cavalry fought gallantly, the other regiments of the brigade fled disgracefully, and left their comrades to make a hopeless fight against superior numbers.

Paroled men tell me that many of the persons who had come within our lines at Hartsville, and claimed protection as refugee conscripts, were in the enemy's ranks, and employed guarding them on their way to Murfreesborough.   They assure me that there can be no mistake, for they recognized them distinctly.   Does not this convey the lesson that none of those who come to us and claim protection as refugees, or ask privileges as citizens, are to be trusted?   Clothed in the peaceful garb of the citizen, they enter our camps and pass through our lines, and the citizen's dress is generally but the disguise of a spy.

Very respectfully, your obedient servant,

EDWARD M. McCOOK,
Colonel, Commanding Brigade.

Lieut. M. B. CHAMBERLAIN,
Actg. Asst. Adjt. Gen., First Cavalry Division.

No. 6.

Report of Maj. Samuel Hill, Second Indiana Cavalry.

CAMP ROSECRANS, NEAR NASHVILLE,
December 13, 1862.

COLONEL: In obedience to your request, I submit the following statement of facts in relation to the disaster at Hartsville, Tenn., on the 7th instant:

On the 6th, scouts were made on all the roads approaching Hartsville, and, at 4 o'clock of that day, Lebanon, Tenn., was not occupied by the enemy, nor were there any indications of an advance of their forces.

At 6.30 o'clock on the morning of the 7th, the couriers announced the approach of the enemy on the old Lebanon road, and immediately after they appeared in view at a distance of three-fourths of a mile, and commenced to form their columns for attack. The Second Indiana Cavalry, commanded by Lieutenant-Colonel Stewart, was ordered out, dismounted, to defend the camp, with the exception of Company G, which was mounted, and was ordered forward, to commence skirmishing with the enemy. The infantry was ordered to form line, their flanks resting on the heads of two ravines; and, on the line being formed, the Second Indiana was ordered to return to camp, mount, and then take position to protect the flanks of the infantry. Up to this time, from a half to three-fourths of an hour, no attack had been made on our lines, and no fighting done, except by the skirmishers of Company G, Second Indiana, a portion of whom were captured by venturing too far, among them Lieutenant Parsley, who commanded the company.

The attack was made by the enemy's infantry and artillery simultaneously, while overwhelming numbers of their cavalry showed themselves upon the flanks and rear of our position. These we managed to hold in check during the engagement, and prevented them from materially assisting their infantry in their attack on ours.

I have thus stated the part the Second Indiana Cavalry took in the engagement, though they resisted the enemy between a quarter and half an hour after our main force had surrendered.

The enemy's force consisted of the Second and Ninth Kentucky and Eighteenth Tennessee Infantry; Colonel Duke's, Colonel Gano's, and Colonel Bennett's cavalry, and one battalion Texas Rangers. Their artillery force consisted of four rifled 6-pounders, two 12-pounder howitzers, and two small rifled pieces, caliber unknown.

On the opposite side of the river there were in view one regiment of cavalry, two of infantry, and a battery of six pieces, two of which were rifled. The artillery on the south side of the river during the engagement was occupied in shelling our camp and cavalry.

In consequence of my hand being disabled by a gun-shot wound, I authorize John Schooler to affix my signature.

Very respectfully, your obedient servant,

SAMUEL HILL,
Major Second Indiana Cavalry.

Col. E. M. McCook,
Commanding First Cavalry Brigade.

No. 7.

Report of Col. Absalom B. Moore, One hundred and fourth Illinois Infantry, commanding Thirty-ninth Brigade.

HEADQUARTERS 104TH REGIMENT ILLINOIS INFANTRY,
Camp Douglas, Chicago, Ill., February 25, 1863.

GENERAL : Having been exchanged as a prisoner of war, and released from my confinement in a rebel prison, I hasten to give you my report of the battle of Hartsville, Tenn., which occurred December 7, 1862.

The Thirty-ninth Brigade, consisting of the One hundred and fourth Illinois Infantry, One hundred and sixth and One hundred and eighth

Ohio Infantry, the Second Indiana Cavalry, one company of the Eleventh Kentucky Cavalry, and a section of Captain Nicklin's Indiana battery, was placed under my command on the 2d day of December, 1862, in consequence of Colonel Scott, of the Nineteenth Illinois, who was commanding the brigade, returning to his regiment.

I entered upon my duties, and did all that I could to be in readiness if we should be attacked. Our position on the banks of the Cumberland River was the same occupied by the brigade that was there before our arrival from Tompkinsville, Ky. The vedette and picket stations were selected by Colonel Scott before he gave up the command. Upon my taking command, I increased the vedette and picket force, and every possible avenue of approach to our camp was well guarded, the vedettes being about 1½ miles and the pickets one-half mile from camp. The country for miles was scouted every day by the cavalry force of my command, and every precaution was used to give us timely warning of the approach of the enemy, should they attempt to attack us.

On Saturday night, December 6, 1862, General John H. Morgan, of the rebel army, started from Baird's Mills, 8 miles south of Lebanon, Tenn., and 25 from Hartsville, for the purpose of attacking me at Hartsville. His force consisted of six regiments of cavalry, two regiments of infantry (the Second and Ninth Kentucky), and fourteen pieces of artillery. Besides this overwhelming force, the citizens between Hartsville and Lebanon joined the rebel force, until they numbered between 5,000 and 6,000 men. This force, with the exception of about 1,000 cavalry, crossed the Cumberland River, under cover of night, between our position and that of the force stationed at Castalian Springs. The advance guard of the rebels were dressed in the Federal uniform, and succeeded in deceiving my vedettes and capturing them without firing a gun. The enemy then pushed on with their entire force toward our camp. The pickets gave the alarm, and held the rebels in check until my force was in line of battle and ready to receive them. The brigade [fell] promptly in line, and commenced the battle by attacking the enemy before he had time to form. The infantry force of the rebels were mounted on horses, behind the cavalry. The entire rebel force dismounted about 1 mile from camp and fought as infantry, with the exception of Bennett's cavalry, which dashed into the town of Hartsville to capture Company A, of the One hundred and fourth Illinois, who were acting provost guard of the town. The 1,000 cavalry before mentioned parted from the main body and crossed the river 8 miles north of the camp, but this latter force did not arrive in time to participate in the fight, but succeeded in capturing the cowards who had deserted us in the time of need.

My force consisted of about 450 men of the One hundred and fourth Illinois, 250 effective men each of the One hundred and sixth and One hundred and eighth Ohio, 280 men of the Second Indiana Cavalry and the Eleventh Kentucky Cavalry, and a section of artillery—1,800 men. I had sent on Saturday, December 6, 1862, to Gallatin, as a guard to our provision train, three companies of infantry, one company of cavalry, and 30 mounted infantrymen, amounting to nearly 200 men, and a great many being sick in hospital at the time of the attack, left me but the small force of about 1,200 men to contend with 5,000 of the rebels and their artillery of fourteen guns, and some of them 12-pounders.

The battle commenced about 6.45 a. m., and continued until 8.30 a. m., one hour and three-quarters. The One hundred and fourth Illinois fought heroically, and maintained their position. The Second Indiana Cavalry and the Eleventh Kentucky Cavalry also did nobly. The One **hundred and sixth Ohio** acted shamefully, and left us in the midst of the fight, many of the men running for shelter in the tents of the One hundred and eighth Ohio, which were in the rear of our line of battle. All efforts of myself and Lieutenant-Colonel Stewart, of the Second Indiana Cavalry, to rally them were unavailing.

The One hundred and eighth Ohio, being entirely destitute of field officers, fought well for a short time, but were soon thrown into confusion and retreated, although Captain Piepho and other officers of the regiment did their utmost to keep the men in front of the enemy and to stand their ground. The section of artillery under command of Lieutenant Green did good execution, and all men connected with the battery did their duty nobly and bravely.

After the battle had raged furiously for some time, and seeing the rebels in front commence wavering under the severe and deadly fire of my men, I gave the order to charge, feeling confident that we could cut our way through the rebel ranks. Immediately upon giving the order, the stampede of the One hundred and sixth commenced, which then brought a tremendous fire upon the One hundred and eighth Ohio; they being the center, and were soon flanked on the right, and gave way in confusion. I withdrew the order to charge, and directed the One hundred and fourth to hold the rebels in check until I drew our guns, now entirely unsupported on the right, to another position. They did so. The guns were moved on the top of the bluff, on the edge of the river, about 200 yards from their former position. I then ordered the One hundred and sixth and One hundred and eighth to form by the guns, but they were so scattered that it was impossible to expect any further assistance from them. I then ordered the One hundred and fourth to fall back to the guns, which they did in good order, contesting every inch of the ground. After arriving at the guns, and forming in our new position, and many of the One hundred and fourth being killed and wounded, and being now completely surrounded, and one-half my force captured by deserting their position without orders, I was compelled to surrender, as fighting longer would only increase the number of killed and wounded, as we were contending against a force of ten to one after forming in our new line of battle. I am unable to give you a list of killed and wounded, but presume that during my absence as a prisoner of war you have received intelligence from other sources. The rebel loss, according to their own statement to me, was about 400 in killed and wounded, the greater part of whom were carried from the field.

I have given you a correct history of the battle, and I did suppose that after fighting for one and three-quarter hours we would certainly receive re-enforcements, and had they come to us promptly from Castalian Springs the result would have been different. I indulged the hope, and encouraged the men to fight one hour and we would be re-enforced, but, after one and three-quarter hours' hard fighting, we were compelled to surrender, and another hour passed before we were marched out of camp, and still no help. To Lieutenant-Colonel Stewart and Major Hill, of the Second Indiana Cavalry; Captain Slater, of the Eleventh Kentucky Cavalry; Lieutenant-Colonel Hapeman and Major Widmer, of the One hundred and fourth Illinois, and all the officers and men of the foregoing regiments and companies, who acted with great coolness and bravery upon the battle-field, and to each and to all of them, I feel indebted for aiding and assisting me in our struggle to overcome the enemy, and had our comrades remained firm we could have held out until re-enforcements arrived. Captain Piepho, of the One hundred and eighth, also performed his duty well. Capt. W. Y. Gholson, my acting assistant adjutant-general, while attempting to rally the

One hundred and sixth Ohio, was shot, and soon expired. He was a brave and noble young man. Lieut. Jacob Dewald, my aide-de-camp, was very active in carrying my orders to all parts of the field. And, in conclusion of this part of my report, I will say I love every man that fought; I hate every dog that ran. It was the first time that any of the infantry regiments engaged in the battle were under fire.

I respectfully request that, when the officers of the Second Indiana Cavalry are released as prisoners of war, and the lieutenant-colonel and major of the One hundred and fourth Illinois Infantry are also released, you will give me a court of inquiry in the matter; and if I have done anything wrong, or neglected any duty, I am willing to be censured, but I have a consciousness that I did my duty the best I could. I also wish to have the conduct of every officer who ran like a coward from the field fully inquired into. I took the command of the brigade on the 2d of December, and on the morning of the 7th the fight occurred. I had never received any orders from any source to take command, nor instructions from any source whether I was to have command, or otherwise, except as the command was handed over to me by Colonel Scott.

I have the honor to submit this report direct to you, learning that General Dumont had resigned.

I have the honor to be, your obedient servant,

A. B. MOORE,
Colonel 104th Illinois Infantry, and Comdg. 39th Brigade.

Major-General ROSECRANS.

No. 8.

Report of Capt. John Wadleigh, One hundred and fourth Illinois Infantry.

DECEMBER 7, 1862.

DEAR SIR: In absence of any field officer of the One hundred and fourth Regiment Illinois Volunteer Infantry, I have the honor to make the following report of the action, as seen by myself. I would refer to the accompanying reports, as handed in by the officers commanding companies, and designated A, B, C, &c., according to the letters of said commands:

Early on the morning of December 7 our camp was alarmed by the report that the enemy were in sight, and approaching with the intention of attacking; soon after which the pickets were fired upon, and returned the fire smartly, contesting the ground until the cavalry and minute-men could be deployed as skirmishers.

Company A was doing provost duty in town, and Company H was thrown forward as skirmishers on the extreme right of the cavalry. I would refer to letters A and H for more full particulars of their actions. Companies B, C (D in part), E, F, G, and I were early on the ground, and in line on the immediate right of the battery, composed of one section of the Thirteenth Indiana. Company K was thrown forward as skirmishers, but soon returned into line. The One hundred and eighth Ohio Volunteer Infantry was placed on the left, and to support the battery. The One hundred and sixth Ohio Volunteer Infantry was ordered to the right. Thus formed, we awaited the approach of the enemy.

Soon the batteries of the enemy, which, until this time, had remained masked, opened upon us furiously with six guns. The action then became general all along the lines. Soon the artillery complained that their support on the left had given way. It also became apparent that the right had also given way, so that the One hundred and fourth was completely flanked.

The artillery then placed one gun on the right of the One hundred and fourth, and this regiment undertook to support both guns; but, after sustaining the united fire of two regiments of Kentucky infantry (the Second and Ninth veteran troops), for something like thirty minutes, they were compelled to fall back, and did so in some little confusion, not, however, until orders had to be given to fall back by the field officers. The artillery failed for some reason to remove the gun from the right flank, and the officers of Company B, with a little help, dragged the gun from its position down the declivity, and attempted to conceal it; but the movement being discovered by the enemy, a shower of balls was poured upon them, and they were compelled to abandon the idea. The order to fall back was immediately followed by an order to retire to the hill and support the remaining gun, and most of the One hundred and fourth immediately repaired to the hill and attempted to stay the storm, which was now setting so strongly against us; but it was of no avail, for after a very severe engagement of musketry and cannonading for one hour and twenty-five minutes, the command was compelled to surrender to the forces of John Morgan and one Duke.

Total killed 23
Total wounded 100
Total missing 12

    Aggregate* 135

I would say that Company A had a very warm fight, killing 5 and wounding 8 of the enemy while in town, and losing 1 killed and 2 wounded.

Captain Leighton (Company A) reports that he was attacked by one regiment of cavalry and two companies of mounted infantry.

I also add that, during the time the One hundred and fourth were in the hands of the enemy, they were shamefully abused by the said enemy, by not being half fed, and by having their clothing stripped from them, by order of one John Morgan. Not being satisfied with taking the overcoats and blankets from the well, they stooped to the meanness of stripping the blankets from the sick, even after their own entreaty had been accompanied by that of the officers of the One hundred and fourth.

All of which I would most respectfully submit.

JOHN WADLEIGH,
Captain, Commanding Company I.

Lieutenant-Colonel GARESCHÉ,
    Chief of Staff, &c.

No. 9.

Report of Lieut. Robert V. Simpson, One hundred and fourth Illinois Infantry.

Just before sunrise, on the morning of December 7, the long-roll was beaten. Formed my company, and took my position in line of battle.

---

* But see revised statement, p. 45.

Regiment, under command of Lieutenant-Colonel Hapeman, marched from color-line, and took position in the edge of some heavy timber. The One hundred and sixth Ohio on the left, One hundred and fourth in the center, and One hundred and eighth Ohio on the right. Artillery (two guns) supported by One hundred and sixth Ohio. Skirmishers thrown out in proper order to feel for the enemy, who were engaged but a few minutes, when the engagement became general. Being at too great a distance to do any execution, we were ordered to lie down, the enemy still firing volley after volley, our artillery playing splendidly upon them. As soon as the enemy appeared, the officer commanding the artillery complained that the One hundred and sixth had fired one volley and run. The One hundred and fourth still kept firing, doing fine execution. After we had been engaged half an hour, one of my men shot down the enemy's color-bearer. At this I observed the enemy fall back in good order. About this time, or rather while this was taking place, the word came along our line that the One hundred and eighth had retreated on the run and surrendered. The enemy then closed in upon our front and flanks, and poured in upon us an unceasing shower of bullets. The artillery was ordered to the rear, and, when out of the way, the One hundred and fourth was ordered to fall back, which it did, with some confusion. We returned to the bank of the Cumberland River. We again rallied to the support of the artillery, but it was in vain; we were alone, and the enemy was upon us in numbers not less, I think, than three to one. Our men stood up bravely under the galling fire, and fought like veterans instead of raw volunteers. We have been in the service but little over three months, and most of that time we have been on the march.

To save the lives, which would have been a vain sacrifice, Colonel Moore, commanding the Thirty-ninth Brigade, surrendered the One hundred and fourth and the artillery, the remainder having surrendered themselves. The action lasted one hour and twenty-five minutes.

Of our lieutenant-colonel and major I think they deserve the highest praise; they were at all times doing their utmost to encourage the men. Of Colonel Moore, I think his bravery cannot be questioned, and I am proud of being an officer in the One hundred and fourth Illinois Infantry.

I heard the rebel General Morgan say that he had never fought any Federal troops who stood so determinedly as did the One hundred and fourth; and I also heard him say that had the other regiments fought as we did, our re-enforcements would have arrived, and he should have had to retreat, and several of his officers said the same. Of the cavalry in our command, I can say nothing, as I did not see them during the engagement.

ROBERT V. SIMPSON,
First Lieut., Comdg. Co. G, One hundred and fourth Illinois Infty.

No. 10.

Report of Lieut. Col. Gustavus Tafel, One hundred and sixth Ohio Infantry.

NASHVILLE, TENN., *December* 12, 1862.

SIR: I respectfully submit the following report of the part taken by my regiment in the battle of Hartsville, on Sunday, December 7, instant:

The first intimation we had of any threatened attack was by some one crying out at the top of his voice, at about 6.30 a. m., "Fall in; they are coming." Some few shots followed the warning. I immediately formed my regiment, then consisting of six companies (one company being off on special duty to Gallatin and one more on picket and brigade guard-duty, in the opposite direction to the place of attack). The regiment fell in promptly, and formed in line to the left of the One hundred and fourth Illinois Regiment, as indicated by Adjutant-General Gholson. We then saw the enemy's cavalry formed in line of battle on top of a hill, in the direction of the Gallatin road, separated by a wide gulf from our position. It occurred to me that a bald hill, commanding both positions, which ran out on our right, ought to be taken possession of, and suggested such a movement to Colonel Moore, commanding Thirty-ninth Brigade. He concurred, and ordered me to move in that direction. When I had marched my command past the One hundred and fourth Illinois, I noticed that a portion of the One hundred and eighth Regiment had then occupied the position in question. On reporting this, I was ordered by Colonel Moore to stay where I was, thus forming, with the One hundred and eighth Regiment, the right of our line of battle. We were not quite done taking this position when our right wing was attacked with impetuosity by the enemy's infantry, which, meantime, had deployed in our front. This attack was preceded by the firing of their artillery, which, on account of its bad aim, produced no effect whatever. The men behaved very well, and our line advanced somewhat from our original position, as the nature of the ground directed. One gun of the Thirteenth Indiana Battery now arrived on the ground, and was posted right in the center, on the left of my command. Colonel Moore then ordered the whole line to fall back to the rear of the gun, and he experienced some difficulty in making my left conform to such order.

Meanwhile I noticed a falling back on my right, which I found was occasioned by a part of the One hundred and eighth Regiment, in order to meet a flank movement by the enemy's dismounted cavalry, which advanced on us through the wood. Thus the fight stood for some time, until our piece of artillery, after achieving fine results, and blowing up one of the enemy's caissons, was forced to retire, on account of its loss of men and horses, caused by its exposed position. The cannon was withdrawn to the top of a rocky hill in rear of the camps of all the regiments from where the other piece was playing across the river. Simultaneously Colonel Moore ordered the men to fall back upon said hill. The flanking movements of the enemy, however, necessitated me to move the greater part of my men along the edge of the wood on the right, where the enemy had long tried to effect an opening.

The train of the One hundred and eighth Regiment afforded me a fine opportunity to check the enemy's advance on our right flank, and there they were punished severely. When, however, the camps of the One hundred and fourth and One hundred and eighth Regiments had fallen into the hands of the enemy, my position became untenable, and I fell back with the men upon the ridge occupied by brigade headquarters. At that time Colonel Moore had already surrendered the battery and that part of the brigade which had rallied on the hill back of the camps.

At this juncture men came riding up, wearing United States uniforms, waving their hats and telling us to surrender like the rest; but I cried out to the men not to listen, and that General Dumont was near with re-enforcements. The men accordingly made another stand, but were quickly surrounded by the then otherwise wholly disengaged aggregate force of the enemy. A part only made their escape across the road, and saved the regimental colors by tearing them off the staff and hiding them on their persons.

With one solitary exception, all the officers performed their duty unflinchingly ; and the men also, with very few exceptions, fought like veterans. Out of a force of about 250 men, I had 22 killed, 42 wounded, and 10 missing.*

The Second (rebel) Kentucky Infantry, with which we had to contend, according to their account, shows a loss of 75 killed and wounded.

The above is a true and correct statement of the fight from its beginning, and, as in this connection I cannot help noticing the scandalous and entirely unfounded reports which got into the papers, I would respectfully ask you to cause a strict investigation of the facts to be made.

GUSTAVUS TAFEL,
Lieut. Col., Comdg. One hundred and sixth Ohio Vol. Infty.

Colonel GARESCHÉ,
A. A. G., and Chief of Staff of Maj. Gen. Rosecrans,
Commanding Army of the Cumberland.

No. 11.

Report of Capt. Carlo Piepho, One hundred and eighth Ohio Infantry.

GENERAL : Allow me to state to you the part which the One hundred and eighth Regiment Ohio Volunteer Infantry took in the battle at Hartsville, Tenn., on December 7, 1862.

The One hundred and eighth, which formed a part of the Thirty-ninth Brigade, was encamped on the west side of the brigade, forming the right flank of the battle-line. The camp of the brigade, which was situated on a rocky hill, about 1 mile from Hartsville, rested, to its left, on a very steep and rocky bank of the Cumberland, close to a ford, which ford was protected by two pieces of artillery; in front of the camp, a dense grove of beech wood; on the right, the turnpike leading from Hartsville to Lebanon. Another ford in the Cumberland, between the camp and town, was left without protection. The outposts were thrown out about a half mile from camp, and formed a line from the bank of the Cumberland about one-half mile above camp to another point of the river bank, about one-half mile below. There were no outposts or vedettes posted on the opposite side of the river, where several roads connected at the above-mentioned ford, between camp and town. The road leading from Hartsville to Gallatin was also left without protection.

Soon after reveille, on Sunday morning, December 7, a negro servant of one of the officers of the One hundred and eighth ran into camp, shouting at the top of his voice, " The rebels are coming." I ordered the long-roll to beat, formed my battalion in line, and went out in front with Companies A and B, which two companies I threw out as skirmishers. I found the enemy thrown up in line of battle on the summit of a low hill, ready to rush on us, in shooting range of our camp. The rest of the battalion (five companies) I left under command of Adjutant

------
* But see revised statement, p. 45.

Huhn, of the One hundred and eighth, and sent word to him to follow me as reserve, and take position on a place to the left of our regimental camp, but by mistake the order was not communicated verbally, so he took position on the extreme right, and soon was in close contact with the rebels. The position he took was good, but I could not thereby accomplish my intention of charging the enemy at the point of the bayonet. By this time the two other regiments of infantry (One hundred and sixth Ohio and One hundred and fourth Illinois) formed in line, and the action began to become very lively. The enemy opened his batteries, throwing a great mass of shells and canister. Our artillery took position on the left of our line, and opened on the enemy. Soon the line of skirmishers, which protected our left, fell back behind the artillery, by which movement the artillery was exposed and soon disabled. My battalion held its position firmly for about one hour, when the commander of the brigade waved a white handkerchief and surrendered. Our left wing broke, and I came pretty near being outflanked. I now changed front toward our right, from which direction the enemy came rushing in on the Hartsville road. Under a heavy fire, the enemy demanded my surrender, which I denied; but soon I was compelled to fall back to a small creek, on the right of the Hartsville road, where I made another stand. By this time the enemy had full possession of our camps, Colonel Moore having surrendered before I knew anything about it. The position I held on the creek above mentioned I soon found totally surrounded by the enemy. Here I was demanded the second time to surrender, and, seeing that I could not accomplish anything with the small force which was left to me, I finally consented to the demand.

My command numbered, besides myself and my adjutant, 4 captains, 7 lieutenants, and 400 enlisted men. (The rest of the officers were disabled by sickness to take part in the action.) They all showed a bravery and gallantry unexpected for new troops. The arms which were used by my command were the Austrian rifle, an arm totally worthless, and condemned on different occasions, the locks of said guns having springs of so weak construction that many of the men had to snap the cock three or more times before the piece would discharge. The men also were provided with ammunition a good deal too large for the pieces; the caliber of the guns .58, and that of the ammunition .54. Notwithstanding these calamities, the men stood like veterans, and most of them fired 20 to 25 rounds. Our loss was 66 killed, wounded and missing.*

Your most obedient servant,

CARLO PIEPHO,
Capt., Comdg. One hundred and eighth Regt. Ohio Vol. Infty.
General ROSECRANS.

No. 12.

Report of Capt. Joseph Good, One hundred and eighth Ohio Infantry.

The battle commenced at 6.30 a. m. The first notice I had of the enemy approaching I heard, "Company, fall in." I ran to my company parade-ground; ordered my men to fall in; formed my company in

----

* But see revised statement, p. 45.

about two minutes ready for action; received orders from Captain Piepho, commanding the One hundred and eighth Regiment, to march my company at double-quick to the right, and join Company A. I arrived, deployed on the right, and formed the reserve with part of my company. I noticed on my right, on the ridge, two companies of cavalry (the Second Indiana and Eleventh Kentucky). The enemy at this time had formed line of battle in the open stubble-field. We opened fire on them; they repeated with musketry and cannon. At this time I noticed one section of our artillery firing about four or five shots. At the commencement of the firing, our cavalry on the ridge gave way and ran to camp; that unmasked the right wing of our skirmish line, and we had to fall back about 100 yards, in order that they could not outflank us. At this instant I noticed one of the regiments fire one volley and retreat in confusion. I could not say what regiment this was, but I think the One hundred and sixth Ohio. At this time the Second Indiana Cavalry Regiment took post on the left of the main column, awaiting orders, when the enemy brought their artillery to bear on our column in the open field. The main column gave way at this time in confusion, and retreated to the camp of the One hundred and fourth Illinois, when the rebels came over the open field and fired very rapidly, when Col. A. B. Moore, commanding the Thirty-ninth Brigade, ordered the white flag to be raised, and surrendered. I, at this time, was with our skirmishers, when I heard from one of the orderlies that the brigade had surrendered, with the artillery.

We then marched our men (about 150) to the right, about three-quarters of a mile, to the creek running through Hartsville; found it to be frozen over, with a thin skim of ice not strong enough to bear us crossing it. I wanted to countermarch down the stream about a quarter of a mile to where a small bridge crossed, when the rebel cavalry came up and demanded our surrender.

Among us were the major and two or three officers of the One hundred and sixth Regiment Ohio Volunteer Infantry; also Captain Piepho, commanding One hundred and eighth Regiment, and three lieutenants of the One hundred and eighth. When the major of the One hundred and sixth Regiment stepped up and acknowledged the surrender, and marched his men to camp, I fell to the rear of our men, and tried to escape, when I was halted by one of the cavalry, asking where I was going. I told him that I was going up to my men to surrender, and I followed the man until I came within 5 or 6 paces of the men going to camp. I met three officers of the One hundred and eighth Regiment Ohio Volunteer Infantry, asking me if I did not want to make my escape. I told them to come on, and we started back about 20 paces, when we met Captain Piepho, who asked where we were going; we told him that we were going to try to make our escape, when he told us there was no use to try to make our escape, as the enemy was all around us.

While we were standing there and talking over the matter, we were hailed by some 20 cavalry. They demanded our revolvers and swords, and then marched us to camp. When near camp we got scattered among the horses of the rebels, when I was asked by one of the rebel officers whether we were prisoners (myself and Lieutenant Hebel, of Company A). I told him that we were. He then told me that we had to go to the river and cross. I then asked if I could go up to camp and get my books, &c. He told me that I could not; that he wanted us to cross immediately, as he feared the Yankees would come; so we started to go to the river. When I got near the river I stepped to the right about

5 paces, followed by Lieutenant Hebel. Then I told the lieutenant to stand still for a few minutes until I got away. Then I leaped off the bank in a by-road leading to the ford; walked quick time down the river, when I met 1 cavalryman with 2 wounded rebels on a cart, with a negro driving the cart. They seemed to be in dispute about something— the road, I think. I told them that they were on the wrong road to ford the river, and that they had to go to the upper road to ford the river, and I passed on about 10 or 15 paces, when I leaped down the bank, ran up the ravine, and got under the roots of a tree, followed by the lieutenant. Remained there until our re-enforcements came up— the Second Brigade, commanded by Colonel Harlan. Just at the time the rebels had the trains over the river he ordered the artillery up. The artillery was brought to bear on the rear of the rebels, they replying twice, and then left. A company of the Eleventh Kentucky Cavalry followed and recaptured 3 wagons, loaded with muskets.

Our killed numbered about 80; wounded, about 120.* About 30 or 40 of the rebels were killed, and about 100 wounded.

Our men acted bravely, but the commander of the brigade not being competent to command, caused the defeat, I think.

JOSEPH GOOD,
Captain Company B, One hundred and eighth Regt. Ohio Vols.

No. 13.

Reports of General Braxton Bragg, C. S. Army, commanding Army of Tennessee, with instructions to Brigadier-General Morgan, and congratulatory orders.

MURFREESBOROUGH, TENN., December 8, 1862.

An expedition sent under Acting Brig. Gen. John H. Morgan attacked an outpost of the enemy at Hartsville, on the Cumberland, yesterday morning, killed and wounded 200, captured 1,800 prisoners, two pieces of artillery, and 2,000 small-arms, and all other stores at the position. On the previous day a small foraging train was captured by General Wheeler, near Nashville, with 50 prisoners, and on the 5th Colonel [P. D.] Roddey, Alabama cavalry, also captured a train near Corinth with its escorts and a number of negroes. Our loss at Hartsville was about 125 killed and wounded; none at either of the other places.

BRAXTON BRAGG,
General, Commanding.

General S. COOPER.

HEADQUARTERS ARMY OF TENNESSEE,
Murfreesborough, Tenn., December 22, 1862.

SIR: Having been informed by Acting Brig. Gen. John H. Morgan, whose cavalry brigade covered my front in the direction of Hartsville, Tenn., that the enemy's force at that point was somewhat isolated, I yielded to his request and organized an expedition under him for their attack.

---

* But see revised statement, p. 45.

On the 5th instant, Hanson's brigade, of Breckinridge's division, was moved forward on the road toward Hartsville, and halted at Baird's Mills, a point nearly due east from Nashville, and half way to Hartsville, where it was joined by Morgan's cavalry force. Two regiments (the Second and Ninth Kentucky Infantry), with [Robert] Cobb's (Kentucky) artillery, moved from this point with the cavalry at 10 p. m. on the 6th, to attack the enemy at Hartsville. Early on the morning of the same day, Hanson, with the remainder of his brigade, moved, as directed, on the road toward Nashville for the purpose of a reconnaissance, and to cause a diversion. At the same time that the troops above named left their camps near here, Major-General [B. F.] Cheatham, with two brigades, moved out on the Nashville road, halted all night at La Vergne, 15 miles, and on the next day, in conjunction with General Wheeler's cavalry, made a strong demonstration on the enemy's front. These movements had the desired effect, and completely distracted the enemy's attention from the real point of attack. Learning that a foraging train of the enemy was on his right flank, Cheatham detached Wheeler, with a cavalry force, to attack it, which he did in his usual dashing and successful manner, capturing 11 wagons and 57 prisoners. Under cover of these feints, Morgan, by an extraordinary night march, reached the point of his destination about sunrise, and, in a short but warmly contested engagement, killed, wounded, and captured the entire command of more than 2,000 officers and men.*

I inclose herewith the reports of General Morgan and the subordinate commanders, and take great pleasure in commending the fortitude, endurance, and gallantry of all engaged in this remarkable expedition. It is a source of personal and official gratification to perceive that the Department has recognized the services of the gallant and meritorious soldier who led the expedition by confirming my previous nomination of him as a brigadier-general. Two sets of infantry colors and one artillery guidon, taken at Hartsville, are also forwarded with this report. A third set of infantry colors was presented by its captors to the President on his recent visit to this place.

I am, sir, very respectfully, your obedient servant,

BRAXTON BRAGG,
General, Commanding.

General S. COOPER,
Adjutant and Inspector General, Richmond, Va.

HEADQUARTERS ARMY OF TENNESSEE,
Murfreesborough, Tenn., December 1, 1862.

Brig. Gen. JOHN H. MORGAN,
Commanding Cavalry at Baird's [Mills]:

GENERAL: The general commanding directs me to say that, when relieved from your present duties, you will proceed with your whole command, by the most practicable route and with the least delay, to operate on the enemy's lines of communications in rear of Nashville. You will assail his guards where your relative force will justify it; capture and destroy his trains; burn his bridges, depots, trestle-work, &c. In fine, harass him in every conceivable way in your power. When practicable,

---

* But see inclosure A to Bragg's report of the battle of Stone's River, p. 673.

send all prisoners to the rear, so as to conceal your operations. When it is necessary, parole them, sending lists by first mail to these headquarters. You are authorized to increase your command to the extent of your captured arms and horses, assigning the men to your old regiments. Do everything to prevent the enemy from foraging north of the Cumberland River, and especially toward Clarksville. If practicable, communicate and co-operate with Brigadier-General [N. B.] Forrest. You are not limited in the extent of your operations, every confidence being reposed in your zeal, discretion, and judgment. You will make weekly reports of your operations, sending with each a return of your command. It is reported that the enemy is obstructing the fords of the Cumberland.

Brigadier-General [J.] Wheeler has been ordered to relieve you as soon as Brigadier-General [J.] Pegram can be placed in position with a sufficient command.

I am, general,* very respectfully, yours,

GEORGE WM. BRENT,
Assistant Adjutant-General.

—

GENERAL ORDERS, }   HEADQUARTERS DEPARTMENT NO. 2,
No. 155.   }   *Murfreesborough, Tenn., December 12, 1862.*

With pride and pleasure, mingled with gratitude to the Supreme source of all our victories, the general commanding has the satisfaction of announcing to his troops the signal triumph of our arms at Hartsville, Tenn., on the 7th instant. This brilliant exploit was achieved by a portion of Morgan's cavalry brigade, together with detachments from the Second and Ninth Kentucky Regiments of Infantry, under Colonel Hunt, the whole under Brigadier-General Morgan. After a remarkable march of more than 40 miles, through snow and ice, they forded the Cumberland under cover of darkness, and at daylight precipitated themselves upon the enemy. Our success was complete. With a force of not more than 1,200 men in action, we inflicted a loss upon the enemy of 500 killed and wounded, and captured 1,800 prisoners, with all their arms, munitions, and other stores. Our own loss was small compared with the result, not exceeding 125 in killed and wounded. The memory of the gallant men who fell to rise no more will be revered by their comrades, and forever honored by their country. To Brigadier-General Morgan and to Colonel Hunt the general tenders his thanks, and assures them of the admiration of his army. The intelligence, zeal, and gallantry displayed by them will serve as an example and an incentive to still more honorable deeds. To the other brave officers and men composing the expedition the general tenders his cordial thanks and congratulations. He is proud of them, and hails the success achieved by their valor as but the precursor of still greater victories. Each corps engaged in the action will in future bear upon its colors the name of the memorable field.†

By command of General Bragg:

GEO. G. GARNER,
Assistant Adjutant-General.

---

* Copy to General Wheeler same day.
† The U. S. colors of the One hundred and fourth Illinois were captured by Private William H. Carson, Second Kentucky (Confederate) Infantry, and the regimental colors by Corp. Augustus Reynaud, Ninth Kentucky (Confederate) Infantry.

No. 14.

Return of casualties in the Confederate forces at Hartsville, Tenn., December 7, 1862.

[Compiled from nominal lists.]

Command.	Killed.		Wounded.		Missing.		Aggregate.	Remarks.
	Officers.	Enlisted men.	Officers.	Enlisted men.	Officers.	Enlisted men.		
Morgan's brigade:								
Staff			1	1			2	
Gano's regiment						1	1	
Cluke's regiment	1	1	4	20	1	5	32	Lieut. W. S. Kendall killed.
Chenault's regiment		1		4			5	
Bennett's regiment		1	1	2			4	
Total	1	3	6	27	1	6	44	
Hanson's brigade:								
2d Kentucky	2	6	3	51		6	68	Lieuts. John W. Rogers and Charles H. Thomas killed, and Lieut. Thomas M. Horne mortally wounded.
9th Kentucky	1	5	1	9		1	17	Lieut. Dandridge S. Crockett killed.
Cobb's battery		3		7			10	
Total	3	14	4	67		7	95	
Grand total	4	17	10	94	1	13	139	

No. 15.

Report of Brig. Gen. John H. Morgan, C. S. Army, commanding expedition.

MORGAN'S HEADQUARTERS,
Cross-Roads, near Murfreesborough, Tenn., December 9, 1862.

SIR: I have the honor to lay before you, for the information of the general commanding, a report of the expedition against the Federal force at Hartsville:

I left these headquarters at 10 a. m. on the 6th instant, with 1,400 men of my own command, under the orders of Colonel Duke; the Second and Ninth Kentucky Infantry, commanded by Colonel [T. H.] Hunt; Captain [Robert] Cobb's battery of artillery, two small howitzers, and two rifled Ellsworth guns belonging to my own command. At Lebanon I received information that no change had been made in the number of the Federals at Hartsville, their number being still about 900 infantry and 400 cavalry, with two pieces of artillery. I found afterward that their force had been considerably underrated. I proceeded with the infantry and artillery to Purier's Ferry, on the Cumberland River, sending the cavalry, under the orders of Colonel Duke, to pass at a ford some 7 miles below the point where we were to rendezvous. I passed my troops with great difficulty, there being but one boat, and about 5.30 on the morning of the 7th I arrived at Hager's Shop, 2 miles from the Federal camp. I found that Colonel Duke, with his cavalry, had only just marched up, having crossed the ford with difficulty, and that one regiment of his command, 500 strong (Colonel [R. M.] Gano's), had not yet reported. Major [R. G.] Stoner's battalion had been left on the other side of the Cumberland, with the two mountain howitzers, to prevent the escape of the enemy by the Lebanon road, and Colonel [J. D.] Bennett's [Ninth Tennessee Cavalry] regiment had been ordered to proceed to Hartsville to picket the road leading to Gallatin, and to attack any of the Federals they might find in that town, to take possession of the Castalian Springs, Lafayette, and Carthage roads, so as to prevent the escape of the enemy. This reduced my force considerably, but I determined to attack, and that at once. There was no time to be lost; day was breaking, and the enemy might expect strong re-enforcements from Castalian Springs should my arrival be known. Advancing, therefore, with the cavalry, closely followed by the artillery and infantry, I approached the enemy's position. The pickets were found and shot down. The Yankee bivouac fires appeared to cover a long line of ground, and gave me to suppose that their numbers were much greater than I anticipated. On nearing their camp the alarm was sounded, and I could distinctly see and hear the officers ordering their men to fall in, preparing for resistance. Colonel Duke then dismounted Colonels Cluke's and Chenault's regiments (in all about 450 men), drawing them up in line in a large field in the front and a little to the right of the enemy's line, which was then forming, and seeing that the artillery and infantry were in position, he ordered his men to advance at the double-[quick], and directed Colonel Chenault, who was on the left, to oblique, so as to march on the enemy's flank. His men then pressed forward, driving the Federals for nearly half a mile, without a check, before them, until their right wing was forced back upon their own left wing and center. Colonel Duke then ordered a halt until the infantry had commenced their attack on the Federal left wing, which caused a retreat of the whole line. At this juncture Lieutenant-Colonel [J. M.] Huffman and Major [Theophilus] Steele, of Gano's regiment, came up with about 100 men of that regiment, who had succeeded in crossing the ford, and threw their small force into the fight. My dismounted cavalry, under Colonel Duke, had only been skirmishing previously to this for about twenty minutes; but seeing that Colonel Hunt, with the infantry, was pressing hard upon the Federal left, he ordered an advance upon the right wing and flank of their new line. It gave way and ceased firing, and soon after surrendered.

Colonel Duke reports that his men fought with a courage and coolness which could not be surpassed.

Colonels Cluke and Chenault led on their men with the most determined bravery, encouraging them by voice and example.

The timely arrival of Lieutenant-Colonel Huffman and Major Steele, and the gallant manner in which they threw themselves into the fight, had a very decided effect upon the battle at the point at which they entered.

The artillery under Captain Cobb did most excellent service, and suffered severely from the enemy's battery, which fired with great precision, blowing up one of his caissons and inflicting a severe loss on that arm.

The infantry conducted themselves most gallantly, the Second Kentucky suffering most severely.

Colonel Bennett's regiment, as I said before, was not in the fight, having been sent on a special service, which was most efficiently performed, 450 prisoners having been taken by them and 12 Federals killed.

Thus, sir, in one hour and a half the troops under my command, consisting of 500 cavalry (Colonel Gano's and Colonel Bennett's regiments and Major Stoner's command not participating in the fight), 700 infantry, with a battery of artillery (in all about 1,300 strong), defeated and captured three well-disciplined and well-formed regiments of infantry, with a regiment of cavalry, and took two rifled cannon—the whole encamped on their own ground and in a very strong position—taking about 1,800 prisoners, 1,800 stand of arms, a quantity of ammunition, clothing, quartermaster's stores, and 16 wagons.

The battle was now won. The result exceeded my own expectation, but still I felt that my position was a most perilous one, being within 4 miles in a direct line, and only 8 by the main Gallatin road, of an enemy's force of at least 8,000 men, consisting of infantry, cavalry, and artillery, who would naturally march to the aid of their comrades on hearing the report of our guns. I, therefore, with the assistance of my staff, got together all the empty wagons left by the enemy, loaded them with arms, ammunition, and stores, and directed them immediately to Hart's Ferry. There was no time to be lost. The pickets placed by my assistant adjutant-general on the Castalian Springs road sent to report the advance of a strong body of Federals, estimated at 5,000 men. I sent Colonel Cluke's regiment to make a show of resistance, ordering Colonel Gano's regiment, which had arrived, in support. In the mean time I pressed the passage of the ford to the utmost. This show of force caused a delay in the advance of the enemy, who had no idea of the number of my men, and probably greatly overrated my strength, and gave me time to pass the ford with infantry, artillery, and baggage-wagons, the horses of my cavalry being sent back from the other side of the Cumberland River to carry over the infantry regiments.

It was time to retreat. The enemy attacked our rear, but was kept at bay by the two regiments before specified, aided by four guns I had previously ordered to be placed in position on the south side of the Cumberland, looking forward to what was now taking place. The banks of the river on both sides are precipitous, and the stream breast-deep, but our retreat was effected in excellent order. We lost not a man, except 3, badly wounded, that I was reluctantly forced to leave behind. Cavalry, infantry, guard, guns, and baggage-train safely crossed, with the exception of four wagons, which had been sent by another route, and which are still safely hidden in the woods, according to accounts received to-day.

In justice to my brave command, I would respectfully bring to the notice of the general commanding the names of those officers who contributed, by their undaunted bravery and soldier-like conduct, to the brilliant success which crowned the efforts of the Confederate arms: To Colonel Hunt, of the Ninth Kentucky, commanding the infantry, I am deeply indebted for his valuable assistance; his conduct and that of his brave regiment was perfect; their steadiness under fire remarkable. The Second Kentucky also behaved most gallantly and suffered severely; 62 men killed and wounded, 3 regimental officers left dead on the field, sufficiently testified to their share in the fight and the resistance they had to encounter. Colonel Cluke's regiment paid also a high price for its devotion. It went into the field 230 strong; had 6 officers, with 21 non-commissioned officers and privates, killed and wounded, besides 6 missing. Colonel Duke, commanding the cavalry, was, as he always has been, "the right man in the right place." Wise in counsel, gallant in the field, his services have ever been invaluable to me. I was informed by my adjutant-general that Colonel Bennett, in the execution of the special service confided to him, and in which he so entirely succeeded, gave proof of great personal gallantry and con·

tempt of danger. I owe much to my personal staff: Major [D. H.] Llewellyn, Capts. Charlton H. Morgan, [Rufus K.] Williams, and Lieut. Robert Tyler, acting as my aide-de-camp, gave proofs of great devotion, being everywhere in the hottest fire.

Major Llewellyn received the sword of Col. Robert R. Stewart and the surrender of his regiment. Captain Morgan's and Captain Williams' horses were killed under them, and Lieutenant Tyler was severely wounded. My orderly sergeant, Craven Peyton, received a shot in his hip and had his horse killed by my side. I must crave forgiveness if I add, with a soldier's pride, that the conduct of my whole command deserved my highest gratitude and commendation.

Three Federal regimental standards and five cavalry guidons fluttered over my brave column on their return from this expedition. With such troops, victory is enchained to our banners, and the issue of a contest with our Northern opponents, even when they are double our force, no longer doubtful!

I have the honor to be, sir, with the highest respect, your most obedient servant,

JOHN H. MORGAN,
Brigadier-General.

Colonel [GEORGE WILLIAM] BRENT,
Chief of Staff.

No. 16.

Report of Col. Roger W. Hanson, Second Kentucky Infantry, commanding First Brigade, Breckinridge's division.

HEADQUARTERS BRECKINRIDGE'S DIVISION,
December 11, 1862.

SIR: I have the honor to forward a report from Col. R. W. Hanson, commanding First Brigade, of my division, covering the report of Col. Thomas H. Hunt, who commanded the Second and Ninth Kentucky Regiments and Cobb's battery in the recent expedition (under command of Brigadier-General Morgan) against Hartsville; and also the reports of Major [James W.] Hewitt and Captain [James T.] Morehead, commanding, respectively, the Second and Ninth Kentucky, and of Captain [Robert] Cobb, commanding the battery.

I beg to call attention to the officers and men specially named for gallantry, and to suggest respectfully that the troops engaged in this expedition deserve mention in orders for conduct which in fortitude and daring has not been surpassed during the war.

Very respectfully,

JOHN C. BRECKINRIDGE,
Major-General, Commanding.

Maj. THOMAS M. JACK,
Assistant Adjutant-General.

[Inclosure.]

HEADQUARTERS FIRST BRIGADE,
Camp near Murfreesborough, Tenn., December 11, 1862.

In pursuance of the order of General Bragg, I proceeded with my command on the 5th instant to Baird's Mills, and remained two days, making, as directed, reconnaissance toward Nashville. General Morgan designated the Second and Ninth Kentucky and Cobb's battery as the troops he desired to accompany him upon the Hartsville expedition. They were detached under the command of Colonel Hunt. I inclose herewith his report of the battle of Hartsville and the reports of his subordinate officers. I wish to call attention to the honorable mention that is made in Major [James W.] Hewitt's and Colonel Hunt's report of the gallant conduct of Sergeant Oldham, of the Second Kentucky Regiment, with the hope that the proper steps may be taken to procure for him the proper reward for his conduct. Sergeant Oldham was the color-bearer of the Second Kentucky Regiment at the battle of Donelson, and acted with great gallantry upon that occasion. He is a suitable man for a lieutenancy, being well qualified as well as truly brave.

R. W. HANSON,
Colonel, Commanding Brigade.

Colonel [J. A.] BUCKNER,
    Assistant Adjutant-General.

No. 17.

Report of Col. Thomas H. Hunt, Ninth Kentucky Infantry, commanding detachment First Brigade.

CAMP NEAR MURFREESBOROUGH, TENN.,
December 9, 1862.

CAPTAIN: I have the honor to report that the detachment from the First Brigade, Breckinridge's division, consisting of the Second Kentucky Regiment, Maj. James W. Hewitt commanding, 375 strong; Ninth Kentucky, Capt. James T. Morehead commanding, 320 strong, and Cobb's battery, placed under my command as senior officer, with orders to report to General Morgan, left Baird's Mills, where the brigade was in bivouac, on Saturday, the 6th instant, about 1.30 p. m. Marching in the rear of the cavalry force until we arrived in the vicinity of Lebanon, an exchange was made, when the infantry mounted the horses and rode 5 or 6 miles. The command reached Cumberland River about 10 o'clock; the infantry, artillery, and a small portion of cavalry [crossed] at —— Ferry, the balance of the cavalry crossing at a ford a few miles lower down the river. The two boats used for crossing were of small capacity, and in miserable condition, but, by constant bailing, they were kept afloat, and by 5 o'clock in the morning the command was safely over. The march of 5 miles to Hartsville, where the battle was fought, yet to make over bad roads for artillery, was not accomplished until after sunrise, and the purpose of General Morgan to surprise the enemy was defeated. When we approached in sight of their camp, we found their infantry already formed, occupying a very strong position on the crest of a hill, with a deep ravine in front and their artillery in battery. The troops of my command were placed in position west of the enemy's camp while under a heavy fire from their battery and sharpshooters thrown out from their right, but these latter were quickly driven in by the dismounted cavalry. The Second Regiment, having been formed on the left of the Ninth, was now ordered forward to support and follow up the success gained by the cavalry skirmishers. That they had hot work to accomplish is shown by their heavy loss in killed and wounded.

In the mean time Captain Cobb with his battery was not idle. He was doing good execution, and the enemy responded with effect, one of their shells striking and blowing up a caisson. As the ground was cleared of the enemy opposite our left, he (Captain Cobb) was ordered to take a new position with his battery in that direction, and at the same time the Ninth Kentucky Regiment was ordered forward to engage the enemy's left. My whole command was now engaged. The crest of the hill was reached, and here commenced a desperate struggle, as the contestants were only from 30 to 50 paces apart, where they fought for the space of ten minutes, when the order to charge was given, and most nobly was the command responded to. The enemy broke and were driven to the river cliff, where they were completely surrounded by my force in front and the dismounted cavalry on their flank and rear, and where they surrendered at discretion. It was a continued success from the commencement of the engagement. In about an hour and a quarter from the time the first gun was fired they surrendered, and more prisoners were brought off than we had men in the action. Large quantities of commissary and quartermaster's stores were also secured, a section of artillery, and a large number of small-arms, with the usual supply of ammunition. General Morgan had made most skillful dispositions, which, with the good fighting qualities of the troops engaged, secured success.

I cannot speak in too high terms of praise of the troops, and I scarcely know which most to admire, their patient endurance on the march or courage in battle. They marched 50 miles in cold winter weather, the ground covered with snow; crossed and recrossed the Cumberland River; fought a largely superior force strongly posted within 6 miles of their supports, and brought off the prisoners, all within the space of thirty hours. Captain Cobb with his officers and men had a most laborious time in getting their pieces and horses across the river, and it was only by the best-directed executions they succeeded at all.

Where officers and men all behaved so well, it is impossible for me to single out individual cases as peculiarly worthy of commendation. I cannot, however, refrain from mentioning Lieut. Joseph Benedict [Company B, Ninth Kentucky Infantry], who acted as my aide on the occasion. He was the right man in the right place.

I inclose herewith copies of the reports of Major Hewitt, Captains Morehead and Cobb, and would bring to your attention the fact that the former commends Color-Sergt. John Oldham for his gallant bearing.

The following is a summary of the loss sustained by my command:

Command.	Killed.	Wounded.	Missing.
2d Kentucky Regiment	8	54	3
9th Kentucky Regiment	7	10	1
Cobb's battery	3	7	......
Total	18	71	4

Included in the above are: Of the Second Kentucky Regiment—Charles H. Thomas, first lieutenant, and John W. Rogers, second lieutenant, Company C, killed; T. M. Horne, first lieutenant, Company A, mortally wounded; Second Lieut. A. J. Pryor, Company D, and Lieutenant [E. B.] Harding, Company K, wounded. Of the Ninth Kentucky—Second Lieut. Dandridge S. Crockett [Company K], killed, and First Lieut. J. W. Cleavland [Company I], wounded.

I am, sir, very respectfully, your obedient servant,

THOS. H. HUNT,
Colonel, Commanding Detachment.

Capt. JOHN S. HOPE,
Acting Assistant Adjutant-General.

No. 18.

Report of Maj. James W. Hewitt, Second Kentucky Infantry.

CAMP MURFREESBOROUGH, TENN.,
December 9, 1862.

SIR: I have the honor to report that, in pursuance of your orders, I formed my regiment on the left of the Ninth Kentucky, opposite the enemy's camp near Hartsville, a portion of General Morgan's cavalry being at the same time on my left. When the order came for me to advance, I ordered my regiment forward, and, after passing the fence, the nature of the ground was such that I deemed it advisable to deploy my regiment, and therefore gave the order to deploy. In this way we drove the enemy from their first camp, and continued to drive them until they surrendered.

The officers, without an exception, behaved in the most gallant style. They were continually in advance of their men, urging them forward, and where all behaved so well it would be impossible to particularize. Each seemed to vie with the other in deeds of gallantry. The whole command, I am pleased to say, behaved in a most unexceptionable manner.

I cannot conclude my report without referring to Color-Sergt. John Oldham, whose conduct and carriage during the whole engagement elicited the encomiums of both officers and men.

Appended is a list of killed, wounded, and missing, all of which I respectfully submit:

Killed	8
Wounded	54
Missing	3
Total	65

Very respectfully, your obedient servant,

JAMES W. HEWITT,
Major, Commanding Second Kentucky Regiment.

Col. THOMAS H. HUNT.

No. 19.

Report of Capt. James T. Morehead, Ninth Kentucky Infantry.

CAMP NEAR MURFREESBOROUGH, TENN.,
December 10, 1862.

SIR: At 12 o'clock on Saturday, the 6th instant, I, as senior captain, was placed, by your orders, in command of the Ninth Kentucky Regiment, which had the day before moved to Baird's Mills, 18 miles from

Murfreesborough, and was at that time about to march against the enemy, reported to be at Hartsville, Tenn. The weather was excessively cold, the snow having fallen the day before to some depth, and the road was very rough. Notwithstanding, the men marched steadily during the day and all night, and reached the immediate neighborhood of the enemy's camp near Hartsville at sunrise. The enemy occupied a strong position in front of his encampment, his line of battle stretching along the crest of a hill, which was separated from our forces by an intervening hollow or ravine. Our line of battle was formed, with Cobb's battery on the right, supported by the Ninth Kentucky Regiment directly in its rear. On our immediate left was the Second Kentucky Regiment, and still farther to the left a portion of two regiments of dismounted cavalry, under Colonel Duke. The enemy occupied with his sharpshooters the woods and ravine in front of the left wing of our line, and opened a brisk fire on us. Against them the dismounted cavalry deployed as skirmishers, and soon succeeded in dislodging and driving them back upon the main body of the enemy. The Second Kentucky Regiment was ordered forward, and the Ninth Kentucky left in support of the battery. In a few minutes after, I was ordered to advance, and moved the regiment in double-quick in the direction of the main body of the enemy, going over in our route very rough ground and through a deep ravine. Ascending the hill, the regiment advanced to the right of the Second Kentucky, halted, and immediately became engaged, at less than 50 paces, with the enemy. After fighting for a short time, I ordered a charge, which was made with such gallantry by the regiment that the left wing of the enemy's line gave way and commenced retreating in confusion. Pressed closely by the Ninth Kentucky, they passed through their camps, and took refuge under the brow of a hill on the bank of the river and in rear of their artillery. The regiment continued to move rapidly on, and captured the two pieces of artillery and a stand of colors, charged the line of the enemy, and drove them to the brink of the river, compelling their immediate surrender. Here we captured Colonel Moore, commanding brigade, who, in reply to a question from Captain [N. A.] Crouch [Company B], answered that he surrendered himself and all the men around him, meaning the whole force.

The battle was now fairly won. The firing had ceased, save a few scattering shots here and there. I immediately formed the regiment again in line of battle, had order restored, stragglers collected, and the men kept in their places.

I sent details from all the companies to look after the dead and wounded, and detailed Company H, Captain [Chris.] Bosche, to guard the One hundred and sixth Ohio Regiment, captured by us. The prisoners being collected, I was ordered to detail Companies A and C to guard them, and afterward Company G. The regiment recrossed the river, and began its march toward Lebanon, Tenn.

Too much praise cannot be given to the officers and men for their spirit and patient endurance under a march of almost unexampled hardship and rapidity, and for their gallantry and good conduct in action.

The regiment had in battle an aggregate of 320 men. The casualties were as follows, viz :*

All of which is respectfully submitted.

JAS. T. MOREHEAD,
Captain, Commanding Ninth Kentucky Regiment.

Col. Thomas H. Hunt, *Commanding Infantry.*

---

* See p. 65.

DECEMBER 9, 1862.—Skirmish at Dobbins' Ferry, near La Vergne, Tenn.

REPORTS.

No. 1.—Maj. Gen. Thomas L. Crittenden, U. S. Army.
No. 2.—Surg. M. C. Woodworth, Fifty-first Ohio Infantry.

No. 1.

Report of Maj. Gen. Thomas L. Crittenden, U. S. Army.

HEADQUARTERS LEFT WING,
December 9, 1862.

COLONEL : I am this moment in receipt of a note from your headquarters, asking me if General Stanley has come in yet. I presume this must refer to the foraging expedition of Col. Stanley Matthews. As soon as I arrived at camp I sent an order to General Van Cleve to return to me a full report; but it has not yet been sent. As soon as it comes in it shall be forwarded. Eight wagons from my headquarters accompanied the party. They have all returned, well filled, but report that Colonel Matthews had a sharp skirmish, having quite a number killed and wounded, but that the wagons were filled and none lost. Since your orderly arrived, the inclosed note from Colonel Grose has been received through General Smith.* I declined to permit him to attack, for fear it might interfere with the proposed reconnaissances. Should you think differently, advise me, and I will yet direct the attack to be made.

A prisoner, taken by some of our troops and brought to me, reports that the attack was made by six regiments of cavalry, under Wheeler, who fought principally as infantry, being armed with Enfield rifles and navy revolvers; that the regiments are, however, greatly reduced, and do not number, all together, over about 1,500 men, and that this is the only force about La Vergne; also that Bragg left last week for Richmond; that Johnston is in command, and is camped some 4 miles this side of Murfreesborough; that his force numbers about 35,000 men. I will send him to you in the morning.

Most respectfully, your obedient servant,
T. L. CRITTENDEN,
Major-General, Commanding.

Col. J. P. GARESCHÉ, *Chief of Staff.*

P. S.—Since writing the foregoing, Colonel Matthews' report has come in, which is herein inclosed.*

No. 2.

Report of Surg. M. C. Woodworth, Fifty-first Ohio Infantry.

HEADQUARTERS TWENTY-THIRD BRIGADE,
December 12, 1862.

CAPTAIN : Pursuant to orders just received, I have the honor to report the result of my journey within the enemy's lines, under a flag of truce, to recover our wounded in the skirmish of the 9th. I left our outpost, accompanied by Drs. Russell and Mills, with an orderly and three ambulances, about 10 a. m., on the road passing from the Murfreesborough and to the Chicken pike, about 1 mile beyond the insane asylum.

---

* Not found.

I passed about 5 miles on the Chicken pike, in the direction of Stone's River, to a house where we had left one of the enemy's wounded—he being too severely wounded to move—which we left on the evening after the engagement. I found that a flag of truce had just removed his body to the enemy's lines. I left the Chicken pike just this side of the burned bridge crossing Stone's River, leaving the road to my left, and passed on about 1½ miles, to a house where I had left 6 of our men, who were wounded when the enemy made their last attack on the rear of our train. I found that the enemy had buried one of our dead left upon the field, also one of our wounded, who had died from a wound of the abdomen. I sent the remaining five in two ambulances back to our lines. I then took the remaining ambulance and passed on about 1 mile in the direction of La Vergne, where I came to the enemy's out-posts. I here waited one-half hour for the arrival of a proper officer to receive the flag, when Lieut. Col. William S. Hawkins, of General Wheeler's staff, came and escorted me to the house of Dr. Charlton, where I found one of our wounded, also one of the enemy's wounded, fatally.

They spoke of it as a battle rather than a skirmish, and admitted a loss of 8 killed upon the field. The picket at the outpost said they had carried away a large number of wounded, but would not state how many. I took our wounded man in the ambulance, and left their lines to return about 4 p. m. Colonel Hawkins assured me they had but one of our men prisoner, a lieutenant of the Eighth Kentucky Volunteers, who was slightly wounded in the back, and that he had been well cared for by their surgeons, and would soon be sent to our lines. The wounded on the field were all from the Eighth Kentucky Volunteers, and had all been paroled the day previous. Colonel Hawkins accompanied me about 2 miles from their lines on my return. I saw no force of the enemy this side of their outposts.

I am, captain, very respectfully, your obedient servant,

M. C. WOODWORTH,
Surgeon 51st Ohio Vols., Acting Medical Director 23d Brigade.

Capt. E. A. OTIS,
Assistant Adjutant-General, Fifth Division.

DECEMBER 9, 1862.—Reconnaissance toward Franklin, and skirmish near Brentwood, Tenn.

REPORTS.

No. 1.—Col. John A. Martin, Eighth Kansas Infantry.
No. 2.—Brig. Gen. John A. Wharton, C. S. Army, commanding Cavalry Brigade.

No. 1.

Report of Col. John A. Martin, Eighth Kansas Infantry.

CAMP NEAR NASHVILLE, *December* 9, 1862.

SIR: I have the honor to report that, in obedience to orders from head-quarters Ninth Division, I ordered the Twenty-fifth Regiment Illinois Vol-unteers, Lieutenant-Colonel McClelland, and the Eighth Kansas Battalicn, Captain Block, to proceed on a reconnaissance to the front, in the direction of Franklin, at 2 p. m. to-day. The regiments left at the hour, and I rode with them as far as the outside pickets, which had a short time before been fired into by a small body of the enemy. Here I received an order from headquarters to send out another regiment and a section of artillery, and, in obedience, I immediately ordered the Eighty-first Indiana Regiment, Major Woodbury, and two pieces of Captain Carpenter's Eighth Wisconsin Battery to join the reconnaissance, and then went forward to join the force in advance. Colonel McClelland had already deployed four companies of the Twenty-fifth and Eighth as skirmishers on each side of the road, and these had engaged in a brisk running fight with the enemy, also thrown out as skirmishers. The latter fell back rapidly, some of them abandoning their guns and clothing in their hasty flight. I directed the battery to move up the road behind the infantry. Captain Pease, of General Davis' staff, had meantime joined the command, and was doing valuable service in reconnoitering to the right and front.

The whole command then moved forward, the skirmishers keeping up an occasional firing, until we were about 5 miles beyond Brentwood, when a considerable body of the enemy's cavalry was seen in the road about a mile ahead. I had the battery placed in position, and fired several rounds at them. The enemy disappeared in great haste at the first shot. We remained at this point until just before sundown, when, in accordance with our orders, we returned.

From the best information to be obtained along the road, the enemy's force is all cavalry, and numbers 250 or 300 men. We drove them from their camp, finding their camp-fires yet burning brightly when we came up. One private of the Twenty-fifth Illinois is reported slightly wounded. What loss the enemy sustained I was unable to ascertain, although several are supposed to have been wounded.

I am, very repectfully, your most obedient servant,

JNO. A. MARTIN,
Colonel Eighth Kansas Volunteers, Commanding.

Lieut. T. W. MORRISON,
Acting Assistant Adjutant-General, Ninth Division.

No. 2.

Report of Brig. Gen. John A. Wharton, C. S. Army, commanding Cavalry Brigade.

HEADQUARTERS SECOND CAVALRY BRIGADE,
Nolensville, Tenn., December 10, 1862—6 p. m.

GENERAL : I moved a forced reconnaissance yesterday, with a regiment of cavalry and one piece of artillery, on the Owen and Wilson, or Liberty pike. Found the enemy's camp near the junction of that pike with the Nolensville pike. Threw solid shot into their camp and aroused them sufficiently to induce re-enforcements to be sent to their aid. They showed no disposition to follow. The field officers and captains of Howard's regiment desire it to remain with me, and I am anxious for it to do so. I have never seen Colonel [James R.] Howard; the taking of it now would prevent me from picketing properly. Let me know if there is any probability of that regiment, or any other I have, being taken at any time, as I wish to know, on account of distributing clothing and drawing pay.

Most respectfully, your obedient servant,

JNO. A. WHARTON,
Brigadier-General, Commanding Cavalry Brigade.

Brig. Gen. JOSEPH WHEELER, *Chief of Cavalry.*

DECEMBER 11–12, 1862.—Reconnaissance from Nashville to Franklin, Tenn., and skirmishes on the Wilson Creek pike (11th) and at Franklin (12th).

REPORTS.

No. 1.—Brig. Gen. David S. Stanley, U. S. Army, commanding cavalry.
No. 2.—Col. Edward M. McCook, Second Indiana Cavalry, commanding brigade.
No. 3.—Brig. Gen. John A. Wharton, C. S. Army, commanding cavalry brigade.

No. 1.

Report of Brig. Gen. David S. Stanley, U. S. Army, commanding cavalry.

HDQRS. CAV., 14TH A. C., ARMY OF THE CUMBERLAND,
Near Nashville, December 13, 1862.

COLONEL: I have the honor to submit an account of a scout I made from this place on Thursday. I started at daylight, moved down the Franklin pike to Brentwood. At that point I took the Wilson pike, with the design of striking the road from Franklin to Murfreesborough, expecting to destroy the supply trains I had learned were moving on that road. We had not, however, passed Brentwood but 2 miles when our advance guard engaged the enemy's pickets, and soon encountered a full regiment. The enemy fled south, and, at a point on the pike due west from Triune, turned off toward that place. I designed to pass on after driving the enemy 2 miles from the road, but they grew bold, and dismounted to fight our men on foot. Upon my endeavoring to close in on them, they again fled. This delay caused me to change my plan, and I took the old Liberty road to Franklin. Night came on when we had reached the Widow Waters' plantation, and I bivouacked at 9 o'clock. One of the enemy's pickets fired upon mine, wounding, probably mortally, a private in Captain Julian's company, First Middle Tennessee Cavalry. At midnight they again fired upon my pickets.

Leaving at 4 o'clock next morning, I reached Franklin a little after daybreak. The enemy's pickets were met 1½ miles east of the place. Upon getting up to the town, I found the enemy in considerable force on the bank of the Harpeth, and in the mill and houses. The Fourth Michigan, Colonel Minty, and the Seventh Pennsylvania, Major Wynkoop, were dismounted, and were soon sharply engaged with the enemy. The latter soon fled, and before I could get Colonel McCook's brigade behind them. We killed 4 of the enemy, including 1 officer; wounded some 8 or 9, and took 11 prisoners. I intended to burn the mill, which has been turning out 100 barrels of flour daily for the rebel army, but I found that to do so would destroy part of the town ; I had the machinery and burrs of the mill entirely destroyed. My loss is 1 man mortally wounded and 4 horses killed. I captured 10 horses, 4 wagons loaded with flour, and destroyed one wagon-load of brandy and whisky on its way to the rebel army. I am happy to be able to report that my men behaved well. The officers and men of the Seventh Pennsylvania Cavalry, who did the fighting principally, are brave and good troops. Reports from division and brigade commanders will be sent in.

Respectfully submitted.

D. S. STANLEY,
Brigadier-General, Commanding Cavalry.

Colonel GARESCHÉ.

No. 2.

Report of Col. Edward M. McCook, Second Indiana Caval y, commanding brigade.

HEADQUARTERS FIRST CAVALRY BRIGADE,
Camp Rosecrans, December 13, 1862.

SIR: I have the honor to report that, in pursuance to orders, I moved with my command, consisting of the Third Kentucky, Seventh Pennsylvania, and Fourth Michigan Cavalry, at daylight on the morning of the 11th instant, taking the advance of the division and moving on the Wilson Creek pike. My advance guard, consisting of two companies of the Seventh Pennsylvania, found the enemy's pickets about 6 or 7 miles south of Brentwood, and drove them back on to a squad of about 50 of the enemy's cavalry. After some skirmishing, the enemy ran off over the hill. Lieut. Frederick H. Geety, Seventh Pennsylvania Cavalry, was wounded in the left shoulder.

We turned off on a by-road and bivouacked for the night. The next morning we moved upon Franklin, my brigade still having the advance. The advance guard struck the enemy's pickets 2 miles from the town and drove them in. The enemy had formed their line of battle to the left of the mill and near the creek. I was ordered by General Stanley to take two of my regiments and form in the field on the left of the road. I ordered Major Wynkoop to take his command and attack them, which he did, advancing to the top of the bluff and opening fire, which the enemy returned with spirit. He had but 50 men with him, the rest of his command constituting the advance, and being on the right with the artillery. The firing continued about fifteen minutes, when the enemy broke and ran.

The Third Kentucky came up and formed on the right of the Seventh Pennsylvania, but had no opportunity to engage. The Fourth Michigan was still farther to the right, under the immediate supervision of General Stanley or Colonel Kennett; consequently I cannot report the part taken by them in the engagement.

By order of General Stanley, I moved over on to the Murfreesborough road, in order to intercept the enemy's retreat after they broke. When they saw my column approaching, part of their force went off on some little road on the other side of the river. We had to make a circuit in order to cross, and by the time we got over they were out of the reach of pursuit.

I saw 3 of the enemy dead and 1 wounded. My loss was nothing. The Seventh Pennsylvania had 4 horses killed. I saw 6 prisoners with the Fourth Michigan.

Very respectfully, your obedient servant,
EDWARD M. McCOOK,
Colonel, Commanding Brigade.

Lieut. M. B. CHAMBERLAIN,
A. A. A. G., First Cav. Div., Fourteenth Army Corps.

No. 3.

Reports of Brig. Gen. John A. Wharton, C. S. Army, commanding cavalry brigade.

HEADQUARTERS WHARTON'S CAVALRY BRIGADE,
Nolensville, Tenn., December 12, 1862—3.30 p. m.

GENERAL: The enemy attacked Franklin this morning just before daylight. Colonel [Baxter] Smith, who was there with 400 men, engaged them. The enemy forced him to retire, with a loss of 3 men killed and 6 wounded. Colonel Smith lost one of his most valuable officers. Colonel Smith reports the enemy's force to be two regiments of cavalry and one of infantry. The colonel is still near Franklin. I had put a force of 400 men there instead of 200, as I was ordered. I had also ordered one more regiment to his assistance, which did not reach him in time. General Cleburne is now moving on Franklin, on the Triune and Franklin dirt road, and I have sent Colonel [Thomas] Harrison, with his rangers, and [John R. Davis'] battalion of cavalry on the Franklin and Nashville pike, to hold the enemy in check until the arrival of General Cleburne's force. I advised General Wheeler last evening of the movements of the enemy; also this morning that I thought the enemy designed moving on that place.

I have the honor to be, yours, respectfully,

JNO. A. WHARTON,
Brigadier-General, Commanding Cavalry Brigade.

Lieut. Gen. LEONIDAS POLK,
Comdg. Polk's Corps d'Armée, Army of Tennessee.

—

HEADQUARTERS WHARTON'S BRIGADE,
POLK'S CORPS D'ARMÉE, ARMY OF TENNESSEE,
Nolensville, Tenn., December 12, 1862—7.30 p. m.

GENERAL: I dispatched you this morning, advising [you of] the occupation of Franklin by the enemy, who, after breaking the stones and destroying the machinery of the mill, left, via the Nashville pike, about 11 o'clock. Colonel Smith has returned to Franklin and reoccupied the place. The force of the enemy engaged this morning was 2,000 cavalry and two pieces of artillery, being five times as much as Colonel Smith's force. Their loss was 3 killed and 6 wounded. General [Colonel John] Kennett was in command. The infantry sent over there has been recalled, but the cavalry are in pursuit of the enemy. I have learned that the infantry now in my rear will soon be recalled, and I beg to call your attention to the exposed condition of my left and rear which will result therefrom. For this reason I would like to recall the force from Franklin, so as to have my forces more concentrated. The mill being destroyed, the only object to be attained would be to prevent illicit communication with the enemy, which could be done by having my forces this side.

I have the honor to be, general, very respectfully, your obedient servant,

JNO. A. WHARTON,
Brigadier-General, Commanding Cavalry Brigade.

Lieutenant-General POLK,
Commanding Corps d'Armée, Army of Tennessee.

DECEMBER 14, 1862.—Attack on forage train and skirmish on the Franklin pike, near Nashville, Tenn.

REPORTS.

No. 1.—Col. Joseph R. Scott, Nineteenth Illinois Infantry.
No. 2.—Lieut. Sylvanus H. Stevens, Stokes' (Chicago Board of Trade) Illinois battery.

No. 1.

Report of Col. Joseph R. Scott, Nineteenth Illinois Infantry.

HDQRS. NINETEENTH REGIMENT ILLINOIS INFANTRY,
Camp near Nashville, Tenn., December 15, 1862.

SIR: I respectfully report having taken command of the division forage train yesterday, in accordance with orders from brigade headquarters. The Nineteenth Illinois, Sixty-ninth Ohio, and a section of artillery, Fourth Kentucky Battery, detailed as escort, proceeded on Franklin pike some 7 miles, securing the desired amount of forage. I placed the artillery in position to command forage train and the approaches thereto. Being apprised of the immediate presence of the enemy, I sent the Sixty-ninth Ohio and one piece of artillery to the junction of a road leading into the pike to my rear, with the intention of holding that point until my train was formed. Shortly after my command had started for camp, firing was heard about half a mile to the left and rear. I immediately ordered back the Nineteenth Illinois and one piece of artillery, and found that the firing had been caused by a party of rebel cavalry, numbering about 20, attacking a forage party, consisting of 3 wagons, with an escort, consisting of 10 men, under command of Lieutenant Stevens, of the Chicago Board of Trade Battery. The rebels succeeded in capturing 5 men and 4 horses from one of the teams. The lieutenant and the balance of the men escaped. Our loss was 1 man wounded, 5 taken prisoners, 2 horses killed, and 4 captured.

Having no cavalry with me, I could not pursue the enemy to advantage.

Very respectfully, your obedient servant,
JOS. R. SCOTT,
Colonel, Commanding Nineteenth Illinois Infantry.

Col. A. V. SCHRADER,
Chief of Staff, Eighth Division.

[Indorsement.]

HEADQUARTERS TWENTY-NINTH BRIGADE,
Camp Hamilton, December 15, 1862.

Respectfully forwarded. The attack mentioned was not upon any part of the train under Colonel Scott's command, but an independent party, and the loss mentioned was of that party, not of Colonel Scott's.

Colonel Scott brought in his train and men all right. There was a delay in starting, owing to wagons of Seventh Brigade and Division not reporting in time. Very few of the teams had any men detailed to load, except my brigade.

T. R. STANLEY,
Colonel, Commanding.

No. 2.

Report of Lieut. Sylvanus H. Stevens, Stokes' (Chicago Board of Trade) Illinois battery.

IN CAMP ON FRANKLIN PIKE,
Near Nashville, Tenn., December 14, 1862.
(Received headquarters Eighth Division, Dec. 15, 1862.)

SIR : I have the honor to report that, in obedience to your orders, I proceeded with 3 wagons and a detail of 6 men to obtain forage on the Franklin pike; that before leaving the lines I had the pass from General McCook approved by General Negley, authorizing such commands. While on the road I was informed by Lieutenant Wood, of General Negley's command, commanding a party of forage wagons, that he had just obtained a quantity of forage at a place about 2½ miles outside of the pickets, and that other teams, under an escort commanded by Colonel Scott, had gone beyond this place. Before commencing the loading of the wagons, I made a thorough reconnaissance of the position, and placed my sergeant on an eminence to observe the country around. While proceeding to load, about 20 or 30 guerrillas, mounted and well armed, surrounded my men. They fought as long as there was a chance of a defense, and then surrendered. Rather than be taken prisoner, I fought my way through, escaping on foot. In consequence of the gateway being blocked up by one of my wagons, the sergeant and myself held the party at the gate with our pistols while the teams were escaping. Five privates and 1 corporal were taken prisoners; 1 private wounded in the back. This man we brought away. Five horses were captured and 2 killed. The guard under Colonel Scott with train had passed without my knowledge, leaving my party about a half mile in the rear.

I am, captain, very respectfully, your obedient servant,

S. H. STEVENS, JR.,
First Lieutenant.

Capt. JAMES H. STOKES, *Commanding Battery.*

The date of this report is the date of the matters therein set forth, viz, December 14, 1862.

S. H. STEVENS, JR.,
First Lieutenant.

DECEMBER 15–16, 1862.—Violation of flag of truce.

REPORTS, ETC.

No. 1.—Maj. Gen. Thomas L. Crittenden, U. S. Army, commanding Left Wing, Army of the Cumberland.

No. 2.—Capt. George G. Knox, aide-de-camp.

No. 3.—Brig. Gen. Horatio P. Van Cleve, U. S. Army, commanding Fifth Division.

No. 4.—Col. Robert H. G. Minty, Fourth Michigan Cavalry.

No. 5.—Correspondence between Major-General Rosecrans, U. S. Army, and General Bragg, C. S. Army.

No. 1.

Report of Maj. Gen. Thomas L. Crittenden, U. S. Army, commanding Left Wing, Army of the Cumberland.

HEADQUARTERS LEFT WING, *December* 16, 1862.

COLONEL : I spent the entire day yesterday visiting the front of our lines. Found all quiet; very orderly and exceedingly wet. Late in the evening, whilst a flag from the enemy was waiting for an answer from General Rosecrans, the forces of the enemy came in and captured the cavalry pickets, numbering about 45 men, which had been placed by General Stanley in front of the Fifth Division, it being all the cavalry in front of my command. By 9.30 the enemy occupied the station where the cavalry had been captured, and were signaling from it. Another regiment was promptly ordered to the front, to strengthen our outposts, and the night passed quietly. The divisions all report no absentees without passes, and guard vigilant. I inclose a report from General Palmer requiring attention.*

Most respectfully, your obedient servant,

T. L. CRITTENDEN,
Major-General, Commanding.

Col. J. P. GARESCHÉ.

No. 2.

Report of Capt. George G. Knox, aide-de-camp.

HEADQUARTERS LEFT WING,
December 25, 1862.

MAJOR: By permission of the general commanding, I accompanied a command on the 16th instant, numbering 111 men, of the Fourth Michigan Cavalry, commanded by Lieutenant-Colonel Dickinson, who was ordered to go with his command 2 miles beyond our outpost on the Murfreesborough pike. Arriving at our outpost, which is just at the 8-mile post, we found a party just ready to go out with a flag of truce to escort Lieutenant-Colonel Hawkins, of the Confederate Army, outside our lines. The command of Colonel Dickinson was ordered to dismount and remain inside our line until the flag returned. This we did, and remained there until the party bearing the flag returned and reported the way open for us. Our order required us to go as far as the 10-mile post. On our way, just this side of the 10-mile post, we came upon Lieutenant-Colonel Hawkins, who had stopped at a house to have his horse fed and to get his dinner. He at once got on his horse and proposed to go with us, but Colonel Dickinson not desiring a white flag, and being so near the point to which he was directed to go, refused to let the colonel accompany him, and required him to remain where he was until he had returned. To prevent any insult or injury being offered him, a commissioned officer and two privates of the Fourth Michigan Cavalry were left with him. Returning in less than half an hour to where he was, we released him, after having expressed our regrets for having found it necessary to detain him as long as we did.

I am, major, very respectfully, your obedient servant,

GEO. G. KNOX,
Aide-de-Camp.

Maj. LYNE STARLING,
Assistant Adjutant-General.

---

*Not found.

No. 3.

Reports of Brig. Gen. Horatio P. Van Cleve, U. S. Army, commanding
Fifth Division.

HEADQUARTERS FIFTH DIVISION,
December 16, 1862.

MAJOR: The first report of the capture of our cavalry pickets yesterday evening was from a private who was on post at the time and made his escape. He stated that while a flag of truce from the enemy was waiting to receive an answer from headquarters, a body of rebel cavalry dashed in and captured our cavalry reserve. This statement was afterward corroborated by Lieutenant Rowe, of the Fourth Michigan Cavalry, who reported, in addition, that he had learned from some who had escaped that Captain Abeel, who commanded the cavalry, had been very remiss in suffering his men to dismount and leave their ranks while the rebel party with the flag of truce were there. Lieutenant Rowe belonged to the company of cavalry on duty, but was not present at the affray, having been sent to these headquarters on business.

If the facts are as reported, it was a disgraceful outrage on the part of the rebels. At the same time, those bearing the flag of truce may have borne no part in it, and the conduct of Captain Abeel was very culpable and unsoldierlike.

Very respectfully, your obedient servant,
H. P. VAN CLEVE,
Major-General, Commanding Fifth Division.

Maj. LYNE STARLING,
Assistant Adjutant-General, Left Wing.

—

HEADQUARTERS FIFTH DIVISION,
Near Nashville, Tenn., December 25, 1862.

MAJOR: Pursuant to directions from Major-General Rosecrans, I have the honor to report the circumstances connected with the capture of a portion of the outposts in my front on the 15th instant, and the alleged detention of Lieutenant-Colonel Hawkins, of the Confederate Army, while at my lines with a flag of truce. Colonel Hawkins came to my outposts about 2 p. m. of the 15th instant, with communications for the general commanding, accompanied by several civilians and ladies, who desired to go to Nashville. Word was immediately sent to department headquarters, but, before a messenger could return, a scouting party of the First Alabama Cavalry attacked and captured all the cavalry outposts, and immediately retreated to the rebel lines. Colonel Hawkins was at this time waiting at my outposts for the arrival of a staff officer from the general commanding, and, when the enemy retreated, went with them beyond my lines. He presented himself the next morning at my infantry outposts, when he was placed under guard by Colonel Knifler [Knefler?], Seventy-ninth Pennsylvania [Indiana?] Volunteers, and the case reported to me for instructions. Colonel Knifler [Knefler?] believed Colonel Hawkins was in some respects responsible for the attack on the pickets the day before, and proposed to guard against a repetition of the occurrence. Soon after, Lieutenant-Colonel Hepburn, of General Rosecrans' staff, arrived, and Colonel Hawkins' dispatches received, and he sent beyond our lines. Of his subsequent arrest by Captain Knox and Lieutenant-Colonel Dickinson I know nothing, no report of the occurrence having been made to me. Colonel Hawkins, while at my outpost, was treated with the utmost courtesy, and was not placed under arrest until he presented himself at my infantry outposts under suspicious circumstances, before the position formerly occupied by my cavalry had been retaken, and was very shortly released.

Very respectfully, your obedient servant,

H. P. VAN CLEVE,
Brigadier-General, Commanding Fifth Division.

Maj. LYNE STARLING,
Assistant Adjutant-General, Left Wing.

No. 4.

Col. Robert H. G. Minty, Fourth Michigan Cavalry.

HEADQUARTERS FOURTH MICHIGAN CAVALRY,
Camp Rosecrans, December 16, 1862.

SIR: I have to report, for the information of the colonel commanding, that Companies H and M, of my regiment, while on picket on the Murfreesborough pike yesterday, were, under cover of a flag of truce, captured by the enemy's cavalry, numbering about 150 men. Company H had 38 men and Company M 20 men, but of these 22 were on duty, forming the chain of pickets. Second Lieutenant Rowe, with an orderly, was at General Van Cleve's headquarters, and one orderly had been sent to Nashville. The first sergeant of Company H and one of the pickets have escaped. I have heard of 2 of our men being wounded and 1 rebel killed.

General Stanley has ordered me to send out four companies to bring in our wounded men, and to scout the road for 3 or 4 miles.

I am, respectfully, your obedient servant,

ROBT. H. G. MINTY,
Colonel, Commanding Fourth Michigan Cavalry.

Lieutenant WOOLLEY,
Actg. Asst. Adjt. Gen., First Brigade, Cavalry Division.

[Indorsements.]

Will Colonel Minty state more explicitly the circumstances of this capture; by whom and what the flag of truce was used for; how the two companies were captured, &c.?

If a flag has been violated while being used for a legitimate purpose, I will call the attention of higher authorities to the outrage. I desire a circumstantial report of this affair.

EDWARD M. McCOOK,
Colonel, Commanding Brigade.

Lieutenant-Colonel Hawkins, with a flag of truce, had arrived at our outer pickets, and, while waiting for an officer of equal rank to receive the dispatches, a party of rebel cavalry dashed in from the left of the road, surprising and overpowering our pickets. Eight men have now returned to camp, and I have hopes of the escape of 6 more. One of my men was killed and 1 wounded. The rebels, so far as I can learn, met with the same loss, 1 killed and 1 wounded. When the scout returns, I may be able to give more particulars.

ROBT. H. G. MINTY,
Colonel, Commanding Fourth Michigan Cavalry.

HEADQUARTERS FIRST CAVALRY BRIGADE,
December 16, 1862.

Respectfully forwarded.

I would call the attention of the general commanding to this apparent violation of the usages of war.

EDWARD M. McCOOK,
Colonel, Commanding.

No. 5.

Correspondence between Major-General Rosecrans, U. S. Army, and General Bragg, C. S. Army.

HEADQUARTERS FOURTEENTH ARMY CORPS,
DEPARTMENT OF THE CUMBERLAND,
Nashville, December 15, 1862.

General BRAXTON BRAGG:

You will see by the copies of reports to me, herewith inclosed,* that another outrage of the grossest character has been perpetrated by your troops, in the presence of your own flag, commanded by a lieutenant-colonel in your service, who but yesterday was courteously received. I cannot believe you had authorized, or will permit to go unpunished or without prompt reparation, such barbarous conduct, hardly paralleled by savages. You cannot restore life to my men who have been inhumanly murdered, but I shall leave to your own head and heart to devise such reparation as is demanded by your own honor and the honor of our common humanity.

Very respectfully, your obedient servant,

W. S. ROSECRANS,
Major-General, Commanding.

—

HEADQUARTERS ARMY OF TENNESSEE,
Murfreesborough, Tenn., December 23, 1862.

Maj. Gen. W. S. ROSECRANS,
Commanding U. S. Forces, Nashville, Tenn.:

GENERAL: I have the honor to acknowledge the receipt of your communication of the 15th instant, in which you complain of the capture of your pickets, near Nashville, pending a flag of truce, and demand their restoration to your lines.

I have delayed my reply until a full and thorough investigation could be reported. As its result, I respectfully, but firmly, decline to accede to your demand.

The flag was sent from my lines for a specific purpose, and was reasonably expected back within a few hours. The movements of my force in front were directed accordingly, and there was no intention to avail themselves of the existence of the flag to cover an attack. The delay of the flag was caused by the reprehensible and criminal conduct of some of your subordinates, who placed its bearer under arrest, and kept him twenty-four hours before permitting him to return. Upon being finally permitted to leave, he was again arrested, menaced, and insulted by soldiers with drawn weapons at the command of an officer who placed him under strict arrest, notwithstanding the accompanying presence of his flag. The officers most active in perpetrating this outrage gave

---

* Not found.

their names as Capt. George [G.] Knox and Lieutenant-Colonel Dickinson, who represented themselves as belonging to the Fourth Michigan Cavalry, a part of which command was near by. The reason assigned for his detention was that they intended making an attack on our pickets, and did not wish them notified.

With these facts before me, I consider myself as justly entitled to apology and reparation for this unprecedented disrespect and outrage. To claim that a truce existed while my flag was forcibly detained by you is preposterous. By parity of reasoning, it would only be necessary to capture a flag and hold it indefinitely in custody in order to secure immunity from attack. The detention of a flag by you is incontestably proven. When so detained, it ceased to be my flag, and was yours by unlawful capture. It lost its sanctity by reason of your violence, and you ought to be the last one to seek a refuge beneath its folds.

To avoid the danger of future complications of a similar character, I have directed that hereafter flags shall be sent only on Mondays and Thursdays, between the hours of 12 m. and 4 p. m. They will also be received on the same days and between the same hours, unless the necessity is urgent and the urgency of the case manifest.

Trusting that this arrangement will preclude the recurrence of any further misunderstanding, I am, general, very respectfully, your obedient servant,

BRAXTON BRAGG,
General, Commanding.

[Indorsement.]

HEADQUARTERS DEPARTMENT OF THE CUMBERLAND,
Nashville, Tenn., December 25, 1862.

Respectfully referred to Major-General Crittenden, who will have General Van Cleve investigate this, and report result of investigation to-night.*

By order of General Rosecrans:

CHAS. R. THOMPSON,
Captain and Assistant Adjutant-General.

DECEMBER 20, 1862–JANUARY 5, 1863.—Carter's raid into East Tennessee and Southwest Virginia.

SUMMARY OF THE PRINCIPAL EVENTS.

Dec. 29, 1862.—Passage of Moccasin Gap, and capture of Confederates on the Blountsville road.

    30, 1862.—Capture of Confederates at Blountsville.

        Capture of Union, Tenn., and destruction of the railroad bridge across the Holston River.

        Capture of Carter's Depot, and destruction of the Watauga railroad bridge.

Jan. 2, 1863.—Skirmish at Jonesville, Lee County, Va.

REPORTS.†

No. 1.—Maj. Gen. Horatio G. Wright, U. S. Army, commanding Department of the Ohio, with congratulatory messages.

---

* See report No. 3, p. 82.
† See also Confederate correspondence, January 1 to 5, inclusive, Part II.

No. 2.—Brig. Gen. Samuel P. Carter, U. S. Army, commanding expedition.
No. 3.—Col. Charles J. Walker, Tenth Kentucky Cavalry, commanding Cavalry Brigade.
No. 4.—Lieut. Gen. E. Kirby Smith, C. S. Army, commanding Department of East Tennessee.
No. 5.—Maj. Gen. Samuel Jones, C. S. Army, commanding Department of West Virginia.
No. 6.—Brig. Gen. Humphrey Marshall, C. S. Army, of operations December 30–January 7.
No. 7.—Col. H. L. Giltner, Fourth Kentucky Cavalry, of operations December 30–January 2.
No. 8.—Lieut. Col. E. F. Clay, Third Battalion Kentucky Mounted Rifles, of operations December 30–January 1.
No. 9.—Lieut. H. H. Duncan, Company A, Third Battalion Kentucky Mounted Rifles, of operations December 29–30.
No. 10.—Capt. William W. Baldwin, commanding cavalry squadron, of operations December 29–January 2.
No. 11.—Col. Hiram Hawkins, Fifth Kentucky Infantry, of operations December 29–30.
No. 12.—Col. Campbell Slemp, Sixty-fourth Virginia Infantry, of operations December 29–January 1.
No. 13.—Maj. Isaac B. Dunn, relative to operations December 29–January 1.

No. 1.

Reports of Maj. Gen. Horatio G. Wright, U. S. Army, commanding Department of the Ohio, with congratulatory messages.

CINCINNATI, OHIO, *January 7, 1863.*

GENERAL: I have just received a dispatch from Maj. Gen. G. Granger that the cavalry force of about 1,000 men which he sent to East Tennessee on the 21st ultimo, by my order, under the command of Brig. Gen. S. P. Carter, to destroy the East Tennessee Railroad bridges, &c., has been heard from. General Granger has just received a dispatch from General Carter at Manchester, Ky., on his return, stating that on the 30th ultimo he entirely destroyed the Union and Watauga Bridges, with 10 miles of railroad. Five hundred and fifty rebels were killed, wounded, and taken prisoners. Seven hundred stand of arms and a large amount of flour, salt, and other rebel stores, also a locomotive and two cars, were captured and destroyed.

A brisk skirmish took place at the Watauga Bridge and another at Jonesville. We lost but 10 men. This expedition, as characterized by General Granger, has been one of the most hazardous and daring of the war, attended with great hardships and privations, owing to the almost impracticable nature of the country, the length of the route (nearly 200 miles each way), and the inclement season. The important results of this expedition can hardly be overrated, severing, as it has, Virginia and the Southwest; and General Carter, his officers and men, deserve the thanks of the country. Great credit is also due to Major-General Granger, under whose immediate supervision the expedition was fitted out, and whose long cavalry experience was a guarantee that nothing tending to its success would be neglected or forgotten.

H. G. WRIGHT,
Major-General, Commanding.

Major-General HALLECK.

HEADQUARTERS DEPARTMENT OF THE OHIO,
Cincinnati, Ohio, January 7, 1863.

Maj. Gen. G. GRANGER, *Lexington, Ky.:*

General Carter has done well. He has severed the great rebel artery of communication between the North and South, the importance of which at this time can hardly be overestimated; has killed, wounded, and captured more than half of his own numbers, with the loss of only 10 men; has destroyed large amounts of rebel stores, arms, &c., and has brought back his own command in safety. The result of the expedition has been telegraphed to the General-in-Chief, with an expression of my views as to the importance of the results accomplished. While waiting a reply from Washington, please present to General Carter, his officers and men, my congratulations upon the success of their efforts, and my full appreciation of the hardships and privations endured by them on their long and hazardous march over an almost impracticable country.

H. G. WRIGHT,
Major-General, Commanding.

—

WAR DEPARTMENT,
Washington, January 9, 1863.

Major-General WRIGHT, *Cincinnati, Ohio:*

The daring operations and brilliant achievements of General Carter and his command are without a parallel in the history of the war,* and deserve the thanks of the country. This expedition has proved the capacity of our cavalry for bold and dashing movements, which I doubt not will be imitated by others.

H. W. HALLECK,
General-in-Chief.

—

HEADQUARTERS DEPARTMENT OF THE OHIO,
Cincinnati, Ohio, January 20, 1863.

GENERAL: I have to transmit herewith a letter from Maj. Gen. G. Granger, commanding Army of Kentucky, inclosing the reports of Brig. Gen. S. P. Carter and Col. C. J. Walker, relating to the late expedition into East Tennessee, which resulted in the burning of bridges on the Virginia and East Tennessee Railroad at Union and Watauga, and of Majors Foley and Brown, commanding expedition into Middle [East] Tennessee.†

In submitting these reports, General Granger takes occasion to recommend Brigadier-General Carter for promotion to major-general, on the grounds of his valuable services in command of the East Tennessee expedition, and also to recommend Brigadier-General Gillmore for major-general, and Col. S. A. Gilbert, Forty-fourth Ohio Volunteer Infantry, for promotion to brigadier-general. General Carter's claims speak for themselves. As regards General Gillmore and Colonel Gilbert, I would say that I fully indorse all that is said in their favor. Few men can be found combining the qualifications necessary to important commands in a higher degree than these two officers.

In stripping Kentucky of all available troops, and sending them to support General Rosecrans, I have retained both these officers, much against their wishes and interests, believing that the interests of the

---

* See Maynard to Halleck, January 10, and reply, January 12, in Part II, pp. 313, 319
† See December 24, 1862–January 1, 1863, pp. 159–163

nation required officers of reliable character to command in Kentucky at this particular juncture in the affairs of the State.

General Gillmore will be assigned to the command of the Central District of the State, and Colonel Gilbert will command the most reliable brigade of his force, and neither should suffer in their prospects of advancement by being kept back from the field.

I have the honor to be, very respectfully, your obedient servant,

H. G. WRIGHT,
Major-General, Commanding.

Maj. Gen. H. W. HALLECK,
General-in-Chief, Washington, D. C.

No. 2.

Report of Brig. Gen. Samuel P. Carter, U. S. Army, commanding expedition.

LEXINGTON, KY., *January 9,* 1863.

GENERAL: I have the honor to submit the following report of the operations of the expeditionary force to East Tennessee, which was intrusted to my command:

Although a movement on East Tennessee was proposed as early as November 25 last, it was not until December 19 that arrangements were completed and the necessary orders given for the movement of the troops. It was hoped that the force to be sent on this hazardous, but most important, expedition would have been much larger than that which the commander of the department felt could be detached for such service when the final arrangements were made. My original design was to have divided the force into two columns, and strike the East Tennessee and Virginia Railroad at two points at the same time, distant 100 miles apart, and, by moving toward the center, have completely destroyed the road for that distance; but, on the junction of the different detachments, I found that the number was too small to risk a division, and I was reluctantly compelled to keep them united, or within easy supporting distance during the whole of my operations.

Having given orders for the junction of the forces, consisting of two battalions Second Michigan Cavalry, Lieutenant-Colonel Campbell, the Ninth Pennsylvania Cavalry, Major Russell, and First Battalion Seventh Ohio Cavalry, Major Reaney, near the mouth of Goose Creek, Clay County, Kentucky, I left this place with my staff on the 20th ultimo for that point. By your order, Col. Charles J. Walker, of Tenth Kentucky Cavalry, was placed in command of the cavalry brigade, and I here take occasion to tender my thanks for the appointment, and to express my commendation of the manner in which Colonel Walker discharged his arduous duties. The troops were ordered to move without baggage, with ten days' rations and a hundred rounds of ammunition, but, as it was feared some difficulty would be met with in obtaining forage, a supply train was ordered to proceed some 60 miles on the route, and then transfer forage and rations to a train of pack mules.

On the 22d ultimo I came up with the two battalions Second Michigan and Ninth Pennsylvania at McKee, Jackson County, Kentucky, where we were detained a day waiting for the arrival of the supply train and pack saddles.

On the 25th ultimo we effected a junction with the remainder of the troops (First Battalion Seventh Ohio Cavalry) at Heard's, on Goose Creek. I then found, to my surprise, that the whole force amounted to only about 980 men, and of that number a considerable portion were in the field for the first time. The marches, owing to the roughness and narrowness of the roads (being mere bridle-paths along the banks of creeks and over steep and rugged mountains), were, of necessity, slow and tedious, and their length had to be governed by the distance to the several points at which forage could be obtained.

It was not until about meridian of the 28th ultimo that we reached the foot of the Cumberland Mountains (on the north side), opposite Crank's Gap, and 12 miles to the south and east of Harlan Court-House. The horses were there fed, a day's forage prepared, and the pack train sent back under charge of a detachment of the Kentucky State Guard. A little before sunset we reached the summit of Cumberland Mountains, and had the field of our operations, with its mountains and valleys, spread out before us. I there held a consultation with the officers of the command, and it was the unanimous opinion that the force was entirely too small to venture on a division, according to the original plan. This decision seemed to be the more necessary, from the news we had received through East Tennessee refugees at the foot of the mountain, relative to the disposition of the rebel force along the line of railroad.

Soon after dark, the advance commenced the descent of the mountain, hoping to make a long march before sunrise, but, owing to the steepness, narrowness, and roughness of the way, the rear of the column did not reach the foot of the mountain until 10 p. m., having consumed four hours in the descent. Here I was told there were some 400 rebel cavalry in the vicinity of Jonesville, 5 miles distant. As it was important to move through Lee County, Virginia, without exciting suspicion, I moved down Cove Creek, crossing through a gap in Poor Valley Ridge, and crossed Powell's Valley, about 5 miles east of Jonesville. On leaving the valley road, our guides were at fault, and valuable time was lost in finding the way. The march was continued through the night, and at daylight we reached the top of Waller's Ridge, 22 miles distant from the foot of Cumberland Mountain, and halted to feed the horses. Thus far we had advanced without giving any alarm, or even exciting any suspicion as to our character. The village of Stickleyville lay immediately below us, and, but for the imprudence of some of the officers in allowing the men to visit the village, we could have passed on as rebel cavalry. A number of rebel soldiers, belonging to Trigg's battalion, came within our lines, supposing we were their friends, and were captured.

In a short time we were again in the saddle, passed through Stickleyville, across Powell's Mountain, and through Pattonsville. Before sunset we crossed Clinch River, 12 miles from Estillville, Scott County, Virginia, and halted for a couple of hours to feed. News of our approach had gone before us, but few of the rebels were inclined to credit it, believing it impossible that a Government force would venture so far within their territory.

Upon arriving at Estillville, at 10 p. m., we were told that a considerable rebel force was in possession of Moccasin Gap, prepared to resist our passage. I could not afford to lose time. The Michigan battalions were dismounted, and, under command of Lieutenant-Colonel Campbell, a portion were deployed and moved through the gap. Being unacquainted with the ground, and having to guard against an ambuscade in this strong pass, which could have been held by a small force of determined men against greatly superior numbers, we advanced with great caution. It was midnight ere the rear of the column had passed through. The enemy, deterred by the resolute advance of our brave men, fled toward Kingsport, East Tenn. (as I afterward learned), without firing a gun. A rebel lieutenant and several soldiers, with their arms, were captured on the south side of the gap, on the Blountsville road.

During the remainder of the night we moved forward, as rapidly as was practicable over unknown roads, picking up rebel soldiers by the way. Owing to the darkness of the night, a portion of the command lost their way and became separated from the main body. A small force of rebel cavalry, which was hovering about our rear, killed a sergeant of the Second Michigan and captured two others who had wandered from the road.

At daylight on the morning of the 30th we reached the town of Blountsville, Sullivan County, East Tennessee, surprised and took possession of the place, captured some 30 soldiers belonging to the Fourth Regiment Kentucky (rebel) Cavalry, in hospital, and paroled them. We were informed that at Bristol, 8 miles distant, there was a large amount of stores, besides the meat of a considerable number of hogs, belonging to the rebel authorities, but as the place was guarded, according to the best information we could receive, by a regiment of infantry, under Colonel Slemp, said to be 900 strong, a cavalry force, under Colonel Giltner, and a battery, we were reluctantly compelled to leave it to our left and move toward the railroad bridge at Union, 6 miles from Blountsville. I accordingly sent forward Lieutenant-Colonel Campbell with a portion of the Second Michigan, under the direction of Col. James P. T. Carter, of the Second East Tennessee Infantry, toward Union, with orders to take the place and destroy the railroad bridge across the Holston River. As soon as the remainder of the troops, which got separated from us during the night, came up, I moved them rapidly forward in the same direction. When we reached Union, I found the town in our possession, and the railroad bridge, a fine structure some 600 feet in length, slowly burning. The rebel force, about 150 strong, consisting of two companies of the Sixty-second North Carolina troops, under command of Major McDowell, had surrendered without resistance, the major himself having been first captured by our advance while endeavoring to learn if there was any truth of our reported approach.

The prisoners were paroled, and a large number of them were that afternoon on their way to the mountains of North Carolina, swearing they would never be exchanged. Their joy at being captured seemed to be unbounded.

The stores, barracks, tents, a large number of arms and equipments, a considerable amount of salt, niter, a railroad car, the depot, &c., were destroyed, and also a wagon bridge across the river, a few hundred yards below the railroad bridge. As soon as the work of destruction was fairly under way, I dispatched Colonel Walker, with detachments from the Second Michigan, Ninth Pennsylvania, and Seventh Ohio Cavalry (in all 181 men), the whole under guidance of Colonel Carter, toward the Watauga Bridge, at Carter's Depot, 10 miles west of Union. On their way they captured a locomotive and tender, with Colonel Love, of Sixty-second North Carolina troops, who, having heard of the approach of the Yankees, had started on the locomotive to Union to ascertain the truth of the rumor.

On reaching the station, about sunset, they found the enemy, consisting of two companies Sixty-second North Carolina troops, estimated by Colonel Walker at nearly 200 men, falling into line. Colonel Walker gallantly attacked them, and, after a brief but firm resistance, they broke and fled to the wood. The gallant Major Roper, of the Sixth Kentucky Cavalry, with two companies of the Ninth Pennsylvania Regiment, under Captain Jones, of that regiment, made a dashing charge, and captured and destroyed many of their number.

Our loss was 1 killed, 1 mortally and 1 severely wounded, and 2 slightly wounded. The rebel loss was 12 to 16 killed.

Dr. McMillan, of First East Tennessee Infantry, acting brigade surgeon, reports that he dressed the wounds of 13, several of which were mortal. Owing to the darkness of the night, it was impossible to learn with certainty their entire loss.

The railroad bridge across the Watauga River, some 300 feet in length, was soon in flames, and entirely destroyed; also a large number of arms and valuable stores. The captured locomotive was run into the river and completely demolished, destroying in its passage one of the piers of the bridge.

The men and horses, especially the latter, were much worn and jaded from constant travel and loss of rest. The alarm had been given; the rebels had the road open to Knoxville, and could move up a strong force to resist us. I also learned that some 500 cavalry and four guns, under Colonel Folk, were within 3 miles of us; that an infantry force would be concentrated at Johnson's Depot, 6 miles west of Carter's Station, by daylight; and, further, that Humphrey Marshall, who was at Abingdon, was moving his troops to occupy the passes in the mountains, and thus cut off our egress. It was deemed prudent, therefore, to return.

We left Watauga about midnight, and, after a hard march, reached Kingsport, at the mouth of the North Fork of the Holston River, at sunset on the 31st ultimo. After feeding and resting a short time, and issuing a ration of meat to the men, we were again in the saddle. We passed some 8 miles north of Rogersville, and reached Looney's Gap, in Clinch Mountain, late in the afternoon; passed through without opposition, and about 11 p. m. of January 1 reached a place in the edge of Hancock County, Tennessee, where forage could be obtained, and bivouacked for the night. This was the first night's rest we had been able to take since the night of the 27th ultimo. The command had been annoyed during the day and night by bushwhackers, but we, providentially, escaped with only 2 men slightly wounded.

Soon after daylight, on the morning of the 2d instant, we resumed our march toward Jonesville, Lee County, Virginia, with the intention of reaching the foot of the Cumberland Mountains, on the Kentucky side, before we halted. Our march was much impeded during the day by bushwhackers, who constantly annoyed our front and rear. Just before we reached Jonesville, they endeavored to check us by occupying the hills in our front with two companies (supposed to be Larmer's and Staley's), but they were soon driven from their strong positions by the skirmishers of the Second Michigan.

We reached Jonesville late in the afternoon, but, before the rear guard had passed, they were attacked by about 200 rebels. Colonel Walker took charge of the rear guard, re-enforced by two light companies, and drove them back to the wood. Several of their number were killed; 1 in the village of Jonesville. Some 20 were captured during the day. We sustained no loss. From prisoners we learned that the passes in Clinch and Powell's Mountains, through which we marched in going to Union, had been blockaded, and were occupied by three or four companies of infantry. We reached the foot of Cumberland Mountains, passing through Crank's Gap at 11 p. m., and bivouacked, men and horses completely jaded and worn, having been, in the last five days and seventeen hours, out of the saddle but thirty hours.

On the 5th instant the command reached Manchester, Clay County, and rested on the day following. The march was resumed on the morning of the 7th, and on the 8th I received your order directing the several detachments to be sent to their respective camps.

After reaching Richmond, on the 9th instant, they separated, the First Battalion Seventh Ohio moving on to Winchester, and the two battalions Second Michigan and Ninth Pennsylvania to Nicholasville.

Notwithstanding the inclemency of the weather, the severity of the marches, and the scanty supply of rations for no inconsiderable portion of the time, both officers and men bore their hardships without a single murmur or a word of complaint. They returned, after a journey of 470 miles, 170 of which were in the enemy's country, in high spirits and in good condition, proud to think they had accomplished a feat which, for hazard and hardships, has no parallel in the history of war.

Where all were so ready and willing to do their duty, and performed it with so much cheerfulness and alacrity, it is no easy matter to select a portion for special commendation, but the two battalions of the Second Michigan, under command of Lieutenant-Colonel Campbell, deserve particular notice for their drill, discipline, and efficiency. From the superiority of their arms, and their skill in their use, they seemed to feel themselves invincible, and, whenever there was an enemy to meet, they advanced against him with the coolness and steadiness of veterans.

I desire to make special mention of the following officers, who were temporarily attached to my staff, and to whose zeal and faithful services I bear willing testimony. I hope that you will bring them to the favorable notice of the proper authorities: Col. James P. T. Carter, Second Regiment East Tennessee Infantry; Col. T. T. Garrard, Third Regiment Kentucky Infantry; Maj. W. P. Roper, Sixth Regiment Kentucky Cavalry; Capt. L. D. Watkins, Fifth U. S. Cavalry, and chief of cavalry; Capt. T. B. Brooks, New York Volunteer Engineers; Capt. T. McNish, Third Regiment East Tennessee Infantry, and Capt. T. H. Easley, Third Regiment East Tennessee Cavalry.

To Colonel Carter's knowledge of the people and country in the vicinity of the railroad bridge is mainly due our success at those points, with so small a loss of life.

Colonel Garrard, an officer of sound judgment and great discretion, was of invaluable service in passing through the mountains of Eastern Kentucky. He gave his whole heart to the work, and was of great service to the expedition.

To the members of my staff, Capt. C. W. Cowan, assistant adjutant-general; Dr. C. W. McMillan, acting brigade surgeon, and Lieut. S. H. Robinson, aide-de-camp, my special thanks are due for the satisfactory manner in which they at all times performed their (under the circumstances) difficult duties.

I inclose the report of Colonel Walker, commanding cavalry brigade, and also the list of paroled prisoners.

I am, general, respectfully, your obedient servant,

S. P. CARTER,
Brigadier-General of Volunteers.

Maj. Gen. GORDON GRANGER,
Commanding Army of Kentucky.

No. 3.

Report of Col. Charles J. Walker, Tenth Kentucky Cavalry, commanding Cavalry Brigade.

HEADQUARTERS CAVALRY BRIGADE,
Richmond, Ky., January 9, 1863.

CAPTAIN: I have the honor to state that, pursuant to instructions from Headquarters Forces in the Field, dated Lexington, Ky., December 19, 1862, I proceeded to Nicholasville on the 19th ultimo and assumed command of that portion of the cavalry brigade (Ninth Pennsylvania, 430 men, two battalions Second Michigan, 320 men) stationed at that place.

On the 20th this force marched from Nicholasville to Kirksville; on the 21st to Big Hill, and on the 22d to McKee. Here we were delayed by the non-arrival of our provision train until about 10 a. m. on the 24th. This delay I do not hesitate to attribute to the incompetency and lack of energy in the officer in command of the escort. The delay was inexcusable. I regret that I am not able at present to furnish the name of the officer.

On the 24th we marched from McKee and encamped at Julius Robinson's, about 10 miles north of Manchester, and on the 25th to Metcalf's, on the Red Bird. We were joined during the day by one battalion of the Seventh Ohio Cavalry, under command of Major Reaney.

On the 26th we marched to Asher's, and again encamped on Red Bird. On the 27th, taking the road up Philips' Ford, of Red Bird, we crossed the Pine Mountains and encamped at Britton's, on the south ford of the Cumberland River, 12 miles from Crank's Gap.

On the 28th we marched to the top of Cumberland Mountains through Crank's Gap, from which point we marched night and day until our return to this side of the mountains.

Leaving the gap on the night of the 28th by a road passing about 5 miles to the north of Jonesville, we crossed Waller's Ridge, passed through Stickleyville, Pattonsville, Estillville, and arrived at Blountsville, Tenn., on the morning of the 30th. Here Lieutenant-Colonel Campbell, Second Michigan Cavalry, was, by order of the general commanding, detached with his command, and ordered to march at once on Union, now called Zollicoffer. The force at this place, about 150 strong, surrendered without firing a shot. Our entire force reached this place soon after Lieutenant-Colonel Campbell had taken possession of it, when we at once proceeded to destroy the wagon and railroad bridges over the Holston. We also destroyed the railroad depot, several cars, and a quantity of salpeter and salt found here. I then proceeded, by General Carter's order, with six companies of the command, making in all 181 men, to Carter's Depot, 10 miles below this point. On the way down we captured a locomotive and tender and several rebel prisoners, including one colonel.

The credit of this capture is due entirely to Colonel Carter, Second Tennessee Infantry, who, throughout the whole expedition, rendered the most invaluable service.

We arrived at Carter's Depot a few minutes before sunset, and immediately attacked the place. The affair was short, but brisk. The enemy made a spirited resistance for a few minutes and then fled to the brush. Major Roper, Sixth Kentucky Cavalry, in command of two companies of the Ninth Pennsylvania, under Captain Jones, did good service, and by a well-timed charge completed the rout of the enemy.

We lost 1 killed (Seventh Ohio), and 4 wounded (2 from Second Michigan and 2 from Ninth Pennsylvania). The enemy lost 12 killed, 15 or 20 wounded, and 138 prisoners. This force is said to have been about 200. In consequence of the darkness and of our short stay at this place, it was impossible to ascertain the exact strength or loss of the enemy.

We destroyed the railroad over the Watauga, burned their camp, together with all their arms and accouterments, and at 12.30 p. m. on the 31st started on our return. We were undisturbed, except by bushwhackers, who fired on us from almost every hill until we reached Jonesville. Here our rear guard had quite a brisk skirmish with a party of the enemy, about 150 strong. The enemy lost 2 killed in this skirmish; we were unharmed.

On the night of the 2d we recrossed the mountain through Crank's Gap, and, by easy marches, reached this place to-day, when, in accordance with the order of the general commanding, I divided the brigade, sending the Seventh Ohio to their old camp, at Winchester, and the Second Michigan and Ninth Pennsylvania to theirs, at Nicholasville.

Our loss during this expedition, I find by the reports of the regimental commanders, to be—killed, wounded, and missing, 19. Of this the Ohio battalion lost 1 killed and 8 missing; the Michigan, 1 killed and 7 missing, and the Ninth Pennsylvania, 2 wounded. Total, 19. In this number are included 2 men who were accidentally crippled by the falling of their horses, 1 man left sick, and 5 men who were left at different points to take care of our sick and wounded. The others missing were, no doubt, picked up by the enemy's scouts.

For my command it is but proper to say that for their patient endurance of hardships and cheerful submission to all the privations attending this expedition, both officers and men deserve the highest commendation.

I am, captain, very respectfully, your obedient servant,

C. J. WALKER,
Colonel Tenth Kentucky Cavalry, Commanding Brigade.

Capt. C. W. COWAN,
Assistant Adjutant-General, Lexington, Ky.

No. 4.

Report of Lieut. Gen. E. Kirby Smith, C. S. Army, commanding Department of East Tennessee.

KNOXVILLE, TENN., *January* 1, 1863.

A large cavalry force, consisting of the Tenth Pennsylvania and Second Ohio and Seventh Ohio, from Rosecrans' army, I suppose, has passed through Southern Kentucky, Russell and Scott Counties, Virginia, seized the railroad, and burned the bridges between Jonesborough and Bristol. I think they are striking at the salt-works. I have no cavalry at my disposal to meet them. On November 15 I ordered the First Louisiana, the First Georgia, and Adrian's battalion of cavalry to proceed, via Monticello and Somerset, across the mountain toward London and Mount Vernon, to obtain information of the enemy's movements, and ascertain if any forces were approaching from these directions, and return through Cumberland and Big Creek Gaps. General Bragg ordered back this cavalry. I arrested the commanding officer, and directed the next senior officer to proceed to Montgomery and report by letter. I communicated this to General Bragg in a letter dated December 9, instant; requested him to enforce my order, and added that the non-compliance of Colonel [J. J.] Morrison with my instructions, ordering him into Kentucky, may have endangered this department. I have, up to this time, had no report from these troops.

E. KIRBY SMITH,
Lieutenant-General, Commanding.

General [S.] COOPER,
Adjutant and Inspector-General.

No. 5.

Report of Maj. Gen. Samuel Jones, C. S. Army, commanding Department of West Virginia.

DUBLIN, TENN., *December* 31, 1862.

General [H.] Marshall reports that a brigade of the enemy's cavalry, estimated from 2,000 to 4,000, passed Pendleton Gap on the 28th instant and burned the bridge over Watauga, at Union, East Tenn., yesterday. I have sent all my troops immediately available to General Marshall to protect the salt-works and the road within this department, and, if possible, to intercept the enemy.

SAM. JONES,
Major-General.

General S. COOPER,
Adjutant and Inspector General.

No. 6.

Reports of Brig. Gen. Humphrey Marshall, C. S. Army, of operations December 30–January 7.

ABINGDON, VA., *January* 7, 1863.

DEAR SIR: You will understand my delay in writing, as I promised to do at our last interview in Richmond, when I tell you that I was much indisposed for nearly a week after my return, and then heard you had passed here going west. I reached here to-day after an absence in the saddle since December 30, during which time I made a pursuit of the Yankee force under General Carter, which did not prove quite a success, if catching them and thrashing them means alone success. They were 2,000 strong, and splendidly armed with Colt's five-shooting rifles and army revolving pistols. I do not doubt they had twenty shots to my one. I had for action 750 men. I came upon their rear at Jonesville, Lee County, Virginia, at nightfall on the 2d instant, and exchanged a volley as my skirmishers passed into the town and their rear guard retired. They passed out at the gap called Crank's Gap by 11 o'clock that night. I did not pursue past Jonesville except by a picket of 30 men, to watch that they did not encamp, for in 4 miles from Jonesville to the gap the road crosses two high ridges, and then skirts between wooded hills across two very narrow vales, all the way being a succession of the finest places for ambuscades, to which, of course, my men would be subjected, and which I would not subject them to without some compensating reason. I could not bring the enemy to a general engagement. He was retreating as fast as he could out of the State, and did retire from it before me in three hours after I came upon him—superior to me by three to one in numbers and by more than ten to one in armament. I did everything that could be done to intercept him, for, hearing of his raid for the first time on Monday night at 10 p. m., I made dispositions to meet him as rapidly as they could be made. In half an hour my orders to every corps of my command had been dispatched.

The information I received was by telegraphic dispatch, which came by the way of Morristown, Tenn., from Pattsonville, Va., dated Monday, December 29, and reaching me at Abingdon at 9.30 p. m. :

The enemy's cavalry, 4,000 strong, passed this point to-day at 1.30 p. m., marching on Bristol, 45 miles from this place.

This was signed by Captain [S. P.] Larmer, one of [R. C.] Trigg's partisan rangers, who was gathering up deserters in the western counties. If there was anything of truth in it, my first thought was that the raid was meant not for Bristol, but the salt works above this place 18 miles, and Captain Larmer could not possibly tell by the march of the enemy by Pattonsville where his point of attack would be, nor could any one, until he arrived at Estillville. There he would pass Moccasin Gap, in the Clinch Mountains, and from that point he might feint upon Bristol or Holston Bridge, in Tennessee, while, in fact, his main body might be moving on the salt works. At Estillville he could turn up the valley of Moccasin Creek or up the valley of Copper Creek, crossing at Osborne's Ford, or he might come up the Reedy Creek road or up the valley of Holston River and take the Poor Valley road. To meet this possible or probable move of the enemy, I ordered my battalion of Georgia artillery to move from Jeffersonville, in Tazewell County (where it was stationed), 28 miles, with dispatch, and cover Saltville. This order was executed by the evening of the 30th, the information having reached Jeffersonville by the middle of the day on the 30th.

I adopted the road from Abingdon to Pound Gap as my line of defense, and in front of it, looking westward, all the roads leading to Estillville as my lines of observation. I had [H. L.] Giltner's cavalry regiment at Lebanon, in Russell County. I ordered it to hold its position, throwing strong pickets to Russell Old Court-House, and to Hansonville (10 miles on one road and 7 on another), and from these pickets to throw out vedettes along the Copper Creek, Moccasin Creek, and Poor Valley roads, leading toward Estillville. I sent from this place a squad of 20 horses to Holston Ford, 7 miles back, with orders to communicate with the pickets at Hansonville, and at the same time to throw vedettes down the river road leading to Estillville. The mounted battalion of [Maj. V. A.] Witcher [Thirty-fourth Virginia], then at Chatham Hill, in Smyth County, I ordered to move via Saltville and down the Poor Valley until it came to the Abingdon road, leading to Pound Gap, taking its station there just to the south of Little Moccasin Gap. By these arrangements I manned a line of 28 miles from Abingdon, and made reconnaissance of all the roads leading from Estillville toward that line, while I brought my mounted forces within supporting distance of each other, ready to concentrate upon whichever road the enemy might be approaching.

[Col. C.] Slemp's regiment of infantry (about 600 strong) was within 2 miles of Bristol. [Lieut. Col. E. F.] Clay's [Third Kentucky] battalion of mounted rifles (300) was at the Three Springs, in 5 miles of Bristol, on the Reedy Creek road, where the main road to Abingdon and that to Bristol fork. [Major] Johnson's battalion of mounted rifles (250) was at Kingsport, or its vicinity, 7 miles from Big Moccasin Gap, and about 17 miles from Bristol. Johnson himself was in Abingdon on business that night. I telegraphed to Bristol, to Colonel Slemp, immediately what I had heard, and directed him to send a courier to Clay (3 miles from him), with orders to scout the roads leading from Estillville toward Bristol, and that they should co-operate to resist the approach of the enemy toward Bristol, keeping me informed at once of all they ascertained as to his route and purposes. I directed Major Johnson to repair that night to Kingsport, and draw his force back in the direction of Bristol until he formed a junction with Clay. I hoped by this arrangement to have my forces disposed to meet the enemy whichever way he came, and to hold him in check until I could re-enforce at his point of assault, so as to repulse or capture him. This diagram will give you an idea of the relation of places and dispositions :

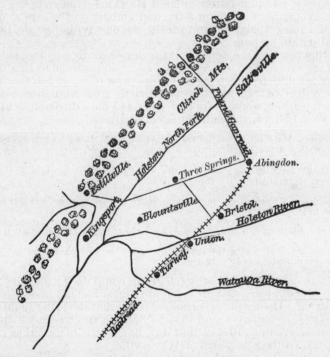

I sent, by telegraph, to Wytheville for Jeffress' and Davidson's batteries to be moved to Abingdon by rail (guns, carriages, and harness) that night. I had at Abingdon about 400 infantry, under Colonel [H.] Hawkins. All the dispositions I have written so much to describe I made before I slept, after receiving Larmer's dispatch.

December 30.—This morning I found that the agents of the railroad had started the rolling stock of the company from Bristol about 3 o'clock in the morning, with Government stores that were in Bristol, and had run them to Abingdon for safety. I approved the proceeding, and expressed my gratification that the cars were just in place should I find it proper to re-enforce the troops at Bristol, which, I stated, I expected I should have to do during that day, after I could hear from the country as to the direction of the enemy, and that I should, at all events, desire to send ammunition to Bristol, which I at once directed my ordnance officer to place on the cars.

By 10 a. m. the scouts from the Abingdon road to Pound Gap reported that the Estillville roads in front of their line had been scouted for some 8 or 10 miles, and no enemy appeared in that direction. Slemp telegraphed me that Clay was observing the enemy, and that he had turned off to Blountsville, which was in 9 miles of Bristol. Johnson communicated that he had passed Clay's camp, making for his own, before day, and had come upon the enemy in front of Clay's pickets; had shot a sergeant and captured two prisoners with his little party, but that he was cut off from Kingsport and could not get to his camp, and that the enemy at day-dawn was making for Blountsville, said by the prisoners to be from 2,600 to 3,000 strong, composed of Ohio, Pennsylvania, Michigan, Kentucky, and Tennessee [troops], under General Carter, of Tennessee. I immediately ordered Hawkins to move to the railroad depot at Abingdon his 400 infantry, and embark on the cars at once for Bristol. I telegraphed Slemp to resist the enemy, and he should be re-enforced within an hour.

Hawkins reached the depot by 11 a. m., when, to my utter surprise, I learned the cars had all left Abingdon and had returned to Bristol about 9 o'clock. I directed the telegraphic operator to telegraph for their immediate return, to transport troops to Bristol from Abingdon. An hour and a half elapsed, when the operator handed me a dispatch to him from a Mr. [W. S.] Minor, the railroad agent at Bristol:

Does General Marshall order the cars to Abingdon ? If so, let him say how many troops he wishes to transport.

I give the substance, possibly not the exact words, of this dispatch. Answered immediately by telegraph :

General Marshall orders the immediate return of cars to transport 400 men from Abingdon to Bristol.

Another hour and a half passed, and then came this dispatch :

If General Marshall wants the cars at Abingdon, he will have to confer with the general superintendent at Lynchburg.

This was done as soon as the telegraph could do it; and now was the first time I was aware that my original request had not taken that direction. Mr. [T.] Dodamead telegraphed to me that the cars should be sent from Bristol immediately, and that he had not received my dispatch of the night before until 10 a. m. that day, but that cars were then (2 p. m.) loading my artillery on board at Wytheville.

I repaired to the depot in person in about an hour, with my staff, to go to Bristol. Slemp telegraphed that the enemy had taken the direction of Union from Blountsville with a part of his force. I then saw he was making for Holston Bridge. I could not arrive in time to stop him. The cars did not come from Bristol until after dark, and my men had been waiting to go since 11 a. m. We reached Bristol after 11 o'clock at night, and learned that the enemy had crossed the Holston, burned the bridge, captured the guard at Union, and had gone before sundown westward, toward the Watauga Bridge, and, doubtless, had destroyed that also, and was, when last heard from, going west.

Before leaving Abingdon I had sent a courier to Colonel [H. L.] Giltuer, and to the officer commanding Witcher's battalion, for both to move immediately to Bristol. My artillery arrived from Wytheville at Bristol as soon as I did, but not the horses, which had been started on the night of the 29th by land. The damage to the bridges was done. It could have been avoided, and would have been, had the railroad agents furnished the cars to send my infantry forward. It rained hard all that evening.

I learned, on arriving at Bristol, that the enemy had cut the telegraph wires leading west, on his reaching there that day (the 30th). I learned further that the telegraph operator, Mr. [J. C.] Duncan, had the night before (29th) refused to let Captain [T. W. W.] Davies, the commandant of the post at Bristol, communicate to General Smith, at Knoxville, the letter or substance of my dispatch to Colonel Slemp until it should be the pleasure of Colonel Slemp to make it known, as it was a rule that the contents of private dispatches should not be made known until it was done by the party to whom addressed. Slemp was 2 miles out of town. Duncan was positive. A courier was sent to Slemp to obtain his permission, though the moments were precious, if force was to be sent from Knoxville to the bridges to strengthen the guards. Before the courier got back from Slemp's camp, Duncan had left his office and had hid his instrument working westward, and neither he nor his instrument could be found until next morning, after the enemy had reached the telegraph wire and had cut off the connection with Knoxville. I inquired as to Mr. Duncan's sentiments, and was told that he was well known as a Union man. I ordered his arrest immediately, and felt very much like arresting Minor also, but did not. · General Smith, I understand, has released Duncan, which, under the circumstances, I consider a very grave mistake, for, if such a case goes unpunished in East Tennessee, we shall have plenty of such cases. I supposed he was in this department. Major-General Jones suggested to me his release, because they said they could not work the railroad without the operator of the telegraph at Bristol. I refused to release him, and ordered the operator at Abingdon to repair to Bristol, which he did. It was discovered that Duncan did not live in this department, and General Kirby Smith, it appears, released him after I left Bristol. It is proper you should be apprised of this whole state of facts. I [have] no interest in the result beyond the public good. I have never seen Duncan, and never heard of him before December 30.

December 31 found me at Bristol; the enemy's whereabouts unknown. The picket of cavalry at Union reported that at 11 a. m. he was encamped at 3 miles from Union, between the Holston and Watauga, but appeared to be preparing to move. I ordered Captain [W. W.] Baldwin, in command of a squadron of Partisan Rangers, to move to Blountsville, and thence to watch the road from Carter's Depot to Kingsport, and to report promptly every movement of the enemy.

By 2 p. m. Giltner's regiment of Kentucky cavalry entered Bristol, having come from Lebanon since midnight—550 men. I should have said that I ordered [Thomas] Johnson's camp at Kingsport to be broken up, and his train to move last night to the Three Springs, so as to get behind our forces. Three companies of Johnson's men came in about 12 o'clock to-day. Clay's men a good deal fagged from active scouting for the past thirty-six hours. In a short time after Giltner's arrival, Captain Baldwin reports from Blountsville that the enemy has encamped, in force of about 500, at Hull's, 4 miles from Blountsville, on the Jonesborough road, and is now there, feeding. The picket from Union reports that the enemy has moved, and seems to be taking the direction of

Blountsville. The road up Beaver Creek comes from Hull's directly to Bristol, without passing by Blountsville, thus:

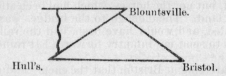

There is a country road (a by-path) leading from Hull's across the country to the Kingsport road; thence crossing Eden's Ridge, at Sheaver's Falls, into the road leading out to Estillville, by Moccasin Gap.

A second and a third dispatch from Captain Baldwin informs me the enemy is encamped at Hull's, though it is believed a part of his force has gone to Kingsport to destroy Johnson's camp. The force of the enemy is reported everywhere at from 1,700 to 2,500. If I move upon Blountsville to intercept his passage by that place, he may move from Hull's to Bristol by a different road; so while I go out to catch him, he may come in and catch me. If I move all upon him at Hull's, he clearly passes off at Moccasin Gap and escapes. I give my own reflections as to the situation. I determine to move my whole infantry force, with a section of artillery, to Blountsville late in the evening; to retain my mounted force until the cars come in, so as not to uncover Bristol until a force I expect from Salem shall have arrived.

At 7 p. m. Baldwin reports from Blountsville that he has reconnoitered the country around that place, and the enemy is still in camp at Hull's, though some 1,500 of his force have crossed the Eden's Ridge. Capt. J. G. Bedford, who was on picket at Union, reports at 7.15 o'clock that he has crossed from Union to Blountsville, and the enemy has taken the direction of Kingsport without coming to Blountsville. I thought it was now plain that it was a race between us for Moccasin Gap, and that if he had gone by Kingsport—making a detour of some 6 miles to the west of the gap, in order to rescue the 30 East Tennesseeans we had captured the day before in trying to go to Kentucky, and some 8 or 10 of his cavalry my men had picked up—I could gain the gap before him with my mounted force, and check him until my infantry and artillery could come up and make the engagement definitive between us. My whole mounted force was advanced rapidly to Moccasin Gap, passing my infantry and artillery at midnight at Blountsville, and gained Moccasin Gap (19 miles from Bristol) before daylight on the 1st. I saw the force from Salem arrive in the cars at Bristol, put Colonel [Ambrose C.] Dunn in command, and, with my mind easy about Bristol, rode on to Blountsville, put my infantry and artillery en route for the gap, and passed on myself to the cavalry force, which I was now informed had reached the gap before the enemy. Scouts from the direction of Kingsport come in early this New Year's morning, who tell me the enemy entered Kingsport after night and stopped awhile, but again moved in the night, and had taken down the south side of the Clinch Range, in the direction of Rogersville, Tenn.

There are several gaps practicable for cavalry to lead over within 12 miles of Kingsport; so, resting my infantry and artillery to hold Moccasin Gap, I took all my mounted force and took down the north side of the same range, intending to meet the enemy should he try the experiment of leading over the mountains, and to intercept his egress, if possible, by whatever route he might go. Passing Estillville, 2 miles behind Moccasin Gap, I took the road to Speer's Ferry (where the enemy had crossed to Clinch River as he came in), and reached it, crossed, and went on to within 4 miles of Pattonsville by midnight. I learned that one road led directly up the valley of the Clinch, another from Sneedsville passed up Stock Creek. I had now passed both of these, and I should feel very silly if the enemy, taking one of these, should cross my trail behind me and pass over to the road from Estillville to Gladesville. He could cross the Clinch at Kyle's Ford (some 14 miles below me), and take either of the roads I have named, or he could take up the North Fork of the Clinch and pass out at Pattonsville, a point 4 miles in front of my present position; or he could pass out by Stickleyville, 12 miles in front of my then position; but where he was or where he intended to go I had not ascertained. My men had ridden all the night before; Giltner's regiment had been in the saddle forty-eight hours. The men had had but once anything to eat, such as they could get in passing Estillville, and the poor fellows were sleeping on their horses as we rode along. I halted in the woods at midnight to let the men sleep until dawn. In a short time scouts came in, who informed me that the enemy had crossed the mountains at War Gap, and had crossed the river 12 miles below Speer's Ferry, and at 8 p. m. was encamped. He had crossed at Kyle's Ford.

It turned out the enemy did not pass the War Gap, but through Looney's Gap (lower down); that he did not cross Clinch River that night, but encamped for a time to rest 4 miles from the river. He crossed Kyle's Ford before day, and reached Hunter's Gap by 12 o'clock on January 2. There he was fired on by some of Larmer's men, and from that point was troubled by bushwhackers. I rested until dawn, supposing the enemy to be in camp, and, not knowing what road he would take, I ordered my infantry to move forward to Speer's Ferry by rapid march, and, if the enemy did not come that way, to come on to Pattonsville, which was 20 miles from Estillville.

I moved at dawn to Pattonsville, and there I was informed that Jonesville was occupied by 400 infantry, with some artillery, and two companies of cavalry, which had been sent up from Cumberland Gap, only 35 miles from Jonesville. I detached my son's (John J. Marshall) company [I, Fourth Kentucky Cavalry] from Giltner's regiment, and sent it down the North Fork of Clinch to find out the trail of the enemy, and, if he was coming up by Pattonsville, to dispatch to me; if he passed through Hunter's Gap, to harass his rear and follow him to Jonesville, and that I would move the rest of the force on the arc to Jonesville, now distant 20 miles. I crossed Powell's Mountain (north side sleek with ice), entered Stickleyville; no news. Sent forward Lieutenant [J. N.] Gibson with 10 men to Jonesville, to let the force there know I was near and coming, should the enemy attack it. Arrived at Powell River, 8 miles from Jonesville; received a dispatch from Gibson that he heard heavy firing in the direction of Hunter's Gap; put my whole force to a trot. Gibson again dispatched at 1½ miles from Jonesville that the firing continued heavy, and he heard artillery. I ordered our speed to increase, if possible. Arrived at 1 mile from Jonesville; met Gibson, who informed me the enemy had entered the town unknown an hour since, having prisoners in charge, and now occupied the town in force. I ordered Clay to open the attack at once. Giltner was now at least 2 to 3 miles behind, his horses so fagged that they could not make the speed, for they had marched 105 miles from Lebanon. The rifles dismounted and formed in about 300 yards of the town, and opened fire at once. The enemy was in the streets and massed at the court-house, and on the

intended to strike by merely seeing them pass Pattonsville going in the direction of Bristol. It was not certain if 4,000 cavalry had passed Pattonsville that it was the only column in the State of Virginia. I knew that from Pattonsville the column might take any one of half a dozen roads that would lead directly to the section of country in which I was then located, and that the salt works in Smyth County (18 miles above Abingdon and near the railroad) would be an interest at which such a force would be most apt to direct its efforts. It might make a feint upon Bristol (an unimportant depot) while the main body might move rapidly upon Saltville, and in an hour might there do damage that would be nearly irreparable. I felt that I owed the duty of taking care that no such effect might be produced. My command was at the time much scattered. Two of my regiments and a battalion had been detached at your own urgent request. I had left a regiment (nearly formed) in Kentucky beyond the Cumberland Mountains. I had only the representatives of two infantry regiments left. One of these (the Sixty-fourth Virginia) had only been formed about one month by adding a battalion of perfectly raw recruits to a battalion which had been in service for a year past. I had never seen this regiment since it had taken a regimental formation. I had ordered it down to take post in front of Bristol, that it might be in a place to be equipped and drilled, and at the same time might be transferred rapidly by rail to any point where its services should be needed. The other infantry force consisted of six companies of minimum size, all recruited during my march into Kentucky last summer, and which I now had near Abingdon to drill and to afford me a chance to swell its numbers to at least the number of companies to make a skeleton regiment. A battalion of Georgia artillery, under my command, was at Jeffersonville, in Tazewell County, about 500 strong, with a battery of twelve pieces. I had a battery of six pieces at Wytheville, where it had been placed under directions from your predecessor in office. Another battery of four pieces was then *en route* for Rocky Gap, in Bland County, by agreement between the major-general and myself. The rest of my force was mounted, and had for some time past been moving about to find a scanty forage, and to draw it from unwilling owners in every part of Southwest Virginia. Still, it had been required to keep in relation to the points of the country demanding defense. I had in November stationed it to forage near Kingsport, Tenn., but the military authority commanding that department had ordered the officers to withdraw from that department, and, under penalty of arrest, not to take corn or other forage or supplies from East Tennessee; and they had furnished me with a copy of this order, in the nature of a demand, that it should meet my acquiescence. In consequence of this, my mounted force had been scattered to hunt forage. The Fourth Kentucky Cavalry had from day to day fallen back to Russell County, Virginia. The First [Third] Battalion of Kentucky Mounted Rifles had encamped near the Three Springs, in Washington County, Virginia. Johnson's battalion of four companies still lingered near Kingsport, but was on the eve of starting to Kentucky to try to find forage and recruits. Witcher's battalion of Virginia riflemen (mounted also) had drifted as far east as Chatham Hill, in Smyth County, a point on the road from Marion to Jeffersonville, and above the salt works. [Capt. John A.] McFarlane's company of Virginia cavalry was posted at the Richlands, in Tazewell, to observe the approaches from the valley of the Sandy. If you are conversant with the geography of this section of the State, you will observe from my statement of the facts that at the time of Captain Larmer's telegram my force of less than 3,000 men was dispersed over about 60 miles square, the most of it principally engaged in trying to keep from starvation the horses so necessary to service in this part of the Confederacy. I felt extremely embarrassed by the condition of affairs, but soon arranged in my own mind a theory upon which to meet the enemy, to learn his intentions and movements, and to ascertain the data by which to regulate my own movements. Several officers of these commands were in Abingdon that night on business, and I had them aroused and summoned to my quarters to receive orders. I at once sent to Colonel Slemp, commanding the Sixty-fourth Virginia Infantry, in camp 1 mile from Bristol, the following dispatch by telegraph:

ABINGDON, VA., *December* 29, 1862—10 p. m.

Colonel SLEMP:

I have a dispatch from Larmer that 4,000 of the enemy's cavalry are marching on Bristol, and were within 45 miles of it to-day at 1 p. m. Be on the alert. Communicate immediately to Lieutenant-Colonel Clay, at the Three Springs, and direct him to throw out scouts to learn the movements of the enemy, which you will immediately communicate to me at this place.

H. MARSHALL,
Brigadier-General.

Also, I sent to Wytheville the following:

ABINGDON, VA., *December* 29, 1862—10 p. m.

Captains JEFFRESS and DAVIDSON:

I have just received a dispatch that 4,000 of the enemy's cavalry were in 45 miles of Bristol at 1 p. m. this day, marching on that place. Your batteries must come to this place immediately.

H. MARSHALL,
Brigadier-General.

In fifteen minutes I received the following:

WYTHEVILLE, VA., *December* 29, [1862.]

GENERAL: Your dispatch received. I shall start the horses by land, and await railroad transportation for the battery, &c. Is this best? Let me know immediately if you can send down any cars. Reply immediately.

W. C. JEFFRESS,
Captain, Commanding Battery.

I instantly returned this reply:

CAPTAIN: Dispatch received. Reserve your harness to come with guns and men. Start horses immediately. Davidson's battery, if at Wytheville, to come also.

H. MARSHALL,
Brigadier-General.

I sent this shortly afterward, referring to same subject:

ABINGDON, VA., *December* 29, 1862—near midnight.

Mr. DODAMEAD, *Lynchburg, Va.*:

It is very important to transport Jeffress' and Davidson's batteries (ten pieces of artillery with caissons and carriages) to Abingdon to-night; also their companies, say 125 men. Can I rely on you to furnish the transportation at Wytheville?

H. MARSHALL,
Brigadier-General.

I may as well say here that the reply to this dispatch was delivered to me next day about 2 p. m., as follows:

LYNCHBURG, *December* 30, [1862.]

General HUMPHREY MARSHALL:

Message not received until 10 this a. m. Have trains now loading at Wytheville.

T. DODAMEAD.

The train aforesaid brought on the batteries the next night to Bristol under the following order :

SPECIAL ORDERS, }   ABINGDON, VA.,
    No. 165.   }   December 30, 1862—6.45 p. m.

Captain Jeffress' and Captain Davidson's batteries, if they arrive at Abingdon to-night, will proceed direct to Bristol without delay.
By order of Brig Gen. H. Marshall, commanding :

EDWD. O. GUERRANT,
Assistant Adjutant-General.

On the night of the 29th, after sending the dispatches set forth above, I sent to Maj. Gen. Samuel Jones the following telegram :

ABINGDON, VA., *December* 29, 1862.
Maj. Gen. SAMUEL JONES, *Dublin Depot :*

GENERAL: Dispatches just received from Captain Larmer, of Trigg's rangers, from Pattonsville, Scott County, Virginia, announce 4,000 cavalry of the enemy in 45 miles of Bristol to-day at 1 p. m., marching on that point. I have ordered my batteries at Wytheville to Abingdon, and shall order the Georgia battalion to fall back to Salt-ville immediately. A regiment of infantry and a battalion of horse of mine 4 miles from Bristol ; one battalion of infantry here ; one regiment of cavalry in front of Hyter's Gap, cover Saltville.

H. MARSHALL,
Brigadier-General.

I aroused Lieutenant-Colonel [M. T.] Pryor, of the Fourth Kentucky Cavalry, and sent him to his camp that night (29th), distant 22 miles from Abingdon, with orders immediately to throw out heavy cavalry pickets to Russell Old Court-House, to Hansonville, and to the mouth of Dump's Creek, with flying vedettes from those pickets to move some 8 or 10 miles down the roads leading in the direction of Estillville and Osborne's Ford, on Clinch River, so as to discover, if possible by morn-ing, on what road the enemy was in fact moving, and whether his main force was threatening Saltville, Lebanon, or Abingdon. He was instructed on his arrival at his camp immediately to dispatch a mounted courier to Major [A.] Leyden, of the Georgia artillery, at Jeffersonville, with orders to conduct his battalion without any delay to Saltville, and to take position so as to defend the salt works. At the same time I or-dered Maj. Thomas Johnson, of Kentucky, to repair without delay to his camp, at Kingsport, Tenn., and to fall back upon Clay's camp at the Three Springs, so as to unite with the troops near Bristol in the de-fense of the place and the railroad. Major Witcher's battalion was at Chatham Hill. He was absent on account of wounds, from which he had not yet wholly recovered; his ranking captain was in Abingdon that night, but could not be found. He was found next morning and the following order was delivered to him :

ABINGDON, VA., *December* 30, 1862.
Captain Harman will move Witcher's battalion with all practicable speed via Salt-ville down Poor Valley to the little Moccasin Gap. Arrived there, throw scouts out to Hanson's, and open communication with Giltner. If the enemy is advancing by Boyd's to Russell Old Court-House, let him proceed, but advise me of his approach. Reach your post by daybreak to-morrow at least, and inform me when you arrive.

H. MARSHALL,
Brigadier-General.

Thus, sir, you will perceive that, receiving the dispatch from Captain Larmer, I had at once advised every one with whom I had any military connection of the approach of the enemy before I slept, and had assigned to my troops, scattered over nearly 60 miles, the duties which would devolve upon them. To those at Abingdon I gave notice to hold themselves in readiness, and I sent a picket of mounted men from a squad waiting at headquarters to Worley's (at the ford of Holston, 7 miles back of Abingdon), with orders to send vedettes down the river road, similar to those I have already detailed. My plan, as you will see, was to accept Abingdon as my post; to adopt the road to Pound Gap as my line of observation, as it ran transversely to every road leading from the direction of Pattonsville to the salt works and the upper country; to throw out my scouts upon those roads, and to learn, before I undertook to move, where the enemy was, so that I might mass my disposable force in his front. At the same time, by dispositions in the direction of Bristol, assumed to be on the other face of the parallelogram that certainly embraced the enemy, I observed him in like manner and with a similar intent to guide my own future actions. After a full opportunity to review what was done, and how it should have been done, I see no reason to regret the determinations I made, or how I could have been more prompt.

On the morning of the 30th, hearing that Major-General [J. B.] Floyd, of the Virginia State Line, was in Abingdon, and had some force near Saltville, I at once addressed him the following note:

ABINGDON, VA., *December* 30, 1862.

Major-General FLOYD:

I think it proper to inform you that I have dispatches which render it more than probable the enemy is making a raid in this direction. It will be well to inform your forces near Saltville of the fact. It will afford me great pleasure to co-operate with you in movements for his arrest and chastisement, to which I think my own force is probably equal, and our united forces will be ample.

Respectfully, &c.,

H. MARSHALL,
Brigadier-General, Provisional Army, Confederate States of America.

Ascertaining that General Floyd had gone to Saltville, I dispatched to him the information I possessed, which he courteously acknowledged the same night. I did not telegraph to Knoxville because, my own dispatch coming by Morristown, I did not doubt the same had already been communicated to headquarters at Knoxville. This was the case, in fact, for the dispatch was sent to both places at the same time, and was received at Knoxville as soon as I received it in another military department.

Early in the morning I learned that the railroad cars had left Bristol in the preceding night about 3 a. m., transporting Government stores to Abingdon for safety, and that they were then at Abingdon. I expressed to the men who had given me this information, and who brought the cars to Abingdon, my gratification that they were at hand, and requested the conductor to remain, for that during the morning I might desire their return to Bristol with ammunition and troops. I understood him to signify his assent, and, indeed, I did not think it probable there would be any inclination on the part of any of those concerned to return to Bristol, unless under my positive orders to do so. At a later hour that morning I had a supply of ammunition for Bristol put on those cars, and I remember that some one called at my room to say to me that the ammunition was aboard the cars, and they were ready to proceed again to Bristol, and they wanted to know if I had any other orders. I replied to this that they should wait a little and I would attend to it, for I was at the time busy with dispatches. They did not wait, but left for Bristol without my knowledge, and so caused me very serious disappointment, and prevented me from reaching Bristol at a time when, the probability is, I should have saved the damage to the railroad bridges that ensued. As the cars were on hand at Abingdon, I never thought of asking any one to send them there, and, as those who had them in charge promised to wait my orders, I never thought of asking Mr. [T.] Dodamead, at Lynchburg, to tell them to do so. I had dispatched him the night before to give me transportation for my artillery, and had received no reply. By reference to his dispatch you will see he did not receive my dispatch until a later hour on the 30th than that at which I saw the cars at Abingdon from Bristol, and if the telegraph had done no better in conveying a dispatch to order those cars to stay than it did in procuring cars for my artillery at Wytheville, I should not have attained the object in view, or have been able to avoid the loss.

On the 30th, about 9 a. m., the following dispatches reached me at Abingdon:

DECEMBER 30, [1862]—2.30 a. m.

General MARSHALL:

Information received at 12 o'clock to-night is that the enemy were 10 miles beyond Estillville at dark, which is 31 miles from this place. The most reliable information is that the enemy is 2,000 in number. One man direct from there counted 490; said to be a detachment. They could arrive here early in the morning, probably at daylight. We will have about 500 infantry, and Clay's battalion; also Johnson's and Giltner's if they have received the information we sent them by courier. You can well see what we are in want of—more men; but we will fight them with what we have. There ought to be another regiment, at least, here, and I think we could thrash them decently. I would like that you could be here in person. More ammunition is wanted—musket-cartridges.

C. SLEMP,
Colonel, Commanding.

Also the following:

DECEMBER 30, [1862]—7.30 a. m.

General MARSHALL:

Enemy advancing, I think, to Bristol; cannot tell which road. I caught 3 stragglers. Sent 7 miles from camp. Part of three regiments, perhaps 1,500 or 2,000 strong.

E. F. CLAY,
Lieutenant-Colonel, Commanding.

I dispatched this reply to Colonel Slemp:

ABINGDON, VA., *December* 30, [1862]—10 a. m.

Colonel SLEMP:

Johnson ordered to join Clay. I think the enemy has divided his force, and may be trying to get to the salt works or to this place. Throw cavalry scouts well forward. You shall have artillery so soon as it arrives from Wytheville. Report every hour to me at this place. If attack on Bristol be certain, I will move Hawkins with 400 to join you in an hour.

H. MARSHALL,
Brigadier-General.

As the morning advanced, I received the following additional telegrams:

BRISTOL, TENN., *December* 30, 1862—10.30 a. m.

General MARSHALL:

Dispatches from Jonesborough state that courier had arrived, and stated enemy in 20 miles of this place last night. Three of their scouts were captured last night 12 miles from here by Clay's cavalry.

T. W. W. DAVIES,
Commanding Post.

BRISTOL, TENN., *December* 29 (30 ?), [1862].

General MARSHALL:

We have 550 infantry and 300 cavalry. Can you send us two pieces of artillery, with canister and shrapnel?

T. W. W. DAVIES,
Commanding Post.

BRISTOL, TENN., *December* 30, 1862.

General MARSHALL:

Send ten boxes musket-cartridges. Enemy, from best information, turned in the direction of Blountsville—1,200 or 1,500 strong. Our force united, I think, can take them. Be glad [to have] your company.

C. SLEMP,
Colonel.

On receipt of these dispatches, the ammunition was ordered to the cars at Abingdon immediately. Unfortunately it afforded an excuse for them to return to Bristol without further notice to me. I received the following note from Major Johnson by courier:

CLAY'S CAMP, *December* 30, 1862.

General MARSHALL:

I passed Clay's camp about 3 o'clock. I proceeded on the Kingsport road. About 7 miles from his camp I met Clay's pickets dashing back, and they reported the Yankees in pursuit. I rode to the rear; it was dark, and 3 Yankees rode up and asked me if we were the Ninth Pennsylvania Regiment. I unhorsed 1; the other 2 surrendered. I learn from these men there are three regiments ahead of the prisoners. Of course they are near by. I am cut off from my command. I have no doubt they are marching for Bristol, and can be there by noon.

THOS. JOHNSON,
Major, &c.

The foregoing was received at 11 a. m. Also the following from Lieutenant-Colonel Clay:

DECEMBER 30, 1862—11 a. m.

I have just received information from Lieutenant [R. T.] Jack (of Johnson's command) that the enemy has gone in the direction of Union; perhaps will go thence to Bristol. Force about 1,500. Johnson's command is near here. Will act together in the direction of Union. His command is only about 80 men. I have scouts in all directions.

E. F. CLAY,
Lieutenant-Colonel.

THREE SPRINGS—11 a. m.

General MARSHALL:

Reliable information. The enemy gone to Union by the Blountsville road. Will be there by 1 o'clock. Major Johnson's command will act in that direction.

E. F. CLAY,
Lieutenant-Colonel.

The pickets sent out to the Holston Ford brought me now a report that the enemy was not seen on the roads leading from Estillville in the direction of the salt works, and as the above telegrams indicated that his movement was really designed for Bristol or its vicinity, I ordered Colonel Hawkins to move his infantry at once to the railroad cars to embark for Bristol, intending to transfer my force to the front of the enemy. The word soon came to me, to my surprise and mortification, that the cars had returned to Bristol. I directed the colonel to wait at the depot until the cars could be ordered to return. I was in the telegraph office, I think, at the time; if not, I was in its immediate vicinity, and requested the telegraph operator to dispatch immediately to have the cars returned from Bristol to transport my troops to that point. I waited a considerable time before I received any reply. Meanwhile the following arrived:

DECEMBER 30, [1862.]

General MARSHALL:

Our pickets were driven in by the enemy's pickets 1 mile this side of Blountsville. Our pickets just here at 12 o'clock.

C. SLEMP,
Colonel

General MARSHALL:

Enemy reported within 3 miles of this place; have moved out to meet him. Send us re-enforcements and ammunition. Detachment is reported moving on Holston Bridge. Johnson's command is on the path.

T. W. W. DAVIES,
Commanding Post.

I was now most anxious, as I had at 12.15 p. m. received the following from Maj. Gen. Samuel Jones, in reply to mine of the preceding night:

DUBLIN, TENN., *December* 30, 1862.

General MARSHALL:

Your telegram this instant received. Presume you have given the officers commanding the troops in 4 miles of Bristol [notice?] of the movements of the enemy on that point, with the necessary directions for uniting them. If you have not done so, do it immediately. Send the battalion of infantry from Wytheville to Bristol, and go there yourself, assume command, and make the best disposition you can for the defense of the place. I will send you 500 or 600 of Jenkins' men (dismounted). Telegraph promptly all the information you get.

SAM. JONES,
Major-General.

Expecting the return of the train from Bristol every minute, I received the following from the telegraphic operator, I think:

BRISTOL, TENN., *December* 30, [1862.]

G. KELLER:

Does General Marshall order trains? If so, answer at once, and say how many troops to come.

W. S. MINOR.

Now, for the first time in my life, did I know such a being existed as Mr. Minor. I learned he was the railroad agent at Bristol, having charge of the trains. This dispatch to Mr. Keller, who, I suppose, is the railroad agent at Abingdon, is evidently the answer to the first request I made to have the trains returned. It was of the first importance they should come at once, and then understanding that the man only wanted to know if it was my order they should come, I dispatched him as follows:

ABINGDON, VA., *December* 30, 1862.

W. S. MINOR, *Agent, Bristol, Tenn.:*

Send me cars immediately to transport 500 men and 8 horses.

H. MARSHALL,
Brigadier-General.

There was another long interval before a reply came, and then I received the following:

BRISTOL, TENN., *December* 30, 1862.

General MARSHALL:

Please communicate with general superintendent at Lynchburg in regard to the cars asked for.

W. S. MINOR.

And very shortly after I received this from Lynchburg:

LYNCHBURG, VA., *December* 30, 1862.

General MARSHALL:

You will please address orders to me for transportation. Subordinate agents have no authority to order the movements of trains. You can at once see the propriety of this; otherwise collisions might occur.

T. DODAMEAD.

Obedient, of course, to the railroad regulations, but intensely anxious to get to Bristol, I requested Mr. Dodamead to have the goodness to order the trains from Bristol, to which he courteously replied:

I have ordered a train at once from Bristol to take the men from Abingdon. Everything shall be done to aid the prompt movement of the troops.

T. DODAMEAD.

This dispatch was received at Abingdon at 3 p. m., which marks the time which had elapsed since I ordered Colonel Hawkins to wait for the return of the train until I obtained by regular approach consent from the proper quarter that one should come at once. But the promised train did not come until nearly 8 p. m., and after the enemy had burned both the bridges and had gone west from the Watauga, and the scouts from Union had made the fact known at Bristol, for the scouts returned by dark (say 5 p. m.), and then the trains came to aid me in "the prompt movement of the troops."

I had received from Colonel Slemp in the afternoon a closing dispatch, which gave me quiet upon the point as to whether the enemy had met:

BRISTOL, TENN., December 30, 1862.

General MARSHALL:

Reliable information received 1.30 p. m. states that the enemy are at Union, and bridge burning. Clay's and my command are here; Johnson is coming. Our strength is 900. We will not advance on them until word from you. Their strength supposed to be large (3,000). Communication stopped in that direction by telegraph.

C. SLEMP,
Colonel, Commanding.

Thus, Mr. Secretary, you will see that to the last, when the enemy had reached the bridge and had burned it, his force was estimated as very superior to any I could command, and you will readily realize the anxiety I labored under to get forward to Bristol the limited re-enforcement I had to furnish from Abingdon. It was raining all that evening very hard indeed. I had been kept in momentary expectation of the arrival of the cars from Bristol. It never occurred to my mind that Minor's dispatch to [George] Keller was in the nature of a protest against my authority to order the cars, for my mind was only bent on getting the transportation, and I supposed the agent would be as anxious as I to afford the protection to Bristol a re-enforcement would furnish. As to collision, that was impossible, for it is only 15 miles from Bristol to Abingdon, and there is no stopping-place between. Cars might run the distance in half an hour, and one hour from Abingdon should have put the troops at Union. Had they been started by 12 o'clock they could have saved the bridge, or, at least, could have contested its possession even with a superior force. I did all, as it seems to me, I could to get there to bring the required relief; but, as you see, I tried in vain.

Before leaving Abingdon on the 30th, I addressed the following order to Colonel Giltner by courier:

ABINGDON, VA., December 30, [1862]—6 p. m.

Colonel Giltner will move his cavalry regiment so as to join the main body of my command before Bristol without delay, unless his scouts inform him of the approach of a force of the enemy on the road to Lebanon. Leave all baggage behind, except a few cooking utensils and ammunition, and hurry. This order extends also to Witcher's battalion, which communicate to them at or near Little Moccasin Gap.

H. MARSHALL,
Brigadier-General.

As my artillery had not arrived from Wytheville, I left an order for it to come direct to Bristol that night, which order I have already set forth in a former page of this report. I embarked on the cars with the troops about 8 p. m., and we arrived at Bristol between 11 and 12 o'clock. I was met at the cars by Colonel Slemp, and from him and Lieutenant-Colonel Clay I learned the existing state of the facts: The enemy had gone to Union; overcome the guard stationed there; had burned the railroad bridge and the county bridge, nearly; had marched away to the Watauga Bridge, 10 miles farther off, and had destroyed that structure also before nightfall, and, when last seen, were going west, in the direction of the railway. It was not known where he was then or what he intended to do. Pickets had been thrown out in every direction from Bristol before night, and one company was then on picket duty 10 miles from Bristol, at Union. I could learn no more, for they knew no more. I could add nothing to the arrangements they had made for the night, for they seemed complete, and were correct; nothing had been overlooked.

Before I slept, I ordered a courier to be sent to Major Johnson's camp, near Kingsport, Tenn., with an order to break up that camp instantly, and for that force, with the baggage and prisoners, to take the Reedy Creek road to Abingdon, and to make good their junction with Clay's camp, at the Three Springs, as soon as it could be done. I impressed on Major Johnson the importance of speed. I then thought it not improbable the enemy, hearing of that camp, which in his entry he had passed, might go from Carter's Depot to destroy it, release the prisoners my men had taken, and make our people prisoners, besides destroying our arms and public property. These duties being all discharged, I retired to rest some time after midnight. I mention the fact of my retiring because that also has been made a subject of impertinent criticism upon my conduct by persons who, I suppose, would have had me talk the rest of the night over what had been done, and over what should be done on the morrow, without either they or I knowing that the enemy was then in 30 miles of us, or that he would ever be seen again. The train from Wytheville brought the ten pieces of artillery that night to Bristol, but the horses had not arrived with which to manage them.

Being a stranger to the country in which I might at any moment be called to act, the first thing to which my attention was directed in the morning was to obtain a room in Bristol where I might see and converse with gentlemen in some degree of privacy. In this I failed, but after so long a time I secured a room in the hotel, and soon was introduced by Col. James Preston to four gentlemen, who, he said, could give me all the information I required about the roads and water-courses in that section. These were Colonel McClelland, Major Dunn, Mr. Blair, and Mr. Sullins, of Jonesborough. I very soon explained to these gentlemen what aid they could furnish me, and Messrs. Dunn and Blair retired, promising to make me a paper sketch of the country around Bristol, though they said they were not accustomed to the art of sketching. I was much obliged, and then Colonel McClelland agreed to ride to Blountsville with a mounted company and observe for me a road which was said to lead from a point lower down the Holston than Union, in the direction of Kingsport. If the enemy intended to retire by the route he came, it was considered probable he might cross the country by that road. Colonel McClelland accompanied Captain [W. W.] Baldwin, a partisan ranger, whom I found at Bristol with some of his men, to discharge this duty. I was soon left alone, Mr. Sullins deferring to those who had undertaken to furnish me with the topography I needed. The locomotive, with a car attached, started, after breakfast, down to the point where one of Clay's companies was on picket. I received the following dispatch (the first of that day, I think) about 12 o'clock:

Lieutenant [E.] Hammond, of Clay's command, reports Federal camp 3 miles west of Union last night, and still there at 11 o'clock to-day. Will move toward Blountsville and for Kentucky. Federal scouts in Union this morning.

E. HAMMOND,
Lieutenant.

I inferred from this report that Mr. [Lieutenant] Hammond was reporting what he had heard at Union as coming from the Federal scouts who were in Union that morning, as he could not otherwise have an idea where the enemy, who was in camp at 11 a. m., intended to march, and this information was not deemed very satisfactory as a basis for my movements.

The next information I received was about 2 o'clock, from Captain Baldwin, at Blountsville. As he addressed me four during the evening, I beg to submit them here in order:

BLOUNTSVILLE, TENN., December 31, 1862.

Brigadier-General MARSHALL:

GENERAL: The Yankees are crossing the Blountsville road *en route* for Kingsport and Estillville, and may be intercepted by way of the Reedy Creek road.
In haste,

W. W. BALDWIN,
Commanding Cavalry, &c.

Appended to the foregoing was the following from one of Major Johnson's captains:

I will get in front of them, and check them until your men can get upon their rear.

JNO. T. WILLIAMS.

BLOUNTSVILLE, TENN.,
December 31, 1862. (Received 2.30 o'clock.)

The Abolitionists are (a portion of them) in camp at Hull's, 4 miles south of this place. My company has gone on the Kingsport road for further discoveries. The camp at Hull's is on the Jonesborough road. Let me know if you have any force moving on the Reedy Creek road.
Respectfully,

W. W. BALDWIN,
Captain, &c.

(Received about 4 p. m.)

General MARSHALL:

Within you find the report of one of my captains. We are pressing them. For God's sake send all your force direct to Kingsport.

W. W. BALDWIN, &c.

Inside was the following:

Major BALDWIN:

SIR: They have been crossing the ridge by Sheaver's, in the direction of Kingsport.

W. G. GLENN.

P. S.—The supposition is they are about 2,000 strong, as they have been passing for two hours.

AT JOHN L. SHEAVER'S, EDEN'S RIDGE, TENN.,
December 31, 1862—6.45 p. m.

General HUMPHREY MARSHALL:

After reconnoitering the country around Blountsville, I am fully convinced that a large portion of the Yankee force is now in camp at Hull's, 4 miles southwest of Blountsville; 1,200 to 1,500 are now, perhaps, in Kingsport, and it is generally believed, from their own statements along the way, that this advanced party is *en route* for Rogersville, in view of plundering the bank at that place. I yet think we can intercept this force, if your force can reach Kingsport by midnight.
Respectfully,

W. W. BALDWIN,
Commanding Cavalry Scouts.

P. S.—The force at Hull's may be moving. If so, they must pass this point. I will watch their movements and try to keep you advised.

About the same time I received this last dispatch (near 8 p. m.), I also received the following from Captain Bedford, of Clay's command, who had left Bristol about noon to relieve Lieutenant [E.] Hammond, at Union. He had passed directly from Union to Blountsville, and as he had neither seen nor heard of the camp at Hull's, I concluded that Captain Baldwin had made a mistake, possibly, as to its existence, and I issued to Colonel Giltner immediately the following order:

DECEMBER 31, [1862]—8 p. m.

Press on to Blountsville with speed. When arrived there, direct your movements by the reports which Baldwin makes. My chief aim is to cut the enemy off from Moccasin Gap; but, remember, your function is only to harass him until my infantry can catch up.

H. MARSHALL,
Brigadier-General.

I will observe that, from the time at which Captain Baldwin made his first report, I was much at a loss how to understand the movement of the enemy by the light of these reports: "The enemy is crossing the Blountsville road." I inferred from that he was making for Moccasin Gap. Had he designed going to Kingsport, he would have taken the road to Kingsport. He would only cross the Blountsville road (coming from Union) if he intended to go to Moccasin Gap, or to get upon the Reedy Creek road and to take that, by which he could go either to the one place or the other. Next came the declaration that he was in camp on the Jonesborough road to Blountsville. If so, he was as near Bristol as he would be at Blountsville, and could approach it directly by the Beaver Creek road. If that was true, it would not do for me to attempt pursuit and leave Bristol uncovered, since I was ordered to look to its defense. When the third dispatch came, announcing that the enemy had been crossing the ridge two hours, I could not tell whether the force at Hull's had gone, nor could I tell that he meant to make for Kingsport, as the road he was said to be taking was the very nighest cut he could take to Moccasin Gap. When the officer reported him still in camp at Hull's at 6.45 o'clock, I should have hesitated to uncover Bristol had I not received Captain Bedford's dispatch. I had determined early in the day that if, in fact, the enemy was intending to retreat, I would try to intercept him, and, with the view to a pursuit, had ordered rations for four days to be cooked, that our movement might commence at nightfall. Considering all I had heard of the sentiments of the population of East Tennessee, and the limited experience I had had, I was not disposed to let my adversary have access to information as to my movements. If he had moved and encamped again, as reported in Captain Baldwin's second dispatch, he would be there that night, and, by going to Blountsville under cover of the night, I should gain his rear. I made no order to move or to cook rations until my cavalry arrived (after 2 p. m.). Until I was satisfied that the probability was strong that he had not encamped at Hull's, or had left there, I would not give marching orders to the cavalry, though I had already started the infantry and one section of artillery; and, to move this, I had to press horses that evening, as mine had not arrived from Wytheville.

I waited after my force was in motion for several reasons: First, to receive the troops promised by General Jones, and to know certainly whether they arrived. Second, because Captain Jeffress' horses came in after nightfall from a day's journey, and I wanted them to rest a little before they were put again on the road to draw the guns I desired to carry with me. Third, because a section of artillery under that officer, which I ordered him to prepare and move, would have no other escort to Blountsville than myself and staff, and a signal corps who were with me. Your correspondent intimates that he knows, but will not tell, the reason I delayed my departure until 1 a. m. of January 1. I was in Blountsville about the hour he fixes for my departure from Bristol, and his pretended concealment of knowledge, I assure you, but discloses to my sense the turpitude of his motives in representing as existing something he affects to desire to conceal. The reasons for my delay are now plainly disclosed, and that delay was not longer than I thought my business required, of which I was the sole judge.

If it was the intention of Major Dunn to intimate that I was intoxicated, my statement is that the assertion can be proved false, not only of that day and time, but of every other day and time since I held your commission, for there is not a more temperate man in the Southern Confederacy than I am and have always been. In this connection, let me remark that the same writer comments upon what he calls my "imbecility." A long personal acquaintance, both with the President and yourself, will enable you to pronounce judgment upon such a charge with more propriety than I can.

I inclose you Major Dunn's map—the result of several hours' labor—which you will perceive places all the points of compass wrong; puts Abingdon west of Bristol, and, in a word, is such a production that no art could explain it. It is possible I may have been inattentive to any explanation of a diagram so wrong as it was, though I have no recollection of it, as it was my purpose, even if *ennuyéd*, to remain polite, and I am not in the habit of conducting myself otherwise. I leave it to the President to judge, however, if my activity in the intelligent discharge of my duty slackened.

Instead of the 1,500 efficient men which it is asserted were at my disposal, you perceive that, up to 2.30 p. m. on the 31st, I had a force as follows:

Sixty-fourth Virginia Infantry	373	
Fifth Kentucky [Infantry]	310	
		683
Clay's Mounted Rifles	250	
Johnson's Mounted Rifles	100	
		350
Total		1,033

Making a total about equal to Colonel Slemp's estimate of 900, though the company on picket should be subtracted, as it was 10 miles from Bristol. After 2.30 p. m. of the 31st, add Giltner, and we have a total of some 1,400 or 1,500 of all arms.

I submit, respectfully, that in the state of my information it was my duty not to leave Bristol sooner than I did, and it was proper, after a ride of 37 miles through mud and rain, to have let my cavalry horses feed before I commenced a pursuit. How effective that cavalry was, I leave you to judge upon the plain statements of Colonel Giltner that his men were in the saddle the night of the 30th and 31st, and in that time (forty hours) never ate, and traversed 66 miles over deep, bad roads in the winter, in a mountain land. When I was at Bristol, before starting on the night of the 31st, I did not know what route the enemy would take. Major Witcher had arrived in person, but not his battalion. I directed him to return that night to Little Moccasin Gap, and lead his battalion to the defile at Hanging Rock, 3 miles from Osborne's Ford, so that, if the enemy tried to turn to the right at Estillville and to go by the ford over to the Pound Gap road, he might check him. I did not know I could intercept him before he would reach that point. If the enemy did not approach the ford next morning, Major Witcher was to lead his battalion down the north side of Clinch River and join me. At the same time I started a reliable messenger to Kentucky with orders to Col. Ben [E.] Caudill, at Whitesburg, to man Pound Gap, Stone Gap, and all the other mountain gaps along his front, and to resist the egress of the enemy, and to say that I would be near and approaching.

After crossing Sheaver's Ridge, the enemy kept on to Kingsport. He could have turned to the right at several places after that and have passed through Moccasin Gap. When I was in Blountsville, everybody there supposed of course he had gone to Moccasin Gap, and lamented our inability to reach the gap before him. I knew no reason for him to go by Kingsport. If he meant to go out at the Moccasin Gap, it was only a detour of about 8 miles to go by Kingsport and then to return into the gap, for they are only 7 miles apart. His only motive to go by Kingsport that I could imagine would be to strike at Major Johnson's camp and to release some prisoners taken by my men the day before. I took the chance if he had made this detour of reaching Moccasin Gap in advance of him. I occupied it by 4 a. m. on January 1. He had passed Kingsport that night and had taken down the south side of the Clinch Range.

Colonel Giltner is mistaken as to the hour of my arrival at Estillville, though possibly not as to the time when he first saw me there. I was at Estillville at dinner-time, and rode into town with his scout, returning from Kingsport, from whom I learned the direction the enemy had taken. Clay and Johnson had moved when I reached there, so that I infer the young officer had reported, and I came in with a squad from his party which had lagged behind. I sent word for my mounted men to halt until the rear came up, because there were bridal-gaps over the mountains a few miles from Estillville, and the enemy might have passed over those, and would turn successfully upon 300 or 350 men and whip them, if beyond supporting distance from the remainder of my force. Besides, I had given no authority to Colonel Giltner to direct the movements of the corps he had ordered to march. Presuming at Estillville the enemy would cross the Clinch Range below me, and might try to go out on the Lee County border somewhere, I at once dispatched Lieutenant-Colonel Pridemore, a native of Scott County, to the front, with directions to rouse the country people, and to dispatch a courier from Jonesville to Cumberland Gap, so as to let the force there know the situation and to request their co-operation, and to have word sent forward to block up the mountain passes. I urged on him to go to Jonesville that night and dispatch the courier instantly thence to Cumberland Gap.

I pressed on now to the Clinch River, at Speer's Ferry (the point the enemy had crossed coming in), and, finding my cavalry in bivouac, ordered the whole forward. I passed over two roads, one leading up the Clinch from Kyle's Ford (some 25 miles below), the other from Sneedsville. I thought the enemy might double and pass out behind me, for now I did not know where he was, save that I was on one side of a mountain range and he on the other.

Before midnight I met Lieutenant-Colonel Pridemore returning. He had advanced as far as Pattonsville, and there learned that the news I wished to convey had gone already; that the movement of the enemy on the south side was known, and that the country people (it was told him at Pattonsville) had that day felled trees across the road on the north side of Powell's Mountain, so as to obstruct passage in the direction of Jonesville; that I was blockaded as well as the enemy. I then determined to halt until daylight. It was intensely cold, and my men were very much exhausted, some of them being in the saddle now for the third night.

I waited until light. Before light, scouts came to me with the information that the enemy had crossed the Clinch Mountains and the river at War Gap, and were encamped at 9 p. m. 15 miles below Speer's Ferry. My conclusion was, then, that he would rest also until day, and that his course would not before be determined. It was quite plain he was at a center to travel the radius and I the arc of a circle; that he had half a dozen ways to go out, and that, if I was not very watchful, I should not intercept him. I ordered my infantry and artillery forward.

On the morning of January 2, I moved to Pattonsville, where another road by which he could pass out crossed my path, and there I learned that 400 infantry and two companies of cavalry from Cumberland Gap had taken position at Jonesville, and that the forces from that quarter were co-operating to prevent his egress. I thought the prize was nearly sure. I detached Captain Marshall's cavalry company, with orders to move down the North Fork of the Clinch as low as Blackwater; thence, if the enemy had gone into Hunter's Gap, to harass his rear, and so on to Jonesville. I sent forward Lieutenant Gibson with 10 men to Jonesville (now 20 miles), to inform the force there of my approach, and to procure rations for my men, if possible (Giltner's regiment had not eaten a morsel since the day before at 2 p. m.). The north side of Powell's Mountain was partially obstructed by a few trees cut across the road, but more so from being very hard frozen and becoming sleek under the horses' feet. We led down it, passed on, and at 8 miles from Jonesville I received a dispatch from Lieutenant Gibson that there was heavy and continuous firing in the direction of Hunter's Gap, on the direct road from Rogersville to Jonesville, and some 4 or 5 miles south of Jonesville. I ordered my force forward to Jonesville as rapidly as possible, all at a brisk trot and many in a gallop. Clay and Johnson were some 2 miles ahead of Giltner. I pressed on between them. At about 3 miles from town another dispatch from Lieutenant Gibson, written at 1 mile from town, announced the continuance of the firing, and that artillery was heard. I knew the enemy had none, and was certain it had come up from Cumberland Gap, and that a brave band from that garrison (which was only 33 miles off) were gallantly resisting the superior force of our enemy. I congratulated myself that our toil would be crowned with success at last and the insolence of our foe would be punished. At 1 mile from town I met Lieutenant Gibson with the information that the enemy had possession of Jonesville, and had a good number of prisoners with them. I asked for the force which had engaged them, what also of the artillery, where the Cumberland Gap men had gone to, but could get no satisfactory response. I ordered my attack on the town to open at once, for it was now near sundown. My Rifles (dismounted) went into action deployed on a hill east of the village, but within rifle range of the court-house. Giltner came up, and I deployed a part of his force on the south side of the village, at about 100 yards from the main street. The enemy was now plainly visible on the hill by the academy, on the northwest side of the village, formed in line some 400 strong. Villagers declared he was flanking me on both sides, and I made some detachments to ascertain the falsity of their apprehensions. I ordered both my lines forward, heard the enemy's bugle-call to the saddle, and my men under Giltner followed to the Harlan road. The enemy was mounted. Our horses were outside the village, some of them nearly a mile. The distance to be traversed to the gap was 4 miles. I learned that the front of the enemy had passed the village an hour or more when we arrived and commenced firing. It was now night, but moonlit partially. Beyond the town the clearings are small, the timber heavy, the undergrowth thick of black-jack, scrubby oak, and chestnut; ground broken; two or three heavy ridges to be crossed and narrow vales. I had never seen it. Deployment would be impracticable at night and the situation most inviting for ambuscades. The enemy would in an hour be out of Virginia. He had the position on me, and I desisted from further pursuit, as I am sure I should have done, and with my present knowledge of the country should, under the same circumstances, do again. As I was returning from Jonesville, I received a dispatch from Major-General Jones and another from Lieut. Gen. E. Kirby Smith, asking me to make pursuit, the latter dated at Knoxville on the day after the enemy passed into Kentucky.

Thus I have at great length submitted all I have to represent touching the raid of the enemy into our country. I think, upon a review of my action, the President will find that if success in overtaking and punishing the enemy was not achieved, it was not for the want of effort upon my part or of the troops I command. My infantry marched 70 miles in some sixty hours over bad roads, mountains, and rivers, and my cavalry pressed night and day on the track of the foe, as I think has not frequently been done before in the war. I have felt that it was better to bear in silence the shafts of impotent and ill-natured criticism, when basing its attacks on false premises, than to make our combinations, forces, and views known to a vigilant enemy by dissertations and defenses before the tribunal of the press, which has no jurisdiction over the subject-matter. When you call me forward, I make my report, abstaining from all that my feeling of indignation might dictate to me to say, but which your dignity and my own position alike forbid. Your own examination will find all the data here on which to form a correct opinion. If the enemy was jaded, it was before he rested after his incendiary effort. His travel daily afterward until he left Virginia proves he had full capacity to move when desiring to do so.

Respectfully,

H. MARSHALL,
Brigadier-General.

Hon. JAMES A. SEDDON,
Secretary of War.

No. 7.

Report of Col. H. L. Giltner, Fourth Kentucky Cavalry, of operations December 30–January 2.

CAMP RICHARDSON, LEE COUNTY, VA.,
January 26, 1863.

GENERAL: On the morning of December 30, 1862, about 3 o'clock, a dispatch from you was received at my camp, near Lebanon, Russell County, Virginia, informing me that a force of the enemy was reported in the neighborhood of Scott Court-House, and ordering me to throw out a picket to the Old Russell Court-House to guard the road from that place to Osborne's Ford; and also a picket to Hansonville, guarding the roads from that point to Saltville, via Poor Valley, and via Lebanon. Your order was promptly obeyed, a strong picket being sent to each of the above-named places.

At 11 p. m. of the same day I received an order from you to repair with my regiment to Bristol immediately. In a very short time my men were in the saddle, and, leaving the camp with the dismounted and otherwise disabled men, under command of Captain [George T.] Campbell [acting commissary of subsistence], I started for Bristol, via Abingdon, with 550 men, and accompanied by three wagons, two containing cooking utensils, the other ammunition. The road via Abingdon was not the shortest to Bristol, but I was compelled to go to Abingdon to draw about 100 guns, which were needed; also ammunition, as that which I had was not suitable for many of the guns in the command. The exceedingly rough and heavy condition of the roads, and the darkness (the night being cloudy and rainy) rendered the march most arduous, yet we arrived in Abingdon, a distance of 20 miles from my camp, before daylight. Proceeding directly to the railroad depot, I procured the needed ordnance stores and sufficient forage to feed my horses. Moving to the outskirts of the town, I fed my horses in the road, and, after a halt of about three-quarters of an hour, I pushed on to Bristol, where I arrived and reported to you about 2.30 p. m. December 31, 1862.

At 8 p. m. I received the following order:

DECEMBER 31, [1862]—8 p. m.

Colonel [H. L.] GILTNER:

Press on with speed to Blountsville. When arrived there, direct your movements by the reports which Baldwin makes. My chief aim is to cut the enemy off from Moccasin Gap; but, remember, your function is only to harass him until my infantry can catch up.

H. MARSHALL,
Brigadier-General.

In obedience to the above order, I proceeded with speed to Blountsville, arriving there at 10 p. m. From information there received, I determined to push on to Moccasin Gap, which point I reached at 4 a. m. January 1, and went into camp, having marched, since 8 p. m. the evening before, a distance of 29 miles.

At daylight I sent a scout of 20 men, under command of Lieut. B. F. Duncan, in the direction of Kingsport, with orders to gain accurate information as to the enemy's position and movements, and report to me as speedily as possible. At the same time I ordered Captains [John G.] Scott and [S. P.] Duncan to proceed with their squadrons to Estillville and procure and have cooked rations for the regiment. Up to that time my men had had nothing to eat since leaving camp at Lebanon; had ridden a distance of 65 miles through the rain and mud without rest, having been in the saddle the whole of both nights since starting, and were consequently greatly in need of food and sleep.

At 12 m. Lieutenant Duncan returned and reported to me at Estillville that the enemy had encamped the night before in the Holston Valley, 7 miles from Kingsport, and had moved at daylight in the direction of War Gap. My own men not having procured anything to eat at this time, I ordered Lieutenant-Colonel Clay, with his own and Major [Thomas] Johnson's battalion (they both having cooked rations for four days), to War Gap, with instructions to occupy the gap should he gain that point in advance of the enemy; but, if he should fall in his rear, to harass him until I could re-enforce him with my regiment.

About 3 p. m. you arrived at Estillville. I reported to you the information I had received of the movements of the enemy and the order I had given to Lieutenant-Colonel Clay. You sent a courier to Colonel Clay, ordering him to halt and await further orders. About sunset, both men and horses having been fed, I moved on from Estillville, with orders from you to halt at Speer's Ferry, 11 miles distant, and await orders.   Passing Colonel Clay, bivouacked on the road a mile from the ferry, I crossed the river and halted.   In about half an hour you came up and ordered the whole command forward.   We marched about 5 miles to Pridemore's, where we halted and remained until sunrise the next morning.   Moving on to Pattonsville, a distance of about 4 or 5 miles, we halted, fed our horses, and again moved on toward Jonesville about 9 a. m.   When within about 7 miles of the latter place, being a mile or two in the rear of the other battalions, I received a message from yourself to move on to Jonesville with rapidity.   I pushed on at a brisk trot until I reached the horses of Colonel Clay's and Major Johnson's commands, a short distance from the town, the men having dismounted for action.   Passing these horses, I halted, dismounted my men, and ordered the guns to be loaded.   I then received an order from you to take the town.   Throwing out a company as skirmishers, I advanced upon the town, and, finding no enemy there, and being told by the citizens that he had formed in line at or near the academy, beyond town, I moved on through the town and past the academy until my line of skirmishers had intersected the Harlan road.   It being then after dark, we saw no enemy, though they were heard by the skirmishers as they passed out of the old field beyond the academy.   Receiving information from the officer commanding the skirmishers that the enemy had taken the road and were certainly gone, I called in the skirmishers, threw out a picket upon the road the enemy had taken, and returned with my regiment to the town, when I was ordered into camp for the night at the academy.   The distance from my camp, near Lebanon, to Jonesville, by the route we marched, is 105 miles, and we were from 11.30 p. m. of December 30 until 4 p. m. of January 2 in going that distance.

H. L. GILTNER,
Colonel, Comdg. Fourth Regiment Kentucky Cavalry.

Brig. Gen. HUMPHREY MARSHALL,
Jonesville, Va.

No. 8.

Report of Lieut. Col. E. F. Clay, Third Battalion Kentucky Mounted Rifles, of operations December 30–January 1.

CAMP LIVESAY, January 24, 1863.

SIR: In obedience to your orders, I submit the following report:

At or about 10 a. m. Tuesday, December 30, 1862, I received information from Colonel Slemp and Major [Lieut. Col. T. W. W.] Davies [Twenty-eighth Alabama Infantry], (the commandant of the post at Bristol), that some 4,000 Yankee cavalry were moving on Bristol, and at 1 p. m. on Monday were distant 45 miles; that they would probably reach that place by morning; that their direction was about west. While I was acknowledging the receipt of these dispatches, two citizens from Lee County rode up to my tent and confirmed the report, and stated by that time the enemy was no doubt at Estillville, some 28 miles distant from Bristol.   I inquired of them why they thought that the enemy was intending a demonstration on Bristol.   They replied, because the soldiers had told it along the road, and had frequently asked the distance to that place, which at once led me to believe that he was certainly making for Bristol.   Immediately on receiving this intelligence

I aroused the camp, ordered horses saddled, and ammunition issued to all who had arms (there being about 75 men without arms). As soon as ammunition was issued to Company A, I ordered it out on duty, with orders to scout rapidly the three roads leading from Estillville, by which the enemy might approach my camp, and find out his position and watch his movements, my camp being between the enemy and Bristol. The scout on the road known as the Reedy Creek road, upon which I was en-camped, had not advanced more than 6 or 7 miles before they met three of the enemy's cavalry—one, a sergeant. Two of them were made pris-oners by the scout, and the other shot from his horse by Major [Thomas] Johnson, who had just overtaken my scout on his road from Abingdon to join his command. Concerning this affair I inclose the lieutenant's report to me,* who was in command of the party, and upon which you can rely. The 2 prisoners were sent to camp, accompanied by Major Johnson, who was very much excited, and yet holding his pistol in his hand. This was about daylight. I questioned the prisoners, and learned from the sergeant one had stopped to fix something about his saddle, and that he (sergeant) had stopped back to bring them up to their com-mand, having been placed in rear of his company by his captain for that purpose. It seems from after developments that these prisoners had fallen in rear of their command just before it had reached the forks of the road, 8 miles from my camp, and that the command had taken the right-hand road, which leads to Union, via Blountsville; that these three men in their hurry to rejoin their command passed this road unnoticed, and ran up to my scout, thinking it a part of their own command. I im-mediately ordered tents struck and wagons loaded, ready to march at a moment's warning. Thinking that the enemy would make a demonstra-tion on Bristol with his whole force, or a part, by the road upon which I was encamped, I ordered the train and sick to Bristol, and determined to hold my position, or, by skirmishing with him, detain him until you could send a sufficient force to Bristol to defend it with complete suc-cess, knowing Slemp's regiment insufficient to do so, as he had reported it to me as only 400 strong.

This brings us up to 7.30 a. m. About this time there rode into camp three citizens, one of whom was introduced to me as Colonel [Maj. I. B.] Dunn by Major Johnson, who gave me some information in regard to two roads leading from Blountsville to Bristol, and suggested that the enemy would likely approach Bristol by one or both of these roads, and proposed to go as a guide with my scouts on these roads. These roads entered the main Bristol and Estillville [road] between my camp and Bristol. I, therefore, ordered Captain [James] White to take his com-pany and scout these roads as far as Blountsville, with all speed, which was promptly obeyed. Colonel Dunn accompanied Captain White a short distance beyond his house and then returned to his domicile.

At 11 a. m. I received a dispatch from Captain White, who was then 1 mile from Blountsville, stating that the enemy had left that place and gone in the direction of Union; that the greater portion had passed the point that he was then at before daylight; that they remained only a short time at Blountsville. This information I telegraphed you at Abingdon, and sent to Colonel Slemp, at Bristol. About this time Johnson's command arrived, I think about 80 strong. Finding that the enemy's whole force had passed to my left, I called in my pickets from my right and moved my command with Johnson's (which was ad-vancing) to Bristol, and covered that place with pickets and scouts in the direction of Blountsville and Union, thinking the enemy would likely attack Bristol from these positions after destroying the bridge at Union. It was about 2 p. m. when I reached Bristol.

On Tuesday night I received information from my scout at Union that the enemy had burned the bridge there and gone in the direction of the Watauga Bridge, some 7 or 8 miles southwest of that place. This information I gave you when you got to Bristol on Tuesday night. Colonel Dunn states in his letter to the Hon. James A. Seddon that he found my camp in a perfect state of disorganization, and that I did not know what to do; that my command was some 450 strong—all confidentially. These statements are infamous, false, and slanderous to the utmost. My command did not exceed 250 men.

I must say, in conclusion, that it is strange, but nevertheless true, that I did not receive any information whatever from citizens except from the two alluded to in the first part of my report.

Yours, very respectfully,

E. F. CLAY,
Lieutenant-Colonel, Commanding Battalion.

Brig. Gen. HUMPHREY MARSHALL.

No. 9.

Report of Lieut. H. H. Duncan, Company A, Third Battalion Kentucky Mounted Rifles, of operations December 29–30.

—— ——, 1863.

SIR: By your order, I submit the following report:

It was on the night of December 29, 1862, that, by your order, I was ordered to take a part of one company and scout down the Kingsport road, as it was reported the enemy's cavalry was coming in the neighborhood. I had gone some 7 miles and stopped the main body, and sent pickets 1 mile in front, with orders to stand until relieved. This was about two hours before daylight. The pickets in the mean time, hearing horsemen advancing, sent one of their number back to me to know what to do, as Colonel [Major Thomas] Johnson's command was encamped in the neighborhood, and they fearing to fire for fear it was Johnson's men falling back. I was sitting in the road, mounted, with my men, when three men rode up to us from the rear, who afterward proved to be Colonel Johnson and two of his men. At or about the same time three of the enemy rode up and asked if the front of the column was ahead. I asked what column. They replied the Ninth Pennsylvania. I replied that we were Confederate troops, and ordered them to surrender, which they did, as I ordered my men to prepare. At or near the same time I heard a pistol shot, which I afterward learned was Colonel Johnson's. He shot one of the prisoners. We then fell back and stationed pickets. I then delivered the prisoners over to you (Colonel Clay). Colonel Johnson was a prisoner himself until he let himself be known. That was about the time of taking the enemy. These are the facts, as well as I remember.

Yours, respectfully,

H. H. DUNCAN,
Second Lieut. Co. A, First [Third] Batt. Ky. Mounted Rifles.

Lieutenant-Colonel CLAY.

No. 10.

Report of Capt. William W. Baldwin, commanding Cavalry Squadron, of operations December 29–January 2.

KINGSPORT, EAST TENN., *January* 6, 1863.

GENERAL : You will, doubtless, have heard of the raid made upon East Tennessee and Southwest Virginia by the notorious renegade Carter and his Abolition crew before this reaches you, but as I was an eye-witness to the whole affair, I propose to give you a brief account of it that you may rely upon.

On Monday night, December 29, I was informed by reliable sources that a large Yankee force was passing through Big Moccasin Gap. I immediately threw out a picket force, and found it to be true that a mounted force of about 2,000 was passing rapidly up the Bristol road. I next proceeded to dispatch to the authorities along the line of railroad. My courier to Bristol being cut off by the head of the enemy's column, I failed to get the news to Bristol, but reached Jonesborough and Rogersville, and, by telegraph, informed General Marshall, at Abingdon, of their approach. General Marshall mustered his infantry and artillery to Bristol Tuesday night, and there lay waiting for the enemy to arrive until he had approached the railroad at Union Depot, burned the bridge and depot; thence moved down to Carter's Depot, burned the bridge at that place, rushed the cars into the river, destroying a large amount of stores, arms, &c. Tuesday evening I tendered my force to General Marshall, at Bristol, but was coolly informed that we would have to provide for ourselves and wait for orders.

Next morning, being very impatient, I went to General M[arshall] and asked leave to follow up the enemy, harass him upon his rear, and report to the general my discoveries. His reply to me was (turning scornfully upon his heels), "By God, when I have orders for you, I will let you know." Captain [B. W.] Jenkins, of his staff, and others, however, interfering, prevailed to induce him to send for me about 9 a. m. Wednesday, and grant me liberty at this late hour to start after him, but with special orders to make no general attack until the word was given by him. Under this sort of orders, I proceeded in search of the enemy in the direction of Union, discovered him 4 miles southwest of Blountsville about 1 p. m., on his backward march, and reported the fact to General Marshall. While harassing him upon his rear, I kept a regular line of couriers to Marshall, advising him fully of all the enemy's movements. At 8 p. m. I learned, by a dispatch from General Marshall, that his whole force was in motion toward the enemy's front. Being encouraged by this information, I pressed close upon him, sent up an advance so close as to fire upon the general and his staff at Kingsport, who were, strangely enough, halting for refreshments in the rear, wounding his aide-de-camp in the hand, took the general's horse, saber, and baggage, saddle, &c., one of his staff's horses and baggage, the balance all making their escape. This produced no small excitement in the enemy's ranks, and, to avoid hastening his retreat in advance of General Marshall's intercepting column, I concealed my force in a neighboring wood until he quieted and went into camp. In this way I pursued him, plucking off a few from his rear every now and then until he reached Jonesville, Va. Here I was full of hope that we should bag up the whole force. But, as might have been expected, Marshall had stationed his force about three-quarters of a mile from where he would pass, and reserved a fire only for the enemy's rear, which, like the old man's tuft of grass, "only made the youngster laugh;" and, pained, disgusted, chagrined, and disgraced, we were compelled to stand, and, feeling our abuses never so deeply and intensely, see our abusers not only flee unhurt, but protected in their flight. Besides the great public damage done us by this raid, an almost irreparable damage is done to private circles in the robbery of horses on the route; almost every serviceable horse on the road has been taken off by these robbers, so that there are not horses left on this route to cultivate the fields.

And now, general, I have a few questions to ask you, and through you to ask the War Department:

First, then, why did General Marshall hold all his infantry and artillery in Abingdon and Bristol until the enemy had burned up the public property at Union and Carter; and why did he still hold his cavalry force in Bristol eight hours after he learned they were returning toward Kentucky?

Second. Why did he not, by means of the railroad, throw all his infantry and artillery along the line of railroad upon their front, and his cavalry upon his rear, and thus not only prevent all this damage, but bag him on the road?

Third. After failing in these, why did he hold his cavalry force at Estillville all night, and wait for infantry and artillery to come up, to intercept a retreating cavalry foe?

Fourth. After being fully advised of the enemy's movements across Clinch Mountain, Powell's Mountain, and Waldron's Ridge, in his rapid flight toward Cumberland Mountains, why did he halt 1,700 cavalry near Pattonsville for nine hours in open daylight?

Fifth. After all these strange proceedings, why did he at Jonesville select a position for attack with musketry and rifle forces at moderate range from the enemy's pass for light artillery, and even then reserve his fire for the rear, the head of the enemy's column being 3 to 5 miles in advance of any force or route to intercept him?

Sixth. And why did he, having his force dismounted, order a charge of infantry upon the enemy's cavalry rear after all these cursed failures?

Seventh, and finally, what will be likely to follow such a raid as this, and what will become of the salt works, and Bristol and Abingdon, and the railroad, and, in a word, the very backbone of our Confederacy, if Humphrey Marshall is continued in command of this department?

I am in a good place for forage, and will go to Kentucky with Col. [Major] Tom. Johnson soon. I could add to my force of cavalry fast enough here from the scattered old Fifth Kentucky, but cannot raise any infantry.

General, will you consent to my raising other companies of ranger cavalry; and will you recommend me to the War Department for majority of such command? I can do but little with this small command, but let me have 400 men, and I will make a raid upon the banks of the Ohio River.

Very respectfully, and fraternally,

W. W. BALDWIN,
Captain Cavalry Squadron.

Brig. Gen. J. S. WILLIAMS,
Commanding Second Brigade, &c.

No. 11.

Report of Col. Hiram Hawkins, Fifth Kentucky Infantry, of operations December 29–30.

JONESVILLE, VA., *January 29*, 1863.

SIR: At your request, I submit the following report of the operations of my command during the late raid made by General Carter:

My regiment (310 effective men) was encamped near Abingdon, Va., when on December 30 last, at 2 a. m., I was informed by an officer from your headquarters that you had information that a large cavalry force of the enemy was in Lee County, destination not known, strength estimated at 4,000; that you desired me to hold my command in readiness to move at a moment's warning. About 11 a. m. same day I received orders to move my command immediately to the depot and take the cars for Bristol. Moved at once to the depot and reported to you that the cars were gone. You seemed much surprised, and remarked that you had informed the conductor not to move the train without your permission, and directed me to remain at the depot until the train could be ordered back. The train arrived about dark, but was not ready for some time afterward to take my command on board. Arrived at Bristol about midnight; left the cars and bivouacked until morning (31st), when you informed me that you would not move from Bristol until you could learn something of the movements of the enemy, which you would likely do by the time the remainder of your mounted men would arrive. Late in the evening, when scouts brought information that the enemy was retreating, you informed me that it was your purpose to move under cover of the night to cut off his retreat, and without further orders I would move my command at dusk on Blountsville, accompanied by Colonel Slemp's regiment (Sixty-fourth Virginia) and a section of [George S.] Davidson's battery, and await further orders; that the mounted men, not yet ready, would move as soon as ready, and that you would remain at Bristol to await the arrival of more troops on the train, and assist Captain Jeffress to start his battery, which would also follow during the night.

When we reached Blountsville, a distance of 9 miles, halted, quartered troops in houses (it being very cold). My men had rested about two hours, when you arrived and ordered the column to move at once to Big Moccasin Gap, the mounted men having passed me on the march, and were to move rapidly to that point, head the enemy, and hold him in check until the infantry and artillery could attack his rear.

Leaving Bristol at dusk, we marched continuously and rapidly (except the two hours' rest at Blountsville), until we arrived at Moccasin Gap, 28 miles; not finding the enemy, we moved to Estillville, and encamped for the night. When I arrived there, Colonel Giltner's regiment was feeding and preparing to move, the remainder of the mounted men having passed on. You informed me that you were expecting Colonel Dunn's regiment and Captain Jeffress' battery at Estillville that night; that you were going to press forward during the night with the mounted force to head the enemy, in which event he might attempt his escape by passing in your rear, in which event I must, if possible, intercept him.

The next morning at 6 o'clock (January 2) I received a dispatch from you, dated *en route*, January 1, 10 p. m., ordering me to move my own and Colonel Slemp's regiments and the two guns from Davidson's battery by the quickest route to Hickory Flats, leaving Colonel Dunn's regiment and Captain Jeffress' battery to guard Moccasin Gap, in the event the enemy should be headed and compelled to turn back and attempt his escape through that gap, a thing thought not improbable.

My column was put in motion early in the morning for Hickory Flats, moving briskly, so as to cover the roads leading from the direction the enemy was taking, by way of Speer's Ferry and Pattonsville. At 8.30 p. m. I received the following dispatch:

Colonel HAWKINS:

The enemy is engaged near Hunter's Gap, as I hear. My force is now in 7 miles of Jonesville. You take the shortest road to Hunter's Gap with your column, so as to intercept the enemy if he attempts to pass by Pattonsville, and to come in his rear if he makes a stand at that point. Follow up through Hunter's Gap; if he is advanced beyond that point, on his rear until you reach him.

H. MARSHALL,
Brigadier-General.

The head of my column was then near Pattonsville, at which place I halted for rest, having marched that day (January 2) 20 miles over a muddy road; had camp fires made, as it was too cold to do without fires, and having no tents or shelter; put out camp guard and a picket on the road leading from Hunter's Gap to Pattonsville and Speer's Ferry, 10 miles from my command. The picket was detailed from my regiment and put under command of Lieutenant [H. D.] Pridemore, of [Company C] Sixty-fourth Virginia, who knew the country, and mounted on horses impressed for that purpose. This was done that the enemy might not only not surprise me, but to prevent him from gaining my rear and making his escape by way of Speer's Ferry by taking the road 10 miles of my command, which, if he had attempted (being warned by my pickets of his purpose), I could have intercepted him by rapidly countermarching my column on the road I had just passed over. I did not retire for rest that night until 2 a. m. of 3d instant, and at 5 o'clock my column was stretched out on the road to Hunter's Gap, animated with high hopes of engaging the enemy.

In the mean time I dispatched to you that if the enemy attempted to pass by Pattonsville I would intercept him. If he made a stand at that point, would attack his rear by 10.30 a. m. at farthest. My column continued the march, passing through Hunter's Gap. On arriving at Jonesville, was directed to go into quarters, the enemy having made his escape.

The men of the Fifth Kentucky and Sixty-fourth Virginia Regiments deserve the highest praise for their patient endurance on this march, having moved in three days and nights 70 miles over rough roads, hills, and mountains, and each day crossing a river—one in a small ferry-boat and two in small canoes—an inclement season, and without tents or camp equipage of any kind.

Very respectfully, your obedient servant,

H. HAWKINS,
Colonel Fifth Kentucky Infantry Regiment.

General [HUMPHREY] MARSHALL.

No. 12.

Report of Col. Campbell Slemp, Sixty-fourth Virginia Infantry, of operations December 29–January 1.

JONESVILLE, VA., *January 30, 1863.*

According to your order [of] December 16, 1862, my regiment was moved near Bristol, Tenn., and was encamped 1 mile north of that place. On the 29th I received your dispatch dated 10.15 p. m. at 11.30 p. m., bearing information that the Federal cavalry were within 45 miles of Bristol at 10 o'clock, same date, 4,000 strong, and were marching on that place. I communicated at once to Lieutenant-Colonel Clay, at Three Springs, 4 miles distant, according to your instructions, and ordered scouts upon all the roads. At 2 a. m. 30th, two reliable messengers came to Lieutenant-Colonel Clay's encampment and reported the enemy on the Estillville road, 35 miles distant, at dusk the night before. This information reached me at or near 3 a. m. I rode immediately to the telegraph office at Bristol to communicate to you the information. The operator could not be found ; the battery and all his instruments concealed, which delayed my information to you until near 8 a. m. No special engine could be had, from the fact that the commander of the post had sent them all off before my arrival, and could not have conveyed you information earlier by horseback. At 8.30 a. m. I received word from Lieutenant-Colonel Clay that the enemy had turned in a southeast direction from the Abingdon road in the direction of Blountsville, Tenn.; forks of the road 13 miles distant; Clay situated on Abingdon road, 4 miles distant; scouts had captured two stragglers near forks of the roads. Enemy reported at Blountsville at 10 a. m. My regiment was then 373 strong, available men, and about 100 men, consisting of citizens and a company of about 5C under Captain Troy, at the post, the latter with very common arms and but very little ammunition. This composed my infantry strength. All the cavalry present was Lieutenant-Colonel Clay's battalion, consisting of about 250 men for duty. This makes my available force at that time but little over 600 men. When it was observed that the enemy had left the Abingdon road at Blountsville, Clay's force was brought upon the Blountsville road, that our whole force might be united for the defense of Bristol, it being the point ordered to defend, and the road by Blountsville being direct to Bristol. At 11 a. m. the enemy was reported within 3 miles of Bristol; we took a position for the defense of the town. At 11.30 a. m. scouts reported the main force gone by way of Union Depot, where one of the bridges was burned, and a picket in force upon the Blountsville road, the enemy in all numbering about 2,000 strong, partly armed with five-shooters. A special train was then ordered to move my infantry to Union, when two scouts came in and reported the bridge burning at 12.15 p. m., and enemy making threats upon Bristol from that point. Cavalry was thrown forward upon that road, and an infantry picket upon a special train to advance as far as possible without being surprised or taken, and to the bridge, if possible. They did advance as far as the bridge, and found it nearly burned down, and the enemy moving in the opposite direction. Bridge fell in before they left. As our force was too small to divide against a superior force like the enemy, at their approach I communicated, through the commander of the post at Bristol, to the commander of the post at Union upon the news of the enemy's advance, to throw scouts forward upon the road from Blountsville to Union, and to be on the alert, stating the circumstances. We received no information from him until late in the evening, stating he and his men (70 available) were surrounded before noon, captured, and paroled. My picket returned between 4 and 5 p. m., and reported Major [Thomas] Johnson arrived with 80 men for duty (mounted). I prepared the command to move in the direction of Blountsville, notwithstanding it would have been hazardous with my inferior force, all not amounting to 800, and two-thirds infantry ; but receiving information that you were on the road to Bristol with re-enforcements, I awaited your arrival, which was between 11 and 12 p. m., being delayed by cars with Colonel Hawkins' regiment and some artillery, Hawkins' regiment not numbering over 300 for duty, but no cavalry, which left us in still a bad condition to pursue cavalry. Colonel Giltner's regiment of cavalry was on the march for Bristol, and arrived about 2 p. m. 31st, to my recollection. In a short time afterward I received orders from you to have my regiment in readiness and to march at dusk with three days' rations. Accordingly, my regiment moved at dark in the direc- tion of Blountsville, and arrived at Blountsville about 1 a. m. January 1, a distance of 9 miles. Within an hour afterward you arrived, and gave orders to resume the march to Moccasin Gap immediately, distant from Blountsville 17 miles. At sunrise we were within 11 miles of the gap, and marched in quick time until within about 6 miles of the gap, when we learned the enemy had gone in the direction of Rogersville, Tenn. I then gave my men a little more time, and arrived at the gap about 1 p. m., the enemy being on the march on the Rogersville road, and proceeded to Estillville without halting. There I received orders to move to Speer's Ferry, 10 miles farther, and all other orders on the march were received from Col. H. Hawkins, senior to myself.

Very respectfully, your obedient servant,

C. SLEMP,
Colonel Sixty-fourth Virginia Regiment.

Brigadier-General MARSHALL.

No. 13.

Report of Maj. Isaac B. Dunn, relative to operations December 29-January 1.

GOODSON, VA., *January* 5, 1863.

DEAR SIR : After my last letter to you, in which I advised you of the disorganized and scattered condition of General Marshall's command, and reporting the doings of a portion of his command near by my resi- dence, but six days had transpired before a courier from Lee County called me out of bed at 2.30 a. m. Tuesday, informing me that a column of Yankee cavalry (variously estimated at from 1,500 to 4,000) had reached Pattonsville at 1 p. m. Monday, and were advancing upon Bris- tol, and would reach the railroad before daylight, passing my house, which is on the public road, 3 miles west of the Bristol depot. I sent runners to all my neighbors, and got them in arms, and then at daylight proceeded to the camp of [Lieutenant-]Colonel Clay, which was, as stated in a former letter, 1 mile from my house. I found them disorganized, confused, and apparently utterly at a loss to know what to do. Colonel Clay had been notified by General Marshall, from Abingdon, that a Yankee force was advancing upon him. He had thrown a picket down the road, for he was encamped upon the road by which they were ap- proaching Bristol. Colonel [Maj. Thomas] Johnson, of Kentucky, who had been at Abingdon, had brought intelligence from General [Marshall] to Colonel Clay of the Yankee approach ; was proceeding with all pos- sible haste to his command (350 men), encamped below Kingsport, 2 miles west, at Ross Camp-Ground, fearful they would be cut off, the Yankees being then 6 miles distant from Colonel Clay's camp, and be- tween Clay and Colonel Johnson's command, the latter being entirely in their rear. Six miles west of Colonel Clay's camp Colonel Johnson met Clay's scouts returning at full speed, cautioning him that the enemy were approaching in very heavy force close by. This was about 5 a. m. Tuesday. Colonel Johnson at once halted with two of his men, who were in company (one unarmed), and waited the advance of the Yankee column. Drawing his revolver, he ordered his armed companion to do likewise, and but a moment had elapsed before three men (the advance of Carter's Abolition army) halted in his front not more than 15 feet from him, asking at the same time if they were not a part of the Ninth Pennsylvania. Colonel Johnson made no reply, but ordered them to surrender. One of them, a sergeant, made a motion to draw his pistol, when Colonel Johnson fired and killed him; the other two surrendered, and were turned back prisoners, and returned with horses and guns (of the dead man also) to Colonel Clay's camp. The main column of the enemy was not over 100 yards in rear of this advance guard. They countermarched immediately, entered an old field a quarter [of a mile] in rear of their turning point, deployed in line of battle, remained until sunrise, then returned by the road they had come some mile or more, and took a right-hand road to Blountsville and Union. No one doubts but their first intention was to burn Bristol and take possession of all the trains, stores, &c., and destroy them first, which could have been as easily done as to take Union and destroy the bridges at that point. The appearance of a force in front on this route deterred them. I suggested, when I reached Colonel Clay's camp, that he should scout all the roads leading to Blountsville and Union, find out where the enemy was, and then act accordingly; and after giving him all the information I possessed in regard to the roads and country, proposed to go with his scouts and place them over all the different routes (three in number) and aid them in finding out what course the enemy had taken. This he consented to, and, after scouting all the roads in the direction of Union and Blountsville, by 12 or 1 p. m. found the enemy at Blountsville; a portion having advanced to Union, burned the depot and railroad bridge and county bridge, proceeding next in the direction of Watauga Bridge, on same evening (Tuesday), and burned that. General Marshall had news, by telegraphic communication from Morristown, Tenn., of their approach at 10 p. m. Monday. He ordered Clay and Colonel Slemp's infantry to take position at Bristol and defend the railroad if attacked. He never reached Bristol until Wednesday morning at 1 o'clock, as he told me. Colonel McClelland and myself called on Colonel Marshall Wednesday morning, gave him an idea of the country, and proposed to map the same for him. This duty devolved upon Mr. Blair and myself, while Colonel McClelland proposed to lead a party of scouts in the direction of Blountsville and Union, and find out enemy's position and report.

General Marshall had at Bristol and near by Clay's battalion (near 450 men, cavalry) and Colonel Slemp's regiment (in 1 mile) of infantry (about 750 men); besides, he had in rear of Yankees at Kingsport Colonel Johnson's command (over 300 men, cavalry); in all, 1,500 efficient men, on the ground, to meet this invasion of not over 1,200 to 1,500 Abolitionists, who were jaded and worn out, sleeping on their horses, and leaving their caps, coats, oil-cloths, and arms along the road. So jaded and worn out were they that the officers had to be traversing the line from one end to the other continually, pricking up the horses with their sabers and closing up the column scattered for 2 to 3 miles along the road, four-fifths of them asleep, having been riding constantly day and night for five days; so say the prisoners taken by Colonel Johnson.

On Wednesday noon Colonel Giltner's regiment of cavalry (800 strong) filed into Bristol and went into camp. Wednesday night General Jenkins' men (1,000 strong) reached [there] by rail, two batteries (Davis' [Davidson's] and Jeffress', eight guns) having reached [there] the day before. I continued with General Marshall throughout Wednesday, and had provided him a map of the railroad and all the stations to Bull's Gap, and all the approaches to same, as well as Mr. Blair and myself could do, and he slept over our explanations in his chair as perfectly imbecile as you could imagine. Wednesday evening scouts reported Yankees returning from Watauga Bridge (which they had burned) to Blountsville or near by (9 miles from Bristol), where they had encamped. Not a man of the command of General Marshall was moved in the direction of the enemy until after nightfall on Wednesday. General Marshall and staff had horses before the hotel at 4 p. m. on Wednesday, and did not get mounted until 1 a. m. Thursday, as I am informed. The cause I will not make known, as it is no purpose of mine to prefer charges.

Wednesday night Marshall moved Clay's battalion, Slemp's infantry regiment, and four pieces under Jeffress and Davis [Davidson] from Bristol in the direction of Moccasin Gap, while he had called in from Kingsport Colonel Johnson's command, and that also returned with the troops first stated.

On Thursday the Yankees encamped at Kingsport, 16 miles west of Blountsville, moving perfectly at their leisure, and, retracing their course, encamped at Kingsport (near by) without even posting a picket guard. Four of Capt. W. W. Baldwin's cavalry scouts went up to Pierce's tavern, in the east end of Kingsport, when General [S. P.] Carter and staff were eating supper, called them out of the house and shot at them, wounding an aide of General Carter in the hand, and, report says, Carter also. The whole Yankee party retreated by the back way of the house and fled on foot, guided by one of Pierce's negroes, leaving their horses hitched to the rack, which were taken by Baldwin's men. Captain Baldwin had stopped to feed and rest his men 4 miles in rear of Kingsport.

Such is the character of the raid upon our country; it is useless to say disgraceful. The damage is small; nothing was interrupted except to take all the horses, watches, &c., of loyal citizens, to seize and parole all the prisoners they could find, and destroy two bridges (worth probably $50,000 to construct them), with small amount of stores at each place, and the injury to one "material" engine, run into the river at Watauga. The greatest injury is the confidence afforded to the Union sentiment in East Tennessee, for already they have commenced bushwhacking in Carter County, and several persons have been killed.

It is no part of my purpose in this letter to find fault with any management or lay blame in any quarter. My report is one of facts, known to myself and the country, and cannot be gainsaid. In conclusion, let us have at least a fighting man to lead our men and our people. No one here will fail to see then that, while nothing has been accomplished by our men for want of proper officers, much could have been effected with active and efficient generalship. General Jones, I learn, reached Abingdon, but made no move west of that point that I know of. General Floyd, of Virginia State Line, was also at Abingdon, as I hear reported. The Yankees were four hours destroying the trestle-bridge at Union. It had been recently constructed of green timber, was uncovered, and they had to cut it down piece by piece, and let it fall into the river.

Please show this to the Secretary of War. You will see I had first directed it to him, but concluded it would look like anticipating Marshall's report, and I send it to you, that you may see how this thing has been butchered. Had we had such a man as Stuart or Forrest or Jones, or any leader at all, not a man of them could have escaped. Our people are disappointed, for they see, with ample force in our midst, a Yankee army can invade us with impunity and stir up the worst feelings of those Union devils who live around and in our very midst.

I have made this letter too long, and hope you will excuse the liberty I take in writing it at all.

Very respectfully, your obedient servant,

ISAAC B. DUNN.

Hon. J. R. TUCKER,
  Richmond, Va.

DECEMBER 21, 1862.—Skirmish on the Wilson Creek Pike, Tenn.

Report of Capt. Frank W. Mix, Fourth Michigan Cavalry.

HEADQUARTERS FOURTH MICHIGAN CAVALRY,
  Camp Rosecrans, December 21, 1862.

COLONEL: In obedience to orders I received last evening, I left camp this morning at 6 o'clock with 24 men of Company B and 25 of Company A, under command of Lieutenant Anderson, to report to General Negley, on the Franklin pike, as an escort for a forage train. I arrived at General Negley's headquarters at 7.30 o'clock, and was informed that I was to take my command out to the fork of the Franklin and Wilson Creek pike for picket duty. I informed the general I did not come prepared, as my men had no rations with them. He then ordered me to go out on the road, until I found the forage train, and to scour the country on both sides of the Wilson Creek pike, and gather what information I could. I found nothing worthy of mentioning until I came up with his train, about 4 miles out on the Wilson pike. There I found two regiments of infantry, one section of artillery, and 30 of the Fifth Kentucky Cavalry, under the command of Colonel Stanley. I reported to him; he informed me that the Kentucky cavalry were skirmishing with some of the enemy's cavalry off at the left of the pike, and wished me to go there with my command, and also take command of the Fifth Kentucky company, and to use my own judgment what course to pursue. I went down there, and found our men in an open piece of timber, firing away, and the enemy in a narrow lane, behind a stone wall. I at first dismounted my men (being armed with Colt's rifles, I could not use them on the horses), and went at them dismounted, but I soon found out that I would have to resort to some other way to get them away from the wall. I accordingly ordered my men to mount, and I started for the road, or lane, which they were in, with Company B in advance, and Third Kentucky in the rear. I started off at a brisk gallop, and as I came up on a line of the wall, I received a volley from them, wounding Sergeant McIntire, of Company B, who was in advance with me. They fired another volley at us, when they broke and ran; some going off to the left of the road, while the main body went down the road, with our boys close to their heels, firing at them at every chance. We soon passed those on the left of us, and I had made up my mind to cut them off at my leisure, and should have done so if it had not been for a lieutenant, who is, I believe, an aide-de-camp for Colonel Stanley, who, seeing those fellows come up, told some of Company B to go in there after them. I did not know anything of it until I had got up to within about four rods of the enemy; had fired every round from my pistol, and was fast gaining on them. I looked back to see if my men were all ready for them, and not a man was with me except Sergeant McIntire, who, although wounded in the leg, kept close to my side. I soon made up my mind I had gone far enough. I went back and found most of the men in the lot, with this lieutenant picking them up there. It was now too late to think of overtaking them, but, thinking some of them might be in the woods, I dismounted Companies A and B, and skirmished through the woods and got 1 prisoner by the operation; in all we got 6 prisoners; killed 2, wounded 1, and came out ourselves with only 1 wounded. The men all behaved nobly, and, although the bullets fell thick and fast, not one faltered, but did his best to keep up. I cannot speak too highly of Sergeant McIntire, who, although wounded, showed coolness and courage not often exhibited by older and more experienced soldiers. Had it not been for the interference of the lieutenant, I am confident that we might have captured a fine lot of them. We went back and reported to Colonel Stanley, who took the prisoners in charge, when we started for camp, arriving here at 5 p. m.

I am your most obedient servant,

F. W. MIX,
Captain Fourth Michigan Cavalry.

Col. R. H. G. MINTY.

DECEMBER 22, 1862–JANUARY 2, 1863.—Morgan's second Kentucky raid.

SUMMARY OF THE PRINCIPAL EVENTS.

Dec. 22, 1862.—Morgan's command sets out from Alexandria, Tenn., and crosses the Cumberland River.

    24, 1862.—Skirmish at Glasgow, Ky.

    25, 1862.—Skirmish on the Burkesville road, near Green's Chapel, Ky.
        Skirmish at Bear Wallow, Ky.

    26, 1862.—Skirmish at Bacon Creek, near Munfordville, Ky.
        Capture of stockade at Nolin, Ky.

    27, 1862.—Capture of Union forces at Elizabethtown, Ky.

    28, 1862.—Skirmish at Muldraugh's Hill, Ky.

    29, 1862.—Skirmish near Johnson's Ferry (or Hamilton's Ford), Rolling Fork, Ky.
        Capture of stockade at Boston, Ky.

    30, 1862.—Affair at Springfield, Ky.
        Skirmish at New Haven, Ky.

    31, 1862.—Affair at Muldraugh's Hill, near New Market, Ky.

Jan. 2, 1863.—Morgan's command recrosses the Cumberland River

REPORTS.

No. 1.— Maj. Gen. Horatio G. Wright, U. S. Army, commanding Department of the Ohio.

No. 2.—Brig. Gen. Jeremiah T. Boyle, U. S. Army, commanding District of Western Kentucky.

No 3.—Col. John M. Harlan, Tenth Kentucky Infantry, commanding brigade, including skirmish near Johnson's Ferry, Ky.

No 4.—Col. William A. Hoskins, Twelfth Kentucky Infantry, commanding brigade, including affair at Springfield, Ky.

No. 5.—Col. Edward H. Hobson, Thirteenth Kentucky Infantry, commanding at Munfordville, including skirmishes at Glasgow, near Green's Chapel, at Bear Wallow, and at Bacon Creek, Ky.

No. 6.—Capt. Frank W. Dickey, Second Michigan Cavalry, of skirmish at Glasgow, Ky.

No. 7.—Col. Isaac P. Gray, Fourth Indiana Cavalry, of skirmish near Green's Chapel, Ky.

No. 8.—Col. William H. Benneson, Seventy-eighth Illinois Infantry, of skirmish at New Haven, Ky.

No. 9.—Brig. Gen. John H. Morgan, C. S. Army, commanding expedition.

No. 1.

Report of Maj. Gen. Horatio G. Wright, U. S. Army, commanding Department of the Ohio.

HEADQUARTERS,
Cincinnati, Ohio, December 31, 1862.

A force of cavalry from Bragg's army having crossed the Cumberland at Hartsville, and proceeding via Glasgow, have made a raid on the Louisville and Nashville Railroad, occasioning considerable damage, and cutting, for a time, the communication with General Rosecrans. The rebels, under Morgan, first made an attack on Munfordville, but are reported to have been three times repulsed. Leaving this place, and penetrating between our forces, they fell upon and captured the smaller posts at Elizabethtown and Muldraugh's Hill, burning the trestle-work near latter. This is the most serious damage to the road. At Rolling Fork the rebels were also repulsed, and at last advices were moving eastward. It is hoped the dispositions made of our forces may result in their capture, though, as our mounted force is inferior, it cannot be looked upon as certain. The Cumberland is now navigable, and supplies are being sent that way to General Rosecrans, so that the result of the raid will not be very important. As soon as the reports called for are received, a full report will be made. Last reports from Nashville were that Rosecrans was in sight of Murfreesborough Monday night, after severe skirmishing, and a battle expected Tuesday.

H. G. WRIGHT,
Major-General.

Maj. Gen. H. W. HALLECK.

No. 2.

*Reports of Brig. Gen. Jeremiah T. Boyle, U. S. Army, commanding District of Western Kentucky.**

LOUISVILLE, KY., *December* 30, 1862.

Colonel Harlan fell on Morgan's rear and killed and wounded a number of rebels. Among them Col. Basil W. Duke was wounded. Captured 1 captain and 6 privates. There was brisk fighting for one hour and a half, when the rebels retreated. We lost 2 killed and 3 wounded—Lieutenant Pollis, of the artillery, since died. Rolling Fork Bridge not injured. Morgan retreated toward Bardstown. My pickets 22 miles in the direction of Bardstown, at Salt River. Saw no signs of the enemy, but heard from many persons that Morgan was in Bardstown last night, and left this morning at 8 o'clock, going eastward, toward Springfield.

---

* See also Correspondence, etc., December 24, 1862–January 3, 1863, Part II.

Three or four hundred of Morgan's men attacked the stockade at New Haven, but were twice repulsed, with some loss, not known. New Haven Bridge safe. At last accounts my men report one or two companies of Morgan's men going to Bloomfield.

J. T. BOYLE,
Brigadier-General.

Major-General WRIGHT.

—

LOUISVILLE, KY.,
January 1, 1863—11 p. m.

Rebel General Morgan crossed Cumberland River, cut off Nashville at Gainesborough, and appeared in front of Munfordville on 25th December. Colonel Hobson, Thirteenth Kentucky, drove part of his force, killing 9 and capturing 16. Morgan crossed Green River above Munfordville, and moved in direction of Elizabethtown, burning bridge at Bacon Creek and Nolin. He destroyed trestle-work at Muldraugh's Hill, and moved for Rolling Fork. Colonel Harlan, of Tenth Kentucky, commanding brigade, overtook at Rolling Fork and attacked him, killing and wounding a number and capturing a captain and some privates. Colonel Duke (rebel) died of wounds, and one of our lieutenants of artillery. Colonel Harlan crossed, pursued, and attacked him at Rolling Fork, Salt River Bridge. This is first instance, I believe, of infantry waiting and attacking cavalry. Morgan fled before Harlan to Bardstown, and from there attempted to escape between Lebanon and Campbellsville. Colonel Hoskins, Twelfth Kentucky, commanding there, attacked him this morning, killing a number and capturing 90 men, his caissons, and ammunition wagons. Morgan is flying precipitately. General Reynolds marched from Glasgow yesterday for Greensburg, and may intercept him. Colonel Halisy, Sixth Kentucky Cavalry, killed. Our casualties not yet reported. Morgan has paid dearly for what he has done.

I have sent boats up Green River to Bowling Green, whence railroad is in order to Nashville, with provisions for Rosecrans' army. Also sent boats up Cumberland. With control of gunboats on Cumberland, can easily supply General Rosecrans' army. General Rosecrans occupies Murfreesborough.

J. T. BOYLE,
Brigadier-General.

His Excellency ABRAHAM LINCOLN,
    President of the United States.

—

No. 3.

Reports of Col. John M. Harlan, Tenth Kentucky Infantry, commanding brigade, including skirmish near Johnson's Ferry, Ky.

BOWLING GREEN, KY.,
December 26, 1862—8.15 p. m.

COLONEL: Delayed to-day by condition of road; loads too heavy for engines. One engine became entirely useless at South Tunnel, and one train delayed there until engine came from Nashville. All the trains will be here by 9 o'clock. You have been advised, as I learn by Colonel Hobson, of the success of the rebels at Bacon Creek stockade, and the destruction by them of 2 miles of road. Not believed here that Morgan has any force south of Green River, and the impression is that the track is all right as far as Cave City and Munfordville, but no certain facts are known upon which to base the opinion. Shall I go on in the cars to-night, under these circumstances, or wait until daylight? General Manson says he has positive information that the track was right last night at Cave City, but knows nothing definite as to track beyond that point.

JOHN M. HARLAN,
Colonel, Commanding Second Brigade.

Col. J. P. GARESCHÉ.

—

MUNFORDVILLE, *December* 29, 1862.

GENERAL : Came up with Morgan to-day—mouth of Beech Fork, on Rolling Fork, 10 miles from Elizabethtown, on Bardstown road. I formed in line, advanced skirmishers, who engaged the enemy's skirmishers with great spirit. Part of Morgan's men had crossed the river before we arrived, and were driven across with some confusion. Many had to swim; many fled up the river to Boston Ford, beyond pursuit. Think Morgan is aiming for Bardstown, and designs to destroy Shepherdsville Bridge, if possible. He destroyed the trestle-work; he did it before I arrived, and I learn that he has destroyed Rolling Fork Bridge, but not certain; will know in a few hours. I had a lieutenant and several men wounded, 2 killed; number of rebel horses were killed by our artillery. If Rolling Fork Bridge is not destroyed, I will go there to-night and save it. I would have saved the road, I think, but for delay occasioned by engines on the road. Skirmishers behaved well.

JOHN M. HARLAN,
Colonel, Commanding.

Major-General ROSECRANS.

—

ROLLING FORK BRIDGE,
December 30, 1862.

GENERAL : On the night of the 26th, I left Gallatin, with orders to come to Cave City and drive Morgan from the railroad. When I reached Bowling Green, I received additional orders to come on to Munfordville, and drove him from that vicinity. As he followed the line of the railroad, I continued the pursuit, and came up with him yesterday morning at 10 o'clock, near Johnson's Ferry, about 5 miles above this point. When my artillery opened, two of his regiments and two pieces of artillery were within a half mile of the bridge here, and about to make an attack. The noise of my guns induced them to move back up the river, and abandon the attempt on this bridge. My close pursuit of him saved this bridge. A part of his force crossed 1½ miles higher up the river, above the mouth of Beech Fork. Two hundred went up the river toward New Haven. After driving them across the river, I rested until 12 o'clock p. m., and then came to this place, reaching it at daybreak. My men were worn out and their rations exhausted, and in the swollen state of the river it would have been difficult for my infantry to cross. I feared, besides, that Morgan would whip around and make an attempt on this point. I am in doubt as to what I should do, and desire you to communicate with me at once. I think the time has come for Morgan either to retreat in the direction of Glasgow or Somerset, or to move on into Central Kentucky.

I am satisfied that, if I abandon this point, the bridge will be destroyed as soon as it is known that there are but two companies here; and hence I do not feel that I ought to go beyond here without orders, under the circumstances by which I am surrounded. I consider myself subject to your orders. All my camp equipage is at Gallatin. Tell me what I must do. If Morgan goes into Central Kentucky, I cannot possibly overtake him by my almost thoroughly exhausted infantry, but it may be that some arrangement could be made to render my brigade serviceable in driving Morgan, and saving particular localities of importance. It is for you to determine what is to be done. I could have saved the road but for defective engines furnished at Nashville and Bowling Green to convey my troops. The engine seemed to get out of order just at the wrong time; that delayed me thirty-six hours. The rear train, conveying the Fourth Kentucky and part of battery, did not arrive at Munfordville until 10 o'clock on Sunday night. The trestle-work was destroyed Monday after dinner. I left Munfordville 3 o'clock Monday morning. The road between Munfordville and Bowling Green is all right; and between Munfordville and Elizabethtown the damage is not very great, consisting mainly in the destruction of the bridges, which can be easily repaired. The telegraph is injured a good deal.

Whether I am to halt here or go on, I need 1,000 pairs of shoes and 2,000 pairs of socks. My men will suffer unless supplied. If it is clear that I have complied with my orders, then I suppose that I should return to Gallatin, unless the higher authorities in Kentucky think that my remaining here is necessary to aid in keeping the army supplied with provisions. Let me hear from you fully, and I will endeavor to communicate with you to-day by telegraph (pocket instrument). May not Morgan also make a dash on the bridge at Frankfort? He could reach that point from Bardstown, but I fear that his main object of attack is the bridge at Shepherdsville. That is the opinion at department headquarters, as I learn. I have now out numerous scouts to ascertain, if possible, whether Morgan is crossing from Boston and Bardstown to Shepherdsville. If I find that he is on his way to Shepherdsville, I will attack him on the way or endeavor to get in his rear.

Yours, truly,

JOHN M. HARLAN,
Colonel, Commanding Second Brigade.

Brig. Gen. J. T. BOYLE.

—

LEBANON JUNCTION, *January* 1, 1863.

GENERAL: A dispatch from Lieutenant-Colonel Holeman, commanding at Lebanon, says Morgan's forces encamped at Muldraugh's Hill, 8 miles from here, on Columbia road, last night. Colonels Hoskins and Reid are pursuing with their commands. When last heard from, Colonel Hoskins was close upon his rear, near Campbellsville, at 12 o'clock to-day. Colonel Halisy, Sixth Kentucky Cavalry, was murdered last night by Morgan's men; his body is here. Was shot, after he had surrendered, by a rebel officer. We have captured about 90 of Morgan's men to-day, considerable quantity of arms, ammunition, &c. I will send messenger to Hobson and Reynolds.

JOHN M. HARLAN,
Colonel, Commanding Second Brigade.

Brig. Gen. J. T. BOYLE.

MUNFORDVILLE, HART COUNTY, KY.,
January 5, 1863.

CAPTAIN: At a late hour during the night of the 25th of December, while encamped at Gallatin, Tenn., I received through the division commander an order from the general commanding the department to proceed with my brigade, by rail, to Bowling Green and Cave City, and drive from the line of the Louisville and Nashville Railroad the rebel cavalry of Morgan, then north of the Cumberland River, and meditating, as was supposed, the destruction of that railroad. At that time Morgan was supposed to be south of Green River, and at some point in the vicinity of Cave City or Glasgow. The cars to convey my troops were to come from Nashville, and on the morning of the 26th instant (and without unnecessary delay after the arrival of the transportation), I left Gallatin with my command, five regiments of infantry, and Southwick's battery of artillery. Simultaneously with this movement the Twelfth Division, under that accomplished and able officer, Brig. Gen. J. J. Reynolds, marched toward Scottsville and Glasgow, with a view to intercept Morgan, in the event that he was driven back in the direction of either of those points. Three trains of cars, each drawn by one engine, was the amount of transportation furnished me by the railroad authorities at Nashville. The cars were barely sufficient to contain the men, horses, and guns of the brigade, and subsequent developments proved either that the engines furnished were very defective or that enough engines were not furnished, for when the rear train, containing the Fourth Kentucky Infantry (Colonel Croxton), three companies of the Seventy-fourth Indiana, the battery horses, and a part of the battery, reached South Tunnel, 6 miles north of Gallatin, the engine attached thereto became entirely useless, and the train was delayed until another engine could be sent from Nashville. While the rear train was halted at South Tunnel, waiting for another engine, the passenger train from Nashville (Conductor Taylor), arrived, but the conductor refused to permit his engine to be used to forward any rear train, notwithstanding Colonel Croxton advised him of the great importance of the expedition upon which the brigade was sent, and the imminent danger which might result to the entire road from any delay.

This I learn from Colonel Croxton. I have no personal knowledge of these facts, since I was in the advance train, some distance ahead of the rear train. Whether the conductor is to be blamed for refusing to permit his engine to be detached for the purpose indicated, I do not pretend to say; that is for others to judge; my duty is simply to state the facts.

It may be proper also to state that the track of the railroad was, when I left Gallatin, in bad condition, from recent rain, though that difficulty might have been obviated had more engines been furnished.

This unfortunate detention delayed the rear train, so that it did not reach Bowling Green until 10 o'clock of the night of the 26th. For that detention I am not in any wise responsible, as those concerned received from me full information as to the number of men, horses, and guns for which transportation would be required.

After my arrival at Bowling Green, I learned that all of Morgan's force was most probably north of Munfordville, beyond the points to which I had been ordered, and it was evident that I must follow him beyond that place, in order to save any part of the railroad from destruction.

It was not certainly known upon my arrival at Bowling Green whether the track was clear to Munfordville; but as soon as it was ascertained to be safe to proceed farther by rail (which I d.d in part through dispatches from Col. E. H. Hobson, commanding at Munfordville, to General Manson, at Bowling Green), I determined to push forward and save as much of the railroad as it was possible to do.

After supplying my command with one day's rations at Bowling Green (which were very kindly supplied by General Manson), I started for Munfordville. When, however, the rear train had gone about 10 miles from Bowling Green, its engine got entirely out of order, and it became necessary to send back to Bowling Green for another one. This second unfortunate detention delayed the rear train, so that it did not reach Munfordville until 10 o'clock at night of the 27th.

My command was disembarked immediately. Here I should state that the battery and other horses of the brigade had been on the cars for nearly forty hours, without a drop of water or a pound of forage. They were fed as well as the supplies would permit; nothing but corn could be obtained at Munfordville to feed them.

My men, wearied and fatigued by loss of sleep and the crowded condition of the cars, as much fatigued as if they had been marching, lay down upon the damp ground, without tents to shelter them, to rest as best they could. Though I had received from the division commander at Cave City a dispatch ordering me to proceed to Munfordville and drive Morgan from that vicinity, I conceived it to be my duty, under my orders, to go even farther, for I believed that Morgan, if unchecked, would destroy every bridge and structure on the entire road, thus interfering very materially with supplies for the main army beyond Nashville. He had then destroyed the Bacon Creek and Nolin Creek bridges, and had probably destroyed the bridge near Elizabethtown, and captured our forces there, as he had already captured those at Bacon Creek and Nolin. My only hope, then, was to save the immense trestle-work at Muldraugh's Hill; and, failing in that, to save the bridges over Rolling Fork, near Lebanon Junction, and over Salt River, at Shepherdsville. These, or any one of these, results I conceived to be of vital importance to the army, and I appealed to the officers and men of my command to bear up under any privations in order to accomplish it.

After resting my men but a few hours, I left Munfordville at 3 o'clock on the morning of the 28th with my brigade, and also with the Thirteenth Kentucky Infantry, Major Hobson, and Twelfth Kentucky Cavalry, Colonel Shanks, in all about 2,900 effective men. These last two regiments constituted a part of Colonel Hobson's command at Munfordville, and were detached at my request to accompany me in the expedition.

On the route from Munfordville to Elizabethtown no enemy was seen; but upon my arrival at Elizabethtown, on the morning of the 29th, I learned that Morgan had destroyed the trestle-work on the very day upon which I left Munfordville, and had, the previous night, encamped 10 miles from Elizabethtown, on the Rolling Fork, where the Elizabethtown and Bardstown road crosses that stream.

I marched immediately in that direction, ordering the cavalry to go far in advance. When I had gone about 5 miles from Elizabethtown, information reached me that the rebels were, in fact, at the place supposed, and would probably soon cross the river. A section of Southwick's battery was ordered to join the cavalry, and, in conjunction with it, to detain the rebels at the crossing until the infantry arrived. When Colonel Shanks arrived within a mile of the crossing, he discovered, in the plain below (our road from Elizabethtown was on a high ridge of Muldraugh's Hill), a body of rebel cavalry, upon whom he ordered the artillery to open, which was promptly executed, resulting in the rapid dispersion of the rebels. The infantry were ordered up double-quick. I went to the front in person, and from a high hill I saw quite distinctly a very large body of cavalry formed in line of battle near the river. Their officers were riding along their line, apparently preparing to give us battle.

Knowing that Morgan had a larger force than I had, I proceeded cautiously, and yet as expeditiously as the nature of the ground and the circumstances admitted. My men were formed in two lines; skirmishers were thrown out from both infantry and cavalry, covering our whole front, and were ordered to advance and engage the enemy, the whole line following in close supporting distance. The firing commenced on the part of the rebels, on our left; it was promptly and vigorously responded to by my skirmishers and the artillery. After a while the rebels were driven away, and they then made some demonstrations to occupy an eminence upon my right. To meet this movement the Tenth Indiana (Colonel Carroll) was ordered to occupy that eminence, from which four companies were ordered to clear the woods on the right of my line. The Fourth Kentucky, Colonel Croxton; Fourteenth Ohio, Colonel Este; Seventy-fourth Indiana, Colonel Chapman, were ordered to form on the left of the Tenth Indiana. A section of the battery was ordered to occupy the eminence, and the Tenth Kentucky, Lieutenant-Colonel Hays, ordered to support it. This left the Thirteenth Kentucky, Major Hobson, on my left, supporting the section of the battery stationed there. The firing now became general all along the right of our line of skirmishers; but the rebels, after an obstinate resistance, broke and fled precipitately in every direction. Some struck out into the woods; some went up the river as far as New Haven; some swam the river with their horses. Farther pursuit that evening was impracticable, and I may say impossible, in the exhausted state of my men, they having left Munfordville Sunday morning and come up with the enemy the succeeding day at 1 o'clock—43 miles distant.

The casualties in my command were as follows, viz: Lieut. Henry W. Pollis, of Southwick's battery (Company C, First Ohio Volunteer Artillery), fell at his post, mortally wounded. He died the succeeding day. He was a promising young officer, and his loss will be severely felt. Private Louis W. Finney, Company I, Tenth Indiana Volunteers, was also mortally wounded, and died the 30th. Private John C. Osborn, Company A, Tenth Indiana, slightly wounded. Thomas J. Burton, Company F, Fourth Kentucky Volunteers, was killed instantly.

The number of killed and wounded among the rebels I have not had an opportunity to ascertain, because, for the most part, they fought under cover of a thick, heavy woods, and we marched away from the scene of conflict shortly after its conclusion, for reasons hereinafter stated. It is certain, however, that among the wounded was General Basil W. Duke, commanding a brigade under Morgan, and who is believed to be the life and soul of all the movements of the latter; and near where he was seen during the engagement 10 dead horses were found within a space of 20 feet square, the work of the section of Southwick's battery on the left. Some of the citizens in the vicinity informed me that the rebel wounded were taken off and some of their dead thrown into the river; whether this is true or not I will not pretend to say.

The rebels encamped that night near Boston, Nelson County. Their camp was equally distant with mine from the Rolling Fork Bridge, which was believed at Elizabethtown to have been destroyed; but not being satisfied that such was the case, I dispatched a messenger to that point, who returned at 11.30 o'clock in the night with the information that that bridge was still safe. My men were immediately aroused, and at midnight I started for the bridge, reaching it before daylight of the 30th, and encamped on the south side of it. Thus was this important structure saved. Its safety is, however, attributable in part to circumstances which may appear singular, but which, nevertheless, actually transpired.

On the morning of the 29th, two of Morgan's regiments and a portion of his artillery marched from their camp, on Rolling Fork, to the bridge (only 4½ miles distant), to destroy it, and at the same time capture our forces there. The garrison at that place constituted only two companies. The rebels reached the vicinity of the bridge, and were about to commence an attack, when the firing by my advance upon the remainder of their forces notified them that an enemy was near at hand. They immediately commenced a rapid movement back to their camp, abandoned the attack upon our forces at the bridge, and joined the remainder of the rebel forces by the time that the infantry came up with my advance. They arrived in time to participate in the scenes already described. Upon my arrival at the Rolling Fork Bridge, I reported to the general commanding the district in which I was operating (General Boyle) for orders. He ordered me to remain in camp at the bridge, rest my men, protect the bridge, and hold myself in readiness to meet an attack on the long bridge over Salt River at Shepherdsville, 20 miles from Louisville.

On the morning of the 31st I crossed over to the north side of the Rolling Fork, in obedience to orders from General Boyle, to resist an attack which the commandant at Shepherdsville believed would be made upon him that day. No attack having been made, I halted, under General Boyle's orders, at Lebanon Junction until January 4, when I received orders to return to Gallatin. I am now *en route* with my brigade for that place, and will leave here as soon as transportation is afforded.

I do not suppose that the engagement which my command had with Morgan's forces could properly be called a battle, the main bodies of the respective forces not being engaged. It was simply brisk skirmishing, exhibiting the utmost willingness, even anxiety, on the part of all the officers and men under my command, though outnumbered by the enemy in every respect, to engage him at all hazards; and, on the part of the rebel chieftain and his men, an entire unwillingness to meet them upon any fair terms. Every circumstance on the occasion indicated to my command that the enemy were disposed to give us battle in force, yet nowhere, along the whole line, was there to be observed any, even the slightest, faltering by either officers or men.

To Colonels Este, Chapman, Carroll, Croxton, and Shanks, Lieutenant-Colonel Hays, Major Hobson, Captain Southwick, of the battery, and to all their brother officers, I return my thanks for the promptness and cheerfulness with which, on the line of march, they executed all my orders. To the members of my staff, Lieutenants Lisle, McKay, and Simpson, and to Capt. Wellington Harlan, volunteer aide, I am indebted for the most valuable services rendered throughout the entire expedition. More efficient and competent officers are not to be found in the service. The men under my command deserve the thanks of the country for the cheerfulness with which, with insufficient food and rest, they bore up under the severest privations, determined to do all within the power of man to perform the important duty assigned them by the general commanding the department.

I claim, for my command, that it saved the Rolling Fork Bridge, and most probably prevented any attempt to destroy the bridge at Shepherdsville, thus saving from destruction property of immense value, and preventing the utter destruction of the line of railway, by which our army, near Nashville, was mainly supplied. And I submit whether the attack upon Morgan's forces, the timely arrival of my command at Rolling Fork, did not prevent a raid upon other important points in Kentucky. It is very certain that after my command drove the rebel chieftain across the Rolling Fork, in such a precipitate manner, he abandoned the railroad, and very soon thereafter fled from the State, hotly pursued by other forces.

I cannot permit this occasion to pass without acknowledging the promptness with which that gallant officer, Col. E. H. Hobson, furnished me all the aid in his power, in the way of men, provisions, and transportation. The rapidity of my marches is due in a great measure to the aid so cheerfully and generously rendered by him. Nor can I close this report without saying that had sufficient engines been furnished to draw the trains, the railroad would have been damaged but very little, because, without accident, I could have reached Munfordville in abundant time to have caught up with the rebels before they reached Elizabethtown; certainly before they reached the trestle-work on Muldraugh's Hill.

As the operations of my brigade were entirely within the Western District of Kentucky, Brigadier-General Boyle commanding, I have deemed it my duty, in compliance with his request, to forward to him a copy of this report, so that he may be officially advised of all that was done by me within his department, in connection with the recent raid into Kentucky.

I have the honor to be, very respectfully, your obedient servant,

JOHN M. HARLAN,
Colonel, Commanding Second Brigade.

Capt. Ed. C. Denig,
Assistant Adjutant-General, First Division.

[Indorsement.]

HEADQUARTERS FIRST DIVISION,
Gallatin, Tenn., January 11, 1863.

Respectfully forwarded. Colonel Harlan, for the energy, promptness, and success in pursuing and driving rebel forces from railroad, is entitled to the gratitude not only of the people of Kentucky, but of the whole Army of the Cumberland. He is, in my opinion, entitled to special notice from the commanding general, and anything he can say or do for him will be thankfully received.

SPEED S. FRY,
Brigadier-General, Commanding Division.

No. 4.

Report of Col. William A. Hoskins, Twelfth Kentucky Infantry, commanding brigade, including affair at Springfield, Ky.

HEADQUARTERS POST,
Lebanon, Ky., January 6, 1863.

GENERAL: I have the honor to submit the following report of operations before Lebanon, commencing on December 26, 1862, at which time

I was notified by Brigadier-General Boyle, by telegram, that the rebel Morgan was in our State, and ending on January 2, 1863, at which time the pursuit of him was abandoned, by order of Brig. Gen. Speed S. Fry, 3 miles beyond Columbia:

At the time I received notice of Morgan's invasion of the State, and movements in the direction of Bardstown or Lebanon, I had under my command the Seventh Tennessee, consisting of 258 men, Twelfth Kentucky Infantry, consisting of 425 men, and Sixteenth Kentucky Infantry, 650. I was informed by the post quartermaster that he had at this post near 3,000 head of loose stock, mules and horses, about 300 wagons, and stock for same, some 200,000 rations, a quantity of ammunition, and 1,600 stand of small-arms. I did not know how soon Morgan would be upon us, and, having no fortifications, as an only means of defense, I ordered all the wagons to be placed in corral. I also ordered guns to be distributed to all the convalescents capable of using them, as also to the teamsters, whom I placed under competent commanders. I ordered an increase of our picket guards, and a thorough inspection of arms, ammunition, &c. Knowing that a force of some ten or eleven regiments was at Danville, I then telegraphed to Brigadier-General Baird for re-enforcements of infantry and a battery of artillery. In reply, he notified me on December 26 that he had ordered to my support a battery of Napoleon guns and two regiments of infantry. From my observation, I know of no place so vulnerable as Lebanon, lying, as it were, in a basin surrounded by commanding positions, as also with approaches from almost every direction, and I was, therefore, satisfied that a fight with equal numbers could not be successfully made within or very near the town, and I accordingly determined, should he move upon the place, to meet him from 1 to 2 miles from the depot.

On the 28th, I was notified by dispatch from General Boyle that re-enforcements from Danville, which I knew were within 4 or 5 miles of me, were recalled. During the day cannonading was distinctly audible in the direction of Elizabethtown or the tunnel. I again urged upon General Baird the necessity of sending forward re-enforcements, and was by him notified that two strong regiments of infantry had been ordered, under command of Colonel Henderson, to join me, and would be at Lebanon on the 3d. I then dispatched General Boyle, in anticipation of such re-enforcements, suggesting the propriety of halting the Thirty-fourth Brigade, which had been ordered to Lebanon, at Muldraugh's Hill. Receiving no answer to this dispatch (in consequence, I presume, of an interruption in telegraphic communication between this place and Louisville), the brigade joined me on the morning of the 29th. On that morning I sent out a scouting party of 25 men, under command of Lieutenant Porter, of the Ninth Kentucky Cavalry, with orders to proceed in the direction of New Haven and Bardstown until he could learn something definite of Morgan's force and movements. I had also sent out a single and reliable citizen-scout with similar instructions.

On the morning of the 30th, the citizen returned to camp with intelligence that he had that morning breakfasted with 15 of Morgan's men at Fredericksburg, distant from us 19 miles.

About 3 o'clock of the same day Lieutenant Porter also returned, confirming the report of the first scout, and stating that the cannonading heard by us was at Rolling Fork, and that at the point from which he had returned he could distinctly hear musketry.

Morgan's force was variously estimated at from 7,000 to 11,000. I had been notified by General Boyle that Colonel Harlan, with a brigade of infantry, a battery of artillery, and two regiments of cavalry, was pressing upon his rear from the direction of Elizabethtown.

So soon as the above information was received by scouts, I ordered strong detachments from the Sixth and Ninth Kentucky Cavalry, under command of Colonel Halisy and Lieutenant-Colonel Boyle, to make a reconnaissance, with a view of ascertaining whether Morgan would pass out by Raywick and to our right, or whether he was yet upon the Springfield and direct road to us. About nightfall this party returned, and reported that the enemy had been found encamped on the Springfield road, distant from us 7 miles. Shortly afterward I received information that Morgan had divided his force and sent 2,000 'n the direction of Haysville. To ascertain the truth of this statement, I ordered out detachments from the Sixth and Ninth Kentucky Cavalry, under command of Majors Fidler and Farris, to reconnoiter in the direction of Barber's Mill, with instructions that, if the enemy had not passed that point, to take the Springfield road and reconnoiter in their rear. In the execution of this order, Major Fidler performed a feat of daring which is worthy of the highest praise, and which, as well as his subsequent conduct, has proven him one of the most fearless and energetic officers in the service.

On arriving at Barber's Mill, and learning that the enemy had not passed up in that direction, he pursued the Springfield road until he came upon one of the enemy's pickets in the streets of that town, whom he captured without attracting notice. He and his men then advanced to within a few yards of a battery planted in the streets, fired a volley into the midst of the enemy, killing 2 of their number, and retreated to camp with their prisoner.

I have omitted to state in the proper order that, after the return of Colonels Halisy and Boyle, and following immediately on their heels, the rebels came up and captured one of our vedette pickets only a short distance from his post.

After receiving information that Morgan had divided his forces, knowing that Colonel Henderson, with his command, consisting of two strong regiments, was within 2 miles of the intersection of the road leading from Springfield to Haysville, I sent, by courier, an order to halt his command near Bethel Church, ambuscade, and await the arrival of the enemy, when he should engage him.

After learning, through Majors Fidler and Farris, that the enemy had sent no force upon that road, I dispatched to Colonel Henderson to join me with all possible speed, having the evening previous sent up 50 wagons to aid in transporting his command. Judge of my surprise when the courier returned and reported that Colonel Henderson had fallen back in the direction of Danville, taking with him my wagons. All my plans were now disconcerted. With the force at my command I did not think that I would be justifiable in attacking Morgan in his chosen position, and more particularly when I had no definite idea of his real strength, which was variously estimated at from 3,000 to 11,000, and I was induced to act even more cautiously than I would otherwise have done, from the fact that I could hear nothing of Colonel Harlan's command. As I knew that he had engaged Morgan at Rolling Fork, and as he did not follow up the pursuit and press him down upon either General Baird or myself, the inference drawn by me was that Morgan had sufficient force to repulse Colonel Harlan, or he would have followed up any advantage that might have been gained by him.

Believing that Morgan's command was suffering for rest, at 3 o'clock in the morning, December 31, I ordered out another reconnoitering party, under command of Major Gratz, of the Sixth Kentucky Cavalry, with instructions to press upon the enemy, cut off and capture his pickets, if possible, fire into his camp and retire, after ascertaining whether he had changed position. This order was executed, and Major Gratz returned with the report that the enemy had advanced 2 miles in our direction.

I have omitted to state that my chosen position for action was on the Springfield road, and I had, on the evening of December 30, selected a position for one section of the battery, which was placed and masked, supported by Company A, Sixteenth Kentucky. The position chosen was in the angle formed by the Springfield road and Cartwright's Creek. This position commanded the Springfield road for 1½ miles, and was strengthened by a precipitous bluff on the right flank. At this point I felt we must meet the enemy; for, if they were permitted to pass it, and gain possession of a copse of timber and the commanding position on the hill, they could shell us in the town, while their riflemen could advance under cover of the timber until they would be in range of any line of battle formed north of town, and which would of necessity leave us fully exposed, as the ground was entirely open. These arrangements having been made, after the report of Major Gratz I ordered Colonel Halisy to make another reconnaissance upon the Springfield road to ascertain whether the enemy was really advancing with a view of attacking us.

Colonel Halisy left camp about 7 a. m. on December 31, and at 11 a. m. sent back a courier with the information that he had proceeded as far as their camp of the night previous, which they had abandoned. Colonel Halisy was then directed in the event they should have moved, with a view of passing either to the right or left of us, to pursue, hang upon their rear, and, if possible, harass them to a stand. Finding they had left, he pressed on to Springfield, and in the direction of Muldraugh's Hill.

About noon citizens came rushing into town with the most extravagant reports regarding Morgan's force, and assuring us that he was advancing on the place, with his right column moving from the direction of Saint Mary's Church, on the Lebanon Branch Railroad. To ascertain the truth of this statement, I ordered another reconnaissance to be made in that direction by Lieutenant-Colonel Boyle, of the Ninth Kentucky Cavalry, who set out to execute the order in command of a detachment of 300 men from his regiment.

In anticipation of pursuing Morgan, in case he should give us the go-by, I had also ordered the commanders of different regiments to draw five days' rations and be in readiness to move without camp or garrison equipage at a moment's warning, and I also ordered all the teams at the post to be in readiness to move at a moment's notice. In the mean time I had heard nothing from Colonel Halisy since 11 a. m., and already felt considerable anxiety in regard to his safety.

At 5 p. m. I received information that Colonel Halisy was still in pursuit of the enemy, who was moving in the direction of Muldraugh's Hill, and from their rear guard he had succeeded in capturing 15 prisoners, whom he sent into camp. About the same time Colonel Boyle returned, bringing into camp some prisoners, with the assurance that Morgan's main body had passed Saint Mary's Church. I knew we had a force at Glasgow, and had been informed that we had a force at or near Greensburg, under command of Colonel Wolford, to whom I had on the 30th started a courier, notifying him that I would pursue Morgan, should he pass west of us, and suggesting the propriety of his moving his command to Pinchinn or Muldraugh's Hill. Unfortunately, however, this courier was captured and paroled before he reached Colonel Wolford

On December 31, at 6 p. m., my command, consisting of a squadron of the Sixth Kentucky Cavalry, under Major Gratz; a squadron of the Ninth Kentucky Cavalry, under command of Major Rue; the Twelfth Kentucky Infantry, the Sixteenth Kentucky Infantry (which two regiments, together with the Seventh Tennessee, had been temporarily brigaded and placed under command of Colonel Craddock, of the Sixteenth Kentucky); the battery of artillery, and the Thirty-fourth Brigade, commanded by Colonel Reid, moved in pursuit. The order of march was as follows: First, the squadron of cavalry, under Major Gratz; second, one section of the battery; third, the Ninth Kentucky Cavalry; fourth, section of the battery, supported by Company A, of the Sixteenth Kentucky; fifth, Sixteenth Kentucky Infantry; sixth, section of the battery, supported by Company I, of the Sixteenth Kentucky; seventh, Twelfth Kentucky Infantry, mounted in wagons; eighth, the brigade of Colonel Reid, unbroken. In the above order we moved on the Campbellsville road until we reached a point near New Market. Here we were informed by a citizen of the death of the gallant, accomplished, and lamented Colonel Halisy, whom I could but admire for his great zeal in the cause of our Union, and the energy and promptness with which he executed every order confided to him. By his death the service has lost one of its most accomplished and chivalrous officers, and the community one of its most useful and honorable citizens. We were also informed by the same person that the rebels were then encamped 2 miles to our right, on the Rolling Fork. A halt of the column was ordered. Major Rue, of the Ninth Kentucky Cavalry, was ordered forward to guard the bridge over Rolling Fork. A strong cavalry picket was sent back upon the road leading from Saint Mary's to Lebanon, and which intersects the Campbellsville road 1½ miles in our rear. This I thought necessary to prevent their passing to our rear upon Lebanon, and thence through Bradfordsville and Somerset, in the event they should discover our movement toward Muldraugh's Hill. I also ordered a reconnaissance of their position, which duty was assigned to Major Rue, his men being familiar with the locality in which they were said to be encamped. I ordered the remaining force to form in line of battle, with the artillery in position, and each section supported by a select company of riflemen from the Twelfth and Sixteenth Kentucky. In this position they were required to bivouac on their arms and without fires.

Near daylight on the morning of the 1st instant, the reconnoitering party returned, with the report that the rebels had left camp. I immediately ordered the column to be in readiness to move, and the march was resumed in the order of the previous night, except the transportation, which was turned over to the Thirty-fourth Brigade, the Twelfth and Sixteenth Kentucky marching.

On arriving at the summit of Muldraugh's Hill, I learned that the enemy's rear guard had passed about 12 o'clock the night previous. From citizens I learned that they had passed up the old Dug road, which intersects the Campbellsville road on the summit of Muldraugh's Hill. We now forwarded with all possible celerity, in the hope that we might come upon them at Campbellsville, or at all events be in supporting distance, should Colonel Wolford's or any other force attack them in front or on the flank. Our cavalry was much worn down by scouting both at Lebanon and on the border. They were also in bad condition to attack a superior force, inasmuch as they were poorly armed, the Sixth Kentucky having no arms but pistols and sabers. Notwithstanding they were thus poorly armed, they manifested a disposition to press forward, which they were allowed to do with as much speed as I deemed consistent with prudence, I endeavoring to keep the infantry within quick supporting distance.

On arriving within 2 miles of Campbellsville, I was informed by citizens and paroled soldiers that the rebel rear guard was still at that place, engaged in destroying commissary goods abandoned by the Thirty-fourth Brigade. The column being well closed up, I ordered the cavalry to charge upon the town, which they did in handsome style, resulting, however, in the capture of but a few prisoners, the main force having left some five hours previous. Knowing that a considerable quantity of forage had been collected at Green River Bridge, and believing that the enemy would halt there to feed and rest his stock, I ordered Majors Gratz and Rue, with one section of artillery, to press forward, hoping to prevent by rapid pursuit the destruction of forage and bridge; also directing the shelling of their rear at every available point, with the further view of attracting the attention of any force that might be to our right, and thus defining to them the route pursued by us.

At 2 o'clock our advance came in sight of the ruins of Green River Bridge, when, believing that further pursuit was cut off, the section of the battery was placed in position and opened fire, not so much with a view of damaging the enemy, but as signal guns to any force which might be in reach of Columbia, trusting to thus give them a cue to the route pursued by the rebels. I ordered the troops to go immediately into camp, feed stock, and make details for cooking, while the men could get that rest they so much needed, after the forty-eight hours heavy duty they had undergone.

I also ordered the company of Pioneers attached to the Thirty-fourth Brigade to be immediately set to work in clearing the obstructions from a dirt road that crossed the river but a few hundred yards below the bridge. In the mean time the whole column closed up, the Twelfth and Sixteenth Kentucky having marched 22 miles in seven consecutive hours. I had not yet abandoned the hope of overtaking the enemy at Cumberland River.

I also learned that Colonel Wolford was certainly at Greensburg, in command of four regiments of cavalry. I immediately dispatched to him, notifying him of our pursuit, and suggesting that he should press on to Columbia, and, in the event that he should find Morgan in camp at the latter place, to quietly await our arrival, which would be some time during the night.

By 10 p. m. of the 1st instant, the obstructions in the road were removed. I then directed that the whole cavalry force under my command should move forward, accompanied by one section of the battery, with instructions to Colonel Boyle that, if he should find Morgan in camp at Columbia, not to disturb him, unless he should attempt to move off, until he was supported by my infantry or Colonel Wolford's cavalry. Following immediately in the rear of the cavalry was the remainder of the force under my command. As soon as I saw the principal part of the Thirty-fourth Brigade across the river, I pressed forward to the front, and, to my surprise, found the whole column halted, at 6 a. m., 6 miles from the bridge, which they had left at 11 o'clock the previous night. The apology for such a direct violation of orders by the cavalry was, that a citizen had told them that Morgan had left Columbia at 8 o'clock the previous night, and that their horses were worn down. The infantry and artillery were moved forward, and reached Columbia about noon on the 2d instant, when, learning that the Cumberland was certainly fordable, I abandoned the pursuit and ordered my men into camp.

Soon after going into camp, General Fry arrived and assumed command of all the troops in the vicinity of Columbia, and ordered the pursuit to be resumed, which order was countermanded at a point 3 miles beyond Columbia. The result of these operations was the capture of about 150 prisoners, a number of horses and trappings, some arms, two caissons, and a quantity of ammunition for artillery and small-arms. It is also reported by a citizen that one of our shells exploded among the rebel rear guard at Green River, and killed 3 of their number.

I regret that there could not be more concerted action between Colonel Harlan and myself, for, had he pressed upon and followed Morgan to Springfield, I could have attacked him in front while he engaged his rear, or we could have attacked him unitedly. I also regret that the re-enforcements from Danville never reached me. My determination was to attack Morgan at Springfield, had they come up.

To Colonel Reid and the officers and men of his brigade I take pleasure in expressing my thanks for the promptness and alacrity with which they executed orders confided to them. It may be proper to state that the aggregate force of this brigade did not exceed 1,800 men, and my whole effective force did not exceed 3,300 men.

To Captain Miller, of Company M, First Illinois Battery, thanks are due for his efficient services as an artillery officer.

My thanks are due to Colonel Craddock for his energy and valuable suggestions, as well as to all the officers on the expedition. But, above all, the gallant soldiers composing the command deserve especial notice for the cheerfulness with which they endured the privations to which they were necessarily subjected and the alacrity with which they obeyed all orders.

To my aides, Captain Letcher, of the Twelfth; Captain Hilpp, of the Tenth; Lieutenant Mannen, of the Sixteenth Kentucky, and Lieutenant Nell, of the First Kentucky Battery, my thanks are due for the efficient manner in which they discharged their duties.

Captain Gaubert, post quartermaster, displayed great energy and efficiency in getting up, on short notice, transportation and rations for the expedition. And while it may seem invidious to make distinctions where all deserve commendation, yet especial thanks are due to Lieutenant-Colonel Gault and Major Harbeson, of the Sixteenth Kentucky; Majors Farris, Rue, and Fidler, of the cavalry, and Dr. S. M. Cartmell, medical director of the expedition; nor should I forget Capts. John S. and Carr B. White, of the Sixteenth Kentucky, and Lieutenant Crozier, of the Twelfth, who, with their companies, supported sections of battery, and were always in place and ready for duty.

I ought, perhaps, to state that I labored under great disadvantage, from the fact that I could get no definite information of Morgan's force. I had been officially notified that Morgan, at the time of his attack on Elizabethtown, had less than 3,000 men, and certainly but two pieces of artillery. I had also been officially notified that simultaneously with his attack on that place an attack was made on Munfordville, supposed to be led by Kirby Smith, whose force was unknown. When I learned that the force advancing on Lebanon certainly had ten pieces of artillery, I inferred that a junction of the two forces had been effected, the whole force being reported by citizens and scouts at 11,000.

Very respectfully, your obedient servant,

W. A. HOSKINS,
Colonel, Commanding Expedition.

Brig. Gen. C. C. GILBERT,
Comdg. Tenth Division, Army of the Cumberland.

No. 5.

Report of Col. Edward H. Hobson, Thirteenth Kentucky Infantry, commanding at Munfordville, including skirmishes at Glasgow, near Green's Chapel, at Bear Wallow, and at Bacon Creek, Ky.

HEADQUARTERS,
Munfordville, Ky., January 4, 1863.

CAPTAIN: I have the honor to submit a report of the disposition of the troops under my command at this point during the recent raid of Morgan on the line of the Louisville and Nashville Railroad.

On December 17, 1862, I received information of a rebel force being in the State. I immediately put my scouts on the alert, and waited for the enemy to make some move by which I could detect his design.

On the 24th I received a dispatch from General Reynolds, at Gallatin, stating that a large rebel force had crossed the Cumberland at Gainesville, and were making for Glasgow. I received dispatches at the same time from Generals Boyle and Gilbert, confirming what I had formerly heard.

On the evening of December 24, Companies C, L, M, and H, Second Michigan Cavalry, under orders from Gallatin to Munfordville, captured a man belonging to Morgan's command, who reported a large force in Glasgow. Company C, Lieutenant Darrow, met the advance of the enemy in the town, and a skirmish ensued, in which our loss was 1 killed, 1 wounded, and 16 prisoners. The loss of the enemy was 1 major, 1 captain, 1 lieutenant, and several privates killed and wounded, and 7 prisoners.

It being nearly dark, and the enemy clothed in our uniform, it was with difficulty that friends could be distinguished from foes. After repulsing the advance guard of Morgan, the Second Michigan fell back to Cave City, their retreat being covered by the Twelfth Kentucky Cavalry, Col. Q. C. Shanks, and both returned to camp, the Twelfth Kentucky Cavalry to get new arms, which had just arrived, and the Second Michigan Cavalry to rest from a march of 60 miles in less than twenty-four hours, men and horses being completely exhausted.

The siege guns, which were anxiously expected, having arrived on the morning of December 25, at 1 o'clock, I immediately put a force to work to manufacture the proper technical fixtures, which I was pained to learn had been entirely neglected in shipping the guns, and place them in position on the north side of the river. At the same time I had the floor of the bridge planked over to render it safe in crossing, should re-enforcements be required on either side. I also telegraphed General Boyle all the information of importance, and asked him for additional ammunition for infantry, and sponges, rammers, sights, elevating screws, &c., for the siege guns.

On the 24th I had taken all pains to learn the real strength of the enemy, which I found variously estimated at from 3,000 to 4,500, commanded by Major-General Morgan, the regiments by Duke, Gano, Cluke, Chenault, Bennett, Stoner, and Breckinridge, with White's battery of eight guns, the largest a 12-pounder. White's name is supposed to be Robinson, formerly of Kentucky.

At 5 a. m., December 25, I again ordered the Twelfth Kentucky Cavalry, Colonel Shanks, to Cave City and beyond to Bear Wallow, with the First and Second Battalions, the Third, under Major Stout, being ordered on the Greensburg road to Burnt Bridge Ford, north of Green River, and two companies each, Fourth and Fifth Indiana Cavalry, Col.

Isaac P. Gray, on the Burkesville road, south of Green River, with instructions to each to give battle, and, if overpowered by largely superior forces, to skirmish the way back to Woodsonville, sending couriers often to my headquarters.

When near Green's Chapel, 6 miles from Munfordville, Colonel Gray attacked the advance guard of Morgan, and about the same time Colonel Shanks attacked the rear guard at Bear Wallow, 12 miles from this point. The advance guard fell back on the main body, with a loss of 9 killed, 22 wounded, and 5 prisoners, our loss being 1 killed, 2 prisoners, and several horses killed. The Twelfth Kentucky Cavalry, in the rear, killed 1, wounded 2, and took 2 officers and 10 men prisoners, with no loss.

The force and position of the enemy being ascertained by these movements, the cavalry was ordered back to camp, leaving vedettes to watch the movements of the enemy. I telegraphed General Granger, General Boyle, and General Gilbert everything of importance, and telegraphed General Boyle the condition of the guns and the want of ammunition. I sent dispatches frequently, but could get no answer from the operator in Louisville to the call of the operator at this point during the afternoon of the 25th, until too late to effect anything by trains from Louisville. I also telegraphed that it was Morgan's design to attack the tunnel and the works beyond.

At 9 p. m. the 25th, scouts brought the information that 100 of the enemy were crossing the river at Burnt Bridge Ford. This was confirmed during the night by reports that the whole force was crossing and moving in the direction of Hammondsville. I immediately ordered Captain Dickey, of the Second Michigan, to proceed to Bacon Creek stockade, reporting to my headquarters by courier at 9 and 10 a. m., and oftener, if necessary, and also ordered the Twelfth Kentucky Cavalry, Colonel Shanks, toward Hammondsville, to report often by courier. Soon after arriving at Bacon Creek and arranging his pickets, Captain Dickey was attacked by the advance of Morgan, and flanked by a large force. Captain Dickey having less than 80 men for duty, on account of the exertions of the 23d and 24th, was compelled to fall back on Munfordville, fighting his way. Learning this by courier, I shifted Colonel Shanks, with the exception of two companies, from the Greensburg road to cover the retreat of the Second Michigan, by attacking the enemy, and, gradually falling back on Munfordville, to draw him in and give play for the skirmishers—the Twenty-fifth Michigan Infantry, Colonel Moore, on the right; Lieutenant-Colonel Carey, Thirty-sixth Indiana, in the center, with the convalescent battalion, and Major Hobson, commanding Thirteenth Kentucky, on the left.

The officers and men of these commands acted with great promptness and ease while performing the various evolutions, but the wary foe would not engage them. A few shots were fired by the Twelfth Kentucky Cavalry, when the enemy fell back to Bacon Creek.

During this skirmish our loss was 21 men and 2 officers taken prisoners. Loss of the enemy not known.

During the night of the 26th, believing that Morgan would make an attack on this place from the other side of the river, I made arrangements for ferrying from the south side the only two field pieces under Lieutenant Hale, Sixth Michigan Battery; also to bring over ammunition by way of the bridge on a hand-car.

I kept the Twelfth Kentucky Cavalry in line of battle between Bacon Creek and Munfordville until after dark on the 26th; and, believing that if an attack was made in the morning the depot would be burned,

I doubled my line of pickets and removed the stores within the fortifications.

The gallant hero of inferior numbers did not attack me on the morning of the 27th, and I was forced to be content with re-enforcing Colonel Harlan with the Thirteenth Kentucky Infantry and nine companies of the Twelfth Kentucky Cavalry, at the urgent request of Colonel Shanks, whose services he will, of course, mention in his report in a proper manner.

The troops were all in readiness for the reception of Morgan. The brass guns (6-pounders), under command of Captain Demarest, Twenty-fifth Michigan Infantry, manned by infantry, were placed in positions commanding Bacon Creek and Greensburg roads, and the siege guns being in the fortifications near the bridge, under special charge of Captain Stacey, inspector-general of the Tenth Division, whose perseverance in overcoming the difficulties of mounting the guns without the proper equipments, deserves the highest praise. The officers and men of my command during these movements bore themselves with the most soldierly behavior.

I cannot speak too highly of the cavalry commands of Colonels Gray and Shanks, Captains Dickey and Twyman, for the valuable services they rendered constantly.

Flegle's sharpshooters were promptly at their post, ready at any time to do their duty as becomes their commands, as also the One hundred and seventh Illinois, Lieutenant-Colonel McComas. The Twenty-seventh Kentucky, Lieut. Col. J. H. Ward, also rendered efficient service south of the river, not forgetting to bring to your notice Lieutenant Hale's sixth section Sixth Michigan Battery, and Captain Hall, commanding battalion of the Thirty-third Kentucky.

I was materially assisted in my duties of the disposition and movements of my command by J. S. Butler, acting assistant adjutant-general, and Captain Stacey, of General Gilbert's staff; also by the energy and efficiency of volunteer aides, Lieutenant Smith, Thirteenth Kentucky, and Lieutenant Dawson, Thirty-third Kentucky; also Post Quartermaster and Lieutenant Cummings.

Very respectfully, your obedient servant,

E. H. HOBSON,
Colonel, Commanding Post.

GEORGE K. SPEED,
Acting Assistant Adjutant-General, Tenth Division.

No. 6.

Report of Capt. Frank W. Dickey, Second Michigan Cavalry, of skirmish at Glasgow, Ky.

CAVE CITY, KY.,
December 24, 1862—8.04 p. m.

GENERAL: The Second Battalion of Michigan Cavalry were attacked at Glasgow at dark this evening. Two of our men killed. Two or three rebels killed. We were on the march from Gallatin to Munfordville. Rebels supposed to be strong—have two batteries.

F. W. DICKEY,
Captain.

General ROSECRANS.

No. 7.

Report of Col. Isaac P. Gray, Fourth Indiana Cavalry, of skirmish near Green's Chapel, Ky.

MUMFORDVILLE, *December* 31, 1862.

COLONEL: In accordance with your order, I took the forces under my command, consisting of two companies of the Fourth Indiana Cavalry and two companies of the Fifth Indiana Cavalry, and proceeded to scout the road. I had just reached the pike with the column when my advance, which was about 1 mile ahead, was fired upon by the advance of the enemy. I immediately ordered the fences to be thrown down on each side of the road, and directed Captain Purdy's company, of Fourth Indiana Cavalry, to proceed through the field on the right of the pike, and form his company in line of battle. He had just got his company formed when the enemy came on at full speed, on a charge, 300 strong, and, when within shooting distance, commenced firing. I sent Lieutenant Smith, in command of Company C, of Fifth Indiana Cavalry, through the field on the left of the pike, and ordered him to proceed down a hollow in the field out of view of the enemy, who did not discover him until he commenced firing at not to exceed 50 yards range, which threw him into confusion and caused him to retreat in disorder, with a loss of 9 killed, and, as near as I can ascertain, 22 wounded and 5 prisoners. My loss was 1 killed and 2 taken prisoners, by being intoxicated and straggling behind the command. I had also several horses shot. I had scarcely got my command reorganized before the main force of the enemy, 4,500 strong, came on at full speed, flanking at both sides for the purpose of surrounding my command, but were not fast enough to effect this object.

Yours, most respectfully,

ISAAC P. GRAY,
Colonel, Fourth Indiana Cavalry.

Colonel HOBSON.

No. 8.

Report of Col. William H. Benneson, Seventy-eighth Illinois Infantry, of skirmish at New Haven, Ky.

HDQRS. SEVENTY-EIGHTH REGIMENT ILLINOIS VOLS.,
New Haven, Ky., January 10, 1863.

SIR: In obedience to the order of General Gilbert, requiring a report of the late affair between the troops of my command at this place and a body of the enemy, I have the honor to report as follows:

The enemy appeared in the vicinity of the stockade at this place on the evening of the 29th ultimo, and displayed a force much superior to my own, but the extent of his numbers I could not ascertain. The weakness of my command, consisting of one company (H, Seventy-eighth Illinois Volunteers) only, numbering 80 guns, and the strict orders I was under to keep within 300 yards of the stockade, and act on the defensive alone, prevented me making any reconnaissance to ascertain his strength. In anticipation of an attack from him the next morning, the stockade and its environs were cleared for action, and every precaution taken to secure the safety of my men as far as possible under the circumstances.

About 9 o'clock the next morning (December 30), after a formal demand for the surrender of the post, and refusal, the enemy, with one piece of artillery (a 12-pounder howitzer), but with a force smaller than he displayed the evening before, emerged from the timber on the north west of our position, advanced along the south side of the railroad to within 1,000 yards of the stockade, and there took his first position.

In the mean time the forces of my command were disposed as follows: Lieutenant Beers, with one-fourth of the command, occupied the rifle-pits on the northwest side ot the stockade; sentinels were placed without the stockade at divers points, commanding views of all surroundings not visible from the stockade itself. The balance of my force, under Captain Allen, were distributed within the stockade, so as to detect the advance of the enemy from any and all quarters he might see proper to attack us.

The enemy bombarded us for some time from his position first taken, as above stated; then changed his position to a point some 200 yards south of his first, threw a number of shells, and changed position again to a point still farther south of his last one, and at the distance of 700 yards from the stockade. He also, at the same time, dismounted a portion of his forces and deployed in the corn-field, situated between the meadow in which he first planted his artillery and the stockade, and sent another portion of his forces to the north side of the railroad, and down the wagon-road leading to the ford at the railroad bridge, with the evident design of occupying if possible the north bank of the railroad, near the ford.

To prevent the accomplishment of this object by the enemy, Lieutenant Simmons was sent, with a few men, to the threatened point, but on reaching it found the enemy in hasty retreat, from the fire of the single sentinel who had been placed there prior to the commencement of the action.

In the mean time the enemy, having thrown a number of shells from his third position, was proceeding to take a fourth, still nearer to us. His forces, deployed in the corn-field, had advanced to within 600 yards of the stockade, and opened upon us with small-arms.

At this juncture we commenced a rapid fire upon the enemy with all our disposable force. The damaging effects of our fire were immediately apparent. The cannoneers abandoned their cannon, and only returned to remove it out of our range. The forces in the corn-field receded from their advanced position. In a few minutes the rout became general, and the enemy, moving at a rapid pace and in a disorderly mass, disappeared from view in the timber from which he had emerged prior to the attack.

The enemy received some punishment, but to what extent we do not certainly know, as he carried his killed and wounded from the field with him. From information obtained since the affair, we have reason to believe he lost 3 killed and 10 or 12 wounded. My command received no damage whatever. The stockade remains uninjured. The affair lasted one hour and a half.

I cannot speak in too high terms of the conduct of my officers and men during the attack. Though not one of them had ever been under fire before, they behaved like veterans.

In concluding this report, I should do injustice to my own feelings should I omit to acknowledge the very great obligations I am under to Captain Allen, Lieutenants Beers and Simmons, and my adjutant, Lieutenant Green, for their efficient support prior to and during the affair.

Very respectfully,

WILLIAM H. BENNESON,
Colonel, Commanding.

GEORGE K. SPEED,
Acting Assistant Adjutant-General, Louisville, Ky.

No. 9.

*Reports of Brig. Gen. John H. Morgan, C. S. Army, commanding expedition.**

HEADQUARTERS ARMY OF KENTUCKY,
Campbellsville, Ky., December 31, 1862.

COLONEL : I have the honor to report that thus far the success of this expedition is complete, and that every object that was contemplated has been attained. My first meeting with the enemy occurred at Glasgow, Ky., on December 24. My advance guard, on entering the town shortly after dark, fell in with four companies of the Second Michigan Cavalry. A slight skirmish ensued, in which I lost 3 wounded (2 mortally), and the enemy had 4 or 5 killed and wounded and some 20 taken prisoners. The enemy passed through town in the direction of Munfordville.

The next morning I moved forward early with my command. About 10 miles this side of Green River, a slight skirmish took place, in which none were hurt on either side, and we captured several prisoners.

The next morning I sent part of my command to take the stockade at Bacon Creek, while I moved on with the main body to Upton and Nolin. By 4 p. m. all the places had surrendered and the stockades and trestles were on fire. That night I encamped at Nolin, having taken and paroled some 200 prisoners, with only 2 or 3 slightly wounded on my side.

The next morning I moved to Elizabethtown. On arriving near the place, much to my surprise, I was met by a flag of truce, informing me that I was surrounded, and demanding an unconditional surrender of myself and command. To this proposition I declined to accede, and made a counter demand for an unconditional surrender. On its being refused, I immediately began to shell the houses in which the enemy had taken refuge. After a brisk firing of three-quarters of an hour from the batteries and skirmishers, the place was surrendered. Eight companies were taken and paroled. Three bridges were burned, and the entire track for miles set on fire.

December 28 I moved toward the long trestles, about 5 and 6 miles from Elizabethtown. I sent Colonel Breckinridge and command toward one trestle, while I moved with the remainder toward the other. I sent in flags of truce, demanding a surrender, which was declined. I then opened fire, and after some shelling and skirmishing for about an hour the stockades surrendered. The stockades, trestles, and a quantity of army stores were destroyed. About 700 prisoners were taken and paroled. No one on either side killed or wounded. I moved on that night to the Rolling Fork and encamped.

Next morning, just as the rear of my command was crossing the fork, the enemy began shelling me in the rear. I immediately threw out some six or seven companies as skirmishers, drove back their line, finished crossing the river, and moved on to Bardstown that same night. Here I turned my course and began to march southward.

On the morning of the 30th I left Bardstown, and reached Springfield the same evening. Hearing at Springfield that there was a large force of the enemy at Lebanon, I determined not to attack them, but to elude them by leaving Lebanon on my left and by making a night march, which I accomplished successfully, and reached this point, leaving the

---

* For General Bragg's letter transmitting this, with Forrest's report, see Series I, Vol. XVII, Part I, p. 591.

enemy in my rear this evening, and am now holding telegraphic communication with him.

I have also to report that the Federal colonel, [Dennis J.] Halisy, of the Sixth Kentucky Cavalry, commanding brigade, while engaged in picking up some stragglers of mine, was killed in a hand-to-hand conflict by Lieutenant [George B.] Eastin, of my command, and a lieutenant accompanying him was captured. The Federal forces are now moving down upon me. They left Lebanon this afternoon. I leave early tomorrow morning.

I am, colonel, very respectfully, your obedient servant,

JOHN H. MORGAN,
Brigadier-General.

Lieut. Col. GEORGE WILLIAM BRENT,
A. A. G., Army of Tennessee, and Chief of Staff.

HEADQUARTERS MORGAN'S DIVISION,
Smithville, Tenn., January 8, 1863.

SIR: I have the honor to submit the following report of the action of the forces under my command during the late expedition into Kentucky:

On the morning of December 22, 1862, I left Alexandria, Tenn., with an effective force of 3,100 guns and seven pieces of artillery, which I divided into two brigades, placing the first under command of Col. B. W. Duke [Second Kentucky Cavalry], and the second under command of Col. W. C. P. Breckinridge [Ninth Kentucky Cavalry]. About dusk I crossed the Cumberland River, which I found easily fordable, and encamped some 3 or 4 miles on the other side. I found the people generally well disposed, and that vague rumors of my coming had preceded me.

On the morning of the 23d I made an early start, and succeeded (though the way for the most part was extremely rough) in making Centreville that evening, a distance of some 30 miles.

The following day (December 24) I marched to within 6 miles of Glasgow, where my first encounter with the enemy took place. I had encamped the main body of my command some 6 miles from the town, and had sent two companies to take possession of it. As they entered the town, they encountered the advance guard of a battalion of the Second Michigan Cavalry. It being quite dark, some little time elapsed before either party became aware of the presence of an enemy, when a skirmish took place, in which Captain [W. E.] Jones [Company A, Ninth Kentucky Cavalry], and a private of Breckinridge's regiment were mortally, and Lieut. Samuel O. Peyton, of Duke's regiment, seriously, wounded, and some 6 or 7 of my men taken prisoners. Not knowing in what force the enemy might be, my squadron fell back, when the enemy passed through town and took the road to Munfordville. Several of the enemy were killed and wounded, and 22 prisoners, including a captain, were captured and paroled.

The next morning (December 25) I passed through Glasgow and took the Bear Wallow turnpike in the direction of Munfordville. About 10 miles from Green River my scouts reported that a battalion of cavalry was drawn up in line, awaiting our approach. I threw forward two companies and a section of artillery to engage them, made my dispositions for an extended engagement, and advanced as rapidly as possible.

The enemy, however, did not wait to receive the charge of the force I had sent forward, but, after firing a few random shots, took to flight and left the road clear. I then made the best of my way through to Green River, which I succeeded in crossing with considerable difficulty, owing to the steep and muddy banks, and reached Hammondsville with my command at midnight. 1 had ordered Colonel Breckinridge, as he passed the cross-road leading to Woodsonville, to send two companies in that direction, with instructions to drive in the enemy's pickets, and immediately on my arrival at Hammondsville I dispatched two companies of Colonel Duke's command, with similar instructions, in the direction of Munfordville. My object was to induce the enemy to believe that I intended to attack the fortifications at Green River, and, by so threatening him, to divert his attention from the combined attack which I intended to make the succeeding day on the stockades at Bacon Creek and Nolin.

The next morning (December 26) I sent Duke's and [R. M.] Gano's [Seventh Kentucky Cavalry] regiments and a section of Palmer's battery, under command of Lieutenant-Colonel [John B.] Hutcheson [Second Kentucky Cavalry], to attack the stockade at Bacon Creek, while I moved on with the main body of the forces to Upton. A heavy rain had fallen during the night, and it was still raining hard, so that it was with the utmost difficulty that the artillery and trains made any progress whatever. It was, therefore, nearly 11 o'clock before I heard Colonel Hutcheson's cannon open. On arriving at Upton, I cut the telegraph wire, and my operator was soon in communication with Louisville, Cincinnati, and other points. No important messages were received, however, except one informing me of the arrival of a train loaded with ammunition, small-arms, and two pieces of rifled cannon, which I immediately took measures to intercept, but unfortunately missed.

It being now nearly 3 p. m., I sent forward to Nolin, under charge of Colonel Duke, the remainder of the forces, with the exception of Johnson's regiment and the other section of Palmer's battery. With these troops—as I was fearful, from the duration of the firing at Bacon Creek, that the stockade had been re-enforced from Munfordville—I moved down to Bacon Creek to assist Colonel Hutcheson. On my arrival there, I immediately sent in a flag of truce, and demanded an unconditional surrender of the place, which, after considerable hesitation on the part of the commanding officer, Captain James, was finally acceded to. Ninety-three prisoners, belonging to the Ninety-first Illinois Volunteers, were captured, including four commissioned officers. The stockade and trestle were immediately fired and destroyed, and I moved on with the command to Nolin. In this affair 3 of the enemy were slightly wounded by our shells, and some 3 or 4 men on our side were slightly wounded in attempting to fire the trestle before the stockade had surrendered. The force at the trestle near Nolin, amounting to 3 officers and 73 privates of the Ninety-first Illinois Volunteers, surrendered to Colonel Duke without opposition. The stockade and bridge at that point were also fired and destroyed. While waiting at Upton, I had caused large fires to be built all along the track for some 3 or 4 miles, in order to warp and destroy the rails, which was most effectually accomplished.

Early the following morning (December 27), having learned the previous evening that some seven or eight companies of United States troops were stationed at Elizabethtown, I moved with my command in that direction. On arriving within sight of the town, the following peremptory document, scrawled in pencil on the back of an envelope, was handed to me :

ELIZABETHTOWN, KY., *December* 27, 1862.

To the COMMANDER OF THE CONFEDERATE FORCES:

SIR: I demand an unconditional surrender of all your forces.   I have you sur-rounded, and will compel you to surrender.
        I am, sir, your obedient servant,

H. S. SMITH,
Commanding U. S. Forces.

To which I replied that I thought the positions were reversed ; that it was his forces, and not mine, which were surrounded, and called upon him to surrender.   He answered that it was the part of a United States officer to fight, and not to surrender.

Leaving one regiment and a howitzer in reserve to guard the trains, I ordered Colonel Duke to deploy his command to the right, and Colonel Breckinridge to deploy his command to the left of the town, and to throw forward skirmishers to discover the position of the enemy.   It soon became apparent that he had taken possession of several brick houses on the outskirts of the town, and expected to make a street fight of it.   I therefore immediately placed my artillery in position on a hill a little to the left of the road, which completely commanded the town, and sent Capt. C. C. Corbett, with one mountain howitzer, to attack the town on the right.   After about half an hour's vigorous shelling, the place surrendered, and 652 prisoners, including 25 officers, fell into our hands.

At this point I wish particularly to notice the excellent service done on this occasion by Capt. Baylor Palmer and his battery, to whose rapid and accurate fire (nearly every shot striking the houses occupied by the enemy) the quick reduction of the place is in a great measure due; and also the gallantry shown by Captain Corbett, who ran one of his howitzers into the town while the enemy were pouring a heavy fire from the houses, and by Lieutenant-Colonel [R. G.] Stoner, commanding Breckinridge's regiment, who at the same time charged into the town at the head of his men.

On the morning of the 28th I moved from Elizabethtown in the direc-tion of Bardstown.   Four miles from Elizabethtown I ordered Colonel Breckinridge to turn with his command to the left and to attack the lower stockade, near Muldraugh's Hill, while I moved on with Colonel Duke's brigade to attack the upper.   After two or three hours' shelling, both places surrendered, and at 7 o'clock that evening I had the satisfac-tion of knowing that the object of the expedition was attained, and the railroad was rendered impassable for at least two months.   These two trestles are the largest and finest on the whole road, being, each of them, some 60 feet in height and from 300 to 350 yards in length.   Neither of them had ever before been destroyed during the war.   Seven hundred prisoners, including 27 officers, were captured, and a large and valuable amount of medical, quartermaster's and commissary stores were de-stoyed.   I encamped that night near the Rolling Fork.

The following morning (December 29) I sent Colonel [R. S.] Cluke's regiment, with one piece of artillery, to attack and burn the bridge over the Rolling Fork; Colonel [D. W.] Chenault's regiment [Eleventh Ken-tucky Cavalry], and one piece of artillery in advance, to burn the stock-ade and trestle at Boston, and three companies of Breckinridge's regi-ment and one mountain howitzer, to attack at New Haven.   Having completed these dispositions, I set my command in motion.   Just as the rear regiments were crossing Rolling Fork, a large force of the enemy—

consisting of cavalry, infantry, and several pieces of artillery, which had followed us from Elizabethtown—came up and began to shell the ford at which the troops were crossing. I immediately sent orders to Colonel Duke, who was in the rear, to send a courier to Colonel Cluke, ordering him to rejoin the command as rapidly as possible, and to hold the enemy in check until the entire command had crossed the ford. Colonel Duke, assisted by Colonel Breckinridge, placed seven companies from different regiments in position and held five in reserve. With this force he several times repulsed the enemy's advance, and very nearly succeeded in capturing two pieces of the enemy's artillery, when he fell from his horse, severely wounded by a shell. Colonel Breckinridge then took command, and maintained the position until Colonel Cluke's regiment had crossed the river, when I ordered him to fall back, which he accomplished in good order and without loss.

In this affair only 3 men were hurt on our side—Colonel Duke, Captain [V. M.] Pendleton [Company D, Eighth Kentucky Cavalry], (who was struck by a ball while gallantly leading a charge on the enemy's artillery), and a private slightly wounded. The enemy lost several officers and men killed and wounded.

Meanwhile Colonel Chenault had captured and burned the stockade at Boston. He rejoined me that night at Bardstown. The force sent to burn the stockade at New Haven was not successful, and did not rejoin the command until the following night at Springfield.

On the morning of the 30th I left Bardstown and marched to Springfield, a distance of some 18 miles, where I arrived at nightfall. On my arrival I learned that the enemy had withdrawn all his forces from the southern portion of the State, and had concentrated them at Lebanon. Troops from Danville, Burkesville, Campbellsville, and Columbia had been collected there to the number of nearly 8,000, with several pieces of artillery. Intelligence also reached me that a column nearly 10,000 strong was moving from Glasgow to Burkesville to intercept me. My position was now sufficiently hazardous. A superior force only a few miles in my rear, a force nearly treble my own immediately in my front, and a vastly superior force, which had only about half the distance to march that I had, moving to intercept my passage of the river. In this emergency, I determined to make a detour to the right of Lebanon, and, by a night march, to conceal my movements from the enemy, outstrip the column moving from Glasgow to Burkesville, and cross the Cumberland before it came within striking distance. Immediately, therefore, on my arrival at Springfield, I sent out two companies on the Lebanon road, with instructions to drive in the enemy's pickets, and to hold the position. This being done, they were to build large and extended camp-fires, so as to induce the enemy to believe that my whole force was in position, and that I was only waiting for daylight to attack. Considerable delay was occasioned from the difficulty in obtaining guides who were sufficiently well acquainted with the country to lead me over the route I desired to march, but at length, by 11 p. m., the whole column was fairly in motion. The night was dark and stormy and the road rough and intricate, so that the morning of December 31 found the command only 8 miles from Springfield and 2½ miles from Lebanon. By 1 o'clock that afternoon, however, the top of Muldraugh's Hill was reached, where I could see Lebanon with a glass distinctly, and the enemy's skirmishers deployed in the valley below. Just as the rear guard of the column had reached the foot of the hills, a remarkable hand-to-hand conflict took place between Colonel [D. J.] Halisy, of the Sixth Kentucky Cavalry, commanding brigade, and two other Federal officers on the one side, and Capt. Alexander Tribble and Lieutenant Eastin, of my command, on the other, in which Colonel Halisy was killed by Lieutenant Eastin, and his companions captured.

Both Captain Tribble and Lieutenant Eastin displayed great gallantry on this occasion, and deserve the thanks of the civilized community for putting to rest such an exponent of the Butler and Turchin school as Colonel Halisy.

I reached Campbellsville late that evening, and found there quite an amount of commissary stores, which was most fortunate, as my command had had but little for two days.

On the morning of January 1, 1863, I started for Columbia, where I arrived at 3 p. m.   By a night march from this place, I reached Burkesville at daylight the following morning.   Here I halted the command for a few hours to rest and feed, and then crossed the Cumberland without molestation.   Traveling, then, by easy stages, I reached this point on the evening of January 5, with my command.

The results of the expedition may be summed up as follows : The destruction of the Louisville and Nashville Railroad from Munfordville to Shepherdsville, within 18 miles of Louisville, rendering it impassable for at least two months; the capture of 1,877 prisoners, including 62 commissioned officers ; the destruction of over $2,000,000 of United States property, and a large loss to the enemy in killed and wounded.

The loss of my entire command was as follows : Killed, 2 ; wounded, 24 ; missing, 64.

In closing this report, I desire to return my sincere acknowledgments to my brigade commanders (Colonels Duke and Breckinridge) and to their subordinate officers for their able and efficient assistance rendered me by them during this expedition, without which it must have failed in effecting many of its principal objects.

I am, sir, very respectfully, your obedient servant,

JOHN H. MORGAN,
Brigadier-General.

Col. GEORGE WILLIAM BRENT,
A. A. G. and Chief of Staff, Army of Tennessee.

DECEMBER 23, 1862.—Skirmish near Nashville, Tenn.

REPORTS.

No. 1.—Maj. Gen. Alexander McD. McCook, U. S. Army.
No. 2.—Brig. Gen. John A. Wharton, C. S. Army.

No. 1.

Report of Maj. Gen. Alexander McD. McCook, U. S. Army.

HEADQUARTERS RIGHT WING,
December 23, 1862.

One of General Sheridan's outposts (a sergeant and 9 men) was captured this evening.   The vedettes were driven in, and gave no alarm. The enemy's cavalry were dressed in our uniform.   Detailed report will be sent in the morning.

A. McD. McCOOK,
Major-General, Commanding.

Col. J. P. GARESCHÉ.

No. 2.

Report of Brig. Gen. John A. Wharton, C. S. Army.

HEADQUARTERS CAVALRY BRIGADE,
Nolensville, Tenn., December 24, 1862.

GENERAL: A detachment of Texas Rangers and Second Georgians, under Lieuts. M. L. Gordon and John F. Trippe, captured the advance picket (14 in number) of the enemy on this pike yesterday evening. Several were left dead and wounded on the ground. We sustained no loss. The prisoners have been sent to Murfreesborough. The enemy promise us a visit to-morrow. Thomas' *corps d'armée* arrived Friday evening, and is encamped on the Charlotte and Granny White pikes. We have annoyed their foraging parties so much that they now send out a very heavy supporting force. Seward, Blair, and Chase have resigned, and things are in a terrible state at Washington. The removal of Halleck has become a military necessity. Banks' forces are to be landed at Ship Island, for the reduction of Mobile. He will command Butler, without Lincoln sends other orders. Please return all papers that have been sent up from these headquarters.

Most respectfully, general, your obedient servant,

JNO. A. WHARTON,
Brigadier-General.

Brig. Gen. JOSEPH WHEELER,
Chief of Cavalry.

DECEMBER 24, 1862–JANUARY 1, 1863.—Expedition into East Tennessee and skirmish at Perkins' Mill, on Elk Fork, December 28.

REPORTS.

No. 1.—Maj. John M. Brown, Tenth Kentucky Cavalry.
No. 2.—Maj. James L. Foley, Tenth Kentucky Cavalry.

No. 1.

Report of Maj. John M. Brown, Tenth Kentucky Cavalry.

CAMP FIRST BATTALION, TENTH KENTUCKY CAVALRY,
Danville, Ky., January 3, 1863.

SIR: I have the honor to report that, having been detached with my battalion to London, Ky., under command of Lieut. Col. H. B. Wilson, Forty-fourth Ohio Volunteer Infantry, and having reached that place on the afternoon of December 25, 1862, I was intrusted by Lieutenant-Colonel Wilson with the independent command of my cavalry, acting under written orders, of which a copy is herewith inclosed.

I judged it prudent to proceed as rapidly as due regard to the condition and efficiency of my horses would permit, and, therefore, leaving London, Ky., at 11.30 p. m. on December 25, rode 9 miles to the Burnt Church, on the Barboursville road, where I rested until sunrise. I easily reached Barboursville by 3 p. m. of the 26th.

That afternoon and night I spent in concerting plans with Capt. Dempsey King and Mr. John Lanman, both men of tried loyalty and extensive information and influence, the former being the recognized head of the Union Home Guards, of Knox and Whitley Counties. Captain King readily agreed to support any inroad I might make into Tennessee with 150 mountaineers, and mounted his horse to assemble them, but just as he was starting he received a dispatch from Brigadier-General Carter (of the purport of which I am ignorant), which must have changed his plans, as I saw him no more. Mr. Lanman, then on his way to Lexington, furnished me with valuable information as to persons and roads.

On the morning of the 27th I left Barboursville, and, taking an unfrequented road on the south bank of the Cumberland River, reached the Pine Mountain, and, crossing its main ridge by a difficult and circuitous route (the former main road being obstructed by numerous trees felled by the mountaineers to impede General Kirby Smith's retreat), reached Lanman's at 4 p. m.

I had been apprised by several reliable men that a rebel camp of cavalry, numbering 250 or 300, lay near Fortner's Mill, a short distance beyond Boston, and 9 miles from Lanman's. I, therefore, advanced cautiously, and having proceeded 2 miles or more toward Rogers' Gap, retraced enough of my route after dark to secure a safe retreat in case the enemy should have received intelligence of my proximity. To guard against this, I posted mountaineers on every path of the road, leaving to them the choice of proper men and positions, and giving only general directions to keep the enemy ignorant of my presence. I must gratefully acknowledge the promptitude and efficiency of their assistance; so completely was every by-path stopped, that, had I chosen to have laid concealed at Jesse Powers' (where I encamped), 1 mile southwest of Lanman's, I could have done so for a week.

I dispatched Dr. Sproule, a native of Whitley County, a refugee from the rebel troops, to approach Boston, and bring back accurate information of the position and force of the enemy on Elk Fork, and availed myself of the volunteered services of Jesse Powers and Huston Collins, whom I furnished with horses to bring intelligence from Rogers' Gap. Dr. Sproule sent me word that the enemy were careless and unsuspicious in the smaller camp; that a large force of, perhaps, 1,200 cavalry, with two pieces of artillery, were this side of the Big Creek Gap, and that Major Foley, with the Second Battalion, Tenth Kentucky Cavalry, was at Williamsburg. Powers and Collins were unable to return, but sent me word that they had sent into Tennessee, as far as Maynardsville, Mrs. Rogers, wife of Lieut. Canada Rogers, now a prisoner in Knoxville, who reported a force of rebel cavalry at Miller's Woodlands, in Powell's Valley, 2 miles from the crest of Rogers' Gap, numbering nearly 300; also 500 cavalry at Rice's Mill, on Lost Creek, near Maynardville, and rumors of half-organized parties at Jacksborough and other points to the westward. I had no time to communicate with Major Foley at Williamsburg, and it seemed to me that an incursion into Tennessee, sufficiently dangerous under the most favorable circumstances, would be foolhardy, with the prospect of an aroused enemy in the rear. I felt forced, therefore, to abandon, though reluctantly, the project of burning the railroad bridge at Strawberry Plains. It seemed to me that the next best thing was to assist Major Foley in the attack, which I felt certain he would make on Sunday morning, 28th.

Accordingly, I moved toward Boston at early daylight, as soon as the crossing of the Pine Mountain was practicable, and came into Boston entirely unexpected at 7 o'clock. I then learned that Major Foley had already attacked, with brilliant success. The enemy were already in pursuit, perhaps 600 strong, in the direction of Williamsburg. With my small force I could not think of another attack on the enemy, now thoroughly on the alert, so I busied myself to cover Major Foley's retreat and draw off the pursuit. I assumed the title and functions of a brigadier, and, after ordering the infantry and artillery of a fictitious brigade to advance, and giving the enemy time to hear of the formidable force on their flank, I retreated to Barboursville, and the next day to London, where I met Major Foley, and we lay expecting the enemy, who, however, seemed to have been deceived, and afraid to pursue.

On the 30th, at midnight, I reached Richmond, and, delaying there a day to shoe my horses, joined the brigade on the night of January 1.

I cannot speak too highly of the devoted and unflinching patriotism of the citizens of Whitley and Knox Counties. Hundreds of them lead the life of wild beasts, lodging in caves and skulking through the mountains, seldom visiting their houses, and all having the certainty of the gallows if they fall into rebel hands. Their only defense against a pillaging and murdering foe is their rifles and an unconquerable love for their homes and their Government. I was implored by numbers of them to represent to headquarters that bushwhacking was with them an inexorable necessity in their present unassisted condition, which could and would cease with the presence of efficient aid.

I have to report the roads to Barboursville good for the season, and practicable for army teams; also a good road, with the exception of two or three points—in my opinion, easily remedied—from Boston to the mouth of Big Poplar Creek—better, I am inclined to think, than the road laid down on the maps, or that leading by the Pine Mountain and Lanman's. There is also a direct road, reported very good, from Boston to London, crossing the Cumberland at Evans' Mill, effecting a saving of 12 to 15 miles, as compared with the route through Barboursville.

My retreat was by Evans' Mill, crossing the Cumberland at that point, recrossing at McNeil's Mill, and entering the main State road 5 miles south of Barboursville. I have observed inaccuracies in the published maps, too tedious, and perhaps unimportant, to mention here. If considered desirable, I can point them out.

My horses suffered much from fatigue and the weather; several died, and others had to be left in the hands of Union men, to be collected by authorized agents of the Government.

I am, sir, very respectfully, your obedient servant,

JOHN MASON BROWN,
Major Tenth Kentucky Cavalry, Commanding First Battalion.

Col. SAMUEL A. GILBERT,
Comdg. Second Brig., Second Division, Army of Kentucky.

[Inclosure.]

HEADQUARTERS UNITED STATES FORCES,
London, Ky., December 25, 1862.

JOHN MASON BROWN,
Major Tenth Kentucky Cavalry:

SIR: The detachment of cavalry from Danville not having arrived, in pursuance of orders, I will return to Richmond, and you will assume command of the forces now here, excepting the detachment of Forty-fourth Ohio Volunteer Infantry. They will turn over their horses to you, and you will mount them with armed volunteer mountaineers that you may induce to accompany you. You will also procure of Lieutenant Jacobs, commanding said detachment, fifteen canteens, and fill them with turpentine. You will, if you find it practicable, proceed to or be-yond Boston, via Barboursville, and ascertain the force and position of the enemy at Big Creek Gap, or in the vicinity of Boston, Ky., or in Scott County, Tennessee. If, however, you find it practicable to do so with the forces you have, you may proceed to Strawberry Plains, about 15 miles from Knoxville, and destroy the big railroad bridge at that place. It is with the hope that you may find it practicable to accomplish this with safety that I have directed the turpentine to be procured. Should you reach the railroad, you will, of course, destroy the telegraph wires as soon as you get there. In my judgment, if you reach the railroad, it will be safe for you to return via Cumberland Gap, but in reference to the route you take, both going and returning, you will be governed by the best information you can obtain, and your operations throughout must necessarily be directed accordingly by your own good judgment and discretion. You will report from time to time to Col. S. A. Gilbert, at Richmond, and on your return will report direct to him.

Very respectfully, &c.,

H. B. WILSON,
Lieutenant-Colonel, Commanding.

No. 2.

Report of Maj. James L. Foley, Tenth Kentucky Cavalry.

HDQRS. SECOND BATT., TENTH KENTUCKY CAVALRY,
Danville, Ky., January 3, 1863.

I have the honor to report that, in accordance with instructions received from headquarters, I proceeded to London, Ky., on the morning of December 25, 1862, with the greater portion of my command, including the force reported to me under command of Captain Buchanan, of Munday's cavalry. Arriving at London, I learned that Major Brown had been ordered to Barboursville by Lieutenant-Colonel Wilson, who likewise ordered that the next morning I should proceed to Williamsburg, in Whitley County, Kentucky. This point was reached at 9 p. m. the following day, where I had made arrangements by my advance guard to select a camp, procure a sufficient quantity of forage, and also to picket all roads leading out of the town until my arrival.

My detachment rested here until the next evening, the 27th instant, during which time I spent in learning the location, numbers, and disposition of the rebel forces. My command was again in motion at 8 p. m., having been informed by scouts that a rebel force, 350 strong, had encamped at a point on Elk Fork, called Perkins' Mill, in Campbell County, Tennessee, 19 miles from Williamsburg. Proceeding cautiously in that direction, I came upon their pickets at 4 a. m. of the 28th instant, which were captured, 16 in number, by my advance guard, under command of Lieutenant Kerr, of Munday's cavalry, without the slightest noise or confusion; in fact, they were fast asleep. From them I learned the location of their camp, numbers, strength, &c., which was very accurate, as I afterward discovered.

Forming my line, I now awaited the approach of daylight, but so intense and heavy was the fog as to prevent anything being seen at the distance of 20 paces. I determined, however, to attack them, and detailed 40 men of Munday's cavalry, under Lieutenant Kerr, armed with carbines and the captured rifles. I deployed this force as skirmishers, with instructions to approach the camps as near as possible before opening fire. The cavalry companies (B and M, Tenth Kentucky), supported these. The order "forward" was now given, and after proceeding a quarter of a mile the skirmishers opened fire. This was returned by the enemy with considerable spirit, but they soon gave way at the approach of the cavalry, after three unsuccessful attempts to form their line. The rout now became general; the enemy, pushed one very side, refused to stand their ground; our forces, elated with the first success, manfully bore down upon them, and in less than one hour we had full possession of their camp.

They lost 30 killed, 17 wounded, and 51 captured. In addition to this, 80 head of horses and mules fell into our hands, together with a large number of Enfield rifles and ammunition. What could not be brought away was destroyed. The number of rifles which fell into our hands amounted to nearly 200 stand. The camp equipage was all destroyed and burned. This, sir, was accomplished in one hour's time, and without the loss of a man killed or wounded.

The fight occurred in such close proximity to a second camp of the enemy's cavalry, estimated by the prisoners at 600 strong, as to cause the assailed party to seek protection in their lines, hotly pursued by our men.

I take occasion, with much pleasure, to compliment Captains Buchanan and Coffman, and Lieutenants Kerr and Taylor, of Munday's cavalry; Captains Rogers, Nute, and Gray, and Lieutenants Thompson, Caldwell, Trumbo, Bierbower, and Taber, of the Tenth Kentucky Cavalry, for their gallantry and cool bearing displayed on this occasion. Great praise is due the men for their bravery, and they deserve alike to share the glory.

I am, sir, with much respect, your obedient servant,

JAMES L. FOLEY,
Major Tenth Kentucky Cavalry, Commanding Battalion.

Capt. B. H. POLK,
Acting Assistant Adjutant-General.

DECEMBER 25, 1862.—Skirmish on the Wilson Creek pike, between Brentwood and Petersburg, Tenn.

REPORTS.

No. 1.—Col. P. Sidney Post, Fifty-ninth Illinois Infantry, commanding brigade.
No. 2.—Brig. Gen. John A. Wharton, C. S. Army, commanding cavalry brigade.

No. 1.

Report of Col. P. Sidney Post, Fifty-ninth Illinois Infantry, commanding brigade.

HEADQUARTERS FIRST BRIGADE, FIRST DIVISION,
December 25, 1862.

LIEUTENANT: I have the honor to report that, in obedience to orders from Brigadier-General Davis, commanding First Division, I started at daylight this morning, with the First Brigade, First Division, and the Fifteenth Regiment Wisconsin Infantry, from the Second Brigade, and the train, reported to me as consisting of more than 200 wagons. We proceeded to Brentwood, and from thence on the Wilson pike, near where we drove in the enemy's pickets. Two miles farther we came to a cross-road leading to Nolensville, on which the enemy were encamped about a mile distant, and at another point about 2 miles distant. The small cavalry force occupying the nearest camp abandoned it, and I stationed the Fifty-ninth Regiment Illinois Infantry and one section of the Fifth Wisconsin Battery in a position to command this road, and prevent the enemy from Nolensville, which was 5 miles distant, establishing themselves in our rear. I then proceeded 2 miles farther with the train, placing the Fifteenth Regiment Wisconsin Infantry and one section of the battery on the right, and commanding a road coming from Franklin, and the Twenty-second Regiment Indiana Infantry, the Seventy-fourth Regiment Illinois Infantry, and one section of the battery in front. Our advance was attended with considerable skirmishing. Two of the enemy were killed, and some wounded were seen being carried off. A few shells from Captain Pinney's battery cooled the Confederate ardor until all the wagons were completely loaded. The wagons of the enemy were hurried out of the field without being loaded, though, I regret to say, their presence was not discerned in time to effect their capture. The captain of one of the skirmishing parties caused some neighborhood negroes to bury the enemy's dead, and we returned to camp without any mishap whatever.

I beg leave to observe in this report that foraging in such a country as this in our front, and so great a distance from camp, while the enemy are so near and from every hill-top estimate the number of the escort and the value of the train, is attended with considerable risk. Our train could not be made to move in a less space than 4 miles, and if it were not possible to throw a superior force in rear of foraging expeditions it would not be difficult to suddenly attack so long a train and destroy some portion of it, especially while threatening it in the rear, as they did much of the way in to-day, unless the escort were very large.

I have the honor to be, very respectfully, your obedient servant,

P. SIDNEY POST,
Colonel, Commanding Brigade.

Lieut. T. W. MORRISON,
    Actg. Asst. Adjt. Gen., First Division, Right Wing.

No. 2.

Report of Brig. Gen. John A. Wharton, C. S. Army, commanding cavalry brigade.

HEADQUARTERS WHARTON'S CAVALRY BRIGADE,
    Nolensville, Tenn., December 25, 1862—9.30 p. m.

GENERAL: We have been fighting the enemy from sunrise until dark. The forage now lies to the left of this pike, in between this and Wilkerson pike. To-day the enemy came out in large force and a heavy supporting force. With what cavalry could be used without disturbing the pickets, we engaged the enemy. The country is very hilly and covered with cedar brakes, which renders it totally unfit for cavalry, and the infantry here has orders to risk nothing. I had 3 men wounded; killed 6 and wounded 14 of the enemy. They thus paid for their forage.

I cannot get the five companies to complete Smith's and Murray's regiments, though they have long been promised me. The service that I am required to perform here is too much for my force, and it will soon be unfit for service. Other cavalry commanders are drilling daily, and I assure you that every day for the past ten days I have engaged the enemy. My force in camp has to be moved forward every day to sustain the pickets, and never return until dark, so, whether on picket or off, they have no rest.

I ordered Colonel Smith to leave a portion of his command at Franklin, and to move last night on a scout on the Hillsborough pike. The result of the expedition is not yet known.

I take great pride in this brigade, and do not intend that it shall be used up without advising you of it. I intend to write to General Wheeler, and ask him to come over and see for himself the amount of labor I have to perform. The enemy were followed beyond our lines, and our pickets are at their usual stands. The enemy will be out early in the morning, and to-morrow will be, as usual, a day for us to fight and not to rest. I have nothing new as to the several movements of the enemy.

Most respectfully, general, your obedient servant,
> JNO. A. WHARTON,
> *Brigadier-General.*

Lieutenant-General LEONIDAS POLK,
> *Commanding, &c.*

DECEMBER 25, 1862.—Skirmish at Prim's blacksmith shop, Edmondson pike, Tenn.

Report of Brig. Gen. Thomas J. Wood, U. S. Army. *

[HEADQUARTERS FIRST DIVISION, LEFT WING,]
> *December* 25, 1862.

The brigade (Colonel Harker's) which went out this morning for forage is coming in. Colonel Harker reports having filled his wagons with corn, but had to fight for it. He was attacked in front and on the flanks, and lost 1 man killed outright and 2 wounded; one seriously, the other slightly. The casualties all occurred in the Fifty-first Indiana Volunteers. Colonel Harker estimates the enemy at 600, and says he was attacked by mounted men and men on foot, but does not know whether the latter were infantry or dismounted troopers. If we should move to-morrow, I beg to be distinctly informed what amount of baggage it is expected we will take. If all is not taken, which, I presume, will hardly be done, what arrangements will be made with the remainder? Will it be ordered to follow, or sent to Nashville? Please be explicit, as it will save much embarrassment. Further, is it expected any forage will be taken? I understand the forage is exhausted on the Murfreesborough road to La Vergne; and if it were there to forage for, scattering our troops so, where the enemy are, would be hazardous. On the other hand, to haul the bulky forage provided from the country will make an immense train. I beg you will furnish the necessary information at your earliest convenience.

> TH. J. WOOD,
> *Brigadier-General, Commanding.*

---

* See also Wharton's report, p. 164.

DECEMBER 26, 1862.—Capture of guerrilla camp in Powell County, Kentucky.

Report of Maj. Gen. Horatio G. Wright, U. S. Army, commanding Department of the Ohio.

CINCINNATI, OHIO,
January 2, 1863—12.15 p. m.

I have just learned from Major-General Granger that Major Stivers, of the Fourteenth Kentucky Cavalry, with 150 men, who were ordered by him upon a scout, to ascertain the whereabouts of a large band of guerrillas in the eastern part of Powell County, Kentucky, on the 26th ultimo, after traveling all night, over obscure and dangerous bridle-paths, came upon their camp as they were preparing to move, dashed upon them, capturing their leader, a noted guerrilla, and 11 men. The rest, though outnumbering Major Stivers' force, were utterly routed, and escaped into the dense brush and mountain gorges. Twenty-five horses and a large amount of clothing, blankets, guns, pistols, &c., that were being transported to Humphrey Marshall's camp, were also captured.

H. G. WRIGHT,
Major-General.

Maj. Gen. H. W. HALLECK,
General-in-Chief.

DECEMBER 26, 1862–JANUARY 5, 1863.—The Stone's River or Murfreesborough, Tenn., Campaign.

SUMMARY OF THE PRINCIPAL EVENTS.

Dec.   26, 1862.—Skirmish at Franklin, Tenn.
                 Skirmish at Nolensville, Tenn.
                 Skirmish at Knob Gap, Tenn.
         26–27, 1862.—Skirmish at La Vergne, Tenn.
         27, 1862.—Skirmish on the Jefferson Pike, at Stewart's Creek Bridge, Tenn.
                 Skirmish at Triune, Tenn.
                 Skirmish at Franklin, Tenn.
                 Skirmish on the Murfreesborough pike, at Stewart's Creek Bridge, Tenn.
         29, 1862.—Skirmish at Lizzard's, between Triune and Murfreesborough, Tenn.
                 Skirmish at Wilkinson's Cross-Roads,* Tenn.
         29–30, 1862.—Skirmishes near Murfreesborough, Tenn.
         30, 1862.—Skirmish at Jefferson, Tenn.
                 Skirmish at La Vergne, Tenn.
                 Skirmish at Rock Spring, Tenn.
                 Skirmish at Nolensville, Tenn.
         31, 1862.—Skirmish at Overall's Creek, Tenn.
Dec.   31, 1862–Jan. 3, 1863.—Battle of Stone's River, or Murfreesborough, Tenn.
Jan.   1, 1863.—Skirmishes at Stewart's Creek and La Vergne, Tenn.
         3, 1863.—Skirmish at the Insane Asylum, or Cox's Hill, Tenn.†
         4, 1863.—Skirmish on the Manchester pike, Tenn.
                 Skirmish at Murfreesborough, Tenn.

---

* Called also Wilkerson's Cross-Roads.   † Called also Blood's.

Jan. 5, 1863.—Murfreesborough occupied by Union forces.
      Skirmish at Lytle's Creek, on the Manchester pike, Tenn.
      Skirmish on the Shelbyville pike, Tenn.

REPORTS, ETC.

ARMY OF THE CUMBERLAND.

No. 1.—Organization of the Fourteenth Army Corps, or Army of the Cumberland.
No. 2.—Maj. Gen. William S. Rosecrans, U. S. Army, commanding Army of the Cumberland, with congratulatory resolutions, orders, &c.
No. 3.—Return of casualties in the Union forces.
No. 4.—Surg. Ebenezer Swift, U. S. Army, Medical Director.
No. 5.—Lieut. Col. Samuel Simmons, U. S. Army, Chief Commissary of Subsistence, of stores lost and captured.
No. 6.—Lieut. Col. John W. Taylor, U. S. Army, Chief Quartermaster, of public animals and means of transportation captured by the enemy, &c., December 26–January 16.
No. 7.—Capt. William M. Wiles, Forty-fourth Indiana Infantry, Provost Marshal, of prisoners captured.
No. 8.—Capt. Jesse Merrill, Chief Signal Officer.
No. 9.—Col. James Barnett, First Ohio Light Artillery, Chief of Artillery.
No. 10.—Capt. James St. C. Morton, U. S. Corps of Engineers, commanding Pioneer Brigade.
No. 11.—Capt. Lyman Bridges, commanding First Battalion.
No. 12.—Capt. Calvin Hood, commanding Second Battalion.
No. 13.—Capt. Robert Clements, commanding Third Battalion.
No. 14.—Capt. James H. Stokes, Stokes' Illinois battery.
No. 15.—Maj. Gen. Alexander McD. McCook, U. S. Army, commanding Right Wing.
No. 16.—Surg. Clarke McDermont, U. S. Army, Medical Director.
No. 17.—Brig. Gen. Jefferson C. Davis, U. S. Army, commanding First Division.
No. 18.—Lieut. Charles B. Humphrey, Fifth Wisconsin Battery.
No. 19.—Lieut. Henry E. Stiles, Eighth Wisconsin Battery.
No. 20.—Col. P. Sidney Post, Fifty-ninth Illinois Infantry, commanding First Brigade.
No. 21.—Capt. Hendrick E. Paine, Fifty-ninth Illinois Infantry.
No. 22.—Col. Jason Marsh, Seventy-fourth Illinois Infantry.
No. 23.—Lieut. Col. John E. Bennett, Seventy-fifth Illinois Infantry.
No. 24.—Col. Michael Gooding, Twenty-second Indiana Infantry.
No. 25.—Col. William P. Carlin, Thirty-eighth Illinois Infantry, commanding Second Brigade.
No. 26.—Maj. Isaac M. Kirby, One hundred and first Ohio Infantry.
No. 27.—Col. William E. Woodruff, commanding Third Brigade.
No. 28.—Capt. Wesford Taggart, Twenty-fifth Illinois Infantry.
No. 29.—Lieut. Col. William P. Chandler, Thirty-fifth Illinois Infantry.
No. 30.—Brig. Gen. Richard W. Johnson, U. S. Army, commanding Second Division.
No. 31.—Capt. Peter Simonson, Fifth Indiana Battery.
No. 32.—Capt. Warren P. Edgarton, Battery E, First Ohio Light Artillery.
No. 33.—Lieut. Albert G. Ransom, Battery E, First Ohio Light Artillery.
No. 34.—Col. William H. Gibson, Forty-ninth Ohio Infantry, commanding First Brigade.
No. 35.—Lieut. Col. Charles T. Hotchkiss, Eighty-ninth Illinois Infantry.
No. 36.—Lieut. Col. Frank Erdelmeyer, Thirty-second Indiana Infantry.
No. 37.—Lieut. Col. Fielder A. Jones, Thirty-ninth Indiana Infantry.
No. 38.—Col. William Wallace, Fifteenth Ohio Infantry.
No. 39.—Col. Joseph B. Dodge, Thirtieth Indiana Infantry, commanding Second Brigade.
No. 40.—Maj. Alexander P. Dysart, Thirty-fourth Illinois Infantry.

No. 41.—Maj. Allen Buckner, Seventy-ninth Illinois Infantry.
No. 42.—Maj. Joseph P. Collins, Twenty-ninth Indiana Infantry.
No. 43.—Lieut. Col. Orrin D. Hurd, Thirtieth Indiana Infantry.
No. 44.—Capt. Thomas E. Rose, Seventy-seventh Pennsylvania Infantry.
No. 45.—Col. Philemon P. Baldwin, Sixth Indiana Infantry, commanding Third Brigade.
No. 46.—Lieut. Col. Hagerman Tripp, Sixth Indiana Infantry.
No. 47.—Lieut. Col. William W. Berry, Fifth Kentucky Infantry.
No. 48.—Maj. Joab A. Stafford, First Ohio Infantry.
No. 49.—Col. Charles Anderson, Ninety-third Ohio Infantry.
No. 50.—Brig. Gen. Philip H. Sheridan, U. S. Army, commanding Third Division.
No. 51.—Capt. Henry Hescock, First Missouri Light Artillery, Chief of Artillery.
No. 52.—Capt. Charles Houghtaling, Battery C, First Illinois Light Artillery.
No. 53.—Capt. Asahel K. Bush, Fourth Indiana Battery.
No. 54.—Col. Nicholas Greusel, Thirty-sixth Illinois Infantry, commanding First Brigade.
No. 55.—Capt. Porter C. Olson, Thirty-sixth Illinois Infantry.
No. 56.—Col. Francis T. Sherman, Eighty-eighth Illinois Infantry.
No. 57.—Lieut. Col. William B. McCreery, Twenty-first Michigan Infantry.
No. 58.—Maj. Elisha C. Hibbard, Twenty-fourth Wisconsin Infantry.
No. 59.—Lieut. Col. Bernard Laiboldt, Second Missouri Infantry, commanding Second Brigade.
No. 60.—Maj. Francis Ehrler, Second Missouri Infantry.
No. 61.—Col. Luther P. Bradley, Fifty-first Illinois Infantry, commanding Third Brigade.
No. 62.—Maj. Gen. George H. Thomas, U. S. Army, commanding Center.
No. 63.—Maj. Gen. Lovell H. Rousseau, U. S. Army, commanding First Division.
No. 64.—Lieut. Francis L. Guenther, Battery H, Fifth U. S. Artillery.
No. 65.—Col. Benjamin F. Scribner, Thirty-eighth Indiana Infantry, commanding First Brigade.
No. 66.—Lieut. Col. Daniel F. Griffin, Thirty-eighth Indiana Infantry.
No. 67.—Maj. Anson G. McCook, Second Ohio Infantry.
No. 68.—Lieut. Col. Stephen A. Bassford, Ninety-fourth Ohio Infantry.
No. 69.—Col. Alfred R. Chapin, Tenth Wisconsin Infantry.
No. 70.—Col. John Beatty, Third Ohio Infantry, commanding Second Brigade.
No. 71.—Col. John C. Starkweather, First Wisconsin Infantry, commanding Third Brigade.
No. 72.—Lieut. Col. Oliver L. Shepherd, Eighteenth U. S. Infantry, commanding Fourth (Regular) Brigade.
No. 73.—Capt. Jesse Fulmer, Fifteenth U. S. Infantry.
No. 74.—Capt. Robert E. A. Crofton, Sixteenth U. S. Infantry.
No. 75.—Maj. James N. Caldwell, Eighteenth U. S. Infantry.
No. 76.—Maj. Frederick Townsend, Eighteenth U. S. Infantry.
No. 77.—Capt. James B. Mulligan, Nineteenth U. S. Infantry.
No. 78.—Brig. Gen. James S. Negley, U. S. Army, commanding Second Division.
No. 79.—Lieut. Alban A. Ellsworth, Hewett's (Kentucky) battery.
No. 80.—Lieut. Alexander Marshall, Battery G, First Ohio Light Artillery.
No. 81.—Brig. Gen. James G. Spears, U. S. Army, commanding First Brigade, of operations January 2-9.
No. 82.—Col. Joseph A. Cooper, Sixth Tennessee Infantry, of skirmish at Cox's Hill.
No. 83.—Col. Timothy R. Stanley, Eighteenth Ohio Infantry, commanding Second Brigade.
No. 84.—Lieut. Col. Alexander W. Raffen, Nineteenth Illinois Infantry.
No. 85.—Col. William L. Stoughton, Eleventh Michigan Infantry.
No. 86.—Lieut. Col. Josiah Given, Eighteenth Ohio Infantry.

No. 87.—Lieut. Col. George F. Elliott, Sixty-ninth Ohio Infantry.

No. 88.—Col. John F. Miller, Twenty-ninth Indiana Infantry, commanding Third Brigade.

No. 89.—Lieut. Col. William D. Ward, Thirty-seventh Indiana Infantry.

No. 90.—Col. James M. Neibling, Twenty-first Ohio Infantry.

No. 91.—Col. Granville Moody, Seventy-fourth Ohio Infantry.

No. 92.—Col. Moses B. Walker, Thirty-first Ohio Infantry, commanding First Brigade, Third Division.

No. 93.—Col. Daniel McCook, Fifty-second Ohio Infantry, commanding brigade, Fourth Division.

No. 94.—Maj. Gen. Thomas L. Crittenden, U. S. Army, commanding Left Wing.

No. 95.—Capt. John Mendenhall, Fourth U. S. Artillery, Chief of Artillery.

No. 96.—Brig. Gen. Thomas J. Wood, U. S. Army, commanding First Division.

No. 97.—Brig. Gen. Milo S. Hascall, U. S. Army, commanding First Brigade and First Division, including skirmishes at La Vergne and on the Murfreesborough pike, at Stewart's Creek.

No. 98.—Maj. Seymour Race, First Ohio Light Artillery, Chief of Artillery.

No. 99.—Lieut. George Estep, Eighth Indiana Battery, including skirmishes at La Vergne and on the Murfreesborough pike, at Stewart's Creek Bridge.

No. 100.—Capt. Jerome B. Cox, Tenth Indiana Battery.

No. 101.—Capt. Cullen Bradley, Sixth Ohio Battery.

No. 102.—Col. George P. Buell, Fifty-eighth Indiana Infantry, commanding regiment and First Brigade, including skirmish at La Vergne, December 27.

No. 103.—Col. Frederick A. Bartleson, One hundredth Illinois Infantry, including skirmishes near La Vergne and at Stewart's Creek Bridge, December 27.

No. 104.—Lieut. Col. James T. Embree, Fifty-eighth Indiana Infantry.

No. 105.—Col. Samuel McKee, Third Kentucky Infantry, of skirmishes near La Vergne and Stewart's Creek Bridge, December 27.

No. 106.—Maj. Daniel R. Collier, Third Kentucky Infantry.

No. 107.—Capt. William H. Squires, Twenty-sixth Ohio Infantry, including skirmishes at La Vergne and Stewart's Creek Bridge, December 27.

No. 108.—Col. George D. Wagner, Fifteenth Indiana Infantry, commanding Second Brigade.

No. 109.—Lieut. Col. Gustavus A. Wood, Fifteenth Indiana Infantry.

No. 110.—Maj. Henry Leaming, Fortieth Indiana Infantry, including skirmish at La Vergne, December 27.

No. 111.—Col. John Q. Lane, Ninety-seventh Ohio Infantry.

No. 112.—Col. Charles G. Harker, Sixty-fifth Ohio Infantry, commanding Third Brigade.

No. 113.—Col. Abel D. Streight, Fifty-first Indiana Infantry.

No. 114.—Col. Gilbert Hathaway, Seventy-third Indiana Infantry.

No. 115.—Col. Michael Shoemaker, Thirteenth Michigan Infantry.

No. 116.—Lieut. Col. Alexander McIlvain, Sixty-fourth Ohio Infantry.

No. 117.—Maj. Horatio N. Whitbeck, Sixty-fifth Ohio Infantry.

No. 118.—Brig. Gen. John M. Palmer, U. S. Army, commanding Second Division.

No. 119.—Surg. Mason G. Sherman, Ninth Indiana Infantry, Acting Medical Director.

No. 120.—Capt. William E. Standart, Battery B, First Ohio Light Artillery.

No. 121.—Lieut. Norval Osburn, Battery F, First Ohio Light Artillery.

No. 122.—Lieut. Charles C. Parsons, Fourth U. S. Artillery, commanding Batteries H and M.

No. 123.—Brig. Gen. Charles Cruft, U. S. Army, commanding First Brigade, including skirmish at La Vergne, December 26.

No. 124.—Surg. James B. Armstrong, Thirty-first Indiana Infantry, acting brigade surgeon.

No. 125.—Col. John Osborn, Thirty-first Indiana Infantry, including skirmish at La Vergne, December 26.

No. 126.—Col. David A. Enyart, First Kentucky Infantry, including skirmish at La Vergne, December 26.

No. 127.—Col. Thomas D. Sedgewick, Second Kentucky Infantry, including skirmish at La Vergne, December 26.

No. 128.—Col. Isaac N. Ross, Ninetieth Ohio Infantry.

No. 129.—Col. William B. Hazen, Forty-first Ohio Infantry, commanding Second Brigade, including skirmishes on the Jefferson pike, near Stewart's Creek Bridge, December 27.

No. 130.—Surg. Mason 'G. Sherman, Ninth Indiana Infantry, acting brigade surgeon.

No. 131.—Lieut. John L. Chilton, Sixth Kentucky Infantry, acting brigade quartermaster.

No. 132.—Col. Thomas S. Casey, One hundred and tenth Illinois Infantry.

No. 133.—Col. William H. Blake, Ninth Indiana Infantry.

No. 134.—Col. Walter C. Whitaker, Sixth Kentucky Infantry.

No. 135.—Lieut. Col. Aquila Wiley, Forty-first Ohio Infantry.

No. 136.—Col. William Grose, Thirty-sixth Indiana Infantry, commanding Third Brigade.

No. 137.—Surg. Silas H. Kersey, Thirty-sixth Indiana Infantry, acting brigade surgeon.

No. 138.—Col. Louis H. Waters, Eighty-fourth Illinois Infantry.

No. 139.—Capt. Pyrrhus Woodward, Thirty-sixth Indiana Infantry.

No. 140.—Maj. Thomas H. Hamrick, Twenty-third Kentucky Infantry.

No. 141.—Col. Nicholas L. Anderson, Sixth Ohio Infantry.

No. 142.—Capt. Armistead T. M. Cockerill, Twenty-fourth Ohio Infantry.

No. 143.—Brig. Gen. Horatio P. Van Cleve, U. S. Army, commanding Third Division.

No. 144.—Col. Samuel Beatty, Nineteenth Ohio Infantry, commanding Third Division.

No. 145.—Capt. George R. Swallow, Seventh Indiana Battery.

No. 146.—Lieut. Alanson J. Stevens, Battery B, Pennsylvania Light Artillery.

No. 147.—Lieut. Cortland Livingston, Third Wisconsin Battery.

No. 148.—Col. Samuel Beatty, Nineteenth Ohio Infantry, commanding First Brigade.

No. 149.—Col. Benjamin C. Grider, Ninth Kentucky Infantry, commanding regiment and First Brigade.

No. 150.—Col. Frederick Knefler, Seventy-ninth Indiana Infantry.

No. 151.—Col. George H. Cram, Ninth Kentucky Infantry, of engagement January 2.

No. 152.—Maj. Erasmus L. Mottley, Eleventh Kentucky Infantry.

No. 153.—Maj. Charles F. Manderson, Nineteenth Ohio Infantry.

No. 154.—Col. James P. Fyffe, Fifty-ninth Ohio Infantry, commanding Second Brigade.

No. 155.—Lieut. Col. Simeon C. Aldrich, Forty-fourth Indiana Infantry.

No. 156.—Lieut. Col. George F. Dick, Eighty-sixth Indiana Infantry.

No. 157.—Maj. Dwight Jarvis, jr., Thirteenth Ohio Infantry.

No. 158.—Lieut. Col. William Howard, Fifty-ninth Ohio Infantry.

No. 159.—Col. Samuel W. Price, Twenty-first Kentucky Infantry, commanding Third Brigade.

No. 160.—Col. Bernard F. Mullen, Thirty-fifth Indiana Infantry.

No. 161.—Maj. Green B. Broaddus, Eighth Kentucky Infantry, of engagement January 2.

No. 162.—Lieut. Col. James C. Evans, Twenty-first Kentucky Infantry, of engagement January 2.

No. 163.—Lieut. Col. Richard W. McClain, Fifty-first Ohio Infantry.

No. 164.—Lieut. Col. John E. Cummins, Ninety-ninth Ohio Infantry, of engagement January 2.

No. 165 —Brig. Gen. David S. Stanley, U. S. Army, Chief of Cavalry, including skirmishes near La Vergne, December 27, at Wilkinson's Cross-Roads, December 29, Overall's Creek, December 31, and Lytle's Creek, January 5.

No. 166.—Col. John Kennett, Fourth Ohio Cavalry, commanding First Cavalry Division.

No. 167.—Lieut. Nathaniel M. Newell, Battery D, First Ohio Light Artillery, of skirmishes near La Vergne and Stewart's Creek, December 26–January 1.

No. 168.—Col. Robert H. G. Minty, Fourth Michigan Cavalry, commanding First Brigade, including skirmishes at La Vergne, December 26, between Stewart's Creek and La Vergne, December 30, at Overall's Creek December 31, and on Manchester pike, January 5.

No. 169.—Capt. Joseph A. S. Mitchell, Second Indiana Cavalry, of operations near La Vergne, December 29–31.

No. 170.—Col. Eli H. Murray, Third Kentucky Cavalry, including skirmishes at La Vergne, December 26, Wilkinson's Cross-Roads, December 31, and on Manchester pike, January 5.

No. 171.—Lieut. Col. William H. Dickinson, Fourth Michigan Cavalry, including skirmish at La Vergne, January 1.

No. 172.—Capt. Frank W. Mix, Fourth Michigan Cavalry, of skirmish at Stewart's Creek Bridge, December 27.

No. 173.—Lieut. Lansingh B. Eldridge, Fourth Michigan Cavalry, of operations between Nashville and La Vergne, January 1–3.

No. 174.—Maj. John E. Wynkoop, Seventh Pennsylvania Cavalry, including skirmishes on the Murfreesborough road, December 26–27, at Overall's Creek, December 31, and on Manchester pike, January 5.

No. 175.—Col. Lewis Zahm, Third Ohio Cavalry, commanding Second Brigade, including skirmishes at Franklin, December 26–27, Wilkinson's Cross-Roads, December 29, Overall's Creek, December 31, La Vergne, January 1, Cox's Hill, January 3, and on Shelbyville pike, January 5.

No. 176.—Maj. James Laughlin, First Ohio Cavalry, of operations January 1–5.

No. 177.—Capt. Valentine Cupp, First Ohio Cavalry, including skirmishes at Franklin, December 26, Wilkinson's Cross-Roads, December 29, and Overall's Creek December 31.

No. 178.—Lieut. Col. Douglas A. Murray, Third Ohio Cavalry, including skirmishes at Franklin, December 26–27, and Overall's Creek, December 31.

No. 179.—Maj. James W. Paramore, Third Ohio Cavalry, including skirmishes at Overall's Creek, December 31, and at La Vergne, January 1.

No. 180.—Maj. John L. Pugh, Fourth Ohio Cavalry, including skirmishes at Franklin, December 26, Wilkinson's Cross-Roads, December 29, and Overall's Creek, December 31.

No. 181.—Capt. Henry B. Teeter, Fourth Ohio Cavalry, of operations December 31.

No. 182.—Maj. Robert Klein, Third Indiana Cavalry (unattached), including skirmishes at Triune, December 27, and near Overall's Creek, December 31.

No. 183.—Lieut. William S. Hall, adjutant Second Tennessee Cavalry.

No. 184.—Capt. Elmer Otis, Fourth U. S. Cavalry, including skirmishes at Overall's Creek, December 31, and on the Manchester pike, January 5.

No. 185.—Col. William P. Innes, First Michigan Engineers, of attack on wagon-train near La Vergne, January 1.

No. 186.—Lieut. Col. John G. Parkhurst, Ninth Michigan Infantry, including skirmish near Overall's Creek, December 31.

No. 187.—Lieut. Col. Joseph W. Burke, Tenth Ohio Infantry, of operations December 31–January 22.

ARMY OF TENNESSEE.

No. 188.—General Joseph E. Johnston, C. S. Army, commanding the Western Department, with congratulatory orders.

No. 189.—Organization of the Army of Tennessee.

No. 190.—General Braxton Bragg, C. S. Army, commanding Army of Tennessee, with congratulatory orders.

No. 191.—Return of casualties in the Confederate forces.

No. 192.—Lieut. Gen. Leonidas Polk, C. S. Army, commanding Army Corps, with resulting correspondence.

No. 193.—Maj. Gen. Benjamin F. Cheatham, C. S. Army, commanding First Division.

No. 194.—Brig. Gen. Daniel S. Donelson, C. S. Army, commanding First Brigade.

No. 195.—Lieut. Col. John H. Anderson, Eighth Tennessee Infantry.

No. 196.—Col. John H. Savage, Sixteenth Tennessee Infantry.

No. 197.—Col. John C. Carter, Thirty-eighth Tennessee Infantry.

No. 198.—Col. John Chester, Fifty-first Tennessee Infantry.

No. 199.—Col. S. S. Stanton, Eighty-fourth Tennessee Infantry.

No. 200.—Lieut. L. G. Marshall, Carnes' Tennessee battery.

No. 201.—Brig. Gen. Alexander P. Stewart, C. S. Army, commanding Second Brigade.

No. 202.—Col. Oscar F. Strahl, Fourth Tennessee Infantry, commanding Fourth and Fifth Regiments.

No. 203.—Col. Francis M. Walker, Nineteenth Tennessee Infantry.

No. 204.—Maj. S. E. Shannon, Twenty-fourth Tennessee Infantry.

No. 205.—Col. E. E. Tansil, Thirty-first Tennessee Infantry, commanding Thirty-first and Thirty-third Regiments.

No. 206.—Capt. T. J. Stanford, Mississippi battery.

No. 207.—Brig. Gen. George Maney, C. S. Army, commanding Third Brigade.

No. 208.—Col. H. R. Feild, First Tennessee Infantry.

No. 209.—Col. James A. McMurry, Fourth Tennessee Infantry.

No. 210.—Maj. John L. Harris, Sixth Tennessee Infantry, commanding Sixth and Ninth Regiments.

No. 211.—Lieut. William B. Turner, Smith's Mississippi battery.

No. 212.—Col. A. J. Vaughan, jr., Thirteenth Tennessee Infantry, commanding Fourth Brigade.

No. 213.—Capt. R. F. Lanier, Thirteenth Tennessee Infantry.

No. 214.—Maj. J. B. Johnson, Twenty-ninth Tennessee Infantry.

No. 215.—Lieut. Col. Michael Magevney, jr., One hundred and fifty-fourth Tennessee Infantry Senior Regiment.

No. 216.—Col. William H. Young, Ninth Texas Infantry.

No. 217.—Capt. W. L. Scott, Tennessee battery.

No. 218.—Lieut. W. M. Polk, Scott's Tennessee battery.

No. 219.—Maj. Gen. Jones M. Withers, C. S. Army, commanding Second Division.

No. 220.—Capt. Felix H. Robertson, Florida battery, Deas' brigade.

No. 221.—Brig. Gen. J. Patton Anderson, C. S. Army, commanding Walthall's brigade.

No. 222.—Capt. Overton W. Barret, Missouri battery.

No. 223.—Capt. David D. Waters, Alabama battery, Anderson's brigade.

No. 224.—Lieut. Gen. William J. Hardee, C. S. Army, commanding Army Corps.

No. 225.—Maj. Gen. John C. Breckinridge, C. S. Army, commanding First Division, with appendix by General Bragg.

No. 226.—Brig. Gen. Daniel W. Adams, C. S. Army, commanding First Brigade.

No. 227.—Col. Randall L. Gibson, Thirteenth Louisiana Infantry, commanding Thirteenth and Twentieth Regiments and Adams' brigade.

No. 228.—Lieut. Col. Henry Maury, Thirty-second Alabama Infantry.

No. 229.—Maj. F. C. Zacharie, Twenty-fifth Louisiana Infantry, commanding Sixteenth and Twenty-fifth Regiments.

No. 230.—Maj. J. E. Austin, Fourth Louisiana Battalion (sharpshooters).

No. 231.—Lieut. W. C. D. Vaught, Fifth Company, Washington Light Artillery.

No. 232.—Col. Joseph B. Palmer, Eighteenth Tennessee Infantry, commanding regiment and Second Brigade.

No. 233.—Brig. Gen. Gideon J. Pillow, C. S. Army, commanding Second Brigade.

No. 234.—Brig. Gen. William Preston, C. S. Army, commanding Third Brigade.

No. 235.—Col. William Miller, First Florida Infantry, commanding First and Third Regiments.

No. 236.—Col. W. L. L. Bowen, Fourth Florida Infantry.

No. 237.—Maj. John T. Lesley, Fourth Florida Infantry.

No. 238.—Col. Joseph A. McDowell, Sixtieth North Carolina Infantry.

No. 239.—Col. T. B. Smith, Twentieth Tennessee Infantry.

No. 240.—Maj. F. Claybrooke, Twentieth Tennessee Infantry.

No. 241.—Lieut. John W. Mebane, Wright's Tennessee battery.

No. 242.—Col. Robert P. Trabue, Fourth Kentucky Infantry, commanding Fourth Brigade.

No. 243.—Lieut. Col. M. L. Stansel, Forty-first Alabama Infantry.

No. 244.—Maj. James W. Hewitt, Second Kentucky Infantry.

No. 245.—Col. Joseph H. Lewis, Sixth Kentucky Infantry.

No. 246.—Col. Thomas H. Hunt, Ninth Kentucky Infantry.

No. 247.—Capt. Robert Cobb, Kentucky battery.

No. 248.—Brig. Gen. John K. Jackson, C. S. Army, commanding brigade.

No. 249.—Maj. Charles P. Daniel, Fifth Georgia Infantry.

No. 250.—Maj. Jesse J. Cox, Second Georgia Battalion Sharpshooters.

No. 251.—Lieut. Col. A. McNeill, Eighth Mississippi Infantry.

No. 252.—Lieut. Harvey H. Cribbs, Lumsden's (Alabama) battery.

No. 253.—Maj. Gen. Patrick R. Cleburne, C. S. Army, commanding division.

No. 254.—Brig. Gen. Lucius E. Polk, C. S. Army, commanding First Brigade.

No. 255.—Lieut. Thomas J. Key, Helena Battery.

No. 256.—Brig. Gen. St. John R. Liddell, C. S. Army, commanding Second Brigade.

No. 257.—Col. Daniel C. Govan, Second Arkansas Infantry.

No. 258.—Lieut. Col. Reuben F. Harvey, Second Arkansas Infantry.

No. 259.—Lieut. Col. John E. Murray, Fifth Arkansas Infantry.

No. 260.—Maj. William F. Douglass, Sixth Arkansas Infantry, commanding Sixth and Seventh Regiments.

No. 261.—Col. John H. Kelly, Eighth Arkansas Infantry.

No. 262.—Lieut. Col. George F. Baucum, Eighth Arkansas Infantry.

No. 263.—Lieut. H. Shannon, Warren Light Artillery.

No. 264.—Brig. Gen. Bushrod R. Johnson, C. S. Army, commanding Third Brigade.

No. 265.—Lieut. James B. Lake, ——, Chief Ordnance Officer.

No. 266.—Lieut. Col. Watt W. Floyd, Seventeenth Tennessee Infantry.

No. 267.—Lieut. Col. R. H. Keeble, Twenty-third Tennessee Infantry.

No. 268.—Col. John M. Hughs, Twenty-fifth Tennessee Infantry.

No. 269.—Lieut. Col. Samuel Davis, Twenty-fifth Tennessee Infantry.

No. 270.—Capt. C. G. Jarnagin, Thirty-seventh Tennessee Infantry.

No. 271.—Col. John S. Fulton, Forty-fourth Tennessee Infantry.

No. 272.—Capt. Putnam Darden, Jefferson Artillery.

No. 273.—Brig. Gen. S. A. M. Wood, C. S. Army, commanding Fourth Brigade, including skirmish on the Nolensville road, December 27.

No. 274.—Col. William B. Wood, Sixteenth Alabama Infantry, including skirmish at Triune, December 27.

No. 275.—Col. Samuel Adams, Thirty-third Alabama Infantry.

No. 276.—Maj. J. F. Cameron, Third Confederate Infantry.

No. 277.—Lieut. Col. R. Charlton, Forty-fifth Mississippi Infantry, including skirmishes near Triune, December 27.

No. 278.—Capt. A. T. Hawkins, Fifteenth Battalion, Mississippi Sharpshooters.

No. 279.—Capt. Henry C. Semple, Alabama Battery.

No. 280.—Maj. Gen. John P. McCown, C. S. Army, commanding division, Smith's corps.

No. 281.—Capt. J. D. Allison, ——, Chief Ordnance Officer.

No. 282.—Maj. George M. Mathes, ——, Chief of Artillery.

No. 283.—Brig. Gen. M. D. Ector, C. S. Army, commanding First Brigade.

No. 284.—Col. M. F. Locke, C. S. Army, Tenth Texas Cavalry (dismounted).

No. 285.—Lieut. Col. J. M. Bounds, Eleventh Texas Cavalry (dismounted).

No. 286.—Col. J. L. Camp, Fourteenth Texas Cavalry (dismounted).

No. 287.—Col. Julius A. Andrews, Fifteenth Texas Cavalry (dismounted).

No. 288.—Capt. James P. Douglas, Texas Battery.

No. 289.—Col. Robert B. Vance, Twenty-ninth North Carolina Infantry, commanding regiment and Second Brigade.

No. 290.—Lieut. Col. M. A. Stovall, Third Georgia Battalion.

No. 291.—Maj. Joseph T. Smith, Ninth Georgia Battalion.

No. 292.—Lieut. Col. William Thedford, Eleventh Tennessee Infantry.

No. 293.—Lieut. W. A. McDuffie, Eufaula Light Artillery.

No. 294.—Brig. Gen. E. McNair, C. S. Army, commanding Third Brigade.

No. 295.—Col. Robert W. Harper, First Arkansas Mounted Rifles, commanding regiment and Third Brigade.

No. 296.—Lieut. Col. James A. Williamson, Second Arkansas Mounted Rifles (dismounted).

No. 297.—Col. H. G. Bunn, Fourth Arkansas Infantry.

No. 298.—Capt. William A. Cotter, Thirtieth Arkansas Infantry.

No. 299.—Maj. J. A. Ross, Fourth Arkansas Battalion.

No. 300.—Capt. John T. Humphreys, Arkansas Battery.

No. 301.—Maj. Gen. Joseph Wheeler, C. S. Army, Chief of Cavalry, including skirmishes at and near La Vergne, December 26 and 30, and January 1; at Stewart's Creek Bridge, December 27; at Stewart's Creek, December 28; at Wilkinson's Cross-Roads, December 29; at Cox's, or Blood's Hill, January 3; at Murfreesborough, January 4; on Manchester pike, January 5; at Mill Creek Bridge, January 8; near Nashville, January 12; and capture of transports, January 13, 14, and 17, and of construction train at Antioch, January 25.

No. 302.—Capt. T. H. Mauldin, Third Alabama Cavalry, Wheeler's brigade, including skirmishes December 26–January 5.

No. 303.—Lieut. Col. J. D. Webb, Fifty-first Alabama Partisan Rangers, including skirmishes December 26–January 5.

No. 304.—Capt. J. H. Wiggins, Arkansas Battery, including skirmishes at La Vergne December 26–27.

No. 305.—Brig. Gen. John A. Wharton, C. S. Army, commanding cavalry brigade.

No. 306.—Brig. Gen. Abraham Buford, C. S. Army, commanding cavalry brigade, including skirmishes December 31–January 3.

No. 307.—The Confederate Roll of Honor.

No. 1.

*Organization of the Fourteenth Army Corps, or Army of the Cumberland, Maj. Gen. William S. Rosecrans, U. S. Army, commanding, December 26, 1862–January 5, 1863.**

ARTILLERY.

Col. JAMES BARNETT.

PROVOST GUARD.

10th Ohio, Lieut. Col. Joseph W. Burke.

GENERAL ESCORT.

Anderson Troop, Pennsylvania Cavalry, Lieut. Thomas S. Maple.

---

* Arranged according to the numerical designation of the divisions and brigades as prescribed in General Orders, No. 41, Headquarters Fourteenth Army Corps, Department of the Cumberland, December 19, 1862.

RIGHT WING.

Maj. Gen. ALEXANDER McD. McCOOK

FIRST (LATE NINTH) DIVISION.

Brig. Gen. JEFFERSON C. DAVIS.

Escort.

36th Illinois Cavalry, Company B, Capt. Samuel B. Sherer,
2d Kentucky Cavalry, Company G:
Capt. Miller R. McCulloch.
Lieut. Harvey S. Park.

First (late Thirtieth) Brigade.	*Second (late Thirty-first) Brigade.*
Col. P. SIDNEY POST.	Col. WILLIAM P. CARLIN.

59th Illinois, Capt. Hendrick E. Paine.
74th Illinois, Col. Jason Marsh.
75th Illinois, Lieut. Col. John E. Bennett.
22d Indiana, Col. Michael Gooding.

21st Illinois:
    Col. J. W. S. Alexander.
    Lieut. Col. Warren E. McMackin.
38th Illinois, Lieut. Col. Daniel H. Gilmer.
101st Ohio:
    Col. Leander Stem.
    Lieut. Col. Moses F. Wooster.
    Maj. Isaac M. Kirby.
    Capt. Bedan B. McDonald.
15th Wisconsin, Col. Hans C. Heg.

Third (late Thirty-second) Brigade.

Col. WILLIAM E. WOODRUFF.

25th Illinois:
    Maj. Richard H. Nodine.
    Col. Thomas D. Williams.
    Capt. Wesford Taggart.
35th Illinois, Lieut. Col. William P. Chandler.
81st Indiana, Lieut. Col. John Timberlake.

*Artillery.**

2d Minnesota Battery, Capt. William A. Hotchkiss.
5th Wisconsin Battery:
    Capt. Oscar F. Pinney.
    Lieut. Charles B. Humphrey.
8th Wisconsin Battery:
    Capt. Stephen J. Carpenter.
    Sergt. Obadiah German.
    Lieut. Henry E. Stiles.

SECOND DIVISION.

Brig. Gen. RICHARD W. JOHNSON.

First (late Sixth) Brigade.

(1.) Brig. Gen. AUGUST WILLICH.
(2.) Col. WILLIAM WALLACE.
(3.) Col. WILLIAM H. GIBSON.

89th Illinois, Lieut. Col. Charles T. Hotchkiss.
32d Indiana, Lieut. Col. Frank Erdelmeyer.
39th Indiana, Lieut. Col. Fielder A. Jones.

15th Ohio:
    Col. William Wallace.
    Capt. A. R. Z Dawson.
    Col. William Wallace.
49th Ohio:
    Col. William H. Gibson.
    Lieut. Col. Levi Drake.
    Capt. Samuel F. Gray.

---

* The Second Minnesota was attached to the Second Brigade, Fifth Wisconsin to the First Brigade, and Eighth Wisconsin to the Third Brigade.

Second (late Fifth) Brigade.

(1.) Brig. Gen. EDWARD N. KIRK.
(2.) Col. JOSEPH B. DODGE.

34th Illinois:
    Lieut. Col. Hiram W. Bristol.
    Maj. Alexander P. Dysart.
79th Illinois:
    Col. Sheridan P. Read.
    Maj. Allen Buckner.

29th Indiana:
    Lieut. Col. David M. Dunn
    Maj. Joseph P. Collins.
30th Indiana:
    Col. Joseph B. Dodge.
    Lieut. Col. Orrin D. Hurd.
77th Pennsylvania:
    Lieut. Col. Peter B. Housum.
    Capt. Thomas E. Rose.

Third (late Fourth) Brigade.

Col. PHILEMON P. BALDWIN.

6th Indiana, Lieut. Col. Hagerman Tripp.
5th Kentucky, Lieut. Col. William W. Berry
1st Ohio, Maj. Joab A. Stafford.
93d Ohio, Col. Charles Anderson.

Artillery.*

5th Indiana Battery, Capt. Peter Simonson.
1st Ohio, Battery A, Lieut. Edmund B. Belding.
1st Ohio, Battery E, Capt. Warren P. Edgarton.

Cavalry.

3d Indiana, Companies G, H, I, and K, Maj. Robert Klein.

THIRD (LATE ELEVENTH) DIVISION.

Brig. Gen. PHILIP H. SHERIDAN.

Escort.

2d Kentucky Cavalry, Company L, Lieut. Joseph T. Forman.

First (late Thirty-seventh) Brigade.

(1.) Brig. Gen. JOSHUA W. SILL.
(2.) Col. NICHOLAS GREUSEL.

36th Illinois:
    Col. Nicholas Greusel.
    Maj. Silas Miller.
    Capt. Porter C. Olson.
88th Illinois, Col. Francis T. Sherman.
21st Michigan, Lieut. Col. William B. Mc-
    Creery.
24th Wisconsin, Maj. Elisha C. Hibbard.

Second (late Thirty-fifth) Brigade.

(1.) Col. FREDERICK SCHAEFER.
(2.) Lieut. Col. BERNARD LAIBOLDT.

44th Illinois, Capt. Wallace W. Barrett.
73d Illinois, Maj. William A. Presson.
2d Missouri:
    Lieut. Col. Bernard Laiboldt.
    Maj. Francis Ehrler.
15th Missouri, Lieut. Col. John Weber

Third Brigade.†

(1.) Col. GEORGE W. ROBERTS.
(2.) Col. LUTHER P. BRADLEY.

22d Illinois:
    Lieut. Col. Francis Swanwick.
    Capt. Samuel Johnson.
27th Illinois:
    Col. Fazilo A. Harrington.
    Maj. William A. Schmitt.
42d Illinois, Lieut. Col. Nathan H. Walworth.
51st Illinois:
    Col. Luther P. Bradley.
    Capt. Henry F. Wescott.

---

* The Fifth Indiana was attached to the Third Brigade, Battery A to the First Brigade, and Battery E to the Second Brigade.
† Formerly First Brigade, Thirteenth Division.

*Artillery.**

Capt. HENRY HESCOCK.

1st Illinois, Battery C, Capt. Charles Houghtaling.
4th Indiana Battery, Capt. Asahel K. Bush.
1st Missouri, Battery G, Capt. Henry Hescock.

CENTER.

Maj. Gen. GEORGE H. THOMAS.

PROVOST GUARD.

9th Michigan, Col. John G. Parkhurst.

FIRST (LATE THIRD) DIVISION.

Maj. Gen. LOVELL H. ROUSSEAU.

First (late Ninth) Brigade.

Col. BENJAMIN F. SCRIBNER.

38th Indiana, Lieut. Col. Daniel F. Griffin.
2d Ohio:
  Lieut. Col. John Kell.
  Maj. Anson G. McCook.
33d Ohio, Capt. Ephraim J. Ellis.
94th Ohio:
  Col. Joseph W. Frizell.
  Lieut. Col. Stephen A. Bassford.
10th Wisconsin, Col. Alfred R. Chapin.

Second (late Seventeenth) Brigade.

Col. JOHN BEATTY.

42d Indiana, Lieut. Col. James M. Shanklin.
88th Indiana:
  Col. George Humphrey.
  Lieut. Col. Cyrus E. Briant.
15th Kentucky:
  Col. James B. Forman.
  Lieut. Col. Joseph R. Snider.
3d Ohio, Lieut. Col. Orris A. Lawson.

Third (late Twenty-eighth) Brigade.

Col. JOHN C. STARKWEATHER.

24th Illinois, Col. Geza Mihalotzy.
79th Pennsylvania, Col. Henry A. Hambright.
1st Wisconsin, Lieut. Col. George B. Bingham.
21st Wisconsin, Lieut. Col. Harrison C. Hobart.

Fourth Brigade.

Lieut. Col. OLIVER L. SHEPHERD.

15th United States, 1st Battalion:
  Maj. John H. King.
  Capt. Jesse Fulmer.
16th United States, 1st Battalion, and Company B, 2d Battalion:
  Maj. Adam J. Slemmer.
  Capt. R. E. A. Crofton.
18th United States, 1st Battalion, and Companies A and D, 3d Battalion, Maj. James N. Caldwell.
18th United States, 2d Battalion, and Companies B, C, E, and F, 3d Battalion, Maj. Frederick Townsend.
19th United States, 1st Battalion:
  Maj. Stephen D. Carpenter.
  Capt. James B. Mulligan.

Artillery.†

Capt. CYRUS O. LOOMIS.

Kentucky, Battery A, Capt. David C. Stone.
1st Michigan, Battery A, Lieut. George W. Van Pelt.
5th United States, Battery H, Lieut. Francis L. Guenther.

Cavalry.

2d Kentucky (six companies), Maj. Thomas P. Nicholas.

---

* Battery C was attached to the Third Brigade, Fourth Indiana to the First Brigade, and Battery G to the Second Brigade.
† Battery A, Kentucky, was attached to the Third Brigade; Battery A, First Michigan, to the Second Brigade, and Battery H, Fifth United States, to the Fourth Brigade.

SECOND (LATE EIGHTH) DIVISION.

Brig. Gen. JAMES S. NEGLEY.

First (late Twenty-fifth) Brigade.

Brig. Gen. JAMES G. SPEARS.

1st Tennessee, Col. Robert K. Byrd.
2d Tennessee, Lieut. Col. James M. Melton.
3d Tennessee, Col. Leonidas C. Houk.
5th Tennessee, Col. James T. Shelley.
6th Tennessee, Col. Joseph A. Cooper.

Second (late Twenty-ninth) Brigade.

Col. TIMOTHY R. STANLEY.

19th Illinois:
    Col. Joseph R. Scott.
    Lieut. Col. Alexander W. Raffen.
11th Michigan, Col. William L. Stoughton.
18th Ohio, Lieut. Col. Josiah Given.
69th Ohio:
    Col. William B. Cassil'y.
    Maj. Eli J. Hickcox.
    Capt. David Putnam.
    Capt. Joseph H. Brigham.
    Lieut. Col. George F. Elliott.

Third (late Seventh) Brigade.

Col. JOHN F. MILLER.

37th Indiana :
    Col. James S. Hull.
    Lieut. Col. William D. Ward.
21st Ohio, Lieut. Col. James M. Neibling.
74th Ohio, Col. Granville Moody.
78th Pennsylvania, Col. William Sirwell.

Artillery.

Kentucky, Battery B, Lieut. Alban A. Ellsworth.
1st Ohio, Battery G, Lieut. Alexander Marshall.
1st Ohio, Battery M,* Capt. Frederick Schultz.

THIRD (LATE FIRST) DIVISION.†

Brig. Gen. SPEED S. FRY.

Escort.

2d Kentucky Cavalry, Company B, Captain Henry E. Collins.

First Brigade.

Col. MOSES B. WALKER.

82d Indiana, Col. Morton C. Hunter.
12th Kentucky, Col. William A. Hoskins.
17th Ohio, Col. John M. Connell.
31st Ohio, Lieut. Col. Frederick W. Lister.
38th Ohio, Col. Edward H. Phelps.

Second Brigade.

Col. JOHN M. HARLAN.

10th Indiana, Col. William B. Carroll.
74th Indiana, Col. Charles W. Chapman.
4th Kentucky, Col. John T. Croxton.
10th Kentucky, Lieut. Col. William H. Hays.
14th Ohio, Col. George P. Este.

Third Brigade.

Brig. Gen. JAMES B. STEEDMAN.

87th Indiana, Col. Kline G. Shryock.
2d Minnesota, Col. James George.
9th Ohio, Col. Gustave Kammerling.
35th Ohio, Col. Ferdinand Van Derveer.

---

* Attached to Second Brigade.
† The First Brigade (except the Twelfth Kentucky) and Church's battery were the only troops of this division engaged in the battle of Stone's River.   All commanders are given as they stood December 31, 1862.

Artillery.

1st **Michigan, Battery D, Capt. Josiah W. Church.**
1st **Ohio, Battery C, Capt. Daniel K. Southwick.**
4th **United States, Battery I, Lieut. Frank G. Smith.**

FOURTH (LATE SEVENTH) DIVISION.

Brig. Gen. ROBERT B. MITCHELL.

First Brigade. *

Brig. Gen. JAMES D. MORGAN.

10th Illinois, Lieut. Col. McLain F. Wood.
16th Illinois, Lieut. Col. James B. Cahill.
60th Illinois, Col. Silas C. Toler.†
10th Michigan, Lieut. Col. C. J. Dickerson.†
14th Michigan:
Lieut. Col. Myndert W. Quackenbush.‡
Lieut. Col. Milton L. Phillips.

Second (late Thirty-sixth) Brigade.

Col. DANIEL MCCOOK.

85th Illinois, Col. Robert S. Moore.‡
86th Illinois, Lieut. Col. David W. Magee.
125th Illinois, Col. Oscar F. Harmon.
52d Ohio, Lieut. Col. D. D. T. Cowen.†

Cavalry.

2d Indiana, Company A, Capt. John G. Kessler.
5th Kentucky, Maj. John Q. Owsley.
3d Tennessee, Col. William C. Pickens.§

Artillery.

2d Illinois, Battery I, Capt. Charles M. Barnett.
10th Wisconsin Battery, Capt. Yates V. Beebe.‖

Unattached Infantry.

8th Kansas (five companies), Col. John A. Martin.
1st Middle (10th) Tennessee, Col. Alvan C. Gillem.

Artillery Reserve.

11th Indiana Battery, Capt. Arnold Sutermeister.
12th Indiana Battery, Lieut. James A. Dunwoody.
1st Michigan, Battery E, Capt. John J. Ely.

FIFTH (LATE TWELFTH) DIVISION.¶

Brig. Gen. JOSEPH J. REYNOLDS.

First (late Thirty-third) Brigade.

Col. ALBERT S. HALL.

80th Illinois, Col. Thomas G. Allen.
123d Illinois, Col. James Monroe.
101st Indiana, Col. William Garver.
105th Ohio, Lieut. Col. William R. Tolles.

Second (late Fortieth) Brigade.

Col. ABRAM O. MILLER.

98th Illinois, Col. John J. Funkhouser.
17th Indiana, Col. John T. Wilder.
72d Indiana, Maj. Henry M. Carr.
75th Indiana, Col. Milton S. Robinson.

Artillery.

18th Indiana Battery, Capt. Eli Lilly.
19th Indiana Battery, Capt. Samuel J. Harris.

---

* Formerly Second Brigade, Thirteenth Division.
† Eight companies Sixtieth Illinois, two companies Tenth Michigan, and five companies Fifty-second Ohio, detached under command of Col. Daniel McCook, and engaged in skirmish at Cox's Hill, January 3.
‡ Detached under command of Brig. Gen. J. G. Spears, January 2 and 3, and, with the First Brigade, Second Division, center, participated in the battle of Stone's River, January 3.
§ Detachments with General Spears and Colonel McCook, January 2 and 3.
‖ Two sections with General Spears, January 2–5.
NOTE.—The exceptions indicated in foregoing notes were the only troops of the Fourth Division taking part in the movement from Nashville to Murfreesborough.
¶ Not engaged at Stone's River. Commanders given as they stood December 31, 1862.

LEFT WING.

Maj. Gen. THOMAS L. CRITTENDEN.

FIRST (LATE SIXTH) DIVISION.

(1.) Brig. Gen. THOMAS J. WOOD.
(2.) Brig. Gen. MILO S. HASCALL.

First (late Fifteenth) Brigade.

(1.) Brig. Gen. MILO S. HASCALL.
(2.) Col. GEORGE P. BUELL.

100th Illinois, Col. Frederick A. Bartleson.
58th Indiana:
    Col. George P. Buell.
    Lieut. Col. James T. Embree.
3d   Kentucky:
    Col. Samuel McKee.
    Maj. Daniel R. Collier.
26th Ohio, Capt. William H. Squires.

Second (late Twenty-first) Brigade.

Col. GEORGE D. WAGNER.

15th Indiana, Lieut. Col. Gustavus A.
    Wood.
40th Indiana:
    Col. John W. Blake.
    Lieut. Col. Elias Neff.
    Maj. Henry Leaming.
57th Indiana:
    Col. Cyrus C. Hines.
    Lieut. Col. George W. Lennard.
    Capt. John S. McGraw.
97th Ohio, Col. John Q. Lane.

Third (late Twentieth) Brigade.

Col. CHARLES G. HARKER.

51st Indiana, Col. Abel D. Streight.
73d Indiana, Col. Gilbert Hathaway.
13th Michigan, Col. Michael Shoemaker.
64th Ohio, Lieut. Col. Alexander McIlvain.
65th Ohio:
    Lieut. Col. Alexander Cassil.
    Maj. Horatio N. Whitbeck.

Artillery. *

Maj. SEYMOUR RACE.

8th Indiana Battery, Lieut George Estep.
10th Indiana Battery, Capt. Jerome B. Cox.
6th Ohio Battery, Capt. Cullen Bradley.

SECOND (LATE FOURTH) DIVISION.

Brig. Gen. JOHN M. PALMER.

First (late Twenty-second) Brigade.

Brig. Gen. CHARLES CRUFT.

31st Indiana, Col. John Osborn.
1st Kentucky, Col. David A. Enyart.
2d Kentucky, Col. Thomas D. Sedge-
    wick.
90th Ohio, Col. Isaac N. Ross.

Second (late Nineteenth) Brigade.

Col. WILLIAM B. HAZEN.

110th Illinois, Col. Thomas S. Casey.
9th Indiana, Col. William H. Blake.
6th Kentucky, Col. Walter C. Whita-
    ker.
41st Ohio, Lieut. Col. Aquila Wiley.

---

* The Eighth Battery was attached to the First Brigade, the Tenth Battery to Second Brigade, and the Sixth Battery to the Third Brigade.

Third (late Tenth) Brigade.

Col. WILLIAM GROSE.

84th Illinois, Col. Louis H. Waters.
36th Indiana:
    Maj. Isaac Kinley.
    Capt. Pyrrhus Woodward.
23d Kentucky, Maj. Thomas H. Hamrick.
6th Ohio, Col. Nicholas L. Anderson.
24th Ohio:
    Col. Frederick C. Jones.
    Maj. Henry Terry.
    Capt. Enoch Weller.
    Capt. A. T. M. Cockerill.

Artillery.

Capt. WILLIAM E. STANDART.

1st Ohio, Battery B, Capt. William E. Standart.
1st Ohio, Battery F:
    Capt. Daniel T. Cockerill.
    Lieut. Norval Osburn.
4th United States, Batteries H and M, Lieut. Charles C. Parsons.

THIRD (LATE FIFTH) DIVISION.

(1.) Brig. Gen. HORATIO P. VAN CLEVE.
(2.) Col. SAMUEL BEATTY.

First (late Eleventh) Brigade.

(1.) Col. SAMUEL BEATTY.
(2.) Col. BENJAMIN C. GRIDER.

79th Indiana, Col. Frederick Knefler.
9th Kentucky:
    Col. Benjamin C. Grider.
    Lieut. Col. George H. Cram.
11th Kentucky, Maj. Erasmus L. Mottley.
19th Ohio, Maj. Charles F. Manderson.

Second (late Fourteenth) Brigade.

Col. JAMES P. FYFFE.

44th Indiana:
    Col. William C. Williams.
    Lieut. Col. Simeon C. Aldrich.
86th Indiana, Lieut. Col. George F. Dick.
13th Ohio:
    Col. Joseph G. Hawkins.
    Maj. Dwight Jarvis, jr.
59th Ohio, Lieut. Col. William Howard.

Third (late Twenty-third) Brigade.

Col. SAMUEL W. PRICE.

35th Indiana, Col. Bernard F. Mullen.
8th Kentucky:
    Lieut. Col. Reuben May.
    Maj. Green B. Broaddus.
21st Kentucky, Lieut. Col. James C. Evans.
51st Ohio, Lieut. Col. Richard W. McClain.
99th Ohio:
    Col. Peter T. Swaine.
    Lieut. Col. John E. Cummins.

Artillery.

Capt. GEORGE R. SWALLOW.

7th Indiana Battery, Capt. George R. Swallow.
Pennsylvania, Battery B (26th), Lieut. Alanson J. Stevens.
3d Wisconsin Battery, Lieut. Cortland Livingston.

CAVALRY.

Brig. Gen. DAVID S. STANLEY.

CAVALRY DIVISION.

Col. JOHN KENNETT.

First Brigade.

Col. ROBERT H. G. MINTY.

2d Indiana, Company M, Capt. J. A. S. Mitchell.
3d Kentucky, Col. Eli H. Murray.
4th Michigan, Lieut. Col. William H. Dickinson.
7th Pennsylvania, Maj. John E. Wynkoop.

Second Brigade.

Col. LEWIS ZAHM.

1st Ohio :
 Col. Minor Milliken.
 Maj. James Laughlin.
3d Ohio, Lieut. Col. Douglas A. Murray
4th Ohio, Maj. John L. Pugh.

Artillery.

1st Ohio, Battery D (section), Lieut. Nathaniel M. Newell.

RESERVE CAVALRY.*

15th Pennsylvania :
 Maj. Adolph G. Rosengarten.
 Maj. Frank B. Ward.
 Capt. Alfred Vezin.
1st Middle (5th) Tennessee, Col. William B. Stokes.
2d Tennessee, Col. Daniel M. Ray.

UNATTACHED.

4th U. S. Cavalry, Capt. Elmer Otis.

MISCELLANEOUS.

PIONEER BRIGADE.

Capt. JAMES ST. C. MORTON.

1st Battalion, Capt. Lyman Bridges.
2d Battalion, Capt. Calvin Hood.
3d Battalion, Capt. Robert Clements.
Illinois Light Artillery, Stokes' battery, Capt. James H. Stokes.

ENGINEERS AND MECHANICS.

1st Michigan, Col. William P. Innes.

POST OF GALLATIN, TENN.†

Brig. Gen. ELEAZER A. PAINE.

Ward's (late Eighth) Brigade.

Brig. Gen. WILLIAM T. WARD.

102d Illinois, Lieut. Col. Frank C. Smith.
105th Illinois, Lieut. Col. Henry F. Vallette.
70th Indiana, Col. Benjamin Harrison.
79th Ohio, Col. Henry G. Kennett.
Indiana Light Artillery, 13th Battery, Capt. Benjamin S. Nicklin.

Cavalry.

1st Kentucky, Col. Frank Wolford.
7th Kentucky, Lieut. Col. John K. Faulkner.
11th Kentucky, Lieut. Col. William E. Riley.

---

* Under the immediate command of General Stanley, Chief of Cavalry.
† Not engaged at Stone's River. Commanders given as they stood December 31, 1862.

No. 2.

Reports of Maj. Gen. William S. Rosecrans, U. S. Army, commanding Army of the Cumberland, with congratulatory resolutions, orders, &c.

LA VERGNE, TENN., *December* 28,
By messenger to Louisville, Ky., December 31, 1862—noon.

Our advance was delayed one day. The right wing, under McCook, drove Hardee's skirmishers 18 miles down the Nolensville pike, and advanced on Triune for battle. A heavy fog delayed this advance, and gave Hardee time to escape toward Murfreesborough. Our left wing drove the enemy on the main Murfreesborough turnpike with heavy skirmishing, and seized all the bridges over Stewart's Creek last night, by dark. Our total loss on both lines does not exceed 20 killed, 100 wounded, and 10 missing. We have some 50 prisoners. Our center crossed from Nolensville yesterday and to-day, and now occupy the north side of Stewart's Creek, 10 miles from Murfreesborough—the right at Triune. Pursuing division went 7 miles toward Shelbyville. We have report from Murfreesborough to 10 o'clock yesterday. All his right wing, closed in, came toward Stewart's Creek. If, under Kentucky and Tennessee influence or orders, they fight as they propose, I think we are in position, by God's help, to win, and McCook will cut off their retreat.

W. S. ROSECRANS,
Major-General.

Maj. Gen. H. W. HALLECK,
General-in-Chief.

—

GENERAL ORDERS, }   HDQRS. DEPT. OF THE CUMBERLAND,
No. —.   } *In front of Murfreesborough, December* 31, 1862.

The general commanding desires to say to the soldiers of the Army of the Cumberland that he was well pleased with their conduct yesterday; it is all he could have wished for; he neither saw nor heard of any skulking; they behaved with the coolness and gallantry of veterans. He now feels perfectly confident, with God's grace and their help, of striking this day a blow for the country the most crushing, perhaps, which the rebellion has yet sustained.

Soldiers, the eyes of the whole nation are upon you; the very fate of the nation may be said to hang on the issue of this day's battle. Be true, then, to yourselves, true to your own manly character and soldierly reputation, true to the love of your dear ones at home, whose prayers ascend to God this day for your success.

Be cool! I need not ask you to be brave. Keep ranks. Do not throw away your fire. Fire slowly, deliberately; above all, fire low, and be always sure of your aim. Close steadily in upon the enemy, and, when you get within charging distance, rush on him with the bayonet. Do this, and the victory will certainly be yours. Recollect that there are hardly any troops in the world that will stand a bayonet charge, and that those who make it, therefore, are sure to win.

By command of Maj. Gen. W. S. Rosecrans:

J. P. GARESCHÉ,
Assistant Adjutant-General and Chief of Staff.

MURFREESBOROUGH, TENN., *January* 3, 1863.

On December 26 we moved from Nashville in three columns. Mc-Cook's corps by Nolensville pike; Thomas' from its encampment on Franklin pike, via Wilson pike; Crittenden's on main Murfreesborough pike. The left and center met with a strong resistance, such as the nature of the country permits—rolling or hilly routes, skirted by cedar thickets, farms, and intersected by small streams, with rocky bluff banks, forming serious obstacles. McCook drove Hardee's corps 1½ miles from Nolensville, and occupied the place. Crittenden reached within 1½ miles of La Vergne. Thomas reached the Wilson pike, meeting with no serious opposition. On the 27th, McCook drove Hardee from Nolensville, and pushed reconnoitering division 6 miles toward Shelbyville, and found Hardee had retreated toward Murfreesborough. Crittenden fought and drove the enemy before him, occupying the line of Stewart's Creek, capturing some prisoners, with slight loss. Thomas occupied the vicinity of Nolensville. On the 28th, McCook completed his reconnaissance on Hardee's movements. Crittenden remained, awaiting the result and bringing up trains. Thomas moved on to Stewart's Creek. On the 29th, McCook moved into Wilkinson's Cross-Roads, 7 miles from Murfreesborough, the end of a short pike, the road rough, through rolling country, skirted by bluffs, covered with dense cedar thickets, tops open timber. Crittenden pushed the enemy rapidly, saved all the bridges, and reached a point within 3 miles of Murfreesborough, his advance driving all their outposts to within sight of town. Thomas, with two divisions, closed up with Crittenden, and took position on the right. On the 30th, McCook advanced on Wilkinson pike, having to make his way through dense woods, meeting with a determined resistance. Got into position 3 miles from Murfreesborough, occupying the extreme right of our line. The left stood fast; the center advanced slightly, and were engaged in cutting roads through an almost impenetrable growth of cedars, which separated them from our right, rendering communication with them exceedingly difficult. The combat and the roughness of the country had brought forward McCook's right division, so as to face strongly to the southeast, instead of being refused to face south, with the reserve division, between the center and right, and sufficiently from the rear to support, and, if necessary, to extend it, the grave consequences of which were developed the next day. The 31st found our left crossing Murfreesborough pike and railroad, one division front, one forming crotchet on Stone's River, and one in reserve. Center, Negley between left and right; Rousseau in reserve. The plan of the battle was to open on the right and engage enemy sufficiently to hold him firmly, and to cross the river with our left, consisting of three divisions, to oppose which they had but two divisions, the country being favorable to an attack from that part of the town. But the enemy attacked the whole front of our right wing, massing his forces on its right flank, which was partially surprised, thrown into confusion, and driven back. Sheridan's division repulsed the enemy four times, protected the flanks of the center, which not only held its own, but advanced until this untoward event compelled me to retain the left wing to support the right, until it should be rallied and assume a new position. [January] 1, the rebels opened by an attack on us, and were again repulsed. On the 2d, skirmishing along the front, with warm threats of attack, until about 3 o'clock in the afternoon. Evening, advanced one small division thrown across Stone's River, to occupy commanding ground. While reconnoitering the ground occupied by this division, which had no artillery, I saw heavy forces emerg-

ing from the woods and advancing in line of battle, three lines deep.
They drove our little division before them, after a sharp contest, in which
we lost 70 or 80 killed, and 375 wounded; but they were repulsed by
Negley's division and the remaining troops of the left wing, headed by
Morton's Pioneer Brigade, and fled far over the field and beyond their
intrenchments, their officers rallying them with great difficulty. They
lost heavily. We occupied the ground with the left wing last night.
The lines were completed at 4 o'clock this morning. The 3d was spent
in bringing up and distributing provisions and ammunition. It has
been raining all day; ground very heavy. To-morrow, being Sunday,
we shall probably not fight, unless attacked. This whole country is a
natural fortification, and worse than Corinth. No great battle can be
fought without regular approaches. Our total loss in wounded, up to
this date, is 4,500; killed, 700 or 800. Our communication with Nashville is open. We have provisions there to last to the 25th instant.
Further report by letter as soon as I can get an opportunity.

W. S. ROSECRANS,
Major-General, Commanding.

H. W. HALLECK,
    General-in-Chief.

—

CAMP NEAR MURFREESBOROUGH, TENN.,
January 4, [1863.]

Following my dispatch of last evening, I have to announce that the
enemy is in full retreat. They left last night. Rain having raised the
river, and the bridge across it, between the left wing and center, being
incomplete, I deemed it prudent to withdraw that wing during the night.
This occupied my time until 4 o'clock, and fatigued the troops. The
commencement of the retreat was known to me at 7 o'clock this morning.
Our ammunition train arrived during the night. To-day was occupied
in distributing ammunition, bringing in the dead, and collecting arms
from the field of battle. The pursuit was commenced by the center, the
two leading brigades arriving at the west side of Stone's River this evening. The railroad bridge was saved, but in what condition is not
known. We shall occupy the town and push the pursuit to-morrow
with the center. Will not, probably, be prudent to advance the army
very far until communication shall be open to Nashville. We labor under
great disadvantages from the inferior number of our cavalry, necessitat-
ing large detachments of infantry to guard our trains. Our medical
director estimates the wounded in hospital at short of 5,500 wounded,
and our dead at 1,000. We have to deplore the loss of Lieutenant-Colonel Garesché, whose capacity and gentlemanly deportment had already
endeared him to all the officers of this command, and whose gallantry
on the field of battle excited their admiration.

W. S. ROSECRANS,
Major-General.

Maj. Gen. H. W. HALLECK,
    General-in-Chief.

—

MURFREESBOROUGH,
January 5, 1863—4.30 a. m.

God has crowned our arms with victory. The enemy are badly beaten,
and in full retreat. We shall press them as rapidly as our means of

traveling and subsistence will permit. Will you please ask the President to have Captain Morton, engineer, made brigadier-general? He has distinguished himself in the fortification and defense of Nashville, after our army left for Kentucky. He has organized a Pioneer Corps of 1,700 picked men, which he now commands, with the rank of captain, and behaved like a hero during the whole battle of Stone's River. He not only deserves the promotion, but it is absolutely necessary to the interest of the service that he should have the rank to command his brigade.

> W. S. ROSECRANS,
> *Major-General.*

Hon. E. M. STANTON,
  Secretary of War.

—

HEADQUARTERS DEPARTMENT OF THE CUMBERLAND,
  Via Nashville, Tenn., January 5, 1863.

We have fought one of the greatest battles of the war, and are victorious. Our entire success on the 31st was prevented by a surprise of the right flank; but have, nevertheless, beaten the enemy, after a three-days' battle. They fled with great precipitancy on Saturday night. The last of their columns of cavalry left this morning. Their loss has been very heavy. Generals Rains and Hanson killed. Chalmers, Adams, and Breckinridge are wounded.

> W. S. ROSECRANS,
> *Major-General.*

H. W. HALLECK,
  General-in-Chief.

—

EXECUTIVE MANSION,
  Washington, January 5, 1863.

Maj. Gen. W. S. ROSECRANS,
  Murfreesborough, Tenn.:

Your dispatch announcing retreat of enemy has just reached here. God bless you, and all with you! Please tender to all, and accept for yourself, the nation's gratitude for your and their skill, endurance, and dauntless courage.

> A. LINCOLN.

—

MURFREESBOROUGH, TENN.,
  January 8, [1863.]

Did not have up trains before close of battle. Bringing up subsistence rapidly. Will have railroad completed here in a few days. Rebels had eight divisions of infantry. Seven have gone by Manchester and one by Shelbyville. Their prisoners and doctors estimate their loss at from 13,000 to 15,000 men. The weight of testimony warrants these figures. Glad to hear of batteries coming. To secure our long lines of communication requires a large force. To fight and maneuver in these regions of roads, ravines, cedar thickets and mountains, against a determined defensive policy, with certainty of success, demand the same. The Cumberland River is now navigable.

> W. S. ROSECRANS,
> *Major-General.*

Maj. Gen. H. W. HALLECK,
  General-in-Chief.

WAR DEPARTMENT,
Washington, January 9, 1863—1.05 p. m.

Maj. Gen. W. S. ROSECRANS,
Commanding Army of the Cumberland:

GENERAL: Rebel accounts fully confirm your telegrams from the battle-field. The victory was well earned and one of the most brilliant of the war. You and your brave army have won the gratitude of your country and the admiration of the world. The field of Murfreesborough is made historical, and future generations will point out the places where so many heroes fell, gloriously, in defense of the Constitution and the Union. All honor to the Army of the Cumberland—thanks to the living and tears for the lamented dead.

H. W. HALLECK,
General-in-Chief.

—

GENERAL ORDERS, ⎱ HDQRS. DEPT. OF THE CUMBERLAND,
No. 7.　　　 ⎰ 　*Murfreesborough, Tenn., January* 31, 1863.

The following resolutions of the General Assembly of the State of Ohio have been received, and, in accordance with the request contained therein, are published to this army:

JOINT RESOLUTIONS RELATIVE TO A VOTE OF THANKS TO MAJOR-GENERAL ROSE-
CRANS.

Resolved by the General Assembly of the State of Ohio, That the thanks of this General Assembly are hereby tendered to Major-General Rosecrans, staff, officers, and the brave men under their command, for the glorious victory resulting in the capture of Murfreesborough and the defeat of the rebel forces at that place.

Resolved, That the sympathies of the General Assembly are extended to the families of the brave and noble patriots that have fallen in defense of freedom and constitutional liberty, and that their memories will ever be cherished by a grateful people.

Resolved, That the Governor be requested to forward a copy of the foregoing resolutions to General Rosecrans, with the request that they be read to his command.

JAMES R. HUBBELL,
Speaker of the House of Representatives.
P. HITCHCOCK,
Pro Tem. President of the Senate.

By command of Major-General Rosecrans:

C. GODDARD,
Assistant Adjutant-General and Chief of Staff.

—

MURFREESBOROUGH, TENN.,
February 9, 1863.

We have now all the reports of the subordinate commanders and staff officers. Will have my report of the battle sent forward in a few days. Some facts in it are worth stating in advance. We have prisoners from one hundred and thirty-one regiments of infantry, twelve battalions of sharpshooters, twenty-three batteries of artillery, and fifty-three regiments of cavalry, giving their fighting force at what all our officers consider a low estimate, near 46,000 infantry, 1,200 sharpshooters, 1,800 artillery, and 13,200 cavalry. Total, 62,000 men. We fought them with 42,000. We hit 165 to their 100. Their loss was 23½, ours 21, per cent. of the fighting force. These figures are significant.

Yours, very respectfully,

W. S. ROSECRANS,
Major-General, Commanding.

Maj Gen. H. W. HALLECK, *General-in-Chief.*

MURFREESBOROUGH, TENN.,
February 11, 1863—11.30 p. m.

Capt. Elmer Otis, Fourth Cavalry, in the recent battle, with 400 men charged the enemy, recaptured 300 prisoners, and greatly distinguished himself. By their consent, and at their request, he is commanding a brigade of three regiments, each with a colonel. I earnestly urge his appointment as brigadier-general, in order that he may continue to command, as cavalry officers are greatly needed.

W. S. ROSECRANS,
Major-General.

Hon. E. M. STANTON,
Secretary of War.

—

GENERAL ORDERS, } HDQRS. DEPT. OF THE CUMBERLAND,
No. 20.   }   *Murfreesborough, Tenn., February* 15, 1863.

The following resolutions of the General Assembly of the State of Indiana having been received, are published to this army, in accordance with the request contained therein :

Resolved by the senate (the house concurring), That the thanks of this General Assembly are hereby tendered to Major-General Rosecrans, and the officers and soldiers under his command, for the well-earned victory of Murfreesborough, Tenn. That they, one and all, merit the lasting gratitude of the nation and the admiration of the world.

Resolved, That the patriotic earnestness, skill, sleepless vigilance, and pertinacity displayed by the commanding general in his advance upon the enemy, his plan of battle, and especially in promptly meeting the exigencies of its varying fortunes, prove that he was "the right man in the right place ;" that the hearty and prompt co-operation, the gallantry and skill of his division and other commanders, the ready obedience, unyielding and hardy courage of the soldiers are worthy of the highest commendation.

Resolved, That the Army of the Cumberland, Murfreesborough, and the name of each fallen and surviving patriot soldier who took part in the perilous struggle, are forever linked together in historic renown, and Indiana will preserve, and gratefully cherish, their memory to the latest generation, as among the brightest jewels of an undivided republic.

Resolved, That the secretary of the senate be directed to forward a copy of these resolutions to Major-General Rosecrans, with the request that they be read at the head of each regiment taking part in the great battle, if consistent with the rules of military propriety and discipline.

We hereby certify that the accompanying resolutions unanimously passed both branches of the General Assembly of the State of Indiana.

PARIS C. DUNNING,
President of Senate.
SAM. H. BUSKIRK,
Speaker of House of Representatives.

JAMES H. VAWTER,
Secretary of Senate.
A. T. WHITLESEY,
Clerk of House of Representatives.

By command of Major-General Rosecrans:

C. GODDARD,
Assistant Adjutant-General and Chief of Staff.

· —

HEADQUARTERS DEPARTMENT OF THE CUMBERLAND,
Murfreesborough, Tenn., February 12, 1863.

GENERAL : As the sub-reports are now nearly all in, I have the honor to submit, for the information of the General-in-Chief, the subjoined report, with accompanying sub-reports, maps, and statistical tables of the battle of Stone's River.   To a proper understanding of this battle it will be necessary to state the preliminary movements and preparations:

Assuming command of the army at Louisville on October 27, it was found concentrated at Bowling Green and Glasgow, distant about 113 miles from Louisville; from whence, after replenishing with ammunition, supplies, and clothing, they moved on to Nashville, the advance corps reaching that place on the morning of November 7, a distance of 183 miles from Louisville.

At this distance from my base of supplies, the first thing to be done was to provide for the subsistence of the troops and open the Louisville and Nashville Railroad.   The cars commenced running through on November 26, previous to which time our supplies had been brought by rail to Mitchellsville, 35 miles north of Nashville, and from thence, by constant labor, we had been able to haul enough to replenish the exhausted stores for the garrison at Nashville and subsist the troops of the moving army.

From November 26 to December 26 every effort was bent to complete the clothing of the army; to provide it with ammunition, and replenish the depot at Nashville with needful supplies; to insure us against want from the largest possible detention likely to occur by the breaking of the Louisville and Nashville Railroad, and to insure this work the road was guarded by a heavy force posted at Gallatin.   The enormous superiority in numbers of the rebel cavalry kept our little cavalry force almost within the infantry lines, and gave the enemy control of the entire country around us.   It was obvious from the beginning that we should be confronted by Bragg's army, recruited by an inexorable conscription, and aided by clans of mounted men, formed into a guerrilla-like cavalry, to avoid the hardships of conscription and infantry service.   The evident difficulties and labors of an advance into this country, and against such a force, and at such distance from our base of operations, with which we were connected but by a single precarious thread, made it manifest that our policy was to induce the enemy to travel over as much as possible of the space that separated us, thus avoiding for us the wear and tear and diminution of our forces, and subjecting the enemy to all this inconvenience, besides increasing for him and diminishing for us the dangerous consequences of a defeat.   The means taken to obtain this end were eminently successful.   The enemy, expecting us to go into winter quarters at Nashville, had prepared his own winter quarters at Murfreesborough, with the hope of possibly making them at Nashville, and had sent a large cavalry force into West Tennessee to annoy Grant, and another large force into Kentucky to break up the railroad.

In the absence of these forces, and with adequate supplies in Nashville, the moment was judged opportune for an advance on the rebels. Polk's and Kirby Smith's forces were at Murfreesborough, and Hardee's corps on the Shelbyville and Nolensville pike, between Triune and Eagleville, with an advance guard at Nolensville, while our troops lay in front of Nashville, on the Franklin, Nolensville, and Murfreesborough turnpikes.

The plan of the movement was as follows: McCook, with three divisions, to advance by Nolensville pike to Triune.   Thomas, with two divisions (Negley's and Rousseau's), to advance on his right, by the Franklin and Wilson pikes, threatening Hardee's right, and then to fall in by the cross-roads to Nolensville.   Crittenden, with Wood's, Palmer's, and Van Cleve's divisions, to advance by the Murfreesborough pike to La Vergne.

With Thomas' two divisions at Nolensville, McCook was to attack Hardee at Triune, and, if the enemy re-enforced Hardee, Thomas was to support McCook. If McCook beat Hardee, or Hardee retreated, and the enemy met us at Stewart's Creek, 5 miles south of La Vergne, Crittenden was to attack him, Thomas was to come in on his left flank, and McCook, after detaching a division to pursue or observe Hardee, if retreating south, was to move with the remainder of his force on their rear.

The movement began on the morning of December 26. McCook advanced on the Nolensville pike, skirmishing his way all day, meeting with stiff resistance from cavalry and artillery, and closing the day by a brisk fight, which gave him possession of Nolensville and the hills 1½ miles in front, capturing one gun by the One hundred and first Ohio and Fifteenth Wisconsin Regiments, his loss this day being about 75 killed and wounded. Thomas followed on the right, and closed Negley's division on Nolensville, leaving the other (Rousseau's) division on the right flank.

Crittenden advanced to La Vergne, skirmishing heavily on his front, over a rough country, intersected by forests and cedar brakes, with but slight loss.

On the 28th [27th] General McCook advanced on Triune, but his movement was retarded by a dense fog.

Crittenden had orders to delay his movements until McCook had reached Triune and developed the intentions of the enemy at that point, so that it could be determined which Thomas was to support.

McCook arrived at Triune, and reported that Hardee had retreated, and that he had sent a division in pursuit.

Crittenden began his advance about 11 a. m., driving before him a brigade of cavalry, supported by Maney's brigade of rebel infantry, and reached Stewart's Creek, the Third Kentucky gallantly charging the rear guard of the enemy, and saving the bridge, on which had been placed a pile of rails that had been set on fire. This was Saturday night.

McCook having settled the fact of Hardee's retreat, Thomas moved Negley's division on to join Crittenden at Stewart's Creek, and moved Rousseau's to Nolensville.

On Sunday the troops rested, except Rousseau's division, which was ordered to move on to Stewartston, and Willich's brigade, which had pursued Hardee as far as Riggs' Cross-Roads, and had determined the fact that Hardee had gone to Murfreesborough, when they returned to Triune.

On Monday morning, McCook was ordered to move from Triune to Wilkinson's Cross-Roads, 6 miles from Murfreesborough, leaving a brigade at Triune. Crittenden crossed Stewart's Creek by the Smyrna Bridge and the main Murfreesborough pike, and Negley by the ford 2 miles above; their whole force to advance on Murfreesborough, distant about 11 miles. Rousseau was to remain at Stewart's Creek until his train came up, and prepare himself to follow. McCook reached Wilkinson's Cross-Roads by evening, with an advance brigade at Overall's Creek, saving and holding the bridge, meeting with but little resistance. Crittenden's corps advanced, Palmer leading, on the Murfreesborough pike, followed by Negley, of Thomas' corps, to within 3 miles of Murfreesborough, having had several brisk skirmishes, driving the enemy rapidly, saving two bridges on the route, and forcing the enemy back to his intrenchments.

About 3 p. m. a signal message coming from the front, from General Palmer, that he was in sight of Murfreesborough, and that the enemy were running, an order was sent to General Crittenden to send a division to occupy Murfreesborough. This led General Crittenden, on reaching the enemy's front, to order Harker's brigade to cross the river at a ford on his left, where he surprised a regiment of Breckinridge's division and drove it back on its main line, not more than 500 yards distant, in considerable confusion; and he held this position until General Crittenden was advised, by prisoners captured by Harker's brigade, that Breckinridge was in force on his front, when, it being dark, he ordered the brigade back across the river, and reported the circumstances to the commanding general on his arrival, to whom he apologized for not having carried out the order to occupy Murfreesborough. The general approved of his action, of course, the order to occupy Murfreesborough having been based on the information received from General Crittenden's advance division that the enemy were retreating from Murfreesborough.

Crittenden's corps, with Negley's division, bivouacked in order of battle, distant 700 yards from the enemy's intrenchments, our left extending down the river some 500 yards. The Pioneer Brigade, bivouacking still lower down, prepared three fords, and covered one of them, while Wood's division covered the other two, Van Cleve's division being in reserve.

On the morning of the 30th, Rousseau, with two brigades, was ordered down early from Stewart's Creek, leaving one brigade there and sending another to Smyrna to cover our left and rear, and took his place in reserve, in rear of Palmer's right, while General Negley moved on through the cedar brakes until his right rested on the Wilkinson pike, as shown by the accompanying plan.* The Pioneer Corps cut roads through the cedars for his ambulances and ammunition wagons.

The commanding general remained with the left and center, examining the ground, while General McCook moved forward from Wilkinson's Cross-Roads, slowly and steadily, meeting with heavy resistance, fighting his way from Overall's Creek until he got into position, with a loss of some 135 killed and wounded.

Our small division of cavalry, say 3,000 men, had been divided into three parts, of which General Stanley took two and accompanied General McCook, fighting his way across from the Wilkinson to the Franklin pike, and below it, Colonel Zahm's brigade leading gallantly, and meeting with such heavy resistance that McCook sent two brigades from Johnson's division, who succeeded in fighting their way into the position shown on the accompanying plan, marked A,* while the third brigade, which had been left at Triune, moved forward from that place, and arrived at nightfall near General McCook's headquarters. Thus, on the close of the 30th, the troops had all got into the position, substantially, as shown in the accompanying drawing, the rebels occupying the position marked A.*

At 4 o'clock in the afternoon General McCook had reported his arrival on the Wilkinson pike, joining Thomas; the result of the combat in the afternoon near Griscom's house, and the fact that Sheridan was in position there; that his right was advancing to support the cavalry; also that Hardee's corps, with two divisions of Polk's, was on his front, extending down toward the Salem pike, without any map of the ground, which was to us *terra incognita*. When General McCook informed the general commanding that his corps was facing strongly toward the east, the general commanding told him that such a direction to his line did not appear to him a proper one, but that it ought, with the exception

---

* To appear in Atlas.

of his left, to face much more nearly south, with Johnson's division in reserve, but that this matter must be confided to him, who knew the ground over which he had fought.

A meeting of the corps commanders was called at the headquarters of the commanding general for this evening. General Thomas arrived early, received his instructions, and retired. General Crittenden, with whom the commanding general had talked freely during the afternoon, was sent for, but was excused at the request of his chief of staff, who sent word that he was very much fatigued and was asleep. Generals McCook and Stanley arrived about 9 o'clock, to whom was explained the following

PLAN OF BATTLE.

McCook was to occupy the most advantageous position, refusing his right as much as practicable and necessary to secure it, to receive the attack of the enemy; or, if that did not come, to attack himself, sufficient to hold all the force on his front; Thomas and Palmer to open with skirmishing, and engage the enemy's center and left as far as the river; Crittenden to cross Van Cleve's division at the lower ford, covered and supported by the sappers and miners, and to advance on Breckinridge; Wood's division to follow by brigades, crossing at the upper ford and moving on Van Cleve's right, to carry everything before them into Murfreesborough. This would have given us two divisions against one, and, as soon as Breckinridge had been dislodged from his position, the batteries of Wood's division, taking position on the heights east of Stone's River, in advance, would see the enemy's works in reverse, would dislodge them, and enable Palmer's division to press them back, and drive them westward across the river or through the woods, while Thomas, sustaining the movement on the center, would advance on the right of Palmer, crushing their right, and Crittenden's corps, advancing, would take Murfreesborough, and then, moving westward on the Franklin road, get in their flank and rear and drive them into the country toward Salem, with the prospect of cutting off their retreat and probably destroying their army.

It was explained to them that this combination, insuring us a vast superiority on our left, required for its success that General McCook should be able to hold his position for three hours; that, if necessary to recede at all, he should recede, as he had advanced on the preceding day, slowly and steadily, refusing his right, thereby rendering our success certain.

Having thus explained the plan, the general commanding addressed General McCook as follows: "You know the ground; you have fought over it; you know its difficulties. Can you hold your present position for three hours?" To which General McCook responded, "Yes, I think I can." The general commanding then said, "I don't like the facing so much to the east, but must confide that to you, who know the ground. If you don't think your present the best position, change it. It is only necessary for you to make things sure." And the officers then returned to their commands.

At daylight on the morning of the 31st the troops breakfasted and stood to their arms, and by 7 o'clock were preparing for the

BATTLE.

The movement began on the left by Van Cleve, who crossed at the lower fords. Wood prepared to sustain and follow him. The enemy, meanwhile, had prepared to attack General McCook, and by 6.30 o'clock advanced in heavy columns—regimental front—his left attacking Willich's and Kirk's brigades, of Johnson's division, which, being disposed, as shown in the map, thin and light, without support, were, after a sharp but fruitless contest, crumbled to pieces and driven back, leaving Edgarton's and part of Goodspeed's battery in the hands of the enemy.

The enemy following up, attacked Davis' division and speedily dislodged Post's brigade. Carlin's brigade was compelled to follow, as Woodruff's brigade, from the weight of testimony, had previously left its position on his left. Johnson's brigades, in retiring, inclined too far to the west, and were too much scattered to make a combined resistance, though they fought bravely at one or two points before reaching Wilkinson's pike. The reserve brigade of Johnson's division, advancing from its bivouac, near the Wilkinson pike, toward the right, took a good position, and made a gallant but ineffectual stand, as the whole rebel left was moving up on the ground abandoned by our troops.

Within an hour from the time of the opening of the battle, a staff officer from General McCook arrived, announcing to me that the right wing was heavily pressed and needed assistance; but I was not advised of the rout of Willich's and Kirk's brigades, nor of the rapid withdrawal of Davis' division, necessitated thereby—moreover, having supposed his wing posted more compactly, and his right more refused than it really was, the direction of the noise of battle did not indicate to me the true state of affairs. I consequently directed him to return and direct General McCook to dispose his troops to the best advantage, and to hold his ground obstinately. Soon after, a second officer from General McCook arrived, and stated that the right wing was being driven— a fact that was but too manifest by the rapid movement of the noise of battle toward the north.

General Thomas was immediately dispatched to order Rousseau, then in reserve, into the cedar brakes to the right and rear of Sheridan. General Crittenden was ordered to suspend Van Cleve's movement across the river, on the left, and to cover the crossing with one brigade, and move the other two brigades westward across the fields toward the railroad for a reserve. Wood was also directed to suspend his preparations for crossing, and to hold Hascall in reserve. At this moment fugitives and stragglers from McCook's corps began to make their appearance through the cedar-brakes in such numbers that I became satisfied that McCook's corps was routed. I, therefore, directed General Crittenden to send Van Cleve in to the right of Rousseau; Wood to send Colonel Harker's brigade farther down the Murfreesborough pike, to go in and attack the enemy on the right of Van Cleve's, the Pioneer Brigade meanwhile occupying the knoll of ground west of Murfreesborough pike, and about 400 or 500 yards in rear of Palmer's center, supporting Stokes' battery (see accompanying drawing). Sheridan, after sustaining four successive attacks, gradually swung his right from a southeasterly to a northwesterly direction, repulsing the enemy four times, losing the gallant General Sill, of his right, and Colonel Roberts, of his left brigade, when, having exhausted his ammunition, Negley's division being in the same predicament, and heavily pressed, after desperate fighting, they fell back from the position held at the commencement, through the cedar woods, in which Rousseau's division, with a portion of Negley's and Sheridan's, met the advancing enemy and checked his movements.

The ammunition train of the right wing, endangered by its sudden discomfiture, was taken charge of by Captain Thruston, of the First Ohio Regiment, ordnance officer, who, by his energy and gallantry, aided by a charge of cavalry and such troops as he could pick up, carried it through the woods to the Murfreesborough pike, around to the rear of the left wing, thus enabling the troops of Sheridan's division to replenish their empty cartridge-boxes. During all this time Palmer's front had likewise been in action, the enemy having made several attempts to advance upon it. At this stage it became necessary to re-adjust the line of battle to the new state of affairs. Rousseau and Van Cleve's advance having relieved Sheridan's division from the pressure, Negley's division and Cruft's brigade, from Palmer's division, withdrew from their original position in front of the cedars, and crossed the open field to the east of the Murfreesborough pike, about 400 yards in rear of our front line, where Negley was ordered to replenish his ammunition and form in close column in reserve.

The right and center of our line now extended from Hazen, on the Murfreesborough pike, in a northwesterly direction; Hascall supporting Hazen; Rousseau filling the interval to the Pioneer Brigade; Negley in reserve; Van Cleve west of the Pioneer Brigade; McCook's corps refused on his right, and slightly to the rear, on Murfreesborough pike; the cavalry being still farther to the rear, on Murfreesborough pike, at and beyond Overall's Creek.

The enemy's infantry and cavalry attack on our extreme right was repulsed by Van Cleve's division, with Harker's brigade and the cavalry. After several attempts of the enemy to advance on this new line, which were thoroughly repulsed, as were also their attempts on the left, the day closed, leaving us masters of the original ground on our left, and our new line advantageously posted, with open ground in front, swept at all points by our artillery.

We had lost heavily in killed and wounded, and a considerable number in stragglers and prisoners; also twenty-eight pieces of artillery, the horses having been slain, and our troops being unable to withdraw them by hand over the rough ground; but the enemy had been thoroughly handled and badly damaged at all points, having had no success where we had open ground and our troops were properly posted; none which did not depend on the original crushing in of our right and the superior masses which were in consequence brought to bear upon the narrow front of Sheridan's and Negley's divisions, and a part of Palmer's, coupled with the scarcity of ammunition, caused by the circuitous road which the train had taken, and the inconvenience of getting it from a remote distance through the cedars. Orders were given for the issue of all the spare ammunition, and we found that we had enough for another battle, the only question being where that battle was to be fought.

It was decided, in order to complete our present lines, that the left should be retired some 250 yards to a more advantageous ground, the extreme left resting on Stone's River, above the lower ford, and extending to Stokes' battery. Starkweather's and Walker's brigades arriving near the close of the evening, the former bivouacked in close column, in reserve, in rear of McCook's left, and the latter was posted on the left of Sheridan, near the Murfreesborough pike, and next morning relieved Van Cleve, who returned to his position in the left wing.

DISPOSITION FOR JANUARY 1, 1863.

After careful examination and free consultation with corps commanders, followed by a personal examination of the ground in rear as far as Overall's Creek, it was determined to await the enemy's attack in that position; to send for the provision train, and order up fresh supplies of ammunition; on the arrival of which, should the enemy not attack, offensive operations were to be resumed.

No demonstration [being made] on the morning of January 1, Crittenden was ordered to occupy the point opposite the ford, on his left, with a brigade.

About 2 o'clock in the afternoon, the enemy, who had shown signs of movement and massing on our right, appeared at the extremity of a field 1½ miles from the Murfreesborough pike, but the presence of Gibson's brigade, with a battery, occupying the woods near Overall's Creek, and Negley's division, and a portion of Rousseau's, on the Murfreesborough pike, opposite the field, put an end to this demonstration, and the day closed with another demonstration by the enemy on Walker's brigade, which ended in the same manner.

On Friday morning the enemy opened four heavy batteries on our center, and made a strong demonstration of attack a little farther to the right, but a well-directed fire of artillery soon silenced his batteries, while the guns of Walker and Sheridan put an end to his efforts there.

About 3 p. m., while the commanding general was examining the position of Crittenden's left across the river, which was now held by Van Cleve's division, supported by a brigade from Palmer's, a double line of skirmishers was seen to emerge from the woods in a southeasterly direction, advancing across the fields, and they were soon followed by heavy columns of infantry, battalion front, with three batteries of artillery. Our only battery on that side of the river had been withdrawn from an eligible point, but the most available spot was pointed out, and it soon opened fire upon the enemy. The line, however, advanced steadily to within 100 yards of the front of Van Cleve's division, when a short and fierce contest ensued. Van Cleve's division, giving way, retired in considerable confusion across the river, followed closely by the enemy.

General Crittenden immediately directed his chief of artillery to dispose the batteries on the hill on the west side of the river so as to open on them, while two brigades of Negley's division, from the reserve, and the Pioneer Brigade, were ordered up to meet the onset. The firing was terrific and the havoc terrible. The enemy retreated more rapidly than they had advanced. In forty minutes they lost 2,000 men.

General Davis, seeing some stragglers from Van Cleve's division, took one of his brigades and crossed at a ford below, to attack the enemy on his left flank, and, by General McCook's order, the rest of his division was permitted to follow; but, when he arrived, two brigades of Negley's division and Hazen's brigade, of Palmer's division, had pursued the fleeing enemy well across the fields, capturing four pieces of artillery and a stand of colors.

It was now after dark, and raining, or we should have pursued the enemy into Murfreesborough. As it was, Crittenden's corps passed over, and, with Davis', occupied the crests, which were intrenched in a few hours.

Deeming it possible that the enemy might again attack our right and center, thus weakened, I thought it advisable to make a demonstration on our right by a heavy division of camp-fires, and by laying out a line of battle with torches, which answered the purpose.

Saturday, January 3, it rained heavily from 3 o'clock in the morning. The plowed ground over which our left would be obliged to advance was impassable for artillery. The ammunition trains did not arrive until 10 o'clock. It was, therefore, deemed unadvisable to advance; but batteries were put in position on the left, by which the ground could be swept, and even Murfreesborough reached by Parrott shells.

A heavy and constant picket firing had been kept up on our right and center, and extending to our left, which at last became so annoying that in the afternoon I directed the corps commanders to clear their fronts.

Occupying the wood to the left of Murfreesborough pike with sharp-shooters, the enemy had annoyed Rousseau all day, and General Thomas and himself requested permission to dislodge them and their supports, which covered a ford. This was granted, and a sharp fire from four batteries was opened for ten or fifteen minutes, when Rousseau sent two of his regiments, which, with Spears' Tennesseans and the Eighty-fifth Illinois Volunteers, that had come out with the wagon-train, charged upon the enemy, and, after a sharp contest, cleared the woods and drove the enemy from his trenches, capturing from 70 to 80 prisoners.

Sunday morning, January 4, it was not deemed advisable to commence offensive movements, and news soon reached us that the enemy had fled from Murfreesborough. Burial parties were sent out to bury the dead, and the cavalry was sent to reconnoiter.

Early Monday morning General Thomas advanced, driving the rear guard of rebel cavalry before him 6 or 7 miles toward Manchester. McCook's and Crittenden's corps following, took position in front of the town, occupying Murfreesborough.

We learned that the enemy's infantry had reached Shelbyville by 12 m. on Sunday, but, owing to the impracticability of bringing up supplies, and the loss of 557 artillery horses, farther pursuit was deemed unadvisable.

It may be of use to give the following general summary of the operations and results of the series of skirmishes closing with the battle of Stone's River and occupation of Murfreesborough:

We moved on the enemy with the following forces: Infantry, 41,421; artillery, 2,223; cavalry, 3,296. Total, 46,940.

We fought the battle with the following forces: Infantry, 37,977; artillery, 2,223; cavalry, 3,200. Total, 43,400.

We lost in killed: Officers, 92; enlisted men, 1,441; total, 1,533. Wounded: Officers, 384; enlisted men, 6,861; total, 7,245. Total killed and wounded, 8,778, being 20.03 per cent. of the entire force in action.*

Our loss in prisoners is not fully made out, but the provost-marshal-general says, from present information, they will fall short of 2,800.*

If there are many more bloody battles on record, considering the newness and inexperience of the troops, both officers and men, or if there has been more true fighting qualities displayed by any people, I should be pleased to know it.

As to the condition of the fight, we may say that we operated over an unknown country, against a position which was 15 per cent. better than our own, every foot of ground and approaches being well known to the enemy, and that these disadvantages were fatally enhanced by the faulty position of our right wing.

The force we fought is estimated as follows:

We have prisoners from one hundred and thirty-two regiments of infantry (consolidations counted as one), averaging from those in General

---

* But see revised statement, p. 207.

Bushrod Johnson's division 411 each, say, for certain, 350 men each, which will give—*

132 regiments of infantry, say 350 men each	46,200
12 battalions of sharpshooters, say 100 men each	1,200
23 batteries of artillery, say 80 men each	1,840
29 regiments of cavalry, say 400 men each, and ⎰ 24 organizations of cavalry, say 70 men each ⎱	13,250
220	62,490

Their average loss, taken from the statistics of Cleburne's, Breckinridge's, and Withers' divisions, was about 2,080 each. This, for six divisions of infantry and one of cavalry, will amount to 14,560 men, or to ours nearly as 165 to 100.

Of 14,560 rebels struck by our missiles, it is estimated that 20,000 rounds of artillery hit 728 men; 2,000,000 rounds of musketry hit 13,832 men, averaging 27.4 cannon-shots to hit 1 man; 145 musket-shots to hit 1 man.

Our relative loss was as follows: Right wing, 15,933 musketry and artillery; loss, 20.72 per cent. Center, 10,866 musketry and artillery; loss, 18.4 per cent. Left wing, 13,288 musketry and artillery; loss, 24.6 per cent.

On the whole, it is evident that we fought superior numbers on unknown ground; inflicted much more injury than we suffered; were always superior on equal ground with equal numbers, and failed of a most crushing victory on Wednesday by the extension and direction of our right wing.

This closes the narrative of the movements and seven days' fighting which terminated with the occupation of Murfreesborough. For a detailed history of the parts taken in the battles by the different commands, their obstinate bravery and patient endurance, in which the new regiments vied with those of more experience, I must refer to the accompanying sub-reports of the corps, division, brigade, regimental, and artillery commanders.

Besides the mention which has been already made of the services of our artillery by the brigade, division, and corps commanders, I deem it a duty to say that such a marked evidence of skill in handling the batteries, and in firing low and with such good effect, appears in this battle to deserve special commendation.

Among the lesser commands which deserve special mention for distinguished services in the battle is the Pioneer Corps, a body of 1,700 men, composed of details from the companies of each infantry regiment, organized and instructed by Capt. James St. Clair Morton, Corps of Engineers, chief engineer of this army, which marched as an infantry brigade with the left wing, making bridges at Stewart's Creek; prepared and guarded the ford at Stone's River on the night of the 29th and 30th; supported Stokes' battery, and fought with valor and determination on the 31st, holding its position till relieved on the morning of the 2d; advancing with the greatest promptitude and gallantry to support Van Cleve's division against the attack on our left on the evening of the same day, constructing a bridge and batteries between that time and Saturday evening. The efficiency and *esprit du corps* suddenly developed in this command, its gallant behavior in action, and the eminent services it is

---

*See Union correspondence, December 16, 1862, Brig. Gen. J. T. Boyle's report of Confederate prisoners received at Louisville, Ky., from October 1 to December 14, 1862, Series I, Vol. XVI, Part II, p. 676.

continually rendering the army, entitle both officers and men to special public notice and thanks, while they reflect the highest credit on the distinguished ability and capacity of Captain Morton, who will do honor to his promotion to a brigadier-general, which the President has promised him.

The ability, order, and method exhibited in the management of the wounded elicited the warmest commendations from all our general officers, in which I most cordially join. Notwithstanding the numbers to be cared for, through the energy of Dr. Swift, medical director, ably assisted by Dr. Weeds and the senior surgeons of the various commands, there was less suffering from delay than I have ever before witnessed.

The Tenth Regiment of Ohio Volunteers, at Stewart's Creek, Lieut. Col. J. W. Burke commanding, deserves especial praise for the ability and spirit with which they held that post, defended our trains, succored their guards, chased away Wheeler's rebel cavalry, saving a large wagon-train, and arrested and retained for service stragglers from the battle-field.

The First Regiment of Michigan Engineers and Mechanics, at La Vergne, under the command of Colonel Innes, fighting behind a slight protection of wagons and brush, gallantly repulsed a charge from more than ten times their number of Wheeler's cavalry.

For distinguished acts of individual zeal, heroism, gallantry, and good conduct, I refer to the accompanying lists of special mentions and recommendations for promotion, wherein are named some of the many noble men who have distinguished themselves and done honor to their country and the starry symbol of its unity. But those named there are by no means all whose names will be inscribed on the rolls of honor we are preparing, and hope to have held in grateful remembrance by our countrymen.

To say that such men as Maj. Gen. George H. Thomas, true and prudent, distinguished in council and on many a battle-field for his courage, or Major-General McCook, a tried, faithful, and loyal soldier, who bravely breasted the battle at Shiloh and at Perryville, and as bravely on the bloody field of Stone's River, and Maj. Gen. Thomas L. Crittenden, whose heart is that of a true soldier and patriot, and whose gallantry, often attested by his companions in arms on other fields, witnessed many times by this army long before I had the honor to command it, and never more conspicuously than in this combat, maintained their high character throughout this action, but feebly expresses my feeling of obligation to them for counsel and support from the time of my arrival to the present hour. I doubly thank them, as well as the gallant and ever-ready Major-General Rousseau, for their support in this battle.

Brig. Gen. D. S. Stanley, already distinguished in four successful battles—Island No. 10; May 27, before Corinth; Iuka, and the battle of Corinth—at this time in command of our ten regiments of cavalry, fought the enemy's forty regiments of cavalry, and held them at bay, or beat them wherever he could meet them. He ought to be made a major-general for his service, and also for the good of the service.

As for such brigadiers as Negley, Jefferson C. Davis, Johnson, Palmer, Hascall, Van Cleve, Wood, Mitchell, Cruft, and Sheridan, they ought to be major-generals in our service. In such brigade commanders as Colonels Carlin, Miller, Hazen, Samuel Beatty, of the Nineteenth Ohio; Gibson, Grose, Wagner, John Beatty, of the Third Ohio; Harker, Starkweather, Stanley, and others, whose names are mentioned in the accompanying reports, the Government may well confide. They are the men from whom our troops should at once be supplied with brigadier-generals; and justice to the brave men and officers of the regiments equally demand their promotion to give them and their regiments their proper leaders. Many captains and subalterns also showed great gallantry and capacity for superior commands. But, above all, the sturdy rank and file showed invincible fighting courage and stamina, worthy of a great and free nation, requiring only good officers, discipline, and instructions to make them equal, if not superior, to any troops in ancient or modern times. To them I offer my most heartfelt thanks and good wishes. Words of mine cannot add to the renown of our brave and patriotic officers and soldiers who fell on the field of honor, nor increase respect for their memory in the hearts of our countrymen.

The names of such men as Lieut. Col. J. P. Garesché, the pure and noble Christian gentleman and chivalric officer, who gave his life an early offering on the altar of his country's freedom; the gentle, true, and accomplished General Sill; the brave, ingenuous, and able Colonels Roberts, Milliken, Schaefer, McKee, Read, Forman, Fred. Jones, Hawkins, Kell, and the gallant and faithful Major Carpenter, of the Nineteenth Regulars, and many other field officers, will live in our country's history, as will those of many others of inferior rank, whose soldierly deeds on this memorable battle-field won for them the admiration of their companions, and will dwell in our memories in long future years, after God, in his mercy, shall have given us peace, and restored us to the bosom of our homes and families.

Simple justice to the gallant officers of my staff, the noble and lamented Lieutenant-Colonel Garesché, chief of staff; Lieutenant-Colonel Taylor, chief quartermaster; Lieutenant-Colonel Simmons, chief commissary; Maj. C. Goddard, senior aide-de-camp; Maj. Ralston Skinner, judge-advocate-general; Lieut. Frank S. Bond, aide-de-camp of General Tyler; Capt. Charles R. Thompson, my aide-de-camp; Lieut. Byron Kirby, Sixth U. S. Infantry, aide-de-camp, who was wounded on the 31st; R. S. Thoms, esq., a member of the Cincinnati bar, who acted as volunteer aide-de-camp, behaved with distinguished gallantry; Colonel Barnett, chief of artillery and ordnance; Capt. J. H. Gilman, Nineteenth U. S. Infantry, inspector of artillery; Capt. James Curtis, Fifteenth U. S. Infantry, assistant inspector-general; Captain Wiles, Twenty-second Indiana, provost-marshal-general; Captain Michler, chief of Topographical Engineers; Capt. Jesse Merrill, Signal Corps, whose corps behaved well; Capt. Elmer Otis, Fourth Regular Cavalry, who commanded the courier line connecting the various headquarters most successfully, and who made a most opportune and brilliant charge on Wheeler's cavalry, routing a brigade and recapturing 300 of our prisoners; Lieutenant Edson, United States ordnance officer, who, during the battle of Wednesday, distributed ammunition under the fire of the enemy's batteries, and behaved bravely; Captain Hubbard and Lieutenant Newberry, who joined my staff on the field and acted as aides, rendered valuable service in carrying orders on the field; Lieut. E. G. Roys, Fourth U. S. Cavalry, who commanded the escort of the headquarters train, and distinguished himself for gallantry and efficiency—all not only performed their appropriate duties to my entire satisfaction, but, accompanying me everywhere, carrying orders through the thickest of the fight, watching while others slept, and never weary when duty called, deserve my public thanks and the respect and gratitude of the army.

With all the facts of the battle fully before me, the relative numbers and positions of our troops and those of the rebels, the gallantry and obstinacy of the contest and the final result, I say, from conviction, and as public acknowledgment due to Almighty God, in closing this report, "*Non nobis Domine ! non nobis sed nomini tuo da gloriam.*"

W. S. ROSECRANS,
Major-General, Commanding.

Brig. Gen. LORENZO THOMAS,
    Adjutant-General, U. S. Army.

Effective force of infantry and artillery, December 31, 1862.

Command.	Strength.	Killed and wounded.	Percentage.
RIGHT WING.			
FIRST DIVISION.			
Brigadier-General DAVIS.			
1st Brigade, Colonel Post	1,418	161	11.33
2d Brigade, Colonel Carlin	1,781	619	34.75
3d Brigade, Colonel Woodruff	1,445	226	15.64
Total division	4,644	1,006	21.66
SECOND DIVISION.			
Brigadier-General JOHNSON.			
1st Brigade, Colonel Gibson	1,650	472	28.66
2d Brigade, Colonel Dodge	2,100	405	19.28
3d Brigade, Colonel Baldwin	2,500	291	11.64
Total division	6,250	1,168	18.68
THIRD DIVISION.			
Brigadier-General SHERIDAN.			
1st Brigade, Colonel Greusel	1,839	479	26.05
2d Brigade, Colonel Laiboldt	1,680	206	12.25
3d Brigade, Colonel Bradley	1,520	443	29.14
Total division	5,039	1,128	20.72
Total right wing	15,933	3,302	20.72
CENTER.*			
FIRST [THIRD] DIVISION.			
Major-General ROUSSEAU.			
1st Brigade, Colonel Scribner	1,588	208	13.10
2d Brigade, Colonel Beatty	1,534	281	18.33
3d Brigade, Colonel Starkweather	1,548	28	1.80
4th Brigade, Colonel Shepherd	1,566	561	35.82
Total division	6,236	1,078	17.28
SECOND [EIGHTH] DIVISION.			
Brigadier-General NEGLEY.			
1st Brigade, Brigadier-General Spears	812	16	2.00
2d [29th] Brigade, Colonel Stanley	1,822	500	27.44
3d [7th] Brigade, Colonel Miller	1,998	410	20.00
Total division	4,632	926	20.00
Total center corps	10,868	2,004	18.44

* Walker's brigade, First Division not accounted for in original.

Effective force of infantry and artillery, &c.—Continued.

Command.	Strength.	Killed and wounded.	Percentage.
LEFT WING.			
FIRST DIVISION.			
Brigadier-General WOOD.			
1st Brigade, Brigadier-General Hascall	1,701	343	20.17
2d Brigade, Colonel Wagner	1,644	329	20.00
3d Brigade, Colonel Harker	1,747	454	26.00
Total division	5,092	1,126	22.11
SECOND DIVISION.			
Brigadier-General PALMER.			
1st Brigade, Brigadier-General Cruft	1,207	255	21.12
2d Brigade, Colonel Hazen	1,385	336	24.25
3d Brigade, Colonel Grose	1,768	516	29.18
Total division	4,360	1,107	25.40
THIRD DIVISION.			
Brigadier-General VAN CLEVE.			
1st Brigade, Col. S. Beatty	1,216	411	33.80
2d Brigade, Colonel Fyffe	798	288	36.09
3d Brigade, Colonel Matthews [Price]	1,822	342	18.75
Total division	3,836	1,041	27.14
Total left wing	13,288	3,274	24.64
PIONEER BRIGADE.			
Captain Morton	1,700	30	1.75
CAVALRY.			
Cavalry	3,200	84	2.60

RECAPITULATION.

Right wing	15,944
Center corps	10,868
Left wing	13,288
Pioneer Brigade	1,700
Total infantry and artillery	41,800
Cavalry division	3,200
Total	45,000
Deducting wagon guard	1,600
Total	43,400

Combined loss, killed and wounded, 8,778, or 20.22 per cent. of the forces engaged.*

—

Names specially mentioned for important services and particular acts, &c., in official reports.

Name and rank.	Regiment or detachment.	Service performed.
R. W. Johnson, brigadier-general. P. H. Sheridan, brigadier-general. Jefferson C. Davis, brigadier-general	Commanding divisions in the right wing.	For gallant conduct during the battle, and for prompt support and conscientious attention to duty during their service with the right wing.

* But see revised statement, p. 207.

Names specially mentioned for important services, &c.—Continued.

Name and rank.	Regiment or detachment.	Service performed.
D. S. Stanley, brigadier-general.	Chief of cavalry	Commanded advance of right wing during its advance from Nolensville; is specially mentioned for energy and skill.
Hascall, brigadier-general.	Commanding 1st Brigade.	Deserves commendation and gratitude of his country.
Cruft, brigadier-general	1st Brigade	For holding an important position, and for extricating his command from the mass of confusion around him.
T. J. Wood, brigadier-general. H. P. Van Cleve, brigadier-general. John M. Palmer, brigadier-general.		Specially mentioned for distinguished gallantry and the skill with which they handled their commands. Generals Van Cleve and Wood were wounded, but remained with their commands until after the battle was over.
J. S. Negley, brigadier-general.		Specially mentioned for the courage and skill displayed in handling his command.
C. McDermont, surgeon	Medical director, staff of Major-General McCook.	For gallant conduct in the field, and great care and consideration for the wounded.
G. D. Beebe, surgeon	Medical director, staff of Major-General Thomas.	For great zeal, energy, and efficiency.
A. J. Phelps, surgeon	Medical director, on staff of Major-General Crittenden.	For prompt attention to the wounded; great energy and efficiency in discharge of his duties.
Minty, colonel, commanding First Brigade.	4th Michigan Cavalry	Deserves credit for the management of his command on the march and in several engagements.
Murray, colonel	3d Kentucky Cavalry	Rendered important and distinguished service, gallantly charging and dispersing the enemy's cavalry in their attack on our train on Wednesday, 31st.
Zahm, colonel	3d Ohio Cavalry	Contributed greatly, by his personal example, to the restoration of order and confidence in that portion of the Second Brigade stampeded by the enemy's attack on Wednesday.
W. H. Gibson, colonel	49th Ohio Volunteers; commanded Willich's brigade.	Has been several times before recommended for promotion, and is again recommended by General Johnson, for meritorious conduct. Is also specially mentioned by Major-Generals McCook and Crittenden.
Charles Anderson, colonel	93d Ohio Volunteers	Honorable mention for gallant conduct, by Major-General Rousseau.
Wallace, colonel. Dodge, colonel. Baldwin, colonel.	15th Ohio Volunteers. 30th Indiana Volunteers. 6th Indiana Volunteers.	Recommended for promotion, for coolness and courage on the field of battle.
G. D. Wagner, colonel	15th Indiana, commanding brigade.	Has commanded a brigade for a year; is recommended for promotion for brave and skillful conduct during the late battles.
C. G. Harker, colonel	65th Ohio Volunteers	Has commanded a brigade for a year; is recommended for promotion, for brave and skillful conduct. He is also specially mentioned by Major-General McCook, for valuable services with the right wing.
John W. Blake, colonel	40th Indiana Volunteers	Recommended to be dishonorably discharged for being so drunk as to be unfit for duty. Before going into action on the 31st, was ordered in arrest by his immediate commander, Colonel Wagner, and was next heard from in Nashville, claiming to be wounded and a paroled prisoner.
Hazen, colonel	41st Ohio Volunteers	Commanded a brigade; is specially mentioned for courage and skill in handling his troops, and for maintaining an important position.
W. Grose, colonel	36th Indiana Volunteers	Commanded brigade; is recommended for coolness and bravery in fighting his troops against a superior force.
Sedgewick, colonel. Enyart, colonel. Ross, colonel. Osborn, colonel.	2d Kentucky Volunteer Infantry. 1st Kentucky Volunteer Infantry. 90th Ohio Volunteer Infantry. 31st Indiana Volunteer Infantry.	Displayed marked gallantry on the field, and handled their respective commands with skill and judgment.
Samuel Beatty, colonel	19th Ohio Volunteer Infantry.	Commanding brigade; for coolness, intrepidity, and skill.

Names specially mentioned for important services, &c.—Continued.

Name and rank.	Regiment or detachment.	Service performed.
Fyffe, colonel..............	59th Ohio Volunteer Infantry.	Is recommended for coolness, intrepidity, and skill. Is also specially mentioned by Major-General McCook, for valuable services with the right wing.
Grider, colonel...............	9th Kentucky Volunteer Infantry.	Commanded brigade, and is specially mentioned for gallantry and coolness under trying circumstances.
C. O. Loomis, colonel........	1st Michigan Artillery......	Rendered most important services throughout the battle.
John C. Starkweather, colonel	1st Wisconsin Volunteer Infantry.	Commanding brigade; especially mentioned for coolness, skill, and courage.
William Sirwell, colonel	78th Pennsylvania Volunteer Infantry.	
Granville Moody, colonel....	74th Ohio Volunteer Infantry.	For the skill and ability with which they handled their respective commands.
Hull, colonel.............	37th Indiana Volunteer Infantry.	
Greusel, colonel	36th Illinois Volunteers ..	Are specially commended for skill and courage.
Bradley, colonel ....,........	51st Illinois Volunteers ..	
Sherman, colonel	88th Illinois Volunteers	Honorably mentioned for distinguished service.
Hotchkiss, lieutenant-colonel.	89th Illinois Volunteer Infantry.	Recommended for promotion for meritorious conduct.
Jones, lieutenant-colonel	39th Indiana Volunteer Infantry.	
W. W. Berry, lieutenant-colonel.	Commanding Louisville Legion.	Specially mentioned for gallant and meritorious conduct. It is also specially mentioned by Major-General Rousseau, for retreating in good order before an overwhelming force, and drawing off by hand a section of artillery he had been ordered to support.
Shepherd, lieutenant-colonel.	18th U. S. Infantry, commanding regular brigade.	Specially mentioned by Maj. Gen. L. H. Rousseau.
Neibling, lieutenant-colonel..	Commanding 21st Ohio Volunteer Infantry.	For skill and ability during the battles.
Laiboldt, lieutenant-colonel..	2d Missouri Volunteer Infantry.	Specially commended for skill and courage.
McCreery, lieutenant-colonel.	21st Michigan Volunteer Infantry.	Honorably mentioned for distinguished services.
Klein, major..................	3d Indiana Cavalry.........	On the 27th engaged the enemy on the Nolensville pike and put them to flight.
Otis, captain..................	Commanding 4th U. S. Cavalry.	With his regiment rendered important and distinguished service, gallantly charging and dispersing the enemy's cavalry, in their attack upon our train on Wednesday, the 31st.
Lyne Starling, major	Assistant adjutant-general.	Specially mentioned by Major-General Crittenden, for gallantry in the battle, general efficiency, and eighteen months' faithful service.
John H. King, major.........	15th U. S. Infantry	Commanding their respective regiments; are specially mentioned for distinguished gallantry and ability. Major Carpenter was killed, and Majors King and Slemmer wounded.
Carpenter, major..............	19th U. S. Infantry	
Slemmer, major................	16th U. S. Infantry	
Townsend, major..............	18th U. S. Infantry	
Caldwell, major...............	18th U. S. Infantry	
Miller, major	36th Illinois Volunteers. ..	Honorably mentioned.
Chandler, major	88th Illinois Volunteers. ..	
Hibbard, major...............	24th Wisconsin Vols......	
John Mendenhall, captain, chief of artillery, and topographical engineer, staff of Major-General Crittenden.	4th U. S. Artillery........	Recommended for promotion, for general efficiency and personal bravery and good conduct in battle.
Chambers, captain............	51st Indiana Volunteer Infantry.	These brave officers, with 120 men, drove a large force of the enemy from a covered position and unmasked his battery.
Gladwyn, captain.............	73d Indiana Volunteer Infantry.	
Standart, captain.............	Company B, 1st Ohio Artillery.	For the gallant manner in which he handled his guns and brought them off the field.
Edgarton, captain.............	Company E, 1st Ohio Artillery.	Was guilty of a grave error in taking even a part of his battery horses to water at an unseasonable hour, and thereby losing his guns.
G. P. Thruston, captain	1st Ohio Volunteer Infantry.	Is specially mentioned by Major-General McCook and others for particular acts of gallantry, skill, and good conduct. Mentioned by Generals Sheridan, Johnson, Davis, and by Colonel Carlin, commanding brigade.

Names specially mentioned for important services, &c.—Continued.

Name and rank.	Regiment or detachment.	Service performed.
Hale, captain	75th Illinois Volunteers... }	Specially mentioned for gallant conduct in skirmishing.
Litson, captain	22d Indiana Volunteers... }	
Crofton, captain	16th U. S. Infantry	These three infantry captains commanded their respective battalions after their majors had been disabled, and behaved with great gallantry and skill, although opposed by an overwhelming number.
Fulmer, captain	15th U. S. Infantry	
Mulligan, captain	19th U. S. Infantry	
Guenther, captain	Company H, 5th Artillery	Deserves great credit and special mention.
Hescock, captain	1st Missouri Battery	Specially mentioned for bravery and skill in the battles and for general efficiency.
Bridges, captain	19th Illinois Volunteers	Continued in command of his regiment after receiving a painful wound.
Belding, lieutenant	Commanding Company A, 1st Ohio Artillery.	Recommended for promotion for saving three guns of his battery. (Goodspeed's.)
Richard Jervis, lieutenant	8th Indiana Battery	Behaved in a cowardly manner, by retiring his section at a critical moment without notifying his company commander. He is recommended for dismissal.
Lamberson, lieutenant	19th Illinois Volunteers... }	Inspectors of Pioneer Brigade. Are specially mentioned in two reports for gallant conduct and energy.
Wyman Murphy, lieutenant	21st Wisconsin Volunteers }	
W. S. Fish, assistant surgeon.	3d Indiana Cavalry	Fled during the battle to Nashville, and is recommended by Major-General McCook for dismissal. This man passed himself off as an assistant surgeon; proved to be a private. Case being attended to.

Enlisted men recommended for gallant conduct during the battle of Stone's River, Tenn.

Quartermaster-Sergeant Colburn, Thirty-third Ohio Volunteers.
First Sergeant German, Eighth Wisconsin Battery.
Sergeant Ferguson, Company G, Fifty-ninth Illinois Volunteer Infantry.
Sergeant Holden, Company G, Sixty-fourth Ohio Volunteer Infantry.
Sergeant McKay, Company E, Forty-first Ohio Volunteer Infantry.
Sergeant McMahon, Company H, Forty-first Ohio Volunteer Infantry.
Sergt. R. B. Rhodes, First Ohio Volunteer Cavalry.
Sergt. Jason Hurd, Nineteenth Ohio Volunteer Infantry.
Sergt. H. A. Mills, Seventy-eighth Pennsylvania Volunteer Infantry.
Sergt. A. R. Weaver, Seventy-eighth Pennsylvania Volunteer Infantry.
Sergt. F. Mechling, Seventy-eighth Pennsylvania Volunteer Infantry.
Sergt. P. A. Weaver, Seventy-fourth Ohio Volunteer Infantry.
Corpl. James T. Slater, Second Indiana Volunteer Cavalry.
Corpl. J. P. Patterson, Company G, Forty-first Ohio Volunteer Infantry.
Corpl. W. Hughes, Seventy-eighth Pennsylvania Volunteer Infantry.
Private R. J. Pindle, Company L, wagoner. (Especially recommended by Colonel Murray, colonel of Third Kentucky Cavalry.)
Private A. F. Freeman, orderly, with Brigadier-General Davis.
Private Abijah Lee, orderly, with Brigadier-General Davis.
Private James Gray, Company E, Thirty-ninth Indiana Volunteer Infantry.
Private William Hayman, Second Indiana Volunteer Cavalry.
Private William Brown, Fifty-ninth Ohio Volunteer Infantry.
Private Nelson Shields, Thirteenth Ohio Volunteer Infantry.
Private S. T. Mitchell, Company B, Thirty-third Ohio Volunteer Infantry.

ADDENDA.

Special mention of gallantry, &c.

Lieutenant-Colonel Housum, Seventy-seventh Pennsylvania Volunteer Infantry.
Captain Brigham, Sixty-ninth Ohio Volunteer Infantry.
Captain Cox, Tenth Indiana Battery.
Capt. James P. Mead, Thirty-eighth Illinois Volunteer Infantry.
Lieut. John L. Dillon, Thirty-eighth Illinois Volunteer Infantry.
Lieutenant Jones, Post's brigade.

1st. Seventy-eighth Pennsylvania Regiment captured a rebel flag from the Twenty sixth Regiment Tennessee, assisted by other regiments of General Negley's division.

2d. Lieutenant Guenther's battery and the Second Ohio Volunteers captured the flag of the Thirtieth Arkansas Volunteers.

3d. Fifteenth Indiana Volunteers, Lieutenant-Colonel Wood commanding, charged and captured 173 prisoners from Twentieth Louisiana Regiment.

4th. Thirteenth Michigan Volunteers gallantly recaptured two guns belonging to Captain Bradley's battery.

5th. Carlin's brigade lost half its field officers in killed and wounded.

6th. Fifth Kentucky Volunteers dragged from the field by hand a section of artillery, through deep mud and under heavy fire.

7th. Four color-bearers of the Twenty-first Illinois were shot down, yet the colors were borne safely through the fight.

—

WASHINGTON, D. C., *February* 27, 1863.

Colonel KELTON,
　　Staff of the General-in-Chief, Washington:

COLONEL : I have the honor to forward to you the inclosed letter of Maj. Gen. W. S. Rosecrans, commanding department. The general desired me to make such verbal explanations as the General-in-Chief might require.

I also inclose a statement of our available force in and about Murfreesborough, which differs considerably from the " paper" army.

I shall remain in the city no longer than to-morrow, as my health will not permit me to put further off that care and treatment which I can only obtain at home.

I have the honor to be, very respectfully, your obedient servant,
　　　　　　　　J. C. PETERSON,
　　*Captain Fifteenth Infantry, and Acting Assistant
　　Inspector-General, Department of the Cumberland.*

[Inclosures.]

HEADQUARTERS DEPARTMENT OF THE CUMBERLAND,
　　　　Murfreesborough, Tenn., February 20, 1863.

Maj. Gen. H. W. HALLECK,
　　Commander-in-Chief, Washington, D. C.:

GENERAL: Captain Peterson, acting assistant inspector-general, being obliged to change climate by medical direction, I avail myself of his zeal and intelligence to send you some details of this army, showing the percentage of absentees and the wear and tear of an army in battle :

1st. I find from careful examination that the average percentage of the present and absent, now present, is :

	Per cent
For the Fourteenth Army Corps	56.01
For the Twentieth Army Corps	50.16
For the Twenty-first Army Corps	50.44

Presuming that each of these corps has fought but one great battle, in which they lost as follows, viz :

	Per cent
Fourteenth Army Corps	18.44
Twentieth Army Corps	20.50
Twenty-first Army Corps	24.64
Average loss for the entire command	20.03

We have before the battle :

	Per cent.
Fourteenth Army Corps	63.42
Twentieth Army Corps	64.60
Twenty-first Army Corps	66.93

Hence, before the battle we have to pay 100 men for the above per cent., and we now have the preceding percentage for each hundred on the pay-roll. Although these are better results than I have expected, they are much worse than they ought to be. I am now endeavoring to bring the absentees to some rule, and reduce their numbers. The inspection system detects the illegal absentees, but it requires in addition the paymasters with the corps to know who ought not to be paid.

Captain Peterson comes to show what means we use to detect absentees, and what even then are our results.

He is also charged to carry on a form of return, which, if adopted in the Adjutant-General's office and throughout the army, will force the various commanders to give such data in their returns as will afford means of knowing the true condition and strength of our forces, which, with the present forms in use, is not the case.

Very respectfully, your obedient servant,

W. S. ROSECRANS,
Major-General, Commanding Department.

STATEMENT OF FORCE.

Fourteenth Army Corps	27,725
Twentieth Army Corps	13,031
Twenty-first Army Corps	13,061
Cavalry not included	4,295
Total	58,112

Detached troops:		
Nashville	7,495	
Gallatin	3,550	
Bowling Green	1,840	
Clarksville	1,674	
Total		14,559

Grand total present	72,671
Strength present and absent February 14, 1863	133,305
Discount	60,634
Detached troops	14,559
Number that cannot be led against the enemy	75,193

—

MURFREESBOROUGH, TENN.,
March 1, 1863—12.23 p. m.

Hon. E. M. STANTON,
Secretary of War:

I see that by your permission the reports of the corps commanders of the battle of Stone's River are published. They are but a partial view of the operations, and an omission in General McCook's report to state the meeting of corps commanders at my headquarters, and his final instructions on Tuesday night, coupled with an erroneous statement in General Johnson's report, are calculated to mislead.* Mine should also be published, omitting such statistics as ought not to be made public.

W. S. ROSECRANS.

---

* See correspondence between Rosecrans and McCook and letters from Stanley and Thomas in March, 1863, Part II, pp. 381–383.

MURFREESBOROUGH, TENN.,
March 23, 1863—10.38 p. m.

Maj. Gen. H. W. HALLECK,
　　General-in-Chief:

Recent reports of the senior surgeon of General Bragg's army, left here in care of the wounded rebels, prepared to be sent to his superior, of the deaths in hospitals, carefully analyzed as to confirm the analytical report of our provost-marshal as to the number of regiments, show that Breckinridge had thirty-six infantry and five cavalry regiments, four batteries, and some minor organizations in his division.

W. S. ROSECRANS,
Major-General.

No. 3.

*Return of casualties in the Union forces in the Stone's River (Tennessee) campaign, December 26, 1862–January 5, 1863, inclusive.**

[Compiled from nominal list of casualties, returns, &c.]

Command.	Killed.		Wounded.		Captured or missing.		Aggregate.
	Officers.	Enlisted men.	Officers.	Enlisted men.	Officers.	Enlisted men.	
FOURTEENTH ARMY CORPS.							
Maj. Gen. WILLIAM S. ROSECRANS.							
Staff and escort	1	3	2	3	......	......	9
RIGHT WING.							
Maj. Gen. A. McD. McCOOK.							
FIRST DIVISION.							
Brig. Gen. JEFFERSON C. DAVIS.							
Escort.							
36th Illinois Cavalry, Company B	......	......	......	2	......	......	2
2d Kentucky Cavalry, Company G	1	......	......	2	......	6	9
Total escort	1	......	......	4	......	6	11
First Brigade.							
Col. P. SIDNEY POST.							
59th Illinois	......	7	......	43	......	30	80
74th Illinois	......	8	1	34	......	42	85
75th Illinois	......	2	2	19	......	59	82
22d Indiana	......	7	5	34	......	18	64
Wisconsin Light Artillery, 5th Battery	......	1	1	5	......	6	13
Total First Brigade	......	25	9	135	......	155	324

* Includes losses at Nolensville and Knob Gap, December 26; La Vergne and Franklin, December 26 and 27; Triune, December 27; Stewart's Creek, December 27; Stone's River or Murfreesborough, December 29–January 4 ; Stewart's Creek and La Vergne, January 1; Insane Asylum or Cox's Hill, January 3; Shelbyville and Manchester roads, January 5.

Return of casualties in the Union forces, &c.—Continued.

Command.	Killed.		Wounded.		Captured or missing.		Aggregate.
	Officers.	Enlisted men.	Officers.	Enlisted men.	Officers.	Enlisted men.	
Second Brigade.							
Col. WILLIAM P. CARLIN.							
21st Illinois	2	55	7	180	......	59	303
38th Illinois	2	32	5	104	......	34	177
101st Ohio	1	19	5	121	......	66	212
15th Wisconsin	2	13	5	65	1	33	119
Minnesota Light Artillery, 2d Battery	......	3	1	5	......	1	10
Total Second Brigade	7	122	23	475	1	193	821
Third Brigade.							
Col. WILLIAM E. WOODRUFF.							
Staff	......	......	1	......	......	......	1
25th Illinois	1	15	3	72	......	5	96
35th Illinois	......	10	2	49	......	25	86
81st Indiana	1	4	2	46	1	15	69
Wisconsin Light Artillery, 8th Battery	1	......	......	4	......	1	6
Total Third Brigade	3	29	8	171	1	46	258
Total First Division	11	176	40	785	2	400	1,414
SECOND DIVISION.							
Brig. Gen. RICHARD W. JOHNSON.							
First Brigade.							
(1.) Brig. Gen. AUGUST WILLICH.*							
(2.) Col. WILLIAM WALLACE.							
(3.) Col. WILLIAM H. GIBSON.							
Staff	......	......	......	......	1	......	1
80th Illinois	1	9	1	45	......	94	150
32d Indiana	......	12	......	40	......	115	167
39th Indiana	......	30	3	116	2	229	380
15th Ohio	......	17	2	68	1	127	215
49th Ohio	2	18	6	88	......	108	222
1st Ohio Light Artillery, Battery A	......	1	......	4	......	24	29
Total First Brigade	3	87	12	361	4	697	1,164
Second Brigade.							
(1.) Brig. Gen. EDWARD N. KIRK.†							
(2.) Col. JOSEPH B. DODGE.							
Staff	......	......	1	......	......	......	1
34th Illinois	2	19	2	98	2	72	195
79th Illinois	1	23	3	68	3	121	219
29th Indiana	1	14	2	66	1	51	135
30th Indiana	1	30	2	108	2	70	213
77th Pennsylvania	1	4	1	28	2	28	64
1st Ohio Light Artillery, Battery E	......	3	......	5	2	22	32
Total Second Brigade	6	93	11	373	12	364	859
Third Brigade.							
Col. PHILEMON P. BALDWIN.							
6th Indiana	......	17	......	50	1	36	104
5th Kentucky	1	18	7	73	......	26	125
1st Ohio	......	8	1	46	......	81	136

* Wounded and captured December 31.
† Wounded December 31.

Return of casualties in the Union forces, &c.—Continued.

Command.	Killed.		Wounded.		Captured or missing.		Aggregate.
	Officers.	Enlisted men.	Officers.	Enlisted men.	Officers.	Enlisted men.	
Third Brigade—Continued.							
93d Ohio		12	3	45		64	124
Indiana Light Artillery, 5th Battery		3	1	18		1	23
Total Third Brigade	1	58	12	232	1	208	512
Cavalry.							
3d Indiana, Companies G, H, I, and K		4		6		15	25
Total Second Division	10	242	35	972	17	1,284	2,560
THIRD DIVISION.							
Brig. Gen. PHILIP H. SHERIDAN.							
First Brigade.							
(1.) Brig. Gen. JOSHUA W. SILL.*							
(2.) Col. NICHOLAS GREUSEL.							
Staff	1		1				2
36th Illinois	1	45	7	144	2	13	212
88th Illinois	1	13	2	48		48	112
21st Michigan		13	7	82		36	143
24th Wisconsin		19	2	55		98	174
Indiana Light Artillery, 4th Battery		6		17		3	26
Total First Brigade	3	101	19	346	2	198	669
Second Brigade.							
(1.) Col. FREDERICK SCHAEFER.*							
(2.) Lieut. Col. BERNARD LAIBOLDT.							
Staff	1						1
44th Illinois	1	28	5	104		17	155
73d Illinois	1	15	3	61	1	7	88
2d Missouri		7		40	1	14	62
15th Missouri	3	9	4	51		5	72
1st Missouri Light Artillery, Battery G	1	5		13		1	20
Total Second Brigade	7	64	12	269	2	44	398
Third Brigade.							
(1.) Col. GEORGE W. ROBERTS.*							
(2.) Col. LUTHER P. BRADLEY.							
Staff	1						1
22d Illinois		21	7	109	2	54	193
27th Illinois	1	8	2	67		25	103
42d Illinois	1	18		96	1	45	161
51st Illinois	1	6	4	37		9	57
1st Illinois Light Artillery, Battery C		5	2	19		25	51
Total Third Brigade	4	58	15	328	3	158	566
Total Third Division	14	223	46	943	7	400	1,633
Total Right Wing	35	641	121	2,700	26	2,084	5,607
CENTER.							
Maj. Gen. GEORGE H. THOMAS.							
Staff and escort		1	1				2

* Killed December 31.

Return of casualties in the Union forces, &c.—Continued.

Command.	Killed.		Wounded.		Captured or missing.		Aggregate.
	Officers.	Enlisted men.	Officers.	Enlisted men.	Officers.	Enlisted men.	
FIRST DIVISION.							
Maj. Gen. LOVELL H. ROUSSEAU.							
Staff and escort			1	1			2
First Brigade.							
Col. BENJAMIN F. SCRIBNER.							
Staff			1		1		2
38th Indiana	1	13	3	91		4	112
2d Ohio	2	9	3	31		7	52
33d Ohio		2		21		11	34
94th Ohio		3	2	21		28	54
10th Wisconsin		3	1	15		6	25
Total First Brigade	3	30	10	179	1	56	279
Second Brigade.							
Col. JOHN BEATTY.							
42d Indiana		17	6	75	2	32	132
88th Indiana		8	4	47		19	78
15th Kentucky	2	8	1	31	1	17	60
3d Ohio		17	1	65		23	106
1st Michigan Light Artillery, Battery A		1		10		2	13
Total Second Brigade	2	51	12	228	3	93	389
Third Brigade.							
Col. JOHN C. STARKWEATHER.							
24th Illinois				4		52	56
79th Pennsylvania		1		9		6	16
1st Wisconsin			1	11		16	28
21st Wisconsin		1	1	4		37	43
Kentucky Light Artillery, Battery A				1		2	3
Total Third Brigade		2	2	29		113	146
Fourth Brigade.							
Lieut. Col. OLIVER L. SHEPHERD.							
15th United States, 1st Battalion	1	10	4	74		17	106
16th United States, 1st Battalion, and Company B, 2d Battalion.		16	7	126		16	165
18th United States, 1st Battalion, and Companies A and D, 3d Battalion.	1	28	6	115		2	152
18th United States, 2d Battalion, and Companies B, C, E, and F, 3d Battalion.	1	30	5	98		5	139
19th United States, 1st Battalion	1	6		57		10	74
5th United States Artillery, Battery H				5			5
Total Fourth Brigade	4	90	22	475		50	641
Cavalry.							
2d Kentucky (six companies)				3			3
Total First Division	9	173	47	915	4	312	1,460
SECOND DIVISION.							
Brig. Gen. JAMES S. NEGLEY.							
First Brigade.							
Brig. Gen. JAMES G. SPEARS.							
1st Tennessee		3		16			19
2d Tennessee			1	6			7

Return of casualties in the Union forces, &c.—Continued.

Command.	Killed.		Wounded.		Captured or missing.		Aggregate.
	Officers.	Enlisted men.	Officers.	Enlisted men.	Officers.	Enlisted men.	
First Brigade—Continued.							
6th Tennessee*.........................							
85th Illinois *.........................							
14th Michigan.........................		2		5			7
Wisconsin Light Artillery, 10th Battery*.........							
Total First Brigade.............		5	1	27			33
Second Brigade.							
Col. TIMOTHY R. STANLEY.							
19th Illinois.........................	1	13	8	75		11	108
11th Michigan.........................	2	28	6	78		25	139
18th Ohio.........................	1	25	8	107		26	167
69th Ohio.........................	1	4	6	47		38	96
1st Ohio Light Artillery, Battery M.........		1	1			1	3
Total Second Brigade.............	5	71	29	307		101	513
Third Brigade.							
Col. JOHN F. MILLER.							
Staff and escort.........			1	3			4
37th Indiana.........................	2	25	5	110		8	150
21st Ohio.........................		24	5	104		26	159
74th Ohio.........................		8	6	92		19	125
78th Pennsylvania.........................	1	15	3	130		39	188
Kentucky Light Artillery, Battery B.........		1	1	2		2	6
1st Ohio Light Artillery, Battery G.........		4		9		3	16
Total Third Brigade.............	3	77	21	450		97	648
Total Second Division.............	8	153	51	784		198	1,194
THIRD DIVISION.							
First Brigade.							
Col. MOSES B. WALKER.							
82d Indiana.........................				5			5
17th Ohio.........................			1	4			5
31st Ohio.........................				6			6
38th Ohio.........................			1	5			6
1st Michigan Light Artillery, Battery D*.........							
Total First Brigade.............			2	20			22
Total Third Division.............			2	20			22
Total Center.............	17	327	101	1,719	4	510	2,678

LEFT WING.

Maj. Gen. THOMAS L. CRITTENDEN.

Staff.........			1				1
FIRST DIVISION.							
(1.) Brig. Gen. THOMAS J. WOOD.†							
(2.) Brig. Gen. MILO S. HASCALL.							
Staff.........			1				1

* No loss reported.   † Wounded December 31.

Return of casualties in the Union forces, &c.—Continued.

Command.	Killed. Officers.	Killed. Enlisted men.	Wounded. Officers.	Wounded. Enlisted men.	Captured or missing. Officers.	Captured or missing. Enlisted men.	Aggregate
First Brigade.							
(1.) Brig. Gen. MILO S. HASCALL.							
(2.) Col. GEORGE P. BUELL.							
100th Illinois	1	6	6	23			46
58th Indiana	1	16	4	93			114
3d Kentucky	2	12	8	77		34	133
26th Ohio	1	11	2	85			99
Indiana Light Artillery, 8th Battery				8			8
Total First Brigade	5	45	20	296		34	400
Second Brigade.							
Col. GEORGE D. WAGNER.							
15th Indiana	2	36	7	136		7	188
40th Indiana		4	5	63		13	85
57th Indiana		11	6	55		6	78
97th Ohio		3		15		6	24
Indiana Light Artillery, 10th Battery		1		4			5
Total Second Brigade	2	55	18	273		32	380
Third Brigade.							
Col. CHARLES G. HARKER.							
51st Indiana		7	2	32		9	50
73d Indiana	2	22	3	48		36	111
13th Michigan		17	2	70			89
64th Ohio	1	23	3	61		17	105
65th Ohio	2	33	8	92		38	173
Ohio Light Artillery, 6th Battery		1	1	8		1	11
Total Third Brigade	5	103	19	311		101	539
Total First Division	12	203	58	880		167	1,320
SECOND DIVISION.							
Brig. Gen. JOHN M. PALMER.							
Staff			1				1
First Brigade.							
Brig. Gen. CHARLES CRUFT.							
31st Indiana		5	1	44	3	34	87
1st Kentucky		13	1	51	1	30	96
2d Kentucky		9	2	56		10	77
90th Ohio		17	5	67	2	46	137
Total First Brigade		44	9	218	6	120	397
Second Brigade.							
Col. WILLIAM B. HAZEN.							
Staff and escort			4	1			5
110th Illinois	1	6	3	46		2	58
9th Indiana	1	10	5	82		11	109
6th Kentucky	2	11	5	85		10	113
41st Ohio	1	13	2	102		6	124
Total Second Brigade	5	40	19	316		29	409

Return of casualties in the Union forces, &c.—Continued.

Command.	Killed.		Wounded.		Captured or missing.		Aggregate.
	Officers.	Enlisted men.	Officers.	Enlisted men.	Officers.	Enlisted men.	
Third Brigade.							
Col. WILLIAM GROSE.							
84th Illinois	2	33	5	119	......	8	167
36th Indiana	2	23	6	85	......	18	134
23d Kentucky	......	8	3	50	......	22	83
6th Ohio	2	23	4	134	......	14	177
24th Ohio	4	10	4	68	......	12	98
Total Third Brigade	10	97	22	456	......	74	659
Artillery.							
1st Ohio Light Artillery, Battery B	......	5	......	12	......	3	20
1st Ohio Light Artillery, Battery F	......	2	1	13	......	2	18
4th U. S. Artillery, Batteries H and M	......	2	......	14	......	6	22
Total artillery	......	9	1	39	......	11	60
Total Second Division	15	190	52	1,029	6	234	1,526
THIRD DIVISION.							
(1.) Brig. Gen. HORATIO P. VAN CLEVE.* (2.) Col. SAMUEL BEATTY.							
Staff	......	......	1	......	......	......	1
First Brigade.							
(1.) Col. SAMUEL BEATTY. (2.) Col. BENJAMIN C. GRIDER.							
79th Indiana	1	10	6	68	......	36	121
9th Kentucky	4	18	7	80	......	3	112
11th Kentucky	......	7	4	81	......	10	102
19th Ohio	3	24	3	122	......	34	186
Total First Brigade	8	59	20	351	......	83	521
Second Brigade.							
Col. JAMES P. FYFFE.							
Staff	......	......	1	......	......	......	1
44th Indiana	......	10	2	54	......	25	91
86th Indiana	1	33	5	55	2	99	195
13th Ohio	2	29	6	79	......	69	185
59th Ohio	......	3	2	35	2	43	85
Total Second Brigade	3	75	16	223	4	236	557
Third Brigade.							
Col. SAMUEL W. PRICE.							
35th Indiana	......	22	5	77	......	33	137
8th Kentucky	2	7	6	69	......	27	111
21st Kentucky	2	10	2	34	......	9	57
51st Ohio	......	24	4	118	......	44	190
99th Ohio	......	12	5	41	1	29	88
Total Third Brigade	4	75	22	339	1	142	583

* Wounded December 31.

Return of casualties in the Union forces, &c.—Continued.

Command.	Killed.		Wounded.		Captured or missing.		
	Officers.	Enlisted men.	Officers.	Enlisted men.	Officers.	Enlisted men.	Aggregate.
Artillery.							
Capt. GEORGE R. SWALLOW.							
Indiana Light Artillery, 7th Battery		4	1	7			12
Pennsylvania Light Artillery, Battery B (Twenty-sixth)		2		7			9
Wisconsin Light Artillery, 3d Battery				4			4
Total artillery		6	1	18			25
Total Third Division	15	215	60	931	5	461	1,687
Total Left Wing	42	608	171	2,840	11	862	4,534
CAVALRY.							
Brig. Gen. DAVID S. STANLEY.							
CAVALRY DIVISION.							
Col. JOHN KENNETT.							
First Brigade.							
Col. ROBERT H. G. MINTY.							
4d Indiana, Company M		1			1	13	15
3d Kentucky		1	1	7		1	10
4th Michigan		1	1	6		12	20
7th Pennsylvania		2		9		50	61
Total First Brigade		5	2	22	1	76	106
Second Brigade.							
Col. LEWIS ZAHM.							
1st Ohio	3	2	1	10	1	14	31
3d Ohio		6		15		13	34
4th Ohio		7		18		31	56
Total Second Brigade	3	15	1	43	1	58	121
Artillery.							
1st Ohio Light Artillery, Battery D (section)		1					1
Total Cavalry Division	3	21	3	65	2	134	228
*Reserve Cavalry.**							
15th Pennsylvania	1	8	1	8		53	71
1st Middle (5th) Tennessee			1	5	1	8	15
2d Tennessee	1	2		10		5	18
Total Reserve Cavalry	2	10	2	23	1	66	104
Unattached.							
4th United States		3	1	9		12	25
Total Cavalry	5	34	6	97	3	212	357
PIONEER BRIGADE.							
Capt. JAMES ST. C. MORTON.							
1st Battalion		4	3	5			12
2d Battalion		4		5			9

* Under the immediate command of General Stanley, chief of cavalry.

Return of casualties in the Union forces, &c.—Continued.

Command.	Killed.		Wounded.		Captured or missing.		Aggregate.
	Officers.	Enlisted men.	Officers.	Enlisted men.	Officers.	Enlisted men.	
PIONEER BRIGADE—Continued.							
3d Battalion		4		10			14
Illinois Light Artillery, Stokes' battery		3	1	9			13
Total Pioneer Brigade		15	4	29			48
1st Michigan Engineers and Mechanics		2		9		5	16
Total Engineers and Mechanics		2		9		5	16

RECAPITULATION.

Command	Officers	Enlisted men	Officers	Enlisted men	Officers	Enlisted men	Aggregate
General headquarters	1	3	2	3			9
Right Wing	35	641	121	2,700	26	2,084	5,607
Left Wing	42	608	171	2,840	11	862	4,534
Center	17	327	101	1,719	4	510	2,678
Cavalry	5	34	6	97	3	212	357
Pioneer Brigade		15	4	29			48
Engineers and Mechanics		2		9		5	16
Grand total	100	1,630	405	7,397	44	3,673	13,249

OFFICERS KILLED.

Brig. Gen. Joshua W. Sill.
Lieut. Col. Julius P. Garesché, assistant adjutant-general.

ILLINOIS.

Capt. Knowlton H. Chandler, 19th Infantry.
Lieut. Joseph C. Alvord, 21st Infantry.
Lieut. Emanuel M. Weigle, 21st Infantry.
Col. Thomas D. Williams, 25th Infantry.
Col. Fazilo A. Harrington, 27th Infantry.
Capt. Mabry G. Greenwood, 34th Infantry.
Lieut. John M. Smith, 34th Infantry.
Lieut. Soren L. Olson, 36th Infantry.
Capt. James P. Mead, 38th Infantry.
Lieut. John L. Dillon, 38th Infantry.
Col. George W. Roberts (commanding brigade), 42d Infantry.
Lieut. Julius Lettman, 42d Infantry.

Capt. Andrew J. Hosmer, 44th Infantry.
Lieut. John S. Keith, 51st Infantry.
Capt. Edwin Alsop, 73d Infantry.
Lieut. Col. Sheridan P. Read, 79th Infantry.
Lieut. Luther T. Ball, 84th Infantry.
Lieut. Henry E. Abercrombie, 84th Infantry.
Lieut. Thomas F. W. Gullich, 88th Infantry.
Capt. Henry S. Willett, 89th Infantry.
Lieut. Morris Worthingham, 100th Infantry.
Lieut. Jesse G. Payne, 110th Infantry.

INDIANA.

Lieut. Henry Kessler, 9th Infantry.
Capt. Robert J. Templeton, 15th Infantry.
Capt. Joel W. Foster, 15th Infantry.
Capt. Frank Stebbins, 29th Infantry.
Lieut. Edwin B. Stribley, 30th Infantry.
Capt. Abram D. Shultz, 36th Infantry.
Capt. James H. King, 36th Infantry.
Lieut. Isaac N. Abernethy, 37th Infantry.
Lieut. Jesse B. Holman, 37th Infantry.

Capt. James E. Fouts, 38th Infantry.
Lieut. Francis B. Blackford, 58th Infantry.
Capt. Miles H. Tibbits, 73d Infantry.
Capt. Peter Doyle, 73d Infantry.
Lieut. Benjamin T. Poynter, 79th Infantry.
Lieut. William M. Morgan, 81st Infantry.
Lieut. George W. Smith, 86th Infantry.

KENTUCKY.

Capt. Miller R. McCulloch, 2d Cavalry.
Col. Samuel McKee, 3d Infantry.
Lieut. Matthew Cullen, 3d Infantry.
Capt. Alexander B. Ferguson, 5th Infantry.
Lieut. Col. George T. Cotton, 6th Infantry.
Capt. Charles S. Todd, 6th Infantry.
Capt. Robert B. Hickman, 8th Infantry.
Capt. John B. Banton, 8th Infantry.

Capt. William T. Bryan, 9th Infantry.
Capt. Demetrius B. Coyle, 9th Infantry.
Lieut. Algernon S. Leggett, 9th Infantry.
Lieut. Frederick F. Carpenter, 9th Infantry.
Col. James B. Forman, 15th Infantry.
Capt. Aaron S. Bayne, 15th Infantry.
Lieut. Sebastian Stone, 21st Infantry.
Lieut. John H. Bevill, 21st Infantry.

MICHIGAN.

Lieut. Joseph Wilson, 11th Infantry.

Lieut. Thomas Flynn, 11th Infantry.

MISSOURI.

Lieut. R. C. M. Taliaferro, Battery G, 1st Light Artillery.
Col. Frederick Schaefer (commanding brigade), 2d Infantry.

Capt. Melchoir Zimmerman, 15th Infantry.
Lieut. Christian Quintzius, 15th Infantry.
Lieut. Charles Kellner, 15th Infantry.

OHIO.

Col. Minor Milliken, 1st Cavalry.
Maj. David A. B. Moore, 1st Cavalry.
Lieut. Timothy L. Condit, 1st Cavalry.
Col. John Kell, 2d Infantry.
Lieut. Richard S. Chambers, 2d Infantry.
Lieut. Albert G. Williams, 6th Infantry.
Lieut. Charles H. Foster, 6th Infantry.
Col. Joseph G. Hawkins, 13th Infantry.
Lieut. James C. Whitaker, 13th Infantry.
Lieut. William W. Blacker, 18th Infantry.
Capt. Urwin Bean, 19th Infantry.
Lieut. Daniel Donovan, 19th Infantry.
Lieut. Job D. Bell, 19th Infantry.

Col. Frederick C. Jones, 24th Infantry.
Maj. Henry Terry, 24th Infantry.
Capt. Enoch Weller, 24th Infantry.
Lieut. Charles R. Harman, 24th Infantry.
Lieut. David McClelland, 26th Infantry.
Lieut. Calvin C. Hart, 41st Infantry.
Lieut. Col. Levi Drake, 49th Infantry.
Capt. Amos Keller, 49th Infantry.
Capt. Joseph B. Sweet, 64th Infantry.
Capt. Jacob Christophel, 65th Infantry.
Lieut. Dolsen Van Kirk, 65th Infantry.
Capt. Leonard Counseller, 69th Infantry.
Lieut. John B. Biddle 101st Infantry.

PENNSYLVANIA.

Maj. A. G. Rosengarten, 15th Cavalry.
Lieut. Col. Peter B. Housum, 77th Infantry.

Lieut. M. J. Halstead, 78th Infantry.

TENNESSEE.

Capt. James H. Morris, 2d Cavalry.

WISCONSIN.

Capt. Stephen J. Carpenter, 8th Battery.
Lieut. Col. David McKee, 15th Infantry.

Capt. John Ingmundson, 15th Infantry.

REGULARS.

Capt. Jacob B. Bell, 18th Infantry.
Capt. Charles L. Kneass, 18th Infantry.

Lieut. John F. Hitchcock, 18th Infantry.
Maj. Stephen D. Carpenter, 19th Infantry.

OFFICERS MORTALLY WOUNDED.

ILLINOIS.

Col. Joseph R. Scott, 19th Infantry.
Lieut. Wellington Wood, 19th Infantry.
Lieut. John H. Hunter, 19th Infantry.
Lieut. Cyrus M. Galloway, 22d Infantry.
Lieut. Daniel Riley, 34th Infantry.
Lieut. Humphrey M. McConnell, 35th Infantry.

Lieut. Peter N. Scott, 38th Infantry.
Capt. Ernst Moldenhawer, 44th Infantry.
Lieut. Silas L. Parker, 44th Infantry.
Capt. Moses W. Davis, 84th Infantry.
Lieut. Charles F. Mitchell, 100th Infantry.

INDIANA.

Lieut. Frank W. Buckmar, 7th Battery.
Capt. Isaac M. Pettit, 9th Infantry.
Lieut. James W. Pickins, 31st Infantry.
Capt. Frank Baggot, 35th Infantry.
Capt. Henry Prosser, 35th Infantry.
Lieut. William Kilroy, 35th Infantry.

Lieut. Thomas S. W. Hawkins, 38th Infantry.
Lieut. Moses M. Neal, 39th Infantry.
Lieut. Samuel Wilde, 81st Infantry.
Lieut. John G. Goheen, 88th Infantry.

KENTUCKY.

Lieut. Daniel Severance, 3d Infantry.
Lieut. Frank Dissell, 5th Infantry.
Capt. Landon C. Minter, 8th Infantry.

Lieut. Wade B. Cox, 8th Infantry.
Lieut. L. Frank Todd, 15th Infantry.

MICHIGAN.

Capt. Clement C. Webb, 13th Infantry.

Capt. Leonard O. Fitzgerald, 21st Infantry.

MISSOURI.

Lieut. Martin Schroeder, 15th Infantry.

OHIO.

Lieut. Lafayette Van Horn, 2d Infantry.
Capt. Henry McAlpin, 6th Infantry.
Lieut. John Murphy, 13th Infantry.
Lieut. John Fox, 13th Infantry.
Capt. George Stivers, 18th Infantry.
Capt. Philip E. Taylor, 18th Infantry.
Capt. Ashbel Fenton, 18th Infantry.
Lieut. Enoch B. Wiley, 21st Infantry.
Lieut. Lester T. Patchin, 41st Infantry.
Lieut. Aaron H. Keller, 49th Infantry.
Capt. Benjamin F. Heskett, 51st Infantry.

Lieut. William H. Massey, 65th Infantry.
Lieut. Joseph W. Boynton, 69th Infantry.
Capt. David Steel, 94th Infantry.
Capt. William C. Scott, 99th Infantry.
Capt. Oliver P. Capell, 99th Infantry.
Lieut. William S. Kishler, 99th Infantry.
Col. Leander Stem, 101st Infantry.
Lieut. Col. Moses F. Wooster, 101st Infantry,
Lieut. Asa R. Hillyer, 101st Infantry.

PENNSYLVANIA.

Maj. Frank B. Ward, 15th Cavalry.

Capt. William S. Jack, 78th Infantry.

TENNESSEE.

Capt. John L. Sneed, 2d Infantry.

WISCONSIN.

Capt. Oscar F. Pinney, 5th Battery.
Lieut. Christian Nix, 24th Infantry.

Lieut. George Bleyer, 24th Infantry.

REGULARS.

Capt. William W. Wise, 15th Infantry.
Capt. Charles E. Dennison, 18th Infantry.

Lieut. James Simons, 18th Infantry.
Lieut. Joseph McConnell, 18th Infantry.

No. 4.

Report of Surg. Ebenezer Swift, U. S. Army, Medical Director.

HEADQUARTERS DEPARTMENT OF THE CUMBERLAND,
Murfreesborough, Tenn., January 25, 1863.

COLONEL : Herewith I have the honor to transmit a brief report of the transactions of the medical department of the Army of the Cumberland, together with the reports of the medical directors of the right, left, and center:

On the morning of December 26 last, pursuant to orders from the commanding general, the army moved forward from camp, near Nashville, toward Murfreesborough, the right on the Nolensville and the center on the Franklin pikes, while the left advanced direct on the Murfreesborough road.

Soon after Major-General McCook, in command of the right wing, left his camp on Mill Creek, he encountered the cavalry of the enemy and skirmished with them till he reached Nolensville. About a mile in advance of this place the enemy made a determined stand, with a battery in position, but was soon routed, with a loss of one of his guns and several prisoners. We had 3 men killed and 7 wounded in Davis' division. The heavy rain of the morning had subsided, and now the country was enveloped in a fog or mist.

The same day Major-General Thomas, in command of the center, moved across the country from the Franklin to the Nolensville pike; sent aid to General Davis, who, he learned, was engaged, and on the following day marched to Stewartsville, on the Murfreesborough pike. He remained here till the morning of the 29th, when he advanced to the support of the left wing, which had preceded him, and was now near Murfreesborough.

On the 30th, General Negley's division, of this portion of the army, joined with Sheridan, who occupied the left of General McCook's command, which had moved up from Nolensville on the Wilkinson pike and now occupied a position nearly parallel with the enemy, the left resting on the Wilkinson pike and the right extending southwesterly in a line in a direction with the river. In this movement of the right from near Nolensville, General Stanley, in command of a division of cavalry in advance, encountered the enemy in considerable force, and drove him beyond Triune. The cavalry lost 1 killed and 5 wounded, and in another affair the much-lamented Major Rosengarten was killed and Major Ward mortally wounded. Of the Anderson Cavalry, 6 privates were also wounded. These were taken with the command in ambulances, and placed in hospital at the cross-roads.

Major-General Crittenden, in command of the left wing, while advancing along the Murfreesborough pike, met the enemy on the 27th at La Vergne and put him to flight. In this engagement we lost 2 killed and 32 wounded. These latter were left in hospital at La Vergne, in charge of medical officers, and were subsequently removed to Nashville.

On the 29th, this grand division of the army moved into position on the extreme left, with General Palmer on the right, resting on the Murfreesborough pike and joining Negley, of the center, and General Wood occupying the ground from Palmer to the river, General Van Cleve in reserve of this, and General Rousseau in rear of the center.

General Rosecrans, with his entire staff, advanced from Nashville on the Murfreesborough pike, and, having reached the head of the column, turned off to the right over a heavy mud road, visited General McCook's command, and returned to his camp, in the rear of La Vergne, about 4 o'clock the following morning. Here he remained, contemplating the movements of the enemy, till the following day, when he moved on to Stewartsville. The next day (the 29th), late in the evening, he visited General Crittenden's headquarters, and remained in consultation all night with the chief officers of his command.

On the following morning, one of our batteries, in position a little to the left and in advance of the general, opened fire upon a battery of the enemy still more to the left and on elevated ground, which, replying, killed one of the escort, Private Dolan, of the Fourth U. S. Cavalry, and wounded the adjutant of the Fifty-seventh Indiana Volunteers in the shoulder. At the same time a private of an infantry regiment not engaged was killed. The general and his staff now fell back 300 or 400 yards to the sloping ground on the left of the road, where he remained all day.

About 11 o'clock the heavy picket firing on our left ceased, and opened generally along our right, where General McCook was being engaged. The enemy was strongly intrenched behind earthworks, extending from the river on our extreme left across our front in almost a direct line; then, far along our right, but receding from the Wilkinson to the Franklin pike, through heavy timber.

The left wing lost to-day 3 killed and 18 wounded; the center 14 killed and 53 wounded, and the right wing 24 killed and 105 wounded.

Field hospitals were established for the left and center in houses and tents along the Nashville pike, and for the right wing in the same manner on the Wilkinson pike and neighborhood.

Before leaving Nashville I had approved of full and complete requisitions, at the suggestion of Surgeon Murray, U. S. Army, my predecessor, for the three grand divisions of the army. I had also, in reserve, tents, bedding, &c., for a field hospital for more than 2,500 men, which I ordered up from the rear on the 29th, as soon as I learned the enemy had made a stand near Murfreesborough. At the same time I ordered forward 20 ambulances—all that we had on hand at Nashville. Surgeons were detailed to perform operations, when decided on after consultation, for dressing, and such other duties as the reception and disposition of the wounded and circumstances required.

Early on the morning of the 31st, the enemy, during the night having massed a heavy force on our right, fiercely attacked Johnson's and Davis' divisions, which he forced back; and Sheridan's, being heavily pressed, was obliged to recede. The hospitals, wounded, and nearly all the medical supplies of this wing of the army thus fell into the hands of the enemy. We were also called on to lament in sadness the loss of General Sill, and many noble and brave officers and men.

About 9 o'clock the commanding general, with his staff, dashed boldly forward to the front of the left wing, and in person directed the movements of troops and placed batteries in position. His daring presence so near the enemy's line brought down upon him an angry and spiteful fire of musketry, round shot, and shell, almost at point-blank range. But utterly disregarding this metallic storm, our brave commander moved calmly on from left to right, cheering and inspiring our faltering troops; and throughout the day, wherever the tide of battle most fiercely raged, General Rosecrans bore his charmed life and ubiquitous presence. The noble Garesché was killed by his side, and his aides, Lieutenant Kirby severely, and Lieutenant Porter slightly, wounded. Sergeant Richmond and 4 privates of his escort were also killed or wounded, the former mortally.

Much the heaviest loss sustained to-day fell upon our regular battalions, brigaded under command of Lieut. Col. O. L. Shepherd, in holding the cedar brake, on the right of the center, against the columns of the enemy sweeping down upon them, after having forced back our entire right wing. This loss amounted to 561 killed and wounded, more than one-third of their numbers; in fact, I might probably better say nearly one-half.

Our casualties in killed and wounded did not fall short of 4,000 men, including about 1,500 of the right wing, 1,200 of whom, wounded, fell into the hands of the enemy.

The ambulance corps, though temporarily organized, worked admirably. As soon as the fire of the enemy slacked at any point along our lines and became only desultory, the ambulances dashed in at a brisk trot, and snatched our wounded from their picket lines. In justice, I should add, the enemy did not fire on these brave men when they knew their humane mission, friend and foe, no longer combatants, being equally the objects of their care.

In the early part of the day, Dr. Weeds, assistant medical director, went to the rear to take charge of the property pertaining to the field hospitals, and placed it in proper position. About 10 o'clock Surgeon McDermont, medical director of the right wing, reported to me that his hospitals and wounded, hospital supplies and medical officers, had fallen into the hands of the enemy, and asked for instructions. I directed him to a cedar brake on the left of the road, half a mile to the rear, where I instructed him to make a temporary field hospital, constructing the shed, roof, and beds for the wounded from cedar boughs, to make his requisition on Dr. Weeds for supplies, and report to me when he could receive the wounded. Visiting his place an hour later, I found it untenble, or, at least, unsafe, on account of round shot and shell from the enemy occasionally falling upon it. I then directed Surgeon McDermont to find suitable buildings on the pike to the rear.

It became necessary, in order to accommodate so many wounded, to make use of tents, and my field hospitals having arrived, I was enabled to afford comfortable shelter for all. In the mean time my attention was drawn to a large number of wagons, ambulances, caissons, &c., moving from different points to the river, more to the left. I soon learned they had come in disorder from the right, and were looking for safety, over an uneven rocky ford, on the opposite river bank. This Babel-like confusion was somewhat augmented by the approach of the enemy, who now charged upon this flank. They were, however, driven back before much property had been destroyed. I had succeeded in drawing out many of the ambulances before crossing the ford. Three were reported to me as having been taken by the enemy and burned. The remainder subsequently did good service.

During the day the enemy's cavalry made a descent upon our hospitals, on the Nashville pike; but, beyond some confusion and embarrassment, they did little harm. Our own cavalry, commanded by Captain Otis, speedily drove them away, and recaptured all we had lost.

During the night I visited the hospitals within our lines along the pike and off of it, to the rear, and was gratified to find the wounded well provided and attended. At daylight, surgeons, nurses, and attendants were busily engaged in the labor they had begun the morning before.

As the fighting on January 1 was confined to brisk skirmishing, and but few casualties resulted therefrom, we were able to complete our organization, and finish the heavy work so suddenly thrown upon our hands the day before. Many of the slightly wounded, and those who were able to ride in empty wagons and walk, I ordered to Nashville, 25 miles to the rear.

After a brisk engagement the following morning, without any marked results, the day passed much as the preceding, till 5 o'clock, when the enemy came down with an overwhelming force upon our left flank, driving, for a while, everything before him; but, emerging from the heavy timber upon the open ground, he was met by terrific volleys of grape, round shot, and shell from fifty-two pieces of artillery, placed in position by Captain Mendenhall, on the opposite river bank. The enemy faltered, then fell back, and soon this living mass was in full retreat. Our loss, not exceeding 500 men, was comparatively small, his being estimated at nearly three times that number.

Then, as on other occasions, the ambulance corps behaved well. It was dark when the battle ceased, but while occasionally only shot fell from the baffled foe, our wounded were on the road, and less than an hour later they were all comfortably provided for in the rear. Lieutenant ———, who had charge of this branch of the medical service, deserves favorable mention for his zeal and industry; for though he could not share, from indisposition, the more bold and daring occupation of his brave comrades, he contributed much to the comfort of the wounded.

Saturday morning found our army bivouacked in mud, drenched with rain, without shelter, and almost without food, but still hopeful and cheerful. None were sick—few complaining. Our heavy lines of pickets on all sides were all day engaged, and at night General Rousseau's division stormed their rifle-pits in front, carried and held them. Our loss in this affair and throughout the day was not large. This proved to be our last encounter with the enemy.

On the following day we were engaged in the mournful task of burying our lamented dead. I visited the hospitals on the Wilkinson pike and neighborhood, now again within our lines, and found the wounded generally well cared for. Surgeon Marks and other medical officers, as also the attendants, left in these hospitals by direction of Surgeon McDermot, medical director of the right wing, I am happy to state, with but few exceptions, did their duty faithfully and well. Their labors were great and harassing, and not unattended with danger.

On the 31st, when the ground was fiercely contested, and only yielded to an overwhelming force, some buildings were pierced by round shot and musketry, wounding attendants in the earnest discharge of their duty.

During the battle of Wednesday a portion of Negley's division, of the center, fell into the hands of the enemy. These have been reported to me as having received the same care and attention as their own wounded by the medical officers of their army. In fact, they have said to me they had been "well treated, and had no reason to complain."

Surgeons Bogue, Johnson, Brelsford, and Wright are highly commended for their gallantry in maintaining their position with their wounded comrades when the hospitals of this portion of the army came within the enemy's lines. In strong contrast with these, and many other brave, devoted, and self-sacrificing men, it becomes my painful duty to say that V. D. Miller, assistant surgeon, Seventy-eighth Pennsylvania Volunteers, is reported to me by the medical director of his corps as having "basely deserted his post."

Surgeon Phelps, medical director of the left wing, is entitled to the highest praise for his zeal and untiring industry in the establishment of the largest field hospital in the rear; for professional skill and devoted attention to the wants of the wounded. Surgeon Blair also deserves credit for the comfortable provision made for those intrusted to his care, in tents, and shelters made of tent-flys. The wounded here, as elsewhere under canvas, did well, and most clearly established, in the opinion of all, the advantages derived from free ventilation thus afforded over hospitals in ordinary dwellings of wood or brick, notwithstanding a liberal provision of windows and doors.

I am gratified to say my conservative views were generally adopted, and that amputations were seldom performed without consultation. Many exsections were made, which are doing well, and some cases were treated as compound fractures with marked success.

Surgeon Muscroft, medical director of General Rousseau's division, established a hospital in the rear, and accommodated comfortably a large number of wounded. Many of the serious cases are in an advanced state of recovery. His zeal, skill, and industry are commendable; also Surgeons James, medical director of the cavalry division, and Comfort, of the Anderson Troop, did faithful service. Assistant Surgeon Failer has been assiduous in his attentions to sick and wounded.

Lieutenant-Colonel Northcott, unable longer to bear the fatigue and exposure incident to duty in the lines, on account of ill-health, aided me greatly in organizing parties of stragglers, with whom he policed camps, and procured wood, water, and straw.

Captain Munger, with his company, was detailed to guard property and enforce discipline in and about the field hospitals, and Captain Stackpole, to provide and issue subsistence stores as required. These gentlemen did their duties well, and gave universal satisfaction. The duties of these officers, like those of the medical department, though not of the brilliant nature of their more fortunate comrades in front, were essential to the comfort of the brave wounded, and deserve well of their commanding general and country.

I must crave your indulgence for again mentioning the ambulance corps and Lieutenant ———.

The service performed was highly creditable. The drivers and assistants—among the former of whom I desire to mention F. M. Figett, private, Company M, Twenty-first Kentucky Volunteers—were kind, prompt, and zealous in the discharge of their duty. This service was often necessarily continued into the night and near the enemy's lines; yet these brave men, unarmed, untiring, and unflinching, in the face of danger, gathered their bleeding comrades from under the guns of the enemy and bore them to the rear.

My orderly, Private Barrett, Fourth U. S. Cavalry, deserves creditable mention for his unceasing devotion to duty, and the prompt manner in which he conveyed my directions on the field. My clerk, William Domer, private in the Anderson Troop, who, I am gratified to know, has been highly recommended for a commission, also served faithfully and assiduously at the hospitals in the rear.

The commissary and quartermaster's departments are entitled to our thanks for timely and efficient aid in furnishing supplies and transportation, and in the preparation of hospitals for the reception of sick and wounded here and at Nashville. My thanks are also due to my assistants, Dr. Weeds and Surgeon Phelps, whom I have previously mentioned, for their prompt and efficient co-operation, and for valuable suggestions conducive to the comfort and best treatment of the wounded; to Surgeon Thurston, assistant medical director at Nashville, also, for his zeal, energy, and rare professional abilities displayed in providing for the wounded sent him from the battle-field. Surgeons McDermot and Beebe were untiring in their labors, and afforded me valuable aid. Their observations on treatment of wounded, &c., as shown in their reports, herewith appended, should receive attention.

From the difficulty of individualizing, where so many are distinguished, I have mentioned but few officers as deserving of commendation for faithful and conscientious attention to duty. I am sorry to say, however, that there are those whose conduct has been bad, whose names at an early day will be forwarded to the commanding general for his action. Among these are two officers, who left the field to look for hospitals beyond Stewart's Creek, and did not soon return, reported to me by Colonel Burke, Tenth Ohio Volunteers.

Under the present standard of professional ability among subordinate medical officers, too much stress cannot, in my opinion, be laid upon the importance of securing supervisory talent of the highest order. The rank now common to corps medical directors is most inadequate to the responsibility, extent of authority, and respect attaching to such a position, while the pay and emoluments pertaining thereto are a poor inducement to skillful practitioners to abandon a lucrative practice at home for the drudgery, exposure, and, at best, brief honors of service with troops in the field. While the medical officers now acting in this capacity are comparatively the best fitted therefor among those open to selection, I am of opinion that the standard of professional administrative capacity of such officers should be elevated, and that increase of rank (it may be local), of pay and emoluments to medical directors will insure the availability to the department of a much higher order of talent than is at present accessible.

It appears to me that the liberality of the Government and the people, which grants such liberal donations of money and supplies for sanitary purposes, might be most advantageously applied to securing more valuable personal attentions to the objects of these laudable efforts.

I append hereto a complete return of the killed and wounded of the various subdivisions of the army, with a tabular statement of the location and nature of the wounds.

Very respectfully,

EBEN. SWIFT,
Surgeon, U. S. Army, Medical Director,
Department of the Cumberland.

———

Tabular statement showing the location of 3,102 wounds received in the Army of the Cumberland during the late battle of Stone's River.

Location of wound.	No.	Location of wound.	No.
Head and face	282	Abdomen	52
Breast	134	Groin	11
Shoulder	259	Hip	159
Arm	347	Side	100
Forearm	21	Thigh	432
Elbow	16	Leg	626
Wrist	22	Knee	94
Hand	245	Ankle	45
Neck	59	Foot	41
Back	57		

The remaining wounds are unknown or too slight in their nature to be mentioned.

EBEN. SWIFT,
Surgeon, U. S. Army, Medical Director.

*General summary of casualties during the battle of Stone's River.**

Corps and detachments.	Officers killed.	Enlisted men killed.	Officers wounded.	Enlisted men wounded.	Total.
Right Wing	30	573	100	2,481	3,184
Center	16	308	94	1,619	2,037
Left Wing	42	527	180	2,663	3,412
Staff and escort of general commanding	1	3	2	3	9
Fourth U. S. Cavalry		3	1	8	12
Chicago Board of Trade Battery		3	1	5	9
Pioneer Brigade		7	3	21	31
Cavalry Division	3	17	3	61	84
Total	92	1,441	384	6,861	8,778

No. 5.

Report of Lieut. Col. Samuel Simmons, U. S. Army, Chief Commissary of Subsistence, of stores lost and captured.

HEADQUARTERS ARMY OF THE CUMBERLAND,
OFFICE CHIEF COMMISSARY OF SUBSISTENCE,
Murfreesborough, February 14, 1863.

COLONEL: I have the honor to submit herewith a statement of stores lost and picked up by the several commissaries of the center and left wing, commanded by Major-Generals Thomas and Crittenden, on the battle-field and between Stone's River and Nashville, during the late action on Stone's River. No report of stores lost in the right wing has been furnished me.

Very respectfully, your obedient servant,
SAMUEL SIMMONS,
Lieutenant-Colonel and Chief Commissary of Subsistence.

Lieut. Col. C. GODDARD,
Assistant Adjutant-General and Chief of Staff.

—

Statement of subsistence stores lost and taken up on and near the battle-field during the battle of Stone's River, about January 1, 1863.

(Fourteenth Army Corps, First Division.—Capt. J. R. Paul, commissary of subsistence.)

LOST.

Fresh beef	pounds..	8,700
Bacon	do....	3,874
Flour	barrels..	39
Hard bread	pounds..	10,123
Beans	bushels..	61¼¼
Rice	pounds..	225
Roasted coffee	do....	891
Tea	do....	187
Sugar	do....	1,380
Adamantine candles	do....	320
Tallow candles	do....	120

* But see revised statement, p. 215.

Soap	pounds..	1,380
Molasses	gallons..	42
Mixed vegetables	pounds..	220

TAKEN UP.

Fresh beef	pounds..	4,500
Bacon	do....	29,873
Flour	barrels..	5$\frac{64}{196}$
Hard bread	pounds..	38,382
Beans	bushels..	32$\frac{18}{44}$
Rice	pounds..	2,537$\frac{6}{16}$
Roasted coffee	do....	4,681
Tea	do....	91
Sugar	do....	6,835
Vinegar	gallons..	80
Adamantine candles	pounds..	360
Soap	do....	1,532

(Fourteenth Army Corps, Second Division.—Capt. W. J. Kane, commissary of subsistence.)

LOST.

Pork	barrels..	4
Fresh beef	pounds..	6,432
Bacon	do....	500
Flour	barrels..	5
Coffee	pounds..	150
Sugar	do....	1,400
Molasses	gallons..	40

(Twenty-first Army Corps, First Division.—Capt. S. D. Henderson, commissary of subsistence.)

LOST.

Head of cattle, estimated to weigh 600 pounds each, net	38

(Second Division.—Lieut. C. C. Peck, acting commissary of subsistence.)

LOST.

Bacon	pounds..	4,500
Hard bread	do....	5,000

(Third Division.—Capt. J. O. Stanage, acting commissary of subsistence.)

LOST.

Bacon	pounds..	1,295
Roasted coffee	do....	3,922
Tea	do....	46
Soap	do....	893

No. 6.

Report of Lieut. Col. John W. Taylor, U. S. Army, Chief Quartermaster, of public animals and means of transportation captured by the enemy, &c., December 26, 1862–January 16, 1863.

HDQRS. DEPARTMENT OF THE CUMBERLAND,
OFFICE OF CHIEF QUARTERMASTER,
Murfreesborough, February 1, 1863.

GENERAL: I have the honor to report herewith a statement of the losses of animals and means of transportation during the battle of

Stone's River; also a list of the animals, means of transportation, and other property captured from the enemy and picked up on the field and at Murfreesborough, as reported by the quartermasters of the several divisions named. A large number of the wagons that were partially burned by the enemy have been recovered and turned into the repair shops. Some wagons and a large number of animals reported as lost have been picked up by the several regiments, and will be taken up and accounted for by the quartermasters in their monthly returns, so that the actual loss is much less than appears by the annexed statement.

Very respectfully,

JOHN W. TAYLOR,
Lieutenant-Colonel and Quartermaster.

Maj. Gen. W. S. ROSECRANS,
Commanding Department of the Cumberland.

—

Statement of public animals and means of transportation captured by the enemy, killed in battle, and lost and destroyed from December 26, 1862, until January 16, 1863.

Command.	Wagons.	Ambulances.	Harness, sets.	Horses.				Mules.	Animals.
				Draught.	Artillery.	Cavalry.	Total.		
RIGHT WING.									
Headquarters	10	1	60					60	60
FIRST DIVISION.									
Headquarters			3	7		1	8	5	13
Ammunition and supply train	35		204	4		3	7	204	211
First Brigade.									
Headquarters			4	3		1	4		4
22d Indiana	1		6			2	2	5	7
59th Illinois	2	1	12			2	2	11	13
74th Illinois	2		12					12	12
75th Illinois	1		6					12	12
5th Wisconsin Battery	2		30		21		21	12	33
Second Brigade.									
Headquarters			24			1	1	24	25
21st Illinois	4		13					13	13
38th Illinois	2		14	1			1	15	16
15th Wisconsin	2	1	28	3			3	25	28
101st Ohio	4		2						
2d Minnesota Battery					13		13		13
Third Brigade.									
Headquarters						4	4	1	5
25th Illinois	1		6			1	1	6	7
35th Illinois	1		6			4	4	6	10
81st Indiana	2		10	4		1	5	6	11
8th Wisconsin Battery			8		18		18		18
36th Illinois Cavalry, Company B						3	3		3
2d Kentucky Cavalry, Company G						7	7		7
SECOND DIVISION.									
3d Indiana Cavalry		1				30	30		30
Supply train	3		18					18	18
Ammunition train	2		12					12	12

Statement of public animals and means of transportation captured by the enemy, killed in battle, lost and destroyed, &c.—Continued.

Command.	Wagons.	Ambulances.	Harness, sets.	Horses. Draught.	Horses. Artillery.	Horses. Cavalry.	Horses. Total.	Mules.	Animals
First Brigade.									
15th Ohio		1	5	4			4	1	5
49th Ohio		2	4						
32d Indiana		1		1			1	1	2
39th Indiana	1	1	4	4			4		4
89th Illinois		2	2	2			2		2
1st Ohio Artillery, Battery A		1	30		62		62		62
Second Brigade.									
Headquarters						7	7	7	14
34th Illinois				1			1		1
79th Illinois	1			2			2	1	3
29th Indiana	1	1	2	2			2	4	6
30th Indiana			1					2	2
77th Pennsylvania				2			2		2
1st Ohio Artillery, Battery E			82	7	75		82	6	88
Third Brigade.									
Headquarters	1		6					6	6
93d Ohio		1	4	5			5		5
5th Kentucky (Louisville Legion)	1		6	1			1	6	7
6th Indiana		1	6	1			1	6	7
5th Indiana Battery			13		24		24		24
THIRD DIVISION.									
Headquarters ammunition and supply train	58		348					348	348
First Brigade.									
36th Illinois	1		6					6	6
88th Illinois	2	1	14	2			2	12	14
24th Wisconsin	1		6					1	1
4th Indiana Battery	1	1	8	2	43		45	6	51
Second Brigade.									
Headquarters	1		6					6	6
2d Missouri	1		4					4	4
15th Missouri									
44th Illinois									
73d Illinois	1		6					6	6
1st Missouri Artillery, Battery G	1		6		37		37	6	43
Third Brigade.									
Headquarters	1		6					6	6
22d Illinois	1		6					6	6
27th Illinois	2	2	16					16	16
42d Illinois	1	2	8					8	8
51st Illinois	2	1	14	18			18	18	36
1st Illinois Artillery, Battery C	1		8		85		85	8	93
CENTER.									
FIRST DIVISION.									
Second Brigade.									
3d Ohio	1							4	4
88th Indiana	1		4	1			1		1
1st Michigan Battery				10			10		10
Fourth Brigade.									
Headquarters				1			1		1
1st Battalion, 18th Infantry, U. S			2					10	10
2d Battalion, 18th Infantry, U. S		1	2					2	2
5th U. S. Artillery [Battery H]					15		15		15

Statement of public animals and means of transportation captured by the enemy, killed in battle, lost and destroyed, &c.—Continued.

Command.	Wagons.	Ambulances.	Harness, sets.	Horses.				Mules.	Animals.
				Draught.	Artillery.	Cavalry.	Total.		
SECOND DIVISION.									
Headquarters and division train	5		90					90	90
Second Brigade.									
Headquarters				1			1		1
18th Ohio				6			6	4	10
Third Brigade.									
Headquarters	2		12	1		1	2	8	10
74th Ohio	1	1	6	2			2	4	6
37th Indiana	4	1	16	1			1	12	13
21st Ohio	4	1	1	6			6		6
78th Pennsylvania	1		14	1		9	10		10
1st Ohio Artillery, Battery G			28		46		46		46
Hewett's Kentucky Battery	1		19		18		18		18
1st Ohio Artillery, Battery M			1		9		9	1	10
FIFTH DIVISION.									
Second [First] Brigade.									
Headquarters	15		88	5			5	84	89
105th Ohio	4		8					16	16
80th Illinois	5		10	1			1	20	21
123d Illinois	4		12					24	24
101st Indiana	4		10					20	20
19th Indiana Battery	2		4		10		10		10
LEFT WING.									
FIRST DIVISION.									
Supply train								2	2
6th Ohio Battery			2		16		16		16
10th Indiana Battery					22		22	1	23
8th Indiana Battery	2		12		18	3	21	12	33
26th Ohio	1	1	8	4			4	6	10
58th Indiana	2		12					12	12
3d Kentucky	1		6					6	6
13th Michigan			6					6	6
SECOND DIVISION.									
Supply train	2		6					12	12
90th Ohio	1								
110th Illinois								1	1
9th Indiana		1	1	2			2		2
THIRD DIVISION.									
Supply train	2		8					7	7
3d Wisconsin Battery					11		11		11
26th Pennsylvania Battery					7		7		7
7th Indiana Battery					5		5		5
DETACHED.									
Michigan Engineers and Mechanics	3		41	21			21	20	41
3d Ohio Cavalry	1		6					6	6
Captain Warren's supply train	6								
Total loss	229	28	1,540	139	555	80	774	1,334	2,108

List of animals and means of transportation and other property captured from the enemy and picked up on the battle-field from January 1 to January 16, 1863, as per reports of division quartermasters.

Command.	Wagons.	Ambulances.	Mules.	Horses.	Total number of animals.	Harness, single sets.	Number of hides.	Pounds of cotton.	Bushels of bran.
RIGHT WING.									
Second Division.............			20	50	70				
Third Division.............				4	4				
CENTER.									
Fifth Division.............	9		18	15	33	12			
LEFT WING.									
First Division.............	1	1	17	7	24				
Third Division.............		1	2	6	8				
DETACHED.									
10th Ohio.............	3		14	1	15	19			
Captain Boyd, assistant quartermaster......				6	6				
First Brigade Pioneers.............	4		4		4	21			
Chief of army police.............	1		143	103	246	2			
Capt. C. T. Wing, assistant quartermaster..								8,680	3,500
Lieut. Col. J. W. Taylor, quartermaster....			5	4	9		1,069		
Total.............	18	2	223	196	419	54	1,069	8,680	3,500

No. 7.

Report of Capt. William M. Wiles, Forty-fourth Indiana Infantry, provost-marshal-general, of prisoners captured.

HDQRS. DEPARTMENT OF THE CUMBERLAND,
OFFICE PROVOST-MARSHAL-GENERAL,
Murfreesborough, Tenn., February 9, 1863.

GENERAL: I have the honor herewith to forward a complete report of Confederate prisoners captured by the army under your command at the late battle of Stone's River, showing the number of regiments and other organizations represented, the number of the same from each State, the number of officers and enlisted men captured from each regiment or organization, the entire number of officers and enlisted men captured, and to what arm of the service they belong. The total number of prisoners captured is shown to be 3,694.*

Taking into account the number and character of the organization, and using the lowest possible estimate of the strength of each, it can be shown, beyond controversy, that the enemy's force exceeded our own by at least one-third. Complete reports of the number captured by the enemy from our own forces have not yet been received. From the best information received up to the present time, the number will not exceed 2,800, and in all probability the estimate is too large.

I am, general, very respectfully, your obedient servant,
WM. M. WILES,
Captain and Provost-Marshal-General.

Maj. Gen. W. S. ROSECRANS,
Commanding Department of the Cumberland.

---

* An earlier report (January 12, 1863) from this officer gave 126 officers and 3,071 men captured; total, 3,197.

[Inclosure.]

OFFICE PROVOST-MARSHAL-GENERAL,
DEPARTMENT OF THE CUMBERLAND,
Murfreesborough, Tenn., February 9, 1863.

The following is a complete report of Confederate prisoners captured by the army under command of Maj. Gen. W. S. Rosecrans at the battle of Stone's River, January 3, 1863, showing the number of regiments and other organizations represented, the number from each State, the number of officers and enlisted men captured from each regiment or organization, the entire number of officers and enlisted men captured, and to what arm of the service they belong:

Confederate officers and enlisted men captured.

INFANTRY.

Organization.	Officers.	Men.	Aggregate.
ALABAMA.			
First		22	22
Second		1	1
Third		5	5
Fourth	1	1	2
Ninth		1	1
Fourteenth		1	1
Sixteenth	2	36	38
Nineteenth	1	22	23
Twenty-second	1	10	11
Twenty-third		2	2
Twenty-fourth		34	34
Twenty-fifth	1	16	17
Twenty-sixth		14	14
Twenty-eighth	1	30	31
Thirty-second	2	79	81
Thirty-third		22	22
Thirty-fourth	1	10	11
Thirty-seventh	1		1
Thirty-ninth	2	14	16
Forty-first	1	93	94
Forty-fourth		1	1
Forty-fifth		18	18
Fifty-first		10	10
Total	14	442	456
ARKANSAS.			
First	5	50	55
Second	3	63	66
Third	1	3	4
Fourth	1	30	31
Fifth	2	33	35
Sixth	3	30	33
Seventh		6	6
Eighth	4	29	33
Thirteenth		3	3
Fifteenth	1	8	9
Nineteenth		1	1
Thirtieth	2	22	24
Total	22	278	300
CONFEDERATE.			
First		3	3
Third		56	56
Fourth		1	1
Fifth	2	18	20
Eighth	8	75	83
Total	10	153	163

Organization.	Officers.	Men.	Aggregate.
FLORIDA.			
First and Third	4	69	73
Fourth	3	99	102
Sixth		1	1
Ninth		1	1
Total	7	170	177
GEORGIA.			
First		4	4
Second	1	2	3
Fifth		10	10
Forty-third		1	1
Total	1	17	18
KENTUCKY.			
Second	1	54	55
Fourth	4	42	46
Sixth	2	32	34
Eighth		2	2
Ninth	2	23	25
Thirteenth		1	1
Total	9	154	163
LOUISIANA.			
First	1	46	47
Eleventh		3	3
Thirteenth and Twentieth	9	239	248
Sixteenth and Twenty-fifth	2	119	121
Fortieth *		1	1
Total	12	408	420
MISSISSIPPI.			
Third		1	1
Fifth		9	9
Seventh	1	15	16
Eighth	1	28	29
Ninth	3	28	31
Tenth		27	27
Twelfth		1	1
Thirteenth		1	1
Seventeenth		1	1
Twentieth		1	1
Twenty-first		1	1
Twenty-fourth	1	33	34
Twenty-seventh	2	12	14
Twenty-ninth	2	23	25

* No record of such regiment.

Confederate officers and enlisted men captured—Continued.

INFANTRY—Continued.

Organization.	Officers.	Men.	Aggregate.	Organization.	Officers.	Men.	Aggregate.
MISSISSIPPI—Continued.				**TENNESSEE—Continued.**			
Thirtieth	4	62	66	Eighteenth	1	32	33
Thirty-second		1	1	Nineteenth		27	27
Thirty-seventh		2	2	Twentieth		24	24
Forty-first		30	30	Twenty-third		45	45
Forty-fifth	5	89	94	Twenty-fourth		16	16
				Twenty-fifth	1	38	39
Total	19	365	384	Twenty-sixth	2	35	37
				Twenty-seventh		4	4
NORTH CAROLINA.				Twenty-eighth	3	24	27
				Twenty-ninth	1	27	28
Sixteenth		11	11	Thirtieth		40	40
Twenty-fifth		10	10	Thirty-first		9	9
Twenty-ninth		15	15	Thirty-second	1	4	5
Thirty-ninth	1	13	14	Thirty-third	1	17	18
Sixtieth	2	45	47	Thirty-seventh	1	12	13
				Thirty-eighth		22	22
Total	3	94	97	Thirty-ninth		4	4
				Forty-first		4	4
SOUTH CAROLINA.				Forty-fourth	3	54	57
				Forty-fifth	4	49	53
Tenth	1	19	20	Forty-seventh	1	27	28
Nineteenth		13	13	Fiftieth	1	4	5
				Fifty-first		16	16
Total	1	32	33	Eightieth	1	2	3
				One hundred and fifty-fourth, senior.	2	16	18
TENNESSEE.							
				Total	48	1,010	1,058
First	1	34	35				
Second		19	19	**TEXAS.**			
Third		26	26				
Fourth	1	34	35	Fourth	1		1
Fifth		22	22	Ninth		28	28
Sixth	1	27	28	Tenth		19	19
Eighth	7	47	54	Eleventh		18	18
Ninth		16	16	Fourteenth		18	18
Eleventh	4	53	57	Fifteenth		11	11
Twelfth	3	38	41	Nineteenth		1	1
Thirteenth		38	38	Twenty-sixth*		1	1
Fifteenth		16	16				
Sixteenth	3	44	47	Total	1	96	97
Seventeenth	5	44	49				

VARIOUS INFANTRY ORGANIZATIONS.

Name.	State.	Officers.	Men.	Aggregate.
Austin's sharpshooters	[Louisiana]	1	1	2
Bluff City Sharpshooters	Tennessee		2	2
Blythe's sharpshooters	Mississippi	1	25	26
Chalmers' sharpshooters			2	2
Cox's sharpshooters	[Georgia]		3	3
Cox's signal corps			1	1
Dake's [sic] regiment			1	1
Georgia Sharpshooters	Georgia		3	3
Hyde's company, Ross' regiment			1	1
Holleman's [sic] regiment			1	1
Mississippi Sharpshooters	Mississippi		4	4
Tennessee Sharpshooters	Tennessee		2	2
Total		2	46	48

* No record of a Twenty-sixth Texas Infantry.

Confederate officers and enlisted men captured.—Continued.

RECAPITULATION OF INFANTRY.

States.	Regiments represented.	Officers captured.	Men captured.	Total captured.
Alabama	23	14	442	456
Arkansas	12	22	278	300
Confederate States	5	10	153	163
Florida	4	7	170	177
Georgia	4	1	17	18
Kentucky	6	9	154	163
Louisiana	5	12	408	420
Mississippi	19	19	365	384
North Carolina	5	3	94	97
South Carolina	2	1	32	33
Tennessee	39	48	984	1,032
Texas	8	1	96	97
Various organizations	12	2	46	48
Total	144	149	3,239	3,388

STATE REGIMENTS.*

States.	Officers captured.	Men captured.	Total.	States.	Officers captured.	Men captured.	Total.
ALABAMA.				**KENTUCKY.**			
First		23	23	First		5	5
Second		5	5	Fourth		2	2
Third		3	3	Sixth		4	4
Eighth		1	1	**TENNESSEE.**			
Fourteenth		2	2	First		43	43
Fifty-first	1	5	6	Second		2	2
ARKANSAS.				Third		4	4
First		4	4	Fourth		14	14
Second	1	1	2	**TEXAS.**			
Fourth		1	1	Fourth	1		1
CONFEDERATE STATES.				Eighth	1	19	20
First		7	7	Tenth		10	10
Third		19	19	Eleventh		5	5
Eighth		4	4	Fourteenth		5	5
GEORGIA.				Fifteenth		1	1
First		1	1	Total, twenty-nine regiments.	4	211	215
Second		12	12				
Third		5	5				
Third Georgia Battalion		4	4				

* Regiments thus classified seem to have been embraced in the preceding tables.

Confederate officers and enlisted men captured.—Continued.

CAVALRY.

Name.	Officers captured.	Men captured.	Name.	Officers captured.	Men captured.
Ashby's cavalry		1	Morgan's Kentucky cavalry		1
Bennett's Tennessee cavalry		2	Morris' battalion		1
Breckinridge's escort		1	Roddey's cavalry		1
Buford's body guard		1	Second Mounted Infantry		1
Buckner's cavalry		1	Tennessee Battalion		1
Cox's Kentucky cavalry		1	Terry's Texas Rangers		1
Douglass' Tennessee battalion		9	Wharton's escort		5
Duke's Kentucky cavalry		1	Wheeler's command		1
Fyffe's battalion		4	Willard's Legion		1
Gilbert's Tennessee battalion		2	Woodward's cavalry		2
Holman's cavalry		1	Aide to General Morgan	1	
Howard's cavalry		1			
McCann's Tennessee cavalry		1	Total	1	41

ARTILLERY.

Name of battery.	Officers captured.	Men captured.	Name of battery.	Officers captured.	Men captured.
Byrne's	1		McTyer's		1
Calvert's		1	Napier's		1
Cobb's		4	Phipps'		1
Darden's		1	Redman's		1
First Kentucky		1	Robertson's		1
First Texas		1	Scott's		1
Fourteenth Georgia		5	Semple's [Marks' artillery]	1	2
Jackson's Florida		4	Steuben Artillery		1
Ketchum's		6	Walton's		2
Lumsden's		1	Washington Artillery		3
Marks' Alabama [Semple's]		1	Wright's		4
Moses'		4			
			Total	2	47

RECAPITULATION.

	Number of regiments represented.	Number of various organizations represented.	Number of batteries.	Entire number of organizations represented.	Officers captured.	Men captured.	Total captured.
Artillery			23	23	2	47	49
Cavalry	29	24		53	5	252	257
Infantry	132	12		144	149	3,239	3,388
Grand total	161	36	23	220	156	3,538	3,694

WM. M. WILES,
Captain and Provost-Marshal-General.

NOTE.—It appears from the official records that many of the organizations enumerated in tables pp. 230–233 were not with the Army of the Tennessee (Confederate) during the Stone's River Campaign.—COMPILER.

No. 8.

Report of Capt. Jesse Merrill, Chief Signal Officer.

HDQRS. SIGNAL CORPS, FOURTEENTH ARMY CORPS,
                    Murfreesborough, January 7, 1863.

MAJOR: We left Nashville on Friday, December 26, in company with the advancing army, and kept well up to the front until Monday, when the troops were pushed vigorously forward, about 11 miles from where we then were, to the place which was afterward the battle-field, the west side of one fork of Stone's River. We kept communication with two columns of the advancing troops, but, as they afterward merged into one, one of the lines was abandoned. The one kept up was with General Crittenden, commanding left wing; the one abandoned, with Negley's division of center, which came in on Crittenden's right, on the same road on which we were.

The right wing of the army, under McCook, consisting of three divisions, marched on a road about 6 miles to our right. We used all our energies in trying to get communication with him, but failed, the intervening country being almost level, and a dense wood.

On Monday night I accompanied Generals Rosecrans and Thomas to the front. Communication was kept from the front to the rear during the night. A copy of the messages sent will be forwarded as soon as the reports are received. On Tuesday we communicated between Generals Rosecrans and Thomas. McCook was then about 10 miles to the right in the woods.

Crittenden's headquarters were beside those of Rosecrans. The skirmishing during the afternoon was very severe. At daylight on Wednesday morning loud reports of artillery and musketry in rapid succession were heard on the right, and at almost the same time an attack was made on the front center. Between 8 and 9 o'clock McCook's line of battle was broken, and his division separated, and, straggling, rushed through the woods to the Murfreesborough pike, 2 miles from their original position. Another line was formed parallel with the pike, and here the enemy were successfully resisted, both on the right and in front. They were pressing us heavily, though, and when the sun went down, and the din of battle and the roar of artillery ceased, all seemed relieved.

Signals could not be used to any advantage on that field; woods and clumps of trees were all around us. Even if this had not been so, it would have been impossible to use them, for General Rosecrans was constantly riding over the field, and other generals seemed equally active. At no one time, and I rode with him during most of the day, do I remember of his having been one-half hour at the same place. The result of this day's fight was, our right wing driven 2 miles, with a loss of thirty pieces of artillery, and a large number of wounded and prisoners, and thousands of stragglers, who were rushing to the rear, and could hardly be driven back to their places in the ranks. On Thursday both armies lay quiet, seemingly worn out by the contest of the previous day. To us it was a day of terrible suspense. On Friday afternoon all our available force was massed on the left, to attack the enemy's right. Happily for us, they attacked us just when we were about to move on them, and they were driven back with great loss and in much disorder. On Saturday evening we again attacked them, and drove them from a strong position. On Sunday morning they had withdrawn their forces across the river, and they began to evacuate this place. The officers of the corps rendered all the assistance they could; the movements of the enemy were watched closely, though but little could be seen of them. Some of them were efficient as aides-de-camp to the generals to whom they were assigned.

I will claim your indulgence for this report, as it has been written under very unfavorable circumstances, and in great haste.

I am, major, very respectfully, your obedient servant,

JESSE MERRILL,
Captain in Charge of Signal Corps, Fourteenth Army Corps.

Maj. ALBERT J. MYER,
Chief Signal Officer, U. S. Army.

No. 9.

Report of Col. James Barnett, First Ohio Light Artillery, Chief of Artillery.

HEADQUARTERS DEPARTMENT OF THE CUMBERLAND,
Murfreesborough, Tenn., February 8, 1863.

SIR: I have the honor to submit, for the information of the general commanding, a summary from the reports of the batteries of this department, of their position, &c., at the late battle of Stone's River.

Right wing, Second Division, composed of the following batteries: Battery A, First Ohio Artillery, Lieutenant Belding commanding, attached to General Willich's brigade; Battery E, First Ohio Artillery, Captain Edgarton, attached to Colonel Kirk's brigade; Fifth Indiana, Captain Simonson, attached to Colonel Buckley's brigade, having the following guns: Nine James rifles, three 6-pounder smooth-bore, two 12-pounder howitzers, two 10-pounder Parrotts, and two 12-pounder light field guns.

On the evening of December 30, Battery A was placed in position in the rear of the brigade, on the extreme right of the right wing, with one section, the other two sections fronting the rear, horses unhitched, but not unharnessed.

At daybreak the horses were sent to water, with the precaution to return at the least alarm; firing commenced; teams returned quickly and hitched. The brigade falling back very fast, the battery retired to a slight eminence in the rear, but the enemy having got so far to the right that the guns were under a cross-fire. Near this point three guns were taken by the enemy. Two other pieces were taken rapidly to the rear, one gun, having horses remaining, was served with effect as opportunity was offered, firing about four rounds at each unlimbering. Upon reaching the Murfreesborough pike, this gun was put in position with Captain Simonson's battery, where about ten rounds were fired. Upon being ordered to return, one wheel-driver and two horses being killed while limbering up, the piece was temporarily abandoned, but was brought off by the Louisville Legion with prolonge attached. This battery the next day was held in position, with two guns, near the Murfreesborough pike, in reserve, where it remained until ordered forward across the river.

Company E, First Ohio Artillery, Captain Edgarton, was posted, on the night of December 30, on the extreme right and in front of Battery A, in position to guard a country road, horses harnessed all night.

At daylight of the 31st, horses were sent to water; at the firing of the pickets, horses were hitched in, or at least one-half, and others immediately returned. Two shells were thrown in the direction of the enemy, still invisible, and, as they appeared, six rounds of canister were thrown with great effect. The vigorous attack of the enemy in front and flank, and the loss of many horses, rendered it necessary to abandon the battery, after, however, a determined resistance, 2 cannoneers being bayoneted at the guns. Captain Edgarton and Lieutenant Berwick were captured.

The Fifth Indiana Battery, Captain Simonson, was first put in position on the morning of the 31st about one-half mile to the right of the Six-Mile pike, upon which the right wing advanced upon an open field, with the battery fronting to the west. Here the right section was temporarily detailed, by order of Colonel Baldwin, and ordered to the left and front about 400 yards. From this position the battery fell back with the division, and was ordered, by Brigadier-General Johnson, to take another position on the crest, about 200 yards to the right of the Murfreesborough pike and near to the right of Major-General Rousseau's division, which position it retained until ordered to retire.

The next ground taken was in the open space to the left, and about 25 yards from the railroad, where it remained until about sunset, when General Johnson ordered the battery to the left of his division, about 185 yards to the right of the Murfreesborough pike, opposite the headquarters of Major-General Rousseau, where it remained until ordered to cross Stone's River, January 5. The battery lost two guns.

The artillery of the First Division is composed of the following batteries, and had the following guns: Fifth Wisconsin, Captain Pinney, attached to Colonel Post's brigade; Second Minnesota, Captain Hotchkiss, attached to Colonel Carlin's brigade; Eighth Wisconsin, Captain Carpenter, attached to Colonel Woodruff's brigade. Four 10-pounder Parrotts, eight 6-pounder smooth-bore, four 12-pounder howitzers. Captain Pinney's battery, which, with his brigade, was on the extreme right of the army, on the 30th, after driving the enemy, to enable the skirmishers to advance to the open fields in front, took position, with horses in harness, for the night. After dark, two brigades of the Second Division took position on the right.

On the morning of the 31st, upon the falling back of these two brigades, the battery changed front to the right, to meet the enemy rapidly approaching by the right and rear, supported by the Fifty-ninth Illinois and posted in a corn-field, where they opened fire with canister, checking temporarily the advance of the enemy. However, being unopposed on the right, the position became untenable, and the battery was withdrawn, leaving Captain Pinney dangerously wounded, with the loss of some 18 horses and one gun. The balance of the battery was dragged to the rear by the assistance of the Fifty-ninth Illinois. Near the Nashville pike it was charged upon by cavalry, who were driven off by the Fourth Cavalry Regiment, and took position behind Overall's Creek, on a hill to the right of the pike, where they remained all night.

The next morning their position was on the left of the pike, where breastworks were thrown up in a position to enfilade the enemy's lines. At this point a rebel battery, opening, was soon silenced by a few Parrott shots.

In the afternoon of the next day the battery, with its brigade, was ordered to cross the Stone's River, where it was put into position, throwing up breastworks, and where it remained until 2 o'clock on the morning of January 4, when it recrossed the river, taking its former position on the right, where it remained until January 6, 1863.

The Second Minnesota Battery, Captain Hotchkiss, moved on the 30th with its brigade to the right of the Wilkinson pike until the withdrawal of skirmishers, when the battery opened with canister and spherical case with effect. When the first line of the brigade had arrived at the point about 180 yards from the house of Mrs. William Smith, two batteries, one about 100 yards west of the house and another on the east of the house, 250 yards distant, opened fire on the Twenty-first Illinois and Fifteenth Wisconsin Volunteers. These batteries were soon silenced, but another to the right, about 500 yards, enfilading the brigade, was driven off by a well-directed fire from this battery.

Before daylight on the morning of the 31st, the battery was retired 200 yards, soon after which the brigade was vigorously attacked and obliged to fall back across the open fields, and entered a wood about 200 yards east of Griscom's house, when several rounds were fired with destructive effect.

The command was again retired about 1 mile, and went into position in the edge of a cedar grove, from whence it again retired to the railroad. The next position was near the Nashville pike, 4 miles from Murfreesborough.

On January 2, under order of Major-General Rosecrans, the brigade and battery were sent to the left, crossing Stone's River at the ford, relieving Colonel Hazen, where they remained until January 4.

The Eighth Wisconsin Battery, Captain Carpenter, at about 11 o'clock, December 30, was posted on the edge of a cotton-field, in front of a wood running parallel with the pike, facing southeast, placed in the interval between General Sill's right and the left of its (Colonel Woodruff's) brigade.

At about 3 o'clock the command was moved forward, with heavy skirmishing. The right of the brigade, being well advanced, was halted, and remained until support should come up. The battery was placed at the angle of the fence, to protect the right and front, when it received a heavy fire, occasionally replying with shell, until toward night, when the enemy opened a heavy artillery fire on the right of Carlin's brigade, which was silenced in handsome style in five minutes. Colonel Carlin's brigade being attacked at about the same time, this battery again opened with such effect as to effectually check the attack.

The enemy on the morning of the 31st made their attack in five lines, the battery opening a full fire of canister with terrific effect. After a determined resistance, being ordered back, several ineffectual attempts were made to get into position, but, owing to the general stampede, no stand could be made until they reached the Murfreesborough pike, where they remained until Friday; being then ordered to the left, crossed the ford, and went into position on the extreme left, about 2 miles from the ford.

On Saturday, January 3, the battery changed position again to the right, where it remained until ordered to Murfreesborough.

The batteries of the Third Division are as follows: Battery G, First Missouri, Captain Hescock, attached to Colonel Schaefer's (Second) brigade; Battery C, First Illinois, Captain Houghtaling, attached to Colonel Roberts' (Third) brigade; Fourth Indiana Battery, Captain Bush, attached to General Sill's (First) brigade, with the following guns: Two

10-pounder Parrotts, four 12-pounder light field guns, two James rifles, six 6-pounder smooth-bore, and four 12-pounder howitzers.

Battery G, First Missouri, Captain Hescock, moved on the morning of the 30th, at 7 a. m., with its brigade, on the right and rear of the division, to the right of the Wilkinson pike, having Bush's battery on the left. Toward evening, Bush moving to the front, Captain Hescock took his place. The three batteries of the division concentrated their fire upon the enemy's batteries, silencing their fire.

In the morning this battery and Captain Houghtaling's opened a heavy fire upon the enemy, who were engaging Generals Sill's and Davis' commands, until the enemy, who were pursuing General Johnson's command, gained their rear, when they moved to the front, to the position first held by the enemy, and then took position on the north side of the road, sending one section to re-enforce Captain Bush, engaging the enemy hotly until their ammunition was expended, when they retired through the cedars with the division. After gaining the open field, their guns were brought into action and fired until all the ammunition was expended.

About 3 o'clock, January 1, they took a position south of the Murfreesborough pike, and were not further engaged.

Battery C, First Illinois, Captain Houghtaling, on the 30th moved on the left of Captain Bush, and next to the Wilkinson pike, south side; opened fire, in concert with other batteries of the division, at the enemy in front.

On the 31st, at the falling back of General Johnson, this battery took position on the right of the pike, just in the edge of the timber, supported by Colonel Roberts' brigade, where he remained until all of his horses were killed and ammunition expended, when he was forced to abandon his guns, falling back and assisting at the guns of the other batteries of the division.

The Fourth Indiana Battery, Captain Bush, on the afternoon of the 30th, being on the right of Captain Houghtaling, moved his battery to the front and opened fire on the enemy at short range, with the other batteries, driving back the enemy. During the night the captain moved to a more commanding position.

On the 31st, the battle opened with this division by an attempt to capture this battery, which was gallantly defended by General Sill, when this brave officer fell between the guns. The battery fell back with the other batteries of the division, and took position on the north of the pike, sending one section, with Lieutenant Flansburg, to re-enforce Captain Houghtaling; one Parrott section, with Lieutenant Taliaferro, was, at this time, sent to Captain Houghtaling, assisted by Captain Hescock, when, after a very warm resistance, and ammunition failing, the battery was compelled to retire, with the loss of two of its guns left in the cedars. The next position taken was on the south of the Murfreesborough pike, with the division.

Center.—The artillery of the First Division consists of the following batteries: Captain Stone, First Kentucky Battery; Lieutenant Van Pelt, First Michigan Battery; Company H, Fifth U. S. Artillery, Lieutenant Guenther, with the following guns: Ten 10-pounder Parrotts, two James rifles, two 6-pounder smooth-bore, and four 12-pounder light field guns.

Captain Stone's First Kentucky Battery was not ordered into position until January 1, when it was posted on the right of the Murfreesborough pike, directly in front of the log-house, one section being stationed in the woods, about 100 yards distant. The battery afterward moved to the front edge of the woods, in rear of the center of the brigade to which it was attached. At night it relieved Lieutenant Parsons' battery, which was stationed outside and in front of the woods, commanding the corn-fields and woods to the right and front, in which position it remained until January 3. At 4 p. m. relieved Captain Cox's half battery, which was about 50 yards to the left, posting a half battery in its place at night; shelled the fields and woods from both points; was not further engaged.

The First Michigan Battery, Lieutenant Van Pelt, took position on the morning of the 31st on the left of the pike, 3 miles from Murfreesborough, where they remained during the day, serving their guns with effect; were relieved on the 1st of January, and took position about half a mile in rear of front line of battle.

On January 2 moved a few hundred yards to the front, and took position on the right of the pike, remaining at this point through the day. On Saturday morning the battery moved to the front, behind earth-works, immediately beyond the pike, fronting the position occupied on Wednesday, remaining there all day and night, shelling the woods at sundown.

On the morning of the 31st, Company H, Fifth Artillery, Lieutenant Guenther, moved through the cedars to the left of the pike with its brigade, but was returned, owing to the impracticability of operating in the woods, and took position in the open ground in time to check a rebel advance. From the cedars it then moved to a position on the rise of ground on the opposite side of the pike. On the appearance of the enemy at close range, a heavy fire with canister shot was opened on them with such effect that they were driven back to the woods in disorder. The battery held this position until the morning of January 1, when it was moved some distance to the rear, and, after several changes of front, was ordered with the brigade to a point on the Murfreesborough pike, beyond Stewart's Creek. This order being countermanded, the battery encamped near its old point.

On the morning of January 3 fire was opened on a battery of the enemy which was annoying our troops, resulting in driving it from its position. During the forenoon the brigade and battery moved forward and occupied rifle-pits and epaulements which had been constructed for them. At dusk the battery opened fire with shell and spherical case shot on the enemy, concealed in the woods and buildings and behind breastworks, &c., which, being followed by infantry, drove them from their position. The battery remained in position during the following day, and on the morning of the 5th removed to Murfreesborough.

The batteries of the Second Division, Brigadier-General Negley, are as follows: Company M, First Ohio, Captain Schultz; Company G, First Ohio Artillery, Lieutenant Marshall; Company M, First Kentucky [Second Kentucky Battery], Lieutenant Ellsworth, with the following guns: Two 12-pounder Wiard steel guns, two 6-pounder Wiard, four 12-pounder howitzers, two James rifles, one 6-pounder smooth-bore, and two 16-pounder Parrotts. The three batteries of this division were posted with the division on a slope of the west bank of Stone's River, in advance, but joining the right, of General Crittenden's line, with General Sheridan on their right; Captain Schultz on the right of Battery G, First Ohio, and Battery M, First Kentucky [Second Kentucky Battery], on the left. The batteries opened fire on the enemy and drove them, holding the position during the day and night.

On the 31st, these batteries, after holding their position under a murderous fire for four hours, having a large proportion of their horses killed, and being out of ammunition, were compelled to retire with the loss of six guns in getting through the cedars.

On January 1, Company M was posted on the left side of the railroad; changed position about 1 o'clock to the right of Murfreesborough pike, where it remained until night.

On January 2, these batteries were posted on the hill at the ford of Stone's River, to resist the attack on the left, which proved successful.

Left Wing.—The batteries of the left wing are the following: Company M, Fourth U. S. Artillery, Lieutenant Parsons; Company H, Fourth Artillery, Lieutenant Throckmorton; Company B, First Ohio Artillery, Captain Standart, attached to the Second Division; Tenth Indiana, Captain Cox; Eighth Indiana, Lieutenant Estep; Sixth Ohio, Captain Bradley, attached to the First Division; Seventh Indiana Battery, Captain Swallow; Third Wisconsin, Lieutenant Livingston; Twenty-sixth Pennsylvania [Battery B, Pennsylvania Light Artillery], Lieutenant Stevens, attached to the Third Division, with the following guns: Four 3-inch rifles, ten 12-pounder howitzers, six James rifles, twelve 6-pounder smooth-bores, and sixteen 10-pounder Parrotts.

The first position taken by Batteries H and M, under command of Lieutenant Parsons, was just to the right of the Murfreesborough pike, $2\frac{1}{4}$ miles from Murfreesborough. During the morning they retired for ammunition, and took a second position between the railroad and pike, and, after firing away all their ammunition, they again retired. On January 2 they were moved to the front, and soon after took position at the hill near the ford, and participated in repulsing the enemy from our left.

Company B, First Ohio Artillery, Captain Standart, on the 31st was posted on the right of Lieutenant Parsons. After firing away his ammunition, he retired for the day. On the 2d he was put in position on the hill on the right of the pike, commanding the corn-field occupied by Stokes' battery the day before. Being under a very heavy cannonading, three pieces were retired to a position under cover, in reserve, to the left of the pike. These three guns were, in the afternoon, moved to the left, to resist the attack of the enemy.

Company F, First Ohio, Captain Cockerill, on the 31st, was placed in position on the left of Parsons' battery, and on the right of the pike; but during the morning retired and took position on the left of the railroad and about 400 yards from it, which position they held until the attack on the left, to which point Lieutenant Osburn moved four pieces, the captain having been wounded.

Captain Bradley, on the morning of the 31st, moved, with Colonel Harker's brigade in its advance, to check the enemy on the right, and held with it its position through the day. On the 2d he held a position on commanding ground near to the right of the railroad. When the attack was made on the left, he changed front to fire to the left.

The Seventh Indiana Battery, Captain Swallow, on the 31st, went into battery a short distance to the right of the pike, $2\frac{1}{2}$ miles from Murfreesborough, and in the afternoon moved to the left of the railroad, going into battery on the right of Cockerill's battery. On the 2d this battery also was placed on the high ground to resist the enemy's attack at the ford.

The Eighth Indiana Battery, Lieutenant Estep, was placed on the opposite side of the pike (left) and rear of Captain Swallow's battery.

On the 2d, having suffered severely from the enemy's artillery in the morning, he retired to repair damages, and, when the attack was made on the left, massed with the other batteries on the hill at the ford.

The Tenth Indiana Battery, Captain Cox, was placed in position in front and on the left of the railroad, which he maintained on the 31st and afterward.   The Twenty-sixth Pennsylvania Battery [Battery B, Pennsylvania Light Artillery], Lieutenant Stevens, was posted on the left and facing the pike, 3 miles from Murfreesborough, when the enemy appeared.   As they fell back he moved forward, crossing the pike, taking position on the ridge, changing several times.

On the 2d he changed front to fire to the left, and opened fire when the attack was made in that direction.

The Third Wisconsin Battery, Lieutenant Livingston, was commanding the ford on the 31st.   They afterward moved across the river at the ford.   When the attack was made on the 2d, they recrossed and took position on the hill in line with the other batteries of the corps.

The Board of Trade Battery, Captain Stokes, attached to the Pioneer Brigade, consisting of four 6-pounders, smooth-bore, and two James rifles, moved, on the 31st, promptly to the front and right of the pike, serving canister with effect.   They afterward moved still farther to the front, holding a good position, commanding a corn-field and the wood beyond.   After having held the position thirty-six hours, the battery was ordered to the rear.

On the 2d, this battery was again put in position with the batteries to resist the attack from the left, and opened, with the artillery force massed at that point, a destructive fire, causing the enemy to retire. The losses in *matériel* and *personnel* I had the honor to report immediately after the battle.

The many gallant actions of battery officers and men are named by their immediate commanders in their reports, to which I respectfully refer for the details of their action.   The practice of the batteries was good, and the precaution of the general commanding to fire low and be sparing of ammunition was heeded.   Owing to the nature of the country, the loss of the guns was unavoidable, as in falling back on the right the horses could not be under cover, and the thick cedar thickets prevented the guns being brought off by hand.

Six guns, 3 caissons, 3 damaged forges, and 2 battery wagons were captured from the enemy, or recaptured; also 5,451 muskets, with bayonets, scabbards, &c.

The whole number of men engaged in serving the batteries was 86 commissioned officers and 2,760 non-commissioned officers and privates.

I remain, colonel, your obedient servant,
JAMES BARNETT,
Colonel and Chief of Artillery.

Lieut. Col. C. GODDARD,
Assistant Adjutant-General and Chief of Staff.

Report of loss sustained by the batteries of the Fourteenth Army Corps.

Designation of battery.	Name of commanding officer.	Officers Killed	Officers Wounded	Officers Captured	Enlisted men Killed	Enlisted men Wounded	Enlisted men Captured and missing	Guns Captured	Guns Disabled	Horses Killed	Horses Wounded	Horses Captured and missing	Harness Sets of lead	Harness Sets of wheel	Battery wagons Lost	Battery wagons Disabled	Forges Lost	Forges Disabled	Number of rounds ammunition expended.
Battery E, 1st Ohio Artillery	Captain Edgarton		2	2	10	5	20	6		75			28	14	1		1		7
Battery A, 1st Ohio Artillery	Lieutenant Belding				1	5	23	3		73			22	11	1		1		25
5th Indiana Battery	Captain Simonson	1	1	1	3	19	2	2		9	14	17	6						213
Battery G, 1st Missouri Artillery	Captain Hescock				4	12	5			20		15			1		1		1,112
Battery C, 1st Illinois Artillery	Captain Houghtaling		1		6	20	24			80		10					1		1,154
4th Indiana Battery	Captain Bush		1		1	17	3	6		17							1		1,160
5th Wisconsin Battery	Lieutenant Hill	1			1	5		2		21									726
8th Wisconsin Battery	Lieutenant Stiles		1			4	1	1		18	5		6	3					375
2d Minnesota Battery	Captain Hotchkiss				3	5	2	2		13			4	2					500
1st Michigan Battery	Lieutenant Van Pelt		1		1	8				5	4		1	1					697
1st Kentucky Battery	Captain Stone				1	5	2			3		4	2						110
Battery H, 5th U. S. Artillery	Lieutenant Guenther																		558
Battery M, 1st Michigan Artillery	Captain Church																		170
Battery M, 1st Ohio Artillery	Captain Schultz				4	4	1	1		9		12							750
Battery G, 1st Ohio Artillery	Lieutenant Marshall		1		4	8	3	4		34									553
Hewett's Kentucky Battery	Lieutenant Nell				2	1	3	1		28									531
Battery B, 1st Ohio Artillery	Captain Standart				3	13				21									1,610
Batteries H and M, 4th U. S. Artillery	Lieutenant Parsons				3	14	3		1	20	4		14	5		1		1	2,299
7th Indiana Battery	Captain Swallow				4	7	6			1	24								406
Battery F, 1st Ohio Artillery	Captain Cockerill					12													1,080
3d Wisconsin Battery	Lieutenant Livingston				2	4	1			9									358
26th Pennsylvania Battery	Lieutenant Stevens				2	7				7									1,650
10th Indiana Battery	Captain Cox				1	4	2			72	4								1,442
8th Indiana Battery	Lieutenant Estep				2	6	1			15									871
6th Ohio Battery	Captain Bradley					2				16	5								500
Board of Trade Battery	Captain Stokes		1		3	8	1			3		1							1,450
Total		2	9	3	61	195	103	28	1	569	60	59	83	36	3	1	5	1	20,307

Respectfully submitted.

JAMES BARNETT,
Colonel and Chief of Artillery.

No. 10.

Report of Capt. James St. Clair Morton, U. S. Engineers, commanding Pioneer Brigade.

HDQRS. PIONEER BRIGADE, FOURTEENTH ARMY CORPS,
Camp, 3 miles north of Murfreesborough, Tenn., January 5, 1863.

MAJOR : According to your order, I have the honor to submit the following report of the part taken in the late battle by my brigade, which is composed of three battalions of Pioneers and Stokes' (Chicago Board of Trade) battery :

On the march hither from Nashville, my brigade constructed two bridges over Stewart's Creek between the hours of 4 p. m. and 4 a. m. December 29 and 30, arriving here on the 30th.

On the morning of the 31st, the brigade was engaged in improving the fords of Stone's River, in which the right battalion sustained the fire of some rebel cavalry, when I was ordered to take position in the line of battle, and formed my brigade, by the orders of the commanding general in person, fronting toward the right, where the enemy appeared on a rise of ground in front of us, from which they had driven one of our batteries. I immediately opened fire with canister from Stokes' battery and drove them back. I then, by order of the commanding general in person, advanced to the said rise, and held it under the fire of three rebel batteries. I supported the battery by the First Battalion of Pioneers on the left, posted in a thicket, and by the Third Battalion on the right. The Second Battalion was placed in a wood still farther to the right.

Shortly after I had formed my line, the enemy appeared across the field, preparing to charge upon some of our troops, who were retiring, but had been rallied by the commanding general. I opened fire upon these from Stokes' battery, which played over the head of the commanding general and our troops, and arrested their advance. My right battalion was soon after attacked, the object of the enemy being to penetrate through the line under cover of the woods. Said battalion changed front so as to obtain a flanking fire, and by a single volley repulsed the enemy, composed of the Eleventh and Fourteenth Texas Regiments. In this the battalion was aided by the Seventy-ninth Indiana, which had rallied on its right.

Toward sundown, the enemy appearing on my left, I brought two sections of Stokes' battery to the left of my First Battalion, and repulsed a brigade of the enemy which attacked that battalion in the thicket. They left their dead within 50 paces of my line. In this affair both the battalion and the battery behaved very creditably.

The brigade slept on their arms the night of the 31st. Early on the 1st instant the enemy appeared on my left, apparently to advance through the gap between it and the pike. I changed my front and occupied the gap, and sustained and returned their volleys of musketry, playing upon them from the battery and preventing their advance beyond the edge of the woods. We held this position till after nightfall, when the brigade was relieved and formed in reserve.

On the morning of the 2d, part of the Pioneers were engaged in making road crossings over the railroad, when the enemy opened a cannonade, which reached our camp. I brought out Stokes' battery and returned the fire. The battalions advanced, supporting it under a fire of solid shot and shell. The cannonade having ceased, I received orders to fall back to my assigned position in reserve, and remained till late in the afternoon, when the commanding general in person ordered me to the left as re-enforcement. I then marched my command at a double-quick and arrived on the line, occupying a gap in it under the fire of a rebel battery, which was, however, soon silenced by Stokes' battery, which was worked with exceeding vigor and skill.

General Negley now approached me and requested me to re-enforce his troops, who, after a violent contest, had gained ground on the opposite side of the river. I accordingly moved my command there at a double-quick, and formed the Third Battalion in second line behind General Davis' command, the First Battalion extending beyond it and throwing out its own advance, occupying the space between it and the river. The battery was posted on a knoll between the First and Third Battalions, the Second Battalion being in second line on the extreme right. In this position we remained till after nightfall, when I received orders to recross the river and again assume a position in reserve, and to furnish the Second Battalion to construct rifle-pits in the front and near the pike, and also on the extreme right. Said battalion worked all night in the rain.

On the 3d, the Third Battalion relieved the First, on duty in the trenches, and on the 4th the Second and Third Battalions began two lunettes on the north bank of the river, and the First Battalion began a trestle bridge across it. On the 5th, the said work was continued, and the Third Battalion, with the advance of the army, in pursuit of the enemy.

The loss of the brigade is as follows: First Battalion: Killed, 4; wounded, 3 commissioned officers and 5 enlisted men. Second Battalion: Killed, 4; wounded, 5 enlisted men. Third Battalion: Killed, 4; wounded, 10 enlisted men. Stokes' battery: Killed, 3; wounded, 1 commissioned officer and 9 enlisted men. Total, killed and wounded, 48.

The force of the brigade actually engaged was 1,600 men, there being ten companies or 1,000 Pioneers employed on the fortifications between Gallatin and Nashville, and 200 detached guarding the implement train. Of the force above mentioned, 95 belong to Stokes' battery.

During the engagement, the Pioneers behaved as well as could be wished, and, when required, worked zealously by night and day, although insufficiently provided with rations, in spite of inclement weather, and under fire. The artillerymen displayed the highest discipline, and worked their guns with extreme rapidity and accuracy. As the commanding general was everywhere present on the field with his staff, he cannot but have remarked the good service done by Captain Stokes, who manifested the greatest zeal, and managed his battery with the utmost precision and success.

I beg leave to mention to the favorable notice of the commanding general my adjutant, Lieutenant Lamberson, of the Nineteenth Illinois Volunteers; my inspectors, Lieutenants Clark, of the Sixteenth U. S. Infantry, and Murphy, of the Twenty-first Wisconsin Volunteers, and my aides, Lieutenant Reeve, of the Thirty-seventh Indiana Volunteers, and Assistant Engineer Pearsall, all of whom exhibited the utmost ardor and alacrity in the performance of their duty.

I beg leave also to mention Captain Hood, of the Eleventh Michigan Volunteers, commanding Second Battalion; Captain Clements, of the Sixty-ninth Ohio Volunteers, commanding Third Battalion, and Captain Bridges, of the Nineteenth Illinois Volunteers, commanding First Battalion, who, though wounded on the first day, retained the command of his battalion throughout.

I have the honor to inclose the sub-reports of the chiefs of battalions, of the commander of the battery, and of the surgeon of the brigade.

I have the honor to be, sir, very respectfully, your obedient servant,

J. ST. C. MORTON,
Captain of Engineers, U. S. Army, Chief Engineer
Fourteenth Army Corps, Commanding Pioneer Brigade.

Maj. C. GODDARD,
 Acting Assistant Adjutant-General.

No. 11.

Report of Capt. Lyman Bridges, commanding First Battalion.

HDQRS. FIRST BATTALION, PIONEER BRIGADE,
  DEPARTMENT OF THE CUMBERLAND,
Stone's River, near Murfreesborough, Tenn., January 5, 1863.

CAPTAIN: In compliance with your order, I herewith furnish a report of the part this battalion took in the recent battle at this place.

I have the honor to report that on the morning of December 30, 1862, having completed the bridge at Stewart's Creek at 4 a. m., I received orders to hold my command in readiness to march at a moment's notice. At 8 a. m., by your order, I moved seven companies, 600 strong, forward upon the Murfreesborough pike, throwing out an advance guard and flankers upon either side, three companies being upon special duty. At 10 a. m., in accordance with orders received from you, I moved to the front and halted, awaiting your order. At 2 p. m. I moved my command to the river, taking position upon the left of Captain Stokes' Chicago Board of Trade Battery, and built an abatis from the river toward General Rosecrans' headquarters, as directed by you. At 4 a. m., December 31, I improved a ford across Stone's River. At 7 a. m. our right wing having been overpowered, and the enemy's advance being within 80 rods of my camp, I fell in with my command and followed Stokes' battery, as previously ordered by you. The battery having been ordered into position on the ridge between the pike and railroad, I forwarded my command in line of battle upon the left of Stokes' battery, the enemy having possession of the parallel ridge upon the opposite side of the pike, about 20 rods distant.

At that crisis General Rosecrans rode along our line, and ordered me to charge and take the knob upon the opposite side of the pike, he sending the same order to Captain Stokes' battery. I moved one wing upon either side of the battery to the hill in good order. Soon after reaching the hill, General Rosecrans ordered me to occupy the skirt of woods upon my left. I moved my entire command upon the left of the battery, the Third Battalion of this brigade relieving my right wing, changing position to the left.

The enemy continued a heavy fire of grape, canister, and musketry upon us as we advanced and they fell back. After gaining our new position, General Rosecrans rode to our front, and rallied the Twenty-first Ohio, First Kentucky, and Seventy-eighth Pennsylvania, which had fallen back upon our right.

At 12 m. the enemy, General McCown's division, came down, upon the double-quick, with their standards flying, in splendid order. They were allowed to come within 300 yards, when the musketry of the entire brigade and the battery opened with grape and canister a most deadly fire, which he returned as earnestly. The column reeled and fell back in disorder, their colors struck down and barely rescued. Lieutenant Ritchie, Company A, of Third Ohio Detachment, was here wounded while encouraging his men. The number of killed and wounded left on the field tells how severe was his loss. Many of his wounded reached our lines during the day and night, all declaring that the 12 o'clock charge was an expensive one for them.

The enemy again rallied his forces at 5 p. m., advancing a brigade upon my left flank through a skirt of wood, attempting a surprise. My pickets being fired upon by the enemy, who took advantage of a train of ambulances being in the vicinity, firing upon ambulances and pickets indiscriminately, I ordered this battalion to change front and commence firing. Lieutenant Stevens, of Stokes' battery, opened fire upon him simultaneously with grape and canister. Our new line fortunately rested upon the crest of the hill. Each volley by us thinned his ranks. He advanced, perhaps 40 paces, discharging repeated volleys of musketry, but his repulse was complete, and they fell back to the wood, 1,000 yards in the rear, cursing their fate. Dozens of their wounded men, found within our lines of skirmishers, all corroborated each other in stating that a brigade was repulsed in attempting to take our position. He left 60 of his men upon the field. Lieutenant Smith, of Company B, in charge of my skirmishers, with his company captured 1 major, 1 captain, and 30 men. I received a slight wound in my left leg, above the ankle, not so severe as to require me to leave the field. My command laid upon their arms during the night, holding the ground gained early in the morning.

Lieutenant Froelich, Twenty-second Illinois, at daybreak next morning, January 1, while in charge of the skirmishers of and in front of my command, reported a large force of the enemy assembling near to the left of the position to which he returned the previous evening. I rode to the front and left flank of my line of battle. The fog being very dense, the enemy could not be seen, but I could distinctly hear his commands, and being satisfied that he was advancing on my left, and there being no support between my left and the Murfreesborough pike, I informed you of my information and position. Receiving orders from you, I immediately changed front, my left resting upon the Murfreesbororough pike. Captain Stokes moved his battery promptly upon my right. The sun had just risen, but the fog had not yet cleared. We took our position without accident. The enemy advanced within 500 yards and opened fire, as he supposed, upon our flank. A few moments' return fire convinced him that we were not unaware of his movements. In half an hour he fell back behind his intrenchment, remaining there during the day.

No demonstration was made upon our front during the day. At 10 p. m. Colonel Buell relieved my command, and I moved, by your orders, 1 mile to the left and rear, having held the one position upon the front thirty-six hours without relief.

At sunrise, January 2, the enemy charged upon our left center, capturing a section of a battery one-half mile in our immediate front, and were forcing our position. I moved my command, as ordered by you, to the left and front, my right resting on the Third Battalion of this brigade, and my left upon an open field near the river; remained an hour in line of battle; was then ordered to take a position at the bend of the river, 40 rods farther down; remained in position until 3 p. m., when, by your orders, I moved forward in good order to the support of

Stokes' battery in the charge upon the hill, above the bend of the river, recently held by our left wing.

Lieut. E. S. Dodd, acting lieutenant-colonel, was wounded in the leg with a 6-pounder ball while the battalion was taking its position. By your order, I moved forward in double-quick, forded the river, and charged up the hill; formed line of battle over the crest of the hill, my left wing occupying an oak ridge, as indicated by you. I remained in position an hour, until the several regiments that had done such gallant service rallied and formed in line of battle again.

By your order I changed position, my right resting upon the river, my left occupying a front of woods, and supported by Stokes' battery. Remained in position until 12 p. m., when I was ordered to move across the river.

January 3, by your order, this battalion commenced building a military bridge at the lower bend of Stone's River, which, I have the honor to inform you, is now completed and in use.

It is with pleasure that I mention with the highest regard and praise the officers and men of this battalion, who all did their duty so promptly and nobly during the past terrible week. To Lieut. George Turner, adjutant, I am under many obligations for repeated and timely assistance.

Annexed is a list of the killed and wounded of this battalion.*

I have the honor to be, very respectfully, your obedient servant,

LYMAN BRIDGES,
Captain, Commanding.

Capt. JAMES ST. CLAIR MORTON,
    Chief Engineer, Fourteenth Army Corps, Comdg. Pioneer Brig.

No. 12.

Report of Capt. Calvin Hood, commanding Second Battalion.

HDQRS. RIGHT BATTALION, PIONEER BRIGADE,
    Camp in the Field, January 5, 1863.

SIR: I have the honor to submit the following report of the part taken in the late battle by my battalion:

On the morning of December 31 we were ordered to improve a ford of Stone's River near camp. Soon after commencing work, we were fired upon by the enemy's cavalry, and retired, as we were ordered not to remain under fire.

At 9 a. m. we marched, and formed line of battle with the brigade between the railroad and pike, near the cedar woods. In front of us was hard fighting, when the enemy finally gave way, and our troops advanced to the field beyond the cedars. We moved forward in line with the brigade, my battalion on the right, and took position about midway of the woods, and about 100 rods from the field. The troops in front of us there gave way, and regiment after regiment came through our lines entirely broken up. We here received orders from Captain Morton to fix bayonets and allow no stragglers to pass our lines, and to hold fire and give the enemy the cold steel. The retreating troops passed on our right, except the Seventy-ninth Indiana, whose commander rallied them on my right and rear. The Eleventh and Fourteenth Texas came on at

---

* Embodied in revised statement p. 214.

a charge, and tried to flank our right, when my battalion changed positions by the right flank and fronted toward them. General Van Cleve here rode up from my right, and asked what troops we were, and said we must fall back. I here learned that a small part of his command was on my right and near the pike. I replied that I was ordered to hold this position at all hazards. I then ordered my men to lie down and wait until the enemy were well upon us. They then rose, gave them a volley, and charged with the Seventy-ninth Indiana, and drove them from the woods.

Our loss here was 4 killed, including my orderly, Bennett Smith, Eleventh Michigan, who was shot from his horse beside me, and several wounded. Lieutenant Sherman, Twenty-fifth Illinois, was wounded in the arm, slightly, but did not leave the field. We remained under arms all night, with one company under Lieutenant Sands, Thirty-sixth Illinois, as advance picket, and brought from the field in front some 25 wounded men of our own and the enemy's.

Early in the morning of January 1, we changed position with the brigade to the front and center of our lines and on the brow of the hill. Here we remained all day under fire of the enemy's sharpshooters, with continual fighting with their skirmishers, our skirmishers being under command of Lieutenant Sands. Late in the evening we were relieved by the Thirty-third Ohio, and retired beyond the brow of the hill and bivouacked. I then gave the immediate command to Lieutenant Hartsough, Forty-ninth Ohio, acting lieutenant-colonel, as I had become so hoarse that I could not speak aloud. Early in the morning of the 2d, while a part of my command were at fatigue duty, the enemy commenced firing solid shot from the center at the battery in front of us and on the hill, but, shooting too high, their shot struck in front of us and ricochetted, and made bad work with us. Our men formed and marched forward to the support of the Chicago Board of Trade Battery, with shot falling among them thick and fast, and, as near as can be ascertained, 3 were killed and several wounded. Lieutenant Hartsough here had his horse shot under him, and the command fell upon Lieutenant Moore, Sixth Indiana, acting major, who commanded them gallantly. Firing soon ceased, and we remained upon the ground until late in the afternoon, when, as the enemy charged across the river upon General Negley's division, we were ordered to his support, and my command charged across the river under Lieutenant Moore. My command was ordered back, and, under the direction of General Thomas, worked all night in the rain on the rifle-pits in front, and without rations.

With few exceptions, officers and men behaved gallantly, and on the 31st behaved like veterans; and, taking into consideration that they are formed of detachments from forty different regiments, and have never drilled together in either company or battalion drills, moved in the face of the enemy splendidly.

I would especially mention Lieutenant Moore, Sixth Indiana, acting major; Lieutenant Baker, Thirty-ninth Indiana, acting adjutant, and Lieutenant Sands, Thirty-sixth Illinois, who rendered me valuable assistance throughout.

Your obedient servant,

CALVIN HOOD,
Captain, Commanding Right Battalion.

Capt. JAMES ST. CLAIR MORTON,
Commanding Pioneer Brigade.

No. 13.

Report of Capt. Robert Clements, commanding Third Battalion.

HDQRS. CENTER BATTALION, PIONEER BRIGADE,
Near Murfreesborough, Tenn., January 5, 1863

SIR: On the morning of December 30, 1862, my battalion was ordered by Capt. J. St. C. Morton to report to General Rosecrans. By 4 a. m. I reported my command to the front ready for duty, when I received orders from the commanding general to report to General Thomas, who ordered me to cut and clear several roads through the thick woods on the right of the pike and in front. We worked all day under the fire of the enemy's guns, and by 5 p. m. cleared several roads for the passage of artillery and infantry. At 6 p. m. I was relieved, and reported my battalion in camp some three-fourths of a mile to the rear, on the left of the Murfreesborough and Nashville pike.

December 31, 1862, Company F, under charge of Acting Lieutenant-Colonel Lingeman, reported to General Negley to finish the previous day's work. Acting Major Stewart, with Companies A, D, I, and E, was ordered to the front of General Crittenden's corps, to cut the east bank, a portion of it on Stone's River, passable for troops. Reaching the river, they found it in possession of the rebels. Leaving a reserve of two companies on this side, in charge of Capt. A. K. Robinson, Major Stewart crossed with the balance of his men, and drove the enemy from the ground, and commenced work. At 8 a. m. heavy firing was heard on our right and in front of General Negley's division. Immediately the left wing of our battalion was ordered to form line, and soon we were on the march toward the direction of the firing, that was becoming more terrific as we advanced. In the mean time Major Stewart was relieved by a portion of the Eleventh Brigade, General Van Cleve's division, and, with the exception of Company F, our battalion moved forward under a fire from the enemy's cannon, and supported Captain Stokes' Chicago battery, that opened, from the top of a slight elevation on the left of the pike, a terrific shower of grape into the enemy's ranks, who were at that moment driving our front line from the woods, on the right of the road, by heavy volleys of musketry. Soon the enemy were forced back, our troops advancing with the battery into an open field some 300 yards.

By this time the rebels had renewed their fire, and were driving our advanced line, that had moved forward into a thick wood, panic-stricken, back upon my men, who were ordered by Captain Morton to fix bayonets and charge upon the first man attempting to pass the line. The order was promptly enforced, and soon hundreds of confused stragglers were formed into line on our right, and, with the shower of shell and grape from our battery, succeeded in driving the enemy from the field. During the day my battalion was kept on the front, and at night threw forward Company H, as advanced pickets and skirmishers, some 400 yards.

The night being very cold, and no fires allowed, the men suffered much from the want of blankets, as well as from the scarcity of rations, many of them having had nothing to eat since the previous night.

At 6 a. m., January 1, I was ordered to change my line and support our battery, expecting an attack from the southeast, as it could be seen the enemy were advancing from the wood in that direction. My line was formed, and opened fire, together with the battery, that checked the enemy's advance, and heavy skirmishing was kept up during the entire day. Benjamin L. Wagner, of Company C, wounded, was the only injury sustained by my men.

At 9 p. m. my battalion was relieved and encamped, after thirty-six hours' duty on the front, one-half mile toward the rear and on the left of the pike.

At 7 a. m., January 2, the enemy commenced shelling our camp, having the night previous planted a battery in direct range of our camp fires. I soon deployed my men from column into line, and moved forward with the battery to a slight rise of ground, and ordered my battalion to lie down, so as to protect my line from the shot and shell that flew over us without doing much damage. Before I could get my battalion deployed, however, Sergt. John F. Burke, Twentieth Kentucky Volunteers, Corpl. Peter Wagoner, One hundredth Illinois, and William Trimble, Third Kentucky Volunteers, were killed, and Samuel S. M. Blankenship, Ninth Kentucky Volunteers, John Desch, Eighty-fourth Illinois Volunteers, John C. Pelser, and Sergt. William Mason, Sixth Kentucky Volunteers, were wounded.

The enemy's guns being silenced, I was ordered to move my men by columns doubled in the center toward the rear, and remained under cover of wood near the river till 2.30 p. m., when a sudden attack by the enemy was made on General Van Cleve's front. We were marched forward to the support of our battery. Reaching the top of a small bluff, I was ordered to halt my battalion. Orders were soon given, however, to advance, and we moved forward on a double-quick to the support of our front, who were obliged to fall back upon this side of the river under cover of our artillery, that was soon brought into position, and played with great execution upon the advancing columns of the enemy, who were repulsed by a heavy cross-fire from our guns. I was then ordered by General Negley to cross the river, and formed line just at dark on the ground occupied in the morning by the rebel skirmishers. In this position my men lay until 9 p. m., suffering much from wet feet and a rain, when we were ordered back and went into camp.

January 3, an order came detailing 200 men for duty. The men, under charge of Lieut. Benjamin F. West, reported to the front, and threw up rifle-pits until 8 p. m., when relieved.

January 4, after spending a cold and rainy night without tents and [on] half rations, I moved my battalion to the east 300 yards from camp, and on a bluff near Stone's River, where I was ordered to throw up a heavy breastwork. While clearing the rubbish from an old building, Amos Hoak, Thirteenth Ohio Volunteers, was killed by the falling of a heavy timber.

At 4 p. m. I was relieved and ordered to report, January 5, to General Thomas, at Murfreesborough, the enemy having evacuated the town.

I need not add that, notwithstanding the inclemency of the weather, to which my men were exposed during the whole engagement, having no tents, few blankets, and without half rations, they went forward to the prompt execution of every order and command with a cheerfulness and bravery commendable only to a prompt and efficient soldier.

Respectfully,

R. CLEMENTS,
Captain, Commanding.

Capt. JAMES ST. CLAIR MORTON,
Commanding Pioneer Brigade.

No. 14.

Report of Capt. James H. Stokes, Stokes' Illinois Battery.

STOKES' BATTERY, IN CAMP NEAR MURFREESBOROUGH,
January 5, 1863.

SIR : I have the honor to report that the battery under my command was called into action Wednesday morning, 31st ultimo, about 8 a. m., and at a time when the left of our right army corps, completely demoralized, was under full retreat.   The battery, by a terrific fire of canister, drove back the enemy, the infantry rallying under its fire.   The battery then moved still farther to the front, and took a position commanding the approaches where our right had been dispersed.   Under a fire, it is said, of three rebel batteries, well served, it held this key to our front during the entire day.   About 4 p. m. a rebel brigade formed under cover of the woods to the right of the battery, and was only known by a foolish discharge of musketry on one of our ambulances, picking up their wounded as well as ours.   The battery, being charged with canister, opened upon this brigade, and, it is said by one of the wounded, entirely annihilated it.   The killed and wounded prove the accuracy of the fire.   This position was held through the night, until next evening. About 10 p. m. it was ordered to the rear to rest, having been thirty-six hours to the front.   In this engagement the battery, with a strength of 98, all told, lost 3 privates killed ; 1 officer, 3 non-commissioned officers, and 5 privates wounded, being 12 killed and wounded, or about one-eighth.

On Friday, the 2d instant, the battery was again called into action, about 4 p. m., by the retreat and threatened destruction of our left. The battery, under the direction of the commanding general, moved to the front through the retreating infantry and artillery, and did not halt to go into battery until it had moved far beyond the front.   The infantry again rallied under its fire.   The battery opened a destructive fire of shell on the rebel battery, so destructive to our troops, completely silencing and destroying it, so that several of its pieces were captured by our advancing infantry.   The battery that night occupied the ground of this rebel battery.

The commanding general, who witnessed the bearing of this gallant little band, will do justice to its discipline and bravery.   All were brave; all nobly did their duty to their country.

I am, captain, very respectfully, your obedient servant,
JAMES H. STOKES,
Captain, Commanding Battery.

Captain MORTON,
Commanding Pioneer Corps, Army of the Cumberland.

No. 15.

Reports of Maj. Gen. Alexander McD. McCook, U. S. Army, commanding Right Wing.

HEADQUARTERS RIGHT WING,
One mile in advance of Nolensville, December 27, 1862.

COLONEL : I am here with my wing in camp.   There is very strong ground in front of my main camp.   I have all the crests heavily defended.   The enemy resisted my advance all day with cavalry and artillery. My casualties are very few. The One hundred and first Ohio charged one battery, and captured one gun and caisson, with teams. The men in glorious spirits, and only want a chance. Negley is here with his division. General Thomas sent a courier here; states that he is somewhere on the Wilson pike. Hardee had a dance given him at Triune last night.

A. McD. McCOOK,
Major-General.

Colonel GARESCHÉ.

—

HEADQUARTERS RIGHT WING,
December 27, 1862.

COLONEL: The fog is so thick in these hills that I cannot see 300 yards in my front. I have ordered a halt until the fog rises. The enemy have resisted our advance for 3 miles this morning, and have a battery posted on the hill in front to enfilade the road. One brigade of the enemy in Triune; the other troops scattered on the Shelbyville road.

A. McD. McCOOK,
Major-General.

Colonel GARESCHÉ.

P. S.—The firing you hear is the enemy's battery. I will apprise you when I move forward. Can do nothing intelligently now.

—

HEADQUARTERS,
Near Triune, December 27, 1862—3 p. m.

GENERAL: The enemy, under Hardee, escaped me this morning in the fog; at times I could not see more than 50 yards. I had reliable information that Hardee was here in person, and that his army lay in line of battle last night. I have yet to pursue them 6 miles before I can well determine whether they have retreated toward Murfreesborough or Shelbyville. Every prisoner I have taken has contradictory statements as to their destination. I will know to-night.

Very respectfully,

A. McD. McCOOK,
Major-General.

Major-General THOMAS,
Commanding Center.

—

HDQRS. RIGHT WING, FOURTEENTH ARMY CORPS,
Triune, December 27, 1862—3 p. m.

COLONEL: Hardee escaped me during the fog to-day. Some reports say he left last night; others, to-day. Our prisoners tell contradictory stories about them. They had two divisions here. I am pursuing with one division, and Stanley has started with his cavalry in pursuit. I will know and promptly inform you what road they have taken. It will be necessary for me to pursue 6 miles on the Shelbyville road to determine upon what road they have marched. From College Grove there is a dirt road running 4 miles and intersecting the Salem pike. My cavalry are all raw, but have done well to-day.

General Rousseau's division did not get up until 12 m. to-day. The weather horrid. Captain Long will explain the country to you.

A. McD. McCOOK,
Major-General.

Colonel GARESCHÉ, Chief of Staff.

HDQRS. RIGHT WING, FOURTEENTH ARMY CORPS,
In Camp, Two and a half miles south of Murfreesborough, Tenn.,
January 8, 1863.

MAJOR: In compliance with telegraphic orders from the general commanding, received at my camp, on Mill Creek, 5 miles south of Nashville, at 4.30 a. m., on the morning of December 26, 1862, I put the right wing of the Fourteenth Army Corps in motion toward Nolensville, Tenn. The First Division, Brig. Gen. Jefferson C. Davis commanding, marched at 6 a. m. upon the Edmondson pike, with orders to move upon that road to Prim's blacksmith-shop, from whence it was to march direct by a country road to Nolensville.

The Third Division, Brig. Gen. Philip H. Sheridan commanding, also marched at 6 a. m., and upon the direct road to Nolensville. The Second Division, Brig. Gen. R. W. Johnson commanding (the reserve of the right wing), followed the Third Division upon the direct road.

The advance guards of Generals Davis' and Sheridan's columns encountered the enemy's cavalry about 2 miles beyond our picket line. There was continuous skirmishing with the enemy until the heads of these columns reached Nolensville.

About 1 mile beyond the town the enemy made a determined stand, in a defile and upon a range of hills that cross the turnpike at this point, lining the slopes with skirmishers and placing a six-gun battery on a commanding position, endeavoring to repel our advance. He was attacked in front and his position handsomely turned by General Carlin's brigade, of Davis' division, capturing one piece of his artillery and several prisoners. After taking possession of the defile and hills, the command was encamped.

On the night of this day, I was visited by the general commanding, who gave me verbal orders to move forward in the morning to Triune, 7 miles distant, and attack Hardee's corps, supposed to be quartered at that place. At this camp I was joined by Brig. Gen. D. S. Stanley, chief of cavalry, with the First and Second Tennessee Regiments, and the Fifteenth Pennsylvania Cavalry.

Preparations were made to move forward at daylight, the cavalry under General Stanley in the advance, followed by the Second Division, under General Johnson. It having rained all the day previous and the entire night, there was a dense fog, which prevented us from seeing 150 yards in any direction. The column having moved about 2 miles to the front, they again encountered the enemy, consisting of cavalry, infantry, and artillery. The fog at this time being so thick that friend could not be distinguished from foe, and our cavalry having been fired upon by our infantry skirmishers, on the flanks, the enemy being conversant with the ground, my troops strangers to it, and from prisoners captured having learned that Hardee's corps had been in line of battle since the night before, I did not deem it prudent to advance until the fog lifted, and I ordered the command to halt until the work could be done understandingly.

The fog having lifted at 1 p. m., an advance was immediately ordered, driving the enemy's cavalry before us.

On nearing Triune, we found that the main portion of their forces had retired, leaving a battery of six pieces, supported by cavalry, to contest the crossing of Nelson's Creek, which has steep and bluff banks. The enemy having destroyed the bridge, it was with difficulty that artillery could be crossed. On the approach of our skirmishers, the battery, with the cavalry, took flight down the Eagleville road. It now being nearly dark, and a severe and driving rail-storm blowing, they were pursued no farther.

Johnson's division crossed and encamped beyond Nelson's Creek, repairing the destroyed bridge.

On the morning of the 28th instant I ordered out a strong reconnaissance, under Brigadier-General Willich, to learn whether the enemy had retired to Shelbyville or Murfreesborough. Pursuing 7 miles down the Shelbyville road, it was found that the enemy had turned to the left, having taken a dirt road which led into the Salem pike, thence to Murfreesborough.

Leaving the Third Brigade of Johnson's division at Triune, I marched, on the 29th, with my command on the Bole Jack road toward Murfreesborough. The road being a very bad one, the command did not reach Wilkinson's Cross-Roads (5 miles from Murfreesborough) until late in the evening.

My command was encamped in line of battle; Sheridan's division on the left of Wilkinson's pike; Davis' division on right of same road; Woodruff's brigade guarding the bridge over Overall's Creek; the two brigades of Johnson's division watching the right.

On that evening, believing that the enemy intended giving our army battle at or near Murfreesborough, I ordered the brigade left at Triune to join the command without delay, which it did on the 30th.

At 1 o'clock on the morning of the 30th I received an order from General Rosecrans to report in person at his headquarters, on the Murfreesborough pike, and arrived there at 3.30 a. m. I received my instructions, which were that the left of my line should rest on the right of General Negley's division, and my right was to be thrown forward until it became parallel, or nearly so, with Stone's River, the extreme right to rest on or near the Franklin road.

My entire command advanced at 9.30 a. m., Sheridan's division moving down the Wilkinson turnpike until its advance encountered the enemy's pickets. The line of battle was then formed, the left of Sheridan's division resting upon the Wilkinson pike and immediately upon General Negley's right; the remainder of Sheridan's division was deployed to the right, the line running in a southeasterly direction. Davis' division, which had already been deployed, moved up, his left resting upon Sheridan's right, Johnson's division being held in reserve. Our front was covered with a strong line of skirmishers, who soon became sharply engaged with the enemy's sharpshooters and skirmishers. The line moved forward but slowly, as the enemy contested stubbornly every inch of ground gained by us. The ground was very favorable to them; they were under cover of a heavy wood and cedar thicket.

At 12 m. on the 30th the house of a Mr. Harding came within our lines. From that point I ascertained where the enemy's line of battle was, our skirmishers being then about 500 yards from it. The right, under General Davis, moved handsomely, but slowly, into position, as the ground over which he had to march was hotly contested by the enemy's skirmishers.

At 1 p. m. word was sent to General D. S. Stanley, chief of cavalry, that Colonel Zahm, commanding three regiments of cavalry on my right flank, was hard pressed by a superior force. I ordered one brigade of my reserve division to report to General Stanley, who conducted it to the Franklin road. On his approach the enemy, pressing Colonel Zahm, retired, and the brigade was ordered back to its former position.

At 2 p. m. a citizen living on the Franklin road, and about one-half mile in front of the enemy's line of battle, was sent me under guard by

General Stanley.   He reported as follows:

I was up to the enemy's line of battle twice yesterday and once this morning, to get some stock, taken from me.   The enemy's troops are posted in the following manner: The right of Cheatham's division rests on the Wilkinson pike; Withers is on Cheatham's left, with his left resting on the Franklin road; Hardee's corps is entirely beyond that road, and his left extending toward the Salem pike.

This man was sent immediately to the general commanding, and subsequently returned to me, with the report that his information had been received.   I also sent a report to the general commanding by my aide-de-camp, Capt. Horace N. Fisher, that the right of my line rested directly in front of the enemy's center.   This made me anxious for my right.   All my division commanders were immediately informed of this fact, and two brigades of the reserve division, commanded, respectively, by Generals Willich and Kirk, two of the best and most experienced brigadiers in the army, were ordered to the right of my line, to protect the right flank and guard against surprise there.

At 6 p. m. I received an order from the general commanding to have large and extended camp-fires made on my right, to deceive the enemy, making them believe that we were massing troops there.   This order was communicated to General Stanley, commanding cavalry, and carried into execution by Maj. R. H. Nodine, Twenty-fifth Illinois, engineer officer of my staff.

On the evening of the 30th, the order of battle was nearly parallel with that of the enemy, my right slightly refused, and my line of battle in two lines.   Two brigades of the reserve re-enforced the right of the line, and the Third Brigade, of the reserve, was posted in column about 800 yards in rear of the right.

On the evening of the 30th, Sheridan's left rested on the Wilkinson road, on the right of Negley's division, and the line then ran in a south-easterly direction through an open wood; thence in front of and partly through a cedar thicket, until General Davis' right rested near the Franklin road.   Kirk's brigade was on Davis' right, Willich's brigade placed on a line nearly perpendicular to the main line, forming a crotchet to the rear, to avoid the possibility of my right being turned by anything like an equal force.   My line was a strong one, open ground in front for a short distance.

My instructions for the following day were received at about 6.30 p. m. on the 30th, which were as follows:

Take a strong position; if the enemy attacks you, fall back slowly, refusing your right, contesting the ground inch by inch.   If the enemy does not attack you, you will attack him, not vigorously, but warmly; the time of attack by you (General Mc-Cook) to be designated by the general commanding.

I was also informed that Crittenden's corps would move simultaneously with my attack into Murfreesborough.   Written instructions were sent by me to each division commander on the night of the 30th, explaining to each what would be required of them on the 31st.

At about 6.30 a. m., on the 31st, a determined and heavy attack was made upon Kirk's and Willich's brigades, on the extreme right.   They were attacked by such an overwhelming force that they were compelled to fall back.   General Kirk being seriously wounded at the first fire upon his main line, General Willich having his horse killed early in the action, and he falling into the hands of the enemy, the two brigades were deprived of their immediate commanders, and gave way in confusion.   Colonel Post's brigade, on the right of Davis' division, and, in fact, my entire line to Sheridan's left, was almost simultaneously attacked by a heavy force of the enemy. The attack in front of Davis and Sheridan was repulsed several times, and had not the heavy turning columns of the enemy on my right succeeded so well, my line could have been maintained, and the enemy driven back to his barricades, which extended from the Wilkinson pike, with but a short interval, three-fourths of a mile beyond the Franklin road. General Sheridan's division was ably maneuvered by him, under my own eye. As soon as it became evident that my lines would be compelled to give way, orders were given to reform my line in the first skirt of timber in rear of my first position. The enemy advancing so rapidly upon my right, I found this impossible, and changed the point of reforming my line to the high ground in rear of the Wilkinson pike. Moving to the left of my line, and in rear of Sheridan's division, I here met General Rousseau in a cedar wood, posting his division to repel the attack. I then ordered my line to fall still farther back, and form on the right of Rousseau. I gave General Johnson orders, in person, to form his division in rear of Rousseau. Rousseau's division having been withdrawn to the open ground in rear of the cedar woods, the last position became untenable, and my troops were retired to the Nashville pike, where my wing, except Schaefer's brigade, of Sheridan's division, was reassembled and replenished with ammunition. On arrival at the pike, I found Colonel Harker's brigade, of Wood's division, retiring before a heavy force of the enemy. I immediately ordered Roberts' brigade, of Sheridan's division, to advance into a cedar wood, and charge the enemy and drive him back. Although this brigade was much reduced in numbers, and having but two rounds of cartridges, it advanced to the charge, under the gallant Colonel Bradley, driving the enemy back with the bayonet, capturing two guns and 40 prisoners, and securing our communication on the Murfreesborough pike at this point. This brigade is composed of the Twenty-second, Twenty-seventh, Forty-second, and Fifty-first Illinois Volunteers. The Twenty-seventh particularly distinguished itself.

About 11 a. m., Col. Moses B. Walker's brigade arrived upon the field, and reported to me for duty. They were assigned to General Sheridan's command, to whose report I refer for the good conduct of his brigade.

On the afternoon of the 31st, the right wing assumed a strong position, its left, composed of Walker's brigade, resting near a commanding knoll, its line running nearly northwest along the slope of a ridge, covered with cedar growth, the right resting upon the Murfreesborough pike. On the slope strong barricades were erected, which could well have been defended by single lines. The second line and Gibson's brigade (late Willich's) was used as a reserve. The right wing, excepting Davis' division and Gibson's brigade, did not participate in any general engagement after the 31st.

There was constant skirmishing in my front until the night of the 3d.

On the 4th, the enemy left his position in front of the right, and evacuated Murfreesborough on the night of the same day.

On the 6th, the right wing marched to its present camp, 2½ miles south of Murfreesborough, on the Shelbyville pike.

The reports of Generals Johnson, Davis, and Sheridan, division commanders, are herewith inclosed.

Accompanying General Johnson's report you will find the reports of the brigade, regimental, and battery commanders, carefully prepared.

I have been thus particular, on account of the commanding general's dispatch to the General-in-Chief, and also from erroneous reports sent to the public by newspaper correspondents.

The attention of the general commanding is particularly called to Colonels Gibson and Dodge; also to Lieutenant-Colonel Jones' report, who commanded the pickets in front of Willich's brigade.

Captain Edgarton, commanding battery of Kirk's brigade, certainly was guilty of a grave error in taking even a part of his horses to water at such an hour. He is in the hands of the enemy; therefore no report can be had from him at present.

In strict compliance with my orders, and the knowledge I possessed of the position of the enemy, which was communicated to my superior, also to the generals under my command, I could not have made a better disposition of my troops.

On subsequent examination of the field, I found the statements of the citizen, referred to in my report, correct, as the barricades extended fully three fourths of a mile beyond the Franklin road.

I am well satisfied that Hardee's corps, supported by McCown's division (late of Kirby Smith's corps), attacked Kirk's and Willich's brigades. About the same time Withers' division attacked Davis, and Cheatham's division attacked Sheridan. Cheatham's and Withers' divisions composed General Polk's corps. I was in the rear of the center of my line when this attack commenced; therefore I did not see all the column that attacked and turned my right; but it can be safely estimated that the rebel force outnumbered ours three to one. After leaving my line of battle, the ground in rear was, first, open fields; second, woods; then a dense cedar thicket; and over such ground it was almost impossible for troops to retire in good order, particularly when assailed by superior numbers.

My ammunition train, under the charge of my efficient ordnance officer, Capt. Gates P. Thruston, First Ohio Volunteers, was at an early hour ordered to take a position in rear of the center of my line. It was there attacked by the enemy's cavalry, which was handsomely repulsed by a detachment of cavalry, under the direction of Capt. H. Pease, of General Davis' staff, and Capt. G. P. Thruston, ordnance officer. The train was conducted safely to the Nashville pike, Captain Thruston cutting a road through the cedar wood for the passage of the train.

To Brig. Gens. R. W. Johnson, Philip H. Sheridan, and Jefferson C. Davis I return my thanks for their gallant conduct upon the days of the battles, and for their prompt support and conscientious attention to duty during their service in the right wing. I commend them to my superiors and my country.

To Brig. Gen. D. S. Stanley, chief of cavalry, my thanks are particularly due. He commanded my advance from Nolensville and directed the cavalry on my right flank. A report of the valuable services of our cavalry will be furnished by General Stanley. I commend him to my superiors and my country.

For the particular instances of good conduct of individuals, I refer you to the reports of division commanders.

I cannot refrain from again calling the attention of my superiors to the conspicuous gallantry and untiring zeal of Col. W. H. Gibson, of the Forty-ninth Ohio Volunteers. He succeeded to the command of Willich's brigade, and was ever prompt to dash upon the enemy with his gallant brigade when opportunity permitted. I have repeatedly recommended him for promotion. He has again won additional claims to his reward.

Colonel Harker, commanding a brigade of Wood's division, performed gallant service, under my supervision, as also did Colonel Fyffe, of the Fifty-ninth Ohio. They are commended to my superiors.

To my staff, Lieut. Col. E. Bassett Langdon, inspector-general; Maj. R. H. Nodine, engineer officer; Maj. J. A. Campbell, assistant adjutant-general; Capt. Gates P. Thruston, ordnance officer; Capt. B. D. Williams, aide-de-camp; Capt. J. F. Boyd, assistant quartermaster; Capt. Orris Blake, provost-marshal; Maj. Caleb Bates, volunteer aide-de-camp, and Capt. Horace N. Fisher, volunteer aide-de-camp and topographical engineer, my thanks are due for their conspicuous gallantry and intelligence on the field. My escort, under command of Lieutenant Thickstun, Second Kentucky Cavalry, and my orderlies behaved gallantly. When my horse was shot, Orderly Cook, of the Second Indiana, promptly replaced him with his own. The officers of the Signal Corps were ever ready to perform any service in their line or as aides.

The report of Surg. C. McDermont, the medical director of the right wing, is also submitted. Surgeon McDermont's gallantry on the field, and his great care for the wounded, is worthy of great praise.

My entire medical corps behaved nobly, except Asst. Surg. W. S. Fish, of the Third Indiana Cavalry, who fled to Nashville. He is recommended for dismissal.

The casualties of my wing are 542 killed and 2,334 wounded.*

The nation is again called to mourn the loss of gallant spirits who fell upon this sanguinary field. First of these, Brig. Gen. J. W. Sill, commanding First Brigade, Third Division. He was noble, conscientious in the discharge of every duty, and brave to a fault. He had no ambition save to serve his country. He died a Christian soldier, in the act of repulsing the enemy.

Such names as Roberts, Schaefer, Harrington, Stem, Williams, Read, Housum, Drake, Wooster, and McKee, all field officers, and many other commissioned officers of the right wing, who fell vindicating their flag, will never be forgotten by a grateful country.

Complete lists of the killed and wounded will be furnished from each regiment. There will be a map of the field sent forward to-morrow.

All of which is respectfully submitted.

A. McD. McCOOK,
Major-General of Volunteers, Commanding Right Wing.

Maj. C. GODDARD,
Chief of Staff, Fourteenth Army Corps.

No. 16.

Report of Surg. Clarke McDermont, U. S. Army, Medical Director.

MEDICAL DIRECTOR'S OFFICE, RIGHT WING,
Murfreesborough, Tenn., January 14, 1863.

SIR: I transmit, for the information of the commanding general, the accompanying report of the casualties that occurred in the right wing during the late battle of Murfreesborough:

While the loss of so many brave men must be a source of profound sorrow to the general, it will afford him some satisfaction to know that the wounded were not neglected. Throughout the severe and protracted struggle our surgeons exerted their utmost energies in alleviating the sufferings and promoting the comfort of their unfortunate brethren, and

---

* But see revised statement, pp. 207-209.

succeeded, as far as it was possible to do so with the means at their disposal.

When, on the second day of the battle, it became evident that the territory occupied by our hospitals would fall in possession of the enemy, I directed a sufficient number of surgeons and attendants to remain in charge, and not to desert the wounded in any event. These officers were exposed to much danger, as the contending armies swept past; but they remained faithfully at their posts, and were unceasing in their attentions to the wounded during the three days that elapsed before the recovery of this territory by our troops.

The enemy took from them a large portion of the medical and hospital stores and instruments, and our men were compelled to seek for dressing materials, bedding, &c., among the families in the rear of the lines. Much kind assistance was received from citizens in the vicinity, and no violence was experienced at the hands of the Confederate soldiers.

It affords me much pleasure to bear testimony to the efficiency and self-denial of the medical officers of the right wing. During that long week of hardship and exposure they labored day and night, regardless of their own safety and comfort, and only anxious for the well-being of the wounded intrusted to their care.

I have the honor to remain, your most obedient servant,

C. McDERMONT,
Surg. U. S. Vols., Medical Director, Right Wing, 14th A. C.

Major CAMPBELL,
Asst. Adjt. Gen., Right Wing, Fourteenth Army Corps.

General summary of casualties of Right Wing.

Regiments.	Killed.	Wounded.	Total.
FIRST DIVISION.			
22d Indiana	7	39	46
5th Wisconsin Battery	1	7	8
15th Wisconsin	15	72	87
74th Illinois	8	33	41
59th Illinois	7	43	50
35th Illinois	11	53	64
25th Illinois	16	79	95
75th Illinois	2	22	24
21st Illinois	47	198	245
2d Minnesota Battery	2	5	7
81st Indiana	6	48	54
101st Ohio	18	125	143
8th Wisconsin Battery	1	4	5
38th Illinois	34	110	144
Total	175	838	1,013
SECOND DIVISION.			
49th Ohio	16	96	112
15th Ohio	17	96	113
93d Ohio	12	41	53
1st Ohio	8	38	46
39th Indiana	30	109	139
32d Indiana	12	41	53
6th Indiana	15	52	67
30th Indiana	29	100	129
29th Indiana	4	22	26
89th Illinois	10	45	55
79th Illinois	19	80	99

General summary of casualties of Right Wing—Continued.

Regiments.	Killed.	Wounded.	Total.
SECOND DIVISION—Continued.			
34th Illinois	18	100	118
5th Kentucky	18	80	98
Battery A, First Ohio Artillery	1	5	6
5th Indiana Battery	3	18	21
77th Pennsylvania	4	29	33
Total	216	952	1,168
THIRD DIVISION.			
36th Illinois	45	159	204
88th Illinois	15	55	70
24th Wisconsin	19	58	77
21st Michigan	18	84	102
42d Illinois	21	109	130
22d Illinois	25	88	113
51st Illinois	6	48	54
27th Illinois	8	55	63
73d Illinois	22	52	74
44th Illinois	6	34	40
15th Missouri	14	44	58
2d Missouri	2	22	24
4th Indiana Battery	5	16	21
1st Missouri Artillery, Company G	6	13	19
1st Illinois Artillery, Company C	5	20	25
Total	217	857	1,074
Aggregate	608	2,647	3,255

Respectfully forwarded.

C. McDERMONT,
Surgeon U. S. Volunteers, Medical Director of Right Wing.

A. McD. McCOOK,
Major-General, Commanding.

—

General summary of killed and wounded at the battle of Stone's River, near Murfreesborough,
Tenn., from December 30, 1862, to January 3, 1863, of Right Wing, Fourteenth Army Corps,
Department of the Cumberland.

FIRST DIVISION.

(JOHN L. TEED, medical director.)

Regiments.	Killed.	Wounded.	Total.
38th Illinois	34	110	144
22d Indiana	7	39	46
5th Wisconsin Battery	1	7	8
15th Wisconsin	15	72	87
74th Illinois	8	33	41
59th Illinois	7	43	50
35th Illinois	11	53	64
25th Illinois	16	79	95
2d Minnesota Battery	2	5	7
75th Illinois	2	22	24
81st Indiana	6	48	54
101st Ohio	18	125	143
21st Illinois*			
8th Wisconsin Battery	1	4	5
Total	128	640	768

* Not reported.

General summary of killed and wounded at the battle of Stone's River, &c.—Continued.

SECOND DIVISION.

(S. MARKS, medical director.)

Regiments.	Killed.	Wounded.	Total.
34th Illinois	18	100	118
77th Pennsylvania	4	28	32
79th Illinois	19	80	99
30th Indiana	29	100	129
6th Indiana	15	52	67
1st Ohio	8	38	46
93d Ohio	12	41	53
5th Kentucky	18	80	98
32d Indiana	12	8	20
39th Indiana	30	109	139
15th Ohio	17	106	123
1st Ohio Artillery, Battery A	1	5	6
89th Illinois	10	45	55
49th Ohio	16	96	112
5th Indiana Battery	3	18	21
Total	212	906	1,118

THIRD DIVISION.*

(D. J. GRIFFITHS, medical director.)

Regiments.	Killed.	Wounded.	Total.
88th Illinois	15	55	70
21st Michigan	18	84	102
36th Illinois	45	159	204
27th Illinois	9	35	44
24th Wisconsin	19	58	77
51st Illinois	6	48	54
22d Illinois	25	88	113
42d Illinois	21	109	130
44th Illinois	6	34	40
73d Illinois	22	52	74
2d Missouri	2	22	24
15th Missouri	14	44	58
Total	202	788	990

General summary of Right Wing, Fourteenth Army Corps, Department of the Cumberland (C. McDermont, medical director).

Divisions.	Killed.	Wounded.	Total.
First Division	128	640	768
Second Division	212	906	1,118
Third Division	202	788	990
Total	542	2,334	2,876

No. 17.

Report of Brig. Gen. Jefferson C. Davis, U. S. Army, commanding First Division.

HDQRS. 1ST DIVISION, RIGHT WING, 14TH ARMY CORPS,
January —, 1863.

MAJOR: I have the honor to submit the following report of the part taken by the division under my command in the recent operations

---

* This division reports no batteries.

against the enemy's forces in the vicinity of Triune and Murfreesborough:

On the morning of the 26th ultimo, in compliance with instructions received from the general commanding the right wing, I broke up camp at Saint James' Chapel, on Mill Creek, and advanced upon Nolensville, via the Edmondson pike, as far as Prim's blacksmith shop; from thence my advance was over a rugged country road, rendered almost impassable by the incessant rain, which had been falling in torrents during the entire morning.

The enemy's pickets were discovered by my cavalry escort, composed of Company B, Thirty-sixth Illinois Volunteers, under command of Captain Sherer, within a few miles of our camp.   This small force of cavalry being the only mounted force under my command, I ordered them to the front, with instructions to drive in the enemy's pickets, and to attack him on his flanks at every opportunity.   So effectually was this done, that the infantry and artillery were enabled to move with little interruption to within a mile of Nolensville.   By this time I had learned, from reliable information, through citizens as well as cavalry scouts, that the enemy occupied the town in some force, both of cavalry and artillery.

The First Brigade, consisting of the Twenty-second Indiana, Seventy-fourth, Seventy-fifth, and Fifty-ninth Illinois Regiments, and the Fifth Wisconsin Battery, commanded by Col. P. Sidney Post, was immediately deployed for an advance upon the town.   Pinney's (Fifth Wisconsin) battery was posted so as to command the town and all approaches from the southwest.   The enemy's cavalry was seen by this time taking position on a range of hills southwest of the town, and was evidently attempting to flank our position.   A few shells from Pinney's battery soon caused them to fall back.   A battery, which by this time they had succeeded in getting into position, opened fire, but was, after a few rounds, silenced by Pinney's guns.

The Second Brigade, consisting of the Twenty-first and Thirty-eighth Illinois, Fifteenth Wisconsin, and One hundred and first Ohio Regiments, and the Second Minnesota Battery, commanded by Colonel Carlin, had by this time formed a line of battle on Post's right, and, moving rapidly forward, soon engaged the enemy's dismounted cavalry in a sharp skirmish.

The Third Brigade, consisting of the Twenty-fifth and Thirty-fif'h Illinois, Eighty-first Indiana Regiments, and the Eighth Wiscon'in Battery, commanded by Colonel Woodruff, was deployed on the right, so as to check any effort which might be made to attack my flank from this direction.   Carlin advanced in excellent order, driving everything before him, until ordered to halt, having dislodged the enemy from his position entirely.

By this time I ascertained that the enemy would probably make another effort to resist our advance about 2 miles farther on; and, notwithstanding it was late in the afternoon, and the men were much fatigued from a hard day's march through rain and mud, I could not forego the opportunity thus offered in giving them another chance to signalize their courage and endurance.   Ascertaining the enemy's exact position as well as I could, I ordered the advance.

Their lines were soon discovered, occupying a range of high, rocky hills, through which the Nolensville and Triune pike passes, known as Knob Gap.   This was a favorable position to the enemy, and well guarded by artillery, which opened fire at long range upon Carlin's lines.   Hotchkiss' and Pinney's batteries were rapidly brought into action and opened fire, while Carlin's brigade charged the battery, carried the heights in his front, and captured two guns. Post's brigade carried the heights on the left of the road with but little resistance, while Woodruff's brigade drove in the enemy's skirmishers on the extreme right.

The day had now closed, and I ordered the troops to bivouac, in accordance with instructions from the general commanding, who arrived at this time upon the ground, followed by Generals Sheridan's and Johnson's divisions.

The steady courage and soldierly zeal displayed on this occasion by both officers and men gave ample assurances of what could be expected of them in the coming struggle at Murfreesborough.

On the 27th, in accordance with the general's instructions, the division took position at the junction of the Bole Jack road with the Nolensville pike, 1 mile from Triune, where it remained in bivouac until the morning of the 29th, at which time the advance was resumed. In compliance with instructions, I moved forward on the Bole Jack road as far as Stewart's Creek, a few miles beyond which it was reported by our cavalry the enemy had shown himself in considerable force. The general commanding arriving at this time in person at the head of the column, ordered a halt until the divisions in rear could be brought up.

Brigadier-General Stanley, commanding the cavalry in advance, soon reported the road clear, and the march was resumed without obstruction until the entire command reached the Wilkinson pike, 6 miles from Murfreesborough. The division bivouacked during the night at Overall's Creek, 3½ miles from Murfreesborough, the left brigade resting on the Wilkinson pike.

On the morning of the 30th the division moved forward and took position on General Sheridan's right, about 300 yards south of and parallel to the Wilkinson pike, in which position it remained until 2 p. m. A few companies of skirmishers thrown to the front in a skirt of timbered land soon found those of the enemy, and for several hours a brisk skirmish was kept up with varying results. About 2 p. m. the general commanding ordered a general advance of the whole line. This the enemy seemed at first disposed to resist only with his skirmishers; gradually, however, as both parties strengthened their lines of skirmishers, the contest became more animated. Our main lines steadily advanced, occupying and holding the ground gained by the skirmishers until about half an hour before sunset, when the enemy's position was plainly discerned, running diagonally across the old Murfreesborough and Franklin road.

The enemy's batteries now announced our close proximity to their lines. Carpenter's and Hotchkiss' batteries were soon brought into position and opened fire. Woodruff's and Carlin's brigades by this time felt the fire of the enemy's main lines, and responded in the most gallant manner. Post's brigade, moving steadily forward on the right, after a most obstinate resistance on the part of the enemy, succeeded in driving his skirmishers from a strong position in our front, forcing them to retire upon his main lines. Night soon brought a close to the contest.

Receiving directions at this time from General McCook to desist from any further offensive demonstration further than what might be necessary to hold my position, I ordered the troops to rest for the night on their arms. Two brigades of General Johnson's division, heretofore held in reserve, arrived and took position on my right, about sunset, thus extending our line of battle beyond the old Franklin and Murfreesborough road.   These brigades were commanded by Generals Willich and Kirk.

The night passed off quietly until about daylight, when the enemy's forces were observed by our pickets to be in motion.   Their object could not, however, with certainty, be determined until near sunrise, when a vigorous attack was made upon Willich's and Kirk's brigades. These troops seemed not to have been fully prepared for the assault, and, with little or no resistance, retreated from their position, leaving their artillery in the hands of the enemy.   This left my right brigade exposed to a flank movement, which the enemy was now rapidly executing, and compelled me to order Post's brigade to fall back and partially change its front.   Simultaneous with this movement the enemy commenced a heavy and very determined attack on both Carlin's and Woodruff's brigades.   These brigades were fully prepared for the attack, and received it with veteran courage.   The conflict was fierce in the extreme on both sides.   Our loss was heavy and that of the enemy no less.   It was, according to my observations, the best contested point of the day, and would have been held, but for the overwhelming force moving so persistently against my right.   Carlin, finding his right flank being so severely pressed, and threatened with being turned, ordered his troops to retire.

Woodruff's brigade succeeded in repulsing the enemy and holding its position until the withdrawal of the troops on both its flanks compelled it to retire.   Pinney's battery, which I had posted in an open field upon my extreme right, and ordered to be supported by a part of Post's brigade, now opened a destructive fire upon the enemy's advancing lines.   This gallant and distinguished battery, supported by the Twenty-second Indiana and Fifty-ninth Illinois Regiments, together with a brigade of General Johnson's division, commanded by Colonel Baldwin, Sixth Indiana Volunteers, for a short time brought the enemy to a check on our right.   Hotchkiss' battery had also by this time taken an excellent position near the Wilkinson pike, so as to command the enemy's approach across a large cotton-field in his front, over which he was now advancing.   The infantry, however, contrary to expectations, failed to support this battery, and, after firing a few rounds, was forced to retire.

In accordance with instructions received during the night, announcing the plan of operations for the day, I desisted from any further attempts to engage the enemy, except by skirmishers thrown to the rear for that purpose, until my lines had reached within a few hundred yards of the Nashville and Murfreesborough pike, when I again determined to form my lines and resist his further advance.   To this order but few of the regiments responded, their ranks being much thinned by killed and wounded; and not a few had availed themselves of the favorable opportunity offered by the dense woods, through which we were compelled to pass, to skulk like cowards from the ranks.   The reserve forces here moved to the front, and relieved my command from any further participation in the engagement until late in the afternoon, when, in compliance with instructions, I took position on the right.   My skirmishers were immediately thrown out, and soon engaged the enemy's, until night brought a close to hostilities for the day.

During the 1st and 2d of January the division occupied this position in skirmishing with the enemy's pickets, until late in the afternoon of the 2d, when I received orders from General Rosecrans to hasten to the support of a part of General Crittenden's command, who had been for some time hotly engaged with the enemy across the ~~river~~, on our extreme left.

Moving as rapidly as possible across the river to the field of battle, I found our gallant troops forcing the enemy back on his reserves. The brigade of Colonel Woodruff, being in the advance, only arrived in time to participate in the general engagement.

After relieving the troops of General Palmer and Colonel Beatty, and particularly the brigade of Colonel Hazen, which had so nobly vindicated their courage in the then closing conflict, I ordered a heavy line of skirmishers to be thrown out. The enemy's lines were soon encountered, and a renewal of the engagement seemed imminent. A few rounds of grape and canister from one of our batteries, however, caused them to withdraw, and night again brought a cessation of hostilities.

During the night I disposed of my troops in such manner as would best enable me to repel an attack, and, in compliance with instructions, I directed rifle-pits and breastworks to be thrown up. This was done, and morning found us well prepared for any emergency, either offensive or defensive.

The following day (January 3) considerable skirmishing was kept up, without abatement, from early in the morning until dark.

During the night I received orders from General Crittenden to withdraw my command from the east bank of the river, and to report with it to General McCook. This movement was executed between the hours of 1 and 4 o'clock in the morning, during which time the rain fell incessantly.

The pickets about this time reported the enemy as having been very active in their movements during the latter part of the night, and their convictions that he was evacuating his position. Further observations, made after daylight, found this to be the case.

The following list of casualties shows a loss in the division during the several engagements above described as follows:

Commissioned officers:

Killed	16
Wounded	34
Missing	2

Enlisted men:

Killed	176
Wounded	784
Missing	399

Total killed, wounded, and missing *1,411

The division lost three pieces of artillery and captured two. In the list of officers killed are the names of Colonel Stem, One hundred and first Ohio; Colonel Williams, Twenty-fifth Illinois; Lieutenant-Colonel Wooster, One hundred and first Ohio; Lieutenant-Colonel McKee, Fifteenth Wisconsin; Captain Carpenter, Eighth Wisconsin Battery, and Captain McCulloch, Second Kentucky Cavalry, of my staff, whose noble deeds of valor on the field had already placed their names on the list of brave men. The history of the war will record no brighter names, and the country will mourn the loss of no more devoted patriots, than these.

Among the wounded are Colonel Alexander, Twenty-first Illinois; Lieutenant-Colonel Tanner, Twenty-second Indiana; Captain Pinney, Fifth Wisconsin Battery, and Captain Austin, acting assistant adjutant-general, on the staff of Colonel Woodruff, whose names it affords me special gratification to mention.

---

* But see revised statement, pp. 207, 208.

From December 26 until the close of the engagement, on the 4th of January, at Murfreesborough, no entire day elapsed that the division, or some part of it, did not engage the enemy. During a great part of the time the weather was excessively inclement, and the troops suffered much from exposure. A heavy list of casualties and much suffering were unavoidable, under the circumstances.

It affords me pleasure, however, to be able to report the cheerful and soldierlike manner in which these hardships and privations were endured by the troops throughout. History will record and the country reward their deeds.

My staff, consisting of Lieut. T. W. Morrison, acting assistant adjutant-general; Capt. H. Pease, inspector-general; Captain McCulloch, aide-de-camp (killed); Lieut. Francis E. Reynolds, aide-de-camp; Lieut. Thomas H. Dailey, aide-de-camp; Surg. J. L. Teed, medical director; Captain Shriver, ordnance officer; Lieut. R. Plunket, provost-marshal, and Private Frank Clark, clerk to the assistant adjutant-general and acting aide-de-camp, deported themselves throughout the entire campaign, as well as on the battle-field, with distinguished zeal and conspicuous gallantry.

While expressing my high regard and appreciation of the general commanding, I desire also to tender my thanks to yourself, major, and to Colonel Langdon, Major Bates, Captains Thruston, Williams, and Fisher, of his staff, for the prompt and efficient manner in which the field duties were performed by them.

During the several engagements in which the division participated the conduct of many subaltern officers attracted my admiration by their conspicuous gallantry, and whose names, I regret, cannot be mentioned in this report. They will be remembered in future recommendations for promotion.

I am, major, very respectfully, your obedient servant,

JEF. C. DAVIS,
Brigadier-General, Commanding Division.

Maj. JOHN A. CAMPBELL,
Asst. Adjt. Gen., Right Wing, Fourteenth Army Corps.

No. 18.

Report of Lieut. Charles B. Humphrey, Fifth Wisconsin Battery.

HEADQUARTERS FIFTH WISCONSIN BATTERY,
January 6, 1863.

COLONEL: In obedience with your commands, I would respectfully submit the following report of the part taken and casualties suffered by the Fifth Wisconsin Battery in the engagements with the enemy since December 26, 1862:

The battery left Camp Andy Johnson, December 26, and marched to Nolensville, where it arrived and engaged the enemy's cavalry about 2 o'clock of the same day.

After firing a number of rounds of shell and canister into the town, the enemy fell back about a mile, where they made a stand in a very strong position, and planted a battery. The battery followed, and were soon playing upon them from all its guns. The enemy soon retired, leaving one of their guns upon the field. Camped upon this ground at night, and the next day (December 27) marched forward about 4 miles and camped until the 29th ultimo, when we were ordered in the direction of Murfreesborough. Advanced about 8 miles and camped in the woods, without tents or fires. The next morning advanced slowly, and camped within sight of the enemy's lines; fired a few rounds from the Parrott guns, and again the men lay by their guns, without tents or fires, all night. At daylight we were up and ready for an attack. As soon as it became light the enemy could be seen from our position, in great numbers, marching upon the right wing. We were soon ordered to its support, and in a short time took position in a corn-field, supported by the Twenty-second Indiana Regiment on the right, and the Fifty-ninth Illinois on the left. The enemy could be seen in heavy force advancing upon us. We opened fire immediately from all our guns. They soon made their appearance over a knoll directly in front of our guns. A few rounds of canister caused them to move to the left, under cover of a thick clump of bushes. They were followed by another line, and they then advanced upon us. After firing upon them for about thirty minutes, the order was given to limber up and fall back. This was done in good order, though we were obliged to leave one gun and two caissons on the field, on account of the horses being killed.

The battery fell back to the Murfreesborough pike in good order, when the rebel cavalry dashed in from the left and captured the whole battery, with the exception of one gun. We were soon relieved by our own cavalry, and the battery was got together, and fired a few rounds at the enemy's cavalry, who were in strong force about 2 miles in rear of our former position ; lay by our guns that night, and the next morning (January 1) were ordered to join our brigade, near our present position. We took position, and lay there until the afternoon of January 2, when we were ordered over the stream to the left of the pike, where we lay within sight of the enemy's lines until the morning of the 4th, when we fell back to our present position. During the time of action the officers and men behaved with coolness and bravery, and though they were exposed to the weather, with uncooked rations, not a man appeared unwilling to do his duty. They were much worn out, but the two days of rest that they have had fitted them for the field.

The following is a list of casualties suffered :* Killed, 1 private; wounded, 1 officer and 5 men; missing, 4; taken prisoners, 2. Total loss, 1 captain and 11 enlisted men, 2 wagons and 12 mules.

Very respectfully, your obedient servant,

CHARLES B. HUMPHREY,
Lieutenant, Commanding Fifth Wisconsin Battery.

No. 19.

Report of Lieut. Henry E. Stiles, Eighth Wisconsin Battery.

HEADQUARTERS 8TH WISCONSIN BATTERY,
3D BRIG., 1ST DIV., RIGHT WING, 14TH ARMY CORPS,
January 9, 1863.

GENERAL : I have to report the following as a detailed account of the part taken by the Eighth Wisconsin Battery in the recent engagements near Murfreesborough, Tenn., December, 1862, and January, 1863:

December 26, 1862, by order of Brigadier-General Woodruff, we formed

---

* Nominal list omitted.

in battery three different times at Nolensville, and fired 38 rounds at the enemy; effects of the shots unknown.

December 30, we took up our line of march with the brigade. By order of Brigadier-General Woodruff, we took position in front about noon and shelled a piece of woods in our front for two hours, when we were ordered to advance. We then came into position on the left of the Third Brigade, in the edge of a belt of timber, near a small corn-field, in the immediate vicinity of the enemy, from which point we shelled them until dark, the enemy only firing two shots at us while in this position, one of which struck a tree over one of our caissons, the other burst in our front, a piece of shell striking the wheel of a gun-carriage. At dark we fell back with three of our guns, by order of General Woodruff, and stationed ourselves over a hill in the rear of the infantry, remaining all night with harness on our horses; one gun on picket.

December 31, as soon as it was light, we took a position to the left of the position occupied the night before, with our three guns. Immediately on taking our position the enemy charged on us in force. We opened on them with canister, with good effect, checking them considerably. Our infantry support here gave way, and we were ordered to fall back. Capt. Stephen J. Carpenter was killed before we ceased firing, and 4 men wounded. Our battery retired in some confusion, with the loss of one 10-pounder Parrott gun, and 11 horses killed and wounded.

By order, we again came into position in a large corn-field in our rear, from which point we opened on the enemy, and continued to fire until our support left us, when we were again obliged to fall back. We then moved a little to the right and rear, when we came into position and opened on the enemy as they advanced out of the woods in our front. We did some execution with canister and shell, but our support again leaving us we were obliged to fall back. By this time the confusion seemed to have become general; our battery fell back to the rear and left, and reported to Brigadier-General Woodruff's headquarters at 3 o'clock in the afternoon with three guns, 50 men, and one gun-limber.

January 1, 1863, by order of General Woodruff, we drew 100 rounds of ammunition, and sent one 6-pounder gun, caisson and limber, to a 10-pounder Parrott gun to the rear, where they were captured by the enemy, with 1 man taken prisoner and 3 horses lost. Went into position with two guns, and remained till next day.

January 2, were ordered to march with the brigade. Moved to the left, and took a position between our brigade and that commanded by Colonel Carlin, by order of General Davis, commanding division. Immediately on coming into position the enemy opened a volley of musketry on us, when we were ordered to fire. Opening on them with canister, they soon fell back.

January 3, we lay in front all day, exposed to the fire of the enemy's sharpshooters.

January 4, at 3 o'clock in the morning, we were ordered to fall back to our former position on the pike, which we did, thus ending the fight on our part. We fired about 400 rounds of ammunition during the engagements.

Respectfully submitted.

HENRY E. STILES,
Lieut., Comdg. Eighth Wisconsin Battery, Volunteer Artillery.

Brig. Gen. JEFFERSON C. DAVIS,
Comdg. First Division, Right Wing, Fourteenth Army Corps.

No. 20.

Report of Col. P. Sidney Post, Fifty-ninth Illinois Infantry, commanding First Brigade.

HEADQUARTERS FIRST BRIGADE, FIRST DIVISION,
RIGHT WING, FOURTEENTH ARMY CORPS,
In Camp, south of Murfreesborough, January 9, 1863.

LIEUTENANT: I have the honor to submit the following report of the part taken by the First Brigade in the late engagements, resulting in the taking of Murfreesborough:

In compliance with the order of Brigadier-General Davis, commanding division, we left camp, at Saint James' Chapel, at daylight December 26, 1862, and marched in the direction of Nolensville, this brigade being in advance. We soon came upon the enemy's cavalry. Company B, Thirty-sixth Illinois Cavalry, under direction of Captain Pease, of Brigadier-General Davis' staff, occupied the road, and the Fifty-ninth Illinois Infantry was thrown out as skirmishers on each side of it. A lively skirmish was kept up until we reached Nolensville, when the enemy appeared in force and opened upon the brigade with artillery.

The left of our line of battle rested upon the pike, the right occupying a hill commanding the town. Captain Pinney's (Fifth Wisconsin) battery opened upon the enemy and drove them from the town.

A large force of cavalry was seen moving to the right and dismounting, with the evident intention of attacking our right and rear and dislodging us from the hill. The Twenty-second Regiment Indiana Infantry was moved to the right to repel this attack, and Colonels Carlin's and Woodruff's brigades deployed, by order of Brigadier-General Davis, upon our right, soon came up, and the enemy were driven from their position and forced to withdraw their artillery.

This brigade, on the left of the line of battle, moved forward up the pike leading to Triune, Pinney's battery being on the pike, the Twenty-second Indiana and the Seventy-fourth Illinois on its right, and the Seventy-fifth and Fifty-ninth Illinois on its left. The enemy were posted in a position of great natural strength, about 2 miles from Nolensville, on the right and left of the pike, with one section of artillery on and the remainder near the road. Pinney's battery, from a knoll to the left of the pike, opened at short range with all his guns, and this brigade, on the left of Colonel Carlin's, marched steadily forward, driving the enemy from the hill, where they were compelled to abandon one piece of artillery. This march had been made in a drenching rain, and the men, exhausted by their exertions upon the muddy road and the excitements of the day, bivouacked on the field, for the possession of which they had fought. The following day this brigade marched in rear of Colonel Carlin's nearly to Triune, it raining constantly and being very cold.

December 29, we marched in rear of Colonel Woodruff's brigade, on the Bole Jack road, toward Murfreesborough. About 2 miles from Overall's Creek, by order of Brigadier-General Davis, I deployed the brigade on the right of the road, and moved forward nearly to the creek, where we bivouacked in the rain, without fires.

On the morning of December 30, we marched across the fields on the right of the Wilkinson pike, the Seventy-fourth and Seventy-fifth Regiments Illinois Infantry deployed on the right of Colonel Carlin's bri-

gade, and being the right of the entire army, the Fifty-ninth Regiment
Illinois Infantry in reserve to support the battery, and the Twenty-second Regiment Indiana Infantry in a position to protect the right flank
from the enemy's cavalry, which were continually hovering about and
engaging the skirmishers.   I directed Captain Sherer, who, by order of
Brigadier-General Davis, reported to me with Company B, Thirty-sixth
Illinois Cavalry, to throw out skirmishers and march upon our right
flank, where he repeatedly engaged and drove back the cavalry threatening our line.   The skirmishing in front grew more brisk, and late in the
afternoon the enemy were found in force, strongly posted, and opened
upon us, with artillery from our front and right, killing 1 and wounding
several men.   Captain Hale, acting as major of the Seventy-fifth Illinois, and Lieutenant Hall, of my staff, each had a horse killed under
him.

General Kirk's brigade at this time moved into position upon our
right.   Captain Pinney's battery drove back the enemy from our front,
and, under cover of his fire, our skirmishers were advanced to the open
field, when night closed the contest.   The men lay down without fires
or shelter, and in the morning were awakened and standing in order of
battle one hour before the first dawn of light.   The battery horses stood
at their pieces during the night, ready for any emergency.

As soon as it became light, the enemy were discovered moving in
great numbers toward our right, and nearly parallel with our line, with
the evident design of turning the right wing of the army.   I immediately dispatched Lieutenant Jones, of my staff, to inform Brigadier-General Davis.

The right of the brigade extended into a dense and almost impenetrable thicket of cedars, connecting there with the left of General Kirk's
brigade, and in that direction nothing could be seen on account of the
thicket.   For more than half an hour the enemy's dark columns flowed
toward our right, where the volleys of musketry and their advancing
cheers from that direction assured me that they had driven the brigades on our right from their position, and were already in our rear,
and I accordingly changed front nearly perpendicularly to the rear to
meet them.

The Seventy-fourth Illinois, Col. Jason Marsh, and the Seventy-fifth Illinois, commanded by Lieut. Col. J. E. Bennett, were stationed
behind a fence in the edge of the timber.   By order of Brigadier-General Davis, several companies were added to our force of skirmishers,
and, under his direction, Pinney's battery took position in a corn-field,
with the Fifty-ninth Illinois Infantry, commanded by Capt. H. E. Paine,
supporting it on the left.   Perceiving that the enemy were still far beyond our right, I deployed my reserve regiment, the Twenty-second
Indiana, Colonel Gooding commanding, on the right of the battery.
The Sixth Regiment Indiana Infantry, having been separated from its
brigade, was placed about 400 paces in rear as a reserve.

Captain Pinney opened upon the advancing line with all his guns,
and when they came within range of his canister and the fire of the
supporting regiment, the execution was so great that the entire line
recoiled before it, but, after temporary confusion, they were rallied and
lay down.   The enemy opened a battery upon the hill and advanced a
second line.

Captain Pinney's guns were splendidly handled, and great credit is
due to Lieutenants Humphrey, Gardner, and McKnight, and to the
men of the company, for their promptness and skill.   No shots were
wasted over the heads of the enemy.   For about thirty minutes this

fierce contest continued, while the enemy on our right had advanced, so as to again endanger our rear.

As those in front rallied and charged upon the battery on the double-quick, the Fifty-ninth Illinois Regiment fixed bayonets to receive them, but, with the large force unopposed upon our right, the position was already untenable, even though that in front was repulsed, and I ordered the battery withdrawn.

Captain Pinney was dangerously, if not mortally, wounded. He fell, and was left on the spot where he executed his most gallant deeds. Lieutenant-Colonel Tanner, of the Twenty-second Indiana, and many others seriously wounded, were left upon the field.

Eighteen of the battery horses were disabled, and one gun, in consequence, could not be brought off. One Parrott gun had but two wounded horses before it. I ordered the Fifty-ninth Regiment to drag the guns to the rear. As the battery reached the Nashville pike, it was charged upon by cavalry, and partially captured, but they were quickly driven away by the Fourth Regiment Regular Cavalry, and, crossing Overall's Creek, it took a position, under the direction of Lieutenant Hall, on a hill to the right of the Nashville pike, from which it repeatedly shelled and drove back the enemy's cavalry, endeavoring to take possession of the road.

The Seventy-fourth and Seventy-fifth Illinois Regiments fell back across the cotton-field, and, under the direction of Lieutenant Jones, who also rallied a number of detachments from other regiments, made a determined resistance, again checking the foe. The fresh troops from the reserves here relieved the brigade, and I proceeded to the pike, reformed my shattered battalions, and supplied them with ammunition.

I was soon ordered by Brigadier-General Davis to move up the pike and take position on the right of the line, and here, exhausted, the men lay down for the night.

The next morning I was ordered to occupy the open field to the left of the pike, where I caused a breastwork to be thrown up, the battery being in position to enfilade the enemy's lines attempting an attack. A strong force of skirmishers was thrown out, covering our front and right. The enemy opened a battery upon us, but, after a few well-directed shells from Pinney's Parrott guns, they ceased firing.

During the following day the constant skirmishing was kept up on our front, and a number of prisoners were taken. Late in the afternoon we were ordered to cross Stone's River. The stream was swollen from the heavy rains, but the entire brigade, hearing the volleys of musketry on the other side, plunged into it with cheers and debouched upon the field, which was still being contended for, and, rapidly forming, hurried to the front. All that stormy night, the men who had been previously soaked in fording the river, stood by their arms without fires, the Twenty-second Indiana and Seventy-fifth Illinois busily engaged in constructing a breastwork. During the night our pickets, under charge of Major Dutcher, of the Seventy-fourth Illinois, contested for the possession of the fields and woods in our front, and advanced a considerable distance.

Substantial breastworks were completed during January 3, under a constant fire of sharpshooters, and at night, in a pouring rain, the men again lay upon their arms.

At 2 o'clock the next morning the battery was ordered to recross the river, and at 4 o'clock, in a torrent of rain, the brigade forded the swollen stream and took its former position on the right, where it remained until January 6, when, passing through Murfreesborough, we encamped at this place.

During the long contest, and notwithstanding the extreme inclemency of the weather and the scarcity of provisions, no word of complaint was heard. Officers and men seemed alike anxious to do their full duty as patriot soldiers. In our advance they pushed forward boldly, and when greatly superior numbers were hurled against them they awaited the onset with the utmost coolness and determination. The temporary confusion which occurred when they fell back was caused, to a considerable extent, by the large force of skirmishers thrown out to check the enemy, having been driven toward the left, instead of directly upon their own regiments. The deliberation and order with which the Seventy-fourth Illinois retired is especially commended.

During the series of engagements the several regimental commanders displayed great persistence and resolution, and everywhere encouraged their men.

Too much praise cannot be awarded to the dauntless and skillful Captain Pinney, whose characteristic conduct elicited compliment even from his foes.

I herewith transmit the reports of the regimental and battery commanders, together with a full list of casualties.

The gallant bearing of Captain Hale, of the Seventy-fifth Illinois, who had chief command of the skirmishers; of Captain Litson, of the Twenty-second Indiana, and of Sergt. P. S. Ferguson, of Company G, Fifty-ninth Illinois, one of the skirmishers, is deserving of mention. Assistant Surgeon Corbus, of the Seventy-fifth Illinois, and Assistant Surgeon Bunce, of the Fifty-ninth Illinois, remained with and took care of our wounded while the fight was raging around them.

The zeal and decision shown by Lieutenants Jones, Hall, Hatch, and Baker, members of my staff, and the intrepidity of my faithful orderly, George Fogle, demand my highest commendation.

The names of the self-constituted messengers, who carried to Nashville, with such unparalleled celerity, the tidings of the battle of December 31, have already been forwarded. In the hour of trial, showing themselves false as the news they manufactured and disseminated, their infamy only makes more bright by contrast the imperishable record of those who nobly struggled or bravely fell in that unequal contest.

I have the honor to be, very respectfully, your obedient servant,

P. SIDNEY POST,
Colonel, Commanding First Brigade.

Lieut. T. W. MORRISON,
Acting Assistant Adjutant-General, First Division.

No. 21.

Report of Capt. Hendrick E. Paine, Fifty-ninth Illinois Infantry.

HDQRS. FIFTY-NINTH REGIMENT ILLINOIS VOLUNTEERS,
In Camp near Murfreesborough, Tenn., January 10, 1863.

SIR: In compliance with an order from brigade headquarters, I respectfully submit the following report:

The regiment which I have the honor to command broke up camp, 7 miles south of Nashville, on the morning of the 26th of December, the men carrying three days' rations in their haversacks, all of our transportation and camp equipage having been ordered within the fortifications at Nashville.

As we approached Nolensville, my whole regiment was deployed as skirmishers, where we did efficient service in feeling for the enemy, and driving in his pickets, who took refuge in the houses on the outskirts of the town until they were finally driven out and repulsed. The regiment was then assembled, and formed the left of the line of battle of the First Brigade, as it moved upon the enemy's batteries and cavalry, south of the town, drawing him from his position with a loss of one or more of his guns. We lay on our arms that night and next day; moved forward and went into camp near Triune, where we remained all the day following. On the morning of the 29th took up our line of march toward Murfreesborough. The continued heavy firing in front gave evidence of the near proximity of the enemy. Bivouacked for the night, and next morning (30th), at an early hour, were on the march, moving by the front in line of battle. By noon it became evident that the enemy were in force in our front. At that time I was ordered, with my regiment, to support Captain Pinney's Fifth Wisconsin Battery. During the p. m. Captain Pinney opened on the enemy's battery, when my men were exposed to the shot and shell of the enemy's fire. After Captain Pinney had silenced or driven his battery from the field, we moved forward and bivouacked until morning. That night was very cold, and the men suffered very much from its effects. At daylight, on the morning of the 31st, we were in line of battle, in full view of the enemy, who appeared to be moving in strong force to our right. I was then ordered, together with Captain Pinney's battery, to hold ourselves as a reserve, and were moved a short distance to the rear; at the same time the line of battle was formed in our front, and the firing became heavy both on our right and left.

It soon became evident that the enemy was closely pressing our right, and our lines were rapidly extended in that direction. At the same time my regiment and Captain Pinney's battery were ordered to the front to engage the enemy across an open field. I immediately faced my command in the direction indicated, and moved forward in good order. At the same time the long lines of the enemy appeared on the opposite side of the field, moving directly to our front. When we approached within short musket range, I gave the order to fire, and lie down and load, which order was promptly responded to; at the same instant the enemy's balls came whistling over us in awful proximity to our heads. I do not know how long we remained in that position, but my men poured a deadly and destructive fire upon the enemy, who had laid down to avoid its terrible effects, until regiment after regiment on our right gave way, when I, reluctantly, received the order to fall back. At the same instant Captain Pinney was severely wounded, and the horses from two of his guns were either disabled or killed, when my men gallantly took hold and assisted to haul the guns from the field by hand, exposed all the while to a deadly fire of the enemy's musketry and grape and canister shot. We continued to move to the rear in reasonably good order, forming twice and firing upon the pursuing enemy, until we were beyond the range of his fire, when we formed and awaited the orders of our brigade commander. When the brigade was reformed, we took our position in line of battle in the front, where we remained during the remainder of the day and the succeeding night.

I cannot speak too highly in praise of the bravery displayed by the officers and men under my command. All nobly did their duty. To Capts. B. M. Veatch and James M. Stookey, acting field officers, I especially return my thanks for the efficient aid they rendered me, and the promptness with which they executed my orders during the series of battles and skirmishes in which we have been engaged during this campaign. My regiment took part in all the subsequent movements made by our brigade up to the present time.

I can't but admire the patience and fortitude exhibited by the officers and men of my command during the present campaign, part of the time on short rations, and all the time exposed to the inclemencies of the weather, without tents or blankets, being compelled to bivouac in the presence of the enemy without fire, yet I heard no complaints uttered. All were willing and anxious to do their duty.

Respectfully submitted.

H. E. PAINE,
Captain, Comdg. Fifty-ninth Illinois Infantry Regiment.
Col. P. SIDNEY POST.

No. 22.

Report of Col. Jason Marsh, Seventy-fourth Illinois Infantry.

HDQRS. SEVENTY-FOURTH REGT. ILLINOIS VOLS.,
In Camp near Murfreesborough, January 7, 1863.

SIR: I have the honor to report that the Seventy-fourth Regiment Illinois Volunteers, under my command, left camp near Nashville on the 26th ultimo, early in the morning, for Murfreesborough, in the advance brigade. Coming up in the afternoon, near Nolensville, with the enemy, apparently in considerable force, mainly of cavalry and artillery, my command was immediately formed in a line of battle and advanced. A brisk cannonading was opened on both sides, the enemy's shots and shell frequently reaching within our lines, occupying an exposed position within shot range, but no damage was done. The enemy soon falling back, a brisk pursuit was kept up until night, when we bivouacked, without fire, keeping up constant and thorough watch against surprise through the night. The next day, being exceedingly rainy, we marched but about 5 miles, without special incident, and bivouacked for the night, my regiment meeting the inclemency of the weather and discomforts of the march with the fortitude and cheerfulness of veteran soldiers. Resting in the camp over the Sabbath, I resumed the march early Monday morning by a cross-road leading from the Nolensville to the Murfreesborough turnpike; bivouacked at night in a drenching rain, on short rations, after our exceedingly toilsome day's march over an almost impassable road. The next morning I had my command in line at 3.30 o'clock, standing at their arms until daylight, when, resuming the march in the direction of Murfreesborough, we came up with the enemy about noon, and a slight firing was kept up between skirmishers during the day, our column slowly and cautiously advancing, the enemy retreating.

Just at night, near the edge of a cedar thicket, as our line was advancing, the enemy opened a brisk fire from a masked battery, within short range, making it necessary for the entire line to fall back a short distance to a line of battle selected for the operations of the day following. My regiment, being directly in range of the enemy's fire, M. C. Felmly, corporal, of Company K, was killed, and J. B. Caspares, corporal, of the same company, was seriously wounded. A strong picket guard was thrown out about 30 rods in front, which occasionally drew fire from the enemy's pickets; their camp-fires being not more than three-quarters of a mile distant, extending along the farther edge of a corn-field, a long distance beyond the extreme right of our division, indicated a strong force of the enemy massed on our front and right. My command was formed in line of battle, close behind a narrow strip of cedar thicket, nearly covering our front, and skirting a strip of open level ground, about 20 rods wide, to the corn-field occupied by the enemy's pickets. Being thus satisfied of the close proximity of the enemy in strong force, and apprehending an attack at any moment, I deemed it necessary to use the utmost precaution against surprise, and, accordingly, in addition to general instructions, bivouacked without fires, and, to maintain a cautious, quiet vigilance, I ordered my command to stack arms, each man to rest at the butt of his musket, and without using his shelter-tent, although the night was dark, chilly, and somewhat rainy, and the men cold, wet, weary, and hungry. I deemed it objectionable to use their shelter-tents, not only because of the hindrance in case of a sudden attack, but even in a dark night they would be some guide to the enemy to trace our line. At a little before 4 a. m. my men were quietly waked up and formed into line; remained standing at their arms until moved by subsequent orders.

As soon as it became sufficiently light to discern objects at a distance, I could plainly observe the enemy moving in three heavy columns across my front to the right, one column striking out of the corn-field and moving defiantly along the edge of the open ground, not more than 60 to 80 rods from and about parallel with my line. It was plainly seen that the fire of my skirmishers took effect in their ranks, and in emptying saddles, to which, however, the enemy seemed to pay no attention. This movement continued from a half to an hour, when a brisk discharge of musketry at considerable distance to my right indicated a rapid advance of the enemy on the right flank, and at the same time their columns were advancing in overwhelming force directly in front, and extending to the left as far as could be seen. At this time my command was ordered to fall back, and to change front to the rear, or nearly so, forming behind a fence. This movement was executed in good order, without the least confusion or faltering. In the course of ten or fifteen minutes the enemy's line approached, but, as previously instructed and ordered, my command reserved their fire until within short range, when they opened with terrible effect upon the advancing ranks, and holding them completely in check until they had delivered 10 to 15 rounds. I maintained this position until the regiments on the right and left of me had fallen back 30 to 40 rods, and, the enemy's line directly in front breaking and deploying right and left and about to flank me, I ordered a retreat, which was effected in tolerable order; at least, without the least appearance of a panic. From this point, having fallen back in a straight line between half and three-quarters of a mile, I effected a stand with a considerable portion of my regiment, but could maintain it only long enough to deliver a few shots.

I should here mention that early in the morning three companies of my command had been thrown out as skirmishers, who, in consequence of the first change of line, and of their fidelity and bravery in discharging their duty, had been cut off from the regiment, and unable to rally upon it, until at this point.

First Lieutenant Leffingwell, in command of Company A, came up with a few of his men, and rendered most efficient aid in rallying the regiment. I commend his conduct on this occasion as indicating an efficient, faithful, and brave officer. Falling back from this line a short distance, I succeeded in rallying about half of the regiment in rear of the reserve force, which was now driving the enemy back, when, being ordered to form on the brigade, my command had no further part in the fighting of the day, except that two companies of my regiment were sent out just at night as skirmishers, under command of First Lieutenant Blakesley, who rendered important service in a brilliant skirmish with a large cavalry force.

The day following my regiment was put in line of battle at an early hour, and stood at their arms till near night, momentarily expecting to make or receive an attack.

On Friday, just at night, my command was put in rapid march across Stone's River, to the extreme left, where a fierce battle was raging, but was closed just before our arrival, by the retreat of the enemy. Late in the evening we bivouacked here, without fires, in such close proximity to the enemy's line as to produce frequent skirmishing between the pickets during the night, which was intensely dark and stormy. Remaining here through the following day and night, suffering the severities of an almost uninterrupted storm, without fires or shelter, until 4 o'clock Sunday morning, I returned with my command to the camp previously occupied.

The hardships, privations, and exposures in the march from Louisville to Crab Orchard, and thence to Nashville, have been regarded nearly unendurable by new troops, and yet while they sink into utter insignificance compared with those of our march and engagements during these eight days, I have the gratification of knowing that my regiment have met and endured them with the utmost promptness, fortitude, and cheerfulness, facing the enemy in the heat of battle with the coolness, courage, and determination of experienced soldiers and true patriots, ready at every call to face new danger without faltering, undergoing the most extraordinary labor and exposure without murmuring, and evincing under all circumstances a spirit of subordination and discipline worthy of the highest commendation.

I have also the pleasure to say that during all these trying hardships the general health of the men has been better than at any time since we left Louisville. While I have such occasion to commend the fidelity, bravery, and good conduct of all the officers of my command, save one, I should fail to do justice were I to omit to make special note of the cool, persistent courage of Capt. J. H. Douglass, in remaining at his post under the fire of the enemy, and of his promptness and efficiency in forming and maintaining the lines during the day. It is not to be presumed that all the meritorious acts of privates will come within the personal observation of the commander of a regiment, but having been eye-witness of the fearless bravery and enthusiastic zeal of Private Charles A. Allen, of Company E, during the operations of Wednesday, as well as at other times, I commend him as worthy of promotion.

I desire also to acknowledge my obligations to Major Dutcher and Adjutant Nieman, for their constant and able assistance during this eventful period.

The casualties in my command, as more fully stated in the report herewith forwarded, are:

Killed	8
Wounded	35
Missing	42
Total	85

I have the honor to be, very respectfully, your obedient servant,

JASON MARSH,
Colonel Seventy-fourth Illinois Volunteers.

Col. P. SIDNEY POST,
Commanding First Brigade.

No. 23.

Report of Lieut. Col. John E. Bennett, Seventy-fifth Illinois Infantry.

HDQRS. SEVENTY-FIFTH REGT. ILLINOIS VOLUNTEERS,
In the Field, January 7, 1863.

SIR: I have the honor to make the following report of the Seventy-fifth Illinois Volunteers since the breaking up of camp near Nashville:

December 26, took up line of march and, same day, engaged in skirmish, with no loss; were ordered to support the battery, and soon drove the enemy from the town of Nolensville, and camped for the night.

December 27, at 10 a. m., marched on, while it rained very hard, to Hardee's old camp.

December 28, staid in camp.

December 29, moved on toward Murfreesborough, and camped near the enemy, and no fires allowed.

December 30, marched in line of battle across fields. Company I was sent in advance, as skirmishers, commanded by Captain Hale. Soon came to the enemy, and fired on them. The enemy returned the fire, and wounded 2 men and killed Captain Hale's horse. Company I fell back, and a general engagement commenced, but with no more loss to the Seventy-fifth Regiment. Camped for the night, and slept on their arms.

December 31, a large number of the enemy attacked our right at daylight, and our men fell back in confusion.

January 1, 1863, in camp all day, and not engaged in any fighting.

January 2, 1863, men rested near their arms till about 4 p. m., when a general engagement commenced. The enemy was driven back with great loss. The Seventy-fifth moved to support our men, but were not engaged in the fight.

January 3, 1863, built breastworks of rails and logs, and the men had laid by their arms for nearly two days, with no fire, and rain most of the time. During the long battle the men behaved gallantly. The officers also performed their part well. Captain Hale, acting major, has shown himself a brave and efficient officer, but was compelled to leave his regiment, after being wounded in the face and thigh. Captain Watson, acting lieutenant-colonel, has taken a prominent part, and is competent to fill any office to which he may be appointed.

Nothing important has transpired since January 3, 1863. We are now camped 2 miles south of Murfreesborough.

I am, sir, very respectfully, your obedient servant,

JOHN E. BENNETT,
Lieutenant-Colonel, Commanding.

Col. P. SIDNEY POST.

No. 24.

Report of Col. Michael Gooding, Twenty-second Indiana Infantry.

HDQRS. TWENTY-SECOND INDIANA VOLUNTEERS,
Near Murfreesborough, Tenn., January 9, 1863.

SIR: In compliance with orders received from brigade headquarters, I have the honor herewith to transmit the following report of the part taken by my regiment in the several late engagements:

On Friday, the 26th of December, I, with my regiment, reached Nolensville, where the enemy were posted in considerable force. I threw my regiment into line of battle on the right of the brigade, occupying a strong position on a high ridge reaching from our extreme right to the town, on our left. The fight had already begun, and the enemy now opened on us a heavy fire of canister and grape, but, fortunately, too high, and no serious injury was done us. The enemy's cavalry now moved to their left, with the evident intention of gaining our right flank or rear, but in this attempt they were foiled, for I now threw out a heavy body of skirmishers, who, with one section of Captain Pinney's Fifth Wisconsin Battery, not only held the enemy in check, but drove them from their ground. With the brigade, my regiment pursued the fleeing enemy, driving them from every position. Night now set in, and we bivouacked till morning, lying on our arms.

From thence we marched toward Murfreesborough. On the morning of the 30th we came in contact with the enemy's pickets, and drove them for 3 miles through a dense thicket of cedar and underbrush. But our advance was now checked by a heavy fire from the enemy's batteries. The cannonading lasted for some hours, but with little effect. Night now again set in, and we laid down on our arms, facing the foe, and only 300 yards distant. We could plainly hear the rebels converse during the night. At daylight next morning they could be seen moving to our right, by thousands, which movements were promptly reported. I now sent out five companies to the front as skirmishers, instructing them to fall back as our lines did, which they did, hotly contesting every inch of ground, and shooting down numbers of the enemy. With the remaining five companies of my regiment I took position on the right of the Fifth Wisconsin Battery. I was now on the extreme right of our lines. The enemy made their appearance in great numbers, advancing in solid column from the dense cedar thickets in our front. On and on they came, nothing daunted at the heavy charges of canister and grape the battery on our left was pouring into their ranks. When they had advanced within 30 yards, I ordered my regiment to fire, which they did, with deliberate aim. Our fire was returned by a raking fire from their extended lines of infantry, while their batteries played on us from our front and right. Our battery being hotly pressed, began to fall back, and I ordered my regiment to fall back. I rallied them again on the right of General Rousseau's command, and took position on the right of a battery, and successfully aided in supporting it. Late in the evening of the same day I was ordered to the right of the division again, where we remained until the evening of the 2d of January, at which time I was ordered, double-quick, to the support of our left across the river. I reached them just as the enemy were giving way and being hotly pursued by our forces. Nothing worthy of note occurred during the night and the following day. On the night of the 3d the enemy retired, leaving us undisputed possession of the field.

I here wish to mention the names of some of the officers of my regiment who distinguished themselves by their courage and bearing: Capt. W. H. Taggart, Company C; Lieut. William F. Riggs, Company F; Lieut. John Gooding, Company A; Lieut. Patrick Carney, Company D. Lieut. Col. T. B. Tanner was severely wounded in the hip while at his post in the performance of his duty. Major Shea and Adjutant Adams rendered themselves highly conspicuous in attempting to rally the regiment, and by their bravery and noble daring. Capt. William Powers, Company H; Lieut. A. D. Sawyer, Company B; Lieut. R. V. Marshall, Company I; Capt. W. H. Snodgrass and Sergt. A. J. Moss, commanding Company G, are brave and good officers, and did their whole duty.   With few exceptions, the men of my regiment fought with a willingness and determination rarely equaled.   But while I make favorable mention of the above-named officers, I cannot but censure the conduct of Capt. N. De Versey, Company A ; Lieut. James McGrayel and Lieut. A. W. Griffith, Company G, and Lieut. L. C. Orrill, Company K, who left the field in the early part of the engagement.   On the morning of the 31st of December they went to Nashville, taking with them quite a number of non-commissioned officers and privates of my command, most of whom were taken prisoners and paroled at La Vergne, and who are still at Nashville.

Very respectfully, your most obedient servant,

M. GOODING,
Colonel, Commanding Regiment.

Lieut. S. M. JONES,
  Acting Assistant Adjutant-General.

No. 25.

Report of Col. William P. Carlin, Thirty-eighth Illinois Infantry, commanding Second Brigade.

HEADQUARTERS SECOND BRIGADE, FIRST DIVISION,
  RIGHT WING, FOURTEENTH ARMY CORPS,
  January 6, 1863.

SIR: I have the honor to submit the following report of the operations of this brigade since leaving Knob Gap, near Nolensville, December 27, 1862 :

The brigade took up the line of march on the morning of the 27th, in a heavy rain, in the direction of Triune, bivouacking within 1 mile of that place, where it remained during the 28th, moving on the morning of the 29th in the direction of Murfreesborough.

That night we bivouacked on Blackman's farm, 4½ miles west of that town.

Early on the morning of the 30th we crossed Overall's Creek, on the right of the Wilkinson pike, and took up position in a heavy wood south of Asa Griscom's house.

At 2 p. m. I was ordered to advance; passed through a corn-field, entering another heavy wood, where my skirmishers first met those of the enemy.   Before making this advance, Brigadier-General Davis, commanding division, informed me that my brigade was to direct the movements of the division, and that Colonels Post and Woodruff, commanding, respectively, the First and Third Brigades, were ordered to keep on a line with me.   My skirmishers, under Lieutenant-Colonel McKee, Fifteenth Wisconsin Volunteers, continued to drive those of the enemy through the wood for about one-fourth of a mile, when I halted and sent a request to Colonels Post and Woodruff to keep pace with my advance.

·At this point my skirmishers, having suffered severely, were withdrawn, and my battery (Second Minnesota, Capt. W. A. Hotchkiss) opened on the enemy with canister and spherical case, inflicting serious damage.   I then threw forward another line of skirmishers, under Lieutenant-Colonel McMackin, Twenty-first Illinois Volunteers, which advanced so slowly that my front line of battle soon closed upon it, driving in, however, the skirmishers of the enemy. My first line of battle was now within 180 yards of the enemy's line, at the house of Mrs. William Smith.

At this point a battery, about 100 yards west of the house, opened with canister upon the Twenty-first Illinois Volunteers, and another, on the east of the house, 250 yards distant, on the Fifteenth Wisconsin Volunteers, killing and wounding a number of my men. Here it was my intention to halt until the First and Third Brigades should come up, on my right and left, respectively; but Col. J. W. S. Alexander, commanding Twenty-first Illinois Volunteers, without instructions from me, ordered his regiment to charge on the battery in his front. His command was moving, with a shout, at double-quick step, within 80 yards of the battery, already abandoned by its cannoneers, when a very heavy fire was opened upon it by infantry, which lay concealed behind fences and outhouses, on the right and left of the battery. This fire killed and wounded a large number of the Twenty-first Illinois Volunteers, and threw the left companies into some disorder, when the regiment was halted and formed on the right of the Fifteenth Wisconsin Volunteers.

The fight was now fairly opened, and continued vigorously until night by the front line of my infantry and the battery which had been placed between the two regiments. The batteries in our front were soon silenced, but another was then opened on my right flank, distant about 500 yards, which completely enfiladed my lines and considerably injured us; but this, too, was driven out of sight by Captain Hotchkiss, after a vigorous and well-directed fire.

Again I sent a request to Colonels Post and Woodruff to come up, but they continued to remain in rear of my lines. I maintained my position during the night, having at dark relieved my front line by the Thirty-eighth Illinois and One hundred and first Ohio Volunteers.

My loss during this day, in killed, wounded, and missing, was about 175 officers and men. Before daylight on the morning of December 31, perceiving indications of an advance by the enemy, I retired my battery about 200 yards. At daylight the enemy advanced. Seeing that the troops on the right and left of my line would not come up, I fell back, with my infantry on a line with my battery, and made a stand; the Twenty-first Illinois Volunteers about 200 yards to the rear, and on the right of the One hundred and first Ohio Volunteers; the Fifteenth Wisconsin Volunteers were posted on the rocks in front of my battery, and the Thirty-eighth Illinois Volunteers on the left of the One hundred and first Ohio Volunteers.

My men were falling rapidly on the front line, and, wishing to increase the fire on the enemy, I sent an order to Colonel Alexander to advance and form on the right of the One hundred and first Ohio Volunteers, and to Colonel Heg, Fifteenth Wisconsin Volunteers, to form on the left of the Thirty-eighth Illinois Volunteers, and to my battery to retire. To my surprise, I received a reply from Colonel Alexander that he was already so hotly engaged that he could not come forward. The startling intelligence was also at this moment communicated to me, by one of my orderlies, that all our forces on our right had left the ground. Immediately afterward a heavy fire of musketry and artillery from the enemy, from my right flank and rear, unmistakably announced that I was also attacked from that direction.

On my left Woodruff's brigade had left the ground. My command was thus exposed to fire from all points, except the left of my rear. When too late to retire in good order, I found that I was overpowered, and but a moment was wanting to place my brigade in the hands of the foe. I decided to retreat by the left flank, when my horse was shot under me and myself struck, and all my staff and orderlies dismounted or otherwise engaged, which prevented me from communicating the order to the regimental commanders. The rear line, then consisting of the Twenty-first Illinois Volunteers, was the first to withdraw, by the order of Lieutenant-Colonel McMackin, then commanding, Colonel Alexander having been wounded. Colonel Stem and Lieutenant-Colonel Wooster, of the One hundred and first Ohio Volunteers, having been shot down, and the ranks of the regiment dreadfully thinned by the fire of the enemy, it gave way and retreated. The Thirty-eighth Illinois Volunteers held its position until the enemy was within a few steps, and then retired. This regiment would have suffered far more severely in its retreat had not a heavy fire from the Fifteenth Wisconsin Volunteers, judiciously posted by Colonel Heg to its left and rear, kept the enemy in check until it had left the wood and partially reformed along the fence, on the right of the Fifteenth Wisconsin Volunteers, where an effective fire was kept up, holding the enemy at bay.

This only gave the foe on our right and left the more time to envelop us. All that now remained of my brigade crossed two open fields and entered a wood about 200 yards east of Griscom's house.

The regiments were painfully reduced in numbers, but I formed a line at this point, and several volleys of musketry and artillery were fired with destructive effect upon the ranks of the enemy ; but the foe was still on our right at Griscom's house, with none of our forces at that point to oppose them, and being informed that General Davis had ordered a still farther withdrawal, I retired my command about half a mile to our rear, and again endeavored to rally the men, but it was evident that they were so utterly discouraged that no substantial good could result, while no supports were in sight.

At another point, about half a mile farther to our rear, I rallied all who could be found, and took a strong position in the edge of a cedar grove, holding it until the enemy came up, when my men fired one volley, and broke without orders. I conducted them to the rear, passing through the lines of our reserves, and halted at the railroad, where we remained during the afternoon collecting our scattered men.

During the two days' fight the loss of officers was so great that some companies had not one to command them, and others not even a sergeant. Our regimental colors were all borne off the field flying, though four color-bearers in succession, of the Twenty-first Illinois Volunteers, were shot down, and two of the color-guard of the Thirty-eighth Illinois Volunteers, three of the color-guard of the Fifteenth Wisconsin Volunteers, and four of the color-guard of the One hundred and first Ohio Volunteers fell. Our artillery was all brought off in safety.

I have to report the loss of many officers, who were ornaments to our army, and who will be mourned by all who knew them. Col. L. Stem, One hundred and first Ohio Volunteers; Lieut. Col. David McKee, Fifteenth Wisconsin Volunteers, and Lieut. Col. M. F. Wooster, One hundred and first Ohio Volunteers, were unsurpassed in all the qualities that make up the brave soldier, the true gentleman, and the pure patriot. Capt. James P. Mead, Thirty-eighth Illinois Volunteers, fell, shot three times, while bravely fighting the enemy with his revolver after his regiment had retired. Lieut. John L. Dillon, Thirty-eight Illinois Volunteers, commanding Company E, fought with a musket until he was shot once, when he drew his sword and cheered on his men till he fell dead. Other instances of equal gallantry were observed in the other regiments, but to recount all would give my report an undue length. The long, sad list of killed and wounded forms the truest eulogium on the conduct of the troops composing this brigade, and it is by that list I wish it to be judged.

Of the 10 field officers of the regiments, 3 were killed and 2 wounded. Seven horses were shot under the regimental, field, and staff officers. Of my orderlies, Private Pease, Company B, Thirty-sixth Illinois Volunteers, had his horse shot under him while carrying my orders. Private Knox, same company, also had his horse shot under him, and while endeavoring to procure another horse for me was wounded by a grape-shot and again by a Minié ball, and Corporal Hart, Thirty-eighth Illinois Volunteers, was stunned and disabled by a cannon ball.

I deem it my duty to call the special attention of the general commanding the Fourteenth Army Corps to Col. John W. S. Alexander, Twenty-first Illinois Volunteers, and Col. Hans C. Heg, Fifteenth Wisconsin Volunteers. While every field officer under my command did his duty faithfully, Colonels Alexander and Heg, in my opinion, proved themselves the bravest of the brave. Had such men as these been in command of some of our brigades, we should have been spared the shame of witnessing the rout of our troops and the disgraceful panic, encouraged, at least, by the example and advice of officers high in command.

Lieut. Col. D. H. Gilmer, commanding Thirty-eighth Illinois Volunteers, was always at his post and attending to his duty. Maj. Isaac M. Kirby, One hundred and first Ohio Volunteers, took command of the regiment after the fall of the brave Colonels Stem and Wooster, and conducted it to the rear, reduced to about 100 men.

Capt. W. A. Hotchkiss, commanding Second Minnesota Battery, and all his officers and men, deserve credit for their gallantry in the fight, and energy in preventing the loss of the battery.

Among the staff officers of this army who made themselves useful in rallying the scattered men, Dr. L. F. Russell, Second Minnesota Battery; Lieut. S. M. Jones, Fifty-ninth Illinois Volunteers; Captain Thruston, aide-de-camp to Major-General McCook, and Chaplain Wilkins, Twenty-first Illinois Volunteers, came especially under my observation.

On the night of December 31 this brigade was ordered to take up position near the Nashville pike, 4 miles from Murfreesborough.

January 1, 1863, slight skirmishing with the enemy continued during the day, in which we killed several, capturing 13 prisoners and paroling 11 others, wounded.

At 3.30 p. m. January 2, while hard fighting was progressing on our left, I received orders from General Rosecrans to report to him in person. He directed me to take my command to the left, form it in two lines, and, should I find our forces repulsed by the enemy, to allow our men to pass through my lines, and, on the approach of the enemy, give a whoop and a yell, and go at 'em. With a brigade which, in three days' hard fighting, had been reduced from 2,000 to 700 and greatly discouraged, I felt serious apprehension that I would not be able to fulfill the expectations of the general, and, to prepare him for such a result, I informed him of the condition of my brigade. He said, "Tell them they must do it for us and for the country." I told him I would do my best. My men fell into ranks with the utmost alacrity and marched to the scene of the conflict, a great portion of the way on the double-quick, crossing Stone's River at a ford. All apprehensions that I had previously entertained now vanished. I felt confident that they would not only charge the enemy, but would repulse them. Before reaching the ground designated, however, I learned that the enemy had already been driven back in confusion. I continued my march, and, under the direction of Brigadier-General Davis, placed my command in the advance, relieving the command of Colonel Hazen. It was now dark. We maintained our ground till the morning of January 4, when we returned to our position on the right.

My loss in killed, wounded, and missing in the engagement at Knob Gap, near Nolensville, December 26, and the battles of December 30 and 31, 1862, and in front of the enemy east of Stone's River, January 2 and 3, 1863, is as follows:

Command.	Killed.		Wounded.		Missing.		Total.
	Officers.	Men.	Officers.	Men.	Officers.	Men.	
21st Illinois	2	55	7	180	......	59	303
38th Illinois	2	32	5	104	......	34	177
101st Ohio	4	19	2	121	......	66	212
15th Wisconsin	2	13	5	65	1	33	119
2d Minnesota Battery	......	3	1	5	......	1	10
Total	10	122	20	475	1	193	821

I cannot close this report without expressing my obligations to the following-named officers of my staff for their zeal, fidelity, and courage in all the severe engagements embraced in this report, viz : Capt. S. P. Voris, Thirty-eighth Illinois Volunteers, acting assistant adjutant-general ; Capt. W. C. Harris, Thirty-eighth Illinois Volunteers ; Lieut. Albert Woodbury, Second Minnesota Battery, and Lieut. Walter E. Carlin, Thirty-eighth Illinois Volunteers. Also to my faithful orderlies, Pease, Knox, Amick, and Hart. Private Alexander C. Hosmer, One hundred and first Ohio Volunteers, my clerk, though not required to go into the battle, was constantly at my side to carry my orders.

Regimental reports and lists of casualties are herewith inclosed ; also a report of the engagement at Knob Gap, near Nolensville, December 26, 1862.

A topographical sketch, showing the ground passed over and positions occupied by this brigade on December 30 and 31, 1862, is herewith inclosed.

Very respectfully, your obedient servant,

W. P. CARLIN,
Colonel Thirty-eighth Illinois Volunteers, Commanding.

Lieut. T. W. MORRISON,
Acting Assistant Adjutant-General.

No. 26.

Report of Maj. Isaac M. Kirby, One hundred and first Ohio Infantry.

NEAR MURFREESBOROUGH,
January 5, 1863.

CAPTAIN : On the morning of December 26, 1862, in our proper position in the brigade, the regiment (Colonel Stem commanding) marched from our camp, near Nashville, out on the Edmondson pike. Commissioned officers reported for duty, Col. Leander Stem, Lieut. Col. M. F. Wooster, Maj. I. M. Kirby, Adjt. Leonard D. Smith, First Surg. T. M. Cook, Asst. Surg. Walter Caswell, Second Lieut. D. H. Fox, Company A; First Lieut. S. B. Beckwith, Company B; Capt. B. B. McDonald and Second Lieut. John B. Biddle, Company C; Second Lieut. John M. Latimer, jr., Company D; First Lieut. Lyman Parcher and Second Lieut. R. D. Lord, Company E; First Lieut. A. R. Hillyer, Company F; Capt. John Messer and First Lieut. John P. Fleming, Company G; Second Lieut. J. I. Neff, Company H; Capt. N. M. Barnes and Second Lieut. H. A. Taggart, Company I; Second Lieut. P. F. Cline, Company K, and 441 enlisted men.

Early in the afternoon of the same day the regiment formed in line of battle to attack the enemy near Nolensville. Deploying a line of skirmishers, we moved to the front about a half a mile, with some little firing on the part of our skirmishers, who succeeded in capturing 2 prisoners. While halting at this point, the enemy was discovered attempting to plant a battery on a hill one-half or three-quarters of a mile distant. By order of Colonel Carlin, the regiment was wheeled into line, bayonets fixed, and moved forward to take that battery at all hazards. The enemy retired on our approach. We were again moved forward, by the right of companies to the front, on the enemy in their new position, a mile distant from this point. Forward we marched, under a heavy fire of shell. Arriving within a quarter of a mile of the enemy's battery, we formed into line, and, led by Colonel Stem, charged at double-quick, succeeding, together with the rest of the brigade, in taking one gun and 4 prisoners. We were again ordered forward a short distance, but soon called off to rest for the night. Our loss was 3 men wounded. Second Lieutenant Cline fell from the ranks on the last charge; afterward reported himself stunned by concussion of shell.

The next day, December 27, we marched out near Knob Gap, where we rested till Monday morning, December 29, when we again took up our line of march on the Murfreesborough road, going into camp, near this place, soon after dark.

At or near 10 o'clock, Tuesday morning, December 30, the regiment was moved forward in "double column at half distance," supporting the Twenty-first Regiment Illinois Volunteers. About 3 o'clock in the afternoon the Twenty-first became engaged with the enemy, the One hundred and first lying a short distance to the rear, supporting the Second Minnesota Battery, which was engaging a battery of the enemy. Just at dark the Twenty-first fell back through our lines, leaving us in front. This day our loss was 2 men wounded. Before moving forward, Second Lieutenant Cline reported himself unfit for duty, and permission was granted him to go to the rear. Immediately upon taking the front for the night, we advanced a picket line. The regiment was ordered to sleep on their arms. Ten men were kept on guard immediately in front of the regimental lines, and one field officer constantly on the watch during the night.

At early daylight, Wednesday morning, December 31, the enemy was discovered moving in heavy force to our right; soon after their skirmishers opened fire on us from the front. By order of Colonel Carlin, Colonel Stem moved his line forward about a hundred yards, when the firing became quite brisk. Soon after, Colonel Stem was ordered to fall back to his former position, sling knapsacks, and form a new line a short distance to the rear, which he performed in good order. Here the firing was very severe. Our forces falling back on our right, without our knowledge, the enemy turned our right flank, and poured a terrific cross-fire upon our lines, which we were unable to stand; consequently the regiment fell back in some disorder. It was at this time Colonel Stem and Lieut. Col. Moses F. Wooster fell, mortally wounded, while gallantly and nobly attempting to hold the regiment in line. Colonel Stem fell just as he had called out, "Stand by your colors, boys, for the honor of the good old State of Ohio." We again succeeded in rallying the regiment at the fence, just at the edge of the woods, where we stood under a terrific fire until we had permission from Colonel Carlin to retreat. Then the march became quite disorderly, through the corn-field and cotton-field, to the edge of the timber, where we again rallied; were in turn driven from there; rallied again in the woods; marched in good order to a new line of battle; were finally ordered from that position, and formed in front of a dense cedar thicket, from which position we were soon driven in some confusion; but we rallied about 30 men on the colors, and led them back into the cedars, but were driven from that, and rallied for the last time on the railroad, from which position we were marched with the brigade a short distance to the rear, and rested till near 3 o'clock in the afternoon. At this time there were present Captain McDonald, Captain Messer, Captain Barnes, Adjutant Smith, Lieutenant Fox, Lieutenant Latimer, Lieutenant Neff, Lieutenant Parcher, and Lieutenant Beckwith, all of whom performed their whole duty nobly during the entire day.

We were moved from here to a position in front, west of the railroad, which we occupied till Friday afternoon, January 2, about 4 o'clock, when we were taken on double-quick to the left of the lines, and lay in line of battle during the night and till the afternoon of Saturday, January 3, at which time, being quite sick, Colonel Carlin granted me permission to go to the fires in the rear. Captain McDonald, assuming command, reports to me that the regiment was not actively engaged from that time till 3 o'clock a. m. Sunday, January 4, when they were relieved and marched to this place, where I joined the regiment early Sunday morning, though not able for duty.

The loss in the regiment, so far as I have yet ascertained, is, Col. Leander Stem, mortally wounded, died at 6 o'clock January 5, 1863; Lieut. Col. Moses F. Wooster, mortally wounded, died January 1, 1863; First Lieut. Asa R. Hillyer, mortally wounded, died January 4, 1863; Second Lieut. John B. Biddle, killed on the field; First Lieut. John P. Fleming, wounded in the arm, supposed to be a prisoner; Second Lieut. R. D. Lord, slightly wounded; killed, 15 enlisted men; wounded, 122; missing, 92.*

Second Lieut. Henry A. Taggart I have not seen since early in the morning, December 25, 1862, but think he has gone to Nashville. He was quite unwell, and excused by the surgeon, and may have been taken to Nashville on account of sickness. It is difficult to make selections of commanding officers for gallant conduct, when all who are now present performed their duty so gallantly, but cannot lose this opportunity to thank Capt. John Messer and First Lieut. Lyman Parcher for their determined efforts during the battle to serve their country and sustain the reputation of the regiment. To Adjt. Leonard D. Smith I am particularly indebted for valuable assistance and the heroic examples he gave others. Color Sergt. James M. Roberts deserves mention here for gallant conduct. He never faltered, always planted the colors promptly where directed, and never moved them till ordered. My thanks are due to Orderly Sergt. Samuel Strayer, commanding Company K, for managing his company well till he fell, wounded, on the

_____
* But see revised statement, p. 208.

field, and to Orderly Sergt. Isaac P. Rule, for taking command of Company I from January 1 to January 5, Captain Barnes being sick and unfit for field duty.

First Lieut. Asa R. Hillyer and Second Lieut. John B. Biddle fell while heroically attempting to rally their men. The regiment has lost in them officers whose places cannot be filled, and the country patriots who served faithfully to the last.

The regiment is particularly indebted to Asst. Surg. Walter Caswell for gallantly staying by them under the heaviest fire.

We have now present for duty 10 commissioned officers and 178 enlisted men. Present, on detached service, 15 enlisted men, and report 19 enlisted men known to have gone to Nashville.

Respectfully,

I. M. KIRBY,
Major, Comdg. One hundred and first Regt. Ohio Vol. Infty.

Capt. SAMUEL P. VORIS,
Acting Assistant Adjutant-General.

No. 27.

Report of Col. William E. Woodruff, commanding Third Brigade.

HEADQUARTERS THIRD BRIGADE, FIRST DIVISION,
RIGHT WING, FOURTEENTH ARMY CORPS,
January 5, 1863.

SIR: I have the honor to report the operations of the Third Brigade, First Division, of the right wing, in the five days' battle before Murfreesborough.

This brigade having held the advanced position on Overall's Creek in the afternoon and night of Monday, December 29, was the base of formation for the line of battle on Tuesday morning. At an early hour on the morning of the 30th, I received instructions that we would move forward in line of battle.

I was directed to join my left with Brigadier-General Sill's brigade, holding the right of the Second Division, under Brigadier-General Sheridan, and that Colonel Carlin, commanding the Second Brigade of the First Division, would connect his line with my right.

This brigade was accordingly formed in two lines, the Thirty-fifth Illinois Regiment, Lieutenant-Colonel Chandler, on the right; the Twenty-fifth Illinois Regiment, Col. T. D. Williams commanding, on the left, in the first line of battle, and the Eighty-first Indiana Regiment, Lieutenant-Colonel Timberlake, in the second line in reserve, the extreme left on the right of [the Wilkinson?] turnpike; the Eighth Wisconsin Battery, of four guns, Captain Carpenter commanding, being placed in the interval between Brigadier-General Sill's right and my left. My front was curtained with two companies of skirmishers, detailed from the Twenty-fifth and Thirty-fifth Illinois Regiments, under the command and immediate supervision of Major McIlwain, of the Thirty-fifth Illinois Regiment. The commands to my right and left were formed in the same manner.

We moved forward on the morning of Tuesday, the 30th, at about 10 o'clock, and halted on the edge of a large cotton-field, immediately in front of a wood running parallel with the turnpike, our lines facing Murfreesborough, which was in a southeasterly direction. This was about 11 a. m.

No enemy being visible in our front, I caused a few shells to be thrown into the woods beyond, but met no response. The topography of the country in this line and in my front was a cotton-field, which we then occupied, at the farther end of which was a belt or strip of timber, ending at a corn-field on my left and front, and immediately in front of Brigadier-General Sill's right. This corn-field extended to a narrow, heavy-timbered wood, bordered by a rail fence. Beyond this timber was a corn-field, receding toward a ravine, terminated by a bluff wood bank, along the foot of which, in the ravine, was the enemy's line of battle, with its supports and artillery on the elevation.

We remained in position until about 3 p. m., when my skirmishers were ordered forward to occupy the belt of timber, which they did. Major McIlwain, who was in command, reported to me that the enemy's skirmishers were in the farthest wood to our front and left, and desired me to send him a further support of one company, which was sent him, with orders to press their skirmishers back. The skirmishing soon commenced briskly, and my brigade was ordered to advance, which it did in admirable order, and was halted in the first belt of timber.

Desiring to know the position of the enemy's line, and the situation of their skirmishers, I proceeded to the line of skirmishers, to assist in directing their movements and urge them on, and, having given them directions in person, returned to my command, to be ready to move forward to their support. The wood was so thick and brushy on my right that it was difficult to see farther than the left of the Second Brigade; but as I discovered it advancing, we moved forward also, to protect its flank. Sheridan's division had halted some 100 yards in rear of my brigade, his line of skirmishers joining my line of battle.

At this juncture my skirmishers commenced falling back rapidly, and I endeavored to get the officer in command of those of Sheridan's division to advance to their support, as those of my brigade had not only driven the enemy from my front, but General Sill's also; but, as he had no orders to move forward, he refused. The emergency being imminent, Colonel Williams was ordered to detach the left company of his regiment, and deploy it forward as skirmishers, to relieve or strengthen those engaged, as circumstances might require, while the brigade was advanced to support them.

The command pressed forward in splendid order, and soon became hotly engaged, and drove the enemy back through the wood and corn-field in their own lines. As we were now far in advance of any support upon the left, I deemed it advisable to halt and wait for them to come up, and, therefore, took position in rear of the rail fence, my right nearly at right angles to my line of battle, thereby obtaining an oblique, as well as direct, fire; but the space to be occupied by this brigade was so great that the Eighty-first Indiana Regiment was ordered up to complete my line, thereby leaving me no reserves.

The battery was placed in the angle of the fence to protect my right and front. Shortly after taking this position, Brigadier-General Sill joined me on the left. We remained in position, receiving a heavy fire, and occasionally replying with shell, until toward night, when the enemy opened a heavy artillery fire, apparently on the right of Colonel Carlin's brigade. Thus, discovering their battery, and mine being in good range and position to enfilade theirs, Captain Carpenter was ordered to silence their battery, which he did in handsome style in about five minutes.

An attack of infantry was then made from the same point on Colonel Carlin, and as their lines presented the same advantage, Captain Carpenter again opened fire with such terrific effect that their yells of pain, terror, and anguish, as our shells exploded in their dense ranks, could be distinctly heard where we stood. So well was the battery served that their attack ceased, and darkness closed the conflict.

We slept on our arms without fires, prepared for the battle which we well knew would open on the morrow. During the night we discovered what appeared to me to be a continued movement of troops, which led me to believe that the enemy were massing troops on our right, which information I had the honor to report to my immediate superior, Brigadier-General Davis.

As soon as day dawned I examined the line of battle, and, as I had no supports, placed three pieces in battery on my left, and pointed out to Brigadier-General Sill the weakness of the line at this point, and requested him to order up some regiments of his brigade, held in reserve, to strengthen his right and protect my left, feeling certain that the enemy meditated an attack, and that it would be made at that place. He agreed with me, and immediately ordered up two regiments, which remained there but a short time, and then resumed their former positions as reserves. Deeming the knowledge of this fact of paramount importance, I dispatched a staff officer to Brigadier-General Davis to give him the information. Afterward the general informed me that I must hold the position as best I could, for he had no supports to send me.

Almost simultaneously with the withdrawal of the reserves ordered up by Brigadier-General Sill, the enemy made their attack in five heavy lines, and we were immediately engaged. Captain Carpenter's battery opened with terrific effect with grape and canister, and they were mowed down as grass beneath the sickle, while the infantry poured in a well-directed and very destructive fire. Sheltered by the rail fence, they were partially protected, and fired with the coolness of veterans.

As soon as the battle became general, the Twenty-fourth Wisconsin, which joined my left, gave way, leaving my battery and left flank exposed to an enfilading fire. I finally succeeded in rallying them as a reserve. At this moment the right of Brigadier-General Sill's brigade commenced to swing to the rear, and Colonel Carlin's was discovered falling steadily back.

I then received orders to take position to the rear, some 300 yards, in the belt of timber. I informed the staff officer who brought the order that we could maintain our position if supported. He said the order was peremptory, and I hastened to execute it, but not until I was flanked both on the right and left. The brigade moved to the rear in good order, and halted on the new line; but the right and left continuing the march, and being severely pressed, we made a vigorous charge and drove the enemy back in our front, and, strange to say, not only carried our point, but swung the enemy's lines upon right and left with it.

Had we been supported here, they would have been routed; as it was, we regained our position occupied when the battle opened, but could hold it but a moment, when we were forced to yield to superior numbers, and steadily fell back to the ground from which the charge was first made. From this point we charged a second time, compelling the enemy to yield ground, but our ammunition beginning to fail, and no wagons to be found from which to replenish the stock, the brigade was ordered to hold its position as best it could, and, if pressed too hard, to fall steadily back until the battery could be got into position to protect their movement across the cotton-field. I placed the battery in position, and gave the officer in command (Sergeant German) directions where to fire, pointing out to him the position of the brigade, and what he was required to do.

The ammunition of the regiments now entirely failing, and a perfect rout appearing to have taken place, the brigade fell back to the ground occupied by them on the morning of Tuesday. At this time the whole wing was in the utmost confusion, and I used every endeavor to rally and organize them, but without avail. There seemed to be no fear, no panic, but a stolid indifference, which was unaccountable. Officers and men passed to the rear; no words or exhortation could prevent them. In three different positions I used every exertion to reform our lines, but it became impossible. Reaching the Murfreesborough pike, a stampede or panic commenced in the wagon-train, but, succeeding in getting a regiment across the road, it was stopped, and, by a vigorous charge of cavalry, saved from the enemy.

We were then placed in reserve to our division along the Murfreesborough pike, and there waited in anxious expectation to make or repel attacks until the afternoon of Friday, when we were ordered to move in double-quick to the extreme left, to support the division which was being driven in by the enemy, and, although fatigued and worn out by exposure to the rain, without tents or blankets, for seven days, and want of sleep (two days of which time we had had nothing to eat but parched corn), the command, with yells of joy, rushed forward, and, after fording the river three times, pushed the enemy back with the greatest rapidity, the ground being covered with rebel dead and wounded. We went into position about 2 miles from the ford, and on the extreme left. During the night we threw up an abatis of rails, and laid on our arms, without fires, in a drenching rain.

The next morning (Saturday, January 3) we expected an attack, but none occurred during the day. That night we changed position to the right again, nothing but picket skirmishing having occurred during the day. When the morning of Saturday passed without an attack, I became satisfied in my own mind that the enemy were evacuating Murfreesborough, and so expressed it.

I cannot speak in too high terms of the gallant conduct of the officers and men under my command. If indomitable daring, cool courage, and invincible bravery in the midst of the turmoil of such a battle, when all space seemed occupied by some deadly missile, amid carnage and noise, be any proof of heroism, they certainly possess it. Many instances of personal daring and feats of individual prowess were visibly performed, but I must refer you to the reports of subordinate commanders for names and instances.

To the officers and men of the Twenty-fifth and Thirty-fifth Illinois Regiments and Eighth Wisconsin Battery I owe especial thanks for the determined bravery and chivalric heroism they evinced throughout; and also to the officers and men of the Eighty-first Indiana, a new regiment, the first time under fire, who, with but a few exceptions, manfully fronted the storm of battle, and gave earnest proof of what may hereafter be expected of them.

I desire to call the attention of the commanding officer to the gallant conduct of Lieutenant-Colonel Chandler, commanding the Thirty-fifth Illinois, whose cool, steady courage, admirable deportment, and skillful management evinced the soldier, true and tried, and who at all times proved himself worthy of the trust he holds. Major McIlwain, of the same regiment, I cannot praise too much; his good management and skillful handling of the skirmishers, of which he was in charge, elicited encomiums of well-merited compliment—at all times cool, determined, and persevering. Lieutenant-Colonel Timberlake and Major Woodbury, of the Eighty-first Indiana, displayed manly courage, and held their regiment firm and steady under heavy fire; for officers young in the service their efforts are worthy of imitation. Capt. W. Taggart, who succeeded to the command of the Twenty-fifth Illinois Regiment, behaved as a soldier should, everywhere efficient, and ever ready to execute orders. First Sergeant German, of the Eighth Wisconsin Battery, merits much praise for the cool, skillful, and determined manner in which he served his battery after he succeeded to the command.

To my staff, Capt. George Austin, acting assistant adjutant-general; Capt. A. C. Keys, Lieut. C. P. Ford, Lieut. John F. Isom, Lieut. William R. McChesney, and Lieut. H. S. Park, I owe especial thanks for the manner they served upon the field, carrying my orders, wherever required, through a storm of shot, shells, and bullets, regardless of all save the performance of their duty.

During the conflict it became necessary, in the absence of staff officers on duty, to make use of orderlies to supply their places. In connection herewith I take great pleasure in testifying to the brave conduct of Orderlies A. T. Greeman and Abijah Lee, on my escort.

Amid the glorious results of a battle won, it gives me pain to record the names of the gallant men who offered up their lives on the altar of their country; but we must drop the tear of sorrow over their resting-place, and offer our heartfelt sympathies to their relatives and friends, trusting that God will care for them and soothe their afflictions. And while we remember the noble dead, let us pay a tribute of respect to the gallant Col. T. D. Williams, Twenty-fifth Illinois Regiment, who died in the performance of his duty. He fell with his regimental colors in his hands, exclaiming, "We will plant it here, boys, and rally the old Twenty-fifth around it, and here we will die." Such conduct is above all praise, and words can paint no eulogium worthy of the subject. And here let me call the attention to the conduct of Captain Carpenter, of the Eighth Wisconsin Battery, who fell gallantly serving his guns until the enemy were within a few yards of their muzzles. He died as a soldier would wish to die, with his face to the foe, in the smoke and din of battle.

The casualties of the command are small in comparison to the fire they received and the service done.

The Thirty-fifth Illinois lost 2 commissioned officers wounded, 8 privates killed, 49 wounded, and 32 missing; the Twenty-fifth Illinois, 1 commissioned officer killed and 3 wounded, 14 privates killed, 69 wounded, and 35 missing; the Eighty-first Indiana, 2 commissioned officers killed, 2 wounded, and 1 missing, 3 privates killed, 40 wounded, and 39 missing; the Eighth Wisconsin Battery, 1 commissioned officer killed, 4 privates wounded, and 19 missing. Total, 4 commissioned officers killed, 7 wounded, and 1 missing; 25 privates killed, 162 wounded, and 125 missing. Aggregate killed, wounded, and missing, 324.*

I hope a portion of those missing may yet return, as all cannot have been made prisoners.

I have the honor to submit the above report to your consideration, and remain, dear sir, yours, most respectfully,

W. E. WOODRUFF,
Colonel, Commanding Third Brigade.

Lieut. T. W. MORRISON,
Acting Assistant Adjutant-General, First Division.

---

* But see revised statement, p. 208.

No. 28.

Report of Capt. Wesford Taggart, Twenty-fifth Illinois Infantry.

HDQRS. TWENTY-FIFTH REGIMENT ILLINOIS VOLS.,
THIRD BRIGADE, FIRST DIVISION, RIGHT WING,
Camp near Murfreesborough, Tenn., January 8, 1863.

SIR : I have the honor of submitting to you the following report of the operations of the Twenty-fifth Regiment Illinois Infantry during the late battle before Murfreesborough, Tenn. :

The regiment left camp, near Nashville, Tenn., at 6.30 a. m. December 26, 1862, under command of Maj. R. H. Nodine, and, after a march of 10 miles, in company with balance of brigade, encountered a force of the enemy near Nolensville.

About 3 p. m. were deployed on the right of the brigade; Companies A, I, and K were thrown out to the front as skirmishers. After sharp action, of about two hours' duration, the enemy were driven back, and we bivouacked for the night on the field, the rain falling in torrents. Took 1 prisoner of the Eighth Texas Cavalry.

At 7 a. m. on the 27th resumed the march at a distance of 10 miles, encamping near Triune, Col. Thomas D. Williams assuming command early in the morning, Major Nodine being detailed on the staff of Major-General McCook.

At 6 a. m. on the 29th resumed the march; encamped on Stone's River. Distance marched, 15 miles. Detailed five companies as advanced picket.

At 3 p. m. on the 30th fell into line. At 8 a. m. marched in close column, by division, in company with rest of brigade. After marching a distance of 1½ miles, arrived at the front; deployed in line of battle, the men stripping knapsacks. Company A, under command of Lieut. T. H. West, was deployed to the front as skirmishers, and immediately afterward joined by Companies I and K, under command of Capt. Samuel Houston and Lieut. M. B. Thompson. These companies, in conjunction with others of the brigade, continued skirmishing until dark, driving the enemy's skirmishers into his main line, Company A losing 6 men wounded, Company I 2 killed and 3 wounded, and Company K 1 wounded.

The regiment advanced in line of battle into a strip of timber, and, covered under shelter of a rail fence, a corn-field of about 150 yards in width separating our forces from that of the enemy, Company A was thrown out to the front as skirmishers a distance of 60 yards. The regiment lay in this position until 3 a. m. of the 31st, at which time it was called into line, the Thirty-fifth Illinois on our right and the Eighty-first Indiana on our left, supporting the Eighth Wisconsin Battery. At daybreak a line of the enemy's skirmishers advancing, opened fire on our skirmishers, and were followed immediately afterward by their main body advancing in four consecutive lines of battle diagonally on our left. A change of front was ordered by Colonel Williams, which was executed under a heavy fire of musketry. Our regiment then opened a murderous fire on the enemy, completely checking him, and finally driving him back in confusion. The enemy immediately made another advance, and were received with a terrific fire of musketry. Our regiment was, however, forced back a short distance.

At this time, while bravely rallying his men, Colonel Williams fell mortally wounded by a musket-ball passing through his right breast. He was carried from the field immediately. I then assumed command of the regiment, which by this time had fallen back a distance of 150 paces from the first position. I rallied the men, and, finding them almost destitute of ammunition, immediately dispatched a messenger to General Woodruff to report the fact; then ordered bayonets to be fixed, and charged on the enemy once more, driving him from the field and retaking one Parrott gun, which had been taken by the enemy from the Eighth Wisconsin Battery; also capturing a number of prisoners.

At this time, finding all our supplies gone, and flanked on the left, the enemy's lines having passed us on the right, and being unable to communicate with General Woodruff, I assumed the responsibility of withdrawing the regiment in good order to the rear of a battery placed on a commanding eminence, taking with us the piece retaken from the enemy, but which we were forced to leave after taking it about 300 yards, on account of a destructive fire being opened on us from one of the enemy's batteries.

At this point I reported in person to Major-General McCook that we were out of ammunition, and was ordered by him to retire to the ammunition train in the rear. Did so, and supplied ourselves with ammunition. Then, in obedience to orders, took position on the Murfreesborough pike, remaining there until 10 a. m. of January 1, 1863.

At this time received orders from General Woodruff to fall back a distance of 300 paces and erect barricades. Did so, remaining there until 4 p. m. of the 2d instant.

At this time received orders to fall in line, cross Stone's River, and participate in the action going on on the left. Moved forward at a double-quick a distance of 1½ miles, wading the river three times, the last time under a heavy fire of shot and shell from the enemy's battery, placed on an eminence directly in front of our regiment; formed line of battle, and moved forward at a double-quick, charging on the enemy, who, however, speedily retreated. After going a distance of 300 yards in the open field, I halted the regiment, threw out a party of skirmishers in front, built a strong line of barricades, and bivouacked on the field of battle.

At daylight of the 3d instant the enemy's sharpshooters, who were concealed in the timbers, opened fire on the regiment, keeping it up until dark, wounding 2 of our men. Remained on the field until 4 a. m. of the 4th instant; then received orders to recross the river and go into camp on the Nashville pike, which we did.

Col. Thomas D. Williams acted with great courage, coolness, and bravery until he fell. Capt. Samuel D. Wall was severely wounded while gallantly doing duty as a field officer. He was carried from the field. Lieutenants Dickson and Hastings were also severely wounded while nobly discharging their duty, and were carried from the field.

To the officers and men of the regiment I am deeply indebted for the coolness and bravery shown on every side, all doing nobly.

There were present with the regiment the following commissioned officers: Capts. S. D. Wall, S. Houston, B. F. Ford, Z. Hall, and J. Smart, Adjt. G. W. Flynn, First Lieuts. T. H. West, T. J. McKibben, E. Hall, A. Varner, W. J. Sallee, J. H. Hastings, and Second Lieuts. A. Martin, J. C. Gundy, M. B. Thompson, Thomas W. Braselton, S. Dickson, and A. H. South. Our loss is: Killed, 15; wounded, 68; missing, 25.*

Very respectfully,

WESFORD TAGGART,
Captain Twenty-fifth Illinois, Commanding Regiment.

Lieut. G. W. FLYNN,
Acting Assistant Adjutant-General.

---

* But see revised statement, p. 208.

No. 29.

Report of Lieut. Col. William P. Chandler, Thirty-fifth Illinois Infantry.

HEADQUARTERS THIRTY-FIFTH ILLINOIS VOLUNTEERS,
Camp near Murfreesborough, Tenn., January 3, 1863.

SIR: I have the honor to submit the following report of the part taken by this regiment in the movements and battles occurring from the time of taking up camp at Saint James Chapel, on December 26, 1862, to the evacuation of Murfreesborough by the enemy, on January 3, 1863:

December 26, the regiment was on picket duty, and, after the division passed outside the lines on the Nolensville pike, formed the rear guard. The roads being very bad, the train did not close up at night, and the command was placed in position to protect it.

December 27, moved forward at daylight and joined the brigade before marching. Moved forward on the road to Triune, about 6 miles, and halted for the night.

December 28, remained in camp.

December 29, marched at daylight on the road to Lane's Store. Brigade formed the advance at Stewart's Creek, and slept on our arms at night.

December 30, formed line of battle at 10 a. m. and advanced on the enemy's lines. Major McIlwain was placed in command of skirmishers of the brigade, and toward night was sharply engaged. Had 4 men wounded. Laid on our arms at night.

December 31, skirmishing commenced at daylight. About sunrise the enemy advanced obliquely in strong force, striking first the Eighty-first Indiana and next the Twenty-fifth Illinois Volunteers, causing them to retire from their position. Soon coming within range of our rifled muskets, we opened a murderous fire on their flank, checking their advance, and enabling the Twenty-fifth and Eighty-first to regain the ground lost. Our loss in the first charge of the enemy was light, owing to a strong position we had on the cedar ridge. Soon, however, the enemy reformed his broken lines, appearing with fresh troops on our right, and made a second desperate charge on our lines, causing them to waver and fall back, but again they were repulsed with terrible slaughter and our original position regained, except on the right, from which I had been retiring, by orders of the brigade commander, and, in obedience to those orders, I retired to the point of timber in rear of the cotton-field, my right being hotly pressed by the enemy, and the whole line under heavy fire of the enemy's batteries. On reaching the timber, the regiment was halted, and messengers sent for ammunition, but, owing to the confusion on our right, where the train had been parked, none could be procured. Having received no orders from the brigade commander in relation to the point to which I should retire, I governed my movements by the left of Carlin's brigade, and so continued to do until nearly reaching the Nashville pike, when other troops and batteries crowding in, separated us. I directed Major McIlwain to report to Colonel Carlin and find out his position, with the intention of forming the brigade (then acting under my orders) on his left; but before his return was obliged to change my position, to give room to other troops then forming in line of battle. I moved the troops a short distance to the rear, procured and distributed ammunition, and, moving to the right and front, formed on the left of Carlin's brigade, and remained in that position until nearly night, when Colonel Woodruff, returning, assumed command, and we took position on the west side of the Nashville pike, and laid on our arms at night.

Our loss during the day was First Lieut. H. M. McConnell, Company H, killed, and Second Lieutenant Kagay, Company K, slightly wounded; 9 men killed and 39 wounded.

January 1, 1863, changed position to rear of the pike, and laid on our arms at night.

January 2, about 4 p. m., moved across the river to our left, to repel the enemy's assault in that direction. After coming under fire of the enemy's batteries, formed line of battle, and advanced, under heavy artillery fire, to within musket range of their battery, and silenced it. Took the adjutant of the Forty-first Alabama and 12 men prisoners. Lost 1 man killed and 1 wounded. Laid on our arms at night.

The officers and men deserve great credit for their patience and endurance, being exposed to drenching rain, cold, and hunger, without fire nearly all the time, for a week. No officer failed in his duties. All did well and deserve commendation.

Major McIlwain had command of the skirmishers of the brigade on the 30th and on the morning of December 31, and deserves great credit for the bravery and skill he displayed in handling them; and, after they were driven in and the action became general, he returned to his command, and by his cool courage and gallantry, shown throughout the entire conflict, deserves my highest commendation.

Recapitulation of casualties.

	Killed.	Wounded.	Missing.	Total.
Commissioned officers	1	1	......	2
Enlisted men	10	49	25	84
Total	11	50	25	86

Very respectfully, your obedient servant,

WM. P. CHANDLER,
Lieutenant-Colonel, Commanding Regiment.

Lieutenant FLYNN,
Actg. Asst. Adjt. Gen., Third Brigade, First Division.

No. 30.

Report of Brig. Gen. Richard W. Johnson, U. S. Army, commanding Second Division.

HEADQUARTERS SECOND DIVISION, RIGHT WING,
January 8, 1863.

SIR: I have the honor to submit the following report of the operations of the Second Division, under my command, beginning December 26, 1862, the day on which it left Nashville, and terminating on January 6, 1863:

The Second Division is composed of the following troops:

First Brigade, Brig. Gen. A. Willich commanding: Forty-ninth Ohio, Colonel Gibson; Fifteenth Ohio, Colonel Wallace; Thirty-ninth Indiana,

Lieutenant-Colonel Jones; Thirty-second Indiana, Lieutenant Colonel Erdelmeyer; Eighty-ninth Illinois, Lieutenant-Colonel Hotchkiss, and Goodspeed's battery, First Ohio Artillery.

Second Brigade, Brig. Gen. E. N. Kirk commanding: Twenty-ninth Indiana, Lieutenant-Colonel Dunn; Thirtieth Indiana, Colonel Dodge; Seventy-seventh Pennsylvania, Lieutenant-Colonel Housum; Thirty-fourth Illinois, Lieutenant-Colonel Bristol; Seventy-ninth Illinois, Colonel Read, and Edgarton's battery, Ohio Artillery.

Third Brigade, Col. P. P. Baldwin commanding: Sixth Indiana, Lieutenant-Colonel Tripp; Fifth Kentucky (Louisville Legion), Lieutenant-Colonel Berry; First Ohio, Major Stafford; Ninety-third Ohio, Colonel Anderson, and Simonson's (Indiana) battery.

Major Klein's battalion, of Third Indiana Cavalry, was assigned to duty with the Second Division.

Agreeably to orders, the three divisions constituting the right wing of the Fourteenth Army Corps marched from their camps, near Nashville, taking the Nolensville pike, and arrived in that village the same day at 4 p. m.

On the following day the same divisions, with mine in advance, marched to Triune. The rebel rear guard contested the ground inch by inch, and the day was passed constantly skirmishing with them, with no loss on our side, but several casualties on their part. Triune was occupied by my division about 4 p. m.

The following day, December 28, the command remained in Triune. A reconnaissance to ascertain the direction the enemy had retreated was made by a brigade of my command, commanded by Brig. Gen. A. Willich. It having been ascertained that the enemy had retreated toward Murfreesborough, I was ordered to leave a brigade at Triune, and on the 29th to march on Murfreesborough, on what is known as the Bole Jack road. Col. P. P. Baldwin's (Third) brigade was left at Triune.

The command arrived at Wilkinson's Cross-Roads about 8 p. m. on the 29th, and an order was sent at once to Colonel Baldwin to move forward his brigade, which arrived early on the afternoon of the 30th. My division was in reserve on the 29th.

On the following morning, December 30, General Sheridan's division was ordered to advance in line of battle, covering the Wilkinson pike, while General Davis' division marched in the same order on the right of General Sheridan. My division, being held in reserve, was marched in column on the pike. There being no troops on General Davis' right, and General Sheridan's left being guarded by General Crittenden's left wing, I was ordered to oblique to the right, covering the right of General Davis' division.

About 2 p. m. I received an order from Major-General McCook to look well to my right, as General Hardee (rebel), with his corps, was on the right flank of our column. I ordered Brigadier-General Kirk, commanding the Second Brigade, to take position with his brigade, his left resting against the right of General Davis, his right refused, so as to cover our right flank.

About dark I placed General Willich's brigade on the right of Kirk's, refusing his right, and directing a heavy line of skirmishers to be thrown forward, connecting on the left with those of General Davis, and extending to the right and rear, near the Wilkinson pike. This line of skirmishers was thrown forward about 600 yards, and near those of the enemy. My Third Brigade, Colonel Baldwin commanding, was held in reserve.

At dusk on the evening of the 30th the troops occupied the position as indicated by the accompanying map. In consultation with Major-General McCook, late in the afternoon of December 30, he informed me that he had reliable information in the effect that the center of the rebel line of battle was opposite our extreme right, and that we would probably be attacked by the entire rebel army early on the following morning. His prediction proved true. He also informed me that he had communicated this information to the commanding general.

I expected a change in the programme for the following day, but none was made. My brigade commanders were called together, and the operations of the following day fully explained to them. Every arrangement was made for an attack. Two gallant and experienced officers commanded my two advanced brigades, and every precaution was taken against surprise.

At 6.22 on the morning of the 31st the outposts in front of my division were driven in by an overwhelming force of infantry, outnumbering my forces greatly, and known to contain about 35,000 men. At the same time my extreme right was attacked by the enemy's cavalry.

The gallant Willich and Kirk soon opened a heavy fire of musketry and artillery upon the advancing columns, causing wavering in the ranks, but fresh columns would soon replace them, and it was apparent that to fall back was a "military necessity." Edgarton's battery, after firing three rounds, had so many of its horses killed as to render it unmanageable. He, however, remained with it, and continued to fire until he fell by a severe wound, and he and his battery fell into the hands of the enemy. Before falling back, the horse of General Willich was killed, and he was wounded and taken prisoner.

About the same time General Kirk received a severe wound, which disabled him. Seeing the pressure upon my lines, I ordered up my reserve brigade, under the gallant Baldwin. The troops of his brigade advanced promptly and delivered their fire, holding their ground for some time, but they, too, were compelled to fall back. The troops of this division for the first time were compelled to yield the field temporarily, but the heroes of Shiloh and Perryville did not abandon their ground until forced to do so by the immense masses of the enemy hurled against them, and then, inch by inch. The ground over which the division passed, covered with the enemy's dead and those of our own men, shows that the field was warmly contested. Several times the lines were reformed and resistance offered, but the columns of the enemy were too heavy for a single line, and ours would have to yield. Finally the left flank of my division reached the line of General Rousseau's, when it was reformed and fought until out of ammunition, but my efficient ordnance officer, Lieutenant Murdoch, had a supply in readiness, which was soon issued, and the division assisted in driving the enemy from the field in their last desperate struggle of the day. Soon the curtain of darkness fell upon the scene of blood, and all was quiet, awaiting the coming of morn to renew hostilities. Morning came, but the enemy had withdrawn.

January 1 was a day of comparative quiet in camp, few shots being fired, but many preparations made for a heavy battle on the following day. General Crittenden's wing was attacked in force on the 2d, and one of my brigades (Colonel Gibson's) was sent to re-enforce him. For the gallant part taken by it, reference is made to the report of Major-General Crittenden. The enemy evacuated Murfreesborough on the night of the 3d.

On the 6th I was ordered to remove my camp to a point on the Shelbyville road, 4 miles south of Murfreesborough.

The conduct of officers and men under my command was good. (The Louisville Legion, under the gallant Lieutenant-Colonel Berry, brought off by hand one cannon after the horses were killed.) They yielded the ground only where overpowered, offering an obstinate resistance at every point. Some few in each regiment, becoming panic-stricken, fled to Nashville for safety. Captain Simonson managed his battery with skill and courage, and with it did good execution. He lost two guns, but not until the horses had been killed and the guns disabled. Goodspeed's battery lost three guns and quite a number of horses. This battery was handled well, and did good execution, under Lieutenant Belding.

Reference is respectfully made to the reports of regimental and brigade commanders for the list of those who, by their bravery and good conduct, rendered themselves conspicuous.

After the capture of General Willich, his brigade was commanded temporarily by Colonel Wallace, Fifteenth Ohio, but was afterward replaced by Colonel Gibson, Forty-ninth Ohio. General Kirk becoming disabled, was replaced by Colonel Dodge, Thirtieth Indiana, while the Third Brigade was commanded throughout by Colonel Baldwin.

These four colonels have demonstrated their fitness for command on several bloody fields, and are recommended to my superiors for promotion. Their coolness and courage rendered them conspicuous throughout the bloody engagement. Major Klein and his battalion of the Third Indiana Cavalry deserve special mention. Under their gallant leader the battalion was always in front, and rendered efficient service.

To Captains Bartlett, Hooker, Thruston, and McLeland, and Lieutenants Taft, Hill, and Sheets, of my staff, my thanks are due for their efficiency and promptness in carrying orders to all parts of the field.

My medical director, Surgeon Marks, and the medical officers of the division were untiring in their exertions to alleviate the sufferings of the wounded, and to them my thanks are due. My escort, composed of the following-named men of the Third Kentucky Cavalry, who accompanied me throughout the engagement, deserve special mention for their good conduct: Sergt. William C. Miles, Privates George Long, Thomas Salyers, John Christian, John Whitten, James Bowen, B. Hammerstein, and R. A. Norah. Private Bowen's horse was killed by a cannon-ball.

The loss of the division was as follows: Killed, 260; wounded, 1,005; missing, 1,280 (supposed to have been captured).*

Very respectfully, your obedient servant,

R. W. JOHNSON,
Brigadier-General of Volunteers, Commanding.

Maj. JOHN A. CAMPBELL,
Assistant Adjutant-General.

No. 31.

Report of Capt. Peter Simonson, Fifth Indiana Battery.

HEADQUARTERS FIFTH INDIANA BATTERY,
Camp in Field, January 5, 1863.

SIR: I have the honor to report that, on the morning of December 27, this command marched with the brigade from its bivouac on the

----

* But see revised statement, p. 209.

Nolensville pike, half mile south of Nolensville, Tenn. After marching about 2 miles, the battery was ordered forward with the brigade, which was advancing in line of battle on the right of the pike, cannonading being heard directly in our front. Colonel Baldwin, brigade commander, ordered one piece forward, which fired three shots at the enemy's cavalry, which was in sight, retreating, on the opposite hill. We then advanced a short distance, and two Parrott guns were ordered in the woods to the right of the pike, where six rounds were fired at the enemy, who were apparently cavalry, drawn up in line of battle, supported by a battery planted on the left of the pike. Their artillery ceased firing, and their cavalry retreated when we advanced, but too late to properly support the brigade, which had charged through the village of Triune. The cause of delay was a bridge being destroyed, and very heavy ground bordering on each side of the creek, when we passed beyond. With a light 12-pounder we fired two shots at the enemy, retreating through a wood. The command then encamped half a mile south of Triune, where it remained, and was employed in inspecting ammunition, until the morning of December 29, when four pieces of the battery were ordered to report to General Willich, under whom they marched, without any event worthy of notice, to within 4 miles of Murfreesborough, Tenn.

At this place, at about 1 o'clock, the four pieces rejoined the brigade, when the whole command went with the brigade upon a reconnaissance 2 miles to the right of the main body of the division, from which the command returned at about 8 p. m., and went into bivouac in the woods near brigade and division headquarters. We received permission to unhitch the horses, but not to unharness, and, early on the morning of the 31st, an order was sent to us by the brigade commander to hitch, which we did without watering the horses.

At about 7.30 a. m. two light 12-pounder guns were ordered out to a position about 800 yards southeast from the camp, facing a large cornfield, the enemy appearing in a very heavy force. I was then ordered to return and get the other four guns in position as quickly as possible, which was done, placing them to the right and rear of the first pieces posted. The light 12-pounder gun in the advanced position was under command of First Lieut. H. Rankin. The brigade commander is better informed as to their actions than I am, as they were under his immediate eye. I simply noticed that they fired very rapidly, and were the last troops which passed to the rear upon my left. They fired in that position 17 rounds from one piece, and 23 from the other—nearly all canister. Some of the rounds were double charges. The four guns under my immediate command commenced firing shell. We had fired about 15 rounds when a very large body of our own troops appeared to our right-oblique, retreating rapidly; it was the remains of Kirk's brigade. Colonel Dodge, of this brigade, had hardly time to inform me that a very large body of the enemy was in close pursuit, when they appeared. Three of the four guns opened upon them with canister, and checked them in front and to the right-oblique, but more appearing almost directly on our right flank (our infantry were out of sight to the rear), the order was given to leave the field. The command succeeded in getting away with but two of the four pieces. At these two positions there were 3 men killed and 21 wounded; also 23 horses disabled. We retreated through a dense woods, and had great difficulty in getting our carriages through.

I endeavored to go as much to the left as possible, as I noticed that our troops were less disorganized in that direction. With two pieces we made an ineffectual stand in the woods, about midway between the two pikes, at a point 500 or 600 yards to the right of the Murfreesborough pike. Under the direction of the brigade and division commanders, with three of our own pieces and one of Battery E, First Ohio Light Artillery, we succeeded for a time in checking the enemy, but the infantry fell back, and we were ordered to retire the battery. At this point about 42 rounds of ammunition were fired. It was a splendid position, and I regretted leaving it. One man was wounded and several horses disabled. We then fell back across the pike and the railroad, and became again separated from the brigade. I then reported to General Johnson, who ordered me in position on a point to the left of the railroad, where we remained until about 3 p. m., and were then ordered to our present position, on the right of the Murfreesborough pike.

On the following morning we had a short artillery duel with a four-gun battery in front of us. In the afternoon the enemy appeared advancing with about a brigade, and we opened fire, firing about 25 rounds. We have been lying in our present position since.

Very respectfully, yours, &c.,

PETER SIMONSON,
Captain Fifth Indiana Battery.

Lieut. GEORGE H. BURNS,
Actg. Asst. Adjt. Gen., Third Brigade, Second Division.

No. 32.

Report of Capt. Warren P. Edgarton, Battery E, First Ohio Light Artillery.

NASHVILLE, TENN., *June 25, 1863.*

COLONEL: I have the honor to submit, for your consideration, a brief report of the action of my command (Battery E, First Regiment Ohio Volunteer Light Artillery), at and immediately preceding the battle of Stone's River.

I have cause seriously to regret that my capture and subsequent imprisonment have so long delayed the recital of facts which I purpose to embody in this report, known only to myself, by which injustice has been done to the brave men of my command, especially as there seems to have been very generally a misapprehension in regard to my position on the morning of the 31st of last December, and the cause which resulted in the capture of my battery.

We left camp near Nashville on the 26th of December, attached to General Kirk's brigade of General Johnson's division, right wing. We marched on the Nolensville pike. The next day, the 27th, approaching Triune, our brigade was ordered in the advance. After marching about 1 mile, we encountered a battery of the enemy posted in a commanding position. My battery was ordered forward to engage it, and, after a few rounds, we drove them from that position. We took a second position on a hill overlooking the village of Triune, and again discovered the enemy's battery planted in our front, well supported by cavalry. We dislodged them a second time, dismounting one of their guns. The enemy ceased to annoy us here, and we were ordered to bivouac near the village, one section being ordered on picket duty.

The duty of following the enemy on this day was very arduous. We were obliged to leave the traveled roads in order to gain position; we removed fences, dragged our pieces through the soft ground of cultivated fields, through streams of water, and climbed hills, where it became neces sary to call for a detail from the infantry to help us along.

On the 29th we took the direction of Murfreesborough, passed over a very rough and hilly road, and arrived after dark near the scene of the contemplated battle. The utmost caution and vigilance was ordered. We were hitched up and ready for action at daylight of the 30th.

On this day the Second Division was held in reserve. We followed the advance till late in the afternoon, when we were ordered to oblique to the right, to cover the right of General Davis' division. The enemy had posted a battery on the right of General Davis, in a handsome position, enfilading his whole line. General Kirk ordered me forward with a regiment of infantry as support, with instructions to silence, if possible, the rebel battery. Under cover of a cedar thicket, I was enabled to approach within about 700 yards of the enemy. The battery was silenced by six rounds from our pieces. They retreated, leaving a caisson disabled. An attempt was made to gain another position, but we followed them, engaging the infantry that came to their support, and kept up a brisk fire until dark. General Kirk then ordered us to cease firing.

My battery was the only detachment of General Johnson's division engaged in the action of Tuesday, the 30th of December. I here represented to General Kirk that my men were very weary, my horses almost famished; that my ammunition was short in the limber-chests of the pieces, and asked permission to withdraw long enough to prepare for hard work on the following day. Believing horses to be the main dependence of a light battery, and not knowing when I should have an opportunity to feed and water if brought into action, I asked time to prepare for the conflict of the morrow. General Kirk pointed out a spot about 100 yards in the rear of the position I then occupied, sheltered by a heavy growth of timber, and ordered me to bivouac there for the night. I reported to him that I could not place my guns " in battery " there, or defend myself if assaulted. He replied that I should be protected, and that ample notice should be given when I was expected to take a position in the line of battle.

After I had brought my guns into park, the right of the brigade was thrown across the muzzles in front. General Willich's brigade marched up and formed on the flank. I found myself within the angle formed by the junction of the two brigades, retiring about 50 yards, and on a low and narrow piece of ground. I have before stated that it was dark when I arrived at this point. We were not permitted to have lights. The ground in our rear had not been reconnoitered. I rode back some distance, but failed to find water for my horses. I did not consider it safe to push the investigation far outside of our lines that night. I waited until morning. At daylight a small stream was discovered about 100 rods in our rear. It was quiet all along our lines. I could not hear a picket shot, nor any indication that the enemy was in our vicinity. I had no orders to take position. My horses were already harnessed, to hitch on at a moment's warning. I was completely surrounded by veteran troops. I had a right to suppose that our front and flank were so picketed that I should have notice of the approach of the enemy. I ordered a half battery of my horses to go to water on a sharp trot, and return at the slightest indication of danger. The horses had barely reached the water when a fierce shout was heard at the front, and a terrible volley of musketry was poured in upon us. I called the cannoneers to their posts, had a half battery hitched in, put my guns in battery where they were, and in a moment was prepared, as best I could, to fight in that position. The infantry, our support, gave way on the front and flank in disorder, almost with the first volley. I then opened on the enemy with canister, firing from 16 to 20 rounds, with good effect, as I have cause to know, for I passed over the ground in our front a few moments afterward a prisoner.

The assault of the enemy was fierce and overwhelming. After the first fire, in which I had 1 man killed, a number wounded, and 12 horses killed, the enemy charged with an impetuosity which carried everything before him. The battery was taken.

It would have been impossible for me to have saved my battery, even if I had commenced a retreat on the first alarm. The enemy was very near us before discovered, and the fight commenced without any of the preliminary skirmishing before a general engagement. To the best of my judgment, it was not more than five minutes from the firing of the first shot to the catastrophe when my battery was taken and myself a prisoner. In the mean time some of my horses returned, were hitched in, and killed. The rest were driven back by the fierce fire from the front. I deemed it my duty to stay with my guns so long as a single shot could be fired, or a chance exist of their being supported and re-taken. I did not realize the helplessness of the case until I was surrounded and retreat impossible.

In the brief time we were engaged I had 3 men killed, 25 wounded, and 22 taken prisoners.

I wish here to compliment my men for their determined bravery; they obeyed orders implicitly, and stood by their guns to the last.

I would not be understood in this report as casting the slightest reflection on the discretion or vigilance of my brigade commander. I am not capable of criticising his orders, nor would I be permitted to do so had I the disposition. I had learned highly to respect General Kirk as a fine gentleman and accomplished soldier. I reverenced him for his heroic courage in the presence of an enemy. He was dangerously wounded in a desperate attempt to rally his broken regiments to support my battery, riding almost upon the bayonets of the enemy.

As I have been charged with grave errors on the occasion of the battle, I respectfully request that I may be ordered before a court of inquiry, that my conduct may be investigated.

Very respectfully, your obedient servant,

W. P. EDGARTON,
Captain Battery E, First Regiment Artillery, Ohio Vols.

Col. JAMES BARNETT,
Chief of Artillery.

No. 33.

Report of Lieut. Albert G. Ransom, Battery E, First Ohio Light Artillery.

IN CAMP NEAR MURFREESBOROUGH, TENN.,
January 7, 1863.

SIR: I have the honor to report the part taken by Battery E, First Regiment Ohio Artillery, in the movement of the Federal army on Murfreesborough and the battles before that town.

Leaving camp near Nashville, December 26, 1862, but marching in rear of two other divisions, the Second was not that day engaged. We bivouacked south of Nolensville, and early on the morning of the 27th instant started on the road to Triune. Before we had proceeded more than 1 mile, heavy skirmishing was heard in front, and one section of our battery was ordered forward by General Kirk. Our place in the march being in rear of the Second Regiment, when the head of the column had reached the top of a ridge beyond which cavalry skirmishing was still going on, a masked battery of the enemy on the left and commanding the road opened on it. Our pieces were at once unlimbered, and, after firing twelve rounds, got no response from the enemy's guns. The infantry skirmishers had filed off the road to the left, and our entire battery now moved rapidly after them.

Leaving the pike, the skirmishers moved to the top of another ridge, and our battery, following, was at once placed in position there, from which point it opened fire from every gun, driving the rebels out of range. Here we were ordered to await the uplifting of a very heavy fog, and, when the infantry moved forward, again sought the pike, which we followed until the skirmishers reported the enemy again in sight and in line of battle. A fine position, on a hill overlooking Triune, and within the range of the rebel cavalry, in line of battle facing our left, was found here, and four pieces opened from this eminence, throwing shot and shell into and beyond the town, and into the rebels on right and left.

When we first came in sight of Triune, the road was filled with rebel cavalry, and one section, unlimbering in the road, made them its especial mark. The town was soon made untenable, and in an effort made by the rebel battery planted above the village to return our fire, it was driven off with one gun disabled. The enemy again retired before our fire, and the skirmishers, following up as fast as the nature of the ground would admit, threatened the capture of his guns, which he fired rapidly, and which we could not return, as he had cut down a bridge, obliging us to search a crossing more than one-half mile down the creek. When our battery again appeared, the enemy had drawn off, but we threw several shots in the direction of his retreat.

We were not again in action until the evening of December 30, when the Second Brigade was ordered to support the right of General Davis' division, threatened by rebel cavalry. They showed themselves in force, but, having secured a good position, a few shells threw their ranks into confusion and made them retire. The right of General Davis was at this time suffering from the shells of the enemy's battery, to which we turned our attention, and had the satisfaction of silencing the battery after a few rounds. Knowing our danger on the right, we planted two pieces on the road by which it was supposed the enemy would come, kept the horses harnessed all night, and took every precaution we thought necessary to guard against surprise.

At daylight on the morning of the 31st instant the pickets gave the alarm, and skirmishers were firing, but as yet could see no enemy. The horses were quickly hitched, except a few, perhaps one-half of which were on their return from water, and were brought up at once. Failing to distinguish the enemy, two shells were thrown in the direction of their fire, and, when they appeared, canister. Six rounds were poured into the moving mass with great effect, but, attacked in front and flank, we soon saw our horses shot down, the work evidently of sharpshooters, who moved in the advance and on the right and left, until the whole column being now upon us, we had not horses enough to save our guns.

The number of deaths among our men, and particularly the fact that two of them were bayoneted at their guns, will show conclusively the courage and tenacity which influenced them on the occasion. Com-

pletely overpowered, it became necessary to retire with a few horses--
perhaps 30.

In conclusion, allow me to express my heartfelt regret at the loss of
Captain Edgarton, whose manly voice rang out above the din of musketry, encouraging his men, and giving orders coolly and judiciously.
He preferred to go a prisoner with his battery to leaving his much-
cherished pieces. In mentioning the other officers and men, the name
of Lieutenant Berwick comes foremost, who, an adopted citizen, rushed
to arms at the first call, and, in acts as well as words, proved his un-
changeable love of the freedom which enticed him from his bonnie hills.
The sergeants and men behaved with noble devotion, as the death of
three of the former will fully testify, while the alacrity shown by all to
enter the service anywhere, so they could fight for their country, proves
patriotism and courage.

Accompanying this report I append the names of those known to have
been killed and wounded.

Respectfully, your obedient servant,

A. G. RANSOM,
First Lieutenant, Commanding.

Capt. D. C. WAGNER,
Acting Assistant Adjutant-General, Second Brigade.

No. 34.

*Report of Col. William H. Gibson, Forty-ninth Ohio Infantry, command-
ing First Brigade.*

HDQRS. FIRST BRIGADE, SECOND DIVISION, RIGHT WING,
Murfreesborough, Tenn., January 5, 1863.

CAPTAIN: The capture of Brigadier-General Willich renders it my
duty to report to Brigadier-General Johnson, commanding division, the
participation of this command in the events of the last ten days. In
accomplishing this task, I shall address myself to a concise narrative of
occurrences, that " the truth of history may be vindicated," the memory
of our heroic slain honored, and that justice may be done to the brave
survivors, who, by their energy and stubborn courage, maintained a
conflict for six days, and vanquished the great army of our foe.

Leaving camp, near Nashville, December 26, 1862, the first and second
days' march was without incident, and took us through Nolensville to
Triune, 20 miles.

The following day we reconnoitered the country 7 miles to our front,
in the direction of Shelbyville, and developed the fact that the rebel
forces had retreated the day and night previous in the direction of this
place. In that reconnaissance we made 41 prisoners of war.

On the 29th we moved upon this place, reaching the Salem road, 4
miles distant, after dark, and slept upon our arms in rear of General
Davis' division.

On the 30th we advanced upon this position, acting as a reserve to
the right wing, and were not brought under fire that day. In the evening we took up a position on the extreme right of our army on the Franklin road. General Kirk's brigade was in front, with pickets thrown out
to the margin of open fields. To his rear and near his right, in open
woods, was Edgarton's battery in position, with a narrow cleared field
in front. To the right of this battery, and on a line perpendicular to the

rear of General Kirk's right, were the reserves of the Thirty-ninth and Thirty-second Indiana, of this command, portions of each being on picket duty.

The direction of the Franklin road is due east and west at this point, and it was covered by General Kirk's right, his line of battle fronting east and in advance of a lane running north and south, 8 yards wide, and intersecting the road at right angles. In this angle is a field of open woods 330 yards square. South of this is an uninclosed space covered by a few trees and near 100 yards wide, through which the Franklin road is located. At the fence, to the right of Edgarton's battery, five companies of the Thirty-ninth Indiana were camped in line of battle, fronting south. To their right the Thirty-second Indiana occupied a like position. Inside of the wooded field and within 30 yards of the fence the Forty-ninth Ohio was formed in line of battle, fronting south, its left resting within 100 yards of the lane and its right within a like distance of the west inclosure. In its rear the Eighty-ninth Illinois was in double column, closed in mass, fronting south. Perpendicular to the rear of the right of the Forty-ninth was the Fifteenth Ohio, in line near the fence, fronting west, its left wing resting within 60 yards of the Forty-ninth. In the southwest corner of this wooded field Goodspeed's battery was parked in oblong square. North and west of this field and south and east of the uninclosed space were cleared fields. The picket line of General Kirk covered his front and flank, connecting with that of this brigade at a fence 600 yards south of the left of the reserve of the Thirty-ninth Indiana. The pickets of the Thirty-ninth were advanced 700 yards in front of the reserve in an open corn-field. The pickets of the Thirty-second joined those of the Thirty-ninth and covered our flank and rear. At 3 a. m. Colonel Jones was ordered to patrol the woods 600 yards in front of his pickets. No indications of the presence or purposes of the enemy were discerned.

Here I beg leave to call attention to the very concise and satisfactory report of Lieutenant-Colonel Jones, commanding Thirty-ninth Indiana, and also to the report of Lieutenant-Colonel Erdelmeyer, commanding Thirty-second Indiana. These dispositions had been made and these precautions adopted by General Willich.

At dawn of day orders were received to build fires and make coffee. In a few moments after I met General Willich, who remarked that he would be absent a few moments at the headquarters of General Johnson, and in case anything occurred in front of our pickets he directed me to rally the Thirty-ninth and Thirty-second to their support.

At 6.25, and soon after meeting the general, firing was heard on General Kirk's right. The brigade was instantly ordered to take arms, and Lieutenant Miles, of the staff, was dispatched for General Willich. He was found, and started for his command, but his horse was shot under him, and he was made a prisoner before giving an order.

The enemy advanced upon our position with four heavy lines of battle, with a strong reserve held in mass. All these were in full view before the lines of General Kirk gave way. His left extended a great distance beyond our extreme right, and was thrown forward, so that his lines were, to some extent, oblique to ours. To the right of our position, and near the Franklin road, he took position with an immense force of cavalry. In fact, the center of Hardee's corps attacked our right. His lines were advanced with great rapidity, and his force could not have been less than 35,000, besides cavalry.

Portions of Polk's and Smith's corps were engaged. The lines of General Kirk soon yielded to an assault which no troops in the world could have withstood. The Thirty-second and Thirty-ninth moved promptly, but were embarrassed by the retiring forces, and their safety endangered by an assault in overwhelming numbers upon front and flanks. Lieutenant Belding moved back with four guns, but was so hotly pressed that he could not put them in position with safety. He had done nothing in his original position, because the lines falling back in our front were between his guns and the enemy's line. He and his men stood at their pieces until the enemy's lines were within 50 yards, when they fell back, leaving two guns on the field, owing to the killing of horses attached to one and the breaking of the pole of the other.

The Forty-ninth remained in its position until ordered to retire, and fought desperately at every rod. The Fifteenth Ohio, Colonel Wallace, delivered six rounds before falling back, while the Thirty-second and Thirty-ninth Indiana bravely contested the ground on the right. The courage and activity of these regiments kept the enemy in check until our artillery horses could be hitched, and the dead of the foe showed the telling effect of their fire. With cavalry on their right, infantry assailing them on the left, and heavy masses rushing to the assault in front, these regiments were directed to retire as the only escape from annihilation or capture.

Edgarton's battery, after being uncovered by the lines of General Kirk, opened fire, but before three rounds were delivered the enemy reached the guns and captured the pieces. Unchecked, the foe rushed on, and as his advance reached Goodspeed's battery, his second line reached Edgarton's battery, and that gallant officer being wounded and made prisoner, his men continued to defend themselves with their gun-swabs. The Fifteenth Ohio, Colonel Wallace, had got into position, and, under cover of its fire, the Forty-ninth Ohio and Eighty-ninth Illinois were directed to retire by the flank. The Thirty-second and Thirty-ninth were now retiring in good order.

At this juncture, learning nothing of General Willich, I felt it my duty to exert myself as far as possible to save the command. Goodspeed's battery, under command of Lieutenant Belding, was ordered to retire to a position beyond an open field, and Lieutenant-Colonel Drake was directed to place the Forty-ninth Ohio in position at the same point.

Here I had hoped to rally the whole brigade, but Lieutenant-Colonel Drake was killed, and Major Porter, of the Forty-ninth, was severely wounded. My horse was shot, and most of our field officers were disabled or dismounted by the enemy's fire. From my position, looking to our center, I could see our whole line fall back rapidly in some disorder, though a constant fire was kept up to the right.

Lieutenant-Colonel Jones was bravely rallying his men, and large numbers, separated from other regiments, were moving directly west, instead of to our center. Lieutenants Belding and Scovill, with one gun, moved to the center, while Lieutenant Day, in charge of three guns, moved back toward the Wilkinson road, with our extreme right. After retiring for nearly half a mile, and rallying and fighting at every available point, my second horse was killed, placing it again out of my power to communicate with our center.

Soon after, a line was rallied and formed, extending west to a small creek, and Lieutenant Belding's gun was got in position. Beyond the creek Lieutenant-Colonel Jones and myself rallied, under cover of a fence and cedar thicket. As the enemy's columns neared our irregular lines, they were met by a rapid and deadly fire, and Lieutenant Belding opened fire at the same time with terrible effect. The rebel columns were checked and fell back across the open ground. Here they opened on us with artillery and again advanced their infantry, our line falling back.

After thus rallying and meeting the enemy several times, we arrived with our flank on the Wilkinson road, a short distance west of our ammunition train. Here we were charged by the enemy's cavalry and lost one gun, all of us being in the enemy's power. My sword was demanded, but just at that instant a detachment of our cavalry made a dash for our rescue, and in the confusion of the moment most of us fought our way out and escaped.

The division train was got under motion, and we moved rapidly and in considerable disorder to the Nashville road, closely pursued by the enemy's cavalry. Here the colors of the Thirty-ninth Indiana were captured. At this moment I learned that a considerable portion of this brigade had reached the center; that General Willich had been killed or captured, and that General Wallace was in command of the brigade. A complete panic prevailed. Teams, ambulances, horsemen, footmen, and *attachés* of the army, black and white, mounted on horses and mules, were rushing to the rear in the wildest confusion. I exerted myself to arrest this panic, and hastened down the road until I met Colonel Walker with his brigade, who promptly formed in line of battle and put his artillery in position. With this assurance the tide was quite checked, and, placing a strong guard of cavalry across the road, Colonel Walker moved his command to the front, compelling every able-bodied soldier to fall in. I hurried them back to the front, and thus hundreds, if not thousands, were compelled to return to their commands.

In the evening this brigade was reorganized, and, by order of General Johnson, took position on our extreme right, in rear of Colonel Carlin's brigade, of the First Division.

Though repulsed and sustaining severe loss in officers and men the day previous, January 1 found us 1,300 strong, and eager to participate in the dangers and struggles of the field.

I was directed to reconnoiter the woods to the right and rear of our position, which was accomplished under the observation of Major-Generals Rosecrans and McCook. Though within range of the enemy's battery, we reached the woods unobserved, and soon met his sharpshooters, and discovered that he was massing his infantry under cover of these woods, with the apparent design of attacking our extreme right. In withdrawing we were harassed by shot and shell from his batteries, but sustained no loss. We were soon directed to reoccupy the woods, and promptly took up our position with the Fifteenth Ohio and the Thirty-second Indiana and Eighty-ninth Illinois, in line of battle (their front covered by skirmishers), and the Thirty-ninth Indiana and Forty-ninth Ohio, under Lieutenant-Colonel Jones, as a reserve. The enemy's cavalry made a dash upon our position, but were gallantly repulsed by our skirmishers.

The movements of the enemy on the right having averted the serious attention of General Rosecrans, troops were promptly placed in position to our left, and our lines withdrawn to the margin of the woods, our flank covered by a strong force of cavalry. The prompt movements of our forces and the splendid maneuvering of the commander-in-chief defeated the designs of the enemy, and no further attack was made.

Leaving this position on the morning of the 2d, by order of General Johnson, we were placed in an important position, so as to sustain the right, center, or left, in case of a reverse to either.

In the evening a terrible assault was made upon our extreme left, and our forces were repulsed. We were ordered to make a charge with the bayonet. The brigade moved out and deployed in splendid style. It moved with alacrity and perfect order, clearing the field and reaching the river, where we were ordered to halt. Our right flank was exposed to the enemy's infantry, concealed in the woods on our right, while he annoyed us with a battery across Stone's River.

General Palmer attempted to drive the foe from the woods, but, meeting with strong resistance, his aide appealed to me for re-enforcements, and the Thirty-second Indiana was detached for that service. They met and repulsed two regiments, driving them across the river at the point of the bayonet. Nothing could exceed the gallantry and enthusiasm that this heroic regiment exhibited in this emergency. Our brigade changed the fortunes of the hour, and, under cover of our lines, the enemy was driven back and three pieces of artillery captured. Though under arms night and day, and maneuvering, we were not again brought within range of the enemy's musketry.

I must mention the fortitude and good cheer with which the officers and men submitted to the hardships and exposure of four long days and nights, without adequate rations or shelter; they cheerfully subsisted partly on parched corn, and rested in drenching rains.

On visiting the field over which we retired on the 31st, abundant evidence was presented of the desperate struggle. Our men rallied whenever summoned, and delivered their fire with deadly effect. Though the enemy's wounded and many of his dead had been removed, it is safe to affirm that his killed exceeded ours as three to two, and that vast numbers were wounded. It was before our fire that General Rains, of the rebel army, was killed, and a vast number of subordinate officers and men killed and wounded. Every rod of ground over which we retired was marked by the blood of the foe, and our men reached the center with empty cartridge-boxes.

Our loss was terrible, but unavoidable, and is, to a great extent, compensated by the result ultimately obtained. We went into action with 2,458 men and 113 commissioned officers. In killed, we lost 96, including 4 officers; in wounded, we lost 365, including 14 officers, and our missing reach 682, including 6 officers. Many of our missing escaped, and are safe in the rear, but it is probable that 400 were made prisoners.

Lieutenant-Colonel Drake, Forty-ninth Ohio, fell at the post of duty, bravely cheering his men. By his death the State has lost a valued citizen, his community an ornament, his family a noble husband and kind father, and the army a most gallant and faithful soldier.

Captain Keller, of the same regiment, fell as heroes love to fall. A true patriot and accomplished soldier, he carried with him into camp and field all the graces of Christianity.

Captain Willett, of the Eighty-ninth Illinois, fell while bravely leading his command, and such were his accomplishments as a gentleman and soldier that it will be difficult to fill his place.

Throughout these trying days and nights officers and men did their duty nobly, with a few exceptions—a few officers failed to earn the confidence of their men, and some privates sought safety in flight.

The Fifteenth Ohio evinced the greatest courage, and many of its officers deserve special mention. Colonel Wallace, always prudent, energetic, and brave, fully sustained his high reputation as a soldier, and won the admiration of all who witnessed his conduct. Lieutenant-Colonel Askew fell, early on the 31st, while heroically cheering his men.

Captain Dawson was especially distinguished for thrilling heroism and persistent courage. This officer, conspicuous in so many battles, and so well qualified, merits, and should receive, honorable promotion.

Adjutant Dubois, of the same regiment, deserves special mention for gallantry and good conduct.

The Forty-ninth Ohio sustained its high reputation, and, though it lost 10 officers, it faced the foe at every point. Captain Gray, as ranking officer, had charge of a portion of the regiment on the 31st, and proved himself brave, prudent, and competent for any command. Adjutant Norton was especially heroic, and excited general admiration by his inflexible courage and great activity. Both of these officers merit, and I hope will receive, promotion. Captains McCormack and Tyler were ever active, brave, and self-possessed in the midst of dangers, and showed themselves worthy and competent to command.

The splendid conduct of the Thirty-second Indiana fully sustained its claims to confidence. Every officer and man did his duty heroically. Lieutenant-Colonel Erdelmeyer, commanding, and Major Glass and Captain Mank were especially conspicuous throughout the long struggle.

Lieutenant-Colonel Hotchkiss, commanding Eighty-ninth Illinois Volunteers, deserves the highest praise for his coolness and skill in action. He drew off his men in good order, fighting as he withdrew, and showed himself worthy of any command. This gallant officer has given to the service one of its best regiments, and has justly earned promotion. Major Hall and Captain Whiting, brave and valuable officers, I regret to say, were made prisoners. All the officers and men of this regiment did their duty promptly, and earned the confidence of their companions in arms. Captain Williams, commanding during the illness of Lieutenant-Colonel Hotchkiss, is an efficient and competent officer.

The Thirty-ninth Indiana, Lieutenant-Colonel Jones commanding, fought with desperation and terrible effect. Its list of casualties shows that where it moved the battle raged most fierce. Men could not have evinced greater courage and heroism. Captains McClelland, Cody, McCoy, Graham, and Captain Herring, acting major, merit the highest praise for their activity and energy. Lieutenant-Colonel Jones discharged his duties in the most gallant manner; ever active and brave, he rallied his men at every point, and yielded only before overwhelming numbers. He met the foe in hand-to-hand conflict, and owes his escape to the skillful use of his side-arms. I beg leave to urge the name of this most meritorious officer upon the Executive of his State for promotion.

I cannot too highly commend the good conduct of Lieutenants Belding, Scovill, and Day, of Battery A, First Ohio Artillery, and the men under their command. The loss of three guns was from no fault of any one. Lieutenant Belding did splendid execution upon the enemy's column, and proved himself worthy of a command. I cannot too strongly urge his promotion upon the Executive of Ohio.

Surgeons Kunkler, Park, Tuttle, Kelly, and Pitman, as well as Dr. Corey, hospital steward of the Forty-ninth Ohio, remained on the field and labored for days and nights, unaided, in caring for our wounded. For thus faithfully performing their duty, at the risk of maltreatment, and possibly captivity, they have secured the confidence and respect of this command.

On the evening of the 31st, Captain Schmitt, Lieutenants Green, Miles, and McGrath, of General Willich's staff, reported to me for duty, and in all the subsequent operations of the command these gallant officers were vigilant and prompt in every duty, and to them I am under special obligations for suggestions on the field. Though not acting under my personal observation on the 31st, they were in the thickest of the fight, and officers of experience speak of their conduct as being most intelligent and heroic in rallying our forces. James Purdy, mounted orderly, merits especial praise for his activity and courage throughout the week of battles.

I must express the deep regret of officers and men at the capture of Brigadier-General Willich; having the confidence of the brigade, and being a soldier of education and experience, his removal from the command at this juncture is a public misfortune.

To Brigadier-General Johnson we are under obligations for constant vigilance, unremitting energy, and his many acts of kindness and expressions of confidence toward this command.

In the name of the brigade, I am allowed to thank Major-General McCook and the general-in-chief for their flattering attentions on the field, and for their repeated exhibitions of confidence in our efficiency, prudence, and courage.

I am, most respectfully,

W. H. GIBSON,
Colonel, Commanding First Brigade.

Capt. J. R. BARTLETT,
Acting Assistant Adjutant-General.

No. 35.

Report of Lieut. Col. Charles T. Hotchkiss, Eighty-ninth Illinois Infantry.

HEADQUARTERS EIGHTY-NINTH ILLINOIS INFANTRY,
FIRST BRIGADE, SECOND DIVISION, RIGHT WING,
In Camp near Murfreesborough, Tenn., January 7, 1863.

SIR: I have the honor to submit the following report of the part taken by this regiment in the series of engagements between the Federal and rebel forces near Murfreesborough, Tenn., and upon the approaches thereto, commencing on December 26, 1862, and ending on January 4, 1863, when the latter, under General Bragg, were defeated by the army of General Rosecrans and forced to evacuate all their positions in and about Murfreesborough.

This regiment left camp, in front of Nashville, with my brigade on the morning of December 26, taking the Nolensville pike and moving slowly with the column (as the enemy had to be driven by the advance) through Nolensville, Triune, and along the Murfreesborough and Franklin road, arriving, on the night of the 30th, at a point about 3½ miles due west from Murfreesborough, where, just after dark, the brigade was put in position on the extreme right of our right wing, about 200 yards in rear of and at right angles with Kirk's brigade.

My regiment was formed in double column at half distance in rear of the Forty-ninth Ohio, which was formed in line, fronting south. The Fifteenth Ohio formed in line, fronting west, on my right flank, with Battery A, First Ohio Artillery, near the right flank of the Forty-ninth Ohio and the left flank of the Fifteenth Ohio, the Thirty-second and Thirty-ninth Indiana Regiments being on picket covering the front of our position both south and west, thus protecting the rear of the extreme right (Kirk's brigade) of the right wing. In this position my men bivouacked without fires for the night.

At 5.30 o'clock on the morning of December 31, as my men were building fires for cooking, rapid firing was heard on Kirk's front, which was almost instantly followed by the men of his brigade rushing in confusion and indiscriminately through our ranks and over my men, closely followed by a heavy column of rebel infantry. The enemy's fire being very severe and heavy upon us, and the large number of fugitives passing through and covering my front, together with peremptory orders communicated to regimental commanders of his brigade by General Willich the night previous, made it impossible for me to make a deployment or otherwise advantageously change my position.

To protect my men as much as possible from the enemy's fire, I ordered them to lie down. In that position they remained without confusion until my left wing was uncovered of fugitives and the enemy within 50 yards of my position, when I ordered that wing to fire, which was done with good effect, the colors of the leading column of rebels falling. Having received no orders as yet, and seeing the other regiments of the brigade falling back, I gave the order to retire by the right flank, on double-quick, which was done (but with some confusion), to a lane, about 400 yards in a northwesterly direction, where I placed Captains Willett's, Whiting's, and Comstock's, and Lieutenant Wells' companies in a very good position.

But few of our shots were wasted, the colors of the leading column of the enemy again falling under our fire ; but, being closely pressed, I ordered the companies to retire on the same line of direction to a point on a small creek, about 500 yards distant, where I placed Captains Rowell's and Blake's companies under the partial cover of a thicket, and their fire most materially checked the enemy's advancing skirmishers, allowing me time to cross the creek with, and partially reorganize, my command, Captain Rowell's gradually following.

Following the line of the creek, I again crossed to a point some 500 yards southeast of the Second Division hospital, where, in an open field, I joined a portion of each of the Forty-ninth and Fifteenth Ohio and Thirty-second Indiana Regiments. The enemy's cavalry appearing on our right, and their infantry approaching on our left flank, threatening to cut us off, I moved by the left flank, the other regiments following, in a northeasterly direction, to a position in the woods on the south side of the Wilkinson pike, and about equidistant from the hospitals of the First (General Davis') and the Second (General Johnson's) Divisions, a position from which our fire, at short range over an open field, thinned the ranks and partially checked the advance of the rebels' closely pressing columns.

At this point, being informed of the loss of General Willich and Colonel Gibson, the next senior officer, the command of the brigade was assumed by Colonel Wallace, of the Fifteenth Ohio.

The forces (to me unknown) which here formed upon the right and left flanks of our brigade having retired, in obedience to orders I retired my regiment in line and in good order, making several stands in the same woods with the balance of the brigade to and near the right of General Rousseau's division, where I was ordered by General Johnson to take position in a cedar thicket on the right with some troops (to me unknown) who were in front and joining on the right of said division. Soon afterward, the troops on my right and left of the line, which they and I in common held, having unexpectedly and rapidly retired, and my position just then receiving the brunt of the enemy's artillery and musketry fire, and my ammunition being exhausted, I retired my regiment, by the flank, to the rear, there replenishing my ammunition and resting my men, who had up to this time taken and delivered an unceasing fire for nearly five hours.

Later in the day, being informed of the position of the balance of the brigade, I at once rejoined them, when I was put in position on the right of the same, thus unitedly forming the second line of infantry (General Davis' division being in front) on the extreme right of the right wing, where we bivouacked that night without fires.

The operations of the regiment during the subsequent four days were in common with the brigade, and were not of a character to need from me particular mention, with the exception of the part taken by it on the night of Friday, January 2, when, under the command of Captain Williams (myself being unable to take active command), it had the responsible position of guarding the ford and supporting Captain Stokes' (Chicago Board of Trade) battery, while the forces under General Negley made the successful charge upon the enemy's right.

The behavior of the officers and men during this period, particularly in the trying action of the 31st, was, in steadiness and bravery, all that could be required by any commander. This phrase fully expresses my estimate of their conduct: "Every man that day did his duty." Where bravery and obedience were so general it is difficult for me to make personal discrimination; but among my non-commissioned officers I particularly commend, for their gallantry in rallying to my colors fugitives from other commands, Sergt. Maj. John M. Farquhar and Sergt. Erastus O. Young, of Company A; also Capt. Button G. Cody, of the Thirty-ninth Indiana, and Lieutenant Seifert, of the Thirty-second Indiana, who tendered their services to me on the field and fought gallantly in my ranks.

Very respectfully, your obedient servant,

C. T. HOTCHKISS,
Lieutenant-Colonel, Commanding.

Capt. CARL SCHMITT,
Assistant Adjutant-General.

No. 36.

Report of Lieut. Col. Frank Erdelmeyer, Thirty-second Indiana Infantry.

HDQRS. THIRTY-SECOND INDIANA VOLUNTEERS,
Camp near Murfreesborough, Tenn., January 7, 1863.

SIR: I respectfully submit to you the official report of the part taken by the Thirty-second Indiana Volunteers in the late battle at Murfreesborough and in the events of the days preceding.

The regiment left camp, near Mill Creek, on the morning of December 26, 1862, and marched to Nolensville.

On the 27th, the regiment advanced to Triune.

On the 28th, having the advance guard of the brigade, participated in a reconnaissance toward Shelbyville.

On the 29th, we left Triune, crossing over to within 4 miles of Murfreesborough.

On the 30th, the battle having commenced, the regiment moved up to the road and performed picket duty on the right flank of the extreme right of the army corps.

On the morning of the 31st, firing having been heard on our left, Lieut. S. Green, of the staff of General A. Willich, ordered me to draw in the pickets and move up to the brigade. Before I was able to as-semble seven companies of my command and form them in line, facing toward the center, I observed the enemy's columns advancing and firing. At the same time a great portion of our battery, guns, caissons, and battery teams, together with a dense mass of infantry, in disorder, came rushing toward us, and, breaking through the regiment, forced our men to give way and fall back. The confusion and panic having then be-come general, I was unable to reassemble the regiment until we had retreated along the creek for nearly three-quarters of a mile, when we succeeded in rallying about 200 of our men.

I would respectfully state that Lieutenant Belding, of Captain Good-speed's battery, retreated with me with one gun, and, by firing several times on the enemy, checked their flanking columns. We then moved toward the center of the engagement, firing on the enemy's cavalry at different times, and met at a rise of the ground the rest of the division, where Colonel Wallace, of the Fifteenth Ohio, directed me to fall in line with his regiment. The enemy advancing at that time, we fought there for more than an hour, and, being relieved by fresh troops, fell back and joined the brigade.

In the afternoon of January 1 we moved to a strip of wood on the right of the first hospital on the Nashville road, and remained there during the night, picketing.

On the 2d we moved with the brigade as reserve to the center of the right wing.

Toward 5 o'clock the brigade was ordered to charge on the enemy on the left of our center. While the regiment advanced in line of battle toward Stone's River, General Palmer rode up and ordered me to move the regiment by the right flank into a strip of wood on our right, occu-pied by the enemy.

On approaching said wood I received their fire and threw out my skirmishers to cover my advance. We then charged and drove them back to the edge of the hill, where the heavy firing commenced, the enemy contesting every inch of ground. My skirmishers, advancing on the right and left, unexpectedly found themselves within 15 yards of the enemy, lying below the crest of the hill.

At that time a regiment came up to our support on the right. They fired one volley and fell back in disorder. A second regiment (Thirty-first Indiana) came up in fine style, and at the right moment assisted us in driving the enemy from his position, causing him to retreat precipi-tately and in great disorder across Stone's River. It having grown night for nearly two hours, it was impossible to gain more advantages or better results of the fight, keeping our position until relieved by Gen-eral Palmer's pickets, after which we returned to camp.

The casualties of December 31 amount to 2 killed, 13 wounded, and 115 missing; of January 2, 10 killed, 27 wounded, and none missing.

I have the honor to be, very respectfully, your obedient servant,

FRANK ERDELMEYER,
Lieutenant-Colonel, Comdg. Thirty-second Indiana Volunteers.

Col. W. H. GIBSON,
Commanding First Brigade.

No. 37.

Report of Lieut. Col. Fielder A. Jones, Thirty-ninth Indiana Infantry.

CAMP NEAR MURFREESBOROUGH, TENN.,
January 7, 1863.

SIR: I have the honor to submit the following report of the operations of the Thirty-ninth Regiment of Indiana Volunteers since December 25, 1862:

Nothing of note occurred after breaking camp near Nashville, Tenn., until the regiment arrived on the field of operations in the enemy's front, near Murfreesborough, Tenn., where it arrived December 30, 1862.

On the evening of the same day the First Brigade, to which the regiment belongs, was moved to the extreme right wing of the army, the line of battle of the brigade being nearly at right angles with that of the right wing.

I was ordered to detail five companies from the Thirty-ninth Indiana for picket duty during the night. My orders were to join the left of my line with the right of General Kirk, and join my right on the left of the picket line of the Thirty-second, and leave the five reserve companies in line of battle, facing toward my picket line. Companies A, B, C, D, and K were detailed, and, having deployed A, C, and D as skirmishers, with B and K as supports, I joined picket lines with General Kirk and Thirty-second Indiana, as ordered. The following diagram will aid in explaining the operations of the 31st:

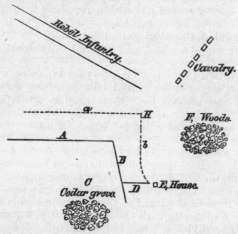

A, line of battle of right wing; B, position of reserve companies of Thirty-ninth Indiana; dotted line a, General Kirk's pickets; dotted line b, picket line of Thirty-ninth Indiana, distant from the reserve one-half mile; line extends through open corn-field from point H to house E; D, fence.

About 3 a. m. December 31, 1862, I received orders from General Willich to throw forward one company to patrol the woods F, in our front, and distant about 600 yards. Captain Herring, acting major, immediately sent Company B forward for that purpose.

At early daylight General Willich ordered me, in case there should be any indication that the rebels had placed a battery in our front, to move my picket line at once to the woods F, and hold it till the brigade could give me support. I went immediately to the picket line, and, learning from the patrol that no indication of the enemy had been seen, I was on the point of ordering Company B from the front, when several shots were fired from the pickets on our left, who gave way at the point H, leaving our flank exposed. I ordered Lieutenant Stanley to reconnect his line with General Kirk and hold his ground. At the same time I ordered all the company reserves on the picket line, forming a very strong skirmish line. Scarcely had this disposition been made when Kirk's pickets again gave way, and three regiments of rebel infantry, moving abreast in line of battle, were interposed between my picket line and the reserve companies. Many of my men were shot down at their post by the enemy who had moved into their rear.

Seeing that the rebel line of battle was oblique to that of our right wing, and supposing that our brigade would either change obliquely on the Thirty-ninth Indiana, or place the batteries in position to enfilade the rebel lines, I, partly to support such a movement, and partly to secure an opportunity to rally the pickets on the reserve, ordered Captain Herring to move the pickets in double-quick time by the right flank and take position behind the fence D, and open fire on the advancing foe, at the same time sending Lieutenant Neal to the house E, to open the fence and show the companies where to commence filing to the right. We succeeded in rallying Company A, and parts of Companies D and K, behind the fence, when the enemy opened upon us a murderous fire. Lieutenant Neal fell mortally wounded, and of the few who took position there, nearly one-half were either killed or wounded. Twice did our fire cause the enemy's lines to halt and waver, but he quickly rallied and moved forward. Had we been supported here, either with infantry or artillery, the enemy would have been repulsed with great slaughter. But no support came. Three rebel standards were within 30 feet of the fence when I ordered the men to double-quick to the cedar thicket C, where they again made a stand and covered the retreat of one piece of Goodspeed's battery.

Here I first learned that my five reserve companies, under command of Captain Cody, senior captain, had charged, front forward, on seven companies, and had bravely held their ground until the regiment on their left had given way, when they were forced to abandon their position. They retired in good order for some distance, when their ranks were thrown into confusion by the rush of stragglers through their lines. Seeing our colors at a distance, I ordered the skirmishers to fall back at once and join them. I met Colonel Gibson near this point, and we selected a ground on which to rally our two regiments; but ignorance of the topography of the country, and the operations of our cavalry, threw me so far over to the right as to separate me from Colonel Gibson and involve me in difficulty with the rebel cavalry, which was swarming on our flank. The division train being threatened by this cavalry, I rallied as many men as possible to its support, and escorted it safely and in good order to the Nashville pike.

Here both myself and the other officers did our utmost to file the regiment to the right and join the center of our army; but at this time the panic on the pike was at the highest, and our men were swept away as by a whirlwind, leaving me but a handful of men and officers. With these, after having been under a murderous fire for over eight hours, with our colors lost and men dispirited, I joined General Johnson, near the rear of the center of our army. Had I been better acquainted with the topography of the country I might have saved more men; but hour after hour elapsed, and I received no orders, and I did not even know where to direct my line of retreat; yet every obstacle, thicket, fence, or ravine was taken advantage of, and at no time was our fire relaxed.

Our loss was terrible. We had 31 killed, including 1 lieutenant; 118 wounded, including 2 lieutenants, and 231 missing, including 1 captain and 1 lieutenant. Of those reported missing, I have reason to believe that very many are wounded, though, perhaps, slightly.

How well the regiment fought let the above fearful list proclaim. Over 30 fell behind the fence D, while opposed to ten times their number, yet no man left his post until ordered. Lieutenant Neal, acting adjutant, fell here. No truer gentleman, no better soldier or braver man belongs to the great patriot army. He fell at his post doing his duty. He is no longer with us, but his name is in his country's history and his memory is enshrined in the hearts of us all who knew him well. Lieutenant Leavell was also wounded while in the discharge of his duty. He is a brave man and good officer. Most of the company officers acted manfully.

I am under obligations to Captains McCoy, McClelland, Cody, and Graham, Lieutenants Foote, Stanley, Mitchell, Clark, Hamilton, and Scott for efficient and timely aid. Of Capt. Thomas Herring, acting major, I cannot say too much in his praise. He was always at the post of danger, brave and cool, aiding here in rallying the men and there in directing the fire, so as to make it most effective. He deserves well of his regiment and his country. Private James Gray, of Company E, behaved nobly. No commissioned officer did more that day to rally the men than he did. He deserves promotion. Sergeants Boyer, Jones, Crozier, Noah W. Downs, Daniel Wilkins, and Mart Mollihan are also worthy of mention. Asst. Surg. John Gray did everything mortal man could do in caring for the wounded, and richly merits the deepest gratitude of the regiment and friends of the wounded.

On January 1, 1863, the Forty-ninth Ohio and Thirty-ninth Indiana were consolidated, at the request of Colonel Gibson, commanding brigade, and the request of the officers of the Forty-ninth. I assumed command of the two.

My command took an important part in the maneuvering in the right wing on January 1, and also in the bayonet charge of the brigade on the evening of January 2. In this charge the men were in excellent spirits, and never in the history of the two regiments did they fight with greater desperation than on that night. Three men of the Forty-ninth Ohio were wounded by shells thrown from the enemy's batteries.

My thanks are due to Captains Hays, Gray, and Tyler; also to Lieutenant Kessler and Adjt. C. A. Norton. Their untiring energy and zeal aroused the drooping spirits of the men, and excited enthusiasm out of despondency.

Very respectfully,

F. A. JONES,
Lieutenant-Colonel, Commanding Thirty-ninth Indiana.

Capt. CARL SCHMITT,
Assistant Adjutant-General.

No. 38.

Report of Col. William Wallace, Fifteenth Ohio Infantry.

HDQRS. FIFTEENTH OHIO VOLUNTEER INFANTRY,
January 7, 1863.

SIR: In accordance with orders from Colonel Gibson, commanding brigade, I have the honor to report to you the part taken by the Fifteenth Ohio in the march from Nashville to Murfreesborough, and the engagements in which the Fifteenth participated.

We were first engaged with the enemy on the morning of December 31, 1862, about 7 o'clock, when I found the enemy approaching in our rear, and received the order from Colonel Gibson to move out and form line of battle. To do this I countermarched the regiment and took up a position about 10 rods in front of my camp. By the time this was accomplished the brigade in rear of the First Brigade had given way, and, with the balance of our brigade, was in full retreat. We held this position only long enough to cover the retreat of our forces, when I gave the order to fall back.

It was at this point that the brave and gallant Lieutenant-Colonel Askew fell, severely wounded in the thigh, and was taken prisoner, and the no less brave Captain Douglass and Lieutenant Hilles also fell— Captain Douglass wounded in the breast, and Lieutenant Hilles in the thigh; both fell into the enemy's hands. None of the above have been paroled, and are now within our lines. Major McClenahan was slightly wounded in the shoulder, but made his escape on foot with the regiment. Five men of the regiment were killed at this point. The retreat was through an open field, with a high fence to cross before we could get under cover of the wood. Most of my killed and wounded occurred at or near this fence.

Having placed this fence between us and the enemy, we fell back in good order, keeping up a brisk and deadly fire on the advancing foe. I rallied the regiment about one-half mile from my camp, being greatly assisted by Captain Dawson and Adjutant Dubois, both of whom showed themselves to be brave and gallant officers.

At this time I found myself in command of the brigade, and my report of the 15th for the balance of the day will be included in that of the brigade, which was rallied here, and, with one piece of artillery, under Lieutenant Belding, we checked the advance of the rebel column.

Lieutenant Belding is deserving of great praise for the admirable manner of handling his piece. From the effects of three shots not less than 100 of the enemy fell.

When in command of the brigade, Adjutant Norton, of the Forty-ninth Ohio, Captain Schmitt, Lieutenants Miles, Green, and McGrath, of General Willich's staff, rendered invaluable assistance in rallying the men, in charging the enemy, and conducting the retreat.

Captain Dawson took command of the Fifteenth Ohio, Major McClenahan not feeling able to do so, and once, when there was danger of the men breaking in wild confusion, he seized the colors of the Fifteenth, and, by a united cheer, the brigade was again formed, and checked again the enemy's advance; the brigade fell back at last in rear of General Rousseau's lines, and formed again, and held the rebel advance in check, but were again compelled to fall back, by the overwhelming numbers of the enemy, in rear of General Van Cleve's division, who put a stop to the further advance of the enemy.

On the evening of this day I learned with pleasure of the safety of Colonel Gibson, who took command of the brigade. Under his direction the Fifteenth took part in the maneuvering on the right the following day, and on the succeeding day was present in the charge made by the First Brigade upon the right of the enemy, and in which but one man of the Fifteenth was injured, Sergeant Malin, who was struck by a piece of shell in the thigh.

Major McClenahan rejoined the regiment on the 3d, having been ordered to do so by the brigade commander. I am pleased to mention with pride the gallant bearing of all the company officers of the Fifteenth who took part in the action of the 31st and the following days of the conflict. They did their whole duty under the trying circumstances under which they were placed.

Lieutenant Fowler was wounded slightly in the right leg and taken prisoner on the 31st, but he is now within our lines.

From December 31 to the evening of January 4 the loss of the Fifteenth was: Killed, 17; wounded, 68; missing, 127.

> Your obedient servant,
>
> WM. WALLACE,
> *Colonel, Commanding Fifteenth Ohio Volunteer Infantry.*

Capt. CARL SCHMITT,
  A. A. G., First Brig., Second Div., Right Wing, Fourteenth A. C.

P. S.—I cannot close my report without speaking in terms of the highest commendation of Dr. Kelly, of this regiment, who remained with our wounded, and by his untiring efforts succeeded in having our unlucky braves made as comfortable as the nature of the circumstances would permit.

[Addenda.]

GENERAL ORDERS, }   HDQRS. DEPT. OF THE CUMBERLAND,
  No. 55.   }   *Murfreesborough, Tenn., March 21, 1863.*

I. At a court of inquiry, convened at Murfreesborough, Tenn., pur suant to Special Field Orders, No. 59, Headquarters Department of the Cumberland, on the request of Maj. John McClenahan, to report on the charges against him during the battle of Stone's River, of which court Col. Stanley Matthews, Fifty-first Ohio Volunteers, was president, and Capt. D. G. Swaim, assistant adjutant-general, was recorder, the following facts were found upon the testimony :

1st. That on the 31st of December, 1862, at the battle of Stone's River, the Fifteenth Regiment Ohio Volunteers was part of the First Brigade, Second Division, Right Wing; that early in the day General Willich, the brigade commander, was taken prisoner by the enemy, and Col. W. H. Gibson, the next ranking officer, with a portion of the command, was cut off from the main body of the brigade, whereby the command devolved upon Colonel Wallace, Fifteenth Ohio Volunteers; that thereby the command of said regiment devolved upon Major McClenahan, the senior officer present; that previously thereto Major McClenahan had been wounded by a bullet passing through the muscles over the scapula, and through the spine of the scapula of the right shoulder; that said wound was sufficient to prevent the ordinary use of the right shoulder and arm, but was not severe enough to disable Major McClenahan from remaining in the field on horseback, or to unfit him, under the circumstances, for the discharge of his field duties; that it was an occasion of great urgency, requiring extraordinary exertion and endurance on the part of every officer and soldier, the whole line of the corps being driven by the enemy from its position, and this brigade, including the Fifteenth Regiment Ohio Volunteers, having been thrown into confusion; that when Major McClenahan was notified that the command of the regiment devolved upon him, he declined, formally, to assume it, on account of his wound, and thereupon Colonel Wallace ordered Captain Dawson, of the same regiment, to assume command thereof, which he did; that Major McClenahan nevertheless remained with the regiment until it had fallen back to a position on the Murfreesborough turnpike, at about

3 p. m., after which it was not again engaged with the enemy, exerting himself, to the best of his ability, to form, rally, and cheer his men, and that, when the regiment reached the position last named, he left, for the first time, to have his wound examined and dressed.

2d. That on the several succeeding days of that week the said regiment was not actually engaged with the enemy, except slightly on the Friday afternoon; that during that period Colonel Wallace, having been relieved by Colonel Gibson from the command of the brigade, had taken command of the regiment, and the necessity for Major McClenahan's presence and services was not so great; that, accordingly, he was not continually present with the regiment after the 31st of December, 1862, until January 3, 1863, nor on duty with it, but went on duty on the date last mentioned, on the order of his brigade commander; and subsequently, upon a medical certificate and by order of the medical director, went to Nashville for treatment, and obtained leave of absence for twenty days on account of his wound.

Upon these facts the court is of the following opinion:

That there was nothing in the conduct of Major McClenahan, on the occasions referred to, that can be construed to support any charge of cowardice, disobedience of orders, or other misbehavior in the face of the enemy, but that he is censurable for not assuming the formal command of the regiment during the actual engagement on the 31st of December, 1862.

II. The finding of the court is approved.

By command of Major-General Rosecrans:

C. GODDARD,
Assistant Adjutant-General.

No. 39.

Report of Col. Joseph B. Dodge, Thirtieth Indiana Infantry, commanding Second Brigade.

HEADQUARTERS SECOND BRIGADE, SECOND DIVISION,
In Camp near Murfreesborough, Tenn., January 8, 1863.

SIR: In compliance with your order of the 7th instant I have the honor to respectfully submit the following report of the operations of this command since the 26th of December last up to the evening of the 31st ultimo:

On the morning of December 26, last, this brigade left camp, near Nashville, under command of Brig. Gen. E. N. Kirk, and marched out on the Nolensville pike about 12 miles, where we encamped during the night. Although there was heavy skirmishing in our front and on each flank, we were in nowise engaged with the enemy during that day, as there was a heavy force of Federal troops in front of this brigade and between it and the enemy.

On the morning of the 27th we were ordered to resume the march, and on that day the brigade was in advance of our whole forces, with the exception of the cavalry, which was thrown out as skirmishers in advance.

About 1 mile from where we had bivouacked for the night the enemy made his appearance in considerable force, composed of cavalry and supported by artillery, all of which opened upon us, and he showed a disposition to contest the ground over which we wished to pass. The

Thirty-fourth Regiment Illinois Volunteers and the Twenty-ninth Indiana were promptly deployed as skirmishers, each regiment retaining a good reserve, and thrown forward, with instructions to push on as rapidly as possible, which order was obeyed with alacrity and skill, and the other regiments of the brigade moved forward in line of battle, the Thirtieth Indiana supporting Edgarton's battery.

Owing to a dense fog, which enveloped everything, so that we could not distinguish the troops of the enemy from our own, it was deemed prudent to halt until the fog partially disappeared, when we again moved forward, with continued skirmishing on our front, until we gained an elevated position overlooking the village of Triune. Here the enemy were in plain view, drawn up in line of battle, the center of their line being in the village. Edgarton's battery opened upon them immediately with splendid effect, soon throwing them into disorder, and disabling at least one piece of their artillery, as I have good reason to believe. While in this position a very heavy rain commenced, accompanied with fog, rendering an advance immediately hazardous.

The fog disappeared again in the course of about an hour, when we again advanced; but, owing to the ground being very much softened by the rain, the men's clothes were so saturated with water that it was impossible to do so at the rate of speed desired. The enemy had destroyed a bridge across a stream that runs through the edge of the town, thus compelling the artillery to make a detour of nearly a mile to a ford, and by this means gained time to collect his scattered forces and withdraw. On that night we bivouacked about 1 mile south of Triune.

During that day this brigade lost none in killed or wounded, but inflicted considerable loss upon the enemy. The officers and men engaged showed themselves to be cool, skillful, and courageous, and behaved splendidly.

We staid at the above-mentioned place all of the 28th, and on the morning of the 29th took up our march for Murfreesborough. During this day nothing of importance occurred. We bivouacked that night in an open field, without fires, and in a cold, drenching rain.

On the morning of the 30th we were ordered out to take position, preparatory to an expected attack upon the enemy. Heavy skirmishing and fighting was going on in front of us during the whole day, in which we took no active part until about 3 p. m., at about which time we arrived at the extreme right of the line of our army.

At that time the enemy had a battery of artillery stationed directly in front of this brigade, which was pouring a destructive fire into some troops on our left, belonging to Brig. Gen. J. C. Davis' division. General Kirk immediately ordered Captain Edgarton's battery to open upon it, which order was complied with, with great execution, dismounting one of the enemy's pieces, and killing quite a number of men in a very few moments, and driving him from his position.

There was no more firing, either from artillery or infantry, that evening or night. The brigade was formed in line of battle, the Thirty-fourth Illinois, Maj. A. P. Dysart commanding, on the extreme right; the Twenty-ninth Indiana, Lieutenant-Colonel Dunn commanding, next on the left; the Thirtieth Indiana, Col. J. B. Dodge, next, and the Seventy-seventh Pennsylvania, Lieutenant-Colonel Housum commanding, on the left; Edgarton's battery (E, First Ohio Artillery) in the rear and to the left of the Thirty-fourth Illinois, in a cedar grove, with a rather dense thicket immediately in front of the three left regiments. A strong picket line was thrown out from 150 to 200 yards in front, with a corn-field in front of their (the picket) line. Every precaution that was possible was taken to prevent surprise, and to give seasonable warning of the approach of the enemy.

The brigade was up and under arms for nearly or quite an hour before daylight. Just after daylight a part of the horses of the battery were unhitched from the caissons and taken to water, which was close by. Just at this moment the enemy made his appearance on our front and right in immense force, and formed in close columns, with a front equal to the length of a battalion in line and ten or twelve ranks in depth. General Kirk immediately ordered the Thirty-fourth Illinois to advance to near where the picket was stationed, in order to check, at least, the advance of the enemy, and save the battery, if possible, which movement was promptly executed under an awful fire, which almost annihilated the picket line or line of skirmishers, which it really was, and killed or wounded a large number in the line, some 150 or 200 yards in the rear. The battery under command of Captain Edgarton immediately opened with canister upon the enemy, and only had time to fire eight rounds before the battery was taken. Nearly or quite one-half of the horses were killed or wounded, so as to be unmanageable, by the first fire from the enemy, and it was impossible to remove it from the ground.

Captain Edgarton and his officers and men fought nobly, as the number of killed and wounded will testify, and did everything possible to maintain their ground against an overpowering force. The captain was taken prisoner while assisting to work his guns, and Lieutenant Berwick was bayoneted and taken prisoner while assisting him. General Kirk was seriously wounded at almost the first fire, and I then succeeded to the command of the brigade.

The fire the enemy received from us, although well directed, and as effective as a fire from two ranks generally is, produced no visible effect upon him as he moved his heavy column forward upon a double-quick. General Rains, who commanded a part of their column, fell dead or mortally wounded at this point.

The enemy then moved to the left oblique, or nearly, by his left flank, until his center was opposite our extreme right, when he moved forward again, changing direction to his right as he did so, so as to bring his whole force upon our most exposed point. We held our ground until our ranks were not more than 20 yards from the enemy, when I was forced to retire, having no support and seeing that it was a needless waste of life to contend in that position with at least twenty times the number of men I then had left, which was done in the best order possible, across a corn-field in the rear and to the left of our first position, to a field one side of which was on rising ground and overlooking the ground over which the enemy must advance to attack.

I here formed the Thirtieth Indiana, at that time under command of Lieut. Col. O. D. Hurd, of that regiment, and the Seventy-ninth Illinois, Col. S. P. Read commanding, that had just reported to me (it having been detailed to guard a train the day before, and had just arrived upon the field), behind a fence on the rise of ground before spoken of. Before the Seventy-ninth Illinois reached the fence, and while it was at least 200 yards distant from it, the enemy made his appearance and instantly poured a terrible fire into their ranks. Although a new regiment, they advanced with a firmness that would have done credit to veterans, and, after reaching the fence, poured a terribly destructive fire into the enemy

Here, assisted by Captain Simonson's (Fifth Indiana) battery, this brigade, unsupported, except by the Third Brigade, which was on our left, and almost alone, succeeded in checking the enemy, bringing his columns to a halt, and requiring the utmost exertions of his officers to keep his men from fleeing in disorder from the field, during all of which time a tremendous fire was kept up. The enemy finally succeeded in throwing his left wing forward across the fence, thus outflanking this brigade and dislodging us from that position; but the number of dead left by him on that ground for five days afterward shows conclusively that it was by far the dearest position to him that he gained that day.

Colonel Read, of the Seventy-ninth Illinois, was killed instantly while bravely urging his men on. In his death the service has lost a fine officer, a brave soldier, and a true man. Adjutant Stribley, of the Thirtieth Indiana, was also killed here. The service contained no braver or cooler officer than he. The Seventy-seventh Pennsylvania, Lieutenant-Colonel Housum commanding, at the time of the occurrences above mentioned was some 600 yards on the left of the troops under my immediate command, acting with a brigade in General Davis' division. While hotly engaged with the enemy, Colonel Housum was wounded severely, from which he died shortly afterward. He was a cool, clear-headed, courageous officer and gentleman.

After being driven from the fence, I retired my command to a piece of woods in the rear of my former position, the enemy closely following up with infantry on our rear and cavalry on our left flank. I halted my command twice, and formed a line and undertook to hold him in check, but it was impossible to do but little, owing to our weakened condition and the absence of all support.

I finally fell back to near the Murfreesborough and Nashville turnpike, and made up my mind that the enemy must be stopped there. I had at that time the Seventy-seventh Pennsylvania, Captain Rose commanding, Twenty-ninth Indiana, Major Collins commanding, and about 100 men belonging to the Thirtieth Indiana, Thirty-fourth Illinois, and Seventy-ninth Illinois; in all, about, at that time, 500 men. By command of Brigadier-General Johnson, I formed my little force on the right of Captain Simonson's battery, which was in action with one of the enemy's batteries, which was soon silenced, immediately after which it (Captain Simonson's battery) was placed in another position.

I wish to be pardoned for testifying here to the skill, efficiency, and courage displayed by Captain Simonson and his officers and men during that day. I then moved my command some 150 yards to the right of where it had been while supporting the battery, into a piece of woods, and took a good position for defense.

Some troops belonging to some other division moved in on my left just at that moment, and a moment after the remains of the column that made the first attack in the morning made its appearance, coming up on a double-quick. I immediately gave the command forward, and my command met them, poured in a deadly volley, and rushed forward. Their advance was stopped, their line wavered, and in a moment was in full retreat, and thus the brigade that received the first attack from this column in the morning had the satisfaction of giving it the first repulse it received during the day. I followed them but a short distance, when I got a regiment to relieve the command I had left, as they were entirely out of ammunition, and, by order of General Johnson, I took them back and formed along the railroad, and got a supply.

I was then ordered back to the bank of the river, where I awaited further orders. While there, an officer rode up and informed me that the enemy's cavalry was attempting to cross the river some distance below, near a hospital, and that it was important that we should have a force there. There was no superior officer near, and I took the responsibility of at once moving to the point designated and forming in line. The enemy, seeing us approach, promptly fell back, but not until he had taken quite a number of prisoners, as I understand.

I then returned to the turnpike, and at dark bivouacked in the woods near by, where we spent the night.

On the morning of the 1st instant I placed my command in line, under your directions, and we immediately threw up a line of breastworks, behind which we bivouacked until the evening of the 3d instant, without any movement of importance on our part, with the exception that on the 2d instant, at about 9 p. m., I was ordered to take four companies from my command and a like number from the Third Brigade of this division, and to advance to our front until I reached the Franklin turnpike or found the enemy in force.

It was a very dark night, and I took my little command according to your orders, deployed the whole as skirmishers, and started. I first crossed an open field or fields nearly to the woods in our front, where I could distinctly hear the enemy chopping and moving either artillery or heavy wagons. When we got about 20 yards from the edge of the woods, I distinctly heard officers giving commands to their men, and, fearful that I was going into a trap, I ordered my men to fire, which was promptly obeyed, and my suspicions confirmed, as the enemy returned a withering volley in reply. Found at least ten times the number I had with me. Having ascertained that the enemy were in heavy force near our lines, thereby accomplishing the purpose for which I was sent out, I ordered my men to retire, which they did in good order, losing but 4 wounded; none killed.

The officers and men under my command, during this terrible battle, behaved with great coolness and courage under the most trying circumstances.

I cannot help but bring to the notice of the commanding general the gallant conduct of Capt. T. E. Rose, of the Seventy-seventh Pennsylvania Regiment, who took command of his regiment after Lieutenant-Colonel Housum was wounded, and who, by his skill, perseverance, and energy, kept his regiment well together, and, by his example, urged on his men to attack the enemy when all around was disorder and confusion.

Major Collins, of the Twenty-ninth Indiana, took command of that regiment about 9 a. m. on the 31st, after Lieutenant-Colonel Dunn had, by some means, become separated from his command, and fought nobly.

Major Buckner, of the Seventy-ninth Illinois, took command of that regiment after the death of Colonel Read, and gallantly rallied his men, and showed himself worthy of a higher position than he now holds.

Maj. A. P. Dysart, commanding the Thirty-fourth Illinois, distinguished himself in his efforts to arrest the enemy's progress, and his regiment stood by him until it was utterly impossible for the same number of men, without support, to do so longer.

Lieutenant-Colonel Hurd, commanding, and Major Fitzsimmons (who was taken by the enemy), of the Thirtieth Indiana, showed that they were worthy of the positions they occupy. Both needlessly, almost, exposed themselves, and were untiring in their efforts to stop the progress of what seemed a victorious enemy.

I can but express my heartfelt thanks to my staff for their conduct on the field—firm, cool, energetic, and fearless, their assistance was inval uable. Capt. D. C. Wagner, acting assistant adjutant-general; Capt. E. P. Edsall, acting assistant inspector-general; Lieut. I. C. McElfatrick, topographical engineer, and Lieutenants Baldwin and Walker, aides, were untiring in their efforts to rally the troops, and to their exertions the whole right wing of the army is, in my opinion, indebted.

Dr. George W. Hewitt, acting brigade surgeon, was untiring in his exertions in behalf of the wounded, and was captured while at his post by the enemy, as was also Dr. Hostetter, of the Thirty-fourth Illinois, Dr. Keen, of the Twenty-ninth Indiana, and Dr. McAllister, of the Seventy-ninth Illinois, were all taken where a surgeon should be in time of action, attending to the duties of their profession. While in the enemy's lines they were engaged night and day in taking care of our wounded. They have been released since, and their horses retained by the enemy, in pursuance, as they report, of order of General Wharton. Surgeon Downey, of the Seventy-seventh Pennsylvania, was fortunately spared, and staid with the brigade. He was of invaluable service to those who were so unfortunate as to require the attention of a surgeon.

The medical department of this brigade was in splendid condition, thanks to Dr. Hewitt and division medical director, Dr. Marks, and, notwithstanding our loss in surgeons, the wounded were well cared for.

Chaplain Bradshaw, Seventy-ninth Illinois, and Chaplain Decker, of the Thirty-fourth Illinois, exposed themselves in the most fearless manner in taking care of the wounded, taking them off the field, &c., and proved themselves to be well worthy, at least, of the positions they occupy.

This brigade met with a serious loss, in the person of General Kirk, early in the engagement. He fell at the head of his brigade, trying manfully to resist and repel the overwhelming force thrown against it.

Accompanying, please find a summary of killed, wounded, and missing of this command. The missing are, a large majority of them, I fear, wounded and in the hands of the enemy; also, please find reports of regimental commanders of this brigade and complete list, by name, of casualties.

Respectfully submitted.

J. B. DODGE,
Colonel Thirtieth Indiana, Commanding Second Brigade.

Captain BARTLETT,
Acting Assistant Adjutant-General.

P. S.—Excuse me for calling the attention of the general commanding to a gallant charge made by the Seventy-seventh Pennsylvania, while they were separated from this brigade, and were acting in concert with a brigade in Brig. Gen. J. C. Davis' division. A battery in possession of the enemy made its appearance directly in their front and opened upon them. Lieutenant-Colonel Housum immediately ordered a charge upon it, which was obeyed instantly by his command. The cannoneers were either killed or wounded, the horses disabled, so they could not move back. The Seventy-seventh had possession of Captain Edgarton's battery, which the enemy had brought along with them, for a few moments, but before they could do anything more than compel the enemy to spike the guns, a heavy force of infantry made its appearance in their front and flank, and they were compelled to retire, during which movement Lieutenant-Colonel Housum was mortally wounded.

General summary of killed, wounded, and missing in the Second Brigade, Second Division (Right Wing), in the battle before Murfreesborough, Tenn., on December 31, 1862.

Command.	Taken into action.			Field officers.			Company officers.			Enlisted men.			Total loss.		
	Field and staff officers.	Company officers.	Enlisted men.	Killed.	Wounded.	Missing.	Killed.	Wounded.	Missing.	Killed.	Wounded.	Missing.	Commissioned officers.	Enlisted men.	Aggregate.
29th Indiana	6	18	313			1	1	2		14	66	51	4	131	135
30th Indiana	4	21	463			1	1	2	1	30	108	70	5	208	213
34th Illinois	5	19	330				2	2	2	19	98	72	6	189	195
79th Illinois	5	16	416	1				3	3	23	68	121	7	212	219
77th Pennsylvania	3	16	288	1				1	2	4	28	28	4	60	64
Edgarton's battery															
Total	23	90	1,810	2		2	4	10	8	90	368	342	26	800	*826

Very respectfully submitted.

J. B. DODGE,
Colonel Thirtieth Regiment Indiana Volunteers, Commanding Second Brigade.

Owing to the absence of the officers and men of Battery E, First Ohio Volunteer Artillery, I am unable to procure a report of casualties, &c., as required by your order.

Very respectfully, your obedient servant,

D. C. WAGNER,
Captain, and Acting Assistant Adjutant-General.

No. 40.

Report of Maj. Alexander P. Dysart, Thirty-fourth Illinois Infantry.

HEADQUARTERS THIRTY-FOURTH ILLINOIS VOLUNTEERS,
Camp near Murfreesborough, Tenn., January 7, 1863.

SIR : In compliance with circular, dated January 7, 1863, from Headquarters Second Division, requiring a minute statement of regimental commanders of the operations and casualties of their respective regiments from the time of leaving camp, near Nashville, Tenn., up to the expiration of the battle at Murfreesborough, I have the honor to submit the following report :

On Friday, December 26, 1862, this regiment, under command of Lieut. Col. H. W. Bristol, left camp, near Nashville, Tenn., and marched that day to one-half mile south of Nolensville, where we encamped for the night.

Next day, December 27, 1862, the Second Brigade being in advance, the Thirty-fourth Illinois was in advance of the brigade. After advancing nearly three-quarters of a mile, General Kirk ordered Colonel Bristol to throw forward four companies of his regiment on the left of the pike as skirmishers. Companies A, F, G, and B were detailed for that purpose, and placed under command of myself and Captain Van Tassel. We moved forward, the remaining companies of the regiment marching immediately in the rear of the skirmish line, as a support, the skirmish

---

* But see revised statement, p. 208.

line advancing, driving the enemy through Triune, and halting about 1 mile south of that place near dark. The distance skirmished over that day was nearly 5 miles. Although exposed to the enemy's fire from their artillery and musketry nearly all day, we had no one killed, wounded, or missing. We went into camp that night a short distance to the rear of where we had advanced with our skirmish line, and remained in camp at that place the next day (being Sunday) without performing any duties only those required on that day.

On the morning of December 29, 1862, we were ordered back toward Nashville 2½ miles, and turned off the pike on a dirt road to the right, leading in the direction of Murfreesborough, and, after marching 6 miles, went into camp between 10 and 11 o'clock that night. The Thirty-fourth Illinois was rear guard for the brigade teams that day.

On the morning of the 30th, about 10 a. m., we moved forward in the direction of Murfreesborough 3 miles, when we were ordered to the right. The Thirty-fourth Illinois was ordered to support Captain Edgarton's battery, which was moved to the extreme right of our lines, and opened fire on a rebel battery that was firing into the right flank of Davis' division. General Kirk ordered two companies of this regiment to be thrown out as skirmishers (A and B), under the command of Captain Van Tassel, extending the line across an open field to a piece of woods, about 100 rods farther to the right than our troops occupied. Captain Edgarton's battery soon silenced the rebel battery, and it was now near dark.

Colonel Bristol, being unwell, was compelled to leave the regiment, and the command then fell upon myself. I received orders that I was to picket immediately in my front, and that General Willich would join his pickets on the right. This was done shortly after dark. I was then ordered to encamp the remainder of my regiment in the rear of the left of my picket line, and within 30 rods of the same. Everything was quiet through the night.

Just before daylight I had my regiment under arms, and moved it forward some 4 rods in advance of where I was encamped, so that I could more conveniently deploy into line, as I had my regiment in double column. A few minutes after daylight one of my lookouts reported to me that the enemy was moving down on us with an overwhelming force. I immediately sent word to General Kirk, and rode immediately myself to find General Willich, who was encamped in my rear not more than 30 rods. I failed to find the general; they told me he had gone to see General Johnson. I informed some of the officers of his brigade that the enemy was advancing. I hurried back to my regiment, and I then received an order to advance my regiment and try to hold the enemy in check, which was done.

After advancing out in the open field about 15 rods, the enemy opened upon us, my men returning the fire. They were now exposed to the fire of nearly five times their number, as I only had 354 men, including the officers. Ten or twelve of my men were killed, and some 60 odd wounded, before I received an order to fall back in support of the battery. I gave the order for them to fall back. Not one of my men or officers left their post before I gave them the order. When we returned to the battery everything was confusion; the First Brigade was not in position; were engaged, many of them, cooking their breakfast. I endeavored to hold the battery with what few men I had, but it was of no use; the enemy were fast surrounding us, and the only alternative was to retreat or be taken prisoners. I gave the order for them to retreat, and would, I think, have been able to keep them together, but they got mixed up with the First Brigade, and were carried too far to the left, where many of them were taken prisoners.

I rallied some 50 of my men, and made a stand behind a rail fence, about three-quarters of a mile from where I formed my first line, and opened a destructive fire on a regiment of cavalry that was bearing down upon us, but, finding it impossible to hold that position, I had to fall back to near the pike, when I was ordered to assist our train with what few men I had left.

January 1, what was left of my regiment was put in with the Thirtieth Indiana, and took part with that regiment, under the command of Captain Hostetter, Company I, Thirty-fourth Illinois Volunteers, I being sick and unfit for duty. They were engaged in skirmishing from behind breastworks that were erected.

January 2, they were engaged the same as on the 1st, and on the 3d the same routine of duty. The Thirty-fourth Illinois lost no one killed or wounded after the battle of December 31, 1862.

I need not particularize the services of any officers under my command, for both officers and men did their duty nobly ; although being compelled to retreat, they stood firm till we were overwhelmed by superior numbers.

I attach a list of killed, wounded, and missing.* Many of the missing, I have no doubt, are wounded and in the hands of the enemy.

All of which is respectfully submitted.

ALEXANDER P. DYSART,
Major, Commanding Thirty-fourth Illinois Volunteers.

Capt. D. C. WAGNER,
Asst. Adjt. Gen., Second Brigade, Second Division.

No. 41.

Report of Maj. Allen Buckner, Seventy-ninth Illinois Infantry.

HDQRS. SEVENTY-NINTH REGIMENT ILLINOIS VOLUNTEERS,
In the Field, near Murfreesborough, Tenn., January 7, 1863.

SIR : I have the honor to report to you that the Seventy-ninth Regiment Illinois Volunteers left camp, near Nashville, on December 26, under command of Col. S. P. Read, for Murfreesborough, via Nolensville, but was not in action until Wednesday, December 31.

This regiment was detailed on the morning of the 30th as rear guard of the division train, and at night encamped on the right and to the rear of the brigade, as ordered, throwing out a strong line of skirmishers to the front and right.

On the morning of the 31st the men were under arms at daylight, about which time the brigade was attacked in front by such a heavy force that it began to fall back. Colonel Read requested that I should go forward and learn of Colonel Dodge, who was then in command of the brigade, General Kirk having been wounded, what he should do. I did so, and told him that the Seventy-ninth was ready and waiting to do anything it could. He directed me to tell Colonel Read to hurry the regiment forward as soon as possible, which was done, he bravely leading his men on to the field amid a destructive fire from the enemy. The regiment marched up on the double-quick until it arrived on the right of the Thirtieth Indiana, becoming the right of the brigade, and

---

* Embodied in revised statement, p. 208.

commenced pouring a deadly fire into the ranks of the enemy. It was not long before I heard some one say that Colonel Read had fallen. I went immediately to where he was lying, and found that he had been shot directly in the forehead, thus falling at his post and facing the enemy.

My attention was at once called, by one of the officers, to the fact that the enemy was flanking us on our right. I directed the men to fire right-oblique, but could not check them. They rushed forward, opening on us a deadly cross-fire. I saw that in a few moments we would be surrounded, and consequently ordered a retreat, which was made across an open field to the woods, a distance of some 300 yards, exposed all the time to a destructive fire of artillery and musketry, killing and wounding a great many of our men.

At the woods I tried to rally the men, but we were so closely pursued by overwhelming numbers that it was impossible. The regiment became very much scattered, although the officers did all they could to keep them together. Many of them joined other regiments and fought during the day. I was able to keep enough men together in the brigade to form a nucleus around which to rally.

A few of our men acted cowardly, but the regiment, as such, fought as bravely as men could. As to the officers, I must say, to my personal knowledge, that Captains Van Deren, Young, Low, Martin, Lacy, and Pinnell, and also Lieutenants Mitchell, Williams, Patten, Albin, Jacobs, Braddock, and Bigelow, stood to the work, and have gained a name as brave officers. I must speak of Adjutant Lamb, as doing his duty as none but a faithful officer could. Likewise, Assistant Surgeons McAllister and Wheeler, who staid with the wounded and dying, although they were compelled thereby to fall into the hands of the enemy for a time; they have done their part to the utmost, to both officers and men. Last, but not least, the chaplain, C. S. Bradshaw, was with us all day, assisting to carry off the wounded. He conducted himself in such a manner as to command the love and esteem of both officers and men. Sergeant-Major Harding did his part with true courage. Sergeants Boyle, of Company C, and Harding, of Company D, also deserve a great deal of credit for the manner in which they rallied their men, their commanders having been wounded early in the action.

For numbers and names of killed, wounded, and missing, I refer you to report already made.*

Respectfully submitted.

ALLEN BUCKNER,
Major, Commanding Seventy-ninth Illinois Volunteers.

Capt. D. C. WAGNER,
Acting Assistant Adjutant-General.

No. 42.

Report of Maj. Joseph P. Collins, Twenty-ninth Indiana Infantry.

CAMP NEAR MURFREESBOROUGH, TENN.,
January 7, 1863.

SIR: I have the honor to report the part taken by the Twenty-ninth Regiment Indiana Volunteers in the advance on Murfreesborough from Nashville, and the battles before that place.

On the morning of December 26 last, we struck tents, sending the

---

* Embodied in revised statement, p. 208.

train back to Nashville, and left camp, following, in the order of march, the Thirtieth Indiana and Thirty-fourth Illinois. The divisions of Generals Davis and Sheridan preceded the Second, and in the skirmishing with the enemy on the road and near Nolensville we had not an opportunity to take a part.

On the 27th, the Second Division and Second Brigade were the advance forces, and in regular order the Twenty-ninth Regiment Indiana Volunteers followed the Thirty-fourth Illinois. We had not marched over 1 mile when sharp skirmishing was heard ahead, between our cavalry and that of the enemy. Pushing rapidly forward to the summit of a ridge, beyond which the skirmish was going on, we became exposed to the fire of a masked battery of the enemy, which opened on the head of the column, with shot and shell.

Advantage was taken by Generals Johnson and Kirk of a cedar thicket, covering this ridge, to move the Thirty-fourth Illinois and Twenty-ninth Indiana to the left of the road and toward the enemy. Orders were immediately given by General Kirk to Colonels Bristol and Dunn to throw out skirmishers to cover their regiments, the Thirty-fourth Illinois and Twenty-ninth Indiana, which were drawn up in line of battle in front of the thicket, but in an open field.

The skirmishers, being ordered forward, moved over the ground just wrested from the enemy by our cavalry, until they reached the top of another ridge, divided by a narrow valley from the rebel battery. Here we were ordered to halt, to await the issue of an artillery duel between it and Captain Edgarton's battery (E, First Ohio Artillery), attached to the Second Brigade, as well as the lifting of a dense fog, which rendered a hasty movement to the front extremely perilous.

When objects at a distance could be distinctly seen, and the rebel battery silenced, we were again ordered forward, without seeing the enemy, until we had reached a hill overlooking the town of Triune. Large bodies of rebel cavalry were posted in the town and in our front, on the left of the road, about three-quarters of a mile distant. Our artillery was again brought into action, leaving us the privilege of witnessing the hurried retreat of both bodies of the rebels.

When we next advanced they moved their cannon toward us and plied the advancing regiments with shot, shell, and grape-shot. Supporting their artillery we discovered a large force of dismounted cavalry, posted on a hill covered with timber, whose leaden compliments attracted our attention. The skirmishers were ordered forward on double-quick, but the torrent of rain which poured down on us had made their clothing and the plowed field so heavy that the efforts of the men at double-quick were painful and almost futile. They pushed on, however, as rapidly as possible, and by a well-directed fire drove the rebels from the woods, and prevented them again forming within rifle range.

The rebel artillery retreated toward Triune, taking advantage of every rise of ground to check our advance, until the skirmishers of the Twenty-ninth Indiana had almost secured a position in the woods to the rebel right, from which the capture of the rebel guns was perfectly feasible, when the bugle again sounded a halt, and the rebels moved off rapidly. Forward once more, and the line of skirmishers had reached the top of another ridge and halted, leaving the reserve at its base, when we were surprised by the sudden appearance of a regiment of rebel cavalry on our left, within 20 yards, and moving leisurely to the front. I ordered the reserve to wheel to the left and fire, which was heard by the rebels, who instantly quickened their pace to a gallop, but were unable to pass in time to save their entire column. Several were seen to reel in their saddles, and all changed direction by the left flank, making for the woods. Immediately afterward a squad appeared, made a demonstration on the deployed line (Company A, Twenty-ninth Indiana), but failed to intimidate the men or force the line. With a shout, the skirmishers rushed forward, poured in a galling fire, unhorsed 4 or 5, took 1 prisoner, badly wounded, while Company F, Twenty-ninth Indiana, on reserve at the same time, forced another to surrender without a wound.

This cavalry force was the First Confederate Regulars, and I only regret that the fear that this might be Colonel Stokes' cavalry, which had all day supported our left, but of whose personal appearance I was ignorant, rendered their loss so slight. We advanced half a mile farther, when we bivouacked for the night.

After we had reached our final halting place, the Federal (Stokes') cavalry emerged from the woods on our left, but at sufficient distance to leave a gap, through which the rebels escaped.

Until December 30 we were not again engaged in any movement or preparation for the attack on Murfreesborough. On this day we moved in reserve to the column of General Davis until 3 p. m., when the Second Brigade, Second Division, was ordered to the right of General Davis' division, which was threatened by rebel cavalry. The Seventy-seventh Pennsylvania and Thirty-eighth [Thirtieth] Indiana were thrown forward as skirmishers, to the first of which the Twenty-ninth acted as reserve. We moved forward until we reached the reserve of General Davis' right, where the rebel cavalry was distinctly visible in line of battle, but not within range. Captain Edgarton's battery having taken position, soon put them to flight. While in line at this point we were exposed to the fire of the rebel battery supporting their skirmishers, but it was immediately silenced by ours.

About dusk a line of battle was determined upon, and, by order, the Twenty-ninth Indiana took position on the left of the Thirty-fourth, which supported the battery on a lane leading to Murfreesborough and behind a dense thicket of cedars. Steps were at once taken to guard against surprise. A large company (B) of our regiment was sent out as pickets, with instructions to act as skirmishers should the enemy appear, our line connecting that of the Thirty-fourth Illinois on the right and the Thirtieth Indiana on our left, both of which lines were established sufficiently in advance to command a wide range of vision, and enable the regiments to form in time to meet any attack. The night passed without alarm on our line until about 3 a. m., when a shot fired on the picket line, to our right, brought every man to his place in the ranks.

About daylight we were again alarmed by general firing on the picket line, and immediately afterward by shouting in front, but to our right. The men instantly grasped their loaded guns, while I, by Lieutenant-Colonel Dunn's order, rode to the front, along the lane, to ascertain the cause of the firing, and, the force coming down on us emerging from behind the thicket, I saw a heavy column moving rapidly down on the Thirty-fourth Illinois, firing as they advanced, and opposed bravely and vigorously by the pickets and skirmishers. Riding farther down the lane, to obtain a view of the open country beyond the thicket, I saw a column of like proportions moving down on the Twenty-ninth Indiana. I galloped back to the regiment with this information, and found that Lieutenant-Colonel Dunn, anticipating, had thrown forward another large company (C) to support the pickets and skirmish among the cedars. This company, ably and gallantly led by Lieut. S. O. Gregory, pushed forward through the entangled mass until within a few yards of the rebels, and only fell back when overpowered, leaving some of his men killed and wounded. Situated as our regiment was, we dare not fire lest we kill our own men, whom we could not see, from which circumstance we were obliged to receive the storm of bullets without a response; and the resistance of our skirmishers under Lieutenants Gregory, Hess, and Macomber was so obstinate that the rebel column had advanced within 20 yards of our line before they received a shot from us.

Our first fire, delivered lying down, partially checked the advance, and enabled the men to load and fire four or five times; but while engaged in front, the column which pressed on the Thirty-fourth Illinois and the battery had moved so far forward as to uncover our line, giving them the opportunity to deliver a raking fire upon us. The troops on our right had fallen back, and Lieutenant-Colonel Dunn considered that the peril of his situation demanded a retreat. We fell back about 80 rods, and formed behind a corn-field fence, every man loading and firing in retreat, through which field the rebels were pushing vigorously; but as no other troops appeared ready to sustain the shock, the regiment was moved some rods farther to a piece of woods, where we took our position in line of battle.

The Thirtieth Indiana now made its appearance from a corn-field in front and to our left, and, moving still farther to the left, took position behind a fence facing the advancing enemy, who had not yet emerged from the woods at that point. To gain a position beside the Thirtieth Indiana, Lieutenant-Colonel Dunn moved by the flank, under cover of the woods, until directly in its rear, but 40 rods distant, when a section of Simonson's battery came up and unlimbered directly in our front.

The rebel infantry now poured into and through the corn-field, meeting with obstinate resistance from the Thirtieth Indiana and Seventy-ninth Illinois, and the artillery, which the Twenty-ninth now supported. Here we lost Capt. Frank Stebbins, Company G, who was struck by a 12-pound ball in the thigh, causing his death very soon. He had bravely led his men, and by his own conduct inspired them with courage and daring.

Up to this time we had the discreet and tried leadership of Lieutenant-Colonel Dunn, and the valuable assistance of Captain Jenkins, acting field officer; but the former got separated and cut off from the regiment, and the latter, going a short distance to the rear for ambulances to carry off our wounded, of whom we had a great number, was also cut off from us. We did not see Lieutenant-Colonel Dunn again, nor Captain Jenkins until the afternoon; but both, we heard, were busy rallying the runaways and stragglers at the pike and railroad, until the former was taken prisoner, and the latter had turned over his men to their respective regiments.

The artillery limbered up, moved to the rear, passing General Davis' division hospital, which we followed until we reached the wood near the hospital, where we found the Seventy-seventh Pennsylvania, under Captain Rose, in line of battle. I at once formed the Twenty-ninth on its right to await the rebel onset. All seemed pushing to the rear, and, finding our shattered forces unsupported, we again moved in perfect order still farther toward the pike, and again formed our line, having the Ninety-third Ohio on the right, and, I believe, a Kentucky regiment on the left. The artillery did not halt here, and before any enemy appeared in front we found our small force flanked on the right by rebel infantry and cavalry, and on the left by an unknown force.

Again we moved leisurely back to a point designated by General Johnson as one suitable to make a stand. This was on the elevated ground west of the pike, on the east side of which we saw a large force of Federal troops congregated. Colonel Dodge, Thirtieth Indiana, now commanding our brigade, placed us in position in a thicket, our left resting on the section of artillery planted on the most elevated point, and supported on the right by the Seventy-seventh Pennsylvania, its right resting on the woods.

Sharp cannonading ensued; but a few minutes' hot work satisfied our artillerists that they could not contend with two batteries and hold their position. They retired to the pike. Colonel Dodge now directed us along the woods to the road, where we again formed our line. The yells of the rebels coming through the cedar woods became plainer and plainer. The balls rained among us. When within range and in sight, the order to advance was given by Colonel Dodge. With a yell, the line rushed forward, determined to stop the sweeping tide or die. This very unexpected attack on the victorious column entirely changed the aspect of affairs. For the first time that day it was checked. It tried to withstand the withering fire, but soon gave way; at first slowly, but, as our line rushed on, the retreat became a rout. We still pushed on rapidly, few in numbers, but determined, with orders not to waste ammunition, and followed the running horde until every cartridge was expended, when Colonel Dodge, after great exertions, got other troops to take our places. We fell back to the railroad for ammunition, when intelligence was brought that our rear, in the vicinity of the hospitals and train, was threatened by cavalry.

To repel this attack we were marched to a point near the hospitals, where we stood in line half an hour; but no enemy appearing, we again moved to the railroad. After this our force changed its position, as the heavy fire indicated a bloody contest, but we were not again under fire. At night we bivouacked on the pike.

Morning brought with it signs of a renewal of yesterday's fight, and we were placed in position on the edge of the cedar grove, nearest the enemy's line, where the men at once went to work securing their position with breastworks and abatis. The Twenty-ninth had no share in any of the ensuing contests, and was entirely occupied on picket duty, and standing to arms on every alarm to resist any attack on our line.

Volunteers were called for to drive the enemy's skirmishers into the woods and burn some log-houses, in which their sharpshooters found shelter and excellent positions to annoy us. Among the number were several of the Twenty-ninth Indiana, one of whom was killed.

Nothing further of importance occurred, unless I mention the fatigue duty performed by details from this regiment, which succeeded in finding and burying our dead and all our wounded, except those who fell into the enemy's hands.

I cannot close without paying a tribute of praise, well merited and proudly given, to the officers and men of my command, who, Spartan-like, rallied at every call around our glorious old flag, and who would not desert it when all around looked dark and hope had almost fled. Allow me to mention, with feelings of extreme gratification, the names of those who nobly did their duty:

First, Adjutant Coffin, who, exposed more than any other, carrying orders to different parts of the line, never once quailed before the storm. He is an excellent officer, fearless, prompt, and deserving of the highest praise.

Captains Stebbins, Jenkins, and McCaslin Moore. First Lieutenants Melendy, who, though wounded, would not leave until trampled by cavalry; N. P. Dunn, who stuck to the flag, severely wounded, until forced by his companions to retire to a hospital; A. Dunlap, J. E. Houghton, G. W. Maloon, T. J. Henderson, and Hess; also Second Lieuts. S.

O. Gregory, commanding Company C, and Hess, commanding Company B, directed the skirmishers; Irenus McGowan, C. P. Butler, William H. H. McDonald, John Cutler, Macomber, and O. C. Sabin.

While the storm raged without, Surgeon Keen and Rev. Mr. Shaw, chaplain, were busy dressing wounds and doing all they could to alleviate the sufferings of our wounded. Assistant Surgeon Griffith, hospital steward, and corps were elsewhere engaged, but all were busy with their duties. I would not pass over the names of the non-commissioned officers, who, with very few exceptions, were heroes in the fight, giving a noble example to the men, and assisting very materially in maintaining order and discipline; but this report is already too long, and I close.

Accompanying this is a list of casualties.*

Respectfully, your obedient servant,

J. P. COLLINS,
Major, Commanding Twenty-ninth Indiana Volunteers.

Capt. D. C. WAGNER,
   A. A. A. G., 2d Brig., 2d Div., Right Wing, 14th Army Corps.

No. 43.

Report of Lieut. Col. Orrin D. Hurd, Thirtieth Indiana Infantry.

HEADQUARTERS THIRTIETH INDIANA VOLUNTEERS,
Camp near Murfreesborough, Tenn., January 7, 1863.

SIR: In accordance with circular dated January 7, issued from Headquarters Second Division, requiring a minute statement from regimental commanders of the operations of their respective regiments, including casualties, I have the honor to report that on Friday, December 26, 1862, this regiment, under command of Col. J. B. Dodge, left camp, near Nashville, Tenn., marched half a mile south of Nolensville, where we encamped for the night.

Next morning, December 27, the Second Brigade being in advance, we left camp at sunrise, and moved in the same direction on the turnpike as day previous. After advancing 1½ miles we were ordered into line of battle to support Captain Edgarton's battery, in which manner we moved 3 or 4 miles, and until dark, when we were ordered out on outpost picket.

On the next day, December 28, after being relieved from picket, we remained in camp without any actual service.

On December 29, we moved back toward Nashville 2 miles and took a cross-road leading toward Murfreesborough, and, after moving 6 miles, encamped for the night.

On December 30, we moved toward Murfreesborough 3 miles, when we were ordered off to the right, and, after throwing forward two companies each from the right and left flanks as skirmishers, moved forward 1 mile in line of battle, and bivouacked for the night in a cedar thicket.

On the morning of December 31, the enemy moved upon us in force about daylight, driving in our pickets, making it necessary for us to fall back or move out by the flank to the right; the latter movement was made with the loss of 1 man, slightly, and 1 mortally, wounded, except upon the picket line, which, being doubled during the night by two additional companies, to insure vigilance and safety, suffered severely upon being driven in.

---

* Embodied in revised statement, p. 208.

The movement by the flank was a fortunate one for us, for had we remained any longer in that position we would have been cut to pieces or taken prisoners by the enemy, who were in great force on our front. After moving to the right and rear about half a mile, we formed a line of battle in a meadow behind a fence, where we were joined by the remnants of the four companies which were on picket the night before. After sending out two companies as skirmishers across a field to a fence directly in our front, we moved up to the same place, and the action commenced.

General Kirk having been wounded early in the morning, and Colonel Dodge, of this regiment, having taken command of the Second Brigade, the command of this regiment fell upon the undersigned.

After the regiment upon our left and we had sustained the enemy's fire for some time, the Seventy-ninth Illinois Volunteers advanced to our immediate right and supported us gallantly; but being outflanked by a superior force of the enemy, and exposed to a heavy cross-fire, they fell back, and we were obliged to do the same, having no support whatever, and having suffered heavy loss, as hereinafter stated. In retiring, the men became very much scattered, but were mostly collected again, and then we were ordered to the front, on the right of the Murfreesborough turnpike, 3 miles from the town.

January 1, after erecting breastworks we remained behind them, without any further active service, except skirmishing on picket line.

January 2, the same routine of duty as the day previous, except in the evening, when the left wing was sent out with parts of other regiments of this brigade as skirmishers to feel the position of the enemy; but after receiving a severe fire, and supposing the enemy to be in force, we returned their fire briskly for some time and then retired to the breastwork.

January 3, same routine of picket duty as the day previous. It is unnecessary for me to particularize the services of any officer or man, for both officers and men performed their duties well and gallantly.

I have also a statement of the killed, wounded, and missing to submit, as follows:

Killed 30
Wounded 108
Missing and prisoners 70

Number in battle:
    Commissioned officers 24
    Enlisted men 463

All of which is respectfully submitted.

O. D. HURD,
Lieutenant-Colonel, Commanding Regiment.

Capt. D. C. WAGNER,
    A. A. A. G., 2d Brig., 2d Div., Right Wing, 14th Army Corps.

No. 44.

Report of Capt. Thomas E. Rose, Seventy-seventh Pennsylvania Infantry.

HDQRS. SEVENTY-SEVENTH REGT. PENNSYLVANIA VOLS.,
    In Camp near Murfreesborough, January 8, 1863.

SIR: I have the honor to make the following report of the Seventy-seventh Regiment Pennsylvania Volunteers, from the time of leaving

camp, near Mill Creek, Tenn., December 26, 1862, to January 3, 1863, viz:

We broke up our camp, near Mill Creek, December 26; sent our wagon train to Nashville, and took up our line of march in the direction of Shelbyville, on the Nolensville turnpike, and encamped in the evening a short distance beyond Nolensville.

December 27, we continued our march in the same direction and on the same road. At 8 a. m. we encountered the enemy within 2 miles of Triune. We were immediately placed in position with the balance of our brigade on the left of the road. Our front line was composed of the Twenty-ninth Indiana Volunteers on the left, the Thirty-fourth Illinois Volunteers on the right, and the Thirtieth Indiana Volunteers in the center. Our regiment and the Seventy-ninth Regiment Illinois Volunteers were held in reserve, but advanced with the brigade, our regiment covering the Twenty-ninth Indiana Volunteers. Skirmishers were thrown forward by each of the three first-named regiments, as also were two companies of the Seventy-seventh Regiment Pennsylvania Volunteers, which occupied the extreme left of the line. In this manner we advanced toward Triune, driving the enemy from his position, and took possession of the town, the enemy retreating toward Shelbyville. We encamped about 1 mile beyond Triune, near the turnpike.

December 28, we remained in camp, where we stopped the evening before.

December 29, we retraced our march on the same road for 2 miles, and turned off on a dirt road running in an easterly course into the Salem turnpike, at the junction of which two roads we, silently and without fires, encamped for the night.

December 30, we marched toward Murfreesborough, on the Salem turnpike, for about 3 miles, when we were thrown into column, by division, into the woods on the right of the road, with the balance of our brigade and division. At this time heavy skirmishing was going on on our left and in front. We advanced for a short distance, when our regiment and the Thirtieth Regiment Indiana Volunteers were ordered to change front to the right, deploy column, and throw out skirmishers. We then advanced, moving toward the right of the general line of battle for about a quarter of a mile. We then changed front to the left, and occupied a dense cedar grove. The position of our regiment was now on the right of the Twenty-second Regiment Indiana Volunteers, of General Davis' division. It was here that we received a heavy fire from a rebel battery that was stationed to the right and in front of us in an open field by the edge of a woods, at a distance of 500 yards. After a sharp skirmish it was silenced, when we threw out our pickets and remained for the night. Our position was now on the left of our brigade and on the right of Davis' division.

December 31, we were under arms at 4 a. m., and at daylight we discovered the enemy in large force within 60 yards of our pickets, who immediately commenced firing, when the enemy advanced to a furious attack. As the pickets retired, our regiment advanced to meet the enemy, and resisted their attack with desperate valor, repulsing the forces immediately in front, with great slaughter, and compelling them to retire across the brook, where we first found them posted, into a cornfield beyond. This was the first attack that was made on our lines; but almost at the same time the enemy's columns on our left, which were directed on those regiments on our right, pressed furiously onward, bearing down everything before them. Those regiments on our right fell back after a short but desperate resistance, as was shown by the great mortality on both sides. Soon after this, the regiment on our left changed position to our rear, leaving our regiment completely isolated and battling against great odds, with the danger of being surrounded. We were ordered to retire for about 150 yards, and then march to the right, in order, if possible, to reattach ourselves to the balance of our brigade, which had been driven from its first position. While doing this we fell in with a portion of General Davis' division, and were advised that we had better co-operate with that division for the present, as our brigade had by this time retired so far that it would consume much valuable time in finding it that could be used at this particular juncture to great advantage by re-enforcing one of his (Davis') brigades. We posted ourselves on the right of Davis' division, in front of which was a rebel battery, at a distance of about 400 yards. A little to the right and in front of this was Edgarton's battery, which had been previously captured by the rebels in the onset, and was still in their possession.

It was here that our regiment charged alone, recapturing Edgarton's battery, and up to the guns of the rebel battery, through a hurricane of grape and canister, until we were confronted by several thousand of the rebel infantry, when, as we were unsupported, we were obliged to retire to the line from which we started on the charge, leaving our much-loved battery in the hands of the rebels, as we had no means of moving it off. Yet we were repaid for this desperate charge as much as for any we made during the day in damaging the enemy and holding him in check.

We retired in good order, and halted and formed in our previous position, on the right of Davis' division. Here Colonel Housum fell. The battle was here hotly contested for some time, when our forces began to give way, fiercely pursued by the enemy, who came near taking a battery of ours at this place.

As soon as the battery was safely off, we retired to the fence, on the opposite side of the field, where we stood alone for some time contending with the rebels, until they commenced scaling the fence on our right and left, when we retired to the woods, and again made a stand. We thus continued for some time, taking advantage of everything that came in our way, moving slowly, and our line never broke once throughout the day; but we fought every time we could find a line to rest on, or wherever we could gain a position in which we could for a minute successfully make a stand.

When we came near the Nashville and Murfreesborough turnpike we fell in with a portion of the Twenty-ninth Indiana Volunteers, under the gallant Major Collins; also a portion of the Thirtieth Indiana Volunteers. These, with our regiment, were now joined together as the remnant of the old Fifth Brigade, under Colonel Dodge, as brigade commander. We were posted on the edge of the woods by General Johnson, on the right of General Van Cleve's division, which had just come up. The rebels were now coming on with tenfold more impetuosity, and our men were ordered to lie down quietly behind a fence, which partly protected us. We waited here until the rebels were within a short distance, when we up and delivered our fire with such great effect that the rebels began to give way.

We now pitched into them with whoop and yell, all the time delivering a most destructive fire, and soon the whole rebel column was in full retreat. We drove them half a mile, when our ammunition gave out and we were relieved, when we retired to the railroad to obtain a fresh supply. This was the first check of importance that the rebels received, as it saved our ammunition train and secured for our forces an important position. From the break of day until 12 m. our regiment was under constant fire, and terribly our ranks were thinned. At night our regiment went on picket.

January 1, 1863, we remained under arms on the crest of the hill, where we ended our final charge on the 31st ultimo.

At 4 p. m. we received a heavy fire from a rebel battery, which was soon silenced.

January 2, remained in the same position as on the 1st. A heavy battle was fought on our left, in which we took no part. In the evening we went on picket. A heavy skirmish took place immediately in front of our line.

January 3, still remained under arms in our old position. At night, in the midst of the rain, the last final struggle was made, in which we took no part.

During this great battle our little regiment did no discredit to the old Keystone State. Officers and men stood up and did their duty nobly. Among those noted for conspicuous valor I must mention Adjt. S. T. Davis, who rendered me invaluable assistance throughout the battle; also Capt. F. S. Pyfer, Company K; Capt. William A. Robinson, Company E; Capt. A. Phillips, Company G, and Capt. J. J. Lawson, Company C, all of whom cheered and encouraged their men throughout the battle with a coolness which belongs to none but veteran officers. That our line never broke shows that our men fought like veterans.

We went into action with 288 men. We lost, in killed, 5, including Lieutenant-Colonel Housum; in wounded, 29, including 1 commissioned officer; missing, 29, including 2 commissioned officers. Total, 63. Of those missing the greater part are either killed or taken prisoners.

I must not forget to mention the valuable services and noble conduct of Dr. Downey, the assistant surgeon of our regiment. He remained with us throughout the battle, and displayed the most indomitable energy and courage in attending to our wounded, and in superintending the whole medical department, which came within his sphere.

I regret to say that, notwithstanding the great valor displayed by our regiment as a body, there were some miserable cowards who skulked away during the excitement of the battle, and left their comrades to perform their duty. I have carefully obtained their names and rank, however, and shall forward them without delay.

I have the honor to be, most respectfully, your obedient servant,

TOM. ELLWOOD ROSE,
Captain, Comdg. Seventy-seventh Pennsylvania Volunteers.

Capt. D. C. WAGNER,
Acting Assistant Adjutant-General, Second Brigade.

No. 45.

Report of Col. Philemon P. Baldwin, Sixth Indiana Infantry, commanding Third Brigade.

HEADQUARTERS THIRD BRIG., SECOND DIV., RIGHT WING,
In Camp near Murfreesborough, Tenn., January 8, 1863.

I have the honor to submit a report of the operations of this brigade from the time of its leaving camp, December 26, until Saturday, January 3.

This brigade moved with the division, and on the 27th was engaged in the skirmishing about Triune. I deployed the First Ohio and the Sixth Indiana on the right of the road, these regiments being supported by the Ninety-third Ohio and Louisville Legion, the battery taking post on the road, and later in the day being posted near the right of my line. We drove the enemy and bivouacked beyond Triune.

This brigade remained at Triune to cover the extreme right, in obedience to your order, and rejoined the division, on the 30th, in the woods to the right of Wilkinson's pike, about 3 miles from Murfreesborough.

At 2 o'clock this brigade moved off 2 miles to the right, to support a cavalry reconnaissance, Colonel Anderson's regiment being sent forward to support the cavalry, while the remainder of the brigade was held in reserve at a point on the Salem pike.

The brigade returned to the woods, near the headquarters of the division, after dark, and bivouacked there.

At daybreak next morning I was informed by stragglers, who were running across the open field in my front, of the attack on Generals Willich's and Kirk's brigades.

I immediately ordered the brigade under arms, and proceeded to form line of battle in the edge of timber facing the large open fields over which I knew the enemy must come to attack me.

I deployed the Louisville Legion on the right, and was proceeding to post the First Ohio in the center, and the Sixth Indiana on the left, holding the Ninety-third Ohio in reserve, to protect either flank, when you ordered me to move the First Ohio across the open field and post it at the fence. The Sixth Indiana was moved forward and posted in the edge of a skirt of timber to the left of the First Ohio, the Thirtieth Indiana and Seventy-ninth Illinois being posted on the right; a section of the Fifth Indiana Battery was posted between the First Ohio and Sixth Indiana. The Louisville Legion moved to within supporting distance of the First Ohio, and the Ninety-third Ohio held in reserve in the woods near the edge of the field.

These dispositions were scarcely made when the enemy, in immense masses, appeared in my front at short range, their left extending far beyond the extreme right of my line. My infantry and artillery poured a destructive fire into their dense masses, checking them in front, but their left continued to advance against my right. Here four pieces that Captain Simonson had posted near the woods, in rear of my first line, poured in a terrible fire; but the enemy came in such overwhelming numbers that, after half an hour's stubborn resistance, my line was compelled to retire, not, however, until the enemy had flanked my right and were pouring in an enfilading fire. Had my line stood a moment longer it would have been entirely surrounded and captured. Falling back to the edge of the woods, I endeavored to make a stand. I moved the Ninety-third Ohio up to the left of the Louisville Legion, but my line was again forced back, almost before I had got the Ninety-third in position. Ordering Colonel Anderson to retire in good order, I succeeded, after making several short stands in the woods, in forming the brigade near the railroad. Under your orders I took position on the right of the Nashville pike, together with the rest of the division, and held it during the succeeding skirmishes, throwing up a breastwork of logs, rails, &c.

Nothing occurred here but unimportant skirmishing, sometimes quite warm, but always resulting in our driving the enemy. A house about 300 yards from our line was held by the enemy's skirmishers, who annoyed us exceedingly by their fire. It was captured and burned by two companies of the Louisville Legion, after a severe fight.

Too great praise cannot be awarded to the regiments of this brigade and Simonson's battery for the coolness and steadiness with which they resisted the attacks of an overwhelming force, and the readiness with which they rallied and formed again when the enemy had broken their lines. The Louisville Legion gallantly drew off by hand a disabled gun, belonging to Cotter's battery.

It may be proper for me to state here, with reference to the line formed in the woods after leaving the open field, that I am informed by reliable officers that the line could have been held had not the right been ordered to fall back by some general not known to the writer.

I beg leave to refer you to the accompanying reports of regimental and battery commanders for details.

Col. Charles Anderson, commanding Ninety-third Ohio; Lieut. Col. W. W. Berry, commanding Louisville Legion; Lieut. Col. H. Tripp, commanding Sixth Indiana; Maj. J. A. Stafford, commanding First Ohio, and Capt. P. Simonson, commanding Fifth Indiana Battery, displayed the greatest coolness, courage, and skill in the management of their respective commands.

Colonel Anderson and Lieutenant-Colonel Berry were wounded early in the engagement of Wednesday, but refused to leave the field.

Captain Simonson's battery did good service, and was handled bravely and skillfully. Two pieces, under command of Lieutenant Rankin, did effective service in my first line, he continuing to work his guns after being severely wounded. I regret to report the loss of two pieces of the battery, owing to the horses all being killed and the gunners disabled.

I am indebted to Lieut. G. H. Burns, acting assistant adjutant-general, for his valuable assistance, and also to Lieutenant Patterson, First Ohio, and Adjt. J. J. Siddall, for their coolness and readiness in transmitting orders to the hottest parts of the field.

Dr. E. S. Swain, the brigade surgeon, remained with the wounded after the enemy drove us back, and rendered every assistance in his power.

I append a list of killed, wounded, and missing, amounting to 56 killed, 242 wounded, and 137 missing.*

I have the honor to be, very respectfully, your obedient servant,

P. P. BALDWIN,
Colonel, Commanding Third Brigade.

Brig. Gen. R. W. JOHNSON,
Commanding Second Division.

No. 46.

Report of Lieut. Col. Hagerman Tripp, Sixth Indiana Infantry.

HEADQUARTERS SIXTH INDIANA VOLUNTEERS,
In Camp near Murfreesborough, Tenn., January 4, 1863.

SIR: I have the honor to report the part taken by my regiment in the skirmish fight on the 27th; also in the battle of the 31st ultimo.

On the morning of the 27th, while on the march, some 2½ miles north of the village of Triune, on the Nolensville pike, we encountered the enemy near the intersection of the Bole Jack road and pike. I immediately deployed in line of battle on the right of the road, my left rest-

---

* But see revised statement, p. 209.

ing on the road, being supported on my right by the First Ohio and the Ninety-third Ohio in reserve. I at once advanced, as skirmishers, Company A, Captain Kavanaugh, and Company B, Lieutenant McGannon commanding, when a running fight commenced, Captain Simonson, of the Fifth Indiana Artillery, shelling the enemy from the hill tops, being energetically replied to by the enemy's guns. The fight continued until we arrived at Triune, where the rebels made a stand, when we charged double-quick their battery, and drove them from the field. We pursued them some 2 miles, they contesting each rod of ground, when they again made a stand. We again drove them from their position, in precipitate retreat. Night coming on put an end to our day's labor.

I cannot speak in too high terms of commendation of the gallantry of the officers and men of my command during the entire day. When we consider that for eight hours they fought under the hardest rain of the season and mud to the ankles, pressing forward to the mark of their high calling with the utmost cheerfulness, their endurance was worthy the highest commendation.

On the 30th we marched from Triune to the field which was to be the scene of the battle of Murfreesborough, a distance of 16 miles, where we arrived at 5 p. m., when we were at once sent some 2½ miles to the right of the right wing of the army. Being informed that the enemy were in too large force to enable us to maintain our position, we returned at 9 o'clock to the position first taken.

At 7 a. m. on the 31st I was posted in line of battle behind a rail fence, my right resting on an open field; a stalk-field in front, extending far to my left; a wood in rear, and also extending to my left. On my right, some 75 yards to the front, was a section of Simonson's Fifth Indiana Battery. To the right of it lay the First Ohio, behind a fence; also, on my right, some 75 yards to rear, lay the Louisville Legion, also securely posted behind a fence, the whole supported by the Ninety-third Ohio, Colonel Anderson. I promptly deployed as skirmishers the first platoons of Company A, Captain Kavanaugh, and Company B, Lieutenant McGannon commanding. Some half an hour after, my skirmishers returned, being driven in by the enemy, their skirmishers in close pursuit. A few shots from my line served to hold them in check, when their main line advanced, deployed column after column, making some four or five lines approaching our front. When within 100 yards I ordered my men to fire, and they went at it with a right good will, it having been difficult to restrain them so long. Our fire caused the enemy to waver, and checked their advance. They were not idle, but threw upon us their leaden hail, which caused my men to hug closer their frail defense, delivering their fire with the steadiness of veterans. At this time the artillery ceased on my right, and in a few minutes the First Ohio gave way and fell back on the Louisville Legion, which in turn also fell back before an overwhelming force of the enemy, which was passing my right flank in line of battle, their right passing within 50 yards of the right of my regiment, which produced some unsteadiness in one or two companies on my right, they getting out of place for the purpose of firing into the enemy's flank as they passed. I promptly rallied them to the fence. In the mean time the line in front had advanced to within 25 yards of my line. A rebel regiment had crossed the fence on my left. Those advancing on the First Ohio and Louisville Legion, on my right, were already some 100 yards to my rear, and, being closely pressed in front, I gave the order to " Fall back slowly and in good order," which was executed at a double-quick.

At one time I had some wavering in ranks in consequence of some unauthorized person giving an order to fall back to the men instead of to me, but I rallied them without difficulty and continued the fight. I fell back to a point some 200 yards east of the Nolensville pike, when I formed the regiment in line, faced about, intending to renew the fight; but seeing General McCook, reported to him for orders. He ordered me to "march my regiment to the rear," which I did, hauling up on the Nashville pike, thence to the railroad, when I reported to you.

On the 1st, 2d, and 3d instant my command bore a full share of the skirmish fighting on our part of the line. The particulars need not be mentioned here.

I would do violence to my own feelings did I close this report without mentioning the good conduct and soldierly bearing of the men of my command. To the company officers I am greatly indebted for the steadiness of their several companies. I would be glad to name some of them, but where all have so ably done their duty it would be invidious to do so. I must, however, acknowledge the able, prompt, and energetic assistance I received from Maj. C. D. Campbell throughout the engagement.*

I am, sir, very respectfully, your obedient servant,

H. TRIPP,
Lieutenant-Colonel Sixth Indiana Volunteers.

Col. P. P. BALDWIN,
  Commanding Third Brigade.

No. 47.

Report of Lieut. Col. William W. Berry, Fifth Kentucky Infantry.

HEADQUARTERS LOUISVILLE LEGION,
FIFTH REGIMENT KENTUCKY VOLUNTEER INFANTRY,
In Camp, January 8, 1863.

SIR: Having been called upon to furnish a report of the operations of my command from December 26, 1862, to January 4, 1863, inclusive, I have the honor to submit the following:

On the morning of December 26, 1862, being on picket duty with my regiment, I received orders to join the column marching southward on the Nolensville road. We reached Nolensville at 3 o'clock the next morning.

At daylight of the 27th I was ordered forward, and marching 3 miles we found the enemy, with some artillery, prepared to obstruct our march. We were thrown out on the right of the road, and immediately pushed at them, but they fell back to a new position; and this was repeated time and again throughout the day, until we reached a point 1 mile south of Triune. We traversed in line of battle this day some 4 or 5 miles of country, made up of corn and cotton fields, thickets, swamps, and woods. I sustained no loss in this skirmish.

Sunday morning, December 28, I was ordered to support General Willich in a reconnaissance. No enemy was found, and we returned to camp.

On Monday, General McCook's command having moved off toward Murfreesborough, distant some 15 miles, we were left near Triune to prevent the enemy interrupting the march of the main column.

Here we remained till the morning of the 30th, when we marched off

---

* List of casualties, here omitted, embodied in revised statement. p. 208.

toward Murfreesborough and rejoined the division, which we found moving into position beyond Wilkinson's Cross-Roads.

In a short time orders came for us to support a cavalry reconnaissance of the country lying to the right of our front. No enemy was found in this direction, and we returned to the division. We were then placed in position as a reserve for the other two brigades of General Johnson's command, occupying the extreme right of the army.

Early the next morning I received orders to form a line of battle 150 paces in rear of the First Regiment Ohio Volunteers; this done, the command "forward" was given. In this advance, Capt. A. H. Speed, of Company C, was struck in the abdomen by a spent ball and severely injured; but, like a true soldier, he retained the command of his company until late in the evening, when he was ordered to the hospital.

When the First Ohio reached a fence on the crest of a hill, it became hotly engaged. At the same time there was rapid firing from the Sixth Indiana, on the left, and also from some regiment on the right of the First Ohio. A section of Simonson's battery had been moved to the front, to the left and abreast of the First Ohio. A battery of the enemy immediately opened upon it, and their shells killed and wounded many of my men. Presently I observed the regiment to the right of the First Ohio in full retreat, and in a few minutes I saw the First Ohio moving to the rear.

I could see no enemy, on account of the intervening ridge, and supposing that the First Ohio had exhausted their ammunition, I instantly prepared to take its place; but just before it reached my lines, to my utter amazement, a mass of the enemy appeared, moving obliquely upon my right flank. A change of front was imperative. While executing this movement, refusing my right to the enemy, the First Ohio passed through the right of my regiment and threw into great confusion my four right companies. Their officers promptly arrested this, and I here take occasion to thank Capt. John Lucas, commanding Company F, First Lieuts. Thomas Foreman, commanding Company A, and Joseph E. Miller, commanding Company D, and Second Lieut. A. Sidney Smith, commanding Company I, for their steadiness at this trying moment.

In the mean time, my left getting into position, poured its fire into the steadily advancing columns of the enemy; but the troops to my left were giving way, and the enemy, getting a battery into position, almost enfiladed me. The right of the division was completely crushed in, and I had no connection, consequently no protection, here. It was soon manifest that I must fall back or be isolated.

A new position was taken some 200 paces in rear of our first, and here I believe we could have successfully resisted the enemy, but some general, I do not know who, ordered the entire line to fall back still farther, and those who like rapid movements would have been more than satisfied with the celerity with which some of the floating fragments of regiments obeyed him.

Pending this movement my attention was called by Colonel Baldwin to a piece of artillery abandoned by those whose business it was to look after it. A full battery of the enemy was playing on it at the time. I immediately yoked the Legion to it, and, with Huston and Thomasson as the wheel-horses, it was dragged to the railroad, where the new line was forming. I was shortly ordered to move by the flank farther up the railroad, where a position was taken that was not assailed on this day.

I had gone into the fight with 320 muskets, a portion of my command being on detached service; 19 men were killed, including Captain Ferguson, of Company I, who was one of our best officers; 80 were wounded.

Among the latter were 7 commissioned officers, viz: Lieut. Col. W. W. Berry, shot through the wrist; Maj. John L. Treanor, wounded by a shell in the thigh; Capt. A. H. Speed, wounded in the abdomen; Capt. L. P. Lovett, slightly, in the thigh; First Lieut. Frank Dissell, mortally; First Lieut John D. Sheppard, seriously, through the left lung, and First Lieut. William H. Powell, slightly, in the shoulder, and 26 missing. Some of these, I am mortified to say, ran away at the first fire. Their names shall be duly reported.

During the engagement my color-bearer was shot, and down went the flag, but like lightning it gleamed aloft again in the hands of three men, struggling who should have it. Their names are John B. Scheible, Company E; Charles Fleckhammer, jr., Company H, and Sergt. John Baker, Company D. The latter bore it throughout the remainder of the day. Private William Shumaker, of Company G, was badly shot through the thigh, but persisted in fighting with the regiment till he was forced to the rear by order of his captain. I commend him for his devotion. Sergeant-Major Willett deported himself most bravely, and deserves promotion. Adjutant Johnstone rendered me every assistance in his power, and I especially thank him.

On the morning of January 1, I received orders to move farther to the front. There was no general advance of our lines, though constant skirmishing through the day. Captain Thomasson had command of the skirmish line, and by his adroitness was mainly instrumental in the capture of 95 prisoners. The enemy held a dense wood about 300 yards in front of us, in the edge of which were some cabins occupied by sharpshooters. I proposed to push forward my skirmishers and dislodge them, provided those on my right and left were simultaneously advanced. This, though ordered, was not done, and I did not deem it safe to expose my flank; but toward evening the fire of these riflemen became so annoying that I was determined, at any cost, to stop it. I ordered Captains Hurley and Lindenfelser to move with their companies directly upon the houses and burn them. Across the open fields they dashed, the enemy having every advantage in point of shelter. Captain Huston was then ordered to their support, and the place was literally carried by assault, the houses burned, and 5 of the enemy left dead upon the spot. This was the last we heard of the sharpshooters. The daring displayed by officers and men in this affair deserves especial consideration. But one man was hurt—Corporal Moneypenny, shot through the leg.

The skirmishing in which my command took part on the days succeeding this was of an uneventful character, and I forego the details.

Respectfully, your obedient servant,

WM. W. BERRY,
Lieutenant-Colonel, Commanding.

Capt. WILLIAM MANGAN,
Acting Assistant Adjutant-General, Third Brigade.

No. 48.

Report of Maj. Joab A. Stafford, First Ohio Infantry.

HEADQUARTERS FIRST REGIMENT OHIO VOLUNTEERS,
In Camp, January 5, 1863.

CAPTAIN: I have the honor to report the part taken by my regiment in the recent battles and skirmishes about Murfreesborough.

On the morning of December 27, 1863, when about a mile below

Nolensville, the enemy appeared in our front. I was ordered by you to form a line of battle on the right of the pike, my left resting on the right of the Sixth Indiana, and deploy two companies as skirmishers, and to advance. I did so, deploying Company B, Lieutenant Dornbush commanding, and Company D, Lieutenant Hayward commanding. We had severe skirmishing all day, but drove the enemy before us, and encamped near Triune.

On the morning of December 30 we were ordered to join our division, which had preceded us the day before, within about 4 miles of Murfreesborough. We arrived about 4 o'clock, and, after making a reconnaissance on our right, we fell back and bivouacked for the night in a piece of woods in the rear of our division.

On the morning of the 31st, about 6.30 o'clock, I heard what I thought to be heavy skirmishing on our right. I immediately ordered my command under arms, and marched to and halted on the edge of the woods just to the right of where we bivouacked the night previous. A few moments after, by your orders, I moved forward at a double-quick across a large open field, and formed my line behind a rail fence, on a line with the Sixth Indiana (they occupying a piece of woods to my left), with two pieces of Simonson's battery between us, the Seventy-ninth Illinois and Thirtieth Indiana occupying the right, the Seventy-ninth in reserve.

I ordered Lieutenant Hayward, Company D, to deploy the first platoon of his company as skirmishers. This had hardly been done when the enemy appeared in our front in three distinct lines of battle, followed by columns, closed in mass, several batteries of artillery, and a large amount of cavalry, the left of their lines extending not less than one-fourth of a mile to the right of the Thirtieth Indiana. As soon as they arrived within about 150 yards of my line, I opened fire, which checked their advance for about fifteen minutes. Their line then in front of me seemed to separate, and I saw them marching by the flank to the right and left of us. Immediately after this maneuver, the two regiments on my right gave way, and left my flank entirely unprotected. The enemy's left then changed their front to the right and marched diagonally toward my right. At this moment the Sixth Indiana was forced from their position, the enemy immediately taking possession of the fence they occupied. They then again appeared in my front and opened an enfilading fire on my regiment.

Finding it was impossible to hold my position without being annihilated, I ordered my regiment to fall back, intending to take a position in the rear of the Louisville Legion, which was at that time supporting me. My regiment started back in good order, but coming in contact with the Louisville Legion (Colonel Berry having just ordered a change of front forward on first company, to protect our right), we became entangled with them, as we did also with the Ninety-third Ohio, which you had ordered to our support. I then fell back in some confusion to the woods occupied by me some half an hour previous.

Here I tried to form my line, but again became entangled with a part of the First Brigade. My regiment became scattered, and it was impossible to get them into line until we had fallen back through the woods into a cotton-field and into another piece of woods. Here, by your help and the united efforts of my officers, I succeeded in rallying part of my regiment, and took position on the left of Colonel Berry, who had also succeeded in rallying part of his regiment. Here the enemy was checked and driven back a short distance, but soon rallied and came down in a solid mass, and we were obliged again to retire.

In a short time after, I rallied a portion of my regiment, and meeting Captains Trapp and O'Connell, who had succeeded in doing the same (in all, amounting to about 100 men), I halted and formed a line. Here I was joined by a portion of the Ninety-third Ohio, under the command of Lieutenant Harman. I took command of the whole.

At this moment I received an order from General Johnson to proceed immediately to a certain point, but the guide missed the place, so I took a position on the left of a regiment (I do not know what regiment) which was hotly engaged with the enemy. Here I remained until I was ordered to fall in the rear of General Rousseau's division.

Soon after, Colonel Anderson, of the Ninety-third Ohio, came up and took command, and was ordered to proceed in the direction of the river; that we were needed there. Word soon came that our division was again forming on the left of the railroad running toward Nashville. I immediately proceeded to that point, where I found about 100 more men of my regiment, under command of their respective officers.

By your order, I again moved forward with the balance of our brigade to the support of another brigade, which was hotly contesting the ground we now occupied. After a short and severe fight the enemy were driven off, and with considerable fighting and skirmishing it has been held ever since.

The loss in my regiment is heavy, so far as heard from—8 non-commissioned officers and privates killed; 1 officer and 46 non-commissioned officers and privates wounded, and 81 missing; a partial list of which you have already received.

My officers and men behaved most gallantly, and I do not think there are any soldiers in the world that could have done better under the circumstances. I would most respectfully recommend for your favorable consideration Captains Kuhlman, Company B, acting field officer; Trapp, Company G; O'Connell, Company F; Pomeroy, Company E; Prentiss, Company H; Hooker, Company A, and Snodgrass, Company I; First Lieuts. Henry Dornbush, Company B, commanding, and George L. Hayward, Company D, commanding; Adjt. Samuel W. Davies, and Second Lieutenants Kuhlman, Company B, commanding Company C; R. B. Chappell, commanding Company K; Denny, Company G, and Varian, not yet assigned to any company. They are all justly entitled to the thanks of their superiors for their gallant conduct in the past few days. All have been engaged in the service since the breaking out of the rebellion; have been in several engagements, and proved themselves worthy the confidence reposed in them. A more gallant and braver set of officers never entered a field. I would also mention our surgeons, Drs. Wilson and Barr. They performed their duties faithfully and unflinchingly.

I had forgotten to mention that some time during the day a portion of my regiment, under Lieutenant Dornbush and Adjutant Davies, gallantly repulsed a charge of the enemy's cavalry, and drove them off altogether.

Very respectfully, your obedient servant,

J. A. STAFFORD,
Major First Regiment Ohio Volunteers, Commanding.

Captain BURNS,
Acting Assistant Adjutant-General, Fourth Brigade.

No. 49.

Report of Col. Charles Anderson, Ninety-third Ohio Infantry.

HEADQUARTERS NINETY-THIRD OHIO REGIMENT,
Camp near Murfreesborough, Tenn., January 5, 1863.

SIR : In obedience to your order, I beg leave to submit the following report:

At 1 o'clock on the morning of December 27, the regiment left Mill Creek for Nolensville, at which place we arrived at 4 a. m. We went into camp 1 mile south, on the Nolensville road.

At 7 a. m. took up our line of march. The brigade commenced skirmishing with the enemy about 4 miles south of Nolensville. We were then ordered to file to a field on the left of the Nolensville road, and were supports to the Sixth Indiana Volunteers. We marched in the above order until we arrived at Triune. Here quite a brisk skirmish ensued ; but, as the enemy's cavalry retreated before us on the road to Eagleville, my regiment was not engaged. We went into camp on the farm of —— Perkins at 4 p. m.

On the morning of the 28th, was ordered on picket, to relieve the Seventy-ninth Illinois Volunteers, Colonel Read commanding. Remained until 12 m. of the 29th, when the brigade was moved back a short distance beyond Triune.

Here we encamped until 7 a. m. of the 30th, when we started to join our division, which was encamped 3 miles northwest of Murfreesborough. Arrived at 3 p. m. We were then immediately ordered to report to General Stanley, chief of cavalry. After reporting to General Stanley, Company A, of my regiment, was deployed as skirmishers through a cotton-field and drove in the rebel cavalry.

The regiment then advanced through cotton and corn fields and meadows some 1½ miles, when we were drawn up in line of battle, and marched so nearly one-half mile, when a very large cavalry force was seen drawn up in line of battle. We advanced to a fence and commenced firing at them; but, the range being so great and our loads having been long wetted, our shots did no apparent execution.

We were then ordered to fall back, Stanley's cavalry covering our retreat. The rebel cavalry advanced a short distance, but made no demonstration. We were then ordered to go into the division encampment, at the intersection of the Murfreesborough road and a country road, crossing it about 2 miles from Murfreesborough. This we did ; but, finding that our brigade had been in the mean time ordered to act as reserve of the First and Second Brigades, under advice of General Willich, I ordered up the regiment and marched it into the reserve camp, about 1 mile back and near General Johnson's headquarters, and remained in this camp all night.

Upon the attack by the enemy immediately in our front, a little before 7 a. m. on the 31st, the brigade was ordered out to re enforce our front division lines. The other regiments having been placed in their several positions, the Ninety-third Ohio was ordered by myself to form line of battle upon the left of the Fifth Kentucky, in the rear of which it had marched. But this movement was arrested by an order from Colonel Baldwin, with an order for it to remain in its form of column, and to await further orders. This order was obeyed, and the regiment (with two slight changes in advance as the other regiments marched forward into the open field to the second positions) so remained, awaiting orders.

All this time the Ninety-third Ohio was in the wood of our encampment, parallel to the field in which the First Ohio and Fifth Kentucky were marching and forming their lines, while the Sixth Indiana, in line of battle, occupied the fence at the head of this wood, and between it and the adjacent fields on the south. No further orders were given to the regiment, though twice asked for.

In the retreat, the First Ohio fell back from the second position in line of battle. When that event took place, and while the two regiments in the field were retreating back to their first position, I ordered and began a deployment of my skirmishers across the woods and extending from the left flank of these two regiments to the road on the east. While in the actual process of this movement, the colonel commanding the brigade intercepted it, and ordered the regiment to form in line of battle to the left flank of the two other regiments.

I ordered the skirmishers to rally on the right wing, which had not yet begun its deployment, and the colonel commanding the brigade then gave me orders, in person, to retreat. The regiment being still in line of battle, I ordered it to about-face, and to march in slow time. This order was executed for a little time in some regularity. The enemy poured into the woods and pressed on to our rear. The regiment, like the rest of the retreating troops, of course much increased its speed, so that by the time it passed out of the woods into the cotton-field to the northward the march had degenerated into a run.

At this point, and in the cotton-field, the men of my regiment suffered quite severely. Notwithstanding, however, the number of killed, wounded, and scattered, a small remnant of the Ninety-third Ohio was rallied with those of the division, and it may be from some other divisions, and formed in line of battle in the large woods, containing in all several hundred men.

This line was again faced to the front, and marched a short distance against the enemy, which by this time passed the cotton-field, entered the woods, and were again flanking our right in very great force.

Another retreat having been ordered, this whole body of troops retreated once again, under the support of General Crittenden's wing.

No other event of special interest occurred in the regimental history of this day, except that several of its officers and many of its men, after being separated from the regiment, united themselves to other regiments, and fought gallantly during the subsequent conflict. Several of these men were thereby killed and wounded.

In a temporary absence from my regiment, in order to have two slight wounds looked at and dressed by a surgeon, the remnant of mine, with that of his regiment, was left with Major Stafford, of the First Ohio Volunteer Infantry.

Upon rejoining my regiment, I received orders from Lieutenant-Colonel Michler, aide-de-camp of General Rosecrans, to form on the extreme right of the line of battle. This I did, and then rejoined the colonel commanding and what was left at that time of the brigade.

These little and trivial details seem to make a sufficient record of my regiment's share in these great proceedings. For a fuller statement of the various casualties to my command, I beg leave, respectfully, to refer to previous reports and this accompanying addendum.

Total number killed, as far as heard from, 12; total number wounded, as far as heard from, 45; total number missing up to date, 64.

Very respectfully, your obedient servant,

CHARLES ANDERSON,
Commanding Ninety-third Ohio Volunteer Infantry.

Colonel BALDWIN,
Commanding Third Brigade.

No. 50.

Report of Brig. Gen. Philip H. Sheridan, U. S. Army, commanding Third Division.

HDQRS. THIRD DIV., RIGHT WING, FOURTEENTH A. C.,
Camp on Stone's River, Tenn., January 9, 1863.

MAJOR : In obedience to instructions from headquarters right wing, I have the honor to report the following as the operations of my division from December 26, 1862, to January 6, 1863 :

On December 26, I moved from camp, near Nashville, on the Nolensville pike, in the direction of Nolensville. At the crossing of Mill Creek the enemy's cavalry made some resistance, but were soon routed, 1 lieutenant and 1 private of the enemy being captured.

On approaching Nolensville, I received a message from General Davis, who had arrived at Nolensville, via the Edmondson pike, that the enemy were in considerable force in his front, and requesting me to support him. On the arrival of the head of my division at Nolensville, General Davis advanced upon the enemy's position, about 2 miles south of that place, supported by my division. The enemy had here made a stand in a gap of the mountains; but, after a sharp conflict with General Davis' command, were routed and one piece of artillery captured.

On the next day (27th), I supported General Johnson's division in its advance on Triune, where the enemy were supposed to be in considerable force. The town was taken possession of after a slight resistance, the main portion of their forces having evacuated the place.

On December 28, I encamped at Triune.

On the 29th, I supported General Davis' division, which had the advance from Triune on Murfreesborough, encamping that night at Wilkinson's Cross-Roads, from which point there is a good turnpike to Murfreesborough.

On the next day (the 30th), I took the advance of the right wing on this turnpike toward Murfreesborough, General Stanley, with a regiment of cavalry, having been thrown in advance.

After arriving at a point about 3 miles from Murfreesborough, the enemy's infantry pickets were encountered and driven back, their numbers constantly increasing until I had arrived within about 2¼ miles of Murfreesborough. At this point the resistance was so strong as to require two regiments to drive them. I was here directed by Major-General McCook to form my line of battle and place my artillery in position.

My line was formed on the right of the pike, and obliquely to it ; four regiments to the front, with a second line of four regiments within short supporting distance in the rear, with a reserve of one brigade, in column of regiments, to the rear and opposite the center. General Davis was then ordered to close in and form on my right, the enemy all this time keeping up a heavy artillery and musketry fire upon my skirmishers.

The enemy continued to occupy, with their skirmishers, a heavy belt of timber to the right and front of my line, and across some open fields and near where the left of General Davis' division was intended to rest. General Davis was then directed by Major-General McCook to swing his division, and I was directed to swing my right brigade with it until our continuous line would front nearly due east. This would give us possession of the timber above alluded to, and which was occupied by the enemy's skirmishers in considerable force. This movement was successfully executed, after a stubborn resistance on the part of the enemy, in which they used one battery of artillery. This battery was silenced in a very short time by Bush's and Hescock's batteries, of my division, and two of the enemy's pieces disabled.

At sundown I had taken up my position, my right resting in the timber, my left on the Wilkinson pike, and my reserve brigade, of four regiments, to the rear and opposite the center.

The killed and wounded during the day was 75 men.

General Davis' left was closed in on my right, and his line thrown to the rear, so that it formed nearly a right angle with mine. General Negley's division, of Thomas' corps, was immediately on my left, his right resting on the left-hand side of the Wilkinson pike.

The enemy appeared to be in strong force in a heavy cedar wood across an open valley in my front and parallel to it, the cedar extending the whole length of the valley, the distance across the valley varying from 300 to 400 yards.

At 2 o'clock on the morning of the 31st, General Sill, who had command of my right brigade, reported great activity on the part of the enemy immediately in his front. This being the narrowest point in the valley, I was fearful that an attack might occur at that point. I therefore directed two regiments from the reserves to report to General Sill, who placed them in position in very short supporting distance of his lines.

At 4 o'clock in the morning the division was assembled under arms, and the cannoneers at their pieces. About 7.15 o'clock in the morning the enemy advanced to the attack across an open cotton-field, on Sill's front. This column was opened upon by Bush's battery, of Sill's brigade, which had a direct fire on its front; also by Hescock's and Houghtaling's batteries, which had an oblique fire on its front from a commanding position near the center of my line. The effect of this fire upon the enemy's column was terrible. The enemy, however, continued to advance until they had reached nearly the edge of the timber, when they were opened upon by Sill's infantry, at a range of not over 50 yards. The destruction to the enemy's column, which was closed in mass, being several regiments in depth, was terrible. For a short time they withstood the fire, wavered, then broke and ran, Sill directing his troops to charge, which was gallantly responded to, and the enemy driven back across the valley and behind their intrenchments.

In this charge I had the misfortune to lose General Sill, who was killed. The brigade then fell back in good order and resumed its original lines. The enemy soon rallied and advanced to the attack on my extreme right and in front of Colonel Woodruff, of Davis' division. Here, unfortunately, the brigade of Colonel Woodruff gave way; also one regiment of Sill's brigade, which was in the second line. This regiment fell back some distance into the open field and there rallied, its place being occupied by a third regiment of my reserve.

At this time the enemy, who had made an attack on the extreme right of our wing against Johnson and also on Davis' front, had been successful, and the two divisions on my right were retiring in great confusion, closely followed by the enemy, completely turning my position and exposing my line to a fire from the rear. I hastily withdrew the whole of Sill's brigade and the three regiments sent to support it, at the same time directing Colonel Roberts, of the left brigade, who had changed front and formed in column of regiments, to charge the enemy in the timber from which I had withdrawn those regiments. This was very gallantly done by Colonel Roberts, who captured one piece of the enemy's artillery, which had to be abandoned.

In the mean time I had formed Sill's and Schaefer's brigades on a line at right angles to my first line, and behind the three batteries of artillery, which were placed in a fine position, directing Colonel Roberts to return and form on this new line. I then made an unavailing attempt to form the troops on my right on this line, in front of which there were open fields, through which the enemy was approaching under a heavy fire from Hescock's, Houghtaling's, and Bush's batteries.

After the attempt had proved to be entirely unsuccessful, and my right was again turned, General McCook directed me to advance to the front and form on the right of Negley. This movement was successfully accomplished under a heavy fire of musketry and artillery, every regiment of mine remaining unbroken.

I took position on Negley's right, Roberts' brigade having been placed in position at right angles to Negley's line, facing to the south, the other two brigades being placed to the rear and at right angles with Roberts', and facing the west, covering the rear of Negley's lines. I then directed Houghtaling's battery to take position at the angle of these two lines, Captain Hescock sending one section of his battery, under Lieutenant Taliaferro, and one section of Bush's battery, to the same point. The remaining pieces of Hescock's and Bush's batteries were placed on the right of Negley's line, facing toward Murfreesborough. In this position I was immediately attacked, when one of the bitterest and most sanguinary contests of the day occurred.

General Cheatham's division advanced on Roberts' brigade, and heavy masses of the enemy, with three batteries of artillery, advanced over the open ground which I had occupied in the previous part of the engagement, at the same time the enemy opening from their intrenchments in the direction of Murfreesborough. The contest then became terrible. The enemy made three attacks, and were three times repulsed, the artillery range of the respective batteries being not over 200 yards. In these attacks Roberts' brigade lost its gallant commander, who was killed. There was no sign of faltering with the men, the only cry being for more ammunition, which unfortunately could not be supplied, on account of the discomfiture of the troops on the right of our wing, which allowed the enemy to come in and capture our ammunition train.

Schaefer's brigade being entirely out of ammunition, I directed them to fix bayonets and await the enemy. Roberts' brigade, which was nearly out of ammunition, I directed to fall back, resisting the enemy. Captain Houghtaling, having exhausted all his ammunition, and nearly all the horses in his battery having been killed, attempted, with the assistance of the men, to withdraw his pieces by hand. Lieutenant Taliaferro, commanding the section of Hescock's battery, having been killed and several of his horses shot, his two pieces were brought off by his sergeant, with the assistance of the men. The difficulty of withdrawing the artillery here became very great, the ground being rocky and covered with a dense growth of cedar. Houghtaling's battery had to be abandoned; also two pieces of Bush's battery. The remaining pieces of artillery in the division were brought through the cedars with great difficulty, under a terrible fire from the enemy, on to the open space on the Murfreesborough pike, near the right of General Palmer's division. In coming through the cedars, two regiments of Schaefer's brigade succeeded in obtaining ammunition, and were immediately put in front to resist the enemy, who appeared to be driving in our entire lines.

On arriving at the open space, I was directed by Major-General Rosecrans to take those two regiments and put them into action on the right of Palmer's division, where the enemy were pressing heavily.

The two regiments went in very gallantly, driving the enemy from the cedar timber and some distance to the front. At the same time I put four pieces of Hescock's battery into action near by and on the same front. The other two regiments of Schaefer's brigade, and the Thirty-sixth Illinois, of Sill's brigade, were directed to cross the railroad, where they could obtain ammunition. I then, by direction of Major-General McCook, withdrew the two regiments that had been placed on the right of Palmer's division; also Captain Hescock's pieces, that point having been given up to the enemy in the rearrangement of our lines.

These regiments of Schaefer's brigade, having supplied themselves with ammunition, I put into action, by direction of Major-General Rosecrans, directly to the front and right of General Wood's division, on the left-hand side of the railroad.

The brigade advanced through a clump of timber and took position on the edge of a cotton-field, close upon the enemy's lines, relieving the division of General Wood, which was falling back under heavy pressure from the enemy.

At this point I lost my third and last brigade commander, Col. Frederick Schaefer, who was killed. The brigade, after remaining in this position until after it had expended its ammunition, was withdrawn to the rear of this timber, where it was again supplied and joined by the Thirty-sixth Illinois. I was here directed by General Rosecrans to form a close column of attack and charge the enemy, should they again come down on the open ground.

The remaining portion of the evening this gallant brigade remained in close column of regiments and under the fire of the enemy's batteries, which killed about 20 of the men by round shot. In the mean time Colonel Roberts' brigade, which had come out of the cedars unbroken, was put into action by General McCook at a point a short distance to the rear, where the enemy threatened our communication on the Murfreesborough pike. The brigade, having but three or four rounds of ammunition, cheerfully went into action, gallantly charged the enemy, routing them, recapturing two pieces of artillery, and taking 40 prisoners. The rout of the enemy at this point deserves special consideration, as they had here nearly reached the Murfreesborough pike.

On the night of the 31st, I was placed in position on the Murfreesborough pike, facing south, and on the ground where Roberts' brigade had charged the enemy, General Davis being on my right.

On January 1, heavy skirmish fighting, with occasional artillery shots on both sides, was kept up till about 3 p. m., when a charge was made by a brigade of the enemy on my position. This was handsomely repulsed, and 1 officer and 85 men of the enemy captured.

Colonel Walker's brigade, of Thomas' corps, was also placed under my command, temporarily, having a position on my left, where the same character of fighting was kept up.

On January 2, Colonel Walker sustained two heavy attacks, which he gallantly repulsed.

On the 3d, skirmishing took place throughout the day.

On the 4th, all was quiet in front, the enemy having disappeared.

On the 5th, nothing of importance occurred, and, on January 6, I moved my command to its present camp, on Stone's River, 3 miles south of Murfreesborough, on the Shelbyville pike.

I trust that the general commanding is satisfied with my division. It fought bravely and well. The loss of Houghtaling's battery and one section of Bush's battery was unavoidable. All the horses were shot down or disabled, Captain Houghtaling wounded, and Lieutenant Taliaferro killed.

My division, alone and unbroken, made a gallant stand to protect the right flank of our army, being all that remained of the right wing. Had my ammunition held out, I would not have fallen back, although such were my orders, if hard pressed. As it was, this determined stand of my troops gave time for a rearrangement of our lines.

The division mourns the loss of Sill, Schaefer, and Roberts. They were all instantly killed, and at the moment when their gallant brigades were charging the enemy. They were true soldiers, prompt and brave. On the death of these officers, respectively, Colonel Greusel, Thirty-sixth Illinois, took command of Sill's brigade, Lieutenant-Colonel Laiboldt, Second Missouri, of Schaefer's, and Colonel Bradley, Fifty-first Illinois, of Roberts' brigade. These officers behaved gallantly throughout the day.

It is also my sad duty to record the death of Col. F. A. Harrington, of the Twenty-seventh Illinois, who fell heroically leading his regiment to the charge.

I refer with pride to the splendid conduct, bravery, and efficiency of the following regimental commanders and the officers and men of their respective commands:

Col. F. T. Sherman, Eighty-eighth Illinois; Maj. F. Ehrler, Second Missouri; Lieut. Col. John Weber, Fifteenth Missouri; Capt. W. W. Barrett, Forty-fourth Illinois, wounded; Maj. W. A. Presson, Seventy-third Illinois, wounded; Maj. Silas Miller, Thirty-sixth Illinois, wounded and a prisoner; Capt. P. C. Olson, Thirty-sixth Illinois; Maj. E. C. Hibbard, Twenty-fourth Wisconsin; Lieut. Col. William B. McCreery, Twenty-first Michigan; Lieut. Col. N. H. Walworth, Forty-second Illinois; Lieut. Col. F. Swanwick, Twenty-second Illinois, wounded and a prisoner; Capt. Samuel Johnson, Twenty-second Illinois; Maj. W. A. Schmitt, Twenty-seventh Illinois; Captain Wescott, Fifty-first Illinois.

I respectfully bring to the notice of the general commanding the good conduct of Captain Hescock, chief of artillery, whose services were almost invaluable; also Captains Houghtaling and Bush, and the officers and men of their batteries.

Surg. D. J. Griffiths, medical director of my division, and Dr. McArthur, of the board of medical examiners of Illinois, were most assiduous in their care of the wounded.

Maj. H. F. Deitz, provost-marshal; Captain Morhardt, topographical engineer; Lieut. George Lee, acting assistant adjutant-general; Lieuts. R. M. Denning, Frank H. Allen, E. M. De Bruin, J. L. Forman, and [T. H.] Soward, aides-de-camp, officers of my staff, were of the greatest service to me, delivering my orders faithfully, and promptly discharging the duties of their respective positions.

The ammunition train, above alluded to as captured, was retaken from the enemy through the good conduct of Captain Thruston, ordnance officer of the corps, and Lieutenant Douglass, ordnance officer of my division, who, with Sergeant Cooper, of my escort, rallied the stragglers and drove off the enemy's cavalry.

The following is the total of casualties in the division: Officers killed, 15; wounded, 38; missing, 11; total of officers, 64. Enlisted men killed, 223; wounded, 943; missing, 400; total of enlisted men, 1,566. Aggregate, 1,630.* Of the 11 officers and 400 enlisted men missing, many are known to be wounded and in the hands of the enemy.

---

* But see revised statement, p. 209.

Prisoners were captured from the enemy by my division as follows : 1 major, 1 captain, 3 lieutenants, and 216 enlisted men.   Total, 221.

I am, sir, very respectfully, your obedient servant,

P. H. SHERIDAN,
Brigadier-General, Commanding.

Maj. J. A. CAMPBELL,
Asst. Adjt. Gen., Right Wing, Fourteenth Army Corps.

No. 51.

Report of Capt. Henry Hescock, First Missouri Light Artillery, Chief of Artillery.

CAMP OF THIRD DIVISION, FOURTEENTH ARMY CORPS,
Near Murfreesborough, Tenn., January 9, 1863.

SIR : I have the honor to make the following report of the part taken by the batteries of artillery of this division in the battle of Stone's River, and the events during the march from Mill Creek, December 26, 1862, and after the battle, up to January 6, 1863 :

The batteries marched with the several brigades on the morning of December 26, in the following order : Houghtaling's battery, with Colonel Roberts' brigade, on the Nolensville pike ; Hescock's battery, with General Sill's brigade, on the road to the left of the pike, via Patterson's Mill ; Bush's battery, with Schaefer's brigade, on the Nolensville pike, in reserve.   Nothing was done this day by the artillery.   Encamped about 1 mile from Nolensville.

On the 27th, marched at dawn of day toward Triune ; formed line of battle, with expectation of an engagement; the men and horses suffering very much on account of the heavy rains for the last few days, and deep mud.   Did not move on the 28th.   Spent the day preparing the batteries for battle.

Marched on the 29th on the Bole Jack road toward Murfreesborough. Saw but little of the enemy; no fighting.   Encamped near Wilkinson's Cross-Roads, about 7 miles from Murfreesborough.

Marched on the morning of the 30th, at 7 a. m.   Found the enemy strongly posted in our front, about 3 miles from Murfreesborough.

The batteries, having been assigned to brigades as follows—Hescock's battery to Schaefer's brigade ; Houghtaling's battery to Colonel Roberts' brigade, and Bush's battery to General Sill's brigade—took post with their brigades, Houghtaling's on the right of the Wilkinson pike ; Bush's on the right of Houghtaling's ; Hescock's on the right and rear, all supported by their respective brigades.

But little firing was done during the forenoon.   In the afternoon Bush moved with his battery to the front, and opened on the enemy, at short range.   Hescock took the position left by Bush, all three batteries concentrating their fire on the point of timber in front, shelling the enemy's battery and driving back his skirmishers.   The casualties were confined to Bush's battery, he having lost 4 enlisted men and several horses.   His battery was placed in an exposed position and nobly did their duty.

During the night, Bush moved his battery to a more commanding position ; the other batteries remained on the hill facing the enemy.

The events of the 31st relative.to the batteries of this division are difficult to detail, but may be made intelligible to any one conversant with the ground or taking any part in the action. The battle opened in the division by an attempt to capture Bush's battery. It was gallantly defended by General Sill until his brigade was completely turned. The brave general fell dead between the guns. The battery then fell back to the position occupied by the other batteries of the division. In the mean time Houghtaling's and the Missouri batteries were firing into the enemy's ranks and batteries that were engaging General Sill and General Davis, and continued to do fearful execution among them until the enemy, who were pursuing General Johnson's surprised and defeated division, gained the rear of the division, when all the batteries moved to the front to the position just held by the enemy, and from which the division had driven him.

Houghtaling advanced first and took position on the right of the pike (south side), just in the edge of the timber, supported by Colonel Roberts' brigade, where he remained until his last horse was killed or wounded, and his last round of ammunition was expended, and the enemy demanding his men to surrender. He was forced to abandon his battery, after a gallant fight for a most important position. His loss will be found in his statement, already submitted to you.

Bush took position on the north side of the pike, doing his duty bravely; the Missouri battery also on that side of the pike. These two batteries were exposed to a fire of artillery from their front and rear and of sharpshooters on their flank.

Captain Bush re-enforced Captain Houghtaling with one section of his battery, under First Lieut. D. Flansburg. Captain Hescock also sent his Parrott section, under First Lieut. R. C. M. Taliaferro. Lieutenant Taliaferro fell dead, fighting bravely to save his guns, being shot through the head. The two batteries on the north side of the pike engaged the enemy in front and rear until their ammunition was expended, when they retired through the cedar woods with the division. Captain Bush was compelled to abandon two of his guns in the dense cedar trees, for the lack of horses, the enemy charging his cannoneers. After gaining the open ground three guns of the Missouri battery were brought into action and fired on the enemy what little ammunition remained, until ordered to retire and replenish. Thus ended the operations of the 31st.

The batteries took a position, by order of General Sheridan, with the division on the south of the Nashville and Murfreesborough pike, about 3 a. m., January 1, 1863, where they remained until January 6, 1863, nothing of note occurring, except on the 1st, when a brigade of the enemy appeared in our front and was handsomely repulsed in five minutes, leaving 40 of his dead.

The loss of guns, &c., in the division, I believe to be unavoidable, and necessary to the successful resistance of the enemy's attack, which was made in heavy masses; and I do not think the officers can be blamed, as they could not do otherwise without most disastrous results to the army.

The loss of the batteries was severe, but they are in good discipline and ready for service.

I have the honor to be, very respectfully,

H. HESCOCK,
Captain First Missouri Artillery, Chief of Artillery, Third Div.

Lieut. GEORGE LEE,
Acting Assistant Adjutant-General, Third Division.

No. 52.

Report of Capt. Charles Houghtaling, Battery C, First Illinois Light Artillery.

BATTLE-FIELD, NEAR MURFREESBOROUGH,
January 6, 1863.

CAPTAIN: I would respectfully submit the following report of the part my company took in the action on the 30th and 31st ultimo:

As but little was done on the 30th, I will pass over it.

On the morning of the 31st, according to orders, we fell back toward the left, or rather changed front to the west, and my battery was placed in a belt of thick timber south of the pike, and was soon hotly engaged with the enemy's batteries, which cut us up severely. While the battle was raging, I called upon you for re-enforcements, which were promptly furnished. Being still unable to silence the rebel guns, and another battery being opened on me from the left, and being flanked by rebel infantry, I informed Colonel Roberts that unless I moved from that position I should lose my battery, as my horses were falling at every volley, and my men nearly half killed and wounded. He informed me a few minutes afterward that General Sheridan's orders were to hold that position at all hazards, and I did so until my ammunition was nearly expended, when I was ordered to change front and fire to the left, falling back across the pike, which I did, and three of the guns, being out of ammunition, were sent to the rear, while the others took a position and used the last round of canister on the enemy. Here the remainder of my horses were killed, and being flanked both on the right and left, and no possible chance to get the guns off by hand through the heavy cedar timber in the rear, I was forced to abandon them. All was done that could be, under the circumstances, to save them. Thus closed the part my company, as a company, took in the engagement. Lieutenant Wright, with some of the boys, joined your battery; Lieutenant Van Dyke and some more fell in with and joined the Twenty-sixth Pennsylvania Battery, Lieutenant Stevens commanding; some found the Board of Trade Battery, and others took muskets and fell into the ranks as infantry.

All, I believe, did their duty in their various positions, and all behaved with great coolness and gallantry while under my command.

Loss in killed, wounded, and missing, ———.* Total number horses lost, 95.

Very respectfully, your obedient servant,

CHAS. HOUGHTALING,
Captain, Comdg. Company C, First Illinois Light Artillery.

Captain HESCOCK,
Chief of Artillery, 3d Div., Right Wing, 14th Army Corps.

No. 53.

Report of Capt. Asahel K. Bush, Fourth Indiana Battery.

CAMP NEAR MURFREESBOROUGH, TENN.,
January 9, 1863.

SIR: I have the honor to submit the following report of the part

---

* See p. 209.

taken by my command in front of Murfreesborough, Tenn., from and including December 30, 1862, to the morning of January 4, 1863:

On the morning of December 30, 1862, moved near the enemy's lines, and, by order of General Sheridan, opened fire on a rebel battery at 1,500 yards range, and drove it under cover. About 1 p. m. was moved across open fields near the woods occupied by the enemy. A rebel battery opened on us from the woods at about 600 yards range, when General Sill ordered us in position in the woods fronting them, and ordered me to "Silence that battery," which we did after a sharp contest of about two hours, at 450 yards range. We killed about half their horses, completely disabled one gun-carriage, killed 1 of their lieutenants and 12 men, wounded several others, and killed and wounded several of their infantry support, which lay near.

My loss in the contest was 1 sergeant and 3 privates killed, 3 privates wounded, 5 horses killed, two gun-carriage wheels disabled, and two limber-chests damaged.

After dark, by command of General Sill, took position about 300 yards to the right, in open ground, where we remained until the next morning (December 31), and about daylight were attacked by the enemy. We replied with canister at short range until General Sheridan's division was completely flanked, by General Davis' division retreating, and obliged to retire. We fixed prolonges and retired in rear of the brigade, firing canister.

Made another short stand at the first position of December 30, and fired canister from my howitzer and 6-pounder smooth-bores into the enemy in front, and with my rifles drove two of the enemy's pieces from position, which were firing on General Davis' retreating lines; lost one caisson in reaching this position, every horse on it being shot down by the enemy's musketry. Here the under-straps of one of my smooth-bore 6-pounders were broken by firing double charges of canister, and I sent the piece to the rear.

From the above position I retired and took position about 800 yards to the left, adjoining General Negley's division, near which point I remained until my ammunition was expended; then retired to the left. In crossing a dense cedar woods, near the Murfreesborough pike, the infantry were driven rapidly past us, and my two rear pieces (one James 6-pounder and one 6-pounder smooth-bore) were captured by the enemy, after killing all the horses on them, except one wheel-horse on one, and one wheel and two swing horses on the other, and the latter piece fast among the trees and the enemy within 40 yards of them. On reaching the pike, I moved a short distance to the rear and got a supply of ammunition, and reported myself to the front with three pieces for duty. By order of General Rosecrans, we went into park in front and on the left of the pike.

The next morning General Sheridan put us in position, where we remained until Sunday morning without further casualties.

On Saturday, January 3, I got the piece repaired and in position, which was disabled December 31.

Some field officer, on December 31, forced my forge into the train which started for Nashville, and it was captured and burned.

During the above engagement my officers behaved nobly. I can scarcely mention one in particular without doing injustice to the rest. I must, however, mention First Sergt. Willis H. Pettit, whose services in keeping my guns supplied with ammunition and various other duties were invaluable. Joseph E. De Wolf, clerk and private orderly, as usual, showed a clear head and unsurpassed courage, and was always found where the fight was thickest, ready to carry orders, assist in taking out and putting in horses, &c. I must also give great credit to Private Frank Williams, who, with great courage and skill, saved my five remaining caissons, which were at one time cut off and in the rebel lines.

My loss o.̓ men was 6 killed, 17 wounded, 2 paroled, and 1 missing.

I remain, sir, your obedient servant,

A. K. BUSH,
Captain, Commanding Fourth Indiana Battery.

Captain HESCOCK,
Chief of Artillery, General Sheridan's Division.

No. 54.

Report of Col. Nicholas Greusel, Thirty-sixth Illinois Infantry, commanding First Brigade.

HDQRS. FIRST BRIGADE, THIRD DIVISION, RIGHT WING,
Camp on Stone's River, Tenn., January 15, 1863.

SIR: Not being in command of the brigade until General Sill's death, Wednesday morning, December 31, 1862, I am unable to give a very correct report of its operations previous to that time, but have succeeded, from what I observed myself and by reports of other regimental commanders, in getting very near, if not quite, a correct report of the movements of the brigade.

In obedience to orders from General Sill, the brigade was under arms from 4 a. m. Tuesday, December 30, till 8 o'clock, on the Wilkinson pike, about 5 miles from Murfreesborough, and at 9 o'clock we moved forward, this brigade being the center of the division. Skirmishers were deployed and soon were engaged with the enemy's skirmishers.

When within about 2 miles from Murfreesborough, the brigade was ordered by General Sill to the right of the pike, and formed the first line of battle on the edge of the timber, in the following order: The Thirty-sixth Illinois on the right, Eighty-eighth Illinois on the left, Bush's Fourth Indiana Battery in the center, the Twenty-first Michigan supporting the Eighty-eighth Illinois, and the Twenty-fourth Wisconsin supporting the Thirty-sixth Illinois.

Sharp skirmishing was kept up until 3 p. m., when General Sill ordered an advance, and the brigade moved forward (changing front to the left), the regiments keeping their relative positions across a corn-field, and the battery was advanced into the woods beyond, supported by the Thirty-sixth Illinois and five companies of the Twenty-fourth Wisconsin. Soon after the advance into the woods, a battery of the enemy opened on us from the low ground across a cotton-field, and in the edge of a strip of timber, scarce 500 yards distant, and then ensued a terrific artillery duel between our battery and the enemy's, which finally resulted in their battery being silenced and withdrawn. It now being near dark, our battery was moved to the rear, just out of the woods, and the brigade formed in nearly the same relative positions as at first, and lay upon their arms all night, with strong lines of skirmishers out as pickets.

Soon after daylight, on the morning of the 31st, the enemy advanced out of the woods on the opposite side of the cotton-field (referred to before) in great force immediately on our front, but were met by such a fire from our artillery and infantry that they were finally repulsed and driven back with great loss across the cotton-field.

About this time, 7 a. m., while directing the movements of the brigade, our brave General Sill was struck in the face by a musket ball and instantly killed. I then received your order to take command of the brigade. The enemy having turned our right, and again advancing in force, I moved to the rear with the Twenty-fourth Wisconsin and Eighty-eighth Illinois, and across the road, where I formed on the left of the Eighty-first Indiana, Woodruff's brigade, leaving the Twenty-first Michigan to support Hescock's battery, where they were assailed by great numbers of the enemy, but held their ground until the battery was moved, when they retired in good order, losing heavily in killed and wounded. (See report of Lieutenant-Colonel McCreery.) Having expended all the ammunition of the two regiments with me, I retired to and got a supply from the train of General Rousseau, ours having been cut off.

I then reformed my line on the east of the railroad, and moved forward to the Murfreesborough pike. Here I received orders from General McCook to move to the extreme right of our line, to support the cavalry, who were threatened by the rebel cavalry, and in some danger of being flanked. I formed and supported the Fifth Wisconsin Battery and remained in this position until dark, after which I retired the Eighty-eighth Illinois to the rear of the battery, and detailed the Twenty-fourth Wisconsin for picket duty, Colonel Kennett supporting my pickets with his cavalry.

At 2 a. m., January 1, I received your order to move the brigade to the vicinity of your headquarters, when, in accordance with your orders, I formed line of battle in the rear of Colonel Laiboldt's brigade in the following order: The Thirty-sixth Illinois on the right, Fourth Indiana Battery, Eighty-eighth Illinois, and Twenty-fourth Wisconsin on the left, the Twenty-first Michigan being for the time joined to the Third Brigade, Colonel Bradley commanding, where we lay during the 1st, 2d, and part of the 3d of January, 1863, inactive, with the exception of being ordered to form double column on Friday, January 2, to support the left wing (then heavily engaged with the enemy), if necessary, but were not needed.

Saturday, January 3, we moved, by your order, the whole brigade (the Twenty-first Michigan having joined) to the position before held by General Davis' division, to the right and front of our former position, where we remained inactive until Tuesday, January 6, when we moved to our present camp, south of Murfreesborough.

I am unable to give sufficient praise to the officers commanding the different regiments in the brigade; all have done their duty; but I must say that, in regard to Major Miller, Captain Olson, and Adjutant Biddulph, of the Thirty-sixth Illinois; Colonel Sherman and Major Chandler, of the Eighty-eighth Illinois; Lieutenant-Colonel McCreery and Adjt. M. B. Wells, of the Twenty-first Michigan; Major Hibbard and Adjutant MacArthur, of the Twenty-fourth Wisconsin, they behaved with great coolness and presence of mind, ever ready to obey my command. Of my staff, I would especially notice Lieut. J. B. Watkins, acting assistant adjutant-general; Lieut. J. L. Mitchell, aide-de-camp; Lieut. N. S. Bouton, brigade quartermaster, who was very active in procuring ammunition, and Quartermaster Sergt. Frederick Colburn, Thirty-third Ohio, acting as volunteer aide to General Sill, and after his death in the same capacity to me, and who showed great coolness and activity in carrying orders during the thickest of the fight. Brigade

Surg. D. W. Young deserves especial notice for his untiring efforts to care for the wounded.

In General Sill we all feel that we have lost an able commander and a kind friend; though but a short time with us, he had endeared himself to the whole command by his quiet, unassuming disposition, combining gentleness with strict discipline, courageous in action almost to a fault. We all feel that the brigade and the service have lost an officer hard to be replaced.

I inclose with this the reports of the commanders of the different regiments; also a complete list of casualties, the aggregate of which is as follows: Killed, 102; wounded, 369; missing, 200. Total, 671.*

I am, sir, yours, very respectfully,

N. GREUSEL,
Colonel, Commanding First Brigade, Third Division.

Lieut. GEORGE LEE,
Acting Assistant Adjutant-General, Third Division.

No. 55.

Report of Capt. Porter C. Olson, Thirty-sixth Illinois Infantry.

HEADQUARTERS THIRTY-SIXTH ILLINOIS VOLUNTEERS,
January 9, 1863.

The Thirty-sixth Illinois Regiment, Col. N. Greusel commanding, was called into line at 4 o'clock on Tuesday morning, December 30, 1862, and stood under arms until daylight, to the left of the Wilkinson pike, our right resting upon it, and 5 miles from Murfreesborough. At 9 a. m. we moved forward to Murfreesborough; two companies were deployed as skirmishers to the right of the road, and were soon engaged with the enemy's skirmishers. When 2 miles from Murfreesborough the regiment was deployed in the corn-field to the right of the pike, and two companies were deployed forward as skirmishers, as ordered by General Sill. The regiment lay in line in this field until 2 p. m., at which time the whole line was ordered to advance. The skirmishers kept up a sharp fight, the enemy's line retreating and ours advancing. We drove the enemy through the timber and across the cotton-field, a low, narrow strip stretching to the right into the timber. A rebel battery, directly in front of the Thirty-sixth, directed a heavy fire on us. Our skirmishers advanced to the foot of the hill, near the cotton-field, and here kept up a well-directed fire. We were ordered to support Captain Bush's battery, which was brought into position in the point of timber where our right rested, and opened fire with terrible effect upon the enemy. We remained as a support until nearly dark, when Captain Bush went to the rear, the enemy's battery, or, rather, its disabled fragments, having been dragged from the field. In this day's engagement the regiment lost 3 killed and 15 wounded; total, 18. We occupied the hill during the night, and our skirmishers were in line at the edge of the cotton-field.

On the morning of December 31, soon after daylight, the enemy advanced in strong force from the timber from beyond the cotton-field opposite our right. They came diagonally across the field. Upon reaching

----

* But see revised statement, p. 209.

the foot of the hill, they made a left half-wheel and came up directly in front of us. When the enemy had advanced up the hill sufficiently to be in sight, Colonel Greusel ordered the regiment to fire, which was promptly obeyed. We engaged the enemy at short range, the lines being not over 10 rods apart. After a few rounds, the regiment supporting us on our right gave way. In this manner we fought for nearly half an hour, when Colonel Greusel ordered the regiment to charge. The enemy fled in great confusion across the cotton-field into the woods opposite our left, leaving many of their dead and wounded upon the field. We poured a destructive fire upon them as they retreated until they were beyond range.

The Thirty-sixth again took position upon the hill, and the support of our right came forward. At this time General Sill was killed, and Colonel Greusel took command of the brigade. A fresh brigade of the enemy advanced from the direction that the first had come, and in splendid order. We opened fire on them with terrific effect. Again the regiment on our right gave way, and we were again left without support. In this condition we fought until our ammunition was exhausted, and until the enemy had entirely flanked us on our right. At this juncture Major Miller ordered the regiment to fall back. While retreating, Major Miller was wounded, and the command devolved upon me. We moved back of the corn-field to the edge of the timber, a hundred rods to the right of the Wilkinson pike and 2 miles from Murfreesborough, at 8 a. m. Here I met General Sheridan, and reported to him that the regiment was out of ammunition, and that I would be ready for action as soon as I could obtain it. We had suffered severely in resisting the attack of superior numbers. I had now only 140 men. The regiment fought with great obstinacy, and much is due to Col. N. Greusel for his bravery in conducting the regiment before being called away.

Adjutant Biddulph went to find the ammunition wagon, but did not succeed. I then informed Quartermaster Bouton that I needed cartridges, but he failed to find any except size .58, the caliber of most of the arms being .69. I was now ordered by Major-General McCook to fall back to the rear of General Crittenden's corps. I arrived there about 10 a. m. I here obtained ammunition, and dispatched the adjutant to report to Colonel Greusel the condition and whereabouts of the regiment. He returned without seeing the colonel. Lieutenant Watkins soon rode up, and volunteered to take a message to Colonel Greusel or General Sheridan. He also returned without finding either officer. I now went in search of General Sheridan myself; found him at 12 o'clock; reported to him the regiment (what there was left of it) ready to move to the front. He ordered that I should hold the regiment in readiness and await his orders.

At 2 p. m. I received orders from General Sheridan to advance to the front, on the left of the railroad, and connect my command temporarily with Colonel Laiboldt's brigade. We were here subject to a very heavy artillery fire. A 12-pounder shell struck in the right of the regiment and killed Lieut. Soren L. Olson (a brave and faithful officer, commanding Company F) and Corporal Riggs, and wounded 3 others. At dark we were moved by Lieutenant Denning one-quarter of a mile to the rear, where we remained for the night.

At 3 a. m. January 1, 1863, by order of General Sheridan, we marched back to his headquarters, on the Nashville pike, a distance of half a mile, where, at daylight, I reported to Colonel Greusel. As ordered by him, we took position to the right of Captain Bush's battery, fronting west.

We built a barricade of logs and stone, and remained through the day ready to receive the enemy, but no attack was made.

On the morning of the 2d, the regiment was in line at 4 o'clock; stood under arms until daylight. We remained ready for action during the day until 4 p. m., when, by order of Colonel Greusel, we moved to the right, on the line formerly occupied by General Davis. During the night considerable skirmishing occurred on our front.

On the morning of the 3d instant, the regiment stood under arms from 4 o'clock until daylight. At 8 a. m., by order of Colonel Greusel, we changed position to the right, and somewhat to the rear, letting our right rest upon the Nashville pike.

On the morning of the 4th, we were under arms at 4 o'clock; no fighting occurred on our part of the line during the day.

In the action throughout, the regiment behaved in the most gallant manner. The officers, with only a single exception, distinguished themselves for bravery and coolness; the men, with unflinching courage, were always ready, and met the enemy with a determination to conquer. I tender my thanks to Adjutant Biddulph for the gallant and efficient manner in which he assisted me, and also to the other officers for their gallant action throughout the stormy conflict, which resulted in victory.

I append to this report a list of casualties.*

PORTER C. OLSON,
Captain, Commanding Thirty-sixth Illinois Volunteers.

Lieut. J. B. WATKINS,
Acting Assistant Adjutant-General.

No. 56.

Report of Col. Francis T. Sherman, Eighty-eighth Illinois Infantry.

HDQRS. EIGHTY-EIGHTH REGIMENT ILLINOIS INFANTRY,
Camp on Stone's River, Tenn., January 7, 1863.

COLONEL: I have the honor to make report to you of my regiment during the recent battle of Stone's River, near Murfreesborough, Tenn.

On the morning of December 30, at 7 o'clock, by order of Brigadier-General Sill, then commanding your brigade, I marched my regiment on the pike toward the town of Murfreesborough. At 9 a. m. we were ordered to the right of the pike, where skirmishing with the enemy was being had. We formed in line of battle in front of Houghtaling's and Hescock's batteries, and threw out the two flank companies as skirmishers, with Companies F and G as reserves.

We skirmished moderately with the enemy until about 3 p. m., when an advance was made, and I took position with the regiment in a cotton-field on a ridge, just in rear of a strip of bottom land, with my skirmishers a short distance in advance. During the remainder of the day skirmishing was brisk, and Capt. G. W. Smith, of Company A, while bravely directing his company as skirmishers, was wounded in the leg and obliged to leave the field. Night having set in, we were ordered to remain on the field all night and keep our skirmishers out as pickets.

On the morning of the 31st, the men were in line of battle at daybreak, and skirmishing with the enemy began soon after. About 7 o'clock they made an advance across the bottom, one brigade charging

---

* Embodied in revised statement, p. 209.

directly upon my regiment. I ordered the men to hold their fire until the enemy were within short musket range, when, the skirmishers having nearly all rallied on the battalion, I ordered them to rise up and fire, which they did with a coolness and daring worthy of veteran soldiers, and which checked the enemy in his advance and drove him back into the timber. We held our position until forced to retire by the enemy advancing in overwhelming numbers from the timber to our right.

Our retirement was made in good order, but with great loss of men. We reformed our line, when I was informed that General Sill was killed, and that you were in command of the brigade.

The enemy having broken our right, I retreated, under your directions, across the Wilkinson pike into the cedars, where we again made a stand and held our position, checking the enemy's advance, until ordered to retire.

About noon we went out on the Nashville and Murfreesborough pike, to support the cavalry in resisting the attacks of the enemy on our trains. We encamped at night on a hill just beyond Overall's Creek.

At 4 o'clock the next morning (January 1, 1863) we marched back to the battle-field, and took position on the right, where we lay in line of battle all this and the two following days, anticipating an attack from the enemy, but which was not made.

During the engagement I was ably assisted by all my officers present. Lieutenant-Colonel Chadbourne and Lieutenant Ballard, adjutant, being absent, sick, Major Chandler was the only field assistance I had, and I take special pleasure in mentioning Major Chandler, whose conduct throughout the conflict was characterized by calmness and the most determined bravery. His services were invaluable to the regiment, as his gallant example infused itself into the spirits of the men, making them cool and steady when obliged to retire in the face of the enemy. Although wounded, and having his horse shot under him, he remained steadily at his post until the close of the battle.

It gratifies me to be able to make honorable mention of the officers commanding companies, viz: First Lieut. George Chandler, Company A; Capt. W. A. Whiting, Company B; Capt. George A. Sheridan, Company C; Capt. John A. Bross, Company D; Capt. Levi P. Holden, Company E; First Lieut. James A. S. Hanford, Company F; Second Lieut. Dean R. Chester, Company G; First Lieut. Charles T. Boal, Company H; Capt. J. J. Spalding, Company I, and Capt. D. E. Barnard, Company K, all of whom remained steady under fire, always at their posts urging their men on in repelling the enemy. The lieutenants assisting were cool and brave, and worthy of the offices they filled. The conduct of my sergeant-major, N. P. Jackson, was worthy of a soldier, being cool and brave, ever ready to carry out my orders, though bullets were flying thick around him.

During the engagement on the 31st, while at his post, Lieut. Thomas F. W. Gullich, of Company C, fell, shot through the head. In his death his company and country have lost a faithful officer and a gallant soldier.

Herewith you will find a list of the killed, wounded, and missing of my regiment.*

Very respectfully, yours,

F. T. SHERMAN,
Colonel, Comdg. Eighty-eighth Regiment Illinois Volunteers.
Col. NICHOLAS GREUSEL,
Comdg. First Brigade, Third Division, Fourteenth Army Corps.

---

* Embodied in revised statement, p. 209.

No. 57.

Report of Lieut. Col. William B. McCreery, Twenty-first Michigan Infantry.

HDQRS. TWENTY-FIRST REGIMENT MICHIGAN INFANTRY,
Camp on Stone's River, January 7, 1863.

LIEUTENANT: I have the honor to report to you the following as the action taken by this regiment in the recent engagement before Murfreesborough:

On the morning of the 30th ultimo we took position on the hill, between Captains Hescock's and Houghtaling's batteries, to act as a support to the Eighty-eighth Illinois, Colonel Sherman, who had previously taken position a few rods in front. About 3 p. m. we were moved forward into the cotton-field, still retaining the same relative position to the Eighty-eighth. We remained here until after dark, when we were ordered to move to a grass-plot a few rods to our right, where we remained during the night.

Before daylight we were ordered to occupy the same ground we had occupied the evening previous. Soon after daybreak an attack was made in force by the enemy upon our front and to our right. After a fierce contest, the forces on our front and right retired. At this time the enemy were delivering a murderous fire upon our front and right flank. After delivering our fire, and observing him closing in in heavy force upon us, I ordered the regiment to fall back. Owing to a barn and out-buildings which we were compelled to pass, the regiment was for the time being thrown into some confusion; but it was with much difficulty that I could compel the men to leave the cover they had taken behind the fences and buildings, where they were delivering a well-directed fire.

We immediately formed upon the right of the Eighty-eighth Illinois, and were ordered to move a few rods to the rear and left, and were then ordered to support Hescock's battery until further orders, it having taken position a little to our left. The battery soon changed position to a point of woods, where we followed, in support. It was immediately engaged, and a heavy force of the enemy's infantry made their appearance on our front and left.

As soon as they had advanced to within short musket range, I opened a telling fire upon them, which was continued until the battery had retired, when we fought our way back to the woods in good order. We again took position in the woods, but, receiving a heavy fire on our front and flank, we were obliged to fall back. We made another stand farther back in the woods, and fought our way back to the clearing; after which I fell back beyond the railroad, where we remained until along toward evening, when we joined the brigade near Overall's Creek.

The next morning we were ordered to recross the creek, and took position on the right of the pike and to the left of the Twenty-fourth Wisconsin, in support of Colonel Bradley's brigade, where we remained without action until the next morning, when we moved to the right, occupying the ground previously held by the Thirty-sixth Illinois, in which place we remained until we took up our line of march for this place.

Both officers and men, with few exceptions, behaved with coolness and bravery. I am indebted to Major Hunting and Adjt. M. B. Wells for valuable assistance, especially the latter, whom I recommend to your favorable notice.

The list of casualties is as follows:

Officers wounded 7
Enlisted men killed 18
Enlisted men wounded 82
Enlisted men missing 36

Total 143

Very respectfully,

WILLIAM B. McCREERY,
Lieutenant-Colonel, Comdg. Twenty-first Michigan Infantry.

Lieut. J. B. WATKINS,
Actg. Asst. Adjt. Gen., First Brigade, Third Division.

No. 58.

Report of Maj. Elisha C. Hibbard, Twenty-fourth Wisconsin Infantry.

HDQRS. TWENTY-FOURTH WISCONSIN INFANTRY VOLS.,
Camp on Stone's River, Tenn., January 8, 1863.

LIEUTENANT: I have the honor to submit the following report of the part taken by the Twenty-fourth Regiment Wisconsin Volunteers in the late engagements resulting in the taking of Murfreesborough, viz:

On the morning of Tuesday, December 30, 1862, I marched the regiment from camp, right in front, following in rear of Bush's battery, with two companies deployed as flankers, according to orders from General Sill. About an hour's march from camp, and while firing was going on in front, I received an order to add one company to the flankers, and move them out farther from the column, which order was carried out. Soon after, I received an order from General Sill to move my regiment forward, and form line 200 paces in rear of the Thirty-sixth Illinois. These dispositions having been made, an order was received to have the men lie down. I remained in this position, just in the edge of the woods on the left of a white house (afterward used as a hospital), and on the right of Bush's battery.

I remained there until ordered to advance by General Sill, keeping directly in rear and 200 paces distant from the Thirty-sixth Illinois. Advancing to the open field beyond an old log-house, I halted and ordered the men to lie down, the enemy having opened on the advance with artillery, very effectually served.

Soon after, I was directed by an aide to send five companies to the woods in our front to support Bush's battery, which was then hotly engaged with the enemy's artillery. The five companies were sent under the command of the acting field officer. I remained in the field with the balance of the regiment, which was in a very exposed position, and had lost several men from the enemy's artillery, until ordered by General Sill to bring down the balance of my command to the support of the battery, as the enemy were about to make an effort to capture it. The artillery firing then ceased, night having put an end to the action. I was ordered by General Sill to have a picket posted, the balance to lie down on their arms, and allow half of each company to go to the rear and do some cooking. I posted one company as pickets, and allowed the men to boil some coffee; then placed them in line. The night was intensely cold, and the men were nearly frozen.

At 3 a. m. (31st) General Sill came down to the regiment and said we would be supported from the reserve brigade. The men were then awake and ready for action. At early dawn two regiments came into the woods and formed line at right angles with my left. They remained a few moments, and were marched away.

Soon after, firing began, and the pickets were driven in by the enemy's skirmishers directly in my front. Their column of attack came close on the rear of their skirmishers, and I ordered the men to fire. At the same time my attention was directed to a column coming out of the wood on my right flank. They were in line and advancing very rapidly. (I counted five battle-flags.) I immediately sent word to General Sill that the enemy were in force on my flank. About the same time the regiment on my right, formed at right angles, fell back; a battery, which had fired four rounds very effectively, followed them, leaving my flank entirely unprotected. I maintained my position, waiting for orders, until the enemy were in the woods in my rear, and had come on my flank and delivered a cross-fire, doing me considerable damage. No orders having been received, and thinking it improper to remain longer in this position, I ordered the regiment to break to the rear by companies. Some of the officers not hearing the order, the left wing did not move with the right, and the regiment came off in some disorder, but was quickly reformed in the open field to the right of the log-house used for a hospital. No regiment could have formed line more rapidly than they did, after retreating, surrounded on all sides by confused masses of fugitives—the veterans of some of the hardest battles of the war. Where such troops flee, new recruits assuredly deserve praise for standing their ground.

I then received the first orders during the day from Colonel Greusel to move my regiment up to a fence and have them lie down. My left then formed on the right of the Fifteenth Missouri. An order given by Colonel Schaefer for that regiment to move, left me entirely alone, unless I advanced with them, which was done. Moving up to the second fence in my front, I again ordered the men to lie down.

Soon after, an aide from General Sheridan directed me to move my regiment up to the woods. The order was obeyed, when I joined the Eighty-eighth Illinois, and was thereafter under the immediate command of Colonel Greusel. By his direction, we marched through the cedar swamp, a terrific fire of artillery and infantry roaring all around us. I crossed the railroad and marched up the Murfreesborough pike, placed my men, as-per orders from him, in a thicket, with directions to deploy skirmishers and watch for the enemy's cavalry, which was annoying our train. Remained in this position some time. Was ordered up still farther to the right, and placed behind a rail fence, which position I occupied for about one hour. Again moving up the pike, by Colonel Greusel's direction, I supported one gun of the First Ohio Battery. Night coming on, I was directed to post three companies as pickets, keeping the remainder in reserve.

On the morning of January 1, 1863, under direction of Colonel Greusel, I brought the regiment back to the pike, and, following the Eighty-eighth Illinois, marched down to the cedar swamp, a mile beyond Stone's River, with orders to erect temporary breastworks. In this position I remained until the evening of the 2d, when, by directions of the colonel commanding, I moved my regiment on to the grounds occupied by a regiment on my right, which had marched.

On the morning of the 3d, I marched again, by directions of the brigade commander, to the left of Bush's battery, my right resting on the Thirty-sixth Illinois, in which position we remained until we marched to this our present camp.

I cannot too highly speak of the men who passed through all the trials of the two days' fighting and the following four days of suspense, worse than the battle itself. Exhausted and cold, they stood their ground like veterans, and fought as good soldiers.

I desire to make special mention of the conduct of Captains Root, Austin, and Philbrook, and Lieutenants Balding, Chase, Nix, Chivas, Hartung, Goldsmith, Horning, Elmore, Parsons, Battle, Kennedy, Holton, and Greene. The surgeons (Major Hasse and Captain Wheeler) were not under my immediate observation, but I am informed they performed their duties nobly. To the chaplain of the regiment I return thanks for his kind attention to the wounded.

To the adjutant of the regiment (Arthur MacArthur, jr.) I am more than indebted for his aid and efficient service rendered during the engagements. Young and gallant, I bespeak for him an honorable career. Of the sergeant-major (Frank W. Riddle) and Sergeants Drake and Kerston I would make favorable mention. Sergeant Coburn, of Company A, deserves special notice for bringing off the body of Lieutenant Nix, mortally wounded.

Inclosing you a list of the casualties,* and desiring, on behalf of the officers of the regiment, to acknowledge our indebtedness to the colonel commanding the brigade for his care and attention after assuming command, I have the honor to be, your obedient servant,

E. C. HIBBARD,
Major, Commanding Twenty-fourth Wisconsin.

Lieutenant WATKINS,
Actg. Asst. Adjt. Gen., First Brigade, Third Division.

No. 59.

Report of Lieut. Col. Bernard Laiboldt, Second Missouri Infantry, commanding Second Brigade.

HDQRS. SECOND BRIG., THIRD DIV., RIGHT WING,
January 7, 1863.

I have the honor to submit to you a report of the part taken by the brigade I now have the honor to command, in the battle in front of Murfreesborough:

The brigade, then in command of the lamented Col. Frederick Schaefer, was assigned position as reserve of the Third Division on December 30, and took no part in the engagement on the left on that day.

Shortly after daybreak next morning, December 31, Colonel Schaefer received orders to re-enforce General Sill's brigade with two regiments, and the Fifteenth Missouri Volunteers and Forty-fourth Illinois Volunteers, under command of Lieutenant-Colonel Weber, of the Fifteenth Missouri Volunteers, were accordingly sent to General Sill, with orders to report to him for duty.

The Second Battalion of the Seventy-third Illinois Volunteers, under command of Major Presson, was detached to protect Captain Hescock's battery, while the other battalion of the Seventy-third Illinois Volunteers and the Second Regiment Missouri Volunteers were held in reserve.

---
* Embodied in revised statement, p. 209.

The Fifteenth Missouri Volunteers and Forty-fourth Illinois Volunteers had a position assigned to them, about 30 yards in rear of General Sill's brigade, when, after a short interval, Lieutenant-Colonel Weber received orders to advance in double-quick. The order was promptly executed, and Lieutenant-Colonel Weber found himself in front of the enemy, the artillery previously stationed there having retreated, leaving one Parrott gun, supposed to belong to Carpenter's battery, Davis' division, behind. The two mentioned regiments kept up a strong firing, and even when one regiment on their left broke and ran, they held their position until attacked from the flank and front at once. Lieutenant-Colonel Weber then retreated in good order, keeping up a constant firing until he, being heavily pressed by the enemy, reached a corn-field, where he halted.

Soon afterward our troops on the left advanced again on the enemy, when Lieutenant-Colonel Weber also rapidly advanced to a place about 50 yards in advance of his previous position, and formed in line of battle. He had the gun above referred to dragged by his men to the rear of his column, from where it afterward was removed to a safer place. Lieutenant-Colonel Weber contested his ground admirably until the enemy advanced six columns deep, and the ammunition of the Fifteenth Missouri Volunteers gave out, the Forty-fourth Illinois Volunteers having previously withdrawn. Then the order to retreat was given and carried out, without improper haste, until the edge of the timber was reached, when the pressure by the enemy was so hard that it became necessary to resort to the double-quick. By the time the Fifteenth Missouri Volunteers and Forty-fourth Illinois Volunteers rejoined the brigade, orders were given to retreat across the pike toward a piece of cedar woods, and two companies of the Second Missouri Volunteers were deployed as skirmishers to retard the rapid advance of the enemy.

The whole brigade, with the exception of the First Battalion of the Seventy-third Illinois Volunteers, under temporary command of Captain Bergan, and being a short distance from the main body, arrived safely at the woods above mentioned, at the edge of which the Second Missouri Volunteers, behind natural and very favorable fortifications of huge and deeply cut rocks, opened a brisk fire on the enemy, which kept him at bay for a considerable length of time. The First Battalion of the Seventy-third Illinois Volunteers was at the same time attacked by the enemy, but repulsed them. When in the attempt to join the brigade, the battalion was, by the advance of General Rousseau, separated, but, keeping up a constant firing, crossed the pike and took a position in the cedar grove. Here Captain Bergan, commanding the battalion, withstood three different charges of a whole rebel cavalry brigade, and was shortly afterward enabled to join his brigade. By this time the ammunition of the Second Missouri Volunteers had given out, as well as that of the rest of the brigade, and they were ordered into the thicket of the cedar grove.

After the lapse of one hour, the brigade was enabled to receive ammunition, and had a new position assigned to them on the Chattanooga Railroad. Colonel Schaefer ordered the Fifteenth Missouri Volunteers to deploy in a corn-field, while the balance of the brigade held the railroad and kept up such a galling and well-aimed fire that the enemy, though of a strength to which our force was hardly comparable, and fighting with the utmost desperation, was again and again repulsed. The Fifteenth Missouri Volunteers, being in danger of being outflanked, retreated toward the position of the brigade, and it was at that moment, when about giving orders to said regiment, that the true soldier and brave man, my lamented predecessor, Col. Frederick Schaefer, fell. By order of General Sheridan, I assumed forthwith the command of the brigade, the Thirty-sixth Illinois Volunteers, commanded by Captain Olson, having been attached to it; and, after taking up another favorable position on the line of the railroad, I was enabled to hold the enemy in check, in spite of his desperate endeavors, until night broke in and the bloody drama of that day was ended.

On January 1, 1863, at 2 a. m., my brigade was ordered to take a position in front of an open field edged by heavy timber, and I had, as soon as daylight permitted, heavy breastworks erected along the whole front I was to protect; and, keeping a vigilant lookout, I held that position until January 6, when I was ordered to advance to the present camp.

The officers and men of the brigade all behaved as would naturally be expected of veteran soldiers who have heretofore earned the highest praise for their bravery and gallantry, and to enumerate single ones would hardly be in justice to the balance.

Among those who laid down their lives for our holy cause, I particularly lament Captain Zimmerman and Lieutenants Kellner and Quintzius, of the Fifteenth Missouri Volunteers; Captain Alsop, of the Seventy-third Illinois Volunteers; Captain Hosmer, of the Forty-fourth Illinois Volunteers; Lieutenant Taliaferro, of the First Missouri Artillery. May their relatives find a consolation, as their comrades do, in the thought that the death on the battle-field for the righteous cause wins immortal laurels for the slain.

I cannot omit to mention Captain Hescock's battery, which, on December 31, as oftentimes before, did splendid execution. The skill and bravery of its officers is almost proverbial, and need not be further commented on by me than to express my heartiest gratification that they stood by me, as formerly, with a right good will and telling courage.

Inclosed I have the honor to transmit a list of the casualties in my brigade.*

I am, sir, your obedient servant,

B. LAIBOLDT,
Lieutenant-Colonel Second Missouri Volunteer Infantry,
Commanding Second Brigade, Third Division, Right Wing.

First Lieut. GEORGE LEE,
Acting Assistant Adjutant-General, Third Division.

No. 60.

Report of Maj. Francis Ehrler, Second Missouri Infantry.

CAMP BRADLEY, AT STONE'S RIVER,
South of Murfreesborough, Tenn., January 10, 1863.

SIR: I have the honor to hereby most respectfully transmit to you a report, inasmuch as the Second Infantry Regiment of Missouri Volunteers was concerned in the battle in front of Murfreesborough, Tenn., on the 31st ultimo.

We received marching orders on the 24th of December, when in camp near Mill Creek, 7 miles south of Nashville. All the wagons, with tents and other baggage, should, as soon as the troops commenced to move,

---

* Embodied in revised statement, p. 209.

be brought back inside of the fortifications of Nashville. This order was rescinded, when we were ready to march, so far as to remain in camp, to wait until further orders, and not to pitch any tents.

On the 25th of December, early in the morning, the regiment had to go on picket, and on the same evening our outposts repulsed an attack made by the enemy.

At 2 o'clock on the morning of the 26th, we received orders to fall in with our brigade as soon as it should reach the picket line, and to march toward Nolensville. The whole army did move at daylight, and drove in the enemy's pickets from Mill Creek toward Nolensville, where a considerable force of the enemy made a stand, but his position was taken in the afternoon by Davis' excellent division.

On the 29th, at nightfall, we arrived about 6 miles below Murfreesborough. Our cavalry met the enemy, he being in heavy force.

On the 30th day of December the Second Missouri Volunteers was in reserve, and the whole army moving on to Murfreesborough, a distance of about 3 miles. Fast fighting in front, especially on the right wing. The Second Brigade, Third Division, of which we are a part, had to support Captain Hescock's battery (G), First Missouri Artillery, drawn up in line of battle on the right of the Nolensville and Murfreesborough turnpike. At nightfall we received an order to advance into an open wood, in a right-oblique direction, for bivouac.

On the morning of the 31st December the Second Missouri Volunteers had to proceed again (at early daybreak) for support to Captain Hescock's battery. About 8 a. m. the enemy advanced upon the extreme right wing of our army (Davis' and Johnson's divisions) with a number less force, and, overpowered, our troops turned about, and the whole extreme right wing created a very critical confusion. By this time the First Battalion of the Second Missouri Volunteer Infantry, under command of Major Ehrler, was deployed as skirmishers in front of a field, the enemy advancing upon our line with heavy force from the woods opposite. The Second Battalion deployed, and every man of the Second Missouri Volunteer Infantry was engaged. Several times the rebels were repulsed by our energetic fire, but finally came up so thick that the order was given to fall slowly back to the woods, which movement was executed, coolly and promptly, under a heavy flank fire of a rebel battery, the rebels following up, and the two right skirmish companies (H and B) of the Second Missouri Volunteers were cut off and scattered. The remainder of the regiment marched down to the pike, and at the same time advancing toward Murfreesborough, we were ordered to make a stand on the left of the pike, in an oblique line, on a rather rocky ground, which offered excellent natural breastworks for all our fighting men. They received the advancing rebels with a steady and murderous fire, accompanied by the batteries from the hill in the rear of our line. Here we remained, and kept the enemy in check until we were out of ammunition, when another regiment relieved us, and we retired to the cedar woods in our rear. For nearly two painful hours we remained in this dreadful position; then we were marched out into the open air across the other pike, to provide our men with ammunition. After a short rest, we received orders to proceed forward, and to take position behind the embankment of the Chattanooga Railroad, from where we poured a very effective and steady fire upon the desperate enemy.

In this position our worthy and gallant Col. Frederick Schaefer was killed in the execution of his duties as our brigade commander. He fell, a hero, and his fellow officers and his brave soldiers mourn about this heavy loss for the country as well as for ourselves.

For the second time we were out of ammunition, and Lieut. Col. B. Laiboldt, of the Second Missouri Volunteers, now in command of the Second Brigade, Third Division, ordered the Second Missouri Volunteers to fall back into a reserve and get ammunition. One of the rebel batteries on the railroad playing on ours, did do some damage to our very defective ranks, killing 2 and wounding several. At nightfall we were withdrawn to the provision train, and on the morning of New Year's day we had to take our position on the new-formed line, which we strengthened by a ravelin made out of fence rails and rocks. Since that our skirmishers in front only were engaged with the enemy's outposts. The houses in front of our line have been burned, by order of the general commanding, and the enemy's sharpshooters lost every hold.

A special denomination of gallant conduct we do not make. All the officers, non-commissioned officers, and privates have done their full duty, and the Second Infantry Regiment of Missouri Volunteers have preserved and strengthened the good reputation which it already had.

I have the honor to sign,

By order of Major Ehrler, commanding Second Missouri Volunteer Infantry:

CHARLES FUELLE,
First Lieutenant and Adjutant.

His Excellency HAMILTON R. GAMBLE,
Governor of the State of Missouri.

No. 61.

Report of Col. Luther P. Bradley, Fifty-first Illinois Infantry, commanding Third Brigade.

HEADQUARTERS THIRD BRIGADE, THIRD DIVISION,
RIGHT WING, FOURTEENTH ARMY CORPS,
January 8, 1863.

SIR: I have the honor to report, for the information of the general commanding, the part taken by the Third Brigade in the operations before Murfreesborough, ending January 4.

On the morning of December 30, 1862, the brigade, under command of Col. G. W. Roberts, advanced on the Winchester pike, having the right of the column. About 9 o'clock we came on the enemy's skirmishers, engaged with a regiment of General Negley's division. The Twenty-second Illinois was thrown out on the left, and the Forty-second on the right of the pike as skirmishers, and soon forced the enemy back.

Houghtaling's battery was sent to the high ground, just in the edge of heavy timber on the right, and the Twenty-seventh and Fifty-first Illinois formed in line of battle to the rear of the reserves of the Twenty-second and Forty-second, and on the left of the battery. We had active work with the enemy's skirmishers all day, the battery occasionally shelling them, but they were generally out of range. At noon the Fifty-first Illinois relieved the Forty-second Illinois, and occupied the right of the brigade line of skirmishers for the balance of the day. About dark the skirmishers were withdrawn, and the brigade bivouacked on the field. The losses for the day were 7 killed and 35 wounded.

On the morning of the 31st, the brigade was under arms at daylight, and soon after formed line of battle. The enemy's columns opened out from the opposite woods, and Colonel Roberts ordered a skirmishing force to advance and feel the timber on our left. Companies A and B, Twenty-seventh Illinois, were thrown out under Major Schmitt, the balance of the regiment being held in reserve, its left resting on the pike.

About 8.30 a. m. Colonel Roberts ordered the Twenty-second, Forty-second, and Fifty-first to charge the enemy's columns, and gallantly led them in person. The Forty-second and Fifty-first charged in line, with the Twenty-second in rear of the Forty-second, at battalion distance. These regiments went forward at the double-quick, and cleared the wood in front of our lines, the enemy giving way before we reached him. The line was halted, and opened fire in the timber. After some ten minutes, the line on our right giving way, we were ordered to retire to the lane leading at nearly right angles with the pike, and take a new position.

Very soon the whole brigade was moved to the left and rear, and formed in the cedar woods on the pike, east of the hospital. Houghtaling's battery was posted so as to sweep the open ground and timber the brigade had lately occupied. The Forty-second and Twenty-second were thrown to the left and rear of the battery, and the Twenty-seventh and Fifty-first formed on the pike, fronting south. The whole command was soon hotly engaged with the enemy, advancing on the east and south. The Twenty-seventh changed front to rear on first company, and the Fifty-first moved by the right flank, so as to form an angle with the Twenty-seventh Illinois. Company K, Fifty-first Illinois, under Lieutenant Moody, was thrown out in advance of the battery to the east, to skirmish the woods, and remained there until driven in. Houghtaling's battery was worked with great spirit and vigor during the whole action; it, as well as the regiments of the brigade, was exposed to a cross-fire from rebel batteries situated at the brick-kiln, and at the point occupied by Houghtaling on the 30th, as well as a heavy fire of small-arms.

There the brigade met its chief loss; 400 were killed or wounded in two hours. Colonels Roberts and Harrington fell about 10.45 o'clock. At this time the ammunition of the battery and of the infantry was nearly exhausted. Being hard pressed by a superior force, and nearly surrounded, it was thought necessary to retire.

At about 11 o'clock I withdrew the Fifty-first in concert with the Twenty-seventh, under Major Schmitt, both regiments moving by the right flank in good order. Houghtaling's battery was left upon the field, after firing the last round of ammunition and losing more than half the horses; being outflanked on both sides, it was impossible to bring it off in its crippled condition. I was not informed of the fall of Colonels Roberts and Harrington until after the Twenty-second and Forty-second had moved. These regiments, after suffering a loss of half their numbers, retired toward the Nashville pike, striking it near the grounds held by General Palmer's division, and, being separated from the brigade, reported to him.

The Twenty-seventh and Fifty-first were the last regiments to leave the ground, the regiments of General Negley's command having already retired. As soon as I was informed that the command of the brigade devolved on me, I sent Captain Rose, of Colonel Roberts' staff, to report to General Sheridan for orders, and fell back through the timber toward the pike.

Not being able to find General Sheridan, I reported to General Davis, who ordered me to re-enforce Colonel Harker's brigade, then engaged with the enemy, who was endeavoring to turn our extreme right and get possession of the road. I took the Twenty-seventh and Fifty-first in line of battle, just as our troops were falling back in some disorder, and, after delivering a volley or two, charged a rebel brigade of five regiments, routing them completely and taking some 200 prisoners. This was the final effort on the right. About 1 p. m. we stacked arms and supplied the men with ammunition, the Twenty-second and Forty-second joining soon after.

On the morning of January 1 we stood to arms at 3 o'clock, expecting an attack, and after daylight built a breastwork in front of the brigade line. In the afternoon a brigade of the enemy issued from the timber opposite our position and advanced on our line. As soon as they were in range, I opened with small-arms and shell, driving them back in disorder.

Observing that a part of them had skulked in the rocks, I sent out a strong line of skirmishers, under Lieutenant Hanback, of the Twenty-seventh Illinois, and captured 2 lieutenants and 117 men, mostly of the Third Confederate. The brigade occupied the same position on the 2d, 3d, and 4th of January, skirmishing more or less with the enemy every day.

The entire loss of the brigade is 3 commissioned officers killed, 12 wounded; 58 enlisted men killed, 328 wounded; 161 missing; making a total of 562.* This loss occurred on the 30th and 31st. I think there is a considerable number of wounded men in the hands of the enemy, who are now reckoned among the missing; but having no positive knowledge of their condition, we account for them in that way.

I cannot forbear to express the sorrow felt by the whole command at the loss of its senior officers, Colonels Roberts and Harrington. They had served with the brigade since last April, and had each been in command of it for a considerable time. Long service had made the command familiar with them, and inspired them with confidence in their judgment and skill. They fell in exactly the line of their duty, and each met a soldier's death, bravely.

L. P. BRADLEY,
Colonel, Commanding Brigade.

Lieut. GEORGE LEE,
Acting Assistant Adjutant-General, Third Division.

No. 62.

Reports of Maj. Gen. George H. Thomas, U. S. Army, commanding Center.

HDQRS. (CENTER) FOURTEENTH ARMY CORPS,
DEPARTMENT OF THE CUMBERLAND,
Murfreesborough, Tenn., January 15, 1863.

MAJOR : I have the honor to submit to the major-general commanding the Department of the Cumberland the following report of the operations of that part of my command which was engaged in the battle of Stone's River, in front of Murfreesborough :

It is proper to state here that two brigades of Fry's division and Reynolds' entire division were detained near Gallatin and along the Louisville and Nashville Railroad, to watch the movements of the rebel leader Morgan, who had been, for a long time, on the watch for an op-

---

* But see revised statement, p. 209.

portunity to destroy the railroad. Rousseau s, Negley's, and Mitchell's divisions, and Walker's brigade, of Fry's division, were concentrated at Nashville, but Mitchell's division being required to garrison Nashville, my only available force was Rousseau's and Negley's divisions, and Walker's brigade, of Fry's division, about 13,395 effective men.

December 26, Negley's division, followed by Rousseau's division and Walker's brigade, marched by the Franklin pike to Brentwood, at that point taking the Wilson pike. Negley and Rousseau were to have encamped for the night at Owen's store.

On reaching the latter place, Negley, hearing heavy firing in the direction of Nolensville, left his train with a guard, to follow, and pushed forward with his troops to the support of Brig. Gen. J. C. Davis, commanding the advanced division of McCook's corps, Davis having become hotly engaged with the enemy posted in Nolensville, and in the pass through the hills south of that village. Rousseau encamped with his division at Owen's store; Walker with his brigade at Brentwood.

During the night a very heavy rain fell, making the cross-roads almost impassable, and it was not until night of the 27th that Rousseau reached Nolensville with his troops and train. Negley remained at Nolensville until 10 a. m. on the 27th, when, having brought his train across from Wilson's pike, he moved to the east, over an exceedingly rough by-road, to the right of Crittenden, at Stewartsborough, on the Murfreesborough pike. Walker, by my orders, retraced his steps from Brentwood, and crossed over to the Nolensville pike.

December 28, Negley remained in camp at Stewartsborough, bringing his train from the rear. Rousseau reached Stewartsborough on the night of the 28th. His train arrived early next day.

December 29, Negley's division crossed Stewart's Creek, 2 miles southwest and above the turnpike bridge, and marched in support of the head and right flank of Crittenden's corps, which moved by the Murfreesborough pike to a point within 2 miles of Murfreesborough. The enemy fell back before our advance, contesting the ground obstinately with their cavalry rear guard. Rousseau remained in camp at Stewartsborough, detaching Starkweather's brigade, with a section of artillery, to the Jefferson pike crossing of Stone's River, to observe the movements of the enemy in that direction. Walker reached Stewartsborough from the Nolensville pike about dark.

December 30, a cavalry force of the enemy, something over 400 strong, with two pieces of artillery, attacked Starkweather about 9 a. m., but was soon driven off. The enemy opened a brisk fire on Crittenden's advance, doing but little execution, however, about 7 a. m.

During the morning Negley's division was obliqued to the right, and took up a position on the right of Palmer's division, of Crittenden's corps, and was then advanced through a dense cedar thicket, several hundred yards in width, to the Wilkinson Cross-Roads, driving the enemy's skirmishers steadily and with considerable loss. Our loss comparatively small.

About noon Sheridan's division, of McCook's corps, approached by the Wilkinson Cross-Roads, joined Negley's right, McCook's two other divisions coming up on Sheridan's right, thus forming a continuous line, the left resting on Stone's River, the right stretching in a westerly direction, and resting on high, wooded ground, a short distance to the south of the Wilkinson Cross-Roads, and, as has since been ascertained, nearly parallel with the enemy's intrenchments thrown up on the sloping land bordering the northwest bank of Stone's River. Rousseau's division (with the exception of Starkweather's brigade), being ordered up from Stewartsborough, reached the position occupied by the army about 4 p. m., and bivouacked on the Murfreesborough pike in rear of the center.

During the night of the 30th I sent orders to Walker to take up a strong position near the turnpike bridge over Stewart's Creek, and defend the position against any attempts of the enemy's cavalry to destroy it. Rousseau was ordered to move by 6 a. m. on the 31st to a position in rear of Negley. This position placed his division with its left on the Murfreesborough pike, and its right extending into the cedar thicket through which Negley had marched on the 30th. In front of Negley's position, bordering a large open field, reaching to the Murfreesborough pike, a heavy growth of timber extended in a southerly direction toward the river. Across the field, running in an easterly direction, the enemy had thrown up rifle-pits at intervals, from the timber to the river bank, to the east side of the turnpike. Along this line of intrenchments, on an eminence about 800 yards from Negley's position, and nearly in front of his left, some cannon had been placed, affording the enemy great advantage in covering an attack on our center. However, Palmer, Negley, and Sheridan held the position their troops had so manfully won the morning of the 30th against every attempt to drive them back, and remained in line of battle during the night.

December 31, between 6 and 7 a. m., the enemy, having massed a heavy force on McCook's right during the night of the 30th, attacked and drove it back, pushing his division in pursuit *en échelon*, and in supporting distance, until he had gained sufficient ground to our rear to wheel his masses to the right and throw them upon the right flank of the center, at the same moment attacking Negley and Palmer in front with a greatly superior force. To counteract this movement, I had ordered Rousseau to place two brigades, with a battery, to the right and rear of Sheridan's division, facing toward the west, so as to support Sheridan, should he be able to hold his ground, or to cover him, should he be compelled to fall back.

About 11 o'clock General Sheridan reported to me that his ammunition was entirely out, and he would be compelled to fall back to get more. As it became necessary for General Sheridan to fall back, the enemy pressed on still farther to our rear, and soon took up a position which gave them a concentrated cross-fire of musketry and cannon on Negley's and Rousseau's troops at short range. This compelled me to fall back out of the cedar woods, and take up a line along a depression in the open ground, within good musket-range of the edge of the woods, while the artillery was retired to the high ground to the right of the turnpike. From this last position we were enabled to drive back the enemy, cover the formation of our troops, and secure the center on the high ground. In the execution of this last movement, the regular brigade, under Lieutenant-Colonel Shepherd, Eighteenth U. S. Infantry, came under a most murderous fire, losing 22 officers and 508 men in killed and wounded, but, with the co-operation of Scribner's and Beatty's brigades and Guenther's and Loomis' batteries, gallantly held its ground against overwhelming odds. The center having succeeded in driving back the enemy from its front, and our artillery concentrating its fire on the cedar thicket on our right, drove him back far under cover, from which, though repeatedly attempting it, he could not make any advance.

January 1, 1863, repeated attempts were made by the enemy to advance on my position during the morning, but they were driven back before emerging from the woods. Colonel Starkweather's brigade of Rousseau's division and Walker's brigade of Fry's division having re-enforced us during the night, took post on the right of Rousseau and left of Sheridan, and bore their share in repelling the attempts of the enemy on the morning of the 1st instant.

For the details of the most valuable service rendered by these two brigades on December 30 and 31, 1862, and January 1, 2. and 3, 1863, I refer you to their reports. In this connection I also refer you to the report of Lieutenant-Colonel Parkhurst, commanding Ninth Michigan Infantry (on provost duty at my headquarters), for the details of most valuable services rendered by his command on December 31 and January 1 and 2. Negley's division was ordered early in the day to the support of McCook's right, and in which position it remained during the night.

January 2, about 7 a. m., the enemy opened a direct and cross fire from his batteries in our front, and from a position on the east bank of Stone's River to our left and front, at the same time making a strong demonstration with infantry, resulting, however, in no serious attack. Our artillery (Loomis', Guenther's, Stokes', and another battery, the commander's name I cannot now recall) soon drove back their infantry. Negley was withdrawn from the extreme right and placed in reserve behind Crittenden's right.

About 4 p. m. a division of Crittenden's corps, which had crossed Stone's River to reconnoiter, was attacked by an overwhelming force of the enemy, and, after a gallant resistance, compelled to fall back. The movements of the enemy having been observed and reported by some of my troops in the center, I sent orders to Negley to advance to the support of Crittenden's troops, should they want help. This order was obeyed in most gallant style, and resulted in the complete annihilation of the Twenty-sixth Tennessee (rebel) Regiment and the capture of their flag; also in the capture of a battery, which the enemy had been forced to abandon at the point of the bayonet. (See Negley's report.)

January 3, soon after daylight, the Forty-second Indiana, on picket in a clump of woods about 800 yards in front of our lines, was attacked by a brigade of the enemy, evidently by superior numbers, and driven in with considerable loss. Lieutenant-Colonel Shanklin, commanding the regiment, was surrounded and taken prisoner while gallantly endeavoring to draw off his men from under the fire of such superior numbers. From this woods the enemy's sharpshooters continued to fire occasionally during the day on our pickets.

About 6 p. m. two regiments from Col. John Beatty's brigade, Rousseau's division, co-operating with two regiments of Spears' brigade, of Negley's division, covered by the skillful and well-directed fire of Guenther's Fifth U. S. Artillery and Loomis' First Michigan Batteries, advanced on the woods and drove the enemy not only from their cover, but from their intrenchments, a short distance beyond.

For the details of this gallant night attack I refer you to the reports of Brigadier-General Spears, commanding Third Brigade of Negley's division, and Col. John Beatty, commanding Second Brigade of Rousseau's division. The enemy having retreated during the night of the 3d, our troops were occupied during the morning of the 4th in burying the dead left on the field. In the afternoon one brigade of Negley's division was advanced to the crossing of Stone's River, with a brigade of Rousseau's division in supporting distance, in reserve.

January 5, my entire command, preceded by Stanley's cavalry. marched into Murfreesborough and took up the position which we now hold. The enemy's rear guard of cavalry was overtaken on the Shelbyville and Manchester roads, about 5 miles from Murfreesborough, and, after sharp skirmishing for two or three hours, was driven from our immediate front.

The conduct of my command from the time the army left Nashville to its entry into Murfreesborough is deserving of the highest praise, both for their patient endurance of the fatigues and discomforts of a five days' battle, and for the manly spirit exhibited by them in the various phases in this memorable contest. I refer you to the detailed reports of the division and brigade commanders, forwarded herewith, for special mention of those officers and men of their commands whose conduct they thought worthy of particular notice.

All the members of my staff, Maj. G. E. Flynt, assistant adjutant-general; Lieut. Col. A. Von Schrader, Seventy-fourth Ohio, acting inspector-general; Capt. O. A. Mack, Thirteenth U. S. Infantry, acting chief commissary, and Capt. A. J. Mackay, chief quartermaster, were actively employed in carrying my orders to various parts of my command and in the execution of the appropriate duties of their office. Capt. O. A. Mack was dangerously wounded in the right hip and abdomen while conveying orders from me to Major-General Rousseau.

The officers of the signal corps attached to my headquarters did excellent service in their appropriate sphere, when possible, and as aides-de-camp, carrying orders. My escort, composed of a select detail from the First Ohio Cavalry, commanded by First Lieut. J. D. Barker, of the same regiment, who have been on duty with me for nearly a year, deserve commendation for the faithful performance of their appropriate duties. Private Guiteau was killed by a cannon-shot on the morning of January 2. Surg. G. D. Beebe, medical director, deserves special mention for his efficient arrangements for moving the wounded from the field and giving them immediate attention.

Annexed hereto is a consolidated return of the casualties of my command. The details will be seen in the accompanying reports of division and brigade commanders.

Very respectfully, your obedient servant,

GEO. H. THOMAS,
Major-General of Volunteers, Commanding.

Maj. C. GODDARD,
Assistant Adjutant-General and Chief of Staff.

—

Consolidated report of casualties of the Center, Fourteenth Army Corps, in the five days' battle before Murfreesborough, Tenn., commencing December 31, 1862, and ending January 4, 1863. *

| | In action. | | | | Lost in action. | | | | | | | | | | |
| | Commissioned officers. | Enlisted men. | Horses. | Guns (artillery). | Killed. | | Wounded. | | Missing. | | Horses. | | | Guns. |
					Commissioned.	Enlisted.	Commissioned.	Enlisted.	Commissioned.	Enlisted.	Killed.	Wounded.	Missing.	Lost.	Disabled.
First Division, Major-General Rousseau.	303	5,883	....	18	8	171	43	903	3	324	8	5	....	....	....
Second Division, Brigadier-General Negley.	237	4,632	257	13	11	167	47	704	1	308	62	24	9	6	1
First Brigade, Third Division, Col. M. B. Walker.	97	2,243	....	6	....	....	4	19	....	1	....	....	....	....	....
	637	12,758	257	37	19	338	94	1,626	4	633	70	29	9	6	1

* But see revised statement, pp. 209–211.

HEADQUARTERS FOURTEENTH ARMY CORPS,
Murfreesborough, Tenn., May 16, 1863.

COLONEL : My attention having been called by Major-General Rousseau to the fact that Col. B. F. Scribner's brigade had not been men
tioned by the major-general commanding the department, for the part
it took in the battle of Stone's River, I cheerfully submit the following
statement, premising that in my official report of the battle of Stone's
River it was my earnest endeavor to do equal justice to the commands
of Colonels Beatty, Scribner, and Lieutenant-Colonel Shepherd, as well
as to all the other troops under my command, and thought the best way
of so doing, without extending my report to too great a length, was to
give a succinct narrative of the events of the battle, and then refer to
the reports of the subordinate commanders for more detailed information.   This I did, with the more confidence in the justice of that course,
from the fact that, after a careful reading of the different reports, I perceived no discrepancy in the accounts given in these reports of the events
of the battle in which different portions of my command acted together.
In my official report is the following :

As it became necessary for General Sheridan to fall back, the enemy pressed on still
farther to our rear, and soon took up a position which gave them a concentrated cross-
fire of musketry and cannon on Generals Negley's and Rousseau's troops at short range.
This compelled me to fall back through the cedar woods and take up a line along a depression in the open ground, within good musket-range of the edge of the woods, while
the artillery was retired to the high ground on the right of the turnpike.   From this
last position we were enabled to drive back the enemy, cover the formation of our
troops, and secure the center on the high ground.   In the execution of this last movement, the regular brigade, under Lieutenant-Colonel Shepherd, Eighteenth U. S. Infantry, came under a most murderous fire, losing 22 officers and 508 men in killed and
wounded, but, with the co-operation of Scribner's and Beatty's brigades and Guenther's and Loomis' batteries, gallantly held its ground against overwhelming odds—

thus connecting these three gallant brigades together in the honorable
and distinguished work of covering the formation of the troops on the
elevated ground in their rear, when the enemy was straining every nerve
to gain possession of the same point.

I now quote Colonel Scribner's report of the part taken by his brigade
at this period of the battle : *

*   *   *   *   *   *   *

Colonel Scribner's brigade was at this time to the right of the regular brigade, and advanced into the cedars.

It gives me much pleasure to be able to testify, further, that the efficiency of this brigade, so long commanded by Colonel Scribner, is second
to none in this army.

Very respectfully, your obedient servant,

GEO. H. THOMAS,
Major-General, U. S. Volunteers, Commanding.

Lieut. Col. C. GODDARD,
Assistant Adjutant-General, Hdqrs. Dept. of the Cumberland.

[Indorsement.]

HDQRS. DEPT. CUMBERLAND, *May* 18, 1863.

I forward with pleasure General Thomas' special notice of the part
taken by Colonel Scribner in the battle of Stone's River.   It supplies
an omission in the report of General Rousseau, which was the reason
why a notice of it did not appear in my report.

W. S. ROSECRANS,
Major-General.

---

* See report No. 65, paragraphs 4-7, both inclusive.

HEADQUARTERS FOURTEENTH ARMY CORPS.
DEPARTMENT OF THE CUMBERLAND,
Murfreesborough, February 9, 1863.

Col. C. GODDARD, *Chief of Staff:*

The last semi-weekly return of effective force before the battle of Stone's River, dated December 24, shows as follows, to wit:

Rousseau's division .... 303 + 5,883 = 6,186
Negley's division .... 212 + 5,284 = 5,496

11,682

General Negley's report of the actual force engaged shows a deficiency of 664. This deficiency is in cavalry, which had been assigned to General Stanley between the 24th and 31st of December. I shall certainly hold my officers responsible for all reports differing from the above. The supposition was that the whole effective force was engaged. Please send me the reports showing the discrepancy.

Very respectfully,

GEO. H. THOMAS,
Major-General, U. S. Volunteers, Commanding.

No. 63.

Report of Maj. Gen. Lovell H. Rousseau, U. S. Army, commanding First Division.

NASHVILLE, TENN., *January* 11, 1863.

SIR : I have the honor to report the part taken by my command, the Third Division of the army, in the battle of Murfreesborough, begun on the 31st ultimo and ended on the 3d instant.

Early on the morning of the 30th ultimo, in obedience to the order of General Thomas, my division moved forward toward Murfreesborough from Stewartsborough, on the Nashville and Murfreesborough turnpike, about 9 miles from the latter place. On the march forward, several dispatches from General Rosecrans reached me, asking exactly where my command was and the hour and minute of the day. In consequence, we moved rapidly forward, halting but once, and that for only five minutes. About 10.30 a. m. we reached a point 3 miles from Murfreesborough, where Generals Rosecrans and Thomas were, on the Nashville and Murfreesborough turnpike, and remained during the day and bivouacked at night.

At about 9 a. m. on the 31st, the report of artillery and heavy firing of small-arms on our right announced that the battle had begun, by an attack on the right wing, commanded by Major-General McCook. It was not long before the direction from which the firing came indicated that General McCook's command had given way and was yielding ground to the enemy. His forces seemed to swing around toward our right and rear. At this time General Thomas ordered me to advance my division quickly to the front, to the assistance of General McCook.

On reaching the right of General Negley's line of battle, General Thomas there directed me to let my left rest on his right, and deploy my division off toward the right as far as I could, so as to resist the pressure on General McCook. We consulted and agreed as to where the line should be formed. This was in a dense cedar brake, through which my troops marched in double-quick time, to get into position before the enemy reached us. He was then but a few hundred yards to the front, sweeping up in immense numbers, driving everything before him. This ground was new and unknown to us all. The woods were almost impassable to infantry, and artillery was perfectly useless, but the line was promptly formed ; the Seventeenth Brigade, Col. John Beatty commanding, on the left; the brigade of regulars, Lieut. Col. O. L. Shepherd commanding, on the right; the Ninth Brigade, Col. B. F. Scribner commanding, was placed perhaps 100 yards in rear and opposite the center of the front line, so as to support either or both of the brigades in front, as occasion might require. My recollection is that, perhaps, the Second Ohio and Thirty-third Ohio Regiments filled a gap between General Negley's right and the Seventeenth Brigade, occasioned by the effort to extend our lines far enough to the right to afford the desired aid to General McCook.

The Twenty-eighth Brigade, Col. John C. Starkweather commanding, and Stone's battery of First Kentucky Artillery were at Jefferson Crossing, on Stone's River, about 8 miles below.

Our lines were hardly formed before a dropping fire of the enemy announced his approach. General McCook's troops, in a good deal of confusion, retired through our lines and around our right under a most terrific fire. The enemy, in pursuit, furiously assailed our front, and, greatly outflanking us, passed around to our right and rear. By General Thomas' direction, I had already ordered the artillery (Loomis' and Guenther's batteries) to the open field in the rear. Seeing that my command was outflanked on the right, I sent orders to the brigade commanders to retire at once also to this field, and, riding back myself, I posted the batteries on a ridge in the open ground, parallel with our line of battle, and as my men emerged from the woods they were ordered to take position on the right and left, and in support of these batteries, which was promptly done. We had, perhaps, 400 or 500 yards of open ground in our front. While the batteries were unlimbering, seeing General Van Cleve close by, I rode up and asked him if he would move his command to the right and aid in checking up the enemy, by forming on my right, and thus giving us a more extended line in that direction in the new position taken. In the promptest manner possible his command was put in motion, and in double-quick time reached the desired point in good season. As the enemy emerged from the woods in great force, shouting and cheering, the batteries of Guenther and Loomis, double-shotted with canister, opened upon them. They moved straight ahead for a while, but were finally driven back with immense loss.

In a little while they rallied again, and, as it seemed, with fresh troops, and assailed our position, and were again, after a fierce struggle, driven back. Four deliberate and fiercely sustained assaults were made upon our position and repulsed.

During the last assault I was informed that our troops were advancing on the right, and saw troops, not of my division, led by General Rosecrans, moving in that direction. I informed General Thomas of the fact, and asked leave to advance my lines. He directed me to do so. We made a charge upon the enemy and drove him into the woods, my staff and orderlies capturing some 17 prisoners, including a captain and lieutenant, who were within 130 yards of the batteries. This ended the fighting of that day, the enemy in immense force hovering in the woods during the night, while we slept upon our arms on the field of battle. We occupied this position during the three following days and nights of the fight. Under General Thomas' direction, I had it intrenched by rifle-pits, and believe the enemy could not have taken it at all.

During the day the Twenty-eighth Brigade, Colonel Starkweather, was attacked by General Wheeler's cavalry in force, and some of the wagons of his train were burned before they reached him, having started that morning from Stewartsborough to join him. The enemy were finally repulsed and driven off with loss. Starkweather's loss was small, as will be seen by his report of the action. In this affair the whole brigade behaved handsomely. The burden of the fight fell upon the Twenty-first Wisconsin, Lieutenant-Colonel Hobart commanding. This regiment, led by its efficient commander, behaved like veterans.

From the evening of the 31st until the ensuing Saturday night no general battle occurred in front of my division, though firing of artillery and small-arms was kept up during the day, and much of the time, of small-arms, during the night. The rain on the night of the 31st, which continued, at intervals, until the Saturday night following, rendered the ground occupied by my command exceedingly sloppy and muddy, and during much of the time my men had neither shelter, food, nor fire. I procured corn, which they parched and ate, and some of them ate horse-steaks, cut and broiled, from horses upon the battle-field. Day and night, in the cold, wet, and mud, my men suffered severely, but during the whole time I did not hear one single man murmur at hardships, but all were cheerful and ever ready to stand by their arms and fight. Such endurance I never saw before. In this severe trial of their patience and their strength they were much encouraged by the constant presence and solicitous anxiety of General Thomas for their welfare.

On the evening of Saturday, 3d instant, I asked permission of General Thomas to drive the enemy from the wood on our left front, to which he gave his consent. Just before night I directed the batteries of Guenther and Loomis to shell the woods with six rounds per gun, fired as rapidly as possible. This was very handsomely done, and ended just at dusk, when the Third Ohio Regiment, Lieut. Col. O. A. Lawson, and the Eighty-eighth Indiana, Col. George Humphrey, both under command of the brigade commander, Col. John Beatty, moved promptly up the woods. When near the woods they received a heavy fire from the enemy, but returned it vigorously, and gallantly pressed forward. On reaching the woods a fresh body of the enemy, attracted by the fire, moved up on their left to support them. On that body of the enemy Loomis' battery opened with shell. The fusilade was very rapid, and continued for, perhaps, three-quarters of an hour, when Beatty's command drove the enemy at the point of the bayonet and held the woods. It turned out that the enemy was posted behind a stone breast-work in the woods, and, when ousted, about 30 men were taken prisoners behind the works. This ended the battle of Murfreesborough.

On the morning of the 31st, six companies of the Second Kentucky Cavalry, Maj. Thomas P. Nicholas commanding, were ordered down to watch and defend the fords on Stone's River, to our left and rear. The cavalry of the enemy several times, in force, attempted to cross these fords, but Nicholas very gallantly repulsed them, with loss, and they did not cross the river. I should have mentioned that on Friday evening, late, I was directed by General Thomas to place a regiment in the woods on our left front as an outpost, and with a view to hold these woods, as they were near our lines, and the enemy could greatly annoy us if allowed to hold them. Our skirmishers were then just leaving the woods. I ordered the Forty-second Indiana, Lieutenant-Colonel Shanklin commanding, to take that position, which he did; but early next morning the enemy, in large force, attacked Colonel Shanklin, first furiously shelling the woods, and drove the regiment back to our lines, taking Shanklin prisoner. It was this woods that was retaken on Saturday night, as before described.

The troops of my division behaved admirably. I could not wish them to behave more gallantly. The Ninth and Seventeenth Brigades, under the lead of their gallant commanders, Scribner and Beatty, were, as well as the Twenty-eighth Brigade, Colonel Starkweather, veterans. They were with me at Chaplin Hills, and could not act badly. The Twenty-eighth Brigade held a position in our front after the first day's fighting, and did it bravely, doing all that was required of them, like true soldiers. The brigade of United States infantry, Lieut. Col. O. L. Shepherd commanding, was on the extreme right. On that body of brave men the shock of battle fell heaviest, and its loss was most severe. Over one third of the command fell, killed or wounded; but it stood up to the work and bravely breasted the storm, and, though Major King, commanding the Fifteenth, and Major Slemmer ("Old Pickens"), commanding the Sixteenth, fell, severely wounded, and Major Carpenter, commanding the Nineteenth, fell dead in the last charge, together with many other brave officers and men, the brigade did not falter for a moment. These three battalions were a part of my old (Fourth) brigade at the battle of Shiloh.

The Eighteenth Infantry, Majors Townsend and Caldwell commanding, were new troops to me, but I am now proud to say we know each other.

If I could, I would promote every officer and several non-commissioned officers and privates of this brigade of regulars, for gallantry and good service in this terrific battle. I make no distinction between these troops and my brave volunteer regiments, for, in my judgment, there never were better troops than those regiments, in the world. But the troops of the line are soldiers by profession, and, with a view to the future, I feel it my duty to say what I have of them. The brigade was admirably and gallantly handled by Lieutenant-Colonel Shepherd.

I lost some of the best and bravest officers I had. Lieutenant-Colonel Kell, commanding the Second Ohio, was killed. After he fell his regiment was efficiently handled by Maj. Anson G. McCook, who ought to be made colonel of that regiment, for gallantry on the field.

Colonel Forman, my brave boy colonel, of the Fifteenth Kentucky, also fell; Major Carpenter, of the Nineteenth Infantry, fell in the last charge. His loss is irreparable. Many other gallant officers were lost, whose names will appear in the list of casualties.

Of the batteries of Guenther and Loomis I cannot say too much. Loomis was chief of artillery for the Third Division, and I am much indebted to him. His battery was commanded by Lieutenant Van Pelt. Guenther is but a lieutenant. Both of these men deserve to be promoted, and ought to be at once. Without them we could not have held our position in the center.

I fell in with many gallant regiments and officers on the field not of my command. I wish I could name all of them here. While falling back to the line in the open field, I saw Col. Charles Anderson gallantly and coolly rallying his men. Colonel Grider, of Kentucky, and his regiment efficiently aided in repulsing the enemy. The Eighteenth Ohio, I think it was, though I do not know any of its officers, faced about and charged the enemy in my presence, and I went along with it. The Eleventh Michigan and its gallant little colonel (I do not know his name certainly, but believe it is Stoddart) [Stoughton] behaved well, and the Sixth Ohio Infantry, Col. Nick Anderson, joined my command on the right of the regular brigade, and stood manfully up to the work. I fell in with the Louisville Legion in retreat, Lieutenant-Colonel Berry commanding.

This regiment, though retreating before an overwhelming force, was dragging by hand a section of artillery which it had been ordered to support. A part of General McCook's wing of the army (it had fallen back with the rest, but through the woods and fields with great difficulty) bravely brought off the cannon it could no longer defend on the field. When I met it, it faced about and formed line of battle, with cheers and shouts.

To Lieutenants McDowell, my assistant adjutant-general, Armstrong, Second Kentucky Cavalry, and Millard, Nineteenth U. S. Infantry, inspector-general; Captain Taylor, Fifteenth Kentucky Infantry, and Lieut. Alf. Pirtle, ordnance officer, my regular aides, and to Capt. John D. Wickliffe and Lieut. W. G. Jenkins, both of the Second Kentucky Cavalry, aides for that battle, I am much indebted for services on the field.

The wounded were kindly and tenderly cared for by the Third Division medical director, Surgeon Muscroft, and the other surgeons of the command. Captain Paul, my division commissary, rendered valuable services during the whole time of the battle. The musicians of the division carried the wounded from the field, faithfully and fearlessly.

Lieutenant McDowell was wounded. My orderlies, Damas, Emery, and the rest, went through the whole fight, behaving well; Emery was wounded. Lieutenant Carpenter, of the First Ohio Infantry, one of my aides, was so badly injured by the fall of his horse that I would not permit him to go on the field. Lieutenant Hartman, of the Seventy-ninth Pennsylvania Infantry, a member of my staff, was ill with fever and unable to leave his bed.

It should be mentioned that the Eighty-eighth Indiana, Colonel Humphrey commanding, being placed at one of the fords on Stone's River, where our forces were temporarily driven back, very opportunely rallied the stragglers and promptly crossed the river and drove the enemy back. In this he was aided by the stragglers, who rallied and fought well. The colonel was wounded by a bayonet thrust in the hand in the attack of Saturday night on the enemy in the wood in our front.

I inclose herewith the reports of brigade commanders, which will show the list of casualties.

I have the honor to be, &c.,

LOVELL H. ROUSSEAU,
Major-General.

Maj. GEORGE E. FLYNT,
　　Chief of Staff (Center), Fourteenth Army Corps,
　　　　　Department of the Cumberland.

No. 64.

Report of Lieut. Francis L. Guenther, Battery H, Fifth U. S. Artillery.

HEADQUARTERS BATTERY H, FIFTH ARTILLERY,
　　　　　January 10, 1863.

SIR: I have the honor to make the following report of the operations of the battery under my command in the recent engagements near Murfreesborough, Tenn. :

The battery arrived near the battle-field with the brigade of regulars, of which it forms a part, on the morning of December 30, 1862. On the morning of December 31 it was moved forward with the brigade, and, after a short halt, proceeded through a dense grove of cedars to take a position. Finding it impossible to operate with the battery in so dense a wood, I reported to General Rousseau, who, after seeing the impossibility of taking up a proper position, ordered the battery into action in the open field, which it had previously left. The battery was formed in time to check the advance of the enemy from the cedars, and was then moved to a position on a rise of ground on the opposite side of the pike. A heavy column of the enemy advanced from the cedars, but was finally driven back in disorder by the fire of canister from the battery.

On the afternoon of the 31st the enemy again moved forward in heavy force from a position to our left and front, but were unable to advance under the fire of the different batteries which was concentrated upon them. Though the battery changed positions several times, in order to follow up the movements of the troops, its main position was on the rise of ground already spoken of, and on which it camped at night.

On the morning of January 1, 1863, the battery was moved some distance to the rear, and after several changes of position was ordered back with the brigade of regulars toward a point on the Murfreesborough pike beyond Stewart's Creek. After proceeding some miles, the order being countermanded, the brigade and battery returned, and about nightfall camped in the woods near the old position.

On the morning of January 2, the battery moved forward and took position, remaining in position during the day, and camping on the same ground at night. On the 3d, the brigade and battery were moved forward and occupied rifle-pits and epaulements which had been constructed for them. At dusk the battery opened fire with shell and spherical-case shot on the enemy concealed in the woods, in buildings, and behind breastworks, &c., and the attack being followed up by the infantry, the enemy were driven from the position and the grounds occupied by our troops, who were subsequently withdrawn. The battery remained in position during the following day, and on the morning of January 5 took up the line of march toward Murfreesborough, encamping some distance beyond the town in the evening.

To Lieutenant-Colonel Shepherd, Eighteenth Infantry, commanding brigade, and to Majors Carpenter, Nineteenth Infantry; King, Fifteenth Infantry; Caldwell and Townsend, Eighteenth Infantry, and Slemmer, Sixteenth Infantry, commanding battalions, and to their officers and men, I am indebted for the gallant support afforded me during the series of engagements. My officers, Second Lieuts. Israel Ludlow and J. A. Fessenden, deserve honorable mention for their display of coolness, gallantry, and judgment.

Sergeants Egan, Reed, Metcalf, Brode, Bickel, Ervin, and Manbeck behaved with conspicuous courage, and to the other non-commissioned officers and privates of the battery, without exception, I am indebted for faithful services.

I have the honor to append the following list of casualties in my command: Wounded: Corpl. Charles Allitzon and Privates Thomas Burns, James F. Mohr, Michael McGrath, and Benjamin F. Burgess; total wounded, 5; total of horses killed, 10; total of horses wounded, 5; rounds of ammunition expended, 558.

Very respectfully, your obedient servant,

F. L. GUENTHER,
First Lieutenant, Commanding Battery H, Fifth Artillery.

First Lieut. ROBERT SUTHERLAND,
Eighteenth Infantry, A. A. A. G., Brigade of Regulars.

No. 65.

Report of Col. Benjamin F. Scribner, Thirty-eighth Indiana Infantry, commanding First Brigade.

HEADQUARTERS FIRST BRIGADE, FIRST DIVISION, CENTER,
Near Murfreesborough, Tenn., January 9, 1863.

I have the honor to submit the following report of the part borne by my command in the engagements before Murfreesborough on December 31 and three succeeding days:

At daylight we left our bivouac, and moved about 1 mile to the front, and formed the second line of your division, two regiments extending into the cedar thicket on the right, and the left extending to the Murfreesborough and Nashville pike. My line was disposed from right to left, in the following order: The Tenth Wisconsin Volunteers, Col. A. R. Chapin; Ninety-fourth Ohio, Col. J. W. Frizell; Thirty-eighth Indiana, Lieut. Col. D. F. Griffin; Thirty-third Ohio, Capt. E. J. Ellis, and Second Ohio, Lieut. Col. John Kell. Having just finished loading arms, I received your orders to proceed, in double-quick time, to the assistance of the right wing, and to follow the Seventeenth Brigade, on the pioneer road, into the woods. When the Seventeenth Brigade halted in the woods, I was ordered by General Thomas to move to the right, and soon after formed my line of battle near the Wilkinson pike, when we were opened upon by the enemy's battery.

When near this position, the Thirty-third and Second Ohio were, by your order, detached and moved back near to the position we first occupied, to support our batteries stationed there, and nobly did they defend them; for soon after the enemy fiercely charged them, and were handsomely repulsed, the Second Ohio capturing the colors of the Thirtieth Arkansas—a victory dearly bought by the loss of the gallant Lieutenant-Colonel Kell, commanding.

From near the Wilkinson pike I was ordered to move back in great haste to near our position on the Nashville pike, which order was faithfully obeyed. My right had just emerged from the woods, when the enemy, who had just been repulsed in their efforts to take the batteries before mentioned, were seen retreating in disorder in a northwesterly direction through a narrow neck of woods, and were opened upon by the Ninety-fourth Ohio and the two right companies of the Thirty-eighth Indiana. I then threw my skirmishers forward, and advanced about 600 yards into the woods, where my lines became masked by General Negley's division, which was falling back under a heavy fire from the enemy, who appeared to be advancing from a point south of the direction taken by their retreating column. I opened my line to permit that portion of General Negley's command who had expended their ammunition to pass through, which was done in good order, a portion of them forming in my rear.

Here the Ninety-fourth Ohio was ordered to the pike, leaving me but two regiments, Thirty-eighth Indiana and Tenth Wisconsin, the former now on the right. General Negley having halted his regiments some 25 paces obliquely in front of my line, I wheeled my right under heavy fire to connect with him. Here I appeared to be nearly surrounded, a heavy column turning my left, to prevent which I ordered the Tenth Wisconsin to change front to the rear on their first company, thereby forming a right angle with the Thirty-eighth Indiana Volunteers. This position was scarcely taken when the enemy came down on us in great fury. They appeared to be massed in several lines, and their heads seemed to be in terraces not 25 yards before us. For twenty minutes these two regiments maintained their ground, completely checking the advance of the enemy's column.   Here the Thirty-eighth Indiana lost their brave captain, J. E. Fouts, besides nearly one-third their number in killed and wounded.

Lieut. Col. D. F. Griffin and Major Glover both had their horses shot under them, and their clothing perforated by balls.   The Tenth Wisconsin nobly vied with their comrades on the right, and I am convinced that both regiments would have suffered extermination rather than have yielded their ground without orders.   But the order came, and we fell back, and formed on the pike fronting the woods, but the enemy did not venture to follow us farther than the skirts of the timber.

Having reformed my brigade, I soon after advanced my right to the woods from which we had just emerged, deploying skirmishers from the Ninety-fourth Ohio through the neck of the timber, with my left resting on the pike.   Here we remained the rest of the day under the fire of the enemy's sharpshooters, and ever and anon the shot and shell from their batteries on our left fell among us.   A ball from the former struck Colonel Frizell on the shoulder, so wounding him that he was borne from the field on which he had nobly performed his duty.

At 4 o'clock on the morning of January 1, you ordered me to take my command back to a point on the pike, near the place we occupied before the battle, in order that they might build fires, and warm themselves, and get something to eat.

Upon receiving your caution to protect myself from an attack on the left, and from your allusion to a ford in that direction, I ordered Lieut. Alexander Martin, assistant inspector-general on my staff, and Lieut. M. Allen, topographical engineers, to reconnoiter the position.   Upon their reporting the feasibility of the crossing, I ordered Lieutenant Martin to conduct the Second Ohio, Major McCook, to the position.   Soon after, firing was heard in this direction, and a stampede occurred among the wagons and hospitals.   I ordered the Tenth Wisconsin to support the Second Ohio, and placed them behind the embankment of the railroad.   These dispositions had scarcely been made when your order came for me to hurry to the front again with my command.   Having obeyed this order, and after some maneuvering, we were placed in position, the Thirty-third Ohio extending across the neck of woods into which my right threw out skirmishers the evening before, with a battery on the right and left, commanding the fields on either side of the woods.   On the right of the Thirty-third Ohio came the Ninety-fourth Ohio and Thirty-eighth Indiana in the edge of the undergrowth on the crest of the slope from the field west of the Nashville pike.   On the right of the Thirty-eighth Indiana was another battery.   The Tenth Wisconsin and Second Ohio were held in reserve, in order to re-enforce any part of the line that was menaced.   This position was maintained without material change during the subsequent days of the fight.   Our skirmishers were kept out during the time, and employed in discovering and dislodging the sharpshooters, who, during the hours of daylight, almost continually annoyed us.   I cannot too highly praise Captain Ellis, commanding Thirty-third Ohio, for the vigilance of himself and men in their exposed position in the woods.   At times the enemy from the woods below would essay to advance, when every man would be at his post, and often the batteries would open upon them.   While here Captain Ellis had his horse shot under him.   Breastworks of logs and rocks had been constructed to protect the line; also a few rifle-pits dug.

On the evening of the 2d, when the enemy so vigorously attacked our left, the moving of their forces in that direction could be seen from my position, which fact was promptly reported.   I caused my skirmishers to advance and take precaution against demonstration upon my position. The attempt was made just before dark, the enemy forming in the edge of the woods in our front, where Captain Cox's Tenth Indiana Battery, on the right of the Thirty-third Ohio, opened fire upon them, driving them back.

I deem it improper to close this report without commending in high terms the manner in which my command bore the hardships of this terrible conflict. They suffered from cold, rain, fatigue, and hunger without a murmur. These attributes, when added to their bravery, make soldiers of which the country may be proud. I also feel it my duty to praise the courage and efficiency of my staff—Lieutenant Fitzwilliam, acting assistant adjutant-general and aide-de-camp; Lieutenant Martin, inspector, who was wounded above the knee by a shell; Lieut. George H. Hollister, acting assistant commissary of subsistence, missing, after displaying great gallantry in his transmission of your orders to me; Lieut. Mundy Allen, topographical engineer—all of whom have endeared themselves to me by their prompt and intelligent performance of their appropriate duties. I would, in an especial manner, mention the name of one of my orderlies, Josiah F. Mitchell, Company B, Thirty-third Ohio Volunteers, who displayed marked courage and intelligence.

I went into the fight with 1,646 officers and men, minus two companies Thirty-third Ohio, under Major Ely, and Tenth Wisconsin, who were detached to guard the train.

My losses are:

Thirty-eighth Indiana.—Killed: Capt. J. E. Fouts and 14 enlisted men. Wounded: Lieuts. T. S. W. Hawkins, M. T. Davis, and 84 enlisted men. Missing (wounded), 3.

Thirty-third Ohio.—Killed, 2; wounded, 19; missing, 4.

Second Ohio.—Killed: Lieut. Col. John Kell and 9 enlisted men. Wounded: Captains Hazlett and Maxwell, Lieutenant Van Horn, and 29 enlisted men. Missing, 3.

Ninety-fourth Ohio.—Killed, 2. Wounded: Colonel Frizell, Captain Steel, and 25 enlisted men. Missing, 29.

Tenth Wisconsin.—Killed, 3. Wounded: Capt. J. W. Roby and 15 enlisted men. Missing, 6.

Total killed, 32; wounded, 180; missing, 45.*

Your obedient servant,

B. F. SCRIBNER,
Colonel Thirty-eighth Indiana Vols., Comdg. First Brigade,
First Division, Department of the Cumberland.

Capt. M. C. TAYLOR,
Acting Assistant Adjutant-General.

No. 66.

Report of Lieut. Col. Daniel F. Griffin, Thirty-eighth Indiana Infantry.

HDQRS. THIRTY-EIGHTH INDIANA VOLUNTEERS,
On the Field, in front of Murfreesborough, Tenn., January 4, 1863.

SIR: I have the honor to report the following as the part taken by my command in the action of December 31, in front of Murfreesborough, and subsequent operations in the field since that date:

At daylight on the morning of December 31, the command, occupying

---

* But see revised statement, p. 210.

the center of your brigade, moved to the front, on the Nashville turnpike, and about 8 a. m. moved, through a dense cedar forest, toward the right wing of the army, which was then hotly engaged by the enemy. After maneuvering for about an hour, we were ordered to retire, left in front, through the same forest, to near the position first occupied, on the right of the pike, in the timber. Here the enemy was discovered in strong force on our right and rear, charging toward the turnpike. The command was, by your order, immediately faced by the rear rank, and moved down on the flank of the enemy, who was now retiring before a column of our troops moving from the pike.

In this movement the Ninety-fourth Ohio was on our right and the Tenth Wisconsin was on our left. Company H, Captain Poindexter commanding, and Company B, First Lieutenant Lenau commanding, were deployed forward as skirmishers, moving steadily on the skirmishers of the enemy, capturing 6 of them, who were sent to the rear. Continuing our movements about 600 yards, we met the left of General Negley's command, which was now retiring before a heavy column of the enemy, and moved into position to their support. The left of this command having passed to the rear through our ranks, their center came into position on our right, and some 60 yards to the front. By your command the battalion was wheeled to the left, and moved forward with our left, now our right, joining their line. Before we were fairly in position, the enemy opened a heavy fire, and the troops on our right fell back, leaving the left of the battalion, now the right, exposed. I then moved the line by the flank, striving to continue the connection. The enemy now opening on our line, we at once faced to the front, and kept up a continuous fire for the space of twenty minutes, checking the enemy's advance, and holding him in check until your orders to retire to the pike were received. This was done in order, forming there on the right of the Second Ohio Volunteers. The enemy now appearing in force on the front, by your orders we changed front forward on left company, and advanced into the corn-field in front of the Chicago Board of Trade Battery. Lying down in this position, we remained, from 2 p. m. until dark, exposed to the fire of the enemy from the woods in front, awaiting their expected advance. Night closing the engagement, we lay in this position, with pickets advanced, until daylight, when we were relieved, and retired to the woods in our rear.

At 7.30 o'clock the engagement again opened on the front, when, by your orders, we moved forward on the double-quick, and were assigned to position on the right, to support Guenther's battery. In this position we have remained to present date, exposed to the fire of the enemy's sharpshooters and from their batteries on the front.

In the engagement of December 31, the command lost, in killed, Capt. James E. Fouts and 13 men; wounded and missing, supposed to be in the enemy's hospital, 3 men; wounded and in our hospital, Second Lieut. M. T. Davis, Company C; Second Lieut. Thomas S. W. Hawkins, Company I, and 81 men. Total killed, 14; wounded 86.[*] For list of names of killed and wounded, I respectfully refer you to accompanying report.

I cannot close without commending, for their coolness and bravery on the field, each officer and soldier of my command engaged during the five days. Though suffering at times severely from cold, hunger, rain, and fatigue, yet not a murmur was heard nor a duty flinched from. To Maj. J. B. Glover I am indebted for every support. In command of the skirmishers, and during the hottest of the fight, he was ever at his post. His horse received two wounds, himself escaping. My adjutant, George

---

* But see revised statement, p. 210.

H. Devol, was ever on the alert, and rendered much valuaoie assistance. Of our chaplain, Rev. L. E. Carson, too much cannot be said. In his attention and devotion to the wounded he was untiring, making this his especial duty. We have the satisfaction of knowing that all were cared for properly and efficiently.

In the death of Captain Fouts we lament the loss of a brave officer, a true patriot, and a warm friend.

Very respectfully,

D. F. GRIFFIN,
Lieutenant-Colonel, Comdg. Thirty-eighth Regt. Indiana Vols.
GEORGE H. DEVOL,
Actg. Asst. Adjt. Gen., First Brig., First Div., Center.

No. 67.

Report of Maj. Anson G. McCook, Second Ohio Infantry.

CAMP AT MURFREESBOROUGH, TENN.,
January 7, 1863.

COLONEL: I have the honor to report, briefly, the part taken by the Second Regiment Ohio Volunteers in the action of December 31, 1862, and the following days.

On the morning of the 31st, after being ordered into the woods on our right center, with the balance of the brigade, and before being engaged, Lieutenant-Colonel Kell, then in command of the regiment, was ordered by Captain McDowell, assistant adjutant-general on Major-General Rousseau's staff, in person, to leave the position assigned us in the woods, and move to the support of Captain Guenther's battery (H), [Fifth] United States Artillery, then stationed on the left of the main Murfreesborough turnpike. He did so without, I believe, reporting to you, as the exigency of the case would not admit of it. The regiment was formed on the flank of the battery, and, in conjunction with it, successfully repulsed the efforts of a brigade to capture it, killing and wounding many of the enemy, and capturing about 30 prisoners and a stand of colors belonging to the Thirtieth Regiment Arkansas Volunteer Infantry. At this time you made your appearance from the woods with the balance of the brigade, and from that time until we occupied this place we were under your eye.

Our loss was 11 officers and men killed and 34 officers and men wounded; among the former, Lieut. Col. John Kell, commanding the regiment, and First Lieut. Richard S. Chambers, Company F; among the latter, First Lieut. Lafayette Van Horn, Company I, mortally, and Captains Maxwell and Hazlett severely. I cannot refrain from expressing my regret at the loss of Lieutenant-Colonel Kell and Lieutenant Chambers, particularly the former. Brave, competent, and energetic, he had proven himself on several occasions well qualified for the position he held. His death is greatly to be deplored, and his loss will be severely felt by the regiment.

With very few exceptions, the regiment behaved well, and at some future time I will particularly recommend deserving men for promotion.

I have the honor to be,

A. G. McCOOK,
Major Second Ohio Volunteers, Commanding.
Col. B. F. SCRIBNER,
Commanding Ninth Brigade.

No. 68.

Report of Lieut. Col. Stephen A. Bassford, Ninety-fourth Ohio Infantry.

HDQRS. NINETY-FOURTH REGIMENT OHIO VOLUNTEERS,
ARMY OF THE CUMBERLAND,
In the Field, January —, 1863.

In obedience to orders from headquarters, I have the honor to forward the following report of the part taken in the battle of Wednesday, December 31, 1862, and the following days, by the Ninety-fourth Regiment:

My command, forming part of the Ninth Brigade, was ordered to move forward toward Murfreesborough, on the Nashville and Murfreesborough pike. After marching about 1½ miles, we turned to the right, and went a quarter of a mile and halted in the woods. After waiting a short period, we were again moved forward to the right and front in double-quick, halted, formed in line of battle, and for the first time came under fire of the enemy. Shells bursting over and around us, soon we were ordered to move to the right. After marching a short distance, we were halted. Remaining in that position about twenty minutes, we were again ordered to move by the right.

We then marched toward the Murfreesborough pike, and halted at the edge of the woods at the time the enemy left the woods and charged one of our batteries. The foe broke and fled precipitately. We commenced firing on our right, and threw Company B out as skirmishers on our left.

We were then ordered into the open field in line, halted, and delivered several rounds at the retreating foe. Received orders to fix bayonets, which done, we moved in double-quick across the field, following the enemy. We halted at the edge of the woods, remaining but a short time; threw out Company G as skirmishers, advanced into the woods about 75 yards, and halted.

After remaining here for some time, we received orders to move out to the right and up to the top of the hill, which we did, passing one of our batteries there. From this point we crossed the pike, forming in line along the east side. From this point I was ordered back to bring up ammunition. The regiment remained here about thirty minutes. We had several wounded at this point by the enemy's artillery.

The regiment was then ordered forward over the crest of the hill and into the woods, by order of General Rousseau. Companies B and G were advanced from this point, as skirmishers. They were soon brought in, and the whole command marched by the left flank, to join on the right of the Thirty-eighth Indiana, then in the open field. In this position we were ordered to lie down. Many of our men were wounded by the enemy's sharpshooters.

We did not remain long in this position, but returned to the woods, and after a very brief stay we were ordered out again, but not quite so far advanced and less exposed to the sharpshooters. Shortly after this, our gallant colonel, whose cheerful courage and constantly encouraging presence had contributed effectively to the calmness and prompt obedience of the entire command, was severely wounded and instantly carried from the field.

At this juncture the command fell for a short time upon Major King. Our left here joined on the right of the Thirty-eighth Indiana. This position we held during the night, throwing out pickets to the front. No disturbance occurred of any importance.

On Thursday, January 1, 1863, 5 a. m., we were ordered to report ourselves on the Murfreesborough pike, which being done, we were marched back to about the position we started from the morning before ; but we did not have long to remain at this point. We had hardly stacked arms and broken ranks till we heard that familiar sound, "Fall in." We were marched back again toward Murfreesborough in double-quick. After going about 1 mile, we were ordered off to the right of the pike, and formed into line.

Soon General McCook ordered us over to the left of the pike. We were, however, soon ordered back to the point at which we left the pike, at which place we were formed into column of companies, then marched forward to the right and front, to the crest of a hill, and halted, facing south, forming a line. In a few moments we were ordered to change front forward on first company, which being done, we marched forward and were halted in the edge of a thicket. Here we remained till 3 p. m., when we were pushed to the farther edge of the thicket, facing southwest.

During the night and day following we threw up breastworks of such material as was at hand.

On the evening following (January 2) we threw out heavy pickets, and this position we occupied, with nothing to disturb us, excepting the annoyance of the enemy's sharpshooters, until January 5, when ordered to march.

During the five days we were on the field, among those wounded was Captain Steel, bold and brave, who, though suffering from severe sickness, commanded his company with praiseworthy success until removed from the field. The officers, without exception, acted well their parts, and in perfect concert. The men, obedient and prompt, were easy to command, and are worthy of high commendation.

Of our chaplain, Rev. William Allington, I do not think too much can be said. I wish there were more such in our army. He followed the regiment wherever it went, picking up the wounded and carrying them off the field ; and after we were through with the day's fight, he would spend his nights at the hospitals administering to the wounded.

The above report is as near correct as I am able to make it.

Yours, most respectfully,

S. A. BASSFORD,
Lieut. Col., Comdg. Ninety-fourth Regiment Ohio Vol. Infantry.

Col. B. F. SCRIBNER,
  Commanding Ninth Brigade, Third Division.

No. 69.

Report of Col. Alfred R. Chapin, Tenth Wisconsin Infantry.

HDQRS. TENTH WISCONSIN VOLUNTEER INFANTRY,
  Camp at Murfreesborough, Tenn., January 9, 1863.

SIR : I would most respectfully report that on December 30, 1862, at 12 m., the Tenth Regiment Wisconsin Volunteer Infantry, with the other regiments of the brigade, had arrived at a point on the Nashville and Murfreesborough pike 3½ miles from Murfreesborough. Heavy skirmishing was going on at the time in the cedar wood to the right of the pike. We did not get engaged that day.

On December 31, at 7 a. m., we got under arms, and shortly after moved on the pike toward Murfreesborough about one half mile.   We then moved toward the wood on the right, and soon engaged the enemy. After some hot work they gradually retired, followed up by our brigade. About this time the Second Ohio and Thirty-third Ohio were detached, and my regiment, with the Thirty-eighth Indiana and Ninety-fourth Ohio, continued to advance under a pretty hot skirmish fire.   After having advanced some distance, we were attacked by a strong force, which we held for some time, until we began to receive a flank fire from the right.   Orders were received to retire behind the line of the Seventeenth Brigade, which we did; and as I was about to get my regiment into line I saw that the Seventeenth Brigade was also retiring.   I moved to the rear with them, and formed my line on their right and the left of Loomis' battery.   There I remained until retired by your order, about daylight the next morning.

On the morning of January 1, at about 7 o'clock, we were again moved rapidly forward on the pike to near our old position, where we remained all through the battle, but did not have any general engagement with the enemy after December 31.

I went into the battle with 11 officers and 250 men.   My loss is 3 killed, 1 officer slightly wounded, 15 enlisted men wounded, and 6 missing.

My loss would probably have been larger, but the nature of the ground where we were engaged in the woods was such that the men had some protection.

Very respectfully, your obedient servant,

A. R. CHAPIN,
Colonel Tenth Regiment Wisconsin Volunteer Infantry.

ACTING ASSISTANT ADJUTANT-GENERAL,
Ninth Brigade.

No. 70.

Report of Col. John Beatty, Third Ohio Infantry, commanding Second Brigade.

HEADQUARTERS SECOND BRIGADE, FIRST DIVISION,
Murfreesborough, Tenn., January 9, 1863.

SIR: In the recent engagement before Murfreesborough the casualties in my brigade were as follows: *

Colonel Forman, Fifteenth Kentucky, was killed in the cedar woods on the morning of the 31st ultimo.   He was a brave man and an excellent officer.   Captain Bayne, of same regiment, fell at the same time, while urging his men forward.

Lieutenant-Colonel Shanklin, Forty-second Indiana Volunteer Infantry, was surrounded by a superior force on the morning of January 3, and taken by the enemy.   Col. George Humphrey, Eighty-eighth Indiana, was wounded on the night of January 3, in expelling the enemy from the woods in our front.   He behaved gallantly throughout the fight.   Capt. L. S. Bell, Third Ohio Infantry, wounded at the same time, conducted himself with great courage.

Lieutenant-Colonels Lawson, Third Ohio, and Briant, Eighty-eighth Indiana; Capt. J. H. Bryant, Forty-second Indiana; Lieutenants Du-Barry and Wildman, Eighty-eighth Indiana; J. B. McRoberts, Third

---

* Embodied in revised statement, p. 210.

Ohio; Horrall and Orr, Forty-second Indiana; Mr. James K. Patterson, Evansville, and Actg. Asst. Adjt. Gen. James S. Wilson, deserve especial praise. Capt. C. O. Loomis and Lieutenants Van Pelt and Hale, of the First Michigan Battery, rendered most important service throughout the entire battle. No men could have conducted themselves with more courage and ability. There are other officers and men who should be mentioned favorably, but the reports of regimental commanders have failed to reach me, and it is impossible, therefore, to give them the credit they deserve.

My brigade had three separate encounters with the enemy on the first day. On the second and third days it was in front a portion of the time.

Skirmishing on the night of January 3, two regiments, led by myself, drove the enemy from their breastworks in the edge of the woods in our front.

I trust the conduct of the brigade throughout may be satisfactory.

I am, captain, very respectfully,

JOHN BEATTY,
Colonel, Commanding Second Brigade.

Capt. M. C. TAYLOR,
Acting Assistant Adjutant-General, First Division.

No. 71.

Reports of Col. John C. Starkweather, First Wisconsin Infantry, commanding Third Brigade.

HEADQUARTERS TWENTY-EIGHTH BRIGADE,
Camp at Jefferson, near Stone's River, Tenn., December 31, 1862.

SIR: I have the honor to report that on the 30th* instant the train of the Twenty-eighth Brigade, consisting of 64 wagons, loaded with camp equipage, stores, officers' baggage, knapsacks, &c., was sent from Stewartsborough at 8.30 a. m. for this point, unprotected, save by the convalescents and a small guard left to the rear for protection, 10 wagons loaded with rations. The head of the train had just arrived in camp, and while in process of being parked, the rear and center of the same was attacked by a portion of General Wheeler's cavalry brigade; while the remainder of his brigade, he being in command, as also a part of a brigade under command of Colonel Allen, advanced on both sides of the highway for the purpose of attacking the brigade force and destroying the whole train. The outposts and pickets, however, being on the alert, met the enemy at the front and held them in check until the brigade was formed and ready for battle.

I immediately ordered the train at double-quick to be parked; sent the Twenty-first Wisconsin, under Colonel Hobart, to the front and rear of train; ordered the First Wisconsin, Colonel Bingham, to deploy right and left from the center as skirmishers, and to press forward; moved one regiment, the Twenty-fourth Illinois, under Colonel Mihalotzy, to the bridge crossing the river, together with one section of artillery, and then advanced to the front with the Seventy-ninth Pennsylvania, Colonel Hambright, and two sections of artillery, First Kentucky, Captain Stone.

My advance, the Twenty-first Wisconsin, was soon hotly engaged, and, being pressed severely by the enemy in front and on the left, they

---

* See Wheeler's report, No. 301; Mauldin's report, No. 302.

passed to the right of the highway and occupied a hill, upon which was a log-house, giving them a good fighting position. The Second Kentucky Cavalry, Captain Craddock, about 50 strong, was then sent to the left and front to feel the enemy, and at once became engaged. The right wing of the First Wisconsin was rallied on the right, and placed in rear of the first section of artillery, which was then upon the hill occupied by the Twenty-first Wisconsin, opening with shell. The Seventy-ninth Pennsylvania was placed in rear of the left wing of the First Wisconsin, which was skirmishing to the front. One section of artillery opened upon the enemy in front as between my infantry on the right and left.

The engagement at this time became general, as between the enemy and the First and Twenty-first Wisconsin Volunteer Infantry and two sections of the First Kentucky Battery, the enemy acting principally on foot, supported by two field howitzers. The enemy was, however, finally repulsed, and left the field after severe fighting, the engagement lasting two hours and ten minutes, the brigade following 1½ miles, when, deeming my rear unsafe, I ordered the command to retire, and went into camp on the north side of Stone's River, near Jefferson.

The enemy's force, as near as could be ascertained, was some 3,500 strong; strength of my force was about 1,700. The enemy's loss in killed, as learned from prisoners taken since the fight, was 83. Their loss in wounded must have been very severe; but as the wounded and dead were carried away mostly by the cavalry upon their horses, it is impossible to give their loss with certainty. Eight prisoners were taken and paroled, two of whom were mortally wounded. A lieutenant-colonel of Wheeler's brigade was also mortally wounded.

Casualties upon our side were as per recapitulation, the chief part of the loss being convalescents, who were with the train when attacked. Twenty wagons from the rear of the train were taken and destroyed by fire, with the contents thereof, consisting of camp and garrison equipage, officers' and men's clothing, &c.

The troops under my command acted with great coolness and bravery; no flinching, no running, but the utmost coolness shown by all, adding another creditable mark to the old Twenty-eighth Brigade.

Staff officers and orderlies carried orders fearlessly to different parts of the field, entitling them to great credit and to my thanks.

Casualties.

Command.	Killed.	Wounded.	Missing.	Prisoners.	Total.
79th Pennsylvania		1	1	5	7
21st Wisconsin	1	3	37		41
1st Wisconsin		4	13	3	20
1st Kentucky Battery			1	1	2
24th Illinois			52		52
	1	8	104	9	122

The missing are prisoners taken with train, most of them being convalescents, and will undoubtedly be paroled.

Yours, respectfully,

JOHN C. STARKWEATHER,
Colonel First Wisconsin Vols., Comdg. Twenty-eighth Brigade.

Capt. M. C. TAYLOR,
Acting Assistant Adjutant-General, Third Division.

HEADQUARTERS TWENTY-EIGHTH BRIGADE,
Camp near Murfreesborough, Tenn., January 6, 1863.

SIR : I have the honor to report that, on the 31st ultimo, the Twenty-eighth Brigade left Jefferson, in accordance with orders, and reported at 5 p. m. for duty, bringing in one field howitzer belonging to the Fifth Wisconsin Battery, and some 250 cavalry of different regiments, as also many stragglers from infantry regiments that were found on the Jefferson and La Vergne pike and roads adjacent thereto, who had participated in the fight in front of Murfreesborough that day or the day previous.

On the 1st instant the brigade was maneuvered, changing positions, fronts, &c.; going into camp, formed in line, with battalions doubled on the center, the left resting on the Nashville and Murfreesborough pike, right on the left of General Johnson's troops. The following morning the brigade was ordered by General Rousseau to deploy into line and advance to the front to the support of our batteries, then in action. The change of position was made, and the gallant Twenty-eighth Brigade moved to the front to give such support, with unflinching courage, amid a most tremendous rebel fire of solid shot and shell, and remained in such supporting position until another change was made, when it was sent to the extreme front, and ordered to hold the same, which post it occupied the 2d, 3d, and 4th, changing position from time to time, as the nature of circumstances seemed to require, supporting batteries, pioneer corps, &c., in digging trenches; and although not brought into place where its own fire could be made to tell effectively, yet, from the duties performed by it, under the continued and severe fire of shot and shell of the enemy, it is entitled to all praise. Casualties as per recapitulation.

Yours, respectfully,

JOHN C. STARKWEATHER,
Colonel First Wisconsin, Comdg. Twenty-eighth Brigade.

Capt. M. C. TAYLOR,
Acting Assistant Adjutant-General, Third Division.

Recapitulation of casualties.

Command.	Killed.	Wounded.	Missing.	Total.
24th Illinois	1	3		4
79th Pennsylvania	2	8		10
1st Wisconsin		4	3	7
1st Kentucky Battery		1		1
Total	3	16	3	22

No. 72.

Reports of Lieut. Col. Oliver L. Shepherd, Eighteenth U. S. Infantry, commanding Fourth (Regular) Brigade.

HEADQUARTERS BRIGADE U. S. REGULAR TROOPS,
THIRD DIV. (ROUSSEAU'S), CENTER, 14TH ARMY CORPS,
Camp at Murfreesborough, Tenn., January 10, 1863.

SIR : I have the honor, respectfully, to report the operations of this brigade, under my orders, during the recent five days' battle before this place.

The brigade, on going into action, consisted of the First Battalion Fifteenth U. S. Infantry, comprising 16 officers and 304 enlisted men for duty, Major King commanding; the First Battalion Sixteenth U. S. Infantry, and Company B, Second Battalion, same regiment, attached, comprising 15 officers and 293 enlisted men, Major Slemmer commanding; Battery H, Fifth U. S. Artillery, comprising 3 officers and 120 enlisted men for duty, Captain Guenther commanding; the First Battalion Eighteenth U. S. Infantry, and Companies A and D, Third Battalion same regiment, attached, comprising 16 officers and 272 enlisted men, Major Caldwell commanding; the Second Battalion Eighteenth U. S. Infantry, and Companies B, C, E, and F, Third Battalion same regiment, attached, comprising 16 officers and 298 enlisted men, Major Townsend commanding; six companies, A, B, C, D, E, and F, First Battalion Nineteenth U. S. Infantry, comprising 10 officers and 198 enlisted men, Major Carpenter commanding; making a total of 77 officers and 1,485 enlisted men, not including the staff officers and the commanding officer of the brigade, 4 in number, and 1 acting sergeant-major (Commissary-Sergeant Gill, Third Battalion).

The balance of the brigade, including the sick, were left behind to guard the brigade and battalion trains, where they did good service, under their respective battalion quartermasters, in repelling the attacks of the enemy's cavalry, saving thereby the entire trains of the brigade. The musicians were under the orders of the various surgeons.

The brigade, thus constituted and in the order enumerated, went first into action under your eye and general supervision at about 9.30 a. m. December 31, 1862, forming line in the dense cedar forest to the right of the turnpike and railroad, with design of succoring the right wing of the army, under Major-General McCook. After being placed partially, in quick time, in position and line, the rebel enemy attacked briskly the two battalions (Fifteenth and Sixteenth) on the right of the battery. On observing that the battery and the three battalions to the left were separated from, and not in view of, these two battalions, I sent my acting assistant adjutant-general, Lieutenant Sutherland, with orders to Major King to take the command on the right, while I proceeded toward the center and left of the brigade to bring them into this contest, which was shortly terminated by the Fifteenth and Sixteenth being forced to retire with considerable loss; not, however, without having checked the advance of the enemy, who soon succeeded in possessing the flank by their long extended line, and having at first been deceived by the enemy, who advanced dressed in American uniform, and without firing till within a short distance, supported by a heavy line behind. (See official report of Capt. J. Fulmer, commanding First Battalion Fifteenth Infantry.)

A regiment, believed to be the Sixth Ohio Volunteers, withstood the fire of the enemy along with these two battalions.

On arriving on the left of the brigade, I found that the battery had fortunately received your orders to retire by the same narrow cut in the cedar forest by which the brigade first entered. The three battalions of the Eighteenth and Nineteenth were directed to accompany this movement just in time to save the battery from capture, and under fire of the advancing enemy.

In this first conflict in the cedar forest, Captain Bell, of the Fifteenth, was killed, and Captain York and Lieutenant Occleston, Fifteenth, severely wounded, and also about 8 enlisted men were killed and 42 wounded.

After emerging from the cedar forest, the battalions of the brigade drew up in their proper positions to the right and left of the battery, which had taken position, from which, by its effective fire, the advancing lines of the enemy were driven back and dispersed from view in the forest.

While waiting in this position, the enemy's batteries to the front, along the turnpike and railroad, were throwing shot and shell upon our ground, by which Captain Dennison, Second Battalion, Eighteenth, lost his leg, and the heroic first sergeant, George F. White, of Company F, Third Battalion, his life. Other men of the brigade were also killed and wounded.

At about 12 m. the brigade, including the battery, was again directed to advance to the front along the railroad and turnpike, and, after reaching the farther side of the open ground, was suddenly directed to the right, to enter again the cedar forest, to sustain the troops which were receding, exhausted of ammunition. This movement was made in pursuance of orders directly from yourself and Major-General Thomas. The brigade being halted just along the edge of the forest, the battery was ordered to retake the former slightly elevated site near the railroad.

The brigade, having the battalion of the Nineteenth shifted, at the request of its commanding officer, Major Carpenter, from extreme left to position in line between the battalions of the Fifteenth and Sixteenth, was projected about 50 yards into the dense cedar forest toward the enemy, and, after allowing our retiring regiments to pass through the lines to the rear, the fire was opened in return to that of the pursuing enemy. The excellence of the firing by file by all the battalions of the brigade could not be excelled, and was terrifying and destructive to the enemy, who were brought to a stand for about twenty minutes.

During this stubborn combat most of our losses in killed and wounded took place; Major Slemmer, commanding Sixteenth, wounded at its commencement. The enemy's lines extending, however, beyond both flanks of the brigade, enabled them to pour an incessant fire from three directions—the front, left, and right flanks; and the brigade being unsupported by any other forces on either flank, and having secured the required time for the receding regiments to reform, I thought it proper to order a retreat, which was probably quite long enough deferred.

Just after the order to retreat was given, a regiment came up in line in the open field on the extreme right of the brigade, but its fire, though brisk, came too late, and was unavailing against so large a force as filled the forest, three lines being discernible.

It is proper here to remark that, notwithstanding the loss in the brigade had been nearly half its strength, the battalions evidently gave ground with reluctance, probably not having looked to such result, and being too much engaged to know the full extent of their losses. The retreat of the brigade across the open field was done handsomely, and with as much order as was desirable, having in view to prevent further loss of life. On this retreat Major King, commanding the Fifteenth, and Captain Douglass, acting field officer of the First Battalion Eighteenth Infantry, were wounded, causing them both to retire to the hospital.

The brigade was at this time reformed in line near the railroad, in proper place, to the right and left of the battery, as directed in previous orders, for the formation in line of battle, and in this position it remained the balance of the day and during the following night, within reach of the enemy's cannon.

In this last terrific combat in the cedar forest many brave men and officers perished; 4 officers killed and 18 wounded, and 78 enlisted men killed and 430 enlisted men wounded, exclusive of the missing.

At the moment of retreating a few steps, the brave and gallant Major Carpenter, commanding the Nineteenth Infantry, fell from his horse with six mortal wounds, regretted by all who knew him. The left wing of the brigade, First and Second Battalions Eighteenth Infantry, was, during the remainder of the battle, committed mostly to Major Townsend, the right wing, deprived of its field officers, requiring, as I thought, more of my attention.

About the middle of the afternoon an extended line of men was discovered far to our front, advancing with our national colors, and, having passed over a slight rise, descended into a corresponding depression, partially concealing them, when a white flag with a dark ball in its center was substituted, after which they unfurled the rebel flag; whereupon Captain Guenther directed the fire of his battery, causing the line to break in double-quick time to their left flank and disappear into the cedar forest.

Though occasionally visited by the enemy's shot, but little heed was given to it, and thus closed the action of the brigade the first day, being the last of the year, December 31, 1862. During the night our wounded were gathered together, as far as the enemy's pickets would permit.

A short time before daybreak of New Year's day the brigade retired, according to orders, to a point in the rear of the commanding general's headquarters, to meet an attack on our right. Some shiftings of position took place until about 2 p. m., when it marched toward Stewart's Creek, and on arriving near there it was ordered back in double-quick time, which being executed, and night coming on, the brigade bivouacked on the left of the roadway and near the commanding general's headquarters.

On the third day (the 2d instant) the brigade marched, before breakfasting, to the front to meet the enemy's attack, and we retained this position during the day and following night, the battery assisting to silence the enemy's batteries and effect the repulse of the enemy in their attack on the left wing of the army, under General Crittenden, in the afternoon.

On the 3d instant (the fourth day) the brigade and battery moved forward to the standpoint of the first day, December 31, 1862, where slight epaulements were thrown up, principally by the men of the brigade, and encamped within them, though rendered almost untenable by heavy rains, which filled them partially with water and made the adjoining grounds miry. As this day closed, and at dark, a severe attack was made by some portion of the division upon the enemy in front, which resulted in gaining possession of the enemy's first line of breastworks for a time, and subsequently abandoning them, owing to exhausted ammunition.

On the 4th instant I reported, at 7.30 a. m., that the enemy had evacuated our front. The brigade held the same position, employing the day and following night in the sad duty of collecting our dead, who were interred with military honors just in front of our intrenchments, and on the standpoint of the brigade and battery, maintained from the first to the last day's conflict.

The heavy rains of the 2d and 3d instant covered this position and the trenches with mud and water, in which the whole brigade had to stand or recline while seeking to obtain a little rest. Not a murmur escaped the lip in all this trying and painful as well as arduous and dangerous service. On the contrary, cheerfulness and alacrity were evident on their countenances, and this while subsistence was so scarce as to force a consumption of horses killed in the battle.

It is hoped that the bearing and whole career of this brigade of regular troops during the five days' conflict were of a character to meet the approbation of the major-general commanding the division.

The brigade was not without the ambition of deserving also the commendation of Major-General Thomas, commanding the center, whose experience has been so successful and so long, and likewise of the commander-in-chief, whose uniform success inspired confidence. In fine, the brigade having combatted so well, we need hardly search for examples, but should rest satisfied that there are none to excel it in courageous action and mournful losses.

Of 77 officers with the battalions, 5 were killed and 21 wounded, some mortally; and of 1,366 enlisted men, 90 men were killed and 469 wounded, many mortally, besides 47 missing, supposed to be prisoners. The casualties of the battery were not so great, on account of its position and of its fire dispersing every line of the enemy approaching sufficiently near, at one time completely routing the Second Arkansas (rebel) Regiment, causing it to abandon its colors, which were picked up by skirmishers of the Second Regiment Ohio Volunteers before the officer sent for it reached the ground where the regiment was broken; and 22 rebel prisoners were taken during the day.

Captain Guenther's battery, attached, could scarcely have been excelled for the skill and effectiveness of its fire, and the cool, brave conduct of its officers and men. For six days and nights the harness was never taken from the horses either for food or water, the horses being kept patiently on the alert at the pieces.

Appended is a list of the officers killed and wounded, and a consolidated report of the total killed and wounded; also the reports of chiefs of battalions and of the battery. They are admirably drawn, and exhibit more minutely the operations of the particular commands, and are of great interest.

The honor of this brave conduct of the brigade belongs properly to the chiefs of battalions and of the battery, respectively, Majors King, Carpenter, Slemmer, Townsend, and Caldwell; and, after Majors King and Slemmer were wounded and Major Carpenter was killed, to their successors, Captains Crofton, Sixteenth, Fulmer, Fifteenth, Mulligan, Nineteenth Infantry, and also to Captain Guenther, commanding Battery H, Fifth Artillery. Great credit is reflected by the good condition of their respective commands.

The brigade staff, Captain Kinney, quartermaster; First Lieutenants Mills, commissary, and Sutherland, Eighteenth Infantry, acting assistant adjutant-general of the brigade, accompanied me into action with the brigade, and performed the duties of carrying orders and all the other duties required of them with courage, zeal, and ability. Assistant Surgeon Lindsly, acting brigade surgeon, and Acting Surgeons Patton and Henderson were actively and zealously occupied at the various hospitals during the whole time. Dr. Lindsly visited at different times the field.

Resting in the hope that this brigade, but recently organized, has displayed in this great battle of five days' duration a career worthy the approbation of the Government and the cause in which engaged, I have the honor, respectfully, to subscribe myself, very truly, your humble servant, &c.,

O. L. SHEPHERD,
Lieutenant-Colonel Eighteenth U. S. Infantry, Comdg. Brig.

Maj Gen. LOVELL H. ROUSSEAU,
Comdg. Third Division, Center, Fourteenth Army Corps.

List of commissioned officers killed and wounded.

HEADQUARTERS BRIGADE U. S. REGULAR TROOPS,
THIRD DIVISION, CENTER, FOURTEENTH ARMY CORPS,
January 10, 1863.

Killed.—Maj. S. D. Carpenter, Nineteenth Infantry; Capt. William W. Wise, Fifteenth Infantry; Capt. J. B. Bell, Fifteenth Infantry; Capt. Charles L. Kneass, First Battalion Eighteenth Infantry; Second Lieut. J. F. Hitchcock, Second Battalion Eighteenth Infantry.

Wounded.—Maj. John H. King, Fifteenth Infantry; Maj. A. J. Slemmer, Sixteenth Infantry, severely; Capt. Joseph S. York, Fifteenth Infantry, slightly; Capt. Robert P. Barry, Sixteenth Infantry, severely; Capt. John C. King, Sixteenth Infantry, severely; Capt. Newton L. Dykeman, Sixteenth Infantry, slightly; Capt. Henry Douglass, First Battalion Eighteenth Infantry, slightly; Capt. D.•L. Wood, First Battalion Eighteenth Infantry, slightly; Capt. R. B. Hull, First Battalion Eighteenth Infantry, severely; Capt. Charles E. Dennison, Second Battalion Eighteenth Infantry, severely; Capt. A. B. Thompson, Second Battalion Eighteenth Infantry, severely; Capt. Henry Haymond, Third Battalion Eighteenth Infantry, slightly; First Lieut. W. B. Occleston, Fifteenth Infantry, severely; First Lieut. W. H. Bartholomew, Sixteenth Infantry, severely; First Lieut. John Power, adjutant Sixteenth Infantry, severely; First Lieut. James C. Howland, Sixteenth Infantry, slightly; First Lieut. Joseph McConnell, First Battalion Eighteenth Infantry, severely; First Lieut. Morgan L. Ogden, Second Battalion Eighteenth Infantry, severely; First Lieut. James Simons, Second Battalion Eighteenth Infantry, severely; Second Lieut. G. S. Carpenter, First Battalion Eighteenth Infantry, severely; Second Lieut. John I. Adair, First Battalion Eighteenth Infantry, slightly.

O. L. SHEPHERD,
Lieut. Col. Eighteenth Infantry, U. S. Army, Comdg. Brigade.

—

Consolidated report of casualties in brigade U. S. regular troops, Third Division, Center, Fourteenth Army Corps, in the five days' battles before Murfreesborough, Tenn., commencing December 31, 1862, and ending January 4, 1863.[*]

Command.	Officers.			Enlisted men.						Horses.	
	In action.	Killed.	Wounded.	In action.	Killed.	Wounded.	Prisoners.	Missing.	Total enlisted.	Killed.	Wounded.
Brigade headquarters........	4			1							
Battery H, 5th Artillery	3			120		5			5	8	5
1st Battalion, 15th Infantry	16	2	3	304	10	74	2	15	101		
1st Battalion, 16th Infantry	15		7	293	16	147		16	159		
1st Battalion, 18th Infantry	16	1	6	272	28	115	2		145		
2d Battalion, 18th Infantry	16	1	5	298	30	98	3	2	133		
1st Battalion, 19th Infantry	10	1		198	6	55		7	68		
Total.................	80	5	21	1,486	90	494	7	40	611	8	5

* But see revised statement, p. 210.

HDQRS. FOURTH BRIG., FIRST DIV., 14TH ARMY CORPS,
Camp at Murfreesborough, Tenn., February 18, 1863.

SIR : I desire respectfully to state that, owing in part to Capt. H. Douglass, First Battalion Eighteenth Infantry, not being a commander during the recent battle, I have forgotten him in my reports ; therefore I desire respectfully to give an outline of his service.

He was commander of the First Battalion from its organization, in the fall of 1861, and continued so through all the trying campaign of Mill Springs, up to May 26, 1862, just before entering Corinth, and has ever since been acting field officer.

In the performance of said duty he was distinguished in the battle of Perryville, and wounded in the great battle of Stone's River, during the heavy conflict in the cedars, on December 31, 1862.

Having his wound dressed, and with his arm in a sling, he reported for duty as the brigade moved to the front, January 2, but was directed shortly after to go again to the hospital.

He has always been brave and zealous, and is again in command of his battalion, which owes much of its instruction to him. I hope it may not be too late to have justice done him.

I am, colonel, very respectfully, your obedient servant,

O. L. SHEPHERD,
Colonel, U. S. Army, Commanding Brigade.

Col. O. GODDARD,
Asst. Adjt. Gen. and Chief of Staff, Dept. of the Cumberland.

No. 73.

Report of Capt. Jesse Fulmer, Fifteenth U. S. Infantry.

HDQRS. FIRST BATT. FIFTEENTH U. S. INFANTRY,
Camp at Murfreesborough, Tenn., January 10, 1863.

SIR : I have the honor to report that, on the morning of December 31, 1862, the First Battalion Fifteenth U. S. Infantry, comprising eight companies, entered into action before Murfreesborough, Tenn., under the command of Maj. John H. King.

The number of enlisted men present and entering into action was 304; Lieutenant Ogilby, battalion adjutant, and the following company officers, to wit, Captains Fulmer, Wise, Bell, Keteltas, and York, and Lieutenants Jewett, Wikoff, Woodward, Occleston, King, Semple, Galloway, and Gray, were present and participated in the engagement.

The aggregate strength of the battalion on entering into action was 319, officers and men.

This battalion, with the others of the brigade of regulars, commanded by Lieutenant-Colonel Shepherd, Eighteenth U. S. Infantry, advanced several hundred yards into a dense forest of cedars, about 9 o'clock on the morning of the 31st ultimo, to engage the enemy. The Fifteenth, with the First Battalion of the Sixteenth Infantry on the left, were moved a short distance from the other battalions of the brigade and formed in line of battle. Captain Keteltas' company was immediately ordered forward as skirmishers, and, as such, advanced them some 400 yards beyond our line. He had been enticed thus to advance by the action of scattering rebels in our front, who, wearing our style of uniform, feigned to be of us.

This piece of deception, however, was timely detected, and a heavy firing between the skirmishers was immediately commenced. Ours were driven back, and the enemy, in two or three lines of battle, hurriedly advanced, with a strong line of skirmishers in front. Our line of battle suffered somewhat by mistaking a body of rebels dressed in our uniform for our troops. When commanded to open upon the enemy, the battalion poured in a heavy fire upon them, but were soon compelled to give way to the vastly superior numbers of the enemy. We fired, retreating, until we reached the rear of the position just that moment taken by the Sixth Regiment Ohio Volunteers. Here we halted to reform our line, but, while so doing, the overwhelming numbers of the rebels, and the fierce onslaught they made on the Sixth Ohio, forced those gallant volunteers to fall back also; whereupon we moved out of the woods, returning the enemy's fire, and, under cover of Guenther's battery, succeeded in taking favorable position and reforming our line. It was in this engagement that Captain Bell was killed, Captain York wounded, and, I fear, mortally, and Lieutenant Occleston severely wounded.

The battalion reformed, advanced, and again took position in the woods, as also the others of the brigade. This was done promptly, and with a zeal highly creditable to men who had only a few moments before been under a most galling and terrible fire. Very soon we were again engaged with the enemy, and, after a spirited engagement for a while, were ordered to fall back. Then it was that Major King was wounded, and the command of the battalion devolved upon me. I continued the movement, firing upon the enemy, and moved up to the support of Guenther's battery. In this affair Captain Wise fell, mortally wounded, and has since died.

For the remainder of that day we acted in support of Guenther's battery, and remained on the front of our lines that night until nearly daybreak, when we moved to the rear. Later in the morning we moved forward again, first supporting the center, then the right.

Friday morning we again moved to the front, supporting Guenther's battery, and remained there until the battle of that day ended.

Advancing a short distance on Saturday morning, we threw up intrenchments in face of the fire of the enemy's skirmishers and sharpshooters. These we occupied Saturday night, supporting Guenther's battery during the brilliant and successful attack made upon the enemy's lines that night.

In addition to the casualties already named, the battalion had 84 enlisted men killed and wounded, 10 of whom are positively known to have been killed outright, 2 captured, and 15 missing, who have, doubtless, either been killed, wounded, or captured. The aggregate casualties to officers and men number 106.

The conduct of the officers and of the men engaged merits commendation, and the battalion, in all of the advanced movements into the cedars, and in the several actions engaged, did well in aiding to check and drive back the largely superior numbers of the enemy confronted by the brigade of regulars.

I am, sir, very respectfully, your obedient servant,

JESSE FULMER,
Captain Fifteenth U. S. Infantry, Commanding First Battalion.

First Lieut. ROBERT SUTHERLAND,
Eighteenth Infantry, Actg. Asst. Adjt. Gen., Brig. of Regulars.

No. 74.

Report of Capt. Robert E. A. Crofton, Sixteenth U. S. Infantry.

HDQRS. FIRST AND SECOND BATTS., SIXTEENTH INFTY.,
Camp at Murfreesborough, Tenn., January 10, 1863.

COLONEL: I have the honor to submit the following as a report of the part taken by the First Battalion, and Company B, Second Battalion Sixteenth Infantry, under my command, in the late actions before Murfreesborough during December 31, 1862, and January 1, 2, 3, and 4, 1863:

At 7 o'clock on the morning of December 31, 1862, this command (then under Maj. A. J. Slemmer, Sixteenth Infantry) was ordered to move to the front from the bivouac where we had rested the night previous. We marched about a mile in the direction of Murfreesborough, and were then marched into line of battle on the right of the turnpike, the First Battalion Fifteenth Infantry being on our right, and the First Battalion Eighteenth Infantry on our left. Here we stacked arms and rested for some time.

About 9.15 o'clock we were ordered into a thicket of cedars. When we had arrived about three-quarters of a mile from the edge of the thicket, we moved into line of battle, changing our front to the right, to oppose the advancing columns of the enemy. Company B, First Battalion, under command of First Lieutenant Bartholomew, was thrown to the front in skirmishing order, to cover the front of our line. In about five minutes these skirmishers were driven in, and formed on the right of the battalion. The enemy was now seen advancing in line, and at the same moment opened a deadly fire on our ranks. The command, however, succeeded in checking their advance, the men behaving with the greatest possible coolness, and aiming with accuracy. The battalion on our right having moved to the rear, it became necessary to fall back, which we did, by the right of companies, to the rear. The men performed this movement with the same order and regularity they would in an ordinary drill.

Having fallen back about 100 paces, we came into line, faced to the front, and returned the enemy's fire. Again, for want of support, we were obliged to retire, and did so, as before, for about another 100 yards. Maintaining this position for some minutes, we found it necessary to make a retreat to where we could be supported, as the enemy was moving his line on our right and left, and threatening to surround us.

We then moved, by the right of companies, to the rear, out of the woods and across a cotton-field, where the enemy poured musketry and round shot upon us, but without doing much injury. We continued our retreat across the turnpike to the railroad, where we joined the remainder of the brigade, and were ordered to support Battery H, Fifth Artillery.

We remained in this position till about 11.30 a. m., when we were again ordered into the cedars. We advanced this time about 30 yards from the edge of the woods, when we became engaged, and a most terrific conflict ensued. Almost at the commencement of this action Maj. A. J. Slemmer was so seriously wounded as to be obliged to fall to the rear. About the same time Adjt. John Power was dangerously wounded.

After remaining in this position for about twenty-five minutes, and seeing the right of the brigade retire in order, we were compelled reluctantly to fall back, as the enemy outflanked us on our right and left. The men moved out of the woods by the right of companies with great regularity, notwithstanding the fearful fire to which they were exposed. As we crossed the open field between the woods and railroad, the fire was terrible, and the men fell before it in great numbers, until the enemy were driven back by the fire from Battery H, Fifth Artillery, attached to the brigade. Arriving at the railroad, we again formed and remained with the rest of the brigade in support of the above battery. We continued in this position all the afternoon, continually exposed to artillery fire from the enemy's batteries.

About 4 o'clock next morning we were ordered to the rear about a mile, where we obtained some rest. About 8 a. m. we were again put in position on the right center. From this position we were ordered to the right. In the afternoon we were ordered to proceed to Stewart's Creek, and, on arriving within a mile of the creek, were ordered back at a double-quick, when we immediately faced about and retraced our steps in double-quick time.

About sundown we arrived near our original position, the men being very much exhausted by hardships they had undergone, and the rapidity of the march. We were moved into bivouac in a belt of woods near the center of the general position.

Next morning found us again near the front and center, supporting Battery H, Fifth Artillery. Here we remained in reserve, until about 2 p. m., when we moved back to our bivouac of the night before. Here we remained about half an hour, when we were again ordered to the position occupied by us during the morning, owing to an impetuous attack on the left, under General Crittenden, by the enemy. In this position we remained all the afternoon and that night.

Next morning a battery opened on us from the enemy, but was soon silenced by Battery H, Fifth Artillery. We then moved still farther to the front, where we threw up a line of earthworks, and the men slept on their arms in the trenches. That night, so completely were the men exhausted, from want of rest and food, that they slept in about 6 inches of water.

Next morning it was discovered that the enemy had abandoned their position and were in full retreat. The command remained guarding these trenches till the morning of January 5, when we marched to Murfreesborough.

During these five days the men suffered very much for the want of food, and were so much reduced that some of them ate roasted horse-flesh. Fifteen officers and 293 enlisted men went into action.

The following is a list of the officers of the command who were engaged : Maj. A. J. Slemmer, Capts. R. E. A. Crofton, R. P. Barry, James Biddle, N. L. Dykeman, and J. C. King; First Lieuts. A. W. Allyn, E. McConnell, W. H. Bartholomew, John Power (battalion adjutant), W. W. Arnold, J. C. Howland, and E. R. Kellogg; Second Lieuts. S. E. St. Onge and W. G. Wedemeyer.

All the officers and men behaved with great coolness and courage, and, notwithstanding the great sufferings it was necessary for them to endure, they performed their duties without a murmur.

Subjoined you will find a list of killed, wounded, and missing.* Of the latter number I am convinced that few, if any, are stragglers, as some who were at first reported missing it has since been discovered are wounded and were unable to avoid being taken by the enemy.

I have the honor to remain, very respectfully, your obedient servant,

R. E. A. CROFTON,
Captain Sixteenth Infantry, Commanding.

Lieut. Col. O. L. SHEPHERD, *Comdg. Brigade Regular Troops.*

---

* Embodied in revised statement, p. 210.

No. 75.

Report of Maj James N. Caldwell, Eighteenth U. S. Infantry.

HDQRS. FIRST BATTALION EIGHTEENTH INFANTRY,
Camp near Murfreesborough, Tenn., January 6, 1863.

SIR: Herewith I have the honor to transmit a list of the killed and wounded in my battalion in the battle of the "Cedars," near Murfreesborough, December 31, 1862.

I went into the battle with 1 adjutant, 1 sergeant-major, 6 captains, 8 lieutenants, and 272 enlisted men; aggregate, 288. Captain Kneass was killed; Captains Douglass, Wood, and Hull, wounded; Lieutenants McConnell, Carpenter, and Adair, wounded; 1 sergeant and 3 corporals killed, 6 sergeants and 4 corporals wounded, 23 privates killed and 99 wounded; total and aggregate loss, 145. All did their duty well; were cool, deliberate, and firm under the terrific fire that thinned our ranks, and not one gave way until the order to rejoin the battery attached to our brigade was given.

We were under fire on the 1st, 2d, and 3d of January, 1863, and in the trenches on the day and night of the 3d instant, but sustained no loss. During the four days and nights on the battle-fields near Murfreesborough, notwithstanding the cold, mud, and rain, and want of rations part of the time, not a murmur was heard; all exhibited the same coolness and unflinching devotion to their country and flag that they had shown on the battle-field at Perryville, Ky., when composing a part of General Steedman's brigade, which was exposed to a terrific fire on that field.

Captain Douglass acted as field officer on December 31, 1862, and rendered valuable service, and, notwithstanding his painful wound, joined the battalion on the 2d of January, and remained on duty with it during that day. My battalion adjutant, Lieut. R. L. Morris, rendered valuable service on the field; his horse was wounded. My horse was wounded and disabled. My battalion quartermaster, Lieutenant Benham, Quartermaster-Sergeant Price, and Commissary-Sergeant Livsey, with a small escort and the teamsters, all did their duty well, in defending and conducting the battalion train in safety to Nashville.

In conclusion, I beg leave, respectfully, to recommend the following-named non-commissioned officers for promotion, for their bravery and meritorious conduct in the battle of December 31, 1862, near Murfreesborough, Tenn.: Sergt. Maj. Reuben F. Little, Sergt. Allen C. Barrows, Company F; Sergt. Ralph Horton, Company H, and First Sergt. Isaac D'Isay, Company A; and also Sergt. E. C. Beach, Company A; Sergeant Carpenter, Company F; Quartermaster-Sergeant Price, and Commissary-Sergeant Livsey, for certificates of merit.

Very respectfully, your obedient servant,

J. N. CALDWELL,
Major Eighteenth Infty., Comdg. First Batt. Eighteenth Infty.

ACTING ASST. ADJT. GEN., *Brigade of Regulars.*

No. 76.

Reports of Maj. Frederick Townsend, Eighteenth U. S. Infantry.

HDQRS. SECOND BATTALION EIGHTEENTH U. S. INFTY.,
Camp at Murfreesborough, Tenn., January 10, 1863.

SIR: I have the honor to report that, pursuant to the orders of the lieutenant-colonel commanding the brigade, about 7 o'clock on the morning of December 31, 1862, my battalion, comprising 16 officers and 298 enlisted men, being one of the battalions of the brigade of regulars, accompanied that brigade into action.

My orders were to support and defend Lieutenant Guenther's battery (H), Fifth Artillery. While thus employed, Capt. Charles E. Dennison, commanding Company B, and the right general guide, Sergt. Joseph Matthew, were severely wounded, and First Sergt. George F. White, of Company F, Third Battalion, was killed.

Subsequently the brigade and battalion took position in a dense forest of cedars, for the purpose, as was understood, of holding in check the advancing enemy, while a rearrangement of our own line of battle might be effected. We maintained this position for over twenty minutes, when we received the orders of the brigade commander to retire, having, however, achieved the result expected and required, but not without great loss—nearly one-half of the command, as will be observed in the annexed list of casualties.

During the subsequent days of the battle we were continuously under arms and under the fire of the enemy's cannon, and were moved from place to place wherever our presence seemed to be required. The last thirty-six hours of the battle we assisted in throwing up and holding intrenchments commanding the central portion of the field, the occupancy of which, owing to the heavy rains, became one of hardship and trial.

It affords me pleasure to state that there was not a single instance of cowardice in the battalion, and that both officers and men did completely and effectively their whole duty.

The names of the officers of the battalion in the engagement of the 31st are as follows: Maj. Frederick Townsend, commanding battalion; First Lieut. Frederick Phisterer, adjutant of the battalion; Capt. Henry R. Mizner; Capt. Charles E. Dennison, wounded severely; Capt. Henry Belknap; A. B. Thompson, wounded severely; Capt. William J. Fetterman; Capt. Henry Haymond, wounded slightly; Capt. A. B. Denton; First Lieut. M. L. Ogden, wounded severely; First Lieut. H. G. Radcliff; First Lieut. James Simons, wounded severely; First Lieut. Henry B. Freeman; Second Lieut. William H. Bisbee; Second Lieut. John F. Hitchcock, killed, and Second Lieut. Wilbur F. Arnold. Total, 16.

First Lieut. William P. McCleery, quartermaster of the battalion, was with the train, where he displayed conspicuous gallantry in defending it from capture with its guard and the sick.

I beg to call the attention of the brigade commander to the following enlisted men of my battalion, who were conspicuous for their gallantry in the engagement on the 31st: Sergt. Maj. John S. Lind; Sergt. Samuel C. Williamson, Company D, Second Battalion; Sergt. Charles B. Meredith, Company D, Second Battalion; Corpl. Sylvester S. Bartlett, Company C, Second Battalion; Lance Corpl. Paul Fisher, Company D, Second Battalion; Private William H. Maxwell, Company A, Second Battalion; Private Jacob Kline, Company D, Second Battalion; Private James McKenzie, Company B, Third Battalion, and James Hofler, Company C, Third Battalion.

I have the honor to remain, very respectfully, your obedient servant,

FREDERICK TOWNSEND,
Major Eighteenth U. S. Infantry, Commanding.

First Lieut. ROBERT SUTHERLAND,
Acting Assistant Adjutant-General, Brigade of Regulars.

WASHINGTON, D. C., *February* 23, 1863.

GENERAL : I neglected, in my report of the doings of the Second Battalion of the Eighteenth U. S. Infantry, in the recent battles in front of Murfreesborough, Tenn., to mention among the names of certain enlisted men, conspicuous for good conduct on the field and at all times, the name of my mounted orderly, Private Jacob Troutman, of Company D. He was of very great assistance to me in carrying and bringing orders, and displayed a degree of intelligence and bravery worthy of strong commendation. In justice to this excellent soldier, I trust, general, that you will permit this notice of him to be appended as supplemental to my official report.

I have the honor to be, general, your obedient servant,

FREDERICK TOWNSEND,
Major Eighteenth Infantry, Commanding Second Battalion.

Brig. Gen. LORENZO THOMAS,
Adjutant-General U. S. Army.

No. 77.

Report of Capt. James B. Mulligan, Nineteenth U. S. Infantry.

HDQRS. FIRST BATTALION NINETEENTH U. S. INFANTRY,
Camp near Murfreesborough, Tenn., January 8, 1863.

SIR : I have the honor to report that six companies of the First Battalion of the Nineteenth Regiment U. S. Infantry, under command of Maj. S. D. Carpenter, with the regular brigade, under command of Lieut. Col. O. L. Shepherd, Eighteenth Infantry, were ordered to the front, and entered into action on the morning of December 31, 1862, before Murfreesborough, at 9.30 a. m.

The battalion was ordered by the brigade commander to take its position in the brigade on the left of the Eighteenth Infantry, supporting the left of Guenther's battery (H), Fifth Artillery.

About 10 a. m. the brigade, with the battery, was ordered into the cedars to assistance of Negley's division ; but, after finding there was no possibility of securing a position, the battalion, in company with the battery, retired from the cedars in excellent order, under a most destructive fire.

After taking our position on the hill near the railroad, we were again, about 12 m., ordered, with the remainder of the brigade, to advance in line of battle into the cedars. We there engaged an overwhelming force of the enemy for full twenty minutes. It was as we received the order to retire that Major Carpenter fell, receiving six mortal wounds, dying instantly. The fire from the enemy at this time was terrific. Our men were falling on all sides.

At this point the command of the battalion devolved upon myself, being the senior officer present. We fell back, in pursuance of orders, to the support of Guenther's battery, which had taken its position on the hill near the railroad, which position we maintained throughout the day.

The next day, January 1, 1863, at daybreak, we were ordered, with the brigade and battery, to the right, to assist McCook's corps, where we remained in position until after midday, when we were ordered to proceed up the Murfreesborough pike, in the direction of Nashville, to

Stewart's Creek, to protect a provision train which was threatened by the enemy. After proceeding about 4 miles up the road, we were ordered to the right-about, and double-quicked to the center of the line of battle.

On January 2, at daybreak, we took our position on the hill by the railroad, in front of the cedars, which we held during the day and throughout the night.

The next day, the 3d, we commenced intrenching the front and center, under cover of our skirmishers, and that night our breastworks, being completed, were occupied and held by us until after the enemy had left our front, which fact was reported by me to the colonel commanding the brigade shortly after sunrise on the 4th instant.

The battalion lost 1 commissioned officer killed (the major commanding); enlisted men, 6 killed, 55 wounded, and 7 missing. The greater part of the latter known to be in the hands of the enemy.

Twenty-two of the enemy fell, on the 31st, into our hands, and were turned over to an escort of cavalry, by order of Lieut. H. Millard, of General Rousseau's staff, by Lieutenant Stansbury.

The following officers participated: First Lieutenants Andrews, Stansbury, and Jones; Second Lieutenants Wagoner, Lowe, Curtis, Miller, Johnson, and Carpenter.

The conduct of the officers and men throughout the five days' battle was excellent, the battalion taking part and sharing with the brigade in all its hardships, deprivations, and arduous duties in its movements over the entire field, at one time supporting the right of General McCook's corps, at another assisting General Crittenden's, and on the last day and night intrenching and holding the center of our own division.

I take pleasure in mentioning the energy and efficiency displayed by Dr. Henderson, of this battalion, and Dr. Lindsly, of the Eighteenth Infantry, acting brigade surgeon, in the care and treatment of our wounded, all of whom, I am credibly informed, are well cared for and in comfortable hospitals.

I inclose herewith a consolidated list of the killed, wounded, and missing of the battalion during the five days' battle; also copies of the reports, from the commandant of companies, of casualties,* &c.

Very respectfully, your obedient servant,
JAMES B. MULLIGAN,
Captain Nineteenth U. S. Infantry, Commanding First Battalion.

Lieut. ROBERT SUTHERLAND,
Acting Assistant Adjutant-General, Brigade of Regulars.

No. 78.

Report of Brig. Gen. James S. Negley, U. S. Army, commanding Second Division.

HEADQUARTERS EIGHTH DIVISION,
Camp near Murfreesborough, Tenn., January 8, 1863.

SIR: I have the honor to submit the following report of the operations of the troops of my command in the engagements with the enemy on Stone's River:

On Tuesday morning, December 30, 1862, the Eighth Division, composed of the Seventh and Twenty-ninth Brigades, Schultz's, Marshall's,

---
* Embodied in revised statement, p. 210.

and Nell's batteries, was posted on the rolling slopes of the west bank of Stone's River, in advance, but joining the extreme right of General Crittenden's line and the left of General McCook's.

In the rear and on the right was a dense cedar woods, with a broken rocky surface. From our position several roads were cut through the woods in our rear, by which to bring up the artillery and ammunition trains. In front a heavy growth of oak timber extended toward the river, which was about a mile distant. A narrow thicket crossed our left diagonally, and skirted the base of a cultivated slope, which expanded to the width of a mile as it approached the Nashville pike. This slope afforded the enemy his most commanding position (in the center), on the crest of which his rifle-pits extended, with intervals, from the oak timber immediately in my front to the Nashville pike, with a battery of four Napoleon and two iron guns placed in position near the woods, and about 800 yards from my position. Behind this timber, on the river bank, the enemy massed his columns for the movements of the next day. Their skirmishers were driven from our immediate front after a sharp contest, in which the Nineteenth Illinois and Seventy-eighth Pennsylvania Volunteers displayed admirable efficiency. The position of my command was held under a heavy fire until darkness terminated the skirmishing in our front, by which time we had inflicted considerable loss upon the enemy.

In the mean time General Sheridan's division came up and formed line of battle, his left resting on my right, and began to advance, driving the enemy until he had passed the center of my right brigade. While General Sheridan was in this position, I changed my front slightly, bearing it more to the left, to avoid masking a portion of Sheridan's command. The troops remained in this position, and in order of battle, all night, cheerfully enduring the rain and cold, awaiting the morrow's sun to renew the contest.

Early the next morning, and before the heavy fog had drifted away from our front, the enemy in strong force attacked and surprised General McCook's right, commencing a general action, which increased in intensity toward his left. Sheridan's division stood its ground manfully, supported by the Eighth Division, repulsing and driving the enemy at every advance. The enemy still gained ground on General McCook's right, and succeeded in placing several batteries in position, which covered my right. From these and the battery on my left, which now opened, the troops were exposed to a converging fire, which was most destructive. Houghtaling's, Schultz's, Marshall's, Bush's, and Nell's batteries were all ordered into action in my front, pouring destructive volleys of grape and shell into the advancing columns of the enemy, mowing him down like swarths of grain. For four hours the Eighth Division, with a portion of Sheridan's and Palmer's divisions, maintained their position amid a murderous storm of lead and iron, strewing the ground with their heroic dead. The enemy, maddened to desperation by the determined resistance, still pressed forward fresh troops, concentrating and forming them in a concentric line on either flank.

By 11 o'clock Sheridan's men, with their ammunition exhausted, were falling back. General Rousseau's reserve and General Palmer's division had retired in rear of the cedars to form a new line. The artillery ammunition was expended; that of the infantry reduced to a few rounds; the artillery horses were nearly all killed or wounded; my ammunition train had been sent back to avoid capture; a heavy column of the enemy was marching directly to our rear through the cedars; communication with Generals Rosecrans or Thomas was entirely cut off, and it was manifestly impossible for my command to hold the position without eventually making a hopeless, fruitless sacrifice of the whole division. To retire was but to cut our way through the ranks of the enemy. The order was given and manfully executed, driving back the enemy in front and checking his approaching column in our rear.

All the regiments in my command distinguished themselves for their coolness and daring, frequently halting and charging the enemy under a withering fire of musketry. On approaching General Rousseau's line, the battalion of regulars, under command of Major King, at my request gallantly charged forward to our assistance, sustaining a severe loss in officers and men in the effort. Colonels Stanley and Miller now promptly reformed their brigades with the remaining portions of the batteries, and took position on the new line, as designated by Major-General Thomas. Shortly afterward the Twenty-ninth Brigade was ordered to the left to repel an attack from the enemy's cavalry on the trains. The troops remained in line all night and the next day in order of battle until noon, when the division was ordered to the right of General McCook's line, in expectation of an attack upon his front.

The next day, January 2, at 1 p. m., my command was ordered to the support of General Crittenden on the left, and took position in the rear of the batteries on the west bank of Stone's River. About 3 p. m. a strong force of the enemy, with artillery, advanced rapidly upon General Van Cleve's division, which, after sustaining a severe fire for twenty or thirty minutes, fell back in considerable disorder, the enemy pressing vigorously forward to the river bank. At this important moment the Eighth Division was ordered to advance, which it did promptly, the men crossing the river and charging up the steep bank with unflinching bravery.

The Twenty-first, Eighteenth, Sixty-ninth, and Seventy-fourth Ohio, Nineteenth Illinois, Eleventh Michigan, Thirty-seventh Indiana, and Seventy-eighth Pennsylvania Volunteers displayed their usual promptness and gallantry.

Four pieces of artillery and a stand of colors, belonging to the Twenty-sixth (rebel) Tennessee, were captured at the point of the bayonet, and a large number of prisoners, the enemy retreating in disorder.

It is proper to mention here that the artillery practice of Schultz's, Mendenhall's, Standart's, Nell's, Marshall's, and Stokes' batteries, which were acting temporarily under my orders in this engagement, was highly satisfactory, giving the enemy great tribulation. The promptness displayed by Captain Stokes in bringing his battery into action, by my orders, and the efficient manner in which it was served, affords additional evidence of his marked ability and bravery as an officer and patriot. In the same connection I feel permitted to speak in complimentary terms of the gallant Morton and his Pioneer Brigade, which marched forward under a scathing fire to the support of my division.

The enemy having fallen back to their intrenchments, my division recrossed the river and resumed its former position.

On the evening of the 4th, the Twenty-ninth Brigade was moved forward to the north bank of Stone's River, near the railroad, as an advance force. On the same day General Spears' First Tennessee Brigade was assigned to the Eighth Division. This brigade distinguished itself on the evening of the 3d, in a desperate charge on the enemy, a report of which is included in General Spears' report, annexed.

On the morning of the 5th I was ordered to take command of the advance and pursue the enemy toward Murfreesborough.

By 9 a. m. the Eighth Division, Colonel Walker's brigade, Pioneer Brigade, and General Stanley's cavalry force had crossed the river and taken possession of Murfreesborough without having met any resistance, the rear guard of the enemy retreating on the Manchester and Shelby-ville roads, our cavalry pursuing, supported by the Twenty-ninth Brigade, on the Shelbyville pike, and by Colonel Byrd's First East Tennessee Regiment, on the Manchester pike.

The rear guard of the enemy (three regiments of cavalry and one battery) was overtaken on the Manchester pike, 5 miles from Murfreesborough. Colonel Byrd fearlessly charged this unequal force of the enemy, driving him from his position, with a loss of 4 killed and 12 wounded ; enemy's loss not ascertained.

Our army marched quietly into Murfreesborough, the chosen position of the enemy, which he was forced to abandon after a series of desperate engagements.

The joyful hopes of traitors have been crushed, treason receiving another fatal blow.

My command enthusiastically join me in expression of admiration of the official conduct of Generals Rosecrans and Thomas. During the most eventful periods of the engagements their presence was at the point of danger, aiding with their counsels and animating the troops by their personal bravery and cool determination.

I refer to my command with feelings of national pride for the living and personal sorrow for the dead. Without a murmur they made forced marches over almost impassable roads, through drenching winter rains, without a change of clothing or blankets, deprived of sleep or repose, constantly on duty for eleven days, living three days on a pint of flour and parched corn. Ever vigilant, always ready, sacrificing their lives with a contempt of peril, displaying the coolness, determination, and high discipline of veterans, they are entitled to our country's gratitude. Pennsylvania, Ohio, Kentucky, Indiana, Illinois, Michigan, and Tennessee may proudly inscribe upon their scrolls of fame the names of the Seventy-eighth Pennsylvania Volunteers, Eighteenth, Twenty-first, Sixty-ninth, and Seventy-fourth Ohio, Schultz's and Marshall's batteries (Ohio), the Eleventh Michigan, Nineteenth Illinois, Thirty-seventh Indiana, Nell's section, Kentucky battery, and Spears' East Tennessee Brigade.

I respectfully refer to the reports of General Spears, Colonels Miller and Stanley, which I approve and append hereto, for a detailed account of the part taken by each portion of the command, and for special reference to the meritorious conduct of individuals in their respective commands. In addition to which I make honorable mention of the bravery and efficient services rendered by the following-named officers and men, for whom I earnestly request promotion:

Brigadier-General Spears, commanding East Tennessee Brigade; Col. T. R. Stanley, Eighteenth Ohio Volunteers, commanding Twenty-ninth Brigade; Col. John F. Miller, Twenty-ninth Indiana Volunteers, commanding Seventh Brigade; Capt. James St. C. Morton, commanding Pioneer Brigade; Capt. James H. Stokes, commanding Chicago Battery; Maj. John H. King, commanding Fifteenth U. S. Infantry ; Captain Bush, commanding Fourth Indiana Battery; Capt. W. E. Standart, commanding Ohio battery; Capt. James A. Lowrie, assistant adjutant-general, Eighth Division; Lieut. Frederick H. Kennedy, aide-de-camp;

Capt. Charles T. Wing, assistant quartermaster; Maj. F. H. Gross, medical director; Capt. James R. Hayden, ordnance officer; Lieutenants W. W. Barker, aide-de-camp; Robert H. Cochran, provost-marshal; Thomas Riddle, acting assistant commissary of subsistence; Charles C. Cook, acting aide-de-camp; W. D. Ingraham, topographical engineer; Capt. Frederick Schultz, Lieuts. Joseph Hein, Battery M, First Ohio Artillery; Alexander Marshall, John Crable, Robert D. Whittlesey, Battery G, First Ohio Artillery; A. A. Ellsworth, W. H. Spence, Nell's section, Kentucky Artillery; H. Terry, Third Ohio Cavalry; Sergt. H. B. Fletcher, Company K, Nineteenth Illinois Volunteers; Corpl. R. G. Rice, Company K, First Wisconsin Volunteers; Private James A. Sangston, Company C, Seventy-ninth Pennsylvania Volunteers; Sergt. Charles Rambour, Company K, Seventy-fourth Ohio Volunteers, and Private William Longwell, orderly, Seventh Pennsylvania Cavalry; Sergt. George C. Lee, Corpl. E. H. Dougherty, and Privates Henry Zimmerman, Henry Schwenk, John Higgins, Leon Starr, Daniel Walker, John D. McCorkle, Abraham Kepperly, George Gillen, and John Cunningham, of the escort.

The following is an approximate report of the casualties [*] of my command during the battles before Murfreesborough, Tenn., December 30 and 31, 1862, and January 2 and 3, 1863:

Command	Went into action				Lost in action										
	Commissioned officers	Enlisted men	Horses	Guns	Killed Comm.	Killed Enl.	Wounded Comm.	Wounded Enl.	Missing Comm.	Missing Enl.	Horses Killed	Horses Wounded	Horses Missing	Horses Lost	Guns Disabled
SECOND DIVISION, CENTER, FOURTEENTH ARMY CORPS.															
First East Tenn. Brigade...	66	734	8	....	....	3	1	22	....	....	....	1	....	....	....
Twenty-ninth Brigade......	93	1,719	37	....	8	77	25	259	....	94	5	3	5	....	....
Seventh Brigade...........	71	1,948	....	....	3	79	20	415	1	93	....	....	....	....	....
Infantry	230	4,401	45	....	11	159	46	696	1	187	5	4	5	....	....
Schultz's battery...........	2	75	56	4	....	1	1	....	....	1	5	4	....	1	....
Marshall's battery..........	3	110	116	6	....	5	....	5	....	14	34	12	....	4	....
Nell's battery..............	2	47	40	3	....	1	....	3	....	6	18	6	4	1	1
Artillery	7	232	212	13	...	7	1	8	....	21	57	22	4	6	1
Total..............	237	4,633	257	13	11	166	47	704	1	208	62	26	9	6	1

My command captured from the enemy upward of 400 prisoners, four brass pieces of field artillery, and one stand of regimental colors.

I have the honor to remain, very respectfully, your obedient servant,

JAS. S. NEGLEY,
Brigadier-General.

Maj. GEORGE E. FLYNT,
Chief of Staff.

---

[*] But see revised statement, p. 211.

No. 79.

Report of Lieut. Alban A. Ellsworth, Hewett's (Kentucky) battery.

HDQRS. HEWETT'S BATTERY, KENTUCKY VOL. ARTY.,
Murfreesborough, Tenn., January 12, 1863.

SIR: In obedience to orders received from Headquarters Seventh Brigade, Eighth Division, Fourteenth Army Corps, I have the honor to make the following report of the part taken by Hewett's battery, Kentucky Volunteer Artillery, in the recent engagement before Murfreesborough, Tenn.:

On the evening of December 29, 1862, in obedience to orders from General Negley, I placed the battery in position near the old toll-gate, and on the right of Battery G, First Ohio Volunteer Artillery, commanded by Lieutenant Marshall.

Early on the morning of the 30th, I received orders from Colonel Miller to move about three-fourths of a mile to the right and front, through a dense cedar thicket, and over a rough and newly made road. Here I remained partly under cover of the cedars until about 10 a. m., when I received orders from General Negley to move a short distance to the left and front, taking a position fronting an open field, where the enemy had a battery of four guns bearing on us. During the day fired about 50 rounds of shell and solid shot at his battery and intrenchments without receiving any reply. As night approached, withdrew the battery and placed it under cover of the wood, where we remained during the night.

Early in the morning of the 31st, received orders from Colonel Miller to bring my command in position on the left, and near an old log-house, supported on my right and front by the Twenty-first Ohio Volunteer Infantry, where I remained without further orders for about fifteen minutes, when, observing the enemy in large column marching on a battery and some infantry stationed about 300 yards to my left, I opened an oblique fire on him, and soon discovered him retiring to his intrenchments, where I kept up a brisk and well-directed fire, receiving, at the same time, a heavy fire from his artillery for about fifteen or twenty minutes, when a cessation occurred.

I soon after noticed a heavy mass of his infantry moving on our support to my right and front, accompanied by a section of artillery, which was brought into position about 500 yards to my right and front; also a section placed to my left and front, at about the same distance. Here we were subject to a heavy cross-fire of canister. I immediately ordered a return fire of canister, double-shot, firing as rapidly as possible for about twenty minutes, doing good execution. The enemy was soon seen retiring, and I ordered the use of shell to follow his retreat, briskly kept up for about fifteen minutes, when the enemy commenced a well-directed fire from his artillery direct upon my command. After shelling him rapidly for about three-fourths of an hour, one of my guns (a small rifled gun) was disabled. I continued shelling as rapidly as possible for some time after, and finding my horses were fast being crippled by the shells continually exploding in our midst, I ordered a change of position of the battery to the left, that I might break the range of his artillery, bearing heavily upon us.

While my order was being executed, I noticed that our infantry and artillery were retiring, at the same time that a heavy fire was being poured into our right, and almost into our rear. Receiving no orders to retire, made the change of position of the battery to the left, and opened fire on the enemy, now fast approaching; but I soon found it impossible to do more without losing the whole battery, and ordered it limbered to the rear, and to retire into the cedar thicket, now being cut off from the road we came in the day previous. Being principally in the rear of our retiring forces, was subject to a heavy fire from the enemy following our retreat, and having all except one horse that moved my 6-pounder smooth-bore gun shot, was compelled to leave it; also one caisson belonging to the 10-pounder Parrott gun, containing about 50 rounds of ammunition. The remainder of the battery we succeeded in saving. Some of the carriages moved out with two horses, having had over half my horses killed and crippled. Fired during the day 493 rounds of ammunition, losing 2 men killed and 1 wounded.

Early on the morning of January 1, reported to General Negley the Parrott gun, and sent it on the field in charge of Lieutenant Spence. I then took the remainder of the battery, now unserviceable, to the rear; at the same time procuring 22 rounds of Parrott ammunition, and was subsequently ordered to move the unserviceable portion of the battery to Nashville, which I did, and immediately returned; but, while on the road, was attacked, and lost the rear chests of one caisson.

Lieutenant Spence was placed on the left center for a short time; then receiving orders to move to the right and take position with Marshall's battery, where he remained until about 12 m. January 2, when ordered to move to the left center and take position as on the day previous.

About 4 p. m. a heavy force of the enemy was discovered moving on our left and front, driving in our skirmishers. He immediately ordered shell to be fired into him as rapidly as possible, and at the same time receiving a heavy cross-fire from the enemy's artillery. Not long after the batteries on his right and left retired, and retired about 40 yards to the rear; found that the limber contained about 10 rounds of shell and few canister; immediately ordered the gun to its former position, using all the shell, and reporting the same to Captain Lowrie; was ordered to remain and use the canister in case a second attack was made; but the enemy being repulsed and driven beyond their intrenchments, he retired, moving the gun about one-fourth of a mile to the rear. Forty-two rounds of ammunition were expended, receiving little damage, except a few horses wounded.

On the morning of the 3d, I failed to procure ammunition, and remained as on the night previous.

Early on the morning of the 4th, procured 75 rounds of ammunition, and reported to Colonel Miller, who ordered me to move to the left center, and placed my gun in position with Marshall's battery.

About 3 p. m., was ordered to advance on Murfreesborough, and moved about 1 mile and remained during the night.

Early on the morning of the 5th, forded the river and passed through Murfreesborough.

I take great pleasure in referring to the valuable assistance rendered by Lieutenant Spence, whose heroic bravery inspired the men with courage, and his conduct is deserving of public commendation.

My non-commissioned officers and privates deported themselves like veterans who fight for the cause of their country.

Our loss in killed was 2—Godfrey Hautt, Ninth Ohio Volunteer Infantry, on detached duty with the battery, and Lewis Sagers, Seventy-eighth Pennsylvania, on detached duty with the battery; wounded, 1— Milton Crawhorn.

A. A. ELLSWORTH,
Lieutenant, Comdg. Hewett's Battery, Kentucky Vol. Artillery.

H. M. Cist, *Acting Assistant Adjutant-General.*

No. 80.

Report of Lieut. Alexander Marshall, Battery G, First Ohio Light Artillery.

HDQRS. BATTERY G, FIRST OHIO VOL. ARTILLERY,
Murfreesborough, Tenn., January 11, 1863.

SIR : In obedience to orders from Headquarters Seventh Brigade, Eighth Division, Fourteenth Army Corps, I have the honor to report the part taken by Battery G, First Ohio Volunteer Artillery, in the late engagement before Murfreesborough, Tenn.

On the morning of December 29, 1862, the battery was ordered out on a reconnaissance. Leaving the Murfreesborough pike at Stewartsborough, followed up Stewart's Creek 1 mile; discovered the enemy's cavalry in the woods on the opposite side of the creek; fired 12 rounds from rifled 12-pounder, causing them to disperse.

We then moved forward and to the right, taking position as indicated, until 2 p. m., when we crossed the creek with the brigade, advancing on a by-road running nearly parallel with the Murfreesborough pike. Entering the pike at Wilson's Creek, about 5 miles from Murfreesborough, advanced on the pike 2½ miles ; took position on a slight elevation on the right of the pike, where we remained during the night, with horses harnessed and hitched in.

At daylight on the 30th, per order of Colonel Miller, moved about three-fourths of a mile to the right and front over a new and rocky road through a cedar thicket. Remained in this vicinity during the day, occupying several positions in a narrow corn-field and in the thicket, within range of the enemy's battery and rifle-pit, located in an open field in front.

At 4 p. m., fired about 50 rounds, shelling the woods on our right occupied by the enemy's skirmishers, whose fire was severe; also the battery and rifle-pit in front. Some of our shells falling into the rifle-pit caused considerable scattering. We remained in this position in the corn-field during the night. We elicited no reply from the enemy's battery during the whole day.

At 6 p. m., removed the right section out on the right of the section in the corn-field, and remained in this position, hitched in, during the night.

At daylight of the 31st, opened with the four guns stationed in the corn-field, shelling the woods to the right and the battery and rifle-pit in front, as the night before. About 8 a. m., moved the center section down to the left about 40 rods, taking position near two log-houses in rear of the corn-field, a dense thicket across the corn-field directly in front, open country to the left and front, where the enemy was in position. Remained in this position about thirty minutes without firing; then moved this section up and took position in center of the battery; worked the battery till about 11 a. m. The enemy up to this time fired but few rounds from their batteries in our front, firing being mostly from their skirmishers in the woods, when, in obedience to Colonel Miller's order, moved to the right; partially changed front. The batteries of the enemy opened over the advancing infantry a heavy fire before we had fairly got into position. Ordered caissons under shelter. a short distance in the rear, and opened upon the rapidly advancing enemy with canister. As our support advanced, we moved our pieces forward by hand and worked them as rapidly as possible.

One of our 12-pounder howitzers being disabled, the trail having been cut nearly off by a shot, ordered it to the rear. Went to work with canister, the enemy advancing in the woods close upon us. As our infantry support advanced we advanced our pieces by hand to the fence close to the woods, that we might hold an interval in their lines, and continued firing canister as fast as possible. During this time our horses were suffering severely from fire from the enemy; had them replaced by the teams from battery and forge wagon, which I had ordered up the day before, leaving the battery and forge wagon 1½ miles in the rear, in charge of artificers. All of my spare horses were soon used up and several taken from the caissons. Had 3 men killed and several wounded.

Saw the enemy moving down the open field in masses on our left flank, and firing extending far to our rear on our right flank, and one of our 12-pounder rifles having a shot wedged and but three horses remaining, I ordered Lieutenant Crable to take the two disabled pieces and caissons to the rear through the cedar swamp, and ordered the remaining four pieces to fix prolonge, to fire retiring. The enemy had already been twice repulsed, when they moved upon both our flanks and front with renewed ranks and vigor, which caused our support to give way. I ordered the battery to retire to the woods in our rear, two pieces having but three horses and two four horses each.

My own, Lieutenant Whittlesey's, and one sergeant's horse were killed; three of the guns moved off as ordered; prolonge of the left piece, 12-pounder Wiard, broken; at the same time the lead rider was shot; the gunner mounted his team, when the off wheel horse was killed and the off lead horse wounded, which prevented us from using the limber. I then ordered a limber of one of the pieces already in the woods out, to draw the remaining 12-pounder off the field into the woods.

We had no sooner started back when I found the right and center of the brigade had fallen back, and the left (Twenty-first Ohio) was coming in, leaving the pieces about 40 yards outside of our lines, between us and the enemy, which was fast closing in on us, with a heavy fire. Saw that it was impossible to reach the gun. I ordered the limber back and gun limbered up; moved back through the cedar swamp in rear of brigade. There being no road, I was considerably bothered to work my way through. As the brigade was moving rapidly and the enemy pressing close upon us, two more of my wheel horses were shot and one rider, when I was obliged to leave two more guns, having but one wheel and middle horse on each piece. Sergeant Farwell, together with Sergeant Bills, took the remaining piece, passed the pieces left, and worked their way through and took position on the right of Captain Stokes' battery, where I found them and went to work, using up the balance of our ammunition—about 40 rounds.

As soon as joining this piece I sent to inform Lieutenant Crable where I was, and to get that portion of the battery which had succeeded in getting out, together with the battery and forge wagon, which was a short distance in the rear. After expending the ammunition of the piece I was with, moved to the rear, and left it in charge of Lieutenant Whittlesey, with the battery and forge wagon. I then proceeded to find Colonel Barnett or Lieutenant Edson, in relation to ammunition, when I met Lieutenant Crable, who informed me that our piece and four caissons had moved up the pike. I ordered him to have the carriages all halted, and to send back the 6-pounder ammunition. After waiting some time, sent my orderly back to hurry up the 6-pounder ammunition.

At dark, moved over to the left of the railroad, and remained during the night with the First Kentucky Battery, Lieutenant Ellsworth commanding, having previously reported to General Negley and Colonel

Miller the condition of the battery, and where I was; was ordered to remain in that vicinity.

Early on the morning of January 1, I proceeded out the pike; met sergeant with the 6-pounder caisson, who had been unable the night previous to find the gun. Sent sergeant forward with the caisson, when the piece in command of Lieutenant Whittlesey moved up and took position on the left of Captain Schultz's battery, in an open field on the left center, joining General Crittenden's corps. I soon met Lieutenant Crable with the 12-pounder howitzer, who informed me that when he came up with the 12-pounder howitzer, the afternoon of the 31st, the enemy was about making a charge upon our transportation, when he placed the piece in position, fired 15 rounds of shell, doing good execution, where he remained during the night with a brigade of cavalry.

I found that our loss for December 31, 1862, summed up 43 horses, 4 guns, 3 limbers, 2 caissons and limbers; 3 men killed, 8 wounded, and 12 missing. I then moved the 12-pounder howitzer to the front and took position with the other piece. Receiving 50 rounds for howitzer and 80 rounds for 6-pounder Wiard, immediately reported to Colonel Miller, commanding brigade, and General Negley, commanding division.

About 10.30, shifted our position about 200 yards to our front and left; remained in this position about an hour, when we received orders to move immediately to the right, across the pike, into a cedar thicket, and took position in center of Missouri battery.

About 3 p. m., was ordered to move with division to the rear and right; finally took position in corn-field on the extreme right, in company with Captains Standart's, Schultz's, and Ellsworth's batteries (fixed prolonge), where we remained until dark, when we moved back close to the pike under cover of an elevation, where we remained during the night.

At daylight on the morning of January 2, again moved up on the elevation. At about 12 m., received orders to move over and take position on left center, same as day previous. The skirmishers kept up a lively fire along our front until 4 p. m., when I observed the enemy moving in masses through the open country on the opposite side of the river, on our left and front, driving back our forces on the opposite side of the river, when we commenced shelling them as fast as possible, receiving a cross-fire from the enemy's artillery. Soon Captain Schultz's on our left, and Captain Swallow's batteries on our right, fell back. I then ordered prolonge fixed, and retired about 40 yards; commenced firing, when I had 1 man and 3 horses killed on the piece. At the same time the enemy was repulsed, and the ground retaken.

January 3, held the same position as the day previous; fired several rounds on the enemy, shelling the woods to the right and front as our men advanced.

Late on January 4, advanced with the division on Murfreesborough pike about 1 mile; encamped on the right of pike. Early on the morning of the 5th, forded the river and passed through Murfreesborough.

Our losses are:* Horses killed, 34; horses captured by the enemy, 12. Total horses killed and captured, 46.

I take pleasure in referring to the valuable assistance rendered me by Lieutenants Crable and Whittlesey. Their gallant and heroic bearing not only inspired the men with courage, but is deserving of public commendation.

Orderly Sergeant Sliney and Sergeants Bills, Farwell, and Mitchell,

---

* Embodied in revised statement. p. 211.

by their promptness in the execution of orders, and by their unflinching courage in scenes of danger, merit particular mention. Others in the command evinced soldierly qualities of no common order. To mention their names might seem invidious.

I wish to make special mention of Quartermaster Treat, who showed great energy and perseverance in keeping the men supplied with rations during the severe weather of seven days that we were separated by miles from our transportation, and his promptness in looking after, collecting together, and reporting to me property and men, which in the confusion of falling back had separated from the command.

Respectfully submitted.

ALEXANDER MARSHALL,
Lieutenant, Comdg. Battery G, First Ohio Volunteer Artillery.

H. M. CIST,
Lieutenant and Acting Assistant Adjutant-General.

No. 81.

Report of Brig. Gen. James G. Spears, U. S. Army, commanding First Brigade, of operations January 2–9.

HEADQUARTERS FIRST TENNESSEE BRIGADE,
Hawthorn's, near Murfreesborough, Tenn., January 9, 1863.

GENERAL : I herewith beg leave to submit the following report, which is intended to embrace the action of the troops under my command from the 2d instant up to the present date :

At 12 m. on January 2, 1863, when at Nashville, Tenn., I was ordered by Brigadier-General Johnson, military governor of the State, to immediately take command of the First and Second East Tennessee Volunteer Infantry, and such other troops as would be assigned me by Brigadier-General Mitchell, commanding post, which were the Fourteenth Michigan Volunteer Infantry, about 300 men strong, commanded by Captain ———; the Eighty-fifth Illinois Volunteer Infantry, Colonel Moore commanding, 350 to 400 men strong, together with two sections of the Tenth Wisconsin Battery, commanded by Captain Beebe, and a company of cavalry, under Lieutenant ———; also Colonel Pickens, commanding 300 mounted volunteers of the Third Tennessee Cavalry, which forces were placed under my command for the purpose of conducting and protecting a train of 303 wagons, loaded with commissary stores for the army, then before Murfreesborough.

I assumed command of the said forces at the junction of Market street and Murfreesborough pike at 5 p. m., at which place I took up the line of march, throwing out skirmishers and otherwise disposing the forces under my command in such manner as I believed would best protect the train.

After marching all night I reported myself and command at Major-General Rosecrans' headquarters at 5 o'clock on the morning of the 3d instant, and by his order turned over the train to his commissary.

Major-General Rosecrans then ordered me to report to General McCook, which I complied with, and, after receiving orders and instructions from General McCook, I placed the artillery under my command in position, drew up the infantry in line of battle, and the enemy failing to make any demonstrations in front, on the right wing, we stacked arms and took refreshments. At this time I was ordered by General Rosecrans to turn the cavalry in my command over to General Stanley, which was done.

The skirmishing in front of General Thomas' division becoming heavy, I was ordered by General Rosecrans to change my position and report to General Thomas, which I did, and by his order took a position in front of his division, relieving troops that had held said position during the night.

I received further orders from General Thomas to place my artillery in reserve, and to throw up an intrenchment with my force, in doing which two of my men, privates in the First and Second East Tennessee Regiments, were wounded.

I was also authorized by General Thomas, if I thought proper, to throw out skirmishers, consisting of three or four companies, and retake and drive the enemy from a piece of woods in our front.

After my force had finished the intrenchments, I was informed by an aide of General Rousseau that he would co-operate with me in throwing out skirmishers and in retaking the woods, and driving the enemy from the same, as soon as the artillery had begun shelling the woods, which was to be the signal for advance. In accordance to this, I threw out two companies (Company A, Captain Duncan, and Company B, Captain Sawyers) from the First East Tennessee Regiment; also Company A, Captain Marney, of the Second East Tennessee Regiment, and one company of the Eighty-fifth Illinois, and one company of the Fourteenth Michigan, as skirmishers, at the same time that skirmishers were thrown out from General Rousseau's division.

Shortly after sundown, the signal was given by shelling the woods, and the skirmishers advanced. The skirmishing becoming heavy, my force advancing in front and General Rousseau's upon the right, it was soon discovered, as they approached the woods, that the enemy were there in strong force, and intended to maintain his position with the greatest obstinacy—so much so that I thought fit to order up Lieutenant-Colonel Melton, commanding Second East Tennessee Regiment, to support the skirmishers in front. By this time the skirmishers had driven the enemy back and gained the edge of the woods. Colonel Melton was ordered to advance as near as possible to the woods, and then to order his men to lie flat on the ground. By that time darkness had set in. I ordered Colonel Byrd, with the First East Tennessee Regiment, to take his position behind the intrenchments, while I ordered Lieutenant-Colonel Phillips, of the same regiment, to take command of the Fourteenth Michigan Regiment, and to flank the enemy upon the left and rear, and I ordered the skirmishers to withdraw in good order and retreat behind the Second East Tennessee Regiment, which, at this time, was pouring a galling fire into the enemy, while a hot fire was kept up by General Rousseau's skirmishers on the right and from the Michigan regiment on the left, which was kept up until the enemy abandoned his position, being completely routed. The engagement lasted from 6 to near 8 o'clock, during most of which time Major-General Thomas was a spectator on the field. I then ordered my forces to retire behind the intrenchments, throwing an advance picket forward to hold the position we had taken.

The force under my command in this engagement was composed of regiments and parts of regiments: Of the First Regiment East Tennessee Volunteer Infantry, 400 men; of the Second Regiment East Tennessee Volunteer Infantry, 400 men; of the Fourteenth Regiment Michigan Volunteer Infantry, 300 men; of the Eighty-fifth Regiment Illinois Volunteer Infantry, 350 men.

The loss in my command of Tennessee troops was 4 wounded from the First Regiment and 7 wounded from the Second Regiment East Tennessee Volunteers. None killed or missing. The Fourteenth Regiment Michigan Volunteers, commanded by Lieutenant-Colonel Phillips, of the First East Tennessee, reported 2 killed and 3 wounded. The regiment left for Nashville as soon as the engagement was over, with the Eighty-fifth Illinois Regiment, which, during the engagement, was held in reserve and had no casualties.

Nineteen prisoners were taken and sent to corps headquarters. The loss of the enemy is not known, but said to be considerable, his strength being variously estimated at from one to two brigades.

On the morning of the 4th instant, I received an order from Major-General Rosecrans informing me that I, together with my command, had been permanently attached to the Eighth Division, commanded by Brigadier-General Negley.

On the evening of the same day, I was ordered by General Negley to hold myself in readiness to march at a moment's warning.

At 10 o'clock at night, I received an order from General Negley to order one of my regiments to report to Colonel Miller, commanding Seventh Brigade, for picket duty, which order was complied with by sending forward Lieutenant-Colonel Melton, in command of the Second East Tennessee Regiment, at 1 a. m. on the 5th.

On the morning of the 5th, I received a verbal order from General Negley to immediately move forward with the remaining force under my command, consisting of the First East Tennessee Infantry, Col. R. K. Byrd, and Sixth East Tennessee Infantry, Col. Joseph A. Cooper; also two sections of a battery (Tenth Wisconsin) commanded by Captain Beebe, and support Colonel Miller, who was in advance, engaged in building a bridge over Stone's River for the purpose of crossing infantry, the railroad bridge having been burned and injured by the enemy to such an extent as to render it unsafe. Being detained, Colonel Byrd and Colonel Cooper set their men to repairing the railroad bridge, and crossed about the same time that Colonel Miller's rear crossed the other bridge, marching through the town of Murfreesborough, with my force in rear of Colonel Miller's brigade. I was there ordered by General Negley to take and occupy a position near the crest of the ridge on the Manchester pike, which position I now occupy.

In the mean time, the cavalry having advanced upon the rear of the enemy then in our front, and the skirmishing becoming heavy, I was ordered by General Negley to support the cavalry with one regiment of infantry and one section of artillery, which I did by immediately ordering Colonel Byrd's regiment of East Tennessee, 400 strong, and Captain Beebe, with one section of artillery, to go forward and report to Brigadier-General Stanley, commanding the cavalry in front.

The enemy had retreated to a point in the woods near the Manchester pike, 5 miles from Murfreesborough, where they had stopped and formed line of battle.

On the arrival of Colonel Byrd's and Captain Beebe's commands, a sharp fight took place, both sides using artillery and small-arms, which resulted in a complete rout of the enemy, not, however, without some loss to us, Colonel Byrd losing 3 killed and 12 wounded, mostly slight.

About the time the fight was going on between our infantry and cavalry force of the enemy, I received a verbal order from General Negley to advance to the front with the remaining force under my command, which I did as rapidly as possible; but before I could arrive on the battle-field General Stanley, with his brigade of cavalry, and Colonel

Byrd, with his gallant Tennesseeans, aided by Captain Beebe's shells, had succeeded in driving the enemy, so that not one could be seen.

All the troops under my command behaved well, and Col. R. K. Byrd, of the First East Tennessee, and Lieutenant-Colonel Phillips, of the same regiment, are both said to have distinguished themselves, Colonel Byrd having his horse shot and wounded, and several balls passing through his clothes. Several prisoners were taken.

The loss of the enemy has since proved to be some 30 in killed, besides wounded, which he took off.

The two sections of the Tenth Wisconsin Battery were not permanently attached to my command, and have since been ordered back to Nashville.

Herewith I inclose the reports of Colonel Cooper, Sixth East Tennessee Regiment Volunteer Infantry, describing the march from Nashville to this point, and his encounter with the enemy on his way.

The following is a list of casualties: Went into action, commissioned officers, 66; enlisted men, 734; horses, 8. Lost in action, killed, enlisted men, 3; wounded, commissioned officers, 1; enlisted men, 22; horses, wounded, 1. The Fourteenth Michigan and Eighty-fifth Illinois, which were ordered out of my command immediately after the action, I have no reports of.

All of which is respectfully submitted.

I am, general, your obedient servant,

JAMES G. SPEARS,
Brigadier-General, Commanding First Tennessee Brigade.

Brig. Gen. J. S. NEGLEY,
Commanding Eighth Division, Fourteenth Army Corps.

No. 82.

Report of Col. Joseph A. Cooper, Sixth Tennessee Infantry, of skirmish at Cox's Hill.

HEADQUARTERS SIXTH EAST TENNESSEE VOLUNTEERS,
Camp near Murfreesborough, Tenn., January 9, 1863.

SIR: Permit me to submit this my official report of the march of my regiment from Nashville to Murfreesborough, in obedience to Special Orders, No. 8, as follows:

SPECIAL ORDERS, }   HDQRS. FIRST BRIGADE, TENNESSEE VOLUNTEERS,
No. 8.   {   *Nashville, Tenn., January 3, 1863.*

Colonel Cooper, with his entire command for duty, will at once take up the line of march upon the Murfreesborough pike. They will take two days' rations. They will report on said road to Col. Daniel McCook.

By command of General Spears:

D. C. TREWHITT,
Assistant Adjutant-General.

Complying with the above order, we took up the line of march at 8 o'clock. We marched out to the junction of the pike, where we lay in the rain about three hours, waiting for the commanding officer, Col. Daniel McCook. He arrived about 12 o'clock, and gave the following order:

The two regiments in advance of you will march in front with the regiment of regular cavalry, all except 50; the remaining 50 will act as rear guard for the whole. Your regiment, the Sixth East Tennessee, will march immediately in rear of the train.

We then took up the line of march to Murfreesborough. We marched, without halting, about 6 miles, arriving this side the lunatic asylum.

There we, together with a part of the Second East Tennessee Cavalry, which had come up with us, met a body of the enemy. The cavalry, filing to the right, engaged the enemy, who consisted of two or three regiments of cavalry, supported by a small piece of artillery. The cavalry fired one or two rounds and fled in confusion, running through the trains.

Just previous to this occurrence, I received orders from Colonel McCook to move my regiment forward, on the left, to the loss of the rise. [sic.] I moved forward in double-quick, gaining the point designated just in time to arrest the charge of the enemy. I engaged the enemy in a smart skirmish for some ten or fifteen minutes, killing some 6 or 8, wounding several, and capturing 10 prisoners. I met the enemy and repulsed them without assistance from the front. Immediately after the skirmish a battalion of infantry came up on the left, and assisted us in holding the position. We met the enemy and whipped them without the loss of a man, either in killed, wounded, or missing. My men acted with great coolness and bravery.

The train was soon reorganized, and we were again on the march. We arrived at La Vergne without interruption. At that point the two regiments in advance and the battalion, which came up during the skirmish, were mounted on the train, leaving my command on foot in rear of the train. I rode forward and asked Colonel McCook what I should do. He first said I had better encamp there with my command. I then told him it was "most too far from shore for me to cast anchor." He then ordered me to march on as fast as I could on foot, so that if they were attacked we could come up to their assistance, and said "he was ordered to go through that night." I obeyed said order, keeping in my rear the 100 cavalry first mentioned and a portion of the Second East Tennessee Cavalry until we arrived inside the lines. I then halted, let the cavalry pass, and went into camp for the night.

Next morning at daylight I took the line of march and marched to headquarters of Major-General Rosecrans, where I reported to Brig. Gen. James G. Spears.

I had in all when I went to the skirmish, and also when it ended, present, 12 commissioned officers and 213 enlisted men.

All of the above I respectfully submit.

I am, very respectfully, your obedient servant,

JOSEPH A. COOPER,
Colonel Sixth East Tennessee Infantry.

Capt. D. C. TREWHITT,
Asst. Adjt. Gen., First Brigade, East Tennessee Vols.

No. 83.

Report of Col. Timothy R. Stanley, Eighteenth Ohio Infantry, commanding Second Brigade.

HEADQUARTERS TWENTY-NINTH BRIGADE,
Battle-field, near Murfreesborough, Tenn., January 4, 1863.

SIR: Before the smoke of battle is over, and while the dead lie uninterred, I desire to make the following important report:

On the 30th of December the Eighth Division occupied the extreme right of the advance of the army at this point, my brigade occupying the right. The enemy were in our immediate front and extending to our right. It was expected that General McCook would occupy our right and first engage the enemy there. I directed Colonel Scott, with his regiment (Nineteenth Illinois), as skirmishers, to protect our right flank, but not to bring on an engagement, as you had orders not to do so at that time. It, however, became necessary to occupy some buildings in a field, from which we were annoyed by the enemy, and Colonel Scott drove them from the place and afterward held it. We were then annoyed from a barn and brick-kiln in our advance and right, and Colonel Scott charged and drove them away. Quite a number of the enemy were killed in these skirmishes and some two or three of our men.

During the day General McCook came up on our right and sharply engaged the enemy. At night we lay on our arms, and early on the morning of December 31 our skirmishers advanced and drove the enemy's skirmishers partly through the woods in our front, and General McCook engaged them on our right, but eventually fell back, and then a very heavy force was precipitated on our front and right, and on the Seventh Brigade, to my left. This infantry force was supported by a battery on our front and one in intrenchments on our left, and the fire was very severe; but the brigade (as also did the Seventh Brigade, on my left) sustained the fire without falling back, and poured such a well-directed fire upon the enemy that they faltered, and their ranks were thin and stayed; but the troops on our right and left had fallen back so far as to bring the enemy on three sides of us and fast closing on our rear. At this time General Negley directed the division to cut its way through, to join our other troops in the rear. This we did in good order, halting at two points and checking the enemy by a well-directed fire, which by this time they had learned to fear.

After we had formed in line behind the crest of a hill, an officer from another division rode to the front of the Eighteenth Ohio and ordered them forward, himself leading the way, and made the charge upon the enemy in the woods; but the enemy was so strong there that the regiment was compelled to fall back with heavy loss. As soon, however, as I saw the move, I called upon the Eleventh Michigan to follow me to their support, which they did most gallantly; but I soon called them off, as they had no support and the fire was murderous. I exceedingly regretted this order from an officer not having command over me, and without consulting yourself or me. Many of my men were left on the field.

Early in the action of this day I discovered that Colonel Cassilly, of the Sixty-ninth Ohio Volunteers, was so drunk as to be unfitted to command, and I ordered him to the rear in arrest, and placed Major Hickcox in command, who soon after was injured by the concussion of a shell, so as to be unfit for duty, and thus the regiment was left without a commander. I, however, knew nothing of this for some time after; but members of my staff found them scattering, rallied them, and directed the senior officer present, Captain Putnam, to take command. Captain Brigham, the senior captain of the regiment, had been out with skirmishers, and was not at this time with the regiment. The regiment did but little service in the action, but the company officers did what they could, and in that way helped us some.

I recommend the dismissal of Colonel Cassilly from the service. I cannot for a moment tolerate or pass over such flagrant conduct. I saw nothing of him after the action, but have learned that he was wounded and has gone to Nashville. A man who will come to the field of battle, having the lives of so many in his keeping, in such a situation, no matter what his social position, is totally unfit for any command.

On January 2, the enemy attacked the left flank of our army in strong force of infantry and artillery, and soon drove our scattered forces to the rear. General Rosecrans and General Negley were both on the ground occupied by the Eighth Division, and ordered my brigade forward across Stone's River to stay the advancing forces. This was done with a will, the Nineteenth Illinois leading, accompanied by the Seventh Brigade. They met the enemy with cheers, and with such determination that very soon the enemy gave way, followed closely by us, and were driven from every position up the hill through the woods, and through an open field to woods beyond.

In this gallant charge my brigade charged a battery and took three brass pieces. We occupied the field, and soon re-enforcements came to our relief, but it was nearly dark, and I did not deem it prudent to advance further without orders, as there was a battery in the woods beyond, which took effect upon us at short range. I here rallied my men and formed a little in rear of the crest of the hill. It was now about dark, and upon your order I withdrew my command to our former position.

In this engagement, as also in the one of December 31, the Seventh Brigade acted in concert with my own, and sometimes the two, to some extent, were intermingled, but fought together without confusion, and thus the troops from Pennsylvania, Ohio, Indiana, Illinois, and Michigan stood side by side, each vying with the other in the conflict.

With the exception of Colonel Cassilly, I know of no conduct worthy of censure, but much to commend. They acted with that bravery expected of well-disciplined troops fighting in a just cause. They stood manfully and bravely the appalling fire of a much larger force, and in the last engagement met and repulsed the enemy in superior force, elated with a supposed victory. The officers and men, almost without exception, behaved with the most determined bravery.

Colonel Stoughton, of the Eleventh Michigan, was in the thickest of the fight, encouraging his men, and throughout both engagements acted with the most distinguished gallantry. Good judgment was also displayed by him in rallying his own men and others of my brigade at the crest of the hill in the last engagement, during my temporary absence on another part of the field. Colonel Scott, of the Nineteenth Illinois, was also where danger was most imminent, and by his coolness and bravery aided his regiment in their gallant defense the first day, and charge, the second. He was seriously wounded in the second engagement, and carried off the field cheering and encouraging his men.

Lieutenant-Colonel Given, of the Eighteenth Ohio, was also at his post, and the thinned ranks of that regiment show how well they exposed themselves to the missiles of the enemy. He was cool, brave, and judicious.

Those officers, by their coolness and bravery, as well as good judgment and promptness of action, aided me in all my orders, and thus, by combined action and cool bravery, the brigade sustained the most determined shocks and repulsed the enemy at all points.

It would be invidious in me more particularly to specify individual cases of bravery. Where all do well it is hard to particularize.

It is but just, however, to speak in commendation of Captain Brigham, of the Sixty-ninth Ohio. Under his leadership a part of the regiment was in front of the battle in the last engagement, and behaved most gallantly. The regiment is a good one, and only needed a leader the first day to have taken a more active part in that engagement.

The members of my staff, Lieutenants Bishop, Temple, Platt, Sweeny, Rarick, and Cunningham, all were prompt and efficient in carrying my orders and aiding me, no matter what the danger. The same may also be said of my orderlies and clerks, Coffin, Mercer, and Adams, and Agnew and Riley, who were prompt and efficient.

I deem it but an act of simple justice to say of our division commander that in all he was cool, prudent, and determined. In the first engagement, when we were surrounded on all sides by the enemy (the right and left having retired far to our rear), he said to me, " We must cut our way through," and gallantly led the division for that purpose; but the enemy wisely opened a way for us, and only closed upon us at a respectful distance. If we have acquitted ourselves with honor, much of it is due to his careful training, his cool self-possession, and the confidence we all feel in him.

Surgeons Bogue, Johnson, and Elliott, and their assistants, rendered all the aid in their power in alleviating the sufferings of the wounded. It is claimed by some of my men that the Nineteenth Illinois took the enemy's colors on the second day. The same is also claimed by the Seventh Brigade. Suffice it to say that the colors were taken, the two brigades acting in concert. And while I desire for my brigade all credit for gallantry, I would not in the least detract from the other, which was side by side with us.

In these engagements many of my valuable officers and men were killed and wounded.

Our thinned ranks show how well they faced the enemy. The last engagement was against the enemy's best troops in superior force. They had never before been beaten, but now they were driven in confusion, leaving hundreds of their dead and dying on the field.

Captain Schultz, with his battery, rendered me efficient service, and was ready and enthusiastic in executing my orders. He did his duty well. On the first day one of his pieces became entangled in the woods, and was abandoned. We more than compensated this loss the second day.

I append a list of the casualties, and propose hereafter to make a more detailed report.

Very respectfully, your obedient servant,

T. R. STANLEY,
Colonel, Commanding.

Capt. JAMES A. LOWRIE,
Asst. Adjt. Gen. and Chief of Staff, Eighth Division.

HEADQUARTERS TWENTY-NINTH BRIGADE,
Camp near Murfreesborough, Tenn., January 10, 1863.

Command.	Went into action.				Lost in action.									
					Killed.		Wounded.		Missing.	Horses.			Guns.
	Commissioned officers.	Enlisted men.	Horses.	Guns, artillery.	Commissioned.	Enlisted.	Commissioned.	Enlisted.	Enlisted.	Killed.	Wounded.	Missing.	Lost.
Brigade staff	7		7							1	1	1	
18th Ohio	23	423	4		3	26	6	112	23	1			
19th Illinois	23	350	5		2	18	7	75	8		2		
11th Michigan	17	423	14		2	28	6	72	25	2		4	
69th Ohio	23	523	7		1	6	6	45	38	1			
Battery M	2	75	56	4		1	1		1	5	4		1
Total*	95	1,794	93	4	8	79	26	304	95	10	7	5	1

Respectfully submitted.

[T. R. STANLEY,]
Colonel, Commanding.

M. D. TEMPLE,
Lieutenant and Acting Assistant Adjutant General.

* But see revised statement, p. 211.

HEADQUARTERS SECOND BRIGADE,
SECOND DIVISION, FOURTEENTH ARMY CORPS,
Murfreesborough, March —, 1863.

His Excellency Governor BLAIR, *Michigan :*

S. R: I deem it but an act of simple justice to an efficient and brave officer to say to you, as the Governor of the State from which he comes, what I have said in my official report of Col. William L. Stoughton, commanding the Eleventh Michigan, a part of my brigade. In the late battles of Stone's River, General Negley's division, of which my brigade was the right, on Wednesday, the 31st December, and Friday, the 2d January, was placed in prominent and important positions, and nobly and heroically acted its part.

On Tuesday, the 30th, we had some severe skirmishing, first by the Nineteenth Illinois and Eighteenth Ohio, the last relieved by the Eleventh Michigan. Each regiment had men killed and wounded on that day, and well sustained its position. Tuesday night the Eleventh was detailed by me for most arduous and important duty—the care of the extreme front in face of the enemy. I gave the matter wholly into the hands of Colonel Stoughton, and during all that cold, bitter night he watched, and, with his regiment, without fires, kept the front, and were not nor could they have been surprised. In the morning they were relieved, but only to be soon called again into more terrible conflicts. In that terrible carnage—death, bull-dog fighting—my brigade bore a conspicuous part, being uncovered on our right by our associates being driven to the rear, and falling back only when flanked—in fact surrounded—in that falling back, in good order, fighting every step of the way, repulsing the enemy at every available point. In all these the Eleventh was in the right place in the midst of danger, never for a moment flinching. Colonel Stoughton was in his place, handling his men with ease and to the purpose. After we had formed a new line at the rear, one of my regiments was called upon by a major-general from another command to make a desperate charge upon the enemy in the woods, and, seeing them in close quarters, I called to the Eleventh to follow me to their rescue, which they did most gallantly, led by their gallant commander, and fought until called off by myself. From that time until Friday we were ready, as at all times, for the foe, but it was not until Friday evening that we had an opportunity to show our teeth. Then our extreme left was being driven before the enemy; a whole division (three brigades) was falling back in disorder, followed by a superior force. Our gallant commander, General Rosecrans, saw it in person, and rode to me, ordering me forward with my brigade, which was responded to with cheers and immediate action. Colonel Stoughton, with his regiment, took the extreme right, charging and driving the foe in terrible confusion, and exactly at the right point, halting and rallying his own men and others in his vicinity, thus forming a new line at the right time and in the right place. I was at this moment in another part of the field, but quickly there, and found him holding his position, having routed the enemy out of his sight. This was a most gallant exploit, and reflects the highest credit on Colonel Stoughton and his command. I bespeak for him your influence at Washington to make him a brigadier-general, a position to which he is entitled, and which he would fill with credit to himself and the country. In addition to his gallantry and judicious management, his heart is in his country's cause.

This is written wholly without any suggestion from Colonel Stoughton or any one for him, but on my own sense of justice to a deserving officer. For the last two months Colonel Stoughton has been provost-marshal of Murfreesborough, a difficult task, but has done his duty well.

Very respectfully, Your Excellency's obedient servant,

T. R. STANLEY,
Colonel Eighteenth Ohio Volunteer Infantry, Commanding.

No. 84.

Report of Lieut. Col. Alexander W. Raffen, Nineteenth Illinois Infantry.

HDQRS. NINETEENTH REGIMENT ILLINOIS VOLUNTEERS,
Camp near Murfreesborough, Tenn., January 10, 1863.

SIR: I would respectfully submit to you my report of the part taken by the Nineteenth Regiment Illinois Infantry in the late engagements before Murfreesborough.

On Tuesday morning, December 30, the regiment, under the command of its colonel, Joseph R. Scott, was, by your orders, deployed as skirmishers, to take possession of and hold certain buildings on the Nolensville pike. On the north side of said pike, on our front and right, opposite the above buildings, was a brick-yard, in which we found the enemy in strong numbers. We succeeded, after a short struggle, in driving in their line of skirmishers, which had been thrown out, taking possession of the designated places. We held the position thus gained until relieved, about 12 m., by the Forty-second Illinois on our right and the Eighteenth Ohio on our left. We then retired, and were held as a reserve, remaining in that position until next morning, the 31st.

At about 9 a. m. of the 31st we became engaged with a large force of the enemy. By your orders we changed our position, for the purpose of protecting and preventing, if possible, our right wing from being turned, which after some two hours' hard fighting, the enemy succeeded in doing. We retired, falling back in line of battle to the cedar forest, where we halted, but were ordered to fall back still farther. We again made a stand some 50 yards from the edge of the forest, engaging the enemy alone. We held our position, perhaps, half an hour, but our colonel, seeing that we were in danger of being outflanked, ordered a retreat, which was done in good order, falling back to the railroad. By your orders we changed our position several times during the day, but we were not engaged in action.

On Thursday, January 1, 1863, we changed our position several times, but did not become engaged with the enemy.

On the 2d, about 3.30 p. m., the enemy suddenly attacked our left with great fury, and after some severe fighting the left gave way. We were then ordered forward to their support. Charging upon the enemy, we drove them back. Crossing Stone's River, we forced them beyond their batteries, capturing four of their guns, remaining masters of the field.

Early in the engagement our colonel, while gallantly leading his men, fell, severely, but not dangerously, wounded, the command then devolving upon me; and I here take great pleasure in testifying to the bravery and good conduct of both officers and men in my command. But where all did their duty so nobly, it would be unjust to discriminate.

Inclosed please find list of casualties in my command.*

Trusting the above may prove satisfactory, I am, very respectfully, your obedient servant,

ALEX. W. RAFFEN,
Lieutenant-Colonel, Comdg. Nineteenth Illinois Infantry.

Col. T. R. STANLEY,
  Commanding Twenty-ninth Brigade.

No. 85.

Report of Col. William L. Stoughton, Eleventh Michigan Infantry.

HDQRS. ELEVENTH MICHIGAN VOLUNTEER INFANTRY,
In the Field, near Murfreesborough, Tenn., January 4, 1863.

SIR: Agreeably to orders, I submit the following report of the part taken by the Eleventh Regiment Michigan Infantry in the recent engagement:

On the morning of December 31, heavy firing was heard to our right and front, and apparently rapidly approaching the position occupied by the Twenty-ninth Brigade. My regiment was immediately formed and marched to the brow of the hill, near brigade headquarters. The skirmishing soon after indicated the approach of the enemy to the right of this position, and, under orders from Colonel Stanley, and at the request of General Rousseau, the regiment was formed in line of battle under cover of a ledge of rocks, about 100 yards in this direction. The skirmishing continued with much spirit for about half an hour, when a heavy roar of musketry and artillery indicated that the principal attack of the enemy was being made immediately to our left and rear. I immediately gave orders to change front to the rear on the first company, which was promptly executed under a heavy fire, and the regiment advanced to the brow of the hill, from which Schultz's battery had first been drawn, under a galling fire, and poured a well-directed fire into the advancing columns of the enemy, and continued to load and fire with great coolness and bravery until the orders came to fall back. The fire of the enemy was apparently concentrated upon this point, and was terrific. The slaughter was great, and men and officers fell on every side. The regiment fell back about 100 yards, and was again formed and poured a fire into the enemy as he raised the brow of the hill, and then retired to the cover of the cedars in our rear. Here some confusion was at first manifested. A large number of regiments had fallen back here for protection, and the enemy's artillery and infantry opened upon us from all sides, except to our left, toward the Murfreesborough pike. Order was, however, promptly restored by our division and brigade commanders, and then my regiment, with the others, moved back in good order, keeping up a steady fire on the enemy. When near the cleared field, to the right of the Murfreesborough pike, the regiment was rallied and held the ground for twenty or thirty minutes, checking the advance of the enemy. It was then marched about half-way across the open field to the pike, when orders came to charge back into the cedars. My regiment promptly obeyed my orders, rallied on their colors, and charged back into the woods with great gallantry, checking the enemy by their sudden and impetuous charge. **After delivering**

---

* Embodied in revised statement, p. 211.

our fire, orders came from the brigade commander to retire, and the regiment fell back, in good order, to the left of the Murfreesborough pike. Here closed the active operations of the day.

On the 2d of January the regiment was again called into action. In the afternoon of that day we were posted in an open field in the rear of ——— battery, on the left wing of the army, and about 100 yards to the right of Wilson's Creek. Between 3 and 4 o'clock the enemy made a heavy attack with artillery and infantry on our front. My command was kept lying on the ground, protected by a slight hill, for about thirty minutes. At the expiration of this time the enemy had driven back our forces on the opposite side of the creek, and one regiment crossed in great disorder, many without arms, and rushed through our ranks. As soon as the enemy came within range across the creek, my regiment, with the others of this brigade, rose up and gave him a destructive fire, and immediately charged over the creek, the enemy falling back under cover of the woods. In crossing the creek, my line of battle was necessarily broken, and I led them forward to a fence on a rise of ground and formed them in line, when they immediately opened an effective fire on the enemy, who, in a short time, retreated through the woods. The regiment promptly advanced to the edge of the woods and delivered a rapid fire on him, as he retreated across the open field.

The Eleventh was among the first who crossed the creek and assisted in capturing four pieces of artillery abandoned by the enemy in their flight. At this time my ammunition was nearly exhausted, and I, with the other regiments in the advance, formed a line of battle, and held our position until recalled across the creek.

I cannot speak too highly of the bravery of the troops under my command. They fought with the coolness of veterans, and obeyed commands under the hottest fire with the precision of the parade ground.

Lieutenants Wilson and Flynn were killed while gallantly discharging their duties as company commanders. Major Smith and Lieutenants Hall, Briggs, and Howard were wounded, the two former severely, and are prisoners of war.

The officers of my command, without exception, behaved with great gallantry, coolness, and fortitude. Where all nobly discharged their duty, it would, perhaps, be unjust to discriminate.

The following are the casualties, as far as known at this time: Killed, 25; wounded, 70; and missing, 23; aggregate loss, 118.*

I am, very respectfully, your obedient servant,

WILLIAM L. STOUGHTON,
Colonel Eleventh Regiment Michigan Infantry.

M. D. TEMPLE,
Acting Assistant Adjutant-General.

No. 86

Report of Lieut. Col. Josiah Given, Eighteenth Ohio Infantry.

HDQRS. EIGHTEENTH REGT. OHIO VOLUNTEER INFANTRY,
Before Murfreesborough, January 4, 1863.

I have the honor to report that on December 30 the Eighteenth Ohio Volunteers, under my command, with Capt. A. Fenton, acting major,

---

* But see revised statement, p. 211.

and Lieut. A. W. S. Minear, adjutant, took position with the reserve on the left of the center wing.

At 1 p. m., under your orders, I took position in the woods to the west of the Wilson pike, joining with the left of the right wing. At the instance of the commander of the left flank regiment of the right wing, I relieved three of his companies, then deployed as skirmishers and engaging the enemy. My skirmishers soon started the enemy, and would have cleared the woods but for an order received from the right not to advance our part of the line; whereupon I fell back to the first position, preserving an alignment with my right. At 5 p. m. I was relieved by the Eleventh Michigan, and I moved to the rear, where I remained all night.

On the morning of the 31st I again took position with the reserve, but was soon ordered forward to support the battery. At — a. m. I was ordered to take position in rear of the position and fronting to the rear, it having been discovered that the enemy had turned our right. No enemy appearing at that point, I was ordered to take position again on the hill to support the battery. I found the batterymen much endangered by the enemy's skirmishers to the right. I deployed a company and soon removed them.

I was then ordered to take position in the woods on the left, the enemy having made his appearance in that direction. When moving to that position, a very considerable consternation was observed among our forces, many of the regiments moving to the rear. Observing that a regiment still held the position, I moved rapidly to its rear; that regiment was lying down, so that my men were enabled to remain in their rear and engage in the firing. This position was rendered necessary, other regiments having moved into the only available position on the right and left. By the combined efforts of the forces there, the enemy was driven from the woods, but very soon a piece of artillery was brought into position against us. I hastened to where our battery was, to ask that it might be brought to bear against the enemy's piece that was then doing fearful havoc among our ranks. I learned that for want of ammunition none of our pieces were available. In the midst of this terrible fire I received your order to fall back, which I did, my men preserving perfect order.

During this engagement Capt. A. Fenton, who was acting major, and whose services proved of inestimable value, fell, wounded, and was placed on a horse and started to the rear; since that nothing has been heard of him, and I have reason to fear that he has fallen into the enemy's hands. After falling back, as ordered, to the point near the Nashville pike, I received your order to take a position in line with the Nineteenth Illinois, and in rear of a line formed, as I understood, by a part of General Rousseau's command. We had scarcely taken our position when the enemy engaged the first line, which, after some minutes, retired, under a terrible fire from the enemy. Anticipating the movement, I caused my men to lie down, and cautioned them to hold their fire until the enemy closed on them. The first line passed over my men, closely followed by the enemy. My men, observing well the caution I had given, poured a well-directed fire into the enemy, which checked them; but soon their second line pressed upon me, when I, with the rest of the line, fell back.

Immediately on the appearance of the enemy, the Nineteenth Illinois was moved to another position on his flank, so that no other regiment remained on the line with me. I moved to the rear gradually, returning the enemy's fire, until I found myself on open ground, when I ordered my men to move double-quick to a point covered from the enemy's fire, where I rallied my men and reformed my ranks, which had become somewhat broken in the retreat.

Just as I had accomplished this, General Rousseau ordered me to charge the woods again, encouraging the men to charge by taking the lead in person. The men, already breathless from fatigue, approached the close woods, but slowly, yet in perfect order, notwithstanding the enemy from the cover of the woods met us with a withering fire. My men bravely charged upon the hidden enemy and drove them back into the woods, where they held them at bay for some twenty minutes. Seeing that I was unsupported, and standing against a much stronger force, and that some 50 of my command had already fallen, I ordered a retreat, returning to the same place from which I had started under General Rousseau's order.

In this engagement Capt. P. E. Taylor fell, mortally wounded; also Lieutenant Minear, adjutant, fell, severely wounded. I was then, with the balance of the brigade, withdrawn from the field for that day.

My command was not actually engaged again until the afternoon of the 2d instant. I took position in rear of the battery in our center about 4 o'clock, when the enemy appeared to our left. I was ordered by General Negley to move to the support of the battery on the left, and to take covering behind the buildings near the position. When I arrived there, I saw the enemy's columns advancing under cover of the woods to our left, the head of his column almost to the creek. I immediately deployed my column and moved my line forward to a fence, from which my men sent a well-directed fire against the enemy.

At this point Capt. J. M. Welch, who was acting major, was carried from the field, severely wounded; also Sergt. L. D. Carter, aiding me as adjutant. Seeing that our fire brought the enemy to a halt, and that our forces were advancing, I ordered my men forward across the stream, which was promptly under execution when I discovered the enemy moving on our right in the woods in heavy force, evidently intending to attack us on our flank. I immediately ordered a halt, and rallied my men who had not already crossed the stream, leaving those who had crossed, as I supposed, to the command of Captain Welch, of whose wounds I was not informed. I rallied my men, getting many men from other regiments, and moved toward the woods on the right. Finding my ranks very imperfectly formed, I called a halt to allow the men a moment's rest, and to prepare my ranks for a charge bayonet. Just as I halted, a regiment arrived in my rear and passed on. Just then I received an order from General Palmer to move forward, which I did, taking position on the right of the other regiment. The line soon pressed the enemy back, discovering which I moved my line forward; but finding that the other regiment did not advance, I caused my bugler to sound a retreat, so as to align my forces with the other regiment. Just as the line was moving to the rear, a man on the right called out, "They are flanking us from the woods on the right." This caused some of the men to retreat hastily. I hastened to the open ground, from which I saw that the report was false, when I rallied those that had fled, and returned to the woods again. We continued to reply to the enemy's fire until darkness set in, when I withdrew, other forces having arrived to hold the ground.

In this charge Capt. George Stivers, a most valuable officer, fell, mortally wounded. The behavior of all my officers in these various engagements was such as that I may only say every one did all that he could, or that any one in his position could have done, and as to my men, I can praise no one above another. All did well alike, except three or four cowards, who deserted their posts and went back to Nashville

I hereto append a list of our loss.*

Your obedient servant,

JOSIAH GIVEN,
Lieutenant-Colonel, Comdg. Eighteenth Ohio Volunteer Infantry.

Col. T. R. STANLEY,
Commanding Twenty-ninth Brigade.

No. 87.

Report of Lieut. Col. George F. Elliott, Sixty-ninth Ohio Infantry.

HDQRS. SIXTY-NINTH OHIO VOLUNTEER INFANTRY,
Camp near Murfreesborough, Tenn., January 10, 1863.

Agreeably to orders, I submit the following report of the part the Sixty-ninth Regiment Ohio Volunteers took in the battle of Stone's River, omitting all the incidents up to the morning of December 31, 1862:

The Sixty-ninth Regiment occupied the left of the Twenty-ninth Brigade, Negley's division, and was ordered to advance about 6 a. m. across the Nolensville pike. Did so, and sent out three companies to the front. Remained in that position one and a half hours. Received an order to fall back to the right of Schultz's battery, which was executed in good order, the regiment sustaining a heavy fire from front and flank during that time. Remained in that position, fighting, until the division was ordered to retire back as far as the pike. There the regiment was reformed.

During all these moves and fighting we had many killed and wounded. During this time Colonel Cassilly was wounded through the arm, severely. Major Hickcox had his horse shot under him, falling on him, and so severely bruising him as to compel him to leave the field. The command was then turned over to Captain Putnam, he being the senior officer present. Was ordered up to the front, and sustained a heavy fire. Was then ordered to retire by General Negley, in person.

During this day's fighting I was back at Stewart's Creek; left there with a detachment of 200 men. Arrived on the battle-field at 5 p. m. and took command.

Thursday was occupied in skirmishing with the enemy on our right. Nothing of special interest occurred during the day.

Friday, January 2, was ordered to the left, where we took up a position and kept it until 3 p. m. At this time the division on the left of Stone's River was attacked by the enemy, and, after a short fight, fell back.

At this time we were ordered out into a corn-field, and lay down until the enemy came within 300 yards. We then arose, fired, and charged up to the bank of Stone's River, and halted a few minutes and fired across the river. Then crossed the river and reformed, and charged them for half a mile, and assisted to take a battery. The enemy having fallen back, we slowly retired to the woods and took care of our wounded and dead, which, I am sorry to say, was heavy. (A full list has already been forwarded to brigade headquarters.) It was now dark, and we were ordered out on picket in front.

---

* Embodied in revised statement, p. 211.

Saturday, January 3, nothing of interest occurred. January 4, was on picket. Relieved in the evening. January 5, came on through Murfreesborough, since which time we have been encamped in our present camp.

I am, colonel, your obedient servant,

G. F. ELLIOTT,
Lieutenant-Colonel, Comdg. Sixty-ninth Ohio Volunteer Infantry.

Col. T. R. STANLEY,
Commanding Second Brigade, Second Division, Center.

No. 88.

Reports of Col. John F. Miller, Twenty-ninth Indiana Infantry, commanding Third Brigade.

HEADQUARTERS SEVENTH BRIGADE, EIGHTH DIVISION,
Murfreesborough, Tenn., January 6, 1863.

SIR: In compliance with your request, the following report of the operations of my command before Murfreesborough is respectfully submitted:

On the evening of December 29, my command took a position in a field on the right of the Nashville pike, in the rear of General Palmer's line, and bivouacked for the night.

At daylight on the 30th, by order of General Negley, I took a position on the right of General Palmer's division, on the edge of a dense cedar woods fronting to the south, and deployed skirmishers from the Seventy-eighth Pennsylvania and Thirty-seventh Indiana in front, across, and to the left of the Six-mile pike, to act in conjunction with the skirmishers of Colonel Stanley's brigade, on my right. A brisk fire was kept up between the skirmishers and the enemy's sharpshooters, in the open field to the left and in the woods in front, until the arrival of General Sheridan's division on the right, when our skirmishers were withdrawn for Colonel Roberts' command.

During the day General McCook's forces advanced on the right, so that his left rested on our right flank, when a change of front to the left was made by General Negley's division.

The enemy had remained quiet on the open field (now almost directly in my front), in his intrenchments, which were plainly visible, and had kept a battery of four pieces in position at his works all day without firing.

Marshall's and Ellsworth's batteries, attached to my brigade, and posted in a small open field, fired an occasional shot into the works without eliciting reply. My command lost about 20 men, killed and wounded, during the day.

Skirmishers were kept out well to the front during the night, and two regiments of my command, with the batteries, were posted in the open field.

On the morning of the 31st, skirmishing was resumed along our line, and heavy firing was heard on the right along General McCook's line. The firing on our right gradually increased and neared our position, until a continuous roar of artillery and musketry was heard directly in our rear, and the advancing columns of the enemy were seen on our right and front.

Here I received orders from General Negley to hold my position to the last extremity. For this purpose I executed a partial change of my front, and placed my troops in the convex order, as follows: The Seventy-eighth Pennsylvania, Colonel Sirwell, on the right, at the brow of a small hill, the right resting near Schultz's battery, of Colonel Stanley's brigade; the Thirty-seventh Indiana, Colonel Hull, on the right center; the Seventy-fourth Ohio, Colonel Moody, on the left center, behind a rail fence; Marshall's battery on a small hill in the open field, to the left of the Seventy-fourth Ohio; the Twenty-first Ohio, Lieutenant-Colonel Neibling, on the left, in a thicket fronting the enemy's works, and Ellsworth's battery near the log-house, between Palmer's right and the Twenty-first Ohio. Simultaneously with the advance of the enemy from the right, a heavy force advanced from the enemy's works on my left wing.

The batteries at the enemy's works were manned and opened over the heads of the enemy's infantry. Before my regiments were properly in position, a most terrific fire was opened upon every part of the line by infantry and artillery, but there was no wavering, and, as the advancing columns of the infantry approached, they were met by a well-directed and terribly destructive fire from our line.

The batteries were worked with admirable skill, and the firing along our whole line was executed with creditable precision. The enemy halted, but did not abate his fire. The roar of musketry and artillery now became almost deafening, and as the unequal contest progressed it became more terrible. Once the strong force in the open field in front of my left wing attempted a bayonet charge on the Twenty-first Ohio, but were gallantly met and repulsed with great slaughter. On one of the flags was inscribed "Rock City Guards." The battle continued with unabating fierceness on both sides until the 60 rounds of ammunition with which my men were supplied were nearly exhausted.

The Thirty-seventh Indiana was the first to report a want of ammunition, and withdrew a short distance to the rear for a supply, the Seventy-fourth Ohio and Seventy-eighth Pennsylvania filling up the interval. The teamsters of the ammunition wagons had moved to the rear, and when ammunition was being brought forward they turned and fled. Colonel Hull again led his regiment forward and fired the few remaining cartridges on the persons of the men, taking also such as could be had from the dead and wounded.

At this juncture the troops on our right retired, and some unauthorized person ordered Colonel Sirwell to retire his regiment. This regiment was fighting gallantly and holding the position on the crest of the hill, but, on receiving the order, retired to the cedars in the rear. Seeing this, I immediately ordered Colonel Sirwell forward to the same position. This order was obeyed promptly, and the men again took position in admirable order. Soon after this a heavy force was observed to advance on General Palmer's left, and a hard contest ensued.

General Palmer's right brigade held their ground for a short time, and then began to retire. Just at this time I received orders from General Negley to retire slowly with my command into the woods. My troops were nearly out of ammunition; the enemy was advancing on my right flank and on my left, and the fire in front was no less destructive than it had been during the engagement.

The movement was executed in good order by the infantry, but it was impossible for the artillery to obey; nearly all the horses had been killed; the ground was soft and muddy; the men had not the strength to haul away the pieces. Five guns were lost; four were saved by the men of the batteries, assisted by the infantry.

On reaching the woods, I halted the command and formed a line of battle, faced by the rear rank, and delivered several well-directed volleys into the enemy's ranks, now crossing the open field over which I had retreated. This checked the advance of the enemy for a short time, strewing the ground with his dead. Being closely pressed on both flanks, and receiving fire from three directions, I again retired my command, the men loading while marching, and firing to the rear as rapidly as possible. In this way my command retreated for the Nashville pike, in a northeasterly direction.

While in the forest, being closely pressed in the rear, the enemy in strong force was encountered on the line of retreat, when a destructive fire was opened upon my column, which caused them to break to the right. My men did not run, but marched to the pike, carrying many of our wounded. When near the pike, and when rallying his men, Colonel Hull, of the Thirty-seventh Indiana, was severely wounded and disabled. He had fought bravely and gallantly during the whole engagement.

The Twenty-first Ohio, Lieutenant-Colonel Neibling, rallied near the pike, and, at the request of General Rousseau, took a position for the support of a battery then at work near the road. Ammunition was furnished, and the regiment fought with the battery over an hour, and then rejoined my command on the left of the road, where I had organized and obtained ammunition.

During this entire engagement, and under all these terribly appalling circumstances, both officers and men of my command behaved with admirable coolness and bravery. Examples of heroic daring and gallantry were everywhere to be seen, but where all acted so well it is difficult to make special mention without doing injustice to many.

The cool courage and distinguished gallantry of Col. William Sirwell, Seventy-eighth Pennsylvania Volunteers; Col. Granville Moody, Seventy-fourth Ohio (who was wounded early in the engagement and refused to leave the field); Col. J. S. Hull, Thirty-seventh Indiana, and Lieut. Col. James M. Neibling, Twenty-first Ohio, regimental commanders, deserve the highest praise, and the skill and ability with which these brave officers performed their responsible duties cannot be too highly applauded. The other field officers and company officers, and also Lieutenants Marshall and Ellsworth, of the artillery, displayed that high courage and determined bravery which mark the veteran soldier. Too much cannot be said in praise of both officers and men.

The losses in my brigade, killed and wounded in action, amounted to over 500 men.

In the evening of the 31st I was ordered by General Negley to take a position on the center front across the Nashville road for support to the batteries in position at that place. My command remained in this position until the next morning, when I was ordered to take position, as reserve for General Hascall's division, to the left of the railroad. In the afternoon of January 1, I received orders to march my command to the support of the right of General McCook's corps. I took position as directed, and remained there all night in the open field, and until about 1 p. m. on the 2d, when I was ordered to the support of General Crittenden's corps, on the left. I took position, as ordered by General Negley, in an open field, in rear of the battery on the left of the railroad and near the bank of Stone's River.

About 4 p. m. a furious attack was made by the enemy upon General Beatty's (or Van Cleve's) division, then across the river. The fire of the enemy was returned with spirit for a time, when that division retired across the river and retreated through my lines, which were then formed near the bank of the river, my men lying down partly concealed behind the crest of a small hill in the open field.

As soon as the men of Beatty's division had retired entirely from our front, I ordered my command forward—the Seventy-eighth Pennsylvania on the right; the Twenty-first Ohio on the left, to advance under cover of the hill along the river bank; the Thirty-seventh Indiana and Seventy-fourth Ohio in the center. The Twenty-ninth Brigade moved forward in the same direction, the Eighteenth Ohio on the right, and formed partly in the intervals between the regiments of my right wing. The enemy advanced rapidly, following Van Cleve's (Beatty's) division, and gained the river bank, all the time firing rapidly across at my line. My troops opened fire from the crest of the hill; the enemy halted and began to waver. I then ordered the men forward to a rail fence on the bank of the river. Here a heavy fire was directed upon the enemy with fine effect, and although in strong force, and supported by the fire of two batteries in the rear, he began to retreat. Believing this an opportune moment for crossing the river, I ordered the troops to cross rapidly, which they did with great gallantry under fire from front and right flank.

Here the Eighteenth Ohio, part of the Thirty-seventh Indiana, and part of the Seventy-eighth Pennsylvania were ordered by some one to proceed up the river on the right bank, to repel an attack from a force there firing on my right flank. The colors of the Seventy-eighth Pennsylvania, and, I think, Nineteenth Illinois, were the first to cross the river; the men followed in as good order as possible. While my troops were crossing, a staff officer informed me that it was General Palmer's order that the troops should not cross. The enemy was then retiring, and many of my men across the stream.

I crossed in person and saw the enemy retiring. Taking cover behind a fence on the left bank, the men poured a heavy fire into the ranks of the retreating force. The Twenty-first Ohio had crossed the river on the left, and was ascending the bank and fast going into the woods. When in this position I received another order, purporting to come from General Palmer, to recross the river and support the line on the hill. The force on the right of the river was then advancing in the cornfield and driving the enemy, thus protecting my right flank, and, having no inclination to turn back, I ordered the troops forward. Colonel Stoughton, of the Eleventh Michigan, formed his regiment and moved along the bank of the river, while the other troops moved forward to his left. The Twenty-first Ohio came in on the extreme left, and advanced in splendid style.

In crossing the river the men of the different regiments had, to some extent, become mixed together, yet a tolerable line was kept on the colors of the Seventy-eighth Pennsylvania, Nineteenth Illinois, Sixty-ninth and Seventy-fourth Ohio, and the men moved forward with spirit and determination.

The enemy's batteries were posted on an eminence in the woods near a corn-field in our front, and all this time kept up a brisk fire, but without much effect. His infantry retreated in great disorder, leaving the ground covered with his dead and wounded.

When within about 150 yards of the first battery, I ordered the Seventy-eighth Pennsylvania Volunteers to charge the battery, which was immediately done by the men of that regiment, and the Nineteenth Illinois, Sixty-ninth Ohio, and, perhaps, others. The Twenty-first Ohio coming in opportunely on the left, the battery, consisting of four guns, was taken and hauled off by the men.

The colors of the Twenty-sixth Tennessee (rebel) at the time of the charge were near the battery, and were taken by men of the Seventy-eighth Pennsylvania and brought to the rear. Another battery, farther to the front, all this time kept up a heavy fire of grape and canister upon our forces, but without much effect.

Seeing my troops in the disorder which follows such success, and being nearly out of ammunition, I sent a staff officer back to General Negley for re-enforcements with which to pursue the enemy. I ordered the troops to halt and reform, so as to hold the ground until relieved by other troops. This being done, a large body of troops were soon brought to our lines, when I withdrew my command to reform and procure ammunition. At this time Colonel Stanley crossed the river and took command of the regiments of his brigade on that side of the river. I brought my troops across to the right bank of the river, by order of General Negley, reformed them, supplied them with ammunition, and took position as support for the batteries on the hill in front.

The troops in this action behaved most gallantly, and deserve the highest credit for their bravery. Of the officers who participated in this engagement, honorable mention should be made of Col. William Sirwell, Seventy-eighth Pennsylvania; Col. Joseph R. Scott, Nineteenth Illinois, who was severely wounded while leading his regiment; Col. William L. Stoughton, Eleventh Michigan; Col. Granville Moody, Seventy-fourth Ohio; Lieutenant-Colonel Neibling, Twenty-first Ohio; Lieutenant-Colonel Elliott, commanding Sixty-ninth Ohio; Maj. T. C. Bell, Seventy-fourth Ohio; Lieutenant-Colonel Ward and Major Kimble, Thirty-seventh Indiana; Capt. William Inness, Nineteenth Illinois; Captain Fisher and Lieutenant McElravy, Seventy-fourth Ohio. The gallantry of these officers, and of many others, cannot be excelled.

To my staff officers I am greatly indebted for their efficient and valuable services in both these engagements, as well as for their general efficiency and faithfulness.

Maj. A. B. Bonnaffon, Seventy-eighth Pennsylvania Volunteers, topographical engineer; First Lieut. Henry M. Cist, acting assistant adjutant-general; Lieut. Alfred Ayers, Seventy-eighth Pennsylvania Volunteers, aide-de-camp; First Lieut. S. F. Cheney, Twenty-first Ohio, aide-de-camp; First Lieut. F. I. Tedford, Seventy-fourth Ohio, brigade inspector, all deserve the highest credit for the ability displayed in the discharge of their duties, and for their distinguished gallantry and cool courage on the field. I am also under many obligations to Lieut. Robert Mungen, brigade quartermaster, and Lieut. Frank Riddle, brigade commissary, for the able manner in which they discharged their duties.

Chaplain Lozier, of the Thirty-seventh Indiana, rendered valuable service by his labor for the comfort of the men and in taking care of the wounded. His bravery and kindness were conspicuous throughout.

I am informed that Surgeon Anderson, Thirty-seventh Indiana, brigade surgeon, performed his duties in a highly satisfactory manner.

Privates Nicholas J. Vail, Nineteenth Illinois, and W. J. Vance, Twenty-first Ohio, acted as orderlies, and deserve honorable mention for their efficiency and bravery. They are both worthy of promotion to the rank of lieutenant. I also recommend for promotion Sergts. H. A. Miller, A. R. Weaver, F. Mechling, Corpl. W. Hughes, Seventy-eighth

Pennsylvania, and Sergt. P. A. Weaver, Seventy-fourth Ohio, for deeds of valor on the field. There are many others whose names have not been furnished.

You will please find appended a list of killed and wounded, amounting in the aggregate to 531.

I am, captain, very respectfully, your obedient servant,

JNO. F. MILLER,
Colonel Twenty-ninth Indiana Volunteers, Comdg. Brigade.

Capt. JAMES A. LOWRIE,
Assistant Adjutant-General.

Addenda.

Command.	Went into action.				Lost in action.									
					Killed.		Wounded.		Missing.		Horses.			Guns.
	Commissioned officers.	Enlisted men.	Horses.	Guns, artillery.	Commissioned.	Enlisted.	Commissioned.	Enlisted.	Commissioned.	Enlisted.	Killed.	Wounded.	Missing.	Lost.	Disabled.
78th Pennsylvania	15	540			1	17	4	123	....	45					
74th Ohio	18	381			....	12	5	66	1	84					
37th Indiana	17	437			2	28	6	105	....	9					
21st Ohio	21	590			....	22	5	121	....	55					
Battery G, 1st Ohio Volunteer Artillery.	3	110	116	6	....	5	....	5	....	14	34	12	....	4	....
1st Kentucky Battery	2	47	40	3	....	1	....	3	....	6	18	6	4	1	1
Total*	76	2,105	156	9	3	85	20	423	1	213	52	18	4	5	1

JNO. F. MILLER,
Colonel Twenty-ninth Indiana Volunteers, Commanding Seventh Brigade.

H. M. CIST,
Acting Assistant Adjutant-General.

HDQRS. THIRD BRIG., SECOND DIV., FOURTEENTH CORPS,
Murfreesborough, Tenn., March 6, 1863.

SIR: I respectfully ask leave to amend my official report of the part taken by my command in the battle of Stone's River so as to include the names of Lieut. Col. D. M. Stoughton and Maj. G. F. Walker, Twenty-first Ohio Volunteers, in the special mention made of field officers, who were distinguished for gallantry in the engagement of Friday afternoon, January 2. Justice to these officers requires this amendment. At the time the report was written there was a dispute with respect to the conduct of those officers on the occasion referred to, which occasioned the omission. Full investigation has since been made.

I am, colonel, very respectfully, your obedient servant,

JNO. F. MILLER,
Colonel Twenty-ninth Indiana Volunteers, Comdg. Brigade.

Col. C. GODDARD,
Assistant Adjutant-General.

---

* But see revised statement, p. 211.

No. 89.

Report of Lieut. Col. William D. Ward, Thirty-seventh Indiana Infantry

HDQRS. THIRTY-SEVENTH INDIANA VOLUNTEERS,
Camp near Murfreesborough, Tenn., January 10, 1863.

SIR : I have the honor to submit the following report of the part taken by the Thirty-seventh Indiana Volunteers in the engagement at Stone's River, near Murfreesborough, Tenn., commencing December 30, 1862, and ending January 3, 1863 :

On the morning of the 30th the regiment, Colonel Hull commanding, moved through the cedar thicket to the right to bivouac, and there rested, only two companies (D and E) taking part in skirmishing.

On the morning of the 31st the regiment was moved to the open field to support Marshall's battery, where it remained until about 9 a. m., when we changed front, still supporting same battery. While there one piece was disabled by the horses all being killed and cannoneers leaving. The regiment then advanced to the woods on the front, which position was held until 12 m.

The troops on the right giving way, Colonel Hull called up three pieces of artillery while in that position, which did great execution in the center. He also ordered two pieces on the right, which were of great support to the maintaining of the position. We were assisted at one time by the Seventy-fourth Ohio Volunteers; also by the Seventy-eighth Pennsylvania Volunteers, which passed over us. During the entire time we were in this position the cross-fire of the enemy from each flank, in addition to that we were meeting in front, was exceedingly galling.

About 12 m. we were ordered to retire in support of Nell's battery. As we approached the thicket the fire from the enemy's batteries became extremely harassing—so much so that the battery which we supported was compelled to retire. We then moved by left flank to engage the enemy, who was approaching by brigade, at which time we were broken up by a regiment passing through our lines. We again collected our men, when the Eleventh Michigan Volunteers also passed through our lines, causing some confusion.

The regiment again formed near the center of the woods and moved in column of battle to the outer edge, where Colonel Hull was wounded by a musket ball passing through his left hip, entirely disabling him for duty, at which time the command was turned over to me. I moved the regiment to the pike, where I received ammunition, which we were en-tirely out of. The brigade then being again formed, we rested, not being placed in action again that day.

On the morning of January 1, 1863, we were moved to the right, where the enemy was expected to press. There we remained during the day and night following, resting on arms, but unengaged.

On the afternoon of the 2d we were moved to the left center, where we were placed to support a battery or batteries. While there the forces across the river gave way. The Seventh Brigade then being ordered to charge, I crossed the brow of the hill and engaged the enemy that had approached the river; drove them back, and held the position under extremely heavy fire from cannon and musketry. I remained in that position until dark, when I was ordered back about 200 yards, where I remained in that position until after noon of the 4th, when the forces moved for Murfreesborough.

Colonel Hull's actions during the engagement of the 31st were such

have won the highest regards by their eminently good conduct before the enemy and in the fiery ordeal through which they have passed. Lieuts. William McGinnis, commanding Company H ; Richard King, commanding Company B ; Robert Stevenson, commanding Company C ; Robert Hunter, commanding Company D ; Capt. Joseph Fisher and Lieut. H. H. Hering, of Company E ; Capt. Walter Crook, and Lieuts. M. Peters and Joseph Hamill, of Company F ; Lieut. T. C. McElravy, commanding Company G, with Lieut. George Bricker, of the same company ; Capt. Joseph Ballard and First Lieutenant Snodgrass, of Company H ; Lieut. Robert Cullen, of Company I, and William H. Reed, second lieutenant of Company K—these officers, sir, all did their duty bravely ; there was no flinching in any one of them ; each faced the iron hail unmoved ; each was in place superintending the movements and cheering his men in the terrible work they were called on to perform.

Lieutenant Peters was severely wounded in the wrist, and was compelled to retire about the middle of the action on the 31st. Lieutenant Snodgrass was last seen just before the closing struggle, cheering his men, clapping his hands, saying, " Work away, my lads ; we are gaining ground !" Noble fellow ! He was wounded shortly afterward, and is reported among the missing. We fear he was mortally wounded. Captain Crook and Lieutenant Cullen were also wounded in the action of the 31st, the latter dangerously. Captain Ballard was wounded in the shoulder slightly.

In the action of January 2 the Seventy-fourth Regiment occupied its position in the brigade, and aided in the decisive repulse of the rebel forces under Generals Cheatham and Hanson, in which they were driven over Stone's River, and over the hill and through the fields beyond, where our soldiers made the successful charge on the rebel batteries as they belched their fiery fury on the Federal forces. At the close of that eventful onward movement, the flag of the Seventy-fourth was waving on the outer lines amid the rejoicings of its stern supporters, and there remained until recalled by the order of General Negley to reform his division in the rear of the artillery in the center.

The review which I have made of the battle-fields over which we have together made our way during this nine days' struggle shows the awful effectiveness of our arms, the desperate obstinacy which characterizes our troops, and warrants the belief that, though our pathway may be over bloody fields and thickly planted grave-yards, yet the flag of Washington, Jefferson, Jackson, and the heroes of our glorious Union, endeared by a thousand precious memories, and the symbol of greater, grander destiny, shall be upheld and be borne along and aloft till it shall again float in unquestioned supremacy over all its ancient domain.

The following reports I have just received from our company commanders, and forwarded by Sergt. James Worden to headquarters.

Allow me to say, in behalf of the Seventy-fourth Regiment, officers and men, that with such commanders as Major-General Rosecrans, General Negley, and Col. John F. Miller, we are prepared to go forward and follow the fortunes of the flag with increasing confidence in the cause of our country against its rebel foes.

I have the honor to be, your obedient servant,

GRANVILLE MOODY,
Colonel, Comdg. Seventy-fourth Regiment Ohio Vol. Infantry.

H. M. CIST,
Acting Assistant Adjutant-General.

No. 92.

Report of Col. Moses B. Walker, Thirty-first Ohio Infantry, commanding First Brigade, Third Division.

HEADQUARTERS FIRST BRIGADE, THIRD DIVISION,
FOURTEENTH ARMY CORPS, DEPT. OF THE CUMBERLAND,
Camp before Murfreesborough, Tenn., January 11, 1863.

MAJOR: On the night of the 30th ultimo the First Brigade made a night march from Nolensville to Stewartsborough. The road was very heavy, rough, and intricate, and most of the night was occupied in the march. The Fourth Michigan Battery, belonging to the brigade, got through without accident, but in a manner unknown to the oldest inhabitant.

On the 31st the brigade was ordered to join the forces near Murfreesborough. This order would have been promptly obeyed, but at the moment it was received a messenger came into camp with the news that a body of rebel cavalry, numbering from 1,000 to 2,000 men, had attacked and were burning the supply train belonging to General McCook's corps, at La Vergne. I immediately ordered the Seventeenth, Thirty-first, and Thirty-eighth Ohio Regiments, and one section of the Fourth Michigan Battery to move with all possible haste to the relief of the train. Lest an attack might be made upon our camp in the absence of the troops, I left the Eighty-second Indiana Volunteers drawn up in line of battle, with four pieces of the Fourth Michigan Battery for its defense.

The distance from my camp to La Vergne was a little more than 2½ miles, and, though the infantry moved with great rapidity, we were unable to reach La Vergne before nearly all the wagons and their contents had been destroyed. By pushing forward the artillery with all haste, I was able to get the two guns which I had taken into position on the hill about one-third of a mile on this side of the town before the rebels had succeeded in paroling near all the men connected with the train. Many of the rebel cavalry were engaged in trying to drive away the mules belonging to the train, but the timely administration of shells by Lieutenant Wheat put an effectual stop to driving away the mules, but drove the rebels pell-mell into the woods on the right and left of the road.

Captain Patten, of the First Ohio Cavalry, who had joined me on the march with 20 of his men, supported, as well as could be done, by the Thirty-first Ohio Volunteers, now made pursuit, and succeeded in capturing 5 prisoners. The other two regiments having come up, a sufficient detail was made, under the direction of Major Ward and Captain Stinchcomb, to secure all the mules and harness, with two wagons, which were not burned, and a considerable amount of camp and garrison equipage, all of which was for the time being secured, and has since been sent back to Nashville. The rebels had broken and rifled the trunks and valises of the officers, taking everything in the way of clothing and other property of value from them.

Having done the best that I could, under the circumstances, in the way of saving property, and, as I have since learned, having killed several and wounded others, I marched my command back to camp; on reaching which I immediately ordered Colonel Hunter, of the Eighty-second Indiana Volunteers, to move with his regiment on the road leading to Nashville, to collect together and bring forward all the trains which he might meet coming this way. This was accordingly done, the regiment making a forced march to Nashville the same night and returning the next day to rejoin the brigade at this place at about 8 o'clock at night. This regiment rendered important service, checking and forcing back fugitives.

About 11 p. m. of the 30th I was ordered to move forward as soon as relieved by General Stanley. At 7.30 a. m. of the 31st General Stanley relieved me, and again ordered me to move to the front. While on the march, and near the crossing of Stewart's Creek, I received an order from Major-General Rosecrans to take up a strong position and defend the trains at the creek. I hastened forward, and at the creek was met by a large number of fugitives, fleeing to the rear, and spreading most exaggerated reports of disaster to the right wing of our army. I immediately brought the Fourth Michigan Battery into position on the high hill east of the road, and formed my infantry in line of battle to support it. The Tenth Ohio Volunteers, commanded by Colonel Burke, was drawn up in line of battle on the west side of the road. Our position was such as to completely command the road, as well as a wide area stretching off to the front. I here stopped the first stampede, compelling men who had thrown away their guns to pick them up again and return to the field.

We had remained here but a few moments until I received an order from Major-General Thomas, again directing me to move to the front and join my brigade to General Rousseau's division. I was also at this point notified by General Stanley that he would move forward on my right flank with a force of cavalry. It was about 9 a. m. when I again moved forward, throwing a line of skirmishers to the front, for the two-fold purpose of driving back fugitives and giving me timely warning if an enemy should approach.

About 10 a. m. I reached the headquarters of Major-General Thomas, and here, learning from you that but a short time previous a large body of rebel cavalry had menaced that part of the field, I again took up a position in the corn-field, fronting the headquarters, throwing my battalions into squares, and masking a section of guns in the center of each square.

I remained in this position but a few moments until another stampede of mules, negroes, fugitives, and cowards of every grade were seen swarming to the rear. At this moment Captain Mackay, of Major-General Thomas' staff, rode up and requested me, if possible, to check the stampede. I at once reduced my squares, forming line of battle with my right resting upon the road. The appearance of this force appeared to reassure and give confidence to the runaways. Men and mules all stopped.

Again receiving your instructions to move to the front, I advanced on this side of the creek, but was here again met by an order directing me to watch my right flank with great vigilance, as the rebel cavalry was again in strong force menacing that part of the field. I again formed a line of battle, taking advantage of a piece of woodland lying to the right of the road, from a piece of high land immediately in front of which I had a good view of the field to our right. I remained here a short time, and, no enemy approaching, I moved forward to the front.

At 1 o'clock I reached the point on the turnpike in front of General Rosecrans' headquarters, on the field. Here, in accordance with instructions, I reported to General McCook, who ordered me to take up a position on his left, which I did, and remained here comparatively inactive until about sundown, when I was ordered by General Johnson to move to the front, which I did, forming a double line of battle and throwing out a strong body of skirmishers. We remained in this position all night without fires. My skirmishers were busy all night, almost constantly exchanging shots with those of the enemy.

At 3 a. m. January 1, I was sent for to report at General Thomas' headquarters in person, which I did, and was there instructed to watch my front with great vigilance, and keep a strong body of skirmishers in advance to prevent any surprise. This I did, and daylight had no sooner broken upon us than I saw the wisdom of the warning that I had received, as the enemy showed himself in strong force upon the margin of the woodland immediately on my front. General Johnson had in the mean time ordered me to move to the left, about the distance of a brigade front, and form in two lines. The ground I then occupied was covered with a somewhat dense cedar forest. I directed my men to throw up a breastwork upon our front, which they very soon did, constructing it of loose rocks and logs gathered together for that purpose. So well was this work constructed, and with such rapidity, that by 10 o'clock we had a strong line of defenses, which were continued by other troops on our right, who evinced equal energy, skill, and industry.

The Fourth Michigan Battery, under command of Captain Church, assisted by Lieutenants Wheat, Corbin, and Sawyer, acted an important part in this morning's operations. Twice during the early hours of the morning the enemy showed himself upon our front. Captain Church had placed his guns in the most commanding positions, and, whenever the opportunity offered, the most destructive fire I ever witnessed from artillery was poured upon the rebel masses as they thickened upon the margin of the opposite woods. Other batteries, however, to our right and left opened their fire with, perhaps, equal effect.

It is not my business to speak of what they did, further than to admit the noble part that they took in the work. I watched the progress and observed the effect of my own shot, and saw the rebel masses torn down and scattered before it like leaves before a storm.

One rebel battery on our extreme right, and one or two guns in front of our center, replied with shell and round shot, many of which struck in the timber, and fell crashing and bursting in dangerous proximity, but not a man of the brigade was injured by them. The day was spent in skirmishing upon the front and in these artillery duels, in one of which a rebel gun on our right front was dismounted in a very handsome manner by a shot from Lieutenant Wheat's section of the Fourth Michigan Battery, which was sent with the accuracy of a rifle ball.

About 8 o'clock on the night of the 1st, I was ordered by General Sheridan to send a strong reconnoitering party to the front, which I did. The enemy were found in force but a short distance in front of our line, and apparently engaged in the same business.

In this reconnaissance I had 3 men from the Seventeenth Ohio Volunteers wounded—John Zeigler, of Company A, and Corpl. Edward Lacy and W. R. Sain, of Company B. The first two were severely, the third but slightly wounded.

On the morning of the 2d, the enemy could again be seen threatening our front, but so vigorous and well-directed was the fire from Church's battery and others upon the right and left of our position that no body of soldiers could have attacked our front successfully, covered as it was by the batteries. Heavy skirmishing continued upon our front all through the fore part of the day, until the action on our left appeared to command silence upon every other part of the field. There being no firing on our front, I reported in person to Major-General Thomas that the enemy appeared to have withdrawn, upon which he ordered me to advance to the front with my brigade and test the fact. I immediately obeyed his order. My men leaped over their breastworks, formed their lines, and moved to the front with a veteran steadiness and determination. The enemy had again shown himself upon our front, and that at closer proximity than at any time during this or the preceding day.

Stone's battery had opened fire upon such a line as to compel me to move my left directly under it; and finding that the elevation of his guns was not such as to enable me to do so in safety, I sent an officer to him with the request that he would change the direction of his pieces. The officer in command of the battery seems not to have understood my message, and for a few moments the fire from this battery threatened to do us greater injury than anything coming from the front, knocking the branches of trees to pieces and scattering them around us. Several shells from this battery also burst in our very midst, but, fortunately, did us no injury.

We had not advanced more than 300 yards beyond our breastworks when the rebel infantry opened a rapid fire on our right from the cornfield adjacent, and from the pickets in front of our center. My lines advanced under this fire, with the utmost steadiness and good order, a distance of 75 or 80 yards before a shot was returned. I then gave the order to commence firing. The front line, composed of the Seventeenth and Thirty-first Regiments, delivered a steady and well-directed fire. Then, as previously instructed, falling upon the ground to load, the Thirty-eighth Ohio and Eighty-second Indiana immediately advanced and delivered their fire, lying down to load. I then gave the order to fix bayonets, intending to finish the job with that weapon. The enemy, however, had fled precipitately before our volleys behind their breastworks in the woods. There being no corresponding movement on my right, and the battery on our left keeping up a most pertinacious fire, which put my lines in great peril should I advance, I withdrew the brigade again behind the breastworks.*

About 7.30 in the evening I was again ordered by General Sheridan to make a reconnaissance in front. For this purpose I detailed two companies from each of the Ohio regiments under my command, and placed them under the command of Lieutenant Colonel Choate, of the Thirty-eighth Ohio Regiment, assisted by Lieutenant-Colonel Davis, of the Eighty-second Indiana Volunteers, and Captain Stinchcomb, of the Seventeenth Ohio Volunteers. This force had not advanced above a quarter of a mile to the front before they were fired on by the enemy. A brisk skirmish ensued, which was kept up for about half an hour.†

On the morning of the 3d, being ordered to maintain great vigilance in watching the movements of the enemy to our front, I placed the brigade under arms, advancing my rear line and massing it upon the front under the breastworks. Here we remained pretty much all day, exposed to the inclemency of the weather and suffering a good deal, but without complaint.

The officers and men uniformly behaved well while under my command, and I find no lack of zeal, patience, or courage.

With the night of the 3d closed the active struggles of this great conflict. The First Brigade has sustained few casualties compared with others. We have tried to perform our duty. We have done the work

_____

* Nominal list of casualties in this advance reports 11 men wounded, viz: Eighty-second Indiana, 4; Seventeenth Ohio, 1; and Thirty-first Ohio, 6.

† Nominal list of casualties in this affair reports Capt. James W. Stinchcomb, Seventeenth Ohio, and Lieut. Thomas B. Hanna and 4 men, of the Thirty-eighth Ohio, wounded.

assigned us in the best manner we knew how.   We are in good condition to perform any service which may be required of us, and will do it cheerfully, whatever it may be, as we have ever heretofore done.

Respectfully submitted.

M. B. WALKER,
Colonel, Commanding First Brigade.

Maj. GEORGE E. FLYNT.

No. 93.

Report of Col. Daniel McCook, Fifty-second Ohio Infantry, commanding brigade, Fourth Division.

HDQRS. FIRST BRIGADE, SEVENTH [FOURTH] DIVISION,
Nashville, January 5, 1863.

SIR : In accordance with orders received from Generals Mitchell and Morgan, I proceeded, with eight companies of the Sixtieth Regiment Illinois Infantry, two companies of the Tenth Regiment Michigan Infantry, the Sixth Tennessee Infantry, and the left wing of the Fifty-second Ohio Volunteers, together with detachments of the Third and Fourth Ohio, and Second Tennessee Cavalry, to escort an ammunition and hospital train of 95 wagons to the main army lying in front of Murfreesborough.

Within 7 miles of Nashville, General Wheeler and [Colonel] Wade, with 3,000 men and three pieces of artillery, attacked the train. I ordered Colonel Toler, with the Sixtieth Illinois Regiment and two companies of the Tenth Michigan Regiment, to seize some wooded and high ground on the right of the road, the side upon which the attack was being made.   Orders were sent to hurry up the Sixth Tennessee and the Fifty-second Ohio.   The enemy soon drove in the cavalry flankers, and about 60 of them reached the train.   That portion of our cavalry upon the flank could not be rallied, and I endeavored alone to stem the tide—was completely surrounded by the rebels—wounding at least one with my pistol.   While in this position Colonel Zahm and First Lieut. E. L. Anderson, Fifty-second Ohio, with about 20 men, charged upon the body of rebels at the train and drove them off.   As soon as Colonel Toler got into position he opened a destructive fire upon the main body of the rebels, and put them to flight.   The Sixth Tennessee and the Fifty-second Ohio did not get up in time to take any active part in the struggle, but are worthy of all praise for the alacrity with which they double-quicked to the scene of action.   Too much praise cannot be given to Colonel Zahm for his good judgment and dashing bravery during the fight.   Colonel Toler and Lieutenant-Colonel Anderson, with officers and men under their command, behaved with commendable gallantry.   To Major Lee, One hundred and twenty-fifth Illinois, acting upon my staff; Lieutenant Anderson, my aide, and Lieutenant Swift, Fifty-second Ohio, brigade inspector, I am under many obligations for their judgment in delivering and gallantry in carrying orders.   The rebels lost 2 officers and 13 men killed, 2 officers and 12 men taken prisoners, and 11 wounded, Our loss was 2 wounded, one of whom has since died.   The train proceeded without further molestation to Murfreesborough.

I am, very respectfully, your obedient servant,

DANIEL McCOOK,
Colonel, Commanding Brigade.

Lieutenant WISEMAN,
Acting Assistant Adjutant-General.

No. 94.

Reports of Maj. Gen. Thomas L. Crittenden, U. S. Army, commanding Left Wing.

HEADQUARTERS LEFT WING,
December 26, 1862.

COLONEL: The left wing marched this morning, in conformity with orders, for La Vergne, Brigadier-General Palmer, commanding Second Division, taking the advance, preceded by three regiments of cavalry, under Colonel Kennett. When approaching the eleventh mile-stone, our cavalry encountered the enemy's pickets. The skirmish was sharp, but quickly ended by our cavalry driving them from their cover in the cedars, and capturing 6 prisoners. Two of our men were severely wounded, but are doing well. Two miles from La Vergne the enemy met us in considerable force. We occupied some time in artillery firing, without much result (we having 1 killed and 1 wounded), until Brigadier-General Cruft, with two regiments, the First Kentucky and Thirty-first Indiana, with the cavalry securing his left, and a section of artillery pressing down the road, passing under cover of the woods to the right of the enemy, attacked them, and, with great spirit, drove them across the creek into the town. He reports 1 killed and 5 wounded. At the same time Colonel Whitaker, with two regiments, attacked the enemy's left, and, after an animated contest, drove them from the thick woods toward the village, but, night coming on, he withdrew to the camp, having 7 men wounded, none killed. In all these skirmishes the enemy fought with such determination as to induce the belief that there must have been a large force in the neighborhood. Our troops are in excellent condition, and manifest the finest military spirit and enthusiasm.

The rebel force in the beginning is reported by prisoners to have consisted of four regiments of cavalry, one of infantry, and eight pieces of artillery (we saw only four pieces), but during the affair five other regiments came up. We could not ascertain the loss of the enemy.

Recapitulation: Killed of our troops, 2; wounded, 16; prisoners captured, 12.

Most respectfully, your obedient servant,
T. L. CRITTENDEN,
Major-General, Commanding.

Col. J. P. GARESCHÉ,
Chief of Staff.

P. S.—I am waiting anxiously to hear from you and of the fight which took place on the right. The firing for a time was apparently heavy. My command is all ordered to be under arms and ready at daylight.

—

ONE MILE NORTH OF LA VERGNE,
December 26, 1862—4.30 o'clock.

COLONEL: I must camp here. It will be dark before my first division can get into camp. The enemy are now skirmishing briskly on the ground where I propose to camp one division. I have no reason to think there is a heavy force near me but that I have obstinately opposed for several hours, they giving way slowly and taking advantage of every favorable position. I will move up in the morning early to Stewartsborough with a division, and try to save the bridge, but with little hope. I will also send out as directed on Jefferson pike. I hope to hear from you to-night. My headquarters will be about 1½ miles north of La Vergne, on Nashville road.

What about the heavy firing toward Nolensville?

Respectfully,

T. L. CRITTENDEN,
Major-General.

Col. J. P. GARESCHÉ.

—

HEADQUARTERS LEFT WING,
December 27, 1862.

COLONEL: I detached (as ordered) Colonel Hazen, with the Second Brigade, Second Division, down the Jefferson pike, supported by a battery and battalion of cavalry. I sent with him a guide, and placed the First and Second Brigades, Third Division, Van Cleve's, at the junction of the Jefferson pike with the Murfreesborough road. Very soon after leaving the Murfreesborough road the firing commenced, and continued with but little intermission until almost dark. The guide sent has just returned with a verbal message that he had taken, and now holds, the bridge, camping just by it. Colonel Hazen lost several killed and wounded, with 3 or 4 cavalry taken prisoners by the enemy, and took 7 prisoners. As soon as accurate details are returned by Colonel Hazen I will promptly report them.

Most respectfully, your obedient servant,

T. L. CRITTENDEN,
Major-General, Commanding.

Col. J. P. GARESCHÉ.

—

HDQRS. LEFT WING, ARMY OF THE CUMBERLAND,
One mile and a half North of La Vergne,
December 28, 1862—2.30 p. m.

COLONEL: Have this moment received your two dispatches, asking if all my division had moved, and where General Stanley was. I came on with the division, which marched in the center. Van Cleve was to follow, and I doubt not is close up. We have been skirmishing over the last 3 or 4 miles; had 2 men wounded and captured several prisoners. Have had a brisk cannonading here, in sight of La Vergne; no one hurt as yet on our side, we moving up cautiously. Some reports of infantry in sight, but not well authenticated.

Respectfully,

T. L. CRITTENDEN,
Major-General.

Col. J. P. GARESCHÉ,
Chief of Staff.

P. S.—Have heard pretty sharp cannonading toward Nolensville for about one hour, beginning about 12 o'clock.

—

HEADQUARTERS LEFT WING,
December 29 [28?], 1862.

COLONEL: I have the honor to inclose the reports of General Hascall and the officers of his command.

A very difficult task was very handsomely performed on yesterday by General Hascall and his brigade. Ability, activity, and courage marked the conduct of the general commanding, and the brigade showed itself worthy of such a commander. I respectfully call the attention of the general commanding to the particularly handsome conduct of the troops in charging at La Vergne, in seizing the bridge at Stewart's Creek, and in repulsing the cavalry.

Most respectfully, your obedient servant,

T. L. CRITTENDEN,
Major-General, Commanding.

Col. J. P. GARESCHÉ.

—

HEADQUARTERS LEFT WING,
January 15, 1863.

COLONEL: In obedience to orders, I left camp, near Nashville, on December 26, and reached the point where the battle of Stone's River was fought just before dusk on the evening of the 29th.

The march from Nashville was accompanied by the skirmishing usual when any army moves toward any enemy posted near by and in force. The gallant and handsome things done by several portions of my command during this march have been mentioned in detail by the immediate commanders conducting the advance and leading the skirmishers. The seizure of two bridges, one by General Hascall and the other by Colonel Hazen; the gallant charge of the troops of Hascall's brigade at La Vergne, and the counter-charge and capture of 25 of the enemy by a company of the new regiment (One hundredth Illinois), when charged by the enemy's cavalry, are worthy of notice.

It was about dusk, and just at the moment when Generals Wood and Palmer had halted to gather up their troops, that I reached the head of my command. These two generals had their divisions in line of battle, General Wood on the left and General Palmer on the right, the enemy in sight, and evidently in heavier force than we had yet encountered them; it was evident they intended to dispute the passage of the river and fight a battle at or near Murfreesborough.

At this moment I received an order to occupy Murfreesborough with one division, encamping the other two outside. I immediately gave the order to advance, and the movement was commenced. Wood was ordered to occupy the place, General Palmer being ordered, at General Wood's suggestion, to keep in line with Wood's division, and advance with him until we had forced the passage of the river. At this time it was dark. General Wood had declared, when he received the order, that it was hazarding a great deal for very little to move over unknown ground in the night, instead of waiting for daylight, and that I ought to take the responsibility of disobeying the order. I thought the movement hazardous, but as the success of the whole army might depend on the prompt execution of orders by every officer, it was my duty to advance. After General Wood had issued the order to advance, and General Palmer had received his also, they both came to see me, and insisted that the order should not be carried out. I refused to rescind the order, but consented to suspend it for one hour, as General Rosecrans could be heard from in that time. During the interval the general himself came to the front and approved of what I had done.

In the mean time Colonel Harker had, after a sharp skirmish, gallantly crossed the river with his brigade and Bradley's battery, and Hascall was already in the river advancing when the order to suspend the movement was received. As soon as possible I recalled Harker, and, to my great satisfaction, this able officer, with consummate address, withdrew from the actual presence of a vastly superior force his artillery and troops, and recrossed the river without any serious loss.

During the night General McCook came over to see the commanding general, and reported that he was on the Wilkinson pike, about 3 miles in the rear of our line, and that he should advance in the morning.

The next morning (the 30th) early, my line of battle was formed. Palmer's division occupied the ground to the right of the turnpike, his right resting on General Negley's left, General Negley having advanced into the woods and taken a position on the center, to connect with General McCook when he should come into line. General Wood was to occupy that part of our front to the left of the turnpike, extending down the river. General Van Cleve was held in reserve, to the rear and left.

This position of our forces was, without material change, maintained all day, though the skirmishing during part of the day was very heavy, particularly on our extreme right, where McCook was coming up. Then, when it apparently assumed almost the proportions of a battle, I proposed to cross the river with my corps and attack Murfreesborough from the left, by way of the Lebanon pike, but the general, though approving the plan of attack, would not consent that I should move until McCook was more seriously engaged.

On the morning of the 31st, when the battle began I occupied the front near the turnpike, General Palmer's division on the right, General Wood's on the left, General Van Cleve in reserve, to the rear and left.

About 8 o'clock, when my troops under Van Cleve were crossing the river, as ordered, and when all was ready for an advance movement, it became evident that our right was being driven back. Orders were received and immediately issued recalling Van Cleve, and stopping the advance. Van Cleve was ordered to leave a brigade to guard the ford (Matthews' brigade, Colonel Price commanding in Colonel Matthews' absence, was left), and to hurry with all possible dispatch to try and check the enemy to the right and rear. One brigade of his division, Colonel Fyffe's, had already been ordered to protect the train then threatened near the hospital; and General Van Cleve moved at once, and quickly, to the right with Beatty's brigade. He arrived most opportunely, as his own and Colonel Beatty's reports show, and checked the enemy.

The confusion of our own troops, who were being driven from the woods at this point, hindered him for some little time from forming his men in line of battle. This difficulty, however, was soon overcome, his line rapidly formed, and one small brigade, commanded by the gallant Colonel Beatty, of the Nineteenth Ohio, under the direction of General Van Cleve, boldly attacked vastly superior forces of the enemy, then advancing in full career, checked their advance, and drove them back.

Being soon re-enforced by Fyffe's brigade and Harker's brigade, of Wood's division, the enemy were pressed vigorously too far. They came upon the enemy massed to receive them, who, outnumbering them and outflanking them, compelled them to fall back in turn. This they did in good order, and fighting with such effect that the enemy drew off and left them, and they were able to hold their position during the remainder of the day. From this time the great object of the enemy seemed to be to break our left and front, where, under great disadvantages, my two divisions, under Generals Wood and Palmer, maintained their ground. When the troops composing the center and right wing of our army had been driven by the enemy from our original line of battle to a line almost perpendicular to it, the First and Second Divisions of the left wing still nobly maintained their position, though several times assaulted by the enemy in great force. It was evident that it was vital to us that this position should be held, at least, until our troops, which had been driven back, could establish themselves on their new line.

The country is deeply indebted to Generals Wood and Palmer for the sound judgment, skill, and courage with which they managed their commands at this important crisis in the battle. The reports of my division commanders show how nobly and how ably they were supported by their officers; and the most melancholy and convincing proof of the bravery of all who fought in this part of the field is their terrible list of the killed and wounded, for with them there was no rout and no confusion. The men who fell fell fighting in the ranks.

Generals Wood and Van Cleve being wounded on the 31st, their commands devolved, of course, on other officers, General Hascall taking command of Wood's division and Colonel Beatty of Van Cleve's, on the 1st of January. It was a fortunate thing that competent and gallant officers took command of these noble divisions. On the night of the 31st, with the consent of the general commanding, I reunited my command, bringing them all together on the left of the turnpike; and before daylight, by orders from the general commanding, we took up a new line of battle, about 500 yards to the rear of our former line. Hascall's division was ordered to rest their right on the position occupied by Stokes' battery, and his left on General Palmer's right. General Palmer was to rest his left on the ford, the right extending toward the railroad and perpendicular to it, thus bringing the line at right angles to the railroad and turnpike, and extending from Stokes' battery to the ford.

On the morning of January 1, Van Cleve's division again crossed the river and took position on ground the general considered important we should hold, extending from the ford about half a mile from the river, the right resting on the high ground near the river, and the left thrown forward, so that the direction of the line should be nearly perpendicular to it. These changes in position having been accomplished, the day passed quietly, except continued skirmishing and occasional artillery firing.

The next day, January 2, large forces of the enemy's infantry and artillery were seen to pass to their right, apparently contemplating an attack. Lieutenant Livingston, with Drury's battery, was ordered over the river, and Colonel Grose's brigade, of Palmer's division, was also crossed over, taking post on the hill near the hospital, so as to protect the left and rear of Beatty's position.

On the evening of the 2d, about 4 p. m., a sudden and concentrated attack was made on the Third Division, now commanded by Colonel Beatty. Several batteries opened at the same time on this division. The overwhelming numbers of the enemy directed upon two brigades forced them, after a bloody but short conflict, back to the river. The object of the enemy (it is since ascertained) was to take the battery which we had on that side of the river. In this attempt it is most likely they would have succeeded, but for the sound judgment and wise precaution of Colonel Beatty in changing the position of his battery.

It was so late when the attack was made that the enemy, failing in their enterprise to capture our battery, were sure of not suffering any great disaster in case of a repulse, because night would protect them. They not only failed to capture our battery, but lost four of their guns in their repulse and flight.

As soon as it became evident that the enemy were driving Colonel

Beatty, I turned to my chief of artillery, Capt. John Mendenhall, and said, "Now, Mendenhall, you must cover my men with your cannon." Without any show of excitement or haste, almost as soon as the order was given, the batteries began to open, so perfectly had he placed them. In twenty minutes from the time the order was received, fifty-two guns were firing upon the enemy. They cannot be said to have been checked in their advance—from a rapid advance they broke at once into a rapid retreat. Re-enforcements soon began to arrive, and our troops crossed the river, and pursued the fleeing enemy until dark.

It is a pleasant thing to report that officers and men from the center and right wing hurried to the support of the left, when it was known to be hard pressed. General J. C. Davis sent a brigade at once without orders; then applied for and obtained orders to follow immediately with his division. General Negley, from the center, crossed with a part of his division. General McCook, to whom I applied for a brigade, not knowing of Davis' movement, ordered immediately Colonel Gibson to go with his brigade, and the colonel and the brigade passed at double-quick in less than five minutes after the request was made. Honor is due to such men.

On the night of the 2d, General Hascall, with his division, and General Davis, with his, encamped a little in advance of the position which Beatty had occupied. General Palmer, commanding the Second Division, encamped with two brigades in reserve to Hascall's and Davis' divisions and the remaining brigade on this side of the river.

In this position these troops remained until Saturday night, when, the river beginning to rise and the rain continuing to fall, it was feared we might be separated from the rest of the army, and all recrossed the river, except Palmer's two brigades, which remained, and did not come back until it was ascertained the next day, Sunday, that the enemy had evacuated Murfreesborough.

I feel that this report of the part taken by my command in the battle of Stone's River is very imperfect. I have only endeavored to give a general outline of the most important features of the battle. The reports, however, of the division, brigade, and regimental commanders, together with the report of the chief of artillery, accompanying this report, give a detailed and good account of the memorable incidents which occurred in this protracted fight.

Reports of the division commanders show how nobly they were sustained by their subordinate officers, and all reports show how nobly the troops behaved. Generals Wood and Van Cleve, though wounded early in the battle of the 31st, remained in the saddle and on the field throughout the day, and at night were ordered to the rear. General Palmer, exposing himself everywhere and freely, escaped unhurt, and commanded the Second Division throughout the battle.

To these three division commanders I return my most earnest and heartfelt thanks for the brave, prompt, and able manner in which they executed every order, and I very urgently present their names to the commanding general and to the Government as having fairly earned promotion.

After the 31st, General Hascall commanded Wood's division (the First) and Colonel Beatty (the Third) Van Cleve's. To these officers I am indebted for the same cheerful and prompt obedience to orders and same brave support which I received from their predecessors in command, and I also respectfully present their names to the commanding general and the Government as having earned promotion on the field of battle.

There are numerous cases of distinguished conduct, in brigade as well as regimental commanders, mentioned by my division commanders as meriting promotion. I respectfully refer the general commanding to division, brigade, and regimental reports, and solicit for the gallant officers and men who have distinguished themselves for conduct and bravery in battle the honors they have won. We have officers who have commanded brigades for almost a year, though they have but the rank of colonel. In such cases, and in all like cases, as where a lieutenant commands a company, it seems, if the officers have capacity for their commands on the field, that they should have the rank the command is entitled to.

The report of Captain Mendenhall, chief of artillery to the left wing, shows the efficiency, skill, and daring with which our artillery officers handled their batteries. Division and brigade commanders vie with each other in commendations of our different batteries; some of these batteries, fighting as they did in all parts of the field, won praises from all. To these officers also attention is called, with a sincere hope that they may be rewarded as their valor and bearing deserve.

Maj. Lyne Starling, assistant adjutant-general to the left wing, has been for nearly eighteen months the most indefatigable officer I ever knew in his department. His services to me are invaluable. On the field here, as well as at Shiloh, he was distinguished even amid so many brave men for his daring and efficiency.

Capt. R. Loder, inspector-general of the left wing, has entitled himself to my lasting gratitude by his constant and able management of his department. It is sufficient to say that the gallant and lamented Colonel Garesché told him in my presence, but a short time before the battle, that he had proven himself to be the best inspector-general in the army. On the field of battle bravery was added to the same efficiency and activity which marked his conduct in the camp.

Capt. John Mendenhall, who has been mentioned already as chief of artillery to my command, but of whom too much good cannot be said, is also topographical engineer on my staff. In this capacity, as in all where he works, the work is well and faithfully done. His services at Shiloh, of which I was an eye-witness, his splendid conduct as chief of artillery of the left wing, his uniform soldierly bearing, point him out as eminently entitled to promotion.

To the medical director of the left wing, Dr. A. J. Phelps, the thanks of the army and country are due, not only for his prompt attention to the wounded, but for his arrangements for their immediate accommodation. He took good care not only of the wounded of my command, but of more than 2,000 wounded from other corps and from the enemy. Since the battle I have visited his hospitals, and can bear testimony to the efficiency of the medical department of this wing.

Capt. Louis M. Buford and Lieut. George Knox, my aides-de-camp, were brave, active, and efficient helps to me all through the battle. Captain Buford was struck just over the heart, fortunately by a ball too far spent to penetrate, and which only bruised. The captain and Lieutenant Knox were frequently exposed to the heaviest firing as they fearlessly carried my orders to all parts of the field.

Captain Case, of the Signal Corps, tendered his services as a volunteer aide, and proved himself a bold soldier and an efficient aide.

Two other officers of the same corps, Lieutenants Jones and ———, tendered their services as aides, and were placed on my staff during the battle, and I thank them sincerely for their services.

Lieutenant Bruner, of the Third Kentucky Cavalry, who commanded my escort, was as quietly brave on the battle-field as he is mild and gentlemanly in the camp. I thank him and the brave men he commands for the fearless discharge of their duties amid so many hardships and perils.

Before concluding this report, it will be proper to add that when I speak of a quiet day, I mean to speak comparatively. We had no quiet days; no rest from the time we reached the battle-field until the enemy fled; skirmishing constantly, and sometimes terrible cannonading.

On the 2d, which we call a quiet day until about 4 p. m., the First Division, under Hascall, laid for a half hour in the early part of the day under the heaviest cannonading we endured. Many men were killed, but he and his brave soldiers would not flinch.

The appended summary of the killed and wounded, furnished by my medical director, demonstrates with what fearful energy and earnestness the battle was contested in my command.

Report of killed, wounded, and missing, Left Wing.

Divisions.	Killed.	Wounded.	Missing.
First Division:			
Officers	11	56	......
Enlisted men	200	859	167
Total	211	915	167
Second Division:			
Officers	15	49	6
Enlisted men	191	1,031	257
Total	206	1,080	263
Third Division:			
Officers	17	52	4
Enlisted men	216	854	387
Total	233	906	391
Grand total*	......	......	4,372

Most respectfully, your obedient servant,

T. L. CRITTENDEN,
Major-General, Commanding.

Col. C. GODDARD, *Chief of Staff.*

No. 95.

Report of Capt. John Mendenhall, Fourth U. S. Artillery, Chief of Artillery.

HDQRS. LEFT WING, FOURTEENTH ARMY CORPS,
January 10, 1863.

MAJOR : I have the honor to submit the following report of the operations of the artillery in the left wing from December 26, 1862, to January 2, 1863:

This army marched from camp, near Nashville, December 26, the left wing marching on the Murfreesborough pike.

December 26, about 3 p.' m., our advance was brought to a stand-still,

---

* But see revised statement, pp. 211-214.

near La Vergne, by a rebel battery. It was opposed by a section of artillery serving with the cavalry, which, being unable to dislodge the enemy, our advance battery (Captain Standart's, Battery B, First Ohio) was, after a little delay, put in position and opened fire, soon silencing the enemy's battery.

December 27, General Hascall took the advance with his brigade and Lieutenant Estep's Eighth Indiana Battery. They marched steadily forward until the enemy was driven across Stewart's Creek, the battery halting only when it was necessary to fire ; two pieces were posted near, covering the bridge.

December 28, some artillery was so disposed as to check the enemy, should he attempt to destroy or retake the bridge.

December 29, Lieutenant Parsons, commanding Batteries H and M, Fourth Artillery, being in a commanding position, threw a few shells about 9 a. m., driving the enemy's pickets from the opposite woods. Our column advanced across the bridge at 10 a. m., meeting with little resistance until within about 3 miles of Murfreesborough. Our troops were placed in line of battle as they came up, the artillery remaining with their divisions.

December 30, about 9 a. m., the enemy opened upon Captain Cox's Tenth Indiana Battery (which was between the pike and the railroad, and in front partially covered by woods). Captain Bradley's Sixth Ohio Battery at once took a position to the left of the woods and in a cornfield. The two batteries soon silenced that of the enemy. One shot killed a man near where a number of general and staff officers were standing, and another, passing through Battery H, Fourth Artillery, killed one man and wounded another, besides disabling a horse.

December 31, the left wing started to cross Stone's River about 8 a. m., but before a division had crossed, intelligence was received that the right was falling back. Colonel Fyffe's brigade, which was about crossing, was ordered to countermarch and move at double-quick to the right. Captain Swallow's Seventh Indiana Battery operated for a time with this brigade, shelling the rebel cavalry from the brick hospital, &c. Colonel Beatty's brigade, having recrossed the river, advanced to the support of the right wing, but the Twenty-sixth Pennsylvania Battery, Lieutenant Stevens commanding, being unable to follow the brigade through the woods, took a position near the pike, and received the enemy with shot and shell as he advanced after our retreating columns, and, I think, did his part in checking him. He advanced as they retreated, and took a position in a corn field on the right of the pike, near the three-mile post, and again opened upon the enemy. The position of this battery underwent several changes during the rest of the day, but remained in the same immediate vicinity. Lieutenant Livingston, having recrossed the river with the brigade, took a position commanding the ford, and about 12 m. opened upon the enemy's cavalry, while attempting to drive off some of our wagons which had crossed the river, and were near a hospital we had established on the other side. They were driven away with little booty.

The batteries of General Wood's division (Cox's Tenth Indiana, Estep's Eighth Indiana, and Bradley's Sixth Ohio, all under command of Major Race, of the First Ohio Artillery) fought with the brigades with which they were serving. I had no occasion to give special orders to either of them during the day. The batteries of General Palmer's division served with it during the morning, rendering good service. Captain Standart's battery (B, First Ohio) fell back with General Cruft's brigade, and was not again engaged during the day.

Captain Cockerill during the afternoon was ordered to the front, and he took a position in the corn-field on the left of the woods, where the enemy was making such desperate attempts to force back the left. At this place Captain Cockerill was severely wounded in the foot, and the command of the battery devolved upon Lieutenant Osburn. Two guns of this battery were disabled from their own firing, the axles being too weak. One of the limbers of this battery was blown up during the day. Lieutenant Parsons, commanding Batteries H and M, Fourth Artillery, was ordered up to support the left about 4 p. m., and took a position in rear of the woods near the railroad, and after he had expended all his ammunition I sent Captain Swallow's (Seventh Indiana) battery to replace him. These batteries did much to repel the enemy, as he advanced with the evident determination to drive us back at all hazards, if possible.

During the night the batteries were resupplied with ammunition, and I directed them to take positions as follows, before daylight, viz: Lieutenant Livingston (Third Wisconsin), commanding ford on the extreme left; Captain Swallow (Seventh Indiana) on his right near the railroad; Lieutenant Stevens (Twenty-sixth Pennsylvania) also near railroad, but on the left of Captain Swallow. The batteries of the First Division between the railroad and the pike. Captain Bradley (Sixth Ohio) on the left; Captain Cox (Tenth Indiana) on the right, and Lieutenant Estep (Eighth Indiana) in the center. The Second Division batteries near the pike, in reserve.

During the morning Lieutenant Livingston was directed to cross the river; he was assigned a position by Colonel Beatty, and Captain Swallow took his place commanding the ford. Lieutenant Parsons was ordered to a position on General Rousseau's front by General Rosecrans, and Captain Cox was moved across the pike, near the Board of Trade Battery, to support the right of his division, which had moved its right to that point. After dark, Captain Standart was ordered to relieve the Board of Trade Battery. No firing, except now and then a shell at the enemy's pickets was fired, during the day.

January 2, early in the forenoon, the enemy opened his batteries, first upon our left, which was not responded to, their shot and shell doing no harm. They then opened more furiously upon the troops and batteries near the railroad and pike. Several of our batteries replied and soon silenced them. When the enemy had nearly ceased firing, the Board of Trade Battery (Captain Stokes) opened with canister upon Captain Bradley's battery and Colonel Harker's brigade, wounding several men and horses.

Captain Standart, with three pieces, Captain Bradley, Sixth Ohio, and Lieutenant Estep, Eighth Indiana, retired a short distance to fit up, they having received more or less injury from the enemy. Captain Bradley fell back on account of being fired into by Captain Stokes. He returned to his former position after a little while, but Captain Standart and Lieutenant Estep remained in reserve. I then ordered Lieutenant Parsons, with Batteries H and M, Fourth Artillery, to a position on the ridge, to the right of Captain Swallow (who was on the highest point of the ridge covering the ford), and Lieutenant Osburn, Battery F, First Ohio, to a position perhaps 100 yards to the right of Lieutenant Parsons. During the afternoon Colonel Beatty changed the position of Lieutenant Livingston's (Third Wisconsin) battery to near the hospital, across the river.

About 4 p. m., while riding along the pike with General Crittenden, we heard heavy firing of artillery and musketry on the left. We at once rode briskly over, and, arriving upon the hill near the ford, saw our infantry retiring before the enemy. The general asked me if I could not do something to relieve Colonel Beatty with my guns. Captain Swallow had already opened with his battery. I ordered Lieutenant Parsons to move a little forward and open with his guns; then rode back to bring up Lieutenant Estep, with his Eighth Indiana Battery. Meeting Captain Morton, with his brigade of Pioneers, he asked for advice, and I told him to move briskly forward with his brigade, and send his battery to the crest of the hill, near the batteries already engaged. The Eighth Indiana Battery took position to the right of Lieutenant Parsons.

Seeing that Lieutenant Osburn was in position (between Lieutenants Parsons and Estep), I rode to Lieutenant Stevens (Twenty-sixth Pennsylvania Battery), and directed him to change front, to fire to the left and open fire; and then to Captain Standart, and directed him to move to the left with his pieces; and he took position covering the ford. I found that Captain Bradley had anticipated my wishes, and had changed front to fire to the left, and opened upon the enemy; this battery was near the railroad. Lieutenant Livingston's (Third Wisconsin) battery (which was across the river) opened upon the advancing enemy, and continued to fire until he thought he could no longer maintain his position, when he crossed over, one section at a time, and opened fire again. The firing ceased about dark.

During this terrible encounter of little more than an hour in duration, forty-three pieces of artillery, belonging to the left wing, the Board of Trade Battery of six guns, and the batteries of General Negley's division, about nine guns, making a total of about fifty-eight pieces, opened fire upon the enemy. The enemy soon retired, our troops following; three batteries of the left wing, besides those of General Davis, crossed the river in pursuit.

During this engagement Lieutenant Parsons had one of his howitzers dismounted by a shot from the enemy, but it was almost immediately replaced by one captured from the enemy, and brought over by the Nineteenth Illinois Regiment.

The following are the casualties, &c., in the several batteries:

Designation of battery.	Commanding officer.	Commissioned officers wounded.	Enlisted men. Killed.	Enlisted men. Wounded.	Enlisted men. Missing.	Horses. Killed.	Horses. Disabled.	Horses. Missing.	Guns. Disabled by enemy.	Guns. Disabled by firing.	Rounds of ammunition expended.
Batteries H and M, 4th Artillery.	Lieut. C. C. Parsons.	......	2	14	6	20	....	....	1	......	2,299
Battery B, 1st Ohio	Captain Standart	......	3	13	3	21					1,610
Battery F, 1st Ohio *	Captain Cockerill	1	2	12	....	24				2	1,080
7th Indiana Battery	Captain Swallow	1	4	7	....	1	4	4			406
3d Wisconsin Battery	Lieutenant Livingston.	....	....	4	....	9					358
26th Pennsylvania Battery.	Lieutenant Stevens.	......	2	7	....	7					1,650
8th Indiana Battery	Lieutenant Estep			6	6	15	4				871
10th Indiana Battery	Captain Cox		1	4	....	12				2	1,442
6th Ohio Battery	Captain Bradley.	......	2	2	1	16	5				500
Total		2	16	69	16	125	13	4	1	4	10,216

*This battery had a limber blown up on the 31st.

Captain Cockerill and Lieutenant Buckmar were both wounded on the 31st. The former commanded Battery F, First Ohio, and the latter belongs to the Seventh Indiana Battery.

Major Race, First Ohio Artillery, chief of artillery in the First Division, and the several battery commanders, with their officers and men, all, with one exception, deserve most grateful mention for their coolness and bravery throughout the battle.

Lieutenant Parsons, commanding Batteries H and M, Fourth Artillery, and his officers, Lieutenants Cushing and Huntington, deserve great credit for their courage under the hottest of the enemy's fire; they were probably under closer fire and more of it than any other battery in the left wing, and perhaps in the army. I am more than pleased with the way they behaved, as well as the brave men that were under them. Captain Bradley, Sixth Ohio Battery, deserves particular notice for the manner in which he handled his battery.

The one exception above referred to is Lieut. Richard Jervis, of the Eighth Indiana, who is represented to have acted in a very cowardly manner, by retiring a section of the battery at a critical moment, without orders or notifying his battery commander.

I am, major, very respectfully, your most obedient servant,
JOHN MENDENHALL,
Captain Fourth Artillery, Chief of Artillery.

Maj. LYNE STARLING,
Assistant Adjutant-General.

No. 96.

Reports of Brig. Gen. Thomas J. Wood, U. S. Army, commanding First Division.

NASHVILLE, TENN., *January 6, 1863.*

SIR: On the morning of the 26th ultimo, the left wing of the Fourteenth Army Corps broke up its encampment, in the vicinity of Nashville, and moved toward the enemy. Reliable information assured us that he was encamped in force at and in the vicinity of Murfreesborough; but as his cavalry, supported occasionally by infantry, had extended its operations up to our outposts, and as we had been compelled for some days previous to the movement on the 26th ultimo to fight for the greater part of the forage consumed by the animals, it was supposed we should meet with resistance as soon as our troops passed beyond the line of our outposts. Nor was this expectation disappointed.

The order of march on the first day of the movement placed the Second Division, General Palmer, in advance, followed by my own. Several miles northward of La Vergne, a small hamlet nearly equidistant between Nashville and Murfreesborough, parties of the enemy were encountered by our advance guard, a cavalry force, and a running fight at once commenced. The country occupied by these bodies of hostile troops affords ground peculiarly favorable for a small force to retard the advance of a larger one. Large cultivated fields occur at intervals on either side of the turnpike road, but the country between the cultivated tracts is densely wooded, and much of the woodland interspersed with thick groves of cedar. The face of the country is undulating, presenting a succession of swells and subsidences. This brief description is applicable to the whole country between Nashville and Murfreesborough, and it will show to the most casual observer how favorable it was for covering the movements and designs of the enemy in resisting our progress.

The resistance of the enemy prevented our troops from gaining possession of the commanding heights immediately south of La Vergne during the first day's operations, and delayed the arrival of my division at the site intended for its encampment until some time after nightfall. The darkness of the evening and the lateness of the hour prevented such a reconnaissance of the ground as is so necessary in close proximity to the enemy; but, to guard effectually against surprise, a regiment from each brigade was thrown over forward as a grand guard, and the front and flanks of the division covered with a continuous line of skirmishers.

The troops were ordered to be roused an hour and a half before dawn of the following morning, to get their breakfast as speedily as possible, and to be formed under arms and in order of battle before daylight. An occasional shell from the opposing heights, with which the enemy commenced to greet us shortly after the morning broke, showed these precautions were not lost.

As it was understood from the commanding general of the corps that the right wing was not so far advanced as the left, the latter did not move forward until 11 a. m. on the 27th. At this hour the advance was ordered, and my division was directed to take the lead. The entire cavalry on duty with the left wing was ordered to report to me. Being satisfied, however, from the nature of the country, that its position in advance would be injudicious, and retard rather than aid the progress of the infantry, I directed it to take position in rear of the flanks of the leading brigade. I ordered Hascall's brigade to take the advance and move in two lines, with the front and flanks well covered with skirmishers. The other brigades, Wagner's and Harker's, were ordered to advance on either side of the turnpike road, prepared to sustain the leading brigade, and especially to protect its flanks. These two brigades were also ordered to protect their outward flanks by flankers. In this order the movement commenced.

Possession of the hamlet of La Vergne was the first object to be attained. The enemy was strongly posted in the houses and on the wooded heights in our rear, whence he was enabled to oppose our advance by a direct and cross fire of musketry. Hascall's brigade advanced gallantly across an open field to the attack, and quickly routed the enemy from his stronghold. This was the work of only a few minutes, but more than 20 casualties in the two leading regiments proved how sharp was the fire of the enemy. The forward movement of Hascall's brigade was continued, supported by Estep's Eighth Indiana Battery.

The enemy availed himself of the numberless positions that occur along the entire road to dispute our further progress, but he could not materially retard the advance of troops so determined and enthusiastic. They continued to press forward through the densely wooded country, in a drenching rain-storm, until they reached Stewart's Creek, distant some 5 miles from La Vergne. Stewart's Creek is a narrow and deep stream, flowing between high and precipitous banks. It is spanned by a wooden bridge with a single arch. It was a matter of cardinal importance to secure possession of the bridge, as its destruction would entail much difficulty and delay in crossing the stream, and, perhaps, involve the necessity of constructing a new bridge. The advance troops found on their arrival that the enemy had lighted a fire on it, but he had been pressed so warmly there had not been time for the flames to be communicated to the bridge. The line of skirmishers and the Third

Kentucky Volunteers, Colonel McKee's regiment, dashed bravely forward, though exposed to a fire from the opposite side, threw the combustible materials into the stream, and saved the bridge. While this gallant feat was being performed, the left flank of the leading brigade was attacked by cavalry. The menaced regiments immediately changed front to the left, and a company of the One hundredth Illinois, Colonel Bartleson's regiment, succeeded in cutting off and capturing 75 prisoners, with their arms, and 12 horses, with their accouterments.

The result of the day's operations was some twenty-odd casualties (wounded) in Hascall's brigade, and some 35 prisoners taken from the enemy. The enemy fell back in great disorder from Stewart's Creek. He left tents standing on the southern bank of the creek, and on this encampment the ground strewn with arms.

Sunday, the 28th ultimo, we remained in camp, waiting for the troops of the right wing and center to get in position.

Monday, the 29th, the advance was resumed. Wagner's brigade, of my division, was deployed on the left or eastern, and a brigade of General Palmer's division on the right or western side of the road. Cox's Tenth Indiana Battery supported Wagner's brigade. Moving *pari passu*, the two brigades advanced, clearing all opposition till we arrived within 2½ miles of Murfreesborough. Harker's brigade was disposed on the left of Wagner's in the advance, and Hascall's held the reserve.

On arriving within 2¼ miles of Murfreesborough, the evidences were perfectly unmistakable that the enemy was in force immediately in our front, prepared to resist seriously and determinedly our farther advance. His troops, displayed in battle array, were plainly to be seen in our front. Negley's division, which was to take position in the center and complete the connection between the right and left wings, was not up, but 7 miles in the rear. Van Cleve's division, which was to support the left, was in rear of Negley's, nor had the right wing, McCook's command, got into position. Consequently I halted the troops in advance, reported the fact to General Crittenden, commanding the left wing, and desired further orders.

Up to this moment the information received had indicated, with considerable probability, that the enemy would evacuate Murfreesborough, offering no serious opposition. But observations assured me, very soon after arriving so near to the town, that we should meet with a determined resistance, and I did not deem it proper to precipitate the force in advance (two divisions, my own and General Palmer's) on the entire force of the enemy, with the remainder of our troops so far in the rear as to make it entirely possible, perhaps probable, that a serious reverse would occur before they could support us. Furthermore, the afternoon was well-nigh spent, and an attempt to advance would have involved us in the obscurity of the night, on unexamined ground, in the presence of an unseen foe, to whom our movements would have rendered us fearfully vulnerable.

The halt being approved, my division was disposed in order of battle, and the front securely guarded by a continuous line of skirmishers, thrown out well in advance of their reserves. The right of the division, Wagner's brigade, rested on the right of the turnpike, and occupied a piece of wooded ground with an open field in front of it. The center, Harker's brigade, occupied a part of the wood in which Wagner's brigade was posted, and extended leftward into an open field, covered in front by a low swell, which it was to occupy in case of an attack, and General Hascall's brigade was posted on the left of the division, with its left flank resting nearly on Stone's River. The entire division was drawn up in two lines. Stone's River runs obliquely in front of the position occupied by the division, leaving a triangular piece of ground of some hundreds of yards in breadth in front of the right, and narrowing to almost a point opposite the left.

Such was the position occupied by my division Monday night. It remained in this position Tuesday, the 30th, the skirmishers keeping up an active firing with the enemy. In this encounter of skirmishers, Lieutenant Elliott, adjutant of the Fifty-seventh Indiana, was very severely wounded.

In the afternoon I had three days' subsistence issued to the men, and near nightfall, by order, 20 additional rounds of cartridges were distributed to them. Commanders were directed to instruct their men to be exceedingly vigilant, and report promptly any indication of a movement in the front by the enemy. The artillery horses were kept attached to the pieces.

Between midnight and daylight Wednesday morning I received a message from Colonel Wagner to the effect that the enemy seemed to be moving large bodies of troops from his right to his left. I immediately dispatched the information to the headquarters of the left wing, and I doubt not it was sent thence to the commanding general, and by him distributed to the rest of the corps.

The division was roused at 5 o'clock on Wednesday morning; the men took their breakfasts, and before daylight were ready for action. Shortly after dawn I repaired to the headquarters of the left wing for orders. I met the commanding general there, and received orders from him to commence passing Stone's River, immediately in front of the division, by brigades. I rode at once to my division and directed Colonel Harker to commence the movement with his brigade, dispatching an order to General Hascall to follow Colonel Harker, and an order to Colonel Wagner to follow General Hascall. While Colonel Harker was preparing to move, I rode to the front to examine the ground. A long wooded ridge within a few hundred yards from the stream extends along the southern and eastern side of Stone's River. On the crest of this ridge the enemy appeared to be posted in force.

During the morning some firing had been heard on the right, but not to a sufficient extent, however, to indicate that the troops were seriously engaged; but the sudden and fierce roar and rattle of musketry which burst on us at this moment indicated that the enemy had attacked the right wing in heavy force, and soon the arrival of messengers, riding in hot haste, confirmed the indications. I was ordered to stop the movement of crossing the river, and to withdraw two brigades to the rear, for the purpose of re-enforcing the center and right. General Hascall's and Colonel Harker's brigades were withdrawn, and the latter, under an order from the commanding general, moved to the right and rear.

I ordered Colonel Wagner to hold his position in the wood at all hazards, as it was an important point, and, so long as it was held, not only were our left, front, and flanks secured, but the command of the road leading to the rear preserved. The vigorous attack on our right and center extended to the left, and our whole line became seriously engaged. Not only was the extreme left exposed to the attack in front, but it was much harassed by the enemy's artillery posted on the heights on the southern side of Stone's River, but the troops nobly maintained their position, and gallantly repulsed the enemy. Cox's battery was most splendidly served, and did most excellent service in repulsing this attack. A slackening of the enemy's fire at this moment in the attack on our center and left, and other indications that his forces were breaking in the center, rendered the juncture apparently favorable for bringing additional and fresh troops into action.

Hascall's brigade was now brought forward and put in position on the right of Wagner's brigade; but the abatement of the enemy's fire was but the lulling of the storm, soon to burst with greater fury. The attack was renewed on our center and left with redoubled violence. Hascall's brigade had got into position in good season, and aided, in gallant style, in driving back the enemy. Estep's battery, generally associated with Hascall's brigade, had been detached early in the morning and sent to the right and rearward to aid in driving back the enemy from our center and right.

The falling back of the right wing had brought our lines into a crotchet. This rendered the position of the troops on the extreme left particularly hazardous, for had the enemy succeeded in gaining the turnpike in his attack on the right, the left would have been exposed to an attack in reverse. This danger imposed on me the necessity of keeping a rigid watch to the right, to be prepared to change front in that direction should it become necessary. Again the enemy was seen concentrating large masses of troops in the fields to the front and right, and soon these masses moved forward to the attack. Estep's battery was now moved to the front to join Hascall's brigade. The artillery in the front line, as well as that placed in the rear of the center and left, poured a destructive fire on the advancing foe, but on he came until within small-arm range, when he was repulsed and driven back.

But our thinned ranks and dead and wounded officers told, in unmistakable language, how largely we were suffering in those repeated attacks. Colonel McKee, of the Third Kentucky Volunteers, had been killed, and Colonel Hines and Lieutenant-Colonel Lennard, of the Fifty-seventh Indiana, and Colonel Blake and Lieutenant-Colonel Neff, of the Fortieth Indiana, with others, wounded.

During this attack the Fifteenth Indiana Volunteers, commanded by Lieutenant-Colonel Wood, counter-charged one of the enemy's regiments and captured 173 prisoners. The capture was made from the Twentieth Louisiana. While this attack was in progress, I received a message from General Palmer, commanding the Second Division of the left wing, that he was sorely pressed, and desired I would send him a regiment if I could possibly spare one. I sent an order to General Hascall to send a regiment to General Palmer's assistance, if his own situation would warrant it. He dispatched the Fifty-eighth Indiana Volunteers, Colonel G. P. Buell's regiment, to report to General Palmer. The regiment got into position, reserved its fire until the enemy was in close range, and then poured in a withering discharge, from which the foe recoiled in disorder.

Our extreme left next became the object of the enemy's attention. His skirmishers were seen descending the slope on the opposite side of the river, and also working their way down the stream, apparently with the design of gaining our left flank and rear. A few well-directed shots of grape and canister from Cox's battery drove them back. This battery did most useful service in counter-battering the enemy's artillery posted on the heights on the southern side of the river.

The afternoon was now well advanced, but the enemy did not seem disposed to relinquish the design of forcing us from our position. Heavy masses were afresh assembled in front of the center, with a view evidently of renewing the onset, but the well-directed fire of the artillery held them in check, and only a small force came within range of our small-arms, which was readily repulsed.

The enemy concluded his operations against the left, as night approached, by opening on it with his artillery. Cox's and Estep's batteries gallantly and effectually replied, but darkness soon put a conclusion to this artillery duel, and when the night descended and brought a period to the long and bloody contest of this ever-memorable day, it found the First and Second Brigades, Hascall's and Wagner's, occupying, with some slight interchange in the position of particular regiments, the ground on which they had gone into the fight in the morning. Every effort of the enemy to dislodge them had failed; every attack had been gallantly repulsed.

I cannot speak in too high terms of the soldierly bearing and steadfast courage with which the officers and men of these two brigades maintained the battle throughout the day. Their good conduct deserves, and will receive, the highest commendation of their commanders and countrymen. The commanding general of the enemy has borne testimony, in his dispatch, to the gallantry and success of their resistance.

Cox's and Estep's batteries were splendidly served throughout the day, and did the most effective service. They lost heavily in men and horses, and it was necessary for Estep to call on the One hundredth Illinois Volunteers for a detail to aid in working his guns.

I have previously remarked that the Third Brigade, Colonel Harker, was detached early in the day and sent to re-enforce the right. It remained on that part of the field during the entire day. I am unable, consequently, to speak of its services from personal observation; but its extremely heavy list of casualties shows how hotly it was engaged and what valuable service it rendered. I am sure it fully met the expectations I had ever confidently entertained of what would be its bearing in the presence of the foe.

Bradley's Sixth Ohio Battery was associated with this brigade during the day; was skillfully handled, and did most effective service. It lost two of its guns, but they were spiked before they were abandoned. They were subsequently recaptured by the Thirteenth Michigan Volunteers, attached to the brigade.

From all I have learned of the service of the Third Brigade and Bradley's battery, I am sure they deserve equal commendation with the two brigades and batteries which so stoutly held the left.

An official report of events so thrilling as those of the battle of the 31st ultimo, made from personal observation, amid the din and roar of the conflict, and unaided by the reports of the subordinate commanders, must necessarily present but a brief and meager outline of the part enacted by the troops whose services it professes to portray. A report so prepared may, unintentionally on the part of the writer, do injustice to particular troops and officers. From inability of reference to the reports of subordinate commanders, I cannot give any detail of the heavy casualties of the battle of the 31st. I must leave them to be reported, with the subsequent casualties, by my successor in command. The absence of such reports prevents me from signalizing by name such regimental and company officers as particularly distinguished themselves; but, where all did so well, it would be difficult, perhaps invidious, to discriminate among them.

To my brigade commanders, Brigadier-General Hascall, commanding First Brigade; Colonel Wagner, Fifteenth Indiana Volunteers, commanding Second Brigade, and Colonel Harker, Sixty-fifth Ohio Volunteers, commanding Third Brigade, my warmest thanks are due for their valuable assistance, their hearty co-operation, and intelligent performance of duty throughout the whole of that trying day. For these services, and for their gallant and manly bearing under the heaviest fire, they richly deserve the highest commendation and the gratitude of their countrymen. Colonels Wagner and Harker have long and ably commanded brigades, and I respectfully submit it would be simply an act of justice to confer on them the actual and legal rank of the command they have so long exercised.

To Surg. W. W. Blair, Fifty-eighth Indiana Volunteers; Capt. M. P. Bestow, assistant adjutant-general; First Lieut. J. L. Yaryan, Fifty-eighth Indiana Volunteers, aide-de-camp; Capt. T. R. Palmer, Thirteenth Michigan Volunteers, inspector-general, and Major Walker, Second Indiana Cavalry, volunteer aide-de-camp, my thanks are due and cordially given. Capt. L. D. Myers, division quartermaster; Capt. S. D. Henderson, commissary of subsistence to the division, and First Lieutenant Martin, Twenty-first Ohio, signal officer, but for some time engaged in performing the duties of acting assistant quartermaster, great credit is due for the intelligent and efficient performance of duty in their respective departments. Captain Bruce, Fifty-eighth Indiana Volunteers, ordnance officer of the First Brigade, deserves credit for valuable services rendered in the ordnance department, for the entire division, during the absence of the division ordnance officer.

My division is composed of regiments from the States of Illinois, Indiana, Ohio, Michigan, and Kentucky. To the relatives and personal friends of those who have fallen in defense of their country, I would respectfully offer my sympathy and condolence.

About 10 o'clock Wednesday morning, during one of the heaviest attacks, I was struck by a minie ball on the inner side of the left heel. Fortunately the ball struck obliquely, or the injury would have been much severer. My boot was torn open, the foot lacerated, and a severe contusion inflicted. I did not dismount from my horse until 7 o'clock in the evening.

The coldness of the night, combined with the injury, made my foot so painful and stiff as to render it evident I would not be effective for immediate service. I was ordered by the commanding general of the corps to repair that night, by ambulance, with an escort, to this city. It was with extreme regret I found myself in a condition to make it necessary, on account of my injury, to leave the division I had formed and so long commanded; but the regret was alleviated by the reflection that I had left the division in command of an able and experienced officer, one who had long served with it, knew it well, and in whom it had confidence.

I am still confined to my room, but trust ere long to be able to resume my duties.

I am, very respectfully, your obedient servant,

TH. J. WOOD,
Brigadier-General of Volunteers.

Maj. LYNE STARLING,
Asst. Adjt. Gen., Left Wing, Fourteenth Army Corps.

—

DAYTON, OHIO, *January* 28, 1863.

SIR: In my official report of the operations of my division, from the time it moved from Nashville, on the 26th ultimo, to the date of my relinquishing command of it, I omitted to mention the passage of Stone's River the evening of the 29th ultimo by the Third (Harker's) Brigade.

After the division had marched within 2½ miles of Murfreesborough, in obvious view of the enemy's battle array, halted, as explained in my report, and precautionary dispositions commenced for the night, an order was received to continue the advance on Murfreesborough. The order was received just at nightfall, when darkness was beginning to shroud the ground to be passed over with obscurity. The movement was at once commenced, but was subsequently suspended by General Crittenden until further communication could be had with the commanding general of the army. Before, however, the order was suspended, Harker's brigade had crossed Stone's River under a galling fire, driven in the enemy's outposts, and seized a strong position, which it held until nearly 10 o'clock that evening.

The commanding general having approved the suspension of the order, and it not being prudent to leave the brigade in so exposed a position, it was ordered to recross the river. It performed the retrograde movement handsomely, in good order and with perfect success, though confronted by an entire division (Breckinridge's) of the enemy. This fact was learned from a prisoner, captured when the brigade first crossed the river. Bradley's (Sixth Ohio) battery accompanied the brigade in the entire movement.

I desire to repair the omission in my previous report, and request that this communication be made part of it. It will readily be perceived how the omission occurred when it is remembered that my original report was prepared without the aid of the reports of subordinate commanders, and written under the compound embarrassment of inconvenience from my wound and suffering from a quotidian intermittent fever, with which I had been afflicted for ten days previous to the battle of the 31st ultimo.

I am, sir, very respectfully, your obedient servant,

TH. J. WOOD,
Brigadier-General of Volunteers.

Maj. LYNE STARLING,
Asst. Adjt. Gen., Chief of Staff, Crittenden's Corps.

No. 97.

Reports of Brig. Gen. Milo S. Hascall, U. S. Army, commanding First Brigade and First Division, including skirmishes at La Vergne and on the Murfreesborough pike, at Stewart's Creek Bridge.

HDQRS. FIRST BRIGADE, FIRST DIVISION, LEFT WING,
Stewart's Creek, Tenn., December 28, 1862.

Yesterday, about 11 a. m., while General Wood's division was lying about three-fourths of a mile beyond La Vergne, near the Murfreesborough pike, I received notice from General Wood that General Crittenden's command (being the left wing, Fourteenth Army Corps) would again advance, General Wood's leading, and that my brigade had been directed by him to take the advance. My instructions were to advance by the Murfreesborough pike, and reach Stewart's Creek and save the bridge at that point if possible.

The enemy had been throwing shells at us at intervals all the morning from an eminence a little this side of La Vergne, wounding some of our men, so that we knew the town and the hills beyond were occupied by the enemy. Accordingly, I at once formed my brigade in order of battle in two lines, the Fifty-eighth Indiana on the right of the first line, supported by the Third Kentucky, and the Twenty-sixth Ohio, commanded by Maj. William H. Squires, on the left of the first line, supported by the One hundredth Illinois, the Eighth Indiana Battery, commanded by Lieut. George Estep, occupying the intervals between the infantry. This disposition having been made, and the front well covered, with the flank companies of the first line as skirmishers, the order to advance was given. We had to pass over an open field the entire distance to the town.

Before we had been five minutes in motion, a brisk fire was opened by the enemy in and about town upon our skirmishers, which soon became effectual upon the first line also. The fire was vigorously returned by our skirmishers, but, I presume, with little effect, owing to the cover the town, fences, and bushes afforded the enemy.

Not wishing to try and cope with the enemy under such unfavorable circumstances any longer than was absolutely necessary, I ordered the skirmishers and the first line to charge at a double-quick and get possession of the town at all hazards. The front line was lying flat on their faces at the time of receiving the order; but in the twinkling of an eye the entire line sprang to their feet, fixed their bayonets, and, rushing forward with a yell, had, in five minutes' time, possession of the town and the crest beyond. The manner in which this was done left nothing to be desired.

Our entire loss, though skirmishing all day, was sustained at this point. Twenty of the Twenty-sixth Ohio and 7 of the Fifty-eighth Indiana were lying around with wounds of greater or less severity to tell the tale.

Leaving our wounded to be cared for by the rear brigades, we pushed forward, skirmishing nearly all the time. After advancing about 1½ miles beyond the town, I discovered that the front line was becoming much exhausted, and many of the Twenty-sixth Ohio were throwing their knapsacks away. I, therefore, relieved it with the second line, sent a detail back to collect the knapsacks, and pressed on to this point, skirmishing all the way through a drenching rain, and through almost impassable thickets of cedar, and over muddy and sloppy plowed fields. At half a dozen points on the way we were resisted by the enemy's artillery; but Lieutenant Estep's battery, assisted by Maj. S. Race, in command of the artillery of the division, soon dislodged them, and we moved forward without allowing ourselves to be even temporarily detained, until we came to the eminence just in front of our camp, and which overlooks the bridge at Stewart's Creek.

Here we found the enemy had a battery planted on the hill beyond Stewart's Creek. We had no sooner planted a section of Estep's battery and opened upon them than they promptly returned our fire. The fearful accuracy of their fire soon convinced us that this was a different battery from that with which we had been contending all day, as every shot from them either struck our pieces or came within close proximity. Having no long-range guns in Estep's battery, I sent to the rear for some out of another battery, and as soon as they had got in position the enemy's fire was silenced.

It was during this artillery duel that my skirmishers, who were concealed near the banks of Stewart's Creek, discovered that the enemy had loaded the bridge with rails and other combustible material and had set fire to it. Volunteers being called for to extinguish the flame at all hazards, the entire line of skirmishers from the Third Kentucky, assisted by Company B, Captain Ewing, of the Twenty-sixth Ohio, rushed in and threw the combustibles from the bridge, and saved it. Great credit is due for this act, as the loss of the bridge would have delayed the movement of the army till another could be constructed, the stream not being fordable at or near that point.

Shortly after this the enemy retired, and the Third Kentucky was ordered to hold the bridge, which they do at this time. Having accomplished the work set before me, I was about arranging my men in camp, and had got the One hundredth Illinois in position to cover the front of my proposed camp, and the Twenty-sixth Ohio in position, when I found myself suddenly attacked on my left flank by a force of the enemy's cavalry, who were endeavoring to cut their way to the bridge. I immediately ordered the Twenty-sixth to change front forward on the left company, to resist the attack in that direction. This repulsed the attack. Captain Munger's company, of the One hundredth Illinois, had been sent to the left to protect the flank of the regiment, and the enemy endeavored to cut them off and take them prisoners. The company turned upon them, fired, and demanded their surrender; which, being declined, they pressed upon them, drove them into the fence corners, and captured 24 of them, including Lieut. J. J. Seawell. They called themselves "Alabama Partisan Rangers." With them were captured 12 horses and saddles and 12 guns. The residue of them made their escape by flight. We took 10 or 12 other prisoners during the day, which I sent to the rear. I am not aware how much force we were contending with during the day, but we took prisoners from six or seven different regiments, principally Tennessee regiments.

For more minute particulars of the parts performed by the different regiments and the battery, I refer you to their reports, inclosed.

All my officers and men did their duty nobly, and I feel that it would be unjust to particularize. How much credit we all deserve, I leave for yourself and others to determine.

To my staff officers, Capt. Edmund R. Kerstetter, assistant adjutant-general; Captain Roberts, of the Third Kentucky, commissary; Lieut. James R. Hume, aide-de-camp, and Lieutenant Warner, inspector-general, I am under peculiar obligations.

The casualties are as follows:

Command.	Wounded.	Missing.	Total.
58th Indiana	7	1	8
26th Ohio	20		20
100th Illinois	2		2
3d Kentucky			
Estep's battery			
Total	29	1	30

One of the wounded has since died, and 4 or 5 more are thought to be mortally wounded.

The enemy's loss, that fell into our hands, were 4 killed and 5 wounded. We hear of many other killed and wounded being taken to the rear by them.

All of which is respectfully submitted.

MILO S. HASCALL,
Brigadier-General of Vols., Comdg. First Division. Left Wing.

Capt. M. P. BESTOW,
Assistant Adjutant-General, First Division, Left Wing.

HDQRS. FIRST BRIGADE, FIRST DIVISION, LEFT WING,
Near Murfreesborough, Tenn., January 6, 1863.

SIR : I have the honor to submit the following report of the operations of my brigade (formerly the Fifteenth Brigade, Sixth Division, but
under the new nomenclature the First Brigade, First Division, left
wing) on the eventful 31st of December, 1862 :

During the night of the 30th, I had received notice, through General
Wood, our division commander, that the left wing (Crittenden's corps)
would cross Stone's River and attack the enemy on his right. My brigade was posted on the extreme left of our entire line of battle, and was
guarding and overlooking the ford, over which we were to cross.

On the morning of the 31st, heavy firing was heard on the extreme
right of our line (McCook's corps), but as they had been fighting their
way all the distance from Nolensville, as we had from La Vergne, no
particular importance was attached to this, and I was getting my brigade into position ready to cross as soon as General Van Cleve's division, which was then crossing, was over. All this time the firing on the
right became heavier and apparently nearer to us, and our fears began
to be aroused that the right wing was being driven rapidly back upon
us. At this juncture Van Cleve halted his division, and the most terrible state of suspense pervaded the entire left, as it became more and
more evident that the right was being driven rapidly back upon us.

On and on they came, till the heaviest fire was getting nearly around
to the pike leading to Nashville, when General Rosecrans appeared in
person, and ordered me to go with my brigade at once to the support of
the right, pointing toward our rear, where the heaviest fire was raging.
General Van Cleve's division and Colonel Harker's brigade, of our division, received the same order. I at once changed the front of my brigade
to the rear, preparatory to starting in the new direction, but had not
proceeded more than 200 yards in the new direction before the crowd
of fugitives from the right wing became so numerous, and the fleeing
mule teams and horsemen so thick, that it was impossible for me to go
forward with my command without its becoming a confused mass. I
therefore halted and awaited developments.

General Van Cleve and Colonel Harker, not meeting with so much
opposition, pressed forward and got into position beyond the railroad,
ready to open on the enemy as soon as our fugitives were out of the
way. They soon opened fire, joined by some batteries and troops belonging to the center (General Thomas' corps) and Estep's battery, of
my brigade, and, after about one hour's firing along this new line, during which time I was moving my command from point to point, ready
to support any troops that most needed it, the onslaught of the enemy
seemed to be in a great measure checked, and we had reasonable probability of maintaining this line. During all this time my men were exposed to a severe fire of shot and shell from a battery on the other side
of the river, and several were killed.

About this time an aide of General Palmer came galloping up to me
and said that, unless he could be supported, his division would have to
give way. Palmer's division formed the right of General Crittenden's
line of battle on the morning of the 31st. After consulting with General Wood, he ordered me to send a regiment to support General Palmer; accordingly I sent the Third Kentucky Regiment, commanded by
Lieut. Col. Samuel McKee.

Before the regiment had been ten minutes in its new position, Captain
Kerstetter, my adjutant-general, reported to me that Colonel McKee had

been killed, and the regiment badly cut up.   I therefore moved at once, with the other three regiments of my command, to their relief.

The line they were trying to hold was that part of our original line of battle lying immediately to the right of the railroad.   This portion of our original line, about two regimental fronts, together with two fronts to the left, held by Colonel Wagner's brigade, was all of our original line of battle but what our troops had been driven from; and if they succeeded in carrying this they would have turned our left, and a total rout of our forces could not then have been avoided.

Seeing the importance of the position, I told my men it must be held, even if it cost the last man we had.   I immediately sent in the Twenty-sixth Ohio, commanded by the gallant Maj. William H. Squires, to take position on the right of the Third Kentucky, and support them, and dispatched an aide for Estep's Eighth Indiana Battery to come to this point and open on the enemy.   No sooner had the Twenty-sixth got into position than they became hotly engaged, and the numerous dead and wounded that were immediately brought to the rear told how desperate was the contest.

The gallant Lieutenant McClelland, of that regiment, was brought to the rear mortally wounded, and expired by my side in less than five minutes from the time the regiment took position; still the fight went on, and still brave men went down.   The Third Kentucky, now reduced to less than one-half its original numbers, with ten out of its fourteen remaining officers badly wounded, were still bravely at work.

In less than ten minutes after the fall of Lieutenant-Colonel McKee, the gallant Maj. Daniel R. Collier, of that regiment, received two severe wounds—one in the leg and the other in the breast.   Adjutant Bullitt had his horse shot under him; but nothing could induce either of them to leave the field.   Equally conspicuous and meritorious was the conduct of Major Squires and Adjutant Franklin, of the Twenty-sixth Ohio. Major Squires' horse was shot three times through the neck; nevertheless, he and all his officers stood by throughout, and most gallantly sustained and encouraged their men.

Estep's battery came up in due time, and, taking position on a little rise of ground in rear of the Twenty-sixth Ohio and Third Kentucky, opened a terrible fire of shot and shell over the heads of our infantry.

In about one hour after the Twenty-sixth Ohio got into position this terrible attack of the enemy was repulsed, and they drew back into the woods, and under cover of an intervening hill, to reform their shattered columns and renew the attack.

I now took a survey of the situation, and found that along the entire line to the right and left of the railroad, which had not yet been carried by the enemy, I was the only general officer present, and was, therefore, in command, and responsible for the conduct of affairs.   Colonel Hazen, commanding a brigade in General Palmer's division, was present with his brigade, to the left of the railroad, and Colonel Grose, commanding another brigade in the same division, was also present with what there was left of his brigade, and most nobly did he co-operate with me with the Sixth and Twenty-fourth Ohio, to the right of the railroad, while Colonel Wagner, commanding the Second Brigade, in the First Division, left wing, nobly sustained his front, assisted by Colonel Hazen, to the left of the railroad.

I now relieved the Third Kentucky Regiment, which was nearly annihilated and out of ammunition, with the Fifty-eighth Indiana Regiment, of my brigade, commanded by Col. George P. Buell, and this, being a much larger regiment than the Third Kentucky, filled up the entire space from where the right of the Third Kentucky rested to the rail-road. I then threw forward the right of the Sixth Ohio Regiment, of Colonel Grose's brigade, which was on the right of the Twenty-sixth Ohio, so that its line of battle was more nearly perpendicular to the railroad, and so that its fire would sweep the front of the Twenty-sixth Ohio and Fifty-eighth Indiana, and supported the Sixth Ohio with Estep's battery, on a little eminence to its right, and brought up the Ninety-seventh Ohio, Colonel Lane, from Wagner's brigade, to still further strengthen the right.

This disposition being made, I galloped a little to the rear, and found General Rosecrans, and called his attention to the importance of the position I was holding, and the necessity of keeping it well supported. He rode to the front with me, approved the disposition I had made, spoke a few words of encouragement to the men, cautioning them to hold their fire till the enemy got well up, and had no sooner retired than the enemy emerged from the woods and over the hill, and were moving upon us in splendid style and in immense force. As soon as they came in sight, the Sixth and Twenty-sixth Ohio and Estep's battery opened on them, and did splendid execution. But on they came till within 100 yards of our line, when Colonel Buell, of the Fifty-eighth Indiana, who lost 3 men, but had not fired a shot, ordered his men to fire. The effect was indescribable. The enemy fell in windrows, and went staggering back from the effects of this unexpected volley.

Soon, however, they came up again and assaulted us furiously for about one and a half hours; but the men all stood their ground nobly, and at the end of that time compelled the enemy to retire as before.

During the heat of this attack a heavy cross-fire was brought to bear on the position I occupied, and Corpl. Frank Moyer, Third Ohio Volunteer Cavalry, in command of my escort, was shot through the leg, and my adjutant-general, Capt. E. R. Kerstetter, was shot through his coat, grazing his back.

The regiments all behaved splendidly again, and the Fifty-eighth Indiana won immortal honors. Lieutenant Blackford, of that regiment, was shot dead, and several of the officers, including Captains Downey and Alexander, badly wounded.

Estep's battery was compelled to retire from the position assigned it after firing half a dozen rounds, but it did terrible execution while there.

The Sixth and Twenty-fourth Ohio did noble service, as did the Ninety-seventh; but their immediate commanders will, no doubt, allude to them more particularly. Thus ended the third assault upon the position.

I should have remarked that the One hundredth Illinois Regiment, the other regiment composing my brigade, which was in reserve during the first engagement described above, had, under instructions of Colonel Hazen, moved to the front, on the left of the railroad, where they fought splendidly in all the actions that took place on the left of the road. There was no formidable attack made on them, though they were almost constantly under fire of greater or less severity, particularly from shot and shell, and suffered quite seriously in killed and wounded. Lieut. Morris Worthingham, of that regiment, was killed while gallantly sustaining his men, and 6 other commissioned officers, including Major Hammond, were wounded. Their operations being to the left of the railroad and in a wood, did not so immediately come under my personal observation; but their conduct, from Colonel Bartleson down, was such as leaves nothing to be desired.

The Fifty-eighth Indiana having now been over three hours in action, and the Twenty-sixth Ohio about four hours, were exhausted and very nearly out of ammunition. I, therefore, relieved the Fifty-eighth Indiana with the Fortieth Indiana, from Colonel Wagner's brigade, and the Twenty-sixth Ohio was relieved by the Twenty-third Kentucky. There was now not more than an hour of day left, and though the enemy was continually maneuvering in our front, no formidable attack was made upon us, except with artillery. The enemy having been three several times repulsed from their attack on that position, seemed satisfied to keep at a respectful distance, and the sun set upon us as masters of the situation.

We had sustained ourselves and held the only position of the original line of battle that was held throughout by any portion of the army. To have lost this position would have been to lose everything, as our left would then have been turned, and utter rout or capture inevitable.

To the "fearless spirits who hazarded and lost their lives on this consecrated spot" the country owes a deep debt of gratitude. No purer patriot, more upright man, and devoted Christian than Colonel McKee, of the Third Kentucky, ever offered up his life in defense of his country.

To the members of my staff present with me on the field—Capt. Edmund R. Kerstetter, assistant adjutant-general; Lieut. James R. Hume, aide-de-camp, and Lieut. James R. Warner, inspector-general—I am under the greatest obligations. They were constantly with me in the thickest of the fight, ably and gallantly assisting me in every way possible. My escort was also faithful and efficient. With the exceptions already alluded to, all of us were so fortunate as to get through unscathed.

The casualties in our brigade were as follows: The Third Kentucky Regiment went into action with 13 officers and 300 men, and lost—officers killed, 1; wounded, 9; enlisted men killed, 12; wounded, 77; missing, 34. The Fifty-eighth Indiana Regiment went into action with 19 officers and 386 enlisted men, and lost—officers killed, 1; wounded, 4; enlisted men killed, 16; wounded, 91. The One hundredth Illinois went into action with 27 officers and 394 enlisted men, and lost—officers killed, 1; wounded, 6; enlisted men killed, 5; wounded, 33. The Twenty-sixth Ohio went into action with 12 officers and 374 enlisted men, and lost—officers killed, 1; wounded, 2; enlisted men killed, 9; wounded, 77.

RECAPITULATION.*

The brigade went into action with 71 officers and 1,454 enlisted men and lost—officers killed, 4; wounded, 21; enlisted men killed, 42; wounded, 278; missing, 34. Total killed, wounded, and missing in brigade, 379.

For more minute particulars of the parts performed by the different regiments I transmit herewith their respective reports.

During the evening of the 31st I was notified that, in consequence of the indisposition of General Wood and a wound received during the day, he was relieved of the command of the division, and that the same would devolve upon myself. I, therefore, turned over the command of the brigade to Col. George P. Buell, of the Fifty-eighth Indiana, and assumed the command of the division.

All of which is respectfully submitted.

MILO S. HASCALL,
Brigadier-General of Volunteers, Commanding Brigade.

Capt. M. P. BESTOW,
Acting Assistant Adjutant-General, First Division, Left Wing.

HEADQUARTERS FIRST DIVISION, LEFT WING,
Murfreesborough, Tenn., January 10, 1863.

I have the honor to submit the following report of the operations of this division during the recent battles, after the command devolved upon me, on the evening of December 31, 1862:

At that time the division was considerably scattered, as Colonel Harker's brigade had been in action during the 31st on the extreme right, and had not returned. Colonel Wagner's was in position to the left of the railroad, where it had been in action during the day, and my brigade was to the right of the railroad.

About 11 **p.** m. of that day Colonel Harker returned with his brigade, and the division was once more together. At this time I received an order to send all the wagons of the division to the rear, and, shortly after this was executed, I received an order from General Crittenden to fall back, so that my right should rest on the position occupied by Stokes' battery, and my left on the right of General Palmer's division. This brought the new line of the division about 500 yards to the rear of the one of the day before. The line of the division was now nearly at right angles with the railroad, with the center of the line resting on it— the First Brigade, Colonel Buell, on the right; the Third, Colonel Harker, in the center, and the Second, Colonel Wagner, on the left.

In this position we lay all the next day, January 1, with nothing more to break the silence than picket firing and an occasional artillery duel. The division lost, however, several killed and wounded during the day. Each of my brigades was in line of battle, and I was occupying so much front that it kept the men constantly on the alert. Most of the other divisions had one or two brigades in reserve, and could, therefore, relieve their men some.

We maintained this position during the night of the 1st, and till about 8 o'clock in the morning of the 2d, the battery occupying the intervals between brigades. At this time the enemy opened upon us the most terrific fire of shot and shell that we sustained during the entire engagement. It appears that during the night before they had massed and masked several batteries in our front, so they opened on us from a line of batteries one-quarter of a mile long, all at once. They had our range perfectly, so that their fire was terribly effective from the first.

Estep's battery, on the right of my line, being in an exposed position, and receiving a very heavy fire, had to retire at once; not, however, till so many horses had been killed as to render it necessary for two of the pieces to be hauled to the rear by the infantry. Bradley's battery, with Colonel Harker in the center, having a better position and longer-range guns, opened a brisk fire on the enemy in return, and had every probability of maintaining their position until Stokes' battery, in their rear, undertook to open on the enemy with grape, which took effect on Bradley's men instead of the enemy, and compelled Bradley to retire. The infantry, however, along my entire line, though suffering severely from the enemy's fire, all maintained their position.

After about half an hour this firing ceased, and nothing further worthy of note happened till about 4 o'clock in the afternoon of that day. At this time General Van Cleve's division, which was stationed across Stone's River to our left, was suddenly attacked by a heavy force of the enemy under Breckinridge, and so fierce was the onslaught that the division was compelled to give way almost immediately. General Jefferson C. Davis and General Negley were immediately ordered to their relief with their divisions, and, as soon as they had time to get over, the attack was checked and the enemy began to retire.

At this time I received an order from General Crittenden to cross with my division, and immediately put the different brigades in motion. While crossing at the ford, one or two pieces of the enemy's artillery were playing upon us, but as it was then dusk, their firing was not accurate, and I think we sustained no loss in crossing. By the time we were over it was quite dark, and the firing had nearly ceased. Negley's division was returning, and Davis' had taken up a position a little in advance of where Van Cleve's division was attacked, his right resting on the bank of the river. I moved up and went into position on the left of Davis, my left inclining somewhat to the rear, to prevent it from being turned.

General Davis and myself then fortified our fronts as well as we could with the logs, stones, and rails at hand, and remained in this position that night, the next day (January 3), and till about 12 o'clock that night, without anything more than picket firing transpiring. I should remark that it rained very hard all day of January 3, and during the night, so that our men and officers suffered severely.

By this time the rains had so swollen the river that General Crittenden became apprehensive that it would not be fordable by morning, and we might be cut off from communication with the main body of our army. He, therefore, ordered us back, and my division took up a position in reserve, near General Rosecrans' headquarters, arriving there about 2 o'clock at night, completely drenched with mud and rain. They had now been on duty four days and nights, some of the time with nothing to eat, and all the time in the front, where they had to be constantly on the alert. The next morning we heard that the enemy had retreated, and the battle was over.

The conduct of the division throughout was admirable, and it can be truthfully said concerning it that it held its original position and every other position assigned to it during the whole four days, and this is more than can be said of any other division in the entire Fourteenth Army Corps.

I am under great obligations to my brigade commanders, Colonels Wagner, Harker, and Buell. Colonel Wagner had his horse shot under him on the 31st, and his clothes completely riddled with bullets. He, nevertheless, stood by throughout, and ably and gallantly performed his duty. The conduct of Colonel Harker was equally brave and efficient. They have each commanded brigades for nearly a year now, and it seems to me that common justice demands that they now receive the promotion they have so gallantly earned. Colonel Buell came in command of the First Brigade in consequence of my taking command of the division, and, although comparatively inexperienced, he performed every duty gallantly and well.

All the officers of the division, with a single exception, behaved gallantly and well; therefore I need not discriminate. The exception was Col. John W. Blake, of the Fortieth Indiana, and I consider it my duty to draw the line of distinction broad and deep between those who do well and those who prove recreant. He became so drunk as to be unfit for duty before going into action on the 31st, and was sent to the rear, in arrest, by his immediate commander, Colonel Wagner. The next that was heard of him he was in Nashville, claiming to be wounded and a paroled prisoner. For this bad conduct I recommend that he be dishonorably discharged from the service.

For minute particulars, and for a complete report of the part performed by the different brigades, I refer you to the reports of brigade commanders, herewith inclosed.

My staff officers, including Captains Palmer and Bestow, of General Wood's staff, not heretofore mentioned by me, all performed their duty gallantly, and ably assisted me in every way possible.

I would also refer to my report as brigade commander, as that gives more in detail and more truthfully than any other report the operations of Colonel Wagner's and my brigade on the 31st, they being both under my personal observation and control after the heavy fighting commenced that day.

The casualties in the division were as follows:

The First Brigade went into action with 71 officers and 1,454 enlisted men, and lost—officers killed, 4; officers wounded, 21; enlisted men killed, 42; enlisted men wounded, 278; enlisted men missing, 34.

The Second Brigade went into action with 86 officers and 1,389 enlisted men, and lost—officers killed, 2; officers wounded, 18; enlisted men killed, 54; enlisted men wounded, 269; enlisted men missing, 32.

The Third Brigade went into action with 97 officers and 1,790 enlisted men, including the Sixth Ohio Battery, and lost—officers killed, 5; officers wounded, 17; enlisted men killed, 104; enlisted men wounded, 312; enlisted men missing, 101.

RECAPITULATION.

The division went into action with 254 commissioned officers and 4,633 enlisted men, and lost—officers killed, 11; officers wounded, 56; enlisted men killed, 200; enlisted men wounded, 859; enlisted men missing, 167. Total killed, 211; wounded, 915; missing, 167. Total killed, wounded, and missing in the division, 1,293.

All of which is respectfully submitted.

MILO S. HASCALL,
Brigadier-General of Vols., Comdg. First Division, Left Wing.

Maj. LYNE STARLING,
Assistant Adjutant-General, Left Wing.

—

HEADQUARTERS FIRST DIVISION, LEFT WING,
Murfreesborough, Tenn., January 11, 1863.

Having just received the report of the batteries attached to my division,* I hasten to forward them to the general, in order that he may allude to them in his report as their merits deserve. It will be seen by their reports that they all did their duty nobly, with perhaps a single exception on the part of one of the officers attached to Estep's battery. I allude to Richard Jervis, second lieutenant of that battery, who behaved badly throughout the entire four days' action. I recommend that he be dishonorably discharged the service, on account of his bad conduct.

I have already alluded to the distinguished services of these batteries, both in my brigade and division reports, and only desire further to add that, with the exception above alluded to, the conduct of both officers and men was admirable. Particular credit is due to Major Race, in command of the batteries, for the gallantry and good judgment displayed by him throughout the entire four days. The conduct of Stokes'

---

* See Nos. 98–101.

battery, in firing upon Bradley's battery on January 2, was such as, in my judgment, demands immediate investigation, in order that the parties guilty of such gross carelessness may be properly punished.

I am, sir, most respectfully,

MILO S. HASCALL,
Brigadier-General of Vols., Comdg. First Division, Lef. Wing.

Major STARLING,
Assistant Adjutant-General, Left Wing.

—

HEADQUARTERS FIRST DIVISION, LEFT WING,
Murfreesborough, Tenn., January 17, 1863.

In the hurry of making out my official report as division commander, I neglected to allude to the very valuable services rendered by Surg. W. W. Blair, medical director of this division, during and since the recent battles. His services were such as merit special commendation, and I desire that this may be forwarded as a part of my report, in justice to Dr. Blair. He reports to me that all the regimental surgeons were efficient and rendered valuable service.

I am, sir, respectfully,

MILO S. HASCALL,
Brigadier-General of Vols., Comdg. First Division, Left Wing.

Major STARLING,
Assistant Adjutant-General, Left Wing.

———

No. 98.

Report of Maj. Seymour Race, First Ohio Light Artillery, Chief of Artillery.

HDQRS. ARTILLERY FIRST DIVISION, LEFT WING,
January 7, 1863.

DEAR SIR: I have the honor to submit to you the official reports of the commanding officers of the batteries of this division.

About 9 a. m. of December 31, 1862, Capt. Cullen Bradley, Sixth Ohio Light Battery, by orders, moved his battery, with Harker's brigade, to the extreme right of our lines, where they engaged the enemy's artillery (two four-gun batteries, supposed) and infantry in a most severely contested battle. Before superior numbers of the enemy, the brigade and battery (after repulsing the first attack of the enemy) were obliged to retire, but not without disputing every inch of ground, Captain Bradley being obliged to leave two of his guns on the field. They were soon after retaken by the Thirteenth Michigan, Colonel Shoemaker, whose timely support forced the enemy to retire.

Captain Bradley's battery was under my immediate observation, and the conduct of Captain Bradley, his subordinate officers, and men was such as to entitle them to great credit. The conduct of this battery on January 2, under the fire of three batteries of the enemy, was gallant in the extreme. The enemy's batteries were nearly silenced, when Captain Stokes' battery opened, 300 yards in rear of Bradley, with canister, at a distance of at least 2,200 yards from the enemy's guns. Captain Bradley had 5 men and 5 horses wounded by their fire, and was obliged to retire.

I respectfully ask an investigation into the conduct of Stokes' battery on this occasion. Capt. J. B. Cox, Tenth Indiana Battery, and Lieut.

George Estep, commanding Eighth Indiana Battery, were closely engaged during the battle of December 31, on the left of our lines, supported by General Hascall's and Colonel Wagner's brigades. Captain Cox was under the fire of three batteries of the enemy for seven hours during the day, but succeeded in administering to them all in a manner perfectly satisfactory to me, and to the great discomfiture of the enemy.

On January 2, when in position on the right, he repulsed, with canister, a desperate charge of a brigade of the enemy's infantry. Captain Cox, his officers, and men behaved with great gallantry and bravery. Lieutenant Estep's battery, by a free use of case-shot and canister, on December 31, succeeded in repulsing three successive charges of the enemy's infantry, and otherwise, during the three days' battle, did most excellent service. Lieutenants Estep, Voris, and Winsor, and the non-commissioned officers and men of this battery, with few exceptions, behaved with commendable coolness and bravery. Lieut. Richard Jervis acted in a most cowardly manner. I will devote a special communication to his case.

For full particulars of the engagements and losses, I respectfully refer you to the accompanying reports of battery commanders.

Respectfully submitted.

S. RACE,
Major, Chief of Artillery, First Division, Left Wing.

Capt. E. R. KERSTETTER,
Assistant Adjutant-General.

No. 99.

Reports of Lieut. George Estep, Eighth Indiana Battery, including skirmishes at La Vergne and on the Murfreesborough pike, at Stewart's Creek Bridge.

IN THE FIELD, *December* 28, 1862.

GENERAL: While connected with your brigade yesterday, on the march from the camp of the previous night, I could at no time (on account of the disposition of the enemy to retire) get an opportunity to fire more than two or three shots. I fired in all 42 rounds; that these were damaging to the enemy or his guns I am unable to tell. In the last position which I took, commanding the Stewart's Creek Bridge, I fired 8 rounds, and received about the same number in return; one of the enemy's shots took a spoke from the wheel of one of my gun-carriages. I am happy to say no other damages were done. The officers of my battery behaved with commendable coolness.

I am, very respectfully, your obedient servant,

GEORGE ESTEP,
First Lieutenant, Commanding Eighth Indiana Battery.

Brigadier-General HASCALL,
Commanding Fifteenth Brigade.

HEADQUARTERS EIGHTH INDIANA BATTERY,
In the Field, near Murfreesborough, Tenn., January 4, 1863.

I have the honor, respectfully, to submit the following official report of the Eighth Indiana Light Battery, on December 31, 1862, and 1st and 2d days of January, 1863:

I put my battery in position on Wednesday morning about 9 o'clock, by order of General Rosecrans, on the west side of the railroad, supported on the right by two batteries, and on the left by the Nineteenth Infantry (regulars); fired 114 rounds (at a range of 800 yards) at the enemy, who were driving back our infantry advance. I then advanced the battery 75 or 80 yards, supported, as in the first position, by the two batteries on my right and the Nineteenth Infantry on my left.

At this position the enemy in three lines made three desperate charges, and were as often repulsed by my battery. I expended 70 rounds of canister, and was compelled four or five times to double-charge the pieces in order to drive the enemy; this beginning at a range of 90 yards, and increasing as the enemy became confused and retired. I also fired from this position 106 rounds of shrapnel and solid shot, at a range of about 800 yards, at the lines of the enemy advancing on our right.

I then received an order from General Hascall, commanding the First Brigade of the division, to take a position on the left of the pike in the direction of Murfreesborough, which I did, supported by his entire brigade, as good soldiers as ever went to battle. I commenced firing at a range of 400 yards, the enemy bringing up his forces in three lines, and making desperate charges on the center, but was repulsed by my battery and the gallant men of General Hascall's brigade. I was twice in this position, and fired 226 rounds, my men all the time exposed to a galling fire of musketry.

Late in the afternoon I was ordered to a position on the east side of the railroad, supported by three regiments, the Twenty-sixth Ohio, Fifty-seventh Indiana, and an Illinois regiment. Here I expended 66 rounds, shelling the enemy from the woods, near the creek, from which he had driven a portion of our troops during the afternoon. I remained in this position until after dark, and then retired to the camp of the previous night. Loss during the day, 8 horses killed and disabled and 4 men wounded.

On the morning of January 1, I was put in position before daylight, in line of battle, by Major Race. An hour or two after daylight the enemy commenced an advance on our front. I opened fire, in connection with other batteries, and drove him back. No loss during the day; expended 46 rounds.

Remained in position all night, and on the morning of the 2d expended 34 rounds, shelling the woods at different points, where the enemy could occasionally be seen from my position. About 9 o'clock my battery was fired upon by two rebel batteries (twelve guns, supposed) at a range of 2,000 yards; it being beyond my range, I was forced to retire my battery, leaving for the time being two pieces on the field. Some of the horses of one of the limbers were severely wounded, and became so badly frightened by the bursting of the enemy's shell that the drivers were unable to control them; they ran to the rear in spite of every effort made to bring them to the piece. I was not long, however, in recovering both pieces. After repairing the loss of horses in the battery from the battery and forge wagons, I remained quiet in line until about 4 o'clock. I was then ordered to take a position on the left, which I did. I was well supported by infantry, but do not know what troops they were. I commenced firing, at a range of about 700 yards, at what I supposed to be a brigade of the enemy's infantry holding a point of woods. I am positive that my battery from this position did the enemy great injury; expended 123 rounds. I retired the battery for ammunition, and again took a position to the left of my first and near the creek. Here I engaged a rebel battery at a range of 900 yards, and succeeded in silencing it, expending 86 rounds. We soon after crossed the creek, and remained during the night.

I am sorry to say that Second Lieut. Richard Jervis, on Wednesday, at a trying and critical moment, retired a section of my battery without my order or knowledge, and that he otherwise behaved badly during the day. He claimed, on the morning of the second day's fight, to be unwell, but said (this was before daylight) if he should feel better in the course of an hour or two he would come out to the field and report for duty. This was the last I saw of him until the fight was over. I am informed that he went back to the rear to one of the hospitals.

First Lieut. Jeremiah Voris and Second Lieut. Samuel Winsor have my thanks for their efficient service at all times during the engagement; they were brave and unflinching in the discharge of duty. I am also indebted to Orderly Sergt. William Stokes for the promptness with which he supplied the battery with ammunition. My sergeants, corporals, and men, with three exceptions, behaved with commendable coolness and bravery.

I am, very respectfully, your obedient servant,

GEORGE ESTEP,
First Lieutenant, Commanding Eighth Indiana Battery.

Maj. S. RACE,
Commanding Artillery of First Division, Left Wing.

P. S.—I neglected to state that my loss on the third day was 4 men wounded, 11 horses killed and disabled.

No. 100.

Report of Capt. Jerome B. Cox, Tenth Indiana Battery.

JANUARY —, 1863.

On the morning of December 31, I was ordered to move my battery across the railroad (my left was then resting on the railroad) and prepare for battle. I immediately obeyed by crossing and placing the right section immediately on the left of the railroad, and the left and center sections about 200 yards farther north. The entire battery then engaged a battery of the enemy immediately in front, which we compelled to cease firing. Simultaneously with this, two other batteries opened upon us, and shortly afterward were joined by the one that had been silenced. They completely showered the shot and shell, but with little damage. This unequal contest was kept up for about four hours, and was only deviated from on the appearance of heavy columns of their troops, upon which we would open the entire battery and disperse them in great disorder. We would then resume the work on their artillery.

About 1 p. m. I relieved one section of the battery at a time for a short time to retire for ammunition. They came up again to the work supplied with ammunition, when the engagement was renewed somewhat similar to the fight in the forenoon, except that more frequently we had to drive back their infantry.

About 3 o'clock my ammunition was exhausted, with the exception of canister, which I ordered they should hold to disperse a large force then bearing down on us in front. We held our fire until they were within 400 yards, when we could completely see the devices on their colors. We completely broke up their lines and scattered them in great disorder over the field in front. Being then only under fire of their batteries, and having no projectiles to reach them, I withdrew from the field. When near the hospital, about one-fourth of a mile in the rear of my former position, I discovered the enemy's skirmishers deployed out and advancing. I at once drove them back with canister. During the day I silenced each one of the batteries in my front and on my flank several times. They had a cross-fire on us during the entire day. We were at one time fighting four batteries, but my men, not the least disheartened, were determined to hold their position at all hazards, which one, I believe, was the only one held by any battery on the field. On this day I had 1 man killed and 6 slightly wounded.

On January 1, I was removed to the right wing, and about 10 o'clock drove back a brigade of infantry, which was advancing.

On January 2, in the evening, our skirmishers were thrown forward and drew the fire of a brigade in ambush. This we expected, and had prepared by cutting the fuses the proper length and getting the proper elevation and range, and showered their ranks with shrapnel, every one bursting precisely at the spot needed. They became badly disorganized and fled in great disorder.

To Lieutenants Naylor, Cox, Cosner, and Clifford I return my warmest thanks for their coolness, gallantry, and promptness in obeying commands. Their actions deserve the highest commendation.

To my sergeants and corporals, and to the members of my battery, too much could not be said. They fought gallantly for seven hours, and until they were completely exhausted from their excessive labor; but it is enough to say that the whole battery, men and officers, did their whole duty as soldiers, and maintained their original position on the 31st against three, and part of the time four, batteries, and the determined charges of the enemy's troops. The battle-field in front is the witness of their execution.

All of which is respectfully submitted.

J. B. COX,
Captain Tenth Indiana Battery.

Major RACE,
Chief of Artillery, First Division, Left Wing,
Army of the Cumberland.

No. 101.

Report of Capt. Cullen Bradley, Sixth Ohio Battery.

HEADQUARTERS SIXTH OHIO BATTERY,
On Battle-field, near Murfreesborough, Tenn., January 5, 1863.

SIR: I have the honor to submit the following official report of the engagement of December 30 and 31, 1862, and January 1 and 2, 1863, viz:

At 8 a. m., December 30, the battery was put in position on the left bank of Stone's River and near camp, and engaged a four-gun battery of the enemy at a range of 1,500 yards, who held a high, strong, and commanding position on the opposite bank of the river, and silenced the enemy's battery after an engagement of fifteen minutes, expending 72 rounds of shell and solid shot, sustaining no damage, except the loss of one sponge-bucket, struck by an enemy's shot.

At 8 a. m., December 31, the battery, in accordance to orders, proceeded to the right of our lines. At 10.30 a. m. engaged two four-gun batteries of the enemy, supported by two brigades of infantry, at a range of 250 yards. We received a galling fire from the infantry as well as the batteries. We held our position twenty minutes, pouring a heavy and destructive fire upon the infantry, at the same time engaging the batteries with good effect, expending 150 rounds of case-shot and canister, and sustained a loss of 1 man wounded and 2 horses killed.

Our left flank having been turned, I retired my battery and took a position 500 yards in the rear. Again opened upon the enemy (with case and canister), who were advancing in force. After an engagement of five minutes, and expending 12 rounds of ammunition, I was again compelled to retire my battery and abandon two pieces of the battery, one of which I had spiked (since removed), and sustaining a loss of 1 man killed, 2 men wounded, and 1 man missing; also 8 horses killed and 3 wounded. About this time Colonel Shoemaker charged the enemy with the Thirteenth Michigan Regiment, driving them off the field and recovering the guns, and for which Colonel Shoemaker should receive full credit.

About 8 a. m., January 1, I again changed position to the front lines, and, in conjunction with several batteries, opened upon the enemy with case-shot and shell at a range of 2,000 yards, driving them back, expending 54 rounds of ammunition and sustaining no damage.

January 2, while occupying a position on the front line, the enemy advanced eighteen guns (supposed), and opened fire upon my battery with solid shot and shell. About 8 a. m. I was supported upon the right by two six-gun batteries, which gave way early in the action and retired. I silenced the enemy's guns and held the position, expending 177 rounds of ammunition, and sustaining a loss of 5 men wounded, 5 horses killed, and 3 horses wounded. About this time Captain Stokes' (Chicago) battery opened upon my battery several rounds of canister from a position 250 yards in rear, and from which I sustained much damage.

At 2 p. m. the enemy advanced a heavy column upon our left lines, and supported by two four-gun batteries. My battery took a strong position and opened on the enemy at a range of 3,000 yards with good effect, expending 35 rounds of shell, and sustaining no damage.

I take pleasure in noticing the promptness and coolness displayed by First Lieut. O. H. P. Ayres, Second Lieut. A. P. Baldwin, and First Sergt. G. W. Smetts for the manner in which they managed their respective sections; Lieutenant Ayres having been slightly wounded, also his horse being wounded, and Lieutenant Baldwin having his horse shot.

The following non-commissioned officers and privates greatly distinguished themselves, viz: Sergts. G. W. Howard, H. Hartman, T. O. Casey, S. Miller, and J. Hersh; Corpls. N. Poole, H. A. Collier, and Acting Corpl. S. O. Kimberk. Corpl. E. H. Neal is entitled to much credit for the promptness and carefulness he displayed in keeping the caissons well screened, and for keeping the battery well supplied with ammunition. Privates W. C. Stough, J. Robinett, D. H. Evans, J. G. Barger, and Frank Leslie greatly distinguished themselves. The whole company, with but few exceptions, displayed great coolness, and are entitled to much credit.

Respectfully,

CULLEN BRADLEY,
Captain, Commanding Sixth Ohio Light Battery.

Maj. S. RACE,
Comdg. Artillery, First Division, Fourteenth Army Corps.

No. 102.

Reports of Col. George P. Buell, Fifty-eighth Indiana Infantry, command
ing regiment and First Brigade, including skirmish at La Vergne,
December 27.

HDQRS. FIFTY-EIGHTH REGIMENT INDIANA VOLS.,
December 28, 1862.

SIR: I have the honor to report that preparatory to an advance upon the enemy in the town of La Vergne, Tenn., this regiment, in accordance with orders received, was, on the 27th instant, formed in line of battle on the right of the advance line of the Fifteenth Brigade, with Companies A and B in the advance as skirmishers, covering the front and right of the regiment.

When the line of skirmishers had advanced to within about 150 yards from the town, the enemy's skirmishers, supported by one piece of artillery, opened fire upon them, which was promptly and vigorously returned by our skirmishers, who were steadily advancing, closely followed by the regiment. The enemy, being protected by the houses of the village, for a short time seemed to check the advance of the two companies acting as skirmishers, when Company F was also advanced as skirmishers to their assistance, and the regiment ordered to charge bayonets, and thereupon the enemy made a hasty retreat. After pursuing the enemy for about the distance of 2 miles from the town, during the whole of which time a constant skirmish was going on, this regiment was relieved by the Third Kentucky Infantry and took its position in the second line of the brigade.

The following persons were wounded, to wit:* Number of wounded, 7; but 4 of the above wounded are disabled from service. I have to report 1 missing, to wit, George W. Thompson, of Company B. Four of the enemy are known to have been killed by the skirmishers of this regiment and 1 captured.

The entire regiment, officers and men, conducted themselves calmly and bravely during the entire action; but I would beg to make special mention of Maj. Joseph Moore, who commanded the skirmishers, and also of Captains Davis and Cain, and Lieut. James A. Smith, who commanded their respective companies as skirmishers, for the brave determination evinced by them in their respective positions.

Respectfully,

GEO. P. BUELL,
Colonel, Commanding.

Captain KERSTETTER,
Assistant Adjutant-General.

—

HEADQUARTERS FIRST BRIGADE, FIRST DIVISION,
LEFT WING, ARMY OF THE CUMBERLAND,
Near Murfreesborough, Tenn., January 5, 1863.

SIR: Brigadier-General Hascall having assumed command of the division on the night of December 31, 1862, the command of this brigade devolved upon me, by orders issued to that effect. At the time of assuming this command the position of the brigade was on the right of the division, in front, which point we held until the morning of the 1st instant, when we fell back, before daylight, to the rear, as reserve for the division.

---

* Nominal list omitted.

This position we retained until 8 p. m. of the same day, when we again moved forward to the front, occupying the ground then held by the Pioneer Brigade, on the right of the division. Pickets were then thrown forward, so that the enemy's advance was within easy range of their guns, and the brigade lay on their arms during the night.

Early on the morning of the 2d instant sharp skirmishing began between our advance posts and the enemy, followed shortly afterward by a most terrific shower of shell and shot in our midst, from guns having been massed and masked against us during the night, killing 3 and wounding 10 men of the brigade. During the day there was considerable skirmishing, and occasional shells fell among us.

Half an hour before dark we formed line of battle, by order, and moved forward some 600 yards; but, finding no enemy, were ordered to cross Stone's River, where we lay during the night in reserve, under arms, in a drenching rain-storm.

On the morning of the 3d instant we moved into the works thrown up during the night, taking position on the right of the division, relieving the Twentieth Brigade, where we remained quietly during the day and night, lying on our arms. But nothing worthy of note transpiring, and being ordered, we recrossed Stone's River at 2.30 o'clock on the morning of the 4th instant, taking up the position in the rear, which our brigade now occupies, as reserve.

The list of casualties from the night of December 31, 1862, in this brigade, to this date, is: Enlisted men killed, 3; wounded, 10. No commissioned officers killed or wounded.

It gives me great pleasure to state that all the officers of the brigade conducted themselves with true spirit and becoming bravery, and were keenly alive to the great dangers of their respective commands, each endeavoring to guard them from the fire of the enemy. Where all do nobly, no individual case of bravery need be cited.

For more minute details I would respectfully refer you to the individual reports of the regimental commanders, on file.

Very respectfully,

GEO. P. BUELL,
Colonel, Commanding.

Captain KERSTETTER,
Assistant Adjutant-General, First Division.

HDQRS. FIFTY-EIGHTH REGIMENT INDIANA VOLUNTEERS,
Near Murfreesborough, Tenn., January 5, 1863.

SIR: I have the honor to report that the Fifty-eighth Regiment Indiana Volunteers, under my command, entered the late action near Murfreesborough, Tenn., at 11.30 a. m. December 31, 1862, with 386 men, exclusive of commissioned officers.

This regiment, in the battle, was posted on the right of the railroad, fronting toward town, forming a part of the left wing of the army engaged. Each man was, prior to the action, furnished with from 60 to 80 rounds of cartridges, and, after engaging the enemy under very severe fire for three hours and twenty minutes, the regiment was relieved by the Fortieth Indiana Volunteers.

It gives me great pleasure to state that during the action both officers and enlisted men showed no desire nor symptom to retire from the contest, but all stood firmly at their posts and fought nobly and bravely.

I would also state that John J. Hight, chaplain of the regiment, deserves commendation for his efficient services rendered on the field and in the hospitals, caring for the wounded.

I have to report the following loss in this day's engagement, to wit: Second Lieut. Francis B. Blackford, of Company E, was killed while bravely encouraging his men to fight for their cause. Capts. William A. Downey and Ashbury H. Alexander, Second Lieut. William Adams, and Lieut. Charles C. Whiting were all wounded while performing their duty with great zeal and efficiency at their respective posts. Of enlisted men killed in action, there were 16, and 73 wounded in such a manner as to disable them for present service. There were also 24 men slightly wounded. I have also to report 3 men captured by the enemy, with the regimental wagons, at some distance from the field of battle, and also 3 men missing; making a total loss to the regiment as follows: Killed—commissioned officers, 1; enlisted men, 16. Wounded—commissioned officers, 4; enlisted men disabled, 73; enlisted men missing, 3. Total loss in this day's action, 97; enlisted men captured (not in action), 3. Total, 100.

At the close of the action this day, Brigadier-General Hascall being called to the command of the division, I took command of the brigade, and left the command of the regiment to Lieut. Col. James T. Embree, who has since commanded it.

Respectfully,

GEO. P. BUELL,
Colonel, Commanding.

Captain KERSTETTER,
Assistant Adjutant-General.

No. 103.

Reports of Col. Frederick A. Bartleson, One hundredth Illinois Infantry, including skirmishes near La Vergne and on the Murfreesborough pike, at Stewart's Creek Bridge.

IN THE FIELD, AT STEWART'S CREEK,
December 28, 1862.

SIR: I have the honor to report as follows of the part taken by my regiment in the advance on Stewart's Creek on the 27th December, 1862:

We advanced on La Vergne in rear of the Twenty-sixth Ohio. After passing La Vergne some distance, we took the place of the Twenty-sixth Ohio, relieving their skirmishers. The march in line of battle was very difficult, owing to the obstacles in the way, and the rain had made the ground in places very fatiguing to be traveled over; the men, however, advanced very well. After arriving at the point where we are now bivouacked, near the creek, while the artillery was interchanging shots with the enemy, by direction of General Hascall, I moved a little to the left. In a short time, hearing firing toward the left of our rear, I sent Captain Munger's company (G) to protect our left flank, instructing him to take up his position near the crest of a rise of ground. He did so, and had just got ready for deploying his men when a force of the enemy's cavalry, numbering, perhaps, 50 or 60, came dashing along. Seeing them coming, Captain Munger ordered his men to fire, and received some shots in return, when he ordered them to surrender, which they did, some, however, with great reluctance. All were taken that came up near his company, but some, who were behind, seeing those in advance surrender, wheeled to the left behind a house and escaped. The number, including Lieutenant Seawell, Fifty-first Alabama Partisans, who was in command, taken was 24, besides 12 horses and saddles and 12 guns. A number of the prisoners, when they saw they must surrender, threw away their guns. One was wounded fatally and 2 slightly.

Company B, while skirmishing, took 1 prisoner, who is in charge. Some of the horses were taken, I understand, by some other skirmishers, into whose line they ran, and some got away. None of our men were wounded, although one or two were struck by spent balls.

Respectfully, yours,

F. A. BARTLESON,
Colonel One hundredth Illinois.

Capt. E. R. KERSTETTER,
Actg. Asst. Adjt. Gen., Fifteenth Brigade, Sixth Division.

—

HDQRS. ONE HUNDREDTH ILLINOIS VOL. INFANTRY,
On the Battle-field, near Murfreesborough, Tenn., January 5, 1863.

SIR : I have the honor to submit the following report of the part taken by the One hundredth Regiment Illinois Volunteer Infantry during December 31, 1862 :

On the morning of December 31, 1862, while a portion of General Van Cleve's command were returning from the ford of the creek (which up to that time had been guarded by the One hundredth Illinois and Fifty-eighth Indiana), not carrying out their original intention of crossing, my regiment was ordered to follow, in column of companies, the Twenty-sixth Ohio, which we did, and, moving with them toward the right, we at last took our position in line of battle on the right of the Fifty-eighth Indiana and in the rear of the Twenty-sixth Ohio, amid a scene of almost indescribable confusion, other regiments moving among us, ambulances and wagons hurrying to the rear, and scattered cavalrymen and negroes, urging their horses to their utmost speed, seeking a place of safety. We moved with the brigade farther on, until we came within the range of the enemy's cannon, and were exposed for a time to a heavy cross-fire of artillery.

After remaining thus for a short time, the fire on the right becoming momentarily heavier, I moved, in pursuance of orders, across the railroad, the regiment resting at right angles with the road, the right wing on the right of the railroad, and the left wing on the left of it. I noticed at this time, and shortly before, that our troops on the right were falling back, belonging, I presume, to General McCook's corps, and I was ordered to throw my men parallel to the railroad, which I did.

The bank of the excavation being too high for a part of the regiment to fire in that position, I ordered them to get out of it and lie down on the left side of the railroad. The firing in this direction was pretty heavy, but my men were not called on to reply. I observed some troops falling back in considerable confusion. Some of them were rallied and formed in the excavation we had left, toward my right, but not in any considerable number. I am unable to say who they were. At this point a shell, which killed 5 men of an adjoining regiment, so affected my sergeant-major that he is bent to the ground with an injury that will probably affect him for life.

I had noticed about this time that the firing was drawing near on the left of the position I then occupied, parallel with the railroad, and was apprehensive that our troops on the left side of the road might be taken on the flank. About this time Colonel Hazen, of the brigade, directed me to file to the left. Asking him his name, and being myself convinced of the necessity of the movement, I complied, and moved forward in a line at right angles with that just left, until I came up with the One hundred and tenth Illinois, Colonel Casey. We halted here, and for a short time participated in a sharp fire of musketry, which finally ceased, leaving us to bear nothing except a cannonade, which gradually lulled. There was another regiment at this time behind us, but what one I know not. After a short time this was withdrawn, and I was left alone with the One hundred and tenth Illinois.

There was at this point an open space (a cotton field) in our front, and in a short time I discovered a large body of the enemy on the other side, across the field, apparently moving to attack us. The One hundred and tenth at this time formed on my left. I regarded the situation as extremely perilous, and informed General Hascall, who was not far distant, of the same. He replied that he saw it likewise, but we must hold it.

Shortly after, a force of our own was thrown across the field in our front, but was soon withdrawn. Informing my men that this was a good time to show what they were and make a reputation, and announcing my determination to them that they should stay there, I ordered them forward, and halted them at the edge of the wood. The One hundred and tenth said they would stay with us, and moved likewise. I commanded the men to lie down, but the enemy, having necessarily discovered us, opened upon us with a perfect storm of shot, shell, and grape. A battery of our own in a short time replied behind us, and for the space of three or four hours the scene was fearful.

Although so much exposed, I cannot but be thankful that we suffered so little, commensurate with our danger. The most of our loss, however, was incurred here. Second Lieutenant Worthingham was instantly killed by a shell. Second Lieutenant Mitchell, Company A, was mortally wounded in the hip by a musket or rifle ball, of which he afterward died. They were both deserving officers, and did their duty nobly. Major Hammond had a narrow escape, having the skirts of his coat torn and a slight wound in the calf of his leg. First Lieut. George Bez and Second Lieutenant McDonald, both of Company C, were somewhat wounded, but I think not severely. First Lieutenant Kelley, Company K, was wounded severely in the right shoulder. Second Lieutenant McConnell, Company I, was somewhat bruised by the limb of a tree striking him on the head, but has since returned to duty. The list accompanying this report will show the number of enlisted men and others killed and wounded.

Night at last closed in and ended this unequal combat—unequal, because our men were compelled, to a great extent, to be spectators and sufferers without being allowed to be actors in the scene. I threw out skirmishers to the front of the regiment, and the men were ordered to lie down on their arms and forbidden to make fires. Our skirmishers soon came upon the enemy seeking his wounded, and, through misapprehension, some of my men took the horse of a rebel surgeon and 4 prisoners. I sent the horse back, and directed the messenger to say, without mentioning from whom the message came, that it was regretted that the men were taken, but, under the circumstances, they could not be released at present, but would be at the first fitting opportunity. The men themselves were quite pleased at the idea. Two more were brought in to me, being reported to have given themselves up and to be anxious to leave the Confederate service. I questioned them, and finding that it was entirely voluntary on their part, I sent them to General Hascall, who took charge of them. I also sent out an ambulance, under charge of Dr. Woodruff, who brought in a number of our own wounded from the field. The others the next day I sent to the rear. I had no paper on which to express the facts; but if they can be identified hereafter (as they can be by some of my regiment) they ought to be returned.

Recapitulation of killed and wounded.

	Killed.	Wounded.
Commissioned officers	1	6
Enlisted men	5	32
Non-commissioned staff		1
Total	6	39
Aggregate		45

Of the above, one commissioned officer died shortly after. I have not included in the above some of those who have been killed and wounded from among men detailed from the regiment in other parts of the service.

Troops, I think, could not have behaved better than did the One hundredth. Considering that it was a new regiment; that since being mustered into the United States service its time has been almost entirely consumed in marching, precluding proper opportunities of drilling, and that its officers generally were new, it must be confessed, I trust and think, it did well. Where all did well, then, it is unnecessary to specify individual cases.

Respectfully,

F. A. BARTLESON,
Colonel One hundredth Illinois Infantry.

Capt. EDMUND R. KERSTETTER,
Assistant Adjutant-General, Fifteenth Brigade.

—

HEADQUARTERS ONE HUNDREDTH ILLINOIS INFANTRY,
January 5, 1863.

The following is a continuation of my report after December 31, 1862, commencing with the operations of January 1, being supplementary to a report just made to General Hascall, through his adjutant-general:

Very early the next morning (January 1, 1863) we were ordered to change our position, which we did, but nothing was done that day. About 9 or 10 p. m. an order came to proceed to the front, which we did, in conjunction with the rest of the brigade, and relieved the Pioneer Corps, which was on duty there. Everything passed off quietly at night, but in the morning, while my regiment, which had been in the front line all night, was being relieved by the Twenty-sixth Ohio, the enemy opened upon us with artillery.

We took up our position, notwithstanding, and were subjected, for a considerable space of time, to one of the most severe fires that troops can experience. The men lay in that position all day, without rations that day or the night before, and sunk deep in the mud. This made the second night without sleep, and, one might say, almost without food. Private George H. Atkins, Company K, was killed by a solid shot, which penetrated him and severed his arm from his body.

We were here the spectators, to a considerable extent, of the fight on the left, which took place on the afternoon of the 2d. Near dark our regiment, with the remainder of the brigade, after being formed in line, and our skirmishers skirmishing with the enemy, proceeded to ford the creek on the left, which we did, and at last bivouacked in a terrible rain for the night.

On the morning of January 3, with the rest of our brigade, we took our position behind the rail barricades or breastworks, relieving the Twentieth Brigade. Nothing transpired, except one of the most constant rains, lasting day and night. Early the next morning we recrossed to our present position.

Troops could not have behaved better than did the One hundredth. Considering that it is a new regiment; that its time has been mostly occupied heretofore in marching, furnishing but small opportunity for drilling; that most of its officers were new, it must be acknowledged that it did good service. Where all do well, it is unnecessary to specify individual cases.

The following is a list of the killed: Private George H. Atkins, Company K.

The above brings down the report to the time of occupying this present camp.

Respectfully,

F. A. BARTLESON,
Colonel One hundredth Illinois Infantry.

Capt. J. G. ELWOOD,
Acting Assistant Adjutant-General, Fifteenth Brigade.

No. 104.

Report of Lieut. Col. James T. Embree, Fifty-eighth Indiana Infantry.

HDQRS. FIFTY-EIGHTH REGIMENT INDIANA VOLUNTEERS,
January —, 1863.

SIR: I have the honor to report that the Fifty-eighth Regiment Indiana Volunteers came under my command on the evening of December 31, 1862, after the close of that day's action, George P. Buell, colonel of the regiment, having been called to the command of the brigade.

About daybreak, January 1, 1863, this regiment received orders and took position as part of the reserve on the left wing of the army, and retained that position during the entire day, and consequently was not in action.

At 10 p. m. of the same day the regiment was posted on the front line, in the left wing of the army, and retained this position until 9 p. m. January 2.

During this time the regiment was not engaged in action, but was, about 10 a. m., January 2, subjected to a severe fire from the enemy's artillery, discharging into its ranks a large number of solid shot and shell, by which 2 enlisted men were severely wounded.

About 5 p. m. of this day an attack was made by the enemy on the right flank of the regiment, while the regiment was being moved to a new position, which it had been ordered to occupy. The front of the regiment was immediately changed, and skirmishers thrown forward to meet the skirmishers of the enemy, and soon succeeded in driving the enemy from the field without loss to the regiment. At 9 p. m., January 2, the regiment, in pursuance of orders received, crossed the river on the left, and took position on the front line of the left wing of our army, which position it held until the morning of January 4, when it was moved to its present position in the field, in the rear of the army.

During the time the regiment held position south of Stone's River—the night of the 2d and the day and night of January 3—the regiment was not engaged in action.

The loss of the regiment during the time covered by this report was but 2 enlisted men, wounded.

Respectfully,

JAMES T. EMBREE,
Lieutenant-Colonel, Comdg. Fifty-eighth Regt. Indiana Vols.

No. 105.

Report of Col. Samuel McKee, Third Kentucky Infantry, of skirmishes near La Vergne and Stewart's Creek Bridge, December 27.

HEADQUARTERS THIRD KENTUCKY INFANTRY,
Stewart's Creek, Tenn., December 28, 1862.

SIR: In obedience to the command of Brig. Gen. Milo S. Hascall, commanding Fifteenth Brigade, about 10 o'clock a. m. on yesterday, at a point about one-half mile west of the town of La Vergne, I posted my regiment in the rear of the Fifty-eighth Indiana Volunteers, forming the right of the rear line of the Fifteenth Brigade. In this position I moved forward through the town to a point about 1½ miles east, along the right of the Murfreesborough pike. Here my regiment was ordered forward to relieve the Fifty-eighth Indiana. On taking the position in advance, thereby becoming the right of the front line, Companies A (Lieutenant Powell), B (Lieutenant Hogan), and C (Captain Ralston), all under the command of Major Collier, were deployed, and at once thrown forward to relieve the skirmishers of the Fifty-eighth Indiana. These companies had no sooner taken their positions and commenced to advance than they were met by a galling fire from the rebels, ambuscaded behind a dense thicket of cedar. Their fire was promptly returned with such effect as to drive the enemy at once in confusion from their hiding place. But they being mounted, whilst we were afoot, were enabled readily [to avail themselves] of every advantage of position that presented itself from the time we first met them until we reached this place. Driven from one shelter they quickly sought another, but at no point tarried longer than to receive one or two rounds from their pursuers.

Major Collier was constantly, and with great gallantry, riding from one end of the line to the other, encouraging the skirmishers forward, and to him is attributable the fact that we were enabled to steadily [press] forward, though the ground over which we had to pass was a continuous succession of dense thickets and soft corn ground, both rendered almost entirely impassable, except by the most devious routes, by a drenching rain, which fell upon us in torrents, from the time my regiment took the front until reaching this point, a distance of about 3½ miles.

During the advance the enemy were dislodged from not less than five or six of their hiding places. They frequently retained their fire until we had approached within less than 100 paces. They having the advantage of both short range and deliberate aim, yet we were so shielded by an overruling Providence that not a single casualty happened my entire regiment, though several were known to befall the enemy. But their number I have no means of ascertaining.

Of all the achievements of the day, that happening at this point was the most fortunate for the successful advance of the army, and the one for which the parties engaged should be most commended. On approaching Stewart's Creek, which at this place it is almost impossible to ford at this season, the skirmishers discovered that the retreating rebels had, some moments before, fired the bridge; the flames were already reaching high in the air; our battery and one of the enemy, both posted on the pike on opposite sides of the bridge, were shelling each other, many of the missiles from both falling on and near the bridge, and within rifle shot on the east of the creek stood a company of rebel cavalry. The moment was critical. Captain Ralston called for volunteers to extinguish the flames. Without the least hesitation, Major Collier's entire line, with a number of the Twenty-sixth Ohio, then near the same point, rushed forward, and in a moment extinguished the flame and saved the bridge, all escaping unhurt.

I was soon after ordered by General Hascall to post my entire regiment as a guard to the bridge. I at once moved up the rest of my command, and have them now posted at this point.

Very respectfully,

SAM. McKEE,
Colonel, Commanding Third Kentucky Infantry.

Capt. EDMUND R. KERSTETTER,
Assistant Adjutant-General.

No. 106.

Reports of Maj. Daniel R. Collier, Third Kentucky Infantry.

HDQRS. THIRD REGIMENT KENTUCKY VOLUNTEERS,
Camp near Murfreesborough, Tenn., January 5, 1863.

SIR: By order of Brig. Gen. Milo S. Hascall, commanding brigade, I herewith submit a report of the part taken by the Third Regiment Kentucky Volunteers in the action at this place on Wednesday, December 31, 1862.

At 10 a. m. the regiment was ordered to form, and was marched to its first position on the east of the railroad, fronting toward the right of our army, where the battle was raging fiercest, and our forces, overwhelmed by superior numbers, were falling back, contesting stubbornly, inch by inch, the ground which they were forced to give up. Our regiment, with the Twenty-sixth Regiment Ohio Volunteer Infantry on our right, formed the front line, while the Fifty-eighth Regiment Indiana Volunteers, with the One hundredth Illinois Volunteers on its right, formed the second line.

We lay in that position until about 10.30 o'clock, when we were ordered to the front to the support of Colonel Hazen's brigade, which was being attacked by greatly superior numbers. We crossed the railroad, and, marching by the right flank at double-quick, filed to the right across the turnpike, and formed in an open field on the right of the Ninth Indiana, of Colonel Hazen's brigade, our left resting on the turnpike. The men were ordered to lie down, and immediately the firing commenced, the enemy having advanced in two lines to within 200 yards of our position.

We held our position under a galling cross-fire until 1 p. m., when, a regiment which had formed on our right giving way, we were ordered to fall back about 25 yards across the turnpike, to guard against a flank movement which the enemy threatened from the woods on our right.

We occupied our new position about an hour, when, our ammunition having been entirely expended and the guns becoming so foul that it was impossible to load them, we were ordered to fall behind the railroad, about 50 yards in rear of our old position, to fix bayonets and receive the enemy, should they approach nearer, with cold steel.

We lay in this position until 4 p. m., when we were ordered to the rear to replenish our stock of ammunition and clean the guns. We marched half a mile to the rear, and had scarcely filled our cartridge-boxes and wiped out the guns when we were called upon by the commanding officer of ———— battery to support him against a strong force of the enemy, who were approaching our left from the east side of the river. A few rounds from the battery caused the enemy to retire.

We were in line on the left of the battery when General Rosecrans came up, and in person ordered us to advance and take position in a corn-field within about 200 yards of the river. This position we held until about 2 a. m. of Thursday, the men lying on their arms.

The regiment went into the fight with Samuel McKee, colonel commanding; Maj. Daniel R. Collier, acting lieutenant-colonel, and Adjt. W. A. Bullitt, acting major. There were in the regiment 13 officers of the line and 300 men, rank and file.

Colonel McKee fell at 11 o'clock, after we had been engaged half an hour, and when the contest was at his height. A minie ball striking him over the right eye, he fell from his horse and expired almost immediately. A truer patriot, a braver man, or better Christian never fell fighting in defense of truth and liberty—worshipped by his men, respected and loved by the officers, our colonel would have desired no fitter mausoleum than that in the midst of dead and dying comrades.

I was wounded twice during the engagement, but did not leave the field. The horse of Adjutant Bullitt was shot under him. Our hospital was captured by the enemy about 12 m., and our surgeon, Hector Owens, was taken prisoner, but released after having been kept four days. Our men and officers, without exception, acted bravely, and to give you a list of those who distinguished themselves would be but to give you our muster-roll.

Out of 13 officers of the line, 9 were disabled; of the enlisted men, there were killed, 12; wounded, 77; missing, 34. Total, 123.

Many of the wounded have died since the report was compiled. The number of killed and wounded is here stated as it was the day of the fight.

Respectfully,

DANIEL R. COLLIER,
Major, Commanding Third Kentucky Volunteer Infantry.

Capt. EDMUND R. KERSTETTER,
Assistant Adjutant General, Fifteenth Brigade.

HEADQUARTERS THIRD KENTUCKY VOLUNTEERS,
Near Murfreesborough, Tenn., January 5, 1863.

SIR: By order of Col. George P. Buell, I herewith submit a report of the part taken by the Third Regiment Kentucky Volunteers in the action on Thursday, January 1.

By order of Colonel Buell, I moved my regiment, at 2 a. m., west of the railroad, and formed on the right of the One hundredth Illinois, the Fifty-eighth Indiana and Twenty-sixth Ohio in our rear. We remained here all day, ready at any time to meet an attack, but nothing of note took place, with the exception of an occasional shell passing over the regiment, which we shielded ourselves from by lying flat on the ground.

At 8 p. m. we moved to a skirt of woods about 500 yards to the front, and relieved the Third Battalion of Pioneers, where we remained during the night.

Friday, January 2, we remained in the position occupied the night previous, and during part of the time were under a heavy fire from the enemy's batteries.

About 5 p. m. we marched, with the balance of the brigade, across the river, where we formed in line in an open field. After standing under arms for some time in a drenching rain, we withdrew to a skirt of woods on the right of our position, where we bivouacked for the night.

Saturday, January 3, about 7 a. m., we marched to the front, and took position in the second line in rear of the fortifications, where we remained until about 1 p. m., when we moved forward and occupied the position previously held by the Fifty-eighth Indiana, where we remained until about 2 a. m.

Sunday, January 4, we recrossed the river about 2 a. m., and went into camp on the west of the railroad. The day was mostly spent in gathering up and burying the dead.

Respectfully, yours,

DANIEL R. COLLIER,
Major, Commanding.

Capt. J. G. ELWOOD,
Acting Assistant Adjutant-General, Fifteenth Brigade.

No. 107.

Reports of Capt. William H. Squires, Twenty-sixth Ohio Infantry, including skirmishes at La Vergne and on the Murfreesborough pike, at Stewart's Creek Bridge.

HDQRS. TWENTY-SIXTH OHIO VOLUNTEER INFANTRY,
In Field, near La Vergne, December 28, 1862.

SIR: I have the honor to report the following as the part performed by the Twenty-sixth Ohio Volunteer Infantry, under my command, on the 27th instant:

Between 11 and 12 o'clock I first received orders to form the regiment in line of battle, and deploy my flanking companies as skirmishers. This being executed, and the order to advance being given, my skirmishers were ordered to enter La Vergne at a double-quick. On reaching the edge of the town, the firing on them became very severe, and at this point I received the order to advance my regiment at a double-quick and clear the town. This was performed by the regiment to my entire satisfaction. Having passed the town, the regiment, owing to the dense woods and the difficulty of seeing our proper position, obliqued too far to the left, and a part of it was thrown on the left of the railroad, and encountered considerable opposition from a force of the enemy's cavalry, which were finally driven forward. After dispersing this body of cavalry, I received orders to move over to the turnpike, which I did, and was there relieved by the One hundredth Illinois Volunteers, which I was then ordered to support. I then advanced on a line with the Fifty-eighth Indiana to the present point, and, in obedience to orders, was moving my regiment to the rear for the purpose of camping, when I received orders to change front and form on line with the One hundredth Illinois, to cut off the retreat of the enemy's cavalry, which, at this time, were endeavoring to escape by cutting their way through to the turnpike in advance of our forces. This force of the enemy having escaped by passing to the left of the line, I was ordered to camp my regiment. I regret to report the following loss of enlisted men in my regiment, nearly all of which occurred during the execution of the order to charge through the town, viz: Company A, 1 man wounded; Company B, 2 wounded; Company C, 1 wounded; Company D, 2 wounded; Company F, 1 killed and 2 wounded; Company H, 4 wounded; Company I, 3 wounded; Company K, 2 wounded; total, 17 wounded and 1 killed. In considering the circumstances under which the regiment went into the engagement, to wit, with but 1 acting field officer, 1 acting staff officer, 11 commissioned line officers, and 380 men, under arms, and the fact of the men being heavily laden, their clothes and contents of knapsacks being very wet, I have every reason to be satisfied with their conduct. I would also report the fact that Captain Ewing, of Company B, and in command of my skirmishers, not having received the order to return to the regiment when relieved by the companies of the One hundredth Illinois, remained in advance of the skirmishers of the One hundredth, and, with the men under his command and the assistance of a few of the skirmishers of the Third Kentucky, saved the bridge a half a mile to our front and on the main pike. Not having received any report from the surgeons in charge of my wounded, I am unable to state the character of their wounds, though most of them are reported to be severe. In numbers, however, I believe the list of casualties to be perfectly correct.

My company officers deserve my most sincere thanks for their efforts and the success attained in keeping the men well in hand and perfectly cool.

I have the honor to be, yours, very respectfully,
W. H. SQUIRES,
Commanding Twenty-sixth Ohio Volunteer Infantry.
Capt. EDMUND R. KERSTETTER.

—

HDQRS. TWENTY-SIXTH OHIO VOLUNTEER INFANTRY,
In Field, January 5, 1863.

SIR: I have the honor to report the following movements on the part of the Twenty-sixth Ohio Volunteer Infantry on January 1:

At an early hour in the morning I was ordered to fall back with my regiment from the position in which I had been placed by Colonel Wagner and join the Fifteenth Brigade. We were then drawn back and formed a reserve near and at right angles to the railroad.

At night the regiment was thrown across the railroad and into a hollow, for the purpose of allowing the men to build fires.

At 9 p. m. we were ordered forward to relieve the Pioneer Brigade, and the regiment was formed in rear of the Fifty-eighth Indiana as a support. This position was held all night. There were no casualties in the regiment on this day.

On the morning of January 2, the regiment was ordered forward to relieve the One hundredth Illinois and support the Eighth Indiana Battery, on our left flank, and the Board of Trade Battery, on the center and right. Immediately after taking this position the batteries of the enemy opened on our artillery, and severe fighting ensued.

During the day the enemy's skirmishers, advancing under cover, annoyed our line, and were twice driven back by our own skirmishers. Immediately after sundown the regiment, with the brigade, were thrown across the creek, and, being held in reserve, were thrown back into the woods and allowed fires.

The casualties of this day were 2 men killed and 8 wounded, most of which were caused by the artillery of the enemy.

On the morning of January 3, the regiment was ordered to relieve the Sixty-fourth Ohio Volunteer Infantry and occupy the breastworks built during the previous night. In this position the regiment remained during the day and night, nothing of interest occurring and no casualties taking place.

On the morning of January 4, the regiment recrossed the creek and was placed in camp in the present position.

In conclusion, I will add that the Twenty-sixth Ohio Volunteer Infantry entered into the engagement of December 31 with 374 guns, and lost during the interval a total of 1 commissioned officer killed and 2 wounded, and 9 enlisted men killed and 72 wounded. Many others were struck, and so slightly wounded as not to unfit them for duty, and are, therefore, not mentioned in this report.

I cannot mention in particular any of my officers, as each one seemed to vie with the other in deeds and examples of good conduct. The men, with a very few exceptions, behaved nobly, though a few, I regret to say, skulked to the rear.

I have the honor to be, yours, very respectfully,

W. H. SQUIRES,
Captain, Commanding Twenty-sixth Ohio Volunteer Infantry.

Captain ELWOOD,
Acting Assistant Adjutant-General, Fifteenth Brigade.

No. 108.

Report of Col. George D. Wagner, Fifteenth Indiana Infantry, commanding Second Brigade.

HDQRS. SECOND BRIG., FIRST DIV., LEFT WING,
DEPARTMENT OF THE CUMBERLAND,
On the Field, near Murfreesborough, Tenn., January 6, 1863.

SIR: I have the honor to report the following as to the position and part taken by my brigade in the great battle of the last few days:

On the morning of the 31st ultimo my command was formed in order of battle, the right resting on the Murfreesborough road, about 2 miles from the town, and the left resting to the left of the railroad; one section of Cox's battery commanding the pike, the remainder of the battery posted so as to command either side of the railroad.

While in this position I received an order to move forward. My skirmishers immediately became engaged with the enemy, and the enemy's artillery shelling my lines. There was a fearful battle going on at this time on our extreme right. I received orders to proceed no farther, but, if attacked, to hold my position. General Hascall's and Colonel Harker's brigades were posted on my left, but were soon after withdrawn; this made it necessary to extend my lines to the left, so as to prevent the enemy crossing Stone's River at a ford which had been held by Colonel Harker, and that I was now ordered to hold at all hazards by General Wood.

I accordingly moved all my brigade to the left of the railroad, with one section of Cox's battery at the railroad; the other sections were posted directly in front of the ford, on the crest of a hill, supported by the Fifty-seventh Indiana Volunteers, and in such position as to rake the front both to the right and left. Directly in front of this position, on the opposite side of the river, on an elevation defended by earth-works, were posted two of the enemy's batteries and a large force of infantry, under command of General Breckinridge. This was mainly the position of my command when the enemy made the first vigorous assault in front, which, after a long and continued struggle, was repulsed with great slaughter of the enemy, but to return in still greater force.

Learning that General Hascall, on the right of the road, was hard pressed, I sent the Ninety-seventh Ohio to re-enforce him, which did good service as they took position on the flank, and were sheltered by the nature of the ground from the fire of the enemy, and which prevented the enemy from raking our lines from the woods on the right. Colonel Lane maintained this position throughout the day. The enemy at this time had gained the woods on this side of the river, and I ordered the Fifteenth Indiana, supported by the Fifty-seventh Indiana, to advance to meet them. Captain Cox's battery, supported by the Fortieth Indiana, opened on them with canister and soon drove them back. At the same time they were repulsed in front by General Hascall, but only to return, as before, in greater force, this time evidently determined to carry my position, as a brigade was thrown on this side of the river, under cover of the woods in my front, at only about 300 yards distant.

Cox's battery had exhausted nearly all of their ammunition, and had tried in vain to procure more, which made it necessary for me to rely mainly on the infantry to dislodge the enemy from this position. I preferred making the attack myself rather than waiting an assault from them. I ordered forward the Fifteenth Indiana, supported by the Fifty-seventh Indiana, being all the troops I had in hand, the Fortieth Indiana being hotly engaged on the right of the railroad, with the left resting upon the river, so as to completely enfilade the enemy's line.

At this time Colonel Hines and Lieutenant-Colonel Lennard, of the Fifty-seventh Indiana, were severely wounded, and had to leave the field. From this position I directed Lieutenant-Colonel Wood, commanding Fifteenth Indiana Volunteers, to charge the enemy at a double-quick, and nobly did he and his men execute the order, killing, wounding, and capturing nearly one entire regiment, and driving two others in utter rout from the field; and nobly was the movement seconded by the Fifty-seventh Indiana Volunteers, although they had lost all their field officers; they poured volley after volley into the enemy, thereby aiding greatly to the success of the movements. Captain Cox's battery gave them the last shot they had in the locker, thereby making the rout complete.

The Fifteenth Indiana lost in this charge about 30 killed and near 100 wounded; but the rebels were not yet whipped, as they returned again in force, my infantry slowly retiring and fighting their way back. By this time we were prepared for their reception, as Captain Cox had procured some ammunition, and I ordered Lieutenant Estep's Eighth Indiana Battery into position with four guns; when the enemy came within canister range, they were literally swept away and driven back in utter confusion. The artillery was supported at this time by the Twenty-sixth Ohio, under command of the gallant Major Squires.

Night coming on put an end to the conflict; and allow me to say I found my command as far to the front as they were in the morning, and the noble dead of this brigade lay nearer the enemy's position than that of any other. It must be remembered that during the entire day the enemy's guns directly in my front, at 1,000 yards distant, and defended by earthworks from the effect of our artillery, kept up a continual fire of shot and shell, and every movement of my troops had to be made under this fearful fire. And I desire thus publicly to state of the men of my command that in this trying ordeal they proved themselves soldiers of the highest order. They remained in this position during the night without fire, shivering with cold as they lay upon the bloody field, yet not a murmur escaped them.

To Captain Cox's battery, officers and men, I am greatly indebted for the result of this day; they were under a continual fire, and much of it a cross-fire from the enemy's artillery, which was securely protected, while Captain Cox was in an open field, without even a tree to screen him from view; yet when their ammunition was exhausted the only cry of the captain and his men was for more ammunition.

The morning of the 1st, in accordance with orders from General Hascall, I formed my command on the right of Colonel Beatty's division, whose left rested upon the river, some half a mile to the rear of the position of the day before, with Colonel Harker upon my right. Soon after daylight the enemy attacked us warmly, but were soon driven off by the artillery.

My advance still held the grove on the left of my position of the 31st ultimo, which the enemy seemed determined to drive me from. I re-enforced this point and held it during the day, although repeatedly attacked by the enemy.

Things remained in this position until the morning of the 2d. The enemy having, during the night, thrown across the river in our front a large force, they opened upon our lines with a fearful storm of artillery, which, however, did but little execution on my lines, but was directed to Colonel Harker's command, on my right. They were soon silenced and driven off by our artillery. The enemy again attempted to drive my men from the woods on the left. I obtained re-enforcements for that position from General Cruft, which enabled us to hold that position until the attack in the evening, made upon Colonel Beatty, when I was ordered by General Hascall to cross the river to his support. When we arrived on the opposite side the enemy were already repulsed.

Night coming on, we lay upon the field. The troops under my command were not engaged on the 4th.

Allow me, in closing this report, to say that, with one single exception, the commanders of regiments and field officers showed themselves worthy of the positions they hold. Lieutenant-Colonel Wood, Fifteenth Indiana, had his horse shot under him; Colonel Lane, Ninety-seventh Ohio, behaved with the coolness of a veteran; Lieutenant-Colonel Neff, commanding Fortieth Indiana Volunteers, unfortunately was wounded early in the action, devolving the command on Major Leaming, to whom I am under obligations for the manner in which he handled his regiment; Colonel Hines, Fifty-seventh Indiana, was wounded about the middle of the afternoon, while at the head of his regiment, gallantly leading them to the attack of the enemy.   Lieutenant-Colonel Lennard was wounded about the same time, devolving the command of that regiment on Captain McGraw, who deserves special commendation for the manner in which he performed his trust.

It is impossible for me to name the officers who did well, as they nearly all did so, but will leave with the regimental commanders the duty of doing them justice, but must be allowed to pay one last tribute to the noble dead, Captains Foster and Templeton, of the Fifteenth Indiana, who fell while leading their men in the charge upon the foe. May their country not forget them.

The exception above alluded to in my commendation of officers was Col. J. W. Blake, Fortieth Indiana Volunteers, who, upon the field, became so intoxicated as to be entirely unfit for duty.   I ordered him to report to General Wood under arrest, since which time I have not seen him, but report says he is in Nashville a paroled prisoner.   This was about noon on the 31st, before his regiment had become engaged.

The casualties are as follows:

The Fifteenth Indiana Volunteers—officers killed, 2; wounded, 7; enlisted men killed, 36; wounded, 136; missing, 7.   Total killed, wounded, and missing, 188.

The Fifty-seventh Indiana Volunteers—officers wounded, 6; enlisted men killed, 11; wounded, 55; missing, 6.   Total killed, wounded, and missing, 78.

The Fortieth Indiana Volunteers—officers wounded, 5; enlisted men killed, 4; wounded, 63; missing, 13.   Total killed, wounded, and missing, 85.

The Ninety-seventh Ohio Volunteers—enlisted men killed, 3; wounded, 15; missing, 6.   Total killed, wounded, and missing, 24.

Total number of men of the brigade killed, wounded, and missing, 375; total number of men engaged, 1,475; number of men for duty on the morning of the 2d, 1,100.

The Fifteenth Indiana Volunteers captured 171 prisoners, most of them belonging to the Thirteenth Louisiana.

The members of my personal staff present on the field, Capt. Henry C. Tinney, acting assistant adjutant-general; Captain Warren and Lieut. W. M. Casterline, aides-de-camp, and of my escort, rendered me efficient service during the engagement, frequently carrying orders through such a storm of bullets that it was extremely doubtful whether they would live to deliver them.

Which is respectfully submitted.

Your obedient servant,

G. D. WAGNER,
Colonel, Commanding.

No. 109.

Report of Lieut. Col. Gustavus A. Wood, Fifteenth Indiana Infantry.

FIFTEENTH REGIMENT INDIANA VOLUNTEERS,
Camp near Murfreesborough, Tenn., January 9, 1863.

SIR: I have the honor to present you herewith a report of the operations of the regiment during the late engagements before Murfrees-borough.

During the advance on the enemy's position the regiment was not actually engaged prior to the 31st ultimo.

On the 29th, Companies B and F were in advance as skirmishers, and Company F had 1 man wounded.

On the morning of the 31st, while supporting Cox's battery, we were ordered to take and hold a point of woods on the (then) extreme left of the line. Companies G and F were thrown forward as skirmishers. Finding the enemy so strong that the skirmishers could not dislodge him, I ordered the regiment to fix bayonets and charge, which was ex-ecuted in a most brilliant style, driving the enemy out in confusion, killing and wounding a large number, and taking over 200 prisoners from a Louisiana brigade, having in it the Thirteenth, Sixteenth, and Twentieth Louisiana (among others). Being unable, from insufficient force, to send a proper guard, a portion of the prisoners escaped while on the way to the rear. We, however, delivered over to the provost-marshal 170.

The enemy having been completely driven out, skirmishers were left to hold the position, and the regiment was withdrawn in order to escape the heavy raking fire which the enemy's batteries were pouring on us. On the last grand advance of the enemy, when their right was in fair range of the woods, the regiment again took the position and held it under a most terrific fire, until the enemy was finally routed for the day, when it was withdrawn, for the same reason as before. By your order it was soon after placed in a grove to the left of our last position, where we bivouacked for the night.

In the subsequent engagements the regiment was not actually engaged, but at different periods was exposed to a very heavy fire from the enemy's batteries, during which several men were killed and wounded. All be-haved nobly.

It cannot be expected that I should mention names where all did so well. Captains Foster and Templeton died gallantly performing their duty, as did their dead comrades. The more fortunate living were fit compeers for the noble dead. Major Comparet was very active wherever duty called him. Adjutant Nicar fearlessly faced the fire to which the command was exposed, and, in addition, volunteered to bear mes-sages to the battery and other exposed places in the rear (I having no mounted man for that purpose). Captain White, Company F, having skirmishers in charge, performed his duty well during the day, and at night cheerfully volunteered to do the picket duty for the command. It may be proper for me to say that during the entire time of privation and fatigue (being ten days' continuous duty in a very inclement season) the cheerfulness and fortitude of the men was only equaled by their courage on the field of battle.

The regiment went into action with 24 commissioned officers and 416 enlisted men; aggregate, 440. The list of killed, wounded, and missing is appended.*

Respectfully submitted.

G. A. WOOD,
Lieutenant-Colonel, Comdg. Fifteenth Indiana Volunteers.

Col. G. D. WAGNER,
Commanding Twenty-first Brigade.

---

* Embodied in revised statement, p. 212.

No. 110.

Report of Maj. Henry Leaming, Fortieth Indiana Infantry, including skirmish at La Vergne, December 27.

HEADQUARTERS FORTIETH INDIANA VOLUNTEERS,
Near Murfreesborough, Tenn., January 9, 1863.

SIR : On the 26th ultimo the Fortieth Indiana Volunteers, commanded by Col. John W. Blake, marched from Nashville, in the direction of Murfreesborough, and camped near the village of La Vergne, the pickets from this regiment covering the right of the brigade, and one-half of the regiment having been thrown forward for this purpose, the entire picket line of the brigade being made the charge of Lieutenant-Colonel Neff, of this regiment.

The night passed quietly, but early on the morning of the 27th firing commenced between our outposts and those of the enemy who occupied the village, which was kept up briskly for some time, and terminated with a few rounds of artillery firing on either side. The regiment had 1 man wounded in this skirmish.

At about midday we again took the road, and without further casualty marched to Stewart's Creek and encamped, remaining till the morning of the 29th, when we crossed the creek and moved forward amid occasional skirmishing till arriving about 2½ miles from Murfreesborough, where we halted, our right resting on the turnpike at the toll-gate, and the left resting on the railroad.

We remained at this point till the morning of the 31st without casualty, having picketed the front on the nights of the 29th and 30th.

On the 31st firing was heard off to our right from both artillery and small-arms, indicating an important movement in that direction; but the regiment made no change of position, keeping the men ready for instant action.

About 9 a. m. the troops to our right were discovered to be falling back, and we were ordered to retire and move to a position from which we could advance to their support. The enemy were soon repulsed, however, and we were then ordered to take position in rear of Cox's battery, and on a line with that the regiment occupied in the morning, our right resting on the railroad, the left extending nearly at right angles from it. In this position we were exposed to the fire from the enemy's guns, and lost some men, wounded.

We remained here but a short time, when we were ordered to retire the regiment slowly, which order was about being executed when General Palmer, mistaking the Fortieth for the Ninth Indiana, ordered it to remain. Some time was consumed in explaining the mistake, which kept the regiment to the rear of the line of the retiring brigade. The movement on the part of the Fortieth Indiana was being executed with much confusion and greatly to the dissatisfaction of the company officers, as well as to Lieutenant-Colonel Neff and myself, the confusion arising from the intoxication of Colonel Blake, who was discovered to be utterly unfit to command. These facts were reported to Colonel Wagner, who promptly put Colonel Blake in arrest, and ordered Lieutenant-Colonel Neff to assume command.

Shortly thereafter an order came from Colonel Wagner directing that the regiment advance at once and engage the enemy; but this order was found to be impracticable, as there were at that moment two lines immediately in front of us. Lieutenant-Colonel Neff, however, directed the adjutant to say to the officer commanding the front line that the

Fortieth was ready to relieve him; but it was ascertained that the enemy's guns engaging this line were silenced, and that our assistance was not required. In a few minutes another order came from Colonel Wagner, directing the regiment to the support of General Hascall's brigade, which was now engaging the enemy and occupying the ground which we had been resting on in the morning.

The regiment was reported to General Hascall, and was by him ordered to take a position, with the right resting at the old house near the toll-gate, and the left extending across the railroad, which struck the line about the colors, and lie down. This ground being elevated several feet above that occupied by the front line, placed the regiment in a position much exposed to the fire of the enemy, which was at this time very heavy, both artillery and musketry. Many of our men were wounded here, 1 mortally, and 3 were killed outright.

It was while lying here that I was advised that Lieutenant-Colonel Neff was severely wounded in the arm, and had quit the field in consequence thereof. After having laid about three-fourths of an hour on this spot, we were ordered to relieve the Fifty-eighth Indiana, which occupied the advance line in our front. I called up the regiment and advanced at once, notifying the officer commanding the Fifty-eighth of my purpose. The Fifty-eighth was withdrawn and the Fortieth took their place.

For some minutes after getting into position we were only annoyed by artillery fire, but soon we observed a brigade of the enemy moving toward us in order, with the evident intention of attacking us. On nearing the ruins of the burned brick building in our front, one regiment was detached from the brigade and bore down upon us. I allowed them to gain a point within easy range of musketry fire, and directed the regiment to open upon them, which they did with great briskness, and with such effect as to repulse the enemy handsomely.

When I found the enemy had been effectually driven back, I ordered my command to cease firing, and immediately set about replenishing the cartridge-boxes with ammunition, and quietly awaited any further advance on the part of the enemy, which, however, was not made. Nightfall found the regiment occupying the same ground upon which we had bivouacked since arriving, on the 29th.

The regiment remained in position, with a picket thrown forward, till 4 a. m. of the 1st instant, when we were ordered to retire, which we did quietly, and took a position a few rods to the left of the railroad, and about half a mile to the rear of the one abandoned. Nothing of any moment occurred to the regiment on the 1st. We kept the front well covered with skirmishers, and kept in readiness for any attack.

On the 2d, early in the day, we were subjected to a vigorous artillery fire from the enemy, which, however, had no serious result. On the evening of the 2d, at nearly sundown, the enemy attacked the troops on the left of our position, and the regiment threw forward an additional skirmishing company to support our line, which, being in the open field, was much exposed, and had been subjected throughout the day to a vicious fire from the outposts of the enemy, who were concealed by the timber in front, which resulted in wounding Captain Wallace and two of his men. The enemy were repulsed on the left, and the regiment was directed to move to that part of the field.

Crossing the river we moved forward to the advance line, and taking position remained till the evening of the 3d, when we were relieved and retired to the skirt of woods on the bank of the river, where we bivouacked till 4 a. m. of the 4th, when we were withdrawn to the rear, recrossing the river and taking position on the turnpike 1 mile in advance of the general hospital. Shortly after arriving here we learned that the enemy had evacuated.

Our loss during the engagement was 4 killed and 68 wounded. Among the latter were Lieutenant-Colonel Neff, Captains Wallace and Harvey, First Lieutenant Griswold, and Second Lieutenants Coleman and Hazelrigg.

In conclusion, I must state that the conduct of the regiment under the most trying circumstances was worthy of all praise. The coolness and quiet determination of officers and men were admirable, and not less so the cheerfulness of spirit with which the hardships and exposure to cold and rain were borne. The regiment did its duty faithfully. I know no higher praise that can be given it.

HENRY LEAMING,
Major, Commanding Regiment.

Capt. H. C. TINNEY,
Acting Assistant Adjutant-General, Twenty-first Brigade.

No. 111.

Report of Col. John Q. Lane, Ninety-seventh Ohio Infantry.

JANUARY —, 1863.

SIR: I have the honor to report to you the part taken by the Ninety-seventh Regiment Ohio Volunteer Infantry in the late engagement in front of Murfreesborough, commencing December 31, 1862, and ending January 3, 1863.

On the night of December 30, we were, by your order, placed in the front, our advance pickets being deployed on the left bank of Stone's River.

On the morning of the 31st, at the commencement of the engagement, our position was on the north side of the Nashville and Chattanooga Railroad, one-fourth of a mile from the river.

At 9 a. m. the enemy commenced feeling for our position with shot and shell, and by your order I moved my regiment by the left flank to a position in an open field, one-fourth of a mile from the railroad, and deployed one company to the river as skirmishers. We remained in this position under a fire from the enemy's artillery and infantry until 11 a. m.

Our casualties up to this time were: Wounded, Jacob G. Brill, private Company A; Matthias Tapier and Samuel Browning, privates Company I, the latter having since died from the effects of his wound.

By your order I now moved to the south side of the railroad to re-enforce General Hascall. We found the enemy vigorously assaulting his lines with artillery and infantry. Our place here was assigned us by General Rosecrans in person, who ordered us to take the position and hold it. We advanced to the place designated, which was on the south side of the Nashville and Murfreesborough turnpike, returning the fire of the enemy until near sundown, when he withdrew to the cover of the woods, leaving us in possession of the ground.

At nightfall I threw out one company as pickets 100 paces to the front, instructing the officer in command to avail himself of the opportunity to carefully note any movement of the enemy. Near midnight he informed me that he could distinctly hear the tramp of horses and rumbling of artillery moving from our right to our left. Upon investigation I was satisfied that the enemy was massing his forces on our left, and forthwith informed you of the fact.

At 2 o'clock on the morning of January 1, I informed General Rosecrans of this movement of the enemy, when he immediately arranged to relieve us from this position, which we had held since noon of the preceding day.

Our casualties during our absence from your brigade were: Wounded, Isaac McDonald, private Company B; Israel Garrett and J. C. Huffman, privates Company C; Austin Harvey and Evan Foulke, privates Company D; Lewellyn Echelberry, sergeant Company E; George Robinson, private Company G, and John Moore, private Company H. Killed: A. M. Hasom, color sergeant; August Reinsch, private Company B, and John Rodecker, private Company G.

At 3 o'clock on the morning of the 1st, I reported my regiment to you, and was assigned a place in the front line, about a half mile to the rear of the position occupied by me at the beginning of the engagement. We remained here during the day, with no other annoyance than an occasional shot or shell from the enemy's guns. At night we bivouacked on the spot.

On the morning of the 2d, our skirmishers were advanced a half mile to the front, where they remained undisturbed until 2.45 p. m., when the enemy attacked our forces across the river and our skirmishers were driven back. We were here subjected to a cross-fire from the enemy's guns for more than an hour, wounding Charles H. Claspbell, corporal Company K; Purley Dickson, sergeant, and Benjamin Kinsey, private Company D.

At 5 p. m. we crossed Stone's River and remained on its right bank until the morning of the 4th without further event.

Our loss during the whole engagement was 3 killed, 15 wounded, and 6 missing.

The officers and men in my command everywhere acquitted themselves nobly, and we never lost a position after once taking it.

I have the honor to be, colonel, your obedient servant,

JOHN Q. LANE,
Colonel Ninety-seventh Regiment Ohio Volunteer Infantry.

Col. G. D. WAGNER,
Commanding Twenty-first Brigade.

No. 112.

Report of Col. Charles G. Harker, Sixty-fifth Ohio Infantry, commanding Third Brigade.

HDQRS. THIRD BRIGADE, FIRST DIVISION, LEFT WING,
FOURTEENTH A. C., DEPT. OF THE CUMBERLAND,
Murfreesborough, Tenn., January —, 1863.

SIR: I have the honor to submit the following report of the operations of the troops under my command from the 29th ultimo to the 4th instant, inclusive:

The Third Brigade, First Division, left wing, Fourteenth Army Corps, Department of the Cumberland, formerly the Twentieth Brigade, Sixth Division, consisting of the Fifty-first Regiment Indiana Volunteers, Col.

A. D. Streight commanding; the Thirteenth Regiment Michigan Volunteers, Col. M. Shoemaker commanding; Seventy-third Regiment Indiana Volunteers, Col. G. Hathaway commanding; Sixty-fourth Regiment Ohio Volunteers, Lieut. Col. A. McIlvain commanding; Sixty-fifth Regiment Ohio Volunteers, Lieutenant-Colonel Cassil commanding, and the Sixth Ohio Independent Battery, commanded by Capt. Cullen Bradley, left Stewart's Creek about 10 a. m. on Monday, the 29th ultimo, marching most of the time in line of battle, with the right of the line a little in the rear of the left of the Second Brigade, Colonel Wagner commanding.

Our skirmishers soon came upon the enemy's cavalry, engaging them briskly and driving them slowly before them. We proceeded in this manner, cautiously feeling our way until our left arrived at the left bank of Stone's River, which was reached about 4 p. m.

Up to this time we had suffered no casualties from the enemy's skirmishers. We took up a position near Stone's River, about 400 yards to the left of the Nashville and Murfreesborough pike, the Second Brigade, Colonel Wagner commanding, being on the right, and the First Brigade, General Hascall commanding, being on the left, and somewhat to the rear, owing to the conformation of the ground.

We remained in this position until about dark, when we received orders to proceed to Murfreesborough. Stone's River being fordable in our front, we at once commenced crossing the stream. Throwing a strong line of skirmishers over the stream, orders were given to the Fifty-first Indiana, Thirteenth Michigan, and Seventy-third Indiana Volunteers to cross simultaneously, form on the opposite bank, press forward, and seize the commanding heights beyond, while the Sixty-fourth and Sixty-fifth Ohio, with Bradley's battery, were directed to follow as rapidly as possible.

The skirmishers had barely left the bank of the river before they were vigorously attacked by those of the enemy, concealed in a thicket and behind a fence in our front. Our skirmishers, in no way daunted by this fierce assault of the enemy, pressed gallantly forward, driving the foe until they came upon the enemy in force. The skirmishers were soon supported by the front line of the brigade. The enemy seemed to have been entirely disconcerted by this bold movement of our troops, and fell back in confusion. In this movement our loss was 2 men killed and 3 wounded. This slight loss must be attributed to the able manner in which the officers of the brigade conducted their commands. A prisoner taken reported an entire division of the enemy on my front; movements along my entire front and flanks indicated that a strong force was near me. I reported this to the general commanding the division, at the same time stating that I could hold the position until re-enforced.

I soon received orders to recross the stream, which I did, occupying nearly the same ground as before crossing. This movement was so quickly executed as not to excite the suspicion of the enemy.

Too much praise cannot be accorded to the brave officers and men of this brigade for their bravery and skill in driving a concealed enemy from a strong position after nightfall, and holding their ground in the face of an enemy three times their numbers. Though little was accomplished by this feat, it nevertheless made manifest the indomitable courage of the men under the most trying circumstances, and augured well for the more severe work which awaited them.

On December 30, the Sixty-fourth Ohio, being on picket and outpost duty, was somewhat annoyed by the enemy in the slight skirmishing in the front, losing 1 man killed.

About 8 a. m. the enemy's battery, stationed on an eminence near the right bank of Stone's River, opened a severe fire of shot and shell upon my camp. Bradley's battery was ordered into position to engage that of the enemy. After a severe engagement of fifteen minutes, Captain Bradley succeeded in silencing the enemy's battery. My command sustained no loss in this engagement. Aside from this, it was generally quiet on my front during the day.

About 8 a. m., December 31, I received orders from General Wood, commanding division, to cross the river with my command. The movement was commenced, in obedience to General Wood's order, but was suspended for a few moments by an order emanating from Major-General Crittenden, commanding the left wing. While awaiting further orders, Major-General Rosecrans passed my command, and gave me direct instructions to proceed immediately to the support of the right wing of our army, which was yielding to the overwhelming force of the enemy at that point.

We had hardly commenced moving toward the right, when a Confederate battery, located on the south bank of the river, opened upon us, killing 1 man and wounding 2. Not stopping to reply to this battery, we pressed steadily forward. On approaching the right, much confusion was visible; troops marching in every direction; stragglers to be seen in great numbers, and teamsters in great consternation endeavoring to drive their teams they knew not whither. My progress was impeded by the confusion, while the enemy was pouring shot and shell upon us from at least three different directions, wounding several men in my command. The brigade was, however, extricated from this perilous position as soon as possible, and pressed on to a position on the extreme right of our line, Colonel Fyffe's brigade, of General Van Cleve's division, being immediately upon our left.

After reaching this last position, my brigade marched in two lines, the Fifty-first Indiana on the right, the Sixty-fifth Ohio on the left, the battery a little retired and opposite the interval between the Sixty-fifth and Fifty-first, the Sixty-fourth Ohio on the right of the second line, the Seventy-third Indiana on the left, with the Thirteenth Michigan in rear of the caissons. We marched in this order about half a mile, when our skirmishers came up with those of the enemy, and the fire became brisk in front. About this time a battery from the enemy, situated in a cornfield, and nearly opposite my right flank, opened upon my command with canister. In order to get a commanding position for artillery, and at the same time guard well my right flank, which I was fearful the enemy would attempt to turn, I moved the command a little to the right.

While this movement was being executed, a staff officer from the command upon my left reported a strong force of the enemy in his front. I replied that my right was in danger, and that a strong force and battery was in front. No sooner had I taken a position on the crest of the hill than a most vigorous engagement commenced. The position selected for my brigade proved a most fortunate one. The enemy was completely baffled in his design to turn my right; not only were the batteries in my front silenced and the enemy there repulsed, but a most destructive fire from Bradley's battery played upon the heavy columns of the enemy then pressing the troops upon my left. This engagement had continued about twenty minutes, when it was reported to me that the troops on my left had given way, and that the enemy was already in rear of my left flank, and about 200 yards from it, pouring a destructive cross-fire upon my troops.

At this time my command was in a most precarious situation, with a strong foe in front, which, though repulsed, could not be followed up for want of support; my right threatened, and my left already turned. It therefore became necessary to change the disposition of my command and fall back. The commander of the Sixty-fifth Ohio anticipated my order, when he found his left turned, and fell back in good order. I directed this regiment to make a stand behind a rail fence running obliquely to the first line of battle.

During this movement this regiment was subjected to a most galling fire from the enemy, but they stood up under it nobly and fought desperately. While this movement was being executed, the Seventy-third Indiana was left in position on the second line, and the battery retired to a position about 400 yards to the rear, when it again opened. The Sixty-fourth Ohio was now ordered to change its front to the left and charge the enemy. The direction was indicated to the commanding officer, but, unfortunately, he moved too far to the right. Though this regiment handsomely repulsed the enemy in its front, it did the work of the other regiments already in position, leaving the left of the Seventy-third Indiana exposed, and permitting the enemy to advance much farther than could have been done had my design been carried out.

I do not, however, desire to censure the commanding officer of this regiment, who acted most gallantly through the engagement, but attribute it to a misunderstanding of the order. Bradley's battery, having taken its second position, opened again, with great effect, upon the advancing enemy, but, being in an exposed position, it was again ordered to withdraw, being badly crippled by loss of horses; two pieces were abandoned, one of which was spiked.

The command was now ordered to fall back and form on a rocky eminence covered with cedars, being a very strong position. The Thirteenth Michigan, from their position, opened upon the enemy with telling effect, and, having caused his ranks to waver, followed up the advantage with a charge, supported by the Fifty-first Illinois Volunteers, who had now come to our relief. They completely routed the enemy. The Thirteenth Michigan retook two pieces of artillery, abandoned by our battery, and captured 58 prisoners. For this act of gallantry Colonel Shoemaker and his gallant regiment are deserving of much praise.

The enemy thus driven from our right did not again attempt to annoy us in that quarter. How far the brave troops of this brigade contributed toward repulsing the strong columns of the enemy designed to turn the right flank of our army, and thus preventing most disastrous consequences to our army, must be inferred by the position occupied by this command and the part it took in the engagement.

Too much praise cannot be bestowed upon Colonel Shoemaker, commanding the Thirteenth Michigan Volunteers; Colonel Hathaway, commanding the Seventy-third Indiana Volunteers; Lieutenant-Colonel McIlvain, commanding the Sixty-fourth Ohio Volunteers; Lieutenant-Colonel Cassil, who commanded the Sixty-fifth Ohio Volunteers until injured by the falling of his horse, and Major Whitbeck, though wounded in action, remained in command of the Sixty-fifth Ohio Volunteers after Lieutenant-Colonel Cassil was injured, and Captain Bradley, commanding Sixth Ohio Battery, for their bravery and good conduct during this engagement.

My thanks are also due to Col. A. D. Streight, commanding Fifty-first Indiana Volunteers, for valuable information of the movements of the enemy during this engagement. From the less exposed position of his regiment it suffered less than any other regiment of my command.

On the evening of the 31st, I received orders from the major-general commanding to rejoin the First Division, which was done about 11 p. m.

On January 1, this division was moved a little to the right and rear. My brigade occupied a central position in the division, on the front line of battle, and a short distance to the left of the Murfreesborough pike. We were hardly in position before the enemy drove in our skirmishers. Bradley's battery, in conjunction with several others in our front, opened a most destructive fire of case-shot and shell, driving the enemy from our front and sustaining no loss.

On January 2, Bradley's battery being in position on a small eminence on our front, supported on the right by the Sixty-fourth and Sixty-fifth Ohio, behind a small clump of trees, and on the left by the Fifty-first Indiana Volunteers, lying in a skirt of timber, while the Thirteenth Michigan and Seventy-third Indiana were in reserve, three batteries of the enemy opened upon us. They were promptly responded to by Captain Bradley and other batteries on my right, when the most fearful artillery engagement ensued which I had yet had the experience to witness. The enemy, having our range quite perfectly, poured upon us a most destructive fire, causing the battery on our right to be abandoned; but Captain Bradley continued his well-directed firing until the enemy's batteries were silenced.

While this engagement was going on, Captain Stokes' battery, posted in our rear, opened upon us, mistaking us for the enemy. It is due to Captain Stokes, however, to say that I believe this firing was commenced without his orders, and was stopped by him as soon as it was possible for him to do so, but not until we had sustained some injury.

During the engagement we had 1 man killed and 11 wounded.

On the evening of the same day, when the enemy attacked the left flank of our army with great vigor, Bradley's battery was again placed in position, and did good service in silencing those of the enemy.

About-dark on the evening of the 2d instant we were ordered to cross Stone's River. My brigade was placed in the front line, my right resting on the left of General Davis' division. We were hardly in position before the enemy opened upon us, killing 1 man of the Sixty-fourth Ohio.

During the night we constructed a musket breastwork of rails, and remained on the front until about 9 a. m., January 3, when we were relieved and ordered to the rear in reserve, where we remained until about 3 p. m., when we were again ordered to the front to relieve Colonel Wagner's brigade, and occupied a position on the left of the First Division.

We remained in this position until about 1 a. m., January 4, when we received orders to recross Stone's River. We crossed the stream and took a position in rear of the main body of our force, and about 500 yards to the left of the railroad, where we remained until our troops had occupied Murfreesborough.

The loss in killed, wounded, and missing during these six days' engagements was as follows:

The Fifty-first Indiana—officers wounded, 2; enlisted men killed, 7; wounded, 32; missing, 9. Total, 50.

The Sixty-fourth Ohio—officers killed, 1; wounded, 3; enlisted men killed, 23; wounded, 61; missing, 17. Total, 105.

The Thirteenth Michigan—officers wounded, 2; enlisted men killed, 17; wounded, 70. Total, 89.

The Seventy-third Indiana Volunteers—officers killed, 2; wounded, 3; enlisted men killed, 22; wounded, 48; missing, 36. Total, 111.

The Sixty-fifth Ohio Volunteers—officers killed, 2; wounded, 8; enlisted men killed, 33; wounded, 92; missing, 38.   Total, 173.

The Sixth Ohio Battery—officers wounded, 1; enlisted men killed, 2; wounded, 7; missing, 1.   Total, 11.

Total loss in killed, wounded, and missing, 539.

The following is a correct list of the killed and wounded officers of my command:

Of the Fifty-first Indiana, Capt. Francis M. Constant, Company G, and Second Lieut. Alfred Gude, wounded.

Of the Sixty-fourth Ohio, Capt. Joseph B. Sweet, killed; First Lieuts. Warner Young, Joseph B. Ferguson, and Chauncey Woodruff (regimental adjutant), wounded.

Of the Thirteenth Michigan, Capt. Clement C. Webb, Company E; Second Lieut. John E. McIvor, Company E, wounded.

Of the Seventy-third Indiana, Capts. Miles H. Tibbits, Company F, and Peter Doyle, Company H, killed; Maj. William Krimbill, wounded; Second Lieuts. Emanuel Williamson, Company I, and John Butterfield, Company K, wounded.

Of the Sixty-fifth Ohio, Capt. J. Christophel and Second Lieut. Dolsen Van Kirk, killed; Lieut. Col. A. Cassil, Maj. H. N. Whitbeck, Capt. R. M. Voorhees, Company F, First Lieut. A. A. Gardner, Second Lieut. and Regimental Adjt. William H. Massey, Second Lieuts. Peter Markel, Joel P. Brown, Frank Pealer, and Acting Lieut. R. S. Rook, wounded.

Of the Sixth Ohio Battery, First Lieut. O. H. P. Ayres, wounded.

From the 29th to the 2d, inclusive, my brigade occupied some portion of the front, and during each day some portion of the forces under my command were engaged with the enemy, and sustained greater or less losses.   For the cheerful manner in which they stood up under these fatigues and exposures they are entitled to commendation.

I cannot close this report without paying a tribute of respect to the memory of the soldierly Sweet, the conscientious Christophel, and the intelligent and noble-hearted Van Kirk, who fell while manfully encouraging their men in the trying hour of battle.   The country will do justice to the memory of the brave soldiers who so gloriously fell on the morning of December 31.

Great praise is due to Dr. J. M. Todd, Sixty-fifth Ohio, acting brigade surgeon, for the care and professional skill extended to our wounded after the battle.

Where all behaved so gallantly it would be unjust to particularize, but I cannot refrain from mentioning in terms of special praise the name of Capt. Cullen Bradley, of the Sixth Ohio Battery, attached to my brigade.   This gallant officer, ever at his post, was always ready to engage the enemy whenever he opened upon our troops, and managed his battery with so much judgment and skill as to silence those of the enemy in every instance.   Such valuable services and such meritorious conduct, I believe, will not be overlooked.   I therefore take great pleasure in recommending Captain Bradley for some position commensurate with his merit and ability in the artillery branch of the regular service.

Of both officers and men under my command I can speak in tones of unqualified praise for their bravery and good conduct throughout the engagement in front of Murfreesborough.   I must also mention a circumstance worthy of notice which occurred on Friday, the 2d instant. The enemy's sharpshooters, taking advantage of the woods in our front and to the right and left, had crept up sufficiently near our camp with the evident intention of picking off our general and field officers.   They annoyed us exceedingly, firing at every mounted officer or man who appeared near the front. Desirous of dislodging this concealed foe, I directed the skirmishers to advance and clear the woods if possible. Captain Chambers, of the Fifty-first Indiana, had command of the skirmishers, consisting of 40 men from his own company; Company B, Seventy-third Indiana Volunteers, Captain Gladwyn commanding; Company D, Seventy-third Indiana, Lieutenant Grimes commanding; Company H, Sixty-fifth Ohio, Lieut. Joel P. Brown commanding; Company E, Sixty-fifth Ohio Volunteers, Lieutenant Hinman commanding; Company K, Sixty-fifth Ohio Volunteers, Lieutenant Mathias commanding, and Company E, Sixty-fourth Ohio Volunteers, Sergeant Holden commanding. The little detachment numbered only 120 men. The enemy's force was much larger. Our skirmishers drove them until they were checked by the enemy's batteries.

Thus these brave men not only drove a concealed enemy from a strong hiding place, but elicited valuable information concerning the position of his masked batteries. This act of gallantry elicited the praise and admiration of all who witnessed it.

To my personal staff, Capt. S. L. Coulter, acting assistant adjutant-general; Lieut. A. B. Case, acting assistant inspector-general, and D. L. Wright, aide-de-camp, I am indebted for valuable assistance throughout this memorable battle.

For details I would most respectfully refer you to the reports of regimental commanders.

I have the honor to be, sir, very respectfully, your obedient servant,

C. G. HARKER,
Colonel Sixty-fifth Regiment Ohio Volunteers, Comdg. Brigade.

Brigadier-General HASCALL,
Comdg. First Division, Left Wing, Fourteenth Army Corps.

No. 113.

Report of Col. Abel D. Streight, Fifty-first Indiana Infantry.

On the Battle-field,
Near Murfreesborough, Tenn., January 4, 1863.

Sir: I have the honor to submit the following report of the part taken by my regiment in the battle near Murfreesborough, from the 29th ultimo to the 2d instant, inclusive:

At about 4 p. m. I arrived on the west bank of Stone's River, about one-half mile north of the Murfreesborough and Nashville pike, and 2 miles from Murfreesborough, where I was ordered to halt until further orders. Here I remained until about dark, when I received orders to cross the river, preparatory to moving upon Murfreesborough. Being fully aware that the enemy occupied the opposite bank, and as none of our troops had at that time crossed the river, it became necessary to proceed somewhat cautiously, in order to avoid the danger of running into an ambuscade; consequently I deployed Companies A and F to act as skirmishers, and ordered them to cross in advance and engage the enemy briskly, and, if possible, to seize the heights on the east side of the river.

No sooner had my skirmishers crossed than the enemy opened a brisk fire from under cover of a strong fence but a few yards distant.

My skirmishers were ordered forward at a double-quick, and charged upon the enemy, who instantaneously fled from their hiding places. At this moment it became evident, from the brisk firing of the enemy, that large numbers of them were concealed in the standing corn on the hill side; and fearing that my skirmishers would be overwhelmed, I ordered the whole regiment forward at a double-quick, but before the regiment had entirely crossed the river, Captain Russell informed me that the enemy was advancing in line of battle just beyond the crest of a ridge, about 400 yards to our front.

I at once determined to seize the crest before the enemy could get there, if possible; consequently the whole line was ordered forward on the run, and although the whole ridge seemed to issue forth a continuous flame of fire, not a man faltered, but each seemed to strive to reach the desired point in advance of his comrades. The boldness of the movement, and the alacrity with which it was executed, together with the brisk and well-directed fire of my men, struck terror to the enemy, who fell back in great confusion at our approach. I was at this moment ordered to advance no farther, but hold my position. I then ordered my men to lie down, so as to conceal them as much as possible, and in a few moments the enemy were plainly seen advancing upon our position. They were allowed to advance to within 30 paces, when fire was opened upon them with such effect that they hardly waited to reply, but broke and fled again. Re-enforcements soon arrived on my right and left.

We remained in our position without further molestation until about 10 o'clock at night, when I was notified that orders had been given to retire to the opposite bank of the river. After waiting until the balance of the troops had recrossed, my regiment was marched by the rear rank to the river, when it recrossed also. In the mean time my skirmishers were gradually withdrawn. The regiment was marched about 500 yards from the ford, where it bivouacked for the night.

Slight skirmishing was all that occurred of interest until the morning of the 31st, when it became evident from the terrific roar of artillery and musketry that the enemy was turning the extreme right of our army. We were at once ordered to the right and rear at double-quick. We had moved but a short distance, when we came within range of the enemy's artillery; and, although several were wounded when we had no chance of striking a blow at the enemy, yet my men moved a distance of over a mile as regularly as they could have moved had we been on drill; and even when we came in contact with excited teams and teamsters, every command was promptly obeyed without confusion. After marching about 2½ miles we reached the extreme right of the army.

We had hardly reached our position, when we were ordered forward in line of battle across open cotton and corn fields. Companies A, B, and F were deployed as skirmishers to cover my extreme right and front. We had proceeded in this order but about one-half mile, when my skirmishers, approaching the crest of a ridge in front, running at an angle of about fifteen degrees to the right, were fired upon by a large force of the enemy concealed in the standing corn to my front and right. I at once ordered the whole line forward at a double-quick. My skirmishers came in sight of the enemy in a moment, when our well-directed fire soon put them to flight. I was here again, by rapid movements, particularly fortunate in getting the advantage of the enemy in my position. We had a fair chance at them while they were retreating some 400 yards, and large numbers of them were killed and wounded. Although the troops to my left were attacked desperately, the enemy did not attempt to bring infantry against me after his repulse.

Shortly after I had obtained full possession of the ridge, I was informed by Lieutenant-Colonel Colescott, then in command of the skirmishers, that large masses of troops were seen moving toward a piece of woods to my left and front. I at once notified Colonel Harker, and requested that the Sixth Ohio Battery, Captain Bradley, be sent to the ridge occupied by my regiment. The battery was promptly on the ground, but not too soon, for by the time it was in position the enemy had engaged the troops to my left. Captain Bradley opened a most terrific fire, thus enfilading their ranks (they were in column four regiments deep) at a distance not to exceed 500 yards. Their dead were literally piled in heaps by the terrific fire from the battery. Nothing else could have saved our troops to my left from total destruction.

The battle had been raging for about three-quarters of an hour when I was notified that the division on our left was falling back; consequently my position would have to be abandoned. At this moment Colonel Harker ordered me to fall back, which was done in good order, bringing off all my wounded.

Having received no orders as to what point I should fall back to, I formed in line of battle on the first advantageous ground, expecting to give the enemy battle, but was again ordered to fall back to the position first occupied on the extreme right, and at once deployed Companies H and C as skirmishers. The enemy again approached our lines on the left, which formed an angle of about fifteen degrees to the front of our position. My skirmishers and the troops to my left were but handsomely engaged, when the enemy broke and fled from the field in great confusion. It was now nearly night, and the contest was ended for the day. Other troops were brought up, and we were again ordered to the position occupied on the previous day and bivouacked for the night.

Early the next morning we were ordered into position about one-half mile to our right and rear, where we remained through the day. Companies A and G, and one company from the Seventy-third Indiana, were sent forward as skirmishers to drive the enemy from a piece of woods about one-half mile to our front, which was occupied in short order. This was all the engagement my men were in on that day.

January 2, I took Company H, together with several volunteers from my regiment, and drove the enemy from the woods formerly occupied by the Twenty-first Brigade. The contest was severe in the extreme for a short time, but the boys soon got the advantage, and the woods were ours. Ten of the enemy were left dead on the ground. This was the last engagement in which my men participated.

Our entire loss is 7 killed, 34 wounded, and 9 missing. Members of my regiment took 19 rebel prisoners—1 a major and 1 a captain. From careful observation on the various grounds fought over by my men, I am convinced that we have killed not less than 60 of the enemy, and by adding five times that number, the usual proportion of the wounded to the killed, we have a grand total of 360. These figures, though seemingly large for the amount of loss sustained by us, I feel confident could be fully verified by the facts.

Most of the ground fought over by my regiment has not been covered by other troops, and in nearly every case we have been placed where it was easy to decide which were our killed. The success attending us in most cases, and our small loss, I think, is attributable in a great measure to the advantage taken of the ground.

Feeling grateful beyond expression for the brave soldierly bearing and prompt manner in which both officers and men performed every duty assigned them, I feel a great delicacy in mentioning names, being fully convinced that it is more owing to the difference in circumstances than to the difference in men. Nevertheless, Captains Russell, Company A; Chambers, Company H, and Flinn, Company F, and the officers and men under them, are justly entitled to honors for distinguished services at different times during their various engagements with the enemy, though I do not wish to detract one star from the imperishable glory won by other worthy members of my regiment.

I have the honor to be, your obedient servant,

A. D. STREIGHT,
Colonel Fifty-first Indiana Volunteers.

Col. C. G. HARKER,
Sixty-fifth Ohio Volunteers, Commanding Twentieth Brigade.

No. 114.

Report of Col. Gilbert Hathaway, Seventy-third Indiana Infantry.

CAMP NEAR MURFREESBOROUGH, TENN.,
January 4, 1863.

SIR: In compliance with your request, I have the honor to report that the Seventy-third Regiment Indiana Volunteers, under my command, left Nashville on the morning of the 26th, taking the Murfreesborough road, encamping that night near La Vergne.

The next day we marched in line of battle through the fields and cedar thickets amidst a drenching rain, encamping at night on the camping-ground of the enemy, which bore abundant evidence of having been hastily evacuated. In the course of the day we passed several of his camp grounds, strewed with many signs of very recent occupation. Some sharp skirmishing was had to-day by one of my flanking companies.

The next day being Sunday, we remained quiet in camp. The enemy had been here in considerable force, and, in this connection, I may be permitted to mention that a company from my command, and one from that of Colonel Streight's, crossed the river to a camp still in possession of the enemy's pickets, where we found more than 100 cavalry sabers, several rifles, and other arms, which were taken possession of without much resistance, and brought to our camp.

On Monday morning the line of march was resumed. Passing through the same kind of country as on yesterday (very rough and broken), we came to Stone's River, not far from where the railroad crosses the stream, and about 2 miles from Murfreesborough, the enemy being strongly posted on a rise of ground on the opposite bank.

After nightfall my command waded the river amidst a shower of balls with which our reception was greeted. My command was quicky formed and marched in line of battle up the hill, during which time my skirmishers kept up a vigorous fire with those of the enemy, who retired at our approach. Halting under the brow of the hill, we waited the attack, which we had reason to expect, and doubtless would have experienced, had it not been that the very boldness of our advance intimidated him. We were near enough to distinctly hear his officers urge their men forward, appealing in the name of their " country and their rights" to make the attack ; but they came not. We then recrossed the stream and bivouacked for the night near its bank.

The next day skirmishing was indulged in with successful issues. Heavy firing was kept up on our right and left most of the day.

On the morning of the 31st ultimo, the enemy apparently making a more vigorous attack on the right wing of the army than at any time before, we were sent in that direction, and were soon engaged with him. The Sixty-fifth Ohio had taken position in a piece of woodland. In obedience to orders, I took my command to their support. They soon became engaged with a heavy column, which was pressing against it with great force. Well did they sustain themselves, till, by great superiority of number, they were compelled to give way. Passing over my command, which at the time was lying down, we, in turn, were instantly engaged. Twelve rounds were fired with great spirit and effect, when it was seen that the enemy was retreating in disorder, taking an oblique direction to the left. I ordered an advance, and well, indeed, was it obeyed—pressing forward on the double-quick; the ground recently occupied by the Sixty-fifth Ohio was attained, the enemy still fleeing before us. There being no support for us on our left, and the battery on our right (which in the beginning of the engagement had rendered good service) having been withdrawn, the enemy bringing up his reserve, crossed an open field on our left, and subjected us to an enfilading fire for several moments of a most destructive character.

Being thus left entirely alone, and finding it impossible to withstand such fearful odds, I withdrew in a somewhat disordered state, but soon rallied and again took position in front. My horse having been shot in the early part of the engagement, I was compelled to remain on foot the remainder of the day, when, by your kindness, I was furnished with another. That night we bivouacked on the same ground as the night before.

From that time to the evening of the 3d we were in the front, being more or less exposed to the shells of the enemy, sustaining some loss thereby.

We took no active part in any of the actions that ensued, with the exception of having 20 men engaged, with others of the brigade, in gallantly driving about 300 sharpshooters from a piece of woodland, where they had annoyed us for a day or two.

It affords me great pleasure to say to you that all of my command behaved most nobly through all the trying scenes they were called to pass; and where all behaved so well, it would be invidious to make especial mention of any.

In conclusion, I would remark that my command numbered, on the morning of the 31st ultimo, 309 enlisted men, 19 line officers, and 3 field and staff. The casualties of that day were as follows: Enlisted men killed, 22 ; wounded, 49. Capts. Miles H. Tibbits, Company F, and Peter Doyle, Company H, killed ; Second Lieuts. Emanuel Williamson, Company I, and John Butterfield, Company K, wounded; also Maj. William Krimbill, slightly wounded in the knee, and 36 missing. My judgment is that fully one-half those missing are killed or wounded, and part of the others taken prisoners.

Respectfully submitted.

G. HATHAWAY,
Colonel Seventy-third Indiana.

Col. C. G. HARKER,
    Commanding Third Brigade, First Division.

No. 115

Report of Col. Michael Shoemaker, Thirteenth Michigan Infantry.

HDQRS. THIRTEENTH REGIMENT MICHIGAN VOLS.,
In Camp, near Murfreesborough, Tenn., January 8, 1863.

SIR: My report of the 5th, having been made in great haste, was necessarily very brief. I would, therefore, for the better understanding of the movements of this regiment during the several days of battle, commencing on the 29th ultimo and ending on the 3d instant, submit the following:

On the evening of the 29th, when ordered to cross the river, we were on the left, the Fifty-first Indiana in the center, and the Seventy-third Indiana on the right. My regiment commenced crossing as soon as our skirmishers were fairly on the other side. The skirmishers were Company A, commanded by Lieutenant Van Arsdale, and Company F, commanded by Lieut. James R. Slayton. They drove the enemy rapidly, the regiment following quite closely upon them.

When in line in the corn-field, and receiving the third volley from the enemy, we were ordered to fix bayonets and prepare to receive a charge of cavalry. As my regiment was somewhat in advance of the Fifty-first Indiana, and my right covering their left, I moved my regiment to the left and rear, so as to connect with the Fifty-first Indiana, but still leaving my left somewhat in advance, and in such a position as would have enabled us to enfilade any force which might charge the center. Our position was now a very strong one, being in the edge of the woods. Here we remained until ordered to recross the river.

On the 31st, being in reserve when our brigade was placed in position on the extreme right of the army, we occupied an open field just in rear of where the Sixty-fourth and Sixty-fifth Regiments Ohio Volunteers and Seventy-third Regiment Indiana Volunteers were engaged with the enemy. When the battery retired, we were ordered to fall back to the position we held when the enemy advanced upon us. When they opened fire upon us, the other regiments of the brigade had passed by our right to the rear, and we did not see them again until after the close of the engagement.

My regiment was in line during the battle, and delivered their fire with such precision and rapidity that the whole force of the enemy was brought to a stand at the fence in our front, and held there for at least twenty minutes, when their left, which extended considerably beyond my right, having advanced so as to make it apparent that they would soon turn my right flank, I gave the order to retire, but again formed the regiment within 12 or 15 rods of the first line. The enemy advanced so as to occupy our first line, but broke and retreated precipitately when charged by us. The Fifty-first Illinois advanced only to within 3 rods of our first line, and then threw forward skirmishers.

My regiment charged past the first line, and to the right down to near the fence, and full 30 rods in advance of our first position, overtaking and capturing the enemy, from the place where the guns were recaptured, which was to the right and in front of our first line of battle, to the houses in our front, and into a corn-field, on a line with the houses. The artillery ceased firing a short time before we opened upon the enemy, and fell back out of sight, with all but the guns which had had their horses killed, and were captured. The enemy broke up the guns of our dead on the first line of battle while they occupied it. **A** lieutenant, whom we captured, informed me that our fire was very destructive, and that their loss in wounded must largely exceed ours.

On the 1st instant my regiment was exposed to a scattering fire all day, but was not actually engaged. At night we were ordered to the extreme front, to protect the Sixth Ohio Battery, and lay all night on our arms.

On the 2d instant, while supporting our battery, my regiment was exposed to a terrible fire from the artillery of the enemy, the number of guns playing upon us at one time being, as stated by Captain Bradley, eighteen. Though necessarily inactive, my regiment steadily maintained their position for over an hour, when one of our batteries commenced playing upon us from the rear. I then withdrew my regiment a few rods to the left, to a less exposed situation.

In the afternoon we crossed Stone's River with our division, and remained there doing duty both Friday and Saturday nights.

On Sunday morning we recrossed the river and bivouacked near the hospitals.

I am, sir, very respectfully, your obedient servant,

M. SHOEMAKER,
Colonel, Commanding.

Capt. S. L. COULTER,
Actg. Asst. Adjt. Gen., Third Brig., First Div., Left Wing.

No. 116.

Report of Lieut. Col. Alexander McIlvain, Sixty-fourth Ohio Infantry.

HDQRS. SIXTY-FOURTH REGIMENT OHIO VOLUNTEERS,
In the Field, January 5, 1863.

SIR: I have the honor herewith to report the number of killed, wounded, and missing in this command, from December 27, 1862, to January 3, 1863, inclusive, so far as can be ascertained from company commanders now present.*

The command arrived on the south bank of Stone's River on the evening of December 29, 1862, and crossed to the opposite or Murfreesborough side after nightfall on the same evening, and formed as reserve to the remainder of the Twentieth Brigade. Recrossed the river during the same night, and next morning, while on duty on the front, had 1 man killed by the enemy.

On the morning of the 31st was ordered from the left to the right of the line, and occupied the second line on the right. It was discovered that the enemy was approaching on the left flank; I ordered the command forward on tenth company, and, by order, fixed bayonets and successfully drove them for some distance, when the command became isolated and was ordered to fall back.

Among the casualties of officers of my command, I seriously regret the loss of Capt. Joseph B. Sweet, who fell while bravely leading his company into the thickest of the engagement. As an officer and true and devoted soldier, Captain Sweet bore the well-merited love and respect of all those who knew him. Having adopted military life as a profession, and for a long time served in the regular army, he was proficient in all the high qualifications that pertained to his calling. In him his country and cause have lost a brave and patriotic officer.

---

* Nominal list omitted. It shows 24 killed, 66 wounded, and 17 missing.

Of those wounded, honorable mention is justly due to First Lieuts. Warner Young and Joseph B. Ferguson, and First Lieut. and Regimental Adjt. Chauncey Woodruff, all of whom exerted themselves to their utmost to press forward their respective commands to the charge, and only ceased their labors when overcome by the exhaustion occasioned by their wounds. I learn with pleasure that, although seriously, none were mortally wounded.

The officers who survived the battle did honor to the State they hail from and the cause they nobly fought for. Of those who commanded companies, the names of each can be honorably mentioned in justice to them: Capt. R. C. Brown, of Company C; First Lieuts. Samuel Wolf, of Company A, and Henry H. Kling, of Company D; Second Lieuts. Norman K. Brown, Company F, and T. Eugene Tillotson, Company B; and First Sergts. James L. Hall, of Company G, and David Cummins, of Company H; also Lieut. George R. Hall, of Company K, and Sergeants Kuneman and Holden, of Companies I and E, respectively, who commanded the companies to which they were attached, after their immediate commanders had been either killed or wounded; also Second Lieut. Thomas E. Ehlers, who assisted in the command of Company A. The above-named officers did their duty regardless of the danger to which they were exposed at every step while gallantly leading their men forward to meet and charge the enemy.

The file-closers, without exception, manfully stood up to their work, and I cannot, in justice to them all, single out any one for special subject of remark, and too much praise cannot be attached to their patriotism and heroic military bearing. The men in the ranks all did their duty, and did it well, and they are heroes, all.

While we deeply regret and truly sympathize with the friends of those who were either killed or wounded, we are, as they can be, consoled with the thought that they all fell while bravely battling for their country's right and the overthrow of rebellion.

ALEXANDER McILVAIN,
Lieutenant-Colonel, Commanding.

Col. C. G. HARKER,
   Commanding Twentieth Brigade.

No. 117.

Report of Maj. Horatio N. Whitbeck, Sixty-fifth Ohio Infantry.

IN CAMP, NEAR MURFREESBOROUGH, TENN.,
January 6, 1863.

SIR: The Sixty-fifth Ohio Volunteers, under command of Lieutenant-Colonel Cassil, left its bivouac, near Duck Creek, on Monday morning, December 29, 1862. In the advance its position was on the left wing of the front line of the brigade. Two companies were deployed as skirmishers, who very soon encountered a strong cavalry picket of the enemy. This force contested our advance at times sharply, but disappeared near Stone's River. When within a couple of miles of the same river, several shells were thrown at us from cannon, which soon retired. In this skirmishing we sustained no loss, but several of the enemy's saddles were seen to have been emptied and the horses straggling.

We reached the heights on the north side of the river about 3 p. m., where we lay in line till after sundown. Orders were received to advance upon Murfreesborough that night. I was in command of the companies of skirmishers, and immediately threw them across the river, and commenced the ascent of the opposite heights.

Passing the skirt of woods, we encountered the enemy's skirmishers strongly posted to the front on the crest of the hill, and on my left behind a rail fence. A galling fire brought our line to a halt, but we soon cleared the hill, and, advancing over the crest, we found ourselves within 30 paces of a regiment of rebels, who, in their confusion, were rallying with great difficulty. I at once retired the line to the woods, where we remained till the whole brigade had recrossed, when we were quietly withdrawn.

Sergeant Snider, acting orderly, was wounded in the face, which was the only injury our regiment suffered. The regiment itself crossed the stream in good order, under fire of the rebel skirmishers, and remained in line behind the skirt of woods till it recrossed with the brigade.

Tuesday we lay in bivouac near the river, and went on picket at night. In accordance with Colonel Harker's order, we were ready to move at daybreak, with 60 rounds of cartridges to a man.

We received marching orders about 8 a. m., and moved at once forward. The enemy's sharpshooters and a battery on the opposite hill began a fierce fire of ball and shell upon us as we returned up the heights. When on the summit, a shell exploded in the ranks of Company B, killing 1 and wounding 2. We double-quicked, under a storm of shell, after the brigade, which was some distance ahead, moving to the support of the right wing. When the brigade was formed to advance through the open field to the right of General Van Cleve's division, our regiment was placed on the left of the front line, with the Fifty-first Regiment Indiana Volunteers on our right and the Seventy-third Regiment Indiana Volunteers to our rear. Company I, Captain Christophel, was deployed to the front as skirmishers, but, having suffered severely, was, in a short time, relieved by Company H, Lieutenant Brown. When near the skirt of timber protruding from the main forest, we marched by the right flank to support the Sixth Ohio Battery. We were again moved toward the enemy and placed behind a rise of ground. We suddenly found them in line at a short distance, and immediately commenced firing. The enemy, though in brigade front, three columns deep, staggered, concealed himself as far as possible, and did not venture to advance under our fire.

Meanwhile, General Van Cleve's division giving way, the line of the enemy on our left advancing, completely outflanked us, and we were suffering under a raking cross-fire. We held the position for about thirty minutes, and fell back, in accordance with orders; formed behind the Seventy-third Regiment Indiana Volunteers, and moved by the flank to oppose the advancing right of the enemy. We took our position behind a rail fence, and again held the enemy in check for about twenty minutes. At length, being nearly cut off by the enemy on the right, we retired behind the line of battle, resting in the wood near the pike.

We had suffered severely; out of 16 officers with the regiment, 2 had been killed and 8 wounded. Second Lieutenant Van Kirk, commanding Company A, fell in the advance; Captain Christophel, of Company I, some time in the retreat. Both were doing their duty unflinchingly and manfully. Lieutenant-Colonel Cassil having been disabled by the fall of his horse at the second stand of the regiment, I then took command. We rejoined our division at night near the position we left in the morning.

On Thursday, January 1, we lay in front, in support and to the right of the Sixth Ohio Battery, during the furious cannonading, and were annoyed by sharpshooters during the whole day. We picketed at night.

Our skirmishers covered the front on Friday. The regiment lay in a little clump of wood, in support of the battery, and exposed to the most terrific shelling during the morning. In the afternoon our skirmishers, in conjunction with those of the brigade, cleared the wood in front of rebel skirmishers and sharpshooters; were in turn shelled out, and again took possession and held it.

Near night, and the close of the engagement on the left, we moved over the river, threw up a defense of rails to the front, and remained there through the rain till morning. We were retired till Saturday night, when we again picketed the left front. About 2 a. m. Sunday we were marched back to our present bivouac.

The following is the list of the casualties of the regiment: Lieutenant-Colonel Cassil, severe sprain by the fall of his horse; Major Whitbeck, slightly wounded in the neck; Adjutant Massey, severely in leg and slightly in face and hip; Capts. Jacob Christophel, killed, and Voorhees, through the side; First Lieutenant Gardner, through side; Second Lieutenants Van Kirk, killed; Markel, through hip; Brown, in the shoulder, and Pealer, through thigh, and Acting Second Lieutenant Rook, in thigh.

Of 382 enlisted men in the engagements during the week, 34 were killed, 100 wounded, and 38 missing; total, 172. Of the missing, some are known to be prisoners, others are serving in hospitals, and a few stragglers are still coming up.

I will not particularize when all, officers and men, conducted themselves so coolly and fought so determinedly against such desperate odds; nor need I mention their patience under such privations and exposures in midwinter.

HORATIO N. WHITBECK,
Major, Commanding Sixty-fifth Regiment Ohio Volunteers.

Captain COULTER,
  Acting Assistant Adjutant-General, Third Brigade.

No. 118.

Report of Brig. Gen. John M. Palmer, U. S. Army, commanding Second Division.

HDQRS. SECOND DIV., LEFT WING, FOURTEENTH A. C.,
DEPARTMENT OF THE CUMBERLAND,
Camp near Murfreesborough, Tenn., January 9, 1863.

MAJOR: I have the honor to submit, for the information of the general commanding, the following report of the operations of this division from and including December 27 up to and including January 4, instant:

At 11.20 a. m., December 27, while in camp near La Vergne, I received orders to move forward, following the division of General Wood, and to detach a brigade, to proceed by the Jefferson pike, and seize the bridge across Stewart's Creek. The duty of conducting this operation was assigned to Colonel Hazen. How well and skillfully it was done will be seen by his report, which is herewith forwarded.

The brigades of Cruft and Grose reached the west bank of Stewart's

Creek late in the afternoon of the 27th, and bivouacked there until the morning of the 29th.

During all the day (Sunday, 28th) the enemy's pickets were in sight across the creek, firing upon us occasionally at long range, but did us no harm.

On Monday morning, December 29, at 9 o'clock, I was ordered to deploy one regiment as skirmishers; to dispose my other troops so as to support it, and move forward at 10 o'clock precisely, and continue to advance until the enemy were found in position. This disposition was made. A few minutes before 10 o'clock, Parsons was ordered to shell the woods to our front, and at 10 o'clock Grose's brigade moved forward, skirmishing with the enemy, supported by the First Brigade, Hazen not having yet joined me.

The command advanced steadily, driving the light force of rebel skirmishers before it to the top of the hill, some 1½ miles on this side of Stewart's Creek; and, being under the impression that the divisions of Wood and Negley were to advance with me, to my right and left, I halted for them to come up.

In a few minutes Wood's advance came up on the left of the pike, and the two divisions moved forward, constantly skirmishing (though much heavier on Wood's front than my own), to the ground occupied that night, afterward the theater of the battle of the 31st.

During the day the casualties were 10 wounded in Grose's brigade; none severely.

On the morning of the 30th, my division was formed as follows: The Third Brigade (Grose's) in two lines, the left resting on the pike; First Brigade (Cruft's) to the right, extending across the point of woods, his extreme right retired to connect with General Negley's left, and Hazen's brigade in reserve. There was considerable skirmishing during the day, the greater portion of which fell upon Cruft's brigade, which was in rather unpleasant proximity to a point of woods, to his front and right, held by the enemy in strong force.

About 4 o'clock, I was ordered to advance and open upon the enemy with all my artillery. This was not done, probably, as soon as the order contemplated. The ground occupied by the batteries at the time the order was received was low and confined. Upon pushing forward the skirmishers of the First Brigade to clear the way to a good artillery position, in the open field to the front, the rebels were found numerous and stubborn. Learning very soon that a mere demonstration was intended, all my batteries opened, and I am satisfied damaged the enemy considerably. The skirmish attending this movement was quite brisk, the troops engaged doing themselves great credit. This closed the operations of the day.

On the morning of the 31st, Cruft's brigade retained its position of the day before. Hazen's brigade had relieved Grose, who had fallen back to a point some 200 yards to the rear, and was formed in two lines nearly opposite the intervals between the First and Second Brigades, Standart's battery on the extreme right, and Parsons' near the center.

Early in the morning I rode to the right of my own command, and then the battle had commenced on the extreme right of the line. Soon afterward, near 8 o'clock, General Negley, through one of his staff, informed me he was about to advance, and requested me to advance to cover his left. I gave notice of this to the general commanding, and a few minutes later received orders to move forward. I at once ordered General Cruft to advance, keeping closed up well toward Negley; Colonel Hazen to go forward, observing the movements of Wood's right, and

Grose to steadily advance, supporting the advance brigades, and all to use their artillery freely.

My line had advanced hardly 100 yards, when, upon reaching my own right, I found that General Negley had, instead of advancing, thrown back his right, so that his line was almost perpendicular to that of Cruft, and to his rear; and it was also apparent that the enemy were driving General McCook back, and were rapidly approaching our rear.

Cruft's line was halted by my order. I rode to the left to make some disposition to meet the coming storm, and by the time I reached the open ground to the south of the pike, the heads of the enemy's column had forced their way into the open ground to my rear.

To order Grose to change front to the rear was the work of a moment, and he obeyed the order almost as soon as given, retiring his new left so as to bring the enemy under the direct fire of his line. He opened upon them in fine style and with great effect, and held his ground until the enemy was driven back.

In the mean time General Negley's command had, to some extent, become compromised by the confusion on the right, and my First Brigade was exposed in front and flank to a severe attack, which also now extended along my whole front. Orders were sent to Colonel Hazen to fall back from the open cotton-field into which he had moved. He fell back a short distance, and a regiment from Wood's division, which had occupied the crest of a low wooded hill between the pike and the railroad, having been removed, he took possession of that, and there resisted the enemy.

At that time, near 11 o'clock, as I think, my command was all engaged with the enemy; Hazen on the railroad; one or two regiments to the right; some troops in the point of woods south of the cotton-field, and a short distance in advance of the general line, among whom I was only able to distinguish the gallant Colonel Whitaker and his Sixth Kentucky. Still farther to the right Cruft was fighting, aided by Standart's guns, and to the rear Grose was fighting, with apparently great odds against him.

All were acquitting themselves nobly, and all were hard pressed. I could see that Grose was losing a great many men, but the importance of Hazen's position determined me, if necessary to do so, to expend the last man in holding it. I gave my attention from that time chiefly to that point.

The One hundredth Illinois came up on the left of the railroad, and fought steadily. As soon as Colonel Grose was relieved of the enemy in his rear, he again changed front, moved to the left, and co-operated with Colonel Hazen. One regiment was sent to my support from General Wood's command, which behaved splendidly. I regret my inability either to name the regiment or its officers. Again and again the attack was renewed by the enemy, and each time repulsed, and the gallant men, who had so bravely struggled to hold the position, occupied it during the night.

For further details of the day's operations, I respectfully refer to the reports of the brigade and regimental commanders, which are herewith forwarded, and confess my obligations to them all for their assistance during the day.

Brigadier-General Cruft deserves great praise for so long holding the important position occupied by him on our right, and for skillfully extricating his command from the mass of confusion around it.

Standart fought his guns until the enemy was upon him, and then brought them off safely, while the Second Kentucky brought off by hand three guns abandoned by General Negley's division.

Colonel Hazen proved himself a brave and able soldier by the courage and skill exhibited in forming and sheltering his troops, and in organizing and fighting all the materials around him for the maintenance of his important position.

Colonel Grose exhibited great coolness and bravery, and fought against great odds. He was under my eye during the whole day, and I could see nothing to improve in his management of his command.

I shrink from the task of specially mentioning regiments or regimental officers. All did their duty, and from my imperfect acquaintance with regiments, I am apprehensive of injurious mistakes.

I recognized during the battle the Forty-first Ohio, which fought until it expended its last cartridge, and was then relieved by the noble Ninth Indiana, which came into line under a heavy fire with a shout which inspired all with confidence. The Eighty-fourth, One hundredth, and One hundred and tenth Illinois I knew—all new regiments, and all so fought that even the veterans of Shiloh and other bloody fields had no occasion to boast over them. The Eighty-fourth stood its ground until more than one-third its numbers were killed or wounded. The Sixth and Twenty-fourth Ohio, the Twenty-third Kentucky, and the Thirty-sixth Indiana were pointed out to me, and I recognized the brave Colonel Whitaker and his fighting men doing soldiers' duty. I only saw the regiments of Cruft's brigade fighting early in the day. I had no fears for them where valor could win. Indeed, the whole division fought like soldiers trained under the rigid discipline of the lamented Nelson, and by their courage proved that they had caught a large portion of his heroic and unconquerable spirit.

During the whole day I regarded the battery, under the command of Lieutenant Parsons, assisted by his lieutenants, Cushing and Huntington, as my right arm, and well did the brilliant conduct of these courageous and skillful young officers justify my confidence. My orders to Parsons were simple: "Fight where you can do the most good." Never were orders better obeyed.

The reported conduct of the other batteries attached to the division is equally favorable. They were in other parts of the field.

My personal staff, Captain Norton, acting assistant adjutant-general; Lieutenants Simmons and Child; Croxton, ordnance officer; Hayes, division topographical engineer, and Shaw, Seventh Illinois Cavalry, were with me all day on the field, and carried my orders everywhere with the greatest courage. Lieutenant Simmons was severely injured by a fragment of a shell.

On January 1, this division was relieved and placed in reserve.

On Friday, the 2d, Grose's brigade was ordered over the river to the left, to support the division of Colonel Beatty, and during the action the brigade of Colonel Hazen was also ordered over to co-operate with Grose; while the First Brigade (Cruft's) was posted to support a battery on the hill near the ford. For an account of the part the Second and Third Brigades took in the affair of Friday afternoon, reference is had to reports of the officers in command.

During the heavy cannonade the First Brigade maintained its positions with perfect coolness. While the engagement was going on across the river, a rebel force of what seemed to be three small regiments entered the clump of woods in front of the position of our batteries on the hill near the ford. These troops were in musket range of our right, across the creek, and I determined at once to dislodge them.

Seeing two regiments, one of which was commanded by Colonel Given, and the other by Colonel Altemire, I ordered them to advance to the edge of the woods and deploy some companies as skirmishers. They obeyed me cheerfully and pushed in. Not being willing to leave the repulse of the enemy a matter of doubt, or to expose the brave fellows to the danger of heavy loss, I ordered up two of Cruft's regiments, and upon approaching the edge of the woods halted them—told them it was my purpose to clear the woods at the point of the bayonet. To inspire them with coolness and confidence, the preparations for the charge were made with great deliberation. To get the proper direction for the line, guides were thrown out and the proper changes were made, bayonets fixed, and these two regiments, Thirty-first Indiana and Ninetieth Ohio, ordered to clear the woods. They went in splendidly. It was done so quickly that the rebels had hardly time to discharge their pieces. They fled with the utmost speed. All these regiments behaved handsomely.

With this report will be forwarded a list of the casualties of my command, and from its fearful proportions demonstrates its hard service.

List of casualties.

Command.	Killed.			Wounded.			Missing.			Aggregate.
	Officers.	Enlisted men.	Total.	Officers.	Enlisted men.	Total.	Officers.	Enlisted men.	Total.	
First Brigade		44	44	9	218	227	6	120	126	397
Second Brigade	5	41	46	17	318	335		52	52	433
Third Brigade	10	97	107	22	456	478		74	74	659
Standart's battery		5	5		12	12		3	3	20
Parsons' battery		2	2		14	14		6	6	22
Cockerill's battery		2	2	1	13	14		2	2	18
Total*	15	191	206	49	1,031	1,080	6	257	263	1,549

I have the honor to be, very respectfully,

J. M. PALMER,
Brigadier-General, Commanding Division.

Maj. LYNE STARLING,
Assistant Adjutant-General and Chief of Staff, &c.

No. 119.

Report of Surg. Mason G. Sherman, Ninth Indiana Infantry, Acting Medical Director.

HOSPITAL OF THE SECOND DIVISION, LEFT WING,
ARMY OF THE CUMBERLAND,
January —, 1863.

SIR: As acting medical director of your division, I have the honor to respectfully submit the following report of casualties in the several days' battle before Murfreesborough:

Number of killed in the First Brigade 43
Wounded 185
Number of killed in the Second Brigade 50
Wounded severely, 77; slightly, 215 292
Number of killed in the Third Brigade 89
Wounded severely 484

Total killed and wounded* 1,143

* But see revised statement, pp. 212, 213.

From the fact that our hospital was nearer the battle-field than any other, we were during the fight necessarily crowded with hundreds of the wounded from other divisions, making our duties very responsible and laborious; and I cannot, in justice, submit this report without making honorable mention of all the medical officers in your division. They have shown themselves equal to their responsible duties, and have been untiring in their efforts both day and night to alleviate the sufferings of the wounded who have come under their notice; and more especially would I make honorable mention of Dr. J. B. Armstrong, acting brigade surgeon of the First Brigade, and Dr. S. H. Kersey, acting brigade surgeon of the Third Brigade, who were selected as operating surgeons, and they have proved themselves abundantly competent to the task, and have not allowed themselves one moment's rest while the suffering needed their attention.

Their devotion to their suffering fellow-soldiers should win for them the esteem and unbounded confidence of all who know them.

Very respectfully,

M. G. SHERMAN,
Acting Medical Director, Second Division, Left Wing,
Department of the Cumberland.

Brig. Gen. J. M. PALMER,
Commanding Division.

No. 120.

*Report of Capt. William E. Standart, Battery B, First Ohio Light Artil-
lery.*

JANUARY —, 1863.

On December 26, was ordered to march; took up line of march toward Murfreesborough; in the afternoon moved to the front, and fired on the enemy at and in the vicinity of La Vergne. One man wounded by premature discharge.

December 27, 28, and 29, no casualties.

December 30, was ordered to the right of the Twenty-second Brigade, and in the afternoon fired at long range for one hour; 1 horse killed.

December 31, in the morning took same position; was soon ordered to advance and move in connection with Brigadier-General Negley's division, which was on my right, the battery being on the right of the Twenty-second Brigade. General Cruft's brigade, General Negley's division, not moving to the front, and the artillery that was on my left being moved off, changed our section from the right to the left of the Twenty-second Brigade.

The fight at this time was general along our front and right and left of our position near the fence. The enemy showing himself in great numbers on the left, brought all the guns to bear on the cotton-field. The division of General Negley at this time gave way; we received a heavy fire from our right, held our position for a short time, and, the ammunition being expended, were forced to retire, the enemy following us close.

The caisson was ordered out and pieces followed. Had 86 rounds in the boxes when went to the supply trains, filled up the limbers of the pieces, and sent the caisson to the rear, it being all the ammunition that I could get.

Loss: Killed, 1; wounded (3 since died), 9; missing, 2; 15 horses killed.

In the afternoon of January 1, I was ordered up the pike by General Rosecrans. Not having anything to do, was ordered to relieve Captain Stokes' (Chicago Board of Trade) battery. Lieutenant Baldwin took the same position with three pieces, and Lieutenant Sturges, with three pieces, as was occupied by Captain Stokes' battery.

In the morning the enemy opened a heavy fire on the three pieces of Lieutenant Baldwin, who was soon forced to retire. Lost 1 man killed and 5 horses. Lieutenant Sturges, not replying to the enemy's fire, retained his position. In the afternoon was ordered to the left with three pieces, and opened fire as the enemy was being successfully repulsed. Remained on the field for the night.

On January 3, in the evening, Lieutenant Sturges opened fire on the woods in his front, and the enemy's pickets being driven back, was relieved from picket duty. One thousand six hundred and ten rounds of ammunition expended. The battery wagon, being among the wagon trains, was broken down; the axles have been used to repair carriages, and contents have been taken by different batteries. Lieutenants Baldwin and Sturges, as well as every one in the battery, did their whole duty.

Very respectfully, your obedient servant,
W. E. STANDART,
Captain Battery B, First Ohio Light Artillery.

Brigadier-General PALMER,
Commanding Second Division, Left Wing of the Army.

No. 121.

Report of Lieut. Norval Osburn, Battery F, First Ohio Light Artillery.

HDQRS. BATTERY F, FIRST OHIO LIGHT ARTILLERY,
January —, 1863.

SIR: I have the honor to submit the following report of the part taken by Battery F, First Regiment Ohio Volunteer Artillery, in the march from Nashville, and the recent engagements near Murfreesborough, Tenn.:

Our battery numbered on the morning of December 26, 1862, 125 enlisted men and 3 commissioned officers, Capt. Daniel T. Cockerill commanding.

We left our camp, near Nashville, about 9 a. m. December 26, 1862, receiving orders from you to march with the Nineteenth Brigade, commanded by Col. W. B. Hazen. Went into camp late in the evening near La Vergne, having taken no part in any of the skirmishing during the day.

December 27, received orders to move with the Nineteenth Brigade on the Smyrna pike. We came upon the enemy's cavalry at the crossing of the railroad. Colonel Hazen ordered a section of our battery to the front. Our cavalry made a brilliant charge, and drove the enemy beyond the Stewart's Creek Bridge, when the enemy rallied, under cover of a wood, and formed. We threw a few well-directed shell into their lines, which dispersed them, killing some 2 or 3, as we afterward ascertained. Bivouacked near the bridge for the night.

December 28 (Sunday), remained on the same ground during the day.
December 29, we moved with the Nineteenth Brigade to the Murfrees-

522 KY., MID. AND E. TENN., N. ALA., AND SW. VA. [Chap. XXXII.

borough and Nashville turnpike, joined our division, and encamped for the night on the right of the turnpike, about 3 miles from Murfreesborough.

December 30, heavy cannonading and brisk skirmishing during the day, but we, being held in reserve, did not take any part.

December 31, we were ordered forward with the Nineteenth Brigade early in the morning to take a position near a burnt brick house on the right of the turnpike, but before we gained the position designated we discovered the right wing giving way so rapidly before the enemy that it was deemed imprudent to advance farther. We received orders from Colonel Hazen to fall back. We then took up position between the railroad and turnpike. The enemy opened a destructive fire of shot and shell from two batteries before we got into position. Captain Cockerill, deeming it prudent, ordered the caissons to the rear under cover, but the drivers, misunderstanding the order, did not go where ordered, excepting one. Five of them got entirely separated from the battery, and could not be found until 12 m. We opened upon the enemy and maintained our position, with the support of the gallant Nineteenth Brigade, which suffered terribly from an enfilading fire of the enemy's artillery, until our ammunition was exhausted.

In the mean time we had 1 man killed and 6 wounded; we had 16 horses killed and disabled, Captain Cockerill having a horse shot under him. One limber was blown up by a shell from the enemy's artillery, killing and disabling the team, so as to render it impossible for us to bring the piece off the field, but was saved from falling into the enemy's hands by the unflinching courage of our supporting infantry. Two of our other pieces, upon examination, were found to be unfit for service, the axles being badly shivered.

After finding our caissons, replenishing our limbers, and repairing one of the disabled pieces, we discovered the enemy's cavalry attacking our train on the opposite side of the river, and we brought our guns to bear upon them, fired a few rounds, when a field officer ordered us to cease firing; that we were firing upon our own men; but we afterward found that he was mistaken. We were then ordered by Captain Mendenhall to take position in a corn-field to the left of the railroad, supported by the Nineteenth Brigade on our left, and the Tenth Brigade, Colonel Grose commanding, on our right.

No sooner had we taken our position than the enemy opened upon us with two batteries, one in front, the other on our left. Our fire for a short time was directed at the enemy's advancing columns of infantry with marked effect, but our attention was soon drawn to the enemy's artillery, which was doing much damage. Our fire was now directed at their batteries. We soon succeeded in silencing the battery on our left, but the one in our front kept up a destructive fire.

Our ammunition again becoming exhausted, we drew off the field, with the loss of 1 man killed. Our gallant and much esteemed captain was severely wounded in the foot by a 12-pounder solid shot, and had to be borne from the field, to the great mortification of his whole command. Eight enlisted men wounded, also 8 horses killed and disabled. We retired to the rear to replenish our ammunition chests and prepare some refreshments, also to seek some rest, which was so much needed. The command of the battery now devolved upon me.

January 1, we were held in reserve with the Nineteenth Brigade.

January 2, we took position early in the morning to the left of the railroad, by order of Captain Mendenhall, supported by the Twenty-first Brigade, Colonel Wagner commanding, the Seventh Indiana Battery on our right. Our skirmishers advanced across the field in our front, when, nearing the wood on the opposite side of the field, about 1,000 yards distant, the enemy opened upon them with artillery, to which we promptly replied, silencing the enemy's guns in a very few moments. We remained silent until 3 p. m., when the enemy made an advance on our left on the opposite side of the river. We opened fire on a battery in our immediate front, which was operating against our infantry, which was on the opposite side of the stream. We then received orders from Captain Mendenhall to change front, to fire to the left on the advancing columns of infantry which were pressing our left wing back. We here fired several shots, when we received orders from one of General Rosecrans' aides to take position in an open field to our left, on the right of the Chicago battery. We here kept up a continuous fire until ordered to cease. We then bivouacked for the night upon the field.

January 3, we were ordered to take the same position that we occupied the morning of the 2d instant. We were ordered inside the fortifications in the evening, where we remained during the night.

Not expecting to be called upon at the beginning of the recent engagements to make a report of the part taken by us, I am not prepared to give it as minutely as I desire, but I sum up our casualties as follows : Two enlisted men killed, 1 commissioned officer and 13 enlisted men wounded, 2 enlisted men missing, 24 horses killed and disabled ; lost 2 sets wheel harness, 6 sets lead harness, 6 Sergeant's saddles and bridles, 7 navy revolvers, and 12 paulins ; 2 gun-carriages disabled and 1 limber blown up.

I cannot speak too highly of the non-commissioned officers and men of the battery, who, with a very few exceptions, displayed great coolness throughout the entire contest, being the first time they were ever under fire of any consequence.

N. OSBURN,
Lieutenant, Comdg. Battery F, First Ohio Vol. Artillery.

Capt. W. E. STANDART,
  Chief of Artillery, Fourth Div., Army of the Cumberland.

No. 122.

Report of Lieut. Charles C. Parsons, Fourth U. S. Artillery, commanding Batteries H and M.

CAMP NEAR STONE'S RIVER, TENN.,
January 5, 1863.

CAPTAIN: Agreeably to instructions of yesterday, I have the honor to report the part taken by Batteries H and M, Fourth U. S. Artillery, under my command, in the recent operations against the enemy at this point.

These batteries opened fire for the first time on the morning of December 29, from their position commanding Stewart's Creek. After a few rounds of shell, the enemy's pickets were dislodged from their shelter, in the opposite heights, when, upon receiving information from General Palmer that our own infantry had forded the creek, I returned to the pike, crossed the bridge, and moved forward with our first line of reserves. About 1 mile from the creek I observed indications that the enemy had taken position with his artillery, awaiting our approach. With General Palmer's permission, we opened fire with our rifles, and again dislodged him, after which the advance was continued. We fired no more during the day, and at night moved into park, in rear of the line of battle, 3 miles from Murfreesborough.

On the morning of the 30th the enemy's artillery opened upon Cox's battery, to our left and front. During a spirited cannonading one of his shells struck in Battery H, killing 1 private, 1 horse, and wounding 1 sergeant. We moved at once into the position assigned us by General Palmer, and formed the batteries *en échelon*, supported on the left by the Tenth, and on the right by the Twenty-second Brigade. I found no occasion, however, to open fire until about 4 p. m., when, upon receiving information that an artillery demonstration from the left wing to support our right, then hotly pressed, was necessary, we commenced shelling the enemy's rifle-pits beyond the brick house; at the same time elevating the range of the rifled pieces, in order, if possible, to awaken the enemy's batteries. The latter effort was successful; but after exchanging a few shots, during which but 1 of my men was wounded, the enemy's fire was silenced. Satisfied that my position was an unfit one for artillery at night, I retired from the cedars after dark and went into park in the open field behind them.

On the morning of the 31st I thought it most in accordance with my instructions from General Palmer to remain in the position where I then was, in order to check the advance of the enemy, should he turn our right. At about 8 a. m. our infantry came falling back from the pine wood in this direction, when our batteries were swung around and brought at once into action. The approach of the enemy was parallel, instead of perpendicular, to our front, and when he had arrived within about 300 yards we opened upon his first line and column of reserves an enfilade fire of canister. The attempt to advance was continued for a few moments; then an effort to change front was followed by a feeble charge upon the batteries, when, upon being repulsed, the enemy fell back beyond our view. He reappeared shortly afterward to our left; but again, upon receiving our fire, fell back, and a portion of our infantry. I then took position upon the slight elevation, nearer the pike, in season to assist in checking the enemy's advance upon General Rousseau's position; after which both batteries changed front and opened fire, by order of General Palmer, upon the brick house, to co-operate with Colonel Hazen's brigade. So soon as I believed the enemy dislodged from this position, our pieces were moved to the front and directed upon his infantry, advancing into the cedar wood formerly held by the Twenty-second Brigade. The enemy, meanwhile, directed one of his batteries upon us, but I did not think it proper to reply, so long as our ammunition could be used with better effect upon his infantry. At about 12 m., just as I had nearly given out of ammunition, I received orders from Captain Mendenhall to retire.

At about 4 o'clock I moved to the front, by order of General Palmer, and from the elevation on either. side of the railroad opened upon the enemy's infantry. His advance was effectually checked, and at sunset I was ordered to retire and refit.

At daylight, January 1, we moved to a position on General Rousseau's front, where I was ordered by General Rosecrans. Except for the fire of the enemy's sharpshooters, whom we dispersed at intervals by firing spherical case, we were not actively engaged during the day, and at night retired to a position near the pike, where our horses were fed and watered.

During the night and on the next morning I was ordered by different officers to resume my previous position. I was obliged to decline obeying these orders, owing to those I had received from Captain Mendenhall, directing me to await his own. The position in which I was placed by this conflict of orders was exceedingly painful, but I found myself justified by subsequent events.

At about 4 p. m. of the 2d instant, after I had been placed in position by Captain Mendenhall on an elevation near Negley's division, two of the enemy's batteries opened upon us from the front, while a third gave signal for his last attack upon our left. I advanced the four rifles, holding my howitzers in reserve for the shortest range. The batteries around me were silenced far too soon, for when my rifled ammunition was exhausted I found that some scoundrel had led off my caissons, and I was left only with the howitzers to reply to the enemy's concentrated artillery fire. Fortunately, Captain Swallow's battery came up beside us, and the crest of the hill was held until our re-enforcements came up, when, with the assistance of Captain Stokes' battery, the enemy's guns were silenced.

We ceased firing, with our last shot exhausted. We have not again been engaged or under fire. I have to remark, in this connection, that if through the five consecutive days, during which we were thus more or less severely engaged, we expended an unusual amount of ammunition, it must be recognized that we have been longer, and, in general, more closely engaged than perhaps any other batteries of the army, and that nearly all our ammunition has been expended at short range.

The following are our casualties, &c.: Number of men killed, 2; number of men wounded, 14; number of men missing, 6; horses killed, 20; pieces disabled, 1; rounds of ammunition fired, 2,299.

In place of the piece disabled, the Nineteenth Illinois gave me one captured by them from the enemy.

I do myself honor, sir, in asking your attention to the efficient and meritorious services of Lieuts. Harry C. Cushing and Henry A. Huntington, both of the Fourth U. S. Artillery. Disregarding all personal exposure under all circumstances, and especially during the hottest fires of December 31 and 2d instant, these gallant officers discharged their duty with such coolness and fidelity that they deserve my most grateful mention.

My brave men look for their reward to the generous appreciation which has been freely offered them by the troops with whom they fought and the general commanding the division in which they serve.

I am, captain, very respectfully, your obedient servant,

CHAS. C. PARSONS,
First Lieutenant Fourth U. S. Artillery, Comdg. Battalion.

Capt. D. W. Norton,
Assistant Adjutant-General.

No. 123.

Reports of Brig. Gen. Charles Cruft, U. S. Army, commanding First Brigade, including skirmish at La Vergne, December 26.

Hdqrs. First Brigade, Second Division, Left Wing,
In the Field, before Murfreesborough, Tenn., January 8, 1863.

CAPTAIN : I herewith submit, for the consideration of the general commanding the division, the following report of the operations of this brigade in the recent action before Murfreesborough, Tenn.:

The brigade broke camp, near Nashville, on the morning of the 26th ultimo. The effective infantry strength of the command on leaving camp was 1,207. It consisted of the First Kentucky Volunteers, Col. D. A. Enyart; Second Kentucky Volunteers, Col. T. D. Sedgewick; Thirty-first Indiana Volunteers, Col. John Osborn, and Ninetieth Ohio Volunteers, Col. I. N. Ross. Captain Standart's Ohio battery, Company B, First Regiment, was attached to the command for temporary service.

After passing the picket lines near Nashville, this brigade had the advance, preceded by a portion of Colonel Kennett's cavalry command. After various trifling skirmishes and some artillery firing, the enemy's skirmishers were forced into the village of La Verne. Here quite a force of cavalry, artillery, and infantry (or dismounted cavalry) of the enemy disputed the occupancy of the place. General Palmer ordered me to drive the enemy from the woods on the left and take possession of the village from that quarter if daylight would permit. The Thirty-first Indiana and First Kentucky Volunteers were placed under command of Colonel Enyart and sent by me to accomplish this. Colonel Murray, of the Third Kentucky Cavalry, having been ordered to report to me for temporary duty, was placed upon the left flank of these regiments, and with his command acted very handsomely in protecting it and scouring the woods beyond.

The regiments above named advanced, toward nightfall, under cover of the cedars on the left, and finding the enemy in force near the frame church on the west of Stony Creek, attacked him, and, after a sharp discharge of musketry, ran in on a bayonet charge and routed him, forcing him across the creek and occupying the west bank. Our line of skirmishers was then placed in the field beyond the creek and along the outskirts of the village. The conduct of both regiments and all their officers in this skirmish was excellent.

The casualties in my command were 8 wounded.

The Thirty-first Indiana was withdrawn to the rear to encamp, and Colonel Enyart, with his regiment (First Kentucky) and a section of artillery, under Lieutenant Newell, was left to occupy the position until morning.

On the 27th ultimo the brigade reached Stewart's Creek, and went into camp at night.

On the 28th (Sunday), the command lay at Stewart's Creek, one-half of the brigade on picket duty.

On the 29th, the brigade advanced from Stewart's Creek in line of battle across the field, and at night took position in the front, on the right of the Nashville turnpike, in the cedars, near Cowan's burnt house, about 3½ miles west from Murfreesborough. An effective line of skirmishers was thrown forward and the open ground to our front firmly held.

On the 30th, the brigade rested in position, holding the point of woods where it was bivouacked, and the line of pickets to the front during the fierce engagement which occurred on the right of our line. During the night the Second Kentucky Volunteers (Colonel Sedgewick) was on picket duty.

This regiment succeeded in driving the enemy's picket from the crest in the field near the burnt house. His temporary shelters along the row of peach trees on the lane, some 60 yards east of the burnt house, were occupied by my troops after a sharp night skirmish, and held by them against two charges of cavalry until daylight the following morning. No pains were spared to explain my position during the night. Support was promised on my left, but did not come. If re-enforced on the flank, this position could probably have been held. One-half the effective force of my brigade was kept out all night on picket, trying to hold this advanced line. The attempt was partially successful. It was suspected that the enemy had rifle-pits and a large force beyond the crest; but the best reconnaissance I could make by night could not furnish the facts. Subsequent knowledge evinced the correctness of the supposition, and also demonstrated the fact that 5,000 troops could not have taken and held the crest which my brigade of 1,200 attempted to reach and hold.

On the 31st ultimo an order was received from the general commanding division, about 8 a. m., to advance in line, with the brigade supporting me on the right and left. The brigade was promptly put in motion, formed in two lines, as follows: The Second Kentucky and Thirty-first Indiana Volunteers (under general charge of Colonel Sedgewick as ranking officer) constituting the front line, and First Kentucky and Ninetieth Ohio (under general charge of Colonel Enyart as ranking officer) forming the second line; Captain Standart's artillery was formed in half-battery on each flank of the front line. The brigade, by this formation, exhibited a front of, say, 600 men, or less than a full regiment. Colonel Hazen's brigade was in position on my left and rear, and brigades of General Negley's division on the right. Upon giving the orders to advance, my skirmishers ran rapidly forward from the wood and engaged those of the enemy in the open field. They drove them, and my front line advanced promptly up to the rail fence in the margin of the woods. The enemy pushed toward us rapidly, and charged my line in great force and in solid rank. The fight became very severe and obstinate about 9 a. m.

My troops fought with heroism. Every officer and soldier acted well, and seemed to me to accomplish more than could be expected of him. For sturdy endurance, stalwart bravery, and manly courage, it does not seem to me that the conduct of these two regiments here could be surpassed. The enemy were driven back, although superior in numbers His charge was made in two lines, with the appearance of a four-rank formation, and in most admirable order and discipline.

After the first repulse, and before my line could be advanced, the enemy made a second charge (reserving fire until a close approach was had), which was more furious than before. The Second Kentucky and Thirty-first Indiana nobly held their ground, and, after some thirty minutes' well-directed fire, drove him back again for a short distance.

A respite of a few minutes in active firing enabled me to execute a passage of lines to the front, to relieve the first line, the ammunition of which was nearly exhausted. This maneuver was well executed, considering that it was done under a brisk fire of the enemy's skirmishers, the cross-fire of flanking parties that had already passed to the right and left of the line, and in face of two of the enemy's batteries.

The rear line (now front) was soon actively engaged. I attempted with it to assail the enemy, and ordered an advance. The First Kentucky, Colonel Enyart, on the right of the line, made a gallant charge, and drove the enemy before it, rushing forward to the crest of the hill, clear beyond and to the right of the burnt house. The fire was so severe from the enemy's force at the burnt house, on the left, that the order to move up the Ninetieth Ohio was countermanded; not, however, until many of the officers and men of this gallant regiment had pressed forward over the fence in line with the old First Kentucky.

The sad list of the killed and wounded of the Ninetieth and First Regiments speaks loudly of the courage and manhood they evinced in this charge. Standart, with his gallant gunners, was throwing in grape and canister from the flanks as my men ran forward to the charge, and thinning the enemy's ranks. He was too strong for us, however, and soon my gallant advance was beaten back to the point of woods. This point was still held. The brigade on the left was never pressed up to my front, and left me exposed from this quarter. General Negley's brigade, on the right, first advanced with me, but, yielding to the impulsive charge of the enemy, broke up, and a portion of it drifted in disorder immediately to my rear, and left me exposed to the cross-fire of the enemy from the woods on the right. We were now completely flanked. Our own troops impeded my retreat. Cannon, caissons, artillery wagons, and bodies of men in wild retreat filled the road and woods to my rear, precluding everything like proper and orderly retreat. Captain Standart's artillery ammunition was failing rapidly. He was shifting front constantly to keep off the enemy. The cartridges of my men were becoming short. Messages were sent to the rear for re-enforcements and for the reserve brigade of the division. The enemy's fire was upon three sides of my position, and apparently exactly to the rear, in the woods. It was impossible to get ammunition up, to communicate with the general commanding the division, or to obtain re-enforcements.

In this condition the ground was still held for some forty minutes longer than seemed right or proper. My command had some cover in the edge of the woods from the enemy's bullets, and still kept up a fire sufficiently strong to keep them from rushing into the woods. Seeing my little brigade failing rapidly, and many of its best men carried wounded to the rear, without hope of support, or further ability to hold on, I withdrew it in as good order as practicable. The enemy pressed closely, firing constantly into the retreating mass. We faced to rear, and covered the retreat of General Negley's men as well as could be done. The Second Kentucky Regiment brought off three pieces and the Ninetieth Ohio Volunteers one piece of abandoned artillery by hand which the enemy were rushing upon and about to capture.

Standart's battery was saved, with a loss of 3 men and 7 horses. It had but 16 rounds of ammunition when the order to retire was given. Upon falling back to the edge of the wood, on the west side, I met Major-General Thomas and reported to him, and, with his consent, continued to fall back across the open ground to the turnpike with my shattered forces, now numbering about 500. After forming in line along the turnpike (about 12 m.), the brigade was ordered, by a member of General Rosecrans' staff, to the left, to support a battery on the railroad. It took this position and held it during the remainder of the day and the night following.

On the 1st instant, the brigade was placed in line on the right of the division, in rear of the interval between the First and Third Divisions. After remaining thus until noon, it was advanced to the front to support Swallow's (Indiana) battery, posted on a commanding elevation to the left of the railway, and near the ford across Stone's River. During the day it was exposed to occasional shelling from the enemy's batteries.

On the 2d instant, rude breastworks were constructed back of the batteries, and the brigade held the same position behind them. It lay here during the severe fight across the creek on our left, supporting the batteries, and exposed to a heavy cross-fire from the enemy's guns A higher scene of cool moral courage, perhaps, has not been evinced during the war than that exhibited by my brigade on this memorable day. The line lay still and quiet behind the frail works we had been able to construct, with the shot and shell of the enemy coming from three directions and bursting above, in front of it, and all around it, while our own massed batteries were belching out their contents in front of and over it. The roar of artillery was terrific. The smoke from our own pieces and the bursting shell of the enemy at times obscured the line from view. By some wonderful Providence but three men of the brigade were killed here by the enemy's shells.

About dark, and when the enemy were driven upon our left, the brigade was advanced by General Palmer, he gallantly leading two regiments, the Thirty-first Indiana and Ninetieth Ohio, to the point of woods, a half mile to the front and left of our artillery position, and in line with our advance on the left, across the creek. I followed rapidly with the residue of the brigade across the open field to the general's right, and on line with him. Knowing nearly the position of a masked battery of the enemy hid by a crest in the field, I ordered the men to cheer loudly as we approached the latter. It had now become dark. As the noise of the last cheer died away, the enemy opened a fire of shrapnel from four small guns. The line immediately laid down under shelter of the crest, and for some thirty minutes the enemy continued to play at us. His shot passed just over our heads and struck the ground not to exceed 100 feet to the rear of our line.

Only a single casualty occurred here—the death of one man, struck by a shell. He was a straggler, not connected with my command, who was attempting to get to the rear. A strong picket, from my brigade, was posted in the wood and across the field, and the residue brought back to camp near the artillery. The latter position was maintained by the brigade until the evacuation of the enemy.

The following statement, condensed from the report of the medical officer of my staff, and the returns of the regimental commanders, exhibits the casualties of the brigade and battery, to wit:

Command.	Killed.		Wounded.			Missing.			
	Non-commissioned officers and privates.	Total.	Officers.	Non-commissioned officers and privates.	Total.	Officers.	Non-commissioned officers and privates.	Total.	Aggregate.
31st Indiana	5	5	1	44	45	3	34	37	8.
1st Kentucky	13	13	1	51	52	1	30	31	96
90th Ohio	17	17	5	67	72	2	46	48	137
2d Kentucky	9	9	2	56	58		10	10	77
Standart's battery	5	5		12	12		3	3	26
Total*	49	49	9	230	239	6	123	129	417

It may be observed that the above statement includes as wounded only those disabled from duty; slight hurts and trivial injuries are not included. Of those rated as missing, about one-half the number are stated by their officers to have been captured by the enemy in the battle of the 31st ultimo. The number of casualties, it will be noted, reaches nearly one-third of my effective strength.

Herewith are inclosed the reports of Colonels Enyart, Sedgewick, Osborn, and Ross, commanding the various regiments of the brigade,

* But see revised statement, p. 212.

and the report of Surg. J. B. Armstrong, medical officer of my staff. These reports will convey to the general commanding the division a better knowledge of many of the details of the recent actions than can be embraced in this general statement. They make honorable mention of many line and subaltern officers, which is deserving, and to which I crave special attention.

Before concluding, I beg to say to the general commanding the division that the officers and men of all the regiments under my command behaved uniformly well. Three of the regiments are veterans, and have left their impress upon former battle-fields. The Ninetieth Ohio, though for the first time thrown into a severe engagement, behaved admirably, and achieved for itself a right to rank with its associates in the old Twenty-second, or any brigade where high-toned valor is displayed.

Colonels Sedgewick, Enyart, Ross, and Osborn displayed marked gallantry on the field during the engagement, and handled their commands with courage, skill, and prudence. Their associates, field and staff officers, nobly seconded them. It is not in my power to make distinctions among these, where all performed their duty so bravely and cheerfully.

To Captain Standart and his gallant battery I am under peculiar obligations. This brave officer and his command have long been associated with this brigade. Although chief of artillery to the division, he preferred to fight his own battery, and was with it constantly. It rendered most effective service whenever put in action. His associate officers, Lieuts. N. A. Baldwin and E. P. Sturges, acted nobly throughout, and, with the gunners, drivers, and artillerymen of all grades, stood bravely to their work in the fight on the 31st ultimo, almost against hope, and safely brought away their battery. The battery was chiefly instrumental in saving the brigade in this position.

Of my personal staff, it affords me pleasure to say that Capt. W. H. Fairbanks, of the Thirty-first Indiana Volunteers, acting assistant adjutant-general, was at his post constantly, and, as on former occasions, behaved gallantly. Lieut. John Wright, of the First Kentucky, acting aide-de-camp, displayed high courage on the field and most soldierly bearing throughout. I recommend his promotion for gallantry in the action of the 31st ultimo. Lieut. J. C. Beeler, of the Thirty-first Indiana Volunteers, acting quartermaster to the brigade, discharged his duties properly and fearlessly; staid with his transportation while under fire, took care of it, and lost no Government property.

Surg. J. B. Armstrong made very ample and efficient arrangements for the wounded of the brigade, and, by his care and attention, in conjunction with the regimental surgeons, got them speedily from the field, and had them as well cared for as those of any other command. He reports to me good conduct on the part of all regimental surgeons.

The department of Captain Robinson, commissary of subsistence, was well managed. Though absent himself, it was left in good hands, and my troops were at all times during the days of the battle furnished with proper rations, regardless of the danger of conveying them.

Two orderlies from my escort (Corpl. James T. Slater and Private William Hayman, both of the Second Indiana Cavalry) deserve notice for their good conduct on the field, and are worthy of promotion.

With assurances of esteem to the brigadier-general commanding the division, I am, captain, very truly, yours, &c.,

CHARLES CRUFT,
Brigadier-General, Commanding First Brigade.

Captain NORTON,
   Actg. Asst. Adjt. Gen.. Second Div.. Left Wing. Fourteenth A. C.

HDQRS. SECOND DIV., TWENTY-FIRST ARMY CORPS,
DEPARTMENT OF THE CUMBERLAND,
February 6, 1863—8 p. m.

COLONEL: In reply to note of Lieutenant Stone, acting assistant adjutant-general, received an hour since at these headquarters, addressed to General Palmer, I will say that the records of the division adjutant's office do not contain data for an accurate statement of the effective force of this command, which went into the actions of 31st December and 2d ultimo. I am able to make an approximate statement only (in time limited by the note for reply), which is presumed to be substantially correct. One of the brigades of this division is at Readyville and another at Cripple Creek, and it is impossible to communicate with them without the lapse of some hours.

General Palmer has been absent since the 31st ultimo, and may have such statement among his private papers, which I have not examined.

The following, I think, nearly correct. It is as near as can be arrived at from figures here:

Brigades.	Commanding officers.	Effective strength December 31.	Effective strength January 2.
First	General Cruft	1,207	801
Second	Colonel Hazen	1,285	975
Third	Colonel Grose	1,768	1,139
Total		4,360	2,915

A more accurate statement can be furnished upon giving time to regimental commanders.

I am, colonel, very respectfully, yours, &c.,
CHARLES CRUFT,
Brigadier-General, Commanding.

C. GODDARD, *Lieut. Col. and Asst. Adjt. Gen.*

No. 124.

Report of Surg. James B. Armstrong, Thirty-first Indiana Infantry, Acting Brigade Surgeon.

HEADQUARTERS FIRST BRIGADE,
Hospital Second Division, January 9, 1863.

DEAR SIR: I have the honor to forward to you the following report of casualties of the First Brigade in the late battle near Murfreesborough, Tenn.:

Command.	Killed.	Wounded.
31st Indiana	5	46
1st Kentucky	13	52
2d Kentucky	1	31
90th Ohio	17	72
Total*	36	201

* But see revised statement, p. 212.

I cannot close this report without mentioning the names of Surg. B. H. Tipton, of the Ninetieth Ohio, Asst. Surgs. James E. Cox, of the Second Kentucky, and John Dickson, of the First Kentucky, who were regularly detailed as assistant operative surgeons in the hospital of the Second Division, and who most cheerfully performed their entire duty, aiding and assisting the wounded in all cases of emergency, and assisting in all the grave operations necessary to the relief of the wounded. Their untiring exertion, as well as great care and judgment in their duty, require an honorable mention to be made of them.

Perhaps it is inappropriate, yet I do not feel willing to close this brief report without mentioning the name of our superior surgeon in charge of this hospital—Surg. M. G. Sherman, acting medical director Second Division—whom I cannot make too high mention of for his high medical knowledge as a skillful surgeon and careful operator, ever ready and willing at all times, day and night, to render any service in his power to aid and comfort the wounded and dying. Indeed, it is not saying too much when I say, never have I seen a physician and surgeon more attentive to his duty, and, without exception, he has rendered entire satisfaction to all. He has endeared himself by the most tender ties to both patients and surgeons, and we shall ever feel grateful that he was in charge of this hospital during this most trying time.

Excuse the great brevity of this report, as time is precious, and we are yet very, very busy in the performance of our many duties to the afflicted.

With the most profound respect, I am, respectfully, your obedient servant, &c.,

J. B. ARMSTRONG,
Actg. Brigade Surg., 1st Brig., 2d Div., Army of the Cumberland.

Brig. Gen. CHARLES CRUFT,
First Brigade.

No. 125.

Report of Col. John Osborn, Thirty-first Indiana Infantry, including skirmish at La Vergne, December 26.

HDQRS. THIRTY-FIRST REGIMENT INDIANA VOLUNTEERS,
Camp near Murfreesborough, Tenn., January 7, 1863.

CAPTAIN: I have the honor of submitting to you the following report of the part this regiment participated in in the late action with the rebel army before Murfreesborough, commencing December 26, 1862, at the town of La Vergne, and ending before Murfreesborough January 3, 1863:

On the morning of December 26, when the United States forces were put in motion, our regiment was on picket duty some 6 miles southeast of Nashville. Before the pickets could be called in, and the regiment in line of march, the brigade to which they belonged was some 4 miles in advance. The regiment had a very fatiguing march through mud and rain. In passing the forces we had to take the fields; that made the march more arduous.

At 3 p. m. we joined the brigade 1 mile west of La Vergne. We were ordered to the advance, the First Kentucky Regiment on the right and our regiment on the left, the Second Kentucky Regiment and the

Ninetieth Ohio Regiment our support. We were ordered across a field to a woods to the left of the Murfreesborough road. Shortly after we had taken our position, the enemy commenced throwing shell into the woods. We immediately sent out two companies (E and K), and deployed them as skirmishers in advance of our line, and moved on the enemy in line. After advancing about 1 mile, we came in reach of the enemy's rifles. They opened a heavy fire from their rifles and two pieces of artillery, which overreached our line. Our men rushed forward with a shout, which caused the enemy to leave in great confusion.

We remained in this position until dark. We then moved a short distance to the right and bivouacked for the night.

Both officers and men conducted themselves with coolness and bravery, without receiving any injury whatever.

The next day we moved forward in line of battle, which was continued from day to day until the evening of December 29. We arrived at nightfall within a few miles of Murfreesborough, our brigade filing to the right of Murfreesborough pike about one-quarter of a mile, when we bivouacked for the night. Nothing occurred during the night, except heavy skirmishing in our front.

Early on the morning of December 30, 1862, we were ordered forward to the front of the grove in which we were bivouacked, which order was promptly executed, our regiment on the right and the Second Kentucky on our left, the Ninetieth Ohio supporting the Second Kentucky and the First Kentucky supporting our regiment. Upon arriving at this position, I was ordered by you to report to Colonel Sedgewick, of the Second Kentucky, whom you informed me would command the front line. I was ordered to deploy two companies in front of our line as skirmishers, connecting with a like corps from General Negley's division on the right, and the Second Kentucky on the left, which was immediately done by sending out Companies C and E. Before our lines were established the enemy opened on us a brisk fire of shell and ball, which continued all day, the balls of the enemy's sharpshooters reaching our lines.

About 4 o'clock in the evening we were ordered to advance our line to support a battery, which was done, and we remained in that position during the night, Companies A, B, I, D, and H relieving alternately C and E as skirmishers.

Early on the morning of the 31st we were again ordered to move our lines forward, which was done. Shortly after, our skirmishers were driven in by the enemy, our men reserving their fire until all their comrades had joined the line.

At this time a heavy force of the enemy appeared in our front, in an open field on a piece of rising ground, when they opened a severe fire upon our line, which was returned with a steady nerve by our men, which soon made them fall back. In a few moments they again returned to the crest of the field and attempted to charge our line, but the steady nerve of our boys and their deadly aim caused them again to retire. Our men getting short of ammunition, the First Kentucky Regiment came to our aid, and, passing our line, followed the enemy up into the field; but the heavy force of the enemy in front, and the regiment being exposed to a cross-fire from the enemy's battery, they were compelled to fall back with considerable loss. Our regiment remained in its former position, and held their fire until their Kentucky friends had passed to the rear. They again, with the coolness of veterans, poured another volley into the lines of the enemy, thinning their ranks, and making them the third time fall back to their former hiding place.

In a short time the enemy changed their point of attack, and appeared in great force on the left of our brigade and on the right, between our regiment and General Negley's forces. Both our right and left falling back, I was forced to order the regiment to fall back. The men obeying the order so reluctantly, and our left being so far turned before orders to fall back were received, caused our list of missing to be so large. We were also exposed to a cross-fire of the enemy's artillery.

Our regiment occupied the front line from the morning of the 30th until 11 a. m. on the 31st, with the exception of a few moments, when the First Kentucky occupied the front. The brigade, falling back through a dense growth of cedar, became scattered somewhat, but were formed again in line ready for any emergency.

Next morning (January 1) the regiment, with the brigade, took a position farther to the left, as a reserve.

January 2, the regiment again took a front position, sending out Company F as skirmishers, and during this day they laid in rifle-pits, exposed to a terrific fire from the enemy's artillery. Late in the evening Lieutenant-Colonel Smith and Capt. J. T. Smith, acting major, with General Palmer, led them in a splendid charge on the enemy, cleaning out a piece of woods occupied by them in force, both officers and men acting heroically, to the entire satisfaction of the brave general. I herewith send you a list of casualties.*

I cannot close this report without calling your attention to the gallant conduct of the officers under my command during the action. Lieutenant-Colonel Smith was always on the alert, cheering the men, passing along the line of skirmishers and the regiment; wherever duty called him, there he was during the whole engagement. Captain Smith, acting major, was always at his post, calm and collected, cheering the men and directing them where to strike the hardest blow. Captain Hallowell, acting adjutant, was always on duty, visiting the outposts and cheering the men, and where the balls flew thickest he appeared the oftenest. Captain Waterman, of Company A—I cannot speak too highly of his bravery. When one of his men fell, he picked up his gun and nobly kept it still in use. Captains Neff, of Company D, and Grimes, of Company G, were always at their posts, discharging their whole duty. Lieutenants Pickins, of Company B; Ray, of Company C; Scott, of Company E; Lease, of Company F; Brown, of Company H; Pike, of Company I, and Hager, of Company K, were in command of their respective companies during the whole action, and conducted themselves like old veterans, cheering their men and directing them to fire with deliberation.

Lieutenant Ford, of Company A, after the regiment fell back, on the morning of the 31st, after Captain Waterman was missing, took command of his company, and nobly imitated the gallant conduct of his veteran captain. Lieutenants Clark, of Company D; Hatfield, of Company H; Brown, of Company F; Fielding, of Company E; Roddy and McPhetridge, of Company G, and Haviland, of Company B, were at their places throughout the whole action, vying with each other in noble deeds of valor.

Assistant Surgeon Morgan was ever attentive to his profession, close in the rear of the regiment; close thereby he established his hospital, and refused to leave the wounded soldiers, but nobly remained with them, suffering himself to be taken prisoner rather than leave them to suffer. The same is also true in regard to Dr. McKinney, hospital steward, who was also taken prisoner.

---

* Embodied in revised statement, p. 212.

I cannot speak in too high terms of the conduct of Sergeant-Major Noble, who gallantly buckled on the cartridge-box and took a rifle, and was in the front rank of the line dealing out lead pills for the secesh. Sergeant Douglass, of Company K, who was discharging the duties of a lieutenant, was active in leading his brave men to the post of honor. And, indeed, it is not necessary for me to speak of individuals; every commissioned officer and non-commissioned officer and private of my command did his whole duty, without an exception, as did all the officers and men that came under my notice of the entire brigade.

Brigadier-General Cruft was at his post, ever watchful of his command, fearing no danger where duty called him; frequently riding along the line, waving his hat and cheering his command in the hottest of the contest.

Of the few killed on the field, three were of the color-guard.

JOHN OSBORN,
Colonel, Comdg. Thirty-first Regiment Indiana Volunteers.

Capt. W. H. FAIRBANKS,
  Captain and Acting Assistant Adjutant-General.

No. 126.

Report of Col. David A. Enyart, First Kentucky Infantry, including skirmish at La Vergne, December 26.

HDQRS. FIRST REGIMENT KENTUCKY VOLUNTEERS,
  Camp near Murfreesborough, Tenn., January 8, 1863.

GENERAL: I have the honor to make the following report of the operations of the First Regiment Kentucky Volunteer Infantry during the late engagement:

Pursuant to orders we left our camp, near Nashville, on the morning of the 26th ultimo, and proceeded toward Murfreesborough on the direct road. Arriving within 1 mile of La Vergne about 4 o'clock that evening, a considerable force of the enemy were discovered on the left of the road, and the First Brigade, Second Division, left wing, was ordered to operate against them. General Cruft ordered the First Kentucky to the front, and after considerable skirmishing with the enemy we charged and drove him across the creek into the woods near the town, with a loss of 2 men wounded.

The position thus gained was picketed and held during the night by the First Kentucky Regiment. Soon after dark a force of the enemy's cavalry attacked the left of our picket line, but were repulsed by Companies I and C, losing 1 man wounded.

On the 27th ultimo the regiment marched with the division as far as Stewart's Creek, where we bivouacked until the morning of the 29th; we then moved forward slowly and bivouacked about 2½ miles from Murfreesborough.

On the 30th, the regiment was assigned its position in line of battle, being on the right of the second line of the brigade, the brigade (General Cruft's) being on the right of the division (General Palmer's), and of General Crittenden's command. The Ninetieth Ohio was on our left, and the Thirty-first Indiana on our front in the first line. We lay on our arms during the day.

On the morning of the 31st ultimo, about 8 o'clock, General Negley's division took position on our right, and soon after the engagement commenced on our right wing. About 9 o'clock our front was hard pressed, and the brigade moved forward, the first line to the edge of the woods and the First Kentucky to support Standart's battery. The right of our army was being driven back, and the engagement was getting warm in our front, when General Cruft ordered the First Kentucky to move forward, and march over the Thirty-first Indiana into the corn-field, 300 yards in front of them, where we were exposed to the fire of two pieces of artillery, supported by a regiment of infantry, about 100 yards distant, and directly on our left flank.

Our position here was in advance of that held by any other regiment in the army. Being in danger of being cut off by a heavy column of the enemy advancing on our right, we retired in good order to the woods, where we took a new position behind a fence. We remained here but a short time, when the brigade fell back through the woods slowly and reformed on the road.

About 12 o'clock we were ordered forward to the support of a battery; remaining there but half an hour, the brigade was moved to the railroad, and in the evening formed a new line in rear of the division, where we lay during the night.

On the morning of the 1st instant we were again moved to the left to a new position, our left resting on the bank of Stone's River. About noon we were ordered farther to the left, to support Captain Swallow's battery, which was posted on an eminence. Here the regiment remained during the night.

On the 2d we threw up a breastwork of rails and stones, behind which we remained during the attempt of the enemy to turn the left of our line. After the signal defeat of the enemy at this point, we were ordered forward by General Cruft, until, coming in range of a battery of the enemy, we lay down until the fire had ceased. It being dark and nothing further to do, we retired to our former position, where we remained until the 4th instant.

A fuller and more definite report of the operations of the regiment will be made hereafter.

Very respectfully, your obedient servant,

D. A. ENYART,
Colonel, Commanding First Kentucky Volunteer Infantry.

No. 127.

Report of Col. Thomas D. Sedgewick, Second Kentucky Infantry, including skirmish at La Vergne, December 26.

HEADQUARTERS SECOND KENTUCKY VOLUNTEERS,
Camp near Murfreesborough, Tenn., January 18, 1863.

DEAR SIR: In compliance with orders, I have the honor herewith to submit a report of the part taken by the Second Kentucky Regiment in the operations before Murfreesborough, from December 26, 1862, to January 4, 1863, and also my report as commander of the front line of the First Brigade, composed of the Second Kentucky Regiment and Thirty-first Indiana, forming the extreme advance of the Second Division in the action of December 31, 1862.

Leaving our camps beyond Nashville on the morning of December 26, 1862, the brigade being the advance of the division, the division forming the advance of the left wing, my regiment, being the advance of the brigade, was deployed as skirmishers on each side of the road. This position was observed until we arrived within 1 mile of La Vergne, when, meeting with an obstinate resistance from the enemy's artillery and infantry, our cavalry and several regiments of infantry were sent forward, who drove the enemy from his ground. Here we bivouacked for the night.

On the morning of the 27th, we took our position in the line of march, and in the evening bivouacked on Stewart's Creek, remaining in said position until the morning of the 29th, when I was placed in command of the Second Kentucky and Thirty-first Indiana Volunteers, acting as reserve to the Third Brigade, in the general advance, in line toward Murfreesborough.

Arriving within 3 miles of Murfreesborough, we halted for the night, and on the morning of the 30th the brigade moved to a position about half a mile to the right of the pike. The two regiments under my command were thrown forward in the extreme advance of the division, in a cedar wood, and fronting an extensive open field, in which the enemy had thrown up upon commanding crests two rows of rifle-pits, and placed in position and embrasures two batteries.

Upon our right my front line skirmishers were supported by General Negley's division, and upon the left by Colonel Grose, commanding Third Brigade of our division.

Upon the crest of the first hill, immediately in front of and about 200 yards distant from my front line, the enemy had posted a number of sharpshooters, who annoyed us considerably during the day.

This position I determined to take, and, with General Cruft's consent, I strengthened my skirmishers and advanced toward that point, driving the enemy from it. The skirmishers of General Negley kept up the alignment and support on the right, but, through some misunderstanding, or otherwise, we had no support on the left, and during the night the enemy, being re-enforced, advanced and drove my outposts (holding this commanding and important position) back some 25 yards. This position, which would have been of immense advantage to us on the succeeding day, could not have been held or regained by the First Brigade (without the support on the left) without bringing on a sharp and unwished-for engagement.

On the morning of the 31st, the entire line of General Negley, immediately upon our right, became seriously engaged, and at 8 a. m. I received the command from you to move forward. I pushed forward the skirmishers until they had driven the enemy from and gained the crest of the second hill in our front; the front line of the brigade moved forward to a fence at the edge of the woods and at the foot of the first hill. At this juncture I found that the skirmishers and front line of General Negley's division had fallen back to a point in our rear, and that those on the left had come to a halt, and were engaged 200 yards in my rear.

By this time the enemy commenced emerging in heavy force from the woods in our front and on the right, and advanced in column, driving my skirmishers back to the front line. They moved forward in splendid style until they reached the crest of the first hill in our front, there halted, and delivered a well-directed volley full upon us. Captain Standart's battery immediately on my right, and my two regiments in front, simultaneously opened upon them, and with such effect that their front line gave way and fled to the rear; another line was forced up to the same position only to share the same fate; again fresh troops were advanced to the same point in the most perfect order. They planted their colors in the ground, and then extended their line by deploying to the right and left. The entire line threw themselves upon the ground and at once opened upon us and kept up a murderous fire. Here I reported the position of affairs in the front to General Cruft, and, in obedience to his order, hastened to the left, where I found that our support on the left had fallen back to a point near half a mile in the rear and farther to the left. In returning to report to the general, I discovered that General Negley's entire line had apparently given way, and his troops, artillery and infantry, were then hurrying through the woods in our rear to some point on the left, thus leaving our entire right flank open and unprotected.

Our position at this moment was one of great peril and danger. The enemy having driven back the brigade on our left, and gained possession of the high grounds around the burnt house, had there posted a battery, one section of which was turned on our position, hurling with fearful accuracy perfect showers of grape and shell. On the right they had pressed closely upon the retiring forces of General Negley, and had gained a point within 150 yards of our position, when Captain Standart, wheeling one section of his battery to the right, opened upon them with such effect that they were checked, but immediately opened upon our position a terrible fire of musketry.

Meanwhile their batteries and infantry in our front kept up an incessant firing. Thus we were completely exposed to an enfilading fire of artillery and musketry, rendering our position untenable, and our capture or annihilation almost certain if we remained. The men, however, stood up nobly, preventing several different attempts to gain our position from the front. At this moment I was informed that the Second Kentucky and Thirty-first Indiana, who had for over two hours held their position at the fence, fighting against superior numbers, had nearly exhausted their ammunition. I immediately informed General Cruft of the fact, and also of our situation in the front and on the flanks, and asked permission to withdraw. He refused, saying that it was necessary for us to hold our position, in order to protect the retreat of General Negley's artillery. I immediately went forward and relieved the Second Kentucky at the fence by the Ninetieth Ohio, the Thirty-first Indiana being relieved by the First Kentucky. The passage of lines by the advancing and retiring regiments was executed in the most perfect manner and in good order.

By the time the line had again been formed at the fence, the enemy, re-enforced, were pressing steadily forward on our flanks, and a force, eight columns deep, was advancing directly to our front. The First Kentucky sprang over the fence and advanced to meet them, but after delivering several volleys was forced to fall back to the fence. Here this regiment and the Ninetieth Ohio kept them in check. I returned to the rear line, and found that all efforts to obtain a fresh supply of ammunition for the Second Kentucky and Thirty-first Indiana had proved fruitless. I informed the general of the fact, and also that it was impossible for the two regiments, then hotly engaged in the front, to hold their position against such odds.

He again sent me to see the situation on our left and in the rear. I found the Second Brigade still holding their ground far in our rear, and one brigade of Negley's division formed in line facing immediately to our rear, and firing at the enemy, who appeared to be advancing in that direction. Of these facts and our isolated position I informed General Cruft, when he reluctantly gave me the order to have the brigade fall slowly back. After returning through the woods about 200 yards, I took command of my regiment, which was then reformed and faced to the front, and again advanced; but, having little support, and seeing the enemy advancing in strong bodies, I determined to withdraw and rejoin the brigade.

Just here I was informed that three pieces of artillery, belonging to Negley's division, had been abandoned in the woods some 400 yards to my right, and were about falling into the hands of the enemy. I immediately moved my regiment by the flank double-quick to the spot, and, having cut the traces, I brought them off in safety; and, placing them out of danger, I rejoined the brigade, which was formed on the railroad, in rear of former position.

The brigade remained near this place until 4 a. m. next morning, when we were advanced farther to the front, where we remained but a short time, when we returned to our former position.

After daylight my regiment moved with the brigade to a position farther to the left, where we remained until the afternoon, when we were moved still farther to the left, near Stone's River, to the support of Swallow's battery. Here we built small breastworks in our front and around the guns of the battery, and remained in an exposed condition, amid the rain, until the evening of January 3.

During the severe battle of that day on the left, my regiment was exposed to a terrible fire from the enemy's batteries, which had engaged those of Swallow and Parsons, which the brigade was supporting. Here I had 1 man mortally wounded by the explosion of a shell.

From that time to date we have participated with the brigade in all its movements. From the time our forces left Nashville up to this date my regiment has been in the advance, never in reserve; and on all occasions, and under all circumstances, both men and officers have performed nobly and heroically the task allotted them.

In the action on the 31st, and during the fight on January 2, soldiers never displayed more undaunted courage than those of the Second Kentucky. Those that live are heroes, every one; those that died are martyrs to their country's cause.

Lieut. Col. Warner Spencer, Maj. J. R. Hurd, and Capt. A. J. M. Browne deserve special mention and commendation for their gallantry and daring. In fact, every officer of the regiment is deserving of the greatest praise. Colonel Osborn, Lieutenant-Colonel Smith, and Captain Hallowell, of the Thirty-first Indiana Volunteers, merit great praise for the manner in which they discharged their various duties during the action of the 31st.*

RECAPITULATION OF CASUALTIES.

Killed	8
Mortally wounded	2
Seriously wounded	30
Slightly wounded	27
Missing	10
Total	77

Nine wounded were taken prisoners.

I have the honor to be, with much respect, your obedient servant,

T. D. SEDGEWICK,
Colonel Second Kentucky Volunteers.

Capt. W. H. FAIRBANKS,
Acting Assistant Adjutant-General.

_____

* Nominal list omitted

No. 128.

Report of Col. Isaac N. Ross, Ninetieth Ohio Infantry.

CAMP NEAR MURFREESBOROUGH, TENN.,
January 8, 1863.

SIR: I herewith furnish a report of the part taken by the Ninetieth Regiment Ohio Volunteer Infantry, First Brigade, Second Division, left wing of the Army of the Cumberland, in the series of movements beginning with the crossing of Stewart's Creek on Monday, December 29, 1862, and closing with the final repulse of the enemy on Saturday, January 3, 1863.

Monday forenoon the regiment moved across Stewart's Creek, on the Murfreesborough pike, deployed to the right of the pike, and formed in double columns, closed at half distance, in the rear of the Second Kentucky Regiment and on the left of the First Kentucky Regiment. It then moved parallel with the pike, and met no resistance during the day.

Monday night it bivouacked within 3 miles of Murfreesborough, still to the right of the pike, and nothing worthy of notice occurred during the night.

Tuesday morning the regiment moved by the right flank into a cedar forest still farther to the right of the pike, and took position, the Thirty-first Indiana and Second Kentucky Regiments forming the first line, while the Ninetieth Ohio, with the First Kentucky on the right, formed the second line, about 150 paces in the rear. The regiment maintained this position during the day, and was frequently under the fire of shells.

Tuesday night it bivouacked in the same position and in line of battle.

Wednesday morning, about 8 o'clock, the battle opened all along the right wing with both cannonading and musketry, with indications that our forces were being pressed back. About 10 o'clock the brigade moved forward in the order previously named; the Ninetieth Ohio being ordered to support the Second Kentucky, in case it needed assistance, and immediately the front line was engaged with the enemy. Firing continued to increase in rapidity and fierceness until the Second Kentucky sent back word that they needed support, when the Ninetieth Ohio was ordered forward on double-quick. It moved to the front, and was immediately engaged with the enemy, who appeared in great force, with two batteries planted within 150 yards of our position, which raked us with grape and canister.

In noticing the movements of the enemy, I observed him massing a heavy force behind a large house in our front and left, and preparing to plant a battery in the same position, and I also observed that our support on the left had given way. After consulting with Lieutenant-Colonel Rippey, I determined to report the situation of affairs to Brigadier-General Cruft, commanding the brigade, who was on the field, and asked support. Receiving no support, I immediately returned to the regiment and ordered it to fall back, we having maintained our position until the enemy, in overwhelming masses, were within at least 25 yards of us.

The regiment now fell back in considerable disorder through the cedar forest, in which it held position in the morning, to the railroad, where it rallied, and formed on the left of the brigade, supporting a battery. This position it maintained until dark, when the engagement closed. It then moved with the brigade to the right, toward the pike, and bivouacked for the night.

Thursday morning it moved to the left of the railroad and lay in line of battle all day, during which time it was exposed to the enemy's artillery, which frequently sent shell and shot into our ranks. The same day the brigade was moved forward to a small eminence, where it formed the advance line of battle, and supported the batteries which had taken position here. The regiment was on the right of the brigade. About 9 o'clock that evening it was moved back into a skirt of woods, where it bivouacked for the night.

Friday morning, at 7 o'clock, we moved to the same position, and in the same order of the day previous. Here we threw up a hasty breastwork, the enemy firing a scattering shell into our ranks until about 11 a. m., when he opened a fierce cannonade, which lasted about an hour.

About 4 o'clock that evening the enemy attacked our position in great fury, with both musketry and artillery, manifestly endeavoring to turn our left. The regiment held its position on the right of the brigade, behind the breastworks, which formed a protection from the enemy's shot and shell, which fell now in abundance all around us and once drove our artillery to the rear. Many of the shells struck our works, but none of the regiment were wounded.

Just before dark the brigade was ordered to fix bayonets and charge across the plain and clear a wood, in our front, of the enemy. This charge was made in gallant style, and for its behavior during this movement the Ninetieth received the thanks of the division commander. After dark the regiment returned to the position it had occupied during the day, and there remained all night. The charge just mentioned was the closing operation of the day's work.

All day Saturday the regiment was held in the same position until late at night, when it moved into a skirt of woods just in the rear of its former position.

It was not again brought into action, but held the position in the wood all day Sunday, when the information came that the enemy had evacuated Murfreesborough.

Where there was a general effort to perform their duty, it would be difficult to designate individual acts of bravery; yet I would say of the field officers that Lieut. Col. C. H. Rippey was at his post during the series of engagements, doing his whole duty, and doing it well. Maj. S. N. Yeoman was also at his post, cheering on the men and discharging his duty fully.

With one or two exceptions, the line officers performed their duty in a praiseworthy manner. Some of them exposed themselves to great danger in their efforts to save our artillery. Under the direction of Lieutenants Rains and Crow, a piece of artillery that had been abandoned was brought off the field in the very face of the enemy, and delivered to Captain Standart. Lieutenant Welch was wounded early in the engagement of Wednesday; Lieutenant Rains was injured by the concussion of a ball, but kept the field during that day; Captain Rowe and Lieutenants Baker and Selby were also wounded in the same action, while Captain Perry and Lieutenant Cook were taken prisoners.

In all the movements of the regiment the general commanding the brigade was present on the field, and, better than myself, can judge of its efficiency and the manner of its behavior during the entire series of engagements.

The following is a list of the killed and wounded in the Ninetieth

Regiment in the recent battles of December 31, 1862, and January 2, 1863.* The regiment went into this engagement with about 300 men, and came out with 176.

The foregoing report is respectfully submitted.

I. N. ROSS,
Colonel, Commanding Ninetieth Regiment Ohio Volunteers.

Capt. W. H. FAIRBANKS,
Acting Assistant Adjutant-General.

No. 129.

Reports of Col. William B. Hazen, Forty-first Ohio Infantry, commanding Second Brigade, including skirmishes on the Jefferson pike, near Stewart's Creek Bridge, December 27.

HEADQUARTERS NINETEENTH BRIGADE,
Stewart's Creek, December 28, 1862.

MY DEAR GENERAL: We found the enemy, about 300 strong, after leaving the main pike, about 1 mile. After getting them fairly started, my cavalry (90 strong) were directed to pursue at full speed, not giving them time to form. This was done, and a general stampede effected of all across the creek. They, by that time, had five times my cavalry force. As soon as my artillery arrived, they shelled them vigorously, driving them far beyond range. We made several prisoners, killed an officer, and lost 3 prisoners. Had I had a regiment of cavalry, I would have captured full 100. I have out now patrols in all directions, but nothing has been reported to me.

From various remarks and inquiries, made by the people here, I am of the opinion that Hardee is somewhere on our flank, and had we any sufficient knowledge, advantage could be taken of it. I can, however, learn nothing with any degree of certainty.

I am, respectfully, your obedient servant,

W. B. HAZEN,
Colonel, Commanding at Stewart's Creek.

General PALMER,
Commanding Second Division, Left Wing.

—

HDQRS. 19TH BRIGADE, ARMY OF THE CUMBERLAND,
SECOND BRIGADE, SECOND DIVISION, LEFT WING,
Camp near Murfreesborough, Tenn., January 5, 1863.

SIR: I have the honor to submit the following report of the operations of troops under my command since leaving Nashville, December 26, 1862:

The Nineteenth Brigade, which I have commanded since its organization in January, 1862, is now composed as follows: The Sixth Kentucky Volunteers, Col. Walter C. Whitaker; the Ninth Indiana Volunteers, Col. William H. Blake; the One hundred and Tenth Illinois Volunteers, Col. Thomas S. Casey, and the Forty-first Ohio Volunteers, Lieut. Col.

----

*Nominal list, omitted, shows 17 killed, 70 wounded, and 37 missing. But see revised statement, p. 212

Aquila Wiley, and upon leaving Nashville numbered an effective aggregate of 1,391, officers and men.

Being summoned before the commission, then sitting for the investigation of the official course of Major-General Buell, I did not, until evening, join the brigade, which had marched to within 2 miles of La Vergne. Just before my arrival, two regiments of the brigade had been thrown forward to the right of the road into a dense cedar brake; and—as its temporary commander did not think it necessary to throw forward skirmishers—the flank was marched upon a force of the enemy, who, firing from under cover upon the head of the column, killed one of the Ninth Indiana, wounded another, and wounded two of the Sixth Kentucky.

At 12 m., December 27, I was ordered to proceed, via the Jefferson pike, to Stewart's Creek, and save, if possible, the bridge crossing it. Ninety cavalry, of the Fourth Michigan, under Captain Mix, were sent to me. I placed these under charge of my assistant inspector-general, Capt. James McCleery, Forty-first Ohio Volunteers, with directions to keep me thoroughly informed of all that transpired, and as soon as the advance of the enemy was started to put spurs to his troop, and not slack rein until the bridge was crossed. The distance did not exceed 5 miles, and by disposing flankers, for perfect security, and urging the artillery and infantry to its fullest speed, I was enabled to keep within supporting distance all the time.

The enemy was not 3 miles from the bridge, and, by closely following my directions, a steeple-chase was made of the whole affair, the rebel force amounting to full five to our one. By the time the bridge was reached they had formed upon the opposite side of the creek, but were soon dispersed by a few discharges from our artillery.

In this affair we lost 1 cavalryman killed and 2 captured by the enemy. We took 10 prisoners, one of whom an officer, and killed 1 commissioned officer and several men.

Too much credit cannot be given to Captain McCleery, of my staff, and Captain Mix, of the Fourth Michigan Cavalry, for spirit and daring in this affair. On reaching the bridge my little party were upon the heels of the fugitives, and had they been armed with sabers, in place of rifles, by slashing upon their rear the rout would have been pushed to a panic.

On the 29th, I was ordered across to the Nashville and Murfreesborough pike, and, joining the division, proceeded to within 3 miles of Murfreesborough.

On the night of the 30th, the brigade was ordered to the front line, to relieve the Tenth Brigade.

This position we held at the commencement of the general action of the 31st, and it deserves special notice. It was in a cotton-field, 2½ miles from Murfreesborough, on the place of Mr. Cowan, the line being at right angles with the Nashville and Murfreesborough pike, the left resting on the pike at a point about 500 yards toward Nashville, from the intersection of the pike with the Nashville and Chattanooga Railroad. The railroad and pike at this point cross at a sharp angle. The position was utterly untenable, it being commanded by ground in all directions with covers of wood, embankment, and palisading at good musket range in front, right, and left. My brigade was formed in two lines, the right resting against a skirt of woods, which, widening and extending to the right, gave concealment to the Twenty-second Brigade, which was adjacent to mine, and, farther on, the entire division of Negley. On the left of the pike was Wagner's brigade, of Wood's division. The

Sixth Kentucky and Forty-first Ohio were in the front line, the Sixth being on the right and the Forty-first on the left. The Ninth Indiana and One hundred and tenth Illinois were in the second line, the Ninth being on the right and the One hundred and tenth on the left.

A fierce battle had commenced at daylight on our right, and progressed with ominous changes of position until about 8.30 a. m., when it could no longer be doubted that our entire right was being driven around in rear to a position nearly at right angles to its proper line. At this moment authority was given to move forward to seize the commanding positions in front, and the burnt house of Mr. Cowan. The line advanced about 20 yards, when orders were given to face to the rear, the necessity of which was apparent, the enemy having by this time pushed forward quite to our rear. He at the same moment broke cover over the crest in front, at double-quick in two lines. I faced my two right regiments to the rear, and, moving them into the skirt of woods, commenced to engage in that direction. My two left regiments were retired some 50 yards, and moved to the left of the pike to take cover of a slight crest, and engaged to the front, the regiment of Wagner's brigade occupying that ground (the Fortieth Indiana, Colonel Blake) having fallen much to the rear of it.

The enemy had by this time taken position about the burnt house, and the action became at my position terrific. The efforts of the enemy to force back my front and cross the cotton-field, out of which my troops had moved, were persistent, and were prevented only by the most unflinching determination upon the part of the Forty-first Ohio and One hundred and tenth Illinois Volunteers to hold their ground to the last. All the troops of General Wood, posted on our left, except two regiments guarding a ford some distance to our left and rear, were withdrawn to repel the assault upon the right, so that the Nineteenth Brigade was the extreme left of the army.

Upon this point, as a pivot, the entire army oscillated from front to rear the entire day. The ammunition of the Forty-first Ohio Volunteers was by this time nearly exhausted, and my efforts to replenish were up to this time fruitless. I dispatched word to the rear that assistance must be given, or we must be sacrificed, as the position I held could not be given up, and gave orders to Lieutenant-Colonel Wiley to fix his bayonets and to Colonel Casey (without bayonets) to club his guns and hold the ground at all hazards, as it was the key of the whole left. The responses satisfied me that my orders would be obeyed so long as any of those regiments were left to obey them. I now brought over the Ninth Indiana from the right, and immediately posted it to relieve the Forty-first Ohio Volunteers.

It is proper to state here that, in advancing to this position under a galling fire, a cannon-shot passed through the ranks of the Ninth Indiana, carrying death with it, and the ranks were closed without checking a step. The Forty-first Ohio Volunteers retired with its thin ranks in as perfect order as on parade, cheering for the cause and crying for ammunition.

A few discharges from the fresh regiments sufficed to check the foe, who drew out of our range, and at 9.30 lull and rest came acceptably to our troops upon the left, their advance upon the right having also been checked.

At about 10 a. m. another assault was made by the enemy, in several lines, furiously upon our front, succeeding in pushing a strong column past the burnt house, covered by the palisading, to the wood occupied by the Twenty-second Brigade and the Sixth Kentucky. All of our troops occupying these woods now fell back, exposing my right flank, and threatening an assault from this point that would sweep away our entire left. General Palmer seeing this danger, and knowing the importance of this position, sent the Twenty-fourth Ohio Volunteers, Colonel Jones, and a fragment of the Thirty-sixth Indiana, under Captain Woodward, to my support. I posted these with the Forty-first Ohio Volunteers, with the left of the line resting upon the Ninth Indiana, and extending to the right and rear, so as to face the advancing column. It was a place of great danger, and our losses were here heavy, including the gallant Colonel Jones, of the Twenty-fourth Ohio Volunteers; but with the timely assistance of Parsons' battery the enemy was checked, and the left again preserved from what appeared certain annihilation.

The enemy now took cover in the wood, keeping up so destructive a fire as to make it necessary to retire behind the embankment of the railroad, which only necessitated the swinging to rear of my right, the left having been posted on it when the action commenced in the morning. A sharp fight was kept up from this position till about 2 p. m., when another assault in regular lines, supported by artillery, was made upon this position in force. This assault was resisted much more easily than the previous ones, there being now a large force of our artillery bearing upon this point. The enemy also extended his lines much farther to the left, causing something of a diversion of our troops in that direction. The One hundredth Illinois, Colonel Bartleson, was sent to me by the general commanding the army, which was posted with the One hundred and tenth Illinois and Ninth Indiana, in line to the front, with the right resting on the railroad. Here, with a German regiment (I think the Second Missouri), these regiments fought the remainder of the day, the troops previously occupying this position retiring on the last approach of the enemy.

A period of about one hour now ensued with but little infantry firing, but a murderous shower of shot and shell was rained from several directions upon this position, which was covered by a thick growth of timber. A portion of Wood's division, now commanded by General Hascall, was also posted in these woods, in rear of my troops.

At about 4 p. m. the enemy again advanced upon my front in two lines. The battle had hushed, and the dreadful splendor of this advance can only be conceived, as all description must fall vastly short. His right was even with my left, and his left was lost in the distance. He advanced steadily, and, as it seemed, certainly to victory. I sent back all my remaining staff successively to ask for support, and braced up my own lines as perfectly as possible. The Sixth Kentucky had joined me from the other side some time previously, and was posted just over the embankment of the railroad. They were strengthened by such fragments of troops as I could pick up until a good line was formed along the track. A portion of Sheridan's division was also but a few hundred yards in rear, replenishing their boxes. A portion of General Hascall's troops was also on the right of the railroad.

The fire of the troops was held until the enemy's right flank came in close range, when a single fire from my men was sufficient to disperse this portion of his line, his left passing far around to our right. This virtually ended the fight of the day.

My brigade rested where it had fought, not a stone's throw from where it was posted in the morning, till withdrawn at dawn next day.

The Sixth Kentucky was not under my immediate observation from the first assault till late in the day, but the portion of time it was with me (and I have reason to believe at all other times) it fought unflinchingly, and is deserving of all praise. It repelled three assaults of a rebel brigade from the burnt house, endeavoring to reach the wood, and only retired when its ammunition was exhausted. Among its killed are Lieutenant-Colonel Cotton and Captain Todd, men possessing in the highest degree the esteem and confidence of their brothers in arms, and who will be deeply lamented by a large circle of friends.

The One hundred and tenth Illinois, a new regiment never before under fire, displayed that fearless courage one admires in veterans. Its losses from artillery were heavy. The Ninth Indiana and Forty-first Ohio maintained fully their well-known reputation of perfect discipline, dauntless courage, and general fighting qualities. Their steadiness under fire was incredible. The latter regiment was taken by its commander while resting, without orders, to repel an assault of the enemy's cavalry upon our train, which object it effected and returned to its position.

The casualties of this day were as follows:

Command.	Killed.		Wounded.		Missing.	Total.
	Officers.	Men.	Officers.	Men.		
41st Ohio	1	12	4	98	17	132
110th Illinois	1	6	3	43	12	65
9th Indiana	1	9	5	89	13	117
6th Kentucky	2	11	5	85	10	113
Total	5	38	17	315	52	427

A large list also occurred among the other troops under my immediate control on the field, but they will be reported by their proper brigade commanders. I am under many obligations to the commanders of these troops (many of their names I do not know) for their implicit obedience to my orders, but particularly to Colonel Bartleson, of the One hundredth Illinois, for valuable services.

To the officers commanding regiments of this brigade too much consideration cannot be given, both by their commanding generals and their country. Besides the actual service rendered their country this day, such heroic and daring valor justly entitles these men to the profound respect of the people of the country. To them the commander of the brigade feels that he owes everything this day, as there were times when faltering upon their part would have been destruction to the left of the army. He owes the success of this day not only to proper conduct on the field, but more to strict obedience to orders, and a manly co-operation in bringing this brigade to its present high state of efficiency and discipline, through constant care, labor, and study, for a period of over twelve months. This alone has insured this proud result. To Lieutenant-Colonel Suman also, of the Ninth Indiana, twice wounded, great credit is due for gallantry.

Captain Cockerill, Battery F, First Ohio Volunteer Artillery, showed, as he always has, great proficiency as an artillery officer. He was also severely wounded. Lieutenant Osburn, of the same battery, being at the rear to fill his caissons when the train was menaced, turned his pieces upon the enemy, and greatly assisted in dispersing them.

Lieutenant Parsons, of the Fourth U. S. Artillery, who was in the thickest of the fight near my position all day, is also deserving of the warmest consideration of the Government for the efficient manner in which his battery was maneuvered.

To my staff, also, everything can be said in their praise. To Maj. R. L. Kimberly, Forty-first Ohio Volunteers, acting assistant adjutant-general; to Lieuts. William M. Beebe and E. B. Atwood, of the same regiment, aides-de-camp; to Capt. L. A. Cole, Ninth Indiana, topographical officer, for intelligently carrying orders and assisting to post troops, under a galling fire, the whole day; to Capt. James McCleery, Forty-first Ohio Volunteers, acting inspector-general, for assisting to bring forward ammunition even after being wounded; to Harry Morton, Sixth Kentucky, volunteer aide-de-camp, for similar service; to Lieut. F. D. Cobb, Forty-first Ohio Volunteers, acting commissary of subsistence, for keeping me intelligently informed of what was transpiring beyond my immediate vision—all, for unqualified bravery, are deserving, as they have, my warmest thanks, and the consideration of the Government.

Dr. M. G. Sherman, Ninth Indiana, surgeon of the brigade, was acting medical director of the division, and removed from my immediate notice, yet I have reason to call favorable notice to this officer.

Lieut. J. L. Chilton, Sixth Kentucky, acting brigade quartermaster in the absence of Captain Johnson, exercised great capacity in caring for and keeping from the enemy the train of the brigade.

I am under many obligations to the general commanding the division for the confidence reposed in me in vesting with me the management of so important a portion of the field. By seizing the little crest occupied by my troops early in the morning, not exceeding 2 feet in height, and later the railroad embankment, hundreds of lives were saved, the strength of my brigade doubled, and the position successfully held. This will account for the smaller list of casualties than that of some brigades which did less fighting.

I am happy to report, with some 20 miserable exceptions, no straggling in this brigade.

The casualties of my *personnel* were as follows: The colonel commanding the brigade was bruised by a ball upon the shoulder, and his horse was killed; Capt. James McCleery, Forty-first Ohio Volunteers, acting inspector-general, shot through the leg; First Lieut. William M. Beebe, Forty-first Ohio Volunteers, aide-de-camp, wounded in the head, and horse shot; Capt. L. A. Cole, Ninth Indiana, topographical officer, slightly wounded in the foot; Orderly [Henry] Diedtrich, sergeant Fourth Kentucky Cavalry, mortally wounded, and horse shot, and Bugler Lehmann, Sixth Kentucky, horse shot.

Close observation of the conduct and character of our troops for the past few days has confirmed me in a long-settled belief that our army is borne down by a lamentable weight of official incapacity in regimental organizations. The reasonable expectations of the country can, in my opinion, never be realized until this incubus is summarily ejected, and young men of known military ability and faculty to command men, without regard to previous seniority, are put in their places. I saw upon the field company officers of over a year's standing who neither had the power to or knowledge how to form their men in two ranks.

On the 2d instant my brigade was ordered across the river to support Colonel Grose, commanding the Tenth Brigade, then in reserve to General Van Cleve, whose division (the only one on that side of the river) had been vigorously attacked by the enemy. I reached the field about 4 p. m., finding his entire division put to rout. The enemy had been checked by Colonel Grose and a portion of Negley's division, and the several batteries from the point occupied by General Cruft's brigade. It was difficult to say which was running away the more rapidly, the division of Van Cleve to the rear, or the enemy in the opposite direction. I found myself in command of all the troops on that side of the river.

Leaving three of my regiments in position as a reserve, I pushed forward with the portion of Colonel Grose's brigade already moving, and the Forty-first Ohio Volunteers, pursuing the enemy beyond all the ground occupied by our forces before the fight. I here formed the best line circumstances would admit of, the Forty-first Ohio Volunteers being the only regiment wholly in hand. The others were badly broken; the only idea of their officers seeming to be to push on pell-mell, which, if carried beyond the point occupied, might have resulted disastrously. I succeeded in checking the straggling to the front, with the aid of Colonel Grider, of the Ninth Kentucky, who came forward and performed this valuable service after his regiment had gone to the rear.

I was relieved by the fresh division of General Jefferson C. Davis, who arrived just at dark. When far advanced in the pursuit, a portion of General Negley's batteries, far in the rear, were firing on my line, and continued to (without damage) till an aide-de-camp was sent to ask that it be discontinued.

After forming my advance line, a battery of the enemy, about 400 yards in front, continued to fire upon us with great rapidity. I ordered the Forty-first Ohio Volunteers to fire one volley upon it. No more firing took place on either side, and the weakness of my line prevented my going farther.

The next day three caissons and several dead men and horses were found at this point. It was in this fight that the famous rebel General Roger W. Hanson was killed and General Adams was wounded, whether in their advance or retreat I never knew.

First Lieut. F. D. Cobb, Forty-first Ohio Volunteers, acting aide-de-camp, comported himself with great gallantry on the field. Seizing the colors of the Thirty-sixth Indiana, that had been shot down, he galloped forward, rallying many stragglers, who, though going in the right direction, were doing so inefficiently, and on their own account.

My casualties in this action were slight, and, in all, since leaving Nashville, are:

	Killed.	Wounded.	Total.
Commissioned officers	5	17	22
Enlisted men	41	318	359
Total missing			52
Aggregate	46	335	433

I would respectfully call the attention of the general commanding the division to accompanying reports of regimental commanders, and of Lieutenant Chilton, in charge of train; also to explanatory sketch.*

I am, very respectfully, your obedient servant,

W. B. HAZEN,
Colonel, Comdg. 19th Brig., Second Brig., Second Div., Left Wing.

ASSISTANT ADJUTANT-GENERAL,
Fourth Div., Army of the Cumberland, Second Div., Left Wing.

---

* Not found.

No. 130.

Report of Surg. Mason G. Sherman, Ninth Indiana Infan.ry, Acting Brigade Surgeon.

HOSPITAL OF SECOND DIVISION,
Left Wing, near Murfreesborough.

SIR: As brigade surgeon of your brigade, I have the honor to submit the following report of the casualties in the brigade during the several days' fight before Murfreesborough:

One hundred and tenth Illinois: Killed, 7; wounded, 28; total, 35. Ninth Indiana Volunteers: Killed, 14; wounded, 93; total, 107. Sixth Kentucky: Killed, 12; wounded, 71; total, 83. Forty-first Ohio Volunteers: Killed, 17; wounded, 100; total, 117. The whole number killed in the brigade, 50; wounded, 292; total, 342.*

In consequence of our hospital being nearer the battle-field than any other during the time of the engagement, our hospital was necessarily crowded with hundreds of the wounded from other divisions, making our duties very responsible and laborious.

And I cannot in justice submit this report without making honorable mention of all the medical officers in your brigade. They have been untiring in their exertions, night and day, to relieve the suffering of all who came under their notice. After looking after the wounded in their respective regiments, they devoted their skill and attention cheerfully to others, relaxing no effort to make them comfortable. Their unwearied attention to duty during this engagement merits the esteem and confidence of all who know them.

Very respectfully,

M. G. SHERMAN,
Brigade Surgeon, Second Brigade, Second Division, Left Wing.

Col. W. B. HAZEN,
Commanding Second Brigade, Left Wing.

No. 131.

Report of Lieut. John L. Chilton, Sixth Kentucky Infantry, Acting Brigade Quartermaster.

CAMP NEAR MURFREESBOROUGH, TENN.,
January 8, 1863.

DEAR SIR: In compliance with an order from you of this morning, I herein submit to you a report of what transpired with the train of your brigade during the engagement near Murfreesborough, Tenn., on Wednesday, January 1.

Having arrived on the field Monday, December 30, 1862, at a late hour in the night, I parked the train near to, and on the left of, where the brigade was then lying.

On Tuesday, December 31, 1862, early in the morning, believing that the train was too near to what I supposed to be our line of battle, I moved the train to the left and rear of where the brigade had rested the night previous, a distance of about one-fourth of a mile, where it remained until the fight began on Wednesday, January 1. Soon after

---

* But see revised statement, p. 212.

the fight began I received an order from a lieutenant (whom I supposed to be an aide of General Rosecrans) to form the train into a hollow square. I had not more than completed the work before I received another order to move the train toward Stone's River, and to the rear of the left of our army; the several trains of the army were ordered to the same place. Arriving at the crossing over the railroad at the same time, there seemed to be a disposition among the teamsters to crowd through and break the trains. I halted my train until others crossed. During this time of waiting I put several men, who seemed to have nothing to do, to work carrying rails to make another crossing, which by the time it was completed the way was clear. I moved my train over and near the river, and had it drawn up in park, when a shell from a gun of the rebels fell among the wagons, wounding a mule of the train—so much so that it had to be cut loose and left. Then I moved nearer to the river, when an order came for us to cross the river and to halt, which was not more than accomplished before an order came to recross the river, which was done. I recrossed, held the train in moving order, and in a few minutes a squad of rebel cavalry came in view, causing a panic among the teamsters and stragglers who had by this time gathered along the train. I cautioned the teamsters of my train to be composed, while I moved up and assisted in clearing the road, which was soon done. I then moved my train off in good order into the woods to the rear of the center of our army, where I held it until late in the evening, when I moved it to the side of the pike.

When night came on, Lieutenant Blythe, quartermaster Forty-first Ohio Volunteers, and myself rode along to the right of our army to see if we could not pick upon some place to park the train that it might be safe during the next day, and thought best to move near the hospital of our division, which we did; but at 1 o'clock at night I received an order from General Palmer to issue all rations on hand and return to Nashville with the train, which was done, leaving the field at 8 a. m. January 2, arriving at Nashville at 5 p. m. of the same day without any loss or disturbance, save the threatening of an attack from rebel cavalry; the casualties in all amounting to the loss of one mule belonging to the One hundred and tenth Illinois Volunteers, and one single set lead harness belonging to same.

Yours, respectfully,

J. L. CHILTON,
First Lieut. and Actg. Quartermaster Sixth Kentucky Vols.

Col. W. B. HAZEN,
Commanding Second Brigade.

No. 132.

Report of Col. Thomas S. Casey, One hundred and tenth Illinois Infantry

HDQRS. ONE HUNDRED AND TENTH ILLINOIS VOLS.,
Camp near Murfreesborough, Tenn., January 8, 1863.

As commander of the One hundred and tenth Regiment Illinois Volunteers, I have the honor to submit the following report of its operations and casualties in the recent engagements before Murfreesborough:

On the morning of December 31, the regiment, which was in double column in reserve, was advanced to take position in the second line of battle, its left resting on the right of and near the Murfreesborough and Nashville pike.

About 8 a. m. the regiment began its advance on Murfreesborough. Just then the firing, which had been heard at an early hour on our right, appeared to be rapidly nearing our right and rear, and the regiment had advanced scarce its front, when the right-about was ordered, and it was moved to its former position, faced to the front, and almost immediately after moved by the left flank to a slight elevation on the right of the railroad, the highest point of which joins the railroad embankment, and there faced to the front, its left extending across the railroad, its entire right wing about 20 paces in rear of, and parallel to, the left wing of the Forty-first Ohio Volunteers, which was then engaged with the enemy, who had advanced upon the front of our brigade.

This position was maintained for a considerable time. I advanced the left wing of the regiment to the crest of the hill, where they became immediately engaged with the enemy, who had broken cover at the burnt brick house. Twice the enemy came forward as if intending to charge, when Colonel Hazen directed me to have my command fix bayonets. I replied that we had no bayonets, and received the answer that we should club muskets if attacked; but the enemy did not charge our position. The whole right of the army having apparently given way, I was ordered to cross the railroad. Having crossed the road, we took a position perpendicular to it, and in front of the wood facing the enemy, the One hundredth Illinois Volunteers being on our right. This position had hardly been taken before the enemy appeared in force beyond the fence and across the cotton-field, directly in our front. The firing began at once. Here the fire of small-arms was incessant and terrific. My command suffered mostly from the rebel batteries to the left and rear of the burnt brick house. Here the enemy appeared twice on our front, in column, but failed to cross the fence.

Night ended the conflict. My command slept on the ground we fought on, in the extreme advance, until the early dawn of the 1st instant, when we, with the rest of the brigade, took a position on the bank of Stone's River. My command was not again engaged with the enemy.

On Friday, the 2d instant, with the rest of the brigade, my command crossed the river to repel the attack of the enemy, but did not become engaged, the enemy having retired from before the assaults of the Third Brigade, commanded by Colonel Grose.

I subjoin the following list of casualties :* Killed, 7; wounded, 49; missing, 2. Total, 58.

Respectfully submitted.

THOS. S. CASEY,
Colonel One hundred and tenth Illinois Volunteers.

Maj. R. L. KIMBERLY, *Acting Assistant Adjutant-General.*

No. 133.

Report of Col. William H. Blake, Ninth Indiana Infantry.

HEADQUARTERS NINTH INDIANA VOLUNTEERS,
In Camp, near Murfreesborough, Tenn., January 6, 1863.

CAPTAIN: I have the honor to submit the following report of the part taken by the Ninth Indiana Infantry in the battle of Stone's River, December 31, 1862:

Bivouacking in the dense cedars on the right of the Nashville pike

---

* Nominal list omitted.

the night preceding the engagement, I moved, at dawn, in double column to the front, relieving the Thirty-sixth Indiana Infantry, of the Third Brigade. As there was no indication of an immediate advance, I stacked arms, and permitted my men to build fires.

At 6.30 a. m. heavy cannonading and continued discharges of musketry were heard on our extreme right, which gradually approached our position, and were borne rapidly to our rear, until the sound of conflict was immediately in our rear, on the Nashville pike.

At 7 a. m. I received an order to advance in line of battle, supporting the Sixth Kentucky Infantry. Moving forward but a short distance, received orders to face by the rear rank and march to the rear. At this time the enemy's artillery, in our rear, had opened fire on our columns; was halted, and moved by the left flank in the direction of the pike and railroad. I here received orders to move rapidly to the support of Colonel Grose's brigade, then hotly engaged with the enemy's infantry, but a few paces to my right and rear. While forming on the left of the Third Brigade, I lost 2 men killed and several wounded by an enfilading fire from the enemy's artillery on my former front. The Third Brigade was closely engaged firing obliquely to their right.

The enemy did not appear in my front, and, by orders, I changed front to the rear on first company, and ordered my men to lie down. The enemy had advanced in our front, occupying the burnt house and grounds with a force of infantry and a battery of artillery. Remaining in this position but a short time, I was ordered to relieve the Forty-first Ohio Infantry, whose ammunition was said to be exhausted at this early hour in the action. I marched by the left flank at double-quick time, passing under the enemy's fire. Five men of Company H were knocked down by a single shell, two of whom were mortally wounded. Forming on the left of the pike, with my right resting near it, my left on the railroad, I moved forward in line of battle to the low crest, and relieved the Forty-first Ohio Volunteers.

The rebels then occupied the burnt house with one battery and their infantry, partially covered by the out-houses and a stockade fence extending to the pike. I at once opened fire on them, and but a short time intervened until their artillery limbered up, and retired in confusion to the rifle-pits on the ridge, where they went to battery and opened fire. After three-quarters of an hour the fire from the infantry in our front slackened, and many of them ran to the rear, in disorder. At this time a brigade of the enemy's infantry advanced from their rifle-pits, and marched obliquely in the direction of my position. Although at long range, I at once opened fire on them, which thinned their ranks as they continued to approach. As they drew nearer, one of the regiments moved to the front, and advanced at the charge step upon my position. My men poured upon them a galling and deliberate fire that halted them within 75 yards of our line, where they lay down, covered somewhat by the cotton furrows, and opened fire on us, from which we suffered. Their colors had been struck down three times during their advance, and every field officer of the regiment was killed. (The regiment was the Sixteenth Louisiana, Colonel Fisk, of General Chalmers' brigade, composed of the Ninth and Tenth Mississippi and Sixteenth Louisiana. These facts were obtained from prisoners and burial parties that evening, and, I presume, are reliable.*) I received orders to fix

---

* The Sixteenth and Twenty-fifth Louisiana Regiments (consolidated) were in D. W. Adams' brigade.

bayonets and hold the position until details could be sent to the rear for cartridges. My 60 rounds were almost entirely exhausted.

At this period of the engagement Lieutenant-Colonel Suman received a wound in the arm and side; Lieutenant Kessler was mortally wounded; Captain Pettit was severely wounded in the thigh, and borne from the field; Lieutenants Brinton and Criswell were both severely wounded; also Sergeant-Major Armstrong, severely wounded in the leg, and many enlisted men killed and wounded.

The One hundred and tenth Illinois Infantry, Colonel Casey, were in reserve directly in my rear, quietly awaiting an opportunity to render me support, which was not needed.

Captain Cockerill advanced one section of his battery to my support, and opened on the enemy with marked effect, and continued his fire until his ammunition was exhausted. He had his horse shot under him while directing the fire of his guns, and displayed the utmost coolness and courage.

At 11 a. m. our forces were being driven from the cedar grove on the right of the field. The enemy began to cross troops from the burnt house to the timber. Being well within range, I opened fire on them as they marched by the flank. The whole line was subjected to a severe fire as it passed successively the open space. At 11.30 a. m. the enemy's fire in my front had grown feeble; many had retired in disorder; many were killed and wounded, as the ground where they fought clearly attested at the close of the day. I picketed the ground near their line that night.

The enemy occupying the heavy timber on my right, and the whole line on my right having retired, I received orders to withdraw my right and open fire on the forces in the timber, who were then opening fire on us. In performing this movement my brave color-bearer, Charles Zellers, was killed. My left and center still engaged the enemy in front. I was compelled again to withdraw my right from the severe flanking fire from the timber, which brought me to the railroad, where I received orders to cross and open fire upon the enemy moving upon my left and near me. Facing by the rear rank, I opened fire upon the enemy obliquely to my left, then my right, detaching at the same time Companies K, G, and B, in charge of Major Lasselle, to occupy the elevation on the right of the railroad, that had just been held by my left.

At this time Lieutenant Braden fell, severely, if not mortally, wounded. He was an officer brave and without reproach. The One hundred and tenth Illinois Infantry were ordered up to my support and formed on my right.

At 1.30 p. m. General Rosecrans appeared in person on this part of the field, and ordered the Second Missouri and Seventy-third Illinois Infantry to assist in holding the position. The Second Missouri came into action gallantly, both forming on the railroad. The colonel of the Second Missouri was killed at this point.

At 2.30 p. m. these regiments were withdrawn, and the Sixth Kentucky Infantry forming on my right, I was ordered to open fire over the railroad track upon heavy bodies of the enemy then occupying the timber opposite, then directly in our front. Maintained this fire until the enemy (re-enforced) again appeared on my left and rear. I again faced by the rear rank and opened obliquely to my left.

During the time my regiment occupied the position on the left of the railroad we were subjected to a cross-fire from two of the enemy's batteries on their right and center; but, owing to the nature of the position, did not suffer severely. At 4 p. m. the fire of the enemy's musketry ceased, while that of their batteries continued until the close of the day.

Before twilight I sent details to collect and bury my dead upon the ground where they fell. A mutual truce was granted, in which the soldiers of both sides, without arms, gathered their fallen comrades without interruption. The fierce acerbity of the deadly strife had given place to the mutual expression of kindness and regard. While thus engaged, one gun of Captain Cockerill's battery was abandoned well to the front by the explosion of a caisson, and I had it removed well to the rear. The movement drew a fire from one of the enemy's batteries, but without effect.

For the brave men who stood by their colors from 7 a. m. until 4 p. m., continually under fire, no word of mine could do justice to their unfaltering courage. The officers of the Ninth Indiana Infantry I regard as among the bravest of the brave. Many of the captains and commandants of companies exhibited the highest courage and capacity under a severe and long-continued fire; but where, perhaps, none failed in doing their duty, it would be an invidious distinction to name any one for marked honor. Lieutenant-Colonel Suman stood gallantly at the post of duty until wounded, and retired from the field. Major Lasselle exhibited great courage, coolness, and efficiency throughout the day; Adjutant Willard repeated his heroism of Shiloh; Sergeant-Major Armstrong was wounded severely while executing an order. A sergeant, 10 enlisted men, and 1 corporal deserted their colors during the action. I will take prompt measures to publish the infamy of their conduct and bring them to punishment.

I regret to say that when the action opened with such violence the arrangements made with the surgeons and musicians for carrying the wounded to the rear utterly failed. They were borne with the tide of terrified stragglers so far to the left that many of them were captured by the enemy's cavalry, who penetrated their hiding places. Dr. Gilmore, assistant surgeon, with some hospital attendants and one ambulance, fell into the hands of the enemy. The surgeons were subsequently released, and I am told rendered efficient service in their attention to the wounded after the engagement. By reason of this most criminal neglect, many of my wounded had to crawl with shattered limbs to the rear, while others, unable to be removed, lay under the enemy's fire.

I am glad to report two bright exceptions to the base conduct of the hospital corps. Mr. Hurlburt, from the beginning to the close of the action, continually entered our line of fire and bore back the wounded. He exhibited a heroism worthy of all praise, because it was voluntary and out of the line of his duty; and William Morgan, chief bugler, displayed courage and efficiency in the discharge of his duty.

The regiment, in addition to the 60 rounds to the man, fired, during the day, 16,000 rounds of cartridges. The regiment entered the action with 345 enlisted men and 27 commissioned officers.

Loss: Officers killed, 1; enlisted men, 10; total, 11. Officers wounded, 5; enlisted men, 82; total, 87. Enlisted men missing, 11. In aggregate, loss of 109.

I remain, with great respect, your obedient servant,

W. H. BLAKE,
Colonel, Commanding.

Capt. R. L. KIMBERLY,
Acting Assistant Adjutant-General, Second Brigade.

No. 134.

Report of Col. Walter C. Whitaker, Sixth Kentucky Infantry.

HEADQUARTERS SIXTH KENTUCKY INFANTRY,
Battle-field of Stone's River, Tenn., January 5, 1863.

The undersigned, Walter C. Whitaker, colonel commanding Sixth Kentucky Infantry, of the Second Brigade, late the Nineteenth, commanded by Col. W. B. Hazen, of the Second Division, late the Fourth, commanded by General Palmer, makes the following report of the part taken by the Sixth Kentucky Infantry in the battle of Stone's River:

On the night of December 30, the Sixth Kentucky and Forty-first Ohio Volunteers were drawn up in line of battle, fronting east and toward Murfreesborough, in advance of the army, on a cotton-field lying south of the Nashville and Murfreesborough turnpike road, and near where the same crosses the Nashville and Chattanooga Railroad, and also near where both roads strike the bank of Stone's River. On the east, some 250 yards in front of the Sixth Kentucky, on a high piece of ground, in a curtilage, surrounded with a strong palisade of cedar timbers, some 7 or 8 feet high, firmly set in the ground, stands the burnt brick dwelling-house of Mr. Cowan; in the rear of this house the enemy had their rifle-pits. Beyond the house the ground gently rose higher for some 300 yards to the crest of the ridge, on the top of which, in a southeasterly direction, the enemy had a battery. Beyond the crest of the hill, and toward the river from the house, the ground gently sloped until it reached the river and a grove of timber in the rear. On this slope, concealed from our view, the enemy had an earthen breastwork for infantry and artillery. On the right and south of the position of the Sixth was a dense wood of oak and tall cedar. In the same direction, his left resting on the right of the Sixth, with an interval of 250 yards between them, General Cruft had his brigade drawn up in line of battle. Immediately in rear of, and west of, the Sixth was an open field, with a few old houses, some scattered trees, and large surface rocks, through which the turnpike and railroad ran. Directly north of this line of battle was an embankment of the railroad, some 7 or 8 feet in height. On the edge of this field the gallant Ninth Indiana and One hundred and tenth Illinois were drawn up as reserve. Company D, Captain Proctor, and Company I, Lieutenant Patchin, from the Forty-first Ohio Volunteers, and Company C, Captain Todd, and Company I, Captain Stein, of the Sixth Kentucky, were acting as pickets, Companies C and I occupying the curtilage of the brick house, with a small interval between them and the enemy's pickets.

Shortly after sunrise on the morning of the 31st, the pickets were attacked by the enemy, but maintained their position. Heavy firing was soon heard on the right of our army and gave indications of the rapid advance of the enemy. The enemy soon made a most furious attack upon our left. The pickets of the Sixth were driven in by a large force, which, protected by the palisade and out-buildings of Mr. Cowan's house and the high ground, opened a galling fire on the Sixth, which was in the open ground. They gradually advanced under cover, with the intention of flanking the Sixth on the right. Changing position by the right flank, the regiment was formed in line of battle in the skirt of timber south of the cotton-field—an advantageous position—under cover of the timber. Here we were assaulted by a large body of the enemy; from their numbers I estimated them as a brigade. Three times they advanced, and as often were they driven back with great slaughter.

From this position the Sixth was enabled to protect the left flank of the Twenty-second Brigade, General Cruft, who was gallantly maintaining his position. Some of the enemy's skirmishers having, after two hours' hard fighting, gained position in the edge of the wood, the Sixth was thrown forward to drive them from their cover. While in the act of advancing, the enemy, who had driven in General Negley's force on the right, opened a fire on the right flank of the Sixth, by which my lieutenant-colonel (Cotton) was killed. After some hard fighting the enemy were driven from their cover. Then, changing front, the right wing defending one flank and the left wing the other, the Sixth fought the advancing foe until their ammunition was exhausted. Changing position in good order, they took another position in rear of the railroad, where, having replenished their ammunition, they formed in line of battle on the north side of, and under cover of, the embankment of the railroad, the Ninth Indiana being on their left, and the Forty-first Ohio and One hundred and tenth Illinois being in reserve in the rear. The battle had been furiously raging from 8 o'clock in the morning until noon.

About 2 p. m., the right of the army having been driven back, the enemy appeared in heavy force on the crest of the ridge east of Mr. Cowan's burnt dwelling. Massing their forces, they intended, if possible, to crush the Nineteenth Brigade, which had maintained its position during the day against overwhelming numbers. Onward they came; the colors of five or six regiments advancing abreast in line of battle were visible on the crest of the ridge. A further view of this line was intercepted by intervening inequalities of ground and woods. Firmly they advanced until within good range of the guns of the Sixth and Ninth. A most destructive fire was opened upon them by these regiments, by Captain Cockerill's and Captain Parsons' batteries, and by the Fortieth Indiana Regiment, commanded by Colonel Blake. They broke in confusion, but, rallying, advanced again. Three or four times they rallied and advanced to the attack. Each time they were driven back with great loss, the last time in such confusion that it became a rout. The day was ours. We encamped that night on the position that had been so ably and successfully defended.

The Sixth has to regret the loss of two of her bravest and most gallant officers: Lieut. Col. George T. Cotton was killed, nobly encouraging the men on the right, and Capt. Charles S. Todd, commander of Company C, the color company, fell, pressing his men on to victory—scion of illustrious patriots, a braver spirit has not been offered up on the altar of his country.

The total loss in killed is 2 officers and 11 enlisted men; 6 commissioned officers were wounded—Lieutenants Bates, Company A; Dawkins, Company B; Armstrong, Company F; Frank, of Company I, and others; 88 enlisted men were wounded. Total killed and wounded, 107.

Lieutenant Dawkins, acting as adjutant, rendered me very great assistance, until he was so severely wounded as to be carried from the field. Lieutenant Rockingham, of Company A, deserves the highest commendation for courage, coolness, and efficiency as an officer. Sergt. William Jones, of Company A; Captain Dawkins, of Company B; Lieutenants McCampbell, of Company D, and Armstrong, of Company F; Captains Marker, of Company G, and Johnston, and Lieutenant Whitaker, of Company H; Captain Stein and Lieutenant Frank, of Company I; Lieutenant Campbell and Sergeant Furr, of Company K, are specially noticed for gallant conduct and efficient services. I can speak in the most approving manner of the soldierly bearing and courage of the men of the Sixth Kentucky. Three or four times regiments, retreating in confusion, would break through their lines, yet they never faltered in their duty, but obeyed implicitly the orders of the officer commanding.

I was personally cognizant of very gallant conduct on the part of Lieutenant Meeker, of the signal corps, under very heavy fire, in endeavoring to rally some of the fugitive regiments that were breaking through my lines. I was attracted by his bearing, inquired of him his name, and give him merited commendation.

On Friday, in the evening, January 2, the enemy made a most violent and determined attack upon the left of our forces, which had been advanced beyond Stone's River. The Sixth Kentucky was ordered, with the brigade, by Colonel Hazen, to cross the river and aid the forces engaged. This order was immediately obeyed. In double-quick time the Sixth advanced through a heavy shower of solid shot, shell, grape, and minie balls, cheering as they went. The timely aid brought inspired the forces engaged with the enemy, who, pressing forward, drove the enemy, with great slaughter, from the field. While they were advancing, great numbers of one of the divisions attacked (said to be General Van Cleve's) ran in great affright. Throwing down their arms, they broke through the ranks of the Sixth, saying, "All is lost." This did not throw the Sixth into confusion. Steadily they advanced, every man and officer doing his duty.

In the advance, 2 men of Company G were killed by rifled cannon shot, and 2 from Company H were wounded.

The regiment remained encamped on the opposite side of the river till January 4, when it moved to its present quarters, where it learned of the flight of the enemy.

A detail was made, and all its noble dead entombed, with their soldier's honor, in a soldier's grave, on the ground where the Nineteenth Brigade made its memorable, determined stand against such overwhelming numbers.

Great credit is due to the talented and indefatigable surgeons of the Sixth Kentucky, Drs. Joseph T. Drane and E. T. Long, for their faithful and indefatigable attention to the wounded. They not only cared for and attended the wounded of their regiment, but many others besides. They were on the field in discharge of their duty amid the thickest of the fight.

Respectfully submitted.

W. C. WHITAKER,
Colonel, Commanding Sixth Kentucky Volunteers.

Major KIMBERLY,
Actg. Asst. Adjt. Gen., Second Brigade, Second Division.

No. 135.

Report of Lieut. Col. Aquila Wiley, Forty-first Ohio Infantry.

HEADQUARTERS FORTY-FIRST REGT. OHIO VOLS.,
Camp near Murfreesborough, Tenn., January 6, 1863

As commander of the Forty-first Regiment Ohio Volunteers, I have the honor to submit the following report of its operations and casualties in the recent engagements before Murfreesborough:

On the evening of December 30, the regiment (which was then in double column in reserve) was ordered to take position in the first line of battle, its left resting on the right of and near the Murfreesborough and Nashville turnpike, with two companies deployed as skirmishers about 150 yards in advance, covering its front.

A little before daylight on the morning of the 31st, Companies D and I were deployed as skirmishers, and relieved Companies A and F, which were then assembled and took their position in line.

About 8 o'clock the signal " forward" was sounded, and the regiment commenced to advance toward Murfreesborough. At this time the firing, which had commenced at an early hour on our right, appeared to be nearing the pike to our right and rear, and the regiment had not advanced more than about 100 paces when the command "right-about" was given, and it returned to its former position and again faced to the front. At this time the enemy appeared advancing in line across the open country direct in our front.

The regiment was then moved by the left flank across the turnpike, its left resting on a slight elevation to the right of and near the railroad. The enemy, then moving by his left flank, to gain cover of a wood on our right, made an oblique change of front to rear on the left company. The skirmishers, who (during this time under the command of Capt. J. H. Williston, acting major) had been engaged with the enemy, with slight loss, were now rallied and put in position on the right of the regiment. In this position the regiment opened fire, and continued firing until its ammunition was about exhausted, when it was relieved by the Ninth Indiana, and retired a short distance and replenished its boxes. It then took up position on the right of the brigade, extending obliquely across the turnpike, and again opened fire.

It here continued firing until a battery of the enemy opened upon our right flank, when it retired across the railroad and took up position on the left of the brigade, the right resting near and perpendicular to the railroad, the rest of the brigade having taken position behind and parallel with the railroad. After remaining in this position for some time—the enemy not being within effective range of infantry, and suffering considerably from his artillery, one shell from which, exploding in the ranks, killed and wounded 8 men—it retired about 50 yards behind a ridge, which afforded some protection.

Shortly after, hearing that the enemy's cavalry was attempting to cross the creek to our left and rear, and seeing a section of artillery, unsupported, opening in that direction, without waiting for orders I placed the regiment in position on the right of the artillery. A few discharges from the artillery, however, repulsed them. I was here met by a member of the staff of the colonel commanding the brigade, and directed to remain there until further orders.

Shortly after, by direction of General Rosecrans, the regiment took its former position in the field, behind a crest of the hill, which it occupied during the remainder of the day, sustaining some loss from the enemy's artillery, but without opportunity of returning its fire.

During the following day the regiment was not engaged, remaining in double column in reserve on the left of the railroad and near the creek, as it did also during Friday, until in the afternoon, when the enemy made his attack on our left. The column was then moved by the left flank across the creek to our extreme left, where it was deployed. The enemy was at this time repulsed, and retiring in confusion. I was ordered to advance the regiment in line, and did so without firing until ordered to halt at the skirt of a wood. The enemy having retreated across an open field and disappeared in a wood beyond, a single battery of the enemy, posted in the skirt of the wood, was continuing its fire. The regiment was directed to fire one volley in the direction of the battery, and did so, immediately after which the firing on both sides ceased. It being now dark, the regiment remained in this position until relieved by the Twenty-first Illinois, when it was ordered into position to the rear, which terminated its part in the engagement.

The following is the list of casualties :* Total commissioned officers killed, 1; wounded, 2. Total enlisted men killed, 13; wounded, 102; missing, 6. Total engaged—commissioned officers, 19; enlisted men, 394.

Of the above list, five were wounded in the engagement on Friday evening. Sergeants Titus and Huston were carrying the colors at the time they were wounded. Lieutenant Blythe, quartermaster, was with the regiment during the engagement on Wednesday, and rendered efficient service. Both officers and men displayed great coolness and steady bravery throughout the entire engagement, performing all maneuvers with accuracy and precision, and, even when not engaged and suffering severely from the enemy's artillery, not attempting to move until ordered to do so.

Sergeant McKay, of Company E, commanding the company from the commencement of the engagement, and Sergeant McMahon, temporarily in command of Company H, displayed great coolness and courage, and are eminently deserving of promotion. Corpl. J. P. Patterson, of the color-guard, seized the colors when Sergeant Huston fell, and bore them gallantly during the remainder of the engagement.

I have the honor to be, your most obedient servant,

AQUILA WILEY,
Lieutenant-Colonel Forty-first Ohio Vols., Comdg. Regiment.

Maj. R. L. KIMBERLY,
Acting Assistant Adjutant-General.

No. 136.

Report of Col. William Grose, Thirty-sixth Indiana Infantry, command-ing Third Brigade.

HEADQUARTERS THIRD BRIGADE, SECOND DIVISION,
LEFT WING, ARMY OF THE CUMBERLAND,
Near Murfreesborough, Tenn., January 8, 1863.

SIR : In accordance with duty, I have the honor to submit the report of the part this brigade, under my command, took in the recent battles before Murfreesborough.

The five regiments—Thirty-sixth Indiana, Major Kinley; Twenty-fourth Ohio, Colonel Jones; Sixth Ohio, Colonel Anderson; Eighty-fourth Illinois, Colonel Waters; Twenty-third Kentucky, Major Hamrick; aggregate officers and men, 1,788—left our camp, near Nashville, December 26, 1862, with the division; bivouacked that night in front of La Vergne, 12 miles distant.

Next day, 27th, we moved to the west bank of Stewart's Creek, 5

---

* Nominal list omitted.

miles, and my brigade was put in position in front, to the right of the
pike. The pickets of the enemy were separated from ours by the creek.
With light skirmishing, we rested here until Monday morning, the 29th,
when we received orders, and moved forward in double lines of battle on
the right of the pike, the Thirty-sixth Indiana and Eighty-fourth Illinois
in the front line, wading Stewart's Creek, waist-deep to most of the men,
to within 2½ miles of Murfreesborough, where we arrived near sunset,
with skirmishing all the way, which was only ended by the close of the
day. We there rested for the night.

At early morn skirmishing again commenced, and continued during
the day with more severity than before, the artillery taking a heavy
part. This ended again with the day. Up to this time the loss in my
brigade was 10 wounded. During the night it was relieved from the
front by the brigade of Colonel Hazen, and retired to the rear to rest,
and to be held in reserve.

Thus, on the bright Wednesday morning, December 31, the division,
under command of its brave general, at early day was in battle line.
The brigade of General Cruft on the right, that of Colonel Hazen on the
left, both in double lines, with my brigade in reserve in rear of the center, in supporting distance, with the batteries of Cockerill and Parsons
in position to support the lines. While we were perfecting our lines in
the morning, the divisions of Generals Negley and Rousseau filed by my
rear through a heavy cedar grove, which lay in rear of General Cruft's
brigade, and immediately up to the right of my brigade; the brigade of
Colonel Hazen in an open cotton-field, the pike dividing his left from
the division of General Wood, the lines of these two divisions resting
nearly perpendicular to the pike.

The engagement had been raging fiercely some distance to our right
during the early morning, and at near 8 o'clock the clash of arms to our
right had so far changed position that I saw the rear of my brigade
would soon be endangered. Hence I set to work changing my front to
rear, which was done in quick time, with the left, when changed, a little
retired, to support the right of Colonel Hazen's brigade, then closely
engaged with the enemy, our two brigades forming a V. My brigade
was not more than thus formed to the rear before the enemy appeared
in heavy lines, pressing the forces of ours that had been engaged to the
right of our division on our front in fearful confusion. In this new formation the Sixth Ohio and Thirty-sixth Indiana were in the front lines,
the latter on the right, supported in the second line by the Eighty-fourth
Illinois and Twenty-third Kentucky, with the Twenty-fourth Ohio in an
oblique form, a little to the right of the rear line. In this shape the
Thirty-sixth Indiana and Sixth Ohio advanced into the woodland about
250 yards, and there met the enemy in overwhelming numbers.

Here Major Kinley and Captain Shultz, of the Thirty-sixth Indiana,
fell, the former-named badly wounded, the latter killed ; Colonel Anderson, of the Sixth Ohio, was here wounded, and his adjutant, A. G. Williams, and Lieutenant Foster, fell dead, with several others of their comrades. These two regiments were forced from the woodland, and retired
to the right, in the direction of the pike, while the other three regiments,
aided by the eight-gun battery, commanded by Lieutenant Parsons, with
the efficient aid of Lieutenants Huntington and Cushing, poured a galling
fire into the ranks of the pursuing enemy, causing them to break in
confusion and retire back to the woods out of our reach, leaving the
field covered with their dead and dying, with the heavy loss of the
Thirty-sixth Indiana and Sixth Ohio lying with them on the bloody •

field. After some half an hour or three-quarters the enemy renewed his attempts to advance, but was again repulsed with heavy loss on both sides.

After this, then, between 11 and 12 o'clock, the enemy not appearing in our immediate front, the lines of our forces that had retired or been driven from the right by this time were reformed parallel with the pike, so that the front of the brigade was again changed, so as to assist the brigade of Colonel Hazen in the direction as formed in the morning. The Twenty-fourth Ohio and Thirty-sixth Indiana were soon thrown forward near the pike and had a terrible conflict with the enemy. Here Colonel Jones and Major Terry both fell, and were carried off the field in a dying condition.

Each regiment of the brigade, from this until night closed the awful scene, alternately took its part in holding the position that we occupied in the morning. The enemy having gained the heavy cedar woods to the right, where we first took position in the morning, it became necessary to so change our position as to not be in reach of small-arms from that woodland; hence, at nightfall the center of the front line of the brigade laid on the pike and diagonally across the same, fronting to the southeast, our left resting at the right of the lines of General Wood's division. We were then a little retired, and the center of the brigade about 250 yards to the left of where we commenced in the morning. We ceased fighting for the night, with the front lines on the pike. During the day each of the regiments, having exhausted, had to replenish, their ammunition, many of them having fired over 100 rounds.

When Major Kinley, of the Thirty-sixth Indiana, fell, nearly at the commencement in the morning, the command devolved upon Captain Woodward; and upon the fall of Colonel Jones and Major Terry, of the Twenty-fourth Ohio, Captain Weller was left in command.

Although I was at Shiloh, and commanded in that battle at the head of General Buell's army, and fought throughout that battle with that army, yet this battle, the last day of the old year, was by far the most terrible and bloody in my command that I have ever witnessed.

During the latter part of the night, or, rather, early in the morning of January 1, our whole line was retired, for a more eligible position, 600 or 700 yards, and my brigade was relieved from the front, and retired for rest.

During Thursday, January 1, we were ordered to cross the north bank of Stone's River, to support a division on the extreme left of our line, an attack being anticipated in that direction, but returned to our resting place before night, no attack being made that day.

On the next day, January 2, in the forenoon, we were again ordered across the river to support the division there in position, with its right resting on the river bank, and its lines (double lines) formed at right angles to the river, extending therefrom about one-half mile. The river below the right of the division line, about 800 yards, changes direction, running about one-half mile in the rear, and nearly parallel to the lines of the division, formed as above. When my brigade arrived on the ground, I was requested to put it in position so as to protect the left flank of the division referred to, and repel any attack that might be made in that direction.

The Twenty-third Kentucky was posted to the left of the division spoken of about 200 yards, retired; the Twenty-fourth Ohio 300 yards to its rear, fronting the same way; the Thirty-sixth Indiana, to the rear of the Twenty-fourth Ohio, fronting diagonally to the flank of the other two, the right of the Thirty-sixth Indiana distant from the left of the Twenty-fourth Ohio about 150 yards, and with directions specially given to each of these regiments to change front as the exigencies of the case might require in case of an attack. The Eighty-fourth Illinois and Sixth Ohio were placed 150 yards from the left of the Thirty-sixth Indiana, in one line, fronting the same direction as the Twenty-fourth and Twenty-third, as well as in the same direction of the division so posted (as above) to our right and front, the right of the Eighty-fourth Illinois resting on the bluff at the river, with the Third Wisconsin Battery near the left and front of the Eighty-fourth; the Sixth Ohio on the left of the Eighty-fourth Illinois. Thus in position, I took the precaution to have each regiment hurriedly throw before them barricades of such materials, fences, buildings, &c., as were at command.

About 3.30 p. m. the enemy came in against the division in front and right (as above shown in position) in strong force, perhaps in three lines, and with three batteries distributed along the front, and a heavy contest ensued, which lasted from one-half to three-fourths of an hour, when the lines of the division gave way in considerable confusion, retiring toward the river, and many of them breaking through the lines of my brigade. I went to my front regiments and superintended the changing of their fronts, respectively, so as to meet the enemy the best we could, coming from an unexpected direction, which, to some extent, threw the Twenty-third Kentucky and Twenty-fourth Ohio, my advanced front regiments, into confusion, and caused them to retire toward the left of the main line of the brigade, but they kept up a strong fire on the advancing enemy as they retired. The Thirty-sixth Indiana changed its front, and, as the enemy's lines came near, opened on them a deadly fire; but on they came, until in reach of the Eighty-fourth Illinois and Sixth Ohio, behind their barricades, when both these regiments saluted them with a terrible fire, and by this time all my regiments were engaged, and the masses of the enemy began to falter, and soon broke in disorder, and commenced their flight back over the farm they had so fiercely advanced upon, pursued by the Thirty-sixth Indiana, Twenty-third Kentucky, and Twenty-fourth Ohio to the line occupied by the out-picket posts of the division before the battle commenced.

Here night overtook us, the battle was over, and the enemy was gone beyond the reach of our guns. Colonel Hazen's brigade crossed the river to our rear to support us about the time of the enemy's retreat, and moved closely after my pursuing regiments, to give assistance if needed. Some other forces collected or crossed the river to my right, and moved up the river bank in pursuit of the enemy as my regiments advanced. What forces these were I have not learned. The battery posted near the brigade at the commencement of this day's fight fired a few rounds and took a hasty leave from the field, and I have not made its acquaintance since.

Artillery from the opposite side of the river rendered valuable aid by playing upon the enemy in his advance and retreat.

Our loss this day was not large compared with that of the 31st. That of the enemy was very heavy.

I cannot too favorably notice the coolness and promptness of each and every field officer of the brigade. They seemed to vie with each other which should most promptly execute every command, without regard to danger; and the line officers and men of the respective regiments appeared not to fear or know danger. New and old regiments alike acted the heroic part and braved every peril.

Captain Weller, in command of the Twenty-fourth Ohio, fell at his post on the last battle-field, and left Captain Cockerill in command, who bravely and skillfully performed his whole duty; and as much may be said of Captain Woodward, who succeeded to the command of the Thirty-sixth Indiana upon the fall of Major Kinley at a critical and perilous moment in the first day's engagement.

I am under lasting obligations to my staff and orderlies for their efficient assistance during these several days' fighting. Captain Peden, Thirty-sixth Indiana, is entitled to great credit for his aid rendered me up to the time he fell, wounded, on the 31st.

Lieut. J. P. Duke, of the Twenty-third Kentucky, also on my staff, deserves a high meed of praise for promptness and aid rendered me at all times during the whole of these engagements. Dr. Silas H. Kersey, acting brigade surgeon, with unsurpassed industry and skill, has rendered invaluable assistance to the wounded.

My mounted orderlies, Frank Brough, Frank Webb, Albert Woods, William D. Smith, Martin Mann, and Louis Miller, of the Second Indiana Cavalry, George Shirk and Isaac Biglow, of the Thirty-sixth Indiana Infantry, rendered me valuable service. But I am left to remember and lament with friends the fall, in this mighty struggle for human prowess, of such brave spirits as Colonel Jones, Major Terry, Captains Weller, Shultz, King, Adjutant Williams, Lieutenants Foster, Ball, Abercrombie, and others, whose earthly conflicts have closed with these battles I may truthfully add that I mourn with those who mourn over these irreparable losses.

To the brave wounded, whose fate may or may not be uncertain, you have my earnest prayers for a speedy restoration to health and usefulness.

The casualties of the brigade, as near as can be ascertained, are as follows:

Command.	Killed.		Wounded.		Missing.	Total.
	Officers.	Men.	Officers.	Men.		
24th Ohio	4	10	4	68	12	98
23d Kentucky		8	3	50	22	83
84th Illinois	2	33	5	119	8	167
36th Indiana	2	23	6	85	18	134
6th Ohio	2	23	4	134	14	177
Total	10	97	22	456	74	659

List of which, with the reports of the regimental commanders for further details, are herewith respectfully forwarded.

I have the honor to remain, your obedient servant,

WM. GROSE,
Colonel, Commanding Third Brigade (Old Tenth).

Capt. D. W. NORTON,
Acting Assistant Adjutant-General, Second Division.

The following shows the position on January 2, before the battle over the river, of Colonel Beatty's division and Colonel Grose's brigade. Barricades before regiments of brigade.

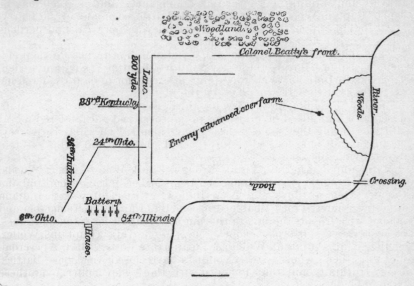

No. 137.

Report of Surg. Silas H. Kersey, Thirty-sixth Indiana Infantry, Acting Brigade Surgeon.

HEADQUARTERS MEDICAL DEPARTMENT THIRD BRIGADE,
January 9, 1863.

DEAR SIR : I have the honor to transmit the following list of casualties suffered by your command in the recent series of engagements with the enemy before Murfreesborough, to wit : *

Before closing this report, permit me, respectfully, to call attention to the faithful manner in which the regimental medical officers of the several regiments composing the Third Brigade have discharged the arduous duties incumbent on them under circumstances the most trying, viz: T. S. Bayse, assistant surgeon Thirty-sixth Regiment Indiana Volunteer Infantry, was assigned the duty of administering anæsthetics, which he has so far accomplished in every operation without producing any untoward symptoms in a single case, and at the same time attended to the dressing of all the slighter wounds of his own regiment, thus performing double duty by day and night since the commencement of the battle.

I would also make honorable mention of A. M. Morrison, assistant surgeon Twenty-third Regiment Kentucky Volunteers, who was appointed to keep the register, which necessarily occupied a large portion of his time, notwithstanding which, by constant industry and energy, his wounded have been well cared for.

Assistant Surgeon McDill, of the Eighty-fourth Illinois, had so large a list of wounded that his time has been almost wholly occupied with them ; they, too, have been as well attended as circumstances would permit.

---

* Table, here omitted, embodied in No. 136. p. 563.

We have, up to this date, a smaller proportional list of deaths from wounds after entering hospital than any other division hospital in the left wing of this army corps. Two cases of erysipelas have appeared in stumps—one of the arm, near the shoulder; the other the leg. They were immediately separated from the other inmates and cared for in a tent to themselves. The utmost care and vigilance is constantly exercised over the wounded that the limited room and means will permit.

I have, sir, the honor to be, respectfully, your obedient servant,

S. H. KERSEY,
Acting Surgeon Third Brigade.

W. GROSE,
Colonel, Commanding Third Brigade.

No. 138.

Report of Col. Louis H. Waters, Eighty-fourth Illinois Infantry.

HEADQUARTERS EIGHTY-FOURTH ILLINOIS VOLUNTEERS,
Near Murfreesborough, Tenn., January 6, 1863.

SIR: Early in the morning of December 31, by direction of Colonel Grose, commanding Third Brigade, my command took position on the left of the brigade, front perpendicular to the pike, with the Twenty-third Kentucky on my right and the Twenty-fourth Ohio in my rear. In a short time it became evident that the division on our right was being rapidly driven in, whereupon I changed front to the right, and got my command under the protection of a ledge of rocks. The enemy soon appeared in the cedar woods in our front, and we opened fire upon him. We here had 5 men severely wounded. Lieutenant Parsons' battery having changed position from our left to the pike in its rear, I retired my left to support the battery, moving my right to the position before occupied by my left.

About 12 o'clock, the battery having moved forward on the pike nearly to the cotton-field in front, by direction of Colonel Grose we moved forward to support the battery on the right, and immediately commenced firing upon the enemy lying across the cotton-field and meadow in our front. During this time there were two regiments of some other division upon my right, engaging the enemy somewhat to their right, and Stevens' Pennsylvania battery was in rear of my center. Both these regiments gave way, and left the field in considerable confusion, leaving Stevens' battery without any support.

I immediately retired the right of my regiment, so as to protect this battery as far as possible until it could be taken from the field. It had done excellent service, and was not to be lost without a struggle. As soon as it was started from the field, I again retired my right, so as to have the protection of a ledge, some 60 paces to the rear. From this ledge we kept up a steady fire upon the enemy, now occupying the skirt of the cedar woods in our front, until Lieutenant Parsons' battery, for want of ammunition or support on his left, was compelled to retire beyond the pike. While occupying this position we suffered terribly from the fire of stragglers, who had sought cover behind some cabins in our rear, and were firing wildly at the enemy over our line.

Captain Higgins and others of my command called to me that their men were being wounded by the firing from the cabins. I reluctantly withdrew my command to the railroad, some 350 yards distant, and from thence, by Colonel Grose's direction, to some woods to the left, where we rested for the night. At the ledge where we made our last stand we left 24 of our dead.

In the fight on the 2d instant we were posted by Colonel Grose on the left of his brigade line, and I cannot report anything that did not occur under the observation of Colonel Grose, who on this occasion, as on the 31st, was wherever duty called him, regardless of danger. After the enemy commenced retreating, I advanced my command to the corn-field in our front, and there learned, to my surprise, that our ammunition was exhausted. We had fired 50 rounds.

My command, on the morning of the 31st ultimo, consisted of 3 field and staff and 21 company officers and 336 enlisted men. Lieutenants Ball and Abercrombie, two as gallant gentlemen as ever fought beneath the stars and stripes, fell at their posts in the first engagement.

On the 31st we lost in killed 35 officers and men, and had wounded 121. On the 2d we had 5 wounded. On both occasions my command, as well as the other regiments of Colonel Grose's brigade, was nearly crushed by the herd of officers and men of other divisions, as they fled, panic-stricken, before the enemy; yet it stood like a "human wood," and officers and men vied with each other in beating back the fugitives.

To the coolness and fearlessness of Lieutenant-Colonel Hamer, Major Morton, and my company officers, and the bravery of our men, are we indebted for whatever of credit the regiment may deserve. In this connection I cannot omit the opportunity of bearing testimony to the gallantry of Lieutenant Parsons and the efficiency of his battery.

I herewith inclose a list of my killed and wounded,* which is as nearly correct as I can now make it. Many slightly wounded are not included in the list.

Very respectfully, your obedient servant,

L. H. WATERS,
Colonel, Commanding Eighty-fourth Illinois Volunteers.

Capt. R. SOUTHGATE,
Acting Assistant Adjutant-General, Third Brigade.

No. 139.

Report of Capt. Pyrrhus Woodward, Thirty-sixth Indiana Infantry.

HDQRS. THIRTY-SIXTH REGIMENT INDIANA VOLUNTEERS,
January 6, 1863.

SIR: It devolves upon me, as the temporary commander of the Thirty-sixth Regiment, to report the part taken by it in the recent engagements before Murfreesborough, and on the march thither.

On the 28th ultimo we were bivouacked on the west bank of Stewart's Creek, 10 miles from Murfreesborough, in sight of the enemy's cavalry pickets. At an early hour the next morning, 29th ultimo, we moved forward in line of battle, and arrived within sight of the enemy's rifle-pits, 2½ miles from Murfreesborough, at 4 p. m. There we retained our position in front, the regiment doing picket duty the night of the 29th, and losing 1 man of Company D, wounded. We retained our position in front during the day and night of the 30th ultimo, losing 1 man wounded in Company I.

---

* Embodied in revised statement, p. 213.

We were relieved on the morning of the 31st ultimo by the Ninth Indiana Regiment, and at daylight of the same day our regiment was called out under arms, expecting to participate in a general attack on the enemy's positions at Murfreesborough. Just as we had formed our line, and were preparing to advance, a terrific fire on the right of our position disclosed the fact that the battle had opened. In compliance with orders from you, my regiment countermarched, changed front, and advanced to the edge of a cedar thicket, to the right and rear of our first position, forming the right flank of the brigade, where it was evident our services would soon be needed. Hardly had we taken our position when the enemy was upon us. Concealed from the view of my men by the thick undergrowth of cedar, the first indication they had of his presence was a volley from his muskets, which riddled our ranks. It was my impression that the Fifteenth U. S. Infantry was in my front, as we had been informed that such was the fact on entering the thicket; hence the precaution of throwing out skirmishers had not been taken.

Up to this time Maj. Isaac Kinley retained command of the regiment, but at this point was seriously, perhaps fatally, wounded, being struck in the thigh by a musket-ball. Here, too, Capt. A. D. Shultz, of Company B, fell, mortally wounded, while bravely encouraging his men; and every mounted officer of the regiment, except the adjutant, had his horse shot under him.

After delivering a few well-aimed volleys at the enemy, it became apparent that our position could not be held, the line having been already confused by the Fifteenth Regulars passing out between my left and the right of the Sixth Ohio, and our right and left flanks, as well as our front, being exposed to the enemy's fire.

He quickly discovered his advantage, and, charging upon my regiment with four times its number, compelled it to retire, cutting it off from the brigade, and separating two of my companies (A and C) from the regiment. The strongest efforts were made by all the officers of my regiment to rally the men, and, though their bravery was unquestioned and they exhibited a strong disposition to maintain their ground, the fire of the enemy was too hot to admit of it, and they were retired to a point a short distance from the scene of our first conflict. Here, with the valuable assistance of Capt. Gilbert Trusler and Adjt. J. H. McClung and other officers of the regiment, I succeeded in forming our line, and again advanced under a heavy fire to the front. Not a man of my command flinched, and for eight long hours we assisted in maintaining our position against the furious assaults of the enemy.

First Lieut. J. W. J. Smith and Second Lieut. J. C. Byram, both of Company G, were wounded in the early part of the day, and compelled to retire from the field.

At 4 p. m., the fire having slackened, we noted our condition and strength, and found that out of 430 commissioned officers and men, with whom we had entered the battle in the morning, 213 remained. This number was increased, by the arrival of those who had become separated from the regiment during the day, to 283.

On January 1 we rested, and, although my men were exposed to a heavy fire from the enemy's artillery during several hours of the day, none of them were killed or wounded.

On the morning of the 2d, by your order, we moved across the river, taking a position on its northeast bank, behind a barricade constructed by my men. We had remained here but a few hours when the enemy made a strong and sudden attack on our position from the direction of our right flank, while his batteries to our right gave my line a raking fire. Then, by your order, I changed position, moving by the left flank a distance of 200 yards. It was a terrible struggle, but the terrific fire to which the enemy was exposed for an hour compelled his lines to break and retire in disorder. At this juncture my men were ordered to charge the enemy, which they did with alacrity, halting not until darkness put an end to the pursuit. Capt. J. H. King, of Company G, was killed in this last engagement while gallantly encouraging his men at the barricade. He died nobly, bravely.

Our loss, colonel, in this series of engagements, is as follows:* Killed, 25; wounded, 91; missing, 18. Total loss in killed, wounded, and missing, 134.

In concluding my report to you, colonel, I wish again to call your attention to the bravery and gallant conduct of both the officers and men of my regiment, and to thank them for their noble conduct and bearing throughout all the trying scenes from December 28 to January 3. They are worthy of immortal honor.

Too much cannot be said in praise of the glorious dead. Captains Shultz and King still live with us, though their bodies molder in the earth. The enemy encountered no braver or truer spirits in those trying battles.

> How sleep the brave who sink to rest,
> By all their country's wishes blessed!

I am, colonel, with great respect, your most obedient servant,
PYRRHUS WOODWARD,
Captain, Comdg. Thirty-sixth Regiment Indiana Volunteers.
Col. W. GROSE,
Commanding Third Brigade.

No. 140.

Report of Maj. Thomas H. Hamrick, Twenty-third Kentucky Infantry.

HEADQUARTERS TWENTY-THIRD KENTUCKY INFANTRY,
Camp in front of Murfreesborough, Tenn., January 5, 1863.

SIR: I hereby beg leave to make my report of the part taken by the Twenty-third Kentucky Infantry in the two battles before Murfreesborough, December 31, 1862, and January 2, 1863:

On December 26, 1862, we left our camp, near Nashville, with 282 men, and took up our line of march with the brigade, under the command of Col. William Grose, in the rear of the Sixth Ohio. Halted near La Vergne at dusk, where we bivouacked during the night.

On the morning of the 27th, my regiment was detailed as guard to General Palmer's division train. At night we took up our position with the brigade.

On the 28th (Sunday), we moved to the front with our brigade, and were placed as reserve to the Eighty-fourth Illinois.

On the 29th, we moved forward, crossed Stewart's Creek, waist-deep, and followed the Eighty-fourth Illinois in line of battle. Remained in front all night with the brigade.

On the 30th, I was ordered forward some 400 yards, to support Parsons' (regular) battery, on the right, where we remained until dark,

---

* Nominal list omitted.

when we were relieved, and ordered some 400 yards to the rear and into the timber, for rest.

On the 31st (Wednesday), I was ordered to form in line on the left of the Sixth Ohio, fronting the enemy's battery in front, when, the fire becoming heavy upon our right and rear, Colonel Grose ordered me to change my front, which I immediately did, facing the direction of the enemy's fire, when I was ordered to unsling knapsacks. I was then ordered to move forward and support the Sixth Ohio, which I did, moving as far as the skirt of the wood on my left, when General Palmer rode up and ordered me to retire to the support of Parsons' battery.

At this time the stampede from the right became general from the woods in our front. I had some fear of being carried away with it, but found no difficulty in moving my men to the support of the battery, forming my right on the battery, and my left resting on the wood. The enemy appeared on our front, and poured in a galling fire upon us, with the intention, it seemed, to charge the battery. Some regiment formed upon my left, resting in the woods. The battery opened a cross-fire upon the enemy, as did also my regiment and the one upon my left, driving him back in great confusion and with heavy loss. The battery retired, when I was ordered to change my front and form behind a ledge of rocks, and cause my men to lie down and await the approach of the enemy. The enemy's fire becoming very heavy, I was ordered to fall back with my command to the railroad, in rear of the Twenty-fourth Ohio, which I did slowly and in good order.

After remaining there for some thirty minutes, I was ordered to move forward and relieve the Twenty-fourth Ohio, whose ammunition was exhausted. This I did under a heavy fire from the enemy. That position I held for fifty-five minutes, driving the enemy back with my superior guns under cover of the woods, when we were relieved and ordered to the rear for ammunition.

At 5.30 p. m. I was again ordered to the front, when I took the position in the wood, in front of the railroad, occupied by me before I was ordered to the rear, which point I occupied until I was relieved, at 1 a. m., when I was again ordered to the rear for refreshments and rest.

On January 1, I was ordered to the rear and center of Van Cleve's and Wood's divisions, where I remained until 12 m., when I was ordered to cross the river to our left, where I remained until 2.30 p. m., when I was ordered to recross the river and go into camp for a night's rest.

On January 2, I was again ordered with the brigade to cross the river, when Colonel Grose ordered me to take a position behind a fence, on the extreme front and left. I threw out three companies as skirmishers. I remained in position until 3.30 p. m., when the enemy appeared, driving back the forces on my right. The Fifty-ninth Ohio broke and ran across my front, and some of them over my men, who were lying behind the fence in line. I saw that the enemy were driving back the forces upon my right, so I changed my front and opened upon him. I had no sooner done so than a battery opened upon my left with grape, and at the same time a fire of small-arms was opened upon my left and rear, placing me within a cross-fire. I then attempted to move my men back to the brigade, when some stragglers raised the cry, " We are surrounded," and I found it was impossible to keep my men in order. They then fell back in confusion. I succeeded in rallying most of them in the woods on the left of the brigade. The balance, with a few exceptions, rallied and returned.

The enemy was then driven back with heavy loss. I then moved forward beyond my original position, keeping open a heavy fire upon him.

When we halted we were 500 yards in advance and to the right of our original position, and occupying the ground of our former picket line, which position we held until dark, when, being relieved, we returned to our position occupied before the engagement, having lost in the two days' engagements 8 killed, 51 wounded, and 22 missing.

Chaplain William H. Black deserves especial praise for the manner in which he acted, being always at his post, and rendering aid and comfort to the wounded, both while the fight was going on and during the two succeeding nights. Dr. A. M. Morrison also deserves great praise for his kindness and attention to the wounded at all hours, day and night.

My officers, line and staff, acted with great coolness and bravery, with a few exceptions, which I cannot particularize in this report.

I have the honor to remain, your most obedient servant,

THOMAS H. HAMRICK,
Major, Commanding Regiment.

Capt. R. SOUTHGATE,
Acting Assistant Adjutant-General, Third Brig., Second Div.

No. 141.

Report of Col. Nicholas L. Anderson, Sixth Ohio Infantry.

NASHVILLE, TENN., *January 7*, 1863.

COLONEL : In accordance with orders from headquarters, I have the honor to make the following report of the part taken by the Sixth Regiment Ohio Volunteers in the late series of battles, beginning on the morning of December 31 :

At about 8 a. m. on that day we were drawn up in line of battle in the open field to the north of the burnt brick house, and to the west of the cedars, while Rousseau's division filed by us to get position. Scarcely had the rear of that column passed when heavy firing was heard to our right, coming from the cedars and approaching rapidly. I was ordered with my regiment into the woods. I immediately changed front and advanced some 200 yards, when I saw our troops flying in wild disorder, and hotly pursued by the enemy. I formed my line and awaited the escape of our men and the nearer advance of the enemy. In a few moments a terrible fire was opened on us, scarce 100 yards distant, from a rebel line apparently four deep. This fire we returned, and a dreadful carnage ensued on both sides. Finding myself hotly pressed, I had determined on a charge, and the order was already given to fix bayonets, when I saw my regiment flanked almost completely on both sides by two rebel regiments. I gave the order to fall back, firing. As soon as we reached the edge of the woods, Lieutenant Parsons, of the Fourth (Regular) Artillery, opened on the enemy with terrible effect, and I reformed my line behind his guns, having held my position against tremendous odds, but with great sacrifice, for forty minutes.

I then replenished my ammunition, and was soon after ordered to throw my regiment diagonally across the Murfreesborough pike and hold that position. This I did, under a destructive fire and with much loss, during the rest of the day and until midnight, when I was relieved by the Twenty-fourth Ohio, and took my regiment a short distance to the rear.

During January 1, my regiment was moved from one place to another as the plan of the battle required, but did not get into any general action.

On Friday, the 2d, my regiment was ordered with the brigade across the river, and placed in position on a slight eminence to the rear of and as a support to Van Cleve's division.

All was quiet until about 3.30 p. m., when a tremendous fire was heard along our front, and whole masses of the enemy were hurled against Van Cleve's division, which soon gave way. The enemy came down boldly, when I brought my regiment into action, simultaneously with the Eighty-fourth Illinois, and we opened a severe cross-fire on the enemy. For more than an hour we held the hill, and under our heavy fire, and that of a battery from the other side of the river, the enemy soon gave way, and when re-enforcements poured in for us they were already in full retreat.

We held our position without further molestation till Sunday morning, when we were ordered across the river into camp, the enemy having retreated.

My regiment, both officers and men, behaved throughout with energy, courage, and discipline. The loss was 177 killed, wounded, and missing. Among the former was Adjutant Williams, who fell cheering the men on, regardless of all personal danger. Accompanying is a correct list of the casualties.*

Respectfully,

N. L. ANDERSON,
Colonel, Commanding Sixth Ohio Volunteers.

Colonel GROSE,
Commanding Tenth Brigade.

No. 142.

Report of Capt. Armistead T. M. Cockerill, Twenty-fourth Ohio Infantry.

HEADQUARTERS TWENTY-FOURTH OHIO REGIMENT,
January 6, 1863.

SIR: I have the honor to submit the following report of the part taken by the Twenty-fourth Ohio Regiment in the recent battles before Murfreesborough, Tenn., of December 31, 1862, and January 2, 1863:

Our regiment being one of the five regiments composing the Tenth Brigade, commanded by Col. William Grose, of the Thirty-sixth Indiana Regiment, numbered on the morning of December 31, 1862, 314 enlisted men and 14 commissioned officers (Company A being detached, and was not with the regiment), Col. Frederick C. Jones commanding, Maj. Henry Terry acting lieutenant-colonel, Capt. Enoch Weller acting major, Adjt. H. Y. Graham, Capt. A. T. M. Cockerill, commanding Company D; Capt. George M. Bacon, commanding Company E; Lieut. Charles R. Harman, commanding Company F; Lieut. Benjamin J. Horton, commanding Company I; Lieut. D. W. C. Wadsworth, commanding Company C; Lieut. William C. Beck, Company C; Lieut. Jacob Diehl, commanding Company H; Lieut. August Draeger, Company H; Lieut. John Acker, commanding Company G, and Lieut. Isaac N. Dryden, commanding Company B.

Early in the morning of the 31st ultimo heavy artillery and musketry firing was distinctly heard on our right, and as the sound neared our position it was evident that our forces were falling back, and our position in danger of being flanked, when our front was immediately changed

---

* Embodied in revised statement, p. 213.

to the left and rear, immediately in rear of the Sixth Ohio, which had now become earnestly engaged with the enemy, who was under cover of thick woods. We immediately moved forward to support the Sixth, and were ordered to lie down in the open space, about 50 paces in their rear, being much exposed to a galling fire of rebel infantry.

The deadly fire of the enemy in superior numbers was mowing down the ranks of the gallant Sixth, and they were compelled to fall back. Colonel Jones now ordered the regiment to fall back, which was done in good order. We halted at about 150 paces, and lay down to await the enemy's approach from the cover of the woods into the open space that separated us. On they came like a tornado that would destroy everything in its path. Encouraged by their success in driving the forces upon our right, they charged upon a battery lying upon our right, belonging to General Rousseau's command, when almost simultaneously our forces lying in their front opened upon them with a tremendous fire from our infantry and artillery, mowing them down almost by ranks, causing dismay and confusion, when they broke and fled in disorder to the cover of woods from which they had but just emerged.

We had rested but a few minutes after this terrible encounter, when an orderly of the gallant General Palmer delivered orders for us to move double-quick to the support of the Nineteenth Brigade (Colonel Hazen's), which was at this time gallantly resisting a furious charge of the rebel hordes in an open cotton-field on our left. We almost instantly formed on their right in the field, with Lieutenant Parsons' Fourth (Regular) Battery on our right. We remained in this position about one hour and a half, amid the most terrible shower of ball and shell, encouraged by the cool and daring courage of our brigade commander, who was apparently omnipresent, watching the movements of the enemy and issuing his orders in person, when we were ordered to fall back to the turnpike, where another stand was made.

We had remained in this position but a few minutes, exposed to a severe cross-fire of the enemy, when Colonel Jones was mortally wounded and carried from the field. The command now devolved upon Maj. Henry Terry, who displayed great coolness and bravery during the brief period he was permitted to command. Our position at this time was very much exposed, and it was here that the regiment suffered most. Major Terry was struck in the head and mortally wounded by a fragment of shell; Lieut. Charles R. Harman was almost instantly killed, and Lieut. Benjamin J. Horton had his leg fractured so severely that amputation was necessary. Capt. Enoch Weller now assumed command, assisted by me, when, our ammunition being exhausted, the regiment was relieved, and retired to the rear to replenish our cartridge-boxes, and again moved forward under cover of a cluster of timber, where we remained until dark, under a terrible and dangerous fire of the enemy's artillery, directed at some batteries upon our right and left, which wounded several of our men.

Night closed the terrible carnage, and we retired to the rear to prepare some refreshments and receive some rest, which was so much needed after the fatigues of the day. After resting January 1, on the morning of January 2 our regiment, with the brigade, moved across the river to support the division of General Van Cleve, which was alone on that side of the river. We prepared a small protection by removing the rails from an adjoining fence and constructing a slight breastwork, where we remained until about 3 p. m., when the enemy made a desperate charge upon the division of General Van Cleve, and being in such force they were compelled to give way, our position being in the rear and on the left of Van Cleve, immediately behind the Twenty-third

Kentucky Regiment, which formed the advance of our brigade, the Thirty-sixth Indiana, Sixth Ohio, and Eighty-fourth Illinois being immediately in our rear. The forces of Van Cleve were retreating in confusion, running directly over our artificial covering, drawing the fire of the enemy directly toward us.

Captain Weller, commanding the regiment, displayed great coolness and bravery, ordering us to hold our position. The enemy were now rushing wildly and madly on, and were near flanking our position, when Captain Weller was instantly killed. The regiment now retired in confusion under cover of some buildings and timber, when the Thirty-sixth Indiana, Sixth Ohio, and Eighty-fourth Illinois Regiments poured in such deadly volleys of musketry, causing a check in the enemy's advance, when the regiment rallied and again went gallantly into the fight with her colors in the front. The command now devolving upon me, the regiment was brought back and bivouacked with the brigade upon the spot that but a few moments before had been the scene of havoc and death.

At 3 a. m. the 3d instant I moved the regiment to the front on picket duty, and remained until 12 m., when we were relieved and retired across the river, which was waist-deep to the men.

Too much praise cannot be bestowed upon the heroic and gallant officers who sacrificed their lives in the late bloody encounters; they were true and brave men. What more can be said?

Great praise is due personally to Capt. George M. Bacon, Lieutenants Dryden, Horton, Diehl, Draeger, Wadsworth, Beck, and Adjutant Graham, for gallant and efficient services rendered during the entire engagement, displaying that coolness and bravery so necessary in such emergencies.

The non-commissioned officers of the regiment performed well their part of the drama, several of the companies being commanded by first sergeants, who bravely and ably performed the tasks assigned them. Our killed and wounded were promptly cared for by the corps of musicians under directions of Dr. Orr, of the Thirty-sixth Indiana Regiment, who manifested great zeal and energy in having them comfortably provided for and dressing their wounds.

I cannot omit to notice that the gallant behavior of the regiment is attributable to the brave example of our gallant brigade commander, whose brave and heroic daring on the field of Shiloh was still fresh in their memories. Also Brigadier-General Palmer, whose simplicity of manners and kind words of encouragement to the men, coupled with the cool and daring courage upon the field, cannot fail to inspire the men with confidence in their commanders.

The command devolving upon me when the last engagement was nearly closed, I am unable to make a minute report in detail of the part taken by the regiment in the recent desperate and bloody engagements of December 31 and January 2.

Our loss in killed, wounded, and missing is as follows: Commissioned officers killed, 4; wounded, 4. Enlisted men killed, 10; mortally wounded, 6; severely wounded, 62; missing, 12. Total killed, wounded, and missing, 98. Besides the foregoing, there are 20 slightly wounded, but not disabled for duty.

I have the honor to be, respectfully, sir, your obedient servant,

A. T. M. COCKERILL,
Captain, Commanding Twenty-fourth Ohio Regiment.

Capt. R. SOUTHGATE,
Acting Asst. Adjt. Gen., Tenth Brig., Fourth Div.

No. 143.

Report of Brig. Gen. Horatio P. Van Cleve, U. S. Army, commanding Third Division.

HEADQUARTERS THIRD DIVISION, LEFT WING,
ARMY OF THE CUMBERLAND,
—— —, 1863.

MAJOR: I have the honor to submit the following report of the operations of my division on December 31, 1862:

At 7 o'clock in the morning of that day I received an order to cross Stone's River, on which my left rested, and march toward Murfreesborough. The First Brigade, Colonel Beatty, Third Brigade, Colonel Price, and the batteries, Captain Swallow commanding, were promptly moved over and formed in line. The Second Brigade, Colonel Fyffe, being retained on the south side by a subsequent order, my lines being formed and about to advance, by your order I recrossed the river, leaving the Third Brigade to guard the ford. With the First Brigade I marched rapidly to the support of General Rousseau, whose division was hard pressed by the enemy. We formed in a wood on the south side of the Murfreesborough and Nashville turnpike.

Our lines were no sooner formed than the enemy was seen advancing, driving before him our scattered troops. Our ranks were opened to suffer these to pass, when they closed and opened on the enemy a withering fire, which soon brought him to a halt. A murderous fire was kept up on both sides about twenty minutes, when the enemy began to recoil. Our second line now relieving the first with hearty cheers, the rebels broke and retreated. The Second Brigade, coming up at this moment, formed on the right and joined in the pursuit. We pressed the enemy through this wood, then across an open field to another wood, where they appeared to have met with re-enforcements and reformed.

The Seventh Indiana Battery, Captain Swallow, joined us in the open field and rendered efficient aid.

Here I received information from General Rosecrans that General Rousseau was driving the enemy, accompanied with an order for me to press them hard. At the same time I was notified by a messenger from Colonel Harker, whose brigade was to my right and rear, that the enemy were in force on my right, in a wood, and were planting a battery there. I immediately sent a message to Colonel Harker to press the enemy hard, as I had no reserve to protect my right; to Captain Swallow, who was doing good service with his battery, not to suffer it to be captured; to Colonel Beatty to send two regiments, if they could possibly be spared, to the support of Colonel Fyffe, and a fourth to General Crittenden, to inform him of my critical situation. The enemy now poured a galling fire of musketry, accompanied with grape and shell, on our right. Colonel Fyffe's brigade, supported by Captain Swallow's battery, gallantly returned the fire, but, being overpowered by numbers on front and flank, were soon compelled to retire, followed but a short distance by the enemy.

Captain Swallow, to whom too much praise cannot be awarded, brought off his battery safely. Colonel Beatty, who had been pressing the enemy on the left, as soon as he learned the conditions of affairs, retired in good order. With two of his regiments he was ordered by General Rosecrans to protect a battery on the Murfreesborough road. The remaining two regiments of his brigade and Colonel Fyffe's brigade were reformed and took a position on the left of General McCook's corps, and to the right of the Pioneers; which position we occupied without further adventure till after dark.

I cannot close this report without inviting your attention to the gallantry displayed by those under my command during this engagement. To both officers and men too much praise cannot be awarded. I would particularly notice the coolness, intrepidity, and skill of my brigade commanders, Colonels Beatty and Fyffe, and of Captain Swallow, chief of artillery. To the members of my staff, Capts. E. A. Otis, assistant adjutant-general; C. H. Wood, inspector-general; William Starling, topographical engineer; Lieuts. T. F. Murdock and H. N. Williams, aides-de-camp, I owe much for the promptness, faithfulness, and gallantry with which they executed my orders and conveyed intelligence on the field. Sergt. R. B. Rhodes, of the First Ohio Cavalry, in command of my escort, conducted himself like a true soldier, and deserves honorable mention.

Individual acts of bravery in the different brigades will be brought to your notice in the reports of their respective commanders.

A slight wound, received early this day, becoming exceedingly painful, on the following morning I was compelled to turn over the command of the division to Colonel Beatty and retire from the field.

Very respectfully, your most obedient servant,

H. P. VAN CLEVE,
Brigadier-General.

Maj. LYNE STARLING,
Assistant Adjutant-General, Left Wing.

No. 144.

Reports of Col. Samuel Beatty, Nineteenth Ohio Infantry, commanding Third Division.

HEADQUARTERS THIRD DIVISION, LEFT WING,
Camp near Murfreesborough, January —, 1863.

MAJOR : I have the honor to submit the following report of the operations of this division for the time embraced between January 1 and 3, inclusive :

I was called to the command of the division on the morning of January 1, by General Van Cleve's disability, from the wound received in the battle of the preceding day. At 3 a. m. on that day I received orders to cross Stone's River with my command at the upper ford, and hold the hill overlooking the river, near the ford. Accordingly, at daybreak, the Third Brigade, Colonel Price commanding, crossed the river at the place indicated, throwing out skirmishers and flankers. Colonel Price was quickly followed by Colonel Fyffe's brigade (Second), the forces being formed in two lines, the right resting on the high ground near the river and east of the ford, and the left thrown forward so that the direction of the line should be nearly perpendicular to the river.

In the mean time the First Brigade, Colonel Grider commanding, had been disposed as follows: Two regiments were formed in the hollow, near the hospital, as a reserve, the other two remaining on the other side of the river to support a battery.

The enemy's skirmishers were now discovered in a wood, distant half a mile or so from our first line, and occasional firing took place on both sides. Information of all these movements was sent to General Crittenden, who sent me word that if I needed artillery to order up a battery. The Third Wisconsin Battery, Lieutenant Livingston commanding, was accordingly, at about 10 a. m., ordered to cross the river and remain in the hollow near the ford.

Small parties of the enemy's cavalry and infantry were occasionally seen, and at length a strong line was distinctly visible through the openings in the wood. Lieutenant Livingston was now ordered to bring up his battery. It was accordingly placed in position on the rising ground in front of Colonel Fyffe's brigade. Several shells were thrown at the enemy's line, which caused its disappearance. It was supposed they had laid down. One section, Lieutenant Hubbard commanding, was now moved to the hill on the right, whence also one or two shells were thrown at detached parties. Colonel Fyffe's brigade was moved to the left of the battery, where it was covered by a skirt of woods. Our whole force had been constantly concealed by making the men lie down.

About 1 o'clock the remaining two regiments of Colonel Grider's brigade (the Nineteenth Ohio and Ninth Kentucky) were ordered to cross the river, which they did, forming near the hospital, on the left of the other two regiments of the same brigade, to protect our left flank. The enemy's forces were occasionally seen moving to our left, and Generals Crittenden and Palmer were advised of that fact. Colonel Grose was, consequently, ordered to support me, his brigade formed so as to protect our left, relieving the Nineteenth Ohio and Ninth Kentucky. These two regiments then formed in rear of the right of the second line as a reserve, being posted in the hollow near the ford. No other disturbance occurred during the day, except the occasional firing of the skirmishers, so Colonel Grose's brigade and Livingston's battery recrossed the river.

About midnight we were alarmed by sharp firing from the skirmishers. They reported that it was caused by the enemy's skirmishers advancing and firing upon us. One of our men was killed and one wounded. Nothing else occurred during the night.

On the morning of Friday, January 2, Livingston's battery came across the river again and was posted as before. There was light skirmishing during the earlier part of the day. The Seventy-ninth Indiana Regiment, Colonel Knefler, was ordered to take place in the first line, to close the gap between Colonel Fyffe's brigade and the others.

Nothing of note occurred until about 11 o'clock, when the firing of the enemy's skirmishers became very constant and heavy, as they slowly crept up toward us. The skirmishers now reported a battery being planted in our front, and shortly afterward that fifteen regiments of infantry and three pieces of artillery were moving to our left. Notice of all these movements was given to Generals Crittenden and Palmer, and Colonel Grose's brigade again came over to our support.

About noon the enemy's battery opened with occasional shell, directed at Lieutenant Hubbard's section of artillery, on the hill. The enemy's artillery was now seen moving to our left, and soon another battery opened fire upon Lieutenant Hubbard's section. As the enemy's skirmishers were so near that their fire was annoying and dangerous to the artillery, I ordered Lieutenant Livingston to retire and take a position on the hill near the hospital. A few shells were still thrown by the enemy's battery on our left, and occasional ones from an apparently heavy battery across the river.

As the enemy's skirmishers pressed ours very closely, our line was strengthened by throwing out two more companies. The firing was very sharp, and many of our men, as well as theirs, were wounded.

At about 2.30 o'clock it was reported that four more of the enemy's guns were moving toward our left. Word was sent in this case, as of all other movements, to General Crittenden.

At about 3 p. m. our skirmishers reported that the enemy's skirmishers were throwing down the fence in front of our line. Orders were sent to Colonel Price to let his first line fall back behind the crest of the hill, but before he could receive them the enemy were advancing across the field to the charge. They were formed in column, with a front of apparently two regiments. The first column was three regiments, or six ranks deep. This was succeeded by a second of the same depth, and a third of apparently greater. At the same moment their artillery opened from three or four different points, throwing shot, shell, and canister directly into us.

As the enemy's column approached to within 100 yards or so, the first line rose up and delivered a heavy fire upon their column, which checked it for a moment. They soon pressed on, however. The regiments of the first line (the Fifty-first Ohio, Eighth Kentucky, and Thirty-fifth and Seventy-ninth Indiana) fought gallantly until the enemy were within a few yards of them, when, overpowered by numbers, they were compelled to retire. This movement confused and disorganized the second line, which also was ordered to fall back. The reserve, consisting of the Nineteenth Ohio and Ninth and Eleventh Kentucky, was now ordered up. They advanced most gallantly toward the crest of the hill and poured a destructive fire upon the enemy, whose first column was by this time almost annihilated. Their supporting column soon came up, however, and at the same time a force advanced along the river bank upon our right flank. Our men fought with the most desperate courage, as will appear from their severe loss, until forced back by the actual pressure of the enemy. Even then they broke from the right, file by file, stubbornly contesting the ground. At last, however, the right being forced back, the left was ordered to retire, which it slowly did, until the bank of the river was reached.

Attempts were made to rally the men at several points, but it was impossible, from the heavy fire and the close proximity of the enemy. Most of them were therefore forced across the river, where many of them rallied and returned with the first supporting troops; and I am proud to say that the colors of the Nineteenth Ohio, Ninth Kentucky, and Fifty-first Ohio were the first to recross the stream after the enemy's check. The tremendous fire of our artillery on the south side of the river, with Livingston's battery on the other, with the determined resistance they had met, had stopped the enemy at the river; and now, as our troops pressed forward, they fled in confusion, leaving four of their guns.

Several brave officers had rallied a great number of our men, and were the foremost in the advance. Night now came on and closed the pursuit. The regiments were rapidly reorganized, and in a few hours were in a state of efficiency, and turned out promptly and cheerfully at an alarm.

The Second Brigade, Colonel Fyffe's, was not attacked, the front of the enemy's column not extending to them; seeing the right driven back, they also retired in good order.

Lieutenant Livingston's battery fired constantly and well from the first appearance of the enemy until the very last moment he could remain safely. He then crossed the river without losing a piece.

I cannot too much commend the gallant manner in which my men fought, and the promptness with which, when forced to give way, they rallied and reorganized. Numerous instances of individual courage and devotion appear in the regimental and brigade reports.

To the commanders of the different brigades (Colonels Grider, Price, and Fyffe) my thanks are due for the gallantry and coolness of their behavior under very trying circumstances. Lieutenant Livingston, of the Third Wisconsin Battery, did efficient service and performed his duty ably and handsomely. Lieutenant Smock, Third Kentucky Cavalry, who commanded a detachment of couriers, remained constantly near me, and was of great use.

To the following officers (members of my staff) I tender my thanks for their assistance, and the manner in which it was rendered: Capts. E A. Otis, assistant adjutant-general; C. H. Wood, acting assistant inspector-general, and William Starling, topographical engineer; Lieuts. T. F. Murdock and H. N. Williams, aides-de-camp.

For particulars of the action of the different brigades and detached regiments, I have the honor to refer you to their respective reports, herewith transmitted.

Most respectfully, your obedient servant,

SAMUEL BEATTY,
Colonel, Comdg. Third Div., Left Wing, Fourteenth Army Corps.

Maj. LYNE STARLING, *Assistant Adjutant-General.*

HEADQUARTERS THIRD DIVISION, LEFT WING,
January 16, 1863.

In my official report of the part the Third Division took in the engagement before Murfreesborough, I omitted to mention the valuable services rendered by the acting medical director of the division, Maj. M. C. Woodworth, surgeon of the Fifty-first Ohio Volunteers, and now take advantage of the opportunity to give credit and due praise to him as an able and efficient officer, and thank him for his valuable services rendered to the wounded of this division by his able and energetic efforts in their behalf.

Very respectfully, your obedient servant,

SAMUEL BEATTY,
Colonel, Comdg. Third Div., Left Wing, Fourteenth Army Corps.

Maj. LYNE STARLING, *Assistant Adjutant-General.*

Report of the number killed, wounded, and missing from the Third Division, Left Wing, in the engagement before Murfreesborough, Tenn.

Command.	Killed.			Wounded.			Missing.			Aggregate.
	Officers.	Enlisted men.	Total.	Officers.	Enlisted men.	Total.	Officers.	Enlisted men.	Total.	
Brig. Gen. H. P. Van Cleve				1		1				1
First Brigade	7	59	66	16	303	319		81	81	466
Second Brigade	4	76	80	14	225	239	2	160	162	481
Third Brigade	6	75	81	21	307	328	2	146	148	557
Artillery Corps		6	6		19	19				25
Total*	17	216	233	52	854	906	4	387	391	1,530

Respectfully submitted.

SAMUEL BEATTY,
Colonel, Comdg. Third Div., Left Wing, Fourteenth Army Corps.

---

*But see revised statement, pp. 213, 214.

No. 145.

Report of Capt. George R. Swallow, Seventh Indiana Battery.

CAMP OF THE SEVENTH INDIANA BATT., THIRD DIV.,
January 5, 1863.

On the morning of December 31, I ordered Lieutenant Buckmar to move the battery in rear of the Second Brigade of the Third Division. This brigade was not moved across the river at the time the First and Third crossed and recrossed, but was ordered up the pike in the vicinity of our hospital, where the enemy's cavalry were trying to capture prisoners from our broken and retreating columns. The battery opened upon them with shell, our cavalry at the same time charging upon them, which caused them to retreat in disorder. The brigade then advanced to the right and front, through a cedar thicket into an open field, the battery following immediately in rear. While in the field, and nearly across it, our advance commenced skirmishing with the enemy. I immediately ordered the battery into position, and the firing to commence with shell to our right and front, where the enemy's infantry were rapidly advancing upon us. They soon entered the field, when I ordered the battery to open upon them with canister, at the same time ordering the caissons to the rear.

I soon saw part of the brigade falling back in disorder and the enemy advancing across the field toward the battery, with a yell. I then ordered the battery to limber to the rear and retire as rapidly as possible, which was done in not the best order. We reached the pike and took position near the old block-house, with a loss of 1 lieutenant, F. W. Buckmar, seriously wounded, 1 man killed, and 2 wounded. During the day the battery occupied several different positions, engaging the enemy's artillery and infantry, but with what effect is not known. At night went into park a short distance from the old block-house, having had 1 lieutenant and 4 men wounded, and 3 killed.

On the morning of the 1st instant, by Captain Mendenhall's order, I took position near the ford, supported by General Cruft's brigade. Nothing worthy of note transpired during the day, and the morning of the 2d instant found us occupying the same position. During the day General Negley's command took position in my rear and near the ford. Six guns of the artillery under his command took position on my left, and Captain Mendenhall's battery of eight guns, under command of Lieutenant Parsons, came into position on my right and front.

About 4 p. m. I received word that the enemy were advancing in force to attack the left of our wing. Their lines of infantry soon came in full view, and the batteries on my right and left, together with my own, opened a rapid and vigorous fire upon their advancing columns. They soon opened a galling artillery fire upon us from three different points. The battery on my left retired a short distance, and the one on my right commenced to fire, retiring. Seeing this, I ordered the battery to fix prolonge, to fire retiring. About this time the vent of my left piece became filled with friction primers, and was ordered to the rear for repair without my knowledge. The drivers of the other pieces, seeing this piece moving to the rear, supposed the order had been given to retire, and drove some 40 yards to the rear before they could be halted. The order was then given to advance, and one piece was moved by hand to its first position; the rest were limbered and moved to the position first occupied, except the gun that had been ordered to the rear, where all the ammunition was expended except a few rounds of canister. In this engagement we had 1 man killed and 2 wounded.

January 3 found the battery in the same position. General Negley ordered the battery to open fire upon a line of the enemy's infantry, which did no good, and wounded 1 of my own men by the premature discharge of one of the guns.

During the whole engagement I expended 406 rounds of ammunition; had 1 lieutenant and 7 men wounded; 4 men killed; 4 horses wounded, 1 killed, and 4 missing.

I should have done more firing, but General Rosecrans told me he wanted some ammunition reserved for an emergency.

Respectfully,

G. R. SWALLOW,
Captain Seventh Indiana Battery.

No. 146.

Report of Lieut. Alanson J. Stevens, Battery B, Pennsylvania Light Artillery.

HEADQUARTERS PENNSYLVANIA LIGHT ARTILLERY,
January 5, 1863.

SIR: I have the honor to make the following report of the part taken in the recent action by the Pennsylvania battery:

On the morning of December 31 we were ordered to cross the river with the First Brigade, to take position, which we had barely time to do when we were ordered back again. We then followed the First Brigade toward the right wing, where the battle was raging fiercely. We found everything there in confusion, and it impossible to follow our brigade, and the battery nearly in the lines of the enemy. You then gave me the permission to fight on my own hook, and do the best in my power. I then countermarched the battery and took position on the rising ground on the left of the old block-house, along the line of the railroad, and opened fire on the enemy, who were advancing through the woods on the right of the pike and in our front. We fired as rapidly as possible with spherical case from our smooth-bores and Schenkl shells from our rifles, when, finding the enemy checked and our infantry advancing, we limbered to the front, advanced a short distance across the pike, where we came in position and fired a few rounds, when the Board of Trade Battery advanced and took position on our left, covering all the intermediate ground in our front.

We changed position by moving by the left flank, and occupied the rising ground in the corn-field to the right of the pike, and covering the woods, out of which General Rousseau's and Negley's troops were retiring. We reserved our fire until our own troops were clear of the woods, and the enemy's lines, with banners flying, came in sight on the verge of the timber, within 500 yards of our battery. We opened upon them with spherical case, shell, and canister, and fired briskly for about fifteen minutes, when, seeing no more of the enemy, we ceased firing; some of the enemy's advance fell within 15 or 20 yards of our guns. By General Rousseau's advice, we then fell back on the rising ground between that and the railroad, firing a few shots at the enemy.

By Captain Mendenhall's order, we again advanced to our former position in the corn-field on the right of the pike, and met with a warm reception from the enemy's musketry from the woods in our front, and, the right flank being at the same time under cross-fire from one of the enemy's batteries on our left, we opened fire on the woods in our front and right, soon silencing the enemy's fire, when, finding that we had no support on either flanks or rear, we again withdrew to the rising ground between the pike and railroad. We then were ordered by Captain Mendenhall to take position across the pike, near the old log-house in our extreme front, having to guard against the enemy's advance up the pike and from the woods on our right, from which a continued fire of musketry annoyed us. At the same time a battery opened upon us from the brick house near the pike, injuring one of our trails and limber, to which we replied until our long-range ammunition, the supply of which was small, was exhausted, when I had the smooth-bores withdrawn and took a position to rake the pike with canister, in case the enemy advanced, and kept the two rifles in the advance until night, when the whole battery was withdrawn about 500 yards to the rear, and supplied with ammunition.

On the morning of January 1, by your order, we took position on the left of the railroad, and at a right angle with it, the Sixth Ohio Battery on our left. We did no firing that day, with the exception of a few shots in the morning thrown at the woods in our front, and kept in position ready for action in that vicinity nearly the whole day; at night went into park in rear of the log-house near the railroad.

At sunrise on the morning of January 2, we were saluted with a shower of solid balls from the enemy's batteries, falling in too close a vicinity to be agreeable. We mounted quickly and took position on the left of the railroad, on a small rise commanding the approach of the enemy in our front. Captain Mendenhall then ordered us to the front, to take a position commanding the open field to the left of the railroad. During the forenoon we were several times saluted with shots from the battery of the enemy planted in the woods beyond the opening in our front, to which we remained silent until near noon, when skirmishers of the Fifty-first Indiana, which supported us on the right, advanced across the opening and drove the enemy's pickets, when the enemy opened upon them with canister, at the same time upon us with solid shot. Our skirmishers falling back, we opened with solid shot, when the battery became silent, and remained so until 3 p. m., when it again opened, and, shortly after, heavy musketry was heard upon our left; we opened at the battery in our front, when it became silent.

When we saw the enemy advancing upon our left wing across the river, and our men falling back, we changed front, firing to the left, and opened a cross-fire on them, and continued it until our forces in their front compelled them to fall back beyond our range. We remained in position until 9 p. m., when we ascertained that our supports on our flanks had been withdrawn without we being notified of the fact; and no pickets in front between us and the enemy's lines, I withdrew the battery to the rear of the infantry and parked.

On the morning of January 3 we returned to our position of the previous day, support having returned, where we remained until 3 p. m., when we were ordered across and took the place occupied by the Third Wisconsin Battery, where we remained until near midnight, when we were ordered to recross the river, which we did, and parked on the ground we now occupy. We expended about 1,650 rounds of ammunition, lost 7 horses, 2 men killed and 7 wounded, a few small-arms, and a large quantity of clothing, camp and garrison equipage.

Yours, respectfully,

A. J. STEVENS,
First Lieutenant, Commanding Battery.

Capt. G. E. SWALLOW,
Chief of Artillery, 3d Div., Left Wing, 14th Army Corps.

No. 147.

Report of Lieut. Cortland Livingston, Third Wisconsin Battery.

CAMP OF THE THIRD WISCONSIN BATTERY.
Near Murfreesborough, Tenn., January 5, 1863.

SIR: I would report as follows the part taken in the actions of December 31 and the 1st, 2d, and 3d of January, 1863, by the Third Wisconsin Battery:

At daybreak on the morning of December 31 we moved from camp with our division, and crossed the ford at Stone's River to the east and Murfreesborough side. We took a commanding position in battery. In a short time we were ordered to recross to the west side and take up a position commanding the ford (all the troops that had crossed were ordered to recross). The Third Brigade, under Colonel Price, supported our flanks. Very early in the action the enemy gained on our right wing, and many wagons and ambulances moved across this ford. A hospital was established in some buildings there. I inquired of an officer, and was informed that we had infantry pickets and a small force of cavalry on the other side.

About 12 m. I saw a great stampede among the ambulances, wagons, and stragglers opposite, and was told some rebel cavalry were charging on them. I was fearful of making a mistake and firing on our own cavalry. We could not see the enemy until he got among the wagons and was taking them off. We then opened upon them and disabled 2 wagons, which blocked the lane and obliged them to leave without their booty. I think they got off with only 5 wagons. They left 1 man killed, and carried off their wounded. We shelled the woods in the direction they had taken. We expended 50 rounds of ammunition that day. The only casualty was 1 man, Henry S. Netley, wounded in the thigh, slightly.

January 1, Thursday, the battery was advanced across the river with the Third Division, under command of Colonel Beatty, with orders to protect the left from any flank movement, but not to bring on a general engagement. After moving forward about half a mile we discovered two regiments of infantry on a hill-side. We threw a few shells among them, and they withdrew to the woods on their left. We fired very little that day, only when we saw evidences of their massing troops. We had 1 man (A. J. Uleric) slightly wounded by the sharpshooters.

January 2. This morning we discovered the enemy had erected a fortification on the brow of the hill, 1½ miles to our front. Soon they opened on us with their 24-pounder brass pieces. We did not reply, and they did us no injury. Soon they moved these guns nearer to us, and more to their right. This gave them a flank fire, and we found it very dangerous to remain there. We were ordered to withdraw and take up a position a half mile to our rear and left, near the hospital. About half an hour after we had done so, we saw the enemy had drawn up in line and were advancing in great force. Just then General Rosecrans ordered me to change my position, so that I was a little late in opening my fire. The enemy advanced steadily, driving in our pickets. Our fire was very effective, but their ranks closed up immediately.

Soon I saw our right had given way that rested on the river. A heavy column had advanced under cover of the bank of the river and its skirt of woods, and had flanked the troops stationed there. I then sent my caissons across to the west side, and, seeing everything giving way, I sent one section at a time across, still working those that remained until the others were over. When the last section reached the ford, one regiment of the enemy was within 100 yards of it, and poured a galling fire into us. Many of our horses were shot dead in the river, but our brave boys cleared them from the teams, and everything was got across. We opened fire on them as soon as we had crossed, though many of our caissons had not yet come up. We opened fire at three different positions after we crossed, and soon after the enemy gave back. Were crossed to the east side, to sustain General Davis, and took a position in advance of the one taken the day previous, January 1. We expended this day 300 rounds of ammunition. Our fire was very good, disabling two of the enemy's limbers and killing their horses, but our fire was directed mostly at their advancing lines. We lost 9 horses, 2 sets lead harness, and had 2 men, Sergeants Holenbeck and Daniel Robin, wounded, not seriously.

January 3. We had remained in our position, assigned us by General Davis, all night and until noon this day, before we were relieved. Our horses had had nothing to eat for forty-eight hours, and our men were wet with wading the river, and without shelter from the cold pelting rain; but when I told them it was the imperative order of General Davis and of vital necessity that we should hold out a little longer, they cheerfully obeyed. General Davis kindly divided what little he had to eat with our men, as did also Colonel Beatty the day before.

We had no rations issued since the 30th, and our provision and forage wagon had been sent back by order of some one. At 11 a. m. we were relieved by the Twenty-sixth Pennsylvania Battery, and fell back a little to feed. At 11 p. m. we recrossed the river, by order of Captain Mendenhall, and took up our old position on the west side, commanding the ford.

January 4. Remained at the ford until 5 p. m., when we were ordered to this camp.

We have expended in all 358 rounds of ammunition, lost 9 horses, 2 sets harness, and have 4 men wounded. Present for duty, 3 commissioned officers and 107 men.

Yours, &c.,

CORTLAND LIVINGSTON,
Lieutenant, Commanding Third Wisconsin Battery.

Captain SWALLOW,
Chief of Arty. Brig., 3d Div., Left Wing, Army of the Cumberland.

No. 148.

Report of Col. Samuel Beatty, Nineteenth Ohio Infantry, commanding First Brigade.

HDQRS. 1ST BRIG., 3D DIV., LEFT WING, 14TH A. C.,
In Camp, near Murfreesborough, Tenn., January 9, 1863.

CAPTAIN: I have the honor to submit the following report of the First Brigade, Third Division, left wing, Fourteenth Army Corps, in the action of December 31, 1862:

At 8 a. m., December 31, 1862, the Third Division having crossed Stone's River, on the extreme left of the army, formed line of battle, with the right of the First Brigade resting on the bank of the river. The line was scarcely established when an order was received to recross the stream and march to the right, across the Nashville and Chattanooga Railroad track, and west of the Nashville and Murfreesborough pike.

Here the brigade, marching in advance of the division, was met by retreating columns, bearing unmistakable signs of disaster, who reported
themselves belonging to the command of Major-General Rousseau
They broke through the lines of the brigade—infantry, cavalry, artillery, ambulances, baggage train, &c.—in the greatest confusion, frequently separating the regiments of the brigade, threatening serious
trouble. Line of battle was finally formed upon a point indicated by
Major-General Rosecrans in person, consisting of the Nineteenth Regiment Ohio Volunteers, Maj. Charles F. Manderson commanding, on the
right; the Ninth Regiment Kentucky Volunteers, Col. Benjamin C.
Grider commanding, on the left; in front, the Nineteenth Ohio Volunteers, supported by the Seventy-ninth Regiment Indiana Volunteers,
Col. Frederick Knefler commanding, and the Ninth Kentucky, supported by the Eleventh Regiment Kentucky Volunteers, Maj. E. L.
Mottley commanding. It was with the utmost difficulty that the line
established was maintained. It was impossible to prevent the retreating columns from breaking through and almost destroying it; but the
brigade stood fast and never wavered. The enemy was rapidly approaching in three heavy columns, to reach and capture the train of the army,
immediately in rear and across the pike. Fire had to be reserved on
account of our own troops, who were in front of the line. The front at
last having been cleared by our own men, and the enemy's column appearing at a short distance, a heavy fire was opened by the front line of
the brigade, which was kept up with very destructive effect, and completely checked the enemy's advance, who for some time maintained the
position, inflicting severe loss upon us.

At this juncture the Eleventh Kentucky and Seventy-ninth Indiana
Regiments were ordered to relieve the Nineteenth Ohio and Ninth Kentucky Regiments, in front, who by this time expended many rounds of
their ammunition, wheeled into column, and the two supporting regiments passed through the intervals. The whole movement was accomplished in fine order, under the very heavy fire of the enemy. The new
line immediately opened fire upon the enemy, who commenced falling
back; bayonets were ordered to be fixed, and the Seventy-ninth Indiana and the Eleventh Kentucky were ordered to advance, supported by
the other two regiments. They advanced rapidly, the enemy retreating.
An uninterrupted fire was kept up, and the enemy compelled, after a
pursuit of nearly a mile from the position first occupied by the brigade,
to take refuge behind his works, which could not be assailed for the
want of artillery, which could not advance in that direction, owing to
the very rough and uneven nature of the ground.

While in this position, the Second Brigade of the Third Division,
which had in the mean time advanced on the right of the First Brigade,
and was now on a line parallel with it, was forced back by strongly re-
enforced columns of the enemy again appearing in front. The First
Brigade was ordered to fall back, to prevent a flank movement, which
was accomplished in good order, to a distance of about 300 yards, and
took position in a cedar thicket, where skirmishers thrown to the front
kept up a continual fire.

At this point I was ordered by Major-General Rosecrans to move to
the support of Mendenhall's and the Chicago Board of Trade Battery,
on the left of the brigade. The Ninth and Eleventh Kentucky Regiments were ordered to that point, and the Nineteenth Ohio and the Seventy-ninth Indiana Regiments were ordered to fall back and to join the
Second Brigade, on the right.

In this position the brigade remained until midnight, when the brigade was ordered to recross the pike, and there bivouacked until morn ing. The brigade was hotly engaged for three hours. Regimental reports, which I have the honor herewith to transmit, have accurate lists of casualties, and I refer you to them for particulars.

Commanders of regiments, officers, and soldiers did their duty gallantly, and their splendid conduct, repulsing the enemy when victoriously pursuing our disordered troops, contributed in no small measure to the successful result of the day.

My thanks are due to Lieutenants Sheets and Percival, of my staff, and the soldiers of my escort, for their efficient services in the action.

I have the honor to be, captain, very respectfully, your obedient servant,

SAMUEL BEATTY,
Colonel, Comdg. Third Div., Left Wing, Fourteenth Army Corps.

Capt. E. A. OTIS,
A. A. G., Third Div., Left Wing, Fourteenth Army Corps.

No. 149.

Reports of Col. Benjamin C. Grider, Ninth Kentucky Infantry, commanding regiment and First Brigade.

IN CAMP, NEAR MURFREESBOROUGH, TENN.,
January 1, 1863.

LIEUTENANT: My regiment, the Ninth Kentucky Volunteer Infantry, was early yesterday morning ordered on the south side of Stone's River, and formed in line of battle in the front line, and on the left of the Nineteenth Ohio Volunteers (Major Manderson). We had advanced a short distance down the river, when we were ordered to recross, to support our forces in the center and on the right, understanding that the enemy were driving them, and had turned our right, and probably gained our rear. We moved by the flank, and at a double-quick, to the Murfreesborough pike, and thence along that pike about a half mile to our rear, to a skirt of woods, through which we saw our men retreating, and heard that they had been before forced back through them. We formed on the pike, the Nineteenth Ohio on the right and the Ninth Kentucky on the left, the two composing the front line, supported by the Eleventh Kentucky, Major Mottley, and the Seventy-ninth Indiana, Colonel Knefler, in the rear or second line.

As soon as our retreating troops cleared the woods, our front, the Nineteenth and Ninth, opened upon the enemy a cool, well-aimed, and deadly fire, which brought them to a stand. After a few such rounds we were ordered to advance, which the men promptly did with the alacrity and steadiness of veterans, gallantly led on by all their officers, driving the enemy with great slaughter for half a mile or more. Here, the ammunition of the front line beginning to fail, and the enemy's fire having almost ceased, we were ordered to open our lines for the reserve—the Eleventh Kentucky and the Seventy-ninth Indiana—to pass through, which they did in gallant style, seeing and hearing but little of the enemy for some hundreds of yards, when they found him rallied; but again he was forced to yield to the well-directed fire and gallantry of the Eleventh Kentucky and Seventy-ninth Indiana, and thus, for a time, the advance was continued for some distance, when we found a body of our troops broken, and retreating from our right in a direction which passed them diagonally through our lines. Our men kept firm, and we tried to rally them, but with no effect. Thus our right was exposed and turned, and you gave the order to fall back, which we did in most excellent order under the heaviest shower of balls and missiles that we had encountered during the day. Our loss here was great, and the courage and coolness of men and officers was here put to a severer test than during the advance, and well did they meet the trying emergency.

We came back a short distance, and promptly formed in line to again meet the enemy. Here General Rosecrans in person ordered me to advance my regiment to close range of the enemy, and, after giving him a few fires, to charge. I ordered the advance, but had gone only a short distance when the general ordered us to halt and cause the men to lie down, while a battery in our rear opened over us upon the enemy. After remaining here for a short time, my regiment and the Eleventh Kentucky were ordered to take position to sustain the Chicago Board of Trade Battery and another, the name of which I do not know, then threatened by the enemy. This we continued to do until late in the night, after the battle was all over for the day.

We were during this time under fire from the enemy's artillery, and lost 2 men killed and several wounded. Our loss during the day was 2 commissioned officers—First Lieuts. Silas Clark and W. J. Cram—wounded; 2 sergeants, 1 of whom was the color-bearer, killed; 1 private killed, and 19 wounded. A full list will be handed in as soon as practicable.

I have no terms of praise that can do justice to the noble bearing and unflinching bravery of all the officers and men. I mention the names of them all: Lieut. Col. George H. Cram, Maj. John H. Grider, Adjt. C. D. Bailey; Capts. R. A. Read, Rufus Somerby, D. B. Coyle, William T. Bryan; First Lieuts. A. Sidney Leggett, T. Freely Heeter, W. J. Cram (commanding companies); R. T. Patton, Boyle O. Rodes, Henry W. Mayes, Silas Clark; Second Lieuts. Frederick F. Carpenter, D. C. Downing, John P. Grinstead, James M. Simmons, and Benjamin M. Johnson.

Company A, Capt. Henry F. Leggett, was on detached duty, and, I regret, could not be in the battle, as their services, brave men and well officered as they are, would have been valuable. First Lieut. John H. Wheat was not with the regiment, being detached on duty with the Pioneer Corps.

Respectfully submitted.

B. C. GRIDER,
Colonel Ninth Kentucky Volunteers.

Lieut. W. H. H. SHEETS,
Acting Assistant Adjutant-General, First Brigade.

—

HEADQUARTERS FIRST BRIGADE, THIRD DIVISION,
Camp in front of Murfreesborough, Saturday, January 3, 1863.

COLONEL: I had the honor to be placed in command of the First Brigade, Third Division (formerly the Eleventh Brigade), on the morning of January 1, and being ordered by you as commander of the division, I at once marched with my command to the south side of Stone's River, and bivouacked in the woods and fields belonging, as I learned, to a man named Hoover. Some skirmishing and picket firing was soon heard and some rebel cavalry seen, but nothing worthy of notice occurred during the day. That night the enemy attempted to drive in our pickets, but failed.

Next morning opened with brisk cannonading on the part of the enemy, to which our artillery made no reply. Our skirmishers in front were actively engaged all day. It was then ascertained that the enemy had planted a battery in our front, and a section or more on our left, and that a portion of their guns across the river, which came down in a course parallel with our right, could reach us with a raking fire, and interfere with our crossing at the first ford, if compelled to recross. It was also suggested by myself and other officers, Major Manderson, commanding the Nineteenth Ohio, particularly, that our right, resting on the river, was exposed, and might be attacked and turned, and that neither the depth of the stream nor character of the banks was a sufficient protection; that troops and artillery were needed on the opposite side to sustain our right. You and we all were assured that this was attended to, and we rested on that assurance.

Thus matters stood until about an hour before sundown, when artillery firing on the part of the enemy and heavy skirmishing on both sides commenced. We now supposed that the attack which we had all day expected would be postponed until daylight the next day, but were mistaken. The enemy were seen advancing in three lines, the front composed of a battalion of sharpshooters, and the other lines composed of the whole divisions of Generals John C. Breckinridge and Cheatham. Generals Roger W. Hanson and James E. Rains, of Kentucky,* as I learn, were present in Breckinridge's command. The regiments of my brigade (the Nineteenth Ohio, Major Manderson, on the right; the Ninth Kentucky, Lieutenant-Colonel Cram, in the center, and the Eleventh Kentucky, Major Mottley, on the left) were, by your orders, held in reserve. The Seventy-ninth Indiana had been about noon ordered to form on and sustain the front line, composed of the Third Brigade, Col. S. W. Price commanding, and were not again seen by me during the day. I doubt not they will receive justice at the hands of the colonel under whose command they were placed.

The onset of the enemy, sustained as they were by their artillery, succeeded in breaking and driving back our first and second lines. You now sent me an order to bring up the reserve, which I instantly did, though it was almost manifest, from the character of the fire in front, that the force we had on the ground, unassisted as we at that moment were by artillery, could not check the enemy's advance. Yet our men (the Nineteenth Ohio, Ninth Kentucky, and Eleventh Kentucky), undaunted by the terrible and desperate state of affairs, with bravery that cannot be described, and led on by their officers, the most cool and daring, moved forward, some through a thick undergrowth of wild briers, which to some extent broke their lines, fearlessly meeting the enemy and breaking his first line. Seeing this from my position, between and slightly in front of the Nineteenth Ohio and Ninth Kentucky, and noticing you just in my rear, I said to you, " Colonel, we have them checked; give us artillery and we will whip them." You replied, " You shall have it."

I rode back and soon saw the right regiment (the Nineteenth Ohio)

---

* Of Tennessee.

falling back. Calling to Major Manderson, who halted and came back, I said to him, "Major, the Ninth is still standing; let us rally the Nineteenth and sustain her." The major replied, "We are flanked on our right; we had better fall back and rally at the foot of the hill, if we can." I told him to do so, and I would order the Ninth and Eleventh Kentucky to do the same. I rode forward for this purpose, but just as I was about to give the order to Lieutenant-Colonel Cram, he gave it to his regiment, which was then receiving most of the fire hitherto directed against the Nineteenth. The Eleventh Kentucky moved back about the same time, and both of these regiments, almost in line with some of the enemy's troops, were the last regiments to quit the field—the Nineteenth Ohio leaving first, because first exposed to the flanking fire.

We fell back, fighting, though in some disorder, crossed the river, rallied under a very heavy fire, checked the enemy, and held him in check until we were re-enforced, when I, with the flags of the Nineteenth Ohio and Ninth Kentucky, recrossed the river, followed closely by Lieutenant-Colonel Cram, Majors Mottley and Manderson, men and officers from the Nineteenth Ohio, Ninth and Eleventh Kentucky, Lieut. Philip Reefy holding the colors of the Nineteenth, and Private Moses Rourk those of the Ninth Kentucky. The Twenty-first Ohio, led by Captain ————, acting major, promptly followed. Our troops now crossed rapidly and opened fire on the south side of the river.

Observing that the men would follow and stand by their colors, I here took the flag of my own regiment (the Ninth Kentucky), and, riding forward, called on the troops to advance, to which they gallantly responded, and, rushing upon the enemy, drove them with great slaughter from and past the ground which they had occupied before the attack, the Eleventh Kentucky taking a stand of colors, and the three regiments capturing four of the enemy's guns (the Washington Artillery), the colors of the Nineteenth Ohio and the Ninth Kentucky Volunteers being the first to reach them. Lieutenant-Colonel Cram, of the Ninth, and Major Mottley, of the Eleventh Kentucky, with myself, were the first mounted officers at these guns. All three of the above regiments were represented there, and at all times in the most advanced and exposed positions. Lieutenant-Colonel Cram and Major Mottley ordered off a gun each, and I ordered off two. In short, each and every officer and man in these three regiments was all that could be asked, and far above the reach of encomiums.

Of Lieutenant-Colonel Cram, Ninth Kentucky, Major Manderson, Nineteenth Ohio, and Major Mottley, Eleventh Kentucky, I make special mention as the commanders on that day of their respective regiments. I refer to their reports accompanying this for more special notice than I can here take of the officers and men under their commands.

The result of the day was, the enemy retreated in haste and disorder, acknowledging a defeat, and evacuated Murfreesborough the next day. We bivouacked that night on the battle-field.

The loss of the three regiments under my command, as near as can be ascertained, is 250 officers and men killed, wounded, and missing, about one-third of the effective force which they had engaged. I refer for particulars to the inclosed regimental reports.

Most respectfully submitted.

B. C. GRIDER,
Colonel, Commanding First Brigade, Third Division.

Col. SAMUEL BEATTY,
Comdg. Third Div., Left Wing, Fourteenth Army Corps.

No. 150.

Reports of Col. Frederick Knefler, Seventy-ninth Indiana Infantry.

HDQRS. SEVENTY-NINTH REGIMENT INDIANA VOLS.,
Near Murfreesborough, Tenn., January 8, 1863.

LIEUTENANT: The undersigned has the honor to report that, on December 31, 1862, after having recrossed Stone's River, the regiment was ordered into position west of the Murfreesborough pike, in rear of the Nineteenth Regiment Ohio Volunteers, to check the columns of the enemy then pursuing our forces across the pike. After very heavy firing by the Nineteenth Ohio, and the repulse of the enemy, the regiment was ordered forward to relieve it. By command of the colonel commanding the brigade, bayonets were fixed and the enemy rapidly pursued, with very severe fire, for about three-quarters of a mile, driving them to their position behind works.

At this point an order was received to fall back, as the support on the right had given way before the enemy. Having fallen back in good order a distance of about 300 yards, halted and faced to the front. The regiment was ordered, by Major-General Rosecrans in person, to move by the right flank to an open field, to check the advance of the approaching enemy, and to cover the retreating right; which being accomplished, the regiment was ordered to fall back to the original line, the supports of the right and left having given way, and there joined the Nineteenth Ohio, the only regiment of the brigade remaining, the others having moved to the support of a battery on the left. The regiment remained in that position until ordered to recross the pike at midnight.

The regiment was engaged for three hours, and the loss severe. A report of the casualties is herewith submitted.*

It may not be improper to remark that the behavior of the regiment (only a short time in the field, on a long march, constant and arduous service when in camp, with but few opportunities to drill) may be attributed, in a great measure, to the splendid conduct of the Nineteenth Regiment Ohio Volunteers, Major Manderson commanding, the effect of whose example was not lost upon the officers and soldiers of this regiment.

Very respectfully, your obedient servant,

FRED. KNEFLER,
Colonel Seventy-ninth Regiment Indiana Volunteers.

Lieut. W. H. H. SHEETS,
A. A. A. G., First Brig., Third Div., Fourteenth A. C.

—

HDQRS. SEVENTY-NINTH REGIMENT INDIANA VOLS.,
Near Murfreesborough, Tenn., January 8, 1863.

CAPTAIN: The undersigned has the honor to submit the following report of the Seventy-ninth Regiment Indiana Volunteers in the action of January 2, 1863:

Having marched, on January 1, from the position east of the pike, across Stone's River, the regiment was formed in line on the left of the Eleventh Regiment Kentucky Volunteers, supporting the brigade in front, and remained in that position until the morning of the 2d, when it was detached from the First Brigade, and, by order of Col. S. Beatty,

---
* Embodied in revised statement, p. 213.

commanding the Third Division, took up a position in front, with the Thirty-fifth Regiment Indiana Volunteers on the right and the Forty-fourth Regiment Indiana Volunteers on the left. A company of skirmishers was deployed in an open wood to cover the front of the regiment.

During the day several pieces of artillery were placed in position by the enemy on a rise of ground some 500 yards distant, throwing shell into our lines, severely wounding some of the men. The regiment was sheltered, as far as the nature of the ground would permit, by lying down.

About 4 p. m. the fire of the skirmishers increased, and a column of the enemy, four or five regiments deep, approached rapidly, supported by artillery, which was kept concealed (as it was dragged by men instead of horses) until it opened fire within 100 yards of our lines. The forces on the right soon became engaged, but the regiment was kept lying on the ground until the enemy had approached within 50 yards, when it was ordered to rise up, and commenced firing with very destructive effect upon the enemy, volley after volley, until, the line having given way on the right and left, the regiment being left alone almost surrounded, the enemy in front and on both flanks, it was forced to fall back across Stone's River, where it rallied at the rendezvous of the Third Division.

The regiment went into action on December 31 with 341, rank and file, and lost during both engagements fully one-third of its available force, including more than half the commissioned officers in killed and wounded; but very few men are missing or taken prisoners.

Officers and soldiers conducted themselves well, doing their duty, and there was no shirking or skulking from the field before or during action It would be injustice to many to mention a few, when all behaved well.

Lieut. Eli F. Ritter, adjutant of the regiment, rendered me very valuable service, acting as a field officer in the absence of the lieutenant-colonel.

A report of casualties is submitted herewith.*

I have the honor to be, very respectfully, your obedient servant,

FRED. KNEFLER,
Colonel Seventy-ninth Regiment Indiana Volunteers.

Capt. E. A. OTIS,
Asst. Adjt. Gen., Third Division, Fourteenth Army Corps.

No. 151.

Report of Lieut. Col. George H. Cram, Ninth Kentucky Infantry, of engagement January 2.

JANUARY —, 1863.

I respectfully submit the following as my report of the part my regiment took in the engagement of January 2, 1863, on the left wing of our army, in front of Murfreesborough:

Early in the forenoon Colonel Grider ordered me to hold my regiment in reserve, with another regiment of his brigade (the Nineteenth Ohio), under cover of a hill about 200 yards from the upper ford of Stone's River, and told me that the enemy would probably attack us some time during the day, and ordered me to hold my regiment in readiness to re-enforce our line, if the enemy should attack us in too great force.

---

* Embodied in revised statement, p. 213.

Nothing but heavy skirmishing and artillery firing on the part of the enemy occurred during the day, until about 4 o'clock in the evening, when our whole line was attacked by a heavy rebel force. My men were under arms, and I knew by the firing that our men were giving way. I was ordered forward, and moved up the hill at a double-quick, through briers and undergrowth, tearing our line badly. Arriving at the crest of the hill, we met our troops retreating in great confusion. Nothing could be more discouraging to my men than the aspect of affairs at that time, but they never faltered. I allowed the retreating mass to pass through my lines, the enemy all the time pouring into us a destructive fire, both infantry and artillery. Our lines closed up, and I ordered my men to commence firing. The enemy gave way after the fourth or fifth round, the colors of the regiment in front of us having fallen no less than three times, and had we had but the enemy in front to contend with, our chances of success would have been tolerably certain; but just when the battle was being decided in our favor, we were flanked by a heavy force on our right, causing our support on that flank to give way, leaving us exposed to a raking fire, which was fast decimating my regiment. We had already suffered. Major Grider and Adjutant Bailey wounded; Captains Bryan and Coyle killed; Read badly wounded; Lieutenants Leggett and Carpenter killed; Heeter and Johnson wounded.

I do not hesitate to say that no regiment could have withstood this fresh attack. I ordered the regiment to fall back under the hill. Colonel Grider ordered me in person to rally my men at the foot of the hill. I found the ground almost in possession of a rebel regiment. We continued the retreat across the river, and I there rallied my men. We were here re-enforced by three or four regiments, and the enemy brought to a stand. The firing here was the most terrible I ever heard. The foe fought us bravely, but could not withstand such a terrible fire. He gave way slowly, and we not only retook the lost ground, but drove him over a mile, cutting him up badly and capturing his artillery, changing the result of the battle from a defeat to a splendid victory. The colors of the Ninth Kentucky recrossed the river by the side of those of the Nineteenth Ohio, and under your leadership. The regiments of your brigade, shattered as they were, were the first to wave their flags over the captured guns of the enemy.

My officers and men fought splendidly, under the most discouraging circumstances. Every man in the regiment knew what he had to encounter when we were ordered forward, but not one faltered. They knew that the gallant reserve—the Nineteenth Ohio and Ninth Kentucky—were insufficient to check the victorious enemy.

Major Grider was wounded while gallantly cheering on his men early in the engagement, and Adjutant Bailey soon afterward. I felt the loss of these officers greatly. Captain Bryan was mortally wounded, doing his duty nobly. Captain Coyle was killed while cheering on his men. Lieutenants Leggett and Carpenter were killed at the head of their companies. Captain Read, Lieutenants Heeter and Johnson were wounded while fighting gallantly.

I take pleasure in mentioning the following officers, whose gallant conduct deserves great praise: Captain Somerby, Lieutenants Patton, Downing, Grinstead, Rodes, and Mayes. Private Moses Rourk, of Company C, deserves special mention. When the colors were shot down, in the engagement of the 31st, he grasped them and brought them safely through the fight, and in the battle of January 2 he carried them into the thickest of the fight, and was at times left almost alone.

He is but eighteen years of age, and is one of the bravest soldiers in the army.

Our loss was as follows:* Commissioned officers killed, 4; wounded, 7. Enlisted men, killed, 18; wounded, 80; prisoners, 3 (wounded). Of the above, 3 were killed and 21 wounded on the 31st. (See Colonel Grider's regimental report.)

I have the honor to be, your most obedient servant,

GEO. H. CRAM,
Lieutenant-Colonel, Comdg. Ninth Kentucky Volunteers.

No. 152.

Reports of Maj. Erasmus L. Mottley, Eleventh Kentucky Infantry.

HEADQUARTERS ELEVENTH KENTUCKY VOLUNTEERS,
January 6, 1863.

SIR: I have the honor to report the part my regiment (Eleventh Kentucky Volunteers) took in the action of December 31, 1862.

The night previous we bivouacked in an open field adjacent to the Murfreesborough pike. Next morning, about 8 o'clock, we were ordered to follow the Ninth Kentucky Regiment and cross the river, where we were placed in line of battle, supporting them. We remained in that position about half an hour, when we recrossed the river, still moving in our position as first placed, having marched about half a mile parallel with the pike.

Was then ordered to halt and front, still occupying my position in the rear of the Ninth Kentucky Volunteers. The firing then began by the regiments in front of me, and continued about half an hour, when I was ordered to move forward and relieve the Ninth Kentucky, which was about 100 yards in advance. We did so, moving in line of battle about 500 yards. We then halted, as our farther advance was interrupted by about four regiments of scattered troops rushing through my line. After they had passed we opened a heavy and destructive fire on the enemy, who were advancing against me, and remained in that position, firing, till the right of our division was nearly flanked, when we received an order from you to fall back, which I did (bringing several prisoners with me) in line of battle, till I reached a dense thicket, when I moved by the left flank. We then formed line in an open field, and were ordered by General Rosecrans in person to occupy the thicket through which we had just passed, and hold it at all hazards. We did so.

Just at this moment the enemy were advancing in strong force on our left, when the left wing of the regiment opened an oblique, galling fire upon them, making them fall back. We were then ordered back by you to the large open field on our left, to support two pieces of Terrill's Regular and the Chicago Board of Trade Batteries, where we remained the remainder of the day, my entire regiment, both officers and men, doing their whole duty.

Inclosed find list of casualties.†

Very respectfully,

E. L. MOTTLEY,
Major, Commanding Eleventh Kentucky.

Col. SAMUEL BEATTY,
Commanding First Brigade, Third Division.

---

* Nominal list omitted.   † Embodied in revised statement, p. 213.

HDQRS. ELEVENTH REGT. KENTUCKY VOL. INFANTRY,
January 6, 1863.

SIR: I have the honor to report the part my regiment (Eleventh Kentucky Volunteers) took in the engagement of January 2, 1863.

Having crossed the river the morning of January 1, and bivouacked 150 yards behind the main advance of our lines about 3.30 January 2, the enemy showed himself in strong force, sixteen regiments deep, advancing in column against us; also a brigade on our left. The firing now became general all along the lines. Seeing the regiments on the left giving way, I ordered my regiment to take arms (the arms had previously been stacked). Just then the front was falling back, and I ordered my regiment forward under the most terrific storm of shot, shell, and musketry it has ever been my lot to witness. I advanced about 100 yards, when I ordered a halt and commenced firing. I broke their ranks more than once, their colors shot down several times, but their broken ranks were speedily filled with fresh troops.

Casting my eyes to the right, and seeing I had no support in that direction, and being nearly outflanked, I gave the order to fall back to the wood in our rear, the men being pressed so closely some of them crossed the river.

After crossing the river, I, in conjunction with yourself and other officers, rallied parts of the different regiments of the brigade, and succeeded in putting the enemy to flight before us, and capturing four pieces of the celebrated Washington Artillery.

I must say, in conclusion, that my regiment was one of the very last to leave the grounds. For the gallantry of my entire regiment, they behaved as officers and soldiers should in such a cause.

The casualties of my regiment are as follows:* Killed, 5; wounded, 61; missing, 9. Total, 75.

Very respectfully,

E. L. MOTTLEY,
Major, Commanding Eleventh Kentucky Volunteers.

Col. BENJAMIN C. GRIDER,
Commanding First Brigade, Third Division.

No. 153.

Reports of Maj. Charles F. Manderson, Nineteenth Ohio Infantry.

HDQRS. NINETEENTH REGT. OHIO VOLUNTEER INFANTRY,
Field, near Murfreesborough, Tenn., January 6, 1863.

LIEUTENANT: I transmit you the following report of the participation of the Nineteenth Regiment Ohio Volunteers, U. S. Army (Charles F. Manderson, major commanding), in the action in front of Murfreesborough, on Wednesday, December 31, 1862:

On the morning of that date the regiment was under arms in double column, between the Murfreesborough turnpike and Chattanooga and Nashville Railroad, being the right of the front line of the Third Division, left wing. By order of Col. Samuel Beatty, commanding First Brigade, after deploying column and loading, we moved by the right flank to the left, crossing Stone's River at the ford, and forming line (after throwing Companies A and K out as skirmishers), with the right

---

* Stated by companies in the original.

resting about 100 yards from the river, the Ninth Kentucky Volunteers, which were first formed on our right, being moved to the left.

About 10 o'clock we were ordered to recall our skirmishers and re-cross the river, which being done we moved by the right flank across the open space between the railroad and pike, amid the greatest confusion of retreating batteries, men, teams, and ambulances. At this point General Rousseau ordered the regiment to move across the turnpike, and form line in the woods skirting the west of the pike. From this position we were immediately ordered by Colonel Beatty to march by the left flank back to the railroad, and then by the right flank back to our former position, in the last-named woods, under a fire by which we lost several men.

This scene was one of disorder and panic. Regiment after regiment swept through our lines in the greatest confusion; but through it all our men preserved an unbroken front, and when the pursuing enemy came within 75 or 100 yards, and our front was clear of the retreating and broken columns, at the order to fire by file, poured most destructive volleys into the foe, breaking his lines in disorder.

General Rousseau, who was in the rear of the right of the regiment, cheering our men with his presence and words, then ordered a charge, and our regiment, with fixed bayonets, supported by the Ninth Kentucky Volunteers on our left, and the Seventy-ninth Indiana Volunteers in our rear, drove the foe in splendid style for about one-fourth of a mile, when, our ammunition running low, the front line wheeled into column, and the Seventy-ninth Indiana Volunteers passed through to the front. The regiment, then forming the second line, in the rear of the Seventy-ninth Indiana Volunteers, advanced for about three-fourths of a mile to an open field, where we were separated from our front line by a cedar thicket.

We were here but a few minutes when our right support gave way, and left our regiment greatly exposed to a flanking fire. I sent word twice to Colonel Beatty that the enemy had flanked our position in great force, but received no order. The regiment was suffering most terribly from the fire, and, seeing the enemy within 50 yards of our right and in position to destroy us, I ordered a change of front to the right and rear. Our men, while executing the movement, were thrown into temporary disorder by the scattered regiments on our right pouring through the line, but gathered on the instant, formed an excellent line in good position, and fired with such precision that, with the aid of a battery of artillery in our rear and left, we held the ground and drove the foe from the open field in our front. Being now entirely out of ammunition, and suffering loss from the fire of our own artillery, we moved by the right flank into the woods, and formed line on the left of the Second Brigade, Colonel Fyffe commanding, the second battalion of the Pioneer Corps supporting us on the left. We were here supplied with ammunition by Captain Wood, assistant inspector-general, Third Division, and threw out skirmishers, who met no enemy.

About 4 o'clock we were relieved by the First Brigade, First Division, Colonel Walker commanding; bivouacked where we were until midnight, when we were ordered by Colonel Beatty to report to him on the left of the railroad.

Our loss in this action is as follows, viz: Killed, 1 officer and 11 enlisted men; total, 12. Wounded, 1 officer and 66 enlisted men; total, 67. Missing, 3 enlisted men. Total loss, 82 men. I subjoin as accurate a list as it is possible at this time to gather.

My men behaved with the utmost bravery and coolness. Senior Capt.

Henry G. Stratton, of Company C, assisted as field officer. He was severely wounded about noon. First Lieut. Daniel Donovan, commanding Company B, fell, dead, in front of his company while gallantly leading a charge. Orderly Sergt. Robert D. Wilson, commanding Company D, was killed about the same time.

The cool, manly daring of these gallant officers cannot be spoken of too highly. But the action of all of the Nineteenth Ohio was under the directing eye of the colonel commanding the brigade and the generals commanding, and to them I leave further comments.

Respectfully, yours,

CHARLES F. MANDERSON,
Major, Comdg. Nineteenth Regiment Ohio Volunteer Infantry.

Lieut. W. H. H. SHEETS,
*A. A. A. G., First Brig., Third Div., Left Wing,
Fourteenth Army Corps, Dept. of the Cumberland.*

—

HDQRS. NINETEENTH REGT. OHIO VOL. INFANTRY,
Field, near Murfreesborough, Tenn., January 6, 1863.

LIEUTENANT: On Friday, January 2, the Nineteenth Ohio Volunteers, U. S. Army, under my command, was formed, with the right resting near the high bank on Stone's River, being held with the Ninth Regiment Kentucky Volunteers, which joined us on the left, in reserve of the Second and Third Brigades, Third Division, which position we had assumed on Thursday, January 1, about noon.

Soon after 4 p. m. heavy firing on our front caused us to take arms and stand in line. The firing had continued about fifteen minutes, when Lieutenant Murdock, aide-de-camp to Colonel Beatty, commanding Third Division, rode up to the front and left of the regiment and ordered me to advance. Although the order, coming from that source, was contrary to rule and custom, presuming the occasion to be an emergency requiring such a deviation, I ordered the regiment forward in double-quick time. We advanced up a gradual slope for about 200 yards, the lines in front of us pouring through our ranks in confusion; but the men preserved an excellent front, and rushed upon the enemy. In some parts of the line our pieces crossed those of the foe. His front line received a check of some few minutes, and was thrown into disorder; but a strong flanking party poured over the bank of the river, and broke our right flank to the rear, file after file. Seeing this, and that brave officers and many men of our right wing had fallen, I ordered the left to fall back.

Col. B. C. Grider, commanding First Brigade, here rode up to me from the left and front, and wished me to rally the men. I told him they were falling back by order; that the enemy had flanked me in force, and that I would form line at the foot of the hill. He said, "Do so;" and stated he would give the same order to the Ninth Kentucky Volunteers, on our left. The regiment rallied and formed line twice before the overwhelming force of the enemy drove them across Stone's River. The storm of missiles was terrific, and for a few moments no men could have stood under it. The bank of the river presented a scene of indescribable confusion. The colors of our regiment were seized by Second Lieut. Philip Reefy, of Company F, who gallantly dashed forward across the stream, followed by daring spirits of different regiments.

At the same time Colonel Grider, bearing the colors of the Ninth Kentucky Volunteers, crossed with another party, and these flags, with two belonging to other regiments, rallied under their folds an indiscriminate mass of men and officers of the Third Division, which, supported by fresh troops that had been ordered to the conflict, drove back, in terrible confusion, the columns of the enemy, victorious but a moment before.   The colors of the Nineteenth Ohio and Ninth Kentucky were placed on three pieces of the enemy's artillery, which were captured and brought into our lines by squads composed of the different regiments and brigades of the division.   After this magnificent scene of individual heroism, the different detachments of the regiment formed on the same ground we occupied in the morning, and bivouacked that night.

Again we have to regret the loss of brave officers and men. Capt. Urwin Bean, of Company E; First Lieut. Job D. Bell, commanding Company C, and Sergt. Maj. Lyman Tylee were killed while gallantly performing their duties. First Lieut. Aurora C. Keel, of Company F, was severely wounded; Second Lieut. William A. Sutherland, of Company H, slightly. Capt. William H. Allen, of Company F, rendered most valuable and efficient aid as a field officer. All the line officers vied with each other in deeds of courage.

I wish particularly to note the gallant bearing of First Lieut. Charles Brewer, adjutant; Second Lieut. Albert Upson, commanding Company K, and Sergt. Jason Hurd, commanding Company G. But all have done their duty, and the unpleasant task is not mine to record any acts of cowardice in the Nineteenth Ohio Regiment.

I annex a list of killed, wounded, and missing.*

In this action we had killed 2 officers and 13 enlisted men; total killed, 15. Wounded, 2 officers and 56 enlisted men; total wounded, 58. Missing (supposed prisoners), 31 enlisted men.

Respectfully, your obedient servant,

CHARLES F. MANDERSON,
Major, Commanding Nineteenth Regiment Ohio Volunteers.

Lieut. W. H. H. SHEETS,
A. A. A. G., First Brig., Third Div., Left Wing,
Fourteenth Army Corps, Dept. of the Cumberland.

No. 154.

Report of Col. James P. Fyffe, Fifty-ninth Ohio Infantry, commanding Second Brigade.

HEADQUARTERS SECOND BRIGADE, THIRD DIVISION,
ARMY OF THE CUMBERLAND, LEFT WING,
· *January 5, 1863.*

CAPTAIN : I herewith transmit my report of the operations of the Second Brigade in front of Murfreesborough, where it arrived with the balance of the left wing December 29, 1862, up to January 3, 1863.

December 30, the brigade was under arms in close column of divisions all day; considerable firing in the afternoon in the direction of the right wing.

---

* Nominal list omitted.

December 31, the brigade was ordered across Stone's River. Prior to reaching the same, an order was received from General Crittenden to countermarch the brigade, together with Swallow's battery, in double-quick to the rear, as the train was attacked. Passing quickly through the woods, as the wagons had blocked up the road, we came out into the open field beyond, and formed a line of battle, perpendicular to the road, on the left, in a corn-field, through which the rebels were seen leading off the train slowly, as the ground was soft. Beyond the train, in the same field, was about a squadron of cavalry, guarded by rebels.

On our appearance the cavalry began capturing their guard; one escaped, one was killed. The rebel cavalry were drawn up in line across the field, in the edge of the woods. Captain Swallow, who had managed to get his battery through the obstructions expeditiously, soon had his pieces in position, and opened fire on the rebel lines, which began dispersing, and were charged by a force of our cavalry, which had passed down the road to the right of the train, doing excellent service. The effect of the charge I could not see from where we were. Captain Swallow now moved his pieces to a more elevated position, which commanded the country for a great distance, from whence he opened on their scattered forces, driving them out of view.

At this point an order was received from General Van Cleve to return to the Third Division, and form on the right of the First Brigade in two lines, to support it; that Colonel Harker would support my right. The order was immediately complied with; the division began advancing down the slope of the cedar ridge south of the road, passing Colonel Harker's on my right, beyond the foot of the slope. After passing his brigade, which did not move, my right flank became exposed, with strong indications of a heavy force approaching in front, extending beyond my right flank. As we continued advancing, I sent three different messengers by my aides, calling Colonel Harker's attention to my exposed flank, and at length reported in person to General Van Cleve. While doing this the Sixty-fifth Ohio, which, it appeared, had been lying down at the edge of the field, rose to their feet in the place where a force was needed. Supposing it would remain there, I passed back again to my position, to see the Sixty-fifth march by the right flank back to Colonel Harker's left. The firing in front of my first line, composed of the Fifty-ninth Ohio and Forty-fourth Indiana, was getting to be heavy, and the skirmishers, running in, reported a heavy force advancing through the woods, outflanking my right. Lieutenant Temple, of my staff, was sent at once to Lieutenant-Colonel Dick with orders to wheel his regiment to the right, and place it in the woods to secure my flank. Before the order reached him the enemy appeared coming through the woods.

Seeing the force would have to fall back, I galloped to the battery and ordered it to open fire to the right of my flank into the woods, for the purpose of checking and confusing the outflanking force, to save my brigade from the effects of the cross-fire, while falling back, as much as possible. The order to fire was complied with instantly, the whole battery opening several volleys in quick succession, and with decided effect, into the woods, while the column fell back rapidly, the front line having sustained itself gallantly until outflanked. The artillery came safely out of the field under fire, Lieutenant Buckmar, a gallant officer, being shot from his horse and badly wounded just as he was passing out of the field.

After falling back from the field, the Thirteenth Ohio, under Major

Jarvis, and part of the Eighty-sixth Indiana, Lieutenant-Colonel Dick was formed near the road, the Forty-fourth being placed on duty elsewhere, and ordered to move up the road to meet the force that had followed from the field, which was represented advancing. Going in advance of the force, I found the Fifty-ninth Ohio, under Lieutenant-Colonel Howard and Major Frambes, hotly contesting the cedar ridge and hard pressed, their left flank being exposed, encouraging the men to hold on, and they should have help immediately. The force following me was hurried up. The remnant of the Thirteenth Ohio, though sadly repressed by the death of the gallant and loved Colonel Hawkins, shot dead on the field, answered the command to go forward with a cheer, and got into line on the left, opening fire just as a regiment on the right of the Fifty-ninth marched to the rear, leaving my right flank again exposed, which the enemy were not slow to perceive, and began taking advantage of. Sorely annoyed, I crossed the road and asked the officer in command, whom I do not know, what it meant. He said he had been ordered back, but on my representations he immediately marched his regiment up again, delivering a heavy fire as he reached the crest of the ridge. I then ordered the whole line to charge, which was gallantly done with a cheer, the enemy being driven from the crest of the ridge down the southern slope and back across the field.

One of the skirmishers, William Brown, of Company B, Fifty-ninth Ohio, met me on the edge of the ridge, marching back through the line at the head of 28 prisoners, besides 2 officers (lieutenants) he had captured in a sink-hole. Many other prisoners were captured by the Second Brigade, amounting to 60, as near as can be ascertained.

After the enemy was repulsed, as stated, there was no more fighting on this day by the left wing, General Van Cleve turning over the command of the division to me, he having been wounded, Colonel Beatty being on duty elsewhere.

January 1, crossed with the brigade over the river, where the Second Brigade was placed on the left of the First, in an open field in rear of a belt of timber on a ridge, the Forty-fourth Indiana and Thirteenth Ohio in the front line, with the Thirty-fifth and Seventy-ninth Indiana on their right, the Fifty-ninth Ohio and Eighty-sixth Indiana in reserve. This arrangement left an open space on the left. On the front line, between it and a road running through a lane beyond the road, was an open field unoccupied by troops, except a line of skirmishers from Colonel Grose's command. In the rear, toward Stone's River, was a cornfield, and behind the fence was a Kentucky regiment, with their right resting on the lane. This left a gap between my left and their right of about 500 yards; thus the forces rested during the day, with sharp skirmishing in our front.

January 2, the skirmishing commenced early and was brisk throughout the day, until about 3 o'clock, when the indications of an attack in front became so threatening, a battery having been planted in the woods on my left flank, that I ordered my reserve into the front line, deflecting the Eighty-sixth Indiana back, and placing them behind the fence across the lane to sweep the open field in front of the Kentucky regiment. Company A, of the Fifty-ninth Regiment, under Sergeant Carr, was placed on the left of the Eighty-sixth, connecting the two forces, which gave them a cross-fire over the open field in front.

About 4 p. m. Colonel Beatty, commanding the division, came over and was shown the disposition of the brigade, which he approved, suggesting, in case we were compelled to fall back, we should do so through the low ground. We then went to the point near the ford, where the artillery was stationed, and, while examining that, Major-General Rosecrans arrived at the same point. In a few moments a messenger from the front arrived and reported a large force was being massed in front of our lines. Colonel Beatty and myself immediately started to our respective positions. I was shortly met by Adjutant Holter, of the Fifty-ninth Ohio, with a report that the enemy were in motion, advancing on our front. Sixteen regimental flags had been counted in one column. Actg. Asst. Adjt. Gen. C. F. King was ordered to make report of the facts to General Rosecrans immediately. Passing on to the Eighty-sixth Regiment, it and Company A were ordered to strengthen their position with rails.

Only a short time elapsed when a tremendous fire indicated that the attack had fallen on Colonel Beatty's right. Another column, it appeared, had crossed Stone's River and participated in the attack, while still another was coming on my left, but for some cause its advance was somewhat delayed. The main column of attack moved diagonally across the front of the wood, striking toward a wooded height on the bank of the river where Captain Drury's battery of artillery had been posted in the morning, under the command of Lieutenant Livingston. The weight of the column of attack fell first on the Eighth Kentucky and Fifty-first Ohio in the front line. They stood gallantly for a few moments, but were swept away. The enemy, still pushing on, received a heavy flank and oblique fire from the Thirty-fifth, Forty-fourth, and Eighty-sixth Indiana, and Thirteenth Ohio. The column next encountered the Ninety-ninth Ohio, Twenty-first Kentucky, and Nineteenth Ohio, which were successively borne backward, as were the Ninth and Eleventh Kentucky.

In the mean time, after the giving way of our second line, and as soon as our infantry had gotten out of the way, Lieutenant Livingston opened upon them with his battery with good effect. The enemy's artillery, following their column, took position on the high ground to the right of the wood, which commanded the field of battle, and, as their infantry passed on, driving our right across the river, opened with grape and canister. The Second Brigade, not being exactly in line of their charge, held their ground until the column of attack had passed our second line.

The brigade then fell back through the low ground, as directed (being myself disabled, my horse having thrown and dragged me for a short distance), and took position behind the buildings on the hill.

The artillery, after the giving way of our last line of infantry, recrossed Stone's River. The column of attack, pushing on toward the ford, was exposed to a severe flank fire from Colonel Grose's force, together with those of my brigade who had collected about the buildings upon the hill, and also to our artillery and the infantry that had taken position on the opposite bank of the river; thus extending the fire around their front to the left flank, encircling them on three sides. A cross-fire of artillery and small-arms, delivered for a short time with terrible effect, was too much for them, and their broken and discomfited columns turned back upon their path, closely pursued by the troops which had rallied, together with the fresh troops which General Rosecrans had ordered up, taking a portion of the celebrated Washington Battery. This repulse closed the operations in front of Murfreesborough, the Second Brigade going into camp on the field for the night.

I cannot close this report without favorably noticing many of the officers and men of my command throughout the trying ordeal of so many days' fighting. My acting assistant adjutant-general, C. F. King; J. B. Temple, aide-de-camp; Capt. Charles A. Sheaf, provost-marshal; Lieut. Joseph Dancer, inspector, who was severely wounded in the last day's fight, and Orderlies H. J. Higgins, E. D. Thomas, members of my staff, are entitled to much credit for their conduct on the field. Colonel Williams, Lieutenant-Colonel Aldrich, and Joseph C. Hodges, adjutant, of the Forty-fourth Indiana; Col. J. G. Hawkins (killed in the first day's fight while gallantly doing his duty); Major Jarvis, upon whom the command devolved after the fall of Colonel Hawkins, and Adjt. T. B. George; Lieutenant-Colonel Howard, Major Frambes, Adjutant Holter, of the Fifty-ninth Ohio; Colonel Dick and Major Dresser, of the Eighty-sixth Indiana (severely wounded in the engagement of the first day), are deserving of particular notice.

Colonel Hamilton, although unacquainted with military matters, was present, assisting all in his power; also Surgs. Martin Hays and Gordon, with the assistance of the brigade band, in getting and attending to the wounded, in which Gus. Penn was shot dead, and Dougherty, both of the band, badly wounded; for their good conduct they are especially noticed. Lieutenants Kibler and Woods attracted my attention by their gallantry while in command of the skirmishers on the cedar ridge. I will also notice the gallantry and death of color-bearer, Sergeant Wood, shot dead with the flag in his hand on the first day's fight; also of Nelson Shields, who seized the colors, and bore them aloft, upon the fall of the color-sergeant, until wounded himself, when he delivered them to Private Loyd; all of the Thirteenth Ohio. I also notice Color-Bearers Benjamin Snellinger and Nathan Coffenberry, of the Eighty-sixth Indiana, who were both shot down (the first killed instantly, the latter mortally wounded) in the fight of the first day. Both of these flags were lost. I also notice the good conduct of Sergeants Ely and Thomas Hayden, of the Fifty-ninth Ohio, who, on the last day's fight, were raised in the air by a cannon ball plowing the earth beneath their feet, and thrown violently to the earth.

I recommend that William Brown, of Company B, Fifty-ninth Ohio, who captured the prisoners above referred to, and Nelson Shields, of the Thirteenth Ohio, who saved his regimental flag, as proper persons to receive, each, one of the medals ordered to be prepared by Congress for those who particularly distinguish themselves in battle.

In closing this report, I wish also to tender my thanks to Maj. Lyne Starling, adjutant-general on General Crittenden's staff, for words of encouragement and cheer to a portion of my command when hard pressed on the cedar ridge in the first day's fight; and also to express my gratitude to our commander-in-chief, General Rosecrans, for the same favor at the place and about the same time.

All of which is respectfully submitted, together with the reports of the different regimental commanders, appropriately marked, with a corrected account of the killed, wounded, and missing, which foot up: Officers killed, 4; wounded, 15; missing, 2. Enlisted men killed, 75; wounded, 251; officers missing, 2; enlisted men, 166. Total, 513.*

JAMES P. FYFFE,
Colonel, Comdg. 2d Brig., 3d Div., Left Wing, 14th Army Corps.
Capt. E. A. OTIS,
Assistant Adjutant-General.

---

* But see revised statement, p. 213.

No. 155.

Report of Lieut. Col. Simeon C. Aldrich, Forty-fourth Indiana Infantry.

HEADQUARTERS FORTY-FOURTH INDIANA VOLUNTEERS,
Camp near Murfreesborough, Tenn., January 5, 1863.

DEAR SIR: It becomes my duty to make a brief report of engagements before Murfreesborough.

We went into the field on December 31, 1862, with 316 men, officers included. We took our position, by your order, in brigade on the right, and marched in line of battle through an open field south of the pike. In passing through this field we discovered the enemy making a flank movement on our right, in a wood bordering upon the field. Intelligence was conveyed to you, and, as I understand, by you to our division commander. We made a stand at the edge of the wood in our front, but were soon ordered to advance, which we did.

After entering the woods our skirmishers were ordered in, as the line of the enemy was in sight. We still advanced to within, as near as I could judge, 100 yards of their line, and opened fire. They replied, and advanced their line; at the same time the flanking force opened a galling cross-fire upon us. We held the position as long as we could do so without sacrificing our whole regiment; we then fell back to our battery and formed line of battle. We were ordered by General Van Cleve to remain here till further orders. We soon had orders from you to join the brigade at the right, which we did. Here we formed a new line, and remained till some time in the night, when we were ordered to march to the left again, where we remained through the night.

Permit me to pass over occurrences not important, for want of room, to January 2, when we were in line of battle on the left. About 4 p. m. the enemy was discovered to be advancing. I received orders from you to fall back to low ground, if it was found we could not hold our position. The enemy attacked on our right; Seventy-ninth and Thirty-fifth Indiana engaged, and held their position firm for some time. In the mean time I directed my fire at right oblique. The enemy pressed on, and the Thirty-fifth and Seventy-ninth gave way. I still held my men and kept up the fire till the enemy had passed by us on the right, and then gave orders to fall back, which we did, to a rail fence. Then we rallied again, and gave them a cross-fire; but they still advancing made it necessary to fall back to the ground you designated. I gave the command, and we fell back to the building on the hill. Here Adjutant Hodges and myself, together with other officers, succeeded in rallying a large force, together with our regiment, and opened a destructive cross-fire on the enemy, which soon had its effect upon their extreme left, and assisted very much in their final repulse. We followed them till ordered to fall back.

I must here mention that at the first rally at the rail fence was the last seen of Colonel Williams. I suppose him to be taken prisoner. Our loss, as it stands now, is 56 wounded, 10 killed, and 47 missing.[*]

I must make mention of some officers and men that acted with great bravery: First is our colonel, William C. Williams. Adjt. Joseph C. Hodges was among the most efficient and brave; Acting Lieut. Joseph W. Burch, Company A; Lieutenants Gunsenhouser and Thomas, Company F; Getty and Murray, Company B; Wilson, Company K; Hildebrand, Company E; acting lieutenants, Company G; Lieutenants

---

* But see revised statement, p. 213.

Story, Company C; King, Company H, and Shell, Company D; Acting Lieutenant Belknap, Company I. Color-Bearer Owen L. Shaw, Company C, acted with distinguished bravery, and, with few exceptions, our men and officers acted finely.

Many things I am obliged to omit, for want of room, and poor health. I must, however, not close without giving our brigade commander high praise and credit for his coolness, bravery, and judgment upon those eventful days.

I remain, sir, your obedient servant,

S. C. ALDRICH,
Lieutenant-Colonel, Comdg. Forty-fourth Indiana Volunteers.

Colonel FYFFE,
Commanding Second Brigade, Third Division.

P. S.—I would state that on December 31 I had my horse shot.

No. 156.

Report of Lieut. Col. George F. Dick, Eighty-sixth Indiana Infantry.

HDQRS. EIGHTY-SIXTH REGIMENT INDIANA VOLUNTEERS,
Camp near Murfreesborough, Tenn., January 5, 1863.

SIR: I have the honor to report as follows:

My command arrived in front of Murfreesborough at 8 p. m. December 30, 1862.

On the following morning the regiment numbered 368, rank and file. About noon of December 31, with the brigade, we were marched in line of battle across the Nashville turnpike road, about one-half mile south, across an open field to the skirt of a heavy wood, in which the enemy lay concealed in heavy force. My regiment was on the extreme right of the brigade. We were halted behind a fence at the edge of the wood, to await the arrival of troops to come up to support us on the right, who failed to come. Our right was totally exposed to the enemy, who immediately attacked us in overwhelming numbers in front, our right flank extending around partially to the rear of our right wing.

Our regiment fought bravely until their ranks were being rapidly cut down and thinned, when we fell back to the turnpike road, where a portion of them again rallied, with portions of other regiments of the brigade, and drove the enemy back.

Our loss in the engagement was as follows: Commissioned officers killed, 1; wounded, 5; missing 2. Enlisted men killed, 33; wounded, 54; missing, 99. Total officers killed, wounded, and missing, 8; enlisted men killed, wounded, and missing, 186; aggregate, 194.

Both color-bearers were shot down and the colors left on the field.

On the following morning we were marched some mile and a half across Stone's River to the front, and placed in line of battle early in the day, where we skirmished with the enemy all day, lying on our arms that night.

The next day we occupied the same ground, skirmishing with the enemy till 3 p. m., when the enemy in vast numbers attacked the right of our line, composed of the First and Third Brigades of our division, which maintained the ground, fighting obstinately for some time, when they were forced to yield to superior numbers, and fell back, when our regiment fell back to a high piece of ground, near a house on the hill, some 100 rods to the rear, where we again made a stand, again rallied with other troops, and drove the enemy from the field, retaking and holding our former position. Our loss here was 1 private wounded.

Captains Frazee, of Company A; Dick, of Company C; Lieutenants Hixson, of Company D, and Gillilan, of Company I, were wounded in the fight of the first day and compelled to remain at the hospital.

I take pleasure in saying that Capt. Philip Gemmer was present with his command during the whole of the different actions, rendering efficient service and aid.

Respectfully, your obedient servant,

G. F. DICK,
Lieutenant-Colonel Eighty-sixth Regiment Indiana Volunteers.

Col. JAMES P. FYFFE,
Comdg. Second Brig., Third Div., Army of the Cumberland.

No. 157.

Report of Maj. Dwight Jarvis, jr., Thirteenth Ohio Infantry.

JANUARY —, 1863.

SIR: I have the honor to report the following as the part taken by the Thirteenth Regiment Ohio Volunteer Infantry in the series of battles before Murfreesborough, Tenn., commencing December 30, 1862, and terminating January 3, 1863:

On Wednesday, at 8 a. m., our regiment, under command of Col. Joseph G. Hawkins, was ordered in from outpost duty, and took our place in line. Soon after, we started for the south side of Stone's River, but got but a short distance when, by your orders, we countermarched at double-quick a distance of about 1 mile, to a corn-field on the right of the Murfreesborough road, to repel an attack of cavalry upon our train. Our lines were here formed, my regiment occupying the right of the Second Brigade. The enemy being driven from the field by our cavalry and artillery, my regiment was not engaged, and about 10 o'clock, under your directions, took a position in the woods south of the corn-field.

My regiment was now ordered to cover the Fifty-ninth Ohio, which, with the Forty-fourth Indiana, formed the first line of attack, my regiment, with the Eighty-sixth Indiana, on its right, forming the second line. In consequence of the unevenness of the ground and the density of the thicket, it was difficult to keep our lines properly, but, on emerging from the woods into the open field beyond, we advanced regularly to the edge of the next woods. The first line having advanced some 20 yards into the woods, my regiment was ordered to lie down. Now it became evident that the enemy was attempting to outflank us upon the right; and this was reported to you, but just at that moment our first line was attacked, and it was compelled to fall back in some disorder and over my men, who were lying down close to the fence.

At this moment our gallant colonel fell, mortally wounded, while encouraging the men to keep cool and to fire low; and the command devolved upon myself. I held the position until the enemy completely outflanked us, and was then compelled to fall back in disorder to the line of reserves, where I rallied my command, and this time drove the enemy back, they now being in the open field, while we had the advantage of the cover of the woods. We inflicted considerable loss upon them in killed and wounded, besides capturing some 30 prisoners.

My loss in this engagement was quite severe, Col. J. G. Hawkins and Second Lieut. J. C. Whitaker being killed, together with 27 enlisted men. Capt. E. M. Mast, Lieuts. John Murphy, John E. Ray, S. C. Gould, John Fox (since dead), and Thomas J. Stone were wounded, and 68 enlisted men, besides 39 missing.

No other movement of importance in which my regiment participated occurred until Friday, January 2, when we occupied the extreme left of our lines on the south side of Stone River, having taken our position the day previous under your immediate supervision.

On the morning of the 2d my skirmishers were thrown forward, and by their vigilance I was enabled to report to you the movements of the enemy and the probability of an attack, as the enemy were massing troops on our right and artillery had moved to my front.

At 3 p. m. the firing of the skirmishers on the right plainly indicated the enemy's advance, and in half an hour after their infantry engaged the brigade on our right, their lines being formed diagonally to our front. My regiment was not exposed to the infantry; but a battery opened upon our front with grape and canister, so that I was compelled to order a retrograde movement, which was executed in as good order as was possible. At about 300 yards I made a stand again, but by this time their battery occupied our former position in line, and we were ordered to fall back to the other side of the river, which was done in good order. Our loss in this engagement was 10 enlisted men wounded and 30 missing.

The following exhibits a detailed account of my casualties in both engagements, viz: Killed—Col. J. G. Hawkins, Second Lieut. J. C. Whitaker; enlisted men, 29. Wounded—Capt. E. M. Mast; First Lieuts. John Murphy, John E. Ray, and Samuel C. Gould; Second Lieuts. John Fox (since died) and Thomas J. Stone; enlisted men, 79. Missing—69. Aggregate loss in killed, wounded, and missing, 185.

Respectfully submitted.

D. JARVIS, Jr.,
Major, Comdg. Thirteenth Regt. Ohio Vol. Infantry.

Col. JAMES P. FYFFE,
Comdg. 2d Brig., 3d Div., Left Wing, 14th Army Corps.

No. 158.

Report of Lieut. Col. William Howard, Fifty-ninth Ohio Infantry.

HDQRS. FIFTY-NINTH REGIMENT OHIO VOL. INFANTRY,
Camp near Murfreesborough, Tenn., January 5, 1863.

SIR: I have the honor to transmit to you the report of the Fifty-ninth Regiment Ohio Volunteer Infantry, of your command, of the battles from December 31, 1862, to January 3, 1863.

On the morning of that day my command was formed at 4 o'clock, in accordance with previous orders, and, with the balance of the brigade, started at 8 o'clock to take position on the left, when we received orders to march immediately to defend the wagon train against the attack of the enemy, which was done with promptness, and they were driven back with loss, and the whole train was saved.

We then received orders to march back and take position on the right of Colonel Beatty's command, in front, as our forces were hard pressed at that point, in line of battle, and moved forward to attack the enemy; and after moving across the woods we came into an open field, which we moved rapidly across until we reached the woods, and my skirmishers soon discovered the enemy in heavy force and in strong position in front, and fired upon him and fell back to the line, which I immediately ordered forward and made the attack; and after firing upon them several rounds, and holding them in check for some time, we were forced back by superior numbers about 20 paces, when, by the prompt assistance of my officers, we succeeded in rallying the regiment and took position behind a fence, and then poured volley after volley into the advancing ranks of the enemy, and held them in check until Major Frambes, upon the right, informed me that we were being flanked upon that wing and that the balance of the brigade was falling back, when I gave the order to fall back, inclining to the right in a skirt of woods, and thereby protecting, to a great extent, my command against a most galling fire in rear, and, to some extent, a flanking fire also.

My officers again coming promptly to my assistance, we succeeded in rallying the regiment again, and moved to the right, through the woods in front of the enemy, and by a well-directed fire checked his onward movement, and held him at that position until the balance of the brigade was put in position, when we moved forward and drove the enemy from the field with great slaughter and in complete disorder. We then, by your orders, took a strong position in the woods, and I threw forward my skirmishers; but the enemy, although making several demonstrations on the right, did not dare again to approach. We held our position until darkness closed the controversy for the day.

We then, during the night, moved to the left and went into camp, but were soon ordered to get into line of battle, and there remained until daylight, when we moved across Stone's River and took position upon the extreme left, and during that day had heavy skirmishing, until night ended the fight.

On the next morning we were ordered to form in column of divisions and take position near the woods and throw out our skirmishers, who soon came in collision with the enemy's, and each in turn advanced and fell back until about 11 o'clock, when the enemy got a battery in position and commenced to throw an occasional shell in the direction of our line, evidently feeling our position, when, by your orders, Major Frambes moved my command back and took position upon some low ground, and gave the order to lie close, to protect themselves against the enemy's shells, and there remained until about 2 o'clock, when the skirmishers were driven in, when I gave the orders to Major Frambes to deploy in line and move forward near the woods. About that time the enemy succeeded in planting a second battery directly in our front, and commenced to throw shells, when we again laid close to the ground. The enemy then planted another battery still farther upon his right and our left.

About 3 o'clock our skirmishers were driven in, and it was very soon apparent that the enemy was approaching in force to attack, and at that time he opened with musketry and artillery along his whole line, and moved forward upon our forces in five heavy columns of brigades; but in his movement all in front of us was entirely clear of our army, and his right had passed our right, and we were about wheeling to give him a flank fire, when we discovered emerging from the woods the same number of his columns, moving with his right upon our left and passing us, when Major Frambes was ordered to fall back with the command,

which order was execuied in excellent style until the enemy, by his terrible discharges of musketry and artillery and the weight of his columns,
bore down and threw into disorder our whole lines, when we were thrown
back in confusion, but succeeded in again rallying our line at a fence in
our rear; but all in vain, for no human power of our strength could
withstand such a force.

But about that time the scene was destined to change. Our artillery
and musketry opened upon their advancing ranks and columns with
fearful destruction, but still he moved steadily forward. At that time
every officer in my command seemed aroused to a sudden sense of duty,
and dashed in to rally what he could for a grand stand, without reference to a general rallying of the regiment, and went into this terrible
battle, Major Frambes taking command of one wing, Adjutant Holter
of another, and each officer with all he could gather; and at that time the
fight became terribly fearful, and the enemy was turned and thrown
into complete confusion, and was driven, with awful slaughter, from the
field. And I am proud to say that every officer and soldier in my
command did his whole duty, and we gained, on that day, a magnificent
victory.

We lost, during the several battles from December 31 to January 3,
in killed, 3; wounded, 37, and we had 45 missing, very few of whom
were captured by the enemy, many of them being ordered to guard the
train to Nashville.

My command in the several battles captured 56 prisoners, among whom
were 1 captain and 1 lieutenant. We commenced these battles with 291
officers and soldiers, and we have now for duty 206 officers and men. I
had 2 officers wounded and there are 2 missing. It is due to my command to state that one part of them assisted in taking the battery which
was captured.

I cannot close this report without awarding due praise to my officers,
and in doing this I must name them here, so that the world may know
who have actually played a prominent part in these splendid victories
before Murfreesborough, that must electrify the world, and cause every
true Union man's heart to thrill for joy. I can, under all circumstances,
rely upon Major Frambes, who was everywhere present in the very hottest of the battle, fearless of his own safety. He deserves his country's
praise. Adjutant Holter, amid showers of bullets, carried my every
order to any part of the field, regardless of his own safety. Let his
country do him justice. Lieutenants Woods and Kibbler deserve to be
remembered by those who may live after them. Captains Vanosdol and
Sargent, and Lieutenants Stevens and Smith can be relied upon in any
emergency; and it was truly a source of pleasure to me to see Capt. L.
J. Egbert move steadily forward in battle. He deserves his country's
honor. Lieut. John O'Connor, after being severely wounded in the hand,
bound it up himself, and he continued in command until night, at which
time he had his finger amputated, and was compelled to leave the field.
The name of such a patriot will live after him. Captain Hill was
severely wounded in the face, and was compelled to retire. A better
officer I do not want.

My surgeons, Drs. Hays and Gordon, have my sincerest thanks for
their prompt attention to the wounded.

Companies F, G, and H were commanded by Sergts. Jesse Ellis, Cohen,
Hawkins, and Riley, each of whom deserves a commission, because they
fairly earned them.

My color-bearers did not allow their flags to trail in the dust, but
brought them safely from the field. In a word, I am perfectly satisfied

with my whole command, and believe the Fifty-ninth Ohio Volunteei Infantry has, in those four terrible days, faithfully discharged its duty, and deserves the country's admiration and esteem.

I am, very respectfully, your obedient servant,

WILLIAM HOWARD,
Lieutenant-Colonel, Comdg. Fifty-ninth Regt. Ohio Vol. Infantry.

JAMES P. FYFFE,
Colonel, Commanding Second Brigade.

No. 159.

Report of Col. Samuel W. Price, Twenty-first Kentucky Infantry, com manding Third Brigade.

HEADQUARTERS THIRD BRIGADE, THIRD DIVISION,
LEFT WING, FOURTEENTH ARMY CORPS,
January 6, 1863.

SIR: I have the honor to submit the following report of the part the Third Brigade, which I command (composed of the Fifty-first Ohio, Eighth and Twenty-first Kentucky, Thirty-fifth Indiana, and the Ninety-ninth Ohio Infantry Regiments), took in the action near Murfreesborough since the 31st ultimo:

On the morning of December 31, my brigade was ordered from the position it held on the north of the Nashville and Murfreesborough Railroad, across and on the east side of Stone's River, crossing the river at a ford about 1 mile below where the railroad bridge crosses it. At the top of the hill, and about half a mile distant from the river, on the east side, I formed my brigade on the left of the First Brigade, then commanded by Col. Samuel Beatty. No sooner had I thus formed the brigade than an order came from Brigadier-General Van Cleve, then commanding the Third Division, for my brigade to cross the river at the same ford, and for me to arrange it so as to overlook and command the ford. I accordingly recrossed, and stationed the brigade on the crest of the hill, the Eighth Kentucky Regiment on the right of the front line, Third Wisconsin Battery (commanded by Lieutenant Livingston) on the left of the Eighth Kentucky, Fifty-first Ohio on the left of the artillery, and Thirty-fifth Indiana Regiment on the left of the Fifty-first Ohio. The second or rear line was formed by the Twenty-first Kentucky and Ninety-ninth Ohio Regiments, Twenty-first Kentucky on the right, and the Ninety-ninth Ohio on the left.

During the entire day severe fighting was going on with the right wing and the center. The battle-field was perfectly visible from the position I held, and although frequently in range of the enemy's cannon, and exposed at times to their bursting shells and solid shot, the men and officers of my command were perfectly cool and composed, and remained in ranks and conducted themselves as became soldiers and officers.

About 2 p. m. 300 or 400 rebel cavalry appeared on the east and opposite side of the river, and made a dash at a number of Government wagons containing camp equipage. Before they reached the wagons, Lieutenant Livingston, ever vigilant and prompt in the performance of his duties, opened a sharp fire of artillery on them, killing 3 of them and somewhat confusing the remainder. Notwithstanding, they succeeded in starting off a number of the wagons; but during theii hasty retreat the artillery disabled one of the wagons, thereby blockading the road and saving the wagons in rear.

Expecting that an attempt would be made afterward by the enemy to cross the river, I detached the Eighth Kentucky as sharpshooters, to command (under cover of the bank) the ford, and prevent their success in such an attempt. Afterward nothing unusual occurred on that day, and my brigade remained in *statu quo.*

On the next morning, January 1, I was ordered by Colonel Beatty (who, by reason of General Van Cleve having been disabled by a shell in the action of the day previous, assumed command of the division) to station the brigade again on the east side of the river, which I accordingly did, placing it half a mile up and perpendicular to the river, in two lines, Fifty-first Ohio on the right of the front line, Eighth Kentucky in the center, and Thirty-fifth Indiana on the left; also the Third Wisconsin Battery was in the front line, between the Eighth Kentucky and Thirty-fifth Indiana Regiments, the Twenty-first Kentucky and Ninety-ninth Ohio forming the rear line, the Twenty-first Kentucky on the right and Ninety-ninth Ohio on the left. During the day there was heavy skirmishing in our front, and occasionally bodies of cavalry appeared in the distance in front of my command. Our artillery opened on them at different times and dispersed them; but after the firing ceased they reappeared. At sundown our artillery was ordered back to the rear, to the west side of the river.

The night was passed without any interruption from the enemy, except about 12 o'clock there was very sharp firing on the skirmish line, when one of the skirmishers, a private of the Thirty-fifth Indiana Regiment, was killed.

On the morning of January 2, the Third Wisconsin Battery was ordered up and occupied its former position. Through the day our skirmishers reported at different times the appearance of rebel artillery in our front, and also of fifteen rebel infantry regiments that seemed to pass toward our left, which was promptly reported to the commander of the Third Division, Colonel Beatty. The rebel artillery frequently shelled the woods we occupied, and killed a private of the Eighth Kentucky, at the same time tearing the colors of that regiment in pieces. In the skirmishing of the day a private of the Fifty-first Ohio was killed, and one or two of the Eighth Kentucky and Thirty-fifth Indiana Regiments wounded.

At 3.15 o'clock the rebels advanced in force through the corn-field in our front, supposed to be a division. As they advanced to our skirmish line, Captain Banton, of the Eighth Kentucky, who was in command of the skirmishers of the Eighth Kentucky Regiment, was shot and instantly killed. When they had advanced to within gun-shot of our line, the Fifty-first Ohio Regiment, commanded by Lieut. Col. R. W. McClain; the Eighth Kentucky Regiment, commanded by Lieut. Col. R. May, and the Thirty-fifth Indiana Regiment, commanded by Col. B. F. Mullen, poured into their ranks a deadly and effective fire, which seemed, for a while, to stop their advancing column, but again they advanced slowly, and here the battle raged desperately. The gallantry and coolness there evinced by the officers and soldiers of the Fifty-first Ohio, Eighth Kentucky, and Thirty-fifth Indiana Regiments deserve the highest praise, and heartily do I attribute it to them.

After these three regiments had contended with the enemy, far superior in numbers to my command, for ten or twelve minutes, and under a severe fire of three batteries of the enemy (none on our side to respond to them), and seeing that to oppose them further would only end in the slaughter of my men, I ordered the front line to fall back in order, which it did, as far as possible, and for the second or rear line, composed of the Twenty-first Regiment, commanded by Lieut. Col. J. C. Evans, and Ninety-ninth Ohio Regiment, commanded by Col. P. T. Swaine, to fire on the enemy as they advanced. Their line being broken and confused by the front line retiring, also was compelled, after a few volleys, to fall back. The officers and men of these two regiments also deserve especial praise for their gallantry.

After crossing to the west side of the river, by the perseverance of the officers a great number of the men were rallied and again returned to the scene of action, and aided in the ultimate defeat of the enemy. All the line officers behaved with the greatest coolness and courage during the entire engagement.

I cannot omit to make honorable mention of a circumstance of the scenes of the last day's engagement, which reflects great credit for the daring bravery and coolness of the parties concerned. Corpl. E. C. Hockensmith, of the color-guard of the Twenty-first Kentucky Regiment, and who carried the colors that day, was confronted by a rebel in the retreat, and was ordered, while on the bank of the river, to surrender, to which he replied, " Myself I will surrender, but my colors never," at the same moment throwing them into the water. Sergt. J. T. Gunn, Company E, of the same regiment, seized them and carried them safely through the battle. Corporal Hockensmith escaped, and is safe.

I am indebted in the highest degree to the members of my staff, Lieuts. John Clark, acting assistant adjutant-general, Carter B. Harrison, acting assistant inspector-general, and Edward Noble, aide-de-camp, for their assistance, who at all times performed their duties with intelligence and zeal, and deserve especially the highest praise for valor and efficiency during the action of the 2d instant.

The loss on both sides has been very heavy. My loss in killed is small in proportion to the number wounded. The enemy's loss, compared with ours, was at least four to one.

I am, with great respect, your obedient servant,

S. W. PRICE,
Colonel, Comdg. 3d Brig., 3d Div., Left Wing, 14th Army Corps.
Capt. E. A. OTIS,
 Assistant Adjutant-General, Third Division, Left Wing.

No. 160.

Report of Col. Bernard F. Mullen, Thirty-fifth Indiana Infantry.

HDQRS. (FIRST IRISH) THIRTY-FIFTH REGT. INDIANA VOLS.,
 In the Field, near Murfreesborough, Tenn., January 5, 1863.

COLONEL: In obedience to orders, I have the honor to report officially to brigade headquarters the part my regiment took in the battles since December 31, 1862.

On the morning of December 31 last, my regiment moved with our brigade (the Third) across Stone's River, and took position on the extreme left of the brigade, fronting east. We remained but a short time, when orders came to recross the river and establish my line, the right resting upon the Fifty-first Ohio. When the line was thus established, my left rested upon the bank of the river. When in this position the action commenced on our right, and in an incredibly short space of time I found hundreds of fugitives and numerous wagons and ambulances fleeing in confusion, and attempting to cross the river. Orders came from you to arrest the flight of these fugitives, and to this end I directed my men to fix bayonets and halt the panic-stricken soldiers. To Capt. John P. Dufficy, acting major, and Adjutant Scully I am much indebted, as well as the company officers, for energetic efforts to form the recusants into line. Two small battalions were formed, and under an officer sent back to the right of the line. The confusion was very great, and I feel as if it was due to my officers and men to mention particularly the cool and determined manner [in which] they brought order out of confusion.

A short time after the subsidence of the panic on the west side of the river, I discovered a stampede arising among the teamsters who had crossed on the east side. An officer rode up and informed me that a battalion of the enemy's cavalry was about to charge upon and capture the wagons—among them were two wagons belonging to the general-in-chief—and requesting me, if possible, to save them. I instantly put the regiment in march to the ford, in order to meet the cavalry force. On my road to the ford I was ordered by Acting Assistant Adjutant-General Clark to form line again on the Fifty-first Ohio. I did so, and saw the cavalry coming in full charge on the train. At this juncture I threw the left wing of the regiment back, and opened a severe fire on the enemy, the battery on our right shelling him handsomely at the same time. The result was, the enemy remained but a little while, and managed to get but a few of the rear wagons away with him.

On the morning of January 1, our division (Third) recrossed to the east side of the river. The lines were formed in the following order: First line of our brigade consisted of the Fifty-first Ohio, Eighth Kentucky, and Thirty-fifth Indiana, the latter regiment being posted on the extreme left of the brigade, and just behind a curtain of woodland. In the rear of my regiment was the Ninety-ninth Ohio; on the left was the Seventy-ninth Indiana. In the course of the day I furnished three companies of skirmishers, G, I, and E, under Captains Prosser and McKim. Skirmishing was kept up all day. In the evening I relieved Companies E, I, and G by sending out the other seven companies, under command of Captain Dufficy.

At midnight the enemy undertook to drive in my skirmishers by a vigorous assault. I am proud to report that in this they signally failed. The line of skirmishers never gave an inch. On the contrary, in the gallant ardor of the moment, they drove the enemy beyond his own line and established the Thirty-fifth upon it. In this affair I lost 1 man killed and 2 wounded. Captain Dufficy on the right, and Captain Crowe upon the left of skirmishers, behaved with distinguished gallantry.

At daylight I found it necessary to relieve the line of skirmishers, as they had been all night and part of the preceding day without rest or nourishment. An order came from brigade headquarters for every regiment to throw out in front of their own line two companies of skirmishers. The skirmishers from my regiment were under command of Capt. James McKim, a cool and daring officer.

All day of the 2d instant, skirmishing kept up heavy in the entire front. About 2 p. m. a rebel battery opened upon us and threw solid shot and shell until 4 p. m., when the enemy, in force, advanced upon us. I had directed my men to lie down and fix bayonets, and in no case to fire until I gave the word. The skirmishing became very brisk, and my skirmishers came in, fell into line with the regiment, reporting to me the approach of an immense force. The enemy advanced steadily in column by regiment, *en échelon.*

When within a short distance of the line of the Fifty-first Ohio and Eighth Kentucky, the first brigade of the enemy came into line, and both parties opened a crashing fire of musketry. The enemy's second brigade came up to the work, yelling—they were immediately in my front. I considered it best to let them advance to within 30 or 40 paces of my line, as I believed they had no knowledge of my position, before I opened my fire. When their right flank was immediately opposite my line, I gave the order to rise and fire. With a deafening cheer the order was gallantly obeyed. A plunging volley staggered the advancing columns, and before the enemy could recover his surprise my regiment had reloaded and commenced a well-aimed and telling file fire. The flash and rattle of my musketry gave information to the battery in my front, which opened furiously upon me. The close proximity of the belligerent lines obliged the gunners to throw their shells to my rear and solid shot to my extreme left. This accounts for the left wing suffering so much more than the right. After twenty minutes of a murderous fire from the enemy, and seeing that he was steadily advancing upon the regiments on my right and left, I called for the Ninety-ninth Ohio to come forward and support me. I intended to have tried the virtue of the bayonet, according to the instructions of our much-respected general-in-chief. I regret very much to say, after two appeals to the Ninety-ninth Ohio, that regiment failed to come forward. The right wing of the Seventy-ninth Indiana was now engaged, and the whole of our brigade line on our right. Through all this terrible fire of musketry and shell, I am proud to say not a single officer or man flinched.

The enemy soon pressed forward. In my rear the Ninety-ninth Ohio had gone from the field. The Seventy-ninth Indiana then gave way under this terrific pressure. The regiments on my right, the Fifty-first Ohio and Eighth Kentucky, were slowly retiring, and fighting heroically. At the end of forty-three minutes of a desperate and unequal contest, I found the enemy completely around my flanks. To prevent a useless destruction of life, or entire capture of my regiment, I gave the order to retire. I was obliged to repeat it, and even then the brave fellows complied reluctantly—many refused, and they were either killed or captured.

On reaching the river, in our rear some 400 yards, I rallied the torn ranks of my regiment. Here were the remaining fragments of the Fifty-first Ohio, Eighth and Twenty-first Kentucky, with some other regiments that I cannot now designate. A bold and determined fire was opened by this new-formed line. The enemy paused, fought, and then at last broke and fled, our men pursuing them with cheers and a heavy straggling fire. So deafening was the musketry, I did not hear or know a single piece of artillery was giving us any aid until I reached the crest of the hill in the wood upon our right. The enemy made one stand more on this hill; it was but momentary, for our brave lads were upon them, and they fled, never again to rally.

In my efforts, agreeably to your orders, to ascertain what officer or man particularly distinguished himself for gallantry, or disgraced himself by cowardice, I asked a special report from officers commanding companies. I received but one report: They commanded a body of heroes. My own observation goes to indorse the truthfulness of these officers' reports. In the rush for the advance, portions of the Thirty-fifth Indiana, Fifty-first Ohio, Eighth and Twenty-first Kentucky reached the enemy's battery. The boys of the Fifty-first claim one piece, their comrades of the Thirty-fifth another. To do justice, I think your entire brigade was freely represented in the capture of these pieces. Where 272 men stand unflinchingly, for forty-three minutes, a combined fire of musketry and artillery at close range, it is certainly hard to give to any one a pre-eminence for gallantry. I had but few officers with me; each and every one had some peculiar tact of excellence, some one splendid soldierly virtue.

In conclusion, I feel obliged to call attention to the splendid conduct of my adjutant, John Scully. His escape was a miracle, freely exposing himself, and cheering the men throughout the action to deeds of valor. Serg. Maj. Robert Stockdale fought desperately, but coolly; he deserves particular mention, not only for his conduct on this field, but for the faithful and cheerful manner he has ever performed his duties. To Dr. Averdick, my surgeon, I must acknowledge valuable services; brave and defiant on the field, he is kind and attentive in the hospital wards. Quartermaster Igoe was on the field, attentive to the wounded, using every effort to have them carefully transported to the rear. By 10 o'clock that night not a wounded man of the Thirty-fifth could be found on the field. To Father Cooney, our chaplain, too much praise cannot be given. Indifferent as to himself, he was deeply solicitous for the temporal comfort and spiritual welfare of us all. On the field he was cool and indifferent to danger, and in the name of the regiment I thank him for his kindness and laborious attention to the dead and dying.

B. F. MULLEN,
Colonel Thirty-fifth Indiana.

Col. S. W. Price,
Commanding Third Brigade.

No. 161.

Report of Maj. Green B. Broaddus, Eighth Kentucky Infantry, of engagement January 2.

Headquarters Eighth Kentucky Volunteers,
January 26, 1863.

Sir: I have the honor to make the following report of the part taken by the Eighth Regiment Kentucky Volunteers in the battle of January 2, near Murfreesborough:

On January 1 we took position near the crest of a hill, the Fifty-first Ohio being on our right and the Thirty-fifth Indiana on our left. Nothing of special interest occurred until the morning of the 2d, when brisk skirmishing began along the whole line, and continued until about 2 o'clock, when the enemy advanced with infantry and artillery. The battle soon became general, and, the enemy pressing hard upon the Fifty-first Ohio, forced them to retire, giving the enemy an opportunity to gain our right flank and rear, which they lost no time in accomplishing. Both men and officers of my regiment fought with becoming bravery, coolness, and determination until flanked on the right and left; and, seeing no chance to stay the onward course of the enemy, we retired to the opposite side of the river just in time to save our capture.

Capt. John B. Banton, of Company F, was killed early in the action, while gallantly commanding a line of skirmishers. We lost 7 killed on the field, 7 officers wounded, 2 of whom have since died; 69 men wounded, 12 of whom have since died, and 27 missing.

Very respectfully,

G. B. BROADDUS,
Major, Commanding Eighth Regiment Kentucky Volunteers.

Col. STANLEY MATTHEWS,
Commanding Third Brigade.

No. 162.

Report of Lieut. Col. James C. Evans, Twenty-first Kentucky Infantry, of engagement January 2.

HEADQUARTERS TWENTY-FIRST KENTUCKY VOLUNTEERS,
Near Murfreesborough, Tenn., January 3, 1863.

SIR: In obedience to your orders, I took my position, with the rest of the brigade, on Thursday morning (1st), on the Murfreesborough side of Stone's River, the Fifty-first Ohio, Eighth Kentucky, and Thirty-fifth Indiana in the first line, running nearly north and south and fronting east, and my regiment and the Ninety-ninth Ohio in the second line; my regiment in rear of the Fifty-first, the Ninety-ninth in rear of the Thirty-fifth. During that day nothing of importance occurred, save the continual firing of the skirmishers.

On Friday (2d), Companies F and D, of my regiment, were ordered out on the extreme left of the division, as skirmishers, and Company B on the right, next to the river. During the fight of that day, Companies F and D did not come under my observation, but I am assured by Captain Evans, who commanded the two companies, that the men behaved like true soldiers. Special mention was made of the coolness and bravery of Lieut. Frederick Temple, commanding Company D. All the morning the skirmishing continued. About 1 p. m. the rebel artillery commenced throwing shells among us, greatly to our annoyance. At this time our artillery was withdrawn to the opposite side of the river, to the astonishment of all. It seems that our little brigade had been forgotten, or was left there all alone to be sacrificed, in order to draw the enemy on, which latter turned out to be the case.

Near 3 o'clock the rebel column advanced. I could see Company B, as they slowly fell back, fighting with the coolness and courage of veterans. On they came, and when within 30 or 40 yards of our line the Fifty-first and Eighth arose and poured into them a destructive fire. These two regiments fought like tigers—longer, too, than could have been expected under the circumstances. I, being interested in the fight in front, failed to notice the rebels advancing around our right, until they completely flanked us. By this time the Eighth and Fifty-first were driven back, and I at once ordered my men to rise and fall back, but to fight as they went, which they did.

We were driven back some 200 yards, to the bed of the river, where I rallied my men, but was ordered by Colonel Beatty, who commanded the division, to cross the river, and rally the men behind the batteries. We crossed, but, owing to the firing of our artillery and the fresh troops coming into line, my men were so scattered that it was impossible to rally all of them together; but I am glad to state that they all rallied upon one regiment or another, and again went in, and remained during the fight. I have no censure for a single man of my command, but the highest praise for them all. I did not see the Thirty-fifth and Ninety-ninth during the engagement.

My loss, in killed, wounded, and missing, was 55.

With the greatest respect, I remain, your obedient servant,

J. C. EVANS,
Lieut. Col. Twenty-first Kentucky Vols., Comdg. Regt.

Col. S. W. PRICE,
Commanding Third Brigade.

No. 163.

Report of Lieut. Col. Richard W. McClain, Fifty-first Ohio Infantry.

HDQRS. FIFTY-FIRST REGT. OHIO VOLUNTEER INFANTRY,
Camp near Murfreesborough, Tenn., January —, 1863.

COLONEL: I have the honor to make the following report of the operations of the Fifty-first Regiment Ohio Volunteer Infantry in front of Murfreesborough during the late engagement:

On our arrival at Stone's River, on Monday evening, December 29, 1862, my regiment was ordered on picket duty, to take post to the left of the pickets of General Wood's division, where we remained until Wednesday morning, December 31, when we received orders to rejoin our brigade, which was then *en route* for the purpose of crossing Stone's River. After we had crossed over, the Fifty-first was assigned its position in the center of the first line of battle; the Eighth Kentucky on our right, and the Thirty-fifth Indiana Infantry on our left. We had not been in line of battle over half an hour, when I received orders to re-cross the river and take position opposite the ford, where we remained until 1 p. m., when the enemy's cavalry, with two pieces of artillery, made a dash at our hospital wagons, which had not yet recrossed. Thereupon the Fifty-first was ordered to change position some 40 paces to the rear, in order to open the way for one of our batteries to open fire upon the enemy. We remained in that position until 3 p. m. The enemy's shot commenced falling among us, and we were again ordered to change our position about 100 yards to the rear, and out of range of the enemy's battery, where we remained during the night.

On Thursday morning, January 1, at 5.30 o'clock, I received orders from Col. Samuel Beatty, then commanding the Third Division, "to take the Fifty-first Ohio and throw it across Stone's River immediately; then to deploy four companies as skirmishers, holding the remaining six companies as a 'reserve;'" adding at the same time, "move your regiment forward," and he would throw additional forces to support me, and, if possible, to accomplish this before it was clearly light, which was done. Our line of skirmishers had not advanced far before a spirited fire was opened between them and the enemy's line of skirmishers. In a few minutes I received orders to "halt the line of skirmishers and not bring on an engagement," which I did.

The six companies of reserve were then ordered to take position on the eminence on the right of the first line of battle, my right resting near Stone's River, while the Eighth Kentucky and Thirty-fifth Indiana formed on our left. We immediately discovered a battery of the enemy about 1,200 yards in our front, which I reported to Colonel Beatty, who sent a battery to the front, posting two pieces to my right and four pieces to the left of the first line. Our battery then opened fire on the enemy, consisting of artillery, cavalry, and infantry, who were posted in the edge of the woods in front of us, the enemy feebly replying with their artillery, their sharpshooters at the same time keeping up a brisk fire on our line of skirmishers all day. Thus passed Thursday. In the evening the four companies that were skirmishing were relieved and formed with the regiment, where we lay that night on our arms.

On Friday morning, at daybreak, the enemy's sharpshooters opened on us with increased vigor. Two companies of the Fifty-first were then sent to relieve the front line of skirmishers. At about 12 m. the enemy changed the position of their battery to the left of our front, and opened a heavy fire on us at this elevated point, and, having got range of the two pieces of artillery posted where we were stationed, our pieces had to be withdrawn a short distance to the rear. The enemy's line of skirmishers was then strengthened, and drove our skirmishers back a short distance, and gained possession of some buildings which our skirmishers were unable to hold. Our line then rallied, drove the enemy from the buildings, who set them on fire before leaving them.

Between the hours of 1 and 2 p. m. we could distinctly see in the distance large bodies of infantry forming in our front and moving to our left, accompanied by artillery and cavalry. I immediately notified the proper officers of the movements of the enemy. Soon thereafter we saw large bodies of infantry forming in our front in line of battle, and moving toward us. They advanced to within between 600 and 800 yards of our front and halted, and commenced throwing down a line of fence running parallel to our line. I immediately directed Adjutant Nicholas to report the fact, and he informed Major Starling of the enemy's movements, as well as the brigade and division commanders that the enemy were in the act of attacking us. The enemy's artillery was playing on us up to this time, when it ceased, and their line of battle immediately advanced, their center moving steadily, while their left was thrown around to Stone's River. After advancing in this manner to within 200 yards of our front, they set up a most hideous yell, and charged upon us in two lines of battle, closed in mass, while their skirmishers rallied to their left.

At this period the eight companies of the Fifty-first were lying down, with bayonets fixed, being partially protected by a depression of the ground, the two companies of skirmishers still disputing the advance of the enemy's left, which was in advance of their center, and moving more rapidly, in order to get between us and the river, to outflank us. When their line arrived within 60 yards of our front, so that we could plainly see their breasts, I gave the command to rise and fire, which was done, the enemy at the same time opening a terrific fire upon us; their front line, using revolving rifles, kept up a continuous fire, and advancing. Being pressed heavily, and our right forced back and outflanked, the artillery having been withdrawn previous to the charge, we were compelled to fall back and cross the river, where I rallied portions of the regiment under cover of our artillery, then recrossed the river, and advanced with our colors and assisted in driving the enemy beyond our first position, capturing one piece of artillery belonging to the Washington Battery, our colors being the first to wave over the gun. It being dark, and the enemy driven from the field, we were ordered to seek quarters for the night.

The following is a list of the killed, wounded, and missing in the regiment during the engagement: Killed, 24; wounded, 122; missing, 44. Total, 190.

The following is a list of those especially noted for gallantry and ungallantry:

For gallant conduct: Sergts. Thomas Rodgers (color-bearer) and William Barnes, Company H; Privates Jesse T. Beachler, Company A; M. Morgan, John G. Fox, and John Hilliker, Company F; N. Jones and Theophilus Phillips, Company H, and Nathan A. Carpenter, Company I.

For ungallantry: First Sergt. William A. Himes, Company A; Privates Jacob Lenhart and Martin Hart, Company F.

Great praise is due both officers and soldiers for the manner in which they sustained the first charge of the enemy, and, although compelled to fall back, being pressed by superior numbers, still greater praise is due them for rallying with the advance, and assisting to drive the enemy from the field.

I am, colonel, your obedient servant,

R. W. McCLAIN,
Lieutenant-Colonel, Comdg. Fifty-first Regt. Ohio Vol. Infantry.

Col. STANLEY MATTHEWS,
Commanding Third Brigade, Third Division, Left Wing.

No. 164.

Report of Lieut. Col. John E. Cummins, Ninety-ninth Ohio Infantry, of engagement January 2.

HDQRS. NINETY-NINTH REGT. OHIO VOL. INFANTRY,
Near Murfreesborough, Tenn., January 24, 1863.

SIR: The following is a copy of my remarks accompanying my report of killed, wounded, and missing of this regiment in the battle of Stone's River, which report was made on the 4th day of January, 1863:

SIR: I have the honor to make the following report:

*   *   *   *   *   *   *

The Ninety-ninth Regiment went into action on January 2 with 369 men, rank and file.

The regiment lost, as the foregoing shows, 1 commissioned officer and 11 enlisted men, killed; 3 commissioned officers and 41 enlisted men, wounded; 1 commissioned officer and 35 enlisted men are missing. Of this number some are known to have been wounded on the field, and some to be prisoners in the hands of the enemy.

After the regiment was compelled to fall back, I found that, with but few exceptions, the men rallied and went back into the action. The conduct of the officers and men of the regiment was all that could be asked, and I might do injustice to some to mention particular instances of good conduct. Colonel Swaine, who was in command, and is wounded and absent from the regiment, sends back word that he was well satisfied with the conduct of all the officers and men of his command, and that they obeyed every order which he gave, with promptness.

J. E. CUMMINS,
Lieutenant-Colonel, Comdg. Ninety-ninth Regiment Ohio Volunteer Infantry.

Colonel PRICE,
Commanding Third Brigade, Third Division, Left Wing.

There are several inaccuracies in the report made at that time. It should have reported 12 enlisted men and 1 commissioned officer killed; 1 commissioned officer and 29 enlisted men missing.

J. E. CUMMINS,
Lieutenant-Colonel Ninety-ninth Ohio.

Col. STANLEY MATTHEWS,
Commanding Third Brigade, Third Division.

No. 165.

Reports of Brig. Gen. David S. Stanley, U. S. Army, Chief of Cavalry, including skirmishes near La Vergne, December 27, at Wilkinson's Cross-Roads, December 29, Overall's Creek, December 31, and Lytle's Creek, January 5.

HDQRS. CAVALRY, FOURTEENTH ARMY CORPS,
DEPARTMENT OF THE CUMBERLAND,
Near Murfreesborough, Tenn., January 9, 1863.

MAJOR: I have the honor to submit, for the information of the general commanding the army, the following statement of the part taken by the cavalry under my command in the advance upon and battle of Murfreesborough:

On December 26 I divided the cavalry into three columns, putting the First Brigade, commanded by Colonel Minty, Fourth Michigan Cavalry, upon the Murfreesborough pike, in advance of General Crittenden's corps. The Second Brigade, commanded by Colonel Zahm, Third Ohio Cavalry, was ordered to move on Franklin, dislodge the enemy's cavalry, and move parallel to General McCook's corps, protecting his right flank. The reserve cavalry, consisting of the new regiments, viz, Anderson Troop, or Fifteenth Pennsylvania Cavalry, First Middle Tennessee, Second East Tennessee Cavalry, and four companies of the Third Indiana, I commanded in person, and preceded General McCook's corps on the Nolensville pike. Col. John Kennett, commanding cavalry division, commanded the cavalry on the Murfreesborough pike. For the operations of this column, and also the movements of Colonel Zahm up to December 31, I would refer you to the inclosed reports of Colonels Kennett, Zahm, and Minty.

On the morning of the 27th our cavalry first encountered the enemy on the Nolensville pike, 1 mile in advance of Bole Jack Pass. Their cavalry was in large force and accompanied by a battery of artillery. Fighting continued from 10 o'clock until evening, during which time we had driven the enemy 2 miles beyond La Vergne.

The Third Indiana and Anderson Troop behaved very gallantly, charging the enemy twice and bringing them to hand-to-hand encounters. The conduct of Majors Rosengarten and Ward, the former now deceased, was most heroic.

On the 28th we made a reconnaissance to College Grove, and found that Hardee's rebel corps had marched to Murfreesborough.

On the 29th Colonel Zahm's brigade, having joined, was directed to march upon Murfreesborough by the Franklin road, the reserve cavalry moving on the Bole Jack road, the columns communicating at the crossing of Stewart's Creek.

We encountered the enemy's cavalry, and found them in strong force at Wilkinson's Cross-Roads. Our cavalry drove them rapidly across Overall's Creek, and within one-half mile of the enemy's line of battle. The Anderson Cavalry behaved most gallantly this day, pushing at full charge upon the enemy for 6 miles. Unfortunately their advance proved too reckless. Having dispersed their cavalry, the Troop fell upon two regiments of rebel infantry in ambush, and after a gallant struggle were compelled to retire, with the loss of Major Rosengarten and 6 men killed, and the brave Major Ward and 5 men desperately wounded. With the loss of these two most gallant officers the spirit of the Anderson Troop, which gave such fine promise, seems to have died out, and I have not been able to get any duty out of them since.

On the 30th the entire cavalry force was engaged in guarding the flanks of the army, in position. Some small cavalry skirmishing occurred, but nothing of importance.

At 11 p. m., the 30th, I marched for La Vergne with the First Tennessee and the Anderson Cavalry. Near that place I was joined by detachments of the Fourth Michigan and Seventh Pennsylvania Cavalry.

At 9.30 o'clock on the 31st I received an order from the general commanding, directing me to hasten to the right. I made all possible speed, leaving a strong detachment to protect the trains crowding the road at Stewartsborough and to pick up stragglers. Upon arriving upon the right flank of the army, I found order restored, and took position on General McCook's right, my right extending toward Wilkinson's Cross-Roads, occupying the woods about the meeting-house on Overall's Creek.

In this position we were attacked about 4 p. m. by a long line of foot skirmishers. My first impression was that these covered infantry, but I learned soon that they were only dismounted cavalry. We successfully held them at bay for one-half an hour with the Fourth Michigan and Seventh Pennsylvania, dismounted, when, being outflanked, I ordered our line to mount and fall back to the open field. The enemy followed here, and being re-enforced by detachments of the Anderson and Third Kentucky Cavalry, and the First Tennessee, we charged the enemy and put him to rout. The cavalry held the same position this night they had taken upon my arrival upon the field.

About 9 o'clock New Year's morning the enemy showed a line of skirmishers in the woods to our front, and soon after brought a six-gun battery to bear upon my cavalry. As we could not reach the enemy's skirmishers, nor reply to his artillery, I ordered my cavalry to fall back. A part of Zahm's brigade marched this day to Nashville to protect our train. Colonel Zahm's report is inclosed.

January 2 and 3 the cavalry was engaged in watching the flanks of our position. Upon the 4th it became evident that the enemy had fled. The cavalry was collected and moved to the fords of Stone's River. Upon the 5th we entered Murfreesborough. Zahm's brigade marched in pursuit of the enemy on the Shelbyville pike—marched 6 miles, finding no opposition. With the remainder of the cavalry I marched on the Manchester pike and encountered the enemy in heavy force at Lytle's Creek, 3½ miles from town. We fought with this force till near sundown, pushing them from one cedar-brake to another, when, being re-enforced by General Spears' brigade of East Tennesseeans, we drove the enemy out of his last stand in disorder. We returned after dark and encamped on Lytle's Creek. Our troops all behaved well. The skirmishing was of a very severe character. The Fourth U. S. Cavalry, which was this day first under my control, behaved very handsomely.

Inclosed please find reports of division, brigade, and regimental commanders. Captain Otis' command acted independently until the 5th instant, when they came under my orders.

Inclosed find list of killed, wounded, and missing,* excepting from Anderson Cavalry; the report of this regiment I have not received. A special report of officers and soldiers deserving mention will be submitted. The duty of the cavalry was very arduous. From December 26 to January 4 the saddles were only taken off to groom, and were immediately replaced.

---

* Embodied in revised statement, p. 214.

A consolidated list of casualties, including those of the First Tennessee, Anderson Troop, and Third Indiana, as nearly as ascertained, will be submitted in the morning.

Respectfully submitted.

> D. S. STANLEY,
> *Brigadier-General and Chief of Cavalry.*

—

> HEADQUARTERS CAVALRY,
> *Near Murfreesborough, January 12, 1863.*

SIR: Inclosed please find consolidated report, with list of commissioned officers killed, wounded, and missing, in the operations before Murfreesborough. I send it unsigned, as the general is away.

I am, your obedient servant,

> WM. H. SINCLAIR,
> *Assistant Adjutant-General.*

C. GODDARD,
Assistant Adjutant-General and Chief of Staff.

—

*Report of casualties in cavalry command, Fourteenth Army Corps, from the advance from Nashville on the 26th December, and including the battles before Murfreesborough.**

Command.	Killed.		Wounded.		Missing.		Total.		Horses.	
	Officers.	Enlisted men.	Officers.	Enlisted men.	Officers.	Enlisted men.	Officers.	Enlisted men.	Killed.	Wounded.
2d Indiana Cavalry		1			1	13	1	14		
7th Pennsylvania Cavalry		2		9		50		61		
3d Kentucky Cavalry		1	1	7		1	1	9	7	15
4th Michigan Cavalry		1	1	6		12	1	19	11	17
1st Middle Tennessee Cavalry †			1	5	1	8	2	13	19	8
2d East Tennessee Cavalry	1	2		10		5	1	17		
4th U. S. Cavalry		3	1	9		12	1	24		
15th Pennsylvania Cavalry	1		1	5			2	5		
1st Ohio Cavalry	3	2	1	10	† 1	14	5	26		
3d Ohio Cavalry		6		15		13		34		
4th Ohio Cavalry		7		18		31		56		
	5	25	6	94	3	159	14	278	37	40

List of officers killed and wounded in cavalry command, Fourteenth Army Corps, Department of the Cumberland, in operations before Murfreesborough, Tenn.

Killed.—Col. Minor Milliken, First Ohio Cavalry; Maj. D. A. B. Moore, First Ohio Cavalry; Lieut T. L. Condit, Company L, First Ohio Cavalry.

Wounded.—Captain Wortham, Company C, First Tennessee Cavalry; Capt. Eli Long, Company K, Fourth U. S. Cavalry; Adjt. William H. Scott, First Ohio; Lieut. Thomas V. Mitchell, Company H, Fourth Michigan Cavalry.

—

> HEADQUARTERS CAVALRY,
> *Camp on Bradyville pike, Tenn., January 29, 1863.*

COLONEL: In accordance with Paragraph 743, Army Regulations, I have the honor to submit the names of the following officers deserving, in my opinion, of special notice:

Major Klein, Third Indiana, on the 27th first engaged the enemy on the Nolensville pike, and soon put them to full flight.

---

* But see revised statement, p. 214.   † Fifth Tennessee Cavalry.   ‡ Surgeon.

Majors Ward and Rosengarten (Anderson Troop), both deceased, behaved with great bravery in the two affairs with the enemy.   In the last one, on the 29th, both these gallant young officers received their death wounds.

Colonel Minty, Fourth Michigan, commanding First Brigade, deserves credit for his management of his command on the maich and in several actions.

Captain Otis, Fourth U. S. Cavalry, and Colonel Murray, Third Kentucky Cavalry, with their respective regiments, rendered important and distinguished service, gallantly charging and dispersing the enemy's cavalry in their attack upon our train Wednesday, the 31st.   Maj. John E. Wynkoop was, as always, a model to faithful soldiers.

Colonel Kennett was only a part of the time under my command; he rendered good service.   Colonel Zahm, Third Ohio Cavalry, Second Brigade (though unfortunate with a portion of his command on Wednesday morning), contributed greatly, by his personal example, to the restoration of order and confidence in that portion of the Second Brigade stampeded by the enemy's attack.

Inclosed please find subordinate reports.   Colonel Zahm, having received an injury, has submitted no report.

Respectfully submitted.

D. S. STANLEY,
Brigadier-General and Chief of Cavalry.

Col. C. GODDARD,
Assistant Adjutant-General and Chief of Staff.

No. 166.

Report of Col. John Kennett, Fourth Ohio Cavalry, commanding First Cavalry Division.

HEADQUARTERS FIRST CAVALRY DIVISION,
Camp Stanley, Tenn., January 8, 1863.

SIR: I have the honor of submitting to you the reports of the part taken in the fighting of the two brigades, composing the First Cavalry Division, from December 26, 1862, up to the night of January 5, 1863, from Nashville to Murfreesborough, and 6 miles beyond Murfreesborough, on the Manchester and Shelbyville pikes.

On leaving Nashville, the Second Brigade, under Colonel Zahm, took the road to Franklin; Brig. Gen. D. S. Stanley, with the First and Second Tennessee Cavalry and Anderson Troop, took the Nolensville pike; the First Brigade, Colonel Minty commanding, under my charge, took the Murfreesborough pike.   I reported my command to General Palmer, who placed us in the advance.   Our skirmishers drove the enemy some 5 miles.   The afternoon was well spent, when General Palmer relieved us with infantry skirmishers, the cavalry forming the reserve on the right and left flanks.   The First Brigade marched daily as a reserve to the advanced skirmishers of the army composing the left wing, on their flanks, up to December 30, 1862.

On December 31, 1862, we were posted as reserves on the flanks, throwing out our skirmishers and vedettes, watching the movements of the enemy.   We performed a variety of duty, as scouts on the different avenues leading to our camp and connecting with the roads centering upon Nashville, Tenn., flankers, vedettes, couriers, engaging the enemy daily on the right flank. For the details of each engagement, I beg leave to refer you to the reports herewith. Some few incidents which could not well have fallen under the eye of the brigade commanders, having occurred under my immediate notice, I beg leave to append.

When the enemy charged upon our right wing, scattering a few regiments, which stampeded to the rear, I received orders from Major-General Rosecrans in person to collect all the cavalry at my command, and proceed to rally the right wing and drive the enemy away. I found Colonel Murray, of the Third Kentucky, in command of about a squadron of men. With that we made our way to the right. We found a complete stampede—infantry, cavalry, and artillery rushing to the rear, and the rebel cavalry charging upon our retiring forces on the Murfreesborough pike.

Colonel Murray, with great intrepidity, engaged the enemy toward the skirts of the woods, and drove them in three charges. His men behaved like old veterans. Between his command and the field the space was filled with rushing rebel cavalry, charging upon our retreating cavalry and infantry, holding many of our soldiers as prisoners. I rallied the Third Ohio, some two companies, which was falling back, and formed it in the rear of a fence, where volley after volley had the effect of driving back the rebels upon the run, they (the Third Ohio) charging upon them effectually, thereby relieving the pike of their presence, saving the train, one piece of artillery, and rescuing from their grasp many of our men taken as prisoners. One of my staff, Lieutenant Rilley, being a prisoner in their hands, was released.

Lieutenant-Colonel Murray, of the Third Ohio, displayed energy, coolness, and courage upon this occasion in executing my orders. I also take great pride in mentioning the prompt manner with which my staff conveyed my orders in all these engagements.

Two of my orderlies displayed high order of chivalry. Jaggers charged upon two rebel cavalry, rescuing two men of the Fourth Ohio Volunteer Cavalry, who were being taken off as prisoners. The other, Farrish, shot two of the rebels and came to my rescue in a personal encounter with a rebel, who was in the act of leveling his pistol at my head; but he found a carbine leveled into his own face, and, at my order to surrender, he delivered his pistols, carbine, and horse to me. They both deserve promotion, and would make good officers.

The able, undaunted spirit and ability which Colonel Minty has displayed whenever coming under my eye, I take great satisfaction in noticing. The officers and men all displayed great self-sacrifice.

Major Wynkoop, of the Seventh Pennsylvania Cavalry, and Lieutenant Woolley, assistant adjutant-general of the First Brigade, carried out every order with unhesitating energy and will, displaying the highest order of gallantry.

Captain Otis, of the Fourth Regiment Cavalry, although he does not belong to my division, but being posted on the left wing of our skirmishers on the march on the Manchester road, I feel it my duty, as well as take great pleasure, in stating he is an able and efficient officer.

Brig. Gen. D. S. Stanley being in command of the forces pursuing the retiring rebels on this march, it fell to my lot to convey and see his orders executed. Before closing this report, it is my duty to make honorable mention of the meritorious conduct of Lieutenant Newell, commanding a section of artillery attached to my division. During the first day's engagement, near La Vergne, he placed his two pieces in well-selected grounds, and did great execution, killing 3 horses, dismounting

7. and scattering the rebel cavalry by his well and timely aimed shots. He has on several occasions displayed talents of the first order as an artillerist. It would not be amiss to state at this time that my entire command were short of rations, performing duty night and day in the wet fields, without shelter, exposed to the wet, cold, and hunger without a murmur.

Major Paramore, of the Third Ohio, displayed great presence of mind and determination in maintaining his position on the right flank with his battalion to cover an ammunition train long after the cavalry on his right had been driven away by the enemy's shells. I annex his report, all of which I respectfully submit for your review.

Your obedient servant,

JNO. KENNETT,
Colonel, Commanding First Cavalry Division.

Capt. W. H. SINCLAIR.

No. 167.

Report of Lieut. Nathaniel M. Newell, Battery D, First Ohio Light Artillery, of skirmishes near La Vergne and Stewart's Creek, December 26–January 1.

HEADQUARTERS BATTERY D, FIRST OHIO ARTILLERY,
Camp near Murfreesborough, Tenn., January 12, 1863.

LIEUTENANT: December 26, 1862, Colonel Kennett ordered me to move with the First Brigade, Colonel Minty, from camp, near Nashville, on Murfreesborough pike, toward La Vergne. Two miles from La Vergne we came upon a body of Confederate cavalry, and went into action, dispersing them after firing 4 rounds. We then moved forward a mile; we there took position on the pike and opened fire on a section of rebel artillery, distant about a mile. I fired 60 rounds, losing, during the action, 1 man killed—Private F. T. Coffin—and 1 horse disabled. I then moved into a field on the right of the pike and opened fire. The enemy retired from their position to the left and rear. I then moved to the left of the pike, and took position near a small church, from which position we fired until dark, silencing the enemy after a few rounds. That night I encamped with the brigade on the right of the pike and 1 mile back.

From the night of December 26 to the morning of January 1, I occupied different positions in and around La Vergne and Stewart's Creek.

On January 1, moved from Stewart's Creek to La Vergne with Colonel Dickinson, of the Fourth Michigan Cavalry, to re-enforce Colonel Innes, of the First Michigan Engineers and Mechanics, stationed near La Vergne. About 1 mile from that place I found Wheeler's rebel cavalry on the left of the pike. I went into action and drove them from the field, and then joined Colonel Innes' command, with whom I remained until the 9th instant.

On the 9th instant received orders to report to General Stanley, chief of cavalry, and by him was ordered to report to Colonel Kennett, and am now in camp on Manchester pike, near First Cavalry Brigade.

Very respectfully,

N. M. NEWELL,
Lieutenant, Commanding Battery D, First Ohio Artillery.

Lieut. M. B. CHAMBERLIN,
Acting Assistant Adjutant-General, First Cavalry Division.

No. 168.

*Report of Col. Robert H. G. Minty, Fourth Michigan Cavalry, command-
ing First Brigade, including skirmishes at La Vergne, December 26,
between Stewart's Creek and La Vergne, December 30, at Overall's Creek,
December 31, and on Manchester pike, January 5.*

HEADQUARTERS FIRST CAVALRY BRIGADE,
Camp near Murfreesborough, Tenn., January 7, 1863.

SIR: I have the honor to hand you the following report of the part
taken by the First Brigade, First Division of the Cavalry Reserve, in the
operations from the advance from Nashville to and including the battles
before Murfreesborough:

I marched from Camp Rosecrans, near Nashville, on the morning of
the 26th ultimo, with the Third Kentucky, Fourth Michigan, Seventh
Pennsylvania, and one company of the Second Indiana, and reported to
General Palmer, on the Murfreesborough road. In accordance with
orders received from him through the colonel commanding the division,
I placed the Third Kentucky on the left and the Seventh Pennsylvania
on the right of the road, keeping the Fourth Michigan on the pike, with
a strong advance guard out. Ten miles from Nashville I met the
enemy's pickets, who, as they fell back before us, were continually re-
enforced, until, arriving at La Vergne, they disputed our progress with
a force of 2,500 cavalry and mounted infantry, supported by four pieces
of artillery, under the command of General Wheeler. As the enemy
had us most perfectly in range, after some sharp skirmishing, I moved,
under cover of a slight eminence, on which Lieutenant Newell, of Battery D, First Ohio, had his section planted, leaving two companies of
the Fourth Michigan, dismounted and in ambush, behind a fence to support the battery.

I must here mention that Lieutenant Newell did splendid service with
his two 3-inch Rodmans. Every shot was well planted, and he nobly
fought the four guns of the enemy for over half an hour, when a battery
from General Palmer's division moved up to his assistance. One of the
gunners was killed by a shell from the enemy while serving his gun.

Saturday, December 27, the Seventh Pennsylvania, under Major
Wynkoop, made a reconnaissance in front of General Palmer's division,
which occupied a position on the left of the line. One battalion of the
Fourth Michigan, under command of Captain Mix, was sent out on the
Jefferson pike, and did not rejoin the brigade until the following day.
I beg to refer you to Captain Mix's report for particulars. The army
advanced at about 11 a. m., the Third Kentucky and one company of
the Second Indiana, under command of Colonel Murray, covering the
left flank, and the Fourth Michigan, under my immediate direction,
covering the right flank. Camped near Stewart's Creek this night.

Sunday, December 28, sent one battalion of the Seventh Pennsylvania to relieve the battalion of the Fourth Michigan, on Jefferson pike.

Monday, December 29, army again advanced; Seventh Pennsylvania,
under Major Wynkoop, on the left flank; Third Kentucky on the right
flank, under Colonel Murray; Fourth Michigan in reserve; Second Indiana on courier duty. Light skirmishing with the enemy all day.
Found the enemy in position in front of Murfreesborough at about 3 p.
m. Bivouacked for the night immediately in rear of our line of battle.

Tuesday, December 30, one battalion of the Seventh Pennsylvania
and one of the Third Kentucky formed a chain of vedettes in rear of

the line of battle, with orders to drive up all stragglers. Under orders from the colonel commanding the division, I took the Fourth Michigan and one battalion of the Seventh Pennsylvania back on the Nashville pike, to operate against Wheeler's cavalry, who, a few hours before, had destroyed the train of the Twenty-eighth Brigade on the Jefferson pike. Between Stewart's Creek and La Vergne I met the enemy, about 100 strong, and dressed in our uniforms. The Seventh Pennsylvania drove them until after dark. I reported to Colonel Walker, Thirty-first Ohio, commanding a brigade, and encamped with him that night, 2½ miles south of La Vergne.

Wednesday, December 31, under orders from Major-General Rosecrans, I reported to Brigadier-General Stanley, chief of cavalry, who came up the same morning with the First Middle Tennessee and part of the Fifteenth Pennsylvania. Under orders from General Stanley, we moved rapidly across the country toward the right of General McCook's position (leaving Lieutenant-Colonel Dickinson, Fourth Michigan Cavalry, with 120 men, to support Lieutenant Newell's section of artillery at the cross-roads northwest of Stewart's Creek), the enemy's cavalry falling back rapidly before us. When close to Overall's Creek our own artillery, in position to our left, opened on us with shell, and severely wounded 1 man of the Fifteenth Pennsylvania.

Crossing Overall's Creek, I took up position parallel to, and three-fourths of a mile distant from, the Nashville and Murfreesborough road. The Fourth Michigan dismounted, forming a line of skirmishers on the edge of the woods immediately in our front, out of which they had driven a large force of the rebel cavalry. They were supported by a part of the First Tennessee, also dismounted. Captain Jennings' battalion, Seventh Pennsylvania, and two companies Third Kentucky, under Captain Davis, were posted in the woods to the right and in rear of the Fourth Michigan, with the Fifteenth Pennsylvania in their rear. Our entire force at this time was 950 men.

The enemy advanced rapidly with 2,500 cavalry, mounted and dismounted, with three pieces of artillery, all under the command of General Wheeler. They drove back the Fourth Michigan to the line of the First Tennessee skirmishers, and then attacked the Seventh Pennsylvania with great fury, but met with determined resistance. I went forward to the dismounted skirmishers and endeavored to move them to the right, to strengthen the Seventh Pennsylvania, but the moment the right of the line showed itself from behind the fence where they were posted, the whole of the enemy's fire was directed on it, turning it completely around. At this moment the Fifteenth Pennsylvania gave way and retreated rapidly, leaving the battalion of the Seventh Pennsylvania and the dismounted men almost entirely unsupported, and leaving them no alternative but retreat.

We fell back a couple of fields and reformed in rear of a rising ground, which protected us from the enemy's artillery.

The rebel cavalry had followed us up sharply into the open ground, and now menaced us with three strong lines, two directly in front of my position and one opposite our left flank, with its right thrown well forward, and a strong body of skirmishers in the woods to our right, and threatening that flank.

General Stanley gave the order to charge, and he himself led two companies (K and H) of the Fourth Michigan Cavalry and about 50 men of the Fifteenth Pennsylvania against the line in front of our left, routed the enemy, and captured one stand of colors, which was brought in by a sergeant of the Fifteenth Pennsylvania. Captain Jennings, Seventh Pennsylvania, with his battalion, supported this movement.

At the same time I charged the first line in our front with the Fourth Michigan and First Tennessee, supported on the right by a fire from the Fifteenth Pennsylvania, and drove them from the field. The second line was formed on the far side of a lane, with a partially destroyed fence on each side of it, and still stood their ground. I reformed my men and again charged. The enemy was again broken and driven from the field.

Colonel Kennett, commanding First Cavalry Division, now arrived on the field with re-enforcements. I held the ground that night with the First Tennessee, Fifteenth Pennsylvania, and Fourth Michigan, picketing the whole of my first position.

A sergeant of the Seventh Pennsylvania, who was taken prisoner by the enemy, states that before we charged we had killed 27, including many officers.

January 1, 2, and 3, had the brigade under arms all day, with two regiments on picket and skirmishing with the enemy's pickets.

Sunday, January 4, moved the brigade to Wilkinson's Cross-Roads, and bivouacked there for the night with the Fourth Cavalry.

Monday, January 5, marched through Murfreesborough and took the Manchester pike; 1 mile out met the enemy's pickets; reported to General Stanley, who ordered an advance, and took the lead himself with the Fourth Cavalry. After crossing a small creek, about 2 miles from Murfreesborough, the bridge over which had been destroyed, the enemy commenced shelling us. I sent the Third Kentucky well to the right and front and the Seventh Pennsylvania to the left, keeping the First and Second Tennessee and the Fourth Michigan in reserve. After some little delay, the general again ordered an advance. I placed the five companies, Fourth Michigan, on the right of the road, with one company advanced as skirmishers; the Third Kentucky on the right of the Fourth Michigan, and the First Tennessee on the right of the Third Kentucky, with the Second Tennessee in reserve. In this formation we advanced through a cedar wood with a dense undergrowth, rendering it almost impossible to force our way through. We had occasional skirmishing with the enemy, who continued to shell us as we advanced.

About 6 miles out we met the enemy in force; a sharp skirmish ensued. The Fourth Cavalry, First Tennessee Infantry, and Seventh Pennsylvania Cavalry were chiefly engaged on our side. The enemy were driven from the field, and we returned within 1½ miles of Murfreesborough and went into camp.

I beg to refer you to the reports of regimental commanders for particulars of operations of detached portions of the brigade.

Inclosed herewith I hand you a report of such officers and men as deserve special mention; also the report of casualties.

In explanation of the large number of missing reported by the Seventh Pennsylvania, I would call your attention to the fact that the entire of one battalion was deployed as a chain of vedettes in rear of our line of battle, where the right wing was driven back, and many of the men must have been captured by the enemy while endeavoring to drive up the straggling infantry. I have to call your particular attention to the reports of Colonel Murray, Captain Mix, and Lieutenant Eldridge.

Colonel Murray, with a handful of men, performed services that would do honor to a full regiment.

Captain Mix, with about 50 men, not only drove 200 of the enemy over

2 miles, but he there held his position agains'. an entire regiment of rebel cavalry.

Lieutenant Eldridge, with 18 men, dismounted, attacked the enemy, routed them, and recaptured a wagon full of ammunition.

In the engagement of Wednesday, while leading his company in a charge, Captain Mix's horse was shot under him, and in the same charge Lieutenant Woolley, my acting assistant adjutant-general, was thrown from his horse, severely hurting his leg; notwithstanding which, he immediately remounted and continued to perform all his duties.

The brigade has captured and turned over 192 prisoners.

I am, respectfully, your obedient servant,

ROBT. H. G. MINTY,
Colonel, Commanding First Cavalry Division.

Lieutenant CHAMBERLIN,
Acting Assistant Adjutant-General, First Cavalry Division.

No. 169.

Report of Capt. Joseph A. S. Mitchell, Second Indiana Cavalry, of operations near La Vergne, December 29–31.

NASHVILLE, TENN., *January 2, 1863.*

SIR: I have the honor to report that, in accordance with your order, I reported to Captain Otis, chief of couriers, on the 29th ultimo, and that on the same date, by his direction, my men were posted on the Nashville and Murfreesborough road as couriers, commencing 9 miles from Nashville, and extending to the headquarters of Major-General Crittenden.

On the 31st ultimo, at 3 p. m., the enemy made a raid upon La Vergne, at which point I had made my headquarters, capturing from my command 1 lieutenant and 13 men, and making it necessary for two other courier posts to abandon their stations to prevent capture, all of which I immediately reported to Major-General Rosecrans the same evening. The places of my men were supplied from another command, and I proceeded to this place to collect the few men who still remained of my company. Those who were at General Crittenden's headquarters having been sent here as an escort with his headquarters train, I collected 17 men for duty and reported to Brigadier-General Mitchell, commanding the post, and, by his command, I have placed them as couriers between Nashville and La Vergne.

I have to report, besides the loss already mentioned, 15 Government horses, 10 mules, 2 wagons, all of the equipage, tents, &c., of the company, 15 Colt's revolving pistols and holsters, 11 Colt's revolving rifles, 14 saddles, bridles, and halters, besides all of my own private baggage and personal effects.

Since occupying the present line, I have to report 1 man killed while bearing a dispatch.

I am, most truly, your obedient servant,

J. A. S. MITCHELL,
Captain, Commanding Company.

Col. R. H. G. MINTY,
Commanding First Cavalry Brigade.

No. 170.

Report of Col. Eli H. Murray, Third Kentucky Cavalry, including skir-mishes at La Vergne, December 26, Wilkinson's Cross-Roads, December 31, and on Manchester pike, January 5.

HEADQUARTERS THIRD KENTUCKY CAVALRY,
Camp Stanley, near Murfreesborough, Tenn., January 7, 1863.

SIR: I have the honor herewith to transmit a report of the part taken by my command from December 26, 1862, the day of our advance from Nashville, the engagement before Murfreesborough, and pursuit of the enemy in their retreat.

On passing our outpost before Nashville, on the Murfreesborough road, my command formed the left wing of the advance. We had pro-ceeded but a short distance when we encountered the enemy, and, press-ing them closely, soon engaged in quite a brisk skirmish. Driving them in a lively chase, we succeeded in capturing 5 of the enemy. Skirmish-ing all day long through dense cedar thickets, we found quite a force at La Vergne, with quite an engagement, exposed to the fire of their artil-lery, which resulted only in the loss of 2 horses. Changing my position, my command formed the left, joined to General Cruft's brigade, cap-turing 1 other of the enemy.

We moved from there to Stewart's Creek the following day, forming still the left, and capturing 7 of the enemy. Advancing from thence, my command formed the right. Night found us on the ground afterward occupied by General Negley in the beginning of the general engage-ment. Captain Wolfley, commanding Second Battalion, opened com-munication with Major-General McCook during the day.

Major Shacklett, with his battalion, on the 30th formed a line of couriers (in rear of line of battle) with Major-General McCook. Cap-tain Davis, with squadron, Companies B and D, ordered to report to General Stanley, at Wilkinson's Cross-Roads. This squadron was after-ward with Colonel Minty, and engaged, with his command, the enemy while detached from me. Fifteen men, of Company C, under Lieuten-ant Smock, reported to General Van Cleve.

At 8 o'clock, December 31, 1862, Colonel Kennett, commanding divis-ion, gave me orders to move to Wilkinson's Cross-Roads. Having moved but a short distance, and in the direction of the cross-roads, I found the greatest confusion, caused by the right wing of the army falling back. Going but little farther, I found our whole train of baggage and ammu-nition in possession of the enemy. Captain Wolfley, with part of his battalion, and Captain Breathitt, commanding the First Battalion, with a squad of his command, in all about 80 men, in a moment were engaged charging down the train. We came upon the enemy in all directions. Here were engagements hand-to-hand, but dashing onward my men were doing in earnest the work before them. The open field gave us the place for charging. The enemy were marching about 250 of our men to their rear as prisoners. These we recaptured. We also recaptured a portion of the Fifth Wisconsin Battery; also a section supposed to be the First Ohio. The hospital of General Palmer's division was still held by them. Bringing about 40 men to dash upon them, their whole command fled. At one time it seemed as if my whole command were taking prisoners to the rear. There being no support near, I ordered the prisoners to be given to the nearest infantry, in order that I might bring all my force against them and hold the train. Major Shacklett here rejoined me, and having taken position near the hospital, our cavalry coming to the field, took position on my left. Again the enemy made a dash, but was again repulsed. Near two hours afterward the enemy moved to the right. By order of Colonel Kennett we moved in that direction at the trot, again to find them about to attack the train; but after exchanging shots, and under fire from our artillery, again baffled in their design, withdrew. We took between 50 and 60 prisoners, killing and wounding about 25.

In the engagement the 80 men of my command drove from the field Wharton's brigade of rebel cavalry; saved the baggage and ammunition of a great part of our army; recaptured a portion of the Fifth Wisconsin Battery and a section of, I think, the First Ohio Battery, and, at least calculation, 800 of our men. From that time up to their retreat from Murfreesborough we held our position with the First Cavalry Brigade, under the direct orders of Colonel Minty, commanding.

In the pursuit on Manchester road, moving with the brigade about 1 mile from Murfreesborough, Captain Cummings, with a squadron, was sent out and discovered the enemy just before us. As the brigade moved, he was in advance and engaged the enemy all along. My command carried the right of the pike and had several engagements, exposed several times to the fire of the artillery, capturing 4 prisoners.

The casualties during the whole engagement were 1 killed, 6 wounded, and 1 missing.* Seven horses killed and 15 wounded.

I will make no mention of one officer above another. All did their duty, and led their men nobly to the action; and the men, their actions on the battle-field, are beyond what I could speak of them here. Not one of my command ran to the rear; all acted bravely. In all, we captured 87 prisoners.

Respectfully, your obedient servant,

E. H. MURRAY,
Colonel Third Kentucky Cavalry.

JOHN WOOLLEY,
Actg. Asst. Adjt. Gen., First Cavalry Brigade.

No. 171.

Report of Lieut. Col. William H. Dickinson, Fourth Michigan Cavalry, including skirmish at La Vergne, January 1.

HEADQUARTERS FOURTH MICHIGAN CAVALRY,
Camp near Murfreesborough, Tenn., January 8, 1863.

SIR : In compliance with an order of Colonel Minty, commanding First Cavalry Brigade, I submit the following report of the troops under my command since my separation from the main body of my regiment at the cross-roads near Stewart's Creek, on the Murfreesborough pike, December 31 :

I remained there, by Colonel Minty's order, with two pieces of artillery and four companies of the Fourth Michigan Cavalry, viz, Companies A, D, G, and L, until the morning of January 1, when I was ordered by Colonel Burke, of the Tenth Ohio Infantry, to move with my command in the direction of La Vergne, to engage the enemy who had attacked our baggage train. On arriving within three-fourths of a mile of that place, we found the enemy attacking and burning our train. I

---

* Nominal list omitted.

immediately ordered a part of my men to dismount and protect the two pieces of artillery under my command and the other to attack the enemy from the left. After a brisk fire of about half an hour, the enemy retired, leaving 15 killed and carrying off 15 wounded.

I was then ordered by Colonel Innes to patrol the pike between Stewart's Creek and La Vergne, both day and night, until January 4, when, by General Stanley's command, I escorted Quartermaster Dudley's train to Nashville and back here, where I arrived on the evening of the 7th instant.

On January 2, two prisoners were brought in by our pickets, whom I turned over to Captain Ward, of the Tenth Ohio, commanding detachment at Stewart's Creek. Inclosed you will find a report, made by Lieutenant Eldridge, who was for a few days in command of a separate detachment.

Yours,

W. H. DICKINSON,
Lieutenant-Colonel, Comdg. Fourth Michigan Cavalry.

Lieut. JOHN WOOLLEY,
Acting Assistant Adjutant-General.

No. 172.

Report of Capt. Frank W. Mix, Fourth Michigan Cavalry, of skirmish at Stewart's Creek Bridge, December 27.

HEADQUARTERS FOURTH MICHIGAN CAVALRY,
Camp near Murfreesborough, Tenn., January 8, 1863.

COLONEL: In compliance with your order, on December 27, 1862, I reported to General Palmer with four companies of the Fourth Michigan Cavalry, Companies H, E, L, and B.

I was ordered to take the advance of a brigade of infantry and one battery of artillery and move off on the Jefferson pike, to take and hold the bridge over Stewart's Creek, about 4 miles east of Murfreesborough pike. I sent Company E into the woods, to the left of the road, as skirmishers, and Company H to the right. When about 1½ miles out on the road, our advance came upon their pickets. I immediately started with Companies L and B after them. We were then 2½ miles from the bridge. At every rod their number increased, so that when we came to the bridge we were chasing about 200 of them. Captain Pritchard, with Company L, had the advance, and was so close to them when we crossed the bridge that some of them were pushed off the side of the bridge and taken prisoners.

As soon as we got possession of the bridge, I sent couriers back to hurry up the infantry. While we were waiting they attacked us in strong force, but our boys nobly stood their ground and repulsed them. We heard no report from the infantry. I sent another courier back, and he soon came back to me saying there was about 100 of them in our rear, between the infantry and my command. I then attempted to draw part of my command (Company L) back of the bridge, but I no sooner started them back than they came down on us like bees, yelling as if they had us sure. I had Company B, under Lieutenant Carter, posted on each side of the road, where they had a good sight of them. Company L came back to the bridge on double-quick, with the enemy close at their heels. I ordered them to right-about, which they did handsomely, not a man flinching or wavering in the least. They immediately opened a fire upon the enemy, which soon made them leave for the woods.

I soon heard firing in my rear, and sent Captain Pritchard, with his company, back to find out the cause. As I instantly expected an attack from that quarter, I called Company B in and placed them on the bridge. They again attempted to drive us from the bridge, but our boys were too much for them, and again drove them back under cover of the woods. Lieutenant Leach now came in with Company H; he had run on the party in our rear, and with 20 men drove them to the woods, and joined my command. The artillery soon came up, and my trouble was over.

The officers and men of these four companies are deserving of great praise. With 50 men we charged and drove for 2½ miles 200 of the First Alabama Cavalry, and held the bridge for one-half hour against the whole regiment. The prisoners we took admit that their regiment was all there, and another regiment in Wheeler's brigade was 2 miles in the rear, on Stone's River.

I lost 3 men taken prisoners, between the infantry and my command, and had 1 slightly wounded. We took from them 9 prisoners, wounded 1 lieutenant and 3 privates, and killed 1 lieutenant and 1 private. We also took 4 horses ; two of them the infantry took possession of. We remained on the ground over night, and were relieved by the Seventh Pennsylvania Cavalry, when I immediately rejoined my regiment, all right, and perfectly satisfied with my trip.

I am, colonel, your most obedient servant,

FRANK W. MIX,
Captain, Comdg. Detachment Fourth Michigan Cavalry.

Lieut. Col. W. H. DICKINSON,
Commanding Fourth Michigan Cavalry.

No. 173.

Report of Lieut. Lansingh B. Eldridge, Fourth Michigan Cavalry, of operations between Nashville and La Vergne, January 1–3.

JANUARY 7, 1863.

SIR : On the 1st day of January, instant, I was ordered by Captain Henion to take 20 men of Company K, Fourth Michigan Cavalry, and proceed toward Nashville as an advance guard of the train. At La Vergne the train was attacked, and the Second Tennessee Cavalry formed in line of battle, and I prepared to join them ; but at the discharge of the enemy's second gun the Tennessee cavalry fled, and I, with my men, remained alone to protect the train. I left the pike and went to the right and passed around on to the pike again, and proceeded with the advance of the train to Nashville, while the enemy burned a portion of the rear of the train.

On the 3d, I left Nashville to join my regiment, and at the asylum the train was attacked, and I was ordered up and proceeded at a double-quick, and found that fighting was going on on both sides of the road, and, seeing we were the weakest on the left, I formed on that side, where a portion of the Second Tennessee Cavalry was engaging the enemy, but as we entered the field they broke and fled, and I dismounted my men and advanced as skirmishers, leaving our horses under cover of a hill. I followed the enemy nearly half a mile, and retook one of our wagons loaded with ammunition, and then proceeded to join my regiment, under Colonel Dickinson.

L. B. ELDRIDGE,

First Lieutenant, Company K.

ADJUTANT FOURTH MICHIGAN CAVALRY.

No. 174.

Report of Maj. John E. Wynkoop, Seventh Pennsylvania Cavalry, including skirmishes on the Murfreesborough road, December 26–27 ,at Overall's Creek, December 31, and on Manchester pike, January 5.

HEADQUARTERS SEVENTH PENNSYLVANIA CAVALRY,
Camp near Murfreesborough, Tenn., January 6, 1863.

SIR: I have the honor to report that on the morning of December 26, 1862, I was ordered with my regiment to move on the Murfreesborough road, in rear of the First Cavalry Brigade, the First Cavalry Brigade being the advance of that portion of the Army of the Cumberland. After proceeding on the road about 6 miles, I was ordered with my entire command to the front, with instructions to use one-half in the advance and upon the right as a line of skirmishers, keeping the other half as a support. In this order we proceeded about 3 miles, when we commenced engaging the enemy, they falling back gradually 1 mile to a belt of wood, where they made a stubborn stand. Here there was considerable heavy firing, in which 3 of my men were wounded and 2 horses killed. I ordered one company to charge, which was done with promptness, and which caused the enemy to retire, we pressing and skirmishing with him until night came on.

The 27th was occupied in skirmishing on the left. No casualties in my regiment this day.

Sunday, December 28, but little skirmishing; my command chiefly in camp.

Monday, December 29, was ordered on the left of General Wood's division; throwing out a line of skirmishers to the left, moved with the line of battle. No casualties.

Tuesday, December 30, ordered to form a line of couriers from the extreme left, connecting with those on the right, keeping a reserve in the center, one upon the right center, and one upon the left center. These duties were performed by the Second and Third Battalions, commanded by myself, the First Battalion being with Colonel Minty upon a reconnaissance to La Vergne; the First Battalion commanded by Captain Jennings.

Wednesday, December 31, the First Battalion absent with Colonel Minty; the Second and Third continuing as vedettes and couriers until 9 a. m., when our right fell back, creating much consternation and disorder. My vedettes and line of couriers were compelled to retire, which was done in good order, the men rallying upon their chiefs.

My command being collected together, I used my utmost exertions to press the troops to the front, who were coming back in much confusion. Finding my endeavors almost useless, the greatest confusion prevailing, I dispatched a courier to General Rosecrans to know what position the cavalry should be assigned to. He directed me to take my command to the rear, which I accordingly did, and remained in the rear until about 2 p. m., when I received an order from Colonel Kennett (commanding cavalry division) to bring my command upon the Murfreesborough pike, where a portion of the cavalry were engaging the rebel cavalry. We were thrown upon the front, and were for some time under a heavy fire from the enemy under cover. The officers and men here behaved with great coolness, and deserve much credit.

The First Battalion, under command of Captain Jennings, returned from La Vergne with General Stanley and Colonel Minty. Moving rapidly to the right and front, it took up position on the extreme right of our line. Dismounting, it met the advance of the rebels, and finally fell back. Mounting and reforming, the First Battalion took up a new position on the left of the rest of the cavalry. After a half hour's more fighting, darkness brought a cessation of the fighting.

The loss this day was 2 killed, 4 wounded, and 4 taken prisoners.

Thursday, January 1, I was ordered with my entire command upon the right to watch the movements of the enemy, who was continually moving upon the flank; considerable firing between the skirmishers, several of my horses being killed and wounded. This day my regimental train was burned by the enemy while *en route* for Nashville, having upon it all regimental books, papers, company property, camp equipage, officers' baggage, &c.

Friday, January 2, was placed on the right to watch that flank. Much skirmishing all day. No casualties to-day. This evening went on picket in right and rear.

Saturday, January 3, on picket all day.

Sunday, January 4, relieved from picket. At 2 p. m. was ordered to move with the brigade to Wilkinson's Cross-Roads.

Monday, January 5, ordered to move in rear of brigade toward Murfreesborough; passed through Murfreesborough, 3 miles on Manchester road, when my command was ordered to the front. The position assigned me was on the left, where we immediately commenced engaging the enemy, which lasted with considerable severity for about one hour, we driving them from the ground they occupied to a belt of wood, where they are under cover. I had 1 sergeant wounded severely.

The loss in my regiment since leaving Nashville to the present time was as follows: Killed, 2; wounded, 9; prisoners and missing, 50. Total, 61.

I am, very respectfully, your obedient servant,

JNO. E. WYNKOOP,
Major, Commanding Seventh Pennsylvania Cavalry.

Lieut. JOHN WOOLLEY,
Acting Assistant Adjutant-General.

No. 175.

Reports of Col. Lewis Zahm, Third Ohio Cavalry, commanding Second Brigade, including skirmishes at Franklin, December 26–27, Wilkinson's Cross-Roads, December 29, Overall's Creek, December 31, La Vergne, January 1, Cox's Hill, January 3, and on Shelbyville pike, January 5.

HDQRS. 2D CAV. BRIG., IN CAMP ON WILSON'S PIKE,
Near Nolensville Crossing, December 27, 1862.

GENERAL : In compliance with orders received, I moved from our old camp at Nashville yesterday morning at 8 o'clock with the First, Third, and Fourth [Ohio] Cavalry Regiments, 950 strong in all. I crossed over on the Franklin pike, south of General Thomas' headquarters, as I afterward learned. I passed the immense trains and troops on the Franklin pike, beyond Brentwood. I halted my command, as I had not seen General Thomas yet. I supposed he was on the move with the troops in front. I kept inquiring along the column, and was told that he was in the advance. I proceeded myself on the Wilson Creek pike some 2 miles, almost to the head of the column, but then learning from General Rousseau that General Thomas was in the rear, I immediately started back some 6 miles; there ascertaining that General Thomas had cut across the country on to the Nolensville pike, I thought further pursuit would be useless. I started back to join my command and to carry out the remainder of my instructions. I proceeded to Franklin; encountered the enemy's pickets 2½ miles out; drove them in. Skirmishing continued until within half a mile of Franklin, when a sharp skirmish ensued, we driving the rebels. They then made another halt in town. I dismounted some six companies to act as skirmishers on foot; came round on both flanks with mounted skirmishers, and their reserves finally charged through the river into town, where some considerable firing ensued; drove the rebels out; drove them some 2 miles beyond town; the lateness of the day prevented further pursuit, for by this time it began to be dark. The enemy was taken by surprise; could not get their forces together before we were upon them; therefore made it rather an easy task to drive them, as they were in several directions, formed several lines, but as we advanced and fired they invariably fled. We took 10 prisoners, one of them a lieutenant of General Bragg's escort, who was there on business with 16 men. We captured a private of the same escort. We captured that number of horses, several mules, some shot-guns and carbines, broke up their camps, and burned several tents for them. From the best information received, I made out the force to have been about 900, consisting of Colonel Smith's regiment and an independent battalion. I shall send the prisoners to Nashville this morning.

I learned that quite a force of infantry and artillery were 9 miles out of Franklin, on the road leading to Murfreesborough. I arrived in camp here at nearly 9 o'clock last evening; reported to General Rousseau, in the absence of General Thomas. We learned that the enemy had quite a force at Triune, some 10 miles south of this. General Rousseau and myself came to the conclusion to use my brigade to-day in reconnoitering the front and right, until further orders could be received from you. I shall therefore send some 500 men toward Petersburg and Triune to reconnoiter; shall likewise send a smaller force over toward Franklin, to ascertain whether the enemy has come back again or not. My force will be back in camp toward evening; will remain here and picket Wilson's Creek pike, as instructed, until your further orders are received.

I forgot to mention that we killed 3 of the enemy; could not ascertain the number of wounded; must have wounded some in proportion to the killed. My command behaved nobly, both officers and men.

The Third [Ohio] Cavalry had the advance, and did the principal part of the fighting; there was no flinch to them; they moved steadly onward, and finally made the charge through town.

I am, general, your obedient servant,

LEWIS ZAHM,
Colonel, Commanding Second Cavalry Brigade.

General STANLEY,
    Commanding Cavalry.

HEADQUARTERS SECOND CAVALRY BRIGADE,
Nashville, Tenn., January 2, 1863—11 o'clock.

GENERAL: I have the honor to report that, at 9 a. m. yesterday, I proceeded with the Third [Ohio] Cavalry and the Anderson Troop, as directed, forward to guard the trains in motion on the road to Nashville. I took up every train in front of me which was in motion. At Stewart's Creek I found the Third Division train just putting out. It detained me about one hour; at the same time I learned that a heavy cavalry force was to the left of me. I ordered the train to proceed at a brisk walk. We moved on until we arrived at La Vergne; the train had passed the flats at La Vergne, myself and command resting on the flat, when my flankers discovered the enemy to our left and engaged him. I immediately turned into the field, formed line of battle, and dispatched orderlies to the front to move the train on a trot.

The enemy formed; then ensued skirmishing with the skirmishers. The enemy formed a new line, which I counteracted; kept him at bay ready to receive their charge; they, however, declined to charge— wheeled in column of fours, moved to the left of our train, and forward around a hill in front and to the left of the road, with the intention of heading off the train. By this time the rear of the train was half a mile ahead of us. I immediately followed the train; sent flankers at a rapid pace toward the front to watch and engage the enemy if approaching. The enemy did not succeed in heading the train.

After proceeding about 2 miles farther, discovered the enemy charging up the pike on our rear. I met them and repulsed them. They charged again. I repulsed them again, charged them back for 2 miles, scattered them, killed 9, wounded 11, and took 2 prisoners. I had a few men slightly wounded. After this they troubled my train no more. Not a wagon fell into their hands ahead of the escort. Some four or five wagons broke down, which we left and destroyed. The enemy's forces were Wheeler's brigade, with two pieces of artillery, which they played upon us pretty lively. A short time before we were attacked a large number of the Second Tennessee came running by my column, running away from the front, stating that our forces were in full retreat. I placed a company in the road, halted every one of them, but at the breaking out of the skirmish they ran again like sheep. I am sorry to say that the Anderson Troop, with very few exceptions, as the enemy charged us in the rear, scampered off in most every direction; did not stand up to the work at all; the contrary, caused, together with the negroes, Second Tennessee all running, somewhat of a stampede among the wagons, which caused the few break-downs above mentioned.

I arrived here at 9 p. m. Found no forage for horses. Sent out a train after forage this morning, so it will be 5 o'clock this p. m. before our horses will get a mouthful to eat. Since 3 o'clock yesterday morning they have labored very hard, and consequently are not fit for any service to-day. Both horses and men are very much used up.

I am awaiting further orders. I have ordered the Anderson Troop to report to me early this morning, but they have not done so up to this time. They are very much demoralized. In any work for me to do, I ask you to please not to count them as being any help to me. I would sooner do without them.

I am, very respectfully, your obedient servant,

LEWIS ZAHM,
Colonel, Commanding Second Cavalry Brigade.

General STANLEY,
Commanding Cavalry.

HEADQUARTERS SECOND CAVALRY BRIGADE,
In Camp near Murfreesborough, Tenn., January 6, 1863.

LIEUTENANT : I herewith have the honor to report the part taken and the work performed by my brigade since our departure from Nashville until the close of the battle before Murfreesborough.

I left Nashville on the morning of the 26th ultimo, with three regiments of my brigade, viz, the First, Third, and Fourth Ohio Cavalry, the Fifth Kentucky remaining at Nashville. My force numbered 950 men. We marched out on the Franklin pike, the Third Ohio having the advance. When within 2 miles of Franklin, drove in the rebel pickets, skirmished all the way down to Franklin, drove the enemy out, and pursued him some 2 miles. From the best information received, the enemy were 900 strong (all cavalry), part of Wharton's brigade. We killed 4, wounded several, and took 10 prisoners, among them a lieutenant of General Bragg's escort, several horses and mules, and destroyed their camps, with some tents standing thereon. We retired from Franklin, moved over to the Wilson Creek pike, and picketed said pike.

On the 27th, sent the First Ohio and most of the Fourth Ohio, under command of Colonel Milliken, on the Wilson Creek pike, toward Triune, to reconnoiter. They proceeded within 2 miles of Triune, captured 6 of the rebel pickets, when the enemy opened on them with shells ; threw some 50 without damaging us any ; then my force retired to camp. I likewise had sent a battalion of the Third to Franklin to reconnoiter, which drove in the rebel pickets, who had returned in force after my command had left the evening previous. Quite a skirmish ensued, in which 3 of the rebels were killed and several wounded. After skirmishing some two hours, and the enemy being too strong to drive, the battalion returned to camp in good order without any loss.

On the 28th, moved with the command to Triune without anything occurring worth mentioning.

On the 29th, proceeded toward Murfreesborough, moving between the Franklin road and the road called Bole Jack road, which General McCook's corps moved on. I divided my brigade into three columns, marching parallel with one another and with the main force, the right (the Fourth Ohio) moving on the Franklin road, the Third in center, and the First on the left, the columns being from 1 to 1½ miles apart, throwing out skirmishers, connecting one column with the other, and connecting on the left with the main column. We thus proceeded for 5 miles, when the center column encountered the enemy's pickets, which they drove in, the different columns steadily advancing.

Shortly after, both the right and the left encountered pickets, driving them in before them. After proceeding about 1 mile farther, we came upon the enemy's cavalry (Wharton's brigade), engaged them for three hours, some time the right wing, then the left, then the center, receiving several charges, which were repulsed, driving the enemy some 2 miles, when the brigade concentrated, repelling a heavy charge from the enemy, driving him back under his guns, which were only a short distance from us. We then retired some 2 miles and went into camp.

Some few casualties occurred this day. The officers and men behaved admirably during the whole day. The Fourth had proceeded until the enemy threw shells into them pretty rapidly, when they retired. We were within 4 miles of Murfreesborough.

On the morning of the 30th was ordered to proceed on the Franklin road toward Murfreesborough, to push the enemy hard. We had encamped that night near the brick church, on the road leading from General McCook's headquarters to the Franklin road. I proceeded that morning with my command and the Second East Tennessee, which reported to me that morning, via that road to the Franklin road, at which crossing we encountered the enemy's pickets and drove them in. Sent a party of the Fourth to reconnoiter on the road leading south to Salem, where they soon came upon a stronger force, and a brisk skirmish ensued. I increased the number of skirmishers, especially to the left, skirmished with the enemy for an hour or more, when a courier arrived, saying that the enemy was approaching with a heavy cavalry force and some artillery.

In the mean time I had ascertained, likewise, that a heavy force of the enemy was encamped some little distance south of the Franklin road, and east of where my column halted. I did not think it prudent to advance, and, owing to the bad grounds (being all timber) where my force halted, I retired to my camping-ground, near which were large open fields, well adapted for cavalry movements. I soon formed a line of battle. The enemy made his appearance. Skirmishers engaged him pretty briskly. The enemy maneuvered with the design to outflank us, but did not succeed. I forestalled him every time. With the exception of severe skirmishing, nothing transpired. The enemy retired, when I concluded to join the main body of our army.

After marching about a mile, met General Stanley, with a brigade of infantry and a battery of artillery, to re-enforce me. The general marched the whole command toward the enemy's camp. On reaching its vicinity the enemy drew up in line of battle. Skirmishing ensued. Remained there about half an hour, when the general withdrew, with the remark that we were not ready yet to fight the whole of Hardee's army corps. That night we encamped 1½ miles from the enemy's camp, and laid on our arms all night.

At daybreak on the morning of the 31st, I had my command drawn up in line of battle in the rear of my camp; sent out two squadrons to the front and to the right to reconnoiter. Had been in the line about half an hour, when I heard heavy firing—cannon and musketry—to my left and a little to the front. Soon after I beheld our infantry scattered all over the fields, running toward my line, when I learned that General Johnson's division was repulsed. At about the same time my skirmishers engaged the enemy, when they were driven in, reporting that the enemy were approaching in heavy force. Sure enough, I soon discovered heavy lines of infantry coming toward my front and on the left, where General Johnson's division had been posted; also to my right the enemy's cavalry were coming round in long columns, with the evident design to outflank us.

I concluded to retire slowly toward the main body of our army, the enemy pressing hard on me; kept him at bay with my skirmishers. I retired in this wise for a mile, when I formed a line of battle with the First and Third, when the enemy charged on them with their cavalry, but were repulsed by my men. About this time the enemy began to throw shells into my lines pretty lively. The first shell that landed mortally wounded Major Moore, of the First Ohio. I now fell back, formed a new line, received the enemy's charge, repulsed them, and made many of the rebels bite the dust. Shells coming pretty thick again, I retired farther, when I made another stand, supported by Willich's regiment of infantry; received the enemy's charge, and repulsed him again. I then withdrew my whole command through a large strip of wood to another open lot—shells of the enemy helping us along—passing by a line of rebel infantry, marching parallel with my column, not over 200 yards from us, so that we were nearly surrounded, as the enemy's cavalry were working round our right all the time, and the infantry and artillery following us closely in our rear and to our left. They had cavalry enough to spare to strike, or to take position, when ever required.

When we arrived on the open ground, General McCook's aide told me the whole of General McCook's ammunition train was close by, on a dirt road running by that point, and that I must try to save it. I soon formed my command in line, when the enemy made his appearance in a position occupying two-thirds of a circle. They prepared to charge upon us; likewise commenced throwing shells, at which the Second East Tennessee broke and ran like sheep. The Fourth, after receiving several shells, which killed some of their men and horses, likewise retired from their line, as it became untenable. The First had been ordered to proceed farther on into another lot, to form and to receive a charge from another line of the enemy's cavalry. The Third moved to the left, in the vicinity of a white house. About the time the First was formed, the enemy charged upon the Fourth, which, being on the retreat, owing to the shells coming pretty freely, moved off at a pretty lively gait. The Third moved farther to the left, and, somewhat sheltered by the house and barns, the First charged upon the enemy; did not succeed in driving them back.

On returning from said charge the gallant Colonel Milliken* and a lieutenant were killed, and another lieutenant severely wounded.

At this juncture the First and Fourth retired pretty fast, the enemy in close pursuit after them, the Second East Tennessee having the lead of them all. Matters looked pretty blue now; the ammunition train was supposed to be gone up, when the Third charged upon the enemy, driving him back, capturing several prisoners, and recapturing a good many of our men, and saved the train. I was with the three regiments that skedaddled, and among the last to leave the field. Tried hard to rally them, but the panic was so great that I could not do it. I could not get the command together again until I arrived at the north side of the creek; then I found that only about one-third of the First and Fourth Regiments were there, and nearly all of the Second East Tennessee. These I marched back across the creek, when, joined by the Third, we had several skirmishes with the enemy's cavalry all day long; received several charges, and repulsed them.

All the officers and men behaved well through all the fighting up to the stampede, which was not very creditable. All of them that I brought back into action again behaved well during the rest of the day. I must say the Third deserves great credit for this day's fighting—for the coolness and bravery of its officers and men, and for its determination to save the train, which they accomplished. I do not wish to take any credit away from the other regiments, as they all fought nobly and did first-rate, with the exception of the stampede.

On January 1, after being in line of battle since 3 a. m., I was ordered to take the Third Ohio and the Anderson Troop, proceed to Nashville, and escort the army wagon train through to Nashville. I left about 9 o'clock. A little below La Vergne was attacked by General Wheeler's cavalry brigade; repulsed him twice; killed 9, wounded several, and took 2 prisoners; saved all the train but two or three wagons, which broke down in the excitement; saved several cannon belonging to a Wisconsin battery going along with the train, which were abandoned by the drivers, horses still hitched to the cannon. Some of my men mounted the horses and took the cannon into Nashville. The enemy threw shells at us, but did not succeed in hurting any of the men. The Anderson

---

* See also Wharton's report, No. 305, p. 966.

Troop, I am sorry to say, were of very little benefit to me, as the majority of them ran as soon as we were attacked. Arrived at Nashville at 9 p. m.; found no forage for my horses.

Next day, January 2, had to send out a foraging party. They returned at 5 p. m., when my horses were fed for the first time since leaving the front, the day previous at 3 a. m.

At 1 o'clock on the 3d was ordered to leave at 3 o'clock, to escort a hospital store train and an ammunition train through to the front. When 2 miles out, had to wait for Colonel McCook to come up with two and a half regiments of infantry and some 150 of the Third Tennessee Cavalry. Two companies of the Fourth Ohio, under command of Lieutenant White, were with me likewise. It was 11 o'clock before we got started. All of this force combined formed the escort of the train. We proceeded about 8 miles, when we were attacked by Wheeler's brigade. We repulsed them, taking 12 prisoners, among them 2 lieutenants; killed 15, and wounded many. They did but little damage to the train, which was done through the cowardice of the teamsters. I had 1 man killed and 1 wounded. The enemy tried to attack us the second time, but retired before our forces met. We brought the train through safely, and arrived with it at 1 o'clock the next morning. During my three days' absence the First and Fourth were busily employed reconnoitering, doing picket duty, and skirmishing with the enemy's cavalry.

On the 4th, marched my command to the front, near Murfreesborough, to reconnoiter, the enemy having withdrawn their forces.

On the 5th, marched to the front, some 4½ miles beyond Murfreesborough, on the Shelbyville road, on a reconnaissance, capturing quite a number of rebel stragglers; pushed a squadron of the Fourth some 3 miles farther, to a point where they could overlook the pike for 5 miles ahead, when they discovered that the enemy had entirely disappeared. The skirmishers of the Fourth had some skirmishing with some of the rebel cavalry. By 7 o'clock was back to camp again. You will observe that my command had fought nearly every day from the time we left Nashville up to this time. They worked very hard, and deserve a great deal of credit for what they have done, as both officers and men fought bravely.

Herewith find list of casualties, which are not large, considering the number of engagements we were in.

All respectfully submitted.

I am, very respectfully, your obedient servant,

LEWIS ZAHM,
Colonel, Commanding Second Ohio Volunteer Cavalry.

Lieut. M. B. CHAMBERLIN,
Actg. Asst. Adjt. Gen., 1st Cav. Div., Army of the Cumberland.

———

Return of casualties in the Second Cavalry Brigade (Zahm's), December 26, 1862–January 6, 1863 (Stone's River).

Command.	Killed.		Wounded.		Missing.		Remarks.
	Officers.	Enlisted men.	Officers.	Enlisted men.	Officers.	Enlisted men.	
1st Ohio Cavalry	3	2	1	10	1	14	
3d Ohio Cavalry		6		15		10	3 enlisted men prisoners.
4th Ohio Cavalry		7		18		16	15 enlisted men prisoners.
Total	3	15	1	43	1	40	

No. 176.

Report of Maj. James Laughlin, First Ohio Cavalry, of operations January 1–5.

CAMP FIRST OHIO VOLUNTEER CAVALRY,
Near Murfreesborough, Tenn., January 6, 1863.

SIR: I have the honor to submit the following report of the First Ohio Volunteer Cavalry:

On the morning of January 1, I was ordered to take command of the regiment, and was immediately ordered in the rear of Stewart's Creek and on the right, on picket or outpost duty. In the evening I was ordered back in front of Stewart's Creek and on the right, to stand on picket for the night.

On the morning of the 2d, I was ordered to advance my regiment forward on the right, which I did, and found the enemy in my front, and skirmished with them until dark. I was then ordered into camp for the night.

The morning of the 3d, I was ordered to march my regiment to the rear of Stewart's Creek, which I did. In the evening I was ordered to join my command with the Fourth Ohio Volunteer Cavalry and make a reconnaissance on our left, which was done, and we returned to camp the same night.

Remained in camp on the 4th until evening; was ordered to the front, and left to guard the railroad bridge for the night.

On the morning of the 5th went on scout beyond Murfreesborough, on the Shelbyville pike, and returned, no casualties having happened during the time included.

Your most obedient,

JAMES LAUGHLIN,
Major, Commanding First Ohio Volunteer Cavalry.

Col. L. ZAHM,
Commanding Second Cavalry Brigade.

No. 177.

Report of Capt. Valentine Cupp, First Ohio Cavalry, including skirmishes at Franklin, December 26, Wilkinson's Cross-Roads, December 29, and Overall's Creek, December 31.

HEADQUARTERS FIRST OHIO VOLUNTEER CAVALRY,
January 6, 1863.

December 26, left Nashville for Franklin; arrived at Franklin at 3 p. m.; found the enemy occupying the town; drove them from it and proceeded to Wilson's Creek pike, and encamped for the night.

December 27, left camp at 8 o'clock; proceeded toward Triune; struck the enemy's pickets within 5 miles of Triune; drove in their pickets, captured 6, and returned to the camp occupied the previous night.

December 28, left camp at 8 o'clock for Triune, where we encamped.

December 29, left camp at 9 o'clock on a reconnaissance toward Murfreesborough. Struck the enemy's scouts when within 1 mile of Stewart's Creek, when active skirmishing commenced and continued until sundown, having driven the enemy's cavalry at least 3½ miles. One man missing while crossing Stewart's Creek. At sundown we retired back across Stewart's Creek and encamped.

December 30, skirmished with the enemy all day on the right of General Johnson's division, driving the enemy's cavalry wherever they made their appearance, and retired and encamped in the camp occupied by us the night before.

December 31, at 7 a. m., I was ordered by you to take two companies and make a thorough reconnaissance up the creek in the woods on our right. After throwing out skirmishers into the woods, I received orders from you to withdraw my command as soon as possible, for the enemy were advancing in force on my left. I immediately withdrew at full speed, and passed the enemy's left (infantry) within 150 yards under heavy fire, slightly wounding only 1 man and 2 horses. After passing their flank half a mile, I discovered your brigade formed in line of battle in the corn-field on the opposite side of the creek. Being unable to join my regiment at this point, I proceeded down the creek half a mile and crossed, joining the brigade on the right (my regiment was on the left), retiring slowly in column of fours. After retiring half a mile, we were again formed in line of battle, and remained until we were under a heavy fire from the enemy's artillery, when we were compelled to retire. Here the brave and heroic Maj. D. A. B. Moore fell, mortally wounded. We then retired across a corn-field, the enemy in full and fast pursuit, with at least three times our number, when we again formed, receiving three heavy charges from the enemy's cavalry, but repulsed them every time with a fire from our carbines. Their artillery was still open on us. We then retired through the woods toward the Nashville pike, when we formed in a corn-field. The enemy (cavalry and infantry) immediately appearing, our noble commander, Col. Minor Milliken, ordered our regiment, five companies, to charge them. Being unable to hold his position after the charge, he ordered the regiment to retire, when he received the fatal shot that killed him instantly. About this time Second Lieutenant Condit was killed, and our adjutant, First Lieut. William Scott, fell seriously wounded. The companies then retired to the pike and crossed Stewart's Creek on the pike. I found myself in command, and repulsed the enemy, who had pursued to the creek and taken possession of our wagon train, killing 2 and wounding 4. At this time the brigade came across the creek and organized.

January 1, at 9 a. m., Major Laughlin reported for duty and took command of the regiment.

RECAPITULATION OF CASUALTIES.

Commissioned officers killed	3
Privates killed	2
Commissioned officers wounded	1
Privates wounded	10
Commissioned officers missing (surgeon)	1
Privates missing	14
Total	31

Respectfully submitted.

VALENTINE CUPP,
Captain, Commanding First Ohio Volunteer Cavalry.

Col. L. ZAHM,
   Comdg. Second Cav. Brig., First Div., 14th Army Corps.

No. 178.

Report of Lieut. Col. Douglas A. Murray, Third Ohio Cavalry, including skirmishes at Franklin, December 26–27, and Overall's Creek, December 31.

HEADQUARTERS THIRD OHIO CAVALRY,
In Camp near Murfreesborough, Tenn., January 6, 1863.

COLONEL: In compliance with instructions received from your head-quarters, I have the honor to report, for your information, the part taken by the Third Ohio Cavalry in the several engagements in which the regiment was engaged since leaving Nashville, Tenn., on December 26 last, on which day we proceeded to Franklin, driving the enemy therefrom and taking possession of the town; took some 10 prisoners. Remaining in town some time, we recrossed the river, and marched across the country to Wilson Creek pike, about 14 miles from Nashville, and encamped, arriving in camp at about 10 p. m.

On the 27th, the Third Battalion of the regiment moved toward Franklin, and found that the enemy had in strong force again taken possession of the town; the battalion drove in their pickets under a heavy fire, killing 3 of them. Seeing that the enemy were in such force, the commander deemed it prudent to retire, and rejoined the regiment, which picketed the roads, &c., in the vicinity of its camp.

On the 28th ultimo, proceeded to Triune and encamped, leaving early next morning across the country toward Murfreesborough, proceeding about 5 miles in that direction, when attacked by the enemy's pickets in force, which we drove, skirmishing, they frequently making a stand, which we each time broke, and still drove them about 5 miles.

The 30th ultimo, ordered to proceed to Stone's River; proceeded but a short distance when attacked by the enemy's pickets; the enemy were in force in our front with artillery. We therefore retired, forming on the high ground in our rear to receive them, their pickets, or patrol, advancing, which we repulsed. In the evening our brigade was re-enforced by one battery of artillery and three regiments of infantry, and proceeded in reconnaissance to the left of the enemy's lines, where we found General Hardee's *corps d'armée* ready, in line of battle, to receive us. We retired, and encamped in the woods, about 2 miles in front of the enemy's lines.

On the morning of the 31st we formed; shortly after the enemy appeared in large force, both on our left, center, and right, evidently endeavoring to cut us off. The brigade of infantry to our left gave way, retreating in confusion through our lines, letting the whole force of the enemy's artillery, cavalry, and infantry fall upon us, which compelled us gradually to retire toward the main body of our army. The regiment covering the entire rear of the brigade, supporting one infantry regiment on our right, drove back, with heavy loss, a large force of cavalry which charged upon us, under cover of a piece of artillery, firing well-directed shells, which passed over us. The enemy being in such force, we had to retire about three-fourths of a mile, when an aide-de-camp of General McCook rode up, informing us that the train close by was General McCook's entire ammunition train, which must be saved at all hazards; on intimation of which the regiment was immediately formed for its protection, holding the enemy in check until the entire train, with the exception of a few disabled wagons that could not be moved, was safely withdrawn. The regiment then moved between the enemy and train as far as the Murfreesborough pike, where we found the enemy making a fierce attack upon General Thomas' train, when we again repulsed them at several points, taking many prisoners and saving that entire portion of the train. The attack of the enemy was furious and desperate, which required the greatest firmness and bravery to resist. Colonel Kennett was an eye-witness to the determined bravery of a portion of the regiment rescuing the train from the enemy, which were in force at the hospital on the Murfreesborough pike. The regiment then formed in the field near the hospital, where the brigade soon assembled and reformed, and advanced toward the enemy's left. Soon came up to the enemy's cavalry, supported by artillery, when several other skirmishes ensued during the evening, the enemy's entire object seeming to be to take the train.

On the 1st instant, received orders to proceed to Nashville in charge of train, consisting of some 200 or 300 wagons. When about 2 miles on the Nashville side of La Vergne, we were attacked by General Wheeler's brigade of cavalry, which made several dashes on the train, and were repulsed. They then attacked our rear in force. After a well-contested fight, our regiment put them to flight in disorder, killing 9 of them and wounding several, and arrived in Nashville at 9 p. m. and encamped.

The 2d instant, remained in Nashville and procured forage for our horses, furnishing working party and escort to forage train.

The 3d instant, left Nashville for Murfreesborough in charge of hospital and ammunition trains. Attacked again in force by Wheeler's brigade of cavalry on the Nashville side of La Vergne, which was repulsed with a loss of 15 on their side and some 8 or 9 prisoners taken; among the latter the adjutant of the Third Alabama Cavalry. Two of our non-commissioned officers, I regret to inform you, were severely and dangerously wounded, whom we had to leave in a house on the roadside.

Arrived at camp, near Murfreesborough, at 1 a. m., 4th instant, with the train all safe, with the exception of one wagon of the regiment that was cut off by the enemy, and is now supposed to have returned to Nashville.

On the evening of the 4th, proceeded with brigade toward Murfreesborough as far as Stone's River, and returned to camp.

On the 5th instant, proceeded again with brigade to Murfreesborough, and beyond it about 4½ miles, where we halted, taking several prisoners, and returning to camp about 7 p. m.

I have much pleasure in informing you that the conduct and behavior of both officers, non-commissioned officers, and privates of the regiment have been highly creditable, with not a single instance to the contrary in the regiment.

Inclosed please find list of casualties that have occurred since December 26, 1862, to January 5, 1863.*

I have the honor to be, very respectfully, your obedient servant,

D. A. MURRAY,
Lieutenant-Colonel Third Ohio Cavalry, Comdg. Regiment.

Col. L. ZAHM,
Comdg. Third Cavalry Brigade, First Cavalry Division.

---

* Embodied in revised statement, p. 214.

No. 179.

Report of Maj. James W. Paramore, Third Ohio Cavalry, including skirmishes at Overall's Creek, December 31, and at La Vergne, January 1.

HEADQUARTERS THIRD OHIO CAVALRY,
January 8, 1863.

SIR: There are a few incidents in the recent series of battles in which we were engaged which, not having fallen immediately under your observation or of the regimental commander, have escaped notice; and being under my immediate command, in justice to the brave officers and men engaged, I deem it my duty to make this special report.

In the severe fighting of Wednesday, the 31st ultimo, which fell so heavily upon your brigade, you will recollect, when we had been forced back as far as General McCook's ammunition train, and were drawn up in front of it for its protection, the furious charge of the enemy's cavalry, preceded by a shower of shells, caused a pretty general stampede of our cavalry, led off by the Second Tennessee on our right, and followed by the Fourth and First Ohio, and the First Battalion of the Third Ohio Cavalry. At that juncture an aide of General McCook came up to me, and informed me that "that was their entire ammunition train, and must be held at all hazards." I gave orders accordingly to the left wing of the Third Ohio Cavalry, under my command, and I am happy to report that they held their position and did not break their lines nor join in that stampede, but received the galling fire of the enemy with the firmness of heroes, and maintained their ground till all the wagons, except a few that were disabled or deserted by the teamsters, had safely reached the lines of our infantry.

The enemy, seeing our determination and bold resistance, turned and left us, and pursued the broken columns of our cavalry that had fled. We then wheeled, and charged upon their rear with terrible effect (scattering their columns in worse confusion, if possible, than they had just routed the balance of our brigade), killing a number of men and horses and taking some 10 or 12 prisoners, and releasing a large number of our brigade that they had captured. We pursued them over to the Murfreesborough pike, Captain McClelland, commanding Squadrons E and F, taking the right of the pike, and the balance of the command, with myself, taking the left.

When within a short distance of the hospital we again encountered a large force of the enemy coming back to take possession of the train. We at once engaged them, although at least double our numbers, and after a severe struggle put them to flight, with a loss of several killed, wounded, and prisoners. The bravery and daring of Captains Wood and Colver, and their respective commands on this occasion, challenged my admiration. I also learned that Captain McClelland, with his squadron, engaged the enemy farther up the pike, beyond the hospital, with Colonel Kennett and a portion of the Third Kentucky Cavalry, and, after a fierce contest, repulsed them. We then quietly formed in line and awaited the reassembling of the brigade. Then be it spoken to their praise, that the Second and Third Battalions of the Third Ohio Cavalry did not run nor break their lines during that day's severe fighting.

This result is greatly attributable to the coolness and bravery of Captains McClelland, Wood, and Colver, and their lieutenants. It was also this portion of the regiment that repulsed the attack of the enemy on the rear of our train the next day near La Vergne as we were proceeding to Nashville, and brought safely into Nashville two pieces of cannon, three caissons full of ammunition, and a wagon loaded with new carbines and ammunition, which had been abandoned by their cowardly teamsters.

All of which is respectfully submitted.

J .W. PARAMORE,
Major, Commanding Left Wing, Third Ohio Cavalry.

Col. L. ZAHM,
Commanding Second Cavalry Brigade.

No. 180.

Report of Maj. John L. Pugh, Fourth Ohio Cavalry, including skirmishes at Franklin, December 26, Wilkinson's Cross-Roads, December 29, and Overall's Creek, December 31.

IN CAMP, *January 6,* 1863.

COLONEL : We left camp, near Nashville, December 26, with the Second Brigade of Cavalry, and marched to Franklin, and assisted in driving out a force of rebel cavalry. Next day remained in camp, and on the 28th ultimo marched for Triune.

On the 29th, was ordered by you to march on the dirt road leading to Murfreesborough, and to throw out a line of skirmishers to the front and flank, connecting with skirmishers of the Third Ohio, on our left. We had proceeded but 5 or 6 miles until we came onto the enemy's advanced picket, driving them in, and occasionally had slight skirmishes with squads of the enemy's cavalry, who were evidently sent out for the purpose of ascertaining our number. When within 3 or 4 miles of Murfreesborough came on a battery of two pieces of artillery and a support of infantry or dismounted men, posted in a wood, which opened a fire of grape on our advance. In reconnoitering their position we found a body of cavalry was passing on our flank, and soon discovered they were on our rear and flank. I faced the column about and ordered Captain Johnson to attack a body of cavalry, posted in the road, which he did, driving them into the woods. Then we attacked their whole force posted at the edge of the wood, when a sharp skirmish ensued, resulting in a loss on our part of 2 killed, 7 wounded (one mortally and has since died), and 9 prisoners. We captured 7 prisoners from the enemy. The loss was principally sustained by Companies K and M, Lieutenants White and Megrue commanding, who behaved themselves admirably, as did all the officers.

On the day following we were, together with the First and Third Ohio, engaged during the day reconnoitering and skirmishing with the enemy.

On the 31st were, by your orders, formed in the field on —— Creek. Had been in our position but a short time when the enemy were discovered advancing, with infantry, cavalry, and artillery, in line of battle, capturing two batteries of our artillery and engaging our infantry, who were soon driven back. Our position now became untenable, and we fell back to another position, and had but just got my line formed when we discovered the enemy's cavalry were outflanking us. We then took a position in the woods adjoining, and charged the enemy's cavalry with Company A, Lieutenant Hamilton ; Company B, Captain Teetor ; Company C, Captain Mathews, and Company E, Captain Gotwald, who succeeded in checking their advance and driving them back a short distance. They were re-enforced, and in turn drove our men from the field.

At this point an aide from General McCook rode up and asked me to form my command so as to protect the train, which I did; but soon was driven away from it by shells from the enemy's guns and by his cavalry. The panic now became so general that our regiment in leaving the field got scattered, but the majority of it were in skirmishes of the afternoon. On the days of January 1, 2, and 3, was in line of battle all day.

On the 31st, while in line near the train, and on leaving the field, we lost in killed, wounded, missing, and prisoners some 35 or 36 men; also 3 horses killed and 5 wounded. The enemy had also captured some 20 more, who were afterward released by our own men, having been pre-viously disarmed and dismounted.

On the 5th, crossed Stone's River and proceeded to a distance of 3 or 4 miles south of Murfreesborough. Lost 2 men prisoners, being captured by rebel pickets.

Annexed please find a list of killed, wounded, missing, and prisoners.*
Killed, 7; wounded, 18; missing, 16; prisoners, 15; total, 56.

I am, very respectfully, your obedient servant,

J. L. PUGH,
Major, Commanding Fourth Ohio Volunteer Cavalry.

Col. L. ZAHM,
Commanding Second Brigade.

No. 181.

Report of Capt. Henry B. Teetor, Fourth Ohio Cavalry, of operations December 31.

IN CAMP NEAR MURFREESBOROUGH, TENN.,
January 12, 1863.

SIR : In the action of Wednesday, December 31, 1862, I take pleasure in calling your especial attention to a brilliant little achievement accomplished by a portion of your command while temporarily and unavoidably detached from your immediate supervision.

While there was apparently a general consternation among other cavalry regiments, you ordered the right of your command to rest at a point commanding a road; and while superintending the alignment, which was very difficult at that time, owing to said confusion, a portion of Tennessee cavalry came pursued hotly up the road upon which your right was resting. A regiment of Texas Rangers were in full pursuit, and were endeavoring also to take two pieces of artillery, one ambulance, and six wagons, which were following the fleeing Tennessee cavalry. It was an emergency, and demanded coolness, bravery, and expedition to save the property, as well as change the wavering fortunes of that day. In fact, it was so immensely critical as, for the time being, at least, to waive the precedence of rank or military etiquette of waiting for orders, and seize upon the golden chance of saving the honor of the regiment and, measurably, the fortunes of the day.

Capt. Peter Mathews, being in command of the First Squadron, consisting of Companies A, B, and C, seeing the exigency, and, at the same time, being aware of your attention being preoccupied with the speedy alignment of the left of the regiment, took the authority, ostensibly warranted by the emergency, and ordered his squadron to charge down the road and drive back the enemy, and save the property imperiled. I had the honor to be in the charge, and can testify with pride that I saw the enemy severely repulsed, driven back, the two pieces of cannon saved, and the ambulance and the six Government wagons.

---

* Nominal list omitted.

In that charge I had 1 man killed, 1 wounded, and 1 taken prisoner, and the other two companies suffered proportionately.

I trust to be pardoned for the vanity I display in calling your particular attention to this glorious little episode of that day. I know well the pride you take in anything done meritorious by your command, and this, in addition to the reflection that there seems to be a design somewhere to detract from the old Fourth's glory, induces me to make mention thus. I, moreover, say that "honor to whom honor is due" should apply in the case in which we are all so much interested; and if the old Fourth did anything creditable, it is my duty and your duty, and every man's duty, to see that she meets not with detraction. In your report of the conduct of the regiment, I deem this may justly take a conspicuous part. I was in all the fight, and I can proudly testify as to the conduct of our regiment, whatever else others may say to the contrary notwithstanding.

I am, sir, with much respect, your obedient servant,

H. B. TEETOR,
Captain, Comdg. Company B, Fourth Ohio Volunteer Cavalry.

Lieut. Col. J. L. PUGH,
Commanding Fourth Ohio Volunteer Cavalry.

No. 182.

Report of Maj. Robert Klein, Third Indiana Cavalry (unattached), including skirmishes at Triune, December 27, and near Overall's Creek, December 31.

HDQRS. THIRD BATTALION, THIRD INDIANA CAVALRY,
Near Murfreesborough, Tenn., January 7, 1863.

SIR : I have the honor to submit the following report of the part taken by this battalion in the field since leaving the camp near Nashville, on the 26th ultimo, up to the 3d instant:

The four companies under my command left camp on the 26th, as ordered, and, bringing up the rear of the Second Division, encamped beyond Nolensville.

On the following morning, 27th, having orders, reported to General Stanley, chief of cavalry, who, remarking he "had understood the Third knew how to take these rebels," ordered me to move forward and take the advance of the column of cavalry then moving toward Triune. I succeeded in gaining the advance at about the point where the enemy's outposts were expected to be. I then threw out portions of Company H, Lieutenant Young commanding, on either side of the pike, and, putting out an advance guard, moved smartly down the pike. Our advance soon encountered the enemy in considerable force drawn up in line of battle. The column now moved on to them at a gallop, receiving the whole of their fire into one company (Company G, Captain Herriott), the skirmishers on the flanks not being able to come up for some time, on account of the soft nature of the ground and the fences intervening. Company G held their ground until Company I, Captain Vanosdal, on the right, and Company K, Lieutenant Lieske, on the left, advanced gallantly to the rescue, and, despite superior force, drove them across the narrow valley to a position beyond where their artillery covered them. Here we advanced with the remainder of our cavalry force and drove them from this hill, from which they fell back to Triune. Here we were ordered by General Stanley, with one company of the Fifteenth Pennsylvania Cavalry, to attack the enemy on the right side of the pike. They were posted behind a stone wall, heads only visible, one or more regiments strong. We advanced across the open fields, and were pouring in a steady fire at easy range, when two pieces of artillery on our left, about 500 yards, and two in front, opened on us, obliging us to retire to the cover of the woods from where we advanced. This movement was done promptly, but in good order.

On the following morning my battalion was in advance of the reconnaissance under General Willich; did no fighting, but captured some 16 of the enemy's stragglers. On the Nolensville pike we lost 3 killed and 3 wounded.* We lost also a few horses wounded and disabled, and 1 killed by cannon shot.

On the 29th and 30th nothing worthy of note occurred.

On the morning of the 31st ultimo my battalion was posted with our cavalry force beyond Wilson's Cross-Roads pike, on the right and rear of the Second Division. When our forces first gave way before the overwhelming numbers of the enemy, the efficiency of my battalion was destroyed in being divided by one of our own cavalry regiments running through our ranks and scattering the men. This movement, had it been in the opposite direction, would have been a most gallant charge, and, doubtless, from its determination, an efficient one. We kept falling back, forming and charging at intervals, until forced across to the Murfreesborough pike, where one of my companies was first to form to drive the enemy from our train.

We captured during the retreat 11 of the enemy. One of Company G, Corporal Justice, recaptured our ambulance, containing our surgeon, by shooting down one of its captors and frightening the others away. I regret to say that Corporal Justice was afterward captured.

We were formed near the center of our cavalry, when the enemy, in the afternoon, again attempted to take our train. We participated in the fight and the charge that followed. We lost 1 man on that morning, Private Daniel Gibbons, of General Willich's escort, and 2 others wounded.

On the following days of the fight my battalion was on provost duty.

Our loss sums up: Killed, 4; wounded, 6; missing, 10; captured, 5. Of the missing, doubtless nearly all were captured. Our total loss is 25; horses, 30, and 1 ambulance.

Respectfully, your obedient servant,

R. KLEIN,
Major, Commanding Battalion

Captain BARTLETT,
Captain and Assistant Adjutant-General.

No. 183.

Report of Lieut. William S. Hall, adjutant Second Tennessee Cavalry.

CAMP NEAR MURFREESBOROUGH, TENN.,
January 9, 1863.

SIR: In compliance with your request, I have the honor to report the following operations of which the Second East Tennessee Cavalry took an active part in the late battles before Murfreesborough, viz:

On December 27, 1862, while attached to the command of Colonel

* Nominal list omitted.

Stokes, we engaged a strong party of the rebel cavalry southeast of the Nolensville pike, and after a sharp engagement put the enemy to flight.

On the following day, while under the same command, we encountered the enemy near Triune, and, after an obstinate engagement, drove the enemy in the direction of Shelbyville, Tenn., in which engagement we sustained a loss of 4 horses killed, and captured a first lieutenant and 5 privates belonging to the Fiftieth* Alabama Cavalry. The following day we rested near Triune.

The next day, December 29, we started in pursuit, in the direction of Murfreesborough, taking the mountain path, leaving all our wagons behind, with the exception of the ambulances. On the afternoon of said day, being in the advance, we discovered the enemy strongly posted about 6 miles in front of Murfreesborough, near the Murfreesborough pike. We, in connection with the First Cavalry Brigade, came up in line of battle. The enemy not showing a disposition to engage us, we waited the coming up of our infantry and artillery. We remained in that condition until Major-General McCook came up. At dark, by the order of General Stanley, chief of cavalry, we were placed on the extreme right as a picket.

The succeeding day we were skirmishing with the enemy during the entire day.

Our loss was, in killed and wounded, Captain Morris, of Company L, 1 private in Company F, and 5 slightly wounded. Several horses shot under the men.

During the remainder of the battle we were held in readiness, but not actively engaged, with the exception of Sunday. We were sent to the river to protect the railroad bridge, within about 1 mile of Murfreesborough, which was on fire. We had a slight engagement with the enemy's rear guard. No damage sustained.

I am, sir, respectfully,

WM. S. HALL,
Adjutant Second East Tennessee Regiment of Cavalry.

Captain OTIS,
Brigade Commander, U. S. Army.

No. 184.

Report of Capt. Elmer Otis, Fourth U. S. Cavalry, including skirmishes at Overall's Creek, December 31, and on the Manchester pike, January 5.

HEADQUARTERS FOURTH U. S. CAVALRY,
In Camp near Murfreesborough, Tenn., January 7, 1863.

SIR: I have the honor to make the following report of the Fourth U. S. Cavalry in the late battles in front of Murfreesborough:

On December 30, the Fourth U. S. Cavalry left camp at Stewart's Creek, leaving the train and baggage under charge of a strong guard, commanded by Lieutenant Rendelbrook. The regiment proceeded to join General Rosecrans on the field of battle, and was drawn up in line of battle in rear of the general's headquarters, but took no immediate part in the action. That day, Company L, commanded by Lieutenant Roys, was detached as General Rosecrans' immediate escort (about 10 o'clock in the morning), and so remains at the present time. Company

---

* Fifty-first Alabama Partisan Rangers.

M, strengthened by 50 men detailed from Companies B, C, D, G, I, and K, commanded by Lieutenant L'Hommedieu, proceeded to establish a courier line from General Rosecrans' headquarters to La Vergne, and so remained, doing good service, until relieved January 4, 1863. These details left me with only six small companies, numbering in the aggregate 260 men, rank and file.

On the morning of the 31st, Colonel Garesché informed me that rebel cavalry were appearing on the right flank of the line of battle, and ordered me to proceed with the Fourth U. S. Cavalry to look after them. This must have been between 7 and 8 o'clock in the morning. I crossed the Murfreesborough pike, and drew up the six companies in line of battle in the following way: Each company was in column of fours, led by the company commanders; the companies on a line parallel to each other, company distance apart according to the following diagram, leading the center myself:

This was owing to the wooded country and fences that were obstructions to the ordinary line of battle. Proceeding to the right of the line, I found our entire right flank had given way. Learning from some men of General Davis' division the position of the enemy's cavalry, I made a turn to the right, moving about one-quarter of a mile, and discovered the enemy. I came out of a piece of timber I was in, and, getting over the fence rapidly, charged the enemy with my entire command, completely routing them, with the exception of two pieces of artillery, supported by about 125 cavalry, stationed between my right and the Murfreesborough and Nashville pike, who were not at first discovered. I rallied my men again, and, while rallying, I saw about 300 of the volunteer cavalry on my right. I rode over to them, and asked them to charge the artillery with me and the few men I had rallied to take the pieces. The officer replied that he was placed there to protect a train, and would not charge with me. I have no doubt I could have taken the artillery. Before I could get my command rallied the artillery moved off. About the time I had got my men rallied I received an order from General Rosecrans to proceed to the Nashville and Murfreesborough pike as soon as possible. I did so immediately. I have since thought that the general did not know my position, or he would have allowed me to follow up the enemy. I was much nearer the pike than I thought I was. I saw no more of the enemy's cavalry on the pike that morning.

In this charge I cannot speak in too high terms of the officers and men. Every man charged and kept in position, taking over 100 prisoners of the enemy and releasing a large number of our own captured men. More redounds to their credit, considering that a large majority are recruits from volunteer infantry, and only some five days drilled and mounted. Two companies of infantry were released in a body.

The train on the pike, I have since learned, was in possession of the enemy, with a large number of stragglers, who were being disarmed at the time. These stragglers did nothing at all to protect the wagons, scarcely firing a shot. From prisoners taken I have learned that the Fourth U. S. Cavalry charged at this time an entire brigade of cavalry, and routed them to such an extent that they disappeared from the field at that point entirely.

Later in the day I sent 79 prisoners in one body to the Tenth Ohio

Infantry, stationed in our rear, at Stewart's Creek. Another body of about 40 men started, but, I regret to say, were recaptured. Of the 79 sent to the rear, there was 1 captain and 2 lieutenants. I have no doubt there were other officers, but did not have an opportunity to examine them closely enough to find out.

Of the officers engaged it is almost impossible to particularize, they all did so well. Capt. Eli Long led his company with the greatest gallantry, and was wounded by a ball through his left arm. Lieutenants Mauck, Kelly, Lee, and Healy could not have done better. It was a matter of surprise to me, considering the ground passed over, to find Dr. Comfort so soon on the field with his ambulance, caring for the wounded. He was in time to capture a prisoner himself. First Sergt. Martin Murphy led Company G, and commanded it with great gallantry. He reports having counted 11 dead of the enemy on the ground over which his company charged. Sergt. Maj. John G. Webster behaved gallantly, taking 1 lieutenant, mounted on a fine mare. First Sergt. James McAlpin led Company K after Captain Long was wounded, and reports having killed 2 with two successive shots of his pistol. First Sergt. John Dolan, Company B, captured a captain and received his sword. No one could have acted more bravely than First Sergt. Charles McMasters, of Company I. First Sergt. Christian Haefling, in charge of courier line near headquarters, proceeded in the thickest of the fire and recovered the effects of Colonel Garesché, on his body, killed in this day's fight. Our loss in this charge was trifling. Capt. Eli Long and 6 privates wounded.

Proceeding on the Nashville pike, I was ordered to escort a train to the rear. I afterward got orders to return, to report to General Rosecrans. I returned, and for two hours looked for the general, with my command, but was unable to find him, although I found several of his staff. I then proceeded to the right flank, and formed my regiment in front of some rebel cavalry, who showed themselves in the distance, in order to protect our train. I returned to General Rosecrans' headquarters that night, and bivouacked near him.

The next morning, January 1, I was ordered to make a reconnaissance on the right flank, which I did, making my reports frequently to Major Goddard, acting assistant adjutant-general, that night bivouacking near Overall's Creek, where my command remained watching the movements of the enemy as far as possible, and making reports thereon, until January 4, when my command was moved to Wilkinson's Cross-Roads.

On the 5th my command proceeded, under command of General Stanley, to engage the enemy's rear guard on the Manchester pike, driving them some 2 or 3 miles. Private Snow, of Company L, orderly to General Rosecrans, was ordered, on January 2, to pick up 15 stragglers, which he did, and was then ordered to take them to the front and turn them over to some commissioned officer. Failing to find one, he put them into line and fought them himself, telling them the first one who attempted to run he would shoot. Private Snow reports they fought bravely.*

Lieutenant Rendelbrook was exceedingly vigilant in guarding the train, and of great service in sending forward supplies.

I am, sir, very respectfully, your obedient servant,

ELMER OTIS,
Captain, Commanding Fourth U. S. Cavalry.

Maj. C. GODDARD,
A. A. A. G., Hdqrs. Dept. of the Cumberland, in the Field.

---

* Nominal list of casualties omitted. See p. 214.

No. 185.

Report of Col. William P. Innes, First Michigan Engineers, of attack on wagon train near La Vergne, January 1.

HDQRS. FIRST REGT. MICHIGAN ENGINEERS AND MECHANICS,
In Camp, January —, 1863.

MAJOR: I have the honor to report that, in accordance with your orders, I broke camp at Mill Creek on December 31, at 7 a. m., and took up line of march for this point, sending my wagon train around by the pike, and went into camp at this point, about three-quarters of a mile south of the village of La Vergne, on the Murfreesborough pike.

About 2 o'clock on the following day my command, numbering 391 effective men, was attacked by a rebel force of cavalry under command of Generals Wheeler and Wharton and Colonel Morgan, of Alabama, said to number between 3,000 and 4,000 strong, with two pieces of artillery. They first dispersed the wagon guard and teamsters of the train going north, and fired and plundered about 30 wagons. The enemy attacked us with great fury, making seven distinct charges upon us, attacking us on every side, mounted and on foot, dashing forward in a gallant and determined manner, but were again and again severely repulsed by my gallant regiment. During the interval between their cavalry charges their artillery were throwing shot and shell, some of them causing considerable damage.

At about 5 o'clock the enemy sent in two flags of truce, demanding an immediate surrender of our position, which I peremptorily refused. They sent in another flag of truce, asking permission to bury their dead, which I refused, and returned for answer that I would bury their dead and take care of their wounded.

In the mean time I had dispatched a messenger to Colonel Burke, of the Tenth Ohio Infantry, stationed at Stewart's Creek, asking him for re-enforcements, which was promptly answered by that gallant officer, who immediately came to my rescue with a section of the First Ohio Battery, in command of Lieutenant Newell, and four companies of the Tenth Ohio; and, although he did not arrive until the enemy had retreated, yet too much credit cannot be given to that gallant officer for his promptness in coming to my aid, which he did under the double-quick.

It is impossible for me to make personal mention of either officers or men where all behaved so gallantly. Every officer was at his post and every man did his duty. The coolness and bravery of the officers was only equaled by the promptness and efficiency of the men.

The following is a statement of the casualties, as near as I have been able to learn: Our loss, 2 killed, 9 wounded, and 5 missing. Enemy's loss, 6 killed, buried by our men; 6 wounded, taken to our hospital, and 7 prisoners. From what I have been able to learn from prisoners, the enemy acknowledge their own loss of killed and wounded at between 40 and 50. We lost 41 horses and mules, and had 3 wagons entirely destroyed and others damaged by the bursting of shell.

I have the honor to remain, major, your most obedient servant,

WM. P. INNES,
Col., Comdg. First Regt. Michigan Engineers and Mechanics.

Maj. C. GODDARD,
A. A. A. G., Fourteenth Army Corps, Dept. of the Cumberland.

No. 186.

Report of Lieut. Col. John G. Parkhurst, Ninth Michigan Infantry, including skirmish near Overall's Creek, December 31.

HDQRS. NINTH REGT. MICHIGAN VOLS. (CENTER),
FOURTEENTH A. C., DEPT. OF THE CUMBERLAND,
January 4, 1863.

MAJOR: I have the honor to make the following report of the part taken by the Ninth Regiment Michigan Infantry, in the recent advance of the army and in the five days' battle before Murfreesborough :.

On the morning of December 26, this regiment, as the provost guards to the *corps d'armée* of Maj. Gen. George H. Thomas, marched 2 miles out from Nashville on the Franklin pike, and crossed over to the Nolensville pike, and proceeded upon that road as far as the Edmondson pike, a distance of 7 miles, and marched out 1 mile on the Edmondson pike, and encamped for the night.

On Saturday morning the regiment, with headquarters train, returned to the Nashville pike, and marched to a point 1 mile south of Nolensville, and 17 miles from Nashville.

On Sunday morning the regiment marched across from the Nolensville pike to the Murfreesborough pike, and encamped, with headquarters, about 5 miles south of La Vergne, and remained there until Tuesday morning, when the regiment moved out on the Murfreesborough pike to Overall's Creek, about 2 miles in rear of our front, and established headquarters for the general.

During the several days' marches the regiment picked up many stragglers from the army in front and sent them forward to their commands.

On Wednesday morning, about two hours after the commencement of Wednesday's battle, I noticed many stragglers crossing the fields from the direction of the right wing of our army, and sent out forces and brought them in, until I had from 100 to 200 collected, when I discovered several cavalrymen approaching with great speed from the direction of our front, and very soon discovered that a large cavalry force, together with infantry and a long transportation train, were in the most rapid retreat, throwing away their arms and accouterments, and many of them without hats or caps, and apparently in the most frightful state of mind, crying, "We are all lost."

I at once concluded it was a stampede of frightened soldiers, and before many had passed me I drew my regiment up in line of battle across the road, extending on either side, and ordered my men to fix bayonets, and to take the position of guard against cavalry. This was done with celerity, and with much difficulty. Without firing upon the frightened troops, I succeeded in checking their course, and ordered every man to face about. Within half an hour I had collected about 1,000 cavalrymen, seven pieces of artillery, and nearly two regiments of infantry. Among them was a brigadier-general. The cavalry, or most of it, belonged to the Second Brigade, and, if I am not mistaken, was commanded by Colonel Zahm. The infantry was from different regiments belonging to General Johnson's division. One colonel succeeded in escaping my lines, and passed on toward Nashville.

From the reports made by these troops, I did not know but the enemy were in pursuit in force, and, consequently, I organized the forces I had collected and formed them in line of battle, on the crest of the hill, the other side of Overall's Creek, planting the artillery on the left and center.

In a short time Colonel Walker came up from the rear with a brigade of troops and took position on the left. After we had occupied this position a short time, a small force of the enemy's cavalry appeared on the opposite side of the creek and attacked our transportation train, which I had directed to proceed moderately toward Nashville. I directed a pursuit, by a cavalry force, and about the same time Captain Church, of the Fourth Michigan Battery, and of Colonel Walker's brigade, opened a fire upon them, and they were soon dispersed, losing some few of their men.

During the remainder of the day there were several attacks by the enemy's cavalry, and they were as frequently repulsed, and with considerable loss, by the cavalry force which I had stopped, but the cavalry of the Second Brigade did not seem very determined in their pursuit.

In the afternoon I was ordered by General Thomas to take position with my regiment on the south side of the creek, which I did, and then collected a large force of straggling infantry, and which, during the evening, were, most of them, returned to their regiments.

Late in the evening I was ordered to advance with my regiment to General Thomas' headquarters, near General Rosecrans' headquarters, which I did.

About 3 o'clock on Thursday morning I received orders to proceed to Nashville with my regiment, in charge of headquarters train, and about 4 o'clock I moved with the regiment in charge of the train.

No casualties occurred on the march until about 1 o'clock, when, about 9 miles this side of Nashville, I discovered a general stampede in the train in my rear, which was not directly under my charge. I immediately formed my regiment across the road and stopped the train and fugitives. Very soon there were several cavalrymen came up and reported that the train was attacked at La Vergne, about 6 miles in our rear. I succeeded in checking the stampede and stopping the alarmed cavalrymen, teamsters, and negroes, who had gotten up the stampede. Among the cavalrymen stopped was a Captain Skinner, of the Third Ohio Cavalry. I reached Nashville about 5.30 o'clock with my train, and the long train in my rear, and pitched my camp on the site occupied previous to leaving Nashville. After I had my camp pitched, I received orders from General Morgan's aide to remove my regiment inside the fortifications early the next day, which I did, and about 5 o'clock in the evening received orders from General Thomas to return to the front with eight days' rations, and between 3 and 4 o'clock on Saturday morning I marched from Nashville with my regiment with a small train. When about 9 miles this side of Nashville I rescued a lady, with a carriage, horse, and servant, which a party of rebel cavalry had captured. The cavalry fled on our approach, and I had no means of pursuit.

When I reached La Vergne I was informed by Colonel Innes, of the First Michigan Engineers, that a large body of cavalry were about to attack his regiment, stationed there. I halted my regiment and prepared to assist Colonel Innes in his defense; but after waiting two hours for their attack, I proceeded on my march to this place without any other incident, and reached here last evening about 7 o'clock with the regiment and train.

In stopping the rout which seemed to be prevailing among our troops on Wednesday morning, my officers and men, without one exception, behaved with great coolness, and are entitled to much credit for the determined and successful effort in preventing a disgraceful rout of a large portion of the right wing of the army.

I remain, major, very respectfully, your obedient servant,

J. G. PARKHURST,
Lieutenant-Colonel, Commanding Ninth Michigan Volunteers.

Maj. GEORGE E. FLYNT,
Assistant Adjutant-General and Chief of Staff.

No. 187.

Report of Lieut. Col. Joseph W. Burke, Tenth Ohio Infantry, of operations December 31–January 22.

HEADQUARTERS TENTH OHIO VOLUNTEERS,
Murfreesborough, Tenn., January 28, 1863.

COLONEL : I beg leave to submit the following report of my command, while posted at Stewart's Creek Bridge, from December 31, 1862, to January 22, 1863:

I remained at Stewart's Creek with eight companies of the regiment, in charge of headquarters train, after detaching two companies of my command, under Capt. John E. Hudson, to accompany headquarters in the field.

On December 31, information reached me that the trains of the Twenty-eighth Brigade had been attacked and captured near Smyrna, at 9 o'clock in the morning of that day; and at a later hour, learning that the rebel cavalry were destroying it, I dispatched a party to the scene, and succeeded in saving 8 wagons loaded with supplies.

I had sufficient force to have saved this train entirely, but, owing to the extreme negligence of the quartermaster in charge of the train, in not reporting the fact of capture to me at an early hour, the enemy were enabled to carry away and destroy a large portion of it.

The force that attacked that train was very small, and I understand there was a guard with it, all of whom were paroled.

We were threatened with attack at the bridge during the whole day. I had the large train corraled in close order, and by extreme vigilance prepared to resist any attack during the night.

A large number of stragglers came back from the front, from an early hour of the day. I deployed a line of skirmishers across the country, from the pike to the railroad, with instructions to shoot down every straggler who attempted to force the line, and marched into camp at night over 1,100 of these men.

Regiments of stragglers were organized, officered by my own commissioned and non-commissioned officers, and put on duty.

On January 1, I was re-enforced by four companies of the Fourth Michigan Cavalry, under Lieutenant-Colonel Dickinson, and a section of Company D, First Ohio Battery, under Lieutenant Newell.

Rebel cavalry threatened the post during the day, and their advance guard was twice repulsed by my pickets and reserve. Concluding not to attack at Stewart's Creek, this force, consisting of Wheeler's, Wharton's, Buford's, John H. Morgan's, and McCann's rebel cavalry, with two pieces of artillery, passed on toward La Vergne, where they attacked Colonel Innes, First Michigan Engineers, at 1 o'clock. I apprised Colonel Innes of the movements of this force at an early hour.

About 1 o'clock a squadron of affrighted negroes came charging at full gallop from Murfreesborough toward Stewart's Creek, and with such impetuosity and recklessness that over 100 passed the bridge before I could check the progress of the main cavalcade. They were dismounted and some of them ducked by my men. This was the advance of what seemed to me to be the whole army—cavalrymen with jaded horses, artillery and infantry soldiers, breathless and holding on to wagons, relating the most incredible defeats and annihilation of the army and their respective regiments, came streaming down the road and pouring through the woods on their way toward the bridge. In vain did my small guard stationed on the road try to check this panic. Officers drew their revolvers, but the fugitives heeded them not.

My regiment was in line on the hill-side, and I promptly fixed bayonet, marched at double-quick to the bridge, and drew up a line before it, sending out, at the same time, two companies, deployed as skirmishers, on the right and left, to prevent the passing of the creek by fording. The fugitives crowded in thousands, and at one time pressed closely up to the bayonets of my men. I ordered the battalion to load, and determined to fire if the crowd did not move back; seeing which, many took flight back toward the front. At this critical moment I was rendered most valuable assistance by Lieutenant Rendelbrook, Fourth U. S. Cavalry, and his men, who were stationed at the bridge with their camp and train.

To him I assigned the duty of getting the stragglers into line, and nobly did his men execute his orders. Riding through the panic-stricken crowds, the cavalrymen drove them into a field, where a good line was formed, and every straggler taken and made dress up. When I had a regiment formed in this manner, I assigned it officers and marched it across the bridge, stacked arms, and rested it. In this manner I secured over 4,000 men. I must mention here the fact that the prominent movers in the panic were the quartermasters in charge of trains. There was only one who behaved with anything like courage and coolness—the quartermaster of the Pioneer Brigade.

Later in the day I was notified by Colonel Innes that he was attacked fiercely by rebel cavalry; that a demand for surrender had been made twice, and asking to be re-enforced. I promptly dispatched four companies of the Fourth Michigan Cavalry and the section of artillery (Rodman guns) to his assistance, and ordered them to move up at a trot, holding my own forces ready to support them.

After the lapse of two hours, during which the cannonading of Colonel Innes' stockade was kept up by the rebels (hearing the report of each gun), Mr. Reily, a citizen, made his escape through the rebel lines, bearing a dispatch from Colonel Innes requesting me to re-enforce him, and the astonishing information that the troops I sent up under Lieutenant-Colonel Dickinson were on their way back to me without having fired a shot, and the rebels were burning the trains.

I quickly decided to save the trains and leave the bridge to the protection of the regiments of stragglers, and set out at a rapid pace for La Vergne with my own command. I met the section of artillery returning, as well as part of the cavalry. I ordered them to fall in behind me, and sent in a strong support of infantry to the guns.

The scene on the road was indescribable. Teamsters had abandoned their wagons and came back mounted on their mules and horses; wagons were packed across the road, and many capsized on the side of the pike; horses ran wild through the woods, and, although men were allowéd by me to pass as wagon guards, there were none at their posts. They had left the road and were bivouacking in small parties in the woods, evidently careless of the fate of the trains.

The woods toward La Vergne were filled with small bodies of rebel cavalry, which were quickly dislodged by my skirmishers and driven off. I reached Colonel Innes at La Vergne at 7 o'clock, and assisted him in arranging the trains and forwarding them to Nashville.

I detached four companies of my regiment, and Lieutenant-Colonel Dickinson's command, and sent them back to Stewart's Creek at daylight next morning, remaining myself at La Vergne, collecting supplies from the trains, gathering in cattle abandoned by our men, and sending them to the front.

With the remaining portion of my command I joined the garrison at Stewart's Creek, January 7, and immediately set to work putting it in a defensible condition by erecting a stockade and throwing up a small redoubt to cover the bridge.

I was relieved in command there by Lieutenant-Colonel Carroll, commanding Tenth Indiana Volunteers, on January 22, and reported for duty at headquarters.

In connection with the disgraceful panic of January 1, I would mention the names of the following officers: Lieutenant Gilbert, Second Tennessee Cavalry, who had his horse hitched up to a wagon on the road, and who abandoned it with the teamsters, joining in the stampede; Lieutenant Newell, Twenty-first Wisconsin, and the regimental quartermaster Seventy-ninth Pennsylvania, who abandoned the train of the Twenty-eighth Brigade, and, although within my lines, never communicated the fact of capture until it was too late to pursue the enemy.

Out of a crowd of runaway teamsters I took the names of four men who cut loose their mules from the wagons and left them to their fate: Henry W. Davis, Twenty-fifth Illinois; Scott Cunningham, Twenty-fifth Illinois; Henry Denney, Fifty-ninth Ohio, and Jacob Rohrer, One hundred and first Ohio. A number of commissioned officers came back with the men, but, on seeing the obstacles interposed to their passage, they returned voluntarily to the front.

My officers and men performed their duty faithfully and strictly. I was rendered signal assistance by Lieutenant Rendelbrook, Fourth U. S. Cavalry, and the non-commissioned officers and men of his command, as also Lieutenant Maple, Anderson Troop, who, with their commands, were constantly on duty, reporting the movements of the enemy, and assisting in effectually checking the disgraceful and causeless panic.

I would respectfully mention the name of Captain Perkins, assistant quartermaster, headquarters quartermaster, who evinced the utmost zeal and vigilance, and assisted most materially in the defense of the post, and in restoring order among the trains.

I have the honor to be, colonel, with great respect, your obedient servant,

J. W. BURKE,
Lieutenant-Colonel, Comdg. Tenth Ohio Volunteer Infantry.

Col. C. GODDARD,
Assistant Adjutant-General and Chief of Staff.

No. 188.

Reports of General Joseph E. Johnston, C. S. Army, commanding the Western Department, with congratulatory orders.

JACKSON, MISS., *January* 6, 1863.

General Bragg reports the enemy fell back from the field of battle to intrenchments, which he attacked and was repulsed. On hearing that the enemy was re-enforced, he fell back from Murfreesborough; not followed by the Federals.

J. E. JOHNSTON.

General S. COOPER.

—

JACKSON, *January* 9, 1863.

Colonel Ewell informs me, from Chattanooga, that on the 31st General Bragg had 35,000, including Wharton's cavalry. Lost 9,000; 3,000 sick, since, from exposure. We have not force enough here if the enemy is vigorous. Prisoners tell General Bragg of Federal re-enforcements from West Tennessee.

J. E. JOHNSTON,
General.

The PRESIDENT, *Richmond.*

—

HEADQUARTERS,
Jackson, via Montgomery, January 11, 1863.

I have just received the following dispatch from Colonel Ewell, Chattanooga:

The following is a summing up of what has been done, by the advice of General Bragg, since 1st of December, obtained unofficially, but directly from him, including Hartsville:

Morgan and Forrest have captured 5,500 prisoners, killed and wounded 2,000, destroyed stores and ammunition in immense quantities. Forrest has also fitted out his entire command in splendid style. Wheeler and Wharton captured 1,000 prisoners at Murfreesborough, and 4,000 more prisoners of war taken at the same place, and not less than 12,000 killed and wounded; total, 10,500 prisoners, and 14,000 killed and wounded; 10,000 small-arms, besides 2,000 distributed to our troops, and 30 pieces of artillery were sent to the rear, and 1,000 wagons, mostly loaded, were secured or destroyed, with a large number of mules and harness secured. The losses on our side were, at the most, 9,000 killed, wounded, and missing, and four pieces of cannon.

J. E. JOHNSTON.

General S. COOPER.

—

GENERAL ORDERS, }   HEADQUARTERS,
  No. 4.   }   *Chattanooga, January* 28, 1863.

General Johnston has great satisfaction in expressing to this command his sense of the high services and admirable conduct of the Army of Tennessee, especially in the recent operations near Murfreesborough. In those operations that patriotic army, contending with greatly superior numbers, by its own courage, and the skill of its general, inflicted upon the enemy a loss almost equal to its own number, besides capturing thirty-three cannon and a thousand wagons—an exploit unparalleled in modern battles. For its heroic fortitude in enduring fatigue, privation, and exposure, and bravery in battle, he can, with confidence, promise to it the thanks of the Government and gratitude of the country.

By command of General Johnston:

BENJ. S. EWELL,
Assistant Adjutant-General.

No. 189.

Organization of the Army of Tennessee.

POLK'S CORPS.

Lieut. Gen. LEONIDAS POLK.

FIRST DIVISION.

Maj. Gen. B. F. CHEATHAM.

First Brigade.

Brig. Gen. DANIEL S. DONELSON.

8th Tennessee:
    Col. W. L. Moore.
    Lieut. Col. J. H. Anderson.
16th Tennessee, Col. John H. Savage.
38th Tennessee, Col. John C. Carter.
51st Tennessee, Col. John Chester.
84th Tennessee, Col. S. S. Stanton.
Carnes' (Tennessee) battery, Lieut. L. G.
    Marshall.

Second Brigade.

Brig. Gen. ALEXANDER P. STEWART.

4th Tennessee, } Col. O. F. Strahl.
5th Tennessee, }
19th Tennessee, Col. F. M. Walker.
24th Tennesseee:
    Col. H. L. W. Bratton.
    Maj. S. E. Shannon.
31st Tennessee, } Col. E. E. Tansil.
33d Tennessee, }
Mississippi Battery, Capt. T. J. Stanford.

Third Brigade.

Brig. Gen. GEORGE MANEY

1st Tennessee, } Col. H. R. Feild.
27th Tennessee, }
4th Tennessee (Provisional Army), Col.
    J. A. McMurry.
6th Tennessee, } Col. C. S. Hurt.
9th Tennessee, } Maj. J. L. Harris.
Tennessee Sharpshooters, Capt. Frank
    Maney.
Smith's (Mississippi) battery, Lieut. William B. Turner.

Fourth (Preston Smith's) Brigade.

Col. A. J. VAUGHAN, JR.

12th Tennessee, Maj. J. N. Wyatt.
13th Tennessee:
    Lieut. Col. W. E. Morgan.
    Capt. R. F. Lanier.
29th Tennessee, Maj. J. B. Johnson.
47th Tennessee, Capt. W. M. Watkins.
154th Tennessee, Lieut. Col. M. Magevney, jr.
9th Texas, Col. W. H. Young.
Allin's (Tennessee) Sharpshooters:
    Lieut. J. R. J. Creighton.
    Lieut. T. F. Pattison.
Tennessee Battery, Capt. W. L. Scott.

SECOND DIVISION.

Maj. Gen. JONES M. WITHERS.

First (Deas') Brigade.

Col. J. Q. LOOMIS.
Col. J. G. COLTART.

19th Alabama.
22d Alabama.
25th Alabama.
26th Alabama.
39th Alabama.
17th Alabama Battalion Sharpshooters,
    Capt. B. C. Yancey.
1st Louisiana (Regulars), Lieut. Col. F.
    H. Farrar, jr.
Robertson's battery, Capt. F. H. Robertson.

Second Brigade.

Brig. Gen. JAMES R. CHALMERS.
Col. T. W. WHITE.

7th Mississippi.
9th Mississippi, Col. T. W. White.
10th Mississippi.
41st Mississippi.
9th Mississippi Battalion Sharpshooters,
    Capt. O. F. West.
Blythe's (Mississippi) regiment.
Garrity's (Alabama) battery.

---

*Compiled from the reports. Other officers than those named may have also been in actual command of the organizations ind' cated.

Third (Walthall's) Brigade.

Brig. Gen. J. PATTON ANDERSON.

45th Alabama, Col. James G. Gilchrist.
24th Mississippi, Lieut. Col. R. P. Mc-
    Kelvaine.
27th Mississippi :
    Col. T. M. Jones.
    Lieut. Col. J. L. Autry.
    Capt. E. R. Neilson.
29th Mississippi :
    Col. W. F. Brantly.
    Lieut. Col. J. B. Morgan.
30th Mississippi, Lieut. Col. J. I. Scales.
39th North Carolina,* Capt. A. W. Bell.
Missouri Battery, Capt. O. W. Barret.

Fourth (Anderson's) Brigade.

Col. A. M. MANIGAULT.

24th Alabama.
28th Alabama.
34th Alabama.
10th South Carolina, } Col. A. J. Lythgoe.
19th South Carolina, }
Alabama Battery, Capt. D. D. Waters.

HARDEE'S CORPS.

Lieut. Gen. WILLIAM J. HARDEE.

FIRST DIVISION.

Maj. Gen. JOHN C. BRECKINRIDGE.

First Brigade.

Brig. Gen. DANIEL W. ADAMS.
Col. RANDALL L. GIBSON.

32d Alabama :
    Lieut. Col. Henry Maury.
    Col. Alexander McKinstry.
13th Louisiana, } Col. R. L. Gibson.
20th Louisiana, } Maj. Charles Guillet.
16th Louisiana, } Col. S. W. Fisk.
25th Louisiana, } Maj. F. C. Zacharie.
14th Louisiana Battalion, Maj. J. E. Aus-
    tin.
Washington Artillery(5th Battery),Lieut.
    W. C. D. Vaught.

Second Brigade.

Col. J. B. PALMER.
Brig. Gen. GIDEON J. PILLOW.

18th Tennessee :
    Col. J. B. Palmer.
    Lieut. Col. W. R. Butler.
26th Tennessee, Col. John M. Lillard.
28th Tennessee, Col. P. D. Cunningham.
32d Tennessee, Col. Ed. C. Cook.
45th Tennessee, Col. A. Searcy.
Moses' (Georgia) battery, Lieut. R. W.
    Anderson.

Third Brigade.

Brig. Gen. WILLIAM PRESTON.

1st Florida, } Col. William Miller.
3d Florida, }
4th Florida, Col. William L L. Bowen.
60th North Carolina, Col. J. A. McDowell
20th Tennessee :
    Col. T. B. Smith.
    Lieut. Col. F. M. Lavender.
    Maj. F. Claybrooke.
Tennessee Battery :
    Capt. E. E. Wright.
    Lieut. J. W. Mebane.

Fourth Brigade.

Brig. Gen. R. W. HANSON.
Col. R. P. TRABUE.

41st Alabama :
    Col. H. Talbird.
    Lieut. Col. M. L. Stansel.
2d Kentucky, Maj. James W. Hewitt.
4th Kentucky :
    Col. R. P. Trabue.
    Capt. T. W. Thompson.
6th Kentucky, Col. Joseph H. Lewis.
9th Kentucky, Col. T. H. Hunt.
Kentucky Battery, Capt. R. Cobb.

Jackson's Brigade.†

Brig. Gen. JOHN K. JACKSON.

5th Georgia :
    Col. W. T. Black.
    Maj. C. P. Daniel.
2d Georgia Battalion Sharpshooters, Maj. J. J. Cox.
5th Mississippi, Lieut. Col. W. L. Sykes.
8th Mississippi :
    Col. J. C. Wilkinson.
    Lieut. Col. A. McNeill.
Pritchard's (Georgia) battery.
Lumsden's (Alabama) battery, Lieut. H. H. Cribbs.

---

* Joined brigade December 31; transferred, January 2, to Manigault's brigade.
† Temporarily assigned to Breckinridge's division.

SECOND DIVISION.

Maj. Gen. P. R. CLEBURNE.

First Brigade.

Brig. Gen. L. E. POLK.

1st Arkansas, Col. John W. Colquitt.
13th Arkansas.
15th Arkansas.
5th Confederate, Col. J. A. Smith.
2d Tennessee, Col. W. D. Robison.
5th Tennessee, Col. B. J. Hill.
Helena (Ark.) Artillery, Lieut. T. J. Key.

Second Brigade.

Brig. Gen. ST. JOHN R. LIDDELL.

2d Arkansas, Col. D. C. Govan.
5th Arkansas, Lieut. Col. John E. Murray.
6th Arkansas, { Col. S. G. Smith.
7th Arkansas, { Lieut. Col. F. J. Cameron.
{ Maj. W. F. Douglass.
8th Arkansas:
    Col. John H. Kelly.
    Lieut. Col. G. F. Baucum.
Swett's (Mississippi) battery, Lieut. H. Shannon.

Third Brigade.

Brig. Gen. BUSHROD R. JOHNSON.

17th Tennessee:
    Col. A. S. Marks.
    Lieut. Col. W. W. Floyd.
23d Tennessee, Lieut. Col. R. H. Keeble
25th Tennessee:
    Col. J. M. Hughs.
    Lieut. Col. Samuel Davis.
37th Tennessee:
    Col. M. White.
    Maj. J. T. McReynolds.
    Capt. C. G. Jarnagin.
44th Tennessee, Col. John S. Fulton.
Jefferson (Miss.) Artillery, Capt. Put. Darden.

Fourth Brigade.

Brig. Gen. S. A. M. WOOD.

16th Alabama, Col. W. B. Wood.
33d Alabama, Col. Samuel Adams.
3d Confederate, Maj. J. F. Cameron.
45th Mississippi, Lieut. Col. R. Charlton.
15th Mississippi Battalion Sharpshooters, Capt. A. T. Hawkins.
Alabama Battery, Capt. Henry C. Semple.

McCOWN'S DIVISION.*

Maj. Gen. J. P. McCOWN.

First Brigade.†

Brig. Gen. M. D. ECTOR.

10th Texas Cavalry, Col. M. F. Locke.
11th Texas Cavalry:
    Col. J. C. Burks.
    Lieut. Col. J. M. Bounds.
14th Texas Cavalry, Col. J. L. Camp.
15th Texas Cavalry, Col. J. A. Andrews.
Texas Battery, Capt. J. P. Douglas.

Second Brigade.

Brig. Gen. JAMES E. RAINS.
Col. R. B. VANCE.

3d Georgia Battalion, Lieut. Col. M. A. Stovall.
9th Georgia Battalion, Maj. Joseph T. Smith.
29th North Carolina, Col. R. B. Vance.
11th Tennessee:
    Col. G. W. Gordon.
    Lieut. Col. William Thedford.
Eufaula (Ala.) Light Artillery, Lieut. W. A. McDuffie.

Third Brigade.

Brig. Gen. EVANDER McNAIR.
Col. R. W. HARPER.

1st Arkansas Mounted Rifles: ‡
    Col. R. W. Harper.
    Maj. L. M. Ramsaur.
2d Arkansas Mounted Rifles,‡ Lieut. Col. J. A. Williamson.
4th Arkansas, Col. H. G. Bunn.
30th Arkansas:
    Maj. J. J. Franklin.
    Capt. W. A. Cotter.
4th Arkansas Battalion, Maj. J. A. Ross.
    Arkansas Battery, Capt. J. T. Humphreys.

---

* Of Smith's corps, serving with Hardee.
† The regiments of this brigade serving as infantry.
‡ Serving as infantry.

CAVALRY.*

Brig. Gen. JOSEPH WHEELER.

Wheeler's Brigade.

Brig. Gen. JOSEPH WHEELER.

1st Alabama, Col. W. W. Allen.
3d Alabama :
  Maj. F. Y. Gaines.
  Capt. T. H. Mauldin.
51st Alabama :
  Col. John T. Morgan.
  Lieut. Col. J. D. Webb.
8th Confederate, Col. W. B. Wade.
1st Tennessee, Col. James E. Carter.
— Tennessee Battalion, DeWitt C. Douglass.
— Tennessee Battalion, Maj. D. W. Holman.
Arkansas Battery, Capt. J. H. Wiggins.

Buford's Brigade.

Brig. Gen. A. BUFORD.

3d Kentucky, Col. J. R. Butler.
5th Kentucky, Col. D. H. Smith.
6th Kentucky, Col. J. W. Grigsby.

Pegram's Brigade.†

Brig. Gen. JOHN PEGRAM.

1st Georgia.
1st Louisiana.

Wharton's Brigade.

Brig. Gen. JOHN A. WHARTON.

14th Alabama Battalion, Lieut. Col. James C. Malone.
1st Confederate, Col. John T. Cox.
3d Confederate, Lieut. Col. William N. Estes.
2d Georgia :
  Lieut. Col. J. E. Dunlop.
  Maj. F. M. Ison.
3d Georgia (detachment), Maj. R. Thompson.
2d Tennessee, Col. H. M. Ashby.
4th Tennessee, Col. Baxter Smith.
— Tennessee Battalion, Maj. John R. Davis.
8th Texas, Col. Thomas Harrison.
Murray's (Tennessee) regiment, Maj. W. S. Bledsoe.
Escort company, Capt. Paul F. Anderson.
McCown's escort company, Capt. L. T. Hardy.
White's (Tennessee) battery, Capt. B. F. White, jr.

ARTILLERY.‡

Baxter's (Tennessee) battery.
Byrne's (Kentucky) battery.
Gibson's (Georgia) battery.

No. 190.

Reports of General Braxton Bragg, C. S. Army, commanding Army of Tennessee, with congratulatory orders, &c.

MURFREESBOROUGH, TENN., *December 30, 1862.*
(Received at Richmond, Va., January 1, 1863.)

Artillery firing at intervals and heavy skirmishing of light troops all day. Enemy very cautious, and declining a general engagement. Armies are in line of battle within sight.

BRAXTON BRAGG.

General S. COOPER.

---

* Forrest's and Morgan's commands on detached service
† Probably incomplete.
‡ Byrne's battery mentioned in Breckenridge's report. The others do not appear to have been engaged in the campaign. Baxter's battery reported as at Shelbyville, December 31, and Gibson's was ordered, December 1, 1862, to Chattanooga, Tenn., to be fitted for the field.

MURFREESBOROUGH, TENN., *December* 31, 1862.

We assailed the enemy at 7 o'clock this morning, and after ten hours' hard fighting have driven him from every position except his extreme left, which [where] he has successfully resisted us. With the exception of this point, we occupy the whole field. We captured 4,000 prisoners, including 2 brigadier-generals, 31 pieces of artillery, and some 200 wagons and teams.* Our loss is heavy ; that of the enemy much greater.

BRAXTON BRAGG,
General, Commanding.

General S. COOPER.

—

MURFREESBOROUGH, *January* 3, 1863.
(Received January 4, 1863.)

The enemy retired last night but a short distance to intrenchments in his rear. In a sharp and short contest this evening we drove his left flank from position, but our assaulting party again retired with considerable loss to both sides. Wheeler and Wharton were again in their rear yesterday; captured 200 prisoners, one piece of artillery, and destroyed 200 loaded wagons.

BRAXTON BRAGG,
General, Commanding.

General S. COOPER,
Adjutant and Inspector General.

—

TULLAHOMA, *January* 5, 1863.

Unable to dislodge the enemy from his intrenched position, and learning of re-enforcements to him, I withdrew from his front night before last ; he has not followed ; my cavalry is still close in his front.

BRAXTON BRAGG,
General, Commanding.

General S. COOPER,
Richmond, Va.

—

DECHERD, *January* 6, 1863.

Enemy have not yet followed us in force. My command is now concentrated on line of Elk Run. From papers captured on the field, their force was from 60,000 to 70,000 ; ours not over half that. We hope to check any advance ; but to save East Tennessee, and enable us to advance again, re-enforcements are necessary. They are bringing forward every man from Kentucky.

BRAXTON BRAGG.

General S. COOPER,
Adjutant and Inspector General.

—

DECHERD, *January* 7, 1863.

We shall hold line of Duck River, if possible. Our losses will reach 9,000 ; the enemy has not advanced from Murfreesborough.

BRAXTON BRAGG.

General S. COOPER.

---

* See Series I, Vol. XVI, Part I, p. 1097.

HEADQUARTERS ARMY OF TENNESSEE,
Tullahoma, Tenn., February 23, 1863.

SIR: On December 26, last, the enemy advanced in force from Nashville to attack us at Murfreesborough. It had been well ascertained that his strength was over 60,000 effective men. Before night on that day the object of the movement was developed by our dispositions in front, and orders were given for the necessary concentration of our forces, then distributed as follows: Polk's corps and three brigades of Breckinridge's division, Hardee's corps, at Murfreesborough; the balance of Hardee's corps near Eagleville, about 20 miles west of Murfreesborough; McCown's division (which, with Stevenson's division removed, constituted Smith's corps) at Readyville, 12 miles east of Murfreesborough, the three cavalry brigades of Wheeler, Wharton, and Pegram occupying the entire front of our infantry, and covering all approaches to within 10 miles of Nashville; Buford's small cavalry brigade, of about 600, at McMinnville. The brigades of Forrest and Morgan (about 5,000 effective cavalry) were absent on special service in West Tennessee and Northern Kentucky, as will be more fully noticed hereafter. Jackson's small infantry brigade was in rear, guarding the railroad from Bridgeport, Ala., to the mountains.

On Sunday, the 28th, our main force of infantry and artillery was concentrated in front of Murfreesborough, while the cavalry, supported by three brigades of infantry and three batteries of artillery, impeded the advance of the enemy by constant skirmishing and sudden and unexpected attacks. To the skillful manner in which the cavalry, thus ably supported, was handled, and to the exceeding gallantry of its officers and men, must be attributed the four days' time consumed by the enemy in reaching the battle-field, a distance of only 20 miles from his encampments, over fine macadamized roads.

Fully aware of the greatly superior numbers of the enemy, as indicated in my early reports from this quarter, it was our policy to await attack. The position was selected and line developed with this intention. Owing to the convergence upon our depot at Murfreesborough of so many fine roads by which the enemy could approach, as will appear from the inclosed map, marked 1,* we were confined in our selection to a line near enough the point of juncture to enable us to successfully cover them all until the real point of attack should be developed.

On Monday, the 29th, it was reported that heavy columns moved on both the direct road from La Vergne and on the one leading into the Lebanon road by way of Jefferson, but on Tuesday, the 30th, it was ascertained that the Jefferson pike was abandoned by a countermarch, and the whole forces of the enemy were concentrated on and near the direct road on the west of Stone's River. The dispositions made for the unequal contest will appear from the inclosed map, marked 2,* and the copy of memoranda to general and staff officers, marked 3.* These arrangements were all completed before the enemy crossed Stewart's Creek, 9 miles out, and the infantry brigades were at once called in, and the cavalry was ordered to fall back more rapidly, having most gallantly discharged its duty and fully accomplished the object desired.

Late on Monday it became apparent the enemy was extending his right, so as to flank us on the left. McCown's division, in reserve, was promptly thrown to that flank and added to the command of Lieutenant-General Polk. The enemy not meeting our expectations of making an attack on Tuesday, which was consumed in artillery firing and heavy

---

* To appear in Atlas.

skirmishing, with the exception of a dash late in the evening on the left of Withers' division, which was repulsed and severely punished, it was determined to assail him on Wednesday morning, the 31st. For this purpose, Cleburne's division, Hardee's corps, was moved from the second line on the right to the corresponding position on the left, and Lieutenant-General Hardee was ordered to that point and assigned to the command of that and McCown's division. This disposition, the result of necessity, left me no reserve, but Breckinridge's command on the right, now not threatened, was regarded as a source of supply for any re enforcements absolutely necessary to other parts of the field. Stone's River, at its then stage, was fordable at almost any point for infantry, and at short intervals perfectly practicable for artillery.

These dispositions completed, Lieutenant-General Hardee was ordered to assail the enemy at daylight on Wednesday, the 31st, the attack to be taken up by Lieutenant-General Polk's command in succession to the right flank, the move to be made by a constant wheel to the right, on Polk's right flank as a pivot, the object being to force the enemy back on Stone's River, and, if practicable, by the aid of the cavalry, cut him off from his base of operations and supplies by the Nashville pike. The lines were now bivouacked at a distance in places of not more than 500 yards, the camp-fires of the two being within distinct view. Wharton's cavalry brigade had been held on our left to watch and check the movements of the enemy in that direction, and to prevent his cavalry from gaining the railroad in our rear, the preservation of which was of vital importance. In this he was aided by Brig. Gen. A. Buford, who had a small command of about 600 new cavalry. The duty was most ably, gallantly, and successfully performed.

On Monday night Brigadier-General Wheeler proceeded with his cavalry brigade and one regiment from Pegram's, as ordered, to gain the enemy's rear. By Tuesday morning, moving on the Jefferson pike around the enemy's left flank, he had gained the rear of their whole army, and soon attacked the trains, their guards, and the numerous stragglers. He succeeded in capturing several hundred prisoners and destroying hundreds of wagons loaded with supplies and baggage. After clearing the road, he made his way entirely around and joined the cavalry on our left.

The failure of Major-General McCown to execute during the night an order for a slight change in the line of his division, and which had to be done the next morning, caused some delay in the general and vigorous assault by Lieutenant-General Hardee. But about 7 o'clock the rattle of musketry and roar of artillery announced the beginning of the conflict. The enemy was taken completely by surprise. General and staff officers were not mounted, artillery horses not hitched, and infantry not formed. A hot and inviting breakfast of coffee and other luxuries, to which our gallant and hardy men had long been strangers, was found upon the fire unserved, and was left while we pushed on to the enjoyment of a more inviting feast, that of captured artillery, fleeing battalions, and hosts of craven prisoners begging for the lives they had forfeited by their acts of brutality and atrocity.

While thus routing and pushing the enemy in his front, Lieutenant-General [W. J.] Hardee announced to me by a messenger that the movement was not being as promptly executed by Major-General Cheatham's command on his right (the left of Lieutenant-General Polk's corps) as he expected, and that his line was, consequently, exposed to an enfilade fire from the enemy's artillery in that front. The necessary instructions for prompt movement at that point were immediately dispatched, and in a short time our whole line, except Breckinridge's command, was warmly engaged. From this time we continued to drive the enemy more or less rapidly until his line was thrown entirely back at right angles to his first position, and occupied the cut of the railroad, along which he had massed his reserves and posted very strong batteries. A reference to the map No. 2* will show this second and strong position.

The enemy's loss was very heavy in killed and wounded, far exceeding our own, as appeared from a critical examination of the field, now almost entirely in our possession. Of artillery alone we had secured more than twenty-five pieces.

While the infantry and artillery were occupied in this successful work, Brigadier-General Wharton, with his cavalry command, was most actively and gallantly engaged on the enemy's right and rear, where he inflicted a heavy loss in killed and wounded, captured a full battery of artillery endeavoring to escape, and secured and sent in near 2,000 prisoners. These important successes and results had not been achieved without heavy sacrifices on our part, as the resistance of the enemy after the first surprise was most gallant and obstinate. Numbering at least two to our one, he was enabled to bring fresh troops at every point to resist our progress, and he did so with a skill and judgment which has ever characterized his able commander. Finding Lieutenant-General Hardee so formidably opposed by the movement of the enemy to his front, re-enforcements for him were ordered from Major-General Breckinridge, but the orders were countermanded, as will hereafter appear, and Polk's corps was pressed forward with vigor, hoping to draw the enemy back or rout him on the right as he already had been on the left. We succeeded in driving him from every position except the strong one held by his extreme left flank, resting on Stone's River, and covered by a concentration of artillery of superior range and caliber, which seemed to bid us defiance. The difficulties of our general advance had been greatly enhanced by the topography of the country. All parts of our line had to pass in their progress over ground of the roughest character, covered with huge stones and studded with the densest growth of cedar, the branches reaching to the ground and forming an almost impassable brake. Our artillery could rarely be used, while the enemy, holding defensive lines, had selected formidable positions for his batteries and this dense cover for his infantry, from both of which he had to be dislodged by our infantry alone. The determined and unvarying gallantry of our troops, and the uninterrupted success which attended their repeated charges against these strongholds, defended by double their numbers, fully justified the unbounded confidence I had ever reposed in them and had so often expressed. To meet our successful advance and retrieve his losses in the front of our left, the enemy early transferred a portion of his reserve from his left to that flank, and by 2 o'clock had succeeded in concentrating such a force in Lieutenant-General Hardee's front as to check his further progress. Our two lines had by this time become almost blended, so much weakened were they by losses, exhaustion, and extension to cover the enemy's whole front.

As early as 10 a. m. Major-General Breckinridge was called on for one brigade, and soon after for a second, to re-enforce, or act as a reserve to, Lieutenant-General Hardee. His reply to the first call represented the enemy crossing Stone's River in heavy force in his immediate front, and on receiving the second order he informed me they had already crossed in heavy force and were advancing on him in two lines. He was immediately ordered not to await attack, but to advance and meet

_____
* To appear in Atlas.

them. About this same time a report reached me that a heavy force of the enemy's infantry was advancing on the Lebanon road, about 5 miles in Breckinridge's front. Brigadier-General Pegram, who had been sent to that road to cover the flank of the infantry with his cavalry brigade (save two regiments detached with Wheeler and Wharton), was ordered forward immediately to develop any such movement. The orders for the two brigades from Breckinridge were countermanded, while dispositions were made, at his request, to re-enforce him. Before they could be carried out, the movements ordered disclosed the facts that no force had crossed Stone's River; that the only enemy in our immediate front there was a small body of sharpshooters, and that there was no advance on the Lebanon road. These unfortunate misapprehensions on that part of the field (which, with proper precaution, could not have existed) withheld from active operations three fine brigades until the enemy had succeeded in checking our progress, had re-established his lines, and had collected many of his broken battalions. Having now settled the question that no movement was being made against our right, and none even to be apprehended, Breckinridge was ordered to leave two brigades to support the battery at A, on his side of Stone's River, and with the balance of the force to cross to the left and report to Lieutenant-General Polk. By the time this could be accomplished it was too late to send this force to Lieutenant-General Hardee's support, who was unable to make further progress, and he was directed to maintain his position. Lieutenant-General Polk was directed with these re-enforcements to throw all the force he could collect upon the enemy's extreme left, and thereby either carry that strong point which had so far resisted us successfully, or, failing in that, at least to draw off from Hardee's front the formidable opposition there concentrated. The three brigades of Jackson, Preston, and Adams were successively reported for this work. How gallantly they moved to their task, and how much they suffered in the determined effort to accomplish it, will best appear from reports of subordinate commanders and the statement of losses, herewith. Upon this flank, their strongest defensive position, resting on the river bank, the enemy had concentrated not less than twenty pieces of his heaviest artillery, masked almost entirely from view, but covering an open space in front of several hundred yards. Supported right, left, and rear by heavy masses of infantry, this position proved impracticable, and after two unsuccessful efforts the attempt to carry it by infantry was abandoned. Our heaviest batteries of artillery and rifled guns of long range were now concentrated in front of, and their fire opened on, this position. After a cannonade of some time the enemy's fire slackened, and finally ceased near nightfall. Lieutenant-General Hardee had slightly retired his line from the farthest point he had attained for better position and cover without molestation from the enemy. Lieutenant-General Polk's infantry, including the three re-enforcing brigades, uniting their left with Hardee's right and extending to our extreme right flank, formed a continuous line very nearly perpendicular to the original line of battle, thus leaving nearly the whole field with all its trophies– the enemy's dead and many of his wounded, his hospitals and stores—in our full possession. The body of Brigadier-General Sill, one of their division commanders, was found where he had fallen, and was sent to town and decently interred, though he had forfeited all claim to such consideration by the acts of cruelty, barbarity, and atrocity but a few days before committed under his authority on the women, children, and old men living near the road on which he had made a reconnaissance.

During the afternoon, Brigadier-General Pegram, discovering a hospital and large numbers of stragglers in rear of the enemy's line and across Stone's River, charged them with his cavalry and captured about 170 prisoners.

Both armies, exhausted by a conflict of full ten hours' duration, rarely surpassed for its continued intensity and the heavy losses sustained, sank to rest with the sun and perfect quiet prevailed for the night.

At dawn on Thursday morning, January 1, orders were sent to the several commanders to press forward their skirmishers, feel the enemy, and report any change in his position. Major-General Breckinridge had been transferred to the right of Stone's River, to resume the command of that position, now held by two of his brigades. It was soon reported that no change had occurred, except the withdrawal of the enemy from the advanced position occupied by his left flank. Finding, upon further examination, that this was the case, the right flank of Lieutenant-General Polk's corps was thrown forward to occupy the ground for which we had so obstinately contended the evening before. This shortened our line considerably, and gave us possession of the entire battle-field, from which we gleaned the spoils and trophies throughout the day and transferred them rapidly to the rear. A careful reconnaissance of the enemy's position was ordered, and the most of the cavalry was put in motion for the roads in his rear, to cut off his trains and develop any movement. It was soon ascertained that he was still in very heavy force all along our front, occupying a position strong by nature and improved by such work as could be done at night and by his reserves. In a short time reports from the cavalry informed me heavy trains were moving toward Nashville, some of the wagons loaded and all the ambulances filled with wounded. These were attacked at different places; many wagons were destroyed and hundreds of prisoners paroled. No doubt this induced the enemy to send large escorts of artillery, infantry, and cavalry with later trains, and thus the impression was made on our ablest cavalry commanders that a retrograde movement was going on. Our forces, greatly wearied and much reduced by heavy losses, were held ready to avail themselves of any change in the enemy's position, but it was deemed unadvisable to assail him as then established. The whole day, after these dispositions, was passed without an important movement on either side, and was consumed by us in gleaning the battle-field, burying the dead, and replenishing ammunition.

At daylight on Friday, the 2d, the orders to feel the enemy and ascertain his position were repeated with the same results. The cavalry brigades of Wheeler and Wharton had returned during the night greatly exhausted from long-continued service with but little rest or food to either men or horses. Both commanders reported the indications from the enemy's movements the same. Allowing them only a few hours to feed and rest, and sending the two detached regiments back to Pegram's brigade, Wharton was ordered to the right flank across Stone's River, to assume command in that quarter and keep me advised of any change. Wheeler with his brigade was ordered to gain the enemy's rear again, and remain until he could definitely report whether any retrograde movement was being made. Before Wharton had taken his position, observation excited my suspicions in regard to a movement having been made by the enemy across Stone's River immediately in Breckinridge's front. Reconnaissances by several staff officers soon developed the fact that a division had quietly crossed unopposed and established themselves on and under cover of an eminence, marked B on map No. 2,* from which

---

* To appear in Atlas.

Lieutenant-General Polk's line was both commanded and enfiladed. The dislodgment of this force or the withdrawal of Polk's line was an evident necessity. The latter involved consequences not to be entertained. Orders were accordingly given for the concentration of the whole of Major-General Breckinridge's division in front of the position to be taken, the addition to his command of ten 12-pounder Napoleon guns, under Capt. F. H. Robertson, an able and accomplished artillery officer, and for the cavalry forces of Wharton and Pegram, about 2,000 men, to join in the attack on his right. Major-General Breckinridge was sent for and advised of the movement and its objects, the securing and holding of the position which protected Polk's flank and gave us command of the enemy's by which to enfilade him. He was informed of the forces placed at his disposal, and instructed with them to drive the enemy back, crown the hill, intrench his artillery, and hold the position. To distract their attention from our real object, a heavy artillery fire was ordered to be opened from Polk's front at the exact hour at which the movement was to begin. At other points throughout both lines all was quiet. General Breckinridge at 3.30 p. m. reported he would advance at 4 o'clock. Polk's batteries promptly opened fire and were soon answered by the enemy. A heavy cannonade of some fifteen minutes was succeeded by the fire of musketry, which soon became general. The contest was short and severe; the enemy was driven back and the eminence gained, but the movement as a whole was a failure, and the position was again yielded. Our forces were moved, unfortunately, so far to the left as to throw a portion of them into and over Stone's River, where they encountered heavy masses of the enemy, while those against whom they were intended to operate on our side of the river had a destructive enfilade on our whole line. Our second line was so close to the front as to receive the enemy's fire, and, returning it, took their friends in rear. The cavalry force was left entirely out of the action. Learning from my own staff officers, sent to the scene, of the disorderly retreat being made by General Breckinridge's division, Brigadier-General Patton Anderson's fine brigade of Mississippians (the nearest body of troops) was promptly ordered to his relief.

On reaching the field and moving forward, Anderson found himself in front of Breckinridge's infantry, and soon encountered the enemy's light troops close upon our artillery, which had been left without support. This noble brigade, under its cool and gallant chief, drove the enemy back and saved all the guns not captured before its arrival. Capt. F. H. Robertson, after the disabling wound received by Major [R. E.] Graves (General Breckinridge's gallant and efficient chief of artillery), took the entire charge of all the artillery of the division in addition to his own. To his gallantry, energy, and fearlessness is due the smallness of our loss sustained before the arrival of support—only three guns. His report, herewith, marked 4, will show the important part he played in this attack and repulse. Before the end of the whole movement it was quite dark. Anderson's command held a position next the enemy, corresponding nearly with our original line, while Breckinridge's brigade commanders collected their scattered men as far as practicable in the darkness, and took irregular positions on Anderson's left and rear. At daylight in the morning they were moved to the front and the whole line re-established without opposition. During the night, Major-General Cleburne's division was retransferred to its original position on the right, and Lieutenant-General Hardee directed to resume his command there and restore our line.

On Saturday morning, the 3d, our forces had been in line of battle for five days and nights, with but little rest, having no reserves; their baggage and tents had been loaded and the wagons were 4 miles off; their provisions, if cooked at all, were most imperfectly prepared, with scanty means; the weather had been severe from cold and almost constant rain, and we had no change of clothing, and in many places could not have fires. The necessary consequence was great exhaustion of officers and men, many having to be sent to the hospitals in the rear, and more still were beginning to straggle from their commands, an evil from which we had so far suffered but little. During the whole of this day the rain continued to fall with little intermission, and the rapid rise in Stone's River indicated it would soon be unfordable. Late on Friday night I had received the captured papers of Major-General [A. McD.] McCook, commanding one *corps d'armée* of the enemy, showing their effective strength to have been very near, if not quite, 70,000 men. Before noon, reports from Brigadier-General Wheeler satisfied me the enemy, instead of retiring, was receiving re-enforcements. Common prudence and the safety of my army, upon which even the safety of our cause depended, left no doubt on my mind as to the necessity of my withdrawal from so unequal a contest. My orders were accordingly given about noon for the movement of the trains, and for the necessary preparation of the troops.

Under the efficient management of the different staff departments everything had been secured and transferred to the rear, including prisoners, captured artillery, small-arms, subsistence, means of transportation, and nearly all our wounded able to bear moving. No movement of any kind was made by the troops on either side during this most inclement day until just at night, when a sharp skirmish occurred between Polk's right and the enemy's left flank, resulting in nothing decisive. The only question with me was, whether the movement should be made at once or delayed for twenty-four hours, to save a few more of our wounded. As it was probable we should lose by exhaustion as many as we should remove of the wounded, my inclination to remain was yielded. The whole force, except the cavalry, was put in motion at 11 p. m., and the army retired in perfect order to its present position behind Duck River without receiving or giving a shot. Our cavalry held the position before Murfreesborough until Monday morning, the 5th, when it quietly retired, as ordered, to cover our front.

We left about 1,200 badly wounded, one-half of whom we learn have since died from the severity of their injuries; about 300 sick, too feeble to bear transportation, and about 200 well men and medical officers as their attendants. In addition to this, the enemy had captured about 800 prisoners from us. As the 1,200 wounded are counted once under that head among our losses, they should be excluded in the general total.

As an offset to this loss we had secured, as will appear from the report of my inspector-general, herewith, marked A, considerably over 6,000 prisoners; had captured over thirty pieces of artillery, 6,000 stand of small-arms, a number of wagons, ambulances, mules, and harness, with a large amount of other valuable property, all of which was secured and appropriated to proper uses. Besides all this secured, we had destroyed not less than 800 wagons, mostly loaded with various articles, such as arms, ammunition, provisions, baggage, clothing, medicines, and hospital stores. We had lost three pieces of artillery only—all in Breckinridge's repulse.

A number of stand of colors (nine of which are forwarded with this report) were also captured on the field. Others known to have been taken have not been sent in. The list, marked B, is herewith transmitted.

A tabular statement of our forces, marked C, is herewith submitted, showing the number of fighting men we had on the field on the morning of December 31 to have been less than 35,000, of which about 30,000 were infantry and artillery. Our losses are also reported in this same comprehensive table, so as to show how much each corps, division, and brigade suffered, and, in case of Breckinridge's division, the losses are reported separately for Wednesday and Friday. These reports are minute and suggestive, showing the severity of the conflict, as well as when, where, and by whom it was sustained.

Among the gallant dead the nation is called to mourn, none could have fallen more honored or regretted than Brig. Gens. James E. Rains and R. W. Hanson. They yielded their lives in the heroic discharge of duty and leave their honored names as a rich legacy to their descendants.

Brig. Gens. James R. Chalmers and D. W. Adams received disabling wounds on Wednesday; I am happy to say not serious, but which deprived us of their valuable services. Having been under my immediate command since the beginning of the war, I can bear evidence to their devotion, and to the conspicuous gallantry which has marked their services on every field.

For the sacred names of other heroes and patriots of lower grades who gave their lives, illustrating the character of the Confederate soldier on this bloody field, I must refer to the reports of subordinate commanders and to the lists which will be submitted.

Our losses, it will be seen, exceeded 10,000, over 9,000 of whom were killed and wounded. The enemy's loss we have no means of knowing with certainty. One corps, commanded by Maj. Gen. Thomas L. Crittenden, which was least exposed in the engagement, reports over 5,000 killed and wounded. As they had two other corps and a separate division (third of a corps) and their cavalry, it is safely estimated at 3,000 killed and 16,000 wounded; adding the 6,273 prisoners, and we have a total of 25,273.

Lieut. Gens. L. Polk and W. J. Hardee, commanding corps; Maj. Gens. J. M. Withers and P. R. Cleburne, commanding divisions, are specially commended to the Government for the valor, skill, and ability displayed by them throughout the engagement.

Brig. Gen. J. Patton Anderson, for the coolness, judgment, and courage with which he interposed his brigade between our retreating forces and the enemy, largely superior to him, on Friday evening, and saved our artillery, is justly entitled to special mention.

Brig. Gens. Joseph Wheeler and John A. Wharton, commanding cavalry brigades, were pre-eminently distinguished throughout the action, as they had been for a month previous in many successive conflicts with the enemy. Under their skillful and gallant lead the reputation of our cavalry has been justly enhanced. For the just commendation of other officers, many of whom were pre-eminently distinguished, I must refer to the reports of their more immediate commanders.

To the private soldier a fair meed of praise is due; and though it is so seldom given and so rarely expected that it may be considered out of place, I cannot, in justice to myself, withhold the opinion ever entertained and so often expressed during our struggle for independence. In the absence of the instruction and discipline of old armies, and of the confidence which long association produces between veterans, we have had in a great measure to trust to the individuality and self-reliance of the private soldier. Without the incentive or the motive which controls the officer, who hopes to live in history; without the hope of reward, and actuated only by a sense of duty and of patriotism, he has, in this great contest, justly judged that the cause was his own, and gone into it with a determination to conquer or die; to be free or not to be at all. No encomium is too high, no honor too great for such a soldiery. However much of credit and glory may be given, and probably justly given, the leaders in our struggle, history will yet award the main honor where it is due—to the private soldier, who, without hope of reward, and with no other incentive than a consciousness of rectitude, has encountered all the hardships and suffered all the privations. Well has it been said, "The first monument our Confederacy rears, when our independence shall have been won, should be a lofty shaft, pure and spotless, bearing this inscription, 'To the unknown and unrecorded dead.'"

The members of my staff, arduously engaged in their several duties before, during, and since the prolonged engagement, are deserving a mention in this report. Lieut. Cols. George G. Garner and G. W. Brent and Capt. P. H. Thomson, adjutant and inspector general's department; First Lieuts. Towson Ellis and F. S. Parker [jr.], regular aides-de-camp; Lieut. Col. W. K. Beard, inspector-general; Lieut. Col. A. J. Hays, Provisional Army; Majs. James Strawbridge, Louisiana infantry, and William Clare, late Seventh Alabama Volunteers, acting assistant inspectors-general; Lieut. Col. L. W. O'Bannon, chief quartermaster; Maj. M. B. McMicken, assistant quartermaster; Maj. J. J. Walker, chief commissary; Majs. F. Molloy and G. M. Hillyer, assistants; Lieut. Col. H. Oladowski, chief of ordnance; Capts. W. H. Warren and O. T. Gibbes, and Lieut. W. F. Johnson, assistants; Capt. S. W. Steele, acting chief engineer, and Lieuts. H. C. Force, A. H. Buchanan, and J. K. P. McFall [assistants]; Lieut. Col. J. H. Hallonquist, acting chief of artillery; First Lieut. R. H. S. Thompson, assistant; Surg. A. J. Foard, medical director; Surg. E. A. Flewellen, assistant medical director; Actg. Surg. T. G. Richardson, attendant on myself, staff, and escort; Cols. David Urquhart, of Louisiana, J. Stoddard Johnston, of Kentucky, and G. Saint Leger Grenfell, of England (the two former volunteer aides, long on my staff), served me most efficiently. Maj. E. W. Baylor, assistant quartermaster; Maj. B. C. Kennedy, assistant commissary of subsistence, and Lieut. William M. Bridges, aide-de-camp to the late Brigadier-General [J. K.] Duncan, reported just before the engagement and joined my staff, on which they served through the battle.

Col. M. L. Clark, of the artillery (Provisional Army), being in Murfreesborough on temporary service, did me the favor to join and serve on my staff during the engagement.

His Excellency Isham G. Harris, Governor of Tennessee, and the Hon. Andrew Ewing, member of military court, volunteered their services and rendered me efficient aid, especially with the Tennessee troops, largely in the ascendant in this army. It is but due to a zealous and efficient laborer in our cause that I here bear testimony to the cordial support given me at all times since meeting him a year ago in West Tennessee by His Excellency Governor Harris. From the field of Shiloh, where he received in his arms the dying form of the lamented Johnston, to the last struggle at Murfreesborough, he has been one of us, and has shared all our privations and dangers, while giving us his personal and political influence with all the power he possessed at the head of the State government.

To the medical department of the army, under the able administration of Surgeon Foard, great credit is due for the success which attended their labors. Sharing none of the excitement and glory of the field, these officers in their labor of love devote themselves silently and assiduously to alleviate the sufferings of their brother soldiers at hours when others are seeking rest and repose.

The reports of subordinate commanders not yet received have been specially called for and are soon expected, when they will be promptly forwarded.

During the time the operations at Murfreesborough were being conducted, important expeditions, under Brigadier-Generals Forrest and Morgan, were absent in West Tennessee and Northern Kentucky. The reports already forwarded show the complete success which attended these gallant brigadiers, and commend them to the confidence of the Government and gratitude of the country.

I am, sir, very respectfully, your obedient servant,

BRAXTON BRAGG,
General, Commanding.

General S. COOPER,
Adjutant [and Inspector] General, Richmond, Va.

[Indorsement.]

MARCH 9, 1863.

ADJUTANT AND INSPECTOR GENERAL:

Let this be copied at once for Congress, leaving out the clause of compliment to General Rosecrans.

J. A. SEDDON,
Secretary.

[Inclosure.]

Memoranda for general and staff officers, December 28, 1862.

1st. The line of battle will be in front of Murfreesborough; half of the army, left wing, in front of Stone's River; right wing in rear of river.

2d. Polk's corps will form left wing; Hardee's corps, right wing.

3d. Withers' division will form first line in Polk's corps; Cheatham's, the second line.   Breckinridge's division forms first line Hardee's corps; Cleburne's division, second line Hardee's corps.

4th. McCown's division to form reserve, opposite center, on high ground, in rear of Cheatham's present quarters.

5th. Jackson's brigade reserve, to the right flank, to report to Lieutenant-General Hardee.

6th. Two lines to be formed from 800 to 1,000 yards apart, according to ground.

7th. Chiefs of artillery to pay special attention to posting of batteries, and supervise their work, seeing they do not causelessly waste their ammunition.

8th. Cavalry to fall back gradually before enemy, reporting by couriers every hour. When near our lines, Wheeler will move to the right and Wharton to the left, to cover and protect our flanks and report movements of enemy; Pegram to fall to the rear, and report to commanding general as a reserve.

9th. To-night, if the enemy has gained his position in our front ready for action, Wheeler and Wharton, with their whole commands, will make a night march to the right and left, turn the enemy's flank, gain his rear, and vigorously assail his trains and rear guard, blocking the roads and impeding his movements every way, holding themselves ready to assail his retreating forces.

10th. All quartermasters, commissaries, and ordnance officers will remain at their proper posts, discharging their appropriate duties. Supplies and baggage should be ready, packed for a move forward or backward as the results of the day may require, and the trains should be in position, out of danger, teamsters all present, and quartermasters in charge.

11th. Should we be compelled to retire, Polk's corps will move on Shelbyville and Hardee's on Manchester pike; trains in front; cavalry in rear.

BRAXTON BRAGG,
General, Commanding.

Lieutenant-General POLK,
Commanding Polk's Corps.

[Inclosure A.]

Tabular statement showing the number of prisoners captured by the Army of Tennessee, under General Braxton Bragg, while at Murfreesborough, Tenn. *

At Murfreesborough, during battle before that place	6,273
At Hartsville, December 6, 1862	1,762
By Morgan's expedition into Kentucky, between December 24, 1862, and January 7, 1863	1,873
By Forrest's expedition into West Tennessee, December 20, 1862	1,530
Total	11,438

W. K. BEARD,
Inspector-General.

[Inclosure B.]

List and description of flags taken by General Bragg's army at Murfreesborough.

No. 1.—Bunting Stars and Stripes; regiment not known; date not known; name of captor not reported.

No. 2.— Large silk Stars and Stripes; Thirty-ninth Illinois [Indiana]; date not known; name of captor not reported.

No. 3.—Bunting Stars and Stripes; regiment not known; date not known; name of captor not reported.

No. 4.—Guidon (artillery); regiment not known; date not known; name of captor not reported.

No. 5.—Bunting Stars and Stripes; regiment not known; date not known; name of captor not reported.

No. 6.—Silk Stars and Stripes; regiment not known; December 31, 1862; captured by Private J. K. Leslie, Company C, Fifth Arkansas, Liddell's brigade.

No. 7.—Regimental standard (regulars); regiment not known; December 31, 1862; captured by Sergt. John F. Lovin, Company B, Third Confederate, Wood's brigade.

No. 8.— Silk Stars and Stripes (faded); Thirty-fourth Illinois; December 31, 1862; captured by Colonel Locke's Tenth Texas, Ector's brigade, McCown's division.

No. 9.—Fragment of silk Stars and Stripes; regiment not known; date not known; name of captor not reported.

No. 10.—Battle-flag of a regiment of General Polk's corps, which was left on the field covered with its slain bearers, and recovered by General Adams' brigade, of Breckinridge's division, during his severe engagement December 31, 1862.

These comprise but a small portion of the number of flags actually taken. Nothing is more difficult than to make officers send up these trophies, which the men seem to regard as their own, and are disposed of accordingly. General Cleburne deserves mention for collecting and forwarding his.

A. J. HAYS,
Lieutenant-Colonel and Assistant Inspector-General, Dept. No. 2.

---

* But see Series I Vol. XVI, Part I, p. 1097.

[Inclosure C.]

Tabular statement showing the number present for duty on the morning of December 31, 1862; the number killed, wounded, and missing, and the percentage of loss in the battle of Murfreesborough.

Command.	Present for duty.			Killed.		Wounded.		Missing.			
	Officers.	Men.	Aggregate.	Officers.	Enlisted men.	Officers.	Enlisted men.	Officers.	Enlisted men.	Aggregate.	Percentage of loss.
POLK'S CORPS.											
Cheatham's Division.											
Donelson's brigade	....	....	....	10	98	42	533	1	16	700	....
Stewart's brigade	....	....	....	8	55	23	311	....	2	399	....
Maney's brigade	....	....	....	3	19	12	151		8	193	....
Smith's brigade	....	....	....	7	98	48	516	3	35	707	....
Total	454	5,090	5,544	28	270	125	1,511	4	61	1,999	36
Withers' Division.											
Deas' brigade	....	....	....	6	47	31	502	....	5	591	....
Chalmers' brigade	....	....	....	8	59	32	413	1	35	548	...
Walthall's brigade	....	....	....	12	118	42	578		13	763	....
Anderson's brigade	....	....	....	3	70	34	394	....	16	517	....
Total	617	7,957	8,574	29	294	139	1,887	1	69	2,419	28¼
Total Polk's corps	1,071	13,047	14,118	57	564	264	3,398	5	130	4,418	31¼
HARDEE'S CORPS.											
Breckinridge's Division.											
Pillow's brigade	....	....	....	6	43	32	292	2	50	425	....
Preston's brigade	....	....	....	4	54	28	356	4	93	539	....
Adams' brigade	....	....	....	8	104	24	421	1	145	703	....
Hanson's brigade	....	....	....	10	37	32	241	3	78	401	....
Total	513	6,540	7,053	28	238	116	1,310	10	366	2,068	29⅓
Cleburne's Division.											
Staff	....	....	....			2			...	2	....
Wood's brigade	....	....	....	7	45	20	319	5	108	504	....
Johnson's brigade	....	....	....	5	56	46	442	9	48	606	....
Liddell's brigade	....	....	....	6	80	32	471	....	18	607	....
Polk's brigade	....	....	....	4	26	42	256		19	347	....
Total	840	6,176	7,016	22	207	142	1,488	14	193	2,066	29½
Total Hardee's corps	1,353	12,716	14,069	50	445	258	2,798	24	559	4,134	29⅜
McCown's division	319	4,095	4,414	8	86	101	661	9	97	962	21⅘
Jackson's brigade	89	785	874	1	40	11	251		......	303	34⅔
Total infantry and artillery	2,832	30,643	33,475	116	1,135	634	7,108	38	786	9,817	29⅓
CAVALRY.											
Wheeler's brigade	124	1,045	1,169	5	17	12	49	3	81	167	14⅓
Wharton's brigade	158	1,792	1,950	2	18	11	120	4	109	264	13½
Pegram's brigade (no return)	30	450	480	....	....	....	....	....	....	....	....
Buford's brigade	52	586	638	......	1	2	9	1	5	18	2⅞
Total cavalry	364	3,873	4,237	7	36	25	178	8	195	449	11⅞
Grand total	3,196	34,516	37,712	123	1,171	659	7,286	46	981	10,266	27 4/7

In estimating the percentage of loss, the aggregate, 480, reported by General Pegram, from whom no report of killed, wounded, and missing was received, is to be deducted from 4,237, aggregate of cavalry, and from 37,712, grand aggregate.

GEORGE WM. BRENT.

TULLAHOMA, *February* 2, 1863.

[Inclosure C—Continued.]

Tabular statement of the number present for duty on December 31, 1862; the number of killed, wounded, and missing, and the percentage of loss in the brigades of Breckinridge's division at the battle of Murfreesborough.

Breckinridge's division.	Present for duty.			Commissioned officers.			Enlisted men.					
	Commissioned officers.	Enlisted men.	Aggregate.	Killed.	Wounded.	Missing.	Killed.	Wounded.	Missing.	Total.	Aggregate.	Percentage of loss.
December 31, 1862:												
Pillow's brigade	129	1,446	1,575	1	1	......	1	19	1	21	23	1¼
Preston's brigade....	143	1,808	1,951	2	11	......	14	129	7	150	163	8¼
Adams' brigade......	100	1,534	1,634	7	18	......	75	326	118	519	544	33½
Hanson's brigade*...	141	1,752	1,893	......	......	......	......	......	......	......	......	......
Total	513	6,540	7,053	10	30	......	90	474	126	690	730	10⅔
January 2, 1863:												
Pillow's brigade	......	......	......	5	31	2	42	273	49	364	402	25½
Preston's brigade....	......	......	......	2	17	4	40	227	86	353	376	19¼
Adams' brigade......	......	......	......	1	6	1	29	95	27	151	159	9½
Hanson's brigade....	......	......	......	10	32	3	37	241	78	356	401	21¼
Total	513	6,540	7,053	18	86	10	148	836	240	1,224	1,338	19

RECAPITULATION.

Total force engaged in the several battles	7,053
Total loss	2,068
Percentage of loss	29½

—

HEADQUARTERS ARMY OF TENNESSEE,
Winchester, [Tenn.], January 8, 1863.

SOLDIERS OF THE ARMY OF TENNESSEE! Your gallant deeds have won the admiration of your general, your Government, and your country. For myself, I thank you, and am proud of you; for them, I tender you the gratitude and praise you have so nobly won.

In a campaign of less than one month, in the face of winter, your achievements have been unparalleled. You have captured more than 10,000 prisoners, taken and preserved 30 pieces of artillery and 7,000 small-arms, in addition to many thousands destroyed. You have, besides, captured 800 wagons, loaded chiefly with supplies, which have been destroyed or brought safely to your lines; and in pitched battles you have driven the enemy before you, inflicting a loss at least three to one greater than you have sustained.

In retiring to a stronger position, without molestation from a superior force, you have left him a barren field in which to bury his hosts of slain, and to rally and recuperate his shattered ranks. Cut off from his Government, both by rail and telegraph, and deprived of supplies by the interruption of his communications, we shall yet teach him a severe lesson for the rashness of penetrating a country so hostile to his cause. Whilst the infantry and artillery defy him in front, our invincible cavalry will assail him in flank and rear, until we goad him to another advance, only to meet another signal defeat.

---

* Hanson's brigade not in action, December 31, 1862. Deducting its strength, 1,893, percentage is 14½ on December 31.

Your general deplores, in common with you, the loss of your gallant comrades, who have fallen in our recent conflicts. Let their memories be enshrined in your hearts, as they will ever be tenderly cherished by their countrymen. Let it be yours to avenge their fate, and proudly to emulate their deeds. Remember that your face is to the foe, and that on you rests the defense of all that is dear to freemen. Soldiers, the proudest reflection of your general's life is to be known as the commander of an army so brave and invincible as you have proven. He asks no higher boon than to lead such men to victory. To share their trials, and to stand or fall with them, will be the crown of his ambition.

BRAXTON BRAGG,
General, Commanding.

No. 191.

Return of casualties in the Confederate forces.

[Compiled from nominal lists.]

Command.	Killed.			Wounded.			Missing.			Aggregate.	Officers killed.
	Officers.	Enlisted men.	Total.	Officers.	Enlisted men.	Total.	Officers.	Enlisted men.	Total.		
POLK'S CORPS.											
CHEATHAM'S DIVISION.											
Donelson's Brigade.											
8th Tennessee	4	37	41	17	248	265				306	Col. William L. Moore, Capt. William Sadler, and Lieuts. Thomas O. Blacknall, A. G. Denton, and N. Martin Kerby.
16th Tennessee	1	35	36	8	147	155	1	15	16	207	Capt. D. C. Spurlock.
38th Tennessee	1	11	12	5	68	73				85	Capt. B. H. Holland.
51st Tennessee	1	10	11	7	65	72	...	3	3	86	Capt. T. C. Campbell.
Carnes' battery	...	2	2	...	5	5		...	..	7	
Total	7	95	102	37	533	570	1	18	19	691	
Stewart's Brigade.											
4th and 5th Tennessee	1	7	8	6	62	68			..	76	Lieut J. P. Ferguson.
19th Tennessee	2	14	16	6	105	111			...	127	Capt. S. J. A. Frazier and Lieut. S. G. Abernathy.
24th Tennessee	3	6	9	5	39	44			...	53	Capt. Jesse Irwin and Lieuts. J. B. Arnold and J. S. Hardison.
31st and 33d Tennessee	1	13	14	7	64	71	...	2	2	87	Lieut. W. P. Hutcherson.
Stanford's battery	1	2	3	...	7	7			...	10	Lieut. A. A. Hardin.
Total	8	42	50	24	277	301	..	2	2	353	
Maney's Brigade.											
1st Tennessee	....	8	8	1	74	75			...	83	
4th Tennessee	....	5	5	5	44	49			...	54	
6th and 9th Tennessee	....	5	5	5	27	32	...	5	5	42	
Maney's Sharpshooters	....	1	1	...	4	4			...	5	
Smith's battery	....	1	1	...	4	4	...	1	1	6	
Total	....	20	20	11	153	164	....	6	6	190	
Smith's Brigade.											
12th Tennessee	1	17	18	12	125	137	....	9	9	164	Lieuts. J. S. Fielder and J. H. Patterson.
13th Tennessee	1	12	13	6	82	88	1	8	9	110	Maj. Peter H. Cole.
29th Tennessee	...	27	27	8	74	82		...	....	109	

Return of casualties in the Confederate forces—Continued.

Command.	Killed.			Wounded.			Missing.			Aggregate.	Officers killed.
	Officers.	Enlisted men.	Total.	Officers.	Enlisted men.	Total.	Officers.	Enlisted men.	Total.		
Smith's Brigade—Cont'd.											
47th Tennessee	1	10	11	7	56	63	1	11	12	86	Capt. James H. Sinclair.
154th Senior Tennessee	1	13	14	6	78	84	....	3	3	101	Lieut. C. S. Hall.
9th Texas	2	16	18	8	94	102	1	1	2	122	Lieuts. R. F. Luckett and E. B. Parham.
Allin's Sharpshooters	1	2	3	1	5	6	....	3	3	12	Lieut. A. M. Bunch. Lt. J. R. J. Creighton died of wounds.
Scott's battery	....	1	1	....	....	....	....	....	....	1	
Total	7	98	105	48	514	562	3	35	38	705	
Grand total Cheatham's division.	22	255	277	120	1,477	1,597	4	61	65	1,939	
WITHERS' DIVISION.											
Deas' Brigade.											
19th Alabama	1	7	8	13	130	143	....	3	3	154	Capt. Robert J. Healey, Lieuts. J. N. Smith and J. H. Wall.
22d Alabama	2	9	11	6	77	83	....	....	....	94	
25th Alabama	3	13	16	10	79	89	....	4	4	109	Lieuts. W. C. Gibson, A. A. Patterson, and H. B. Scofield.
26th Alabama	....	4	4	6	70	76	....	....	....	80	
39th Alabama	....	3	3	9	83	92	....	....	....	95	
1st Louisiana Regulars	2	6	8	7	64	71	....	23	23	102	Lieuts. B. C. Cenas and Bringier Trist.
17th Battalion Alabama Sharpshooters.	....	3	3	1	14	15	....	....	....	18	
Robertson's battery	....	....	....	....	19	19	....	1	1	20	
Total	8	45	53	52	536	588	....	31	31	672	
Chalmers' Brigade.											
Staff	....	....	....	1		1	....	....	....	1	
7th Mississippi	3	9	12	9	88	97	....	4	4	113	Capt. R. D. McDowell and Lts. H. J. M. Harrigill and G. W. Jones.
9th Mississippi	....	8	8	5	66	71	....	5	5	84	
10th Mississippi	2	6	8	8	62	70	....	6	6	84	Lieuts. J. F. Moseley and D. W. Owen.
41st Mississippi	3	22	25	8	115	123	....	8	8	156	Lieuts. F. M. Betts, W. G. Kennedy, and P. H. McMahon.
Blythe's (Mississippi) regiment.	....	4	4	1	30	31	1	16	17	52	
9th Mississippi Battalion Sharpshooters.	....	7	7	....	22	22	....	....	....	29	
Garrity's battery	....	3	3	2	18	20	....	....	....	23	
Total	8	59	67	34	401	435	1	39	40	542	
Walthall's Brigade.											
45th Alabama	....	13	13	5	66	71	....	7	7	91	
24th Mississippi	....	8	8	5	103	108	....	....	....	116	
27th Mississippi	2	9	11	5	66	71	....	1	1	83	Lieut. Col. James L. Autry and Lieut. M. C. Edwards.
29th Mississippi	4	30	34	14	188	202	....	....	....	236	Capt. H. J. Harper and Lieuts. W. G. Barksdale, W. A. McDaniel, and R. S. Spencer.
30th Mississippi	6	57	63	10	136	146	....	....	....	209	Lieuts. T. W. Boone, G. W. Hope, W. J. McGuire, J. C. McIntyre, D. R. Patton and E. B. Ridus.
29th North Carolina	1	1	2	3	33	36	....	6	6	44	Lieut. John W. Rhea.
Barret's battery	....	....	....	....	4	4	....	....	....	4	
Total	13	118	131	42	596	638	....	14	14	783	

Return of casualties in the Confederate forces—Continued.

Command.	Killed.			Wounded.			Missing.			Aggregate.	Officers killed.
	Officers.	Enlisted men.	Total.	Officers.	Enlisted men.	Total.	Officers.	Enlisted men.	Total.		
Anderson's Brigade.											
24th Alabama	1	19	20	3	92	95	....	3	3	118	Capt. William D. Smith.
28th Alabama	1	16	17	11	77	88	....	11	11	116	Not ascertained.
34th Alabama	....	11	11	6	71	77	....	....	....	88	
10th South Carolina	....	16	16	6	85	91	....	2	2	109	
19th South Carolina	1	7	8	8	64	72	....	..	....	80	Maj. John A. Crowder and Lieut. J. T. Norris died of wounds.
Waters' battery	....	1	1	....	5	5	....	....	....	6	
Total	3	70	73	34	394	428	....	16	16	517	
Grand total Withers' division.	32	292	324	162	1,927	2,089	1	100	101	2,514	
Grand total Polk's corps.	54	547	601	282	3,404	3,686	5	161	166	4,453	
HARDEE'S CORPS.											
BRECKINRIDGE'S DIVISION.											
Adams' Brigade, December 31.											
32d Alabama	2	19	21	4	80	84	....	21	21	126	Lieuts. J. J. Keith and Hiram Slay.
13th and 20th Louisiana	2	18	20	10	79	89	....	78	78	187	Lieuts. D. C. Levy and R. O. Smith.
16th and 25th Louisiana	3	34	37	3	156	159	...	17	17	213	Colonel Fisk and Lieuts. Henry Gregory and A. Ranlett.
Austin's Sharpshooters	....	4	4	1	8	9	....	2	2	15	
Slocomb's battery	..	..	....	....	3	3	....	....	....	3	
Total December 31	7	75	82	18	326	344	....	118	118	544	
Adams' Brigade, January 2.											
32d Alabama	....	..	....	....	2	2	....	....	....	2	Lieut. Charles Hepburn
13th and 20th Louisiana	1	25	26	5	74	79	1	23	24	129	
16th and 25th Louisiana	....	4	4	1	16	17	....	4	4	25	
Austin's Sharpshooters	....	..	....	....	..	....	....	....	....		
Slocomb's battery	....	1	1	...	2	2	....	....	....	3	
Total January 2	1	30	31	6	94	100	1	27	28	159	
Total December 31 and January 2.	8	105	113	24	420	444	1	145	146	703	
Pillow's Brigade, December 31.											
18th Tennessee	....	..	....	....	13	13	....	....	....	13	
26th Tennessee	....	1	1	....	3	3	....	1	1	5	
28th Tennessee	....	..	....	....	..	....	....	....	....		
45th Tennessee	....	1	1	....	4	4	....	....	....	5	
Moses' battery	....	..	....	....	..	....	....	...	....		
Total December 31	....	2	2	....	20	20	....	1	1	23	
Pillow's Brigade, January 2.											
18th Tennessee	2	15	17	16	91	107	....	8	8	132	Capt. John Dick and Lieut. Sam'l M. Smith.
26th Tennessee	1	8	9	7	71	78	....	17	17	105	Capt. Edwin Allen.
28th Tennessee	3	8	11	7	49	56	....	9	9	76	Colonel Cunningham and Lieuts. J. L. Proffitt and J. M. Saylors.

Return of casualties in the Confederate forces—Continued.

Command.	Killed.			Wounded.			Missing.			Aggregate.	Officers killed.
	Officers.	Enlisted men.	Total.	Officers.	Enlisted men.	Total.	Officers.	Enlisted men.	Total.		
Pillow's Brigade, January 2—Continued.											
45th Tennessee		12	12	2	77	79	1	16	17	108	
Moses' battery					4	4				4	
Total January 2	6	43	49	32	292	324	1	50	51	425	
Total December 31 and January 2.	6	45	51	32	312	344	1	51	52	448	
Preston's Brigade, December 31.											
1st and 3d Florida		2	2	2	13	15	1	1	2	19	
4th Florida		6	6	1	49	50		1	1	57	
60th North Carolina		1	1	2	27	29		4	4	34	
20th Tennessee	2	6	8	5	40	45				53	Capt. J. W. Watkins and Lieut. F. B. Crosthwait.
Wright's battery											
Total December 31	2	15	17	10	129	139	1	6	7	163	
Preston's Brigade, January 2.											
1st and 3d Florida		5	5	4	69	73		41	41	119	
4th Florida		28	28	6	73	79		30	30	137	
60th North Carolina		2	2		29	29		10	10	41	
20th Tennessee		2	2	9	47	56		7	7	65	
Wright's battery	1	3	4	1	7	8		2	2	14	Capt. E. E. Wright.
Total January 2	1	40	41	20	225	245		90	90	376	
Total December 31 and January 2.	3	55	58	30	354	384	1	96	97	539	
Hanson's Brigade.											
41st Alabama	2	14	16	4	90	94		38	38	148	Lieuts. J. T. Hardaway and N. B. Lenderman.
2d Kentucky		13	13	9	61	70		21	21	104	
4th Kentucky	6	6	12	6	43	49		8	8	69	Maj. Willis S. Roberts Capt. William P. Bramblett, and Lieuts. Geo. B. Burnley, Nathaniel D. Clayton, Robert Dunn, and Green F. Higginson.
6th Kentucky	1	1	2	8	21	29		14	14	45	Capt. G. Utterback.
9th Kentucky *											
Cobb's battery		3	3		3	3				6	
Total	9	37	46	27	218	245		81	81	372	
Grand total Breckinridge's division.	26	242	268	113	1,304	1,417	3	373	376	2,061	
CLEBURNE'S DIVISION.											
Staff				2		2				2	
Wood's Brigade.											
Staff				1		1				1	
16th Alabama	5	19	24	8	134	142				166	Lieuts. David E. Bentley, R. W. Garland, Lewis E. Jackson, Robert W. Roebuck, and Benjamin H. Russell.

* NOTE ON ORIGINAL RETURN.—"The Ninth Kentucky, Col. Thomas H. Hunt, being detached at Manchester, Tenn., no report has been received."

Return of casualties in the Confederate forces—Continued.

Command.	Killed.			Wounded.			Missing.			Aggregate.	Officers killed.
	Officers.	Enlisted men.	Total.	Officers.	Enlisted men.	Total.	Officers.	Enlisted men.	Total.		
Wood's Brigade—Cont'd.											
33d Alabama		14	14	3	83	86	....	1	1	101	
3d Confederate		5	5	3	24	27	....	37	37	69	
45th Mississippi	1	4	5	4	35	39	6	64	70	114	Capt. J. D. Frazier.
15th Battalion Mississippi Sharpshooters	1	2	3	....	25	25	....	5	5	33	Capt. D. Coleman.
Semple's battery	....	1	1	1	18	19	....	....	....	20	
Total	7	45	52	20	319	339	6	107	113	504	
Johnson's Brigade.											
Staff				2		2				2	
17th Tennessee	1	16	17	10	154	164	6	20	26	207	Capt. F. M. Orr.
23d Tennessee		3	3	2	38	40	....	8	8	51	
25th Tennessee	1	15	16	11	78	89	2	13	15	120	Lieut. Simpson Isom.
37th Tennessee	1	10	11	6	45	51	....	6	6	68	Maj. J. T. McReynolds.
44th Tennessee	1	13	14	15	121	136	1	1	2	152	Lieut. J. J. Hill.
Darden's battery					6	6				6	
Total	4	57	61	46	442	488	9	48	57	606	
Liddell's Brigade.											
Staff				1	2	3				3	
2d Arkansas		15	15	1	93	94	....	9	9	118	
5th Arkansas	1	11	12	9	126	135	....	1	1	148	Lieut. A. J. Jones.
6th and 7th Arkansas	3	26	29	12	128	140	....	8	8	177	Capt. J. T. Armstrong and Lieuts. J. L. McCollum and Henry Fisher.
8th Arkansas	4	25	29	10	114	124				153	Lieuts. T. H. Beard, S. B. Cole, Calvin East, and H. J. McCurdy.
Swett's battery	....	1	1	....	7	7				8	
Total	8	78	86	33	470	503	....	18	18	607	
Polk's Brigade.											
1st Arkansas		11	11	9	81	90	....	1	1	102	
13th and 15th Arkansas		4	4	2	47	59	....	5	5	68	
5th Confederate		7	7	9	55	64	....	12	12	83	Capt. C. P. Moore and Lieut. J. L. Gifford.
2d Tennessee	2	2	4	6	53	59				63	
5th Tennessee		1	1	1	23	24				25	
Calvert's battery		3	3	....	2	2		1	1	6	
Total	2	28	30	37	261	298	....	19	19	347	
Grand total Cleburne's division.	21	208	229	138	1,492	1,630	15	192	207	2,066	
Grand total Hardee's corps.	47	450	497	251	1,796	3,047	18	565	583	4,127	
McCOWN'S DIVISION.											
Ector's Brigade.											
Staff				2	2	4				4	
10th Texas Cavalry *		10	10	12	81	93	1	14	15	118	Lieuts. M. V. Clary, L. G. Hefner, and J. M. Hopson mortally wounded.
11th Texas Cavalry *		8	8	10	79	89	3	15	18	115	Col. John C. Burks mortally wounded.

* Dismounted.

Return of casualties in the Confederate forces—Continued.

Command.	Killed.			Wounded.			Missing.			Aggregate.	Officers killed.
	Officers.	Enlisted men.	Total.	Officers.	Enlisted men.	Total.	Officers.	Enlisted men.	Total.		
Ector's Brigade—Cont'd.											
14th Texas Cavalry *		5	5	10	42	52	1	11	12	69	
15th Texas Cavalry *		5	5	5	31	36		3	3	44	
Douglas' battery					2	2				2	
Total		28	28	39	237	276	5	43	48	352	
Rains' Brigade.											
3d Georgia Battalion		6	6	5	28	33				39	Lieut. W. L. Prior mortally wounded.
9th Georgia Battalion		1	1	2	9	11				12	
29th North Carolina		5	5	3	47	50		5	5	60	
11th Tennessee		8	8	10	54	64		11	11	83	
Eufaula (Ala.) Artillery					3	3		2	2	5	
Total		20	20	20	141	161		18	18	199	
McNair's Brigade.											
1st Arkansas Rifles		9	9	13	69	82		4	4	95	
2d Arkansas Rifles	1	9	10	17	82	99	4	7	11	120	Capt. Thomas F. Spence.
4th Arkansas		8	8	9	52	61	1	9	10	79	
4th Arkansas Battalion	1	4	5		19	19		5	5	29	Lieut. W. C. Douglass.
30th Arkansas	2	8	10	12	51	63		22	22	95	Capt. S. T. Black and Lieut. D. J. Wright.
Humphreys' battery				1	5	6				6	
Total	4	38	42	52	278	330	5	47	52	424	
Escort company		2	2		2	2		1	1	5	
Grand total Mc-Cown's division. †	4	88	92	111	658	769	10	109	119	980	
JACKSON'S BRIGADE.											
5th Georgia	2	10	12		48	48				60	Col. William T. Black and Lieut. J. W. Eason.
2d Georgia Battalion Sharpshooters		3	3	3	26	29				32	
5th Mississippi	1	5	6	8	66	74				80	Capt. J. H. Morgan.
8th Mississippi	1	19	20	12	101	113				133	Lieut. J. J. Hood.
Total ‡	4	37	41	23	241	264				305	

RECAPITULATION.

Command.	Killed.			Wounded.			Missing.			Aggregate.	
	Officers.	Enlisted men.	Total.	Officers.	Enlisted men.	Total.	Officers.	Enlisted men.	Total.		
Polk's corps	54	547	601	282	3,404	3,686	5	161	166	4,453	
Hardee's corps	47	450	497	251	1,796	3,047	18	565	583	4,127	
McCown's division	4	88	92	111	658	769	10	109	119	980	
Jackson's brigade	4	37	41	23	241	264				305	
Grand total §	109	1122	1236	667	6,099	7,766	33	835	868	9,865	

* Dismounted.

†Notes on original lists indicate that all these casualties, except 4 of the wounded in Rains' brigade, occurred December 31, 1862.

‡ Note on original list indicates that all these, except 1 man wounded January 2, 1863, occurred near Cowan's house, between 12 noon and 4 p. m., December 31, 1862.

§ No nominal lists for Buford's, Wharton's, or Wheeler's cavalry brigades; but see Inclosure C to Bragg's report, p. 674. No returns from Pegram's cavalry brigade.

[Addenda.]

HEADQUARTERS BRECKINRIDGE'S DIVISION,
Tullahoma, Tenn., January 12, 1863.

General BRAXTON BRAGG, C. S. Army:

GENERAL : In answer to your letter of yesterday,* I have the honor to state that, in a council at your headquarters, on the evening of the 3d of January, at which Lieutenant-Generals Polk and Hardee and Major-General Cleburne were the other officers present, I advised you to retire from before Murfreesborough the same night. About 12 o'clock of that day, Lieutenant-General Hardee informed me that a retrograde movement had been resolved upon, and as my division was to cover the movement of his corps, he authorized me to make preliminary arrangements, but directed me not to give a final order; and also desired me to be present at your headquarters at 7 o'clock in the evening. During that afternoon the baggage and ordnance trains were moved down the Shelbyville and Manchester turnpikes, as I understood, by your order. The question at the conference on the evening of the 3d was, not whether the army should fall back (that movement had been determined on, and in part executed, before I was called into council), but whether the movement of the troops should be postponed for twenty-four hours, to communicate with General Wheeler (then supposed to be near La Vergne), and more thoroughly to close up our rear. I advised that the movement should take place that night; and it is just to you to add that if I had been in consultation on the morning of that day, when it was resolved to retire, I would have approved the movement. I do not enter into the reasons which governed my advice, since your communication does not ask for them, but confines itself to the necessity of the retreat at the time it was commenced.

In obedience to your wishes, I have this day had a conference with the brigade commanders of my division, Generals Pillow and Preston and Colonels Trabue and Gibson. These gentlemen were not sure as to the points upon which you desired their views, since they were not called into council on the question of retiring the army. But, after carefully reading your letter, they supposed that you desired their opinion in regard to the retreat, and to the confidence, or want of it, in you as a commander, on the part of the officers and troops. Accordingly, acting with the candor which you invoke, they request me to say that, in their opinion, the conduct of the military operations in front of Murfreesborough made it necessary for our army to retire. They also request me to say that while they entertain the highest respect for your patriotism, it is their opinion that you do not possess the confidence of the army to an extent which will enable you to be useful as its commander. In this opinion I feel bound to state that I concur.

You state as within your own knowledge that staff officers of your generals have persistently asserted that our retreat was made in opposition to the wishes of their chiefs. I can speak only for my own staff, and have the honor to state that, after thorough inquiry, I have reason to believe that representations of the character to which you refer have not been made by any member of my staff.

In closing, general, I have the honor to state that the brigade commanders of my division spoke of you throughout in terms of high personal respect, and to add that in this regard I fully share their feelings.

Very respectfully, your obedient servant,

JOHN C. BRECKINRIDGE,
Major-General.

---

* See Inclosure No. 1, Polk to Davis, February 4, 1863, p. 699.

TULLAHOMA, TENN., *January* 12, 1863.

General BRAXTON BRAGG, *Commanding, &c.*:

GENERAL: I have the honor to acknowledge the receipt of your note of yesterday,* in which, after informing me of the assaults to which you are subjected, you invoke a response in regard to the propriety of the recent retreat from Murfreesborough, and request me to consult my subordinate commanders in reference to the topics to which you refer. You will readily appreciate the delicate character of the inquiries you institute, but I feel, under the circumstances, that it is my duty to reply with the candor you solicit, not only from personal respect to yourself, but from the magnitude of the public interests involved.

In reference to the retreat, you state that the movement from Murfreesborough was resisted by you for some time, after advised by your corps and division commanders. No mention of retreat was made to me until early on the morning of the 3d of January, when Lieutenant Richmond, of General Polk's staff, read me the general's note to you, and informed me of your verbal reply. I told him, under the circumstances, nothing could be done then. About 10 o'clock the same day I met you personally at your quarters, in compliance with your request, Lieutenant-General Polk being present. You informed me that the papers of General McCook had been captured, and, from the strength of his corps (18,000), it appeared that the enemy was stronger than you had supposed; that General Wheeler reported he was receiving heavy re-enforcements, and, after informing us of these facts, suggested the necessity of retreat, and asked my opinion as to its propriety. Having heard your statements and views, I fully concurred, and it was decided to retreat. No preparation was made by me or my division commanders to retreat which was resisted by you for some time, and I recall your attention to the fact. Afterward, in the evening, about 7 o'clock, we met to arrange details, and the retreat being still deemed advisable, and having been partially executed, I concurred in an immediate movement, in view of the heavy losses we had sustained, and the condition of the troops.

You also request me to consult my subordinate commanders, stating that General Smith has been called to Richmond, with the view, it was supposed, to supersede you, and that you will retire without regret, if you have lost the good opinion of your generals, upon whom you have ever relied as upon a foundation of rock. I have conferred with Major-General Breckinridge and Major-General Cleburne in regard to this matter, and I feel that frankness compels me to say that the general officers, whose judgment you have invoked, are unanimous in the opinion that a change in the command of this army is necessary. In this opinion I concur. I feel assured that this opinion is considerately formed, and with the highest respect for the purity of your motives, your energy, and your personal character; but they are convinced, as you must feel, that the peril of the country is superior to all personal considerations.

You state that the staff officers of your generals, joining in the public and private clamor, have, within your knowledge, persistently asserted that the retreat was made against the opinion and advice of their chiefs. I have made inquiries of the gentlemen associated with me, and they inform me that such statements have not been made or circulated by them.

I have the honor, general, to assure you of my continued respect and consideration, and to remain, your obedient servant,

W. J. HARDEE,
Lieutenant-General.

---

* See Inclosure No. 1, Polk to Davis, February 4, 1863, p. 699.

HEADQUARTERS POLK'S CORPS,
Shelbyville, January 13, 1863.

General BRAXTON BRAGG:

Since this army commenced falling back from Murfreesborough, 1 have, upon all occasions, publicly and privately, stated that I, myself, was one of the first to suggest the movement, and fully indorsed it.

B. F. CHEATHAM,
Major-General, Commanding.

—

TULLAHOMA, *January* 13, 1863.

General BRAXTON BRAGG,
Commanding Army of Tennessee :

GENERAL : I have received your communication of the 11th instant,* with inclosures, and will answer candidly, as you desire. I understood the retrograde movement to have been decided upon, and partially executed, before we met in council on Saturday night, the 3d instant, and the only question presented to me, and the only question before us there, to be, whether the movement should be suspended, as far as practicable, for twenty-four hours. To this I replied that, in my opinion, it could be suspended. I offered advice on no other point. Subsequently, on learning fully the condition of General Polk's corps and General Breckinridge's division, I felt it my duty to say to you that in answering as I had just done I had looked only to the condition of my own division; that it had been successful in the fight, and, notwithstanding its losses and weariness, was still capable of making a firm resistance; that I was also influenced by the fact that my men had had no sleep the previous night, having suffered and repelled a night attack of the enemy, and immediately thereafter been moved from the extreme left to the right of the army, which led me to fear that, in case of a retreat, involving, as it must, the loss of another night's rest, large numbers of my men would fall out by the way, and I might in this manner lose as many as in an attack by the enemy in our then position. I further stated that, in case the enemy attacked us, I believed the chances were in favor of our repulsing him, but that it might turn out otherwise, and that it was for you to decide whether our cause should be risked on a cast the issue of which was doubtful; that I believed the final success of our cause depended in a great measure upon the safety of this army.

I have consulted with all my brigade commanders at this place, as you request, showing them your letter and inclosures, and they unite with me in personal regard for yourself, in a high appreciation of your patriotism and gallantry, and in a conviction of your great capacity for organization, but at the same time they see, with regret, and it has also met my observation, that you do not possess the confidence of the army in other respects in that degree necessary to secure success.

I have, general, the honor to be, respectfully, your obedient servant,

P. R. CLEBURNE,
Major-General.

_____

* See Inclosure No. 1, Polk to Davis, February 4, 1863, p. 699.

No. 192.

Report of Lieut. Gen. Leonidas Polk, C. S. Army, commanding Army Corps, with resulting correspondence.

HEADQUARTERS ARMY OF TENNESSEE,
Winchester, Tenn., March 24, 1863.

SIR : I have the honor to transmit the report by Lieut. Gen. L. Polk, with those of division and brigade commanders, of the operations of his corps at the battle of Murfreesborough. This report, though dated February 28, was only transmitted, as will be seen by its accompanying letter, on the 21st, and was received at this office on March 22. The accompanying map* has some inaccuracies in regard to troops and operations not under the general's command, but not to the extent of materially affecting its usefulness. The general requests leave of absence for an officer of his staff to carry this report to Richmond and transact other official business for his corps. I request the officer named be ordered to deliver the report to the Adjutant-General, but be confined to that specific duty. All other official business must be transacted through these headquarters.

I am, sir, very respectfully, your obedient servant,
BRAXTON BRAGG,
General, Commanding.

Col. B. S. EWELL,
Assistant Adjutant-General, &c.

[Inclosure No. 1.]

HEADQUARTERS POLK'S CORPS, ARMY OF TENNESSEE,
Shelbyville, Tenn., March 21, 1863.

I have the honor herewith to transmit my official report of the battles before Murfreesborough, with accompanying statements and map.* I send also copies of the report of Major-General [B. F.] Cheatham, and of the brigade, regimental, and battery commanders of his division; also a list of its casualties. Major-General [J. M.] Withers, having been absent on sick leave since the battle, has not sent me his report. It will be forwarded in a few days. The report of brigade, regimental, and battery commanders of his division, with a list of casualties, have been already forwarded to you. As these papers are of importance, and as I have other matters of interest to my corps to be attended to, I have to respectfully request that I be permitted to send a staff officer with them to Richmond. Lieut. P. B. Spence, who is the bearer of this, is the officer I desire to send. To accomplish this, I ask for him fifteen days' leave of absence.

I have the honor to be, very respectfully, your obedient servant,
L. POLK,
Lieutenant-General, Commanding.

Col. GEORGE WILLIAM BRENT,
Assistant Adjutant-General.

[Inclosure No. 2.]

HDQRS. POLK'S CORPS D'ARMÉE, ARMY OF TENNESSEE,
Shelbyville, Tenn., February 28, 1863.

SIR : I have the honor to submit the following as my official report of the operations of my corps in the battles on Stone's River, in front of Murfreesborough:

One of my brigades (that of General Maney) was on outpost duty in

---

* To appear in Atlas.

front of Stewart's Creek, and, with a cavalry brigade under General Wheeler, was held in observation. The enemy made a general forward movement on the 26th in their immediate front, and they were ordered to retire slowly upon the line of battle which the general commanding had decided to adopt—on Stone's River, a short distance from Murfreesborough.

On the evening of the 28th, my brigades struck their tents and retired their baggage.trains to the rear, and on the morning of the 29th they were placed in line of battle. As the brigades composing the division of Major-General Withers had not been engaged in any heavy battle since that of Shiloh, I placed them in the first line.* They extended from the river, near the intersection of the Nashville turnpike and railroad, southward across the Wilkinson pike to the Triune or Franklin road, in a line irregular, but adapted to the topography. The division of Major-General Cheatham was posted in the rear of that of Major-General Withers, as a supporting force. The division of Major-General McCown, of Lieut. Gen. Kirby Smith's army corps, was in prolongation of that of General Withers, on the left, having that of Major-General Cleburne, of Lieutenant-General Hardee's corps, as its supporting force. Major-General Breckinridge's division, of Lieutenant-General Hardee's corps, occupied the ground on the east side of the river, in the line of Major-General Withers, on the right. The enemy moved forward, and our outposts fell back slowly and took their place in the line of battle on the 29th.

On the 30th, in order to discover the position at which we proposed to offer battle, he moved up cautiously, shelling his front heavily as he advanced. The cannonading was responded to along our line, and the theater of impending conflict was speedily determined. On the left of my line the skirmishing became very active, and my left brigades, front and rear, became hotly engaged with the line which was being formed immediately before them. The enemy pressed forward very heavily with both artillery and infantry, and a sharp contest ensued, in which he attempted, with several regiments, to take one of my batteries by assault, but was repulsed in the most decisive manner. In this preliminary onset many lives were lost on both sides. It was, from its severity, an appropriate introduction to the great battle of the ensuing day and prepared our troops for the work before them. Twilight following soon after, the enemy settled around his bivouac fires for the night.

Orders were issued by the general commanding to attack in the morning at daybreak. The attack was to be made by the extreme left, and the whole line was ordered to swing around from left to right upon my right brigade as a pivot. Major-General Breckinridge, on the extreme right and across the river, was to hold the enemy in observation on that flank.

At the appointed time the battle opened, evidently to the surprise of the opposing army. Major-General McCown, who was acting under the orders of Lieutenant-General Hardee, was upon them before they were prepared to receive him. He captured several batteries and one brigadier-general, wounded another, and drove three brigades—those composing the division of Brigadier-General [R. W.] Johnson—in confusion before him. He was followed quickly by Major-General Cleburne as a

---

* The division of Major-General Withers was placed in the front line by my order. See memoranda to general and staff officers, accompanying my report.

BRAXTON BRAGG,
General Commanding.

supporting force, who occupied the space left vacant by the forward movement of McCown between the left of my front line and McCown's right. Opposing him in that space was the Second Division, of Major-General [A. McD.] McCook's corps, under the command of Brig. Gen. J. C. Davis, to confront which he had to wheel to the right, as the right of General McCook's corps was slightly refused. Cleburne's attack, following so soon on that of McCown, caught the force in his front also not altogether prepared, and the vigor of the assault was so intense that they, too, yielded and were driven.

Major-General Withers' left was opposed to the right of General Sheridan, commanding the Third and remaining division of General McCook's corps. The enemy's right was strongly posted on a ridge of rocks, with chasms intervening, and covered with a dense growth of rough cedars. Being advised of the attack he was to expect by the fierce contest which was being waged on his right, he was fully prepared for the onset, and this notice and the strength of his position enabled him to offer a strong resistance to Withers, whose duty it was to move next. Colonel [J. Q.] Loomis, who commanded the left brigade, moved up with energy and spirit to the attack. He was wounded and was succeeded by Colonel [J. G.] Coltart. The enemy met the advance with firmness, but was forced to yield. An accession of force aided him to recover his position, and its great strength enabled him to hold it. Coltart, after a gallant charge and a sharp contest, fell back, and was replaced by Colonel [A. J.] Vaughan, [jr.], of Major-General Cheatham's division, of the rear line. Vaughan, notwithstanding the difficulties of the ground, charged the position with great energy; but the enemy, intrenched behind stones and covered by the thick woods, could not be moved, and Vaughan also was repulsed. This caused a loss of time, and Cleburne's division, pressing Davis, reached a point where Sheridan's batteries, still unmoved, by wheeling to the right, enfiladed it. Colonel Vaughan was speedily reorganized and returned to the assault, and, in conjunction with Colonel Coltart, drove at the position with resistless courage and energy; and although their losses were very heavy, the enemy could not bear up against the onset. He was dislodged and driven with the rest of the fleeing battalions of McCook's corps.

In this charge the horses of every officer of the field and staff of Vaughan's brigade, except one, and the horses of all the officers of the field and staff of every regiment, except two, were killed. The brigade lost also one-third of all its force. It captured two of the enemy's field guns.

The brigade of Colonel [A. M.] Manigault, which was immediately on the right of that of Colonel Coltart, followed the movement of the latter, according to instructions; but as Coltart failed in the first onset to drive Sheridan's right, Manigault, after dashing forward and pressing the enemy's line in his front back upon his second line, was brought under a very heavy fire of artillery from two batteries on his right, supported by a very heavy infantry force. He was, therefore, compelled to fall back.

In this charge the brigade suffered severely, sustaining a very heavy loss in officers and men, but the gallant South Carolinians* returned to the charge a second and a third time, and, being aided by the brigade of General [G.] Maney, of the second line, which came to his relief with its heavy Napoleon guns and a deadly fire of musketry, the enemy gave way and joined his comrades on the right in their precipitate retreat

---

* See Indorsement No. 2, p. 697.

across the Wilkinson pike. This movement dislodged and drove the residue of Sheridan's division, and completed the forcing of the whole of McCook's corps out of its line of battle and placed it in full retreat. The enemy left one of his batteries of four guns on the field, which fell into the hands of Maney's brigade.

Here I think it proper to bring to the notice of the general commanding an instance of self-sacrificing devotion to the safety of their immediate commands and of our cause, which, for heroic courage and magnanimity, is without a parallel. A battery was pouring a murderous fire into the brigade of General Maney from a point which made it doubtful whether it was ours or the enemy's. Two unsuccessful efforts had been made by staff officers (one of whom was killed in the attempt) to determine its character. The doubt caused the brigade on which it was firing to hesitate in returning the fire, when Sergeant Oakley, color-bearer of the Fourth Tennessee Confederate Regiment, and Sergt. M. C. Hooks, color-bearer of the Ninth Tennessee Regiment, gallantly advanced 8 or 10 paces to the front, displaying their colors and holding themselves and the flag of their country erect; remained ten minutes in a place so conspicuous as to be plainly seen, and fully to test from whom their brigade was suffering so severely. The murderous firing, instead of abating, was increased and intensified, and soon demonstrated that the battery and its support were not friends but enemies. The sergeants then returned deliberately to their proper positions in the line, unhurt, and the enemy's battery was silenced and his column put to flight. The front of Manigault and Maney being free, they swung round with our line on the left and joined in pressing the enemy and his re-enforcements into the cedar brake.

At 9 a. m. Brig. Gen. [J.] Patton Anderson, on Manigault's right, moved, in conjunction with its left brigade, forward upon the line in its front. That line rested with its right near the Wilkinson pike, and is understood to have been General [J. S.] Negley's division, of General [G. H.] Thomas' corps, which constituted the center of the enemy's line of battle. This division, with that of General [L. H.] Rousseau in reserve, was posted in the edge of a dense cedar brake, with an open space in front, and occupied a position of strength not inferior to that held by Sheridan's right. His batteries, which occupied commanding positions, and enabled him to sweep the open field in his front, were served with admirable skill and vigor, and were strongly supported. Anderson moved forward his brigade with firmness and decision. The fire of the enemy of both artillery and infantry was terrific, and his left for a moment wavered. Such evidences of destructive firing as were left on the forest from which this brigade emerged have rarely, if ever, been seen. The timber was torn and crushed. Nothing but a charge could meet the demands of the occasion. Orders were given to take the batteries at all hazards, and it was done. The batteries, two in number, were carried in gallant style. Artillerists were captured at their pieces, a large number of whom and of their infantry support were killed upon the spot, and one company entire, with its officers and colors, were captured. The number of field guns captured in this movement was eight, which, together with four others, from which the gunners had been driven by the heavy firing from Maney's long-range guns and Manigault's musketry on the left, made twelve taken on that part of the field. This was one of the points at which we encountered the most determined opposition, but the onward movement of the Mississippians and Alabamians was irresistible, and they swept the enemy before them, driving him into the dense cedar brake, to join the extending line of his fugitives.

This work, however, was not done without a heavy loss of officers and men. The Thirtieth Mississippi, commanded by Lieutenant-Colonel [J. I.] Scales, in the act of charging, lost 62 officers and men killed and 139 wounded; others lost in proportion. Here the brave Lieut. Col. James L. Autry, of the Twenty-seventh Mississippi, fell while cheering and encouraging his troops.

The supporting brigade of General Anderson, commanded by Brig. Gen. A. P. Stewart, moved with that of Anderson. It was ordered by the division commander (Major-General Withers, who was in command of Major-General Cheatham's two right brigades as Major-General Cheatham was of his two left) to move to the support of the left regiments of Anderson, which were pressed. These regiments, which had suffered greatly, he replaced, and, moving forward, attacked the enemy and his re-enforcements on Anderson's left. After strong resistance they were driven back, shattered and in confusion, to join the host of their fleeing comrades in their retreat through the cedars. In their flight they left two of their field guns, which fell into the hands of Stewart's brigade.

Brigadier-General Chalmers' brigade (the remaining one of those constituting my front line), whose right flank rested on the river, was the last to move. This brigade, owing to its position in the line, was called on to encounter a measure of personal suffering from exposure beyond that of any other in my corps. The part of the line it occupied lay across an open field in full view of the enemy, and in range of his field guns. It had thrown up a slight rifle-pit, behind which it was placed, and to escape observation it was necessary for it to lie down and abstain from building fires. In this position it remained awaiting the opening of the battle for more than forty-eight hours, wet with rain and chilled with cold; added to this the enemy's shot and shell were constantly passing over it. Not a murmur of discontent was heard to escape those who composed it. They exhibited the highest capacity of endurance and firmness in the most discouraging circumstances. In its front lay the right of Brigadier-General [J. M.] Palmer's division, of Major-General [T. L.] Crittenden's corps, which constituted the left wing of the enemy's line of battle.

The general movement from the left having reached it at 10 o'clock, it was ordered to the attack, and its reserve, under Brigadier-General Donelson, was directed to move forward to its support. This charge was made in fine style, and was met by the enemy, who was strongly posted in the edge of the cedar brake, with a murderous fire of artillery and infantry. In that charge their brigade commander (General Chalmers) was severely wounded by a shell, which disqualified him for further duty on the field. The regiments on the left recoiled and fell back. Those of the right were moved to the left to hold their place, and were pressed forward. The brigade of General Donelson having been ordered forward to Chalmers' support, moved with steady step upon the enemy's position and attacked it with great energy. The slaughter was terrific on both sides.

In this charge—which resulted in breaking the enemy's line at every point except the extreme left, and driving him, as every other part of his line attacked had been driven—Donelson reports the capture of 11 guns and about 1,000 prisoners.

The regiments of Chalmers' brigade, having been separated after he fell, moved forward and attached themselves to other commands, fighting with them with gallantry as opportunity offered.

There was no instance of more distinguished bravery exhibited during this battle than was shown by the command of General Donelson. In the charge which it made it was brought directly under the fire of several batteries, strongly posted and supported, which it assaulted with eager resolution. All the line in their front was carried except the extreme right. This point, which was the key to the enemy's position, and which was known as the Round Forest, was attacked by the right of the brigade. It was met by a fire from artillery and musketry which mowed down more than half its number. The Sixteenth Regiment Tennessee Volunteers, under the command of Col. John H. Savage, lost 207 out of 402. It could not advance and would not retire. Their colonel, with characteristic bravery and tenacity, deployed what was left of his command as skirmishers and held his position for three hours. In the Eighth Tennessee, of the right wing, under the lamented Colonel [W. L.] Moore, who fell, mortally wounded, and who was succeeded by Lieut. Col. J. H. Anderson, the loss was 306 men and officers out of 425.

The enemy was now driven from the field at all points occupied by him in the morning, along his whole line, from his right to the extreme left, and was pressed back until our line occupied a position at right angles to that which we held at the opening of the battle. After passing the Nashville and Murfreesborough turnpike, his flight was covered by large bodies of fresh troops and numerous batteries of artillery, and the advance of our exhausted columns was checked. His extreme left alone held its position. This occupied a piece of ground well chosen and defended, the river being on the one hand and a deep railroad cut on the other. It was held by a strong force of artillery and infantry, well supported by a reserve composed of Brigadier-General [T. J.] Wood's division.

My last reserve having been exhausted, the brigades of Major-General Breckinridge's division, and a small brigade of [Brigadier-]General J. K. Jackson, posted to guard our right flank, were the only troops left that had not been engaged. Four of these were ordered to report to me. They came in detachments of two brigades each, the first arriving nearly two hours after Donelson's attack, the other about an hour after the first. The commanders of these detachments, the first composed of the brigades of Generals [D. W.] Adams and Jackson, the second under General Breckinridge in person, consisting of the brigades of General [William] Preston and Colonel [J. B.] Palmer, had pointed out to them the particular object to be accomplished, to wit, to drive in the enemy's left, and, especially, to dislodge him from his position in the Round Forest. Unfortunately, the opportune moment for putting in these detachments had passed. Could they have been thrown upon the enemy's left immediately following Chalmers' and Donelson's assault in quick succession, the extraordinary strength of his position would have availed him nothing. That point would have been carried, and his left, driven back on his panic-stricken right, would have completed his confusion and insured an utter rout. It was, however, otherwise, and the time lost between Donelson's attack and the coming up of these detachments in succession enabled the enemy to recover his self-possession, to mass a number of heavy batteries, and concentrate a strong infantry force on the position, and thus make a successful attack very difficult. Nevertheless, the brigades of Adams and Jackson assailed the enemy's line with energy, and, after a severe contest, were compelled to yield and fall back. They were promptly rallied by General Breckinridge, who, having preceded his other brigades, reached the ground at that moment, but as they were very much cut up, they were not required to renew the attack. The brigades of Preston and Palmer, on arriving, renewed the assault with the same undaunted determination, but as another battery had been added since the previous attack, to a position already strong and difficult of access, this assault was alike ineffectual. The enemy, though not driven from his position, was severely punished, and, as the day was far spent, it was not deemed advisable to renew the attack that evening, and the troops held the line they occupied for the night.

The following morning, instead of finding him in position to receive a renewal of the attack, showed that, taking advantage of the night, he had abandoned this last position of his first line, and the opening of the new year found us masters of the field.

This battle of December 31 developed in all parts of the field which came under my observation the highest qualities of the soldier among our troops. The promptness with which they moved upon the enemy whenever they were called to attack him, the vigor and *élan* with which their movements were made, the energy with which they assaulted his strong positions, and the readiness with which they responded to the call to repeat their assaults, indicated a spirit of dauntless courage, which places them in the very front rank of the soldiers of the world. For the exhibition of these high traits they are not a little indebted to the example of their officers, whose courage and energy had won their confidence and admiration.

January 1 passed without any material movement of either side, beyond occasional skirmishing along the lines in our front. I ordered Chalmers' brigade, now commanded by Colonel [T. W.] White, [Ninth Mississippi,] to occupy the ground in rear of the Round Forest just abandoned by the enemy. This it did, first driving out his pickets

On the 2d there was skirmishing during the morning. In the afternoon, about 3 o'clock, General Bragg announced his intention to attack the enemy, who was supposed to be in force on the north side of the river, and ordered me to relieve two of General Breckinridge's brigades, which were still in my front, and send them over to that officer, who had returned to his post, as he proposed to make the attack with the troops of Breckinridge's division. I issued the necessary orders at once, and the troops were transferred as directed. The general commanding ordered me also to open fire with three batteries, which had been placed in Chalmers' line, to distract the enemy at the time of Breckinridge's attack, and to shell out of the woods which covered his line of movement any sharpshooters who might annoy him while approaching the river. The shelling ordered, which was to be the signal for Breckinridge's advance, was promptly executed and the woods were cleared. Of the particulars of this movement General Breckinridge will speak in his own report.

When the firing of my batteries was opened, as above, there was a forward movement of the enemy's infantry upon my pickets in the Round Forest, and a sharp conflict, which lasted for some time, and ended in the enemy's regaining possession of the forest. This position being of much value to us, I found it necessary to regain it, and gave the requisite orders.

On the following morning, at daybreak, I ordered a heavy fire of artillery from several batteries to open upon it, and, after it was thoroughly shelled, detachments from the brigades of Colonels White and Coltart charged it with the bayonet at a double-quick and put the enemy to flight, clearing it of his regiments and capturing a lieutenant-colonel and 13 men. The enemy, however, knew the importance of the position also, and was occupied during the day in throwing up earthworks for the protection of batteries within easy range. These being completed, he opened fire from three points with batteries of heavy guns, and placed it under a concentrated fire for many minutes. It was a severe ordeal, and was followed by a charge of a heavy force of infantry; but our gallant troops met the advance with firmness, and, after a severely contested struggle, drove back the advancing column with slaughter and held possession of the coveted position.

In this battle we lost several men and officers, especially of the First Louisiana Regiment (Regulars). Among those who fell mortally wounded was Lieutenant-Colonel [F. H.] Farrar, [jr.] This young officer was one of the most promising of the army, intelligent, chivalrous, and brave. His loss will be felt by his country and lamented by his many friends.

This battle closed the operations of my corps in the field in front of Murfreesborough. By orders from the general commanding, after being eight days under arms, and in actual battle or heavy skirmishing, in the rain and cold without tents and much of the time without fires, my troops were retired from the field and ordered to take up a position near Shelbyville. This they did at their leisure, and in perfectly good order. In all the operations in which they were engaged no troops ever displayed greater gallantry or higher powers of endurance. They captured 1,500 prisoners and 26 guns.

For the details connected with these operations I beg leave to refer to the reports of division, brigade, and regimental commanders. To the same reports, also, I respectfully refer for instances of distinguished gallantry in the case of corps and individuals. I beg leave to refer also to the accompanying statement, marked A, containing a list of the number of men and officers of my corps engaged in the battle; also to B, containing the number of killed, wounded, and missing. I refer also to the accompanying map of the field of battle, marked Bb.* This map was prepared with care by Lieutenant [W. J.] Morris, of the engineers of my corps, from actual survey, and from the reports of the corps commanders of the Federal Army. From these sources he has been enabled to fix the relative positions of the corps, divisions, and brigades of both armies at different periods during the battle with great accuracy. The statements D and B I submit as parts of this report; also the accompanying map, marked Bb.*

To Major-Generals Cheatham and Withers, my division commanders, I am under obligations for their cordial support and active co-operation in conducting the operations of my command; also to the brigade commanders, who, without an exception, managed the parts assigned them in the general programme of the battle with great skill, energy, and judgment. Of the conduct of the regimental, battery, and subordinate commands their immediate commanders will speak in their reports, as they were more directly under their eyes. Our artillery also was well handled when it could be used, but the dense cedar brake into which the enemy was driven continuously prevented it from following our advancing columns. This made it necessary to have the work done chiefly with the musket and the bayonet.

To Maj. George Williamson, assistant adjutant-general, who was severely wounded in the shoulder; Maj. Thomas M. Jack, assistant adjutant-general; Lieut. Col. T. F. Sevier, inspector-general; Lieut. P. B. Spence, of the same department; Lieut. John Rawle, acting chief of ordnance; Capt. Felix [H.] Robertson, acting chief of artillery; Capt. E. B. Sayers and Lieut. W. J. Morris, of engineers; Lieut. W. N. M. Otey, chief of the signal corps; Dr. [W. C.] Cavanaugh, medical director;

---

* On file.

Majs. Thomas Peters and R. M. Mason, of the quartermaster's department, and Maj. J. J. Murphy, chief commissary, members of my general staff, I am indebted for their vigilance and activity in the execution of my orders, and the fearlessness with which they exposed themselves in the discharge of their duties.

To my aide-de-camp (Lieut. W. B. Richmond) I am particularly indebted for the intelligence, decision, and energy with which on this, as on other fields, he gave me his support; also to Lieut. Col. Henry C. Yeatman, my volunteer aide, for services of a like character. And our thanks and praise are above all due to Almighty God, the Lord of Hosts, for the success of our arms and the preservation of our lives.

I have the honor to be, respectfully, your obedient servant,

L. POLK,
Lieutenant-General, Commanding.

Col. GEORGE WILLIAM BRENT,
Assistant Adjutant-General.

[Inclosure A.]

Field return showing the aggregate of officers and men belonging to Polk's corps d'armée actually engaged in the battles before Murfreesborough, from December 28, 1862, to January 4, 1863.

Command.	Officers.	Men.	Total.	Remarks.
Cheatham's division *	496	5,863	6,359	Wharton's (commanding cavalry brigade) reported effective total, 2,376, on December 27; weekly return.
Withers' division	537	7,237	7,774	
Total	1,033	13,100	14,133	

L. POLK,
Lieutenant-General, Commanding.

SHELBYVILLE, TENN., *March* 22, 1863.

[Inclosure B.]

List of killed, wounded, and missing in Polk's corps in the battles before Murfreesborough, from December 28, 1862, to January 4, 1863.

Command.	Killed.	Wounded.	Missing.	Total.
Cheatham's division :				
Donelson's brigade	102	570	19	691
Stewart's brigade	50	301	2	353
Maney's brigade	20	164	6	190
Vaughan's brigade	105	562	38	705
Total	277	1,597	65	1,939
Withers' division:				
Deas' brigade	68	600	27	695
Chalmers' brigade	67	445	36	548
Walthall's brigade	130	620	13	763
Anderson's brigade	73	428	16	517
Total	338	2,093	92	2,523
Aggregate	615	3,690	157	4,462

W. B. RICHMOND,
Aide-de-Camp.

HEADQUARTERS POLK'S CORPS, ARMY OF TENNESSEE,
Shelbyville, March 21, 1863.

---

* But see inclosure to Cheatham's report, p. 709.

[Appendix.]

HEADQUARTERS POLK'S CORPS,
Shelbyville, Tenn., April 6, 1863.

In my report of the battles before Murfreesborough there occurs the following passage:

My last reserve having been exhausted, the brigades of Major-General Breckinridge's division, and a small brigade of General J. K. Jackson, posted to guard our right flank, were the only troops left that had not been engaged. Four of these were ordered to report to me. They came in detachments of two brigades each, the first arriving nearly two hours after Donelson's attack, the other about an hour after the first.

I then expressed the opinion that if these brigades could have followed the attack of Chalmers and Donelson in quick succession the result of our operations would have been a complete victory. I have been informed that certain friends of General Breckinridge, who have seen my report, apprehend that the manner in which these statements are made will produce the impression that these brigades were ordered to my support at the time I first desired them, and that they failed to comply with the order, one detachment arriving two hours after it was ordered, and the other an hour later. I desire to say that it was not my intention to produce such an impression. I did not know at what time they were ordered to my support. I perceived that they would be needed, and asked for them before the attack by Chalmers and Donelson was ordered; but whether they would be sent me or not I did not know until just before they reported to me on the field.

With the request that this may accompany and be made a part of my report, I have the honor to be, respectfully, your obedient servant,

L. POLK,
Lieutenant-General, Commanding.

General S. COOPER,
Adjutant and Inspector General, Richmond, Va.

[Indorsement.]

HEADQUARTERS ARMY OF TENNESSEE,
Tullahoma, Tenn., May 2, 1863.

I transmit this explanatory report of Lieutenant-General Polk. In the language of his original report I see no suggestion that the brigades of Breckinridge did not reach the field of action in due time after being ordered. Had I done so I would have corrected it. They moved as soon as ordered, and I ordered them as soon as I ascertained that the fears of an attack on the right were groundless.

BRAXTON BRAGG,
General, Commanding.

—

HDQRS. ANDERSON'S BRIG., WITHERS' DIV., POLK'S CORPS,
Near Shelbyville, June 10, 1863.

Maj. THOMAS M. JACK,
Asst. Adjt. Gen., Polk's Corps, Army of Tennessee:

MAJOR: I have to-day, for the first time, seen the official report of the battle of Murfreesborough, by the lieutenant-general commanding the corps. As I know of no one who would be further from doing the slightest injustice, even by implication, than General Polk, I would respectfully call his attention, through you, to a paragraph in that report which might be construed prejudicially to the well-earned fame of a portion of the troops under my command.

The paragraph to which I allude is as follows:

As the brigades composing the division of Major-General Withers had not been engaged in any heavy battle since Shiloh, I placed them in the first line.

The brigade which I had the honor to command on that occasion (now Walthall's), and a part of Withers' division, composed entirely of Mississippians, except one regiment of Alabamians (Forty-fifth), had been in every important engagement in which any part of General Bragg's army had participated since the battle of Shiloh. They are justly proud of the laurels they won at Perryville.

The brigade I now command (then Chalmers'), also Mississippians, and a portion of General Withers' command at Murfreesborough, had singly and alone made the bloody assault upon the enemy's works at Munfordville, which, although unsuccessful at the time, was essayed with such intrepidity and courage as to reflect the highest credit upon the survivors, as well as the slain.

One regiment of this brigade (the Forty-first) was also in the battle of Perryville.

Both of the brigades thus composing half of General Withers' division at Murfreesborough had been engaged in heavy battles since Shiloh, and will, doubtless, be excepted by General Polk from the class to which he assigns them when the fact is brought to his notice.

I feel confident the lieutenant-general will pardon me for bringing this matter to his attention, since my course has been actuated by a desire that he should do himself, as well as the troops, no injustice by an immaterial paragraph in his report, inserted, perhaps, inadvertently, certainly without design of doing any injustice.

I am, major, very respectfully, your obedient servant,

PATTON ANDERSON,
Brigadier-General.

[Indorsements.]

HEADQUARTERS WITHERS' DIVISION,
POLK'S CORPS, ARMY OF TENNESSEE.

Respectfully forwarded.

The error to which attention is called was not considered by me of sufficient importance to require correction, as it was not in reference to any fact deemed material to the subject-matter of the report. As, however, the ten Mississippi and one Alabama regiments who were engaged either at Perryville or Munfordville composed more than the half of my command participating in the engagement in front of Murfreesborough now seem sensitive under what they consider a reflection in the remark referred to, I have deemed it proper to forward this communication with approval.

J. M. WITHERS,
Major-General.

HEADQUARTERS POLK'S CORPS,
Shelbyville, June 17, 1863.

I am much obliged to General Anderson for bringing to my notice the paragraph in my report to which he calls attention. It was, of course, an inadvertence, and is easily accounted for. In placing my troops in line of battle, the question in my mind was as to which of the divisions I should give the post of honor—the front rank. General Cheatham.

as the senior officer, was entitled to it, but remembering that General Withers' division was not at Perryville (the only general battle fought by this army since Shiloh), I thought it due to him that he should have it, and to satisfy all parties I thought proper to assign the reason for that arrangement.

It will be remembered that Walthall's brigade was only recently transferred to Withers' division. It belonged to Hardee's corps at Perryville, and in thinking of Withers' division in its past history and action, it did not occur to me that there had been any changes in its composition, or that any troops that were at Perryville now belonged to it. The same is true in regard to the gallant brigade of General Chalmers, now commanded by General Anderson. I, of course, know of the distinguished intrepidity with which it assailed the works at Munfordville, and the heavy losses it sustained, but as I was thinking of the brigades as part of a division of which I was speaking, and not as separate brigades, it did not occur to me to make it an exception.

General Anderson does me no more than justice in saying that he regards me as incapable of doing injustice, even by implication, to any one, and, I will add, especially to troops the whole history of whose connection with me has won my highest admiration, and around whose brow I would rather weave garlands of well-earned fame than to be the occasion, even by inadvertence, of the loss of a single leaf from the chaplets with which they deserve to be crowned.

L. POLK,
Lieutenant-General, Commanding.

—

NEAR SHELBYVILLE, *June* 16, 1863.

Maj. THOMAS M. JACK,
 Assistant Adjutant-General, Polk's Corps:

MAJOR: In his recently published official report of the battle of Murfreesborough, Lieutenant-General Polk, referring to the part taken in the action by the Fourth Brigade of Withers' division, uses this language:

> The brigade of Colonel Manigault, which was immediately on the right of that of Colonel Coltart, followed the movement of the latter according to instructions; but as Coltart failed in the first onset to drive Sheridan's right, Manigault, after dashing forward and pressing the enemy's line in his front back upon his second line, was brought under a very heavy fire of artillery from two batteries on his right, supported by a very heavy infantry force. He was, therefore, compelled to fall back.
>
> In this charge the brigade suffered severely, sustaining a very heavy loss in officers and men, but the gallant South Carolinians returned to the charge a second and a third time.

We respectfully suggest that this language is susceptible of a construction which may cause the reader to award to a part of the brigade honors which, to say the least, are merited as well by another part of it. Such was not the intention of the writer. A soldier himself, he would not willingly withhold from a soldier that which is most highly prized by him—credit for gallantry on the battle-field. We, then, do justice alike to Lieutenant-General Polk and to our own respective commands by directing attention to the inaccuracy in the above recited extract.

The brigade of Colonel Manigault is not composed entirely of South Carolinians, as would be reasonably inferred from the report. In it are five regiments, two from South Carolina (Tenth and Nineteenth) and three from Alabama (Twenty-fourth, Twenty-eighth, and Thirty-fourth), and Waters' (Alabama) battery.

The first charge spoken of in the report was led by the three Alabama regiments. The report does not mention them.

All the Alabama regiments were in the second charge, and led in it. They were also in the third charge. The report states that "the gallant South Carolinians returned to the charge the second and third time."

Respectfully submitting this statement of facts, we ask for it that consideration it may seem to merit, feeling satisfied, as we do, that the lieutenant-general commanding will acquit us of any intention to captiously controvert his report, and that he will do what is proper in the premises.

With much respect, your obedient servants,

J. C. B. MITCHELL,
Colonel Thirty-fourth Alabama.
JOHN C. REID,
Colonel Twenty-eighth Alabama.
N. N. DAVIS,
Lieutenant-Colonel Twenty-fourth Alabama.
D. D. WATERS,
Captain Waters' Battery.

[Indorsement No. 1.]

Respectfully forwarded.

The matter to which the attention of the lieutenant-general commanding is called in this communication is reasonable, and is, in justice to the command herein represented, approved by me. The inference drawn from that portion of the report of the battle of Murfreesborough, as cited, is that the brigade which I commanded was composed either entirely of South Carolinians or that only the South Carolinians of the brigade are credited for gallantry, renewing the attacks after being repulsed.

The Alabama regiments partook in all the attacks, as my report will show, and I again take this opportunity of bearing testimony to the heroic courage and fortitude displayed by them on that bloody field.

The general conduct of all the regiments on that occasion was such that I can draw no distinction between them.

A. M. MANIGAULT,
Colonel, Comdg. Fourth Brigade, Withers' Division.

[Indorsement No. 2.]

HEADQUARTERS POLK'S CORPS,
June 22, 1862.

In reply to the within, I have to say to the officers commanding the Alabama regiments, that the ground of their complaint does not exist in my report as written and sent to War Department. It was said by the printer in a misprint. It was written, "the gallant South Carolinian," meaning their brigade commander, Colonel Manigault, not "South Carolinians." Although the troops from the Palmetto State acted with distinguished gallantry, yet they were in no degree more distinguished for gallantry than their comrades from Alabama, who, side by side, shared with them the difficulties and all the triumphs of that bloody field. My object was to compliment their brigade commander, and through him his whole command, for the tenacity of purpose and unflinching bravery with which they returned time and again to the charge, until they carried the position which had so often resisted them.

Respectfully, &c.,

L. POLK,
Lieutenant-General, Commanding.

HEADQUARTERS POLK'S CORPS, ARMY OF TENNESSEE,
February 4, 1863.

His Excellency JEFFERSON DAVIS,
     President Confederate States of America :

MY DEAR SIR : I know that you have been apprised of a correspondence which has taken place between General Bragg and the corps and division commanders of Hardee's corps, of this army, following upon the retreat from Murfreesborough. As the same circular which was answered by the officers of Hardee's corps was received by those of mine, I think it proper to send you a copy of the correspondence which passed between General Bragg and myself. You will find it inclosed with this, as follows :

No. 1. General Bragg's circular.
No. 2. Generals Cheatham's and Withers' note.
No. 3. My indorsement on same.
No. 4. My reply of 30th, asking an explanation of his circular.
No. 5. His letter in reply.
No. 6. My answer to the question he proposed.

This correspondence has been very unfortunate, and its inauguration ill-judged ; but it is now a part of the history of the times, and I feel it to be my duty to transmit to you copies of the letters which have passed between the general and myself. That correspondence speaks for itself. I thought, with the officers of Hardee's corps, that he desired an opinion on two points. Some of my subordinate commanders had thought, and others then thought, that he desired us to reply to but one. As he desired us to consult our subordinates before answering, the difference of opinion as to the construction of his note made it plainly proper to ask him which was the proper construction. To have this was necessary to an intelligible and satisfactory reply. It will be seen what the reply was, which made my final answer plain and easy. I think it would not be difficult from the form of my note for him to have inferred what my answer would have been if he had asked. It was waived and declined. Under the circumstances it would seem to have been natural for him to desire to know the opinions of all, as he had been forced to know those of half of his subordinates of the highest grade, but, as I have said, it was declined. I feel it a duty to say to you that had I and my division commanders been asked to answer, our replies would have coincided with those of the officers of the other corps. You have known my opinions on this subject since my visit to Richmond.

I have only to add, if he were Napoleon or the great Frederick he could serve our cause at some other points better than here. My opinion is he had better be transferred. I remember you having said, speaking of his being transferred from this command, "I can make good use of him here in Richmond." I have thought that the best disposition for him and for the service of the army that could be made. His capacity for organization and discipline, which has not been equaled among us, could be used by you at headquarters with infinite advantage to the whole army.

I think, too, that the best thing to be done in supplying his place would be to give his command to General Joseph E. Johnston. He will cure all discontent and inspire the army with new life and confidence. He is here on the spot, and I am sure will be content to take it. If General Lee can command the principal army in his department in person there is no reason why General Johnston should not. I have, therefore, as a general officer of this army, speaking in behalf of my associates, to ask, respectfully, that this appointment be made, and I beg to be permitted to do this urgently. The state of this army demands immediate attention, and its position before the enemy, as well as the mind of its troops and commanders, could find relief in no way so readily as by the appointment of General Joseph E. Johnston.

I send this by mail, and will send copies by my aide-de-camp, Lieutenant Richmond, whom I send to Richmond on business with the department, and by whom I also send my report of the battle of Shiloh. In it I have taken care that the presence of our valued friend on that field shall not be ignored.

I remain, faithfully, your friend,

L. POLK,
Lieutenant-General, Commanding.

[Inclosure No. 1.]

HEADQUARTERS ARMY OF TENNESSEE,
Tullahoma, Tenn., January 11, 1863.

Lieutenant-General POLK,
Commanding Polk's Corps, Asheville, N. C.:

GENERAL: Finding myself assailed in private and public by the press, in private circles by officers and citizens, for the movement from Murfreesborough, which was resisted by me for some time after advised by my corps and division commanders, and only adopted after hearing of the enemy's re-enforcements by large numbers from Kentucky, it becomes necessary for me to save my fair name, if I cannot stop the deluge of abuse, which will destroy my usefulness and demoralize this army.

It has come to my knowledge that many of these accusations and insinuations are from staff officers of my generals, who persistently assert that the movement was made against the opinion and advice of their chiefs, and while the enemy was in full retreat. False or true, the soldiers have no means of judging me rightly or getting the facts, and the effect on them will be the same—a loss of confidence, and a consequent demoralization of the whole army. It is only through my generals that I can establish the facts as they exist. Unanimous as you were in council in verbally advising a retrograde movement, I cannot doubt that you will cheerfully attest the same in writing. I desire that you will consult your subordinate commanders and be candid with me, as I have always endeavored to prove myself with you. If I have misunderstood your advice, and acted against your opinions, let me know it, in justice to yourself. If, on the contrary, I am the victim of unjust accusations, say so, and unite with me in staying the malignant slanders being propagated by men who have felt the sting of discipline.

General [E. K.] Smith has been called to Richmond, it is supposed, with a view to supersede me. I shall retire without a regret if I find I have lost the good opinion of my generals, upon whom I have ever relied as upon a foundation of rock.

Your early attention is most desirable, and is urgently solicited.

Most respectfully, your obedient servant,*

BRAXTON BRAGG,
General, C. S. Army.

P. S.—I inclose copies of a joint note, received about 2 a. m., from Major-Generals Cheatham and Withers, on the night before we retired from Murfreesborough [No. 2], with Lieutenant-General Polk's indorsement [No. 3], and my own verbal reply to Lieutenant [W. B.] Richmond, General Polk's aide-de-camp.

---

* Similar letters to Breckinridge, Cleburne, Cheatham, and Hardee. For their replies, see "Correspondence, etc.," Part II.

[Inclosure No. 2.]

HEADQUARTERS IN THE FIELD,
Murfreesborough, Tenn., January 3, 1863—12.15 a. m.
General BRAGG, *Commanding, &c.:*

GENERAL: We deem it our duty to say to you frankly that, in our judg-ment, this army should be promptly put in retreat.   You have but three brigades [divisions*] that are at all reliable, and even some of these are more or less demoralized from having some brigade commanders who do not possess the confidence of their commands.   Such is our opinion, and we deem it a solemn duty to express it to you.   We do fear great disas-ter from the condition of things now existing, and think it should be averted if possible.

Very respectfully, general, your obedient servant,
B. F. CHEATHAM,
Major-General, C. S. Army.
J. M. WITHERS,
Major-General.

[Indorsement No. 1.]

JANUARY 3, 1863—1.30 a. m.

MY DEAR GENERAL: I send you the inclosed paper, as requested, and I am compelled to add that after seeing the effect of the operations of to-day, added to that produced upon the troops by the battle of the 31st, I very greatly fear the consequences of another engagement at this place in the ensuing day.   We could now, perhaps, get off with some safety and some credit, if the affair is well managed.   Should we fail in the meditated attack, the consequences might be very disastrous.

Hoping you may be guided aright in whatever determination you may reach, I am, very truly, yours,

L. POLK,
Lieutenant-General.

[Indorsement No. 2.]

I gave the inclosed note, with the above indorsement on it, to General Bragg in his bed at 2 a. m.   After reading one-half of it, he said, "Say to the general we shall maintain our position at every hazard."
W. B. RICHMOND,
Aide-de-Camp.

[Inclosure No. 3.]

HEADQUARTERS POLK'S CORPS,
Murfreesborough, Tenn., January 3, 1863—3 a. m.
Lieutenant-General HARDEE,
Commanding Hardee's Corps:

MY DEAR GENERAL: After due reflection, I deemed it my duty to make the following indorsement [No. 1] upon the accompanying note, signed jointly by two division commanders, Major-Generals Cheatham and Withers, and addressed to General Bragg.   I have sent the note and indorsement to General Bragg by a staff officer, whom I instructed to await any reply the general might be pleased to make.   After reading them, his reply was, "The position will be maintained at all hazards." I think the decision of the general unwise, and, am compelled to add, in a high degree.   I shall, of course, obey his orders and endeavor to do my duty.   I think it due to you to let you know the views of myself and

---

*See Cheatham and Withers to Polk, March 21, 1863, p. 702.

my two division commanders, especially as we all believe the conflict will be renewed in the morning. To insure its safe conduct, I send this by a staff officer.

Very respectfully, your obedient servant,

L. POLK,
Lieutenant-General, Commanding.

[Inclosure No. 4.]

TULLAHOMA, TENN., *January 30, 1863.*

General BRAXTON BRAGG,
Commanding Army of Tennessee:

GENERAL : Your circular of the 11th instant was received by me at Asheville, N. C., on the 17th instant. I dispatched you immediately, saying I would leave for your headquarters in two days thereafter, and would furnish you the reply you desired on my arrival. There seemed to be two points of inquiry embraced in your note : First, whether the corps and division commanders to whom it is addressed were willing to give you a statement in writing of the opinions and counsel which they gave you verbally as to the retreat from Murfreesborough ; second, whether you had lost the confidence of your general officers as a military commander. From the structure of your note the first of the inquiries appears to be its leading object ; the second, though not so clearly and separately stated, nevertheless is, to my mind, plainly indicated. Upon inquiry, I find this indication seems not to have been so clear to the mind of General Cheatham and such other of my subordinate officers as responded when they penned their replies, and since in your note you appeal to our official relations, and to our candor for a frank expression of our opinion, I feel, to avoid being placed in a false position, that it is due to my subordinate officers and to myself, as well as to you, to ask whether the construction I put upon your note is that you design.

Very respectfully, your obedient servant,

L. POLK,
Lieutenant-General, Commanding.

[Inclosure No. 5.]

TULLAHOMA, TENN., *January 30, 1863.*

Lieutenant-General POLK, &c.:

GENERAL : I hasten to reply to your note of this morning, so as to place you beyond all doubt in regard to the construction of mine of the 11th instant. To my mind that circular contained but one point of inquiry, and it certainly was intended to contain but one, and that was to ask of my corps and division commanders to commit to writing what had transpired between us in regard to the retreat from Murfreesborough. I believed it had been grossly and intentionally misrepresented (not by any one of them) for my injury. It was never intended by me that this should go farther than the parties to whom it was addressed, and its only object was to relieve my mind of all doubt, while I secured in a form to be preserved the means of defense in the future when discussion might be proper. The paragraph relating to my supersedure was only an expression of the feeling with which I should receive your replies should they prove I had been misled in my construction of your opinion and advice.

I am, general, very respectfully, &c.,

BRAXTON BRAGG,
General, Commanding.

[Inclosure No. 6.]

TULLAHOMA, TENN., *January* 31, 1863.

General BRAGG:

GENERAL: I am in receipt of yours of the 30th, in reply to mine of the same date. In it you say you designed your circular should contain but one point of inquiry, and that was whether your corps and division commanders would give you for future reference a statement of what transpired between us in regard to the retreat from Murfreesborough. I have, therefore, now to say that the opinions and counsel which I gave you on that subject prior to the retreat are those that are embodied in my indorsement of the note of my division commanders (Generals Cheatham and Withers) of January 3,* which are in your possession, and I have to add that they were deliberately considered, and are such as I would give again under the same circumstances.

Respectfully, your servant,

L. POLK,
Lieutenant-General, Commanding.

—

[Addenda.]

SHELBYVILLE, TENN., *March* 21, 1863.

Lieutenant-General POLK,
Commanding Corps, Army of Tennessee:

GENERAL: To-day for the first we feel assured of a verbal mistake having been committed in the note addressed by us through you to the general commanding, bearing date "Headquarters in the Field, Murfreesborough, Tenn., January 3, 1863—12.15 a. m."† The second sentence, beginning "You have but three brigades," should have been You have but three divisions, &c. We make this correction simply to place ourselves right, not that we consider the mistake of writing brigades when we purposed and believed we had written divisions either did or should have altered the determination at last arrived [reached?].

Will you, general, do us the justice to transmit this explanation to the general commanding, and oblige, very respectfully, &c.,

B. F. CHEATHAM,
Major-General, C. S. Army.
J. M. WITHERS,
Major-General.

—

TULLAHOMA, TENN., *April* 2, 1863.

Lieut. Gen. LEONIDAS POLK,
Shelbyville, Tenn.:

GENERAL: I have your letter of the 31st ultimo, and thank you for the explanations you give me. I never supposed that you intended the construction to be placed on that part of your report which I feared might be.

Still, I apprehend that many persons, not reading critically, may infer that I was responsible for the failure to gain a complete victory, since it is stated that four of my brigades were ordered to report to you; that they came in detachments of two each, at long intervals, and too late to accomplish the result, which would have been the utter rout of the enemy if they had arrived in time.

Many may say, since I was ordered to report four brigades to you, how did it happen that they came in two detachments, the first two

---

* See Indorsement No. 1, p. 700.   † See Inclosure No. 2, p. 700.

hours after the time, and the other still an hour later, when their timely arrival would have changed the face of affairs?

It occurs to me that the inference will be unfavorable to my conduct, although not conclusive against me. Of course, you could not know when I received the orders, nor with what alacrity I obeyed them, except from my own report. All I could request would be the exclusion of an inference that, in obeying an order to report to you with four brigades, I had delayed two hours with half the force, and three hours with the remainder. The question, as it affects me personally, is not, did the brigades arrive too late for the opportune moment, but, is it inferable from the report that I was responsible for it. If an erroneous construction is placed on your report, it may work me great injury, since it will be read by many thousands through the Confederacy.

With the kindness and frankness which has always marked your intercourse with me, you say that if it had occurred to you that this construction might be put upon your language, you would have so shaped it as to make such an interpretation impossible, and that, if I think it of any importance to me, you will endeavor to have the correction made before your report is printed.

Under the circumstances that surround me, it will be grateful to my feelings if you can, in the way you deem best, exclude the construction to which I have referred.

Very truly, your friend,

JOHN C. BRECKINRIDGE.

HEADQUARTERS POLK'S CORPS, ARMY OF TENNESSEE,
June 15, 1863.

Hon. JAMES A. SEDDON, *Secretary of War:*

SIR: The reports of General Polk, of the battle of Shiloh, General Bragg, of Perryville, and Bragg and Breckinridge, of Murfreesborough, have appeared in the public papers, and, it was understood, by permission of the War Department.

The large body of Tennessee troops serving under General Polk were anxious to see his report of the battles of Murfreesborough and Perryville, and as there was no reason to suppose the Government would object to granting permission for the publication of these reports, which has been accorded in the case of those of other general officers, and as many errors appeared in the copy of General Polk's report of Shiloh, I sent to the gentleman through whom these reports were being published in the Knoxville Register, its Richmond correspondent, "S. L.," a corrected copy of General Polk's report of the battle of Murfreesborough, and wrote him, under date of May 5, as follows:

I send you a carefully revised copy of General Polk's report of the battle of Murfreesborough. * * * This report is sent you predicated on the supposition that its publication has been authorized, and that the Secretary of War will give you access to the originals in the Department. Should he, however, refuse, you will not, of course, use the report.

The publication not appearing, I asked Mr. B. B. Minor to call at the War Office and see if there was any objection to its publication. This he did, and I am this morning in receipt of a note from him saying:

I find objections are entertained to the publication of the reports of the battles of Perryville and Murfreesborough. It is now under advisement whether to publish them prior to and outside of the usual mode. No access will be allowed to them at present.

In the mean time, since Mr. Minor left these headquarters for Richmond, the Knoxville Register, of the 6th, announced that it would, the next day, publish General Polk's report of the battle of Murfreesborough, which had been forwarded by its Richmond correspondent, "S. L," the party to whom the corrected copy had been sent, and the report was accordingly published, as inclosed. I have thought it due to myself and to General Polk to make these statements to the Department, in explanation of the appearance of the report.

Since writing the foregoing, I have, in answer to an inquiry, received the following dispatch from the editor of the Register:

I had no express authority of the Government for publishing General Polk's report, but as my correspondent at Richmond had been allowed access to official copies of the other reports, and it expressed no disapproval of their publication, I inferred its consent.

J. A. SPERRY.

I have the honor to be, very respectfully, your obedient servant,

W. B. RICHMOND,
Aide-de-Camp.

P. S.—Mr. Minor, in his communication, informs me that no supplementary report of the battle of Murfreesborough had been received at the War Department. Such a report was made and forwarded to your office, and this postscript is added in explanation of its publication with the main report.

[Indorsement.]

The explanation of this publication is little satisfactory. Express authority of the Department should be obtained before the copy of any official paper is intrusted to the agents of the press, who are under a strong temptation to publish as news whatever may be interesting to their readers.

J. A. S.,
Secretary.

No. 193.

Reports of Maj. Gen. Benjamin F. Cheatham, C. S. Army, commanding First Division.

HEADQUARTERS CHEATHAM'S DIVISION,
POLK'S CORPS, ARMY OF TENNESSEE,
Shelbyville, Tenn., February 20, 1863.

I have the honor to submit the following report of the action of this division in the battles before Murfreesborough, commencing on December 30, 1862, and ending on January 3, 1863:

The division is composed of the following brigades and batteries:

Brig. Gen. D. S. Donelson's brigade: Sixteenth Regiment Tennessee Volunteers, Col. John H. Savage; Thirty-eighth Regiment Tennessee Volunteers, Col. John C. Carter; Fifty-first Regiment Tennessee Volunteers, Col. John Chester; Eighth Regiment Tennessee Volunteers, Col. W. L. Moore; Eighty-fourth Regiment Tennessee Volunteers, Col. S. S. Stanton; Capt. W. W. Carnes' light battery.

Brig. Gen. A. P. Stewart's brigade: Fourth and Fifth Regiments Tennessee Volunteers, Col. O. F. Strahl; Twenty-fourth Regiment Tennessee Volunteers, Col. H. L. W. Bratton; Thirty-first and Thirty-third Regiments Tennessee Volunteers, Col. E. E. Tansil; Nineteenth Regiment Tennessee Volunteers, Col. F. M. Walker; Capt. T. J. Stanford's light battery.

Brig. Gen. George Maney's brigade: First Regiment Tennessee Volunteers, Col. H. R. Feild; Fourth Regiment Tennessee Volunteers, Col. J. A. McMurry; Sixth and Ninth Regiments Tennessee Volunteers, Col. C. S. Hurt; Capt. Frank Maney's company of sharpshooters; Capt. [then Lieut.] W. B. Turner's light battery (Mississippi).

Brig. Gen. Preston Smith's brigade: One hundred and fifty-fourth Senior Regiment Tennessee Volunteers, Lieutenant-Colonel [M. Magev ney, jr.]; Thirteenth Regiment Tennessee Volunteers, Col. A. J. Vaughan, [jr.;] Forty-seventh Regiment Tennessee Volunteers, Major [Thomas R. Shearon]; Twenty-ninth Regiment Tennessee Volunteers, [Maj. John B. Johnson;] Ninth Texas Infantry, Col. W. H. Young; Captain [P. T.] Allin's company of sharpshooters; Capt. W. L. Scott's light battery.

On December 26, General Maney's brigade, being on outpost duty at Stewart's Creek, hearing heavy firing in front, was moved forward by General Maney to La Vergne, 5 miles toward Nashville, where he came in sight of the enemy advancing, who encamped that night 3 miles beyond La Vergne. After a consultation with General Wheeler, who was stationed at this advanced post with his cavalry brigade, they advised the commander-in-chief that a general advance of the enemy had commenced.

On the morning of the 27th the enemy again commenced his advance, our troops, both infantry and cavalry, skirmishing constantly with the enemy, and gradually falling back, the infantry that night halting at Overall's Creek, and next day falling back to Murfreesborough.

On Monday morning, at daylight, the command (having the day previous cooked three days' rations, struck their tents, loaded their wagons and sent them to the rear) commenced crossing Stone's River, and formed line of battle in the following order, from right to left: First Brigade, Brigadier-General Donelson commanding; Second Brigade, Brigadier-General Stewart commanding; Third Brigade, Brigadier-General Maney commanding; Fourth Brigade, Col. A. J. Vaughan, [jr.,] commanding, the line extending from the Nashville Railroad, on the right, to Franklin road, on the left. My division was formed from 500 to 800 yards in rear of Major-General Withers' division, and was the supporting force to that division, which formed the front line of Polk's corps.

Nothing of importance occurred until the middle of the day on Tuesday, when, the enemy having commenced deploying and forming his lines in our front, heavy skirmishing was commenced between the opposing forces and continued to increase until near sunset, when, the enemy having established his lines as far to his right as the Triune road, where my left rested, in a dense cedar thicket, and more than 300 yards in front of Colonel Loomis' brigade, the firing became very heavy. In the mean time Robertson's battery, which had been placed in position in the Triune road, supported in rear by the One hundred and fifty-fourth Tennessee Regiment, which I had detached from Colonel Vaughan's brigade for that special duty, opened upon the enemy a heavy fire, which was promptly answered by two of the enemy's batteries. In a short time afterward, three of the enemy's regiments made a dash on Robertson's battery, but were repulsed by a few rounds of canister from the battery and a well-directed volley of musketry from the One hundred and fifty-fourth Regiment Tennessee Volunteers and two Alabama regiments on Colonel Loomis' left, after losing quite a number in killed and wounded. During this engagement Captain Robertson had 14 men wounded and several killed, and one ammunition chest blown up by the explosion of a shell from the enemy. The One hundred and fifty-fourth Regiment Tennessee Volunteers lost considerably in this engagement, but behaved themselves most gallantly. The enemy's batteries kept up a continual shelling until quite dark. The loss in Loomis' and Vaughan's brigades and Robertson's battery was over 75.

At daylight on the morning of the 31st, the attack was commenced on our extreme left by Major-General McCown's division, supported by Major-General Cleburne's division, of Lieutenant-General Hardee's corps, the plan of the battle being that the attack should be made by brigades, each advancing to the front, attacking the enemy's lines, then wheeling to the right to take him in flank, to be followed up in like manner from left to right.

At 7 o'clock Colonel Loomis' brigade, in the front line, was ordered to the attack, and being not more than 300 yards from the enemy's lines, was immediately engaged. His command had to cross an open woods and a corn-field in order to reach the enemy, who were strongly posted in a cedar wood. He made a gallant dash, but after reaching near the woods was compelled to fall back to his original position, where the command was soon reorganized under my own superintendence.

In the mean time the supporting brigade under Colonel Vaughan had advanced over the same ground and attacked the enemy furiously, driving him away from and capturing two of his guns, but was forced to give orders to his command to fall back, on account of the murderous fire being poured into his front, and particularly a raking fire that was turned upon him from his right, completely enfilading his lines. They, however, retired in good order, and in a few moments after being re-formed were again sent forward by me, with instructions to bear some-what to the right, so as partially to avoid the heavy wood.

In the mean time the Ninth Texas Regiment, under the command of that gallant officer, Col. W. H. Young, who did not hear the order, be-came detached and was farther to the left. It remained in the woods and continued to fight the enemy, and at last charged them on their flank and drove them from the woods on their entire right, losing very heavily. In the first assault made by Colonel Loomis' brigade that officer was so wounded by the falling of a limb cut from a tree that he had to turn over the command to the next senior officer (Colonel Coltart). The brigade suffered very severely in this charge. Colonel Vaughan's brigade also suffered very severely in its desperate charge against the same stronghold. Lieut. Col. W. E. Morgan and Major [Peter H.] Cole, both of the Thirteenth Regiment Tennessee Volunteers, were mortally wounded; also a very large number of officers and men.

At about 8 o'clock, Colonel Manigault's brigade moved out and at-tacked the enemy directly in his front. He met with very strong resist-ance, and after Colonel Loomis was compelled to fall back, and the enemy's fire turned upon his left flank, enfilading his lines, he was com-pelled to retire. He, however, soon rallied his command, made another gallant attack, and was forced to fall back a second time. At this junc-ture General Maney's brigade came up and took position on the left of Manigault's, when they moved forward and took position facing toward the Wilkinson pike, near the Harding house, when two batteries of the enemy opened upon them, one of them in the woods on Manigault's right, and on the west side of the Wilkinson pike; the other on the east side of the pike. At this place I came up with Colonel Vaughan's bri-gade. General Maney had placed Captain [Lieutenant] Turner's bat-tery of Napoleon guns in position near the brick-kiln, which in a short time silenced the battery on the east side of the road. Colonel Mani-gault assailed the one in the woods with two regiments, but did not succeed in capturing it. Having made my dispositions, I ordered Colo-nel Vaughan to move forward with his brigade, and take position on

General Cleburne's right, which was in the woods to my front and left. General Maney and Colonel Manigault I accompanied across the Wilkinson pike, just in front of the enemy's battery last mentioned, which the enemy had abandoned on our approach. The one in the woods to our right was also abandoned, most of the horses having been so disabled that the guns could not be removed. After crossing the Wilkinson pike, I rode forward to the cedar brake toward the Nashville pike, where I found General Stewart's brigade hotly engaging the enemy. He captured three of his guns, drove him through the woods and beyond the field to the Nashville pike. During this encounter, Colonel Bratton, of the Twenty-fourth Tennessee Volunteers, a most gallant officer, was killed. Colonel Vaughan advanced with Cleburne's division, fighting and driving the enemy until he reached the Nashville pike, when the enemy's fire became so heavy he was forced to retire, after having again driven the enemy from two of his guns. Late in the evening I placed him on the Wilkinson pike, in the rear of General Cleburne's division, with instructions to remain there until further orders. This brigade acted most gallantly during the entire day, having had two terrible engagements, losing 705 men out of 1,813.

About 10 o'clock General Donelson's brigade was ordered forward to the support of General Chalmers' brigade, which had been partially driven back. General Donelson pressed forward through the open field in front of the burnt house, under a terrific fire of twenty pieces of artillery and a heavy infantry force. Colonel Savage's regiment (Sixteenth Tennessee) and three companies of the Fifty-first Tennessee passed to the right of the house, extending to the river on the right; the remainder of the Fifty-first, with the Eighth and Thirty-third Regiments, passing to the left of the house, advanced, under a heavy fire of infantry, toward the south end of the cedar brake. During this advance Colonel Moore, of the Eighth Tennessee, had his horse killed under him, and in a few moments afterward that gallant officer fell, dead, having been shot through the heart by a minie ball. The Eighth Tennessee Regiment, now under the command of its gallant lieutenant-colonel, John H. Anderson, dashed forward into the cedar brake, drove the enemy before them, charged and captured a battery, and, in connection with the Thirty-eighth and seven companies of the Fifty-first Tennessee Regiments, fought and drove the enemy out of the south end of the brake, through the open field to his reserves on the Nashville pike, capturing from 600 to 700 prisoners. Colonel Savage, of the Sixteenth Tennessee, advanced beyond the burnt house (Cowan), and took position on the right of the railroad, and for three hours held the columns of infantry in his front in check, and when, after the arrival of General Adams' brigade, he withdrew his regiment, he left 30 dead men in the line he had occupied. The loss of this regiment was 207 out of 402, being over one-half. The Eighth Tennessee, under Lieutenant-Colonel Anderson, lost 306 men and officers out of 472, which shows what they had to contend against. The other regiments of this brigade suffered nearly as badly.

As soon as [it was] discovered that our advanced line had been checked, I immediately commenced forming a double line of infantry in the cedar brake, in order to resist any movement the enemy might make against us. General Stewart's brigade being in the advance, was first aligned. General Maney's brigade was formed on its left, and Colonel Loomis' on its right, with Generals Donelson's, Preston's, Adams', and Manigault's brigades in the rear line. General McCown formed his division on the left of General Maney. In this position they remained until night, a great portion of the time under a heavy fire of the enemy's artillery.

On Friday morning the brigades of Generals Preston and Adams were withdrawn, when the lines were reformed and straightened, and Smith's brigade was brought forward and placed in the lines, he having arrived and taken command on Thursday.

On Wednesday there was but little done by my artillery, on account of the impossibility of advancing it through the cedars and pedregal on my left. Captain [Lieutenant] Turner's battery was brought into action on that day by General Maney and did good service.

On Friday and Saturday Captains Stanford, Scott, Carnes, and [Lieutenant] Turner did excellent service with their guns, which had been advanced up the railroad by order of Lieutenant-General Polk. Lieutenant [A. A.] Hardin, of Captain Stanford's battery, with one section, was sent to the assistance of Colonel Manigault on Tuesday, and, while gallantly working his rifled pieces, was killed by a round shot.

On Sunday morning, at 1 o'clock, preparations having been previously made, my command brought up the rear as the army slowly fell back toward Shelbyville.

Although my division was originally placed in the second line as a supporting force, it was not long before it was all under fire and hotly engaged with the enemy, and I am proud to say that each brigade did good service. I cannot omit this opportunity to express my thanks for the fortitude with which they bore the hardships and their gallant, soldier-like bearing during the eight trying days they were in line of battle, and most of the time under fire.

A list of casualties of my command is herewith inclosed, the loss being 277 killed, 1,597 wounded, and 65 missing. Total, 1,939.*

My staff with me on the field—Maj. John Ingram, assistant adjutant-general; Maj. Joseph Vaulx, [jr.,] assistant inspector-general; Maj. George V. Young, chief quartermaster; Maj. B. J. Butler, chief of subsistence; Maj. J. A. Cheatham, chief of ordnance; Lieut. J. G. Mann, engineer officer, and Lieut. A. L. Robertson, aide-de-camp—all managed their separate departments to my entire satisfaction.

Capt. Robert L. Weakly, who was badly wounded, and Lieutenant [J. H.] Marsh, of the artillery; Lieut. Thomas [H.] Henderson, adjutant of the Sixth Tennessee; Capt. R. A. Alston, of South Carolina, and Capt. J. Webb Smith, volunteer aides-de-camp, all behaved gallantly, and did good service in transmitting orders over the extensive field of operations during the day.

Maj. F. H. McNairy, my aide-de-camp, who had accompanied me on all previous battle-fields, was, unfortunately, absent, having been severely wounded by the accidental discharge of a pistol at Knoxville.

Very respectfully, your obedient servant,

B. F. CHEATHAM,
Maj. Gen., Comdg. Cheatham's Div., Polk's Corps, Army of Tenn.

Maj. THOMAS M. JACK,
     Assistant Adjutant-General.

HEADQUARTERS CHEATHAM'S DIVISION,
Shelbyville, Tenn., January 8, 1863.

SIR: In compliance with orders from corps headquarters, the following report of the number of officers and men killed, wounded, and miss-

---

* See totals in tabulated statement, p. 677.

ing in the recent engagement near Murfreesborough, Tenn., is respectfully submitted:

Brigades.	Killed.		Wounded.		Missing.		Aggregate.
	Officers.	Enlisted men.	Officers.	Enlisted men.	Officers.	Enlisted men.	
Donelson's	10	98	42	533	1	16	700
Stewart's	8	55	23	311	......	2	399
Maney's	3	19	12	151	......	8	193
Smith's	7	98	48	516	3	35	707
Total*	28	270	125	1,511	4	61	1,999

B. F. CHEATHAM,
Major-General, Commanding.

[Inclosure.]

Report of officers and men actually engaged in the battle of Murfreesborough, in Cheatham's division.

Command.	Officers.	Men.	Aggregate.
Donelson's brigade:			
8th Tennessee	38	436	474
16th Tennessee	24	383	407
38th Tennessee	20	262	282
51st Tennessee	23	270	293
Carnes' battery	5	68	73
Total	110	1,419	1,529
Stewart's brigade·			
4th and 5th Tennessee	41	417	458
19th Tennessee	32	348	380
24th Tennessee	31	313	344
31st and 33d Tennessee	34	345	379
Stanford's battery	4	70	74
Total	142	1,493	1,635
Maney's brigade:			
1st and 27th Tennessee	23	434	457
4th Tennessee (Confederate)	34	337	371
6th and 9th Tennessee	38	374	412
Maney's Sharpshooters	3	58	61
Smith's battery	3	78	81
Total	101	1,281	1,382
Smith's brigade:			
12th Tennessee	25	297	322
13th Tennessee	16	236	252
29th Tennessee	30	224	254
47th Tennessee	16	247	263
154th Tennessee (senior)	25	253	278
9th Texas	24	299	323
Allin's Sharpshooters	3	47	50
Scott's battery	4	77	81
Total	143	1,680	1,823
Grand total	496	5,873	6,369
Less 30 men from each regiment, as infirmary detail			510
			5,859

Total loss, 1,939.   Loss, 35 per cent.

Respectfully submitted.

B. F. CHEATHAM,
Major-General, Commanding Division.

* But see tabulated statement on p. 677, agreeing with totals given above.

No. 194.

Report of Brig. Gen. Daniel S. Donelson, C. S. Army commanding First Brigade.

HEADQUARTERS FIRST BRIGADE, FIRST DIVISION,
POLK'S CORPS, ARMY OF TENNESSEE,
Shelbyville, Tenn., January 20, 1863.

I have the honor to submit a report of the part taken by the First Brigade in the late engagement with the enemy before Murfreesborough.

The brigade was composed of the following regiments and battery, viz: The Sixteenth Regiment Tennessee Volunteers, Col. John H. Savage; the Thirty-eighth Regiment Tennessee Volunteers, Col. John C. Carter; the Fifty-first Regiment Tennessee Volunteers, Col. John Chester; the Eighth Regiment Tennessee Volunteers, Col. W. L. Moore; Eighty-fourth Regiment Tennessee Volunteers, Col. S. S. Stanton, and Captain Carnes' battery. The Eighty-fourth Regiment, being a new and very small regiment, was assigned to my command on the morning of December 29, 1862, only two days before the battle.

In obedience to orders, the tents were struck and the wagons packed and sent to the rear Sunday night, 27th ultimo.

At daylight Monday morning the brigade was moved to and assumed its line of battle, which was second and supporting to the first line of battle, two companies of Colonel Savage's, the right regiment, extending across the railroad, and Colonel Carter's, the left regiment, across the Wilkinson pike, its left resting on the right of General Stewart's brigade. This line of battle, with General Chalmers' brigade in front, which mine was to support, was formed on the brow of the hill, about 300 yards in a southeast direction from the white house, known as Mrs. James'. That position was retained under an occasional shelling, with but few casualties, until dark Tuesday evening, when, in obedience to orders from Lieutenant-General Polk, the brigade was moved forward to the front line, to relieve General Chalmers' brigade, which had already held that position three days and nights. Before day the brigade returned to its proper position, and General Chalmers' brigade resumed its place on the front line.

During the night a general order from General Bragg was received directing a vigorous and persistent attack at daylight by our left wing on the right of the enemy, the whole of both lines conforming to the movements of the left wing, gradually wheeling and attacking the enemy as soon as the advance of the left wing should justify it. Orders were received from Lieutenant-General Polk directing me to conform the movements of my brigade to those of General Chalmers' brigade, always keeping in close supporting distance—about 2,000 feet in rear—and to support it promptly when ordered. Orders also came from Major-General Cheatham directing me to obey any orders which I might receive from Major-General Withers, who gave me orders similar to those received from Lieutenant-General Polk.

In obedience to the foregoing orders, I moved my brigade, except Stanton's regiment, forward at 10 o'clock Wednesday morning, December 31 (the right being the directing regiment and the railroad the line of direction), until it reached the front line, from which General Chalmers' brigade had started, where it was halted until orders should be received to advance to the support of General Chalmers. From the moment I moved from my first position in the morning until dark that night my brigade was constantly under the fire of shot and shell from the enemy's batteries, and it sustained more or less loss in killed and wounded on every part of the field to which it was assigned for duty. This ac. ounts to some extent for the heavy loss it sustained.

Colonel Stanton's regiment, being a new and small one, and having received its arms only the day before, I deemed it best to leave it in the rear, in support of Captain Carnes' battery, and I consequently gave the requisite orders for that purpose.

The brigade had occupied its position along the front line (behind Chalmers' breastworks) only a few minutes, when, General Chalmers having received a severe wound, his brigade was broken and the greater part of it fell back in disorder and confusion. Under orders from Lieutenant-General Polk, I immediately advanced my brigade to its support, and, indeed, its relief, under a shower of shot and shell of almost every description. During this advance my horse was shot under me, from which, and another wound received at the Cowan house, he died during the day. In advancing upon and attacking the enemy under such a fire, my brigade found it impossible to preserve its alignment, because of the walls of the burnt house known as Cowan's and the yard and garden fence and picketing left standing around and about it; in consequence of which, Savage's regiment, with three companies of Chester's regiment, went to the right of the Cowan house, and advanced upon the enemy until they were checked by three batteries of the enemy, with a heavy infantry support, on the hill to the right of the railroad, while the other two regiments (Carter's and Moore's), with seven companies of Chester's regiment, went to the left of that house through a most destructive cross-fire, both of artillery and small-arms, driving the enemy and sweeping everything before them until they arrived at the open field beyond the cedar brake, in a northwest direction from the Cowan house, when, having exhausted their ammunition, they retired to the Wilkinson pike in order to reform their regiments and replenish their cartridge-boxes. The two regiments and seven companies that went to the left of the Cowan house charged, drove, and pursued the enemy very rapidly, loading and firing as they advanced, and did great execution.

In the charge immediately upon entering the woods after leaving the Cowan house, we had to deplore the loss of Col. W. L. Moore, of the Eighth Regiment Tennessee Volunteers, when the command of the regiment devolved upon the gallant Lieut. Col. John H. Anderson, who proved himself fully equal to the responsible post he had been so suddenly called upon to assume. Colonel Moore's horse was killed under and fell upon him. Disengaging himself as soon as possible, he advanced on foot with his regiment only a short distance when he was shot through the heart and instantly killed. His fate was that which, if he must fall, he himself would have chosen—dying upon the field of his glory, his regiment fighting most gallantly around him, and he himself in the full and energetic discharge of his whole duty, without a pang and without a struggle. In the death of Colonel Moore the service has lost one of its most valuable officers, the country a devoted patriot, and the community in which he lived an excellent and most estimable citizen.

In the charge through the cedar woods to the left of the Cowan house, Colonel Carter's report shows that his regiment captured seven pieces of artillery and about 500 prisoners; Colonel Chester's, that his regiment captured three pieces of artillery and several hundred prisoners,* and

---

*As explanatory of the capture of the battery by the Eighth Tennessee Regiment, commanded by Lieut. Col. John H. Anderson, of said regiment, it may be proper, under the circumstances, for me to say that the regiment killed the horses when the gunners surrendered as prisoners of war, leaving Col. [George W.] Roberts, who was pointed out by one of the prisoners as their colonel in command of the brigade, dead near the guns. I make this statement in order that the facts may be known.—[D. S. D.]

Lieutenant-Colonel Anderson's, that his regiment captured six pieces of artillery and about 400 prisoners. It is possible that these gentlemen, with the most honest intentions and in perfect good faith, may have counted some of the same guns as being captured by their respective regiments, but I am satisfied, upon a full conversation with them all and a knowledge of the ground over which they passed, and the position and movements of the other troops upon the same field, that the brigade captured at least eleven pieces of artillery and over 1,000 prisoners.

Colonel Savage's regiment, with three companies of Colonel Chester's, held, in my judgment, the critical position of that part of the field. Unable to advance, and determined not to retire, having received a message from Lieutenant-General Polk that I should in a short time be re-enforced and properly supported, I ordered Colonel Savage to hold his position at all hazards, and I felt it to be my duty to remain with that part of the brigade, holding so important and hazardous a position as that occupied by him. Colonel Savage, finding the line he had to defend entirely too long for the number of men under his command, and that there was danger of his being flanked, either to the right or left, as the one or the other wing presented the weaker front, finally threw out the greater part of his command as skirmishers, as well to deceive the enemy as to our strength in his rear as to protect his long line, and held his position, with characteristic and most commendable tenacity, for over three hours. At the expiration of that time Jackson's brigade came up to my support, but instead of going to the right of the Cowan house and to the support of Colonel Savage, it went to the left of the house and over the ground which the two left regiments and seven companies of my brigade had already gone over. After Jackson's, General Adams' brigade came up to the support of Colonel Savage, when, the latter withdrawing his regiment to make way for it, it attacked the enemy with spirit for a short time, but it was soon driven back in disorder and confusion, Colonel Savage's regiment retiring with it. Subsequently, Preston's brigade came up to the same position, one regiment, and perhaps more, going to the right of the Cowan house, and were repulsed, while the remainder of the brigade went to the left of the house and over the same ground which a part of my brigade and all of Jackson's had already traversed.

About this time I rejoined the two left regiments and seven companies of my brigade drawn up in line of battle on the right of Stewart's brigade at the edge of the open field, after passing through the cedar woods to the right of the Wilkinson pike. Here we remained under a very heavy fire from the enemy's artillery, both of shell and shot, until dark, when I withdrew my brigade about 200 yards, for the night, throwing out a strong picket for its protection. During the night I ordered Colonel Savage's command to rejoin the brigade, and collected all that I could of my stragglers, and had them brought to their respective commands.

On Thursday and Friday but little was done, save to keep my men (under an occasional shelling) in line of battle and on the alert, either for any demonstration on the part of the enemy or any movement that might be in the contemplation of my commanding officers. During this interval my dead were buried, and my wounded, which had not already been cared for, properly attended to.

Friday afternoon, under orders from Major-General Cheatham, I moved my brigade forward, parallel with the Wilkinson pike, about half a mile, in order to relieve Maney's brigade on the front line. There we remained, with a strong picket thrown out in front, and skirmishing with the enemy's pickets nearly all the while, until 1 o'clock Sunday morning, January 4, when, in obedience to orders from Major-General Cheatham, we took up the line of March to Shelbyville.

The field officers—Colonels Savage, Carter, Chester, Anderson, and Major [H. W.] Cotter—all distinguished themselves by the coolness and courage they displayed upon the field, and greatly contributed to the successes achieved by their respective commands by the skill and resolution with which they managed and maneuvered them.   Colonel Stanton's regiment was not seriously engaged, though I do not doubt, if an opportunity had presented itself, that both he and his men would have fought most gallantly.   Captain Carnes' battery was separated from my brigade in consequence of the impossibility of its obtaining a suitable position in that part of the field from which to operate, and, therefore, it acted under other orders than my own.   A report from Lieutenant [L. G.] Marshall, herewith transmitted, will show its operations.

We have to mourn the loss of many gallant officers and brave men, who fell in the faithful discharge of their duty on the field of battle.   Capt. L. N. Savage, acting lieutenant-colonel, and Captain [J. J.] Womack, acting major of the Sixteenth Regiment, most efficient officers, were severely, if not mortally, wounded, and Captain [D. C.] Spurlock, of the same regiment, an excellent officer and most estimable gentleman, was killed.   Capt. B. H. Holland, of the Thirty-eighth Regiment, was killed while gallantly bearing the colors of his regiment, and Acting Lieut. Col. R. A. Burford, of the Fifty-first, was wounded.   These are but a part of those who were either killed or wounded, but I must refer for further details to the regimental reports, which I herewith transmit and beg to make a part of my own.   The Eighth Regiment lost most heavily both in officers and men.   In Company D, the gallant Captain [M. C.] Shook was killed, and the lists show that out of 12 commissioned and non-commissioned officers and 62 men who went into the fight only 1 corporal and 20 men escaped.   Other companies suffered almost as heavily.

Of the general conduct of the officers and men of the brigade, I find it difficult to employ terms of too high commendation.   Cool, brave, and prompt in obeying every command upon the battle-field, they exhibited, during the week of hardships they were called upon to endure before Murfreesborough, a patience, fortitude, and cheerfulness worthy of the highest praise.   The long list of killed and wounded, herewith transmitted, is a sad but a glorious testimony not only to their gallantry and courage, but also to their patriotic devotion to their country and its righteous cause.   Entering the field with only about 1,400 men, I have to deplore a loss of 691 in killed, wounded, and missing, with only 19 missing, and a majority, if not all, of those prisoners of war.

I cannot conclude this report without expressing my appreciation of the services of my staff.   I was attended on the battle-field by the following staff officers: Capt. John Bradford, my brigade inspector, acting as assistant adjutant-general; James H. Wilkes, my clerk, acting as aide-de-camp, my assistant adjutant-general, Maj. James G. Martin, and Lieut. Samuel Donelson, my aide-de-camp, being absent on leave.   My volunteer aides-de-camp were Capt. J. L. Rice, formerly of Colonel Battle's [Twentieth Tennessee] regiment; Col. Granville Lewis, of Texas, and Henry Lindsley, of Lebanon, Tenn.   I feel that I am doing but sheer justice to express my entire satisfaction with the conduct of every member of my staff, for they rendered efficient services in carrying orders with promptness in the hottest of the conflict, particularly to that part of the field, on the right of my brigade, which the enemy was attempting to turn during the entire day, but where he was gallantly repulsed by the determined bravery of my troops.   Mr. Lindsley had his horse killed by a cannon ball early in the action, and was so severely wounded himself that he had to retire from the field during the remainder of the battle. My clerk (Wilkes) had his horse killed late in the afternoon near the Cowan house. It is but right that I should say that Colonel Lewis the previous day had obtained a musket, and was fully equipped to take the field in the ranks of Captain [W. G.] Burford's company of Eighth [Tennessee] Regiment, when, being informed of this fact, I invited him to take a position with me as volunteer aide, which he readily assented to do, and conducted himself with great coolness and determined bravery. I have referred to Captain Rice as a relieved officer. I feel, from his efficient services rendered in this battle, and my knowledge of him as a man and an officer, that I am doing but simple justice to him, and a benefit to the cause and service, in recommending that Captain Rice be given a command at the earliest practicable period, knowing him to be qualified in an eminent degree to fill a high position.

Accompanying this you will find an accurate list of both officers and men killed, wounded, and missing in my command.

All of which is respectfully submitted.

D. S. DONELSON,
Brigadier-General, Comdg. First Brigade, Cheatham's Division.

Maj. John Ingram,
Assistant Adjutant-General.

No. 195.

Report of Lieut. Col. John H. Anderson, Eighth Tennessee Infantry.

Camp near Shelbyville, Tenn.,
January 12, 1863.

General: Below you will please find a report of the part taken by the Eighth [Tennessee] Regiment in the late action before Murfreesborough:

On the morning of December 29, the regiment was ordered into line of battle. We were placed in line of battle in an old field on the west side of Stone's River, my left resting on the left of the Wilkinson turnpike road, in which position we remained, subjected during the time to heavy cannonade of shells, which did but little or no harm, until Wednesday morning, the 31st, at which time I received orders to hold my regiment in readiness to move forward at a moment's notice to the support of Brigadier-General Chalmers' brigade, which was in our front. At about 10 o'clock our brigade was ordered forward. The Eighth moved off promptly at the command, under a very heavy cannonade of shot and shell. When we had arrived at the position formerly occupied by General Chalmers' brigade, we were ordered to halt and lie down behind the little fortification constructed by his brigade of logs and rails. We remained in this position about twenty minutes under a perfect storm of shot and shell, causing considerable mortality in my regiment. In this position we lost 15 or 20 men killed and wounded. It soon became apparent to every one that Chalmers' brigade was giving way, for it was with great difficulty that I could keep his men from running over my men; they came running back in squads and companies, and I am satisfied that before we left this position that at least two-thirds of the regiment that had formerly occupied the position we were in had returned. We were then ordered forward to the charge, which was responded to by the Eighth Regiment with a yell, the gallant Colonel Moore leading. We moved forward at a double-quick, under a perfect hail of shot, shell, and grape, when we arrived at the burnt brick house. The regiment was thrown into some confusion, caused by the house and some picket fence and a portion of Chalmers' men that had remained behind the house, there being several fences and the house and a portion of Chalmers' men that were in the way, causing some four of the companies on the right of the regiment to pass around and through the best way they could. At this juncture the enemy in our front opened a terrible fire upon us with small-arms, at a distance of about 75 or 100 yards. Such a fire I do not suppose men were ever before subjected to. At this point the colonel's horse fell, and I supposed that he himself was either killed or wounded. Seeing the condition in which the regiment was placed, with a powerful enemy in our front and on the right and left—for at this time we were then in front of the balance of the brigade, and the enemy were cross-firing me right and left—and seeing so many of my men falling around me, I ordered them forward at a double-quick with fixed bayonets. The gallant Eighth responded with a shout, and leaped forward like men bent on conquering or dying in the attempt. When we had advanced about 50 or 60 yards, and were just entering the woods in our front, the colonel came up with sword in hand. He was not killed or wounded, as I expected; it was only his horse. He had just reached the regiment again, and was urging them forward, when he fell, dead, shot through the heart with a minie ball. The enemy in our front contested stubbornly, and those on our right and left continued to pour a deadly fire into us. The enemy's first line gave way before my men; their second was brought forward, but could not stand the impetuosity of our charge, and they gave way. At this point it was reported to me that the enemy was trying to get away some artillery on my left. I immediately changed direction to the left, and charged them and captured their guns (three at one place), and went 50 yards below. We captured one more by shooting down their horses and stopped the piece. I also captured at this point about 400 prisoners belonging to the artillery and infantry, and we killed Colonel [George W.] Roberts, who was commanding the brigade, as stated to me by the prisoners.

Through the bloody charge I lost many gallant officers and men killed and wounded. The enemy in the woods in my front having come to a halt, and pouring a galling fire into us, I ordered the men forward again at a double-quick; they responded with a shout, and moved forward upon the enemy. At this point I was joined by the colors and about 100 men of the Fifty-first Regiment, who came in on my left. I ordered them forward with my men, which orders they obeyed promptly. We charged the enemy in his position in the woods, under a perfect storm of bullets, and drove him before us.

About this time I was joined by Colonel Chester in person. We then continued driving the enemy before us, when it was reported to me that they were trying to flank me on my right. I then changed direction to the right, and moved forward upon him, and struck his flank and rear, in which position I halted and gave him a deadly fire, being too weak in strength to close in behind him. About this time I heard a heavy fire to right, in front of the enemy, whose flank I was upon. I sent an officer forward to see what it was, and, if it was our force, which I felt confident it was, to inform the commander of my position, that he might not fire into me, and also to tell the commander to charge them at a double-quick and drive them by me, that I might shoot them down, which he did in gallant style; still, when he came up, it proved to be the Nineteenth Tennessee Regiment. I then formed on his left, and moved forward to the point, driving the enemy before us. It was then reported to me that the enemy was flanking me on my left. I immediately changed direction to the left and moved upon him, when he gave way and fled through the old field in front of the woods occupied by us when we left the other night, when we charged him to the old field through which he fled. We halted in the edge of woods, and gave him a deadly fire as he ran through the old field. The effect of that fire was apparent to every one who visited that place, for the edge of the woods and the field for 200 or 300 yards was strewn with his dead and wounded. When we were unmasked by his force, the enemy, from his batteries on the hill in our front, opened upon us a perfect hail of grape and canister, when I ordered the men back into the woods. I then fell back to the old house in the rear of the woods, to gather together the remainder of the regiment, that had somewhat scattered in the charge through the dense woods, and to get a supply of ammunition. I remained there some time, and gathered all the men that I could get up, in company with Colonels Carter and Chester, when we formed line on the right of General Stewart's brigade. The firing in our front being very heavy, we were ordered forward, which order we obeyed promptly, and moved to the front of the woods in front of the enemy, in the old field. In this position we remained under a very heavy fire of artillery until night closed this bloody and eventful day.

Perhaps it is necessary that I should be more explicit in my explanation of my maneuvering in the woods. The reason why I had to change direction so often was that I was not supported either on the right or left. Our regiment drove the enemy in our front before this; consequently, this force on the right and left remained in their position, and when I had got in their rear it seemed as if they were flanking me; but when I changed direction to the right, as you will see in the foregoing report, I struck his flank and rear; and at that time the Nineteenth Tennessee came to my support on the right again, when I changed direction to the left. I then discovered that support had arrived on my left, and was driving the enemy on my left. It was then that I struck the enemy's flank on my left, when he was entering the old field. This force on my left I did not ascertain who it was, but supposed to be the Thirty-eighth Tennessee.

It is generally the case in battles that every regiment that passes a battery claims to have taken it. In this case there can be no dispute, as we shot down the horses attached to the guns, and captured the men belonging to the guns. It is also claimed by my men that there were two pieces more (in addition to the four that I have previously named) captured by the right of the regiment, some 75 yards to the right, making in all six pieces. These two additional pieces I did not see at the time, as I was near the left of the regiment, but I did see them afterward, and they must have been taken by my regiment, as it was the only force in these woods, and those guns, from their position, [were] covered by my regiment.

I can[not] close this report without saying a few words in regard to the gallant Col. W. L. Moore, though he fell early in that bloody charge. A more gallant and noble spirit never lived or died for his country. Loved and honored by his regiment, he fell gallantly battling for his country, and his native soil drank his blood.

It would afford me great pleasure, and be but sheer justice, to speak at length of the many noble spirits among the officers and men of my regiment who gave their lives a sacrifice to their country and native State on that memorable day, but the casualties of the regiment speak more for those noble spirits than I could write in a volume.

Respectfully, your obedient servant,

JNO. H. ANDERSON,
Lieutenant-Colonel, Commanding Eighth Tennessee.

No. 196.

Report of Col. John H. Savage, Sixteenth Tennessee Infantry.

JANUARY 8, 1863.

The following report of the conduct of the Sixteenth Tennessee Regiment in the battle before Murfreesborough, December 31, 1862, is respectfully submitted:

When the advance was ordered, my regiment being the right of Cheatham's division, I was directed by General Donelson (through his aide, Captain [John] Bradford) to move along the railroad, but two companies to its right and eight on its left, taking the guide to the right. The advance was made under a heavy cannonade, and the line of battle and direction maintained, although serious obstructions impeded the march. The eight left companies advanced between the railroad and the turnpike in front of the Cowan house without the slightest protection, engaging a battery and the enemy's infantry in the woods at a distance of less than 150 yards. The right companies advanced through a stalk-field to the edge of a cotton-patch. Here the enemy opened a heavy fire at short range from a line extending to the right as far as I could see. This killed Captain Spurlock, who fell while leading his men in the most gallant manner. At this moment it seemed to me that I was without the expected support on my left, and that the line had divided and gone off in that direction. My men shot the horses and gunners of the battery in front, but I could not advance without being outflanked and ——— by the enemy on my right; I therefore ordered them to halt and fire. In a few moments my acting lieutenant-colonel (L. N. Savage) fell by my side, supposed mortally wounded, and my acting major (Captain Womack) had his right arm badly broken. There were batteries to the right and left of the railroad which literally swept the ground. The men maintained the fight against superior numbers with great spirit and obstinacy. The left companies, being very near and without any protection, sustained a heavy loss. Thirty men were left dead upon the spot where they halted dressed in perfect line of battle. It was on the day following a sad spectacle, speaking more eloquently for the discipline and courage of the men than any words I can employ. Here the Thirty-ninth North Carolina came up in my rear, and I ordered it into line of battle to my right, but before it got into position the lieutenant-colonel was shot down and was carried from the field. Under the command of Captain [A. W. Bell] it continued under my control and did good service until driven from this position, after which I lost sight of it.

Seeing a heavy force of the enemy crossing the field to my right and rear, I ordered the line to fall back to the river, and formed two lines to the front and right. To cover this space the men were deployed as skirmishers. I also ordered forward a portion of Blythe's Mississippi Regiment that had collected near the railroad, and was joined by Lieutenants [J. F.] Williamson and [T. W.] McMurry (Fifty-first Regiment) with three companies, who continued with me and did good service. This force checked and drove back the enemy advancing up the river, and a column that attempted to cut off my whole party advancing along the railroad, but not without loss. Lieutenant [R. B.] Anderson, of the Sixteenth, a valuable officer, while directing the skirmishers was dangerously wounded and carried under the river bank by Privates Thompson and Adcock, all of whom were captured by the enemy upon his subsequent advance. When Adams' brigade advanced I drew back my little force to let it move to the front, which it did in gallant style, but only for a short distance, when it broke and fled in confusion. Most of the men I had been controlling moved with it. I collected the men of the Sixteenth and Fifty-first, and moved to the front *en échelon* of Chalmers' position, and remained during the heavy cannonade on the enemy. While here two of my men were killed by a shell. I afterward moved, in connection with Colonel Stanton, near the burnt gin-house, and, halting the regiment, went on foot to my first line of battle. About dark I sent a party after the body of Captain Spurlock, which captured a Yankee captain from his lines.

I claim for my command great gallantry in action; that it engaged and held in check superior forces of the enemy, who were attempting to turn our right—forces that afterward drove Adams' and Preston's brigades.

My flag-bearer (Sergeant Marberry) was disabled early in the charge. The flag was afterward borne by Private Womack, who was also wounded. The flag-staff was broken and hit with balls in three places; the flag literally shot to pieces. The fragments were brought to me at night. I carried about 400 officers and men in action. The killed amount to 36; the killed, wounded, and missing to 208, a list of which is forwarded. My men did not strip or rob the dead.

The conduct of my recruits was most honorable. Many of them fell in the front rank beside the veteran soldier of the Sixteenth. It is difficult to make distinction where all act well. While others deserve nobly, I feel that I ought not to fail to notice the courage and good conduct of Private Hackett, whom I placed in command of the company after the fall of Captain Spurlock.

I am, major, very respectfully, your obedient servant,

JOHN H. SAVAGE,
Colonel, Commanding Sixteenth Tennessee.

Maj. J. G. MARTIN,
Assistant Adjutant-General.

No. 197.

Report of Col. John C. Carter, Thirty-eighth Tennessee Infantry.

NEAR SHELBYVILLE, TENN., *January* 14, 1863.

MAJOR: In obedience to orders, I have the honor to report that on Wednesday morning, December 31, 1862, between 9 and 10 o'clock, General Donelson's brigade (to which my regiment is attached) was ordered to charge the enemy, drawn up in line of battle fronting Murfreesborough, Tenn. My regiment advanced over an open field and under a very terrific fire. The enemy was strongly posted in a dense cedar thicket, and well supported by artillery. At first he seemed unwilling to yield his ground. We steadily approached him, and soon he broke and fled in confusion. We pursued him rapidly, the men loading as they advanced. We drove him from the woods, never permitting him to reform. We fought him until the fighting on Wednesday ceased. In the charge, my regiment captured seven pieces of cannon and about 500 prisoners, and killed at least 100 of the enemy.

I take pleasure in acknowledging the valuable services of Maj. H. W. Cotter. He behaved very gallantly, indeed, during the entire engagement. Captains [T. H.] Koen, [O. M.] Alsup, [T. G.] Cook, and [S. H.] Sartain, Lieutenants [J. W.] Slaughter, [J. C.] Miller, [J. C.] Sanders,

[M. V.] McDuffy, [R. J.] Pentecost, [G. R.] Scott, [T.] Wilson, [N. H.] Baird, [T.] Barron, [J.] Hicks, [J. T. or J. W.] Doughty, and [W. W.] Bland acted with great bravery and coolness. Adjt. R. L. Caruthers was severely wounded early in the engagement. He was nobly acting his part when the unerring missile struck him. Quartermaster-Sergt. Robert B. Koen deserves much praise for his brave and gallant conduct. The whole regiment fought well, and every member of it, with four or five exceptions, seemed animated with a determination to conquer or die.

I deeply regret the death of Capt. B. H. Holland. He was shot through the brain, and died with the colors of his regiment in his hands. When he died the Confederacy lost one of its best citizens and bravest soldiers.

Color-Sergt. I. M. Rice was shot down. He still clung to the flag, and, crawling on his knees, carried it a short distance. Another bullet pierced his body, and death alone compelled him to yield his trust. A nobler soldier never lived, a braver never died. We return thanks to God for the victory won.

I am, respectfully,

JNO. C. CARTER,
[*Colonel*,] *Commanding Regiment.*

Maj. J. G. MARTIN,
Assistant Adjutant-General.

No. 198.

Report of Col. John Chester, Fifty-first Tennessee Infantry.

NEAR SHELBYVILLE, TENN., *January* 13, 1863.

The following report of the part taken by the Fifty-first Regiment in the action before Murfreesborough on December 31, 1862, is respectfully submitted:

The order was received from General Donelson, through his aide (Captain [John] Bradford), to advance to the position then occupied by Chalmers' brigade, taking the guide to the right, and advance to the support of Chalmers. We advanced with the brigade under a heavy shelling, many shells striking very near my lines. When we had arrived within about 150 or 200 yards of Chalmers' position, a shell exploded so near my colors as to kill one of the guard (Private J. W. Scott, Company I), and wounded two others (Privates S. Lemons and Goss), and knocked down the color-bearer (Sergt. W. M. Bland). We made a short halt at the position recently occupied by Chalmers, when we advanced to the Cowan house under a heavy fire of cannon and minie balls. My acting lieutenant-colonel (Lieut. R. A. Burford, late of the Twenty-third Tennessee Regiment) was knocked from his horse, and so severely concussed as to disable him for several days. I lost several men killed and wounded before we reached the Cowan house. We found the Cowan house and yard filled with men of Chalmers' brigade, in great confusion. Owing to this confusion, my regiment became somewhat scattered. The three right companies—A, F, and D, commanded, respectively, by Lieutenants [T. W.] McMurry, [J. B.] Tate, and [J. F.] Williamson—still kept dressed to the right, and reported to Colonel Savage, and fought with the Sixteenth Regiment through the remainder of the engagement. I refer you to Colonel Savage's report. I took the remaining seven companies and advanced through the field on the left of the Cowan house to the woods,

Just as we entered the woods, Captain [T. C.] Campbell was shot through the head and killed. Captain [J. A.] Russell was wounded through the thigh, and Lieutenant [G. C.] Howard, commanding Company G, wounded severely through the upper portion of the left lung. Captain [James F.] Franklin was so severely shocked with a bomb as to cause blood to flow freely from his mouth, nose, and ears. Several of the men were wounded here. We continued to advance on the enemy, who at this time was in full retreat. We continued to follow and fire on them for a long distance through the woods, taking three cannon and several hundred prisoners, sending to the rear at one time, by my adjutant (R. A. Connally), 153, among them a lieutenant and 2 surgeons. We continued the pursuit until late in the evening, when the engagement terminated.

I went into action with 20 officers, and 8 of them were killed and wounded.

R. T. McKnight, who was first lieutenant in Company F [E] before the reorganization of the regiment, and who has remained with the regiment since, as an independent, did good service as first lieutenant of Company F, bearing himself gallantly through the whole fight.

My color-sergeant (W. M. Bland), though wounded early in the action, continued to bear the colors most gallantly through the entire day.

After the fall of Lieutenant Burford, acting lieutenant-colonel, I had to rely entirely on my adjutant (R. A. Connally) for assistance, which he rendered most efficiently.

When the officers and men all did their duty so well it would be invidious to discriminate.

I went into the fight with 270 men, and lost, in killed, wounded, and missing, 76.

All of which is respectfully submitted.

JNO. CHESTER,
Commanding Fifty-first Tennessee Regiment.

Maj. J. G. MARTIN,
    Assistant Adjutant-General.

No. 199.

Report of Col. S. S. Stanton, Eighty-fourth Tennessee Infantry.

CAMP NEAR SHELBYVILLE, TENN.,
January 13, 1863.

The Eighty-fourth Tennessee Regiment, having been raised last fall and kept at McMinnville until a few days before the battle of Murfreesborough, never drew arms until Monday evening, December 29—two days before the fight. This regiment not having been drilled in the manual of arms (loading, &c.), and deeming this part of the drill as most important at that particular crisis, I drilled the regiment all day Tuesday on the field, under the enemy's shells, and likewise Wednesday morning, until the battle opened regularly, when we were ordered to move forward with General Donelson's brigade, and did so, and remained with his brigade until the aforesaid charge was made. We moved off on the left of Colonel Savage's regiment, after it had advanced to the point formerly occupied by our front line. Prior to this time my regiment had been formed to support Captain Carnes' battery, but were moved forward to the above-named point by orders from General Polk. When the balance of General Donelson's [brigade] moved or charged the enemy, my regiment was ordered to remain at the point last occupied by the brigade, and to guard Captain Carnes' battery. This battery, however, was moved off to the right, and the Washington Battery was located immediately on our left, and did good service, while we staid and guarded it all the while, until the troops engaging the enemy in our front were driven back to our rear, and while there, reforming their lines, orders came for all troops at that point to advance upon the enemy's batteries, to the right of the brick house, near the railroad and turnpike. Having my men already formed, I moved them off some 500 yards to the front, and halted at the bend of the river, behind a bunch of woods on a bluff immediately on the right of the railroad. Colonel Savage soon rallied his regiment, which necessarily had made a gallant charge, but had fallen back with much loss, and often [after] having reformed his lines, he and the Twentieth Tennessee came to our support, and formed near us. We all remained there, waiting for orders, and for another support, necessary to have charged the battery, but got neither support nor orders.

Night came on, and all was still. My men having no blankets, I moved them back to a point where we could make fires, and on the following morning went forward again to my former position, near the brick house, and then reported to Generals Donelson and Polk. The former ordered me to remain there during the day. However, I was ordered to take the regiment, and go to the brick house, and tear down the fencing thereabouts. We did this, and were shelled there while at work; only got 2 men wounded, however. Having completed this work and marched the men back to said point near the woodland bluff, I was ordered to the rear, under arrest, on account of a personal difficulty or fight with a staff officer, and, therefore, was not with the regiment any more until their arrival at Shelbyville.

It is due my regiment that I should state that they showed marked coolness and courage all the while, as they were under heavy shelling for a great portion of three days, and showed no fear or excitement. They kept good order and never scattered, but, on the contrary, some 40 of my men came up from McMinnville, and got arms and accouterments, and came to us in the hottest time of the fight, and while we were under heavy shelling in the open field at an advanced position, however, by lying down. None of our men scattered on our retreat.

The two wounded were George Cook, sergeant Company B, and Thomas Martin, private, Company E, slight wound.*

Respectfully,

S. S. STANTON,
Colonel Eighty-fourth Tennessee Regiment.

No. 200.

Report of Lieut. L. G. Marshall, Carnes' (Tennessee) battery.

NEAR SHELBYVILLE, TENN., *January* 15, 1863.

MAJOR: After occupying a position in rear of General Donelson's brigade for two days—December 29 and 30—on the reserve, Captain Carnes was ordered about noon, on December 31, to move his battery forward, in support of the right wing of our brigade, especially the brave

---

* Revised statements make no mention of these casualties

Sixteenth Tennessee. The battery accordingly took position on the right of the Nashville road, about three-fourths of a mile in advance of its former position, and near the river. Here we halted about an hour, during which we lost 1 man killed and 2 horses without opening fire. The battery was then ordered to advance, in order the better to return the enemy's fire. We therefore proceeded up the road about 200 yards, when we were met by our forces, making a slight retrograde movement, and the battery was compelled to take its former position, nearly. Here we immediately went into battery and fired a few rounds, by order of General Breckinridge, to assist in steadying our own troops, though not having a very fair shot at the enemy. Late in the evening the battery was ordered to cross over to the Wilkinson road, and finally to its old position near the railroad bridge for the night.

On the next day, the 1st instant, we were ordered to occupy a position in line with four or five other batteries on the high ground to the left of the Nashville road, and about the same distance in front as our position the day before. We here fortified our guns as well as circumstances permitted, but did not return the few shots the enemy gave us in this position.

During the evening Captain Carnes, by order, took our two howitzers over to the bluff, on the right of the railroad and pike, near the river, and opened what we afterward learned to be a very destructive fire upon the enemy, compelling them to retire and change their position. The enemy did not reply with artillery, and our immediate front was cleared of his sharpshooters.

The next day, the 2d instant, our whole battery (also [Capt. T. J.] Stanford's and [M.] Smith's) took position in line on the same bluff. To our left, across the Nashville road, were [W. L.] Scott's and [F. H.] Robertson's batteries. We all opened simultaneously to clear our front of the enemy's sharpshooters, who had reoccupied the woods along our front during the night. The enemy replied by several batteries, two of which were composed of rifled guns. The firing continued about twenty minutes. Our caissons, under command of Lieutenant [James M.] Cockrill, were then ordered up to replenish our ammunition chests. Two similar artillery conflicts took place during the day, our caissons being brought up each time to supply our limbers. The caissons were held under such cover as the ground allowed, about 300 yards in the rear.

During the evening Captain Carnes took our two howitzers to the right of our line of batteries, very near the river, and effectually cleared the woods of the enemy in front of our right. At night the battery was ordered back to the rifle-trench running across the field, 200 or 300 yards in rear of the burnt brick house, and supported by General Maney's brigade.

At daylight on the morning of the 3d instant our battery took the same position by itself on the bluff, instructed not to reply to the enemy's artillery, but to repel any advance of the enemy's infantry or sharpshooters. We immediately opened a brisk fire upon the enemy's skirmishers, who had again occupied the woods in our front. We soon cleared the woods of the enemy, though supported, as usual, by their artillery.

Late in the evening the enemy opened a powerful fire of his artillery upon our position, attracted, probably, by the appearance of a regiment going to relieve our pickets in the woods. We lost at this time 1 man killed and 4 wounded. About 7 p. m. we were ordered to return to our old camp, near town.

Our battery had thus stood at strict attention for seven days, during which the harness had not been taken from the horses. Our men behaved with firmness throughout, and handled their guns with admirable skill and quickness.*

Corpl. Martin Armstrong, missing, heard of at home since, near Tracy City.

We lost 4 horses killed. Three caisson wheels were rendered unserviceable.

We fired in all between 300 and 350 rounds. The battery was engaged once on Wednesday, once on Thursday, four times on Friday, and once on Saturday—in all seven times. We used almost entirely spherical case and canister, and in every case so far successful as to have the effect intended. The fuses operated in accordance with the tables, as we had taught the gunners. We used only the Bormann fuse. As to the adjustable sights, we could make little or no use of them, though we ascertained nothing against their character for very long ranges; but on the occasion under discussion our chiefs of pieces much preferred to watch the effect of their shots, and regulate the elevation accordingly.

L. G. MARSHALL,
Lieutenant, Commanding Capt. W. W. Carnes' Battery.

No. 201.

Report of Brig. Gen. Alexander P. Stewart, C. S. Army, commanding Second Brigade.

HEADQUARTERS SECOND BRIGADE, FIRST DIVISION,
POLK'S CORPS, ARMY OF TENNESSEE,
January 13, 1863.

SIR: I have the honor to submit the following report of the part taken by this brigade in the military operations in front of Murfreesborough, Tenn., commencing on Monday, December 29, 1862, and closing on Sunday, January 4, 1863:

The brigade was composed of the Fourth and Fifth Tennessee Regiments, amalgamated and commanded by Col. O. F. Strahl; the Twenty-fourth Tennessee Regiment, Col. H. L. W. Bratton; the Thirty-first and Thirty-third Tennessee Regiments, amalgamated and commanded by Col. E. E. Tansil; the Nineteenth Tennessee Regiment, Col. F. M. Walker, and Capt. T. J. Stanford's Mississippi battery. We struck tents, packed up baggage, and sent the wagons to the rear on Sunday night, December 28.

Early Monday morning we crossed Stone's River and formed line of battle on its north bank, being on the left of Donelson and right of Maney, the right of the brigade being some distance on the left of the Wilkinson pike. An open country lay in front of the line, excepting on the left, where Walker's regiment was covered by the open forest. From 800 to 1,000 yards in front of us lay the first line, Major-General Withers' division, our division forming the second and supporting line. Nothing of special interest occurred on Monday.

On Tuesday morning a few shells from the enemy passed over and near us, wounding one man in Bratton's regiment, and late in the evening we were under a heavy artillery fire for some half hour or more, but without injury. In the course of the afternoon of Tuesday an officer came from Colonel Manigault, of the Tenth South Carolina, who com-

---

* Nominal list shows 2 men killed and 4 wounded.

manded the third brigade from the right in Withers' division. He
stated that Colonel Manigault was in need of a section of long-range
guns to dislodge guns of the enemy, he having only smooth-bores of
short range, and that he had applied to General Maney, whose brigade
was the support of Manigault's, who replied that he had none suitable
for the purpose. He came to me, therefore, for a section of Stanford's
battery. Knowing that Stanford, his officers, and men were always
ready to go wherever needed, two pieces were promptly dispatched in
charge of Lieutenant [A. A.] Hardin. On their return I was informed
they were not properly supported; that they were required to engage,
at a distance not exceeding 600 yards, guns that were throwing shell,
canister, and spherical case; that they accomplished no useful purpose,
but sustained some loss, one or two men being wounded, and Lieut. A.
A. Hardin, commanding a section, a most estimable and gallant young
officer, being killed.

Tuesday night, or early Wednesday morning, was received a copy of
General Bragg's order directing an attack to commence on the left and
gradually extend to the Murfreesborough and Nashville pike, the left
wing to swing round toward the right on a pivot at the pike. I was also
informed both by Lieutenant-General Polk and by a staff officer from
Major General Withers that I was to be directed by the latter, and to obey
his orders.

On Wednesday morning, December 31, about 8 o'clock, I was notified to move forward, gradually wheeling to the right and maintaining
a distance of a few hundred yards (supporting distance) from Anderson's
brigade, Withers' division. After advancing some distance directly to
the front across the open field, the brigade was moved to the left by the
flank, so as to place the entire line under cover of the forest from the
enemy's artillery fire. The ground over which we were then moving
being wet and heavy, Captain Stanford was directed to take the Wilkinson (or Wilkerson) pike. I did not see anything more of him or his battery for a day or two, they having doubtless been employed elsewhere
by the orders of some one of my superiors.

The line of infantry advanced through the woods, gradually wheeling to the right, and occasionally halting to readjust the line, and maintaining its supporting distance from Anderson, General Withers himself
being often with us, and the movements of the brigade corresponding to
his wishes. At one point he sent word that Anderson's two left regiments would be thrown forward, perhaps, to attack the battery that
continued to play upon our advancing lines, and desired me to throw
forward two regiments in a corresponding manner. Fearing this would
scatter the brigade and produce confusion, it was suggested to him that
the entire brigade had better be advanced, to which he assented. We
shortly arrived at the stone wall built by Anderson's men, where they
were placed in line on Sunday, the 28th. Several men were wounded
here by the fire of the battery in front. While in this position the
Twenty-ninth and Thirtieth Regiments Mississippi Volunteers (belonging, as was supposed, to Anderson's brigade) fell back in disorder,
leaving a large number of dead and wounded in the open ground beyond the Wilkinson pike, over which they had charged. They were
rallied in our rear chiefly by Major [L. W.] Finlay, of my staff, and
again sent forward. The Twenty-ninth ultimately formed on my left,
where it remained until the close of the battle, when it moved away to
join its brigade. The brigade moved on from this position to the pike,
where it was faced by the left flank and marched a short distance down
the road, to bring its right under cover of the woods, when it moved

again to the front. It crossed the open ground interven.ng between the pike and the cedar forest beyond, and advanced to the relief of the front line, which was giving way, and, by a rapid fire, commencing with Walker's regiment (the Nineteenth) on the left and gradually extending to the right, repulsed the enemy, who fled in confusion to the dense cedar woods, leaving many dead and wounded behind. Near the edge of the woods we came upon the battery (First Missouri) that had previously annoyed us so much, and which the enemy were now attempting to remove. Our advance was so rapid and fire so destruct-ive that they were compelled to abandon two pieces and one or two caissons. We left them behind, and, pressing rapidly forward, drove the enemy before us. They attempted to make a stand at several points, but, unable to endure our fire, were driven through the forest and across the open field beyond to the high ground in the vicinity of the railroad. Here they took shelter under the guns of three or four batteries, leaving a number of prisoners in our hands and many dead and wounded scattered through the woods and covering the open field over which they fled in double-quick time. These batteries opened upon us, and for some time we were exposed to a terrific fire of shell, canister, and spherical case. Having no battery of our own, and being nearly out of ammunition, it was impossible to proceed farther. Staff officers were dispatched—one to bring up Stanford's battery, another for ammunition. The latter was soon supplied, but word came from Lieutenant-General Polk that Stanford was employed under his own immediate orders, and could not be spared. While moving through the cedar forest the command of Brigadier-General Jackson came up on the right. The Fifth Georgia, immediately on the right, with the Fourth and Fifth Tennessee, advanced beyond the general line and delivered a heavy and well-sustained fire upon the retreating ranks of the enemy, doing fine execution.

About this time Colonel [J. A.] Jaquess, of the First Louisiana (Regulars), rode rapidly up to Colonel [E. E.] Tansil and delivered some order, which I did not hear. Immediately Tansil's regiment began to fall back without waiting for a command, and was gradually followed by the rest of the brigade, and I learned from Tansil that Jaquess brought to him an order purporting to come from Major-General Cheatham to "move by the right of companies to the rear." The order not having been delivered to me, not recognizing Colonel Jaquess as a member of General Cheatham's staff, and satisfied that the movement was demoralizing in a high degree, it was arrested as promptly as possible. The line was halted and reformed, and moved forward again to the edge of the woods, where we remained until dark, when, leaving a strong picket guard, the command was withdrawn a few hundred yards to the rear, to bivouac, taking along a large number of small-arms, ammunition, and equipments, which were removed next day by wagons brought out for the purpose.

Late in the afternoon, Lieut. Col. W. B. Ross, formerly of Col. [J.] Knox Walker's (Second) Tennessee regiment, was wounded by a minie bullet in the right side of the neck and throat. He was removed to the hospital, and subsequently to a private residence in Murfreesborough, where he died on Friday, January 2. He was serving as a volunteer on my staff. He was with his regiment at the battle of Belmont in November, 1861; resigned in January, 1862, and joined me as a volunteer aide at Corinth a few days before the battle of Shiloh, where he behaved well, and was very useful. He was a brave man and a good officer.

While attempting to stop the retrograde movement alluded to, Col. H. L. W. Bratton, of the Twenty-fourth Regiment, had his left leg shattered near the thigh joint by a piece of shell or a grape-shot. The limb was amputated, and he was left in hospital in Murfreesborough, with little hope on the part of the surgeons of his recovery. He was one of the best and bravest officers in the entire army. Always prompt to obey or execute an order, indefatigable in drilling and disciplining his men, he was animated by a lofty courage and patriotism that bid defiance to danger. He distinguished himself by his cool and courageous bearing both at Perryville and Murfreesborough, and was indeed a "knight without fear and without reproach."

The force we engaged in this famous cedar brake was composed, at least in part, of regulars. Some of the prisoners and wounded men stated that they belonged to the Sixteenth, Seventeenth, and Eighteenth Regulars, and that their brigade was commanded by Colonel [George W.] Roberts, who fell while gallantly attempting to rally his men about opposite the center of my line. He was buried Saturday evening, and the spot marked by a stone having his name scratched upon it with the point of a bayonet.

During the three following days (Thursday, Friday, and Saturday) we held our position at the edge of the brake, the enemy occupying the ridge, but a few hundred yards in front, with a heavy force of infantry and artillery, frequently shelling us, and wounding a few men at almost every round. The command remained in line, enduring this trying ordeal with admirable patience and fortitude. At length, on Saturday night, our pickets were relieved by Colonel Carter's cavalry, and about 1 or 2 a. m. on Sunday, the 4th, we left the field for Shelbyville.

Throughout the week officers and men behaved in a manner that is beyond praise.

I desire especially to mention Col. O. F. Strahl, commanding Fourth and Fifth Regiments; Col. H. L. W. Bratton, of the Twenty-fourth; Col. E. E. Tansil, commanding the Thirty-first and Thirty-third, and Col. F. M. Walker, of the Nineteenth, who, with all their field officers, behaved most nobly.

The Nineteenth (Colonel Walker's) suffered more heavily than any other in the brigade. Colonel Walker, in his report, mentions the brave conduct of Orderly Sergt. Joseph Thompson, Company I, who, after the brigade had halted at the edge of the cedar bottom, advanced far into the field and captured 2 prisoners. Our loss was heavy—over one-fourth of those engaged. The list* of killed and wounded has already been sent in.

Besides those already mentioned, Lieutenant-Colonel [J. A.] Wilson and Adjt. H. W. Mott,† of the Twenty-fourth, were wounded, as were also Major [R. A.] Jarnigan, of the Nineteenth, and Captain [T. H.] Francis, of the Fourth. Several valuable officers were killed. Lieutenant-Colonel [Andrew J.] Kellar, of the Fourth, was really too ill for duty; nevertheless, he was at his post.

Many of the enemy's dead, and some of our own, were left on the field unburied. We procured a few spades on Saturday evening, and buried as many bodies as was possible under the circumstances. I would respectfully submit that at least all our own dead might have been buried during the three days we held the field. Attention is also respectfully called to the plundering and stripping of the dead, even our own, and to the propriety of a general order prohibiting it.

I cannot close this imperfect sketch without expressing my obligations to the gentlemen who served on my staff, and who made themselves so

---

* See No. 191, p. 676.   † Register has W. H. Mott killed at Murfreesborough.

intelligently useful and efficient, regardless of danger, viz: Col. [Capt.] W. M. Reed, assistant adjutant-general; Capt. R. A. Hatcher, aide-de-camp; Capt. John A. Lauderdale, formerly of the Fifth, a volunteer aide; Maj. L. W. Finlay, of the Fourth, and Lieut. Paul Jones, jr., of the Thirty-third, supernumeraries by the amalgamation of their regiments with others, but who preferred to be in the field. These officers, and Private Frank C. Usher, of the First Tennessee, acting as orderly, were active and efficient, and contributed not a little to the ease and facility with which I was enabled to handle the brigade.

Having received no report from Captain Stanford, and his battery having been detached from the brigade before it really went into action, it is not in my power to give an account of its services, which I learn, however, were, as usual, valuable.

I am, sir, very respectfully, your obedient servant,

A. P. STEWART,
Brigadier-General.

Capt. JOHN INGRAM,
Acting Assistant Adjutant-General.

No. 202.

Report of Col. Oscar F. Strahl, Fourth Tennessee Infantry, commanding Fourth and Fifth Regiments.

JANUARY 5, 1863.

SIR: On the morning of December 29, 1862, I took command of the Fourth and Fifth Regiments Tennessee Volunteers, and was immediately ordered out to take position in line of battle. The position we occupied was on the west bank of Stone's River and immediately on the left of General Donelson's brigade, the right of which brigade rested on the Chattanooga and Nashville Railroad. We remained in this position until about 9 o'clock in the morning of the 31st, when we were ordered to advance in such a manner as to change direction gradually to the right, keeping dressed to the left. We advanced in this manner until we came to where General Withers' men had thrown up small breast-works. At this point we were halted for a short time, and had several men wounded by grape and canister from the enemy's guns. While remaining here, a regiment from General Withers' division fell back and formed immediately in my rear. We then advanced, first through a cedar thicket and then through an open field for some 400 or 500 yards, where we entered a cedar glade. All this time we were gradually changing direction to the right. In a few minutes after passing into the cedar glade we were engaged by the enemy, but drove them before us, taking quite a number of prisoners. We continued to press the enemy, fighting as we advanced, until we had driven them entirely out of the glade. The slaughter of the enemy was very great just at the edge of the glade, as they were slow to leave the timber and our men were close upon them, and every shot did its work. Then the enemy opened a very heavy fire upon us from a battery within a few hundred yards of our lines. We soon silenced it, however, by sending out some sharpshooters, who so disabled it that the battery retired, leaving one gun and caisson behind. This was on Wednesday evening, the 31st. We remained in the position we now occupied until Saturday night, all the time exposed to the enemy's guns.

The men and officers under my command acted with the greatest gallantry during the whole time and discharged their duties without a murmur.

The number of killed and wounded has heretofore been reported.

Very respectfully,

O. F. STRAHL,
Colonel, Comdg. Fourth and Fifth Regiments Tennessee Vols.

Col. [Capt.] W. M. REED,
Assistant Adjutant-General, Stewart's Brigade.

No. 203.

Report of Col. Francis M. Walker, Nineteenth Tennessee Infantry.

SHELBYVILLE, TENN., *January 10, 1863.*

About sunrise Monday morning, December 29, the Nineteenth Tennessee Regiment, under my command, moved on the left of your brigade to a position previously selected on the north bank of Stone's River, where we were posted in line of battle as the extreme left regiment of the brigade. The regiment numbered in line 348 privates and non-commissioned officers, 30 company officers, 3 field officers, and adjutant; aggregate, 382. We remained at the point above mentioned in line until 9 a. m. Wednesday, uninterrupted except by the occasional explosion near us of a stray shell from the enemy's batteries, when we moved forward in line with the brigade to the attack, in support of the front line of the corps, we being in the second line. On our way we met many stragglers and wounded men from the front lines retiring to the rear, the former demoralized, the latter disabled. The first we tried to turn back, urging them to renew their efforts; the last we could but pity.

Some 400 yards from our first position, we came to the position previously occupied by the front or first lines the day before, and where they had thrown up a temporary breastwork of loose stone and timber. At and behind this the regiment halted for half an hour or more under a heavy fire from some unseen batteries in our front. At this point, while my men were lying behind the loose wall of rock, a shell struck the latter near the center of my left wing, wounding, by the fragments of shell and shattered rock, 6 of my men, all of whom were disabled and 1 of whom soon after died. Moving from this point we came to the Wilkinson pike, up which we moved by the left flank near 300 yards, when, again resuming the movement to the front, we moved forward through a field to the top of a slight elevation, where the battery which had been playing on us is believed to have been posted. But just when we were resuming the march to the front and crossing the Wilkinson pike we could distinctly see by the action of the men in the front line (for we had now come in sight of them) that they were on the eve of being driven back, if, indeed, they had not already entirely given way. Many of them were falling back, and all seemed disorganized. But our line promptly moved up to their support and crossed the field to the elevation. Here, for the first time, we could see the evidences of the conflict in the field beyond the elevation. Numbers of dead and wounded were lying [about], both Confederates and Federals, horses, and arms, and equipments, and here we first felt the fire from the small-arms of the enemy. Pushing forward, we crossed the field and entered the thick cedar woods in which the enemy had taken shelter. In the edge of this woods we came up with three or four pieces of the battery which they had vainly endeavored to withdraw. These are believed to have been the guns posted on the elevation in the field above mentioned, and from which we had received the injury while at the rock wall in the woods. As we entered the woods the enemy gave us a most galling fire, but we moved steadily forward, driving them farther into the thick wood, and now we passed the various pieces of artillery which they were trying to remove, but which, on our approach and under our fire and from loss of horses, thickness of timber, &c., they were forced soon to abandon. These we left in our rear and pressed upon the heavy lines of their infantry, under whose fire we were exposed. Some 200 yards farther into the woods the enemy appeared in great force, rather to my left. They here poured in upon me a most effective and murderous fire. This we returned with all the vigor and rapidity possible, gradually moving forward, swinging, according to orders, a little from left to right. This constant and severe fire continued for near an hour, when, by the persistency and accuracy of our fire, our steady and resistless advance, the obstinacy of the enemy was at last overcome, and, giving way, a perfect rout ensued. Their retreat was rapidly followed up by us through the woods for several hundred yards, and through an old field, through which a ravine and also the Nashville and Chattanooga Railroad ran, within which and behind the embankment of the railroad the enemy took refuge. At these points they were beyond the reach of our small-arms. We pursued no farther than the edge of this field. But before reaching their safe retreat, while they passed through the woods and field, hundreds of them paid the penalty with their lives for their rash act of invasion and wicked occupation of an unoffending country. The marks on the arms and equipments picked up on the field from which we drove the enemy, as well as the statements of prisoners captured, show conclusively that the brigade or division which we fought was regular troops.

By your direction, the entire brigade halted at the edge of the field, for at the time, and all the time of our advance through the woods, there appeared no support upon our left. It is believed if a battery could have been put in position near the point occupied by my left, the enemy could have been shelled from their shelter in the ravine and behind the railroad, and the day might thus have been more completely ours. Six or eight thousand men seemed to be striving for the mastery, in confusion, in this field, and would have been easily driven into the woods beyond. But a battery was out of the question, for we could scarcely get through parts of the woods through which we came. We remained in position here until near night, when we retired with the brigade to the rear a few hundred yards, for rest.

We moved back to the front each succeeding day, keeping skirmishers in front near the edge of the field for three days, but no casualties or engagement of note further occurred until we moved with the brigade in retreat on the evacuation on Sunday morning.

In the engagement my men captured about 50 prisoners, who were sent to the rear. We also brought from the field about three hundred guns besides our own, some of the men bringing off three.

The loss of the regiment in killed and wounded was 136, as will appear from the accompanying report* of my adjutant. My major (Rufus A. Jarnigan) was mortally wounded while leading the left wing in a charge. Captain [J. G.] Frazier, Company D, was killed instantly at the head of his company. Lieutenant [S. G.] Abernathy fell at his post.

---

*Not found, but see No. 191, p. 676.

No braver or more gallant officers than these have given their lives to their country in this war.

I hope, sir, that the conduct of the men and officers of this regiment in the engagement at Murfreesborough and the days and nights of duty and exposure connected with it has been satisfactory to you. I can complain of none of them myself, but might compliment many of them in terms of high encomium. I might with propriety mention the case of Corporal Mayson, of the color-guard, who, when the color-sergeant was wounded and the colors fell from his hand, instantly seized it in exultation, bearing it as a beacon to the regiment through the storm of the battle; and of Orderly Sergt. Joseph Thompson, who, upon reaching the edge of the field where the brigade halted, ran forward, overtaking the retreating enemy, seized a prisoner and started back with him, but this person being shot down in his hands he relinquished him; back to the lines of the still-retreating enemy, and seized a second prisoner, whom he brought off safely.

Before closing this report, sir, I beg leave to congratulate you upon the successful and skillful manner in which your brigade was maneuvered and kept together, and, through you, I congratulate our division, corps, and other commanders for our successful operations against greatly superior numbers. I hope, sir, that yours and their success may never be less marked or less safe to yourselves in all future engagements with our enemies.

Very respectfully, general, yours, &c.,

F. M. WALKER,
Colonel Nineteenth Tennessee Regiment.

Brig. Gen. ALEXANDER P. STEWART.

No. 204.

Report of Maj. S. E. Shannon, Twenty-fourth Tennessee Infantry.

SHELBYVILLE, TENN., *January* 10, 1863.

The following is a report of the battle at Murfreesborough, Tenn., in which the Twenty-fourth Tennessee Regiment was engaged, commencing on December 29, [1862,] and ending on January 4, 1863:

We left camp on the morning of December 29, 1862; crossed Stone's River and formed line of battle on the north side of said river, and there remained under frequent shelling until December 31, 1862, when we were ordered to advance, which we did through a corn-field; thence through a skirt of woods and across the Wilkinson pike, advancing on through a stubble field; thence into a cedar glade, where we engaged the enemy and drove him through the woods before us.

Here we sustained a loss of 9 killed, 3 of whom were commissioned officers (1 captain and 2 lieutenants), also 70 wounded, 4 of whom were commissioned officers (our colonel commanding, lieutenant-colonel, adjutant, and 1 lieutenant), our colonel and adjutant mortally wounded.

On arriving at the edge of an old field in our front, we were ordered back by some one representing himself as aide-de-camp to Major-General Cheatham, which order was obeyed by falling back to the top of the hill, where we reformed, advanced, and took our former position at the edge of an old field, where we remained in line of battle under occasional heavy shelling, which position we held until ordered off on the night of January 4, during which time we lost 1 man killed and several wounded, resulting from the occasional shelling and skirmishing along our line.

The officers and men acted gallantly, except a few who straggled from ranks during the engagement.   The regiment left the field in good order when the retreat was ordered.

S. E. SHANNON,
Major, Commanding Twenty-fourth Tennessee Regiment.

No. 205.

Report of Col. E. E. Tansil, Thirty-first Tennessee Infantry, commanding Thirty-first and Thirty-third Regiments.

ON OUTPOST, MURFREESBOROUGH AND SHELBYVILLE PIKE,
March 13, 1863.

On the morning of December 29, 1862, we left our encampment near Murfreesborough, and crossed Stone's River, where we formed line and remained until the 31st, when we moved to the front, crossing a corn-field and entering a skirt of woods to the breastworks thrown up by General Withers' troops, and remained until his troops were driven back, when we were again moved to the front, crossing a pike, entering a small field and another narrow skirt of woods and another small field, to a dense cedar grove, where we were halted and formed line.   We were then moved again to the front, but had advanced but a short distance until we came upon the battery which had been playing upon us all the time after leaving the breastworks; also the infantry concealed in the woods.   One volley from our well-aimed pieces caused them to abandon two pieces of artillery, which they were trying to get off, and threw the enemy in confusion, who commenced retreating immediately.   The artillery was passed by the right of the Thirty-first and left of the Thirty-third regiments, who pursued the enemy hotly through the woods (in width half a mile, capturing about 20 prisoners) to a field where the enemy were in strong position on the line of the railroad, but were doing good execution, as the enemy were retreating across the field in great confusion, when some one came up, purporting to be on General Cheat-ham's staff, with orders to fall back by right of companies to the rear, which caused some confusion, as it was given publicly.   We fell back some 100 yards and supplied the men with ammunition, and again took our position near the field, where we remained until the night of January 3.

Both men and officers acted very gallantly.   My loss has been reported.

Respectfully submitted.

E. E. TANSIL,
Colonel Thirty-first and Thirty-third Regts. Tennessee Vols.

No. 206.

Report of Capt. T. J. Stanford, Mississippi Battery.

CAMP NEAR SHELBYVILLE, TENN.,
January 12, 1863.

On Monday morning, December 29, 1862, the battery moved from the camp, 1 mile west of Murfreesborough, to its position, with the brigade, in line of battle on the west side of Stone's River, in rear of Mrs. James' house. Here we remained all day, nothing of interest occurring, and the monotony disturbed only by an occasional shot from the rifle batteries of the enemy passing over us.

On Tuesday morning heavy skirmishing commenced on our left, and was kept up with but little intermission during the day, and, though we did not participate in the fight until evening, the battery was more exposed to random shots than on the previous day. About 3 o'clock in the afternoon an order was received to send two of my pieces to the left, to assist in dislodging the enemy from a certain point. Accordingly, I dispatched Lieutenant Hardin with the first section, who promptly went forward to perform the duty. After an absence of about an hour the section returned, but without its leader. Lieutenant Hardin, after having performed the object of his mission, and withdrawn the section with the view of rejoining us, was suddenly killed by a cannon shot. A gallant officer, a true soldier, and a Christian gentleman, he adds another to the long list of martyrs who have given their lives to their country's cause. Private M. Hartsfield received a painful but not dangerous flesh wound in this engagement.

On Wednesday morning about 9 o'clock I moved in rear of the brigade, on the road leading through the wood on our left, and while moving received an order from General Polk to take position in the old field on the right of the Wilkinson pike, and support Captain [O. W.] Barret's battery. This field, you will recollect, is the one extending to the enemy's lines, and, being for the most part level, his works covered and his guns swept every foot of the ground. Here I remained during the day, changing position only as circumstances required, or the retreating enemy invited to follow. Several times during the day the fire of the battery had a telling effect upon their lines of infantry, which were plainly to be seen. At one time they occupied a strong position in front of the little log-house (daubed with red mud), and held in check our forces, who had to march across an open flat of ground to attack them. Arriving in position in time to observe the enemy and the repulse of our forces at the same time, I threw a few well-directed shots into their ranks, which caused them to retreat precipitately. Our lines immediately advanced, occupied the position, and continued to drive them. Again, later in the afternoon, I advanced as far as the Cowan or burnt brick house, on the Nashville pike, from which point, although exposed to a galling fire from their batteries, we succeeded in pouring a very destructive fire into their ranks, causing them to give back from several points, and materially aiding our infantry in their advance. Here we lost 2 men and several horses killed and one limber disabled. All day we were under fire from their batteries, until late in the evening, when we were ordered to resume our original position.

On Thursday morning I moved to a position on the Nashville pike, at the point where the railroad crosses that road, and remained all day and part of the following night without firing a gun. Indeed, there was no fighting and but little skirmishing on our lines during the time. Orders being received during the night, my battery, together with the other batteries of the division, moved, and was placed in the open woods on the right of the railroad, about 500 yards north of the Cowan or burnt brick house. Chalmers' brigade was sent to support us.

Very early in the morning (Friday) it became evident that the enemy would dispute with us for this ground. Twice during the day their skirmishers drove ours in, and the heavy columns of infantry following were only repulsed by our artillery. It having been determined that General Breckinridge should attack them on our right, orders were sent to me that precisely at 4 o'clock I should open with my battery on the left of the woods skirting the river bank, and upon the enemy's batteries, in order, as I inferred, to draw their fire from our right. This I evidently succeeded in doing. They turned all their batteries on me, producing a concentration of shot and shell such as I never before witnessed. During the night I returned to the place I had left in the morning, and on Saturday morning moved to our extreme left, to resist a movement the enemy were supposed to be making in that direction. Here we remained until late in the evening, when orders were given to move to the rear of Murfreesborough. My movements each day of the fight were governed by orders directly from Lieutenant-General Polk. As usual, I did not move with your brigade in the fight, but I do not doubt but that I gave you as much support as though I had, for my positions covered your right and front as effectually as if I had been with you, and perhaps better.

I feel satisfied with the part the battery played, and know that I did our cause some service. Considering the exposed situation of the company, it would appear strange that we lost so few killed and wounded. This must be accounted for from the fact that I kept my caissons in the rear, out of range of the shot, and the limbers and drivers were, for the most part, sheltered. Only the officers and cannoneers were exposed all the time; nevertheless, we have to mourn the loss of 3 killed and 4 wounded—all by cannon shot. There were also 7 horses killed.

To Lieutenants [H. R.] McSwine and [J. S.] McCall I am much indebted for the proper management of the battery in the several engagements in which it participated. The whole company acted bravely, doing no discredit to their reputation gained at Shiloh and Perryville.

I have the honor to be, very respectfully,
T. J. STANFORD,
Captain, Commanding Light Battery.

Brig. Gen. ALEXANDER P. STEWART,
Comdg. Second Brig., First Div., Polk's Corps, Army of Tenn.

No. 207.

Report of Brig. Gen. George Maney, C. S. Army, commanding Third Brigade.

HDQRS. MANEY'S BRIGADE, CHEATHAM'S DIVISION,
POLK'S CORPS, ARMY OF TENNESSEE,
Camp near Shelbyville, Tenn., January 15, 1863.

SIR: I respectfully submit the following report of the action of my command in the battle near Murfreesborough, Tenn., on the 31st ultimo:

It consisted of the First and Twenty-seventh Tennessee Regiments (consolidated), Col. H. R. Feild commanding; Fourth Confederate Regiment (Tennessee), Col. J. A. McMurry commanding; Sixth and Ninth Tennessee Regiments (consolidated), Col. C. S. Hurt commanding Smith's field battery (four guns—two 12-pounder Napoleons and two 12-pounder howitzers), First Lieut. William B. Turner commanding. The battalions were arranged in line of battle from right to left, in the order above mentioned.

My brigade was on outpost duty at Stewart's Creek, on the Nashville and Murfreesborough pike, when the enemy commenced his advance from Nashville, and on the afternoon of Friday, December 26, hearing firing in front, I moved forward with my command to La Vergne, a point on the pike midway between Nashville and Murfreesborough, and about 15 miles distant from each, where Brigadier-General Wheeler was stationed with his cavalry command. Here indications soon convinced me the enemy was engaged in a general forward movement, and, in consultation with General Wheeler, it was determined to so advise the commanding general.

Next morning the opinion was confirmed as to the movement of the enemy, and, according to instructions, in conjunction with the cavalry, I fell back slowly, skirmishing with his advance and retarding his progress, until advised all was ready for action near Murfreesborough.

My command reached its camp near Murfreesborough on Sunday following, prepared rations, and rested there that night.

Next morning I moved to my position in line of battle on the west bank of Stone's River, between the Wilkinson pike and the Franklin road, being the third brigade from the right of Major General Cheatham's division, which was formed in rear of, and as a supporting line to, that of Major-General Withers, my brigade being directly in rear of and supporting the one commanded by Colonel Manigault.

In the afternoon I moved to the left as support to Robinson's [Robertson's] battery, which engaged a portion of the enemy, and bivouacked that night with my left flank resting on the Franklin road.

Next morning I returned to my position in rear of Colonel Manigault, and there remained until I moved into action Wednesday morning.

My understanding of instructions as to our plan of action was that our troops on the extreme left were to attack the enemy on his right flank, and as he was driven down the front of our line toward his center we were to enter the action successively by brigade, each brigade attacking the line immediately in front and swinging to the right, so as to keep up, as far as possible, continued pressing on the enemy's flank, our alignment to be held toward our pivot flank.

Under this order, about 8 a. m. Wednesday, I commenced moving forward in support of Colonel Manigault. In a short time I was under the enemy's fire, and, after advancing about 1,000 yards from my position, met Colonel Manigault, who informed me that, after driving the enemy from his immediate front, he had been compelled to fall back by a ruinous fire on his right flank from two of the enemy's batteries. These batteries were about 600 yards apart, one on quite a high ridge obliquely to my front and right, across open ground toward the Harding house; the other was directly to my right and could be approached under shelter of the woods in which it was planted. The battery on the ridge was firing actively, and the two were so related in support of each other that an attacking force against either singly from our position would be exposed to flank or oblique fire from the other, and to avoid this it was instantly arranged that Colonel Manigault should change his front to the right and engage the battery in the woods, while I attacked the one in the open ground. In accordance with this plan, Colonels Feild's and McMurry's regiments were ordered to change direction to the right for attack upon the battery, and Colonel Hurt, with his regiment, was detached from the line and advanced directly forward to occupy a skirt of woods about 300 yards to his front, for the purpose of protecting the other two regiments from flank fire during their movement upon the battery, with instructions that, if he engaged no enemy in these woods, to move rapidly forward to his place on the left of my line. These movements were executed with spirit and promptness, but the enemy, seeing the approach of a fresh line, hastily withdrew his battery and its support from the ridge. My own battery was hurried into position and delivered several shots upon his retiring force. Seeing the enemy retiring, the movement of my line was changed more sharply to the right, throwing a small part of it into the woods on my right and the remainder moving rapidly forward to the ridge-top he had abandoned. A short delay being necessary for Colonel Manigault to reform his brigade, my own got considerably in advance, and the battery in the woods opened on my right regiment. Colonel Feild at first took this to be our own battery, and ordered his regiment to lie down without firing, though he was within 200 yards of it; nor was this mistake discovered until one messenger to stop its fire had been killed and another narrowly escaped the same fate. His regiment was then ordered to fire, and with the aid of (I think) a portion of Colonel Manigault's brigade, which came up on the right, soon silenced the battery. Meantime my other two regiments, having attained the ridge-top in the open field but just abandoned by the enemy, were met with a furious shelling from a battery in plain view, about 500 yards distant, and just across the Wilkinson pike. The word coming to me from my right that we were being fired on by our own battery, led me to take the one across the road to be alluded to, that in the woods being at the moment hidden from my sight. Under these circumstances my line was ordered to lie down, and staff officers sent instantly to the right for accurate information. My battle-flag was conspicuously displayed from the ridge-top, but instead of diminishing seemed only, to attract the fire of the battery across the road. Next moment suspicion became certainty as to this battery by discovering the flag of the enemy in the woods to the right of and near it. His purpose in withdrawing from the ridge was now plain. The ground between my line and the Wilkinson pike (a distance of from 400 to 500 yards) was an open field, sloping gradually to the pike, on the opposite or north side of which and directly in my front was a thick wood, affording good cover. The enemy had withdrawn from the ridge I now occupied and posted his infantry in these woods, and established his battery so as to rake the field between us with an oblique fire from my front and right. Evidently his dispositions were made in expectation of my moving directly over this field against him. Fortunately, however, the ridge he had abandoned commanded the new position he had taken, and, finding an excellent location for my battery, I got it instantly in position and opened upon him with admirable effect, my infantry line lying down the while for protection. For a short time the artillery fire was hot and spirited, but Turner's Napoleons and 12-pounder howitzers, being in easy range and aided by advantage of position, were more than the enemy could stand. His battery was soon silenced and his infantry in retreat under our fire.

About this time Major-General Cheatham came in person to my line, and Colonel Manigault reported his brigade reformed and again ready to advance. By order of the major-general, Colonel Manigault was moved from my right to my left, and we moved across the field in line together, bearing sharply to the right, General Cheatham accompanying us. In this movement my center regiment passed over the four guns just beyond the pike with which my battery had been engaged, and which were too much disabled to be carried off in the enemy's flight. My line, after crossing the pike, was inclined to the left, and moved down through the cedar brake between the Wilkinson and Nashville pikes. The enemy fled before us without making any stand in these woods, but in a short time opened a furious shelling from his main position near the Nashville pike. My command was halted at the northern margin of this cedar brake, in line with other brigades on my right, and in a short time Major-General McCown's division came forward in prolongation to my left.

During the afternoon the bulk of our left and center forces were concentrated in these woods and formed in two lines, apparently in anticipation of the enemy making an attack to regain the field from which he had been driven. My command remained in position here in the front line until Friday evening, when I was ordered to take position to the right, in support of our batteries near the Cowan house.

At daylight, Saturday morning, I was ordered back to position in the cedar brake from which I came the previous evening, and remained there until our army retired from Murfreesborough, my brigade bringing up the rear on the Shelbyville road.

I cannot close my report of this memorable battle without expressing my highest satisfaction in the conduct of my entire command. During the main engagement, and the frequent and severe shellings to which they were exposed for the three days following, they exhibited the steady and reliable courage of veterans. Exposure to cold and drenching rain, added to the fatigue of the battle, could not fail in wearing, to some extent, their bodies; but under all the dangers and hardships incident to the time, the *morale* evinced was admirable. Truly, they bore themselves as soldiers, comprehending the stake involved.

My battalion commanders—Colonels Feild, Hurt, and McMurry—have my thanks for their gallantry and efficiency during the entire action, and I refer to their reports, filed with this, for particulars as to their officers and men. Also, I feel it proper to mention First Lieutenant Turner, commanding, First Lieut. Chandler [S.] Smith and Second Lieut. Charles [L. B.] Ingraham, of my battery, for their good conduct, and with them thank their command for the excellent manner in which their guns were served.

My staff—Captain [Thomas H.] Malone, assistant adjutant-general; Captain [E.] Cockrill, acting ordnance officer and aide; Lieutenant Keeble, acting assistant inspector-general and aide—all have my thanks for valuable services and assistance.

Capt. R. H. Harrison, of the Ninth Tennessee Regiment, having been temporarily relieved from his regular command by the consolidation of his regiment, and Hon. John F. House, acted on my staff as volunteer aides, and exhibited both promptness and daring throughout the action.

In the latter part of the day, Captain [J. H.] Trezevant, First Louisiana Regiment (Regulars), reported to me, stating himself disabled by a wound for duty on foot, but anxious to render what service he could, mounted. Under these circumstances I accepted his services, and thank him for bearing several orders to different parts of the field.

I have previously furnished a statement of the losses from my command.

Very respectfully,

GEO. MANEY,
Brigadier-General.

Maj. JOHN INGRAM, *Assistant Adjutant-General.*

No. 208.

Report of Col. H. R. Feild, First Tennessee Infantry.

———— —, 1863.

In compliance with orders, I must submit to you the following report of the part my command took in the action before Murfreesborough on Wednesday, December 31, 1862:

Enemy opened fire on me just as our line arrived at the brick-kiln, some 400 or 500 yards south of the Wilkinson pike, from a four-gun battery about 200 yards distant, which I thought at first was our own battery, from its position and our very close proximity to it before it opened fire. With that belief I ordered the men to lie down, and sent Lieutenant [R. F.] James forward to tell them that they were firing on their friends. He approached within 50 yards of the battery, when he was shot dead by its support. I still believed it to be our own battery, and sent another mounted officer to see. I think it was Lieutenant [John H.] Marsh; I do not know. He rode within 40 yards of it, when its support rose up and fired a volley at him, but fortunately missing, when he wheeled his horse and made his escape. Then I became convinced it was the enemy, and ordered my regiment to open fire, which they obeyed with reluctance, the major part of the men thinking it was our own people. But after firing a few rounds they became satisfied it was the enemy, and then opened with great vigor, driving the enemy from his guns, which guns we passed over as we advanced, and also passed over another battery on the other side of the pike.

All the loss my regiment sustained was in the engagement at the brick-kiln, which was some eighty-odd, and was the only place that we actually engaged the enemy.

Great credit is due both officers and men, who behaved themselves with coolness and bravery, and showed themselves worthy of the regiment to which they belong.

Captain Maney and his company was attached to my regiment throughout the whole, and acquitted themselves with equal credit with the rest of the command. Captain [E.] Cockrill was with me during the action and rendered valuable service, for which I tender him my thanks. He had his horse killed under him while riding in front of the regiment encouraging the men.

H. R. FEILD,
Colonel, Commanding First Tennessee Regiment.

[Brigadier-]General GEO. MANEY.

No. 209.

Report of Col. James A. McMurry, Fourth Tennessee Infantry.

NEAR SHELBYVILLE, TENN.,
January 29, 1863.

I respectfully report that my regiment, agreeably to orders from Brig. Gen. G. Maney, commanding brigade, marched from their camps early on the morning of December 29 last, and took their position in line of battle in the center of the brigade before Murfreesborough, on the west bank of Stone's River, and remained there until the morning of the 31st, the day of the general engagement, except the first evening, when it was ordered to march to the left a few hundred yards, when firing from artillery and infantry indicated that a strong attack might be made. The regiment encamped there until the next day, when it was ordered back to its first position in line of battle.

At an early hour on the morning of the 31st, the firing from artillery and infantry gave evidence that all parts of the front line were engaged in battle, when the regiment, as early as 8 a. m., was ordered by the brigade commander to advance, for the purpose of participating in the battle.

The regiment advanced to a distance of some 500 yards, until it reached our front line of battle, when it was halted, where the brigade which occupied our front line of battle, for some cause, had been thrown into disorder and confusion. After halting here some twenty minutes, until the broken brigade had reformed, and being all the while under fire from artillery and infantry of the enemy, in position in a skirt of woods a little in advance of the right of the brigade, near what is called the Wilkinson pike, the regiment again received orders to advance, which was done by making a circle through a cotton-field until the direction was changed to the right, when the regiment encountered a strong battery, well and ably supported by infantry, in position not more than 300 yards in advance of the right of the brigade, and apparently not more than 150 yards distant, when the first battery opened upon the brigade. This second battery was considerably—some say 300 yards or more—in rear of the forces of the enemy. On their right, being driven back a considerable distance, and from the artillery and infantry combined, a most destructive fire was directed against our advancing column; and it being altogether uncertain whether the missiles of death were directed by friend or foe, the regiment was halted and covered, and protected itself as well as possible upon this ground and behind obstacles until it could be ascertained by whom we were being fired upon. Here the brigade commander, who was immediately in the rear of my regiment, sent some of his staff to ascertain this fact; and I here desire to call attention to the skill, gallantry, and cool courage of Sergeant Oakley, color-bearer of my regiment, who, while the regiment was thus waiting and in doubt, volunteered and did march out with the flag of his country some 8 or 10 paces in advance of his regiment, and held aloft the flag, which he bore erect some ten minutes in a conspicuous place for the fire of the enemy, and amid a terrific fire, to test by whose fire the brigade was suffering so severely. The continued heavy firing directed upon our line soon demonstrated that the battery and its support were no mistaken friends of ours, and the battery belonging to the brigade was placed in a position by the brigade commander on an eminence, where it and all the infantry of the brigade opened a well-directed and destructive fire against the hostile battery and infantry, and after a heavy fire from us (continued some fifteen or twenty minutes) we drove the battery and its support from their position, which resulted in the battery (consisting of four pieces of artillery) being carried off by the enemy some 150 yards, when it was captured by and fell into the hands of the brigade, the enemy being unable to carry it any farther, my regiment passing immediately by the captured guns.

The loss to my regiment in dislodging this battery and its infantry support from this well-selected position in the woods (our brigade having to attack them from an open field) was very considerable.

I have to regret the loss of Capt. D. P. Skelton, of Company K, in my regiment, who was here mortally wounded. This was a severe loss to his company; also that Capt. C. Brown was very severely wounded in the thigh—a brave officer, who is disabled from any further field service; and also the loss of 2 non-commissioned officers and 5 privates, and some 40 non-commissioned [officers] and privates were wounded. And here [Lieutenant] John Shane, adjutant in the regiment, was wounded in the arm, who had rendered valuable assistance on the day of the battle, exhibiting much courage.

After driving the enemy from their position. the regiment, with the brigade, under orders from the commander, advanced through a skirt of woods. When they had proceeded about half through the woods, the enemy, from their numerous batteries on the Nashville and Murfreesborough turnpike, began and directed a heavy cannonading against our advancing line, which continued for some twenty minutes, resulting in the wounding of some 2 or 3 men in my regiment, and from here the regiment and brigade, which had been in the present line of attack ever since it had arrived at our front line of battle, advanced under the command of Colonel Feild (General Maney having been assigned to take command of the left) to a field on the Nashville and Murfreesborough turnpike, where it was directed to be halted, and where it opened a fire on the enemy's line on the turnpike, when 1 officer of the regiment was wounded and 1 private killed, which closed the fight on the part of my regiment that day. My regiment encamped here that night on our extreme front line, and remained on our extreme front line, except one night, until our forces were withdrawn on Saturday night, at 2 a. m., the brigade constituting the rear guard of the retiring forces.

During the three days after the fight of the 31st the enemy kept up a brisk but irregular fire on our line, which was not returned in any way, except by some skirmishers, which I kept constantly in front of my regiment, and who, it is believed, did considerable execution against the enemy by the discharge of their small-arms.

I have further to report that the men and officers of the regiment endured considerable hardships and privations during the six days we were in line of battle before Murfreesborough with great patience and fortitude, such as becomes true soldiers, without uttering any complaint, and that the field, staff, and company officers gallantly and with alacrity performed their duties during the whole time, and to whose assistance much is due to the part performed by the regiment during the engagement.

All of which is respectfully submitted.

J. A. McMURRY,
Colonel, Commanding Fourth Tennessee Regiment.

Capt. THOMAS H. MALONE,
Assistant Adjutant-General.

No. 210.

Report of Maj. John L. Harris, Sixth Tennessee Infantry, commanding Sixth and Ninth Regiments.

MARCH 20, 1863.

SIR : I have the honor to submit the following report of the Sixth and [Ninth] (consolidated) Tennessee Regiments in the late action before Murfreesborough on December 31, 1862 :

Having been posted on the left wing of General Maney brigade—which was in the center of the left wing and in the second line, which rested on Stone's River, where we had been for two days before the regular engagement, which began on the morning of December 31—when the firing had become heavy in the front line, which was early in the morning of December 31, we were ordered forward to support it with the balance of the brigade, by General Maney. After marching straight to the front about 300 yards, we were halted in a corn-field about 200 yards in front of a wood lot, in which a **portion** of the enemy were posted. While in that position we had several men wounded. The command was here ordered to lie down, in order to protect themselves as much as possible against a heavy enfilading fire from the right by one of the enemy's batteries. The regiment, then commanded by Col. C. S. Hurt, was ordered from this place by General Maney to move off by the left flank to the left and front, on an angle of about 35° from the original parallel, in rear of a thicket and down a ravine, so as to gain the right of the woods. We were then ordered by the left flank into the woods, and there formed a line of battle perpendicular to the original line. We were then ordered forward. After having gone about 400 yards, we were halted in an open cotton-field near some out-buildings. Our lines were raked here most terrifically by shot and shell from one battery on our right and another situated a little to the left of our right. Here we were ordered to lie down. Believing the battery on our right to be ours, the colors of the regiment were ordered forward to attract their attention, whereupon Sergt. M. C. Hooks, Company E, Ninth Tennessee Regiment, advanced to the front and placed his colors on the top of a crib, whereupon the battery on the right fired at it and struck the crib near the color-sergeant. We were then convinced as to the character of the battery, which still kept pouring a heavy fire upon us. Here we lost 3 killed and several wounded. Among the killed was Lieutenant [W. D.] Irby, then commanding Company D, Ninth Tennessee Regiment. We were then ordered forward, bearing slightly to the right. After proceeding about 600 yards to the fence of a third field, beyond which the enemy were strongly massed in the cedars, with their batteries playing upon us continually, we were halted, and fired one round at the enemy, they returning the fire, killing and wounding several of our men, among whom were Lieutenant [A. J.] Bucey, of Company A, Ninth Tennessee Regiment, and Lieutenant [T. J.] Gilliam, also of Company A, but then commanding Company D, Ninth Tennessee Regiment, killed, and Captain [E. B.] McClanahan, Company G, Sixth Tennessee Regiment, wounded. We were then ordered by Col. C. S. Hurt to our former position, and there formed on a line with Smith's battery, 100 yards in rear of our first line. After Smith's battery had driven the enemy from the woods we were again ordered forward, and continued to the front, bearing to the right, until we reached a cedar glade beyond the Wilkinson pike. Here we were halted, being partially sheltered by the trees from the most terrific fire of shot and shell I ever saw, completely riddling the forest in every direction. We were again ordered forward amid the thunder of artillery and the crash of falling timber, and continued to march to the front until we arrived at the south side of a field, the north side of which rested upon the Nashville pike, and there halted, it then being between 2 and 3 o'clock in the evening, and the enemy being heavily massed both in men and artillery on the opposite side of the field. We remained here until the following morning about 7 o'clock, when we were ordered to fall back 100 yards into the cedar glade and hold our position.

We remained here until the evening of January 2, 1863, keeping up a continued skirmishing with the enemy all the time, both day and night. We were then ordered to the right, and placed in a field near Cowan's dwelling. The next morning before day we were ordered back to our original line in the cedar glade, where we remained until the evacuation, and then assisted in bringing up the rear of General Cheatham's division.

During all the exposure both officers and men behaved with that becoming coolness and courage that has ever made Tennessee troops invincible. Among a few names that stand conspicuous are Color-Sergt. M. C. Hooks and Private Robert [T.] Bond, of Company E, Ninth Tennessee, who was seriously wounded at Shiloh, and at Perryville received a severe wound through his lungs, and was found among the foremost at Murfreesborough during all the exposure with a bullet-hole through his body. Be it said to the honor of the conscripts of Company I, Ninth Tennessee Regiment, they stood to a man, advancing and retreating in perfect good order.

Respectfully submitted.

JNO. L. HARRIS,
Major, Comdg. Sixth and Ninth (consolidated) Tenn. Regts.
Capt. THOMAS H. MALONE,
    Assistant Adjutant-General.

No. 211.

Reports of Lieut. William B. Turner, Smith's Mississippi battery.

SHELBYVILLE, TENN., *January 14,* 1863.

MAJOR: In accordance with Special Orders, No. 2, issued from headquarters artillery, Polk's corps, Army of Tennessee, I have the honor to report that at the battle of Stone's River the company sustained a loss of 1 private killed (Henry Sellers) and 1 sergeant, 1 corporal, and 2 privates wounded, 4 horses killed and 6 wounded. No damage done to carriages or caissons.

The battery was engaged four different times on Wednesday, 31st ultimo, with the batteries of the enemy and firing on their infantry, averaging about half an hour to each engagement.

We were engaged some six times on Friday, 2d instant. We drove back a line of infantry on Wednesday, and on Friday, in conjunction with Carnes' and Stanford's batteries, were engaged with several of the enemy's batteries, and drove back a column of their infantry. The effect of our two light 12-pounders was particularly noticeable. That evening after sundown, Captain Stanford, acting chief of artillery, seeing a line of the enemy's infantry approaching, ordered me to open fire, which I did upon them with my two light 12-pounder guns, firing several rounds and repulsing the enemy. We fired during the two days we were engaged some 800 rounds, composed of solid shot, shell, spherical case, and canister. We noticed nothing inefficient in regard to the projectiles of the Bormann fuses. We were compelled to use a few of the paper fuses. They proved inefficient, not preserving the range. We never used our adjustable sights, it not being necessary.

Very respectfully,

WM. B. TURNER,
Lieutenant, Commanding Light Battery.
Maj. M. SMITH,
    Chief of Artillery, 1st Div., Polk's Corps, Army of Tennessee.

JANUARY 29, 1863.

In accordance with special orders issued from headquarters, I have the honor to submit the following report of the action of Smith's battery during the engagements before Murfreesborough, Tenn., from December 29, 1862, to January 3, 1863, both inclusive :

On the 29th, the battery was ordered to take a position on Stone's River, about 2½ miles from Murfreesborough, on the left wing, and lay in position until late in the evening, when it was ordered to take another position about three-fourths of a mile farther down on the left. In that position it remained until about sunset, when I was ordered to return and park my battery for the night near the first-named position. The battery was not engaged during the day, and did not fire a single shot.

On the 30th, I was ordered to cross Stone's River and take a position in rear of your brigade, which I did. During this day the battery was not engaged, though exposed to heavy shelling from the enemy's guns. In this position the battery remained until late in the evening, when I was ordered to return and park my battery for the night in the same place it occupied on the night of December 29.

On the 31st, I was ordered to cross Stone's River and take a position about half a mile from said river, which was done, and the battery went into action, firing a few rounds. From thence I was ordered about half a mile farther onward, to take another position. At this point the battery went into action a second time, firing upon one of the enemy's batteries, as well as upon their infantry. In this second engagement the battery fired about 200 rounds, and was engaged about forty minutes; succeeded in silencing the enemy's battery, as well as driving back their infantry. The enemy's battery having ceased firing, and their infantry having fallen back, I was ordered to advance farther onward and take a position near the one occupied by the enemy's battery, which had been captured during the second engagement. In this position the battery remained until late in the evening, when I was ordered to another position to the right of the one last occupied, and at this point the battery was engaged about twenty minutes, firing several rounds. I then parked it near by for the night.

On the morning of January 1, I was ordered with my battery to take a position near the one last held the evening before, which was done. The battery lay in this position during the whole day without being engaged. On the night of January 1, it was parked in the same place, and the men, according to orders, went to building fortifications, which occupied them until a late hour.

At 2 o'clock in the morning of January 2, the battery was ordered to the right of the Nashville pike, to take a position on Stone's River, which was done, and during the day it was engaged six times, averaging about a half hour to each engagement. In the action of this day the battery succeeded twice (in connection with those of Carnes, Stanford, and Scott) in driving back a column of the enemy's infantry. The effect of our two 12-pounder Napoleon guns was noticed particularly during the whole day, and late in the evening they succeeded of themselves in driving back a column of the enemy's infantry. Some time after dark I was ordered back across the pike, and parked my battery for the night.

On January 3, I was ordered with my battery to the left on the Wilkinson pike, and lay in position during the whole day without being engaged. In the evening of this day I was ordered to camp about 2 miles from Murfreesborough, on the Shelbyville pike, and there parked my battery until the evening of the 4th, when I was ordered to proceed on toward Shelbyville.

The commander takes great pleasure to include in this report that his men remained steadily at their posts, filling their respective duties during the hottest part of the engagement, and acted in every respect commendable as soldiers.

The list of casualties were 1 killed and 4 slightly wounded; also 8 horses killed and lost.

Respectfully submitted.

WM. B. TURNER,
Lieutenant, Commanding Smith's Battery Light Artillery.

Capt. THOMAS H. MALONE,
A. A. G., Maney's Brig., Cheatham's Div., Polk's Corps, Army of Tenn.

No. 212.

Report of Col. A. J. Vaughan, jr., Thirteenth Tennessee Infantry, commanding Fourth Brigade.

HEADQUARTERS FOURTH BRIGADE, FIRST DIVISION,
POLK'S CORPS, ARMY OF TENNESSEE,
Camp near Shelbyville, January 9, 1863.

CAPTAIN: I have the honor to submit an official report of the action of the Fourth Brigade, First Division, Polk's corps, Army of Tennessee, in the battle before Murfreesborough, temporarily under my command, during the engagement of December 31, [1862,] and the preliminary skirmish of the day before.

The brigade consisted of the One hundred and fifty-fourth Senior Tennessee Regiment, Lieut. Col. M. Magevney, jr.; Thirteenth Tennessee Regiment, Lieut. Col. W. E. Morgan; Twelfth Tennessee Regiment, Maj. J. N. Wyatt; Forty-seventh Tennessee Volunteers, Capt. W. M. Watkins; Ninth Texas Infantry, Col. W. H. Young; Twenty-ninth Tennessee Volunteers, Maj. J. B. Johnson; Capt. P. T. Allin's company of sharpshooters; Lieut. J. R. J. Creighton, and the light battery of Capt. W. L. Scott. Our line was formed, with the left resting on the Triune road, 300 yards in rear of Loomis' brigade, not far behind Smith's house. The One hundred and fifty-fourth Senior Tennessee Regiment, being detached to the support of Robertson's battery, occupied a position near the front line, with its right resting on the same road and opposite the house before named.

About 3 o'clock in the afternoon of the 30th, skirmishing, which had been going on between the pickets along the whole line, was entered into with great warmth in my front, and a battery of the enemy, which had been posted on an advantageous spot, opened upon the woods in which my command was in line, shelling it with great fury and wounding some of my officers and men, at the same time engaging Robertson's battery in an artillery duel of terrible severity. At one time this battery was threatened with an impetuous charge by the enemy, when the One hundred and fifty-fourth Senior Tennessee Regiment, in support, rushed forward, resisting with great gallantry the attempt, losing in killed and wounded several of its officers and men. After a shelling, about dark, of the camp-fires of this regiment by the enemy, the contest closed for the day, and we rested upon our arms for the night.

At daylight the next morning the battle opened, and before sunrise I received information that the front line needed immediate support, and moved my command forward. The Ninth Texas Regiment, having been for safety rested about 100 yards in rear of its position in alignment, was unable, because of that fact and the want of room between the right of the line and the road, it being on the extreme left, to move in line with the brigade. Accordingly, Capt. M. W. Cluskey, assistant adjutant-general, moved it and rested it on the right of Wood's brigade. Moving the balance of my brigade obliquely across the open field to the rear and right of Smith's house under a tremendous artillery and infantry fire, I soon occupied the front of our line, on the left of Manigault's brigade, and engaged a largely superior force of the enemy in a most hotly contested fight, driving him away from two of his guns, which had been prominent in contesting our advance.

About the same time my assistant adjutant-general gave Colonel [W. H.] Young, of the Ninth Texas Infantry, orders to move forward from the position in which he had placed it, on the right of Wood's brigade, and attack the enemy sheltered in the woods in front of him, which he did in most gallant style, and succeeded in driving him, though with great loss, through the woods and open field on the other side. On the right, after driving the enemy from the guns mentioned, Manigault's brigade, not being supported by its reserve, gave way, and my brigade, having none either in reserve or on my immediate left, was forced by the enemy, heavily re-enforced, to withdraw, which it did, after being commanded by me so to do, in good order, rallying on their colors on their original line. I again advanced my command, this time through the woods and to the left of my former line of advance, and reached the large open fields between the Wilkinson and Triune pikes under a heavy fire of artillery. Forming on the left of Maney's brigade, I placed the Ninth Texas Infantry, which had again united with my command, on my right, and rested my men, to shelter them from the severe artillery fire of the enemy, which was being unremittingly hailed upon them. Ordered by Major-General Cheatham, I moved forward, with Maney on my right and unsupported on my left. Reaching the woods near the Wilkinson pike, I encountered Brig. Gen. Bushrod [R.] Johnson's brigade on a line of battle perpendicular to my own. After a delay on this account, I received the order to advance and engage the enemy. Moving through Johnson's line of battle, I changed front and advanced on the enemy, thickly posted in the woods on my right, from which they had been shelling our lines. Upon our near approach, he fled through the skirt of woods across the Wilkinson toward the Nashville pike. I again changed front, and, crossing the Wilkinson pike, moved through the same woods on their left flank with a view of cutting them off. When about half through these woods, engaging the enemy on my right flank as I went along, I met a line of battle somewhat lapping my left, which I found to be Wood's brigade, engaging another force of the enemy in his front. General [S. A. M.] Wood desired my support to save him from being flanked on the right. Accordingly, I moved forward and engaged this force, driving him across the open field and dirt road into the only remaining field between us and the Nashville pike, where a large wagon train of the enemy was distinctly visible. At this point I found myself about to be flanked on my right by a strong force of the enemy posted in the woods to the right of the field. Seeing no signs of any support on my right, which I had supposed was following me to continue my alignment on the right, I concluded to rapidly continue my advance upon the enemy, which had been driven toward the pike and which had again rallied and formed in line, and, by driving him, to force the troops threatening my flank to retire. Such was the spirit and vigor with which my men pursued this object that the troops on my left did not keep up with them, and before I could effect the purpose I had in view, my right flank was so severely enfiladed that I was compelled to retire them after again driving the enemy from one of his batteries, which on that account I was unable to bring off. Withdrawing my troops to the Wilkinson pike, I there remained in line of battle on our extreme left for the remaining short portion of the day and for the entire night. There was no renewal of the engagement on Thursday, and on Friday morning Brig. Gen. Preston Smith having arrived, I turned over his command to him.

The battery of Captain Scott, being otherwise disposed, was not engaged with the brigade in the actions reported on. Its subsequent operations will form the subject of a report from its captain, through Brig. Gen. Preston Smith.

It is scarcely necessary to refer to the gallant conduct of the entire command. Obeying with alacrity every order I gave them to forward; engaging the enemy whenever they met him with a spirit and impetuosity which evinced their earnestness; retiring, even though exposed to the most galling fire, only when I ordered them, and rallying upon their colors whenever they were called upon to do so, they presented an exhibition of heroic valor seldom equaled and never surpassed by any body of men. The report of the fatality in the brigade demonstrates how well they have earned the tribute I pay them. The killed and wounded among officers illustrates how well they stood at their posts through all of the peril. The horses of every one of the general field and staff except one, and of every one of the regimental field and staff except two, were killed under them.

The incidents of conspicuous gallantry were so numerous as to preclude the mention of all of them in this report.

Colonel Young, of the Ninth Texas Infantry, seized the colors of his regiment in one of its most gallant charges and led it through.

When standard-bearer Quinn, a gallant soldier of the One hundred and fifty-fourth Senior Tennessee Regiment, was killed, Major [J. W.] Dawson snatched the broken staff, and carried it with the colors at the head of the regiment during the balance of the fight.

In many instances entire officers of some of the companies were killed and wounded, and they were gallantly led by the non-commissioned officers.

In the Thirteenth Tennessee Regiment Lieutenant-Colonel [W. E.] Morgan was mortally wounded, Major [Peter H.] Cole was killed, and senior Captain [W. J.] Crook was dangerously wounded. Captain [R. F.] Lanier took charge of the regiment and carried it gallantly through the fight.

All the regimental commanders behaved in a manner worthy of the responsible positions they had been called upon to occupy.

The company of sharpshooters was placed to the right of the One hundred and fifty-fourth Senior Regiment and not used as a separate command. Its commanding officer, Lieutenant [J. R. J.] Creighton, was dangerously wounded and Second Lieutenant [A. M.] Bunch was killed while nobly leading their men. Lieutenant [T. F.] Pattison carried them through the remainder of the fight with great credit.

Capt. M. W. Cluskey, assistant adjutant-general, discharged his duty to the fullest extent. Intrusting to him the execution of the most important orders, he carried them out with a promptness and coolness which greatly facilitated me in the direction of the brigade. In one of the warmest charges near the Nashville pike his horse was killed under him.

I must bear especial testimony to the gallant conduct of Lieut. Frank B. Rodgers aide-de-camp, and Capt John W. Harris [Company L, Fifth

Tennessee], assigned to duty on my staff, who rendered most efficient aid in carrying out my orders and in rallying and cheering the men by their own example of personal daring and valor.   Lieutenant Rodgers had a horse killed under him.

Maj. E. A. Beecher, brigade quartermaster, by his attention to the removal of the wounded from the field, the burying of the dead, and the gathering up of the guns and ammunition scattered upon it, and his efficiency in every way necessary to promote the interests of the command, is entitled to special commendation.

Accompanying this you will find a report* of the killed, wounded, and missing in this command, as also the separate reports of Col. W. H. Young, commanding Ninth Texas Infantry, and senior Capt. R. F. Lanier, commanding Thirteenth Tennessee Regiment, to which you are respectfully referred.

Respectfully,

A. J. VAUGHAN, JR.,
Senior Colonel, Commanding Brigade.

Capt. JOHN INGRAM,
   Actg. Asst. Adjt. Gen., First Div., Polk's Corps, Army of Tenn.

No. 213.

Report of Capt. R. F. Lanier, Thirteenth Tennessee Infantry.

SHELBYVILLE, TENN., *January* 9, 1863.

On the morning of December 31, 1862, about 6.30 o'clock, Lieut. Col. William E. Morgan, commanding Thirteenth Regiment Tennessee Volunteers. had the regiment formed to the right of the Triune road, upon which road the left of the brigade rested.   We remained in line but a short while, when we were ordered forward to the support of Brigadier-General Gardner's [S. A. M. Wood's] brigade,† which was then engaging the enemy in a wood on the far side of a corn-field immediately in our front. We marched boldly forward until within 100 yards of the wood, when we were ordered to halt and lie down, as we had come under the enemy's fire.   We remained in this position but a few minutes when the line in our front came retreating back, and we were ordered to rise and move forward, which the men did with a yell.   Here we were under a galling fire, and I regret to state that Lieut. Col. William E. Morgan and Maj. P. H. Cole were mortally wounded, and many of our men were killed and wounded before we entered the woods, but our gallant men did not falter, but rushed forward with a shout and entered the woods, driving the enemy before them and forcing him to leave a steel piece of artillery, which he had used with terrible effect upon us.   We continued advancing until ordered by Colonel Vaughan, commanding brigade, to retire, caused by a terrible cross-fire from the right.   We fell back beyond the field, and quickly reformed the regiment and moved by the left flank up the Triune road, where we were supplied with ammunition, and moved by the right flank in line of battle to the left of Brigadier-General Maney, in an open field, where we were ordered to halt and lie down to protect us from the terrible shelling from the enemy's battery on our right. From this position we moved forward across the Wilkinson pike and

---

* Embodied in No. 191, p. 676.
† Gardner was relieved from duty with the Army of Tennessee, December 14, 1862.

rested a short time, and as we moved from here we changed front forward on first company, first battalion, and marched across an open field into a cedar thicket to the left of Brigadier-General Polk, and engaged the enemy and drove them across a field, and our men followed them, although raked by artillery from the front and right and a terrible fire of musketry. Near the Nashville pike we drove them from two pieces of artillery immediately in our front, with the assistance of the rest of the brigade. We fell back from here to the Wilkinson pike and bivouacked for the night.

On the morning of January 1, 1863, we moved a short distance to the right down the Wilkinson pike in rear of the division, massed, when I turned the command over to Colonel Vaughan, jr.

Without casting any reflections where all did their part nobly, I would here mention Private Ike A. Stone, Company I, who was severely wounded early in the engagement, but, binding up his wounds, he took charge of his company, the captain (Crook) being wounded. He received a second wound, but still fought bravely on. Adjutant [R. M.] Harwell called for some person to take the colors, when Private Leon Joubert, Company G, volunteered and carried them through the remainder of the fight, always in front of the line and among the last to retire.

I herewith submit the list* of killed, wounded, and missing.

Respectfully,

R. F. LANIER,
Senior Captain, Commanding Regiment.

Col. A. J. VAUGHAN, Jr.

No. 214.

Report of Maj. J. B. Johnson, Twenty-ninth Tennessee Infantry.

FEBRUARY 29, 1863.

I have the honor to submit the following report of the part taken by the Twenty-ninth Tennessee Regiment in the recent battle near Murfreesborough :

On Tuesday evening we were posted in line of battle about 60 yards in rear and to the right of Robertson's battery, which was soon after engaged in a furious cannonade with one of the enemy's batteries. We were exposed to the fire of the enemy all during the time, by which we lost several men killed and wounded, including two lieutenants of Company I, wounded.

Early Wednesday morning orders were received to advance and attack the enemy, strongly posted at the extremity of a large field about a quarter of a mile from our position, and, charging through this field, exposed to a brisk fire of shot and shell, the enemy were driven back from this position in disorder; but we not being supported on the flank, when the enemy came up with fresh troops, exposed to an enfilading fire on the left, the regiment and brigade were ordered to fall back to their original position, which they did in excellent order, having suffered the larger part of our casualties during the day at this place. Having rested for ten minutes, and received ammunition, an advance was ordered across the same field, a little to the left, the enemy having been driven back. They were again encountered in about a mile of the first position, and,

---

* Embodied in No. 191, p. 676.

after a short fight, fell back to a thicket of cedars and river bluff, affording protection to the enemy's line, and here the firing was so heavy that, after a short while, seeing that they were too strong for our greatly reduced brigade, orders were given to fall back to the road, half a mile back, where we encamped for the night.

The [conduct of the] officers and men in this regiment was admirable and commendable.

The casualties of the regiment were as follows: Went into the fight with effective force of 220 men; killed and wounded, 102; missing, 10. Total, 112 killed, wounded, and missing.

I noticed that a great many guns (chiefly Enfield rifles) after a short time became so foul that the balls had to be hammered down, thereby causing slow fire.

During the three days subsequent to the Wednesday fight our position was shifted several times in the lines, and, though exposed to an almost continued fire of artillery, no casualties ensued. We were on the extreme left of the line of battle, in the front line, during the last day.

Respectfully,

J. B. JOHNSON,
Major, Commanding Twenty-ninth Tennessee Regiment.

Capt. M. W. CLUSKEY,
Assistant Adjutant-General.

No. 215.

Report of Lieut. Col. Michael Magevney, jr., One hundred and fifty-fourth Tennessee Infantry, Senior Regiment.

CAMP NEAR SHELBYVILLE, TENN.,
February 26, 1863.

SIR: I hereby submit a report of the part which my command took in the battle of Murfreesborough on December 30 and 31, 1862, and following.

On the afternoon of Tuesday, [December] 30, I was detailed by the major-general commanding to support Captain Robertson's battery of artillery, and late in the afternoon the same became warmly engaged with the enemy. I drew up my command in the rear of the battery, extending the left wing of the battalion, and a little forward, to take advantage of a dip in the ground. The enemy's guns opened on our battery, and also their skirmishers were deployed forward, when the left wing of my command became warmly engaged. At this time the enemy came out of the woods in force, evidently intent on charging our battery. As our gunners were in a great measure disabled by the severe fire to which they were subjected, I moved forward the line in front of the guns, determined to meet them with a counter-charge, but they fell back under cover, and I occupied my former position. A few limbers or caissons were blown up, when Captain Robertson limbered to the rear, I opening the ranks to allow of his guns passing through, and then retired. After dark the command was moved, by orders of Colonel Vaughan, to our place on the right of the brigade, and early on Wednesday morning we were brought into action. The command was not again detached from the brigade during the action.

I take pride in bearing testimony to the gallantry and good conduct

of both my officers and men during the battle.   Among those conspicuous for bravery on the field, Maj. John W. Dawson merits a position,
as also Adjt. W. H. Stovall, who took command of Company G after
Captain [B. B.] Hutcheson was carried off the field wounded, and commanded the company with ability.   In fact, it is impossible to discriminate where all nobly performed their part.

The regiment went into action 245 aggregate, and our loss was:

Killed 14
Wounded 83
Missing 3
                                                                                                         ____
    Total 100

I have the honor to be, your obedient servant,
                                      M. MAGEVNEY, JR.,
            Lieut. Col., Comdg. One hundred and fifty-fourth Senior Tenn.
Lieut. F. B. RODGERS, *Aide-de-Camp.*

No. 216.

Report of Col. William H. Young, Ninth Texas Infantry.

JANUARY 6, 1863.

CAPTAIN: I have the honor to submit the following report of the operations of my regiment while separated from the brigade in the action of
December 31, 1862:

The regiment advanced in its proper position with the brigade until
the brigade entered the corn-field in front of the original line of battle
occupied by it.   Here the regiment, by its position, was immediately on
the left of the field when the brigade became engaged.   There being no
enemy in my front, I moved forward, by order of Captain Cluskey, to
the top of the next hill, when the enemy appeared off to my right-oblique
about 200 yards.   I ordered the regiment to fire, upon which they poured
two volleys into the enemy; but perceiving that the brigade had obliqued to the right, and knowing that my fire would be more effective
by a nearer approach to the enemy, I moved by the right flank until my
right was near the Twenty-ninth Tennessee; I then moved by the left
flank and took position behind a tall fence and opened fire on the enemy,
who was posted about 100 yards immediately in my front, behind a ledge
of rocks and a fence.   Here General Wood's brigade, which was on my
left when Captain Cluskey ordered me forward, came up on my left again
and opened fire; but seeing that our combined attack had but little effect
toward dislodging the enemy, I ordered my regiment to cross the fence
for the purpose of charging the enemy's position, which they did, but,
mistaking my intention, advanced 50 paces and again halted and opened
fire.   Here, while endeavoring to get them to hear my command "forward," my horse was shot, as well as that of the lieutenant-colonel, and
for five minutes the regiment received a most murderous fire, which killed
and wounded more than 100 of my men, including nearly all of the
commissioned officers.   Seeing that we were suffering from a cross-fire,
I resolved to charge and rout the enemy from his position.   Passing
down the line, I notified each company of my intention, and then, taking
the colors, I ordered the regiment to move forward with a shout, both of
which they did *a la* Texas.   It was at this juncture that Captain Cluskey,

who had been with the regiment all the time since it became engaged, rode off to the balance of the brigade. Charging with a yell through the cedar brake in our front, the enemy fled at our approach. Having halted at the position formerly occupied by the enemy, we poured a fire into them as they retreated (with great loss) through the open woods which make up into the field in which is situated the first Abolition hospital we passed; but seeing they were getting out of range, and thinking the brigade had advanced on my right, I crossed the second fence and pursued after the enemy, who were completely thrown into confusion in the immediate front of my regiment and Wood's brigade, which had been advancing steadily after my regiment on the left. Here I discovered an extended line of battle moving across the open field a short distance in advance on my right, and, thinking it was my own brigade, ordered the men not to fire on them, but as they advanced up the slope the sun revealed their blue coats, and we opened on them. They, as well as the line (rather mass) in our front, continued to retreat until they entered a wood about a quarter of a mile beyond the hospital above named. We followed them, advancing as far as the upper edge of the woods which make up into the field. Here some half a dozen batteries opened on us from almost every point of the edge of the woods opposite, and, seeing that the troops on the right were not advancing, we fell back a short distance after Wood's brigade and reformed. Here I dispatched a messenger in search of the brigade, but he failing to find it, I advanced with a battalion of sharpshooters, which had attached itself to my left, moving to the right-oblique across the open field and past the Abolition hospital above named some considerable distance, when a staff officer notified me that Cheatham's division was advancing in my rear, and that Maney's brigade, from whom I was concealed by the buildings of the hospital, would fire on me for the enemy's sharpshooters if they saw me. So, requesting him to ride back and notify that brigade, I fell back and formed on General Maney's left, where our own brigade found us upon advancing.

I cannot speak in too high terms of the conduct of my officers and men. My commissioned officers all did their duty bravely, so I will not specify any in particular. Lieutenant-Colonel [Miles A.] Dillard was conspicuous for the zeal, energy, and bravery he displayed during the whole day. My loss has been furnished numerically in another report.

With much respect, I am, captain, your obedient servant,

WM. H. YOUNG,
Colonel, Commanding Ninth Texas Infantry.

Capt. M. W. Cluskey,
A. A. G., Fourth Brig., First Div., Polk's Corps, Army of Tenn.

No. 217.

Report of Capt. W. L. Scott, Tennessee battery.

Hdqrs. Fourth Brigade, First Division,
Polk's Corps, Army of Tennessee,
January 10, 1863.

Capt. John Ingram,
Asst. Adjt. Gen., First Div., Polk's Corps, Army of Tennessee :

Captain : Herewith I submit the report of Captain Scott, commanding light battery, attached to my brigade, of the part taken by his command in the engagement with the enemy on Friday and Saturday, 2d and 3d instant. My brigade remained in line of battle both these days, but, with the exception of skirmishing between our pickets and those of the enemy, nothing worthy of note occurred.

On Saturday night my command, in obedience to orders, was retired in the direction of Shelbyville.

Respectfully, your obedient servant,

PRESTON SMITH,
Brigadier-General, Commanding.

[Inclosure.]

IN CAMP, NEAR SHELBYVILLE, TENN.,
January 9, 1863.

SIR: I have the honor to submit the following official report of the part my battery took in the late engagement before Murfreesborough:

My battery was not engaged until Friday morning, being held in reserve on Wednesday, and there being no engagement with the enemy on Thursday. Early on Friday morning I was placed in position on the right of the Nashville turnpike, in an open field nearly opposite the large burnt house, but somewhat farther to the front. This field lies between the railroad and the turnpike, at the extremity of which (about 400 yards distant), on a slight ridge, is a skirt of woods, at that time occupied by our skirmishers. Robertson's battery was in position immediately in front of the burnt house, on my left. Soon after I took position here, the enemy advanced in line of battle. Robertson's battery first engaged them, and I immediately thereafter opened fire upon them, and in a short time we succeeded in driving them back to their original position. Two batteries of the enemy to my front and one to my left poured a heavy fire upon me, getting my range with great accuracy. I responded to their fire, and in this engagement lost 1 man instantly killed—Sergt. A. L. Townsend, a brave soldier and good officer. I could not see the effect of my shot upon the enemy's batteries, as they were concealed from view by the field immediately in front of me, but have since learned from our skirmishers, in the cedar glade on my left, that I drove one battery from its position, disabling one piece, which had to be left on the field. As the other batteries of the enemy were beyond my range, I was ordered to discontinue firing, which I did. Later in the day the enemy's skirmishers drove ours from the woods on the hill, when I shelled them out of this position, and it was occupied by our skirmishers.

About 4 o'clock in the evening I was ordered to open fire upon the enemy's lines from my position (which was entirely beyond my range), and after firing a few rounds to discontinue the firing, which I did. This caused the enemy to open fire upon me again with their batteries, in which I lost 1 man wounded in the head by a fragment of a shell— Washington McRea. I was then ordered to bring my battery behind the intrenchments.

Friday night, the enemy having again driven our skirmishers from the woods before mentioned, I was ordered during the night to take position at the same place and shell them out at daylight, which I did. In taking position here I lost 1 man (Pat. Jordan) wounded by cannon wheel breaking his leg. I shelled the enemy out of the woods, and it was occupied by our skirmishers, who took several prisoners in this skirt of woods. I was under fire of the enemy's batteries at long range late in the evening, being beyond my range. I withdrew my battery from its position, and ascertained orders had already been sent for me to retire, which I had not received.

Respectfully submitted.

W. L. SCOTT,
Captain, Commanding Light Battery.

Brig. Gen. PRESTON SMITH,
        Comdg. Fourth Brigade, Cheatham's Division, Polk's Corps.

No. 218.

Report of Lieut. W. M. Polk, Scott's Tennessee battery.

JANUARY 20, 1863.

In accordance with orders received, I make the following report of the part taken by Scott's battery in the battle of Stone's River, and of the effect and efficiency of the different kinds of projectiles used:

The battery crossed Stone's River Monday morning and took a position on the river, near the Triune road and in rear of our brigade. We remained with the brigade until Wednesday morning, not having done any firing up to that time. We were separated from the brigade on that morning, Captain Scott being ordered to hold the battery in reserve on the Triune road.

The battery remained on the Triune road until Thursday morning, when we received an order to take position at the breastworks between the Wilkinson and Nashville pikes, where we remained until Friday morning, not having fired a shot up to that time. The battery was then ordered to take a position about 400 or 500 yards in front of the breastworks between the railroad and Nashville pike, Captains Stanford's and Carnes' and Lieutenant Turner's batteries being on our right beyond the railroad, and Captain Robertson's battery being on our left beyond the pike. After being in that position about fifteen minutes, the enemy's infantry commenced an advance, when we opened on them with spherical case and shell at three seconds time. The enemy, after a little, fell back, upon which we increased our range and time, and continued the firing until they were beyond our range. Two of the enemy's batteries were advancing with their line of infantry, both of which returned our fire, but both ceased firing when their line of infantry retired. One of the batteries fell back with the line, the other remained in its position, having, as we afterward learned from our skirmishers, one of its pieces disabled. It, however, fell back after we ceased firing. As soon as the enemy's line commenced falling back, they opened fire on us with two rifle batteries, which were beyond our range. Having received an order to cease firing, we did so, and fell back about 50 yards, under cover of a little rise in the ground. The batteries of the enemy ceased firing soon after we did. In this engagement we lost 1 man killed. About 2 o'clock we shelled the enemy's skirmishers out of a skirt of timber about 250 yards in our front, from which they had driven our skirmishers. Their batteries replied, but did us no harm. That evening we fired a few spherical case at the enemy's line, all of which burst short, they being beyond our range. We then retired to the breastworks for the night.

The next morning we took the position we had occupied the day previous, and shelled the enemy's skirmishers out of the skirt of woods I mentioned before. The enemy's batteries did not reply. From that time until late that evening we occupied the position quietly.

About 4 o'clock Saturday evening the enemy opened a well-directed fire upon us with three batteries, all of which were beyond our range. The battery fell back inside of our intrenchments, and Captain Scott reported to General Cheatham, when he ordered him to bring the battery to his headquarters, where we remained until 2 o'clock that night, when Captain Scott was ordered to cross the river and join the rest of the division, which was on its way to this point.

During the various engagements of the battery we used the pendulum hausses with tolerable satisfaction. The most of our shrapnel and shell did very well. Our friction-primers also did very well. My experience in regard to the table of ranges used by us, which is the one found in the instruction for field artillery, is that it does not answer as well as it should, from the fact that the powder for which it was prepared is so much superior to ours.

During the various engagements of the battery we had 1 man killed, 1 slightly wounded, and 1 man's leg broken by being run over by one of the guns. No horses were lost and the carriages were not damaged. We fired between 200 and 250 rounds, principally spherical case. Killed, Sergt. A. L. Townsend; wounded, W. McRea; missing, none.

Respectfully submitted.

W. M. POLK,
First Lieutenant, Commanding Scott's Battery.

Maj. M. SMITH.

No. 219.

Report of Maj. Gen. Jones M. Withers, C. S. Army, commanding Second Division.

HDQRS. WITHERS' DIV., POLK'S CORPS, ARMY OF TENN.,
Shelbyville, Tenn., May 20, 1863.

MAJOR: This division took position in line of battle in front of Murfreesborough and Stone's River on the morning of December 28, 1862, as directed in "Memoranda for general and staff officers," issued from headquarters of the army. The brigade of Brig. Gen. James R. Chalmers was placed, with its right resting on Stone's River and extending in a direction west of south, nearly across the open field toward the Wilkinson pike; Walthall's brigade, in command of Brig. Gen. [J.] Patton Anderson (by whose name it will be designated in this report), was placed next; and Anderson's brigade, under Col. A. M. Manigault, of the Tenth South Carolina Regiment, was placed next, and on the left of the line then formed. That night Deas' brigade, under Col. J. Q. Loomis, of the Twenty-fifth Alabama Regiment, arrived from outpost and was placed on Manigault's left, extending the line to the Franklin or Triune road. This was the front center division of the line of battle, the division of Major-General Breckinridge being on the right, its left flank resting on the east bank of the river and to the rear of Chalmers' right, and the division of Major-General McCown being on the west side of the Franklin road, with its right some distance in advance of Loomis' left. The general direction of the line from right to left of the division, the initial point being on the river, was west of south, crossing the Nashville rail and pike roads about 1,000 yards from their crossing of the river and near their intersection; thence across the Wilkinson pike, and thence to the Franklin road, on which was placed Robertson's battery. The open fields extending along their fronts and the character of the ground rendered it proper to throw Anderson's left to the front of the general direction, Manigault's left to be retired, and again Loomis' left to be advanced, the greatest angle being formed by Anderson and Manigault, and which would require that Manigault's left should describe an arc of near 60° to bring his front on a line with that of Anderson's.

On the evening of the 29th, skirmishing commenced between Chalmers' admirable battalion of sharpshooters and the enemy, which gradually extended to Anderson's right. About the same time there was a dash made by a portion of the enemy's cavalry on Manigault's skirmishers, which was creditably punished by Companies A and C, of the Tenth South Carolina Regiment. The supporting division, under Major-General Cheatham, now occupied its position from 500 to 800 yards in rear, and near the crest of the river ridge. The character of the country rendering it impossible for the division commanders to give that immediate, personal supervision which would insure the supports being thrown forward when necessary and with the least delay, it was agreed that Major-General Cheatham should take position on the left and the immediate control of the brigades of Manigault and Loomis, giving to me the direction of his two right brigades, Donelson and Stewart.

Early on the morning of the 30th, firing commenced between the skirmishers on the right, and gradually extended throughout the line to the Franklin road. The artillery of the enemy also opened, and the firing was kept up with more or less rapidity through the day. The cannonading was mostly directed against Chalmers' brigade and Anderson's right, which occupied the exposed position across the field from the Wilkinson pike to the river. About 2.30 p. m. the enemy made a dash to capture Robertson's battery, on our extreme left, which was handsomely repulsed and severely punished by a well-directed and rapid fire from the battery and from the Twenty-sixth and Thirty-ninth Alabama Regiments. The attempt, with less vigor, was repeated late in the evening with similar result, the Twenty-fifth Alabama having been thrown forward to the support of the other two regiments. The enemy's line of battle was now established in our front. His left rested on the river bluff, some 1,000 yards from Chalmers' right, in a skirt of woods; thence through the Round Forest, or Mississippian's "half acre"; thence through the south end of the cedar brake, and along the ridges and woodland to the cedar pedregal on the Franklin road, and about 300 yards from Loomis' front. From this point his line seemed to be retired, making quite an obtuse angle with that running back to the river.

The commanding general's order, directing an assault to be made by our left on the right of the enemy the next morning as early as it was "light enough to see," was received at 9 o'clock at night. Chalmers' brigade was to remain stationary, and constitute the pivot on which the movement was to be made; my left to "swing around and correspond with the movement of General McCown's division," on my left.

Early on the morning of the 31st, skirmishing commenced on the extreme left, and was followed by artillery, and then the full volleys of the line, announcing that the stern work of the day had commenced.

About 7 o'clock Loomis' brigade moved forward, and was immediately and hotly engaged. Steadily advancing, it drove back the first line of the enemy, but having no commanding officer (Colonel Loomis subsequently reporting himself as having been disabled), and the enemy being re-enforced by the second line, the brigade was driven back in some confusion. The reserve, being promptly ordered forward by Major-General Cheatham, made a gallant charge, but was also repulsed. Colonel Coltart, of the Twenty-sixth Alabama Regiment, having assumed command of Loomis' brigade, with the assistance of Captains [D. E.] Huger, [J. R. B.] Burtwell, and [E. B. D.] Riley, of my staff, ordered to the left for the purpose, quickly rallied and reformed the line. The two brigades, under Colonels Vaughan and Coltart, being now formed in line, were moved forward under the immediate direction of Major-General Cheatham, and, after a desperate conflict, dislodged the enemy from their strong position, and drove them for more than a mile and beyond the Wilkinson pike. Moving forward to the cedar brake, between the Wilkinson and Nashville pikes, and finding other troops pressing after the enemy in his front, Colonel Coltart, by direction of General Cheatham, moved his command to the right, and, coming into the front line on the east edge and extreme right of the cedar brake, had a sharp engagement with the enemy, occupying a ridge across a narrow cotton-field, and strongly supported by artillery. Manigault's brigade moved promptly at the proper moment, and his left swinging round, drove the enemy from the wooded ridge back on his second line. In the wheel through the open field, and before his command had completed the angle necessary to bring it on a line with Anderson's, a heavy fire from two batteries and a column of infantry was opened on him from his right, which, enfilading his line, checked and finally forced him back to his former position. Col. A. J. Lythgoe, of the Nineteenth South Carolina Regiment, was killed in this charge while gallantly leading his command. He dies well who dies nobly. Manigault, quickly rallying his command, again moved forward, successfully driving the enemy, and with every prospect of being able to hold his position, when the repulse of the troops on his left, leaving both flanks exposed, rendered it necessary for him again to fall back. The position of the forces and character of the ground and movement, however, rendered it impossible altogether to avoid a cross or enfilading fire. The repulse at any point only increased the liability. The supporting brigade, under Brigadier-General Maney, was now moved forward, and, taking position on Manigault's left, both brigades moved forward, meeting comparatively with but little opposition. As Manigault swung round to a line with Anderson, this brigade was put in motion, and soon Manigault's right was engaged in an attack on a battery, with strong supports of infantry. The assault seemed successful, but before the capture was made, a brigade of the enemy moved up from below the hill, forcing back the regiments engaged, but was in turn driven back by Anderson's left, which was sweeping round. This concluded the engagements of Manigault for the day. His command had been subjected to a most trying ordeal, and had suffered heavily. The calm determination and persistent energy and gallantry which rendered Colonel Manigault proof against discouragements had a marked influence on and was admirably responded to by his command.

Anderson's left, being now moved forward immediately after the right of Manigault, was quickly engaged with the strong force in front. No brigade occupied a more critical position, nor were the movements of any invested with more important consequences. Opposite there were three batteries strongly supported by infantry. The capture of the batteries and rout of the supports was a necessity. Anderson was, therefore, directed to take the batteries at every cost. Stewart's brigade had been moved up into the woods within close supporting distance. In rapid succession Anderson threw forward his regiments from left to right, and terrific was the fire to which they were subjected. Time and again checked, and almost recoiling before the tremendous fire, the regiments were as often rallied by their gallant and determined officers, and the brigade advanced by its cool, steadfast, and skillful commander. His right temporarily falling back in some confusion, caused by the fall of the gallant commanders of the two right regiments (Lieut. Col. James L. Autry, commanding Twenty-seventh Mississippi, killed, and Col. W. F. Brantly, of the Twenty-ninth Mississippi, stricken down by the concussion from a shell exploding near him), Brigadier-General Stewart was ordered forward to the support. In splendid order, and with a cheer, this fine brigade moved forward under its gallant and accomplished commander. Anderson's right, quickly rallying and pressing forward vigorously, attacked and drove back the enemy. This completed the rout of his first line and the capture of the batteries. Our loss, however, was very heavy, the Thirtieth Mississippi alone having within the limits of an acre 62 officers and men killed and 139 wounded.

Stewart, having moved his brigade to the left down the Wilkinson pike, now pressed forward on Anderson's left and hotly engaged the enemy. The determined advance and steady fire of our forces was more than the enemy could withstand. The entire force gave way, and in wild confusion rushed through the cedar brake in rear, being pursued to the northeast edge of the brake, and subjected to an irregular but quite effective fire. Within the northeast edge of this cedar brake, nearly parallel with the Nashville pike road and at right angles to the original line of battle, our troops were halted. They required rest and ammunition.

At 11 a. m. Brigadier-General Chalmers received an order direct from the lieutenant-general commanding to move forward and attack the enemy posted in his front. Quickly advancing to the Cowan, or burnt, house, he was there met by a destructive fire, and soon after, while actively engaged in the discharge of his duties, was stricken down by a fragment of a shell and borne senseless from the field. The quick perception, prompt decision, and fearless energy of this gallant officer being lost to his command, and his staff failing to report promptly to the officer next in rank, this veteran brigade became disorganized, the regiments attaching themselves to and serving with other commands until night, when they were brought together and placed in their original position under Colonel [T. W.] White, of the Ninth Mississippi Regiment. The brigade of Chalmers being driven back, the support under Brigadier-General Donelson was ordered to the attack by the lieutenant-general commanding, and moving rapidly forward was warmly engaged, but was repulsed, and, gradually swinging to the left, passed into the cedar brake.

On the morning of January 1, Anderson's brigade was moved to the position originally occupied by Donelson, and in rear of Chalmers. At daylight on the morning of January 1, Chalmers' sharpshooters were ordered forward, to ascertain the position of the enemy. Moving forward, and into the Round Forest, they drove out the skirmishers of the enemy, whose forces had been withdrawn during the night, and could then be seen in a northeast direction. Quiet prevailed until late in the evening, when the enemy sent forward a force and retook the Round Forest, driving back our skirmishers into the skirt of woods above and on the river.

Before daylight on the morning of the 2d, the batteries of Stanford, Carnes, and Smith had been moved up and placed in the north and outer edge of this river skirt of woods by Capt. J. R. B. Burtwell, division chief of artillery, and Scott's battery advanced up the Nashville pike to a line within but some 300 yards south of the others. In support,

Chalmers' brigade, under Colonel White, had been moved up and occupied the crest of the ridge in rear, and the skirmishers thrown forward extended to the railroad on the left.

At dawn the skirmishers advanced and drove out the enemy from the Round Forest, but in turn were forced to retreat before superior numbers. The enemy advancing, opened fire on the artillery, which, promptly responding, soon shelled them into a precipitate retreat, when, with an increased force, we again occupied the Round Forest. Anderson's brigade had been advanced to and now occupied the former position of Chalmers. The brigades of Manigault and Coltart occupied the southern extremity of the cedar brake, and the right of the column facing the Nashville pike.

Shortly after 3 p. m. the batteries on the hill, as previously instructed, opened a brisk fire on the enemy, whose line extended toward the river and beyond, or into the extreme edge of a skirt of woods, the nearest point of which was some 300 yards from that in which our batteries were. The firing was continued as long as it could be with safety to the column of General Breckinridge, advancing on the east side of the river. The left of this column passing across the river into the woods, in or behind which rested the left of the enemy's force, was immediately attacked by it and driven up the river toward the position of Chalmers' brigade. Colonel [T. W.] White immediately threw out supports, with instructions to drive back the enemy. This was followed by a general advance of the enemy along his entire front, and his being driven out of the Round Forest back into the woods on the river. Night closing in, the fighting ceased for the day.

Late in the evening, Anderson's brigade, under orders from the commanding general, was moved rapidly across the river to the support of General Breckinridge, and did not rejoin the division until the morning of the 4th. That night Manigault was moved to the position vacated by Anderson, and Coltart was moved up to White's support, and their commands placed in proper positions for operations the next morning.

At daybreak on the morning of the 3d, the artillery shelled the Round Forest, which was immediately thereafter charged into by the infantry, and the enemy driven out with considerable loss. Brisk skirmishing was kept up through the day, chiefly with Coltart's command, which occupied the Round Forest.

Late in the evening, after subjecting the Round Forest and woods to a terrific cannonading, the enemy advanced in force, and, engaging our troops, succeeded in breaking a part of our line, when the timely arrival of the reserves enabled the line again to advance, and, after a very sharp and well-contested engagement, to repulse the enemy. Lieutenant-Colonel Farrar, of the First Louisiana (Regulars), was mortally wounded in the engagement. He was a bold and gallant officer, and had arrived on the field only in time to assume command of his regiment in this last engagement. Their infantry being driven back, the enemy renewed the cannonading, continuing it some time after dark. Colonels White and Coltart proved themselves deserving of commendation by the admirable conduct of their commands throughout the harassing period of their occupancy of this important and almost isolated position.

The troops were withdrawn on the morning of the 4th without contest or pursuit. For seven days they had cheerfully endured fatigue, exposure, and hardships sufficient to cause despondency in any breast not actuated by the same steadfast determination to dare all and suffer all in defense of the right. In temporary repulses and the most trying positions, the total absence of everything like panic, and the cool self-possession and alacrity with which they rallied, reformed, and moved forward against the enemy, was as truly remarkable as it was most honorable.

The timely preparations made under direction of Surgeon [Carlisle] Terry for the care of the wounded seem to have been as judicious and ample as was practicable, and the infirmary corps for the division discharged its duties fearlessly and well.

To Capts. D. E. Huger, assistant adjutant-general; J. R. B. Burtwell, chief of artillery, and E. B. D. Riley, chief of ordnance, I am indebted for valuable and indispensable services. In extending orders, seeing to their execution, and in rallying and cheering on the troops, they were energetic and untiring, displaying gallantry and capacity. Maj. B. M. Thomas, adjutant and inspector general, reported on the field from sick leave on the morning of the 2d, and immediately entered on the discharge of his duties with intelligence and efficiency. Lieut. R. W. Withers, aide-de-camp, Asst. Surg. J. Paul Jones, and Lieut. Charles L. Huger, First Louisiana (Regulars), were, through the entire engagement, actively, zealously, and most creditably engaged in the discharge of the various duties assigned them. Maj. W. H. Ross, acting commissary of subsistence, and Maj. R. Q. Pinckney, quartermaster, did good service in their respective departments. Captain [T. M.] Lenoir and Lieutenant [H. R.] Gordon, commanding escort, gave valuable assistance in the collecting and sending off captured property, in driving forward stragglers from and laggards in the fight, and in staff duties, which they were several times called upon to perform. Private M. G. Hudson, of the Twenty-fourth Alabama Regiment, long engaged in the assistant adjutant-general's office, and well and favorably known within the command, rendered services on the field evidencing his fitness and capacity for a more responsible position.

The total strength of the division was 7,774; the total loss by casualties, 2,519. Brigade and regimental reports and detailed statement of casualties have heretofore been forwarded.

Very respectfully, yours, &c.,

J. M. WITHERS,
Major-General.

Maj. THOMAS M. JACK,
Asst. Adjt. Gen., Polk's Corps, Army of Tennessee.

No. 220.

Reports of Capt. Felix H. Robertson, Florida battery,* Deas' brigade.

SHELBYVILLE, TENN., *January 12, 1863.*

SIR: By direction of Lieutenant-General Polk, I reported to General Breckinridge on Friday evening, January 2, with Robertson's battery of six Napoleon guns, and Semple's battery of four Napoleon guns; in all, ten guns. My command was formed in rear of the line of the infantry, and finally behind the artillery of the division which was immediately behind the second line. Leaving my caissons, I advanced to the edge of the opening through which the infantry had charged. The highest point of the hill to the left was selected to be the site of Robertson's battery; Semple's was to take the right. So soon as the ground

---

* Robertson's battery claimed both by Alabama and Florida. Finally credited to Florida.

was cleared upon which Semple's battery was to stand, it was at once pushed to its place. The infantry not being able to clear the crest of the hill, and the fire being very heavy on our right, I decided to alter the plan and send my battery to the right, but our line being cramped by unfavorable ground to the right, I only ordered a section up to fill a gap in our line of artillery. By the repulse becoming general, I determined to stop the remainder of my own battery in the field to check the enemy's advance. The artillery of my command was brought off with the loss of one piece of Semple's battery. This only occurred after the infantry supports had given way entirely.

The fighting of this battery (Semple's) was entirely creditable. The confusion was such that it was not to be wondered at that three pieces were left on the field, but that more were not lost. The artillery as it entered the woods was placed, and by a rapid fire checked the enemy's advance. The batteries under my command were subjected to a hot infantry fire and the worst cross-fire I ever saw.

The loss of the two batteries I cannot know, as I have not seen Lieutenant [E. J.] Fitzpatrick, commanding two sections of Semple's battery. My own lost 6 horses and 6 men.

After dark the guns fell back, and Major [R. E.] Graves having been severely wounded, I, at the request of General Breckinridge, placed the artillery upon the new line.

But for the artillery fire the enemy would surely have carried the position entirely, as our infantry was scattered.

The men of the artillery generally behaved spendidly, but individual exceptions were many to this rule, and I found it necessary to draw my revolver in order to make the drivers halt long enough to fix the piece to be limbered up and brought off.

Very respectfully,

FELIX H. ROBERTSON,
Captain, &c.

ASSISTANT ADJUTANT-GENERAL, BRECKINRIDGE'S DIV.

———

SHELBYVILLE, TENN., *February* 18, 1863.

CAPTAIN: On the morning of January 2, I was ordered to accompany Colonel Brent, assistant adjutant-general, and endeavor to find a position from which the enemy's line might be enfiladed with artillery. Such a position having been found, a report of the fact was made to the general at once. The enemy's skirmishers being in possession of the point selected, it was determined to attack and carry it. I received orders from General Bragg to take Robertson's battery (six Napoleons), two sections Semple's battery (four Napoleons), two rifles and two 12-pounder howitzers belonging to Breckinridge's division, and to occupy and hold to the utmost extremity the desired position after the enemy had been dislodged by the infantry. The necessary preparations for the artillery were made at once. The batteries arrived on the ground and were soon in position.

Having to await the arrival of a still absent brigade, I took an opportunity to consult General Breckinridge. I found his ideas of the attack and my own differed materially. He supposed it was to be made by a combination of both arms, while I was positive the general's orders were that infantry alone should take the hill. General Breckinridge then desired me to form my batteries in the space between his two lines of infantry and advance. This I declined to do, stating as a reason the danger both of confusion and loss from such an arrangement. He then desired me to form and advance behind his second line of infantry. I then repeated the general's orders to me, viz, to wait until the infantry had crowned the crest, and then to rush up and occupy it. Knowing the disposition of all commanders to use artillery, I spoke to General Breckinridge and earnestly protested against crowding a field so contracted as the one in which we were to operate with small guns, stating that, in case of a repulse, we would inevitably lose some if they were carried on the field. General Breckinridge, thinking differently, however, formed his batteries and advanced them simultaneously with his infantry and immediately behind it. Colonel Brent, assistant adjutant-general, was present on this occasion and heard the conversation.

After the first reconnaissance, and before the final arrangements for attack, two pieces (of Breckinridge's division) had been moved and had opened fire on the enemy's skirmishers. It called the enemy's attention to the very point we desired to attack, and probably to this development is due the fact that we found the enemy's batteries had been located so as to cover completely all the ground over which we would be compelled to pass, and which operated to such an alarming extent on our lines. One of these batteries, I think, was located near Hoover's house; the other was located in rear of the Round Forest, to the right of the railroad, in front of Chalmers' position. I know they must have been across Stone's River, for I could notice the shells falling, and all had considerable elevation.

All being prepared, the movement began in the following order: Infantry in two lines, interval 200 yards; the batteries of General B[reckinridge's] division formed immediately in rear of the second line; my batteries in rear of all, caisson left at a distance in rear. I followed up the advance with my command until I gained the open field, across which we were to advance; here I halted. The plan for the artillery was as follows: Two 12-pounder howitzers to rake the slopes from the highest point of the hill to the water's edge, firing down the river the heaviest battery; six Napoleons to occupy the highest point; the other battery, four Napoleons, to occupy a station on the ridge running out from the river to the right from the hill top. The two 12-pounder howitzers began early; the ground for the four Napoleons was soon uncovered and occupied by Lieutenant Fitzpatrick, commanding. Before this, however, the enemy's fire had brought the artillery of General B[reckinridge's] division to a halt; had overturned two pieces; the others had begun firing obliquely to the right, but for a time I thought they were firing into their own men. I waited some time for the infantry to clear the crest, so that I could order Robertson's battery up to its place, but saw unmistakable evidences of a retrograde movement, and seeing Colonel [G. St. Leger] Grenfell at this moment, I sent word to General Bragg that I was satisfied the infantry would be unable to hold their position, and changed my plan, so as to bring the guns of Robertson's battery to bear on the enemy. I ordered it up to take position beside Semple's. It had nearly arrived at the new position when the infantry gave back. I at once ordered the commander, Lieutenant [S. J.] Benton, to take his battery to the rear and establish it in the line of timber, to protect the infantry until it could be reformed; the other batteries were ordered to move off, not, however, until all the infantry support had disappeared. At this point occurred our loss in guns. Two pieces of Wright's battery were lost, and one fine piece belonging to Semple's battery. The batteries, having kept up the fight some time after the infantry had abandoned the field, drew to themselves a very heavy fire; they were, therefore, much reduced in men.

In this communication I desire to call the attention of the general commanding to the good behavior of Captain Semple's company under fire, and more particularly would I direct his attention to Lieutenant Fitzpatrick, commanding the two sections. This gallant officer brought off one piece that would otherwise have been left, and would have saved the other had the wheel driver not been shot at the critical moment of limbering up. Lieutenant [J.] Pollard, of this company, behaved with great gallantry, and was severely wounded.

As fast as the pieces came back to the new line they were placed; but the majority, having no ammunition, were ordered back to their caissons to refill their boxes. So soon as our guns were unmasked, fire was opened on the enemy's line and continued until dark, with a very heavy fire of skirmishers upon the artillery. This line had been established, supposing it would be good to rally the broken division, but the hope proved utterly fallacious. Except about 150 fugitives collected in a ravine to my right, I saw no body of troops, and fearing an advance of the enemy, under cover of the darkness I moved to the rear again and established a new line along another skirt of timber. Here I found some few troops of General Breckinridge's division, but many of them had returned to their old places, as I knew from the sound of the cheering and speaking in the rear. Being unable to find General Breckinridge for some time, I proceeded to regulate the artillery according to my own ideas. After a time I met the general; told him what I had done, and he directed me to continue so to act and report to him after I had finished. The contagion of flight had spread to the artillery, and it was with great difficulty that several pieces of artillery were brought away, owing to the drivers being frightened. In more than one instance I found it necessary to cock my revolver and level it in order to bring men to a realizing sense of their duty. I am clearly of the opinion that if there had been no artillery on that field the enemy would have gone into Murfreesborough easily that evening. There was no organization that I could see or hear of until after the enemy had been checked, save in the artillery. I have never seen troops so completely broken in my military experience. I tried myself, and saw many others try, to rally them; but they seemed actuated only by a desire for safety and beyond the reach of other sentiments. I saw the colors of many regiments pass, and though repeated calls were made for men of the different regiments, no attention was paid to them.

I take this opportunity to mention the courage of some man whom I do not know. He carried a stand of colors, and halted frequently, faced the enemy, and called the Sixth Kentucky Regiment; and although he did not receive much attention, he lingered as long as there was any infantry on the field, and then passed to the rear, calling out, "Here's your Sixth Kentucky."

I have the honor to be, very respectfully, &c.,

FELIX H. ROBERTSON,
Captain, &c.

Capt. K. FALCONER, *Assistant Adjutant-General.*

[Supplemental.]

——— —, 1863.

CAPTAIN: I have the honor to submit the following supplementary report of the action of my battery during the battles near Murfreesborough:

The fuses generally operated to my satisfaction. Occasional exceptions to this general rule arose from a faulty manner of driving the paper well into the wood. The Bormann fuses worked to my satisfaction. There were no sights used with my guns; the effects of each shot served to determine the direction of the next. My aim always low, the effect of my shots good. I had an opportunity to examine some practice made at our cavalry by mistake, and again on the evening of December 30, during a little affair with the enemy; everything was satisfactory. I have no means of determining accurately the number of rounds fired from my battery, as my boxes were frequently replenished, though I think I would be within bounds in saying 70 rounds to the gun.

My loss in *matériel* was 1 caisson; the number of horses killed and disabled, 15. My loss in men was severe; 34 men in my company bear the marks of the enemy's missiles upon their persons. Of this number, however, 17 only were unfitted for duty; the remainder continued at their posts. One of the 17 is missing, and supposed dead; seen to fall while advancing to position on the evening of January 2. None killed on the field, though 5 are thought to be mortally wounded.

Very respectfully,

FELIX H. ROBERTSON,
Captain, Commanding Battery.

Capt. J. R. [B.] BURTWELL,
Chief of Artillery, Withers' Division.

No. 221.

Report of Brig. Gen. J. Patton Anderson, C. S. Army, commanding Walthall's brigade.

HDQRS. WALTHALL'S BRIGADE, WITHERS' DIVISION,
POLK'S CORPS, ARMY OF TENNESSEE,
Shelbyville, Tenn., January 26, 1863.

MAJOR: On the evening of December 27, I received an order from corps headquarters to turn over the command of the brigade recently assigned to me to Colonel Manigault, my next in rank, and to assume command of Walthall's brigade, that officer being absent on sick leave. The several brigades of Withers' division had been previously ordered to have three days' cooked rations in their haversacks, and to hold themselves in readiness for action at a moment's notice.

About midnight of the 27th and 28th, orders were received to move out at an early hour on the morning of the 28th, so as to have a line of battle formed by 9 a. m. At daylight, however, corps, division, and brigade commanders were to assemble at a point designated on the Nashville pike, for the purpose of reconnoitering the ground on which the line was to be formed. On assembling at the rendezvous, the fog proved to be so thick as to prevent, in a great measure, a thoroughly satisfactory reconnaissance. The line, however, was determined upon, and the major-general commanding the division designated the positions of the several brigades. They were immediately marched out from their encampments, and drawn up in line of battle at right angles with the Nashville pike, and about 1,000 yards in front of the point where the pike crosses Stone's River, Brigadier-General Chalmers' right resting upon the pike very near the point where the railroad intersects it, and his left reaching up a slope in an open field, and resting about the crest

of the hill, with an interval on the top of the hill of about 80 yards between General Chalmers' left and my right. My line was a prolongation
of his, stretching some 300 yards into a dense cedar forest. Colonel
Manigault was on my left; his line was deflected to the rear at an angle
of about 45°. My command was posted from right to left as follows:
Barret's battery (four guns) on the crest of the hill, in open field; the
Twenty-seventh Mississippi, Col. T. M. Jones commanding; Twenty-
ninth Mississippi, Colonel [W. F.] Brantly; Thirtieth Mississippi, Lieut.
Col. Junius I. Scales; Twenty-fourth Mississippi, Lieutenant-Colonel
[R. P.] McKelvaine, and the Forty-fifth Alabama, Col. James [G.] Gil-
christ. The troops remained under arms during the afternoon and night
of the 28th.

On the 29th, rifle-pits were constructed along the line of the Twenty-
seventh Mississippi, which was in the open field. Captain [Overton W.]
Barret also threw up slight earthworks to protect his cannoneers and
horses against the enemy's sharpshooters. The other regiments, all of
which were in the cedar forest, erected temporary breastworks of stone,
great quantities of which covered the ground about them. A line of
skirmishers had already been thrown out from 200 to 300 yards in front,
connecting on the right with those of General Chalmers, and on the left
with Colonel Manigault's. Some skirmishing took place during the day,
and a few casualties were the result.

On the 30th, the skirmishers were more hotly engaged, killed and
wounded on this day amounting to 35. At 9 p. m. the order for attack
the next morning was received. Regimental commanders were immediately assembled, and the order communicated to them.

On the morning of the 31st, soon after daylight, a few shots on our
extreme left, quickly followed by the thick roll of musketry and then
by booming artillery, announced that the action had commenced. In
pursuing the instructions contained in the order, it was necessary that
the extreme left of our line should advance some distance, swinging
around upon the right, before my command should move beyond the
breastworks. The direction of Colonel Manigault's line on my left, as
heretofore explained, made it necessary for his left to describe an arc
equal to the eighth of a circle, the length of his line being the radius,
before reaching the point where it would be on a prolongation of my
line. The enemy's right was being steadily driven back.

About 9 a. m. Colonel Manigault came to me and informed me that
he intended to charge a battery in his front; wished me to send two
regiments to his support. I consented to do so, and immediately ordered the Forty-fifth Alabama and Twenty-fourth Mississippi forward
to perform that duty. They became hotly engaged soon after leaving
their breastworks, the enemy being in heavy force and strongly posted,
backed by many pieces of artillery, so planted as to enfilade a portion
of our line. In addition to this enfilading fire, Colonel Manigault was
exposed to a cross-fire from a battery in front of his left. In the unequal contest our line halted, staggered, and fell back in some confusion,
but were easily rallied, reformed, and moved to the front. The Thirtieth, Twenty-ninth, and Twenty-seventh Mississippi were now successively ordered forward, with instructions to swing round upon and preserve the touch of elbow to the right. Captain Barret, commanding the
battery, was directed to hold his fire, not to respond to the long-range
guns of the enemy, and only to use his pieces when a favorable opportunity of playing upon the masses or lines of the enemy was presented.
Immediately in front and in short range of these regiments the enemy
had two batteries advantageously posted, so as to sweep an open field

over which they had to pass in their advance. The ordeal to which they were subjected was a severe one, but the task was undertaken with that spirit and courage which always deserves success and seldom fails of achieving it. As often as their ranks were shattered and broken by grape and canister did they rally, reform, and renew the attack under the leadership of their gallant officers. They were ordered to take the batteries at all hazards, and they obeyed the order, not, however, without heavy loss of officers and men.

Not far from where the batteries were playing, and while cheering and encouraging his men forward, Lieut. Col. James L. Autry, commanding the Twenty-seventh Mississippi, fell, pierced through the head by a minie ball. (The evening before, the colonel of the regiment, Thomas M. Jones, had gone to the rear, complaining of being unwell, and had not returned during the action.)

The death of this gallant officer at a critical period caused some confusion in the regiment until they were rallied and reformed by Capt. E. R. Neilson, the senior officer present, who subsequently was seriously wounded on another part of the field.

About the same time that Lieutenant-Colonel Autry fell, Colonel Brantly, of the Twenty-ninth Mississippi, and his adjutant (First Lieut. John W. Campbell) were knocked down by concussion, produced by the explosion of a shell very near them, but the regiment was soon after carried forward by Lieut. Col. J. B. Morgan in gallant style, capturing the battery in their front, and driving the enemy in great confusion into and through the dense cedar brake immediately beyond. On the left of this last regiment was the Thirtieth Mississippi, commanded by Lieutenant-Colonel Scales. Most gallantly did they perform their part. In moving across the open field in short range of grape, canister, and shrapnel, 62 officers and men were killed and 139 wounded, of this regiment alone, all within a very short space of time, and upon an acre [area] not greater than an acre of ground. The Twenty-fourth Mississippi, Lieutenant-Colonel McKelvaine commanding, and the Forty-fifth Alabama, Colonel Gilchrist commanding, respectively, on the left of the Thirtieth Mississippi, also encountered a battery in their front, strongly supported by infantry on advantageous ground. For a moment these regiments appeared to reel and stagger before the weight of lead and iron that was hurled against them. They were encouraged to go forward by the example of their officers, and a battery was taken. A number of prisoners also fell into our hands. Artillerists, who felt confidently secure in the strength of their positions, were captured at their pieces, and others were taken before they knew that their guns had fallen into our hands. One company entire, with its officers and colors, which had been posted in a log-house near the battery in front of the Twenty-ninth Mississippi, was captured by the Twenty-seventh Mississippi, while the pieces were falling into the hands of the Twenty-ninth.

After losing his artillery, the enemy retired through a dense cedar forest in a direction almost parallel to our original [line] and to the right. In this forest they made no obstinate stand, but, owing to the density of the growth and the exhausted condition of our troops, the pursuit was slow and cautious. It was impossible to preserve a regular and continuous line through such obstacles as the fallen and standing cedars presented. After having pushed through this brake a distance of 500 or 600 yards, an open field appeared in front, through which the enemy was fleeing in scattered confusion. The ground in our front was gently ascending for several hundred yards until the crest of the hill was reached, upon which he was now industriously planting artillery and apparently massing heavy forces of infantry. Our second line had come up and occupied the edge of the forest near the open field. It was growing late in the evening, and advance across the open field, where the enemy would have such decided advantage, was not deemed advisable. Indeed, after resting awhile to collect stragglers and replenish cartridge-boxes, and having become satisfied that my first apprehensions of an effort on the part of the enemy to repossess themselves of the forest was not well founded, a staff officer was sent to Major General Withers, commanding the division, suggesting that, with his consent, I would withdraw my brigade to its original position, where the troops could better recover from their exhaustion, and obtain that rest which they so much needed. He returned soon with the reply that the major-general approved the move. Accordingly, about sundown the brigade resumed its position of the morning, leaving the troops of the second line in position at the far edge of the cedar brake, confronting the enemy's line.

We remained here during the night, but moved forward at an early hour the next morning by order of Major-General Withers, and by his direction had begun to deploy the column on the right of the line then formed in the woods, when Colonel Brantly, of the Twenty-ninth Mississippi, informed me that, by continuing the deployment, much of the line would be exposed to a severe fire from the batteries last above alluded to. I communicated this to General Withers, who directed me to withdraw the line to a position in rear of the second (now become the first) line, near where the batteries had been taken on the day before.

We remained in this new position until about noon of this day (January 1), when, by order of Lieutenant-General Polk, we were conducted by one of his staff officers to the position originally occupied by Brigadier-General Donelson's command, in front of Stone's River, and stretching from Wilkinson pike, on the left, to the railroad, on the right.

At an early hour next morning we moved up by order of Major-General Withers, and took the position at first occupied by Brigadier-General Chalmers' brigade. I was soon ordered across Stone's River, to the right, for the purpose of supporting Major-General Breckinridge's division, upon whom it had been reported the enemy were moving. When the two right regiments of the brigade had succeeded in getting across the river, the order, so far as the other three were concerned, was countermanded, and they were directed to resume their positions in Chalmers' old place, and before I had reached General Breckinridge with the two right regiments, an order was received to return and join the balance of the brigade. Soon after resuming Chalmers' position with the whole brigade, the Twenty-fourth Mississippi, Lieutenant-Colonel McKelvaine, was detached, by order of Lieutenant-General Polk, and sent forward to support Scott's battery, then posted on our front line. This was about 2 p. m., January 2. About 4 p. m. I was ordered by the general commanding to hasten with my brigade to the support of General Breckinridge, on the opposite side of the river from where I then was. Not being familiar with that part of the field, Lieutenant-Colonel [G. W.] Brent, of General Bragg's staff, was directed to conduct me to the desired position.

The troops deserve much credit for the alacrity with which they moved, having waded the river and pushed forward at a double-quick for more than a mile to the scene of Breckinridge's bloody conflict. Darkness had separated the combatants when I reached the spot. A staff officer had been previously sent forward to report to General Breckinridge my near approach. My column was conducted by Colonel Brent to a position in an open wood between two fields, where, as I understood from him, Breckinridge's line of battle had first moved forward to the attack. The column was halted, faced to the front, and skirmishers immediately thrown forward. This precaution had become necessary, inasmuch as there was no line at that time between mine and the enemy, as I learned from Colonel [John A.] Buckner, of General Breckinridge's staff. The general himself rode up at this moment, and soon directed me to withdraw my line to one that would be pointed out by one of his staff officers, in a wood some 200 or 300 yards in the rear. The line of skirmishers, however, was not withdrawn.

Having arrived at the new position about 9 p. m., a reconnaissance was made to the right and left, which disclosed the fact that on my left an interval of 800 yards or more existed between it and the right of Hanson's brigade, and that there were no troops on my right at all. Before daylight the next morning, however, the brigades of Generals Pillow, Preston, and Adams, of Breckinridge's division, had prolonged my right and a few hours later the brigade of Brigadier-General Jackson occupied most of the interval between my left and Hanson's right.

The troops remained in line of battle during the day; many, however, were sent to the rear on account of sickness, caused by the fatigues and exposures of the six days and nights past. It rained nearly all day (3d), and at times so violently that fires could not be kept up; blankets and clothing were wet, and cooked rations were in a condition, from the same cause, not at all inviting, even to a half-famished soldier.

About sundown I received an order from Major-General Withers to withdraw my command at 9 o'clock that night from its position, and take up the line of march down the Shelbyville pike. At the moment the hour arrived, and just as the column was about to be put in motion, I was directed to suspend the execution of this order until further notice. At 11 o'clock the order was repeated, the movement to commence at 1 o'clock the next morning.

At 1 o'clock the morning of January 4, my command moved right in front, following the [rear] of Brigadier-General Pillow's brigade, until we reached the public square in Murfreesborough, where I rejoined Major-General Withers' division, to which I belonged, and marched with it to this place without the loss of a man or anything else.

It should have been mentioned elsewhere that, early in the afternoon of the 31st, the adjutant of the Thirty-ninth North Carolina Regiment (Lieutenant [Isaac S.] Hyams, C. S. Army) reported to me on the battlefield that his regiment had become detached from the command to which it had been assigned in the morning, and was at that time out of ammunition and under command of Captain [A. W.] Bell, the field officers having been killed or wounded. I supplied the needed ammunition, and formed the regiment on the right of the Twenty-seventh Mississippi. It participated creditably in all our subsequent movements until, on the evening of January 2, by order of Lieutenant-General Polk, it was detached and ordered to join Colonel Manigault's brigade.

To my staff officers—Captain [W. G.] Barth, assistant adjutant-general; Lieutenant [W. M.] Davidson, aide-de-camp; Captain [W.] Anderson, ordnance; Capt. Lambert May and Lieut. R. H. Browne, of the inspector-general's department, and Capt. J. B. Downing and Mr. Scanlan, volunteer aides—I am much indebted for their active and efficient assistance in all that pertained to their respective positions. Each and every one performed his duty to my entire satisfaction. Captain May was particularly conspicuous in rallying and leading the troops where danger was thickest. To him I am also indebted for the prompt attention of my order to bring from the field the captured artillery. Capt. E. T. Sykes, assistant adjutant-general on Brigadier-General Walthall's staff, temporarily on duty with me, rendered very efficient service throughout the entire engagement. His activity, courage, and intelligence rendered his services invaluable on a field so extended and in a conflict so protracted. Lieutenant [J. H.] Wood, also ordnance officer of Walthall's brigade, performed his duty with the greatest promptness, displaying much good sense and judgment in conforming the movements of his train to those of the troops.

In endeavoring to give a simple statement of the part taken by the troops under my command in this great engagement, the capture of several batteries has been mentioned in passing. I have abstained from making a statement of the number or kind of pieces taken, for the simple reason that I did not stop to count them or to examine their caliber. The Twenty-seventh, Twenty-ninth, and Thirtieth Mississippi, all participating (but the Thirtieth suffering more severely than the others), captured a battery, of from four to six guns, near a log-cabin in the edge of the cedars, on the right of the Wilkinson pike, and not far from a well used by the enemy in procuring their water on the night previous to the battle. This battery included a small iron rifled piece, somewhat detached from, and a short distance to, the right of the other pieces, and lay in front of the Twenty-ninth Mississippi, which took it. In the log-cabins, and strongly supporting the battery, was a company of sharpshooters, all captured by the Twenty-seventh Mississippi. Farther to the left was a battery, nearer the Wilkinson pike, from which the enemy were driven by the Twenty-fourth Mississippi, supported by the Forty-fifth Alabama. Some 15 or 20 prisoners were here captured at the pieces. Another battery was posted still farther to the left, and nearer the Wilkinson pike, close by which the left of the Forty-fifth Alabama (my left regiment) passed simultaneously with the right of Colonel Manigault. This battery, however, was silenced a few moments before we reached it—I think by one of our batteries playing from a direction where I supposed Colonel Manigault's left to be at the time his right reached the battery simultaneously with my left. As the batteries immediately in my front were being passed, I directed Captain May, of my staff, to have the pieces taken to the rear with as little delay as possible. He subsequently reported to me that he delivered to the chief of ordnance in Murfreesborough eight pieces of different caliber; and I afterward learned that there were two or three pieces taken from the same part of the field by other parties, whose names I could not learn.

Our loss in this engagement was heavy, as the long list of killed and wounded will show. An infant nation struggling for existence, and just now fairly disengaging itself from the oppressor's grasp, pauses in the strife to drop a sympathetic tear over the grave of its gallant dead, and long after that nation shall have risen to manhood among great powers of earth, will her free sons and daughters cherish and revere the names and memories of those who fell upon the bloody plains of Murfreesborough.

The loss of this brigade was 766, as follows: Killed, 119; wounded, 584; missing, 63.

I am, major, very respectfully, your obedient servant,

PATTON ANDERSON,
Brigadier-General, Commanding.

No. 222.

Report of Capt. Overton W. Barret, Missouri battery.

————— —, 1863.

[I have the honor to report the] part taken by Barret's Missouri battery (two 6-pounder guns and two 12-pounder howitzers).

Position on December 28, 1862, in main line of battle on the right of Nolensville road, Walthall's brigade on my left, Chalmers' on my right.

On the 29th, having a very exposed position, and apprehending that the enemy would plant long-range guns on the elevations opposite, I threw up some small earthworks.

About 9 o'clock on the 30th, the enemy opened fire upon me from a battery planted near a small house in the cedars, nearly opposite my position. This battery was composed, as nearly as I could judge, of two Parrott guns, two other rifled guns, and two 12-pounder howitzers. I was ordered not to fire unless compelled or until the infantry charged. During the first ten minutes after the enemy opened fire upon me I had 1 horse killed and 2 men and 2 horses wounded at the limbers. I was obliged by the severity of the fire to send my limbers far to rear, behind a hill. The enemy continued to play upon me until night, with only occasional intermissions, when the enemy turned his fire upon our skirmishers or changed his position so as to obtain a cross-fire upon me. Several times I sustained a fire from three different points and from different batteries. The fire of the enemy was very exact and severe, both from his batteries and sharpshooters, and but for my earthworks my position would have been untenable.

On the 31st, the enemy resumed their fire upon me. I still reserved my fire until Walthall's brigade charged, when I received permission to fire, and opened upon one battery in the cedars and upon another in the left end of the field. My limbers being so far from my pieces, and knowing the opposing batteries had by twelve hours' practice upon me obtained accurate range of my position, I ceased firing when I had diverted theirs from our advancing infantry. In this engagement I lost 1 man wounded. After the enemy were driven from the cedars, I advanced my battery to a position between the Nashville pike and Cowan's house, whence I played on the enemy's infantry until our infantry were about to charge, when I was ordered to cease, and, being within range of the enemy's shot, fell back to my original position, where I remained all day of January 1, 1863.

On January 2, took position some distance in rear of Cowan's house, occasionally fired upon by the enemy's long-range guns. Before daybreak on the 3d, took position on the right and left of Cowan's house and threw up earthworks. About 5 p. m. the enemy commenced and continued firing upon me with ten heavy guns until night, when, by order of the chief of artillery of division, I drew off under the cover of the darkness. In this engagement I lost 1 horse killed and 2 wounded.

I have never been furnished with adjustable sights of any kind. Our Bormann fuses, in my opinion, are very inferior. Our powder, also, I think inferior. My shells, ignited by red, green, and black fuses, were the most effective and accurate projectile which I used in this battle. Six-pounder batteries cannot maintain a fight with long-range guns shooting the Hotchkiss and James projectile unless the distance between the opposing batteries be very short.

The following is a list* of casualties : Four enlisted men wounded ; 2 horses killed, 5 wounded.

Trail of piece struck by solid shot and rendered nearly unserviceable ; 2 spokes shot from wheel of another carriage ; 2 lint stocks, 1 shovel, and 1 sponge and rammer broken by the enemy's shot.

Battery engaged twice and under heavy fire every day, except January 1, from the morning of December 30, [1862,] until dark of January 3, 1863.

Fired 73 rounds 6-pounder spherical case, nearly all of which burst short ; 16 rounds 6-pounder solid shot, which struck lines of infantry 1,000 yards distant ; 3 rounds 6-pounder canister ; 84 rounds 12-pounder howitzer shell, which, at 900 yards distance, drove the enemy's infantry into woods farther back ; 10 rounds 12-pounder spherical case, some of which burst short.

Respectfully,

O. W. BARRET,
Captain, Commanding Barret's Missouri Battery.

No. 223.

Report of Capt. David D. Waters, Alabama battery, Anderson's brigade.

CAMP NEAR SHELBYVILLE, TENN.,
February 16, 1863.

MAJOR : I have the honor to submit the following report of the part taken by my battery in the battle of Murfreesborough, Tenn. :

I took the position in line of battle assigned by chief of artillery of Withers' division for my battery, on the left of the Fourth Brigade, about 10 o'clock on December 28, in which position I remained without interruption until the morning of the 30th, when the enemy, having forced in our skirmishers, got possession of a gin-house and other out-buildings, belonging to the farm of Mr. Harding, in front of the line of our brigade, and about 700 yards distant from my position. I was ordered by the colonel commanding brigade to shell them out, which I did, firing 10 or 12 shells and 4 round shot at the house. A few minutes after I ceased firing, the enemy brought up a rifled gun battery and placed it in position about three-quarters of a mile from my position ; opened on me with percussion shell. I immediately ordered my caissons to move to a position to my left, under cover of a wood. Finding that my position was completely commanded by this battery, and that my guns were not capable of doing them damage, I, after consulting my brigade commander, moved my battery to the left, and took a position in the middle of the brigade, covered by the timber on my right. Here I remained without firing until about 3 p. m., when the enemy made a general advance with infantry and artillery, driving in the line of skirmishers in front of the brigade, bringing into position in front of the right of the brigade a battery of six 12-pounder light guns. I opened upon them at a range of about 650 yards, and compelled him to draw off after firing 6 or 8 rounds. He then moved his battery up under cover of a wood opposite to my position, and took position on a hill about 400 yards from me, when he opened with shell and spherical case shot. At the same time a rifle battery, posted to my right, opened, assisted by

---

* Nominal list omitted.

two rifle guns posted in rear of Harding's dwelling, the battery on my right completely enfilading my line, but was firing over me, doing but little damage, except from falling limbs. The battery in my front occupied all of my guns. After a rapid fire of from three-quarters to an hour this battery was driven from its place. I continued to fire at it until they gained cover of a hill.

In this engagement Corporal Burke, while gallantly performing the duties of gunner, had his thumb shot off. Privates Quinn and Brady were slightly hurt by a falling limb.

None of my horses were hurt, and only slight damage done to my guns, viz: One sponge-staff shot in two, one spoke from right wheel of left center gun shot out by piece of shell, and the trail hand-spike of the first gun shot off.

I remained in this position until dark without firing, as the rifle guns to my right were out of my reach. The enemy's skirmishers, having taken a position about 350 yards from our lines, kept up a rattling fire (doing no damage) until dark, when I moved my command to the rear, to feed and rest my men for the night, where I received a supply of ammunition.

At daylight I received orders from the brigade commander to move at the same time the line of infantry charged to my first position, on the left of the brigade, and cover the charge. I moved to the left and came into battery, but found I could do nothing from that position, and, finding that the right of the line was hard pressed, I moved to the right to support the Tenth and Nineteenth South Carolina Regiments, from which point I commenced firing on the enemy's infantry, and was immediately opened on by one of the enemy's batteries, posted in the wood to the right of the Nolensville turnpike. Our infantry having fallen back to the old line, I kept up a regular fire to cover their preparations for a fresh charge. During the time between the first and second charges, some general officer, with staff escort, came to the front of the enemy's line, and in about 500 yards of my position. I gave them a few rounds of shot and shell, when they retired at a run. I think I must have done them some damage, as I saw my shell burst and shot strike among them, and afterward found one of the horses killed with a round shot. Our line being reformed, made a second charge, drove the enemy across a field within short range, where I had a good chance and gave them spherical case and canister.

During this engagement I regret to have to report Private Richard Murphy killed, Private William Shea wounded, and 1 of my lead horses killed and 2 others so badly wounded that I was compelled to leave them.

I was then ordered to report to Brigadier-General Maney, which I did, and was ordered to remain under cover until he could find a place for me, which I did. My command was not again brought into action. I continued to follow in rear of my brigade until dark, when I took a position in the woods to the left of the Nolensville pike for the night, and here received a full supply of ammunition for my 6-pounder guns and some 12-pounder ammunition.

I met with a great deal of trouble from the great number of friction-primers that were worthless. I was compelled to make on the field quill-primers, which answered the purpose. I would here request that a supply of primers be furnished my battery at once, as it would be totally unserviceable in a fight as it is.

I would here request to mention the gallant conduct of First Lieut. Charles W. Watkins, to whom I was greatly indebted for his coolness and close attention to orders while under fire; also Sergeants Martin,

Turner, and Armstrong. In mentioning these names I do not wish to detract from the rest of my command, all of whom acted with great coolness and attention, the gunners firing slowly and deliberately, doing good service.

I found that the lack of long-range guns was a great drawback to our batteries, for the enemy could, at a distance too far for us, fire upon our lines without interruption and in perfect safety, making his aim more accurate and fire more destructive.

I regret to report that, upon the night of the 30th, Quartermaster Sergt. Thomas Maxwell, while attempting to get to the company with rations, passed through a gap in our line of battle between the left of the Fourth Brigade and the right of the First, was fired upon by the enemy's pickets, killing his horse and wounding him very severely in the knee.

Major, I am, respectfully,

D. D. WATERS,
Captain, Commanding Waters' Battery.

No. 224.

Report of Lieut. Gen. William J. Hardee, C. S. Army, commanding Army Corps.

HEADQUARTERS ARMY OF TENNESSEE,
Tullahoma, Tenn., March 11, 1863.

SIR: I have the honor to forward, by the hands of Col. J. H. Kelly, Eighth Arkansas Volunteers, Lieutenant-General Hardee's corps, the report of that general of the part taken by his corps in the battle of Murfreesborough, December 31 to January 3; also the reports of division and brigade commanders, including those of Major-General McCown's division, which was, during the most important part of the operations, under Lieutenant-General Hardee.

Some errors and misapprehensions of Major-General Breckinridge, incorporated in his report, will be corrected by reference to copies of notes received from him on the field of battle, and which are appended to the report, with an order for the cavalry movement, indorsed by Brigadier-General Pegram as "received." To these papers, appended to General B[reckinridge]'s report, I invite special attention.

I am, sir, very respectfully, your obedient servant,

BRAXTON BRAGG,
General, Commanding.

General S. COOPER,
Adjutant and Inspector General, Richmond, Va.

[Inclosure.]

HEADQUARTERS HARDEE'S CORPS,
Tullahoma, Tenn., February 28, 1863.

COLONEL: After the campaign in Kentucky, our forces were collected at Murfreesborough, while the enemy gradually concentrated an army, reported 70,000 strong, around Nashville. Every preparation that forecast could suggest was made by them to crush our army and obtain possession of Central Tennessee. For nearly two months there was apparent inaction, interrupted only by skirmishes, raids, and a successful affair at Hartsville. The enemy occupied Nashville, their right extending toward Franklin and their left toward Lebanon. Our center was at Murfreesborough, under Lieutenant-General Polk, our right at Ready-ville, under Major-General McCown, and our left at Triune and Eagle-ville.

Such was the situation of the armies when information was received, on December 26, that General Rosecrans was advancing with 60,000 men from Nashville against Murfreesborough. The first demonstration was made against Triune by an advance of the enemy on the Shelbyville turnpike. Cleburne's division and Adams' brigade, under my immediate command, were posted in that vicinity. The commanding general having decided to accept battle and to defend Murfreesborough, I withdrew my command the succeeding day by his order, leaving Wood's brigade and Wharton's cavalry to skirmish with the enemy near Triune. This was done boldly and successfully, and they rejoined the command on the 28th at Murfreesborough. My corps consisted of Breckinridge's and Cleburne's divisions (each of four brigades) and Wheeler's brigade of cavalry.

Murfreesborough is situated 30 miles southeast of Nashville, in a fer-tile, gently undulating, and highly cultivated country, in the midst of the great plain that stretches from the base of the Cumberland Mountains toward Nashville. The Chattanooga Railroad, the chief line of commu-nication from Tennessee to the South Atlantic States, passes through it, and numerous excellent turnpikes radiate from it in every direction. Stone's River flows about 2 miles west of the town, through low banks of limestone, steep, and in some places difficult to pass, and gradually trends to the north as a tributary of the Cumberland. At this time the stream could everywhere be passed without difficulty by infantry, and at the usual fords was not more than ankle-deep, but heavy rains in a few hours swell it to an impassable torrent, and it subsides as rapidly. The road to Lebanon passes nearly due north from Murfreesborough; that to Triune nearly west; that to Salem a little south of west, and the Nashville turnpike northwest, crossing Stone's River about 1½ miles from Murfreesborough. The railroad, leaving the depot on the west of the town, crosses Stone's River about 200 yards above the turnpike ford. At 400 or 500 yards beyond this it intersects the Nashville turnpike at a very acute angle, running between it and the river for about 700 yards, when the stream turns to the east by a sharp bend, and then resumes its northern course. The field of battle offered no peculiar advantages for defense. The open fields beyond the town are fringed with dense cedar brakes, offering excellent shelter for approaching infantry, and are almost impervious to artillery. The country on every side is entirely open, and was accessible to the enemy.

On Sunday morning, December 28, the troops were moved into line of battle. The river separated our right from the left. By order of the commanding general, the space between the Lebanon road and the ford on the Nashville road, making the right of the army, was occupied by my corps. I arranged my troops in two lines, Breckinridge's division form-ing the first line and Cleburne's the second. The former was arranged with Adams' brigade resting on the Lebanon road, about 1½ miles from the town. The line was broken by an intervening field about 300 yards wide, which was left apparently unoccupied, but was covered by the Twentieth Tennessee and [E. E.] Wright's [Tennessee] battery, of Pres-ton's brigade, which swept it and the field in front. The remainder of Preston's brigade rested with its right in the woods, and extended along the margin of the grove, with its left toward the river. Palmer's and Hanson's brigades completed the line, with the left of Hanson resting near the ford. Cleburne's division was posted 800 yards in rear of, and parallel to, that of Breckinridge. Polk's corps extended beyond the river, with its right near the stream, and about 200 yards in advance of my left. Withers' division formed the front line of this corps, and Cheatham's the second, while McCown's division was held in reserve near the town.

No movement of importance occurred until Monday evening. It was deemed necessary to hold a hill situated about 600 yards in advance of Hanson's brigade, as it commanded the sloping hill-sides toward the river in front, and from it the right of General Polk's line could be enfiladed. In the evening the enemy attempted to take this position, but was vigorously repulsed by a portion of Hanson's brigade, and the hill was occupied by our batteries.

During Monday night the cavalry of Brigadier-General Wheeler, attached to my corps, was moved from our right by a circuitous route through Jefferson and La Vergne against the communications of the enemy. After making an entire circuit of the enemy's lines, this daring officer, having inflicted severe injury by the destruction of several hundred wagons and many small-arms, and by the capture of several hundred prisoners, returned through Nolensville and Triune to Murfreesborough.

The next day (Tuesday, the 30th) heavy skirmishing took place on our left between the right of the enemy and the command of Lieutenant-General Polk.

In the afternoon of that day I received instructions from the commanding general to proceed to the left, to take command of McCown's division, to place it in position, and to move Cleburne's division from our extreme right in the same direction. The order was communicated to Cleburne, and I proceeded at once to the left. I found McCown's division, consisting of three brigades, in two lines—Ector's and Rains' brigades in the first, and McNair's in the second line, with Rains' brigade so situated as to be enfiladed by a battery from the enemy. Orders were given to rectify the position of Rains, and to place McNair on the first line. Cleburne's division was brought forward and placed 500 yards in rear of McCown, as a second line. During the night, the commanding general having determined to attack the enemy on our left, Brigadier-General Wharton was ordered to report to me, and I was instructed, with the two divisions mentioned and Wharton's cavalry, to commence the attack at dawn the next morning. The new position which my command now occupied is embraced in the angle between the Salem turnpike and the Triune road. About half a mile from Murfreesborough, on the Nashville road, the Wilkinson turnpike diverges to the left, passing nearly equidistant between it and the Triune road. Each of these roads crosses Stone's River about 1½ miles west of the town. The river makes a bend in the shape of a horseshoe to the west, and the roads cross at the bases of the bend. The enemy's right was about three-quarters of a mile beyond the river, with their line south of the Triune road, and extending almost northwardly toward the Wilkinson pike and the Nashville road. The force under my immediate command Wednesday morning was 10,045 infantry and artillery, under McCown and Cleburne, and 2,000 cavalry, under Brigadier-General Wharton.

I ordered Wharton to make a detour of the enemy's right, and to fall upon their flank and rear, while the infantry and artillery moved upon them in front. He dashed forward at a gallop at daybreak, and soon reached the Wilkinson turnpike, 2½ miles in the rear. With Colonel [John T.] Cox's command [First Confederate Cavalry], he charged with great impetuosity and took prisoners the Seventy-fifth Illinois Regiment. Captain [S. P.] Christian, of the Texas Rangers [Eighth Texas Cavalry], with four companies, at the same time charged and took a complete battery of the enemy, with all its guns, caissons, horses, and artillerists. By these dashes 1,500 prisoners fell into our hands. Wharton afterward swept around toward the Nashville turnpike, and found the enemy's cavalry in position to defend their menaced trains. Harrison, Ashby, and Hardy were ordered to charge. This was met by a counter-charge of the enemy, supposed to be the Fourth Regular Cavalry, who were routed in confusion. The entire cavalry force of the enemy was deployed beyond this point. Wharton's entire brigade was now ordered to charge; 2,000 horsemen dashed forward to the assault. The field was favorable, the charge irresistible, the conflict short. The enemy fled in wild dismay 2 miles beyond Overall's Creek, leaving in our hands several hundred wagons, 400 additional prisoners, and several pieces of artillery.

The conduct of Wharton and his brigade cannot be too highly commended. After a day of brilliant achievements, he covered the left of my infantry at night.

Major-General McCown having failed to get McNair's brigade on the line of battle Tuesday night, as directed by me, the brigade was moved into position early the next morning, and McCown advanced with his division against the enemy, about 600 yards distant, with McNair on the right of Ector and with Rains' brigade on the left. The division of Major-General Cleburne was about 500 yards in rear of McCown, as a second line. The two divisions were posted on the left of Lieutenant-General Polk's command. The troops advanced with animation and soon became hotly engaged. The enemy were broken and driven through a cedar brake after a rapid and successful charge by McCown's command, in which Brigadier-General [August] Willich and many prisoners were taken.

A signal instance of courage was shown by Col. J. C. Burks, of the Eleventh Texas. This brave officer, though mortally wounded, still led and cheered on his regiment until he fell exhausted at its head.

Another instance was shown by Sergt. A. Sims, flag-bearer of the Tenth Texas, who, seeing a Federal flag-bearer endeavoring to rally his regiment, sprang forward, seized the standard, and in the struggle both were shot down, waving their flags with their last breath. The Federal flag was captured.

I had ordered McCown and Cleburne, as they crushed the line of the enemy, to swing round by a continued change of direction to the right, with Polk's left as a pivot, while Wharton was to make a diversion on their flank and rear. This was done by Cleburne, but was not so promptly executed by McCown, on account of the position of the enemy in his front. McCown continued westwardly, fighting toward Overall's Creek, far to our left, while Cleburne, executing the maneuver, changed his direction northeastwardly toward the Wilkinson turnpike, which placed him on the right of McCown and filled the interval between McCown and Polk. The line, now single and without support, engaged and drove the enemy with great carnage through the fields and cedar brakes which lie between the Triune and Wilkinson roads. Before this gap in the line was filled by Cleburne, McCown's right flank was exposed. McNair halted his brigade, while Liddell advanced gallantly, filling the interval, covered McNair's unprotected right, and engaged a superior force of the enemy posted behind a rail fence. These two brigades charged the enemy with impetuosity, took their battery, and pursued their broken and fleeing regiments before Ector and Rains could be brought into action.

General McNair left a sick bed to enter the battle, and after conducting his brigade with gallantry, becoming exhausted, was ordered to retire from the field. The command then devolved upon Colonel [R. W.' Harper.

By this time Liddell, who was upon the left of Johnson's brigade, had become separated from Cleburne's division by following the movement of McCown. The command was near the Wilkinson turnpike, at a point where the enemy had established a hospital. They had driven them nearly 2 miles. The men were greatly fatigued and their ammunition exhausted. As soon as this was replenished, I ordered them again to advance. Rains' brigade being fresh, was brought forward to the right to attack a battery, while Ector's, McNair's, and Liddell's brigades moved forward in the direction of the Nashville road. Ector and Harper, though enfiladed by a battery, forced their way through a cedar brake in which the enemy were posted, while Rains advanced upon the battery. Unfortunately, this brave officer and accomplished gentleman fell, shot through the heart, and his brigade recoiled in confusion. Ector and Harper were ordered to fall back under cover, while [J. T.] Humphreys' battery bravely engaged sixteen pieces of the enemy until our infantry were sheltered.

The divisions of McCown and Cleburne in single line had now driven the enemy, with great slaughter, for several miles through the cedar brakes toward the Nashville turnpike. Cleburne (originally formed with Brigadier-General Polk's brigade on the right, Johnson's in the center, and Liddell's on the left, with Wood's in reserve) had engaged the enemy shortly after McCown commenced the attack. Having changed direction toward the northeast, he encountered their first line, posted behind fences and in dense thickets, a little north of the Triune road. In the open ground beyond were other lines and batteries. Limestone rocks in the thickets furnished the enemy admirable natural defenses. The division dashed forward, and, after a bloody struggle of half an hour, hurled the first line back upon the second, which, in turn, was broken, and the mingled lines were driven in disorder toward the Wilkinson turnpike. Wood's brigade dispersed the One hundred and first Ohio and the brigade composed of the Thirty-eighth Illinois, the Twenty-first, Eighty-first, and Fifteenth Wisconsin. The Seventeenth Tennessee captured a Michigan battery, while the Second Arkansas [Mounted Rifles*] again routed the Twenty-second Indiana, capturing its colonel. This regiment is the same that the Second Arkansas had routed at Perryville, and which, during the campaign of last year, had behaved with such barbarity to the people of Arkansas. It was in this conflict that Colonel [A. S.] Marks, of the Seventeenth Tennessee Regiment, was severely wounded while gallantly leading and encouraging his men. It was also in this conflict that Liddell's and Johnson's brigades suffered their greatest loss. The enemy several times attempted to make a stand, but were each time forced back. Our troops were vigorously pressing forward, when a third line, strongly supported by artillery, stood revealed on the south side of the turnpike. The cannonade was fierce, but could not check our advance. After a stubborn combat the enemy were broken, and fled to the cedar brakes between the Nashville and Wilkinson turnpikes.

Cleburne was now in advance of Cheatham and Withers, and as he crossed the open grounds near the turnpike he was enfiladed by a battery posted on an eminence directly on his right flank. Captain [T. R.] Hotchkiss, acting chief of artillery of Cleburne's division, placed [J. H.]

---

* Dismounted.

Calvert's and [Put.] Darden's batteries in position near the Wilkinson turnpike, and boldly engaged some heavy rifled batteries of the enemy. This officer nobly discharged his duty, and was twice wounded. The First Arkansas and the Fifth Confederate afterward charged the batteries, and captured four of the guns. Several colors, a large number of prisoners, medical stores, hospitals, ammunition trains, and caissons, were captured in this conflict. The battle at this point was bloody. Here General [Joshua W.] Sill, of the Federal Army, was slain.

Cleburne had now driven back all the forces of the enemy beyond the Wilkinson road, when another line was displayed in the cover of the cedar woods between the Wilkinson and Nashville turnpikes. Wood, Polk, and Johnson charged this line, receiving a heavy fire. Here Lieutenant-Colonel [Don] McGregor, of the First Arkansas, and Major [J. T.] McReynolds, of the Thirty-seventh Tennessee, two brave officers, fell, mortally wounded. Brigadier-General Liddell attacked the enemy near the left of Brigadier-General Johnson, whom he had rejoined, and, after an obstinate conflict, threw them into confusion. Here Col. Samuel [G.] Smith, of the Sixth and Seventh Arkansas, and Colonel [John H.] Kelly, of the Eighth Arkansas, both gallant officers, were wounded; and here Lieutenant-Colonel [John E.] Murray, of the Fifth Arkansas, courageously bore the colors of his regiment to the front, while Private J. K. Leslie, of the same regiment, captured the colors of the enemy with his own hands. A portion of Cleburne's division was repulsed, but, after a bloody combat, the enemy were finally dislodged. On our right their lines remained unbroken. With our inferior numbers no further advance could be hazarded until all my forces were collected. Wood, having fallen back for ammunition, was detained to protect the ordnance train. The remaining brigades occupied the cedar brakes and fields near the Nashville road. The command of Cleburne was now reformed, and about 3 o'clock he essayed again to rout a fresh line of the enemy near the Nashville turnpike. The enemy were again broken with heavy loss. Johnson's brigade was conspicuous in the conflict, in which the brigade of Preston Smith also shared. It was now past 3 o'clock. In moving through the open grounds to drive the enemy from the last positions they held near the railroad, a fierce and destructive enfilading fire of artillery was poured upon the right of Cleburne's division from batteries massed near the railroad embankments. At this critical moment the enemy brought up a fresh line to oppose our wearied troops. Our ammunition was exhausted. Smith's brigade recoiled in confusion. Johnson and Polk followed, and the division was repulsed. It was rallied and reformed in the edge of the cedar woods, about 400 yards in rear of the most advanced position we had won. Brigadier-General Polk in this conflict suffered very severely, but, while we sustained, we inflicted great loss.

When I withdrew from the extreme right, Tuesday evening, Major-General Breckinridge's division was left in its original position on the Lebanon road. Brigadier-General Jackson having reported to me with his brigade, it was posted on the east side of the Lebanon road, to the right of Adams' brigade. These five brigades, under Major-General Breckinridge, remained in position from Sunday to Wednesday without any material event, except a skirmish for an artillery position, already mentioned.

About 11 o'clock Wednesday the brigades of Adams and Jackson were, in obedience to orders of the commanding general, sent across the river to the assistance of Lieutenant-General Polk, who was reported to be hard pressed. Crossing the ford about midday, they were formed near the intersection of the Nashville Railroad and turnpike, with their right stretching to the river, and were moved down the Nashville turnpike and railroad against the center of the enemy, passing in the direction of the burnt brick building known as the Cowan house. The brigade of Jackson passed by those of Chalmers and Donelson in the direction of the Cowan house, while Adams', extending toward the river, attacked the enemy between 1 and 2 o'clock. A desperate struggle for a passage down the Nashville road ensued just before Cleburne became engaged against their right, 2 miles farther on. The force was unequal to the task. It recoiled after a loss of one-third of the command.

A short time after, Preston and Palmer were ordered to cross the ford, to continue the same movement, and Hanson's brigade alone remained on the east side of Stone's River. They reached the ground just after Jackson and Adams were repulsed, General Adams having been wounded while gallantly conducting his brigade. They were quickly formed under the immediate command of Major-General Breckinridge, and moved across the plain in fine order under the fire of the enemy's artillery.

Many men and officers were killed along the line, the principal loss falling upon Preston's brigade. The Twentieth Tennessee, of Preston's brigade, vainly endeavored near the river to carry a battery, and, after a heavy loss, including their gallant commander, Colonel [T. B.] Smith, who was severely wounded, was compelled to fall back under cover. Palmer, being farther on the left, suffered but little. The remaining regiments of Preston's brigade encountered great difficulty in passing the fences and pickets at the Cowan house, and, being exposed to an enfilading fire of infantry and artillery at short range, were thrown into some confusion. They were soon rallied, and, rushing forward with cheers across the intervening space, entered the cedar brakes in front.

At 4 o'clock our line was almost parallel with the Nashville turnpike for about 2 miles, stretching from the point of woods near the Cowan house toward Overall's Creek. Preston occupied the extreme right of my line, and the divisions of Cleburne and McCown extended northwest, almost parallel with the railroad. Liddell's brigade formed the extreme left. The enemy occupied the ground northwest of the railroad, lying between it and Stone's River, toward Nashville. Here they massed a vast strength of artillery and infantry. Their right had been completely turned, crushed, and beaten back for more than 3 miles. Great confusion prevailed, but their strength was still such that we could not undertake to force the position without unwise hazard. We had lost nearly a third of the commands engaged. If, at the moment when the enemy were driven from the thick woods north of the Wilkinson turnpike, a fresh division could have replaced Cleburne's exhausted troops and followed up the victory, the rout of Rosecrans' army would have been complete. The interval required to collect and reform our lines, now shattered by four successive conflicts, was occupied by the enemy in planting heavy batteries and massing fresh columns of infantry to oppose our further advance. I sent for re-enforcements. The commanding general replied he had none to give me. Hanson's brigade alone remained fresh and unfought. The enemy lay beyond the range of our guns, securely sheltered behind the strong defense of the railroad embankment, with wide, open fields intervening, which were swept by their superior artillery. It would have been folly, not valor, to assail them in this position. I gave the order to hold the wood, 400 yards in rear of the advanced position we had won, and to bivouac for the night.

During the day the men and officers of my command had displayed the most splendid courage. Twenty-three pieces of cannon and more than 4,000 prisoners, with a corresponding number of small-arms, rewarded their valor. With 12,000 men of all arms, we had driven back and utterly routed McCook's corps, ascertained by his captured returns to have been 18,000 strong, and several brigades and divisions which it is known were sent to his support.

For 3 miles in our rear, amid the thick cedars and the open fields, where the Federal lines had been originally formed, their dead and their dying, their hospitals, and the wreck of that portion of their army marked our victorious advance. Our bivouac fires were lighted at night within 500 yards of the railroad embankment, behind which their disordered battalions sought shelter.

Wednesday night was clear and cold. The armies maintained their relative positions. Some picket skirmishing occurred during the night. No action of importance nor material change of position occurred until about 2 o'clock in the afternoon of Friday, January 2. The commanding general, anxious to secure a position on the east bank of the river, from which he could enfilade the lines of the enemy, ordered Major-General Breckinridge, with his entire division, to seize a hill about 1,600 yards in front of the position occupied by Hanson's brigade. At 4 o'clock the division moved forward. It swept over the crest of the hill, routing a division of the enemy, who fled in disorder across the stream, after leaving many killed, wounded, and prisoners. Our men pursued them with great ardor. A division reported to be that of General [J. S.] Negley, and a brigade under General Porter [Palmer], held the opposite side of the river. This fresh force poured a withering fire from an advantageous position upon our men. Breckinridge's division, after a bloody struggle not exceeding forty minutes, in which at least 1,200 men were killed and wounded, was repulsed. Many brave men and able officers fell in the attack. Among the latter Brigadier-General [R. W.] Hanson, a spirited and intrepid officer, was mortally wounded early in the action. As this movement was made without my knowledge, and under the immediate supervision of Major-General Breckinridge, I refer to his report for details.

Friday night, the commanding general, apprehending an attack on our right, east of Stone's River, ordered me to withdraw Cleburne's and McCown's divisions from the left, and to place them in their original positions—the former in rear of Breckinridge's line, the latter in reserve. These divisions did not get into position until late that night. Cold and drenching rain set in and continued throughout the succeeding day. The enemy manifested no disposition to attack, but our troops, being worn down by the hardships of their winter bivouacs and the exhaustion of battle, and the commanding general having received information that the enemy were being largely re-enforced, he determined to re+ire.

In obedience to his orders, on the morning of January 4, I withdrew my command by the Manchester road to Tullahoma, in good order and without molestation.

It is worthy of remark that at Murfreesborough, whenever the fight was confined principally to musketry, and the enemy had no advantage in artillery, we were successful. It was only when they had massed heavy batteries, under cover of the railroad embankments, that we were repulsed. In every form of contest in which mechanical instruments, requiring skill and heavy machinery to make them, can be used, the Federals are our superiors. In every form of contest in which manly courage, patient endurance, and brave impulse are the qualities and conditions necessary to success, we have invariably been successful. Long-range cannon and improved projectiles can be made only by great mechanical skill, heavy machinery, and abundant resources. The enemy is, therefore, superior in artillery. Infantry constitutes the great arm of the service, and its appointments and equipments are simple. The

Federal infantry, unsupported by artillery, has not in a single instance fought successfully with ours when the odds were less than three to two.

I herewith inclose a tabular statement (A), which exhibits the losses sustained by the divisions of McCown, Breckinridge, and Cleburne, and the brigades of Jackson and Wharton, amounting to 5,663 in killed, wounded, and missing.

To the officers and men of my command I return my heartfelt thanks for the ability and striking courage displayed by them at Murfreesborough. The field required that much should be confided to the commanders of divisions, brigades, and regiments, and it is to me a grateful duty to acknowledge how well these officers merited my confidence. The men illustrated the day by a discipline, courage, and devotion never surpassed. In the reports of my subordinate commanders will be found many instances of individual heroism which the limits of this report will not permit me to record.

My thanks are due to the members of my staff, namely: Maj. T. B. Roy, chief of staff; Capt. D. H. Poole, assistant adjutant-general; Capt. D. G. White, acting assistant adjutant-general; Maj. W. D. Pickett, assistant inspector-general; Capt. S. L. Black, assistant inspector-general; Lieut. T. W. Hunt, assistant inspector-general; Lieut. W. W. Wilkins, aide-de-camp; Maj. L. Hoxton, chief of artillery; Maj. J. M. Kennard, chief of ordnance; Surg. A. L. Breysacher, medical inspector; Maj. C W. Gassett, chief quartermaster; Maj. W. E. Moore, chief of subsistence, and to General W. C. Whitthorne, adjutant-general of the State of Tennessee, and Capt. [Maj.] Thomas Claiborne, C. S. Army, who volunteered their services.

My thanks are also especially due to Capts. S. W. Presstman and J. W. Green, of the engineer corps, for active and efficient service, and to Surg. D. W. Yandell, my medical director, to whose good management I am indebted for having both my own and the Federal wounded in Wednesday's fight rapidly removed from the field and cared for before midnight.

I am, colonel, very respectfully, your obedient servant,

W. J. HARDEE,
Lieutenant-General.

Lieut. Col. GEORGE WILLIAM BRENT,
Assistant Adjutant-General.

A.

Tabular statement of killed, wounded, and missing, to accompany Lieutenant-General Hardee's report of the battle of Murfreesborough.

Command.	Commander.	Killed.	Wounded.	Missing.
HARDEE'S CORPS.				
Breckinridge's Division.				
Palmer's brigade *	Colonel Palmer	49	324	52
Preston's brigade	Brigadier-General Preston	58	384	97
Adams' brigade †	Brigadier-General Adams	112	445	146
Hanson's brigade	Brigadier-General Hanson	47	273	81
Total Breckinridge's division	Major-General Breckinridge	266	1,426	376

* Brigadier-General Pillow assigned to command previous to action, January 2.
† Colonel Gibson in command after General Adams was wounded.

Tabular statement of killed, wounded, and missing. &c.—Continued.

Command.	Commander.	Killed.	Wounded.	Missing.
Cleburne's Division.				
Wood's brigade	Brigadier-General Wood	52	336	113
Johnson's brigade	Brigadier-General Johnson	61	488	57
Liddell's brigade	Brigadier-General Liddell	86	503	18
Polk's brigade	Brigadier-General Polk	30	298	19
Cleburne's staff			2	
Total Cleburne's division	Major-General Cleburne	229	1,627	207
McCown's Division (unattached).				
Ector's brigade	Brigadier-General Ector	29	275	39
Rains' brigade	Brigadier-General Rains	21	154	15
McNair's brigade	Brigadier-General McNair	42	330	52
McCown's escort		2	2	1
Total McCown's division	Major-General McCown	94	761	107
Jackson's brigade (unattached)	Brig. Gen. J. K. Jackson	41	262	
Wharton's brigade of cavalry	Brigadier-General Wharton	20	131	113
Grand total Hardee's corps	Lieutenant-General Hardee	650	4,207	803

RECAPITULATION.

Command.	Killed.	Wounded.	Missing.	Total.
Breckinridge's division	266	1,426	376	2,068
Cleburne's division	229	1,627	207	2,066
McCown's division	94	761	107	962
Jackson's brigade	41	262		303
Wharton's brigade	20	131	113	264
Grand total	650	4,207	803	5,663

[Addenda.]

HDQRS. HARDEE'S CORPS, ARMY OF TENNESSEE,
Tullahoma, Tenn., January 17, 1863.

COLONEL: I have the honor to submit the following report of the "present for duty" in this army corps on the morning of the 31st of December, 1862:

Breckinridge's division:
Brown's [Palmer's] brigade ... 1,446
Adams' brigade ... 1,534
Hanson's brigade ... 1,893
Preston's brigade ... 1,951
——— 6,824

Cleburne's division:
Wood's brigade ... 1,150
Johnson's brigade ... 1,922
Liddell's brigade ... 1,709
Polk's brigade ... 1,343
——— 6,124

Total ... 12,948

Discrepancies in the relative strength of the brigades of Breckinridge's division in the present report, as compared with previous reports, are explained by the fact that the reorganization of that division was perfected by several transfers of regiments only on the day previous to the battle of Murfreesborough.

Very respectfully, your obedient servant,

W. J. HARDEE,
Lieutenant-General.

Col. GEORGE WILLIAM BRENT,
Assistant Adjutant-General.

—

HDQRS. HARDEE'S CORPS, ARMY OF TENNESSEE,
Tullahoma, April 20, 1863.

COLONEL: In obedience to instructions from headquarters of the army, I have the honor to forward herewith the names of officers who fell at the battle of Murfreesborough, conspicuous for their valor, to be inscribed on the battery of Liddell's brigade, and on one of the reserve batteries:

Liddell's battery.—Lieut. Col. Don. McGregor, First Arkansas; Capt. James T. Armstrong, Company E, Sixth Arkansas; First. Lieut. H. C. Collier, Company H, Second Arkansas, and First Lieut. H. J. McCurdy, Eighth Arkansas.

Reserve Battery.—Maj. Henry C. Ewin, Forty-fourth Tennessee Regiment; Maj. James T. McReynolds, Thirty-seventh Tennessee Regiment; Capt. E. Eldridge Wright, Wright's battery, and Capt. Edwin Allen, Company C, Twenty-sixth Tennessee Regiment.

Very respectfully, your obedient servant,

W. J. HARDEE,
Lieutenant-General.

Col. GEORGE WILLIAM BRENT,
Assistant Adjutant-General, Army of Tennessee.

—

No. 225.

Report of Maj. Gen. John C. Breckinridge, C. S. Army, commanding First Division, with appendix by General Bragg.

HEADQUARTERS BRECKINRIDGE'S DIVISION,
January —, 1863.

I have the honor to report the operations of this division, of Lieutenant-General Hardee's corps, in the recent battles of Stone's River, in front of Murfreesborough.

The character and course of Stone's River, and the nature of the ground in front of the town, are well known, and as the report of the general commanding will, no doubt, be accompanied by a sketch, it is not necessary to describe them here.

On the morning of Sunday, December 28, the brigades moved from their encampments and took up line of battle about 1½ miles from Murfreesborough in the following order: Adams' brigade on the right, with its right resting on the Lebanon road, and its left extending toward the ford over Stone's River, a short distance below the destroyed bridge on the Nashville turnpike; Preston on the left of Adams; Palmer on the left of Preston, and Hanson forming the left of the line, with his left resting on the right bank of the river near the ford. The right of Major-General Withers, of Lieutenant-General Polk's corps, rested near the left bank of the river and slightly in advance of Hanson's left.

Brigadier-General Jackson, having reported to me with his command, was placed, by the direction of the lieutenant-general commanding, upon the east side of the Lebanon road, on commanding ground, a little in advance of the right of Brigadier-General Adams.

My division formed the front line of the right wing of the army; Major-General Cleburne's division, drawn up some 600 yards in rear, formed the second line of the same wing, while the division of Major-General McCown, under the immediate direction of the general commanding, composed the reserve.

My line extended from left to right along the edge of a forest, save an open space of 400 yards, which was occupied by Wright's battery, of Preston's brigade, with the Twentieth Tennessee in reserve to support it. An open field 800 yards in width extended along nearly the whole front of the line, and was bounded on the opposite side by a line of forest similar to that occupied by us. In the opinion of the lieutenant-general commanding (who had twice ridden carefully over the ground with me) and the general commanding (who had personally inspected the lines), it was the strongest position the nature of the ground would allow.

About 600 yards in front of Hanson's center was an eminence which it was deemed important to hold. It commanded the ground sloping toward the river in its front and on its left, and also the plain on the west bank occupied by the right of Withers' line. Colonel [T. H.] Hunt, with the Forty-first Alabama, the Sixth and Ninth Kentucky, and Cobb's battery, all of Hanson's brigade, was ordered to take and hold this hill, which he did, repulsing several brisk attacks of the enemy, and losing some excellent officers and men. A few hundred yards to the left and rear of this position a small earthwork, thrown up under the direction of Major [R. E.] Graves, my chief of artillery, was held during a part of the operations by Semple's battery of Napoleon guns.

In the afternoon of Tuesday, the 30th, I received intelligence from Lieutenant-General Hardee that the divisions of Cleburne and McCown were to be transferred to the extreme left, and soon after an order came to me from the general commanding to hold the hill at all hazards. I immediately moved the remainder of Hanson's brigade to the hill, and strengthened Cobb's battery with a section from [C. L.] Lumsden's battery and a section from [C. H.] Slocomb's Washington Artillery. At the same time Adams' brigade was moved from the right and formed on the ground originally occupied by Hanson's brigade. Jackson was moved to the west side of the Lebanon road, to connect with the general line of battle.

All the ground east of Stone's River was now to be held by one division, which, in a single line, did not extend from the ford to the Lebanon road. I did not change my general line, since a position in advance, besides being less favorable in other respects, would have widened considerably the interval between my right and the Lebanon road. The enemy did not again attack the hill with infantry, but our troops there continued to suffer during all the operations, from heavy shelling. Our artillery at that position often did good service in diverting the enemy's fire from our attacking lines of infantry, and especially on Wednesday, the 31st, succeeded in breaking several of their formations on the west bank of the river.

On the morning of Wednesday, the 31st, the battle opened on our left. From my front, information came to me from [John] Pegram's cavalry force in advance that the enemy, having crossed at the fords below, were moving on my position in line of battle. This proved to be incorrect, and it is to be regretted that sufficient care was not taken by the authors of the reports to discriminate rumor from fact.

About 10.30 a. m. I received, through Col. J. Stoddard Johnston, a suggestion from the general commanding to move against the enemy instead of awaiting his attack.* I preferred to fight on the ground I then occupied, but supposing that the object of the general was to create a diversion in favor of our left, my line, except Hanson's brigade, was put in motion in the direction from which the enemy was supposed to be advancing. We had marched about half a mile when I received, through Colonel Johnston, an order from the general commanding to send at least one brigade to the support of Lieutenant-General Polk, who was hard pressed, and, as I recollect, two, if I could spare them. I immediately sent Adams and Jackson, and at the same time suspended my movement, and sent forward Capt. E. M. Blackburn, with several of my escort, and Captain Coleman and Lieut. Thomas B. Darragh, of my staff, with orders to find and report with certainty the position and movements of the enemy. Soon after an order came from the general commanding to continue the movement. The line again advanced, but had not proceeded far when I received an order from the general commanding, through Colonel Johnston, repeated by Colonel Grenfell, to leave Hanson in position on the hill, and with the remainder of my command to report at once to Lieutenant-General Polk. The brigades of Preston and Palmer were immediately moved by the flank toward the ford before referred to, and the order of the general executed with great rapidity.

In the mean time, riding forward to the position occupied by the general commanding and Lieutenant-General Polk, near the west bank of the river, and a little below the ford, I arrived in time to see at a distance the brigades of Jackson and Adams recoiling from a very hot fire of the enemy. I was directed by Lieutenant-General Polk to form my line, with its right resting on the river and its left extending across the open field, crossing the Nashville turnpike almost at a right angle. While my troops were crossing the river, and getting into line, I rode forward with a portion of my staff, assisted by gentlemen of the staffs of Generals Bragg and Polk, to rally and form Adams' brigade, which was falling back chiefly between the turnpike and the river. Jackson, much cut up, had retired farther toward our left. The brigade of Brigadier-General Adams was rallied and placed in line across the field, behind a low and very imperfect breastwork of earth and rails. These brigades did not again enter the action that day, which, indeed, closed soon after with the charge of Preston and Palmer. They had suffered severely in an attack upon superior numbers, very strongly posted and sustained by numerous and powerful batteries, which had repulsed all preceding assaults. The list of casualties shows the courage and determination of these troops.

General Adams having received a wound while gallantly leading his brigade, the command devolved upon Col. R. L. Gibson, who discharged its duties throughout with marked courage and skill.

Preston and Palmer being now in line, Preston on the right, Lieutenant-General Polk directed me to advance across the plain until I encountered the enemy. The right of my line rested on the river (and, from the course of the stream, would in advancing rest on or very near it), while the left touched a skirt of woods from which the enemy had been

---

* I find that Colonel Johnston regarded it as an order, but, as I moved at once, it is not material.

driven during the day. At the opposite extremity of the plain a cedar-brake extended in front of Palmer's whole line and two-thirds of Preston's line, the remaining space to the river being comparatively open, with commanding swells, and through this ran the railroad and turnpike nearly side by side. It was supposed that the enemy's line was parallel to ours, but the result showed that, in advancing, our right and his left at the point of contact would form an acute angle. These two brigades, passing over the troops lying behind the rails, moved across the plain in very fine order under the fire of the enemy's artillery. We had advanced but a short distance when Colonel [T.] O'Hara (my acting adjutant-general) called my attention to a new battery in the act of taking position in front of our right, between the turnpike and the river. I immediately sent him back to find some artillery to engage the enemy's battery. He found and placed in position the Washington Artillery. About the same time Capt. E. P. Byrne reported his battery to me, and received an order to take the best position he could find and engage the enemy. He succeeded in opening on them after our line had passed forward.

A number of officers and men were killed along the whole line, but in this charge the chief loss fell upon Preston's right and center. His casualties amounted to 155.

The Twentieth Tennessee, after driving the enemy on the right of the turnpike, and taking 25 prisoners, was compelled to fall back before a very heavy artillery and musketry fire, Colonel Smith, commanding, being severely wounded, but it kept the prisoners and soon rejoined the command. The Fourth Florida and Sixtieth North Carolina encountered serious difficulty at a burnt house (Cowan's) on the left of the turnpike from fences and other obstacles, and were, for a little while, thrown into some confusion. Here for several minutes they were exposed to a destructive and partially enfilading fire at short range of artillery and infantry; but they were soon rallied by their gallant brigade commander, and, rushing with cheers across the intervening space, entered the cedar glade. The enemy had retired from the cedars, and was in position in a field to the front and right. By changing the front of the command slightly forward to the right, my line was brought parallel to that of the enemy, and was formed near the edge of the cedars.

About this time, meeting Lieutenant-General Hardee, we went together to the edge of the field to examine the position of the enemy, and found him strongly posted in two lines of battle, supported by numerous batteries. One of his lines had the protection of the railroad cut, forming an excellent breastwork. We had no artillery, the nature of the ground forbidding its use. It was deemed reckless to attack with the force present.

Night was now approaching. Presently the remainder of Lieutenant-General Hardee's corps came up on the left, and, with McCown's command and a part of Cheatham's, prolonged the line of battle in that direction. Adams' brigade also appeared and formed on the right of Preston. The troops bivouacked in position.

The commanding general, expecting an attack upon his right the next morning, ordered me during the night to recross the river with Palmer's brigade. Before daylight Thursday morning, Palmer was in position on the right of Hanson. No general engagement occurred on this day, the troops generally being employed in replenishing the ammunition, cooking rations, and obtaining some repose.

On Friday, January 2, being desirous to ascertain if the enemy was establishing himself on the east bank of the river, Lieutenant-Colonel

[John A.] Buckner and Major Graves, with Captain [Edward P.] Byrne's battery, and a portion of the Washington Artillery, under Lieutenant [W.] C. D. Vaught, went forward to our line of skirmishers toward the right and engaged those of the enemy, who had advanced, perhaps, 1,000 yards from the east bank of the river. They soon revealed a strong line of skirmishers, which was driven back a considerable distance by our sharpshooters and artillery, the latter firing several houses in the fields in which the enemy had taken shelter. At the same time, accompanied by Major [W. D.] Pickett, of Lieutenant-General Hardee's staff, and by Maj. James Wilson, Colonel [T.] O'Hara, and Lieutenant [J. Cabell] Breckinridge, of my own, I proceeded toward the left of our line of skirmishers, which passed through a thick wood about 500 yards in front of Hanson's position and extended to the river. Directing Captain [Chris.] Bosche, of the Ninth, and Captain [Thomas] Steele, [jr.,] of the Fourth Kentucky, to drive back the enemy's skirmishers, we were enabled to see that he was occupying with infantry and artillery the crest of a gentle slope on the east bank of the river. The course of the crest formed a little less than a right angle with Hanson's line, from which the center of the position I was afterward ordered to attack was distant about 1,600 yards. It extended along ground part open and part woodland. While we were endeavoring to ascertain the force of the enemy and the relation of the ground on the east bank to that on the west bank of the river, I received an order from the commanding general to report to him in person. I found him on the west bank, near the ford below the bridge, and received from him an order to form my division in two lines and take the crest I have just described with the infantry. After doing this I was to bring up the artillery and establish it on the crest, so as at once to hold it and enfilade the enemy's lines on the other side of the river. Pegram and Wharton, who, with some cavalry and a battery, were beyond the point where my right would rest when the new line of battle should be formed, were directed, as the general informed me, to protect my right and co-operate in the attack. Captain Robertson was directed to report to me with his own and Semple's batteries of Napoleon guns. Captain Wright, who with his battery had been detached some days before, was ordered to join his brigade (Preston's). The brigades of Adams and Preston, which were left on the west side of the river Wednesday night, had been ordered to rejoin me. At the moment of my advance, our artillery in the center and on the left was to open on the enemy. One gun from our center was the signal for the attack. The commanding general desired that the movement should be made with the least possible delay.

It was now 2.30 p. m. Two of the brigades had to march about 2 miles, the other two about 1 mile. Brigadier-General Pillow, having reported for duty, was assigned by the commanding general to Palmer's brigade, and that fine officer resumed command of his regiment, and was three times wounded in the ensuing engagement. The Ninth Kentucky and Cobb's battery, under the command of Colonel Hunt, were left to hold the hill so often referred to. The division, after deducting the losses of Wednesday, the troops left on the hill, and companies on special service, consisted of some 4,500 men. It was drawn up in two lines—the first in a narrow skirt of woods, the second 200 yards in rear. Pillow and Hanson formed the first line, Pillow on the right. Preston supported Pillow, and Adams' brigade (commanded by Colonel Gibson) supported Hanson. The artillery was placed in rear of the second line, under orders to move with it and occupy the summit of the slope as soon as the infantry should rout the enemy. Feeling anxious about my right, I sent two staff officers in succession to communicate with Pegram and Wharton, but received no intelligence up to the moment of assault. The interval between my left and the troops on the hill was already too great, but I had a battery to watch it and a small infantry support. There was nothing to prevent the enemy from observing nearly all of our movements and preparations. To reach him it was necessary to cross an open space 600 or 700 yards in width, with a gentle ascent. The river was several hundred yards in rear of his position, but departed from it considerably as it flowed toward his left.

I had informed the commanding general that we would be ready to advance at 4 o'clock, and precisely at that hour the signal gun was heard from our center. Instantly the troops moved forward at a quick step and in admirable order. The front line had bayonets fixed, with orders to deliver one volley, and then use the bayonet. The fire of the enemy's artillery on both sides of the river commenced as soon as the troops entered the open ground. When less than half the distance across the field the quick eye of Colonel O'Hara discovered a force extending considerably beyond our right. I immediately ordered Major Graves to move a battery to our right and open on them. He at once advanced Wright's battery and effectually checked their movements. Before our line reached the enemy's position his artillery fire had become heavy, accurate. and destructive. Many officers and men fell before we closed with their infantry, yet our brave fellows rushed forward with the utmost determination, and, after a brief but bloody conflict, routed both the opposing lines, took 400 prisoners and several flags, and drove their artillery and the great body of their infantry across the river. Many were killed at the water's edge. Their artillery took time by the forelock in crossing the stream. A few of our men in their ardor actually crossed over before they could be prevented, most of whom subsequently, moving up under the west bank, recrossed at a ford three-quarters of a mile above. The second line had halted when the first engaged the enemy's infantry, and laid down under orders; but very soon the casualties in the first line, the fact that the artillery on the opposite bank was more fatal to the second line than the first, and the eagerness of the troops, impelled them forward, and at the decisive moment, when the opposing infantry was routed, the two lines had mingled into one, the only practical inconvenience of which was that at several points the ranks were deeper than is allowed by a proper military formation. A strong force of the enemy beyond our extreme right yet remained on the east side of the river. Presently a new line of battle appeared on the west bank directly opposite our troops and opened fire, while at the same time large masses crossed in front of our right and advanced to the attack. We were compelled to fall back. As soon as our infantry had won the ridge, Major Graves advanced the artillery of the division and opened fire. At the same time Captain Robertson threw forward Semple's battery toward our right, which did excellent service. He did not advance his own battery (which was to have taken position on the left), supposing that that part of the field had not been cleared of the enemy's infantry. Although mistaken in this, since the enemy had been driven across the river, yet I regard it as fortunate that the battery was not brought forward. It would have been a vain contest. It now appeared that the ground we had won was commanded by the enemy's batteries, within easy range, on better ground, upon the other side of the river. I know not how many guns he had. He had enough to sweep the whole position from the front, the left, and the right, and to render it wholly untenable by our force present of artillery and infantry. The infantry, after passing the crest and descending the slope toward the river, were in some measure protected, and suffered less at this period of the action than the artillery.

We lost three guns, nearly all the horses being killed, and not having the time or men to draw them off by hand. One was lost because there was but one boy left (Private Wright, of Wright's battery) to limber the piece, and his strength was unequal to it.

The command fell back in some disorder, but without the slightest appearance of panic, and reformed behind Robertson's battery in the narrow skirt of timber from which we emerged to the assault. The enemy did not advance beyond the position in which he received our attack. My skirmishers continued to occupy a part of the field over which we advanced until the army retired from Murfreesborough. The action lasted about one hour and twenty minutes. As our lines advanced to the attack, several rounds of artillery were heard from our center, apparently directed against the enemy on the west bank of the river.

About twilight Brigadier-General Anderson reported to me with his brigade, and remained in position with me until the army retired. I took up the line of battle for the night a little in rear of the field over which we advanced to the assault, and Captain Robertson, at my request, disposed the artillery in the positions indicated for it.

Many of the reports do not discriminate between the losses of Wednesday and Friday. The total loss in my division, exclusive of Jackson's command, is 2,140, of which I think 1,700 occurred on Friday. The loss of the enemy on this day was, I think, greater than our own, since he suffered immense slaughter between the ridge and the river.

I cannot forbear to express my admiration for the courage and constancy of the troops, exhibited even after it became apparent that the main object could not be accomplished. Beyond the general good conduct, a number of enlisted men displayed at different periods of the action the most heroic bravery. I respectfully suggest that authority be given to select a certain number of the most distinguished in each brigade, to be recommended to the President for promotion.

I cannot enumerate all the brave officers who fell, nor the living, who nobly did their duty; yet I may be permitted to lament, in common with the army, the premature death of Brigadier-General Hanson, who received a mortal wound at the moment the enemy began to give way. Endeared to his friends by his private virtues, and to his command by the vigilance with which he guarded its interest and honor, ne was, by the universal testimony of his military associates, one of the finest officers that adorned the service of the Confederate States. Upon his fall the command devolved on Colonel [R. P.] Trabue, who in another organization had long and ably commanded most of the regiments composing the brigade.

I cannot close without expressing my obligations to the gentlemen of my staff. This is no formal acknowledgment. I can never forget that during all the operations they were ever prompt and cheerful by night and day in conveying orders, conducting to their positions regiments and brigades, rallying troops on the field, and, indeed, in the discharge of every duty.

It gives me pleasure to name Lieutenant-Colonel Buckner, assistant adjutant-general, who was absent on leave, but returned upon the first rumor of battle; Colonel O'Hara, acting adjutant-general; Lieutenant [J. Cabell] Breckinridge, aide-de-camp; Major Graves, chief of artillery (twice wounded and his horse shot under him); Major [James] Wilson, assistant inspector-general (horse shot); Captain [Charles] Semple, ordnance officer; Lieutenant Darragh (severely wounded). Captains Martin and Coleman, of my volunteer staff, were active and efficient. The former had his horse killed under him.

Drs. J. F. Heustis and [John E.] Pendleton [Ninth Kentucky Infantry], chief surgeon and medical inspector, were unremitting in attention to the wounded. Dr. Stanhope Breckinridge, assistant surgeon, accompanied my headquarters and pursued his duties through the fire of Wednesday. Mr. Buckner and Mr. Zantzinger, of Kentucky, attached themselves to me for the occasion, and were active and zealous.

Capt. E. M. Blackburn, commanding my escort, ever cool and vigilant, rendered essential service and made several bold reconnaissances. Charles Chotard, of the escort, acting as my orderly on Wednesday, displayed much gallantry and intelligence.

The army retired before daybreak on the morning of January 4. My division, moving on the Manchester road, was the rear of Hardee's corps. The Ninth Kentucky, Forty-first Alabama, and Cobb's battery, all under the command of Colonel Hunt, formed a special rear guard. The enemy did not follow us.

My acknowledgments are due to Col. J. Stoddard Johnston, Lieutenant-Colonel Brent, and Lieutenant-Colonel Garner, of General Bragg's staff, and to Major Pickett, of Lieutenant-General Hardee's staff, for services on Friday, January 2.

Respectfully, your obedient servant,

JOHN C. BRECKINRIDGE,
Major-General, Commanding.

Maj. T. B. Roy,
Assistant Adjutant-General.

APPENDIX BY GENERAL BRAXTON BRAGG TO THE REPORT OF MAJOR-GENERAL BRECKINRIDGE.

First. A note dated 10.10 o'clock, December 31, saying, "The enemy are undoubtedly advancing upon me."

Second. A note dated 11.30 a. m., December 31, in reply to what he calls in his report "a suggestion from the commanding general," in which he says, "*I am obeying your order;*" but expressing the opinion that the move would expose him "to a heavy force of the enemy advancing from Black's" (on Lebanon road).

Third. A note dated 12.50 o'clock, January 1, 1863 (an error for December 31, 1862, the day it was received), correcting previous report as follows: "It is not certain the enemy is advancing upon me in two lines," &c., and requesting the two brigades asked as re-enforcements against an imaginary danger be held where he could get them. The hour of this note shows, too, an advance of half a mile (see report) in one hour and twenty minutes.

Fourth. A note dated 7 p. m., December 31, an application to re-enforce Hanson in his isolation.

Fifth. An order to Brigadier-General Pegram, commanding cavalry, indorsed "received," directing the cavalry to join in the attack to be made by General Breckinridge.

It is stated in the general's report that he was informed the cavalry was to attack with him; that he failed to communicate with it, yet reported he would be ready precisely at 4 o'clock, and did attack at that hour with nearly a third of his force absent.

The tabular statement No. 7,* February 8, 1863, accompanying my report of the battle, shows the force of this division on Wednesday, December 31, to have been 7,053. The loss of Wednesday, the 31st, was 730, not 440, as made by the division commander; and the loss on Friday, the 2d, was 1,338, not 1,700. The loss of Wednesday, 440, stated by the division commander, deducted from his whole strength, leaves 6,613. Deducting again the regiment and battery he was ordered to leave out, and adding the two batteries of Captain Robertson, leaves him still over 6,000 infantry and artillery, instead of 4,500, with which he says he made the attack; and, correcting his error in making the loss too small on Wednesday and too large on Friday, he still has underrated his force by more than one-fourth.

BRAXTON BRAGG,
General, Commanding.

[Inclosure No. 1.]

DECEMBER 31, 1862—10.10 a. m.

General BRAGG, *Commanding Forces:*

The enemy are undoubtedly advancing upon me. The Lebanon road is unprotected, and I have no troops to fill out my line to it.

JOHN C. BRECKINRIDGE.

[Inclosure No. 2.]

DECEMBER 31, 1862—11.30 a. m.

General BRAGG:

GENERAL: I am obeying your order, but my left is now engaged with the enemy, and if I advance my whole line farther forward and still retain communication with my left, it will take me clear away from the Lebanon road, and expose my right and that road to a heavy force of the enemy advancing from Black's.

JOHN C. BRECKINRIDGE,
Major-General.

On the above was the following indorsement:

HEADQUARTERS ARMY OF TENNESSEE,
Tullahoma, Tenn., March 6, 1863.

The order of which General Breckinridge acknowledges the receipt in his note to General Bragg, of which the within is a copy, was borne and duly delivered by me.

J. STODDARD JOHNSTON,
Colonel, Aide-de-Camp to General Commanding.

[Inclosure No. 3.]

HEADQUARTERS BRECKINRIDGE'S DIVISION,
In the Field, January 1, 1863—12.50 o'clock.

Lieutenant-Colonel BRENT,
Assistant Adjutant-General:

COLONEL: It is not certain that the enemy are advancing upon me in two lines. General Pegram promised to report the true condition of

---

* See Inclosure C to Bragg's report, p. 674.

things.   The two brigades you ordered to me might be held at the ford of the river, subject to further developments.   If necessary, I could get them into position from that point before the enemy could reach me.

Very respectfully,

JOHN C. BRECKINRIDGE,
Major-General.

[Inclosure No. 4.]

HEADQUARTERS BRECKINRIDGE'S DIVISION,
In the Field, December 31, [1862]—7 p. m.

General BRAXTON BRAGG,
Commanding Army of Tennessee:

GENERAL: When I crossed the river this evening with two brigades, I left General Hanson's brigade holding the hill already designated on the commanding position in front of my division.   I have the honor now to report that Hanson's brigade is still in the same position, with three batteries, isolated from the balance of the army.

Very respectfully, your obedient servant,

JOHN C. BRECKINRIDGE.

[Inclosure No. 5.]

HEADQUARTERS IN THE FIELD,
[January] 2, [1863]—1 p. m.

Brigadier-General PEGRAM:

GENERAL: The general is about moving to take by force a position between Hower's house and the right of our line, on the [this] side of the river.   General Wharton will be there.   You will arrange and dispose your command in the vicinity of Hower's, so as to co-operate with this movement.

Respectfully,

GEORGE WM. BRENT,
Assistant Adjutant-General.

[Indorsement.]

Received.

JOHN PEGRAM,
Brigadier-General.

—

[Addenda.]

HEADQUARTERS BRECKINRIDGE'S DIVISION,
Tullahoma, Tenn., March 31, 1863.

S. COOPER,
Adjutant and Inspector General, Richmond, Va.:

SIR: Two days ago I read General Braxton Bragg's official report of the battles of Stone's River, before Murfreesborough, and, after a proper time for reflection, I think it my duty to send you this communication.

I cannot conceal from myself the fact that so much of the report as refers to my conduct and that of my command (except some general compliments to the courage of a portion of my troops on Wednesday, 31st of December) is in tone and spirit a thorough disparagement of both. . This tone runs through all its parts, and lies like a broad foundation underneath the whole.   At the same time the narrative of events is made to sustain the general spirit.

While the report of the commanding general fails, as I think, to do justice to the behavior of my division on Friday, the 2d of January, yet its strictures are chiefly leveled at my own conduct as an officer during all the operations. By direct statement, and by unmistakable innuendo, it is throughout a reflection upon my capacity and conduct.

Without referring to its contents in detail, I have to say, in respectful terms, that neither its material statements nor its equally material innuendoes can be maintained by proof; that its omission of important facts creditable to my division and myself is as remarkable as many of its affirmative statements; in a word, that in spirit and substance it is erroneous and unjust.

I trust that nothing in the foregoing expressions passes the limit of military propriety, and that plainness of statement will be pardoned to one who, even under the weight of superior military censure, feels that both he and his command have deserved well of their country. Having met the commanding general repeatedly on the field, and on three occasions in council, during the progress of the operations, without receiving from him the least indication of dissatisfaction with my conduct, I was not prepared to see a report, bearing a subsequent date, containing representations at variance with these significant facts. Nor was my surprise lessened when I observed that it was written after a correspondence with his corps and division commanders (I being one of the latter), in which he invokes their aid to sustain him, and speaks of them as officers "upon whom I [he] have ever relied as upon a foundation of rock."

The commanding general, having written and forwarded his report before receiving those of his subordinate commanders, could have derived no assistance in its preparation from those usual official aids to the commander-in-chief; and since his position on the field prevented him from seeing many of the movements, especially those of Friday, the 2d of January, it much concerns all affected by his statements to know something of those other, and to them unknown, sources of information to which he has given the sanction of his influence and rank as the head of the army.

I have felt that it would be improper in a paper of this character to enter upon a detailed vindication; yet in view of the fact that the casualties of war may at any time render an investigation impossible, I hope that it has not been improper for me to place on record this general protest against the injurious statements and inferences of the commanding general, particularly since, not anticipating his censures, I may not have been sufficiently minute in portions of my own report.

And in regard to the action of Friday, the 2d of January, upon which the commanding general heaps so much criticism, I have to say, with the utmost confidence, that the failure of my troops to hold the position which they carried on that occasion was due to no fault of theirs or of mine, but to the fact that we were commanded to do an impossible thing. My force was about 4,500 men. Of these, 1,700 heroic spirits stretched upon that bloody field, in an unequal struggle against three divisions, a brigade, and an overwhelming concentration of artillery, attested our efforts to obey the order.

I have the honor to request that a court of inquiry be appointed, to assemble at the earliest time consistent with the interests of the service, and clothed with the amplest powers of investigation. Of course, I do not desire the interests of the service to be prejudiced in the least degree by any matter of secondary importance; accordingly, while an early investigation would be grateful to my feelings, I can cheerfully await the time deemed best by the proper authority.

With great respect, your obedient servant,

JOHN C. BRECKINRIDGE,
Major-General, Provisional Army Confederate States.

HEADQUARTERS BRECKINRIDGE'S DIVISION,
Near Hoover's Gap, Tenn., May 6, 1863.

S. COOPER,
Adjutant and Inspector General, Richmond, Va.:

SIR: Early in April last,* and immediately after reading General Bragg's official report of the battles before Murfreesborough, I had the honor to address a brief letter to you, protesting against its representations in regard to my command and myself, and asking for a court of inquiry. I have received no answer to that letter, and it may be that the interests of the service will prevent the early assembling of a court. In the mean time General Bragg's report has appeared in print, and will be read by many thousands in all parts of the Confederacy. Under these circumstances, I have to request, in respectful, but earnest, terms, that my letter, asking for a court, may be published, as an act of simple justice to myself and my division.

With great respect, your obedient servant,
JOHN C. BRECKINRIDGE,
Major-General, Provisional Army, Confederate States.

—

Abstract from report of ordnance and ordnance stores, on hand and required, of Major-General Breckinridge's division, Hardee's corps, Army of Tennessee, January 11, 1863.

Brigades.	Total enlisted present.	Percussion muskets, caliber .69.	Rifle muskets, caliber .58.	Enfield rifles, calibers .57 and .58.	Mississippi rifles.	To be supplied, percussion muskets, caliber 64.
			On hand.			
Adams'	1,485	455	....	678	.....	....
Pillow's	1,297	608	296	139	1	....
Preston's	1,202	831	....	355	41	....
Trabue's	1,594	190	....	1,052	.....	....
Total	5,578	2,134	296	2,224	42	882

REMARKS.

I cannot account for the want of so many guns otherwise than the wanton carelessness of the troops in leaving them on the field or throwing them away whilst on the retreat. The excuse the officers give is that several arms were put in wagons and lost by being misplaced. I have also to report the absence of two regiments, the Ninth Kentucky, at Manchester, and the Thirty-second Tennessee, at Wartrace, the wants of which regiments I am unable to report.
Respectfully submitted.

CHARLES SEMPLE,
Ordnance Officer.

Captain O'HARA, *Assistant Adjutant-General, Breckinridge's Division.*

No. 226.

Report of Brig. Gen. Daniel W. Adams, C. S. Army, commanding First Brigade.

ATLANTA, GA., *January 12, 1863.*

COLONEL: Owing to a slight wound which I received in the left arm, I have not been able to report sooner the part taken by my brigade in the engagement before Murfreesborough on the 31st ultimo.

---

* See letter of March 31, p. 790.

I now have the honor to report that my brigade, consisting of the Thirteenth and Twentieth Louisiana Regiments, consolidated into the Thirteenth, under command of Col. R. L. Gibson; of the Sixteenth and Twenty-fifth Louisiana Regiments, consolidated into the Sixteenth, under the command of Col. S. W. Fisk; of the Thirty-second Alabama Regiment, under command of Lieut. Col. Harry [Henry] Maury; of two companies of Louisiana sharpshooters, under command of Maj. J. E. Austin, and of the Fifth Company, Washington Artillery, commanded by Lieutenant Vaught, was ordered from the right of General Breckinridge's division, to which it belonged, to cross Stone's River, where I was directed to report to Lieutenant-General Polk. In obedience to this order, received from the commanding general, I crossed the river at the ford above the Nashville pike, and finding Lieutenant-General Polk, reported to him in person, and received from him an order to take a battery of the enemy, which was some 700 or 800 yards in advance of the ford where I had crossed the river, and on an eminence between the Nashville pike and the river. I immediately formed the infantry of my brigade in line of battle in the open plain near the river, and advanced until reaching a place known as Cowan's house, on the pike, where I found the burnt ruins of a large brick house, a close picket fence, and a deep cut in the railroad, which ran parallel with the pike, and the rough and broken ground on the river bank, presented such serious obstacles as prevented my continuing to advance in line of battle. I therefore moved the First (or Colonel Gibson's) Battalion by the right flank through a gateway in the direction of the river, and formed it in line of battle, with its right resting on the river. I then moved the Second (or Colonel Fisk's) Battalion in column of companies up the pike until clear of the obstacles, where I had it formed in line of battle, with its right resting on the railroad. The Thirty-second Alabama, having moved by the left flank so as to avoid the burnt buildings, was again formed in line on the left of Colonel Fisk's battalion. Line being again formed, I gave the command to charge the battery, which was promptly executed.

As the men approached the brow of the hill, they came fully in view and range of the enemy's guns, and were checked by a terrible fire from his artillery, posted on the second elevation, about 150 or 200 yards distant. At my repeated command, however, they continued to advance until the enemy opened with a battery from a cedar thicket on my left, and what appeared to be a brigade of infantry, and at the same time they commenced moving down the river in force, apparently to get in rear of my command. Under these circumstances, I continued the fight for a period of about one hour, in which my men fought most gallantly and nobly. Finding that I was overpowered in numbers, with a force of infantry on my front, on my right, and on my left, supporting a battery of some fifteen or twenty guns, strongly posted in the cedar thicket on the second eminence on my front, and that my men were being rapidly killed and wounded, and the effort to turn my right likely to prove successful, I had reluctantly to give the command to fall back. Owing to the obstacles before mentioned, some confusion and disorder was created in falling back, which caused some delay in reforming the brigade, much to my regret. The conduct, however, of the officers and men in making the charge and holding the position as long as they did deserves the highest praise. No greater courage or determination could have been displayed.

At one time during the engagement a portion of the enemy's line in my front faltered and gave way under the well-directed fire and continued advance of my brigade, and I had strong hopes of success, and pressed the command forward, but the enemy was promptly re-enforced; and, finding it wholly impracticable to take this battery, supported, as it was, on the right and left by heavy forces of infantry and having in its rear apparently the whole Federal Army from which to draw re-enforcements, I was convinced it was more than any brigade could accomplish, and full work for a division, well directed.

My loss in this engagement and that of Friday succeeding was, killed, wounded, and missing (officers and men), 728. The exact proportion of killed and wounded I could not ascertain.

In this engagement of Wednesday and the succeeding one of Friday, the Fifth Company of Washington Artillery, Lieutenant Vaught commanding, was detached, but did important and essential service.

Among the killed I have to report and to regret the death of Col. S W. Fisk, who fell gallantly leading his battalion in the charge. He was a worthy, brave, and gallant officer. Lieut. Col. H. Maury was wounded in the side by a minie ball while leading his men, with his colors in his hand, and deserves praise for his gallant conduct. Colonel Gibson, Major [Charles] Guillet, and Major [F. C.] Zacharie all displayed commendable coolness and gallantry. Lieutenant [John L.] Chandler, adjutant of the Thirty-second Alabama, also deserves great praise for his courage and coolness under the trying circumstances in which he was placed. Capt. Emile P. Guillet, my adjutant, continued with me and was of very great service, displaying undaunted courage, and, notwithstanding he received a severe wound in his left arm, continued on the field in the discharge of his duties.

So far as my observation extended, all company officers remained firmly at their posts, and conducted themselves with courage, gallantry, and coolness.

From the effects of a wound, received from a piece of shell, in my left arm, I found myself unable to take the field on the following day, and my brigade was, therefore, placed under command of Col. R. L. Gibson, he being senior officer, who has, doubtless, already made his report of the engagement of Friday, the 2d instant.

Very respectfully,

DANL. W. ADAMS,
Brigadier-General, Comdg. Adams' Brig., Breckinridge's Div.,
Hardee's Corps, Army of Tennessee.

Colonel [T.] O'HARA,
    Acting Assistant Adjutant-General.

[Indorsement.]

COLONEL: Brig. Gen. D. W. Adams, being absent, requests me by letter to state that his report was written before he had received the reports of his subordinate commanders, and that he desired especially to make special mention of Capt. M. O. Tracy, acting major; Lieut. H. H. Bein, adjutant, and Capt. T. M. Ryan, of the Thirteenth Louisiana Volunteers, and Captain [Thomas W.] Peyton, of the battalion of sharpshooters, who was severely wounded, for gallant conduct.

RANDALL LEE GIBSON,
Colonel, Commanding Adams' Brigade.

No. 227.

Reports of Col. Randall L. Gibson, Thirteenth Louisiana Infantry, commanding Thirteenth and Twentieth Regiments and Adams' brigade.

TULLAHOMA, TENN., *January* 11, 1863.

SIR : I beg leave to submit the following report of the part taken by the Thirteenth and Twentieth Louisiana Regiments in the action of 31st:

We were posted on the right of Adams' brigade, the right of the regiment resting near the river, and the two left companies overlapping the rail track. We advanced in line of battle until we reached the houses destroyed by fire, and the point at which the ground swelled into a considerable hill, stretching toward the line of the enemy, and where the river turned off quite abruptly to the right. We here halted, in order that disposition might be made to pass the obstacles in front of us. The regiments next to the Thirteenth and Twentieth (the Sixteenth and Twenty-fifth) having been thrown into column, we then advanced up the ascent, leaving quite an unoccupied space between the right and the river. Ascending the elevated position, I discovered the enemy moving troops rapidly up the river, on our right, and placing them also in ambush in the corn-field on our front. Riding to the rail track, I saw, not more than 50 yards distant, a line of battle of the enemy, using the embankment as a breastwork and to conceal them from our troops on the low ground to our left. The line of battle on the rail track, as the line of battle along the river bank, was at right angles to our advancing line, and the enemy reserved his fire until the command was flanked. So soon as I discovered the disposition of the enemy, I rode across the railroad and informed General Adams. It was, however, too late to accomplish a timely change in our position. Moreover, from the moment of our advance, in the face of the enemy, his artillery had kept a constant fire upon us, while the fire of his infantry was reserved, rendering it more difficult, in addition to the broken nature of the ground, to make new dispositions. The first fire we received was from the river bank, and directed upon the infirmary corps of the regiment, posted considerably in our rear. I immediately moved the regiment double-quick by the right flank toward the river, but, finding a front as well as a flanking fire open upon us, I commanded a halt, and determined to contest the field. The right of the regiment stood firm for a few minutes, but under the combined fires gave way. The men naturally faced the direction in which the severest fire came, and this caused some confusion. We were enabled to hold the left in its position, the fence in its front affording some protection. I felt the necessity of holding our position until the balance of the brigade, already falling back, should pass the point at which the enemy was pressing us on the right. Should this be prematurely lost, there had been a very much larger force than the rest of the brigade, with every advantage of position, covering its entire front and enveloping its right flank. I called upon Major [J. E.] Austin to form on my line and assist in its defense. In a few moments he disposed his battalion of sharpshooters as I suggested. We were successful in holding the high ground on the right of the railroad until the **left** portion of the brigade, driven back by a storm of artillery and infantry fire on its front and flank, had reached a point beyond our line. The ground was much broken. A continuous line of battle could not be formed on the hill, and this was one of the main reasons why there was some apparent irregularity in falling back.

I should do injustice to the officers and men of the Thirteenth and Twentieth Louisiana Regiments did I not state that they displayed the best qualities as soldiers. It is difficult for troops to stand firm against great odds, under a heavy fire from the front and on the flank. This was not only done for some minutes, but at the outset, and until the full force of the enemy was developed on our right flank, we drove back his line on our front, charging beyond the fence in the corn-field and rescuing the colors of some Confederate regiment which had previously engaged the enemy in this position, and whose dead marked plainly its line of battle. I send the colors, that you may return them to the gallant regiment whose brave dead spoke its eulogy.

Maj. Charles Guillet, commanding the right, contributed very much to steady this exposed flank of the command, acting as lieutenant-colonel.

I am chiefly indebted to Capt. M. O. Tracy, acting major, and in charge of the left wing, for the steadiness with which it moved forward, and for its handsome behavior on retiring. This officer has been mentioned in every report of various battles in which the Thirteenth Louisiana Regiment has been engaged—Shiloh, Farmington, Perryville; and having lost his leg in this action, I would especially commend him to the favorable consideration of our superior officers.

To Captains King, Bishop, and Ryan the praise of having borne themselves with great efficiency and marked courage is especially due.

Adjt. Hugh H. Bein acted with becoming coolness and efficiency, and to the color-bearer, Sergt. Roger Tammure, and Sergt. Maj. John Farrell great credit is due for the disregard of personal danger and soldierly conduct.

We moved to the rear of our artillery, and were no longer on that day under the infantry fire of the enemy. Lieutenants [Charles J.] Hepburn and [R. O.] Smith were killed in this action. They were brave and devoted young soldiers.

A reference to the list* of casualties will show the heavy loss sustained in this action.

I have the honor to remain, your obedient servant,

RANDALL LEE GIBSON,
Colonel, Commanding.

Capt. E. P. GUILLET, *Assistant Adjutant-General.*

—

HDQRS. ADAMS' BRIGADE, BRECKINRIDGE'S DIVISION,
HARDEE'S CORPS, ARMY OF TENNESSEE,
Tullahoma, Tenn., January 18, 1863.

SIR: On Friday, January 2, while in command of Adams' brigade—consisting of the Thirteenth Louisiana Volunteers, Maj. Charles Guillet commanding; Sixteenth Louisiana Volunteers, Maj. Frank [C.] Zacharie commanding; Thirty-second Alabama, Col. Alexander McKinstry, and a battalion of sharpshooters, Maj. J. E. Austin—I was ordered from the left to report to Major-General Breckinridge, our division commander. Crossing the river, I was placed in position by Colonel O'Hara, of the general's staff, about 150 yards in the rear of Brigadier-General Hanson's brigade, as a supporting line. We advanced as soon as the first line moved forward, preserving our distance until the first line became fully engaged, when I halted the brigade, the left resting upon the river. I ordered the officers and men to lie down, and to cover themselves from the batteries of the enemy on the opposite side of the river, whose fire

---

* Embodied in No. 191, p. 678.

we were drawing. I then went forward to consult with Brigadier-General Hanson as to the particular moment when the second line should be moved up to his support, and thus to avoid confusion. I had hardly reached him when he was struck, and, I observed, too seriously wounded to entertain the matter I desired to see him about. The first line was already beginning to yield and some of the men falling back, when I at once ordered the advance of the second line. I ordered the Thirteenth Louisiana Volunteers to oblique to the right, and sent Captain [A. A.] Lipscomb to order Major Zacharie, commanding Sixteenth Louisiana Volunteers, also to move forward. I went forward with the right regiment, moving it rapidly into the woods, and we soon engaged the enemy under very heavy and steady fire. I presumed that the left regiment was coming up under cover of the bank of the river. Our battery moved up to the position we vacated on the bank of the river, in the open field near some houses that had been destroyed by fire. The Thirteenth Louisiana Volunteers, Major Guillet, went into action in perfect order and succeeded in driving the enemy a considerable distance into the woods. Perceiving that the troops on our right were falling back, and that our own losses, especially in officers, were very heavy, I went to the river and found that the Sixteenth Louisiana Volunteers had crossed the river, and was moving up the stream. It then became evident that the Thirteenth Louisiana Volunteers, which was maintaining its position with great steadiness, and on which the enemy was gradually closing, should be retired. Its position was such that in falling back we had to leave nearly all of the wounded in the woods. In several instances those who were bearing the wounded off were shot as soon as they entered the cleared field. Fourteen officers out of the twenty-eight who were in the action were wounded just here, and several of them were dangerously injured. Some companies were left without officers, and many of the men put down as missing were killed or wounded in this position.

The battalion of Louisiana sharpshooters and the Thirty-second Alabama were left, in obedience to the orders of Major-General Breckinridge, as a reserve, and to the position occupied by them the balance of the brigade was collected.

Major Zacharie's position, taken under a mistake of orders, on the opposite side of the river, enabled him to drive in the skirmishers of the enemy and to hold him in check at this particular ford in front of our batteries for some time.

The inclosed report * of the casualties will show with what devotion this command stood by its colors and contested the field with the enemy.

I would make especial mention of the gallant conduct of Maj. Charles Guillet, Captains Lipscomb, Ryan, and [J. M.] King, of the Thirteenth Louisiana Volunteers.

I have the honor to remain, colonel, your obedient servant,

RANDALL LEE GIBSON,
Colonel, Commanding Adams' Brigade.

Col. T. O'HARA, *Acting Assistant Adjutant-General.*

—

HEADQUARTERS ADAMS' BRIGADE,
BRECKINRIDGE'S DIVISION, HARDEE'S CORPS,
Near Tullahoma, Tenn., January 24, 1863.

SIR: On Friday, January 2, while in command of Adams' brigade, I was ordered from the cedar brake on the left, where I was reporting to Brigadier-General Preston, commanding division of two brigades, to

---

* Embodied in No. 191, p. 678.

report to Major-General Breckinridge, our division commander, on the right of Stone's River. I was placed in position by yourself about 150 yards in the rear of Brigadier-General Hanson's brigade as a supporting line in the charge to be made. In obedience to orders from General Breckinridge, I posted a reserve, consisting of the Thirty-second Alabama, Colonel McKinstry, and a battalion of Louisiana sharpshooters (Major Austin), under the command of Colonel McKinstry, in the position occupied by the second line when formed originally. These dispositions had hardly been effected when the general advance began, and I immediately moved forward my line, consisting of the Thirteenth Louisiana (consolidated) Regiment, Major Guillet, and the Sixteenth Louisiana (consolidated) Regiment, Major Zacharie.

The interval between the first and second lines was very well preserved until the first became generally engaged with the enemy, when I at once halted the second line and ordered the officers and men to lie down, so as to cover them from the enemy's batteries, whose fire we were drawing. We drove in his skirmishers from the opposite side of the river. I then rode forward to the first line, to consult with General Hanson as to the particular moment when the second line should come to his support. I had scarcely reached him when he was struck, and, I observed, so seriously wounded as to disable him from conferring with me. I determined not to engage the second line until the first gave way. General Hanson had hardly fallen, however, when his line began to show symptoms of yielding, and after a few moments many of his men were falling to the rear. I saw that they needed support, and, going back to the second line, instantly ordered the right regiment (Thirteenth Louisiana Volunteers, Major Guillet) to move by the right flank, in order to avoid the river, toward which we were marching, and then to advance in line of battle toward the woods, and, having my horse disabled by a wound in riding back, I dispatched Captain Lipscomb to give the same order to Major Zacharie, commanding Sixteenth Louisiana Volunteers, already under the bank. I moved rapidly forward the right regiment, and soon engaged the enemy under heavy fire. I presumed that the Sixteenth was moving under the river bank on our left, as had been the permanent arrangement, and in accordance with the special order sent by Captain Lipscomb. The woods were full of troops, apparently in great confusion. Many of these formed on our line, and we advanced, driving the enemy before us beyond a ravine, on the farther side of which was a picket fence. This ravine was filled with men broken from their commands, who were sheltered from the enemy, but such was their confusion that they could accomplish nothing against him. I formed the fighting line on the near side of the ravine, on the lower side of the crest, and, by a well-directed volley poured into the advancing line of the enemy, broke and dispersed it. When this first compact line gave way, there was a momentary lull, a suspension of fire, and we prepared to charge, but, as if in the twinkle of an eye, another line of the enemy, extending far beyond our right, assumed the lost position. This was dispersed. Presently a number of skirmishers appeared on our right, and we were fired upon from the left, on the opposite side of the river. The men in the ravine broke to the rear under these fires, that were aimed chiefly at them, and from which they appeared to suffer. There was perpetual skirmishing from the moment we entered the woods. Again another line came on our front, which engaged us. I observed that our own right had given way, going through the open field on the right of us to the rear. I moved to our extreme left and saw the enemy were in heavy lines on the opposite bank, and already beginning to cross. I saw at once that we would be enveloped on the right and left.

I ordered my command to fall back. It was a matter of doubt whether this could be accomplished successfully. Scarcely any one could enter the open field to our right and rear without being shot down either by the infantry or by the batteries of the enemy.

I should observe that from the moment we approached the elevated ground near the river, the batteries of the enemy, posted on the opposite side, poured into our ranks without intermission. As soon as he was driven from the high ground on this side, his batteries played upon it. His batteries and infantry concentrated on every spot from which he was driven. It was for this reason that after a sharp conflict of thirty minutes, and having won the position, we were forced to abandon it; and this accounts, too, for the extraordinary loss we sustained, and for the fact that nearly all our wounded and killed were left on the field. Under my own observation several parties bearing off wounded officers were shot down as soon as they entered the open field. Many, therefore, of those put down as missing were killed or wounded in this affair. Out of 28 officers who went into the fight 14 were wounded, and most of them severely, and, as the event may prove, I fear mortally. This was in the Thirteenth Louisiana Volunteers, Maj. Charles Guillet, of whose conduct I cannot speak in terms too high.

The regiment behaved throughout like veterans. Captains Ryan, Lipscomb, King, Bishop, and [John] McGrath, and Lieutenant [D. C.] Levy displayed distinguished steadiness and courage. The loss of this regiment in two short actions, lasting both together not more than an hour, was 19 officers and 332 men killed, wounded, and missing, losing as many as some brigades.

Major Zacharie's position, taken under a mistake of orders, enabled him to drive in the skirmishers of the enemy and to hold him in check in front of our batteries for some time. After entering the woods, the fire of our own batteries, together with that of the enemy just opposite, and the immediate development of infantry in heavy force along the opposite bank below him, prevented any orders of mine from reaching him or his joining us. He moved up the river, recrossed, and joined the reserve. I assembled the whole command on this line and held our position until our battery was secured, and we moved, in obedience to orders, on the right of Brigadier-General Preston's brigade.

Very respectfully, your obedient servant,

RANDALL LEE GIBSON, *Colonel, Commanding.*

Col. T. O'HARA, *Assistant Adjutant-General.*

[Addenda.]

Abstract from morning report of Adams' brigade, Col. R. L. Gibson commanding, January 8, 1863.

Command.	Present for duty.		Aggregate present.	Aggregate present and absent.	Aggregate last return.
	Officers.	Men.			
Field and staff	4	......	4	7	7
32d Alabama	16	180	261	643	......
13th and 20th Louisiana	15	381	452	834	999
16th and 25th Louisiana	25	440	530	1,014	1,075
Austin's (Louisiana) battalion	5	121	148	181	185
Slocomb's (Louisiana) battery	5	132	138	161	162
Total	70	1,254	1,533	2,840	2,428

No. 228.

Report of Lieut. Col. Henry Maury, Thirty-second Alabama Infantry.

TULLAHOMA, TENN., *January 12, 1863.*

CAPTAIN : I have the honor to submit the following report of the part borne by the Thirty-second Alabama Infantry, under my command, in this brigade, in the battle of Wednesday, December 31, 1862, before Murfreesborough:

We were placed on the left of the line of battle, the right of the brigade resting near Stone's River, and advanced in line under severe fire of artillery until nearly up with the burnt buildings, known, I believe, as Cowan's, when we were ordered to move by the right flank some 300 yards. Immediately afterward I was ordered to advance in line toward the enemy, leaving sufficient space on my right for the deployment of Colonel Fisk's regiment (Sixteenth Louisiana), which had been thrown into column of companies. In this order we advanced beyond the fences surrounding the burnt buildings under a very destructive cross-fire of artillery and small-arms, and, owing to a picket fence on my left, there was not quite room for the Sixteenth Louisiana to deploy, causing a temporary confusion, which, however, was speedily remedied by General Adams. At this point we commenced firing, but finding that it was not efficient on account of the excellent cover of the enemy, I ordered the regiment to cease firing and charge. At this moment we were exposed not only to the sweeping fire in front, but to a withering fire of musketry and grape from the cedar brake on our left, not more than 200 yards distant, and also a severe fire from the right, under which my men fell rapidly. Before we had advanced far I received a wound which disabled me for the time, and at the same moment we received the order to fall back, which, as far as I could see, was done in good order.

After having had my wound dressed, I gathered what was left of the regiment, which had suffered very severely (as will be seen by the accompanying report of casualties), and reported them to General Adams. We were not again under fire on that day.

Adjt. John L. Chandler acted with conspicuous gallantry, and rendered efficient service in preserving good order in the regiment.

The officers and men all, as far as I could judge, did their duty, and acted satisfactorily under the galling fire and trying circumstances we encountered.

Very respectfully,

H. MAURY,
Lieutenant-Colonel, Comdg. Thirty-second Alabama Regiment.

[Capt.] E. P. GUILLET, *Asst. Adjt. Gen., Adams' Brigade.*

No. 229.

Report of Maj. F. C. Zacharie, Twenty-fifth Louisiana Infantry, commanding Sixteenth and Twenty-fifth Regiments.

NEAR TULLAHOMA, TENN., *February 9, 1863.*

SIR : I have the honor to submit the following report of the part taken by this regiment in the engagement of December 31, 1862, before Murfreesborough :

The regiment occupied the center of the line of battle of Adams' brigade, formed about the hour of 1 p. m. that day, just beyond the Nashville turnpike ford. The order being given to advance, the regiment did so, with the Thirteenth and Twentieth Louisiana Volunteers on its right and the Thirty-second Alabama Volunteers on the left. Before reaching Cowan's house, General Adams ordered the regiment to be thrown into column of companies on the Nashville pike. In this order it moved forward nearly a quarter of a mile, changing direction to the right, passing through a cotton-field, one of stubble, and a third of light undergrowth. Having passed through this, the regiment was halted and the column thrown forward into line. During its advance to this point the command was exposed, during the whole march, to a heavy fire from an eight-gun battery of the enemy, posted on the spot which they had now reached, two of the enemy's pieces being in our possession, one resting in our line and another a few paces in advance. As we neared the enemy's position we were met by a storm of missiles from small-arms, and, when finally halted, I noticed that some of our men were being wounded in the rear, and being struck on the back myself and turning to the direction of the fire, I discovered that the regiment of the enemy was in our rear while we were being engaged in the front and on the left by a large body of the enemy. These facts were communicated to General Adams, the regiment then being at a halt, engaging the enemy with great coolness.

At this time Colonel Fisk fell, mortally wounded, and Lieutenants [H.] Gregory and A. Ranlett were instantly killed. Shortly afterward, being ordered to retire, I attempted to withdraw my right, which was most exposed, by a flank movement. The order was misunderstood on the left, and the three left companies marched to the left. The line was thrown into confusion by this, and retired in disorder; the three center companies, remaining in good order, escorted the colors from the field in a very orderly and creditable manner. I attempted to rally the regiment several times, but, being unhorsed during the engagement, found it difficult to do so until we had retreated nearly a quarter of a mile. Lieut. T. L. McLean was mortally wounded on the retreat, and Lieutenants [J. M.] Clayton, Louis Stagg, and [W. L.] Sibley seriously wounded.

I cannot speak in too high terms of the bearing of both officers and men during the engagement, exposed to a fire which had placed in one-half hour 217 *hors de combat* out of 457 that we carried into the engagement. Lieut. G. McD. Brumby, acting assistant surgeon, deserves especial mention for the brave and energetic discharge of his duty. He kept with the regiment during the whole engagement, and administered to the wants of the wounded on the field under a hot fire. Thanks to his activity and energy, all the wounded were safely housed in hospital and under treatment on the evening of the engagement.

Your obedient servant,

F. C. ZACHARIE,
Major, Comdg. Sixteenth and Twenty-fifth Louisiana Volunteers.
Captain [E. P.] GUILLET,
Asst. Adjt. Gen., Adams' Brigade, Breckinridge's Division.

No. 230.

Report of Maj. J. E. Austin, Fourteenth Louisiana Battalion (Sharpshooters).

JANUARY 11, 1863.

CAPTAIN: Having deployed my command in front of General Breckinridge's division, in obedience to orders from division headquarters, I was awaiting the approach of the enemy on the morning of December 31, 1862, when I received an order from division headquarters directing me to join my brigade. I immediately assembled my command and marched it rapidly to the place occupied by the brigade a short time before, but found that it had gone across the river for the purpose of attacking a strong position that the enemy had taken up near the railroad and river bank. I accelerated my movements as much as possible, and came up with the brigade as it was marching upon the enemy's position in line of battle, and reported to General Adams, commanding, in person, and asked him where I should take position. The general informed me that he had already made his dispositions for the attack, and ordered me to take position about 100 yards in rear of the brigade, as a reserve. I formed my command as directed, and followed the brigade as it advanced up the hill, upon which the enemy had planted his artillery and disposed infantry. Here a furious fight ensued, which lasted about thirty minutes, when the brigade was forced to fall back before the terrible flank and front fires of the enemy. Learning from Colonel Gibson, commanding Thirteenth and Twentieth Louisiana Regiments, the flank movement of the enemy, I changed front forward and formed along a fence running near and parallel to the railroad. I found the enemy directly in my front, and opened fire upon him with a staggering effect. His attention had been drawn just previous to this to the brigade, which was falling back, and the rapidity of my movement caused a confusion in his ranks, which, I am of the opinion, was fortunate for the brigade, for his fire was directed upon me until the brigade had retreated some distance (almost out of range), when I withdrew with but little confusion from a contest so unequal, and fell back upon our artillery, which had been brought up as a support.

On January 2, I was deployed in front of a portion of General Stewart's line (I think his right), and my command did some excellent service in driving from the field in front of the cedar thicket a body of the enemy's skirmishers.

Late on January 2, I was ordered with my command to join the brigade, which I did, and was placed as a reserve in the celebrated charge of Friday evening, January 2, in which the (Breckinridge's) division participated. My command, together with the Thirty-second Alabama Regiment, constituted the reserves, and were not ordered forward, but when the shattered battalions fell back they formed upon us.

My officers, without an exception, acted in the most gallant manner. Captain [T. W.] Peyton, commanding Company A, was severely wounded while leading his company.

Lieutenants [W. Q.] Lowd and [A. P.] Martin, of Company A, and [S. R.] Garrett and [C. F.] McCarty, of Company B, as well as Adjt. A. O'Duhigg, deserve the highest praise.

My loss was 4 killed, 9 missing, and 2 wounded.

I am, very respectfully, captain, your obedient servant,

J. E. AUSTIN,
Major, Comdg. [Fourteenth Louisiana] Batt. of Sharpshooters.

Capt. E. P. GUILLET,
Assistant Adjutant-General.

No. 231.

Report of Lieut. W. C. D. Vaught, Fifth Company, Washington Light Artillery.

ALLISONIA, TENN., *January 8, 1863.*

COLONEL: At Murfreesborough, on the 29th ultimo, while with this brigade in line of battle on the Lebanon pike, I detached two rifled guns of this battery, commanded by Lieutenant [J. A.] Chalaron, by order of Major Graves, division chief of artillery, who placed them near the river in front of General Hanson's position. This important point Lieutenant Chalaron occupied, under the orders of Captain Cobb, during Tuesday and Wednesday, subjected to a heavy fire from the enemy's batteries and skirmishers and frequent assaults of his infantry.

On Wednesday, with our other four guns and a section of Captain Semple's battery, under command of Lieutenant [J.] Pollard, I crossed the river with the brigade at 12 o'clock, and was ordered by General Adams to remain near the river while the brigade advanced to the charge. When I saw the brigade retiring, I placed the battery upon the hill to the left of the Nashville pike and the railroad, and as soon as the troops were from under our fire, I opened upon the enemy, soon silencing their battery and checking their pursuit. Receiving no further orders, I took a position forward and to the left, continuing to fire upon the enemy wherever he appeared in range, forcing his battery to change position whenever it opened, and checking his movements in the field opposite our fortified point on the eastern side of the river.

When night fell I withdrew to near General Breckinridge's headquarters and reported to Major Graves, Lieutenant Pollard reporting to Captain Semple. Allow me to say here that Lieutenant Pollard's conduct proved him an accomplished officer and a cool and gallant man.

On Thursday morning I took position near General Hanson's right with four guns (having no rifle ammunition), and received a section of Captain Lumsden's battery. Later, three guns were placed in battery there and three on right of General Palmer's brigade.

On Friday morning Captain Lumsden's section was ordered to the left of the lines and 1 to General Palmer's right with this battery.

About noon we were ordered to the position occupied by our skirmishers in front of General Palmer, to drive in their pickets. Here we remained a couple of hours, doing some fancy practice, then fell behind the infantry of this division, formed for the assault. Our lines moved forward and we followed close behind. Two lines of the enemy were met and dissipated. Our infantry passed over the hill. We galloped upon the crest and opened our fire upon the enemy's batteries upon the opposite hill. Their fire had nearly ceased when our ammunition gave out. I sent for a supply and waited there for it. In the meanwhile one of our detachments manned a piece of Moses' battery, near us, which had ceased its fire, the men lying down. Before the ammunition arrived our brave boys, who had done their utmost, were obliged to retire. I remained until the last regiment and last battery were from the field, the enemy swarming upon my front and flank and within 50 yards, pouring volley after volley into us. I retired in perfect line to the strip of timber behind, and took a position beside Robertson's battery. We again opened upon the enemy, who pursued no farther.

This battery suffered the following casualties* in the several engage-

---

* Nominal list omitted.

ments: Killed, 1 enlisted man; wounded, 1 non-commissioned officer and 4 enlisted men; total killed and wounded, 5.

[We had] 4 horses killed and 4 disabled.

I desire to call your attention to the distinguished gallantry of Lieutenant Chalaron, who was selected by Major Graves upon the field to act as temporary chief of artillery; also to the gallantry of Lieutenants [T. M.] Blair and [A. J.] Leverich.

I desire also to mention Corporal Smith for his efficient gunnery and soldiership, and Corporal Adams, Privates Johnson and Walsh, and the detachment (No. 5) which manned a piece of another battery. This is a difficult task where all conduct themselves with remarkable gallantry.

I have the honor to be, your obedient servant,

W. C. D. VAUGHT,
Lieutenant, Commanding.

Col. R. L. GIBSON,
Commanding Adams' Brigade.

No. 232.

Reports of Col. Joseph B. Palmer, Eighteenth Tennessee Infantry, commanding regiment and Second Brigade.

WINCHESTER, TENN., *February* 6, 1863.

SIR: I have the honor to submit this report of the operations of the Second Brigade, Breckinridge's division, Army of Tennessee, in the late battles at Murfreesborough.

The following regiments compose the brigade: Twenty-sixth Tennessee, Colonel [John M.] Lillard; Eighteenth Tennessee (my own), Lieutenant-Colonel [W. R.] Butler commanding; Forty-fifth Tennessee, Colonel [A.] Searcy; Twenty-eighth Tennessee, Colonel [P. D.] Cunningham; Thirty-second Tennessee, Colonel [Ed. C.] Cook (at that time near Wartrace on detached service), and Moses' battery, Lieutenant [R. W.] Anderson commanding. It occupied the left center in the front line of the division, in line of battle, General Hanson being on my left, and Generals Preston and Adams on the right, and took that position on Sunday morning, December 28, 1862. I kept constantly deployed a line of skirmishers covering my front.

On Wednesday morning, learning that a wagon train and a body of Federal troops had appeared at the distance of 1½ miles in front of my line, I ordered forward my skirmishers to investigate their strength and position, and sent Capt. D. H. C. Spence, of my staff, to direct their operations. They soon united with a detachment from General Pegram's cavalry, and the two co-operating captured 18 wagons and 170 prisoners, without any loss on our part. Capt. Gid. H. Lowe, of the Eighteenth Tennessee, and Captain Spence deserve much credit for their gallantry and efficiency on that occasion.

At noon on Wednesday, January [December] 31, I was ordered by General Breckinridge (as was also General Preston) across Stone's River, to the left wing of our general line of battle. Arriving there, we were immediately ordered to move upon the enemy's position just west of Cowan's residence. In this charge General Preston was on the right, while I was directed to form upon and move with his left, and, during the movement, to effect a general change of direction of my line to the right, so as to support the right brigade and flank the enemy.

The several regiments of my brigade moved gallantly and steadily forward in this charge, although exposed to a terrible fire from Yankee artillery for a distance of 400 yards across an open and unprotected field. The movement was successful on our part. The Federal forces abandoned their ground, retreating westwardly back on the main body of their troops, where their position was strongly protected by embankments thrown up in the construction of the railroad, some natural elevations of the ground, and the cover of their artillery. On these accounts we did not pursue them farther.

A list * of the killed and wounded in this engagement has already been furnished, which I respectfully ask may be taken as a part of this report.

In this action both the men and officers of the brigade behaved with most becoming courage and gallantry, displaying a high degree of unfaltering determination and bravery, now mentioned alike in justice to them and with the utmost satisfaction to myself.

At 1 o'clock on the following morning, under orders from General Breckinridge, I recrossed the river and returned to my former position. Nothing occurred on Thursday except slight skirmishing in my front and occasional shelling from the enemy.

At about 10 o'clock on Friday, February [January] 2, under directions from General Breckinridge, I strengthened my line of skirmishers and ordered them forward, under command of Lieut. Col. Alexander Hall, of the Forty-fifth Tennessee. Major Graves was also ordered forward with a few pieces of artillery, which were supported by the left companies of the Eighteenth Tennessee, under command of Capt. William H. Joyner. They soon encountered a very heavy line of Federal skirmishers, and, after a severe contest, drove them back, with a loss of 2 killed and 11 wounded on our part. The enemy's loss was ascertained to be much greater, both in killed and wounded. Shortly after this, General Pillow assumed command of the brigade, whereupon I took charge of my regiment.

In the skirmish on Friday morning Lieutenant-Colonel Hall bore himself with decided gallantry. The men and officers under him acted nobly. Throughout the period covered by this report, Capts. C. K. Vanderford, Natt. Gooch, D. H. C. Spence, F. H. Lytle, and James S. Barton, of my staff, were all prompt, gallant, and efficient in the discharge of their several duties. I am also much indebted to each of these officers for many acts of personal kindness and voluntary services.

I conclude this report with the remark that, in consequence of wounds received in the right leg, knee, and shoulder, in the engagement of Friday evening at Murfreesborough, it has not been possible for me to prepare it earlier; and with the request that it be now received and considered. I have the honor to be, very respectfully, your obedient servant,

J. B. PALMER,
Colonel, Commanding Second Brigade.

Col. T. O'HARA,
Acting Assistant Adjutant-General, Tullahoma, Tenn.

—

WINCHESTER, TENN., *February* 6, 1863.

SIR: In the battle of Friday, February [January] 2, at Murfreesborough, the Eighteenth Tennessee Regiment, numbering 430 for duty,

---

* Embodied in No. 191, p. 678.

was on the right of the Second Brigade, and occupied the extreme right in the front line of Major-General Breckinridge's division, which was ordered forward to engage the enemy at about 3 o'clock in the afternoon. We soon met the Federal forces in largely superior numbers on the right bank of Stone's River. Their line of battle being prolonged farther north than ours, I encountered one of their regiments immediately in my front, while another (both large) made a desperate effort to turn my right. They opened a most deadly and terrific fire upon us for several minutes, and then attempted a charge, but were repulsed and driven back a distance of more than 50 yards, where, with the advantage of the crest of a hill, they made another severe struggle. I then ordered a charge, which was most successfully executed. The Federals fled in utter confusion and disorder, leaving an immense number of their dead and wounded in their rear. Their flight was down the river, whither we pursued them for nearly half a mile, dealing fire and death in their backs at a most destructive and effective rate. In the rout hundreds of them fell (reversing the position of the poet) with their faces (not their backs) upon the field.

It is proper to remark that the entire Federal force on the right bank of the river were completely routed and driven by our division either across or down the stream; but they had massed a force of many thousands on the opposite (left) bank, where they had a large quantity of artillery, so located and arranged as that both their small-arms and batteries could be brought to bear upon and most dreadfully rake all the western portion of the field over which their troops had been driven. It therefore became proper for our forces to withdraw to a safer position, although they were not repulsed. This necessity, however, was not so great on my part, because, being less exposed to fire from the left bank of the river, I could have continued to hold my position beyond doubt; but on seeing the principal body of the division on my left falling back, I ordered my regiment to withdraw, to avoid a flank movement in that direction. At the time there was comparatively little resistance being made in my front. The regiments that had been driven before me had not recovered from disorder. They had not, in fact, reformed in line of battle, but were in a confused and frightened manner, taking cover behind the houses and fences around the late William Mitchell's residence.

I herewith submit a list* of killed and wounded, from which it will be seen that there were 19 killed; supposed to be mortally wounded, 8; not mortally, 108, making, in all, 135.

I report, with the utmost pride and satisfaction, that the men and officers of the regiment in this memorable action displayed a heroic courage and dauntless valor equaled only by the sacredness of their own homes and the inspirations of their noble country's cause, for whose defense they so gallantly and bravely struggled.

Among other instances deserving individual notice, I mention the following: Capt. John Dick, of Company K [G]; First Lieut. Samuel M. Smith, commanding Company C, and Color-Sergt. George K. Lowe, fell dead upon the field, nobly discharging their whole duties. Lieut. Col. W. R. Butler, Maj. W. H. Joyner, Adjt. John M. Douglass, Sergt. Maj. Fletcher R. Burrus (the two latter being wounded), and the company commanders displayed high courage and efficiency in their respective positions. Capts. James S. Barton and Natt. Gooch, formerly of my staff, fought with distinguished gallantry as privates in the ranks. After as

---

* Nominal list omitted.

many as five different persons had been shot down in the attempt to bear the colors, Logan H. Nelson, a private in Company C (who is but a youth), gallantly sprang forward, raised them from the side of dying comrades, and bore them nobly and triumphantly throughout the remainder of this bloody contest.

It will be seen that this report only relates to the conduct of the regiment in Friday's fight. Having been in command of the brigade prior to that time, and not having been able to join the regiment since, I refer to the reports submitted by Lieutenant-Colonel Butler for an account of its operations on other days of the battle of Murfreesborough. Unable to prepare this report earlier, I beg leave now to present it.

Very respectfully,

J. B. PALMER,
Colonel, Commanding Eighteenth Tennessee Volunteers.

[Col.] T. O'HARA,
Acting Assistant Adjutant-General, Tullahoma, Tenn.

———

[Addenda.]

Abstract from morning report of Brown's brigade, Brig. Gen. John C. Brown commanding, for January 19, 1863.

Command.	Present for duty.		Aggregate present.	Aggregate present and absent.	Aggregate last return.
	Officers.	Men.			
Field and staff	7	......	7	7	7
18th Tennessee	26	305	415	708	708
26th Tennessee	32	269	353	527	505
28th Tennessee	30	148	268	446	445
45th Tennessee	30	293	449	853	856
Moses' (Georgia) battery	3	87	107	145	145
Total	128	1,102	1,599	2,686	2,666

No. 233.

Reports of Brig. Gen. Gideon J. Pillow, C. S. Army, commanding Second Brigade.

HDQRS. FIRST [SECOND] BRIGADE, FIRST DIVISION,
LIEUTENANT-GENERAL HARDEE'S CORPS,
Camp near Tullahoma, Tenn., January 11, 1863.

On Friday afternoon (2d instant), by orders of General Bragg, I was assigned to the command of a brigade, composed of the Eighteenth, Twenty-sixth, Twenty-eighth, Thirty-second, and Forty-fifth Tennessee Regiments, with Captain Moses' field battery, now commanded by Lieut. R. W. Anderson. The Thirty-second Regiment, commanded by Colonel [E. C.] Cook, was on detached service and was not in the action. They were all much reduced in strength by past service.

At the time I was assigned to the command it occupied a position on the extreme right of our line, in front of the enemy's left. This brigade constituted the assaulting force, designed to drive the enemy from an eminence on the right bank of Stone's River, a position which prevented his. left flank from being turned, and from which, if in our possession, we could drive him from his strong position on the left bank of the river and enfilade his line of infantry. I was supported on my left by Brigadier-General Hanson's brigade. In the advance, then about to commence, I directed General Hanson to dress upon my left, and the left of my line to dress upon his right, to guard against a separation of the line formed by the two brigades in the advance. These brigades were supported by a line drawn up in the rear about 300 yards, composed of the brigades of Brigadier-General Preston on the right and a brigade commanded by Colonel Gibson on my left.

At the signal for the movements to commence (viz, a report of artillery on the center of our last line), I ordered my line to advance. The entire line moved forward in beautiful order across the strip of woods and open field, driving the enemy's skirmishers and sharpshooters before it, and at the distance of about 300 yards receiving the fire of the main body of the enemy's infantry, hitherto concealed from view. This fire developed a large body of the enemy's sharpshooters in a body of thick woods to the right of the position now occupied by my advanced line. I immediately ordered Lieut. R. W. Anderson to bring up his battery and to drive them out of the wood. Upon opening fire upon this concealed force of the enemy, his artillery responded from the woods with great vivacity to Lieutenant Anderson's fire. The two batteries, confronting each other, kept up an exceedingly hot fire for about fifteen minutes, when my infantry, pressing the enemy's infantry, forced it to retire into and then from a thicket of woods which skirted the bluff; the enemy's body of sharpshooters and battery retreated precipitately from the woods on the right toward the river bluff. I now ordered the infantry to press the enemy and clear the bluff, while I advanced Anderson's battery, and with it occupied the woods from which the enemy's artillery had been driven. This order was promptly executed, the bluff cleared, the enemy's infantry taking shelter under the bluff and in a deep ravine running obliquely into the river. My infantry having thus advanced as far as was possible on account of the bluff, and having forced many broken portions of the enemy's forces across and through the river, his artillery having retired down the river in the direction of the ford, my fire ceased, and the work seemed completed. In a few moments afterward I discovered a large body of the enemy moving rapidly up the river on my side, turning my right wing. It advanced rapidly, and opened upon the flank and rear of my force. Simultaneously the enemy's artillery and infantry in the front of my position, and on the opposite side of the river, opened fire upon my front, uncovered as it was, on the open bluff on the right bank. Thus assailed in flank by fresh forces and in front with a large force of infantry and artillery, which could not be reduced, there was left my force no alternative but to retire from the position it had so gallantly won. It retired in some confusion, but with as little as could have been expected when suddenly surprised by movements of the enemy's fresh forces, which could not have been foreseen, and which we had not the means of meeting. I directed Lieutenant Anderson to protect my line in retiring from the field, which was done. The infantry line retired to the ground upon which it had originally formed for the advanced movement. In this engagement my brigade took about 200 prisoners, whom I passed to the rear under small guard. The entire command performed its duty most gallantly.

My loss in officers and men was severe for the length of the conflict. Colonel Palmer (who commanded Eighteenth Tennessee Regiment) received three wounds, but did not relinquish the command until the conflict was ended; Colonel Cunningham (commanding the Twenty-eighth Regiment) was killed while gallantly leading his regiment in the main assault.

Maj. C. H. Wadley, of the Forty-fifth Tennessee Regiment, is missing, and is supposed to be a prisoner in the hands of the enemy.

Lieut. Col. J. L. Bottles, of the Twenty-sixth Regiment, was wounded by the splinter of a shell, in the hip. Maj. R. M. Saffell, of the same regiment, was severely wounded in the thigh.

In the Eighteenth Regiment, Captain [John] Dick was killed, and seven other captains in the same regiment were wounded.

I transmit herewith list* of the killed, wounded, and missing of the brigade.

My field battery, commanded by Lieut. R. W. Anderson, performed most important service. In this service Sergeant Brown was wounded by a shell, and is reported to me as acting most gallantly.

I ordered Colonel Palmer to report the participation of his regiment in this engagement, but he was reported to be suffering so severely from his wounds that he was unable to prepare a report. He was left in the neighborhood of Allisonia.

I am, respectfully,

GID. J. PILLOW,
Brigadier-General, C. S. Army.

[Col.] T. O'HARA,
Acting Assistant Adjutant-General.

P. S.—I transmit herewith the colors of the Ninth (Federal) Kentucky Regiment of Infantry, taken on the field by Colonel Cunningham's (Twenty-eighth) Tennessee Regiment in the battle of the 2d. It was much torn and mutilated, and stained with blood in the fights, and has many ball holes on it.

—

HDQRS. VOL. AND CONSCRIPT BUREAU, ARMY OF TENN.,
Huntsville, Ala., April 11, 1863.

SIR : In my verbal interview with General Bragg at Tullahoma, the battle of Murfreesborough on Friday being the subject of conversation, giving him an account of what occurred in that battle, I told him my brigade was, by General Breckinridge's orders, placed on the extreme right of our line. The line of battle was formed as directed by the general and on the ground indicated by him. My line advanced, and from the position of its formation necessarily leaving a thicket of timber and undergrowth on its right. When my line reached and was passing the thicket of woodland, the enemy's force, concealed in this thicket, opened a galling flank fire on my right wing, which so interrupted my advance and annoyed the command that I was forced to suspend the advance until the force of the enemy was dislodged from the thicket by artillery. A proper position of the line of battle would have required the line to have extended about 300 yards farther to the right, so as to have embraced this piece of woodland in its advance, and thus by a front advance to have driven out this force of the enemy from the thicket. Another consequence of this error of the position in which the line of battle was placed was, that, as we advanced, the space for General Hanson's brigade was so rapidly diminished by the course of

---

* Embodied in No. 191, p. 678.

the river that his left wing was forced, by the compact formation and resolute advance of my line, into the river. Notwithstanding these sources of embarrassment, resulting from the error of position in which the line was placed, we swept over the eminence held by the enemy and drove him down the bluff and mostly into and across the river, when our forces held the position until flanked by a large force of the enemy which crossed the river some distance below my right, under General [J. S.] Negley, which rapidly turned my position, opened fire simultaneously with a fire on front and from the opposite side of the river, and compelled my command to fall back. At this point in the conversation, General Bragg asked, "Why did not General Breckinridge protect you from the flanking force by the large body of cavalry I had placed under his orders?" I replied I did not know he had any cavalry under his orders. General Bragg then said that he had a large force of cavalry placed under his orders for the express purpose of providing for such a contingency. I remarked to him that I saw a large body of cavalry on the heights to my right and below the ford when Negley crossed the river, but that it did not make any attempt to arrest the advance of the flanking force, and I felt certain it could not have received orders to do so.

The above is the substance of that conversation on the part of those operating. General Bragg gave me the first intelligence that I received of this body of cavalry being under the orders of General Breckinridge. I expressed astonishment that it was not used for the protection of my right flank and rear. I also expressed myself as clear that the position of the line of battle was a most important error of judgment in the operations of the day.

In regard to the supporting force, I stated that the supporting force was placed in line about 400 yards to my rear; that when my line (constituting the assaulting force) commenced the advance, that the supporting force also commenced the advance; that the supporting line advanced so rapidly that, while my line was checked for a time by the enemy's force in the thicket to my right, it overtook my line coming up (the moment it was lying down under my order). It likewise fell down as close in its rear as it could get, thus forming one line of four deep, and exposing both lines to a most destructive fire, at the same time that, thus situated, the rear and supporting line commenced firing over the assaulting line in its front, which fire in the rear greatly alarmed my line, and that my officers expressed the opinion that my men suffered severely from this fire; that, when the advance was again ordered, both lines went forward commingled, the whole becoming from that time forward the assaulting force, and leaving the command without any reserve or supporting force; that being myself, with my staff, about 30 steps to the rear of my line, I ordered the supporting line to halt, repeating the order several times, intending to move it to the right to attack the enemy's force in the thicket, but that no attention was paid to my orders, the supporting line rushing forward and past me, and falling down as near in the rear of the assaulting line as it could get. I said then, and am satisfied now, that, thus disposed of, the force which was intended as supporting force was a positive disadvantage and injury in the operations of the day. I said, further, that in my judgment the supporting force should have been either placed under my orders or else held in hand of the major-general until I called for it to come to my support. In confirmation of the correctness of this opinion, I mentioned the fact that in the assault upon the works of Cerro Gordo, and also in storming Chepultepec, General Scott, in both instances, provided a supporting force (not a part of my own proper command), which was placed under my orders, and which I did bring into the action at the proper time. I further said I had in conversation with General Breckinridge explained to him the serious embarrassment occasioned to my command by the advance of the supporting line, &c.; that his explanation was that the supporting line was ordered to keep the distance of its formation to the rear, but did not obey.

The above are the facts connected with the operations of that day, and my explanation of the work of that day was thus stated in response to inquiries of General Bragg. In my official report I did not deem it proper to state these facts in regard to the handling of the supporting force. That force was never placed under my orders, and I did not feel it my province to reflect upon my senior officer's conduct or disposition. Indeed, I was studious to avoid doing so, and only made the statement when called upon by General Bragg to do so.

GID. J. PILLOW,
Major-General, C. S. Army, &c.

Capt. [JOHN] B. SALE,
Acting Judge-Advocate-General, Army of Tennessee.

No. 234.

Report of Brig. Gen. William Preston, C. S. Army, commanding Third Brigade.

HEADQUARTERS PRESTON'S BRIGADE,
BRECKINRIDGE'S DIVISION, ARMY OF TENNESSEE,
January 12, 1863.

COLONEL: In obedience to the orders of Major-General Breckinridge, I have the honor to transmit a report of the operations of the brigade under my command in the recent battles near Murfreesborough.

The Twentieth Tennessee, the Sixtieth North Carolina, the Fourth Florida, and the First and Third Florida Regiments, with Wright's battery of four pieces, constituted my command, numbering 1,640 effective men.

The enemy having advanced in force against Murfreesborough, dispositions for battle were made, and Breckinridge's division was posted on the extreme right in our front line, with its right near Spence's house, on the Lebanon turnpike, extending toward the ford, where the Nashville turnpike crosses Stone's River. Adams' brigade was on the right, mine next, and Palmer's and Hanson's extended westwardly toward the ford. This position was occupied from Sunday morning, December 28, with some few unimportant changes in our line of battle, until the succeeding Wednesday. On that day, not long after noon, we were ordered to cross the river at the ford, and, under the supervision of Major-General Breckinridge, my brigade, on the right, and that of Palmer on my left, were formed in line of battle on the ground originally occupied by Lieutenant-General Polk's command. The right of my brigade rested near the intersection of the Nashville Railroad and turnpike, and extended nearly at right angles westwardly, about half a mile south of Cowan's, or the burnt house.

These dispositions made, the order was given to advance in the direction of the burnt house toward a cedar forest beyond. Wide and open fields intervened, through which the command passed with great animation, in fine order.   As we came near the farm-house, heavy batteries of the enemy, supported by strong lines of infantry near a railroad embankment, forming a strong defense, were visible obliquely to the right, on the northeast of the Nashville turnpike.   The brigade advanced rapidly and steadily under a destructive fire from the artillery.   The Twentieth Tennessee, passing to the right of the house, engaged the enemy with vigor on the right in some woods near the river, capturing some 25 prisoners and clearing the wood.   The First and Third Florida, on the extreme left, pressed forward to the cedar forest with but little loss. The two central regiments (the Sixtieth North Carolina and Fourth Florida) found great difficulty in pressing through the ruins and strong inclosures of the farm-house, and, retarded by these obstacles and by a fire from the enemy's sharpshooters in front, and a very fierce cannonade, partially enfilading their lines, were for a moment thrown into confusion at the verge of the wood.   They halted and commenced firing, but, being urged forward, they responded with loud shouts and gained the cedars. The enemy turned upon the wood a heavy fire from many pieces of artillery, across a field 400 or 500 yards distant, and, though we lost some valuable lives, the brigade maintained its position with firmness in the edge of the wood.

Having met Lieutenant-General Hardee, he ordered me, with Adams' brigade (under Colonel Gibson) added to my command, to hold the wood. We bivouacked for the night, establishing our pickets far in the field and very near the enemy.   The Twentieth Tennessee, which had been directed by Captain [R. W.] Wooley, assistant adjutant-general, near the river, finding their force insufficient to advance, after losing many men, halted in good order and rejoined the brigade at nightfall in the cedars. Wright's battery, having been detached by General Hardee, took no part in the action.

At roll-call, about dark, it was ascertained that the loss suffered by my command was 155 killed and wounded.   The companies of the Sixtieth North Carolina, under the immediate command of Colonel [Joseph A.] McDowell, were with me; but those separated from his regiment in passing the burnt house, to which I have alluded, fell back without orders to the encampment, with the exception of some of the men and officers who joined the Twentieth Tennessee Regiment, and who did not rejoin their regiment until after night.   Some few prisoners were taken and 400 or 500 stand of arms were secured.

On Friday, about 2 o'clock, the two brigades under my command were withdrawn from the cedars and ordered to take position in line of battle across the river, near the original post of Hanson's brigade. This being done, preparations for attack were made, and Major-General Breckinridge formed his division in two lines, Pillow's and Hanson's brigades being in the front line, with mine 200 yards in the rear of Pillow's, to support his command, and Gibson's on my left, to support Hanson's.

About 4 o'clock, the order to advance being given, the division moved forward rapidly through a wood and an open field beyond to drive the enemy beyond the river and seize a hill that would enable our artillery to enfilade in reverse their batteries.   As soon as the field was entered the engagement commenced, and our men, pressing forward with great ardor, drove the enemy over the crest of the hill and beyond the river. Wright's battery was advanced to the crest of the hill, and was soon hotly engaged.   On our right the enemy far outflanked us, and the Twentieth Tennessee suffered severely, but dashed forward into the woods with its accustomed gallantry and drove the enemy down the hill, capturing some 200 prisoners. A division of the enemy, said to be that of [H. P.] Van Cleve, was driven down the hill-side in utter rout by our division. The enemy then rapidly concentrated large numbers of fresh troops on the other side of the river, and poured upon our dense ranks a withering fire of musketry and artillery. Our lines, originally very close in the order of advance, were commingled near the river, and this new fire from an overwhelming force from the opposite banks of the stream threw them into disorder. The division recoiled over the field in the direction of the wood through which we first passed. When withdrawing from the field, I met Brigadier-General Wharton with his battery and the cavalry, with which he was covering our right. He was about opening fire with the battery, when I advised him not to do so, as he might fire on some of our men. He detached Colonel Harrison, of the Texas Rangers, who, with my brigade, formed and supported Robertson's battery in the verge of the wood until General Breckinridge ordered me to resume my original lines. One of our batteries opened from its verge, and I succeeded in forming my brigade for its support, and was in that position when Major-General Breckinridge arrived and ordered me to resume our original lines, about a mile in the rear, as night had come on.

The loss sustained by my command in this action was 295 killed and wounded, and 90 missing, most of whom were doubtless killed or wounded. The total loss of my command in both actions was 537.

Wright's battery was bravely fought, but lost its gallant commander, who was killed at his guns. Lieutenant [J. W.] Mebane, though wounded, succeeded in withdrawing all of the battery except two of the pieces, which were lost, and which could not be got off, as many of the horses were killed.

For other details I refer to the reports of the commanding officers of the regiments and of the battery, which I inclose.

During the battle both men and officers displayed great intrepidity, and I attribute the repulse on Friday to the manifest hopelessness of the attempt to hurl a single division, without support, against the cardinal position of the whole hostile army. This was apparent to the least intelligent soldier. The line fell back, rallied, and in half an hour was ready to re-engage.

In rallying the troops, I feel it my duty to notice and report the conspicuous zeal and gallantry displayed by yourself, and to testify my appreciation of the valuable assistance you rendered on the field.

Colonel Smith, of the Twentieth Tennessee, a brave and skillful officer, was severely wounded on Wednesday, and the command devolved on Lieutenant-Colonel [Frank M.] Lavender, who has not been heard of since the action on Friday. It is believed that he is wounded or a prisoner.

Colonel Miller, of the First and Third Florida, was wounded on Friday while bravely leading his regiment, which he withdrew, retaining the command, notwithstanding his wound.

The Fourth Florida in both actions bore itself gallantly, and was ably commanded by Colonel Bowen.

In the action of the 31st, Lieut. Edwin Whitfield, of my staff, was severely, if not fatally, wounded by my side while gallantly rendering me the most efficient aid, and Mr. Orville Ewing, a young gentleman of great promise, distinguished in the battle of Mill Springs, was killed nearly at the same moment.

Maj. J. C. Thompson, volunteer aide, and Captain Wooley, assistant adjutant-general, assisted me efficiently on Wednesday.

Mr. [W. R.] Chambliss, acting assistant adjutant-general; Captain [H. P.] Wallace, and Lieut. [J. C.] Wheeler assisted me on Friday on my staff.

To Major [F.] Claybrooke, who volunteered on my staff on Friday, I am greatly indebted for his services.

I recommend for promotion Sergeant Battle for conspicuous gallantry. After four color-bearers of the Twentieth Tennessee had been shot down and the regiment was in confusion, he seized the colors and bravely rallied the men under my eye.

I remain, colonel, with great respect, your obedient servant,

W. PRESTON,
Brigadier-General.

Col. T. O'HARA, *Acting Assistant Adjutant-General.*

[Addenda.]

Abstract from semi-weekly report of Preston's brigade, Brig. Gen. William Preston commanding, for January 12, 1863.

Command.	Present for duty. Officers.	Present for duty. Men.	Aggregate present.	Aggregate present and absent.	Aggregate last return.
Field and staff	6		6	6	6
1st and 3d Florida	34	461	595	1,362	1,377
4th Florida	16	268	385	678	719
60th North Carolina	26	250	354	804	802
20th Tennessee	29	254	338	610	623
Wright's battery	4	71	86	92	95
Total	115	1,304	1,764	3,552	3,622

No. 235.

Report of Col. William Miller, First Florida Infantry, commanding First and Third Regiments.

CAMP NEAR TULLAHOMA, TENN.,
January 12, 1863.

CAPTAIN: In obedience to instructions received from brigade headquarters, I have the honor to submit the following report of the part borne by my command in the actions of December 31, 1862, and January 2, 1863, near Murfreesborough:

About 3 p. m., on December 31, we were ordered into line, marched across the river, and formed on a hill in an open field in line of battle, occupying the left of the brigade. The command "forward" was soon given, and on advancing, our front being masked by a regiment, our left was thrown back out of line. This defect in our alignment caused the regiment to diverge to the left, and to enter a cedar forest to the left of the burnt house, the balance of the brigade passing to the right. In charging over this field we lost several men killed and wounded by the enemy's batteries, which swept the field by an almost enfilading fire. Passing through the cedar, we arrived before the enemy's batteries, and took position on the right of Stewart's brigade, where we were joined by the balance of the brigade. This position of the enemy, supported by heavy batteries, was judged to be too strong to storm; we, therefore, retained our position, skirmishing occasionally with the enemy during that afternoon and the next two following days, up to 2 or 3 p. m. of the 2d instant.

On this occasion the command numbered 36 officers and 495 men, making the aggregate 531.

About 3 p. m. of January 2, we were ordered from the cedars back to the right, recrossing the river, and about 4 p. m. we were formed in line of battle with the balance of the brigade, occupying again the left of the brigade, which was in the second line of battle. At the command "forward," the regiment advanced in excellent order, soon getting in range of a raking fire from the enemy's batteries, until we reached the crest of a ridge in an open field, where the first line of the division was engaged, and here we were ordered to lie down, which we did for a few minutes, and then arose and charged at the command "forward." Upon advancing, on account of the formation of the ground, we were compelled to move by the right flank, passing into the wood that skirted the field through which we had just passed. This combination of movements caused an intermingling of regiments, which led to no little confusion, separating commands, and, again, the men from their commanders. Nevertheless, the troops behaved bravely, driving the enemy before them. As we moved on through the woods, the ground gradually descended, and our left rested on the river, whose high banks were covered by the enemy, who poured a galling fire upon us from the opposite side. Further forward the river, by a sudden bend, appeared in our front, and we found ourselves exposed to a deadly fire from the hills that overlooked us on our left and front. Crossing this hastily, a large portion of the regiment passed the river, under the opposite bank of which it was partially sheltered. I think it is owing to this fact that the First and Third Florida Regiments lost fewer men than other corps which were not so far advanced in the fight. The hopelessness of carrying the opposite heights being now apparent, we were ordered to fall back, and, owing to the commingling of regiments, as before stated, this was done in some confusion and disorder.

Into this fight the regiments carried 32 officers and 424 men, making the aggregate 456.

I respectfully refer you to the report* of casualties already forwarded for an account of the losses sustained by the regiment.

I am happy to have it in my power to state that both officers and men behaved gallantly.

I have the honor to be, sir, yours, very respectfully,

WM. MILLER,
Colonel, Commanding First and Third Florida Regiments.

Captain [R. W.] WOOLEY,
Assistant Adjutant-General.

No. 236.

Report of Col. W. L. L. Bowen, Fourth Florida Infantry.

HEADQUARTERS PRESTON'S BRIGADE,
Tullahoma, Tenn., February 12, 1863.

SIR: In obedience to orders from brigade headquarters, I have the honor to submit the following report of the part borne in the operations

---

* Embodied in No. 191. p. 679.

of Preston's brigade in the battle of **Murfreesborough** by the Fourth Florida Regiment of Infantry:

On Saturday, December 27, 1862, the necessary preparations for battle were made, and at an early hour on Sunday, the 28th, we were moving to the front to take our position in line of battle. My command was assigned to the right center of the brigade, the right flank of which rested upon the Lebanon turnpike, about 1 mile from town. We occupied this position during the day. At night, by order of General Preston, who seemed ever mindful of the comfort of his men, we moved farther to the left and to the rear, in order to get a wood in which to bivouac for the night.

The following day we were ordered into line of battle again, and my command was shifted to the left center of the brigade, which change was permanent during the engàgements. Several unimportant changes in lines and positions occurred, but up to the afternoon of Wednesday nothing occupied our immediate attention, and an apparent restlessness had sprung up among the men to mingle their fortunes with those who were sending back the echoes of their brilliant achievements from the left, and never were men more eager to test their valor for the first time on the battle-field than were the officers and men of my command ; but such suspense was not long unrewarded, for early in the afternoon of Wednesday, the 31st, we were moved to the left across Stone's River, where the brigade was formed on an eminence, in a large, open field, so that the left flank of my regiment rested upon the Nashville Railroad, and at an angle of about 70° with it. My regiment was at no little inconvenience in crossing the railroad embankments, but preserved the alignment. They, however, soon encountered more serious obstacles at a burnt residence, in the shape of out-buildings and strong picket fences, which so retarded our advance as to detach us from the line (only a portion of the Sixtieth North Carolina remained on our right) and throw our part of the line into some derangement. We advanced in this condition under a heavy cannonade from the enemy's batteries, and had not recovered from the derangement when we were ordered to halt and commence firing. Although we remained in this position but a very few minutes, yet the fire from the enemy's batteries with grape and canister, and the fire from his sharpshooters making a partial enfilade upon us, was so terrific that my loss amounted to 55 in killed and wounded. The men becoming a little confused under such a withering fire, General Preston rode forward, seized the colors, and dashed into a cedar glade just to the front and to the left. We, however, had had no command to move forward since halting. It was, nevertheless, a gallant feat in our intrepid brigadier, and met a gallant response by the men, for, with a gladdening shout, they rushed forward to grapple in a hand-to-hand fight with the enemy's sharpshooters, but they fled precipitately to an adjacent wood, leaving several wounded and the killed to fall into our hands. I sent 13 of their wounded off the field, and secured 250 stand of Enfield rifles. We found protection from the enemy's batteries in the glade and behind the rocks, until night put a quiet to the deafening din. We bivouacked in this wood the ensuing night and day, throwing out skirmishers and burying both our own and the enemy's dead.

On Friday, January 2, 1863, we were withdrawn from this position and recrossed the river. We were then formed on the extreme right, in front of our first position. My command in the second line covered the center of Pillow's brigade in the first line, and thus we were moved forward to carry a strong position held by the enemy in force. The front line soon became engaged, and drove the first line of the enemy before them with seeming alacrity. A little confusion ensued in parts of the second line by the pressure from the flanks, but my command did not exhibit the least disorder, and every officer and man seemed to vie with his comrade in coolness and valor. After driving the first line of the enemy to his support, and hotly engaging him for a time, our first line withdrew, and after they had passed through our line to the rear we opened fire, and such was the obstinacy with which our men contended for the supremacy that the best body of the opposing army was held in check for a considerable time; but at length the line began to yield on our left and then on our right, and I mean to detract nothing from other gallant regiments by saying that I soon found the Fourth Florida almost entirely abandoned by the rest of the line. The men still continued to fire with that deliberate accuracy that characterizes the Florida woodsman, and, I am satisfied, with much effect, for we sent a large number of prisoners to the rear, which I estimated at not less than 200. The accidents of the ground which my command occupied afforded a partial protection, and I determined to hold it as long as practicable, that, if possible, we might form a nucleus upon which to rally the broken line, but obstinate valor had to yield to superior force. It was not, however, until the men began to announce their 40 rounds expended that I gave the command to cease firing and fall back. Upon gaining a little eminence, I discovered that the enemy had smartly turned our left flank and were advancing upon our right, subjecting us to a most concentrated and destructive fire. Midway the field through which we had advanced we found our brigade battery. Its gallant commander had just fallen, and Major Graves, chief of artillery, was nobly endeavoring to save the battery from falling into the hands of the enemy. We rallied to his assistance amid a perfect shower of leaden hail, but, owing to the loss of horses and men, only two pieces were saved. It was here my command sustained its heaviest loss, and many valuable officers and brave men fell, either killed or wounded. Among the former was First Lieut. S. D. Harris, commanding Company I, distinguished in both actions for his dauntless bravery. He was wounded and left on the field. Among the latter was Sergt. L. N. Miller, of Company H, whom I ordered, for his cool courage, to take the colors. He and two other color-bearers were shot down. My adjutant (C. C. Burke) rendered much efficient aid until he received a painful wound and was carried off the field.

Much is due to Lieutenant-Colonel [E.] Badger and Major Lesley for their active efficiency in both actions.

Company C, First Lieutenant [J. B.] Parramore commanding, and Company K, First Lieutenant [H. L.] Mitchell commanding, were conspicuous for gallantry and ready compliance with every command. Many remarkable instances of individual valor arrested my attention, but I refrain from particularizing further.

I entered with 423 men and 35 officers. For my loss I refer you to the list* of casualties. We have to regret many valuable lives, but the survivors live to avenge their loss. A little farther to the rear, yet in easy range of the enemy's fire, General Preston, with his accustomed self-possession and valor, soon restored order in his brigade, and night soon closed the bloody scene.

I am, captain, very respectfully, your obedient servant,

W. L. L. BOWEN,
Colonel, Commanding Regiment.

Capt. R. W. Wooley,
Assistant Adjutant-General, Preston's Brigade.

---

*Embodied in No. 191, p. 679.

No. 237.

Report of Maj. John T. Lesley, Fourth Florida Infantry.

JANUARY 10, 1863.

SIR: In obedience to your order of this date, I have the honor to make the following report of the part taken by the Fourth Florida Regiment in the late battles before Murfreesborough:

On the evening of December 31, 1862, the Fourth Florida Regiment, together with the other regiments of the brigade (to wit, General Preston's), was ordered forward, and formed a line of battle on the right of General Palmer's brigade, on the northwest side of Stone's River, the Fourth Florida occupying the center of Preston's brigade. General Breckinridge, commanding in person, gave the command "forward," which was promptly repeated by General Preston, and the whole brigade moved forward in regular order. The Fourth Florida, encountering some picket fences on the route, was compelled to pull them down amid a most galling fire of grape, bomb-shell, and canister. Still preserving perfect order, they marched forward, amid this deadly fire, a distance of 1,000 yards, where they encountered near a thicket a body of sharpshooters, who had taken shelter therein. At this critical moment the command "halt" was given. They were thus subjected to the fire from three different batteries of the enemy's artillery, and a cross-fire from the rifles of the sharpshooters. The command "fire" was given, which was responded to with alacrity. A hot contest ensued; the sharpshooters were soon driven from their lurking place. Our regiment being at a halt, and General Preston, doubtless, thinking they were wavering, rode forward, seized the flag, and called upon the regiment to charge. With a joyous shout our boys sprang forward, and were soon in possession of the wood that had lately covered the enemy. The enemy now turned their battery upon this cedar forest, literally tearing the trees to pieces by their balls, but doing us comparatively little damage. Our loss in this charge amounted to about 55 killed and wounded.

Again, on Friday, January 2, we were ordered to prepare for immediate action. Our brigade, together with Palmer's brigade, was marched to the southeast of Stone's River, to attack a formidable position of the enemy in their rear. The two brigades were formed in an open field, when the command "forward" was again given. Palmer's brigade being the advance, they charged upon the enemy amid a perfect shower of bullets. Balls whistling around us thick and loud, we were ordered to lie down. In ten minutes the order was given, "Up and to the charge." This order was responded to most heartily by our regiment and the brigade. They rushed forward with such impetuosity as to throw the enemy for a moment into confusion. They, however, soon rallied. A fierce and bloody contest now ensued for about one hour. There was one continual rattle of musketry and roar of artillery. The ranks of the enemy were being rapidly thinned when re-enforcements came to their succor, and they were in the act of flanking us on both wings when the order was given to retreat. Thus was valor forced to give ground to overwhelming numbers. I mean no disparagement to other gallant regiments to state that the Fourth Florida was the last to leave the field.

This, sir, is a brief statement of the part taken by our regiment in the actual contest of the great battle before Murfreesborough, to say nothing of the marches and counter-marches we took in rapid succession during several days of the engagement, to defend weak points upon our line where it was thought the enemy might direct their attention.

Our loss in this engagement was about 140 killed and wounded.

Respectfully submitted.

JOHN T. LESLEY,
Major Fourth Florida Volunteers.

R. W. WOOLEY,
Assistant Adjutant-General, Preston's Brigade.

[Indorsement.]

Colonel Bowen being absent when the order was received, Major Lesley made this report. Colonel Bowen having returned and made his own report, supersedes Major Lesley's, and renders it superfluous.

W. PRESTON,
Brigadier-General.

No. 238.

Report of Col. Joseph A. McDowell, Sixtieth North Carolina Infantry.

CAMP NEAR TULLAHOMA, TENN.,
January 11, 1863.

GENERAL: I respectfully submit the following report of the part taken by the Sixtieth North Carolina in the recent battles of December 31, [1862,] and January 2, [1863:]

On Sunday morning, the 28th, we were ordered into line of battle and occupied our position on the right wing, a little to the left of the Lebanon pike. We were moved from point to point without being engaged with the enemy from Sunday morning until Wednesday, the 31st.

On Wednesday, the 31st, about 2 p. m., we marched across Stone's River and formed line of battle near the Nashville pike, the Sixtieth North Carolina occupying the right-center position of the brigade. We were then marched in the direction of the enemy through an open field about three-quarters of a mile. We advanced in good order, under a heavy fire of shell, until we came upon very serious obstructions in the shape of a large brick house, out-buildings, and strong picket fencing, which extended the length of our regimental line of battle. Owing to these obstructions, and the great difficulty of getting through the picket fencing, my regiment was thrown into some confusion and the line was broken. Company E, Lieutenant [S. C.] Wright commanding; Company F, Captain [James M.] Ray; Company H, Captain [James T.] Huff, and Company K, Captain [W. R.] West, succeeded in making their way through the fence, where the line was reformed with these companies, and was obliqued about 200 yards through a cotton-field, taking shelter in a skirt of woods. During our march through the cotton-field we were subjected to a most terrific fire of grape and shell and musketry, losing at this point about 28 in killed and wounded. We remained for some time in this skirt of woods, our men keeping up a brisk fire.

Lieutenant [J. T.] Weaver, commanding Company A, although detached from the regiment by the obstructions above mentioned, took position on the left of the Twentieth Tennessee, and fought with that regiment until he regained his position with my regiment in the skirt of woods. At this point the general commanding came up and seized the flag of a Florida regiment, and advanced, the brigade following him into a cedar thicket, where the enemy had been strongly posted, and from which position he had done us such serious damage; but when we reached there he had ingloriously fled, and we remained masters of the field. Night put a stop to further operations, and we slept that night on our arms.

I desire to make special mention of Captains Ray, Huff, and West; Lieutenant Weaver, commanding Company A, and Lieutenant Wright, commanding Company E, for their brave and gallant conduct, and likewise the cool and deliberate courage exhibited by W. T. White, a private in Company K; H. C. Fagg, Company B; little John [A.] Freshour, Company B, and the color-bearer, Francis [M.] Bailey, Company E, and Corpl. T. J. Garrison and Private H. N. Bridges, of Company A, both of whom were seriously wounded. This being the first engagement the Sixtieth North Carolina has been in, I am gratified to say that with but few exceptions they acquitted themselves in a highly commendable manner.

On Thursday, the 1st, we remained inactive, occupying the ground gained on Wednesday.

On Friday, in the afternoon, we reoccupied Stone's River, and formed line of battle in the rear of Hanson's and Pillow's brigades, to support them in their attack on the enemy. About 4 o'clock we were ordered to advance, which we did in good order; engaged the enemy and kept driving him before us until about sunset, when, it becoming apparent that he was strongly re-enforced and flanking us, we were ordered to fall back. We retired in perfect order about 300 yards, in advance, however, of our original line of battle, and there reformed our line. At this juncture the general commanding came up and ordered us back to our original position.

I regret to announce the death of Acting Adjt. Stanhope S. Erwin, who fell, pierced through the head by a minie ball, while faithfully and gallantly discharging his duties.

J. A. McDOWELL,
Colonel, Commanding Sixtieth North Carolina Volunteers.

Brigadier-General [W.] PRESTON,
Commanding Brigade.

No. 239.

Report of Col. T. B. Smith, Twentieth Tennessee Infantry.

TULLAHOMA, TENN., *January 22,* 1863.

SIR: In obedience to orders received from brigade headquarters, I hereby submit the following report of the part the Twentieth Tennessee Regiment took in the late action near Murfreesborough:

Early Sunday morning, December 28, [1862,] the regiment was formed, the men being fully equipped, their cartridge-boxes filled with ammunition, and two days' rations in haversacks. The brigade being formed, we were marched through Murfreesborough and out upon the Lebanon road about 1½ miles, where we formed line of battle, our right resting on the road, our left extending westward. In this position we remained until near night, when I received orders from General Preston to move my regiment to a skirt of woods still farther west, where we bivouacked for the night.

At noon on the next day the direction of lines was changed; we were then thrown forward into an open field, where we remained all night. As the night was wet and cold, my men made themselves comfortable by building large fires.

The next day was occupied in maneuvering to the front and right until about 2 p. m., when we were moved to the left across the river at the ford, formed in line of battle, and moved forward, the right resting on the river bank. The line moved steadily onward for about 600 yards, when my regiment fell under a heavy and well-directed fire from a large party of the enemy, who were in ambush among the timber and rocks directly on the bank of the river. My regiment, being in the open field and unprotected by any cover, I thought it best to order a charge, which was done by moving by the right flank and then to the front. In this charge I was wounded and was brought off the field. The charge, as I afterward [learned], was successful. The enemy were dislodged and the position held by my men until night.

In this engagement my officers and men acted well, obeying every command with alacrity.

I cannot close without expressing my high sense of gratitude to General Preston for the care he took of his men, and the skillfulness he displayed in maneuvering us on the field and in bringing us into action.

I am, very respectfully, captain, your obedient servant,

T. B. SMITH,
Colonel Twentieth Tennessee Regiment.

[Capt.] R. W. WOOLEY,
Assistant Adjutant-General.

No. 240.

Report of Maj. F. Claybrooke, Twentieth Tennessee Infantry.

CAMP NEAR TULLAHOMA, TENN.,
January 11, 1863.

[The following is] a report of the part taken in the recent battles near Murfreesborough, Tenn., by the Twentieth Tennessee Regiment:

Saturday, December 27, 1862, orders were received to cook rations and be ready to move at a moment's warning, as it was well known that the enemy were approaching in large force. Officers and men were certain of an engagement, and each man felt we would be victorious. Indeed, so far as my observation extended, I have never before seen soldiers in higher spirits than were ours on that occasion. Nor have I ever seen men better bear up under the long-continued privations and hardships incident to every battle.

Very early Sunday morning, orders to that effect having been received, all the camp equipage was packed ready to be placed in the wagons, the regiment formed and marched to the headquarters of General Preston, where the brigade was formed, our regiment taking the position previously assigned us, on the right of the brigade. General Preston marched us through the town and out upon the Lebanon road about 1½ miles. Here our line of battle was formed; we—the right of the brigade, and, indeed, the extreme right of the front line of the army—were formed, our right resting on the road, our left extending in the direction of Stone's River, which at this place runs nearly from east to west. In this position we remained for several hours, when we were ordered to **advance a few hundred yards** to a skirt of heavy timber, where we bivouacked for the night. Near this place we remained until Wednesday at noon, doing very little else but occasionally changing the direction of our line of battle, so as to get into the best position to receive in case the enemy advanced.

At 2 p. m. on Wednesday we were ordered to cross the river, and, forming in line of battle, to advance on the enemy. Our regiment being on the right, we were ordered to advance down the bank of the river. By this order, owing to obstructions in the front—a large house called Cowan's and the railroad embankment—we were separated from our brigade. After an advance of half a mile we encountered the enemy, strongly posted among the rocks and heavy growth of timber on the river bluff. Here the firing was very heavy, and we lost many men (in all, about 67), among whom was Colonel Smith, severely wounded; Captain [John W.] Watkins, of Company I, and Lieutenant [F. B.] Crosthwait, of Company E, killed. We succeeded in driving the enemy from their position, killing many and taking 20 prisoners, and followed them to the brow of the hill. At this place the shot and shell rained upon us. We were in danger of being surrounded; were in very small force, and had no support. Under these circumstances I ordered the men to fall back 200 yards, and at this place we remained until night, when we were ordered to rejoin our brigade, which had taken position under cover of a thick cedar woods on our left. In this cover we lay concealed until Friday, January 2.

At 2 o'clock we recrossed the river and formed line of battle running parallel with the river, with a view to dislodge the enemy, who had crossed over to the south side of the river and had heavy batteries planted on the banks. At the command "forward," our lines steadily advanced, meeting the enemy on the edge of the wood that slopes down to the river. Here for a time the conflict was desperate. Our regiment, being on the extreme right, suffered severely from the enemy, who attempted to turn our right, but we soon drove them back and pursued them to the river, where they sought shelter under its banks. But the opposite bank was soon lined with strong re-enforcements, and as they far outnumbered us and their position was impregnable, our men began to fall back in some confusion; but our general (Preston), amid a storm of bullets, succeeded in rallying his men.

Night closed upon us, and at 8 o'clock we were quietly bivouacked a short distance from the battle-field, in which position we remained until the order to fall back was received.

General Preston, having in the first battle lost many of his aides, by the consent of Lieutenant-Colonel Lavender, commanding the regiment, detached Major Claybrooke from his regiment to act as his aide.

In this battle we lost Lieutenant-Colonel Lavender; whether wounded or not, I am unable to say.

Our loss in killed, wounded, and missing was 67, making a total loss of 134. In this last engagement we took nearly 200 prisoners.

I cannot speak too highly of the efforts of General Preston, who, regardless of danger, went everywhere, encouraging and rallying the men; nor of the many brave men of my command who fought bravely through both engagements.

During the action four color-bearers were shot, our flag-staff thrice shot in two, and the color itself riddled by balls.

Many distinguished instances came under my eye, but I refrain from particularizing, as I would not do so without seeming partial.

I remain, captain, your obedient servant,

F. CLAYBROOKE,
Major, Commanding Twentieth Tennessee Regiment.

No. 241.

Report of Lieut. John W. Mebane, Wright's Tennessee battery

—————— —, 1863.

[I have the honor to report the] part taken in the battle before Murfreesborough by Capt. E. E. Wright's battery, light artillery, General Preston's brigade, General Breckinridge's division:

The battery was ordered out about 8 o'clock Sunday morning, December 28, 1862, and took a position 2 miles from Murfreesborough, on the left of the Lebanon road, in the center of General Preston's brigade. We held the position until 3 p. m., when we retired about a quarter of a mile on the south side of a small branch, where we remained in bivouac until Monday evening, 3 o'clock, when we moved 1 mile to the left of our first position, and took a position in the edge of a thick wood on the south side of a field, opposite some log-houses on the north side, which were burning at the time we took our position. We held the last-mentioned position until near sunset Tuesday evening, when we moved about a quarter of a mile to the left of our second position, and took a position just in the south side of the last-mentioned field, between the brigades of General Preston and Colonel Palmer, General Preston on our right and Colonel Palmer on our left. We held our third position until Wednesday morning about sunrise, when Captain Wright received orders to report with his battery to Lieutenant-General Hardee, on the left of our lines. He reported as ordered, and was ordered to park his battery in a field about half a mile west of Stone's River, on the Franklin road. We remained in park until Thursday evening, 2 o'clock, when we were ordered to take a position on the Wilkinson pike, about 2 miles from Murfreesborough, where we remained until 2 p. m. Friday, when Captain Wright received orders from General Bragg to report with his battery at the Nashville Ford, on Stone's River, where he would be met by a staff officer, who would show him his position. Captain Wright moved his battery to the ford, and no officer making his appearance, Captain Wright moved his battery about a mile northwest from the ford, to where General Breckinridge's division was in line, and, learning that General Breckinridge would make an attack at 4 p. m., Captain Wright moved his battery on the right of the division, and advanced with General Preston's brigade. We passed through an open skirt of woods about 100 yards in width into a cornfield about 400 yards wide. We advanced about 200 yards in the field, and opened fire on a Federal battery about 300 yards obliquely to our right. As we were advancing at a gallop in the field, before taking our first position, the off lead horse in one of our 6-pounder gun teams was struck in the head with a ball and fell dead. Before the team could be halted, the carriage was rushed against the horse and the pole broken, which caused the piece not to be in action in our first position at all. We continued firing on the battery and a column of infantry, which was filing to the right in rear of the battery, about fifteen minutes, when the Federal battery ceased firing on us, and we limbered to the front to advance.

I received a very painful wound in my left arm from a fragment of a shell about the time my section had fired the first round, but remained in the action until the command was given to limber to the front, when Captain Wright ordered me to the rear to have my wound dressed, and ordered Lieutenant [J. C.] Grant up with the limbers of the caissons. I **conducted Lieutenant Grant to the field and pointed out to him the** position of the battery, and went back to have my wound dressed, but, before the surgeon had finished, our lines had fallen back to their first position.

For the report from the time we limbered to the front at our first position until we fell back from the field, I am indebted to Lieutenant [J. W.] Phillips. It is as follows:

After limbering to the front, the battery was ordered by Major Graves by a left-oblique to the left of the field, under the cover of a small hill, where it remained about ten minutes, when it was again ordered by Major Graves by a right-oblique to the right of the field, on the top of a long hill formerly occupied by the enemy. When we reached the top of the hill our men were in full retreat; but we opened on the enemy with spherical case and canister, and continued to fire with effect until the enemy had charged within 75 yards of our pieces. Here it was that Captain Wright fell, mortally wounded, and three men carried his body to the rear. Just after Captain Wright fell, Major Graves gave the command "limber to the rear," and just as the pieces were limbered up he gave the command to unlimber and fire double charges of canister, which command was obeyed by firing about one round to the piece, when the command "limber to the rear" was again given by Major Graves; but only two of the pieces were ever limbered up and the others fell into the hands of the enemy. The gunner and two of the men of one of the lost pieces had gone to the rear with the captain's body, another one had been shot, and the others in the general panic had gone to the rear. This left not one to raise the trail except Sergeant Wright, who was unable to do it. Two horses of the limber of the other lost gun were shot down while moving the limber to the trail, and the men would have been captured had they remained to cut them out, so close had the enemy charged to them. Had our battery gone to the rear when the other batteries of the division did, we would have saved our guns; but being under the immediate supervision of the chief of artillery, we did not move without orders from him. We carried two pieces and four caissons from the field, and were ordered to the rear as unfit for service by General Preston.

Saturday we endeavored to fit out one section for service, but the day was so very rainy that we did not complete it until late in the evening, when we were ordered to prepare to evacuate the place.

The loss of the battery may be summed up thus: Killed—officers, 1; non-commissioned officers, 1; enlisted men, 4. Wounded—officers, 1; non-commissioned officers, 3; enlisted men, 4. Total, 14.

[We had] 10 horses killed and 2 guns lost.

Very respectfully,

JNO. W. MEBANE,
Lieutenant, Commanding Wright's Battery.

[Indorsement.]

HEADQUARTERS PRESTON'S BRIGADE,
BRECKINRIDGE'S DIVISION, ARMY OF TENNESSEE,
Tullahoma, Tenn., February 21, 1863.

The foregoing are official copies of the reports of the commanders of regiments and battery of Preston's brigade, Breckinridge's division, C. S. Army, of the battle of Murfreesborough, from the originals transmitted to division headquarters.

W. R. CHAMBLISS,
First Lieutenant and Acting Assistant Adjutant-General.

No. 242.

*Report of Col. Robert P. Trabue, Fourth Kentucky Infantry, commanding
Fourth Brigade.*

HEADQUARTERS TRABUE'S (LATE HANSON'S) BRIGADE,
Tullahoma, Tenn., January 13, 1863.

SIR: The untimely fall of the gallant and lamented Hanson, brigadier-general commanding this brigade, in the engagement on Friday, the 2d instant, at Murfreesborough, imposes on me the duty of reporting, to the extent of my knowledge, the operations of the brigade prior to and after his fall in the battle before that place.

On Sunday, the brigade having received orders to that effect, marched from their camp in rear of Murfreesborough, at 8 a. m., to the position in the front line of battle indicated for our occupation. This brigade formed the left of General Breckinridge's division, and in line rested with its left on or near Stone's River, extending eastward until the right was united to Colonel Palmer's brigade. The position first taken up (the exact line not having been pointed out) was along the skirt of woods in rear of the open fields east and south of Stone's River, which afforded, by the existence of a small ridge running parallel with the front, and a consequent depression immediately in rear, very good protection against the enemy's long-range artillery.

On Monday, Semple's battery of six Napoleon guns, furnished by the chief of artillery, was placed on the crest immediately in front of the right wing, and Cobb's battery was held to be placed later. Thus formed in line, the Fourth Kentucky was on the right; Second Kentucky second, Major [James W.] Hewitt; Forty-first Alabama third, Colonel [H.] Talbird; Sixth Kentucky fourth, Colonel [Joseph H.] Lewis, and Ninth Kentucky on the left, Colonel [T. H.] Hunt.

On Monday evening it was perceived that the enemy meant to occupy immediately all the advantageous positions in our front, of which he could possess himself, for artillery. A prominent elevation existed 1,000 yards in front of our left, which General Breckinridge desired we should hold, notwithstanding it was liable to assault, being isolated 1,000 yards in front of our lines. To this end, Colonel Hunt, with the Ninth Kentucky, Colonel Lewis, Sixth Kentucky, Lieutenant-Colonel [M. L.] Stansel, Forty-first Alabama, and Cobb's battery, were ordered to occupy it. Throwing out skirmishers, they were soon engaged with those of the enemy. The force above named was then moved up to the front in support of the skirmishers, and succeeded in establishing Cobb's battery on the eminence. This was not accomplished without the loss of two valuable officers—Lieutenants [A. J.] Beale and [O.] Kennard, of Company D, Ninth Kentucky, the former severely and the latter slightly wounded. By this time it was dark, when the enemy endeavored in a spirited effort to retake the position, rapidly driving in our skirmishers, and approaching to within a few yards of the battery. This attempt was frustrated by promptly advancing the Forty-first Alabama, under Lieutenant-Colonel Stansel, when the enemy were driven off in confusion, leaving two of their dead near the battery. Our loss here amounted to not less than 10 wounded, falling mainly on the Sixth Kentucky and Cobb's battery, among whom was Lieutenant [J. B.] Holman, Sixth Kentucky.

On Tuesday night these regiments were withdrawn, and I, with the Second and Fourth Kentucky and Cobb's battery, occupied this position. It was deemed of the last importance to hold this hill, and orders were received to do so at all hazards, it being called the key of the battle-field.

On Wednesday evening the entire brigade was brought up, having been re-enforced by a section of Lumsden's battery, commanded by Lieutenant [J. A.] Chalaron,* and a section of Washington Artillery, commanded by Lieutenant [E.] Tarrant. Semple's battery having taken up a position 600 yards in rear and left of us, a section of this battery replaced for one night Cobb's battery. During the week which followed we were kept here bivouacking in the mud and rain, and exposed to an incessant fire from the enemy's batteries and sharpshooters. A temporary and slight intrenchment was made, which, to some extent, protected the batteries; but the casualties at this place were not inconsiderable (amounting to 40 men), as stated above, and as will appear by reference to regimental reports.

During the engagement of Wednesday, time and again did the gallant Cobb, aided by his not less gallant lieutenants and three sections before referred to, disperse the enemy's columns as they endeavored to succor that part of their force engaged with the right of the left wing of the army. Indeed, during every day of our occupation of this hill our battery did signal service, frequently driving the enemy's artillery away and often dispersing his infantry. All this while the brigade covered more than a mile of front with skirmishers and pickets, using for that purpose from six to ten companies daily. These advanced to within 100 yards of the enemy in many places, and were hourly engaged.

On this hill Cobb's battery lost 8 men; Colonel Hunt, Ninth Kentucky, lost a most excellent officer killed (his adjutant, Henry M. Curd), whose death all lament, and wounded Capt. Joseph Desha, whose subsequent conduct elicited universal praise, together with Lieutenants [G.] Lewis, Company A, and [H.] Buchanan, Company H, wounded, and 3 other officers and 23 privates. (See detailed statement.) Colonel Lewis, Sixth Kentucky, lost slightly here; Lieutenant-Colonel Stansel, Forty-first Alabama, lost here two of his best officers and several men; the Second and Fourth Kentucky, though equally exposed, lost less at this point.

On Friday, the 2d instant, at 3 o'clock, the order came to move to the right and front, and form the left of the front line of General Breckinridge's division to attack that portion of the enemy's left which were posted in the woods and ravines on the south side of Stone's River, opposite the extreme right of our army, which was done. Colonel Hunt, with his regiment, remained at the hill, ordered to support the battery, and six companies were kept out as before on picket duty, thus leaving us for the fight about 1,200 men.

Stone's River in front of this new position runs nearly parallel with the new line, but inclines to the point occupied by the right of this brigade, when, by a change of direction to the north, it runs for some distance nearly perpendicularly from the front of our line. At this point, whence the river changes its direction northward, is a skirt of woods and an elevated ridge, behind which and in the ravine and woods the enemy lay concealed. To the right of our line the enemy were likewise posted in a woods, thus outflanking us. One thousand yards in the front from this first skirt of woods is a ford of the river, while the bank of the river opposite us, between the ford and point of attack, overlooks the

---

* The above account of commanders of sections of artillery is undoubtedly incorrect, as Chalaron belonged to Washington Artillery and Tarrant belonged to Lumsden's battery.

south and east bank. One mile farther down the river is another ford, as I have since learned. This topography, as well as the enemy's strength, was wholly unknown to us.

The two lines of the division having been formed, the signal for attack was sounded at 4 p. m., when this brigade in line moved steadily forward to the attack, with arms loaded and bayonets fixed, instructed to fire once and then charge with the bayonet. The peculiar nature of the ground and direction of the river and the eagerness of the troops caused the lines of General Pillow's (formerly Palmer's) brigade and this brigade to lap on the crest of the hill, but the fury of the charge and the effective fire of the lines put the enemy at once to flight. All in front of us that were not killed or captured ran across the river at the ford and out of range of our fire, as did a battery which had been posted off to our right, and many of the infantry mentioned before as being on the right likewise fled across this ford. A part, however, of this force, double-quicking toward the ford from their position, finding they would be cut off, formed in line to our right on a ridge, and, not being assailed, held this ground. Meanwhile, and from the moment of beginning the attack, the enemy's artillery from the opposite side of the river directed on us a most destructive fire. Very soon, too, the crests of the opposite side of the river swarmed with infantry, whose fire was terrible. Thus exposed to the fire, seemingly, of all his artillery and a large portion of his infantry from unassailable positions, as well as to the flanking fire from the right, it was deemed prudent to withdraw. This was done slowly, though not in the best order, resulting mainly from the confusion consequent upon the too early advance of the second line into the ground already too much crowded by the first. The lines were reformed about 600 yards in rear of the river, and near the line from which we advanced to the attack.

While thus engaged in reforming my own regiment, I received intelligence of the fall of General Hanson, when I took command of the brigade, the other regiments of which had likewise been reformed. This brigade in the battle having advanced to within 80 yards of the ford, a part of Colonel Lewis' Sixth Kentucky and a part of the Second Kentucky having crossed the river a little to the left, when near the ford, slightly protected by a picket fence on this side, they fought the enemy across the river until the rear having fallen back made it necessary to withdraw them also.

I obtained returns on the field showing still in line more than half the men with which we started out, notwithstanding a loss of 33 per cent. I remained in line until 9 o'clock, having replenished the cartridge-boxes, when I received orders to return to my original position on the hill, which was obeyed.

We remained in this position until Sunday morning at 1 a. m., when, having been assigned the duty of bringing up the rear, we moved off, with Colonel Hunt's Ninth Kentucky, Forty-first Alabama, Lieutenant-Colonel Stansel, and Cobb's battery being detailed as special rear guard. My pickets were withdrawn at 3 a. m. by Captain [C.] Bosche, of Ninth Kentucky, under direction of Captain Martin, of General Breckinridge's staff.

I have thus briefly given you a report of the part taken by this brigade, omitting many details and incidents creditable to individuals and to the command.

In the absence of a report from my own regiment (Fourth Kentucky) prior to the time when I took command of the brigade, I will state simply that both officers and men did their duty. Willis [S.] Roberts, major, was killed early in the action by a grape-shot. Than him there was none a more gallant officer. He had not recovered from wounds received at Baton Rouge. Lieutenant Colonel [Joseph P.] Nuckols was wounded in shoulder, near picket fence. Captain [W. P.] Bramblett, First Lieutenant [G. B.] Burnley, Second Lieutenants [Green F.] Higginson, [N. D.] Clayton, [and Robert] Dunn were killed, and Lieutenants [Isham T.] Dudley, Robert Moore (since said to have died), John [B.] Moore, [William] Lashbrooke, and [R. A.] Thompson were wounded, together with privates and non commissioned officers.

One company (Captain [J. L.] Trice's), being on picket duty, was not in the engagement.

The color-bearer (Robert Lindsey), being wounded, refused to allow any one to accompany him to the rear, although bleeding at the mouth and nose. He handed the colors on return to Private Jones, who was killed, when they were borne to the last by Joseph Nichols, of Company F.

Thus it will be seen that of 23 officers of this regiment who went into the fight, 7 were killed and 6 wounded.

The command of the regiment was, on my assuming command of the brigade, turned over to Captain [Thomas W.] Thompson.

The detailed statements heretofore furnished show the casualties to have been as follows:

Command.	Killed.	Wounded.	Missing.
2d Kentucky	14	70	24
4th Kentucky	12	47	11
6th Kentucky	2	60	14
9th Kentucky	1	28	......
41st Alabama	18	89	35
Cobb's battery	3	3	......
Total	50	297	84
Aggregate	......	......	431

The conduct of Colonel Lewis, Lieutenant-Colonel Stansel, Forty-first Alabama; Maj. James [W.] Hewitt, Second Kentucky; Lieutenant-Colonel Nuckols and Captain Thompson, of Fourth Kentucky, as well as that of the other field and company officers engaged, was gallant in the highest degree, and the men repeated also the steadiness and courage which characterized them at Donelson, Shiloh, Baton Rouge, Vicksburg, and Hartsville.

Lieutenants [T. E.] Stake and [Joseph] Benedict and Captain [S. F.] Chipley, of General Hanson's staff, bore themselves with exemplary courage.

My thanks are due, too, to the medical staff and to Captain Semple, division ordnance officer, and Acting Lieut. Presley Trabue, brigade ordnance officer, for their promptness in bringing up supplies of ammunition, and to my adjutant, Robert H. Williams, of Fourth Kentucky.

I cannot close this report without more special mention of one whose gallantry and capacity we all witnessed with pride, and whose loss we and the whole army sincerely deplore. I mean the gallant General Hanson, who fell in the pride of his manhood in the thickest of the fight, nobly doing his duty. His wound was mortal, and death ensued on Sunday morning, at 5 o'clock.

Colonel Hunt, Ninth Kentucky, although not in the engagement of Friday, deserves commendation for his conduct prior and subsequent to that time, as do the other officers and the men of his regiment.

Respectfully,

R. P. TRABUE,
Colonel, Commanding Brigade.

T. O'HARA,
Acting Assistant Adjutant-General.

P. S.—The missing list comprises those who went into the engagement, but were not seen to come out. They must have been killed or wounded. I find, also, I have omitted to mention that Lieutenant-Colonel Stansel received a severe wound in the leg, but did not quit the field, and still commands his regiment.

[Addenda.]

Abstract from morning report of Kentucky Brigade, Col. R. P. Trabue commanding, for January 8, 1863.

Command.	Present for duty.		Aggregate present.	Aggregate present and absent.	Aggregate last return.
	Officers.	Men.			
Field and staff	5		5	6	6
41st Alabama	24	369	521	938	1,055
2d Kentucky	25	290	411	675	713
4th Kentucky	18	283	392	518	544
6th Kentucky	21	187	255	431	451
9th Kentucky *					
Roberts' cavalry *					
Cobb's battery	4	89	104	133	136
Total	97	1,218	1,688	2,701	2,905

No. 243.

Report of Lieut. Col. M. L. Stansel, Forty-first Alabama Infantry.

TULLAHOMA, TENN., January 12, 1863.

SIR: I have the honor to make the following report of the performances of this regiment in the recent seven days' battles in front of Murfreesborough, Tenn.:

On Sunday, December 28, this regiment, together with the other regiments composing Hanson's brigade, acting under orders proceeding from general headquarters, proceeded to Wayne's Hill and formed line of battle in rear and in support of Cobb's battery and a section of the Washington Artillery, as also a section of Lumsden's battery. In this position we remained for several days, exposed to a constant and galling fire both from the enemy's artillery and sharpshooters, awaiting an evidently contemplated attack upon that point. During this time two of our best lieutenants ([James T.] Hardaway and [N. B.] Lenderman) and Private Suddeth were killed and a number of our men wounded; still, however, we held our position against the most terrific assaults the

---

* Absent on outpost duty.

enemy could bring to bear against it— a point called by General Bragg himself the key of the battle-field.

On Friday evening, January 2, this regiment, together with the Second, Fourth, and Sixth Kentucky Regiments, was ordered to the right of our position, and proceeded down Stone's River to a point about 1 mile north of Wayne's Hill, to make an attack upon a strong body of the enemy in force there. In this attack, from which ensued a most terrific battle, my officers and men demeaned themselves most gallantly, driving the enemy before them across the river entirely from the position they held, pushing forward until they came within the raking fire of the powerful batteries of the enemy planted on the opposite bank of the river and supported by almost their entire army.

So gallant was the general conduct of my officers and men in this the hardest struggle of the battle, that it would seem invidious to discriminate between them.

The annexed is a correct list* of the casualties in the battle, which shows the following result: Killed, 18; wounded, 90; missing, 35; total, 143.

Very respectfully, your obedient servant,

M. L. STANSEL,
Lieutenant-Colonel, Comdg. Forty-first Regt. Alabama Vols.

Col. R. P. TRABUE,
Commanding Hanson's Brigade.

No. 244.

Report of Maj. James W. Hewitt, Second Kentucky Infantry.

TULLAHOMA, TENN., *January 10, 1863.*

SIR: I would respectfully report that on Sunday morning, December 28, [1862,] I left camp with my command and proceeded to a position 1½ miles north of Murfreesborough, where, in company with the brigade, I remained until the following morning, when I was ordered about 300 yards in advance, fronting the enemy's left center. I then threw out my flank companies (A and C) as skirmishers half a mile farther to the front, occupying a position in sight and range of the enemy. After remaining in that position about two hours, I received orders to take my command back to their former position.

On the morning of Tuesday, 29th instant, I was ordered to send two companies (Company B, Captain [Joel] Higgins, and Company H, Lieutenant [A. K.] Lair) to support a battery in the field in the rear of Cobb's battery, where they remained until said battery changed position. The same evening I was ordered with my command (eight companies, two companies being still on picket duty) to a hill immediately in front of the enemy, where, in company with the balance of our brigade, we remained until Friday evening as a support to Cobb's battery, a section of the Washington Artillery, and a section of Semple's artillery, exposed continually to a severe fire.

On Friday evening, about 3 o'clock, in company with the other regiments of our brigade, we advanced about a mile to the right of our position, and, forming in line of battle, we advanced across an open field to a piece of woods occupied by the enemy, about a mile from where our

---

* Nominal list omitted.

line was formed. After driving the enemy across the river, we still advanced to a picket fence in the immediate neighborhood of the enemy's re-enforcements and in range of sixteen of their guns, which continually threw among us a shower of shot and shell, which, in addition to heavy re-enforcements, compelled us to fall back to our former position in the woods, where we reformed under your command, General Hanson having been carried off the field mortally wounded.

About 9 p. m., under the command of Captain [James W.] Moss, acting major (I being compelled to leave the field from the effects of a shell), we were ordered back to the rifle-pits, where we remained until Sunday a. m. (1 o'clock), when we took up our line of march for our present position. I would further state that in going into action I had nine companies (Company K, Captain [E.] Joyes, being on picket duty), numbering 346 men and officers, and that we lost in the engagement 108 officers and men killed, wounded, and missing, among whom were Lieutenants [F.] Tryon and [S. B.] Hawes, left on the field, supposed to be mortally wounded; Captains [H.] McDowell and [H. B.] Rodgers, Adjutant [T. E.] Moss, Lieutenants [L. C.] Moss, [W. J.] Hays, [R. H.] Innis, and [C. W.] Kleisendorff wounded and brought off the field. My color-guard, with one exception, were all either killed or wounded.

In conclusion, I beg leave to state that, without an exception, both officers and men behaved with great gallantry and bravery.

Very respectfully, your obedient servant,

JAMES W. HEWITT,
Major, Commanding Regiment.

Col. R. P. TRABUE,
Commanding Hanson's Brigade.

No. 245.

Report of Col. Joseph H. Lewis, Sixth Kentucky Infantry.

CAMP TULLAHOMA, TENN., *January 10, 1863.*

SIR: Herewith is a report of what concerns my own command of the recent battles at Murfreesborough, Tenn.

For a clear understanding of the part taken by this regiment I will, as far as my limited opportunities allowed me to observe, describe the field of its operations. At the ford, 1 mile below the turnpike bridge, the river, whose general course is northward, bends toward the west and continues in that direction half a mile, when, by a curve at right angles, it takes its previous northward course, and continues it for 1 mile or more to a ford at which the enemy crossed during the engagement Friday afternoon. The left of Breckinridge's division and of Hanson's brigade extended to the river a few hundred paces below the first-named ford. At the point of the second curve a rocky bluff sets in and continues to the lower ford, except at a point 600 or 800 yards below, where there is a slight depression. For this distance the ground is timbered sufficiently to afford protection to the enemy. The ground rises gradually from thence 400 or 500 yards to an eminence fully as elevated as the hill on which Cobb's battery was placed. On the opposite [side] of and bordering on the river, 300 yards below the first-named ford, commences a belt of timber about 100 yards wide and extends nearly to the second bend of the river. Bounded on the south and west by the river, on the north by thick woods and partly on the east by a thicket, is a large field, or. rather, two fields, containing between 60 and 80 acres. The field

toward the south was covered with tall weeds, and upon an eminence in
it, about the height of the bluff on the opposite side, a battery was placed
and earthworks thrown up early Wednesday morning. About 400 yards
north of this in the other (a corn-field), was a mound considerably more
elevated, upon which Cobb's battery was placed and rifle-pits dug. North
of this was thick woods extending up to the river and down it about half
a mile to an old field cleared up to the river. Here the east bank was
high and rocky, but less elevated by 30 feet than the bluff on the opposite side. At the termination of this field was a piece of woodland of a
wedge shape, extending down the river about 300 yards and to within
a short distance of the ford. Separating the woodland and old field was
a rail fence running perpendicularly to the river. From this point to
the ford the ground gradually fell away, while the bluff on the opposite
side, though bare of timber, continued nearly the same elevation to the
ford.

Sunday, the 28th ultimo, the brigade commanded by the late brave
and lamented Brig. Gen. R. W. Hanson left the camp and took position
on a ridge opposite the upper ford.

Monday, the 29th, about 2 p. m., the Ninth and Sixth Kentucky and
Forty-first Alabama Regiments and Cobb's battery moved into the field
first described, Company A, under Capt. C. B. McClaskey, of this regiment, being thrown forward to the high mound, in connection with a
company from each of the other two regiments. Very soon thereafter
they became engaged with the enemy, when the regiments and battery
were moved forward to and occupied the mound, this regiment taking
position in a thicket 200 paces to the right, the Forty-first immediately
in rear, and Ninth to the left of the battery, the skirmishers having
taken position beyond in the corn-field. Afterward, about dusk, Company G, Capt. Gran Utterback commanding, was moved to the left of
Company A, but before getting into position the two companies were
attacked by a large force of the enemy and driven back over the brow
of the hill; but upon discovering the presence of the regiments the enemy
precipitately retreated across the river and made no further demonstration that night. The regiments and battery which, previous to the attack, had commenced to move, were then marched about 400 yards to the
rear, leaving our skirmishers in possession of the hill. Two men of Company G, and Lieutenant [J. B.] Holman, of Company E, were wounded
in this attack. Subsequently, during the night, this regiment again
moved forward near the line of skirmishers, and about daylight took
position in the thicket above described.

Tuesday (30th) this regiment continued in the same position, annoyed
considerably by sharpshooters and the enemy's batteries until nightfall,
when, being relieved by the Second Kentucky, it, except the two companies, moved 500 yards to the rear.

Wednesday (31st) the regiment about daylight occupied the belt of
woods before described, in order to watch the enemy on the bluff opposite and to protect the battery placed in the field that morning. We
remained here until 3 p. m., and then, exposed to a fire, moved across
the field to the rear of Cobb's battery, which was then under fire.
While in the woods we were constantly exposed to shells from the enemy, and at one time from our own batteries on our left, endeavoring,
by firing over us, to reach the enemy's battery farther down the river.
While here, 2 men of Company D, 1 of Company C, and 1 of Company
H were wounded.

Thursday (1st) the regiment remained in the vicinity of Cobb's battery.

Friday (2d) we occupied the same position till the afternoon, keeping
two companies forward as skirmishers. Captain [Gran] Utterback and

1 man were wounded, the former mortally, while daringly opposing the enemy's skirmishers. He was a brave man and faithful officer. About 3 p. m. the brigade, except the Ninth Regiment, left to protect the battery, moved by the right flank to within half a mile of the enemy posted in the strip of woods near the lower ford, which has heretofore been described. Here the line of battle parallel to the river was formed, this regiment being on the extreme left. When the forward movement commenced, impediments in front made it necessary for this regiment to move in rear of the Second Kentucky until open ground was reached, causing considerable effort to regain its right position. We were also afterward embarrassed by a pond of water and an impenetrable thicket, causing a movement by the right of companies to the first for a short distance. Besides all this, while the line of battle was at first parallel with the river, at the time of attack the left had been swung around, so that nearly a right angle was made with the stream. The line of battle was so much longer than the front of the position held by the enemy that it was impossible for the whole force to reach the place of attack simultaneously, and on that account several of the regiments overlapped, so that the Second Kentucky, although next to mine on the right, did not have the full space requisite, yet, as it was, its left, when swung around, rested near the bluff, precluding entirely a movement by this regiment any farther in line of battle. Nevertheless, I preserved the line of this regiment until the river was reached. Upon reaching the eminence that hid us at first from the enemy, they were discovered at the distance of 150 yards, posted behind the fence above referred to and in the woods. The order having been previously given by General Hanson, our forces opened fire upon them as soon as discovered, and, with a shout, moved briskly forward to the charge, driving the enemy precipitately from the fence down the river toward the ford. When our line reached the fence, the alternative for me was either to be left entirely in rear of our lines and out of the fight, or to move by the right flank along on the edge of and under the bluff down the river. The second I adopted unhesitatingly, and was carried out with such alacrity and bravery by my officers and men that they pursued the enemy to the ford and even across the river at the ford. On account of the want of space to maneuver, and the considerable change of direction that had to be made to face the enemy, as before stated, some confusion occurred after reaching the woods, and no line of battle was kept, and there was great danger from the fire of our own men. Following my regiment to the ford of the river as soon as my efforts to stop the firing of those in rear would allow me, I discovered a large body of the enemy just in rear behind the crest of the opposite bluff, advancing. A considerable number of men from the different regiments of the brigade had by this time posted themselves behind a picket fence, and were firing on both the advancing and retreating enemy. A large number of the Yankees were at the time sheltered behind the bank of the river, displaying the white flag. Brigadier-General Hanson, on account of his wound, not being at any time present on the left after the fight commenced, and knowing that what I supposed was the object of the attack had been obtained in driving the enemy out of the woods across the river, I did not hesitate to order the firing at that point to cease, with a view to form the men so as to meet the advancing re-enforcements, or to fall back in good order, which I feared would have to be done, for the high bluff on the other side of the river gave the enemy a fearful advantage of position in addition to that of numbers; besides, about midway the timber we were exposed to a murderous fire from their batteries. This

order of mine was for the other object of securing the prisoners spoken of above, who, to the number of at least 100, were captured and sent to the rear. Before any line could be formed, a heavy fire from partially concealed infantry and artillery, against which our firing availed little, was poured in the regiments; consequently it was impossible to restore perfect order.

I am satisfied that, so far as this regiment is concerned, and for it only have I a right to speak, the enemy paid more than double in numbers, though not one tithe in actual worth, for every one of my men struck. About one-third of my entire command was killed and wounded, though it is remarkable, and at the same time gratifying, that of the great number hurt so few are either killed or severely wounded. Companies G and B having previously been sent forward as skirmishers, were not with the regiment. Company B, however, crossed the river above, and behaved well, as I learn.

Accompanying this report, and as a part of it, is a list* of all the casualties since the battle commenced.

Where there was so much bravery, zeal, and good conduct displayed by officers and men of this regiment throughout, I dislike to discriminate. I cannot, however, forbear referring to the unflinching courage of Color-Sergeant Stotts, who carried the standard in the thickest of the fight until struck down, and to the daring and fidelity of Orderly Sergt. J. Beverly Lewis, of Company C, who seized the colors from the wounded Stotts, and with them rallied and encouraged the men until he fell. Both these brave men were left wounded on the field.

Adjt. Samuel H. Buchanan, with the chivalry that ever characterizes him in battle, when Lewis fell took the colors. There is no more faithful and attentive officer in camp or gallant man in action. Taking the colors from Adjutant Buchanan, I called for some one to bear them, when Private Adams, of Company D, promptly took and bravely bore them during the rest of the engagement.

Maj. W. L. Clarke behaved with coolness and bravery, though I can conscientiously say of every officer and man engaged in the action that he behaved worthy of the old senior of Kentuckians.

Fully one-half the regiment crossed the river through water waist-deep, and only fell back when driven by overwhelming numbers and certain capture threatened them.

The regiment left camp Sunday (28th) with 269 officers and men. By sickness, for want of shoes, and casualties, the actual number on Friday was 231 officers and men.

The whole number killed, wounded, and missing during the entire engagements was: Killed, 2; wounded, 66; missing, 10; total, 78.† Of those wounded, several were left on the field and at Murfreesborough, and, of the missing, I fear all are prisoners and some killed or wounded, for they had all crossed the river, and one of them, Lieut. E. P. Thompson—the last seen—he, with pistol, was firing on the advancing enemy. It is due to him to say that, detailed as commissary, he was not required to go into action, but he during that week discharged his duties as commissary, and, as an officer on the field, shared the hardships and dangers throughout.

Very respectfully,

JOS. H. LEWIS,
Colonel, Commanding Sixth Kentucky Volunteers.
Capt. T. E. Stake,
Asst. Adjt. Gen., Trabue's Brigade, Breckinridge's Division.

---

* Embodied in statement on p. 828.   † Nominal list on file

No. 246.

Report of Col. Thomas H. Hunt, Ninth Kentucky Infantry.

MANCHESTER, TENN., *January 11, 1863.*

COLONEL: In pursuance of your orders, under date 10th instant, I have the honor to make this my report of the part taken by the Ninth Kentucky Regiment in late series of engagements on Stone's River, in front of Murfreesborough, Tenn.

On Sunday, the 28th ultimo, Hanson's brigade moved from camp at 8 a. m., and was placed in line of battle on the left of the right wing of the army, the Ninth Regiment being on the left of the brigade, with its left resting near the ford on Stone's River that has been in use since the turnpike bridge was burned.

Nothing further of interest occurred until Monday, the 29th, about 3 p. m., when, under General Hanson's orders, I moved forward the Ninth and Sixth Kentucky and the Forty-first Alabama Regiments, with Cobb's Kentucky battery, and established them in prolongation of our line of battle on the left bank of the river.

By this time our cavalry had been driven in and the enemy's skirmishers began to show themselves. Under orders to occupy with this force a commanding position some 400 yards in advance, I threw out skirmishers, who were soon briskly engaged with those of the enemy. I moved forward the entire force in support of the skirmishers, and succeeded in establishing the battery in the desired position; but this was not accomplished without the loss of the services of two valuable officers—Lieutenants [A. J.] Beale and [O.] Kennard, of Company D; the former severely and the latter slightly wounded.

By this time it was dark, and the enemy with a regiment of infantry made a spirited effort to retake the position, rapidly driving in our skirmishers and approaching within a few yards of the battery. This attempt was frustrated by promptly advancing the Forty-first Alabama Regiment, and the enemy were driven off in confusion, leaving two of their dead on the field.

Our loss here amounted to not less than 10 wounded, falling on the Sixth Kentucky Regiment and Cobb's battery.

Just after this affair I received orders to fall back to the position I had first been advanced to, but I kept out a strong line of skirmishers.

About 3 o'clock Tuesday morning orders came to me to reoccupy the hill and hold it at all hazard, and I again took possession of it, and without opposition.

On Tuesday, the 30th, I was left with this command in charge of the position, which I endeavored to strengthen by throwing up some rifle-pits, which were constructed under the fire of sharpshooters, while the entire command was subjected to heavy artillery fire. I also kept out a strong line of skirmishers, who were constantly engaged. That night we were relieved by the Second and Fourth Kentucky Regiments, and retired to a position where the men could cook rations.

Daylight Wednesday morning found us in our old position, with the brigade reunited and General Hanson in command. This day, with part of the regiment in the pits and the balance held as supports for our artillery, now increased to twelve pieces, we were subjected to a terrible cannonade from the enemy, as well as to an annoying fire from their sharpshooters. In the afternoon the regiment was put in motion to unite in a charge on the enemy's left center, but the order was subsequently countermanded, and we resumed our original position.

It was now we had to deplore the loss of Adjt. Henry M. Curd, killed by a cannon ball; a gallant and meritorious officer, cheerful under all dangers and privations, and endeared to the command by his frank and manly bearing, who nobly fell in discharge of his duty. Capt. Joseph Desha was also struck by a cannon ball and carried off the field, as was supposed, in a dying condition; but he returned the same night with his wound tied up, and has since continued in command of his company.

Thursday the cannonading commenced early in the morning, but was not of long continuance, and, with the exception of some skirmishing, nothing occurred worthy of note.

Friday morning, with the exception of light skirmishing, all was quiet with us. In the afternoon, when the balance of the brigade was moved out to join in the attack on our right, the Ninth Regiment, with Cobb's battery, was ordered to remain and hold the position. We were then subjected to a tremendous shelling, fully as heavy as on any preceding day.

Saturday passed like Friday morning until nearly sundown, when the enemy made a formidable attack on the brigade posted on our left. My regiment was promptly placed in the rifle-pits, and there received some of the shell and ball intended for our neighbors. That night the retreat commenced, and the Ninth Kentucky and Forty-first Alabama Regiments, with Cobb's battery, were detached under my command as a rear guard on the Manchester pike; but the enemy not following closely, there is nothing of interest in this connection to report.

The severity of the weather and the character and long continuance of the struggle were such as to try the endurance of the troops. Nothing tests the courage more than to be subjected to long continued cannonading, and I am proud to say that the conduct of officers and men was worthy of all praise.

In addition to the officers already mentioned, Lieutenant [G.] Lewis, of Company A, and Lieutenant [H.] Buchanan, of Company H, were wounded.

I inclose a list,* furnished by Dr. [W. J.] Byrne, regimental surgeon, of killed and wounded, and showing the character of the wounds. By it will be seen the regiment lost in killed, 1 officer; wounded, 5 officers and 23 privates.

Respectfully submitting the above, I am, colonel, your obedient servant,

THOS. H. HUNT,
Colonel Ninth Kentucky Regiment.

Col. T. O'HARA,
Acting Assistant Adjutant-General.

No. 247.

Report of Capt. Robert Cobb, Kentucky battery.

CAMP NEAR TULLAHOMA, TENN.,
January 10, 1863.

SIR: I have the honor to submit the following report of the operations of my battery in the late engagements near Murfreesborough, Tenn.:

On Sunday, December 28, I moved with the brigade to the field, and

---

* Embodied in statement on p. 828.

during that day and part of the succeeding remained in park about 100 yards in rear of the first line formed by it.

On Monday, the 29th, at about 4 o'clock, the brigade having moved forward so as to occupy a hill in a corn-field overlooking Stone's River, and nearly opposite the right of Lieutenant-General Polk's line, my battery, under the direction of Maj. R. E. Graves, chief of artillery, was posted upon the crest of the hill, the enemy's pickets occupying the bank of the river in front of the position, and distant about 600 yards. Toward night the enemy was seen to strengthen his picket.

At about 7 p. m. they made a bold dash across the stream, driving in our pickets so rapidly that they had, under cover of the darkness at the time prevailing, advanced to within a few paces of my battery and delivered their fire before the supporting regiment (the Forty-first Alabama) could be brought up. As soon as this could be it was done, whereupon the enemy fell back, having wounded Corpl. J. P. Coleman, gunner of the left piece. The battery was then, by order of Col. T. H. Hunt, commanding the force on the hill, withdrawn to a point in an open field bordering on the river, where it remained until near daylight, when the hill was reoccupied and the battery posted in its original position. The battery remained in this position throughout the several engagements.

On Tuesday, at 8 or 9 a. m., the enemy advanced a column, supposed to be a brigade, to within about 700 yards of my position and on the opposite side of the river. I immediately opened the battery upon it and succeeded in repulsing it. This drew up on me the fire of two of the enemy's rifled batteries, one at a distance of 1,200 yards and the other at about 700 yards. Engaging with the latter, I succeeded in driving it beyond the range of my guns. This done, I withdrew the battery behind the crest of the hill, to protect it from the fire of the enemy's pieces, of much longer range than mine. Light earthworks were thrown up in front of the battery during the day.

At night I was relieved by two rifle pieces from Captain Lumsden's battery and two from Captain [C. H.] Slocomb's battery.

On Wednesday, the 31st, at an early hour, I resumed my position of Tuesday, the two sections above alluded to (to wit, section from Lumsden's battery, commanded by Lieutenant [E.] Tarrant, and the section from Slocomb's battery, commanded by Lieutenant Chalaron) remaining with me. During the day the battery, composed of my own and those two sections, was several times engaged, chiefly in support of General Polk's right, and, as subsequent inspection of the ground shows, with good effect.

Lieutenants Chalaron and Tarrant, as also Lieutenants [R. B.] Matthews and [B. A.] James, of my own battery, handled their guns with consummate skill and coolness, the two former with their rifle guns having succeeded several times in forcing the enemy to retire with their batteries behind the shelter of the ridges and heavy timber in our front.

During this day's engagement I had the misfortune to lose Corpl. J. F. Hawes, who had distinguished himself throughout by his courage and the great accuracy of his fire. He fell, while watching the effect of his shot. His loss is not easily repaired.

The battery was not engaged on Thursday, nor on Friday until very late in the afternoon, when, the enemy having deployed a large number of pieces to repel the attack made by General Breckinridge's division against their left, four shots were fired from Lieutenant Tarrant's section of rifled guns, which drove to the rear a distance of over 500 yards the two of the enemy's pieces fired at, being directly in my front, and drew upon me the fire of four or five of the other pieces to my right and front. This accomplished, the firing was not continued.

On Saturday the battery was not engaged, and Saturday night, having been so ordered by General Breckinridge, withdrew from the field as a part of the rear guard.

I have the honor to be, very respectfully, your obedient servant,

R. COBB,
Captain, Commanding Battery.

Capt. T. E. STAKE,
Assistant Adjutant-General.

No. 248.

Report of Brig. Gen. John K. Jackson, C. S. Army, commanding brigade.

HEADQUARTERS JACKSON'S BRIGADE,
January 22, 1863.

MAJOR: I have the honor to report that in the recent battles before Murfreesborough my brigade consisted of the Fifth and the Eighth Mississippi Regiments, the Fifth Georgia Regiment, a battalion of sharpshooters commanded by Maj. J. J. Cox, and [E. E.] Pritchard's battery. They were moved to various parts of the field, and at different times occupied positions in the front line, on the extreme right, on the left of the right wing, on the right of the left wing, and on the extreme left. Pritchard's battery, belonging to my brigade, being insufficiently manned, only two pieces were carried from Bridgeport to Murfreesborough. These, by order of Lieutenant-General Hardee, were left in the earthwork in the town of Murfreesborough, and were never brought into action. The two rifle pieces of Lumsden's battery, which had been ordered to report to me, were, by order of Lieutenant-General Hardee, subsequently ordered to report to Major-General Breckinridge, thus leaving me but two smooth-bore pieces of artillery of Lumsden's battery. These pieces were brought into action on Wednesday, December 31, [1862,] at long range, expending about 50 rounds of ammunition.

I am informed that the two rifle pieces were placed in position by orders from Major-General Breckinridge, and did good service, expending about 200 rounds of ammunition.

There were no casualties in the artillery of my command.

On the morning of December 31, while maneuvering in front of the enemy's left, I received an order to cross Stone's River at the ford and support Brigadier-General Donelson's brigade, reporting for this purpose to Lieutenant-General Polk. Upon doing so, I was directed to leave the two pieces of artillery and push forward with my infantry to a point indicated beyond the ruins of a house (Cowan's), where the battle was raging fiercely. I advanced, passing Brigadier-General Donelson's brigade, a part of Brigadier-General Chalmers' brigade, and a part of the brigade commanded by Colonel Coltart. My command became immediately engaged, and so continued for about three hours. Twice I ordered a charge upon the enemy's strong position, but for the want of support from others, and the smallness of my own numbers, was forced to take the cover of a thick cedar wood. Both times my men fell back in good order and were reformed in line, until they were ordered to retire from the want of ammunition. My command was not afterward brought into action, although frequently under fire, and most of the time in the front line of battle.

It becomes my duty to report the following officer and enlisted men who left the field without permission while their regiment was engaged, and who failed to return to duty when ordered by their commanding officer: The Eighth Mississippi Regiment—Company A, Privates S. G. Grissom, W. T. Meeks, S. J. Copeland; Company G, Private Josiah Walker; Company H, Private W. W. Ritchie; Company D, Corpl. A. T. Perryman; Company E, Private J. M. Tullos; Company K, Lieut. H. Matthis, Privates W. J. McGee, M. V. Shows.

On the other hand, it affords me pleasure to testify to the great coolness and courage of the officers and men of my command.

Col. John C. Wilkinson, of the Eighth Mississippi Regiment, was severely wounded in the breast, and sent to the hospital in Murfreesborough, where, upon retirement of the army, he was left, and it is apprehended he fell into the hands of the enemy, being too badly wounded to be removed. Lieut. Col. W. L. Sykes, commanding the Fifth Mississippi Regiment, was also severely wounded and sent to the rear. Col. W. T. Black, of the Fifth Georgia Regiment, fell, mortally wounded in the head, while gallantly leading his brave regiment; he survived but a few hours. The color-bearer of this regiment, Thomas J. Brantly, Company E, was killed by a minie ball passing through his head, whereupon First Lieut. J. W. Eason, of Company G, seized the colors and was instantly killed by a shot through the head. I have to lament among the gallant slain Capt. J. H. Morgan, of the Fifth Mississippi Regiment, and Capt. E. W. Ansley, of the battalion of sharpshooters.

I bear willing testimony to the gallantry of Maj. J. J. Cox, of the battalion of sharpshooters, and ask especial attention to his accompanying report,* mentioning the names of certain officers and men of other commands who joined his battalion and remained with it during the engagement.

I am much indebted to the officers of my staff for their promptness in conveying orders and for their general efficiency in the discharge of their duty on the field. Capt. J. B. Cumming, assistant adjutant-general, and Lieut. A. M. Jackson, aide-de camp, each had his horse disabled. I desire also to make favorable mention of Capt. Thomas G. Barrett, volunteer aide-de-camp, and Lieut. S. A. Moreno, C. S. Army, acting inspector-general of my brigade. I have already made a special recommendation of the last named officer for promotion, and take occasion to renew and urge it.

I inclose reports in detail from regimental, battalion, and battery commanders; a consolidated report* of killed and wounded by name has already been forwarded.

The annexed tabular statement is made a part of this report, from which it will appear that there were 874 infantry, including details for infirmary purposes, &c., carried into action, of which there were 41 killed and 266 wounded and none missing.

I have the honor to be, very respectfully, your obedient servant,

JOHN K. JACKSON,
Brigadier-General.

Maj. T. B. ROY,
Assistant Adjutant-General.

---

* Not found.

[Inclosure.]

Report of the brigade commanded by Brig. Gen. John K. Jackson at the battle before Murfreesborough on December 31, 1862.

| Command. | Carried into action. | | | Casualties. | | | | |
| | | | | Killed. | | Wounded. | | |
	Officers.	Men.	Aggregate.	Officers.	Men.	Officers.	Men.	Aggregate.
5th Georgia	27	146	173	2	9	4	49	64
5th Mississippi	20	150	170	1	5	7	66	79
8th Mississippi	27	255	282	1	19	12	101	133
2d Georgia Battalion Sharpshooters	13	139	152		4	3	24	31
Lumsden's battery	2	95	97					
Total	89	785	874	4	37	26	240	307

No. 249.

Report of Maj. Charles P. Daniel, Fifth Georgia Infantry.

CAMP MORGAN, ALA., *January* 10, 1863.

CAPTAIN: In conformity with General Orders, No. 71, Headquarters Jackson's Brigade, January 9, 1863, I have the honor to submit the following report:

Col. William T. Black, commanding in the late fight at Murfreesborough, while bravely and gallantly leading his regiment on the center of the enemy, fell, shot with a minie ball on the left side of the head near the top, about 1 p. m., December 31, 1862, and died at 10 p. m. same day.

*   *   *   *   *   *   *

The above casualties* occurred between the hours of 12 m. and 3 p. m., December 31, 1862, in the battle before Murfreesborough, in attacking the left center of the enemy, who were very strongly and advantageously posted.

From the information I can get, I am proud to say that my command acted very bravely and gallantly, no shirking or straggling, but every man gallantly doing his duty.

I am, very respectfully, your obedient servant,

C. P. DANIEL,
Major, Commanding.

Capt. Jos. B. CUMMING,
Assistant Adjutant-General, Jackson's Brigade.

No. 250.

Reports of Maj. Jesse J. Cox, Second Georgia Battalion Sharpshooters.

BRIDGEPORT, ALA., *January* 10, 1863.

CAPTAIN: In compliance with General Orders, No. 71, Headquarters Jackson's Brigade, January 9, 1863, I have the honor to report as follows:

My command went into action (on the center) at 12 m., on December

---

*Embodied in table above.

31, [1862,] and were withdrawn at about 3 p. m., during the whole of which time they were under a heavy fire from the enemy. After taking our position, we fought them one hour (silencing their infantry fire), at which time we received orders to fall back on the brigade. I am proud to say that my men were very calm, and obeyed every order promptly. My color-bearer and 2 privates killed; 27 officers and men wounded.

The casualties* are as follows: Killed—non-commissioned officers and privates, 3.   Wounded—commissioned officers, 3; non-commissioned officers and privates, 24.   Total, 30.

On Friday, January 2, on the extreme left, while skirmishing with the enemy in front of our brigade, Private Harvey Teat, of Company B, was severely wounded in the thigh.

I also take pleasure in mentioning the names of the following officers and men of different commands that remained with us during the engagement on Wednesday:

Captain [B. F.] Moss, Company E, Eighth Mississippi Regiment, bore colors of his regiment with our battalion; Capt. S. E. Melson, Company F, Forty-first Mississippi Regiment; Captain [R. E. V.] Yates, Company D, Forty-first Mississippi Regiment; Corpl. J. A. Allen, Company A, Forty-first Mississippi Regiment; Private F. E. Johnson, Company A, Forty-first Mississippi Regiment (wounded); Privates A. Sanders, Thomas [S.] Patterson, John Moore, Company F, Forty-first Mississippi Regiment; Lieut. A. T. Calhoun and Private T. L. Ribero, of Captain [John F.] Iverson's company, Fifth Georgia Regiment.

All of which is respectfully submitted.

J. J. COX,
Major, Comdg. [Second Georgia] Battalion Sharpshooters.

—

CHATTANOOGA, TENN., January 20, 1863.

CAPTAIN: In obedience to orders of this date, I have the honor to state that the battalion had engaged in the battle of December 31, [1862,] before Murfreesborough, viz, 13 commissioned officers, 30 non-commissioned officers, and 109 privates.

Very respectfully, your obedient servant,

J. J. COX,
Major, Comdg. [Second Georgia] Battalion Sharpshooters.

Capt. JOS. B. CUMMING, Assistant Adjutant-General.

—

No. 251.

Report of Lieut. Col. A. McNeill, Eighth Mississippi Infantry.

—— —, 1863.

*   *   *   *   *   *   *

The above report† is as accurate as can at present be obtained. The regiment entered the engagement with an aggregate of about 270, and the above list of casualties shows that near half of those who went into action were either killed or wounded.

The regiment became engaged on Wednesday, December 31, 1862, about 12 m., and nobly withstood a most murderous fire of shell and shot until about 3 p. m., at which time they were ordered to withdraw.

---

* Nominal list omitted.

† Nominal list of casualties, omitted, is embodied in statement on p. 840.

It formed the extreme right of the brigade line of battle, and is supposed to have fronted the enemy's center at that time. The above casualties all occurred in the cedar grove occupied by the brigade during the fight on Wednesday, and between the hours of 12 m. and 3 p. m. After Colonel Wilkinson was wounded (which was in the early part of the action), the undersigned assumed command of the regiment, and takes great pleasure in testifying to the cool courage and veteran-like heroism with which they bore the terrific fire of shell and shot that was poured almost incessantly into their ranks for near three hours. Indeed, both officers and men as a whole behaved most gallantly. The conduct of those who are reported as deserving censure is thought generally to merit unmeasured disapprobation. An explanation is forwarded in the case of Private J. Walker, of Company G. As he is very young, his conduct is thought to be somewhat excusable. He returned and served with the regiment during the balance of the time, while the others returned, most of them, to the camp at town, and refused to come back, although repeatedly ordered to do so.

All of which is respectfully submitted.

A. McNEILL,
Lieutenant-Colonel, Comdg. Eighth Mississippi Regiment.

No. 252.

Report of Lieut. Harvey H. Cribbs, Lumsden's (Alabama) battery.

BRIDGEPORT, ALA., *January 10, 1863.*

CAPTAIN: I have the honor to report that on Sunday, December 28, 1862, I was ordered to report for duty with Brigadier-General Jackson's brigade, by Lieutenant-Colonel [J. H.] Hallonquist, chief of artillery Army of Tennessee, and on Monday morning the general assigned me a position near Captain Spence's residence, east of the Lebanon pike, and at 12 midnight I received an order to send the two rifled pieces of the battery to General Breckinridge's headquarters to report, which I did, under the command of Lieutenant Tarrant. He was ordered to the knoll on the east side of Stone's River, which position was ordered by General Bragg to be held, as it was a desirable position, from which place the two guns fired 200 rounds in the first of the engagement. One of the pieces had been dismounted at Perryville some time ago, and in the recoil the axle-tree gave way. It was replaced by one of the pieces taken from the enemy. The two rifled pieces were held in the reserve until we reached the river. The smooth-bore was kept with the brigade, and on Tuesday about noon I moved with the brigade to a position on the left of the Lebanon pike and 1 mile nearer the river.

On Wednesday about noon the section accompanied the brigade across Stone's River, when it was halted by General Jackson until it could secure a position while the brigade advanced. When the brigade became engaged, the section took a position on the hill near Cowan's house, and near the railroad, and fired 50 rounds, when the enemy removed the battery at which we had been firing, and night coming on, I moved down to the river, and on Thursday took a position again on the right, where intrenchments were thrown up.

On Friday I joined the brigade on the extreme left near the Wilsonville [Wilkinson or Nashville] pike, and at 12 [o'clock] that night moved to the Nashville pike, where the men remained until daylight exposed to-a drenching rain, after which we moved to the extreme right again, and at midnight Saturday we moved through Murfreesborough to the Nashville pike, marched until Sunday evening, exposed again to the severity of the weather.

The damage done by the firing of the battery—I cannot say what damage was done to the enemy; it is said that one of the rifled pieces blew up a caisson. I am happy to say that no damage whatever was done to the battery by the shots of the enemy. The men all behaved with coolness, and with a determination to do what was in their power to drive back the enemy of our country.

Respectfully submitted.

HARVEY H. CRIBBS,

First Lieutenant, Commanding Lumsden's Battery.

No. 253.

Report of Maj. Gen. Patrick R. Cleburne, C. S. Army, commanding division.

HEADQUARTERS CLEBURNE'S DIVISION,
HARDEE'S CORPS, ARMY OF TENNESSEE,
Tullahoma, Tenn., January 31, 1863.

On December 26, 1862, three brigades of my division were stationed at College Grove, near Eaglesville, about 20 miles west of Murfreesborough. The Fourth Brigade, under command of Brig. Gen. S. A. M. Wood, was stationed at Triune, 4 miles north of College Grove, on the Nashville and Shelbyville turnpike.

On the evening of the same day I had information that the enemy had driven back the cavalry and occupied Nolensville, in my front.

During the night I received orders from General Hardee, who had gone in person to the front, to have everything in readiness for a movement and to be prepared for any emergency. I also received instructions as to the roads to be taken by my train and fighting force, respectively, in case of a retreat on Murfreesborough.

Early on the morning of the 27th, I received orders from the same source to take up a position on the turnpike about 1 mile north of my encampment. While making this disposition, I received orders from General Hardee to move the three brigades with me to Murfreesborough by the routes previously decided upon; also that Wood's brigade would remain at Triune and assist General Wharton's cavalry to retard the farther advance of the enemy.

For the proceedings of Wood's brigade under this order, I respectfully refer you to the report of Brig. Gen. S. A. M. Wood, herewith transmitted.

I immediately moved as directed; marched all day, part of it over a miserable road and through a cold, drenching rain, and encamped after nightfall on the Salem turnpike, within 1 mile of Stone's River.

On the morning of the 28th, General Hardee ordered me to form line of battle north of Murfreesborough and east of Stone's River, my line to face north, its left resting on the river, its right near the Lebanon turnpike, 800 or 1,000 yards in rear of a line already occupied by Breckinridge's division.

Wood's brigade, falling back slowly before General McCook's army corps, impeding his advance wherever opportunity offered, finally reached Stone's River and rejoined the division on the morning of the 29th.

I lay, inactive, in line of battle until the evening of the 30th, when I received orders to move from the right to the left of the army. Arriving at the fording place on Stone's River, I received orders to remain there until General Hardee had examined the ground and determined my position. It was dark when staff officers were sent to order me forward and show me my position. The passage of the river in the night was attended with many difficulties, and my whole division was not in position before midnight. As well as I could judge from the camp-fires, my line was a prolongation to the left of Cheatham's line, and was 400 or 500 yards in rear of McCown's division.

Soon after midnight I received an order from General Hardee, on which I based and issued the following circular, viz:

Generals of brigades will have their respective commands in readiness to move upon the enemy at 4.30 o'clock this morning. The several commands will fall into line without signal of bugle or drum.

Before daylight I formed line, placing Polk's brigade, with Calvert's battery, on the right; Johnson's brigade, with Darden's battery, in the center, and Liddell's brigade, with the Warren Light Artillery, commanded by Lieutenant [H.] Shannon, on the left. Wood's brigade I placed a short distance in rear of Polk's. This brigade had no battery in the fight, its battery (Semple's, of six Napoleon guns) having been detached the day before to support Hanson's brigade, of Breckinridge's division, and having remained with that brigade on the right of the army.

On account of the absence on duty of my chief of artillery, I ordered my chief of ordnance (Captain [T. R.] Hotchkiss) to act as chief of artillery, and Robert [D.] Smith, ordnance officer of Polk's brigade, to act as division ordnance officer.

It was not yet clear day when I received orders from General Hardee to advance. Swinging to the right as I moved forward, I rapidly communicated these instructions to brigade commanders, caused my division to load, and moved forward, stepping short upon the right and full upon the left, so as to swing round my left as directed. General Cheatham's left did not move forward at the same moment as my right, and my division, inclining to the left as it advanced, a gap was soon left between us, which General Hardee directed General Wood's brigade to fill. My whole division (Semple's battery excepted) was now advancing in line of battle, gradually wheeling to the right as it advanced. My left had not moved half a mile when heavy firing commenced near its front, supposed to be McCown's division engaging the enemy. A few moments more, and the enemy's skirmishers opened fire along the right and left center of my division, indicating that instead of being a second line supporting McCown's division, I was, in reality, the foremost line on this part of the field, and that McCown's line had unaccountably disappeared from my front. Skirmishers were immediately thrown forward, and I pressed on, continuing the difficult wheel under fire, through a country cut up with numerous fences and thickets. There was a great deal of crowding and improper opening out in the center of my line. Polk's and Johnson's brigades had to be moved by the flank more than once to regain their true positions. Driving back the enemy's skirmishers in the face of a heavy fire of shot and shell, I encountered his first solid line of battle at an average distance of three-fourths of a mile from the scene of my bivouac of last night. The left of this line (opposite Wood's and Polk's brigades) stretched through a large cedar brake; the right (opposite Liddell's and Johnson's) through open ground. In many parts of the brake the enemy found natural breastworks of limestone rock. In the open ground he covered most of his line behind a string of fence. Opposite my left, where the ground was open, a second line of the enemy, supported by artillery, could be seen a short distance in rear of his first. Here was my first important fight of the day. It extended along my whole line, and was participated in by McNair's brigade, of McCown's division, which had been placed on my left, and which a few moments before had surprised and driven the enemy from the ground over which my left had passed. The fight was short and bloody, lasting about twenty-five minutes, when the enemy gave way, both in the cedars and open ground, and fled back on his second line, which was immediately encountered in the woods, pastures, and open ground in rear of his former position. His second line soon gave way, and both went off together. My first fight may be said to have ended here. Its results were important.

The Eighth Arkansas, of Liddell's brigade, captured two stand of colors. They were handed to Colonel [John H.] Kelly on the field by Private James Riddle, of Company C, and Corpl. N. A. Horn, of Company E. In the rapid pursuit which followed, Colonel Kelly could not carry them ; they were left on the field, and, I fear, appropriated by some person who had no title to them.

The Second Arkansas [Infantry], of Liddell's brigade, again encountered and defeated the Twenty-second Indiana (the same regiment it had so severely handled at the battle of Perryville), wounding and capturing its lieutenant-colonel. This brigade also captured two rifled cannon, with suitable ammunition ; these Lieutenant Shannon added to his battery, and used on the enemy at subsequent periods of the battle. In Johnson's brigade, the Seventeenth Tennessee charged and captured a battery of four guns. In Wood's brigade, the Sixteenth Alabama wounded and captured the colonel and killed the lieutenant-colonel and major of the One hundred and first Ohio. My losses were very severe, especially on my left wing, where Johnson's and Liddell's brigades suffered more than in all the subsequent fighting of the day. In Johnson's brigade, Colonel [A. S.] Marks, of the Seventeenth Tennessee (one of the best officers in the division), was severely wounded. Major [H. C.] Ewin, Forty-fourth Tennessee, was mortally wounded. Colonel [Moses] White and Lieutenant-Colonel [R. D.] Frayser, Thirty-seventh Tennessee, were wounded. Colonel [J. M.] Hughs, Twenty-fifth Tennessee, was wounded. In Polk's brigade, Majors [C. H.] Carlton and [R. A.] Duncan, Fifteenth and Thirteenth Arkansas, were wounded. In Wood's brigade, Lieutenant-Colonel [A. H.] Helvenston and Major [J. H.] McGaughy, Sixteenth Alabama, were wounded. In all, nine field officers, and a proportionate number of company officers, non-commissioned officers, and privates were killed or wounded in this fight.

My division was now engaged in a rapid, but not very orderly, pursuit of the enemy, which was continued until a fresh line of his infantry and artillery came in view. This line was drawn up on the south side of, and parallel to, the Wilkinson turnpike, its right resting in open woods, its left in open fields. It checked or pushed back portions of my command, which, in the ardor of pursuit, had advanced beyond the general line. My whole division (the right of Johnson's brigade, which had delayed to replenish its ammunition, excepted) again engaged the enemy. Advancing steadily in the face of a heavy fire of infantry and artillery, Liddell's brigade, and the Seventeenth Tennessee, of Johnson's brigade, drove back the enemy's right. Wood's and Polk's brigades encountered a more obstinate and protracted resistance to the open fields where they fought; but here, too, success again rewarded the bravery of my men. The enemy were driven across the Wilkinson pike, and took refuge in the woods and heavy cedar brake on the north side. In this fight I captured 2 hospitals, nearly 1,000 prisoners, a train of ammunition wagons, 1 piece of artillery, 3 or 4 caissons, and 2 wagons loaded with medical stores. The Federal General [J. W.] Sill was killed near one of the hospitals. The Seventeenth Tennessee, of Johnson's brigade, and the Second A;kansas, of Liddell's brigade, contend for the honor of having first captured the hospital and killed General Sill.

My line was now far advanced beyond that of Withers and Cheatham. I began to discover from the firing that I was getting in rear of the right flank of the enemy's center. My right wing and left center were exposed to a heavy enfilading fire as they crossed the open ground near the turnpike from a powerful battery planted near the north side of the pike. Captain Hotchkiss, acting chief of artillery, placed Darden's and [J. H.] Calvert's batteries in position, and boldly attacked the Parrott and rifled artillery of the enemy. Wood's brigade having moved back to get a fresh supply of ammunition, Brigadier-General Polk moved forward, but was forced by the enfilading fire to change front forward on his first battalion, so as to place his line at right angles to the pike and facing eastwardly. This done, he advanced and attacked the supports of the battery, while Hotchkiss, though greatly overmatched in number and caliber of guns, continued to fire on them. The enemy abandoned the position, leaving several pieces of artillery, The Fifth Confederate and First Arkansas passed through and beyond these guns, and fairly deserve the honor of having captured them. Colonel [P. B.] Hawkins, of the Eleventh Kentucky, commanding a Federal brigade, was killed by the First Arkansas [Infantry] during this fight. Relieved of the enfilading fire, Brigadier-General Polk again changed front and resumed his original line of advance.

In the mean time Wood's brigade had come up and been ordered by me to the left of Polk's brigade. Johnson's brigade had also come up, and, like Polk's, had been forced by the enfilading fire to change front. I had ordered Brigadier-General Johnson to throw forward a strong company of sharpshooters and advance on the battery to Polk's assistance; but just at this time the firing ceased, and I discovered the enemy had been driven back, as before stated. I then changed the direction of Johnson's advance to correspond with Polk's, and moved his brigade on the right of Polk's, whose guns were again heard in conflict with the enemy. On examination, I found the enemy had made another stand in a heavy cedar brake north of the Wilkinson pike, and in front of where my right crossed it. He had again found natural breastworks of limestone rock, and covered most of his line behind them. He made an obstinate and destructive resistance, during which Polk's brigade suffered a severe repulse; but he was finally dislodged and driven from the cedars. Toward the close of this fight, Smith's brigade, of Cheatham's division, under command of Colonel [A. J.] Vaughan, [jr.,] came up on my left and rendered us material assistance.

In this fight Sergeant Lovin, of the Third Confederate Regiment, of Wood's brigade, captured a stand of colors, which I herewith transmit. Lieut. Col. Don McGregor, of the First Arkansas, fell mortally wounded, and Major [J. T.] McReynolds, the last field officer of the Thirty-seventh Tennessee, was mortally wounded.

The commanding officers of Brigadier-General Wood's regiments again reported their ammunition expended; he moved the brigade in rear of the Wilkinson pike to procure a supply. While there information reached

General Hardee that the enemy was threatening our left flank, and he ordered Wood's brigade to remain in the rear and protect the trains. This was the smallest brigade I had, numbering on the morning of the fight not over 1,100 officers and men. It was without a battery, as before explained; was on the extreme right of my line (the most exposed position) up to the time of crossing the pike, and at this time did not number 500.

The enemy was now driven out of the cedars in our front, but to the right of my division he still remained undisturbed, and as I again attempted to advance I found myself flanked on the right and again exposed to an enfilading fire. I therefore determined to advance on a line farther to the left, and where my right flank would not be so fearfully exposed. With this view, I ordered General Johnson to move his brigade to the left, where Liddell's brigade would again connect with him.

But here it would be proper to give a statement of the doings of Liddell's brigade since last mentioned as having driven back a line of the enemy on the south side of the Wilkinson pike. While my other brigades inclined to the right, as stated, Brigadier-General Liddell moved diagonally to the left for a considerable distance through open woods. He met the enemy on the far edge of these woods and drove him over the crest of the high ground beyond. Throwing forward skirmishers, it was found he had made another stand in the valley of Overall's Creek, 400 or 500 yards beyond the crest. Liddell moved his battery to the crest and drove him back until he disappeared from view behind the embankment of the Nashville railroad. From the high point where his battery now was, Liddell was in full view of the Nashville turnpike and the enemy's trains. He opened with his artillery on one portion of the train, while General Wharton, with the cavalry, charged another. The trains disappeared in haste and confusion. At this time Liddell's brigade was the extreme left of the infantry of the army, and there was a gap of three-quarters of a mile between his right and the left of the other portion of the division. I determined to unite the division opposite this gap and advance. I ordered Johnson to move on the left of Polk's brigade, and at the same time sent orders to Brigadier-General Liddell to move his brigade by the right flank until he had reconnected with Johnson's brigade.

While these commands were being executed, I met a brigade of McCown's division retreating in great disorder. I think this brigade must have attempted to advance through the gap in my division and been repulsed.

By moving inward and uniting in the gap mentioned, my division again advanced on a line midway between the diverging lines which the two portions had before pursued. I advanced with four brigades, disposed as follows: Polk's brigade on the right, Liddell's on the left, Smith's brigade, of Cheatham's division, the right center, Johnson's the left center. I had not moved 100 yards when Liddell's brigade became hotly engaged with a line of the enemy drawn up across a neck of woods and prolonged into the fields on each side. This, I think, was a continuation to the left of the same line which my other brigades had defeated farther to the right, or it may have been the line which had caused the repulse of McCown's division (just mentioned) and which was pursuing. However this be, Liddell met the enemy here in force and engaged in the most obstinately contested and (to the enemy) most destructive fight which had yet occurred. Not until Liddell had closed within 25 paces of him would the portion of his line in the woods give way.

Colonel Kelly, of the Eighth Arkansas, and Colonel [S. G.] Smith, of the Sixth and Seventh Arkansas, were wounded here.

Lieutenant Colonel [John E.] Murray, of the Fifth Arkansas, bore the colors of his regiment through the hottest of the fight, and by his own bright example encouraged his men to despise danger.

J. K. Leslie, a brave and intelligent private of Company C, of this regiment, captured a beautiful stand of colors belonging to one of the enemy's regiments of regulars. This flag I also herewith transmit.

The enemy gave way and fled, leaving a large number of dead behind him. Johnson's, Smith's, and Polk's brigades moved rapidly in pursuit, obliquing to the left as they advanced. Liddell rapidly reformed his line and followed, *en échelon*, about 100 yards in rear of Johnson. My orders, frequently received from General Hardee during the day, being to push the enemy, and, if possible, give him no time to rally or select positions, I did not halt the division or lose any time in rectifying distances or alignments. The line had not advanced a quarter of a mile when a fresh line of the enemy was discovered in open fields. He was supported by numerous and well-served batteries. At this time I had but one battery (Liddell's). Polk's could not follow through the heavy woods and Johnson's had been ordered by General Hardee to remain in reserve near the Wilkinson pike. My line advanced steadily, pouring in a deadly fire, and drove the enemy across a small dirt road. That portion of his line opposite Johnson rallied behind a fence on the far side of the dirt road, but was driven from there also, when his whole line disappeared in the cedar woods, which here border the Nashville pike, and were close behind him. Still another line of the enemy showed itself on the edge of these cedars. A heavy fire of small-arms was immediately directed upon him. He fled back in the woods, leaving the ground in front of Johnson's brigade thickly covered with dead and wounded. Following up their success, our men gained the edge of the cedars—Johnson's brigade capturing a battery of Parrott guns—and were almost on the Nashville turnpike, in rear of the original center of Rosecrans' army, sweeping with their fire his only line of communication with Nashville; but it was now after 3 o'clock; my men had had little or no rest the night before; they had been fighting since dawn, without relief, food, or water; they were comparatively without the support of artillery, for the advance had been too rapid to enable my single battery to get in position and answer the enemy; their ammunition was again nearly exhausted, and our ordnance trains could not follow.

At this critical moment the enemy met my thinned ranks with another fresh line of battle, supported by a heavier and closer artillery fire than I had yet encountered. A report also spread, which I believe was true, that we were flanked on the right. This was more than our men could stand. Smith's brigade was driven back in great confusion. Polk's and Johnson's followed. As our broken ranks went back over the fields before the fire of this fresh line, the enemy opened fire on our right flank from several batteries which they had concentrated on an eminence near the railroad, inflicting a heavier loss on Polk's brigade than it had suffered in all the previous fighting of the day. The division was rallied on the edge of the opposite woods, about 400 yards in rear of the scene of disaster, though some of the men could not be stopped until they reached the Wilkinson pike. Liddell's brigade, *en échelon* on my extreme left, was not engaged in this last fight and was moved back in good order to the line where the other brigades rallied. Here I reformed my division as rapidly as possible, Polk's brigade on the right, Johnson's in the center, and Liddell's on the left. A fresh supply of ammunition was served out, and I waited in momentary expectation for an advance of the enemy in overwhelming force. He never advanced a foot, and the question presented itself, Ought I to again advance? I was now in possession of 3 miles of ground conquered from the enemy, large numbers of prisoners, cannon, and small-arms. Another repulse, and I might lose all these and cause the demoralization and destruction of my division. I immediately reported the situation to General Hardee, and was ordered by him to hold the ground I had won, rest, and reorganize my division and await further orders. Pushing my pickets well forward, I bivouacked in line of battle on the same line which the division rallied on after the repulse.

On the morning of January 1, there were rumors that the enemy was retreating. I was ordered by General Hardee to push forward, feel the enemy, and ascertain the true state of affairs in our front. Liddell's brigade was moved forward and to the left, and drove the enemy's skirmishers back at least a quarter of a mile, and beyond a white house used as a Federal hospital, and situated on the small dirt road near which our last fight of the day before occurred.

During this fight Lieutenant-Colonel [F. J.] Cameron, Sixth and Seventh Arkansas Regiment, was wounded.

Liddell again swept the Nashville turnpike with his artillery, and greatly disturbed the enemy's trains, which could be seen on and near it. Receiving another message from General Hardee to the effect that he had ordered me to feel the enemy, and could not hear my guns, and at the same time receiving information from General Liddell that he was in line of battle near the hospital just mentioned, and needed immediate support on his right, I ordered General Wood to move his brigade forward cautiously, and support Liddell on the right, but I also informed him that the object was merely to ascertain whether the enemy was still in force in our front, not to bring on a general battle. Wood's brigade moved forward, and I moved Johnson's skirmishers forward en échelon on Wood's right flank, so as to protect him as much as possible. Wood's brigade formed line close to the dirt road last mentioned, and immediately became hotly engaged with a very large force of the enemy, which advanced on him out of the cedars where our repulse of the day before occurred. He found that Liddell was not on his left, as expected, having previously fallen back; he also discovered that the enemy were flanking him on the left with another heavy force. At this time he received an order direct from General Hardee not to bring on a general battle. He ceased firing and fell back, leaving several killed and wounded on the ground. Some of the men of the Forty-fifth Mississippi Regiment had gone so far ahead that retreat was impossible; they remained where they were, and fell into the hands of the enemy. Wood must have lost nearly 100 in killed, wounded, and prisoners in this fight. It was now clear the enemy was still in force in my front, and I so reported it.

On Friday morning, January 2, I was satisfied that the enemy was fortifying his position. On consultation with my brigade commanders, I addressed a note to General Hardee, which I requested him to forward to General Bragg, stating this important fact, and that I feared, if my single, and now reduced, line was pushed on the enemy in his fortified position, the result would prove very disastrous, but that I believed I could hold a defensible position against any assault of the enemy.

Semple's battery rejoined me on the 1st. On the 2d, Friday evening, I was ordered to send four of his guns to support an attack about to be made by Major-General Breckinridge's division. My acting chief of artillery, Captain Hotchkiss, having been twice wounded while gallantly discharging his duty, I ordered him to quit the field (which he reluctantly did) and directed Captain Semple to act as chief of artillery. Captain Semple sent four of his 12-pounders, under Lieutenant [E. J.] Fitzpatrick, to General Breckinridge's division. In the desperate conflict which took place on the right that evening, this battery bore a conspicuous part. Out of 45 men and officers, 20 were killed and wounded; among them Lieut. Joseph Pollard, who is represented as having fought most bravely, and only yielded when his leg and arm were both broken; 14 horses were killed and wounded, and one piece of artillery was lost. For details of the noble conduct of this battery in the fight, I refer you to the report of Captain Semple, herewith sent.

About 11 o'clock that night the enemy made a reconnaissance in force in front of my division; he was driven back by my skirmishers. Immediately afterward I received orders to withdraw my pickets and resume the position held by me on the morning of December 30, on the right of the army, in rear of Breckinridge's division. Here I remained, enduring the incessant cold rain of that night and next day, until 11 p. m. of the 3d, when I commenced retreating on Manchester.

After the battles of Wednesday, I collected a large number of guns and sent them to General Bragg's chief of ordnance. I also got several artillery horses, with which I replaced most of the disabled horses in my batteries; also a large quantity of artillery ammunition, harness, and other articles necessary in batteries.

To the courage and patriotism of the officers and men, the good discipline which existed among them, and the unexpected suddenness of the attack, are alone due the success which attended my advance upon the enemy's right. With the exception of the wheel of my division, directed by General Hardee, on the morning of the great battle, there was no strategic movement attempted. It was one determined charge, sometimes checked, and even repulsed, by the enemy; sometimes delayed to procure a fresh supply of ammunition, but ever renewed and successful, until McCook's Federal corps of 18,000 men, composing the right wing of Rosecrans' army, had been swept away, and two or three lines of his successors had shared the same fate.

To Brigadier-Generals Johnson, Wood, and Polk, and Colonel Vaughan, commanding Smith's brigade, of Cheatham's division, the country is indebted for their great exertions on this occasion. Brigadier-General Liddell led his brigade with a skill, courage, and devotion which, I believe, saved my left flank from being turned by the enemy.

I found the following officers of my staff very efficient in this battle; they were at their posts all the time, and discharged their difficult duties with a courage, promptness, and intelligence not often equaled, viz: Col. W. W. Kirkland, chief of staff; Maj. Calhoun Benham, assistant inspector-general; Capt. Irving A. Buck, assistant adjutant-general; Lieuts. J. W. Jetton and J. K. Dixon (the latter was wounded); Capt. T. R. Hotchkiss (wounded); John M. Johnson, chief surgeon; Surg. J. H. Erskine, chief inspector. Dr. Johnson showed the same zeal, courage, and energy in this battle which has distinguished him on every other occasion, and made me feel that my division was very fortunate in having secured his services.

In addition to the officers and men already mentioned in my report, the following officers and men have been brought to my notice for distinguished services on the field. I hope it will be considered no disparagement of the services of other brave men of my division, some of whom laid down their lives or lost limbs on this field, if their gallant deeds have been overlooked in this report.

In Wood's brigade I must specially mention the following officers and men of the Sixteenth Alabama, viz: Col. W. B. Wood and Adjt. B. A. Wilson (wounded); Captain [William] Hodges, Company F; Lieutenant [C.] Davis, Company B; Lieutenant [G. W. W.] Jones, Company G; Lieutenant [G.] Pride, Company A; Lieutenant [C. F.] Carson, Company C, who remained fighting after he was wounded; Lieutenant [D. O.] Warren, Company F; Lieutenant [Thomas J.] Salter, Company D, who was wounded, but returned to the field the moment his wound was dressed; Sergt. Maj. Robert H. Cherry and Private Harvey G. Sargent, of Company H; Privates William Boyce and James Peeden, of Company C; Sergeant Bowen, Company H; Sergt. H. W. Rutland, Company A; Privates Peter White, Company F; Robert Williams, Company B, and H. D. Smith, Company A; the latter, wounded in both legs, deserves promotion. In the Forty-fifth Mississippi: Lieutenant-Colonel [R.] Charlton, Major [E. F.] Nunn, Adjt. Frank Foster, jr., Sergeants Asberry, Doolittle, Morrison, Vaughan, Stewart, Lieut. G. W. Williams, Sergeant-Major Kern, Corporals Mallett, Hackler, and Read, and Private McChadin. Corporal Read volunteered to carry the colors after the color-bearer had been shot down. He is well qualified as an officer, and ought to be promoted. In the Thirty-third Alabama: Colonel [Samuel] Adams, Captains [W. E.] Dodson and Thomas Seay (severely wounded, in advance), Sergeant-Major Mizell (mortally wounded), Corpl. Isaac R. Smith, Company C; Sergeant Stewart, Company H; Privates Byrd, Company I; Foster, Company E, and Riley, Company D. In the Third Confederate: Major [J. F.] Cameron. Wood's Sharpshooters: Captain [A. T.] Hawkins.

Polk's Brigade.—In Fifth Confederate: Col. J. A. Smith and Adjt. F. T. Smith. In First Arkansas: Colonel [John W.] Colquitt, Lieut. Col. Don McGregor, Adjt. S. N. Greenwood, Captain [William A.] Alexander, Company B (wounded); Captain [W. H.] Scales, Company C (wounded); Captain [O. F.] Parrish, Company D (wounded); Lieut. John E. Letson (wounded); Corpls. Green M. McKenzie, Company A (killed); John S. T. Hemphill, Company B (wounded); Privates G. W. Sallee, Company C; J. C. Bogy, Company D; W. W. Chaney, Company E; Hardee J. Bullion, Company F, and A. P. Green, Company G (killed); James Beeson, Company H; John H. Curd, Company I (killed); Ocean C. Choat, Company K (killed). In Thirteenth and Fifteenth Arkansas: Capt. Thomas H. Osborne, Companies B and H, Fifteenth Arkansas; Lieut. John Dolan, Company A, Thirteenth Arkansas, ought to be promoted; Color-bearer Felix E. Lipe, Thirteenth Arkansas (wounded); First Sergt. J. M. Harkleroad, Company F, Fifteenth Arkansas; Private William Sandford, Company E, Thirteenth Arkansas (wounded), ought to be promoted; Lieut. William [H.] Pearce and Captain [W. H.] Kinsey, Fifteenth Arkansas. In Fifth Tennessee: Col. B. J. Hill, well worthy of promotion. Calvert's Battery: Joseph Lemon, color-bearer, deserves promotion.

Liddell's Brigade.—In Second Arkansas: Lieutenants [H. C.] Collier and [B. L.] Clegg, I fear killed; Lieutenant-Colonel [Reuben F.] Harvey, Captain [J. K] Phillips, Company F, ought to be promoted; Lieutenants [C. S.] Emerson, Company A; [M. D.] Brown, Company K, and [R. E.] Smith, Company G. In Eighth Arkansas: Adjutant [H. J.] McCurdy, a brave young sold er (killed); Lieutenant [S. B.] Cole, Company I; Lieut. Calvin East, Company H; Lieut. T. H. Beard, Company F (killed); Lieutenant [W. M.] Bass, Company E; Captain [W. H.] Lankford, Company A; Lieutenant [B. A.] Terrett, Company E. In Fifth Arkansas: Captain [A. B.] Washington, Company K; Privates John Atkinson, Company C; B. W. Maret, Company I, and C. Mattix,

Company F. This soldier was too badly wounded to carry his gun. He asked to be allowed to carry the colors, and did so through the rest of the day. Three color-bearers had been shot down previously. In Sixth and Seventh Arkansas: Captain [J. W.] Martin, Lieutenant [J. A.] Reeves, and Captain [S. C.] Brown, ever foremost in leading their men; Captains [J. G.] Fletcher, [W. E.] Wilkerson, and [M. M.] Duffie (wounded); Sergeant-Major Eddins, Sergeant Bratton, Company H; Private Hulse, Company K; the color-bearer, whose name has not been furnished to me.

Johnson's Brigade.—In Twenty-fifth Tennessee: Capt. A. Green, Company G; Capt. G. H. Swope, Company H; First Lieut. D. S. Walker, Company D. In Forty-fourth Tennessee: Maj. H. C. Ewin and Capt. Samuel Stiles, Company A; Adjt. R. G. Cross, Lieutenants [F. M.] Kelso, Company B; [J. W.] Dickins, Company C; [W. H.] Gibbs, Company F; A. P. Forester, Company K (wounded); Color-Sergt. M. J. Turner and Corpl. I. S. Berry, Company I (wounded); Corpl. John W. Gill, Company F (killed); Privates J. D. Stone, Company B; S. G. Heflin, Company C (killed); B. P. Hargroves, Company E (wounded); James D. Crenshaw, Company H (wounded), and J. M. Sellers, Company K. In Twenty-third Tennessee: Capt. N. R. Allen, Company E; Capt. W. H. Harder, Company G; Privates Henry C. Haynes, Company E, and Stephen M. Foster, Company C. In Seventeenth Tennessee: Adjt. James [B.] Fitzpatrick.

I wish to call particular attention to the gallant conduct of Sergt. William N. Cameron, color-bearer of Twenty-fifth Tennessee Regiment. In the last fight he advanced in front of his regiment so far that when it fell back he was unable to follow, and was captured. He tore the colors from the staff, concealed them upon his person, and made his escape from Bowling Green, bringing with him the flag of the Twenty-fifth Tennessee Regiment.

In conclusion, I would state that I carried into the fight 6,045 men, out of which I lost 2,081 killed, wounded, and missing.

Very respectfully, your obedient servant,

P. R. CLEBURNE,
Major-General.

Maj. T. B. ROY,
Chief of Staff, Hardee's Corps.

No. 254.

Report of Brig. Gen. Lucius E. Polk, C. S. Army, commanding First Brigade.

HEADQUARTERS POLK'S BRIGADE,
January 13, 1863.

SIR: In obedience to circular of January 10, I submit the following report of the operations of my brigade in the battle before Murfreesborough:

My brigade was arranged in the following order from left to right: Fifth Confederate, First Arkansas [Infantry], Second and Fifth Tennessee, and Thirteenth and Fifteenth Arkansas Regiments.

On the evening of December 30, 1862, I received orders from the division commander to move my brigade from its position (the extreme right of our line of battle) across Stone's River to the left of General Cheatham's division. This having been accomplished by 9 o'clock at night, I remained in line of battle until nearly 7 o'clock on the morning of the 31st. At that time I again received orders from division commander to wheel my command to the right, keeping the right connected with General Cheatham's left. General Cheatham's division not moving at same moment, I found if I attempted to keep with his line I should become separated from the division, then advancing. General Wood, about this time, having been ordered to my right by Lieutenant-General Hardee, and General Cheatham having commenced to move up, I continued my move, gaining ground slightly to the left. About 7.30 o'clock, and before I had moved more than 700 yards, I received word from Colonel [B. J.] Hill that my right had commenced to engage the enemy in a grove of cedars near the old Franklin dirt road. I did not believe at first that the enemy could be so near us, having understood that we were supporting General McCown. Riding to the place, I was received by a volley from the enemy, resulting in the severe wounding of my orderly (Mike Connell). In a few moments my entire line advanced across the Franklin dirt road, entered this cedar brake, and engaged the enemy all along the line. In a very short time, by the aid of Captain [J. H.] Calvert's battery, we succeeded in driving the enemy out of the cedars in great confusion. Here Major Carlton, Captain Dixon, and Lieut. William H. Pearce, Fifteenth Arkansas Regiment, were wounded while gallantly leading their men.

Following them closely as we could, we encountered them again in a woods pasture immediately in our front, in direction of Wilkinson Cross-Roads pike. After a few moments fighting, we succeeded in breaking their lines, and again they fell back in much confusion. From this position, after having reformed my line, I advanced in a line parallel to Wilkinson pike, General Wood on my right and General Johnson on my left en échelon, with the exception of the Seventeenth Tennessee Regiment (which was in advance) of his (Johnson's) brigade. Advancing through the pasture, the enemy were seen posted across an open field near one of their hospitals and only a few hundred yards of the pike. My brigade was obliged to move across this open field with the enemy's artillery and infantry playing upon them. This they did most gallantly, causing the enemy to fall back across the pike under heavy undergrowth of cedars. Getting possession at this place of four or five ordnance wagons, which were sent to the rear, I again moved on, but did not proceed far when the enemy's batteries, posted across a corn field on the right of the pike, commenced playing fearfully upon my ranks. Here Captain [Charles P.] Moore, Second Tennessee, was killed, and many other officers of that regiment. (See Colonel [W. D.] Robison's report.*)

The battery was so placed, by moving straight forward my line would have been enfiladed. To prevent this, my brigade was wheeled to the right. At this time, Captain Hotchkiss sending me word that he had three batteries that required supporting, I left two of my smallest regiments and moved the rest farther to the left, for the purpose of trying to move the enemy's batteries. The Fifth Confederate here first engaged the infantry supporting these batteries, and in a few moments (the First Arkansas arriving in position) their infantry gave way and their batteries changed their position, with the exception of four guns that fell into the hands of the Fifth Confederate and First Arkansas, and in eagerness of pursuit were passed over.

From this place I moved on with my brigade, the regiments left in

---

* Not found.

support of the batteries having come up and discovered the enemy again prepared to make a stand, having taken a strong position on a cedar hill, with rocks so placed by nature as to afford great protection.   The enemy in this place made a most obstinate stand, and it was only after a bloody fight and one repulse we succeeded in moving them.   Here Lieut. Col. Don McGregor, First Arkansas, was mortally wounded. General Johnson at this time was on my right.

Moving from that position, I found several batteries of the enemy posted on the railroad, near Nashville turnpike.   Thinking I might succeed by going to the left in capturing them, I moved from here, Generals Johnson's and Preston Smith's brigades on my left, and General Liddell's brigade to the left of Johnson's.   We did not go far before we discovered the enemy half advanced across an open field in our front in good and strong line of battle.   It required the work of only a few moments to break this line and drive them back in cedar brakes to the right of a small dirt road running parallel to the railroad, we pushing on after them, and had reached the cedars, and got almost in rear of their batteries posted on the railroad, when in turn we were driven back in great confusion, and with the heaviest loss we had sustained during the day, their batteries near the railroad and infantry making fearful havoc in our ranks as we retreated.   Here Adjutant [F. T.] Smith, of the Fifth Confederate Regiment, fell, badly if not mortally wounded, cheering his men and bearing the colors of his regiment in advance.

Most of my brigade were rallied on the slope of a hill in a cedar grove near the place.   We remained for two days in line of battle; others could not be stopped until they reached the turnpike.   My men at the time they were repulsed were much jaded, having been fighting since early in the morning, without any rest, and had nearly exhausted their ammunition.   As soon as ammunition could be furnished, I gave the men a full supply, and moved my brigade in the woods and took position, en échelon, on the left from General Preston's brigade.   In this position I received orders from General Cleburne to take my position on the right of his line of battle (I hope it will not be out of place for me to remark here that I believe if between the hours of 12 and 2 o'clock we could have been re-enforced and rested by another line of battle, that we would have succeeded in getting possession of the railroad and Nashville turnpike, thereby cutting their lines of communication and getting directly in their rear), where I remained until the night of January 2, my advanced sentinels being engaged in skirmishing with the enemy night and day.

About 10 o'clock of this night the enemy made a sudden dash in heavy line of skirmishers, supported by a line of battle, upon my advanced line of sentinels.

In this attack I would fail in my duty if I did not mention the gallant behavior of Captain Osborne, Fifteenth Arkansas, and Major [R. J.] Person, Fifth Confederate Regiments.   He was repulsed with considerable loss; how great I cannot say, as before morning I was ordered to move my brigade to its old position, back across Stone's River, to the place I occupied on the morning of December 30, [1862.]

My brigade was not again under fire, and on Saturday night, January 3, I moved on the Manchester pike.

I with pleasure refer to the bearing of officers and men of my brigade.   Colonel [J. W.] Colquitt, First Arkansas; Colonel [W. D.] Robison and Lieutenant-Colonel [W. J.] Hale, Second Tennessee Regiments, were conspicuous among those who distinguished themselves Colonel [B. J.] Hill, Fifth Tennessee, and Colonel [J. A.] Smith, Fifth

Confederate Regiments, acted with great courage and judgment. I recommend both of those gallant officers to your favorable notice as deserving of promotion. I refer you to the colonels' reports of other officers who acted with great gallantry. My thanks are due Capts. W. A. King and H. S. Otey, of my staff, for the assistance they gave me upon the field.

I carried in the fight, in round numbers, 1,343. My loss in killed, 30; wounded, 298; missing, 18; total, 346.

L. E. POLK,
Brigadier-General, Commanding.

Capt. IRVING A. BUCK,
Assistant Adjutant-General.

No. 255.

Report of Lieut. Thomas J. Key, Helena Battery.

ARTILLERY CAMP,
Tullahoma, Tenn., January 23, 1863.

GENERAL: On the morning of December 31, 1862, Captain [J. H.] Calvert's battery moved forward on the left wing of the Confederate Army, supporting General Polk's brigade. Skirmishing began before the shades of night had fled, and by day-dawn the rattle of musketry extended far off to our right, and at the first charge the Abolition hordes gave way, save a brigade which was concealed in a dark cedar grove and behind large rocks, and to dislodge them Colonel Hill sent to my battery for one piece of artillery, which was immediately dispatched, under charge of Lieutenant Fitzpatrick. After the right wing of the enemy had been driven a mile, one of their batteries was discovered firing upon General Polk's lines, and immediately my battery rushed in advance of the brigade in open field and engaged the enemy. So soon as we opened upon the enemy's artillery it returned the fire with deadly aim, wounding 1 man and killing 3 horses. My artillery killed the Abolition captain, 1 sergeant, and 2 or 3 cannoneers, and cut down 1 of his caissons and a number of horses. The battery was silenced and made a hasty retreat. With all possible speed the harness was cut from my dead horses, and [I] moved forward in pursuit of the enemy.

The next point of attack was near the Nashville and Franklin pike, where the Abolition infantry had ensconced themselves in a dense forest of timber, and were awaiting the advance of our forces to mow them down as they pursued over an open field. This battery began shelling the woods, and routed the Abolitionists in front, but they rallied and renewed the attack on our left, and promptly we turned our guns upon them, and they were hurled back in confusion, regiment rushing upon regiment, in disorder, into the immense cedar thickets.

The fourth place of action was, after we had pursued the enemy's batteries into the clustering cedars, near the railroad, where they were masked. At this period the sounds of the battle carnage that proceeded from that gloomy forest of cedars and towering oaks were appalling, grand, and awful as ever fell upon the ear of the "hero of a hundred battles." The contest was unequal and desperate. Their rifle guns could throw canister as far as ours could spherical case, and in order to prevent annihilation we were forced to withdraw.

The fifth position was in the field west of the enemy's concentrated artillery, where we fought them until we had exhausted our ammunition, losing in this engagement one of our bravest and most expert No 1 cannoneers. The enemy turned a triple number of pieces upon us, and the missiles of death fell among us singing, whizzing, bursting, and crashing through the trees, as if Mount Vesuvius had at one instant poured all its pent-up furies into our midst. Our escape from beneath those powerful guns was fortunate, if not miraculous.

The sixth and last action was near that same intertwined and matted grove of cedars. Here also the contest was unequal. It was in this engagement that Lieutenant Fitzpatrick lost his left hand by a canister, and a cannoneer's head was shot off, and a number of horses were killed, and one howitzer slightly damaged. Finding that we could not move the enemy from his strong position, and that smooth-bore guns could not cope with Parrott and rifled guns, we withdrew from the contest.

The battery lost 3 men killed, 1 officer and 4 men wounded, 10 horses killed and wounded, and 4 sets of harness. We drove the Abolitionists from three positions, and in turn were driven from a like number.

The officers on Wednesday, the 31st, passed through the battle-storm with cool and lofty courage, and the men stood firmly to their guns, and showed their devotion to their country's cause by overcoming and extinguishing fear.

Respectfully, yours,

THOMAS J. KEY,
[*Lieutenant*] *Commanding Helena Battery.*

No. 256.

Report of Brig. Gen. St. John R. Liddell, C. S. Army, commanding Second Brigade.

HEADQUARTERS LIDDELL'S BRIGADE,
Wartrace, Tenn., January 10, 1863.

MAJOR : On the evening of the 30th ultimo my command was placed by order of Major-General Cleburne, on the extreme left of the division, on the prolongation of Major-General Cheatham's line, with orders to move, by continued change of direction, to the right, to conform to the movements of General Cheatham's command in advancing upon the enemy. The line of battle I judge to have been over $2\frac{1}{2}$ miles in length, and my movements had necessarily to be rapid to keep pace with the wheel of the line of battle, the pivot being on the right. This movement commenced a little after daylight, and after marching about 1 mile we came upon a brigade of Major-General McCown, which had just repulsed a regiment of the enemy. In a moment's conversation with General McCown, he wished me to take position in advance, as his men were somewhat exhausted by the fight. I proposed, instead, that he should move by the left flank and allow me to move up in line with his command, thus placing him on my left, which was readily consented to and done. We then moved forward in line, and almost immediately engaged the enemy. This, I suppose, was about 8.30 a. m. My battery was immediately placed in position on an eminence in rear of the line, and opened fire upon the enemy, who were posted behind a fence in front of us, about 75 yards distant, with another line 150 yards farther in their rear, in the woods, from which position they had heavy batteries playing upon our line. After a contest lasting about half an hour, we repulsed the front line, driving it back upon the second, which also gave way upon our approach, after a short struggle. Here I lost sight of Brigadier-General Johnson's left, and continued to move straight forward against the enemy, with General McCown still on my left. We continued the pursuit, constantly skirmishing, until we reached a house, which was afterward found to be a hospital, where we re-engaged and drove back the enemy's second line of defense. My battery was here pushed forward within 60 yards of the hospital, and fired upon the retreating foe, now crossing the Wilkinson turnpike. My men continued the pursuit across the turnpike, when they were halted to wait for ammunition, to obtain which I dispatched Lieutenant [J. L.] Bostick, my aide-de-camp, to General McCown, who was near a house some 300 yards to the left of the hospital, with his command. Meanwhile my own ammunition arrived and supplied me.

In passing the hospital in advance, I was called upon by the Yankee officers to protect them, as there were a great many prisoners and wounded men in and around it and among the numerous tents in the inclosure. I left one man in charge of it, and told him to proclaim it as under my protection, and then passed on with my brigade. I refused taking any prisoners, as I did not wish to be delayed in my forward movement, or to lose the men necessary to guard them, but ordered prisoners reporting to me to remain there or move to the rear and proclaim themselves as my prisoners. I do not know what became of them afterward, though I think they were subsequently taken by General Johnson's brigade. It was at this point, in rear of the hospital, that the Federal General Sill was killed by the Second Arkansas Regiment [Infantry], while being engaged with the enemy at the hospital, Colonel Govan ordering his men to fire at officers on horses near the building. I forgot to mention that in the first engagement [Lieutenant-]Colonel [Thomas B.] Tanner, Twenty-second Indiana Regiment, was left wounded on the field and became a prisoner.

The brigade being now supplied with ammunition, after having crossed the Wilkinson turnpike, was rapidly pushed forward through the woods a quarter of a mile or more, and coming up with the enemy on the edge of a field, which opened in view of a church, in some open woods on Overall's Creek, some 500 yards distant on our left, and engaged him, driving him in confusion over the crest of a hill beyond. Finding myself alone at this point, with no support on my right or left, I halted my command in the woods near the fence, and threw forward a line of skirmishers to reconnoiter and develop the enemy, not then visible from our position. Lieuts. J. M. Dulin and [J. L.] Bostick, of my staff, who had gone forward with the skirmishers, immediately returned and reported the enemy in line of battle in the valley of Overall's Creek, some 400 or 500 yards distant from the crest of the hill. I at once ordered forward my battery to the crest of the hill, and directed it to fire upon him, as I was in good supporting distance with the brigade. This was done with decided effect, resulting in turning the enemy back and driving him from view behind the railroad embankment. The turnpike road at this time was filled with trains of wagons moving in the direction of Nashville, which the Texas cavalry charged, and I ordered the battery to fire upon that part of the train to the right of the cavalry, which caused the train to break in confusion and seek shelter behind the embankment of the railroad. While this change of route by the enemy was taking place, I continued firing as long as any of the train and enemy appeared in view.

I then returned with the battery to my command in the woods and moved by the right flank until I got in sight of Brigadier-General Johnson's command, which by this time had come up from the Wilkinson road. Pending this movement, General McCown passed by me, saying he would move his command to the right, which I suppose he did, as I saw no more of him, thus leaving me on the extreme left, which, in effect, had been the case ever since passing the hospital near the Wilkinson turnpike, as I saw no force on my left after that time. I may here state that my position inclined me, in wheeling with the line of battle, to pass off at a tangent from it toward the left, and I was, consequently, often compelled to move back by the right flank to regain my place in the line.

After rejoining General Johnson's left, I moved forward, and almost immediately engaged the enemy, whose right laid across a neck of woods, the left being behind a fence in front of my right. After a very severe engagement of some twenty minutes, we repulsed him on our right, throwing him into confusion, he still, however, maintaining his ground upon our left, on which we concentrated the fire of the Fifth, Sixth, and Eighth Arkansas Regiments, soon breaking, after a sharp contest, his line at that point also. It was here that Lieutenant-Colonel Murray, of the Fifth Arkansas Regiment, took the colors of his regiment and gallantly bore them to the front, encouraging his men to the contest. A beautiful stand of United States colors was captured by Private J. K. Leslie, of his regiment. The brigade still continued to move steadily on, constantly firing upon the broken ranks of the enemy, and, upon reaching a point about opposite a white building on a hill on our left, I ordered my battery forward, and rode to this building with a view of placing it in position to open on the enemy's right.

While waiting for the battery to come up, I captured an ambulance and two horses belonging to Colonel [William L.] Stoughton, Eleventh Missouri [Michigan] Volunteers, and Major [B. F.] Doughty, [Eleventh] Michigan Volunteers, which officers, I suppose, had been wounded and brought to the hospital. Here, again, the officers of the hospital asked my protection, and I gave them my name and took the building under my charge. While this was occurring, which was in an incredibly short space of time, I discovered our lines breaking rapidly to the rear, although there was but little firing going on at the time. I immediately galloped to the rear, to head off the stragglers and check the retreat, not knowing what was the cause of this sudden movement. On halting and rallying the stragglers, I found that they were General Johnson's men, who were passing in rear of my line, and were retreating toward my position, on the left. I directed them toward the right to their proper place, and, riding rapidly in that direction myself, I met with General Johnson in search of his men, who told me that my brigade was not far distant in the neck of woods; and upon going in the direction indicated, I found it in line, the colors in place, with the men rallied on the line. In the confusion of the retreat, while I was at the Yankee hospital, on the left, General Johnson's men had gotten between me and my brigade, they having fallen back on my position, causing me to mistake them for my own. My brigade fell back to the original position from which I had advanced in this last attack, after joining General Johnson in moving to the right from the direction of Overall's Creek, as before mentioned.

On inquiry as to the cause of this retrograde movement, Colonel Govan, of the Second Arkansas, stated that the line on his right gave way, and being left alone, without support on his right, he ordered, during my temporary absence at the hospital, a retreat, although there was but little firing going on at the time. An additional reason with him for doing so was that his ammunition was nearly exhausted.

We were now directed to remain in position and await further orders. We bivouacked that night in the woods where we were, and on the following morning I found that the enemy's skirmishers had retaken the hospital and the hill from which I had fired upon his train on the day previous. I moved into position in front of the hill, and my skirmishers immediately drove the enemy from it. The battery was pushed forward to its crest a second time, and fired upon his retreating cavalry and infantry, driving them back to the turnpike in great confusion.

From this time until the night of the 2d instant but little was done, except occasional skirmishing, when I was ordered back about 10 p. m., with the other brigades of the division, to the right bank of the river, in support of Major-General Breckinridge's line.

During the engagement I captured two pieces of artillery, one Parrott gun and one 6-pounder brass rifle piece, for both of which I obtained an ample supply of ammunition. In the final attack another battery was also captured, but, in the unaccountable retrograde movement before mentioned, was left on the field. Although my position was on the extreme left of our lines, I discovered no enemy attempting to flank me. Their ambulances were passing and repassing at all times during the day on the turnpike, while I was in position to see them from the hill near Overall Church, and at night the roar of wagons passing on the turnpike was incessant. Each night the enemy's artillery played on our lines in the woods, and at the same time firing was going on between the skirmishers.

The battery under command of Lieutenant [H.] Shannon was of infinite service to me throughout the action, the men behaving with the greatest bravery, having the battery always ready, and, oftentimes, at the right place at the right time without receiving or awaiting orders, for which I am indebted to the good judgment and coolness of Lieutenant Shannon, commanding battery.

Colonel Kelly, of the Eighth Arkansas, was slightly wounded in the arm; Colonel Smith, of the Sixth Arkansas, was wounded in the leg; Lieutenant-Colonel [F. J.] Cameron, of the same, was shot through the fore part of the body. Of my staff, W. R. Liddell, volunteer aide, was shot in the thigh; Lieut. W. R. Young, brigade ordnance officer, was shot in the shoulder; Surg. W. R. Kibler was shot through the body while sitting on his horse by my side in front of the brigade.

The officers of my personal staff—Adjutant-General [G. A.] Williams, Lieutenant Bostick, aide-de-camp, and Lieutenant Dulin, brigade inspector—not only behaved with the most undaunted bravery, but assisted me voluntarily, and with the utmost alacrity, in pushing forward the brigade, in placing the battery in positions, and in the deployment of skirmishers in the very face of the enemy, and in the heaviest fire whenever required, oftentimes using their own judgment without waiting for orders, for the good of the service and the success of the day.

My brave bugler, Jake Schlosser, was wounded near me and taken from the field.

Many instances of personal bravery I might mention were it not extending this report to too great a length. The evidence of the undaunted courage of the brigade is attested by the fact that nearly one-third of the whole were killed and wounded—5 officers and 81 men were killed, and 503 men were wounded and 18 missing, making a total of 589 *hors de combat*, besides the missing, out of a grand total of 1,709, including the artillery. The brigade now numbers 1,108.

There were some instances of cowardice stated in the reports of the colonels, which are herewith inclosed.

We lament our brave dead; we feel for our wounded brothers, while we honor them. The heartfelt thanks of those of us who have escaped, unhurt, through the storm of death are due to a kind Providence, to whom we pray for safety and success in all the coming contests for our country's cause.

Respectfully submitted.

ST. JOHN R. LIDDELL,
Brigadier-General.

Col. W. W. KIRKLAND,
Adjt. Gen. and Chief of Staff, Cleburne's Div., Hardee's Corps.

No. 257.

Reports of Col. Daniel C. Govan, Second Arkansas Infantry.

WARTRACE, TENN., *January* 10, 1863.

CAPTAIN: I have the honor herewith to make the following report of the part taken by the Second Arkansas Regiment in the late battles before Murfreesborough:

On the night of December 30, [1862,] the Second Arkansas Regiment was moved with the rest of the brigade to a position on the extreme left.

Early on the morning of the 31st, immediately after daylight, we were advanced at a rapid pace on the enemy. Occupying, as our brigade did, the extreme left of General Cleburne's division, and moving in a circular direction, the right of the division being the point, we advanced in this direction nearly a mile, when, pressing through an open field, exposed to severe cannonade, we encountered the enemy, who were posted behind a fence and in the woods immediately in front. After a severe engagement of half an hour, the enemy were driven from their position and pursued rapidly through the woods, when a running fight took place for some distance. My regiment suffered heavily in this first fight. It was here that the gallant young Lieutenants Collier and Clegg, of Company H, fell, I fear mortally wounded, while nobly doing their duty. The enemy were closely followed through the woods, when we encountered a second line of the enemy, posted behind a fence and in the woods near a house used by the enemy as a hospital. The Second Arkansas Regiment, being on the extreme right of the brigade, engaged the enemy near this building. The right of the regiment rested within 15 or 20 steps of this building, and were exposed to a heavy fire from the enemy in our front, and also from a portion of the enemy who had taken refuge in and behind the buildings adjacent to this hospital. It was near this point that General Sill, of the Federal Army, was killed. After a severe engagement the enemy were driven from this second strong position. The hospital, together with many prisoners who had taken refuge there, were taken possession of by General Liddell, and a guard of two men detailed from my regiment to guard the prisoners. No other brigade or regiment was at this time in sight of the hospital. Our brigade, after moving forward a short distance, was halted for the purpose of replenishing our exhausted supply of ammunition, and were then moved forward in the direction of the enemy, whom we engaged in a neck of woods on the edge of a field. A second line of the enemy showed itself on the opposite side of the field, and advanced some 100 yards into the open field opposite my regiment, but were driven back by one well-directed fire. The enemy having fled immediately in my front, and finding him still making a stubborn resistance to my left, I moved my regiment by the left flank, and then forward on the enemy in the neck of woods. A very closely contested fight here took place, the enemy holding their position until the Second Arkansas Regiment approached within 25 steps of their line, when it gave way in confusion and fled across the field, exposed to a murderous fire from my regiment, which told with effect, as their dead were thick on the ground. It was at this point that the color-bearer was shot down by one of my men, and the colors were lost in the confusion of the fight.

Our brigade then moved forward, and was halted some 50 yards in the open field from the edge of a cedar ridge, being unable to advance, as General Johnson's brigade, which had moved forward on our right, had, after halting, moved by the left flank, which placed a portion of his brigade immediately in our front. At this point (General Liddell having gone to reconnoiter and select a place for a battery) the commanders of the different regiments reported to me that their supply of ammunition was nearly exhausted. I immediately sent an officer (Lieutenant Dulin) in search of the ammunition, and, while awaiting its arrival, General Johnson's brigade, immediately on my right and front, gave way and fell back in confusion. I was at first at a loss what course to pursue. Our success had been all that we wished, and we had not met with a single repulse, but when I reflected, first, that the ammunition of the brigade was nearly, if not quite, exhausted; that the brigade on our right and front had given way; that we had no support either on our rear or left; that our position was an exposed one, being in an open field, while the enemy were concealed under cover of the thick cedars on the opposite ridge, I concluded the only alternative left was to order the brigade to retreat, which I did—not, however, until the brigade on my right had passed me some 100 yards or more. Be it said, to the credit of the whole brigade, that all stood firm, and neither officers nor men showed any disposition to retire until I gave the command to retreat. The brigade retired some 300 yards, and was immediately halted and reformed. The enemy showed no disposition to follow us.

My regiment, both officers and men, behaved with distinguished gallantry, with the exception of a few men, whose names I herewith forward.

To Lieutenant-Colonel Harvey I here make my acknowledgments, and bear willing testimony to his gallantry and bravery during the fight, rendering me great service in the management of the regiment, and setting an example of gallantry worthy of emulation. I deem any mention of the services of any particular officer of the regiment almost invidious, but cannot refrain from calling the attention of the brigadier general commanding this brigade to the particularly distinguished and gallant conduct of Captain [J. K.] Phillips, commanding Company F; of Lieutenant [C. S.] Emerson, commanding Company A; Lieutenant [M. D.] Brown, commanding Company K, and Second Lieutenant [R. E.] Smith, of Company G. They were foremost in the fight, and by word and action encouraged their men to emulate their example.

It is rather a singular circumstance that the Second Arkansas Regiment should again in this fight have engaged the Twenty-second Indiana Regiment, capturing the lieutenant-colonel, the same regiment which it encountered at Perryville, committing such slaughter in its ranks.

On the succeeding days of the fight, little fighting, other than skirmishing, occurred until our forces were withdrawn.

Respectfully, yours,

D. C. GOVAN,
Colonel, Commanding Second Arkansas Regiment.

[Capt.] G. A. WILLIAMS,
Assistant Adjutant-General.

—

WARTRACE, TENN., *March* 4, 1863.

GENERAL: In accordance with your request, and after making diligent inquiry of the men and officers of my regiment in reference to the taking of the Yankee hospital near the Wilkinson pike, in the late battle of Murfreesborough, I beg leave to submit the following statement of facts:

When I made my report, I was under the impression that the right of my regiment passed on the left of the hospital. I have since been informed by Captain [E. G.] Brasher (commanding the right company) and others that one-half of this company passed on the right of the hospital, and a portion of it passed through the yard. One of his men was killed in the yard, within a few feet of the house, and two others wounded. Some dozen or more of my regiment were wounded in close proximity to the hospital. Private Elder, of Company D, Second Arkansas Regiment, left by you to guard the hospital and prisoners, stated as follows: That, in obedience to your orders, he and Private Faidley, of the same company, took possession of the hospital, which he understood was the residence of a Mr. Griscom. The yard was filled with Yankee tents and their wounded, together with about 250 prisoners. Prisoners were continually accumulating there, but were sent to Murfreesborough by General Cheatham's order. He did not see General Johnson's brigade until some time after he had been stationed there as a guard. Your brigade had then passed to the front, and there was no fighting at or about the hospital after that time.

The body of General Sill was brought to the hospital about 11 a. m. He was killed not far from the hospital, near the fence or lane. My regiment passed, still fighting, immediately over the ground where he was killed. Private Guest, of Company D, got General Sill's gloves and gave them to the captain of his company (Captain Brasher). He states that General Sill then had his uniform on, which he would have taken, but it was too large for him.

Private Faidley, of Company D, the man detailed as guard to the hospital, corroborates the statement of Private Elder, except that he says that he saw the Seventeenth Tennessee Regiment, General Johnson's brigade, come up within 75 yards of the hospital about fifteen minutes after your brigade passed on.

Very respectfully,

D. C. GOVAN,
Colonel, Commanding Second Arkansas Regiment.

Brig. Gen. ST. JOHN R. LIDDELL.

[Indorsement.]

GENERAL: The foregoing facts I submit for your consideration, and am personally familiar with most of them. Until it can be established that men from other brigades in our army fell at Griscom's house, or hospital, the credit of its capture and the killing of Major-General Sill, U. S. Army, should justly belong to the Second Arkansas Regiment.

Respectfully, your obedient servant,

ST. JOHN R. LIDDELL,
Brigadier-General.

Major-General [P. R.] CLEBURNE,
Tullahoma, Tenn.

No. 258.

Report of Lieut. Col. Reuben F. Harvey, Second Arkansas Infantry.

WARTRACE, TENN., *March 25, 1863.*

I wish to call your attention to a portion of the report of Colonel Floyd in regard to the capture of the Federal hospital commonly known as the Jenkins house.   You discover from Colonel Floyd's report that there was a farm around the hospital, inclosed by fences, running as follows: On the south side running from southeast to northwest, or nearly so; on the north side running parallel with the above; a lane passing through the farm on the west of the hospital, running north and south to the Wilkinson pike, the pike running parallel with the fence, and that there was a skirt of woods south of the first-named fence south of the hospital, and that when his (Colonel Floyd's) regiment entered this skirt of woods we were some distance to his left and rear, and that Colonel Keeble says (whose regiment was between his left and our right) about this time your brigade passed still farther to the left, and that his line was being enfiladed by the enemy, who seemed to be on a line with his regiment and to his left, and that he ordered the "forward" as soon as that line gave way.   He also states that his regiment (the Seventeenth Tennessee) just before leaving this skirt of woods made a right half-wheel; otherwise would have passed on the west of the hospital; but [Lieutenant]-Colonel Keeble states that when your brigade was last seen it was moving to the left, and also states that he passed up the lane and covered the hospital with three of his companies.   This position would have thrown the Second Arkansas Regiment at least one-quarter of a mile west of the lane at the time of entering the skirt of woods, which was about a quarter of a mile wide, and after obliquing across this skirt of wood we would have been at least half a mile west of the lane.

Now, sir, the facts known to me and the officers of the Second Arkansas Regiment are as follows: First, that we drove a line of the enemy from behind the fences at the south end of the lane referred to and through the field to the hospital, distance about 250 yards, and beyond the Wilkinson pike; that a part of the regiment passed up the lane to the hospital, firing on the enemy retreating; that we were fired upon from and about the hospital; that we saw the enemy pass the hospital and cross the pike; that we did, after halting for some time at a fence running west from the hospital, move forward 300 yards beyond the hospital referred to, and then halted for ammunition.   So you see, according to Colonel Floyd's report, before leaving the wood he was west of the lane when he moved forward, made a right half-wheel, and had to cross the fence south of the hospital; then both fences, making the lane in order to pass on the east of the hospital.   Colonel Keeble being on his left, and we (according to his report) marching still to the left, where could we have gone to?   Then, you see, we had to march by the right flank about half a mile, then by the left flank in line of battle, in order that the right of the brigade might cover the mouth of the lane before entering the field, unless, however, the colonel will deny we approached the hospital by this route, which no man on earth need to deny. Did you, sir, make such a movement as that? No, sir; you pushed your brigade upon the enemy in a run, as straight forward as the nature of the case would admit, without any perceptible change of speed or direction until your ammunition became exhausted. You know that if any change of direction had been made up to this time it was to the right, as you know that General Hardee came to our lines early in the morning, and ordered a general change of direction to the right, which was made by your brigade so far as to lap one or more of the regiments of General Johnson's brigade. This, however, was corrected before any general engagement took place. The brigade rested at the pike about three-quarters of an hour, when General Johnson's brigade moved up and formed on our right. I do not say the Seventeenth Tennessee Regiment had not arrived up to this time to the position referred to in Colonel Floyd's report.

With reference to the capture of the Federal hospital, I should dislike for it to amount to a question of veracity; but it seems strange to me that the hospital had been surrendered by the violent waving of a white flag, as Colonel Floyd states, a half hour before we arrived, and then our men were falling right and left from a fire coming from and about the hospital, and that we should drive a heavy column of the enemy through and from the field and yard, which he had passed half an hour before, and yet we were half an hour behind, according to Colonel Floyd's report. I would further add, that line repulsed from behind the fence, south of the hospital, which was in a position to enfilade General Johnson's brigade, was certainly much nearer the hospital than Colonel Floyd, as Colonel Keeble was on his left, and between the Seventeenth Tennessee and Second Arkansas Regiments. Colonel Keeble states that we were going to his left, which would certainly throw Colonel Floyd considerably to our right; also shows that we repulsed the enfilading line; at the same time proves that we preceded him to the hospital, or that he ran over and left a heavy column of the enemy at the fence, all of whom were mad men, well armed and unhurt, or that he passed considerably to the right of the hospital and left this line in his rear—which he did not do, for in his report he states he ordered the "forward" when his enfilading line gave way, and I know, and a just God at his bar will prove to Colonel Floyd and his officers that we were not half an hour or fifteen minutes getting to that hospital from the time we entered the skirt of wood. I further add, that after we halted some time at the hospital, behind the fence running west from the hospital, General Liddell ordered his men out of the yard, where the Federals were about 250 in number, into line, looking for a charge of the enemy's cavalry from our left, and, on entering the yard a short time after halting, three Confederate prisoners, who said they were captured the day previous, reported to me.

I hope no honor due the Seventeenth Tennessee Regiment will ever be seized by the Second Arkansas Regiment. We have confidently looked upon them as worthy and brave fellow-soldiers (which they deserve to be called) in the day of battle, and if they captured the Federal hospital referred to, or passed it half an hour before we did, that everything that is glorious be inscribed upon their banner, for they are insensible of danger and fearless of numbers, and noted for speed as well as cool courage, to have advanced their colors and general guides, formed a correct line, and obtained a supply of ammunition from the enemy's own wagons between the lines of his proud legions, and no support nearer than twenty minutes' run; but Colonel Floyd would do well to obtain more proof before asserting that no Confederate troops had reached the hospital before his regiment, for there was a sufficient force there when we approached it to have annihilated any three companies; but if he did capture the hospital, may the future establish the fact or prove otherwise, and satisfy him, as well as the just tribunal into whose hands this may fall, that I am his friend and fellow-soldier.

R. F. HARVEY,
Lieutenant-Colonel, Comdg. Second Arkansas Regiment.

General LIDDELL.

[Indorsement.]

HEADQUARTERS LIDDELL'S BRIGADE,
March 25, 1863.

Respectfully forwarded.

It is possible that there is a mistake as to the identity of the Yankee hospital. The one taken by the Second Arkansas Regiment was called the Griscom house. If, however, the Jenkins hospital and the Griscom house are one and the same, and General Johnson claims its capture by the Seventeenth Tennessee Regiment, then I do not understand why the enemy was left still in possession of it, with a long line of battle stretching westward, with which my brigade had to contend, and finally drive away with musketry and cannon shot. In this affair I certainly must attach some credit to the evidences of my own senses, that, too, corroborated by my field and regimental officers; but if these prove unavailing, I have nothing more to say. I see that General J[ohnson] refers the subject to the Secretary of War in his indorsement on Lieutenant-Colonel Floyd's report. I shall be satisfied to let our claim rest with the division commander, who, it is presumed, is familiar with all the facts and persons interested, and if it should be in the way of General J[ohnson]'s glory, I am willing to let it go without further contention, however well assured I am, nevertheless, of what is due my brigade.

ST. JOHN R. LIDDELL,
Brigadier-General.

No. 259.

Report of Lieut. Col. John E. Murray, Fifth Arkansas Infantry.

ESTILL SPRINGS, TENN.,
January 7, 1863.

SIR: I have the honor to report that on the morning of December 31, 1862, after having bivouacked the previous night on the right bank of Stone's River about 2 miles from the town of Murfreesborough, Tenn., my command, with the other regiments of Liddell's brigade, was moved forward, gradually changing direction to the right as we moved-forward. At about the hour of 7.30 a. m. we came in sight of the enemy, strongly posted with artillery and infantry in the edge of a piece of woods about 200 yards in our front, who immediately opened a well-directed and most deadly fire upon our advancing line. My command halted and immediately commenced returning the fire, and for about twenty minutes the command remained in an open field, exposed to a most deadly fire of artillery and infantry. At the end of this time the command to charge was given, and, as the men arose and started forward with a yell, the enemy gave way, falling back in good order to near the Nolensville pike, when a short stand was made, but, as our men showed no signs of wavering or halting for their fire, the enemy soon gave way again. Near this pike our first halt was made after the charge commenced, it having become necessary to obtain more ammunition. As soon as a supply of ammunition was obtained, we again moved forward, and soon came to a brigade of Confederate troops (McNair's, I think), which had just been repulsed by the enemy. Our men passed them, with a cheer, and soon came in sight of the enemy, who were again strongly posted behind fences and trees. Here the enemy made a most determined stand, fighting until our men got in 20 or 30 steps of them, but they could not withstand the impetuosity of our troops, and soon broke and fled in disorder. At this point I think our men fought three or four to one. We were almost flanked on both sides, and had an enemy equal, if not superior, to us in numbers immediately in our front. Every man of my command who was present fought here like a hero—first fighting on the right, then in front, and then on the left, and we actually whipped the enemy by detail.

It was at this point that Private J. K. Leslie, Company C, captured a stand of colors from the enemy, which I have the honor to forward with this report.

Shortly after this Brigadier-General Johnson's brigade relieved ours and passed to the front. We were by this time nearly out of ammunition, but still continued to follow Johnson's brigade, which was pursuing the fleeing and thoroughly demoralized enemy, when all at once, to our surprise, Johnson's brigade, which was about 100 yards in front of us, halted, and in a few moments gave way and fled in a disorderly and disgraceful manner, the men running through our ranks perfectly panic-stricken, and compelling us to fall back with them.

It is proper to state that not a single man that I could see in my command at this time fell back until the order had been given by Colonel Govan (who was then commanding the brigade) and been repeated by me. The enemy did not pursue us, and we soon halted, and, after changing positions several times, encamped for the night.

We remained within shelling distance of the enemy until the night of January 3, skirmishing with them every day without any decided result.

My total loss in the engagement of December 31, 1862, and in the skirmishes succeeding it, was: Killed, 12; wounded, 134, and missing, 1, making a total of 147.

Accompanying this I send a list* of the names of the killed, wounded, and missing. I carried into the fight 336 men.

The men who distinguished themselves for gallantry above all others were: Capt. A. B. Washington, Company K; Privates J. K. Leslie and John Atkinson, Company C; C. Mattix, Company F, and B. W. Maret, Company I.

Captain Washington, though wounded in right leg, continued to fight and cheer on his men throughout the day.

Private Leslie captured a stand of colors with his own hand, and afterward, when wounded badly by a shell, refused to go to the rear until I had to order him to go.

Private Atkinson fought bravely until wounded, and continued to fight as long as the enemy remained in range of his gun.

---

* Embodied in No. 191, p. 680.

Private Mattix was wounded in the left arm so badly that he could not use his gun. He then came to me, and said, "Colonel, I am too badly wounded to use my gun, but can carry the flag; may I do it?" I gave him the desired permission, and he carried it through the rest of the battle, keeping in front of the regiment. Three color-bearers had been shot previous to this.

Private Maret not only fought bravely himself, but compelled a private in his own company who wanted to run to fight by threatening to shoot him if he started to the rear.

In strong contrast to the conduct of these gallant men is that of the following-named individuals, who all left the field either before or after the fight commenced, without cause: Second Lieut. J. K. Pyburn, Company G; Privates R. Arnold and W. J. Dobson, Company A; Privates A. V. Rudder and E. W. Bott, Company B; Privates D. McNiel and W. A. Haywood, Company E; Private Joseph H. Leaptrot, Company F, and Privates S. Woods, J. Woods, D. N. Quails, and W. H. Vann, Company I. With the exceptions above mentioned, all fought well.

Respectfully submitted.

JOHN E. MURRAY,
Lieutenant-Colonel, Commanding.

Capt. G. A. WILLIAMS,
Assistant Adjutant-General.

No. 260.

Report of Maj. William F. Douglass, Sixth Arkansas Infantry, commanding Sixth and Seventh Regiments.

JANUARY 11, 1863.

SIR: In making a report of battles at Murfreesborough, Tenn., commencing December 30, 1862, as ordered, I labor under the necessity of making a very imperfect exhibit of the important part taken by those two combined regiments now under my command, since I was not in command during the first and second days of the engagement, and was, during a part of the 31st, absent from the field owing to a painful contusion on the right arm from the effects of a spent ball, but shall, from my own observation and information received from Captain [J. W.] Martin, now acting lieutenant-colonel, furnish the following:

As our previous movements were only preparatory, I need commence only with the morning of December 31, when McNair's brigade, moving off by their left flank, gave place for our forward movement into an open corn-field, through which we had moved about half way when a continuous line of the enemy was seen advancing from the woods beyond to gain the protection of a fence in our front, when, from the line of infantry and a rifled battery 200 yards immediately in front of my regiment, a most destructive fire was opened, and the action became general on the whole left. In the exposed position occupied by our men our loss just at this point was five times greater than during the rest of the day. About 20 rounds had been fired when the enemy gave way, our men rapidly following past two abandoned guns of the enemy's battery and scores of their dead across the field and into the woods beyond. I may mention here that the advance of McNair's brigade on our left and flanking the enemy was, perhaps, one cause of their giving way on their right, as they had a strong position, and our battery was rendered ineffective by being in our rear on level ground, killing and wounding several of our men while firing over them. After crossing the fence with my regiment and reaching the position occupied by the enemy's abandoned battery, it was observed that that line of the enemy in front of the Fifth and Second Arkansas Regiments had not given way, but still occupied their position behind the fence. Our men were ordered to face obliquely to the rear and deliver an enfilading fire that soon routed them, when the pursuit was maintained by the whole brigade across the wide scope of woods in front to the vicinity of a cotton-field and Yankee hospital, where the enemy again made an attempt at a stand, but were rapidly driven back, the right of our regiment passing near the hospital, across the turnpike and into the woods beyond, where we were halted to rest the men and get a fresh supply of ammunition, the firing still being kept up by brigades on our right. We were soon ordered forward, and encountered the enemy on the borders of an old field, across which we drove them until, General Johnson's brigade coming up to relieve us, we were ordered to halt and reform our disordered lines. As soon as our line formed, we moved forward as a reserve to General Johnson, and found the enemy in the edge of a cedar thicket, warmly contesting the ground with him. Our men, gaining a ridge about 100 yards in rear of General Johnson and in sight of the enemy, raised a shout and started forward at double-quick, when the Yankees faced to the right-about and disappeared in the thicket, General Johnson's brigade pursuing them to the edge of this thicket, where they (Johnson's brigade) had a strong position, protected by rocks and the nature of the ground, while our line had been halted in the rear in an exposed position behind the fence on a ridge. Just at this time, though the firing did not seem heavy in our front, and one of the enemy's batteries had been abandoned and was in our possession, General Johnson's brigade gave way, the movement commencing on their right, and, I think, occasioned by the retreat of Ector's brigade, still farther to the right. After General Johnson's brigade had passed our line, and it was found that we were entirely unsupported on either flank, Colonel Govan gave the order to fall back (Colonel Smith was wounded at this point and the command devolved upon Lieutenant-Colonel Cameron) to a stronger position across the open fields and into the woods in rear, where we reformed our line and awaited the advance of the enemy that was never made, and closed the fighting on our part for the day.

As our subsequent movements on the succeeding days were only intended to develop the enemy, and, if possible, draw him from his strongly fortified position without resulting in any actual engagement, it is needless for me to make any report, though I may state that on the third day we lost two of our men by fire from batteries in the same thicket from which our troops had been repulsed, and that Lieutenant-Colonel Cameron was dangerously wounded by a ball shot from a Yankee hospital, from which their flag was then flying.

Throughout the entire action our men exhibited the most enthusiastic courage, never flinching from any charge, no matter how desperate, well sustaining that reputation they had won at such cost on other fields. Of the action of the Sixth Arkansas Regiment I need only refer to their long list* of killed and wounded to show how gallantly they had acted throughout that day. The Seventh Arkansas Regiment was not behind in gallant deeds, if I except those men reported by their captains as having left the field; those remaining were as true as steel.

---

* Embodied in No. 191, p. 680.

In making this imperfect report I have been greatly assisted by Captain Martin for that part of the engagement when I was not on the field.

Of the gallantry of individual officers and men I would beg leave to defer special mention until the return of Colonel Smith, whose wound will detain him some weeks from the command.

W F. DOUGLASS,
Major, Commanding.

Captain [G. A.] WILLIAMS,
    [*Assistant Adjutant-General.*]

No. 261.

Report of Col. John H. Kelly, Eighth Arkansas Infantry.

CHATTANOOGA, TENN., *January 7*, 1863.

SIR : I have the honor to submit the following report as to the action of my regiment in the late battles at Murfreesborough :

Early on the morning of December 31, [1862,] I received orders from the brigadier-general commanding to advance with my regiment and to conform to the movements of the regiments on my right, which was done by gradually wheeling to the right. A short time after advancing I was ordered to throw forward skirmishers to cover my front. Very soon after the deployment had been made, a brisk fire began, and skirmishers soon succeeded in driving back those of the enemy ; the lines of battle confronted, and the contest began. My regiment was posted in an open field ; the enemy was strongly posted behind a fence. After a continued and obstinate resistance, the order to charge was given (I should have mentioned that at this juncture Brigadier-General Rains' brigade came up on my left), which was obeyed with promptness and alacrity. The enemy fled in confusion ; we pursued rapidly for several hundred yards, when he rallied to make another stand, but the impetuosity with which we followed him up soon hurled him again to the rear. As the second charge was ordered from this point, he was rapidly pursued for over half a mile, when it became necessary for us to halt, in order to refill our empty cartridge-boxes. This was soon accomplished, and again we moved forward. After proceeding several hundred yards, we marched by the left flank for about one-quarter of a mile, and then forward to a position several hundred yards in advance in an open field ; from this point we withdrew to a position in the wood, a little to the rear. The next position taken placed the left of my regiment on a large field, the remaining portion being in the wood. The lines of battle soon met again. The fire at this point was very heavy. The enemy outflanked my left, but the timely arrival of Swett's battery dispensed all apprehension of danger from that quarter. Another charge was made, and the enemy was falling back rapidly under heavy fire. At this juncture I was wounded and retired from the field. I think it was about 1.30 p. m. The action of the regiment after this will be reported by Lieutenant-Colonel [George F.] Baucum, to whom I turned over the command.

Lieutenant [S. B.] Cole, Company I, Lieut. Calvin East, Company H, and Lieut. T. H. Beard, Company F, fell while gallantly cheering and leading their men to victory. Adjt. H. J. McCurdy was also killed ; faithful to the last. He was always at his post ; no shock could discompose him. The coolness, bravery, and good judgment of this gallant boy is highly commendable.   The gallant conduct of tl e noble dead was conspicuous to the whole regiment.

I have the honor to call attention to the gallant conduct of First Lieutenant [W. M.] Bass, Company E, who was wounded in the first fight while bravely cheering his men.   Captain [W. H.] Lankford, Company A, and Second Lieutenant [B. A] Terrett, Company E, also deserve special mention for gallantry on the field.

In the first charge my regiment captured two stand of colors.   These were handed to me by Private James Riddle, Company C, and Corpl. N. A. Horn, Company E, but, owing to the rapidity of the pursuit, I found it impossible to carry these along, and they were left on the field.   Another stand was also captured, but was left in the same manner as the others.

A full list of killed and wounded will be furnished by Lieutenant-Colonel Baucum.

The regiment during the whole engagement was always prompt to move at the command.

Very respectfully,

JNO. H. KELLY,
Colonel Eighth Arkansas Regiment.

Capt. G. A. WILLIAMS,
Assistant Adjutant-General, Liddell's Brigade.

No. 262.

Report of Lieut. Col. George F. Baucum, Eighth Arkansas Infantry.

WARTRACE, TENN., *January* 12, 1863.

SIR : In the late battle of Murfreesborough, on December 31, 1862, where our brigade engaged the enemy, after leaving our camp on Stone's River in the morning, we were ordered forward, and in a short time we engaged the enemy first in a corn-field, where the firing became general along the line of our whole brigade, at which place our regiment suffered severely in killed and wounded.   The firing was kept up for some ten or fifteen minutes in that exposed position, at which time McNair's brigade moved up on our left and on the enemy's right and opened fire, at which time the enemy's right gave way.   Then we were ordered forward, and, after crossing the fence in front of our regiment and the Sixth Arkansas, we saw that the enemy in front of the Fifth and Second Arkansas was still contesting the ground.   At this time the order was given to about-face, and we gave them an enfilade fire, and they soon fell back. We then forwarded to where they had been compelled to abandon two pieces of their artillery.

At this engagement I had my horse shot, and halted for a few moments and ordered the infirmary corps to carry our wounded to the hospital immediately in the rear.   As I moved forward in the edge of the woods I saw Captain Williams, and asked how far the regiment was.   His answer, as well as I remember, was, that it was some distance in the woods and that we were driving them like dogs.   I moved on at double-quick through the woods, when I came to a cotton-patch and saw General Liddell, and he asked me what I was doing so far behind.   I answered him that I had lost my horse and was very near broke down.   He told me to catch up with my command.   I went across the cotton-patch, passing a gin-house, and came to a cross fence, where the brigade was halted. There was some little firing with small-arms.   Then Swett's battery opened on the enemy in the edge of the woods, and we were then ordered forward across a corn-field and into the woods a few hundred yards, and were halted and received a new supply of ammunition. The firing still kept up on our right. After receiving our ammunition, we were ordered forward to an old field, and were moved some distance into the field and halted. Our battery went forward in the field and opened fire. Our skirmishers were moved forward and engaged. The brigade was ordered back to the woods. We then moved by the right flank for several hundred yards, and were then ordered forward, where we engaged the enemy in a neck of woods, where the ground was warmly contested for some time, at which time General Johnson's brigade came up and we were ordered to charge. The enemy was repulsed, we occupying the ground. The order was then given to cease firing. Johnson's brigade moved forward to the edge of a cedar thicket under cover of a cliff of rocks. We moved forward to a fence to the support of Johnson's brigade. As soon as we reached the fence the right of the front line gave way and the brigade in our front came to the rear in double-quick, passing through our lines. I tried to halt the men in front of my regiment, but they all passed through. After all had passed, Colonel Govan gave the order to fall back ; we fell back to the woods under fire from the enemy.

This, I believe, is about as correct account as I can give, which I respectfully submit.

Very respectfully, your obedient servant,

G. F. BAUCUM,
Lieutenant-Colonel, Comdg. Eighth Regiment Arkansas Vols.

Capt. G. A. WILLIAMS,
Assistant Adjutant-General.

No. 263.

Reports of Lieut. H. Shannon, Warren Light Artillery.

ARTILLERY ENCAMPMENT, LIDDELL'S BRIGADE,
Wartrace, Tenn., January 11, 1863.

SIR: I have the honor to report that the battery under my command, attached to Liddell's brigade, moved with the brigade at daylight on the morning of December 31, 1862, against the right wing of the enemy in front of Murfreesborough. After advancing about 1 mile, crossing a lane, and passing through a narrow strip of timber, I posted the battery on an eminence in an open field to the right of the brigade, and within 600 yards of one of the enemy's batteries, in front of Brigadier-General Johnson's brigade, and opened with a well-directed fire of round shot and shrapnel, causing the enemy to retire. Our loss was one horse killed.

I then moved the battery rapidly to the front and left, and took position 100 yards in rear of the brigade, in front of and within 600 yards of one of the enemy's rifle batteries, firing about 20 rounds to the piece with good effect, when the brigade gallantly charged and captured the battery, consisting of one rifle brass 6-pounder (4-inch caliber and 10-pound shot) and one 10-pounder Parrott steel gun (2.9-inch caliber). From some unknown cause a shrapnel shot lodged about half way down one of the howitzers, thus temporarily disabling the piece, which was at once ordered a short distance to the rear. The limber being brought forward, I substituted the brass rifle piece just captured for the disabled howitzer, getting a good supply of ammunition from the enemy's chests. Our loss at this position was, Corpl. Martin Green, killed by a rifle shell; Sergt. John McMullen, severely wounded in the chest by a minie ball; Artificer Charles McDermit, severely wounded in the arm and chest by a minie ball; Private Peter Hogan, severely wounded in the foot by a minie ball; Private Frank Bonengal, slightly wounded in the hand by a minie ball; Private E. H. Duggar, slightly wounded on the hip by the fragment of a shell; also one wheel disabled by the enemy's rifle shot.

I then moved the battery forward through an open field and dense woods into a cotton-field, taking position 60 yards in rear of the brigade, and within 60 yards of a Federal hospital, a little to the rear and left of the same, and within 400 yards of the Wilkinson pike, the right of the brigade resting at the hospital. I fired shrapnel and shell at the enemy, who were posted along the fence and edge of the woods beyond the pike. The fire was directed principally to the left, and with the most satisfactory result, as the number of dead left on this part of the field by the enemy well attested. I fired about 25 rounds to the piece at this position, driving the enemy from his cover, when the brigade advanced and took possession of the woods beyond the pike. Our loss here was 4 horses killed and disabled.

After a few minutes of necessary delay, I was ordered to seek a position to the right, and moved the battery to the right of the hospital, where I found Generals Johnson and Wood, the latter falling back. I therefore moved the battery to the front and left, rejoining my own brigade across the Wilkinson pike. I then moved the battery to the right, down the pike about 700 yards, and, finding our lines falling back, posted the battery so as to protect their retreat. They, however, soon rallied and advanced, and I was ordered to move with the brigade by a flank to the left about 1 mile, and took position on an eminence, in full view of and commanding the Nashville pike, and about 700 yards to the left and rear of a second Federal hospital. I opened fire on the enemy's train of wagons moving rapidly to the rear, dividing and driving a part of the train back. The battery then moved with the brigade by a right flank about 1,200 yards, and advanced on the enemy, concealed behind a fence in an open field. I posted the battery in the corner of the field, on a line with the brigade, and within 150 yards of the enemy. I fired 4 rounds of canister from each piece with the most gratifying result. I then moved the battery quickly to the left through a narrow neck of woods, and, taking position on the left of the brigade, opened on the enemy, but was almost immediately ordered to a more elevated position in an open field about 300 yards to the left of the brigade, in front and within 500 yards of one of the enemy's four-gun batteries. The firing of the battery was remarkably good, compelling the enemy to change his position several times, and that of one of his guns as often as six times, when he abandoned the field. I then directed the fire of the battery on the enemy's lines, advancing to flank the brigade. The enemy fled before the charge of the brigade, and I was then ordered to take my original position, commanding the Nashville pike, which I did, driving the enemy's train from the road the second time. Private John Burcher was here slightly wounded in the shoulder by the fragment of a shell.

At the urgent and repeated requests of Brigadier-General Wharton for artillery, to assist in capturing the enemy's wagon train, I dispatched two guns to that officer and two to the brigade, the latter having possession of the Federal hospital, near the Nashville pike, at that time. Before General Wharton could use the guns sent him, our lines commenced to fall back, when the guns were ordered to rejoin the brigade, which they did in the woods between the Wilkinson and Nashville pikes, when the command bivouacked until morning.

On the morning of January 1, the battery moved with the brigade through the woods to the left, and took position in an open field within 800 yards of Overall's Creek, and fired on the enemy's cavalry along the creek, driving them in the direction of the Nashville pike. The battery was then moved 400 yards to the front and right, and was posted so as to command the Nashville pike, and open fire on a column of infantry passing to the rear, and scattering his cavalry stationed along the road. The battery was then moved 200 yards to the right, to the original position, commanding the Nashville pike, and opened fire on the enemy's train. I was then ordered to place the battery 600 yards to the right and open on the enemy's line to the right of the hospital from the position I occupied in the open field, the enemy being about 1,000 yards distant. I soon drew the fire of his rifle batteries, when I withdrew, the object being simply to develop his position.

Private L. B. Jones was slightly injured from concussion, 2 horses killed, and 1 wheel disabled. Lieut. Thomas Havern had his horse killed under him by a rifle-shot from one of the enemy's guns.

I was then ordered to place the rifle piece in position so as to command the Nashville pike, and fired about 30 rounds at the enemy's cavalry and trains with some effect, when the axle broke, doubtless from the recoil of the gun. I then ordered it to the rear, in charge of Lieutenant Havern, and had it mounted on the howitzer carriage, and the disabled howitzer placed in the rear chests of a caisson and turned over at the depot in Murfreesborough.

The loss of the battery sums up as follows: 1 man killed, 3 severely and 4 slightly wounded, 11 horses killed and disabled, 2 wheels disabled, 1 howitzer disabled, and 1 axle broken.

I have the rifle piece and Parrott gun captured by the brigade, with 74 rounds of ammunition for the former and 187 for the latter, together with some 6-pounder ammunition taken from the enemy's chests. I also secured 8 artillery horses, with a small amount of harness, the rear portion of a caisson, a good forge, and about 200 horseshoes, with blacksmith's, carpenter's, and saddler's tools sufficient to supply the wants of the battery.

The battery fought over about 4 miles of ground, taking fourteen different positions and firing 153 rounds to the piece, making a total of 612 rounds.

Sergt. William P. McDonald commanded a section of the battery, to whom I am indebted for valuable services.

It affords me peculiar pleasure to state that not a man straggled during the battle, or showed evidence of cowardice, but that every officer, non-commissioned officer, and private stood manfully at his post and performed his duty.

I acknowledge my profound indebtedness to Brigadier-General Liddell and staff for much valuable assistance, but more especially am I indebted to the general for his fearless example, and the readiness with which he in person indicated the position for the battery.

All of which is respectfully submitted.

H. SHANNON,
Lieutenant, Commanding Warren Light Artillery.

Capt. G. A. WILLIAMS, Assistant Adjutant-General.

—

ARTILLERY ENCAMPMENT, LIDDELL'S BRIGADE,
Wartrace, Tenn., March 22, 1863.

SIR: My attention having been called by General Liddell to a report of Lieut. Col. Watt W. Floyd, commanding the Seventeenth Tennessee Regiment, dated March 18, 1863, giving some additional facts for the establishment of his claim to the capture of the Federal hospital, known as the Griscom house, at the battle in front of Murfreesborough, I deem it proper to submit a more minute statement of facts touching the matter at issue than was contained in my report of that battle.

When I ceased firing at my second position, which was about 1½ miles in rear of the hospital, the brigade charged and captured the battery referred to in my report, and continued to advance rapidly in the direction of the hospital. I moved the battery promptly to the front and left about 1,200 yards, and took position to prevent the enemy's cavalry from getting in rear of the brigade. I was detained here some fifteen minutes, but did not fire on the cavalry, as I had some doubt as to their being Federal; at the same time I replenished my ammunition chests. The cavalry disappeared, and I moved to the right and front through the open field, and thence forward through a narrow strip of woods into a cotton-field in rear of the hospital. I found the brigade posted behind a fence, the right resting at the hospital. General Liddell in person indicated the position for the battery, which was posted 50 or 60 yards in rear of the brigade, and about 60 or 70 yards to the rear and left of the hospital, on the left, and within 20 yards of the lane running from the Wilkinson pike to the rear of the hospital. From this position I fired 18 or 20 rounds to the piece, driving the enemy from his position behind the fence running parallel to the Wilkinson pike, when the brigade moved rapidly forward in pursuit into the woods across the pike.

I remained in this position at least twenty minutes after the brigade had advanced, when General Liddell, returning from the front in search of his ordnance train, directed me to seek a position to the right. I moved across the lane to the right of the hospital, and, when opposite thereto, halted to receive ammunition from two of my limbers, which had just come up. At this moment General B. R. Johnson rode up to me. I saw a regiment of his brigade at a halt, the left resting at a horse lot, about 80 or 100 yards to the right and front of the hospital, with the right of the regiment somewhat to the rear, or, rather, at almost a right-wheel from our proper front. Finding a confused state of affairs to my right, I moved forward through the regiment and to the left and front to the Wilkinson pike, in order to rejoin the brigade, which was in the advance. I saw a number of dead and wounded Federals in the cotton-field and lane, and near the line house and hospital; also a large number of prisoners in the hospital yard.

Sergt. John McMullen states that it was here he was severely wounded in the chest by a minie ball, and not at the position last occupied by the battery, as stated in my report. I also lost 4 horses killed and disabled.

All of which is most respectfully submitted.

H. SHANNON,
Lieutenant, Commanding Swett's Battery.

Capt. G. A. WILLIAMS, *Assistant Adjutant-General.*

No. 264.

Report of Brig. Gen. Bushrod R. Johnson, C. S. Army, commanding Third Brigade.

HDQRS. JOHNSON'S BRIG., [THIRD,] CLEBURNE'S DIV.,
HARDEE'S CORPS, ARMY OF TENNESSEE,
Tullahoma, Tenn., January 15, 1863.

SIR: I respectfully submit the following report of the part taken in the action before Murfreesborough on December 31, 1862, by the brigade under my command :

In the first position taken by Major-General Cleburne's division at

Murfreesborough, on Sunday, December 28, this brigade was the second one from the extreme right of the second line; was north of Murfreesborough and a little west of the Lebanon pike. Though there had been skirmishing with artillery and small-arms, no regular engagement had taken place between our troops and those of the enemy up to the night of December 30.

Late in the evening of this day my brigade, with the others of Major-General Cleburne's division, was moved from the extreme right to the extreme left of the second line of battle, in order to support Major-General McCown's division, which formed the extreme left of the first line. My brigade consisted of five regiments, whose position from right to left, and whose strength, respectively, on the morning of the battle in front of Murfreesborough, were as follows:

General and staff	6
37th Tennessee, Col. Moses White	225
44th Tennessee, Col. John [S.] Fulton	509
25th Tennessee, Col. John M. Hughs	336
17th Tennessee, Col. A. S. Marks	598
23d Tennessee, Lieut. Col. R. H. Keeble	272
Darden's battery	70
Strength of brigade taken into action	2,016

The Jefferson Artillery (four guns), commanded by Capt Putnam Darden, having been on detached service with Brigadier-General [S. A. M.] Wood's brigade, reported for duty with my command on the morning of December 31 and moved with my brigade. My brigade was posted between Brigadier-General Liddell's brigade (which was on the extreme left of our line) and the brigade of Brig. Gen. L. [E.] Polk.

At early dawn, on the last day of the old year, 1862, a year so full of bloody records, our line was formed, running north and south on the west side of the West Fork of Stone's River, my left resting on the lane leading up to the McCullouch house. The order was immediately given to advance in support of Major-General McCown's division, by wheeling the whole of our division to the right.

My brigade moved first over open fields up a gentle ascent for about 1,200 yards, when we reached the summit of the slope, with my left within about 150 yards of the Triune road. Here the enemy's balls from cannon and small-arms fell around and in our ranks. Though we had moved out on the second line to support Major-General McCown's division, it became evident that there was here nothing before us but the enemy, whose sharpshooters were posted at the fence and in the woods along the north side of the Triune road. We therefore prepared to take our place in the first line. I ordered out skirmishers in front of each regiment, halting and correcting the right of my line, which had been somewhat broken in passing through a small thicket in the field. Col. Moses White and Lieutenant-Colonel [R. D.] Frayser, of the Thirty-seventh, and several men of the Forty-fourth Tennessee Regiment, were here wounded before we had fired a gun. Major [J. T.] McReynolds, a faithful and brave officer, then took command of the Thirty-seventh Regiment Tennessee Volunteers.

Our skirmishers now drove the enemy from the fence and border of the woods, and the brigade advanced to the Triune road in a beautiful line, completing the wheel to the right. My command was here moved to the left on the road, to give room to Brigadier-General Polk's brigade.

In front of the left wing of the Twenty-fifth Regiment Tennessee Volunteers there was, at this time, a lane running nearly perpendicular to the Triune road; and with a narrow opening on the right of this lane there was on either side a cedar glade. The brigade advanced into the glade, and, passing it under a warm fire on the right wing, it entered a wide corn-field on the left and a narrow field on the right of the lane. The conflict now became very severe—perhaps as much so as at any period during the day.

Immediately in front of the Seventeenth Tennessee Regiment, and to the right of a small thicket, was a battery of four guns—afterward found to be a Michigan battery—supported by a heavy force of infantry. Farther to the left was posted a second battery. As soon as the brigade entered upon the open ground it was exposed to a very heavy fire of grape, shells, and bullets. The Twenty-fifth Regiment, on the right of the lane, was especially exposed to a flank fire of the enemy's battery. The Seventeenth advanced steadily to within 150 yards of the battery, halted, and engaged the enemy most gallantly and efficiently for some time. Captain Darden's battery at the same time took position on the south side of the field, and with admirable skill poured in a well-directed fire of shell, shrapnel, and solid shot over the heads of our men upon the battery and infantry in front of my left wing, which soon silenced the enemy's pieces. The Seventeenth then charged and took the battery of four guns in front of it, having, with the aid of the artillery, killed eight men of the battery and many horses, and having wounded the captain and a number of his men and damaged one of his pieces.

As our men advanced, Captain Darden moved his battery to the left and engaged the enemy's battery on the left of the small thicket, which finally moved back from its position. After continuing the fire for a time from the open fields upon the enemy now in the woods beyond, the Seventeenth again charged and gained the woods, where a stubborn resistance continued to be offered by the enemy, who took shelter behind trees and logs. Still the Seventeenth pushed rapidly forward, driving the enemy until its left was exposed to an enfilading fire from the enemy, who occupied a fence some 60 yards to the left. The Twenty-third Tennessee Regiment, in conjunction with the right of Brigadier-General Liddell's brigade, now approached in good time, and gallantly relieved the Seventeenth from this flank fire, enabling it to pass forward and drive the enemy from the woods.

On the right of the lane, where the Twenty-fifth, Forty-fourth, and Thirty-seventh Tennessee Regiments passed, there was much less open ground than on the left. When the enemy gave way in the field on the left of the lane, they fell rapidly back to the woods, and were soon driven from this cover; but on the right of the lane my right wing had to advance much more slowly against artillery and infantry, and gradually drive the enemy step by step, without the aid of artillery, through woods almost equal in extent to the woods and open ground on the left. The consequence was, that the Seventeenth Tennessee Regiment gained the open field beyond the woods and advanced to the woods beyond the Federal hospital before my right had got through the woods in which this protracted struggle took place. This struggle on the right was maintained by our troops with the same gallantry and persistency as by those on the left, though that struggle presented not the same variety of phases in the former as in the latter. A battery of the enemy's artillery was posted in the corn-field in advance of the woods on the right of the lane. This battery was removed before our troops passed out of the woods.

The first serious conflict in which my brigade was engaged in this battle may be considered as closing here. More than half of the whole loss of this brigade, in my opinion, occurred in this conflict. Without attempting to enumerate the loss in men, it is known that in killed and wounded the Forty-fourth lost here its major, 8 officers, and its color-bearer; the Seventeenth lost its colonel, adjutant, and 12 company officers; the Twenty-fifth lost its colonel and 6 company officers; the Twenty-third lost 2 officers; the Thirty-seventh lost its colonel and lieutenant-colonel. One of my staff was also wounded by a shell. The command of the Seventeenth devolved on Lieut. Col. W. W. Floyd, and that of the Twenty-fifth on Lieut. Col. Samuel Davis, after the colonels of these regiments were wounded, which was early in this fight. Colonel [A. S.] Marks, of the Seventeenth Regiment, advanced within sight of the battery, afterward taken by his regiment, and exclaimed, "Boys! do you see that battery? It is ours, is it not?" It was, however, taken after he was wounded.

After clearing the woods, the Seventeenth Regiment was fired on by the enemy stationed in and about the cotton-gin, about 70 yards in front of a large Federal hospital. One piece of artillery was observed just on the left of the hospital and a battery of four guns about 300 yards to its right. This battery was playing on the woods occupied by the right of the brigade, and an undulation in the ground served to conceal from it the movements of the Seventeenth Regiment, while that regiment passed some 50 yards to its rear and about 150 yards from its right. The fire of the enemy in and about the cotton-gin was returned by the Seventeenth Regiment, killing and wounding several of the enemy, and the conflict was kept up on both sides until the regiment had passed the hospital, seven companies passing to the right of the hospital and three to the left. The enemy was now observed forming at a distance of several hundred yards in front. The battery on the right moved off about this time, leaving behind one piece of artillery. When our troops approached the hospital, a second flag was raised, and a man came out with another, a white flag, which he waved with much energy. A large number of prisoners had been passed in the woods, with whom our men were prohibited from leaving the field, and a number were captured with the hospital. The Seventeenth also captured here two wagons, well loaded with ammunition for small-arms, and the cannon on the left of the hospital. It will be observed that the lane which separated my right from my left wing, and along each side of which my men moved, passed immediately by this Federal hospital. The line of march to this hospital for my brigade was shorter than that for any brigade or regiment on my left. The Fifth Confederate Regiment, commanded by Col. J. A. Smith, of Brig. Gen. L. [E.] Polk's brigade, was the first command to reach the hospital after the Seventeenth Regiment Tennessee Volunteers. The officers of the Seventeenth Tennessee Regiment are very confident that this regiment was the first to reach and pass the hospital. Lieutenant-Colonel Floyd remarks that "At the time I ordered the charge into the woods in front of the hospital, I was at least 70 yards in advance of any other troops on my left; that we passed through the woods very rapidly, and certainly had less space to pass over in getting there than any troops on our left." There may be but little importance attached to the taking of this hospital, and but little honor won in reaching this position first, but as it has been made a subject of some conflict in opinion between honorable men, honestly differing in their opinion, it is but proper that the facts in the case should be determined. The only interest which the undersigned can have in the matter arises from an honest wish to have justice done to those who have a right to expect it at his hands, while he trusts and believes they would scorn to appropriate aught that was not their due.*

Of Lieutenant-Colonel [W. W.] Floyd it is just to say that on this field of battle he has shown himself to be a good, faithful, energetic, and gallant officer. His cool judgment and courage, and the steadiness with which he stood to his post in every position of his command, have not, perhaps, been excelled by any officer on the field at Murfreesborough.

In the woods behind the hospital I reformed the brigade in line of battle, and obtained a new supply of cartridges, the Seventeenth having supplied itself mainly from the wagons it captured. Captain Darden's battery also came up here and took position on the left of the brigade.

About this time, finding Brigadier-General Wood falling back from an advanced position on our right, I learned from him upon inquiry that the enemy had a heavy battery in his front, which was doing much damage. Under instructions from Major-General Cleburne, I sent forward a company of sharpshooters, under command of Captain [F. B.] Terry, of the Seventeenth, with instructions to take off the men and horses of the battery. At the same time Captain Darden's battery, by direction of Major Hotchkiss, moved to the right of my brigade and into the woods in advance of Brigadier-General Wood's brigade, and opened fire on the advancing enemy, driving them back. Captain Darden reports that he then moved his battery to the right into a field, in which there was a hospital, about 300 yards from the Wilkinson pike, and, in conjunction with two guns of, he thinks, Captain [J. T.] Humphreys' battery, engaged a battery of the enemy, and, after a hotly contested fight, silenced four of his guns.

In the mean time Captain Terry advanced, with his company deployed as skirmishers, and, passing to the left of the Wilkinson pike, approached the garden fence of the hospital to our right and front on the north side of the Wilkinson pike, driving from that fence the enemy's skirmishers, who took position in the edge of a cedar thicket, to which a heavy force of the enemy's infantry now advanced, when Captain Terry withdrew his men and joined his regiment, now in motion.

In the mean time I was ordered by Major-General Cleburne to move my brigade by the left flank across a corn-field on the north side of the Wilkinson pike. On passing all but the right regiment of my brigade into the woods beyond the corn-field, I was directed to move to the front in support of Brigadier-General Polk's brigade. We descended the slope of a hill and entered the cedars, on a rocky acclivity some 200 yards to the left of the position to which Captain Terry had driven the enemy's skirmishers. My men here opened fire, when I directed them to desist, believing that our friends were in front of our line. Riding now in advance of the right of our line, the enemy's fire was unexpectedly drawn. After a few rounds it was found that a heavy force was flanking our right, where we were unsupported. I consequently moved my command to the rear in good order. The Forty-fourth Tennessee Regiment reports 21 prisoners captured here. Major McReynolds, the last field officer on duty with the Thirty-seventh, was here mortally wounded, and Captain Jarnagin assumed command of the regiment. In our rear there was drawn

---

* NOTE ON ORIGINAL.—In regard to the Federal hospital in controversy, it is hoped it may be found that while this brigade captured the one known as the Jenkins house, the other brigade captured that known as the Widow Smith's house.

The following officers are known to be prisoners in Nashville : Maj. J. C. Davis, Captain [William] Clarke, Captain [G. W.] O'Neal, Second Lieutenant [M. W.] Black, First Lieutenant [H. M.] Kinsey, Lieutenant [M. P.] Marbury (not known), Seventeenth Regiment Tennessee Volunteers.

up a line of several regiments, some of which, at least, belonged to some other corps.

An order now came to me from General Cleburne to move my brigade to support General Liddell. After marching some 400 yards by the left flank, we moved to our front and passed north through a long wood lot projecting into open fields. Having received a message from General Liddell, through Colonel Kelly, who was wounded, to the effect that the aid of my brigade would rout the enemy, we came up with General Liddell's brigade on an ascent beyond the edge of the woods. General Liddell's command now yielded the ground to my men, and reformed under the brow of a small hill, to the top of which my command ascended.

Before us was now an open field, declining in front. At the foot of the declivity, at the distance of about 400 yards, was a battery, strongly supported by infantry. My command steadily advanced, fighting under fire from the battery and infantry. The battery was soon silenced, and our men advanced in double-quick time to a position behind a fence and a ledge of rocks. In front, about 80 yards, was a cedar glade, in the edge of which the enemy were now seen lying close together along a ledge of rocks. Under cover of the fence and rocks our men took deliberate aim and poured upon the enemy a destructive fire, which was returned with spirit. The conflict lasted some twenty minutes, when the enemy arose to retire. At this moment a volley was discharged upon them with remarkable effect, and our men rapidly advanced to the cedars, capturing the fine battery of Parrott guns against which they had been fighting, and which was now in position on the adjacent flanks of the Twenty-third and Seventeenth Tennessee Regiments. The men of my brigade then took shelter behind the ledge of rocks at the edge of the glade, and were well covered from the enemy's fire. All concur in representing the number of dead and wounded in the edge of the cedars as very large. Many were lying side by side along the ledge in the position they assumed to await our approach, while others had fallen as they turned to retreat.

The fire was still being kept up on the part of our troops, when it was observed that the troops on our right, bearing colors with blue ground and red cross, were falling back, and it was reported that our right was flanked by a heavy force. A precipitate retreat immediately followed. My brigade having a strong position, held to it with tenacity, and abandoned it with reluctance, after a delay that led to considerable loss. Here Captain [N. R.] Allen, of the Twenty-third, who was distinguished for his valor and coolness, fell, mortally wounded. Captain [F. M.] Orr, of the Seventeenth, was killed in the advance. The Forty-fourth lost 2 officers; the Twenty-fifth, 2 lieutenants, the color-bearer and colors. Maj. J. C. Davis, of the Seventeenth, with other officers and men, were here captured.

The retreat was made without order. The lines were broken and men of different regiments, brigades, and divisions were scattered all over the fields. The movement was to me totally unexpected, and I have yet to learn that there existed a cause commensurate with the demoralization that ensued. At the moment in which I felt the utmost confidence in the success of our arms I was almost run over by our retreating troops. I contended with the tide step by step, but made no impression on the retreating columns until they had gained the woods, when, by calling on a number of color-bearers, I succeeded in planting the colors of several regiments, and the men then assembled upon them with ranks much thinned. I cannot but think that the whole ultimate fortunes of the field were lost by this backward movement. Our men were in sight of the Nashville pike; some have said they were on it.   The enemy's right was doubled back upon their center.   Had we held this position the line of communication of the enemy would have been cut.   We could have flanked them and enfiladed their whole line, which was no doubt in disorder.   It was unfortunate that our artillery was not promptly moved forward to support us.   My battery was at this time in position, by order of General Hardee.   I do not think that our artillery was sufficiently used on our left.   General Liddell's battery arrived on the ground, and he proceeded to put it in position for the work to be done, but did not succeed in time to open before the retreat commenced.   Had we received re-enforcements we might have returned and regained the ground.   But very soon the enemy planted a formidable battery on an eminence near the railroad, sweeping all the open fields and commanding even the woods in which our lines were formed.   The enemy's infantry was also brought forward and posted in great strength, so as to be protected by the side slopes of the railroad and pike, and the trees and rocks in the cedar glade.   It would then have been very hazardous to assail them with any force by our former approach.   These facts I promptly communicated to Major [Calhoun] Benham, of General Cleburne's staff.   We now threw forward our skirmishers to the fields, and prepared to hold our position. Allowing for the ground we had lost, we had driven the enemy back 2 miles, and now held our position from 3 o'clock on Wednesday afternoon until 10 o'clock on Friday night.   Between the two armies and beyond the available reach of either, the ground was strewn with the dead and wounded, and with their arms and accouterments.   During Wednesday night the enemy's army seemed to be busy with rapid movements of troops, wagons, and artillery.   The very commands of the officers could be distinguished, and the rumbling of wagons seemed to commence on their left and die away in the distance beyond their right.   Toward the dawn of day I felt confident that we could distinguish the peculiar noise of artillery moving away, and, concluding that the enemy were in full retreat, I stated this impression in a note to General Cleburne, with the suggestion that our forces should be pressed forward.

The ground in front of our pickets was mainly occupied by the enemy's wounded and dead, and the groans of the former were appealing for relief throughout the night.   Early in the morning I took with me a number of men of the infirmary corps of my brigade, and went out on the field to carry off the wounded.   A fire had been built for a number of them by our pickets, but others had passed the night in the cold.   We had moved but few of them, when the enemy's pickets fired on us, and one of their balls struck a wounded Federal borne on the shoulders of our men.   Again, later in the day, when one of our men, yielding to natural sympathy excited by the continued cries of suffering humanity, crawled to a wounded Federal, and was endeavoring to place him in a comfortable position, the enemy's pickets shot the good Samaritan, wounding him in the arm.

During the night of December 31, and day and night of January 1, and until 10 p. m. of the 2d, we remained inactive in our position in the woods, occasionally shelled by the enemy's batteries, and aroused by the firing of our skirmishers in front.   I suggested and urged the planting of a heavy battery to my left and front, but my suggestions seemed not to be approved either by artillery officers or my seniors.   My own convictions still approve this suggestion, convinced, as I am, that on the field of battle there should be no repose, and that energetic, judicious, persistent action affords the only reliable means of success.   Had this battery been planted it would have proved a very great diversion in favor of our attacking force on the evening of Friday, January 2, as a concentrated fire could have been thrown upon the enemy's battery at, perhaps, a shorter distance than from any other battery in our lines, and we would then have had a cross-fire upon the enemy's strongest position.

On Friday evening I sent out, by request of Major-General Cleburne, a party of men to bring in the guns lying near our skirmishers in front, and succeeded in bringing in a number, which were carried from the field by the ordnance officer of the brigade, Lieut. J. B. Lake. My men also armed themselves very generally with long-range guns, by exchange.

At 10 p. m. on Friday, January 2, we were withdrawn from the left wing of our army, and placed in support of Major-General Breckinridge's division, on the extreme right. Here we remained in a heavy rain until 11 p. m. on Saturday, January 3, when our retreat commenced, and continued through the very inclement weather of the night. After dark on the evening of the 4th we halted, and rested until 8 a. m. on January 5, within 6½ miles of Manchester, a number of my men having fallen behind from weariness and other causes.

In the progress of this report the conduct of men and officers of the brigade has been indicated with some particularity. I regret to state that, especially after our first serious conflict, a number of men fell behind the command.

Lieutenant-Colonel [R. H.] Keeble, of the Twenty-third Regiment Tennessee Volunteers, is especially worthy of notice for his steady courage and the manner in which he handled his men, and, with the aid of good company officers, kept them together through all the movements of the day of battle.

Col. John S. Fulton and Lieut. Col. John L. McEwen, jr., of the Forty-fourth, bore themselves gallantly, pressing forward, and encouraging their men in all the dangers of the field.

Out of fifteen field officers, twelve were present on the field of battle, and but one of them escaped untouched in person or clothes. The Forty-fourth [Regiment] took into action 28 officers and lost 19 killed, wounded, and missing; the Seventeenth [Regiment] took into action 41 officers, and lost 21 killed, wounded, and missing; the Twenty-fifth [Regiment] took into action 37 officers, and lost 12 killed, wounded, and missing; the Twenty-third [Regiment] took into action 23 officers, and lost 4 killed, wounded, and missing; the Thirty-seventh took into action 25 officers, and lost 6 killed, wounded, and missing; general and staff took into action 6 officers, and lost 2 killed, wounded, and missing.

The following are the casualties which occurred, as determined by comparison of surgeons' and regimental reports:

Command.	Killed.	Wounded.	Missing.	Total.
17th Tennessee	18	176	24	218
23d Tennessee	4	48	11	63
25th Tennessee	13	91	14	118
37th Tennessee	6	39	1	46
44th Tennessee	14	134	26	174
Jefferson Artillery		2		2
General and staff		2		2
Total	55	492	76	623

I cannot close my report without special notice of Capt. Put. Darden and the battery under his command. The ability and zeal of the officers and men as exhibited in the management of the battery, and in the efficiency and precision of its fire on this field of battle, ranks it, in my opinion, among the best batteries with the Army of Tennessee.

My staff served faithfully and creditably in this action. Capt. R. B. Snowden, assistant adjutant-general, was twice struck, and had his horse disabled, and remained actively employed on the field with the command. Capt. William T. Blakemore, aide-de-camp, was with me everywhere on the field, and rendered me all the assistance in his power. Capt. John Overton, volunteer aide, was wounded, and Capt. Jo. H. Vanleer, also volunteer aide, after having his horse disabled, fought in ranks, with a rifle. Lieut. George H. Smith, of the regular army, and my brigade inspector, was wounded before he reported to me on the field.

A rough map, exhibiting the movements of my brigade and battery in the battle before Murfreesborough, is herewith inclosed.

Very respectfully, your obedient servant,

B. R. JOHNSON,
Brigadier-General, Commanding.

Capt. IRVING A. BUCK,
Assistant Adjutant-General.

No. 265.

Report of Lieut. James B. Lake, ———, Chief Ordnance Officer.

HDQRS. ORDNANCE DEPARTMENT, JOHNSON'S BRIGADE,
Tullahoma, Tenn., January 23, 1863.

SIR : I have the honor of reporting that, while on the battle-field near Murfreesborough, Tenn., December 31, 1862, I collected and turned over to ordnance department about one hundred and sixty guns, consisting in Enfield rifles, minie and percussion muskets. I also took from the field one four-horse wagon complete, with fifteen boxes Enfield cartridges, which wagon I now have in my train.

Very respectfully,

JAS. B. LAKE,
First Lieut. and Chief of Ordnance, General Johnson's Brigade.

Capt. R. B. SNOWDEN,
Assistant Adjutant-General.

No. 266.

Reports of Lieut. Col. Watt W. Floyd, Seventeenth Tennessee Infantry.

TULLAHOMA, TENN., *January* 9, 1863.

GENERAL : In obedience to Special Orders, No. ——, I submit a brief report of the part the Seventeenth Tennessee Regiment took in the battle of Murfreesborough, Tenn., on December 31, 1862.

The regiment was led into the action by the gallant Colonel Marks. When you had put the brigade in position to move against the enemy's lines, the Seventeenth occupied a position in a bottom, where a battery had been captured a few minutes before by General McCown's command. Upon being ordered forward, the regiment advanced up a gentle slope to a fence on the crest of the hill. Here our skirmishers were first fired upon, and we discovered a heavy force supporting a battery in a corn-field immediately in front of our lines. The regiment moved up in fine style to within 150 yards of the battery, under a galling fire from the artillery and infantry. We halted and engaged them for some length of time to great effect. Colonel Marks was wounded here at the first fire, and the command then devolved upon me. The enemy's line finally gave way, and the order was given to charge. Never did soldiers obey an order with more alacrity. We captured the battery (four pieces), and drove the enemy back to the edge of a thick woodland. After passing the battery, we halted and engaged the enemy a second time, soon starting him back again. I ordered a second charge, which was well executed under a heavy fire. On gaining the fence from which we had just driven the enemy, I reformed the regiment. Here the enemy made a very stubborn stand, taking shelter behind the trees and logs; here my left suffered severely from an enfilading fire. The enemy's line had not given way on my left. He occupied the opposite side of the fence from me, not exceeding 60 yards from me. Colonel Keeble, with his noble little band, came soon to our relief, with General Liddell on his left. I discovered that the right wing of the brigade was still held in check some distance in our rear by the enemy, strongly posted in a wood in front of it; but my men were so anxious to go forward that I ordered them to clear the wood in front. So soon as I saw the enemy's line break to my left, we kept up a running and a very destructive fire through the wood, which was, perhaps, some 300 yards.

On emerging from the woods, I discovered a Federal hospital imme-diately in front, and one piece of artillery just at the left of it, which was silent, and a battery of four pieces about 300 yards to the right. The regiment at this point made a half-wheel to the right, seven com-panies passing to the right and three companies to the left of the hos-pital. The battery that was on my right was playing on the right of the brigade, and seemed not to discover us. On passing the hospital and clearing the fences, I discovered the enemy in force forming about 300 yards in front of me. I ordered a halt and reformed the regiment, having passed some 50 yards to the rear of the battery that was on my right, and not more than 150 yards distant, but a slight elevation of ground concealed it from me. It silenced, though, about this time, and moved off to my right, leaving behind one piece, There we captured 2 wagons, well loaded with ammunition for small-arms, and 8 mules. At the hospital we captured a large number of prisoners, besides quite a number in the woods, alluded to heretofore ; I think in all not less than 200 unhurt (my officers think more), besides killing and wounding a great number. Many of the wounded had already been collected at the hospital for treatment.

My regiment was fired upon after clearing the woods by a party of Federals posted in a cotton-gin about 70 yards in front of the hospital, and my men returned the fire, killing several of them. The enemy con-tinued to fire upon our line, particularly the left wing, until we had passed the hospital. I feel very certain that my regiment was first at this hospital. At the time I ordered the charge into the woods in front of it, I was at least 75 yards in advance of any troops on my left. We passed through the woods very rapidly, and we certainly had less space to pass over in getting there than any regiment on our left. After pass-ing the hospital and reforming the regiment, we occupied a position nearly out of sight of it. I found upon examination at this point that our stock of ammunition was nearly exhausted. We replenished from the captured wagons by using all that would fit our guns. We remained here full half an hour before any support came up, Colonel Keeble coming first of your brigade. After you reformed the brigade at this point to make a second advance in line, my regiment had but little to do with the enemy until after 12 o'clock, except Captain [F. B.] Terry's company, which was thrown forward as skirmishers near the Federal hospital, north of the Franklin pike. Here Captain Terry drove back the enemy's sharpshooters, killing several and having several of his own men wounded.

The next thing worthy of note was when you brought up your brigade to support General Liddell. In that action my regiment came up with, I think, the Second Arkansas Regiment in a wood lot. That regiment was driving the enemy slowly, but surely, before it. On reaching the fence on the north side of the lot, this regiment faced about and retired through my lines. I immediately gave the command forward, and nobly and gallantly did the boys clear the fence. This brought us into an open field in plain view of a fine battery of the enemy's guns, down at the foot of the hill (we occupied the top), distant about 500 yards. This battery was supported by a heavy line of infantry. The retreating force that Liddell had been driving made one stand against us before reaching the bottom of the hill and did us serious damage. I halted the regiment about half way down the hill, and gave the enemy a few rounds. Meanwhile his battery was playing heavily upon us, but the well-directed fire of our boys soon drove the gunners from their pieces and stopped the trouble from that quarter. Scarcely had I given the command "forward" before I perceived the boys going at a double-quick for the bottom of the hill.

In this charge I lost Captain Orr, killed, and several others wounded. On reaching the foot of the hill, I halted the regiment, discovering a fine position behind a fence in some sinks or basins, bordered by rocks, &c. The men promptly took advantage of these things, and commenced pouring a deadly fire into their ranks as they were lying in the edge of a cedar glade. The distance between our lines ranged from 75 to 100 yards, or less. Here my boys commenced the work of destruction in good earnest. Never have I seen such cool, deliberate aim taken in battle. The enemy stood the fire well, and returned it briskly, but with little effect. The engagement at this point lasted some thirty minutes, when the enemy arose to retreat, but a deadly volley from our boys prevented most of them from escaping. Another "forward," and the boys soon occupied the ground the Yankees had just left.

In this charge we gained full possession of the fine battery that had annoyed us so but a short time before. My men took a position behind a ledge of rocks that bordered the cedar glade, which afforded a fine shelter from the enemy's bullets. Along the edge of the cedar glade was the greatest destruction of Yankees I have seen on any battle-field. I do not claim for my regiment full credit for taking the battery captured at this point. Colonel Keeble did some effective work here, although the battery was opposite the left wing of my battalion. The position I occupied at this point I considered a very safe one, believing that we could hold it against any reasonable force with but little cost; but after remaining there for some time, I was notified that the right was rapidly giving way. On looking in that direction, I saw the brigade on the right of yours had fallen back considerably, and that the right wing of your brigade was falling back also. I turned to the left, and found it giving back, too. I immediately ordered my command to fall back to the fence, which they did in good order, many of them taking the position again from which they had done such noble work a little while before, and commenced firing.   But no one seemed disposed to stop and support me, and I ordered my men to fall back as rapidly as possible.   But by this time the enemy had got so near that I knew my men would suffer severely, having to fall back through an open field for some 500 yards before getting out of danger, and that up hill.   The men were nearly exhausted from six or seven hours' hard fighting and maneuvering.

I herewith submit a list* of casualties; the list of missing, I am sure, not large enough by one-half to cover the real loss.

Too much praise cannot be awarded the officers and men who fought under my command on that memorable day.   The officers all did their duty nobly; the men gallantly, bravely, effectively.

I cannot close this already too tedious report without making special mention of our color-bearer, W. T. Jones, who was lost on the last field. He carried the colors well to the front through every engagement and every charge.   A braver, better soldier never went forth to battle, or offered up his life a sacrifice to the cause of justice than W. T. Jones.

Respectfully submitted.

WATT W. FLOYD,

Lieutenant Colonel, Comdg. Seventeenth Tennessee Regiment.

Brig. Gen. B. R. JOHNSON.

—

TULLAHOMA, TENN., March 18, 1863.

GENERAL: I submit some additional facts in regard to the hospital that I claimed in my report of the battle of Murfreesborough as having been captured by the Seventeenth Tennessee Regiment.

If any Confederate troops reached that hospital before the Seventeenth Tennessee Regiment, I cannot understand when or how they got in advance of us.   When we started into the last skirt of woods, which lies south, or, rather, west of south, from the hospital, the enemy on our left were nearly on the same line with my regiment and enfiladed our line.   General Liddell was some distance to the left and rear of my regiment.   Colonel Keeble, whose regiment was on the left of our brigade, says that about this time General Liddell's brigade had separated from him some distance, and seemed to be moving still farther to the left.   I ordered the "forward" here as soon as the enemy gave way on my left, as stated in my report.   I know that my regiment at this point was in advance of any other portion of our line that was in sight of me. Every officer in my regiment who went through the fight will corroborate this, as well as any other statement I shall make.

On entering the woods above mentioned, my line was perpendicular to the lane which passes to the left and near by the hospital.   Had my regiment continued to march straight forward it would have passed to the left of the hospital, but just before leaving the woods the regiment made a half-wheel to the right.   Now, I am perfectly satisfied that it was impossible for General Liddell's brigade (or any part of it) to start on my left and rear, as it did, separated from me, as it was, by more than the length of Colonel Keeble's regiment, and enter the woods west of south from the hospital, make the circuit on the large exterior curve, which it must have done in the face of the enemy, and yet reach the hospital by this lengthened route before the Seventeenth Tennessee Regiment did, moving, as it did, on the interior curve rapidly and without halting.   After passing from the woods west of south from the hospital, the Seventeenth Regiment was fired on by the Yankees from both sides

---

* Embodied in No. 191, p. 680.

of the old gin-house and the hospital, and this regiment continued to return a brisk fire until a white flag was violently waved by a Yankee advancing from the hospital. The firing pretty well ceased in the regiment after this white flag was exhibited, and two companies (Captains [T. H.] Watterson's and [G. W.] McDonald's) passed through the yard of the hospital and on both sides of it, and Captain [U. C.] Harrison's company passed entirely on the left of the yard. When the regiment reached the hospital, a brisk fire was again opened upon some Yankees who were running toward the Wilkinson pike, but particularly on some Yankees who were trying to get off some ammunition wagons which the Seventeenth Regiment captured, and from which the men of that regiment filled their boxes. Captains Watterson's and McDonald's companies fired from the yard fence in rear of the hospital upon the Yankees retreating toward the pike. After we had entered the woods beyond the hospital, we halted and the regiment was reformed. After we had been reformed about twenty minutes, a Federal officer came galloping up from our left, apparently thinking we were Yankees, and we captured him and his horse. The capture was made by Lieutenant [M. W.] Black, of Company E, Seventeenth Tennessee Regiment. The enemy were now in full view near the Wilkinson pike.

Now, it is proposed to deny, in the face of the men and officers of the Seventeenth [Regiment] who were engaged, that any such a conflict as described occurred at the point indicated. It is claimed that the Second Arkansas Regiment was the first to reach this hospital, and that there was no fighting about the hospital afterward. Private Elder, of the Second Arkansas Regiment Infantry, left to guard the hospital by General Liddell, states that, with Private Faidley, he took possession of the hospital, which he understood was the residence of a Mr. Griscom, and that he did not see General Johnson's brigade until some time after he had been stationed there, when General Liddell's brigade had passed to the front, and that there was no fighting at or about the hospital at that time. Private Faidley, of Company D, Second Arkansas Regiment, says he saw the Seventeenth Tennessee Regiment, General Johnson's brigade, come up within 75 yards of the hospital about fifteen minutes after General Liddell's brigade passed. Thus it is proved that the Seventeenth Regiment had no conflict at the hospital, and that it reached the hospital after General Liddell's brigade had passed. This, I must be permitted to say, proves too much. No combinations of proof can demonstrate to the officers and men of the Seventeenth Regiment that they did not have a fight in and about the yard of the hospital.

The simple explanation of all this, and the fact that the Second Arkansas Regiment had men wounded and killed near the hospital, is to me plainly as follows: The Seventeenth Regiment, after passing the hospital, entered the woods beyond, obliquing considerably to the right, and the regiment was here reformed, with the left resting about 75 or 100 yards to the right of and beyond the hospital. In this position, and after the regiment had passed the hospital, the half of the right company of the Second Arkansas Regiment might, perhaps, have passed to the right of the hospital without touching or seeing the Seventeenth Tennessee Regiment. The enemy were still in the woods, and might have wounded and killed men of the Second Arkansas Regiment by firing from the left, and, perhaps, the front of the hospital. By no other method can it be explained how Privates Elder and Faidley failed to witness the conflict which the Seventeenth Regiment had at the hospital. The regiment which these men saw approach was the Twenty-third Regiment, or, perhaps, some other regiment of our brigade, which came up over half an hour after the Seventeenth Regiment passed the hospital. And I quite agree with Private Elder, of the Second Arkansas Regiment, that there was no fighting at or about the hospital after he was placed there. In common with the officers of my regiment, I am satisfied that there could not have been any Confederate soldiers guarding the hospital at the time we passed it. Indeed, it is evident, from the nature of our conflict at that point, that no Confederate soldiers could have been there at that time.

As already stated, the enemy was in full view near the Wilkinson pike when we halted beyond the hospital. Feeling apprehensive that the enemy might charge upon us, I sent Lieutenant [J. D.] Floyd back, some twenty minutes after we halted, to bring up any of our men who might be at the hospital. He stated that he saw nothing but Yankees there, and that General Liddell's brigade was then being formed in rear of the fence which runs on the north side of the large cotton-field on the left of the hospital. Captain Watterson, of the Seventeenth [Regiment], states that, in passing the hospital at the time when the regiment first came up to it, he got a drink of water from one of the surgeons. The surgeon made some complaint about the hospital having been fired into, but said he could not blame us, as the hospital had not been properly prepared.

It may be proper here to state that the hospital is named on the engineer's maps of the field of battle as the Jenkins house, and not as Mr. Griscom's house.

The following statement, made by Captain Terry, will exhibit circumstantially the length of time which must have elapsed after the capture of the hospital by the Seventeenth Tennessee Regiment before General Liddell's brigade came up to it :

When the Seventeenth Tennessee Regiment halted in the woods beyond the hospital, its guides were thrown out and the line dressed. I then visited the captured wagons, loaded with ammunition, and returned to my company. I then sent Lieutenant [J. H.] Hastings, Company A, Seventeenth Tennessee Regiment, back, on foot, to Brigadier-General Polk's skirmishers, who were advancing on our right, to inform them where we were, that they might not fire on us. Lieutenant Hastings went to the rear, got on a stump to attract the attention of the skirmishers, and was fired at. He then returned to his regiment. I now took the horse captured by Lieutenant Black and the colors of the regiment, and rode back to notify our forces, which were advancing, that the Seventeenth [Regiment] was in front. I communicated with one of the regiments of General Polk's brigade and returned to my regiment. I then went to the hospital, passed through the yard into the first field on the left of the lane and north of the woods already indicated as being west of south from the hospital, met Brigadier-General Johnson here, and notified him where the Seventeenth Tennessee was. Met a battery ; asked some one who seemed to be connected with it (think it was the captain) whose battery that was, and was told that it belonged to General Liddell's brigade ; then saw the infantry of this brigade near the fence on the north side of this first field—the large cotton-field. I am satisfied this was at least half an hour after we halted. I passed on and met the rest of Johnson's brigade just moving out of the woods, told them where the Seventeenth [Regiment] would be found, returned to the regiment, and remained there some minutes, during which time the Fifth Confederate Regiment passed through our lines, which was still halted. I then took 3 men from my company, went to the captured ammunition wagons, and got three boxes of cartridges. While there, Brigadier-General Polk sent some men to guard the ammunition wagons. They told me that General Polk had ordered them not to allow any ammunition to be taken out of the wagons. I replied that I had already as much as I wanted. I then returned to my company and went to the hospital; found General Liddell at the yard gate which faces toward the Wilkinson pike. As I rode up, General Liddell asked a major of his brigade if he was too badly wounded to go on in the fight. The major replied that he was not, and that he would go on. The general then told the major to go ahead to his regiment. The general then ordered the Confederate soldiers that were in the yard to go to their regiments ; spoke to one particular soldier, and, pointing to him, told him to go to his regiment. The soldier replied, "You, General Liddell, just placed me here on guard." The general then said. "Well, remain there." At this time General Liddell's brigade had passed into the second field on the left, was advancing, and was nearly through it.

When the Seventeenth Regiment passed the hospital, the companies of Captains Watterson and McDonald passed through the yard of the hospital, and Captain Harrison's passed entirely on the left of the yard, a number of men of that company passing along the lane, and, as has already been shown, the firing was commenced again in rear of the hospital. General Sill's body was found not far from the hospital, "near the fence or lane," in the words of Colonel Govan, of the Second Arkansas Regiment.

Now, the foregoing statements having, in my mind, conclusively established the fact that the Seventeenth Regiment captured the Federal hospital at the Jenkins house, and that it reached that house some thirty minutes before any other troops, I cannot resist the conviction that the probabilities quite as much indicate that it was the Seventeenth Regiment which killed General Sill as that any other regiment did it. Until other facts are developed in reference to this matter, I am disposed to think that no regiment can establish this claim in its own favor. Sill might have been killed by the Seventeenth [Regiment] from the fence and lane in rear of the hospital, or he might have been killed by the Second Arkansas Regiment, which came up some thirty minutes later. Sill's body was found on the right of the lane, near the fence, and about 75 yards in rear of the hospital, and it appears exceedingly probable that he was killed by the Seventeenth Regiment firing from the fence in rear of the hospital. This is the impression prevailing in the Seventeenth Tennessee Regiment.

In making the foregoing statement, I profess to be actuated by a simple desire to do justice to all parties concerned. I would rather suffer from injustice to myself than to do injustice to a fellow soldier. I am disposed to submit the foregoing facts, with any counter statements that may be made, to the decision of the impartial tribunals into whose hands they may be destined to fall.

WATT W. FLOYD,
Lieutenant-Colonel, Comdg. Seventeenth Tennessee Regiment.

[Indorsement.]

HEADQUARTERS JOHNSON'S BRIGADE,
Tullahoma, Tenn., March 20, 1863.

I respectfully request that this communication may be forwarded to the War Department as a part of the report of the services of my brigade in the battle of Murfreesborough.

I may here add that John Wilson, a private of Company A, of Seventeenth Regiment Tennessee Volunteers, was wounded near this Federal hospital.

[B. R. JOHNSON,]
Brigadier-General, C. S. Army.

No. 267.

Report of Lieut. Col. R. H. Keeble, Twenty-third Tennessee Infantry.

JANUARY 5, 1863.

The following report of the part taken by the Twenty-third Tennessee Regiment in the battle of Murfreesborough is respectfully-submitted:

Having been changed from the right to the left wing on the evening before the batt e, its position was in an open field, the left resting upon the road leading to the McCullouch house. On the morning of the battle, the brigade and division made a right-wheel, in doing which it passed the house above referred to and continued to wheel and march until its course was almost at right angles with the one it held the evening before, marching in its wheel through a large corn-field and a meadow. Down on the edge of the meadow and to our right before we completed the wheel were stationed some of the enemy's sharpshooters, who opened upon us, doing, however, no damage. Having completed the wheel, we marched forward, obliquing to the right to avoid lapping General Liddell; we marched through a hedge-field grown up with cedar undergrowth until we reached a large corn-field. Here we received a most terrific fire from the enemy of canister, grape, and small-arms. The enemy (from where we received this fire, which lasted some time, and wounded [several] of the regiment) were within a thicket beyond the corn-field, considerably to my left and in front of General Liddell. We passed through the corn-field into an open wood, under fire of the enemy's battery, to our left, and small-arms. During all this time the enemy were concealed in the bushes, and but little, if any, firing was done on our part. Having gotten down into the woods, I was told by General Johnson that I was too far to the right, when I moved by the left flank across a road into an open field, faced to the front, and, forming with the rest of the brigade, marched through a skirt of wood across a road, leaving a hospital and old gin-house to our left. Here a change of front was made upon the First Battalion. When this was done we marched into an open field, then by the left flank across a road and into another open field. The enemy were evidently within this field, upon the brow of the hill; their battery was throwing shells upon us from there. From this field we moved by the left flank into the open woods opposite a cedar glade. We here halted and faced the cedar glade, marched into it a piece, and had a sharp brush with the enemy, who were beyond the cedar glade in a field, and marched by the flank toward our left. General Polk's brigade in the mean time had fallen back and taken position on our left. We then moved farther to the left, and, again facing to the front, marched through an open corn-field, fighting the enemy during the time. We halted at the far end of the field, having driven the enemy to the edge of the glade. Here the action continued for about an hour, when the enemy fled into the glade. I immediately advanced to his battery which he had left, when we received a heavy fire from them, concealed in the midst of the glade. It was here that Captain [N. R.] Allen, who deserves to be especially noted for his bravery, gallantry, and coolness, fell, mortally wounded. While they were firing upon us, and we were unable to get to them or see them on account of the [under]growth, my attention was called to the fact that our right had fallen back. We then fell back also, intending to reform at our old position at the fence, which, however, we found occupied by a portion of General Liddell's command (I think). We then fell back to the skirt of woods and reformed. The firing soon after ceased, and nothing else occurred.

Most respectfully,

R. H. KEEBLE,
Lieutenant-Colonel, Commanding Twenty-third Tennessee.

No. 268.

Report of Col. John M. Hughs, Twenty-fifth Tennessee Infantry.

ESTILL SPRINGS, TENN., *January* 7, 1863.

[I have the honor to submit the following] report of the part [taken in] the battle of Murfreesborough, Tenn., [by the] Twenty-fifth Tennessee Regiment:

The regiment moved by daylight in the morning with the brigade to attack the enemy. The enemy's skirmishers having commenced firing on us, Captain [M.] Lowrey's company was deployed and sent forward in advance. After the brigade wheeled to the right, this regiment rested at the end of the narrow lane. The enemy fired on our line of skirmishers as they crossed this lane. The line advanced to the top of the rise and came in plain view of the enemy's line. A hot fire opened. This regiment being fairly on top of the eminence, the Seventeenth [Regiment] was not on a line with it. The enemy seeing the regiment in advance, and on a fair place, I saw them turn their battery on this regiment. This cross-fire is, in my judgment, the cause of the great loss at this place in the regiment. After a few rounds had been fired, I was struck in the head and stunned considerably, so that I did not have strength to continue to command, so I left the field.

So far as I witnessed the conduct of the officers and men, it was highly commendable. The efforts of Captain [G. H.] Hash and Lieut. D. S. Walker were particularly distinguished.

Respectfully submitted.

JOHN M. HUGHS,
Colonel, Commanding Twenty-fifth Tennessee.

No. 269.

Report of Lieut. Col. Samuel Davis, Twenty-fifth Tennessee Infantry.

ESTILL SPRINGS, TENN., *January* 7, 1863.

[I have the honor to submit the following] report of the part taken by the Twenty-fifth Tennessee Regiment in the battle of Murfreesborough:

The regiment moved early in the morning with the brigade, Captain Lowrey's company in front as skirmishers. The brigade made a right-wheel and rested in a lane, with its center (this regiment) fronting another narrow lane. It was up this last lane that the enemy was first discovered. As the skirmishers moved across the lane, the brigade having moved a little by the left flank, the enemy's skirmishers fired upon them. No firing was done by the skirmishers or the regiment until the brigade was in full view of the enemy, on top of the rise. The regiment then commenced firing, and I never saw in any battle a more regular and constant fire, which was kept up until the enemy gave back. Although a great many of our men were killed and wounded at this place, the line was not confused, and the men continued to fire without noticing those killed or wounded. Colonel Hughs was wounded when the line first commenced to fire, and was conveyed away from the field by his friend, J. M. Richardson, a citizen.

When the enemy commenced to retreat, the regiment moved forward, but so many had been left out that it was impossible to keep a line any longer. The space between the Forty-fourth and Seventeenth [Regiments] was then too long for so few men, but the men took advantage of the good room they had and went forward like skirmishers. Most of them went ahead of the brigade, driving the enemy before them, and then shooting obliquely across before the Forty-fourth Regiment at the enemy's line as it retired before that regiment. When the regiment arrived at the corner of that woods on the left and at the corner of a field on the right, I found that the men were some of them too anxious to go ahead in advance of the brigade, and too likely to be captured by doing so, and I therefore halted them; and seeing all the regiments taking ground to the left, I directed the men that way, and, after going about 250 yards, halted and formed the men, taking our place in the brigade. Here it was discovered that most of the men were out of ammunition. They were ordered to gather all they could from the boxes left on the field, and the adjutant was sent to hunt the train. Meeting General Cleburne, he gave the adjutant orders to get ammunition from any train. Ammunition was soon obtained from some wagons. The brigade wheeled to the right, and as soon as the regiment had marched 300 yards the firing begun anew, and continued until the enemy were driven back to that cedar thicket. There a halt was made, but the fight continued some twenty minutes, and the right of the brigade gave back, and the regiment was, therefore, compelled to do the same. There was no one wounded in this firing of this regiment. The brigade then moved by the left flank about half a mile and relieved another brigade. The regiment then moved with the brigade against the enemy, firing all the time, until we crossed a field and came to a rocky cedar bluff. Here the regiment halted to fire at and drive the enemy from the thicket, but it was impossible for us to start his line. It was not many minutes until the right of the brigade left us again and we were compelled to retreat with the brigade.

There were 2 lieutenants and 7 or 8 men lost here. They are reported missing, but in all probability they are killed or wounded. The color-sergeant and colors were lost here. After this retreat the regiment was not engaged any more during the time it remained on the field.

The officers and men behaved themselves well. The regiment fought a destructive fight to the enemy, as was discovered by the dead and wounded Yankees on the part of the line we passed over. Many instances of bravery of officers and men could be mentioned, but as it seems to me that a set of men could not be more unanimous in trying to do their respective duties, no names will be mentioned, but I will only say for the regiment that all did their part with great credit.

Respectfully submitted.

SAMUEL DAVIS,
Lieutenant-Colonel Twenty-fifth Tennessee.

No. 270.

Report of Capt. C. G. Jarnagin, Thirty-seventh Tennessee Infantry.

JANUARY 7, 1863.

[The following is the] report of the part taken by the Thirty-seventh Tennessee Regiment in the engagement at Murfreesborough, Tenn.:

We engaged the enemy on the morning of December 31, 1862, just after daybreak. We were first attacked by the enemy's sharpshooters, who were about 75 yards on our right flank, damaging us considerably, wounding Colonel White and Lieutenant-Colonel Frayser. Major Mc-Reynolds then took command; I was placed second in command. Not having any skirmishers out, we did not know the position of the enemy; consequently we fell back behind a fence, which was about 25 yards in our rear, in order to send out skirmishers and ascertain the position of the enemy. Before this could be done, a forward movement was ordered. We moved forward about 100 yards, and engaged the enemy in a cedar thicket. We drove them back to a fence in a piece of woodland. We engaged them there for a few minutes and then charged them, making a complete rout, at the same time pouring heavy volleys of musketry into their distracted ranks, mowing them down with terrible slaughter. The enemy retreated back to a cedar glade, where they had several pieces of artillery planted. Owing to the advantageous position the enemy held, we did not pursue them immediately, but moved by the left flank into a skirt of woods, where we formed a line of battle and moved forward until we came to a field. We charged across to a cedar thicket and engaged the enemy. We were met with a warm reception, but were able to repel them, taking 40 or 50 prisoners. We drove them back until we were nearly within the enemy's lines. Seeing that we were about to be flanked, we fell back to a skirt of woods. While falling back, Major McReynolds was mortally wounded. I then took command of the regiment. We formed a line of battle in the woodland, changing our direction a little to the west. We then moved forward until we came to a large field. We charged across it until we came to a fence on the right of a log cabin. We opened fire upon the enemy, who occupied a second fence about 75 yards in front of us. We drove them from their position and occupied it for a few minutes. The enemy again fell back gradually. We were all the time pouring heavy volleys of musketry into them. We pressed upon them, taking possession of the crevices in a ledge of rocks the enemy had just occupied. We then poured buck and ball into them heavy. They had commenced running and scattering at a terrible rate, when the troops upon our right and left commenced giving way, with the cry that the enemy were flanking us. I could not see the danger, and did not give way. I got on a very high rock in order that I might make some discovery. I soon saw that Colonel [J. S.] Fulton and others were trying to rally their regiments, but failed. I waited until the enemy were about to close on us, and I gave the command to fall back. We then fell back across a field to the skirt of woods we had previously occupied and formed a line of battle. We did not engage the enemy any more only with skirmishers.

Respectfully submitted.

C. G. JARNAGIN,
Captain, Commanding.

No. 271.

Report of Col. John S. Fulton, Forty-fourth Tennessee Infantry.

ESTILL SPRINGS, TENN., *January 7, 1863.*

The brigade was formed in line of battle by daylight on the morning of the 31st ultimo; the Forty-fourth, occupying its position next on the right, marched from its encampment through a corn-field. When approaching a thicket, the enemy opened a battery upon us in front of the Seventeenth Regiment, of same brigade, wounding some 3 men of my regiment. We advanced beyond the thicket through a corn-field, when the brigade was halted, the right resting near a cedar thicket. Here a severe fire was opened upon us by the sharpshooters of the enemy, wounding several of our men and creating some little confusion. We here deployed a company as skirmishers, who soon drove back the enemy's sharpshooters, not, however, until they had wounded several field officers and many men. We then advanced and crossed the Old Franklin road into a cedar thicket, where we had a very severe engagement, fighting some twenty minutes before the enemy gave way. Here our color-bearer was shot down, and Major Ewin was shot from his horse, and 8 company officers fell—1 killed and the others wounded. We then charged and drove the enemy through a woodland, they offering a stubborn resistance, until they approached a large corn-field. Here the enemy were routed, some going through the field and others on either side thereof. The Forty-fourth Regiment passed into the corn-field several hundred yards, then moved by the left flank and entered a woodland.

When the brigade reformed, and was resupplied with ammunition, it continued to move forward under the fire of the enemy's battery to our right, which firing was very heavy. After marching until we reached the cotton-field, we made a right half-wheel, facing toward the enemy's battery, advancing through the field in its direction. Having sent forward sharpshooters, the battery retired, our skirmishers doing good service, killing and wounding both horses and men. We pressed forward then through the woods, crossing the Nolensville road, moving by the left flank, and, passing through a small field, entered another woodland. Here the brigade, marching in line of battle, engaged the enemy in a cedar bough [brake]. The enemy fell back. We took 21 prisoners and pressed the enemy. We found that we were in advance of our line of battle, and that we were about to be flanked by them on our right in heavy force. One of the prisoners taken said that had we advanced 100 yards farther we would have been surrounded by an entire division in ambush and thus cut off. The Forty-fourth and Thirty-seventh were marched by the left flank and reunited with the balance of the brigade, which fell back, to avoid a flank movement of the enemy, to our own lines.

Under the direction of the general, the brigade was reformed and ordered forward to support a portion of what I supposed was McCown's division, already engaging the enemy. We marched through a long piece of woods, entering a large corn-field, where we found that the enemy had checked that portion of McCown's division, which division was much scattered and disordered. Their officers were endeavoring to rally and carry them forward. At this moment we reached and passed them, passing a small house, and, crossing two fences, we entered a cedar thicket, which was the strongest natural position we encountered through the day, it being one of large ledges of rock of very rugged formation, protected by a heavy growth of cedar. Here we engaged the enemy, driving him back over a fence. A portion of the Forty-fourth crossed over the fence. It was at this juncture—the enemy gradually falling back, stubbornly resisting our advance, and taking advantage of the ground—that the troops on our right were found suddenly to have broken and given back in confusion, without any apparent cause. A mounted officer of that command, passing Lieutenant-Colonel [John L.] McEwen, [jr.,] said that we were under a heavy cross-fire and must retire. Consequently, being without support, and the men witnessing the flight on our right, fell back in disorder, in spite of the efforts of the officers present.

In retiring, our loss was considerable, 2 officers and nearly 20 men. A general retreat took place. We fell back through the field a considerable distance into the woods, where, with great difficulty, the command was reformed at 4 p. m. The brigade remained in line of battle without any more fighting, under the fire of the enemy's artillery of long range.

It affords me pleasure to state that the officers and men of my command behaved with great gallantry, with the exception of a few persons who fled the field under the fire of the enemy, and whose names shall be reported for the consideration of the general.

Respectfully submitted.

JNO. S. FULTON,
Colonel, Commanding Forty fourth Tennessee Volunteers.

R. B. SNOWDEN,
Assistant Adjutant-General.

[P. S.]—A list of the killed and wounded is also herewith submitted.*

No. 272.

Reports of Capt. Putnam Darden, Jefferson Artillery.

NEAR ESTILL SPRINGS, TENN.,
January 7, 1863.

SIR : In obedience to your orders, I have the honor to report the part taken by my battery in the battle of Murfreesborough.

On December 31, 1862, my battery was temporarily detached from your brigade, and ordered to report at Triune to Brigadier-General Wood, for duty.

On December 26, we were ordered into line of battle.

On the 27th, we had an affair with the enemy, and returned toward Murfreesborough, arriving there on the morning of the 30th, with men and horses very much fatigued by the march and exposure, having slept without tents and exposed to the rain most of the time since we left Triune. In this condition we arrived on the battle-field illy prepared to go into an engagement. We were posted on the right. Late in the evening of the 30th we were to the left.

On the morning of December 31, we were ordered by General Cleburne to report to you for duty. We found your lines just ready to move off. We formed in rear of the center of your brigade and followed on. We moved on for nearly a mile, when we came to a halt on the road. The brigade moved by the left flank for a short distance, then by the right through a small skirt of woods. Emerging from the woods we entered a corn-field, when the firing became general along the lines of your brigade. I moved the battery into the field, but could not engage the enemy without endangering our men, who were in front. I immediately moved by the left flank to an elevated position, and came into battery to the right under a murderous fire of canister from one of the enemy's batteries, posted about 400 yards distant. We opened fire with shell, shrapnel, and solid shot (we could not use canister without injuring our own men), and in about twenty minutes had the satisfaction of knowing that we had silenced their guns. Shortly after this a battery on the left opened on the brigade on our left (General Liddell's, I think). We im-

---

* Embodied in No. 191, p. 680.

mediately threw our guns into position, bearing on the battery, but could not open fire for our infantry, which was in front of us. But this obstacle was soon removed by moving by the flank to a position where they were not in our way. We then opened fire on the battery, and in a few minutes it limbered and retired with its supporting infantry through an open field nearly a mile in length. We played on their retreating columns until they were out of the reach of our guns. We then refilled our chests with ammunition and moved on as rapidly as possible. When we arrived near the Federal hospital we received orders from Major Hotchkiss, acting chief of artillery, to move down to the right of your brigade, and in rear of General Wood's brigade, and open fire at first opportunity.

We moved into the woods about midnight, between the two fields on which the Federal hospitals were located, and opened fire on the enemy, who were then pursuing General Wood's brigade, and succeeded in driving them back. We then limbered up and moved round to the right, in the field near the hospital, which is about 300 yards to the right of the pike, and, in conjunction with two guns of Captain Humphreys' battery, engaged a battery of the enemy, and, after a hotly contested fight, silenced four of his guns. By this time our infantry had rallied, reformed, and did the rest of the work for that battery. Our ammunition was then exhausted. We supplied our chests from the captured batteries, and were placed in position by General Hardee about 3 o'clock.

About 4.30 o'clock, reported, by order of General Hardee, to General Stewart (whose brigade was posted in the cedar brake on the left of the pike), to fight a battery of the enemy. After consultation, it was thought improper to open fire.

After dark I was ordered by Major [L.] Hoxton [of Hardee's staff] to the position I held at 3 o'clock. There we remained until next day, when we were ordered to rejoin our brigade. After dark of the same day I was ordered by General Cleburne to a position protecting the left of our division. Here we remained until the night of January 2, 1863, when the division moved over the right of our lines.

Nothing more of importance occurred until we retired toward Manchester. We moved five pieces of artillery off the field to Murfreesborough.

Corpl. H. A. Hendrixson wounded in the foot by explosion of a shell; Private J. T. F. Waters injured on the hip and shoulder-blade by a limb torn from a tree by a solid shot. Four others were slightly [wounded], but not enough to disable them.

I cannot speak too highly of the judgment, prudence, and courage displayed by my three lieutenants—[H. W.] Bullen, [F. W.] Coleman, and [C. B.] Richardson—in the management of their commands in the battle, nor of the deliberation and good judgment displayed by the non-commissioned officers in the management of their pieces, nor of the gallantry, energy, promptness, soldierly bearing of the privates in the discharge of their arduous duties in the ever memorable battle of Murfreesborough.

Respectfully submitted.

PUT. DARDEN,
Captain, Commanding Battery.

General B. R. Johnson.

[P. S.—Captured] Michigan battery, with shot, canister, case, and solid ball. The captain was wounded and taken prisoner, and he stated to men of D[arden]'s battery: "Killed all horses in one caisson and injured the pieces and horses so that he could not remove it. Killed 8 men and wounded a number."

TULLAHOMA, TENN., *January* 23, 1863.

DEAR SIR: I have the honor to make the following report of arms, ammunition, and equipments captured at battle of Murfreesborough, viz:

1st. I removed seven pieces of artillery from the field to Murfreesborough; caliber unknown.

2d. I captured about 300 rounds of fixed ammunition for 12-pounder howitzer, about 100 rounds of which I used in the fight.

3d. I captured about 500 friction-primers, a portion of which I used in the fight.

4th. The gunners captured gauges, rammers, priming-wires, &c., the exact number of which I cannot state, as some were lost.

5th. I captured 8 battery horses and some few pieces of harness.

The pole was shot out of one of my howitzers. I sent it to Murfreesborough and replaced it with a piece we captured from a Michigan battery

I lost 9 horses killed and disabled.

Respectfully submitted.

PUT. DARDEN,
Captain, Commanding Battery.

Capt. R. B. SNOWDEN.

No. 273.

Reports of Brig. Gen. S. A. M. Wood, C. S. Army, commanding Fourth Brigade, including skirmish on the Nolensville road, December 27.

HDQRS. WOOD'S BRIGADE, CLEBURNE'S DIVISION,
HARDEE'S CORPS, ARMY OF TENNESSEE,
Tullahoma, Tenn., January 11, 1863.

SIR: In obedience to orders from division headquarters, I submit the following report of the part taken by my brigade in the recent battles before Murfreesborough, Tenn.:

On the morning of December 27 last, Lieutenant-General Hardee, who was then in person at our advanced post at Triune, ordered me, in conjunction with Brigadier-General [John A.] Wharton, whose command was then within 2 miles of that place, to skirmish with the advancing columns of the enemy.

My brigade consisted of two companies of sharpshooters, the Sixteenth Alabama, the Thirty-third Alabama, and the Forty-fifth Mississippi Regiments; in all, about 950 men and officers.

The Forty-fifth Mississippi was posted at daylight about 1½ miles from Triune, on the Nolensville pike; four companies deployed as skirmishers on the right of the road, three supporting a section of Darden's battery on the left, and one deployed as skirmishers on the left flank.

The enemy appeared at 9 a. m.; our battery opened on him. The enemy attempted three times to place a battery in position on a hill 500 yards from us, but was driven away by our fire. His cavalry now appeared in large numbers on both our right and left flanks, Brigadier-General Wharton, with his command, holding him in check. It was found necessary to retire our guns, which I did, and caused our skirmishers to assemble and fall back under the protection of our cavalry in return to our second line, consisting of the Sixteenth Alabama, deployed as skirmishers on the left of the pike in rear of Triune, the skirmishers, thrown forward on the left behind a stone wall, near the Franklin road; Darden's battery and Captain White's battery, of two pieces, of Brigadier-General Wharton's command, were massed near the turnpike. The enemy soon possessed themselves of the heights near Triune.

In the mean time I had detailed 20 men to report to Capt. J. W. Green, of the engineers, of Lieutenant-General Hardee's staff, who had offered his services to me, and he had totally demolished the bridge across the stream just beyond Triune.

I am deeply indebted to Captain Green for services rendered during this day, in every way evincing a zeal and knowledge, as well as courage, worthy of the highest commendation, bringing his men away from the bridge only when the enemy's shells were falling in their midst, the work having been accomplished.

The enemy's batteries, placed on the hill out of range of our pieces, now opened fire upon us. I ordered the guns behind the crest of the ridge. At this time large masses of cavalry appeared moving toward our left. They were fired upon by the six pieces which were rapidly advanced to the top of the hill. Many saddles were emptied and the whole thrown into confusion.

At this time a heavy storm of hail and rain beat in our faces, concealing the movements of the enemy. It had not abated before he was found to be advancing with a line of infantry extending a mile in length. Our skirmishers fired quickly upon the line, but seeing the overwhelming forces against us, General Wharton and myself concluded at once to retire. The artillery was ordered off. One piece of Darden's had been sent to the left and was 400 yards from the pike. The enemy made great exertions to capture it, but the coolness and courage of Captain Darden; the steadiness of our skirmishers on assembling and firing on the enemy; the gallant conduct of Captain [B. F.] White, jr., in placing a piece of his battery in position on the pike, and firing so rapidly on the advancing lines as to check them (but, above all, the disposition of cavalry made by Brigadier-General Wharton), gave time to bring it off in safety. In consequence of the loss of the bridge, the enemy could bring no artillery to bear on us. One piece of Darden's was now placed on the pike, and, firing upon the enemy, permitted our whole column to retire in good order, covered by the cavalry.

We marched until dark and bivouacked 3 miles from the Eaglesville pike, where I received an order to move at dawn to Murfreesborough, which I did.

In this affair I lost but 6 men; as they were left behind, I cannot say whether killed or wounded. The enemy report their loss to citizens of Triune (and we also have it from prisoners captured at Murfreesborough) at 65.

It is now known that [General A. McD.] McCook's corps, of three divisions, was assailing us on that day.

I am, general, with the greatest respect, your obedient servant,

S. A. M. WOOD,
Brigadier-General, Commanding.

Capt. IRVING A. BUCK,
   Assistant Adjutant-General.

—

HDQRS. WOOD'S BRIGADE, CLEBURNE'S DIVISION,
   HARDEE'S CORPS, ARMY OF TENNESSEE,
     Tullahoma, Tenn., January 11, 1863.

SIR: In obedience to orders from division headquarters, I submit the following report of the part taken by my brigade in the recent battles before Murfreesborough:

Having arrived at Murfreesborough on Sunday night, the 28th instant [ultimo], on Monday morning took my place in line of General Cleburne's division, being the left center brigade, Brigadier-General Liddell to my left, and Brigadier-Generals Johnson and Polk on my right. Remained in this position until Tuesday evening, when I received an order to follow Brigadier-General Johnson's brigade, which I did, passing through Murfreesborough, and across Stone's River to the left of our lines. I was placed in position about 300 yards in rear of Brigadier-General Polk's brigade. The Third Confederate Regiment (that had been detached) joined me. I had now about 1,100 men for duty. My line was as follows: Third Confederate Regiment, Thirty-third Alabama, Forty-fifth Mississippi, Sixteenth Alabama, and sharpshooters.

We were in line at 5 o'clock Wednesday morning. Near daylight I received an order to move forward and support Brigadier-General Polk. When we had advanced half a mile, firing commenced in front; a few shells exploded over my lines. After advancing 400 yards farther, I received an order from Lieutenant-General Hardee, by Colonel Black, to move by the right flank, and fill up any vacancy between Brigadier-General Polk's right and the left of Major-General Cheatham's command. I marched by the right flank until I came to the Ninth Texas Regiment, which I was told belonged to General Cheatham's division. I then marched to the front against the enemy. Skirmishers were thrown out, who quickly returned before a heavy fire. My brigade then advanced to a cedar glade filled with rocky crevices, in which the One hundred and first Ohio Regiment lay concealed, being about 40 yards in advance of a brigade consisting of the Thirty-eighth and Twenty-first Illinois, and Eighty-first [Indiana], and Fifteenth Wisconsin. Firing continued for several minutes. Being unable to see the foe, I ordered firing to cease. The enemy, believing we were going to retire, sprung up, when a volley was poured into them, at once routing the brigade, which fled, leaving the colonel of the One hundred and first Ohio Regiment and the lieutenant-colonel and major dead, and a large number of other field and company officers, on the field. Pursuit was made, driving the enemy half a mile through the thick cedars and open woods. The lines of my brigade became broken in the eagerness of the pursuit, the men of each regiment mixing together. As the enemy retired through a piece of woods extending forward between two fields, a battery directly in front of us was firing on us.

At this point the right of my brigade captured a hospital of the enemy across the Nolensville pike, containing many wounded officers and men. It was held until orders were given to retire. The sharpshooters and Sixteenth Alabama had possession of the house, and were three-quarters of a mile in advance of any part of our lines at this hour, save the left of my brigade and General Polk's brigade. I halted them, put them in line, and ordered, in conjunction with Brigadier-General Polk, a charge on a battery. The battery fled, however, before our men. We captured one caisson. We then pressed on, though now the lines of our men, which should have been on my right, seemed to have halted. We passed across the field and through a wood and across the Nolensville pike, driving the enemy. Here we entered another field and became engaged with a heavy force in our front, while a battery of several guns was enfilading our entire line. The ammunition of several regiments became exhausted, and we returned to the wood for shelter, while we refilled our boxes.

At this place Brigadier-General Johnson's brigade came up, and he formed it and marched off to our right. We soon followed, and, by direction of Major-General Cleburne, took position on the left of Brigadier-General Polk's brigade. The line now marched against the enemy for the third time. He was again posted in a dense cedar brake. From this position our men drove him. At this point the slaughter seemed to be greater than any other. We drove the enemy out of the woods and across a field, under cover of a large number of guns which he had collected at this point. The fire from his artillery became very annoying, and the men took shelter in the timber. By direction of Major-General Cleburne, I sent forward about 100 sharpshooters to pick off his horses and cannoneers, but they could not cover themselves from the fire of his whole line of infantry, and were forced back to the edge of the field.

About this time Colonel [A. J.] Vaughan, [jr.,] came up with his brigade, and I directed it in position on my left. It had a sharp contest with the enemy, driving him back.

My men, as reported by their colonels, having expended their ammunition, I formed them in rear of the cedar brake and collected parts of several regiments, which had become separated from their commands, to wit, about 100 men of the Forty-fifth Alabama, under Lieutenant-Colonel [J. G.] Gilchrist; about 70 of the First Louisiana Infantry, under a captain; a part of a Mississippi regiment of another corps, all of which I conducted to the wood near our ammunition wagons.

At this point I received notice from a staff officer that our left was certainly threatened by the enemy's cavalry and infantry, which I immediately communicated to Lieutenant-General Hardee, who ordered me to take a position and protect our ordnance trains. I ordered the trains to move between my line and Murfreesborough, and threw out a strong picket about 500 yards in advance, facing our left flank, and bivouacked for the night.

Early the next morning I retook my position in line of battle immediately in rear of the cedar brake, where our last fight with the enemy occurred, Brigadier-General Liddell on my left and Brigadier-General Johnson on my right. We remained in line of battle—our skirmishers fighting frequently in front and the enemy shelling the woods at sundown—during the day.

About 2 o'clock I was ordered by Major-General Cleburne to move my brigade forward to a white house, which it had been ascertained the enemy had used as a hospital, to develop his lines and ascertain his force. The brigade moved promptly across a corn-field about half a mile. As soon as we had shown ourselves in the field, a terrific fire of shell, grape, shot, and minie balls fell around us. The brigade pressed on, firing. As soon as it reached a depression in the ground, near the hospital, it was ordered to halt and lie down. The order was obeyed; but in a few moments a part of the Forty-fifth Mississippi, which was on the right, advanced beyond the general line to some out-houses—perhaps for protection. The enemy's whole line opened upon us, and a brigade of four large regiments began to move around our left flank. Our line was now vertical to the general line of our forces and three-quarters of a mile in advance.

Riding to the right to acquaint Major-General Cleburne of these facts, I met Captain White, of Lieutenant-General Hardee's staff, who informed me that the general desired that no general action should be brought on. I immediately ordered the brigade to fall back, passing over the crest of a hill to the rear. This movement was executed in good order, though the command suffered severely from the fire of the enemy, and about 60 men refusing to come back, were left in the hands of the enemy. The brigade was now permitted by the major-general, in consequence of its recent fatiguing duties, to retire to Stone's River, cook rations, and rest for the night.

On the morning of January 2, by order of Major-General Cleburne, the brigade was placed in line of battle on the extreme left of our lines, *en échelon*, supporting Brigadier-General Liddell, in which position it remained awaiting the approach of the enemy, or orders, during the day and night. The enemy shelled the woods in which we were frequently during the day, and at night pushed forward a regiment at different hours on our skirmishers, who were promptly driven back.

Just before daylight, the brigade moved with the division to the right of the army, occupying nearly its original position in the line of battle, where it remained until 11 o'clock that night, when, by order, it retired.

I have to remark that in this battle the brigade, with some few exceptions, which are noted in the reports of my colonels, behaved with great gallantry. The men went into action with a spirit and determination never before so clearly shown, and endured all the fatigues without a murmur.

To my officers commanding I beg leave to call attention. Col. William B. Wood, of the Sixteenth Alabama, was always in the lead. Located on the right, and subjected by our position to a cross-fire—from the fact that the lines to our right were always behind us—he carried his regiment forward, driving the enemy before him. Colonel [Samuel] Adams, of the Thirty-third Alabama, and Lieutenant-Colonel [R.] Charlton, of the Forty-fifth Mississippi; also Major [E. F.] Nunn, of that regiment, and Major [J. F.] Cameron, of the Third Confederate Regiment, are deserving of particular notice.

Captain [A. T.] Hawkins, of the sharpshooters, distinguished himself in this action. I call attention to the remark of Major Cameron with regard to Adjt. Frank Foster, jr., of the Forty-fifth Mississippi.

To my staff I am greatly indebted. Captain Palmer, assistant adjutant-general, was always in the van, and was surpassed by no one in deeds of valor; as also my aide-de-camp, Capt. William Simpson; as also Capts. Joshua Sledge, D. Coleman, and my volunteer aide, Captain Shorter, who was wounded. Lieut. J. Percy Walker, my assistant inspector-general, is deserving of especial notice for gallant services performed on this occasion from first to last.

In conclusion, the brigade commander expresses the opinion that in this battle the 1,100 men he took into action vindicated by their blood the determination of our people to conquer their freedom or die in the struggle—504 having been killed, wounded, or captured in this battle. Many of those who are noted as missing were killed or wounded. The command is ready to meet the enemy again.

With great respect, your obedient servant,

S. A. M. WOOD,
Brigadier-General, Commanding.

Capt. IRVING A. BUCK,
  Assistant Adjutant-General.

No. 274.

Report of Col. William B. Wood, Sixteenth Alabama Infantry, including skirmish at Triune, December 27.

—— —, 1863.

CAPTAIN: In pursuance of the order to report the movements and operations of this regiment in the battles at Triune and Murfreesborough, on the 27th and 31st ultimo, I beg to submit the following:

On the 26th ultimo we were ordered to the front of Triune, to support

General Wharton and repel the advance of the enemy, who was reported to be moving in that direction with a large force. We remained under arms until late in the evening, when we were ordered to return and strike our camps, send the wagons to the rear, and take position on the hill near the Franklin pike.

At 4 o'clock on the 27th we were under arms and moved forward to take position on the hills in front of Triune. We remained in that position, deployed as skirmishers, until 9 o'clock, when we were ordered back to our position in rear of the town. My regiment was deployed as skirmishers just behind the brow of the hill and awaited the approach of the enemy. Captain Darden occupied the hill with his battery. The enemy made an attempt to turn our left flank with cavalry, which was repulsed by the artillery and my skirmishers on the left, the enemy fleeing in confusion. About 1 o'clock a heavy rain commenced and continued for nearly an hour. As soon as it ceased, and we were able to see a few hundred yards to the front, we discovered the enemy advanced nearly up to our lines. We immediately opened fire upon him and held him in check until the artillery was drawn off, when we were ordered to fall back. As we were retreating, I discovered the enemy moving up on our right flank, but we were enabled to gain the turn in the road before they could cut us off. A piece of artillery opened on them from this point and checked their advance. Our line was then formed on the pike and brought off without loss. Our casualties were 2 men slightly wounded.

We reached Murfreesborough Sunday night, and Monday morning were ordered to take position in the line of battle on the right wing near the Lebanon pike. We remained in this position until Tuesday night, when we were ordered across the river and bivouacked for the night on the river bank in an open field.

At daylight on the morning of the 31st, we were in line of battle and moved forward across the field. Before we had advanced 100 yards the enemy opened upon us with shells. Our line was pushed forward across the fields to the woods, where we discovered the enemy in a dense cedar glade, lying down behind the rocks. We commenced firing as soon as the skirmishers fell back, and continued firing for nearly half an hour, neither party yielding any ground. The general gave the order to "charge," and the men, with a yell, made a charge in gallant style, dislodging the enemy from their strong position and killing scores of them as they fled. We continued to push on for more than half a mile, when we came upon another line of the enemy. Again a fierce and stubborn resistance was made. Again the general ordered a charge, which was made with like results, the enemy being driven for more than half a mile until they fell behind a battery planted near a large frame house used as a hospital. Our line was reformed, and, with General Polk's brigade, moved up to charge the battery. As we approached, a few rounds were fired, and the battery was drawn off. We pursued as rapidly as possible, driving the enemy through the woods, across a corn-field, and beyond the Nolensville pike. As we approached the field another battery to our right opened upon us. We charged across this open field more than a quarter of a mile to capture the battery. About the time we reached another house used as a hospital, another battery (planted on the pike) opened a cross-fire upon us, and at the same time a heavy infantry force, supporting the battery, opened its fire. Our ammunition here gave out, and we were compelled to fall back to the woods to obtain a supply. It was now about 11 o'clock. Our line was again formed and moved forward across the pike and into the woods, where we again encountered the enemy and opened fire upon him. We continued to move forward and charge them whenever they made a stand, until they were driven nearly 2 miles. The fighting in the afternoon continued for about three hours. Our ammunition being again exhausted, we fell back out of the reach of the enemy's guns and obtained a fresh supply. The fighting now ceased on the left wing, and night soon coming on we bivouacked on the field.

The morning of [January] 1 we moved to our position and remained in it until the afternoon, when we were moved forward to make a reconnaissance of the position of the enemy. Being found in large force and our position very much exposed to the enemy's artillery, we were ordered back to our original position.

We were again in line of battle on the morning of the 2d, and remained so all day without any engagement with the enemy. That night we were ordered to recross the river and occupy our former position on the right wing, which we did, and remained there until 11 o'clock that night, when ordered on the retreat.

I lost in the battle of the 31st ultimo 24 killed, of whom 4 were lieutenants, and 142 wounded, among whom were Lieutenant-Colonel Helvenston, Major [J. H.] McGaughy, and Adjutant [B. A.] Wilson, and 6 lieutenants. A list* of the killed and wounded is herewith forwarded.

My regiment encountered the One hundred and first Ohio Regiment, commanded by Colonel [Leander] Stem, at the beginning of the fight. We wounded and captured the colonel and killed the lieutenant-colonel. We next fought the Twenty-fifth [Thirty-eighth] and Twenty-first Illinois, and Eighty-first Indiana, and Fifteenth Wisconsin Regiments, killing and wounding a number of the officers and men.

I feel proud in being able to report that most of my officers and men behaved with signal courage and unflinching bravery during the whole action. There were some instances of peculiar gallantry displayed which came under my notice, and no doubt others equally creditable occurred which I may not have observed. I mention Adjt. B. A. Wilson, who, after Lieutenant-Colonel Helvenston and Major McGaughy were wounded, rendered efficient services in leading the left wing of the regiment in the charges which were made, until he fell, severely wounded. Sergt. Maj. Robert [H.] Cherry, finding Company I without an officer during the action, assumed command, and gallantly led them through the fight. Private Harvey G. Sargent, of Company H, is reported as having behaved very gallantly; he lost an arm, and deserves promotion. Privates William Boyce and James Peeden, of Company C; Color-Sergt. [William] Drury Bowen, of Company H; Sergt. H. W. Rutland, of Company A; Private Peter White, of Company F, and Private Robert Williams, of Company B, acted with courage and bravery. Private H. D. Smith, of Company A, received a wound in one leg, but continued on the field, fighting, until he was wounded in the other leg. He is a young man deserving consideration.

Among the officers who displayed signal gallantry I noticed Captain [William] Hodges, of Company F; Lieutenant [C.] Davis, of Company B; Lieutenant [G. W. W.] Jones, of Company G; Lieutenant [G.] Pride, of Company A, and Lieutenant [C. F.] Carson, of Company C, who remained on the field after he was wounded; Lieutenant [T. J.] Salter, of Company D, who was wounded and left the field, had his wound dressed, returned again to his duties, and remained until compelled by suffering to leave. Lieutenants [D. W.] Alexander and [D. O.] Warren, of Com-

---

* Embodied in No. 191, p. 679.

pany F, were with their command from the beginning to the end of the battle. Lieutenants [William S.] Humphries and [J. N.] Watson, of Company K, were also with their command throughout the whole engagement. The gallant dead and wounded fully discharged their duties until they fell.

I mention with pleasure the efficient services of Capt. T. A. Kimball, chaplain of the regiment, who took charge of the infirmary corps, and followed close behind the regiment, removing the wounded as soon as they fell, himself dressing many of the wounds.

Surg. F. S. McMahon and Assistant Surgeon [William M.] Mayes were at their posts, discharging their duties faithfully, promptly, and efficiently.

Respectfully submitted.

W. B. WOOD,
Colonel, Commanding Sixteenth Alabama Regiment.

[Capt.] O. S. PALMER,
Assistant Adjutant-General.

No. 275.

Report of Col. Samuel Adams, Thirty-third Alabama Infantry.

ESTILL SPRINGS, TENN., *January 7, 1863.*

SIR: In obedience to circular of this date, headquarters Wood's brigade, I have the honor to report that on 24th ultimo I arrived at Triune, Tenn., at which place my regiment was encamped, doing outpost duty. On 26th of same month I resumed command of it. At 1 p. m. on that day my regiment was ordered forward to meet the advance of the enemy. The regiment, in accordance with orders, moved forward about 2 miles from Triune and halted until about 4 p. m., when it was ordered to form line of battle about half a mile in rear of Triune, in which position it remained until 4 a. m., December 27, when it was ordered to form line of battle on the road leading from Triune to Murfreesborough, about 300 yards from the village. At this place until about 9 a. m., when it was ordered to move across the bridge on the turnpike road leading to Shelbyville, about 2 miles from Triune, and form line of battle on the range of hills immediately south of it. At this place it remained until 3 a. m., when it was ordered by General Wood to fall back in rear of his brigade on the Shelbyville turnpike.

On night of December 28, it encamped about 1 mile west of Murfreesborough.

On December 29, it formed line of battle near the Nashville turnpike, about 1½ miles from Murfreesborough, about 1,000 yards in rear of the line formed by General Breckinridge's command, on the right wing of the enemy.

On the night of December 30, it moved across the river to the west wing of the army, and about 12 p. m. encamped on the banks of Stone's River, about 1½ miles from Murfreesborough.

Early on the morning of December 31, it was ordered forward, and about sunset attacked the enemy's lines. The enemy were in a thick cedar thicket. Going down, I ordered my regiment not to fire until the enemy could be plainly seen. The Sixteenth Alabama Regiment, which was on the right of my regiment, fired two or three rounds before the enemy in front of my regiment could be seen. When I first saw the enemy he was about 140 yards off, and I immediately gave the command to my regiment to fire. In about ten minutes after the firing commenced the enemy's lines in front of my regiment commenced giving way. I immediately ordered my regiment forward, which order it promptly obeyed, running at a rapid pace and firing as it advanced. It pursued the enemy for about half a mile, when the line became confused by the regiments, both on the right and left, pressing toward the center; it was halted by General Wood and formed. After being formed in order, it moved forward about half a mile, when it was within 200 yards of one of the enemy's batteries, strongly posted in an open field immediately in my front line, in a secure position. I halted the regiment until I ascertained that the battery could not attack, and then moved my regiment back about 75 yards to support one of our batteries on the right of my regiment. This position I held until the pieces were removed, when I ordered my regiment to fall back for the purpose of supplying it with ammunition.

About 12 m. my regiment, with the brigade, was, by order of General Wood, moved forward for about half a mile, when the regiments on the right of my regiment opened fire; but I not being able to see the enemy, ordered my regiment to move forward. When it had advanced about 25 yards, the enemy, who had been lying down, rose and moved rapidly away.

At this time my regiment, by my order, commenced firing. I pursued the enemy for about 400 yards to the edge of the wood. The enemy had taken a position in the open field too strong to be taken.

On January 1, 1863, my regiment moved forward through an open field to a hospital, about 200 yards from the enemy's lines. In this position it remained about twenty minutes under the fire of the large and small arms of the enemy, and was then ordered by General Wood back to its original position.

On January 2, my regiment during the day remained in line of battle in the same position until about 11 a. m., when it was ordered to cross the river and form line of battle near its original position on the right wing of the army.

In this position it remained until about 11 p. m., January 3, at which [time] it was ordered to fall back from Murfreesborough. For nine days my men were continually marching, in line of battle, or actually engaged in fighting; very frequently slept in the rain without tents, and during the whole time not a word of complaint was heard until they learned that they were to fall back from Murfreesborough.

In this battle the regiment, with the exception of a very few men, acted very bravely. Many of them, when the regiment was moving forward, utterly regardless of their safety, were at all times far in advance of the line. When I ordered the regiment forward, it always promptly obeyed, and when it was retiring it as promptly obeyed the command "halt."

In these engagements Capt. W. E. Dodson, commanding Company C, and Capt. Thomas Seay, commanding Company K, acted with much coolness and bravery, being in all forward movements in advance of the regiment, cheering their men forward.

Near the close of December 31, 1862, Captain Seay fell, severely wounded. Sergeant-Major Mizell, at his own request, carried a gun into the action on 31st, and took position near the colors. He fell, mortally wounded, in the first charge, in advance of the regiment, cheering the men forward.

Corpl. Isaac R. Smith, Company C; Sergeant Stewart, Company H; Private Byrd, Company I; Private Foster, Company E; Private Riley, Company D, each acted with much coolness and bravery during the engagements.

Very respectfully, your obedient servant,

SAM. ADAMS,
Colonel, Commanding Thirty-third Alabama Regiment.

Capt. O. S. PALMER,
Assistant Adjutant-General.

No. 276.

Report of Maj. J. F. Cameron, Third Confederate Infantry.

MANCHESTER, TENN., *January* 5, 1863.

SIR: I have the honor to make the following report of killed, wounded, missing, and prisoners belonging to the Third Confederate Regiment, together with the part taken by my command, in action at Murfreesborough December 31, 1862:

My command took position on the left of the brigade on Tuesday, [December] 30, and remained on the field until the army fell back. During the engagement of Wednesday fought in line of battle, but finding my command more efficient when deployed, I moved in front of the brigade about 12 o'clock Wednesday. The brigade was ordered to charge the enemy, strongly posted in a skirt of timber some 500 yards distant, a corn-field intervening. Having no support, it was repulsed. I withdrew my command under cover of a captured hospital, when I reorganized my regiment and rejoined my brigade. During the afternoon the brigade was ordered to the support of General Johnson, being too much to the left of that command. The enemy immediately appeared in our front. I deployed my regiment on the right of the fourth company and opened fire. The enemy's line was posted behind a fence. With the aid of 50 stragglers, I charged the fence, driving the enemy, capturing their colors and about 30 prisoners. The brigade then opened upon the retreating Abolitionists, killing great numbers.

My command being much reduced, General Wood honored me with a position on his staff during the fight of Thursday, Friday, and Saturday.

The conduct of both officers and men of my command, without exception, was worthy of all praise. I would call the attention of the general to the conduct of Lieut. Frank Foster, jr., of the Forty-fifth Mississippi Regiment. Ever by my side, he displayed great gallantry and coolness. Seizing the standard, he rallied hundreds of panic-stricken men, thereby reforming our then thin ranks.

Lieutenant [H. H.] Davis, Company E, was badly wounded and left at hospital at Murfreesborough. All the remainder of my wounded are within our lines.

Very respectfully,

J. F. CAMERON,
Major, Commanding.

Capt. O. S. PALMER,
Assistant Adjutant-General.

No. 277.

*Report of Lieut. Col. R. Charlton, Forty-fifth Mississippi Infantry, includ-
ing skirmishes near Triune, December 27.*

BIVOUAC NEAR MANCHESTER, TENN.,
January 5, 1863.

CAPTAIN: I beg leave to submit the following as a report of the part
my command took in the action at Triune, December 27, 1862, and at
Murfreesborough on December 31, [1862,] and January 1, 1863:

On the 26th ultimo my command moved out on the road leading to
Nashville. We moved in rear of Triune that night and bivouacked. A
detail was sent to cook two days' rations and returned during the night.
At 4 a. m. of the 27th, under direction of Captain Palmer, my command
took position as follows, viz: The four right companies, under command
of Major [E. F.] Nunn, were deployed as skirmishers on the right of the
pike, 1 mile north of Triune, the four remaining companies supporting
a section of Darden's battery, under Lieutenant [F. W.] Coleman. About
9 o'clock the advance columns of the enemy came in sight. Our battery
immediately opened fire on them, and, after firing some 90 or 100 rounds,
the artillery withdrew. I immediately deployed the four remaining companies as skirmishers on the left of the pike. In a few minutes the
enemy's skirmishers came in sight, and my command opened a heavy
fire upon them, and continued until ordered to fall back by General
Wharton to a fence some 300 yards in our rear, where we again opened
fire on the enemy. General Wharton's cavalry behaved in the most
gallant manner, protecting my flanks while retreating.

I then joined the brigade, leaving one company under Lieutenant [Will-
iam] Fox to cut the bridge. Having arrived at my position, two of my
companies were deployed as skirmishers on the right of the line of the
Sixteenth Alabama Regiment, under Captain [E. J.] Marett and Lieutenant [H. P.] Haynes. In a short time the enemy came in sight. Our
skirmishers engaged him while the reserve marched in retreat toward
Murfreesborough. In a few moments the two companies deployed joined
the regiment.

On the morning of December 31, I was placed on the right of the
Thirty-third Alabama and moved forward in line of battle. About 8
o'clock we engaged the enemy and drove him back. Just as we were
entering an open woods the enemy's artillery opened on our lines. The
command was given to halt and repeated by some one as forward. The
men became confused and our lines were again formed. At this point
Major [J. F.] Cameron, of Third Confederate, aided me in forming my
line and attached his command on my left. We next charged the enemy
in an open field and were driven back, the brigade on our left failing to
move forward, and thus leaving our flank exposed. Having exhausted
our ammunition, we were ordered to a hospital of the enemy to fill our
boxes. We again moved forward and engaged the enemy, strongly
posted behind a stone pile and cedar glade, and drove him from his position to an open field, capturing some 60 or 70 prisoners. A brigade of
Cheatham's division moved forward on my left, overlapping my regiment. Part of my command moved forward with this brigade and were
cut off from the regiment for awhile. About 4 o'clock we were ordered
by Capt. William Clare to join the brigade, some 400 yards in our rear.
We did not engage the enemy any more during the day.

January 1, about 2 o'clock, the brigade was ordered forward. Advancing about half a mile, we were ordered to halt. Seeing the left of the

brigade was moving, I gave the command "forward." The enemy were strongly posted behind some stables and a gin-[house]. We charged and drove him from this strong position, aided in part by the Third Confederate Regiment, the enemy pouring a perfect hail-storm of canister and grape upon us. Perceiving the enemy were flanking me on the right, I ordered Major [E. F.] Nunn to report the fact to you. He returned and informed me that the brigade was falling back. I then ordered my men to fall back, covering themselves as far as possible by a line of fence. During this move I am confident many of my men were killed and wounded.

Never did men act more gallantly than these men under my charge in this move, and, with but few exceptions, during all the battles. The actions of Sergeants Asberry, Doolittle, Morrison, Vaughan, and Stewart, Lieut. G. W. Williams, Sergeant-Major Kern, and Corporals Mallett, Hackler, and Read, and Private McChadin are worthy of mention. I take particular pleasure in recommending Corpl. J. D. Read for promotion. When two color-bearers were shot down, he nobly volunteered to bear the colors. He is every way qualified for an officer. Major Nunn and Adjutant [F.] Foster, jr., acted, as usual, cool and deliberate, and aided me materially in controlling the regiment. We entered the fight with 217 men and officers.

	Killed.	Wounded.	Missing.	Total.
Officers	2	5	6	13
Privates	3	35	61	99
Total	5	40	67	112
Total casualties since December 26, 1862				6
Aggregate				118

Of this number 3 officers reported missing were either killed or wounded and 23 men.

Respectfully, your obedient servant,

R. CHARLTON,

Lieutenant-Colonel, Commanding Forty-fifth Mississippi.

No. 278.

Report of Capt. A. T. Hawkins, Fifteenth Battalion Mississippi Sharp-shooters.

JANUARY 7, 1863.

CAPTAIN: In compliance with circulars, I have the honor to submit the following report, viz:

On Wednesday morning, December 31, 1862, about 7 o'clock, General S. A. M. Wood's brigade was formed in line of battle about half a mile back of the position occupied by General McCown. The battalion of sharpshooters, consisting of two companies, numbering 78 officers and men, was formed on the right of the brigade. After advancing three-quarters of a mile, the firing became brisk, and one platoon of the sharpshooters was thrown out to feel for the enemy. They were not long in finding them, and were rallied on the reserve; fell in with the brigade, and moved on into the general engagement. They fought with the brigade during the day, except when the brigade was to the rear procuring ammunition. The sharpshooters remained with some pieces of artillery, commanded by Major [Capt. T. R.] Hotchkiss, amusing themselves by firing at some Yankee cannoneers.

Both officers and men fought bravely throughout the day. Not one commissioned officer was absent from his post, and most of the command, both officers and men, deserve marked attention for their bravery throughout the fight.

On Thursday morning, January 1, 1863, this command was thrown out as skirmishers on the left of General Liddell's skirmishers, and with them succeeded in driving back the enemy's pickets about a mile, leaving us in fine view of the enemy's movements on the Nashville pike, about 4 or 5 miles above Murfreesborough. In this engagement we had no one killed or wounded.

The following is a list* of killed and wounded in the fight on Wednesday:

	Killed.	Wounded.	Missing.	Total.
Company A:				
Officers				
Non-commissioned officers		4		4
Privates	1	11	2	14
Total	1	15	2	18
Company B:				
Officers	1			1
Non-commissioned officers	1			1
Privates		9	3	12
Total	2	9	3	14
Aggregate	3	24	5	32

A. T. HAWKINS,
Captain, Commanding Sharpshooters, Wood's Brigade.

No. 279.

Reports of Capt. Henry C. Semple, Alabama Battery.

JANUARY —, 1863.

SIR: I have the honor to report that my battery of six Napoleon guns was ordered on the 30th [ultimo] to report to General Breckinridge, on the right; that we were put in position on an eminence near the river, commanding the points on the opposite side of the river near the enemy's left. An earthwork had been constructed the night before in which the guns were placed, and shortly after the commencement of the action fire was opened on us by a battery of rifled guns on the opposite side of the river, to which we did not reply, and late in the day, after firing a few rounds at the lines of the enemy, which seemed to be retiring before our men, we were ordered to another position, in which Cobb's battery and a part of Lumsden's were already in position. From this point we were frequently engaged with the enemy's infantry; on several occasions at

---

* Nominal list omitted.

a range to make our fire very effective. Occasionally we replied to a rifled battery on the opposite side of the river, but, under the orders we had received, we were obliged to husband our ammunition carefully, and engaged as little as possible with the artillery of the enemy. Several men were killed and wounded in the batteries near us, but we escaped without other loss than 1 man wounded and 2 horses.

On the next day I was ordered again to report to General Cleburne, and did so. I had asked to be relieved from duty as acting chief of artillery of our division before the engagement of the 31st, and Major Hotchkiss had been appointed to act in my place, but, as he was wounded, General Cleburne again ordered me to act in that capacity.

On Friday, the 2d, I was ordered by General Bragg to send two sections of the battery to report to him at a point ,on the Nashville pike near the river. I accordingly sent two sections, with First Lieutenant Fitzpatrick and Second Lieutenant Pollard, and they were put in position on the ground on our extreme right about 4 p. m., from which the enemy had just been driven by the attack of Hanson's, Preston's, and Adams' brigades. Lieutenant Fitzpatrick, who is now quite unwell, will soon make to you a report of the part taken by the two sections in that fierce and bloody conflict. Our infantry were finally driven back in great confusion, and all the cannoneers, but two, and two of the drivers of one of the pieces being shot down, and three of the horses from the limber, including both the wheel horses, our infantry finding them fleeing in rear of the piece, and the enemy rapidly advancing at not more than 150 yards, the last round of ammunition having been fired from it, the piece was left on the field, and, together with two guns of Wright's battery, in position near it, fell into their hands.

There were only 45 men, including the officers, drivers, and cannoneers, on the field, of whom 20, together with 14 horses, were killed or wounded in the space of thirty minutes.

The killed* and wounded were: Killed—privates, 1. Wounded—commissioned officer, 1; non-commissioned officers, 4; privates, 14. Total, 20.

Respectfully,

HENRY C. SEMPLE,
Captain, Comdg. Light Artillery, Wood's Brigade.

Brigadier-General [S. A. M.] WOOD.

—

TULLAHOMA, TENN., *January* 23, 1863.

SIR: My battery of six 12-pounder Napoleon guns was ordered to report to Major [R. E.] Graves, chief of artillery of General Breckinridge's division, and I requested to be relieved of the temporary appointment of chief of artillery of your staff in order that I might be with it.

On December 30, [1862,] we were put in position on an eminence just in front of General Hanson's brigade, but during the night I was ordered to examine the ground in front of the left of our right wing, and to attend at the construction of an earthwork with two faces in the field near the river, and somewhat to the left and in rear of another earthwork, in which Cobb's battery and a part of the whole of Lumsden's rifle battery were then in position. We went to our position about daylight, and early in the morning a section of my battery, under Lieutenant Pollard, was withdrawn and sent to another part of the field, by order of Major Graves. Although we were frequently under fire of the

* Nominal list omitted.

enemy's batteries, somewhat in front of Cobb's batteries, we covered ourselves as well as we could under the earthwork, and made no reply until a fierce engagement took place on the opposite side of the river, when we had an opportunity of firing into the enemy with an enfilading fire at good range. After about 30 rounds fired from each piece at this point, we were ordered to limber up and advance to the position occupied by Cobb's and Lumsden's batteries, about 500 yards to the right and front. This was about 12 or 1 o'clock, and as soon as we arrived we opened upon a battery of eight or ten rifled guns at about 1,000 yards, which was pouring its fire into our infantry, then advancing on the opposite side of the river, and in a very short time directed their fire to us. Our infantry continued to advance over this hotly contested field, and in about twenty minutes drove the enemy in masses past us at very short range, so that we fired into them several rounds of double-shotted canister at about 550 yards from the eminence above them. The enemy then endeavored to reform their lines under cover of the timber intervening between them and our troops, when we fired into them with spherical case, and caused them to move off farther to their right.

Such was the excellence of the earthwork constructed by Major Graves' orders, and the commanding character of the position, that we did not lose a single man, and had only two horses wounded here. The casualties in Cobb's battery, next to us, were, however, quite serious. We remained in this position until about 4 a. m. on the 1st, when I was ordered to report to you, which I did, at your position on the opposite side of the river, about sunrise. In the march to join you, I met Lieutenant Pollard, who, with one section of my battery, had acted with a part of the Washington Artillery on the opposite side of the river, without any casualty, except the loss of two horses and one man slightly wounded.

Major Hotchkiss, acting chief of artillery in your division, having been wounded on the 31st, I was ordered, on joining you, to act in that capacity.

On the 1st, neither my battery nor any part of the artillery of the division was engaged, except Swett's battery, which advanced on our extreme left with Liddell's brigade, and fired a few rounds into the enemy, who then appeared to be retreating toward and up the Nashville pike.

On the morning of the 2d, I was ordered by General Bragg to send four pieces of my battery to report to him at the junction of the Wilkinson and Nashville pikes, and accordingly I sent two sections (the right and left), under First Lieutenant [E. J.] Fitzpatrick and Second Lieutenant [J.] Pollard. They were engaged in the extreme advance and right of the artillery which supported the attack made on the afternoon of the 2d by a part of Breckinridge's division on the enemy's left wing. Captain [F. H.] Robertson, General Polk's chief of artillery, and Major Graves, chief of artillery General Breckinridge's division, expressed themselves as well pleased with the conduct of the battery, but the infantry fell back in such confusion, and the fire of the enemy was so deadly, that when Mr. [Lieutenant] Fitzpatrick attempted, under Major Graves' orders, to draw off the pieces, one of them was left on the field. Mr. [Lieutenant] F[itzpatrick] reports to me that two of the drivers and four of the horses of this piece were killed or wounded; all the cannoneers except two were killed or wounded. Our infantry had passed them in hurried flight, the last at least 150 yards, and the enemy were advancing in front and on the flank not more than 100 yards distant.

In this short engagement (half an hour), of the 45 men and officers taken on the field, 20 [were either] killed or wounded; 10 (including

Lientenant Pollard, whose right arm and leg were broken by musket shots), were killed or severely wounded, and 10 with 14 horses) slightly wounded.

I found upon the field, and appropriated to my use, about 130 rounds of excellent 12-pounder fixed ammunition, and also the rear part of a caisson, which I took in place of one of mine.

HENRY C. SEMPLE,
Captain Company Light Artillery.

Major-General [P. R.] CLEBURNE.

No. 280.

Reports of Maj. Gen. John P. McCown, C. S. Army, commanding division, Smith's corps.

SHELBYVILLE, TENN., January 16, 1863.

Lieut. Gen. W. J. HARDEE,
  C. S. Army, Tullahoma, Tenn.:

GENERAL: I send in my report of the part my division took in the battle in front of Murfreesborough, Tenn., on January [December] 31, 1862. The accompanying papers, including subordinate reports, I hope will give you all the information you desire.

  Very respectfully, &c.,

J. P. McCOWN,
Major-General.

[Inclosures.]

HEADQUARTERS SECOND DIVISION, SMITH'S CORPS,
Shelbyville, Tenn., January 20, 1863.

Having acted under the orders of Lieutenant-General Hardee at the battle before Murfreesborough, on December 31, 1862, I have the honor to make the following report of the part taken by my division:

My division is composed of three brigades, constituted as follows,† * * * my effective force being about 4,000 men.

My command was located at Readyville, Tenn., 12 miles east of Murfreesborough.

At 12 o'clock, on the night of December 26, I received orders from the general commanding to move at once to Murfreesborough. I arrived at 9 a. m. on the 27th, this march being made in a cold and drenching rain. In obedience to orders, my division was posted near the Nashville pike, behind Stone's River, as the reserve to the Army of Tennessee.

On the 29th, I moved my division to our extreme left, to fill an interval between Lieutenant-General Polk's left and the Triune road. Not finding an interval, I posted my command on the left of the Triune road, in a lane at nearly right angles to said road, and about 150 yards in advance of Lieutenant-General Polk's advance line, with Brigadier-General McNair's brigade in reserve; two batteries in reserve, and one (Eufaula Light Artillery) near my center.

On the 30th, the enemy extended his lines to our left, placing in position several batteries, and later in the day made a determined attack upon Robertson's battery, placed on General Polk's left. I directed the Eufaula Light Artillery to be posted so as to take the enemy's line and one battery in flank. Brigadier-General Rains executed this order, in person, with considerable damage to the enemy.

---

† See Organization of the Army of Tennessee, No. 189, p. 660.

About this time another battery opened upon my front, killing and wounding about 30 of my command, principally from Brigadier-General McNair's brigade. Night closed this almost a battle. During the night the enemy extended his lines, covering my front.

At the dawn of day, in obedience to orders from Lieutenant-General Hardee, I moved my reserve brigade (McNair's) and placed it on my right, and moved upon the enemy in my front, about 600 or 800 yards distant. I will here state that Major-General Cleburne's division was placed in rear of my command as a second line. The Triune road turned square to the left about 150 yards in front of Lieutenant-General Polk's left, and again square to the right about 400 yards from the first turn. An open field on my entire front; on the right of the field and in front of Lieutenant-General Polk's left was a cedar brake.

As I advanced, my right flank received a galling fire from this brake, as well as in my front, from both infantry and artillery. My men advanced steadily, reserving their fire until they were but a short distance from the enemy's position. A volley was delivered, and their position and batteries taken with the bayonet, leaving the ground covered with his dead and wounded, leaving also many prisoners in our hands; among them Brigadier-General [August] Willich, captured by Mr. James Stone, volunteer aide to General McNair, and another officer representing himself as a brigadier-general (name forgotten), captured by General McNair's orderly, volunteer King. The enemy made several attempts to rally, but failed, being closely pressed by my men, their defeat becoming almost a rout. The enemy was pressed near a mile. The force of the enemy in my front prevented me throwing forward my left wing as soon as instructed by Lieutenant-General Hardee.

In the mean time the enemy pushed a force to my right and rear, close upon the battery captured on my right. Captain [J. P.] Douglas coming up with his battery, came close upon this body of the enemy, discovering that the enemy supposed it to be a Federal battery. He obliqued to the left, came into battery, not bearing on the enemy, they waving their flags at him. In an instant he turned his guns upon them and opened with canister. The surprise was complete, and the enemy fell back in considerable disorder.

About this time a heavy force was brought against my right flank. Brigadier-General McNair, commanding the brigade on my right, discovered their movements and halted his brigade. I directed General McNair to face his brigade to the right, and file it to the right to check this movement. The moment was critical. I sent the same order to Generals Ector and Rains, which was promptly obeyed by them, leaving a strong body of the enemy in their front. Seeing General Liddell's brigade in the rear, I brought it forward and placed it on my right to cover this change of front. General Liddell became at once engaged with a largely superior force, the enemy under shelter of a fence, General Liddell in an open field. He gallantly maintained his ground until General McNair's brigade was placed on his left. General McNair at once moved upon the enemy, pushing his right on his center and forcing him from his position for half a mile. The enemy was here posted behind a rail fence. Again General McNair advanced across an open field for nearly 400 yards, and drove them from their position, capturing all but two guns of their battery—one of those afterward captured. General Liddell's brigade co-operated in this action. The enemy was actively pursued for about three-quarters of a mile, where the division was halted and ammunition issued—40 rounds having been nearly exhausted. Brigadier-General McNair, by his skill and energy, defeated the enemy in this last action before I could bring Generals Ector and

Rains into action. Here General McNair became exhausted, having left a sick bed to lead his brigade. I sent him back to camp, Col. R. W. Harper taking command of the brigade. Captain Humphreys, with his battery on my right, engaged one of the enemy's batteries in flank and rear. This battery was soon silenced or captured by our troops in its front.

We were now near the Wilkinson pike. The command was much exhausted, having forced the enemy's left back several miles, and three times defeated the forces sent to check our advance. I may here add that prisoners, except those of rank, were turned to the rear, my command being so small that I could not dispense with a single man, leaving them to be picked up by the cavalry and those in rear. Notwithstanding the exhausted condition of my men, having received orders from Lieutenant-General Hardee, I prepared at once to advance, leaving General Liddell's brigade receiving ammunition, at his request having sent my train to furnish him. I moved General Rains' brigade from the left of my division to the right, being the strongest and least cut up. He was directed to move some distance to the right, so as to take in flank the batteries posted by the enemy near the Nashville pike, at the same time that General Ector and Colonel Harper ([commanding] McNair's brigade) took them in front. General Rains met with a determined resistance, but succeeded in forcing the enemy from the woods and into the fields that lay south of their position on the Nashville pike, General Ector and Colonel Harper moving in a northeasterly direction, General Rains nearly due north. I soon discovered that my left would become engaged before my right could co-operate. I sent to correct my line, directing the men to be placed under cover and hold their ground. But before this order reached the command, General Ector came under a galling fire from infantry, sheltered in a cedar brake, and artillery. General Ector at once charged them, forcing their first line of infantry beyond their second, and their cannoneers from their guns in their front. I directed Colonel Harper (commanding McNair's brigade) to charge the batteries in his front with a like result. These two brigades were coolly firing into their second line of infantry, not 60 yards distant, notwithstanding they were enfiladed by a terrible fire from their batteries on our right. Every moment I expected to see General Rains take these batteries. I was doomed to disappointment. I was informed that General Rains fell, shot through the heart, at the moment the enemy was routed. The fall of this gallant officer and accomplished gentleman threw his brigade into confusion; also about this time General Cheatham gave some orders to a part of the brigade that tended to change their direction to their front. I now directed General Ector and Colonel Harper to fall back under cover, which was accomplished without demoralization or molestation from the enemy. As these brigades fell back, General Liddell was met in the edge of the woods, having replenished his ammunition. I directed them to form on his right. Captain Humphreys during this last contest passed through an interval in our lines and engaged the batteries on the hill on our right. The enemy turned sixteen guns upon him, but he gallantly maintained the fight until my command was under cover. Four of his guns were disabled and sent to the rear. One regiment of General Rains' brigade received orders from Lieutenant-General Hardee and was again in action.

My division had now been under fire from five to eight hours; although exhausted, the men were in good spirits. By direction of Lieutenant General Hardee, the division was moved to the right, connecting with Lieutenant-General Polk's left.

Here the division remained on the defensive, at times skirmishing with the enemy and being shelled by their battery, until the night of January 2, when I was placed in reserve between the Nashville and Lebanon pikes. Here I remained until 1 a. m. on the 4th, when, in obedience to orders from Lieutenant-General Polk, I moved to this place.

During these operations one section of the Eufaula Light Artillery was detached with General [A.] Buford. Capt. L. T. Hardy's company of cavalry (acting as my escort) was thrown out to connect my left with General [J. A.] Wharton, where he suffered severely.

Among the many incidents of this severe and protracted struggle, I would mention the following: Col. J. C. Burks, commanding Eleventh Texas Regiment, though mortally wounded, continued to lead his regiment until exhausted. Colonel Burks was a gallant soldier, and idolized by his command. In the words of his brigade commander, " A better friend, a warmer heart, a more gallant leader than he was never drew the breath of life." Sergt. A. Sims, flag-bearer of the Tenth Texas (Colonel [M. F.] Locke), seeing in one of the charges a Federal flag-bearer with his flag waving his regiment forward, sprang forward and seized the Federal flag, when both fell dead waving their banners with their last breath. The Federal flag was captured. Sergt. James T. McGee, the only man left of the color-guard, seized our colors, but for a moment, when another of our noblest and bravest men fell to rise no more. Private Manning, of Company H, then raised the flag and bore it aloft the remainder of the day. Private James W. Clark, of Company G, carried the flag of the Fifteenth Texas Regiment in the first charge, during which he was killed. The colors were then taken by Lieut. L. De Board, of Company F, who bore them the remainder of the engagement. Private Clark [D.] Jenkins, of Company D, First Arkansas Rifles, seeing a Federal officer making great exertions to rally his command, detached himself from his company, and, taking deliberate aim, shot him from his horse. The saddle had the saddle-cloth of a general officer. In the first charge in the morning, Sergt. J. R. Perry, color-bearer of the Fourth Arkansas Battalion, had his arm paralyzed by a shot striking the staff, and the flag fell to the ground. Sergt. J. C. Davis, of Company A, immediately snatched the colors and bore them until reclaimed by Sergeant Perry. Color-bearer H. W. Hamblen, Second Regiment Arkansas Rifles, gallantly bore his flag until shot down. The colors were immediately seized by Corpl. J. W. Piles, of the color-guard, who bore them gallantly the remainder of the day. Color-bearer J. B. Bryant, of the Fourth Arkansas Regiment, was wounded. Lieutenant [John] Armstrong then took the colors and fell, mortally wounded. Lieutenant [G. D.] Goodner then took them, but was soon afterward wounded. Captain [John W.] Lavender bore the colors the remainder of the day.

In one of the charges of the Thirtieth Arkansas Regiment it had seven company commanders cut down and the color-bearer, yet the men never wavered. Later in the day a second color-bearer was wounded and the colors lost in a cedar brake, but whether found by the enemy or not is not known. The only field officer (Major [J. J.] Franklin) and several lieutenants also fell, and yet this regiment maintained its organization. Seven color-bearers fell in General McNair's brigade and three in General Ector's. Col. G. W. Gordon, Eleventh Tennessee Regiment, fell, dangerously wounded, while most gallantly leading his regiment. I was informed by prisoners that the Federal General [Joshua W.] Sill was killed by my division while endeavoring to rally his defeated troops. My division moved so rapidly, and was so constantly engaged, that the guns captured were never counted; I am satisfied that [there were] at least twenty-three, besides caissons, forges, and other ordnance stores. The division passed, untouched, wagons, knapsacks, &c.

Brigadier-Generals Ector and McNair and Colonel Harper (commanding McNair's brigade in the latter part of the day) exhibited cool and dauntless courage, as well as skill, in the handling of their commands.

I cannot speak in too high terms of the regimental and company officers; all bore themselves gallantly and nobly.

To the non-commissioned officers and soldiers of my division I owe a debt of gratitude. I did not see a single straggler nor a single plunderer up to the attack on the enemy's position on the Nashville pike; every man seemed inspired.

To my staff on the field I am under many obligations for the efficient manner in which they performed their respective duties, viz: Maj. H. S. Bradford, assistant adjutant-general and chief of staff; Maj. G. A. Henry, jr., inspector-general; Maj. Batt. Barrow and Capt. F. S. De Wolff, assistant adjutants-general; Lieut. B. N. Mathes, assistant inspector-general; Lieut. H. S. Foote, jr., aide-de-camp; Mr. R. R. McClure, volunteer aide; Lieut. E. M. Ross, acting aide-de-camp; Capt. G. M. Mathes, chief of artillery.

Capt. J. D. Allison, ordnance officer, performed his duty well, not only supplying ammunition to my division, but to others.

Lieut. Col. W. E. Dyer, acting paymaster to Smith's corps in the field; Maj. M. Cheatham and Capt. C. W. Kennedy, assistant quartermasters, have my thanks for the efficient manner in which they performed duties assigned to them.

Maj. P. F. Glass, division commissary, and Maj. H. Brownson Smith, acting commissary of subsistence, rendered good service in their department in supplying the command in the field and the hospitals.

Division Surg. Gus. B. Thornton was untiring in his labors with the wounded. He is entitled to the thanks of the command.

On several occasions Lieut. D. C. Chamberlain, of my escort, carried my orders on the field to my satisfaction.

My two orderlies, William T. Brabson and William Forbes, bore themselves with great courage, and were useful to me in many ways. Mr. Armstrong, of Knoxville, behaved with great gallantry.

To Brigadier-General Liddell, commanding brigade in Cleburne's division, I am under many obligations. He came into action at my request at a critical moment, gallantly maintaining the fight until I could change my front and bring my troops into action. This was the only active support that I am aware of receiving until I was forced to abandon my purpose of establishing myself on the Nashville pike.

I feel grateful to Lieutenant-General Hardee for the consideration exhibited for my weary and exhausted command, as well as for the confidence (as exhibited by him in sharing our fortunes at one time in rear of the Federal army) reposed in them.

It is with pride and pleasure I record the gallant bearing of my division, but it is with a sad heart that I record the roll of the gallant dead and wounded.

Col. R. B. Vance, Twenty-ninth North Carolina, succeeded to the command of General Rains' brigade. Colonel Vance bore himself gallantly.

After the fall of General Rains, his staff on the field reported to me. Their bearing at all times when under my observation was very gallant. They are as follows: Capt. [Felix] R. [R.] Smith, inspector-general; Lieut. T. B. Thompson, aide-de-camp, and Capt. C. A. Nichols, volunteer aide-de-camp.

I send inclosed the reports of my subordinate commanders and a list* of killed, wounded, and missing, which please append to this report. I also send a topographical sketch of the battle, drawn from memory.

Yours, &c.,

J. P. McCOWN,

Major-General, Commanding.

Maj. T. B. ROY, *Assistant Adjutant-General.*

Confederates.
Federals.
† Batteries.
O Houses.
Position at night 31st.
a Position Liddell came into action.
b McNair.
A A Ammunition issued.
B Rains moving on Nashville pike.
C C Ector and McNair moving on Nashville pike.
D Position night 31st.
R R Federal line of retreat.
K General Rains' file.
F Liddell receiving ammunition.

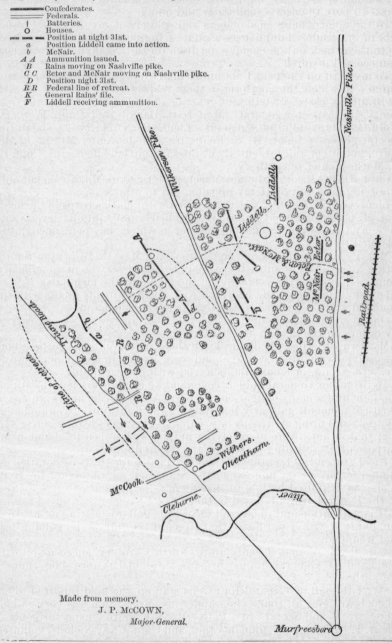

Made from memory.

J. P. McCOWN,

Major-General.

* Embodied in No. 191, pp. 680, 681.

CHATTANOOGA, TENN., *June* 28, 1863.

In General Bragg's report of the battle of Murfreesborough I find the following:

> The failure of General McCown to execute during the night an order for a slight change in the line of his division, and which had to be done in the morning, caused some delay in the general and vigorous assault by Lieutenant-General Hardee, but about 7 o'clock the rattle of musketry and the roar of artillery announced the beginning of the conflict.

This passage conveys to the mind of the reader that I had failed to execute an order, thereby delaying the attack, and that the attack commenced at 7 o'clock. Neither proposition is sustained by the facts in the case. Upon reading General Bragg's report, I applied to him to correct this error, in a communication addressed to his chief of staff, in which I say:

> I received an order on the night of the 30th from General Bragg to change the position of Rains' brigade. The change was made during the night. I also received an order from Lieutenant-General Hardee to change the position of McNair's brigade. General Cheatham was to point out the new position, which he did. The brigade was placed accurately upon the ground indicated by General Cheatham before I left for General Bragg's headquarters. As to the hour of attack, I have to say the attack commenced at 6 o'clock. This fact is sustained by the reports of my subordinates.

I forward inclosed a copy of this application, marked A, together with a copy of the reply thereto, marked B, in which reply General Bragg refuses me the justice to which I am entitled, and, by some strange misapprehension on his part, he bases that refusal on the ground that my application and the certificates therein inclosed sustain his report. This mistake is singular and palpable. He says in his report that I failed to execute an order, whereby the attack was delayed. This statement I deny in my application and sustain the denial by proof. In General Bragg's reply he assumes that this denial constitutes an admission of the fact. His report places the beginning of the conflict at 7 o'clock. My application places it at 6 [o'clock], and the evidence therewith offered proves my statement correct; yet General Bragg in his reply assumes that my application and certificates " fully " sustain his report in this respect, notwithstanding they differ an hour as to the time of the beginning of the attack. When the rules of logic are so far reversed as to make a positive denial an admission of a fact, and when the laws of nature are so far changed as to make 6 [o'clock] in the morning and 7 o'clock one and the same thing, then General Bragg's assumption that my application for a correction of his report sustains the report itself will be comprehensible, and not until then. His report and my application are the reverse of each other, both as to my failure to execute an order and as to the time of attack. General Bragg's reply says that on these points they agree.

General Bragg further says, in his reply, that the statement in his report which I asked him to correct was based on the following paragraph in General Hardee's report:

> Major-General McCown having failed to get McNair's brigade on the line of battle Tuesday night, as directed by me, the brigade was moved into position next morning.

I would respectfully state that I am at a loss to understand how General Bragg could base a statement in his report of February 23, 1863, on a paragraph in the report of General Hardee, dated February 28, 1863, five days after General Bragg's report.

I deem it proper here to relate clearly the facts in the case. Near sundown on the evening of December 30, 1862, Lieutenant-General Hardee came to the left and assumed command, and requested General

Cheatham and myself to explain the location of our commands and the nature of the ground in our respective fronts. On the latter point General Cheatham and myself materially differed. General Hardee, as I understood, accepted General Cheatham's explanation of the ground, and ordered me to change the position of McNair's brigade. I told General Hardee that either he did not understand General Cheatham or I did not understand his order. I then requested General Hardee either to locate the. brigade himself or to order General Cheatham to accurately point out the ground. General Cheatham was directed by General Hardee to comply with my request. I was thus particular because I felt satisfied that an attempt to locate the brigade as I understood General Hardee to direct, would bring on a night engagement, for which I would be held responsible. General Cheatham, by General Hardee's order, went with me and pointed out the position the brigade was to occupy, the right resting at a pile of rails near Mrs. Smith's house, on the Triune road. Inclosed you will find a copy of a note from General Cheatham, with accompanying map, marked C, in which he says:

I was directed by General Hardee to point out to you the position for General McNair's brigade, which I did just before dark on Tuesday evening, placing his right, resting on the Triune road, in a line with Colonel Loomis' brigade, which was in the front line of Polk's corps. You requested that General Hardee would indicate the position for McNair, which I agreed to do at General Hardee's request.

That McNair's brigade was placed as ordered I refer to the following evidence: General McNair's report, the inclosed copies of communications from Generals McNair and Ector and Captain [C. B.] Kilgore, marked, respectively, D, E, and F, and the map accompanying General Cheatham's communication, marked C. General McNair's report contains the following paragraph:

In obedience to orders received from division headquarters at — p. m. December 30, 1862, I formed my brigade in line of battle on the ground designated at the time.

The ground designated was that pointed out to me by General Cheatham. There seems to be a blank in McNair's report as to the hour at which he received this order. I find it so, at least, in the copy before me, the original having been forwarded; but his communication, marked D, fills up the deficiency in his report. In that communication, as you will observe, he says, in reply to an inquiry from me:

On the evening of December 30, about sundown, you ordered me to move my brigade about 200 yards in advance of the line of battle then occupied by me, and in advance of a strip of woods that extended immediately in front of my original line, which order was executed and a new line of battle formed a little after dark.

This statement of General McNair is supported by the letter of General Ector, marked E, and that of Captain Kilgore, marked F.

Now, by reference to the map furnished by General Cheatham, and which you will find with his letter, marked C, you will see McNair's original position—the thicket or woods in front thereof—and the new line for his occupation pointed out by General Cheatham by the direction of General Hardee, and then (in connection with this map), by reference to General McNair's report, together with his letter and the letters of Ector and Kilgore, you will see that I moved McNair forward precisely as ordered, and placed him on the ground designated by General Cheatham by the direction of General Hardee, and it will further appear from the papers referred to that this movement was made early on the night of December 30, 1862, and not delayed until next morning, as I am charged with doing.

As I fully executed the order to move both McNair and Rains, and as those were the only orders I got to alter my position or otherwise change the location of my brigades during the afternoon and night of December 30, 1862, it follows positively that I did not fail to execute an order for a slight or any other change in the line of my division during the night previous to the battle of Murfreesborough. As I placed McNair's brigade on the ground pointed out to me by General Cheatham for that purpose by General Hardee's order, I am not responsible for any misapprehension of my superior in reference thereto. I believed (and so expressed myself at the time) that there was some misconception as to the nature of the ground, and naturally felt desirous of placing the responsibility of any mistake arising therefrom upon those whose duty it was to bear it.

If the attack was delayed, as alleged (which I deny), that delay does not rest on my shoulder. General Bragg, in the paper marked B, says, "The attack was ordered to be made at daylight (dawn), which was then 5 o'clock." This differs materially from the written order which I received from Lieutenant-General Hardee. That order is as follows:

HEADQUARTERS HARDEE'S CORPS, ARMY OF TENNESSEE,
December 30, [1862]—10 p. m.

Major-General McCOWN, *Commanding Division:*

GENERAL: Lieutenant-General Hardee directs that you hold your command in readiness to move upon the enemy at daylight. He will be present to superintend the movement. The general will see you and General Cleburne at 5.45 a. m. at the house on the left of Rains' position—Cleburne's headquarters.

Respectfully,

T. B. ROY,
Chief of Staff.

In this you will see that I am not ordered to commence the attack at daylight (dawn), but to hold myself in readiness "to move upon the enemy at daylight." Now, this plainly is not an order to attack at 5 o'clock, for by it General Hardee directs me to meet him at General Cleburne's headquarters at 5.45 o'clock, which I did, and there received my final orders before commencing the movement upon the enemy. He could not have intended me to attack the enemy three-quarters of an hour before the time appointed by himself for giving me my final instructions for the conduct of that attack. Therefore, if General Bragg issued orders for the attack to commence at 5 o'clock, as he intimates in the paper marked B, General Hardee must have been unaware of them; and the first and only knowledge I have of them is contained in said paper, marked B, written to me long after the battle of Murfreesborough. I was with General Hardee near the hour of 5.45 a. m., as directed by his order, received from him my final instructions, and attacked the enemy about 6 o'clock. That I did so fully appears from the inclosed note of Capt. R. E. Foote, marked G, from the inclosed letters of Generals McNair and Ector, and from the official reports of my subordinates. These papers establish, beyond controversy, that I commenced the attack about 6 o'clock. The sun rose that morning in the latitude of Murfreesborough at from 7.04 to 7.10 o'clock, which brought daylight about 6 o'clock, thus making unvarying nature a witness to the fact that I moved to the attack at the appointed time and without delay.

But, admitting the absurdity that nature on the morning of December 31, 1862, was untrue to herself, and brought daylight at 5 o'clock, you will see that it was impossible for me to commence the attack at that hour, or any sooner than I did, for, by direction of General Hardee, under whose immediate command I was acting, I had to meet him only a few minutes before 6 o'clock to get my final orders for commencing and carrying on the conflict. When I commenced the attack it was just light enough to see from the center to the right and left of each of my brigades.

The announcement that daylight was at 5 o'clock (over two hours before sunrise) in the latitude of Murfreesborough on December 31, 1862, is something not only new to me, but also to the scientific world and the observing farmer. "Daylight (dawn)," the phrase used by General Bragg in the paper marked B, is ambiguous, but simple daylight, the term used in the orders given me preparatory to the battle, is plain, and easily understood.

In addition to the foregoing evidence, Lieutenant-General Polk, in his report of the battle of Murfreesborough, says:

> At the appointed time the battle opened, evidently to the surprise of the opposing army. Major-General McCown, acting under the orders of Lieutenant-General Hardee, was upon them before they were prepared to receive him. He captured several batteries and one brigadier-general, wounding another, and drove three brigades—those composing the division of Brigadier-General Johnson—in confusion before him.

This Federal division was, according to their own accounts, placed to resist just such a movement, and was 6,000 strong. My division numbered about 4,000. This is sufficient evidence of itself, I should think, to show that the attack was well timed, especially when we consider that the enemy was posted in woods, and that my division passed to the attack across open fields, and was flanked by Davis' Federal division.

From the foregoing facts two things clearly appear: First, that I did not fail to execute an order for a change in the line of my division during the night previous to the battle of Murfreesborough, and, second, that I did not thereby, or from any other cause, delay the assault on that day. It follows, then, that the paragraph in General Bragg's report, which charges me with such failure and delay, is erroneous, and manifestly unjust to me.

I have applied to General Bragg, as hereinbefore stated, asking him to correct that error. Instead of so doing, he does me double injustice, by assuming in his reply that I admit the charges. His report will become a part of history, as it now stands, if left uncorrected and uncontradicted; therefore, my honor as a man (which I prize above everything), and my reputation as a soldier (which is only less dear to me than my honor and the welfare of my country), both impel me to ask a court of inquiry, to fully investigate and pronounce upon the justice or injustice of these charges.

Yours, &c.,

J. P. McCOWN,
Major-General, Provisional Army, Confederate States.

General S. COOPER,
Adjutant and Inspector General, C. S. Army.

[Indorsement.]

HEADQUARTERS DEPARTMENT No. 2,
Chattanooga, Tenn., July 24, 1863.

General S. COOPER,
Adjutant and Inspector General, Richmond, Va.:

SIR: The inclosed application of Major-General McCown is forwarded with the hope that the request will be granted as soon as practicable. The whole matter had better be put on record and then neither party will have cause to complain. The only point made by General McCown which requires notice is that of the respective dates of my report and General Hardee's. Before making that part of my report, I called on

General Hardee for the facts and received them from him in writing, together with the correspondence with General McCown, in which the delay was acknowledged and his reasons, unsatisfactory to me, were given.

I am, sir, very respectfully, your obedient servant,

BRAXTON BRAGG,
General, C. S. Army.

[Inclosure A.]

CHATTANOOGA, TENN., *May* 17, 1863.

Brig. Gen. W. W. MACKALL:

General Bragg, in his report of the battle of Murfreesborough, says:

The failure of General McCown to execute during the night an order for a slight change in the line of his division, and which had to be done the next morning, caused some delay in the general and vigorous assault by Lieutenant-General Hardee; but about 7 o'clock the rattle of musketry and roar of artillery announced the beginning of the conflict.

This does me injustice. I received an order on the night of the 30th from General Bragg to change the position of Rains' brigade. The change was made during the night. I also received an order from Lieutenant-General Hardee to change the position of McNair's brigade. General Cheatham was to point out the new position, which he did. The brigade was placed accurately upon the ground indicated by General Cheatham before I left for General Bragg's headquarters. As to the hour of attack, I have to say the attack commenced at about 6 o'clock. This fact is sustained by the reports of my subordinates.

I respectfully request the general commanding to correct the error in his report. I should be pleased to be informed of the action of the general commanding in the premises.

Yours, &c.,

J. P. McCOWN,
Major-General.

N. B.—I send papers marked A, B, C.

[Inclosure B.]

HEADQUARTERS ARMY OF TENNESSEE,
Shelbyville, Tenn., June 5, 1863.

Major-General McCOWN, *Chattanooga, Tenn.:*

SIR: The general commanding directs me to acknowledge the receipt of your note of the 17th ultimo, and in reply to say that the paragraph in his report of the battle of Murfreesborough which you regard as injurious to yourself is fully sustained by your admission and by the certificate you inclose. The paragraph was based on that of General Hardee, which says:

Major-General McCown having failed to get McNair's brigade on the line of battle Tuesday night, as directed by me, the brigade was moved into position early the next morning.

The attack was ordered to be made at daylight (dawn), which was then 5 o'clock. When the action became distinct with artillery and volleys of musketry it was 7 o'clock, as marked by the watch of the commanding general. He had been more than two hours on the field, and felt and exhibited surprise and anxiety at the delay. The order to you admitted of no conditions, and the general commanding cannot understand your right to suspend an important movement ordered by your superior commanders because you supposed it might be seen by the enemy or might cause an engagement. That was a question for your superior. As the commanding general only reported a simple fact communicated by your immediate commander, and which you substantiate and admit, he cannot see that any injustice is done you. Any explanation of the delay you acknowledge will be forwarded to form a part of the report of the battle.

I am, general, very respectfully, your obedient servant,

H. W. WALTER,
Assistant Adjutant-General.

[Inclosure C.]

HEADQUARTERS CHEATHAM'S DIVISION,
Shelbyville, Tenn., June 1, 1863.

Maj. Gen. JOHN P. McCOWN, *Chattanooga, Tenn.:*

GENERAL: In answer to your inquiries, I have to state I was directed by General Hardee to point out to you a position for General McNair's brigade, which I did just before dark on Tuesday evening, placing his right, resting on the Triune road, on a line with Colonel Loomis' brigade, which was in the front line of Polk's corps. The position of McNair's brigade was somewhat of a curved line, as will be seen by the accompanying map. You requested that General Hardee would indicate the position for McNair, which I agreed to do at General Hardee's request. The right of McNair's brigade was on the front line of Polk's corps, but about 100 or 120 yards in rear of the line occupied by General Ector on the lane. His left was in the direction of Ector's right.

Very respectfully,

B. F. CHEATHAM,
Major-General, C. S. Army.

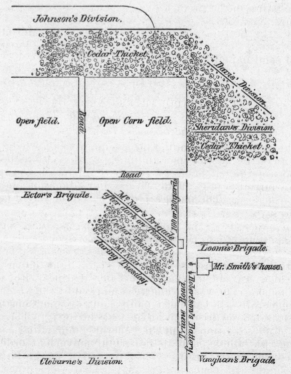

[Inclosure D.]

HEADQUARTERS THIRD BRIGADE, McCOWN'S DIVISION,
Camp Harper, ——— —, 1863.

Major-General McCOWN,
    Chattanooga, Tenn. :

GENERAL : In reply to your inquiry, I have the honor to state that on the evening of December 30, [1862,] about sundown, you ordered me to move my brigade about 200 yards in advance of the line of battle then occupied by me, and also in advance of a strip of woods that extended immediately in front of the original line, which order was executed and a new line of battle formed a little after dark. I then occupied the right of your division, about 300 yards from the enemy's pickets. This position was taken, as I understood, for the purpose of attacking the enemy at daylight the next morning. On the morning of the 31st, by your direction, I moved my brigade forward, and, in connection with the First and Second Brigades, of your division, attacked the enemy. This was about 6 a. m.

    I am, most respectfully, your obedient servant,

                                 E. McNAIR.

[Inclosure E.]

HEADQUARTERS ECTOR'S BRIGADE, McCOWN'S DIVISION,
Shelbyville, Tenn., May 9, 1863.

Maj. Gen. JOHN P. McCOWN:

DEAR SIR : In reply to your letter of May 7, written from Chattanooga, I state that Rains', McNair's, and my brigades were formed in line of battle, and that these three brigades advanced together at the battle of Murfreesborough on December 31, at about 6.06 a. m. General McNair's brigade during the night was moved forward considerably in advance of the position it had occupied during the latter part of the evening before, with its right resting on the Triune road. If it had been moved up on a line with my brigade at the time it first changed its position (from what I know of the enemy's position, and no one had a better opportunity of knowing this than I had), I am confident its movements could not have been concealed from the enemy, and it would, in all probability, have brought on a fight during the night.

    I am, sir, yours, very respectfully,

                                   M. D. ECTOR.

[Inclosure F.]

                            NEWNAN, GA., *May* 4, 1863.

Maj. Gen. JOHN P. McCOWN,
    Chattanooga, Tenn. :

SIR : In compliance with your request, I take pleasure in stating what I know in reference to the movements made by General McNair's brigade on Tuesday night, December 30, 1862.

Returning from General Cheatham's headquarters about 8 o'clock that night, I noticed troops moving forward. I ascertained it was General McNair's brigade moving up near the line occupied by the balance of the division. The first regiment was established a little in advance of Mr. Smith's house, the right resting on the Triune road near a pile of rails and other timbers which had been thrown out of the way during the day. From my knowledge of the enemy's position I do not think the brigade could have been moved upon a line with the other brigades of the division without encountering the enemy's pickets, and probably bringing on an engagement.   On the morning of the 31st, however, it came up on the line, and the whole division moved forward in line of battle about daylight.

I have the honor to be, very respectfully, your obedient servant,
                                    C. B. KILGORE,
                        Assistant Adjutant-General, Ector's Brigade.

[Inclosure G.]

                        CHATTANOOGA, TENN., *May* 11, 1863.

Maj. Gen. JOHN P. McCOWN,
        Chattanooga, Tenn.:

GENERAL: In reply to your question propounded to me this morning, I have the honor to state that on the morning of December 31, 1862, when the line of our division became engaged with those of the enemy at Murfreesborough, I looked at a watch and it was exactly eight minutes to 6 o'clock.

I am, general, very respectfully, your obedient servant,
                                    R. E. FOOTE,
                        Captain, Provisional Army, Confederate States.

No. 281.

Report of Capt. J. D. Allison, ——, Chief Ordnance Officer.

            HEADQUARTERS ORDNANCE DEPARTMENT,
                Shelbyville, Tenn., January 11, 1863.

SIR: Wednesday morning, December 31, 1862, found my ordnance train encamped on the east bank of Stone's River, on the Triune road.   At daylight I received orders from the major-general commanding to follow close behind, and at 8 a. m. I issued to General McNair's brigade; about 9 a. m. to Generals Rains' and Preston Smith's brigades; an hour later to Generals Ector's and Liddell's brigades.   Taking up my position near the hospital, designated by the major-general, I remained until he ordered me to occupy a position in a small grove on the right of the Wilkinson pike, about the center of our division and some half a mile to the rear.   Here I remained but a short time, when I was, by the shot and shell of the enemy, compelled to leave and again take my former position near the hospital.   About 12 o'clock I was ordered up to supply General McNair, also a portion of Generals Ector's and Preston Smith's brigades.   I was then ordered by Lieutenant-General Hardee's ordnance officer to retire some mile or more across the Wilkinson pike toward the Triune road.   About 2.30 p. m. I was ordered to supply a portion of Generals McNair's and Ector's commands.   This done, I supplied a large portion of Generals Wheeler's and Wharton's commands.   Again going to the rear, I remained until the firing of small arms ceased, and after dark I moved up and encamped on the Wilkinson pike, near the mouth of a lane.   My entire train consisted of 23 wagons, one of which (belonging to General Rains' brigade) I lost by its breaking down.

On the next day I procured another wagon and sent for the stores, but found they had been removed.

Three captured Federal wagons and teams were turned over to me, one containing field-gun ammunition and the others small-arm cartridges— 18,000 each.

It affords me pleasure in being able to state that the promptness and energetic manner in which Lieut. J. N. Lane, of General McNair's ordnance; Lieut. H. C. Leigh, ordnance officer to General Ector; Sergt. C. F. Maxey, in charge of General Rains' ordnance, and Sergt. G. W. Morrie, of the division ordnance, moved in execution of orders, did much to assist me in supplying troops and disposing of my train.

I beg the honor, major, to be, very respectfully, your very obedient servant,

J. D. ALLISON,
Captain and Chief of Ordnance to Major-General McCown.

Maj. H. [S.] BRADFORD,
Chief of Staff and Assistant Adjutant-General.

No. 282.

Report of Maj. George M. Mathes, ———, Chief of Artillery.

HEADQUARTERS McCOWN'S DIVISION, SMITH'S CORPS,
Shelbyville, Tenn., January 11, 1863.

MAJOR : I have the honor of submitting the following report of the part the batteries of this division took in the engagements of December 30 and 31, [1862,] before Murfreesborough :

On the 29th, when the division was in position in reserve, in rear of Stone's River, near the Nashville pike, I received an order from the major-general commanding to detach one section of rifled pieces from one of the batteries, with orders to report to Brigadier-General [A.] Buford, on the Salem pike, which was done from the Eufaula Light Artillery, General Rains' brigade (Lieutenant [W. A.] McDuffie commanding), under charge of Lieutenant [W. J.] McKenzie.

When the division was ordered from its reserve position to the left, on the Triune road, the batteries were moved in mass in rear of the division to its new position. The batteries of Captains Douglas and Humphreys were placed in reserve, and Lieutenant McDuffie, commanding Eufaula Battery, was ordered to take position in line to support his brigade (Rains') during the day of the 30th, when the firing became very heavy on Robertson's battery. Lieutenant McDuffie was ordered to take position to support and relieve Captain Robertson, which he did, doing great damage to one of the enemy's batteries, forcing it to change position, and, prisoners state, dismounting one gun and killing several cannoneers. Lieutenant McDuffie kept his battery at 500 yards range until his ammunition was exhausted, when he was ordered to draw off his battery and fill his ammunition chests.

The lieutenant commanding and the men of the battery deserve great credit for the cool and skillful manner in which the battery was handled under the severe fire of two or more batteries. The loss of the battery was 1 man wounded and 1 horse killed.

At daylight on the morning of December 31, all of the batteries of the division were ordered forward. Captain Douglas, of General Ector's brigade, was ordered to take position and go into action on the left of the house on the left of Lieutenant-General Polk's line, which he did, engaging the enemy at short range, throwing the enemy into confusion and greatly facilitating the rout of the enemy on the left. On account of damages received by his battery, Captain Douglas was delayed in following up the division immediately, and was consequently some distance behind by the time he was in condition to move forward, which he did as soon as possible. Captain Humphreys' battery (McNair's brigade) was ordered up to take position on the right of Captain Douglas and to support him; but the enemy having fled before he could arrive, he pushed on his battery and passed to the right of the division, and engaged the enemy near the Wilkinson pike. He was engaged by a vastly superior force of the enemy's artillery, and had four of his guns disabled and five men wounded and several horses killed. He held his position with his two remaining guns until the artillery of the enemy was captured or forced to retire.

Both the officers and men of this battery deserve credit for the gallant manner in which they stood by their guns and served them. The battery commanded by Lieutenant McDuffie not having been furnished with sufficient ammunition, it was left in reserve near the house on General Cheatham's left, where it remained until about 2 p. m., when it was moved across the Wilkinson pike, but was ordered back by Brigadier-General Maney to take position to cover the retreat of our division in case they were compelled to fall back at this place. I put all the batteries of this division in position at the place where they remained until Friday night, when they were ordered to Murfreesborough.

I gathered up and sent to Murfreesborough on this day sixteen pieces of artillery, a number of caissons, and some battery wagons, forges, &c., captured by this division. Major [L.] Hoxton, chief of artillery, Lieutenant-General Hardee's corps, assisted and had others carried off the field. In consequence of the recent rains, the ground was almost impassable for the movements of artillery, and the division was, in a measure, deprived of this arm.

I am, respectfully,

GEO. M. MATHES,
Acting Chief of Artillery, Major-General McCown's Division.

Maj. H. S. BRADFORD,
Assistant Adjutant-General.

No. 283.

Report of Brig. Gen. M. D. Ector, C. S. Army, commanding First Brigade.

HEADQUARTERS FIRST BRIGADE, McCOWN'S DIVISION,
Shelbyville, Tenn., January —, 1863.

In obedience to special orders from division headquarters, it becomes my duty to make a report of the operations of my brigade in the recent battles before Murfreesborough.

During the night of the 30th ultimo, I was ordered to have my command in readiness to move upon the enemy at daylight on the next morning. General McNair's brigade was to move up in position on my right and General Rains' brigade on my left. The enemy were known to be in strong force immediately in front of us, supported by several batteries. These were posted near the edge of the timber. There was a level field between us, about 500 yards across it. A few minutes after 6 a. m. on December 31, the two brigades had arrived in the position indicated, and the command "Forward, march," was given. The three brigades moved off together. When we had arrived within about 200 yards of the enemy's batteries in front of my brigade, they opened fire upon us. Immediately the order was given to charge. The enemy were not expecting such a movement on our part. Their infantry fired into us about this time. None of the three brigades faltered for a moment. When we had arrived within about 100 yards of their batteries, I ordered my men to fire. We poured a hot and deadly fire into them and continued to advance. Such determination and courage was perfectly irresistible. My brigade was within 30 yards of their cannon when they fired the second round. Quite a number of my brigade were killed and wounded, but the gaps made by the canister and small-arms closed up in an instant. In this charge Col. J. C. Burks, commanding the Eleventh Texas Regiment, received a mortal wound. Their infantry gave way about the time we reached their batteries. They attempted to form again behind a second battery. We pressed upon them so rapidly they soon gave way the second time. At a fence they made a short stand, but were driven from it. We passed over two cannon which they had attempted to get off with. They continued to keep up a running fight for awhile, taking shelter behind the farm-houses which lay in the line of their retreat. The rout soon, however, became complete. I soon discovered that we had separated from General McNair's brigade. After pursuing the enemy 2½ miles, I halted my command, faced it to the right, intending to proceed with it in the direction of a heavy firing of small-arms; in that direction I supposed General McNair's brigade had gone. We had captured quite a number of prisoners, who had been sent to the rear. The enemy in their hasty retreat had left their camp equipage; and guns, blankets, overcoats, and knapsacks marked the line of their retreat. General Wharton's cavalry brigade continued in pursuit of those we had been after, and killed and captured (as I have since learned) many of them.

About this time I received an order from the division commander to move my command so as to rejoin General McNair, who, with General Liddell, was engaging the enemy. This order was promptly obeyed by both General Rains and myself. After marching about 1½ miles, we came up with General McNair's brigade. They had driven the enemy some distance, and were halted for the purpose of getting a new supply of ammunition. As most of my men had nearly exhausted their 40 rounds, they were also halted and ordered to supply themselves with ammunition. General Rains thought his men were pretty well supplied, and, after making a short halt, he was ordered to the right of the other two brigades in a northeast direction until he came up with the enemy. He had gone, I would say from the firing in this direction, but little over half a mile before he engaged them. We were ordered forward, and I was told to cause the left of my brigade to oblique to the right. We had marched about 1 mile in this direction. General Rains in the mean time was driving back the enemy, when, unfortunately, he fell, mortally wounded. He had driven them through a dense cedar forest and into a field. Their left wing had either been routed or driven back upon their center; the right of their center had also been driven back some distance, and their forces were thus massed in a very formidable position in a field not far from the Nashville pike. General McNair's and my brigades entered the field near the southwest corner (just above it). About 200 yards from the west side of the fence, immediately before us, was a cedar brake. Near the head of this brake it widened out, where the ground was very rocky. I had thought for some time the left of my command was obliquing too much, and so informed the division com mander. He sent me word that General Hardee, who was in command of that corps of our army, desired I should continue to move in this way. The enemy were in ambuscade in this cedarbrake on the left of my command. They had a very formidable battery planted about 250 yards in a northeast direction from us; one nearly in a north direction about the same distance off, and the third one in a field a quarter of a mile north-west of us. All these batteries turned loose upon us. About the same time their infantry, whose position had been ascertained by my skir-mishers, unmasked themselves and opened fire. The Fourteenth and Fifteenth Texas Regiments were soon in a desperate struggle; the regi-ments on the right of them were equally exposed to their artillery. I im-mediately sent Major [F. M.] Spencer to Colonel Harper, who was in command of the brigade on my right (General McNair having become too unwell), to move his brigade up to my assistance. I hastened to the left of my command. My men had driven back one line of their infantry upon the second line; still behind them was a third line. I have since learned that a short distance behind these was General Rosecrans' head-quarters. The cedars were falling and being trimmed by bombs, canis-ter, and iron hail, which seemed to fill the air. My men had not yielded an inch, but, sheltering themselves behind the rocks, would lie down and load, rise to their knees, fire into the closed blue line not over 60 yards from them. I saw their officers several times trying to get their men to charge us, but they would not. Believing it to be impossible to bring my entire brigade to bear with full force, and that an attempt to do it would be attended with great sacrifice of life, I ordered them to fall back. The enemy did not, so far as I was able to discover, follow us. On reaching the woods, I formed the brigade and ordered the men to rest. In a short time, in obedience to orders, I moved it to the left and took position behind a fence, where my men could rest themselves and check any attempted advance of the enemy in that direction.

It is due to my brigade to say they had been under almost constant fire for eight hours; that one-third, almost, of my command had been killed or wounded, and most of the rest were very much exhausted.

About two hours by sun I was ordered to move farther to the east and to the right. We were halted in a dense cedar forest, where the ground was covered with large rocks. This ground had been three times fought over during the day. The battle continued to rage with uninter-rupted fury until long after dark farther to the right. For over twelve long hours it had continued from the time it had opened on their right wing in the morning. We occupied all the ground at night which had been fought over during the day, except on his extreme left. Most of his dead and wounded were left within our lines. We occupied a very strong position, and one, with a little labor on our part, from which we could not be easily driven. Our line of battle was formed; we threw out our pickets, built small fires—which were very acceptable, as we had been without them for two days and nights—and were permitted to rest undisturbed during the night.

Early the next morning the men made them a secure breastwork of rock. This completed, every man took his position ready to receive the enemy in a proper manner. The day passed off quietly until late in the evening, when an effort was made to shell us out of our position. The timber being so thick and our breastworks substantial, they could effect nothing. Our pickets would exchange shots with them frequently during the day and night.

On the second day, about night, the enemy again shelled the woods for some time. Their pickets advanced, and there was considerable skirmishing with the pickets along the lines. They were prudent enough to keep at a respectable distance from our breastworks.

Captain Douglas' battery, belonging to my brigade, did efficient service in the early part of the engagement. After we had driven the enemy from their guns, and had followed on in pursuit of them, a considerable body of the enemy moved in behind us from our right and formed. About sun-up, Captain Douglas was ordered to move up with his battery toward the enemy's line and join his brigade. He ordered the battery forward immediately; rode himself rapidly in advance to ascertain the position of the troops. After riding to the point where the enemy's first battery was captured, he found that we had captured the b[attery] and were rapidly pursuing. He returned to the battery, and put his horses to their best speed to assist in holding the advanced position attained. When he arrived within 150 yards of the captured battery (his battery being at its best speed), he discovered a body of Federal infantry drawn up in line in front of the position occupied by the captured guns, and not far from his head team. He immediately halted the battery and gave the command, "Front into line." Discovering that the enemy did not know whether he was friend or foe, he gave the command, "Left oblique and action front," thus bringing his guns into positions not bearing exactly on the enemy. During this time Captain Douglas says the enemy waved their flag at him. Seeing no time was to be lost, he ordered the gunners to commence firing with canister. The enemy fired about this time, wounding 1 man, killing 3 horses, and wounding 3 more. He soon threw a rapid and deadly fire into the enemy's ranks. They stood but a few discharges, when they retreated in considerable disorder. As this battery was separated from my brigade throughout the remainder of the day, I would respectfully refer you to his report, herewith inclosed, for a full and complete report of all its movements.

At 10 a. m. on the 3d ultimo [instant] we left our breastworks, and moved near the Lebanon road, just above Murfreesborough.

The officers, non-commissioned officers, and privates, so far as I was able to judge, were at their post and did their duty to my entire satisfaction. They were at all times ready to obey my commands, and at no time during the day gave an inch of ground until they were ordered.

Colonel Burks was gallantly leading his regiment, which had followed him before through the fire and smoke of battle, when he received a fatal wound. He felt that it was mortal. He pressed his hand to it to conceal it, and when within 20 yards of their battery I heard him distinctly say, "Charge them, my boys; charge them." He kept up until, from faintness, he found he could go no farther. A better friend, a warmer heart, a more gallant leader than he was never drew the breath of life. He was idolized by his regiment, and highly esteemed by all who knew him well. He perished in the pride of his life, in the "thunders of a great battle." He went down with his armor on in defense of his country.

The Tenth Texas Regiment captured three stand of colors.

Colonel Andrews and Major [W. E.] Estes, of the Fifteenth Texas Regiment; Colonel Locke, Major [W. D. L. F.] Craig (acting lieutenant-colonel), and Captain [H. D. E.] Redwine (acting major), of the Tenth Texas Regiment, and Lieutenant-Colonel Bounds, of the Eleventh Texas Regiment, together with their entire staffs, acted most gallantly.

The conduct of the different company officers was all that I could have desired.

Captain Kilgore, my assistant adjutant-general, and Major Spencer were conspicuous throughout the day. They were always among the foremost in the charge, leading, directing, encouraging the men, and ready to execute with promptness every order they received. I would especially recommend them for promotion for gallant conduct on the battle-field. They deserve a higher position than they now occupy.

I would speak in the like high terms of the conduct on the battle-field of Capt. R. Todhunter, a volunteer aide. He was slightly wounded in the first of the action, but remained upon the field. I would also specially recommend him for promotion.

Capt. W. H. Smith, acting inspector-general, and Aide-de-camp H. M. Lane rendered me very efficient service. Lieutenant Lane was also slightly wounded.

Maj. Wiley B. Ector, brigade quartermaster, besides discharging his other duties, kept us supplied with cooked rations, and, with a detail, went over the battle-field and collected and buried the dead of the brigade.

Dr. L. J. Graham, the brigade surgeon, was always efficient in caring for, removing, and providing for the wounded. In fact, so far as I have been able to ascertain, all the surgeons deserve credit for the manner in which they discharged their several duties.

I lost 38 killed and 308 wounded in the battle.

In conclusion, I would say that the private soldiers of the brigade have endeared themselves to me by the manner in which they performed the duties and endured the perils they were subjected to during the trying ordeal through which they have just passed.

Respectfully submitted.

M. D. ECTOR,
Brigadier-General, Comdg. First Brig., McCown's Division.

Maj. H. S. BRADFORD,
Assistant Adjutant-General.

No. 284.

Report of Col. M. F. Locke, C. S. Army, Tenth Texas Cavalry (dismounted).

CAMP NEAR SHELBYVILLE, TENN.,
January 10, 1863.

DEAR GENERAL: In compliance with your order (No. —) of the 9th instant, I have the honor to submit the following report, showing the operations of the Tenth Regiment Texas Cavalry in the late battles in front of Murfreesborough:

On Tuesday evening, January [December] 30, [1862,] while our battery and that of the enemy were firing directly across the right wing of my regiment, a ball from a rifle cannon of the enemy struck the cedar-rail barricade in front of the command, and timber from the fence bruised four of the privates and slightly wounded Lieut. J. B. Griffin, of Company C, who was severely [wounded] the following day. Seeing that the situation of the Tenth Regiment was more exposed than that of any other in the brigade on that evening, owing to the facts that a gap of several hundred yards intervened between the right wing (this regiment being on the right of the brigade) and the next command, to wit, General Smith's brigade, on our right, and that powerful efforts were being made by the enemy on that evening to gain a direct range of the line of the Texas Brigade with their artillery, and later in the day the enemy having shifted their position and placed their battery directly in front of this regiment, it was apparent that the fence which had obstructed the sight of the enemy would serve as an auxiliary in the enemy's hands if our position was discovered. Knowing this, although the weather was very inclement and disagreeable, I did not allow any fire, and the blankets having been left at camp, the men suffered very much; and but for the fact that they had been lying on their arms without sleep for two nights previous, sleep would have been impossible.

Having been kept in a silent, still position for two days and nights during disagreeable weather, on the morning of December 31, 1862, when orders came that the command would move forward, it was difficult to restrain the expression of joy and outburst of feeling manifested by the men at an opportunity being presented upon an open field (such as lay before us) of relieving ourselves from this unhappy condition, and of deciding the fate of the Confederacy to the extent that a little regiment was able to go. It will be remembered that, in the first charge made on the morning of the 31st, my orders required that I should keep close on General McNair's brigade, who had just moved into the gap alluded to on the right of my regiment, and that in doing so it threw the center of the Tenth Regiment directly in front of the enemy's battery, consisting of six brass pieces of superior quality, which opened upon our lines immediately after leaving the cedar-fence barricade; and as there was no obstruction between this command and the enemy's lines in that direction, it must be that the houses, shade trees, and fencing on the left and the cedar timber and fencing on the right sheltered to some extent the brave troops on each side of us, causing the disparity in the number killed and wounded in the different regiments of the division and brigade. For some 400 yards before we drove the enemy from their position immediately in rear of the first battery and captured the same, my regiment marched in full view of the infantry and artillery, and before the sun rose we numbered of killed and wounded some 80 men.

At this point I will mention an incident in this bloody conflict: The enemy's lines having been formed immediately in our front, their standard-bearer, directly in front of mine, was waving his flag, casting it forward, and, by various motions, urging the Abolition column forward, when Sergt. A. Sims, flag-bearer of this regiment, discovered him and pressed forward with incredible speed directly toward the enemy's banner, and, on reaching within a pace or less of his adversary, he planted the Confederate flag firmly upon the ground with one hand and with a manly grasp reached the other after the flag-staff held by his enemy; but the other gave back, and in that moment they both fell in the agonies of death, waving their banners above their heads until their last expiring moments. My flag-bearer having fallen, and there being but one of my old color-guard left, Sergt. James T. McGee was only spared to advance a few paces toward his banner, when another of our noblest and bravest men fell to rise no more until aroused by the Trump of God to come to judgment. At this moment Private Manning, of Company H, gathered the flag-staff and rushed to the front with a spirit and nerve sufficient for any calling, and bore the same aloft throughout the day.

Two stand of colors are known to have been taken by this regiment, and, it is believed, three; but as all were sent to the rear by the wounded and the infirmary corps, I have not had opportunity to look them up.

Of Major (Acting Lieutenant-Colonel) Craig and senior Captain (Acting Major) Redwine and Adjutant [J. J.] Jarvis, I will say that they all of them proved themselves fully equal to the emergency on that occasion; and, in my opinion, the display of valor and unflinching bravery in the conflict on December 31, 1862, has not been surpassed upon this continent.

The loss sustained by this command will foot up as follows, to wit: The number of comm[issioned officers] engaged was 20, and of that number 11 were killed, wounded, or left in the enemy's lines. The total number in battle was about 350 men. Of that number 117 were either left in the enemy's lines, killed, or wounded.

As stated, we captured, it is confidently believed, three stand of the enemy's colors and at least six pieces of brass cannon.*

In conclusion, I wish not by the mention of names to make distinction between men where all acted so nobly, but it is with peculiar pride I state the fact that all of my men knew their rights and dared to defend them, reckless of hazard or consequence.

All of which is most respectfully submitted.

M. F. LOCKE,
Colonel, Commanding Tenth Regiment Texas Cavalry.

Brig. Gen. M. D. ECTOR,
Comdg. First Brigade, McCown's Division, Army of Tennessee.

No. 285.

Report of Lieut. Col. J. M. Bounds, Eleventh Texas Cavalry (dismounted).

SHELBYVILLE, TENN., *January* 10, 1863.

SIR: In compliance with Special Orders, No. —, I would respectfully report that our regiment was called into line of battle before Murfreesborough, Tenn., on the evening of December 29, 1862, and took a position within 500 yards of the enemy's line, and established temporary breastworks out of fence rails, where they remained under range of the enemy's guns (and heavy shelling at intervals) until 7 a. m. of the 31st, at which time we were ordered to move forward on the enemy; and the regiment responded promptly, under command of our late gallant colonel, John C. Burks, and charged the enemy's lines, and repulsing them, taking (or running over) three of their batteries, killing and wounding many, routing and putting to flight their reserve, and pursuing them about 3 miles, and making great havoc on their lines, and was then called off (there being no formidable enemy in our front) and marched back in column, inclining to the left, until it was discovered that the enemy had a strong position on the Nashville pike, to our left, and we were ordered to halt and form in line of battle, preparatory to a charge, which was done, and the charge made with gallantry and heroism. But owing to the fatigued condition of the men, and obstructions from the rough conformation of the ground we had to pass over, our line was thrown into confusion and ordered to fall back, which was done in moderate, fair order, and we were ordered to a position on our right, which we took and held until 1 a. m. of January 3, when we were ordered back to Murfreesborough.

In the early part of the first engagement I regret to have to say that our gallant colonel was mortally wounded, though at his post leading his men on to a glorious victory, and the officers and men that were under my immediate command on that day and during the siege acted promptly and gallantly.

---

* The colors of the Thirty-fourth Illinois were captured by this regiment.

Our loss was serious, viz, 8 killed, 2 mortally wounded, 35 severely wounded, 49 slightly wounded, 2 captured, and 15 missing.

All of which is respectfully reported.

Respectfully, yours, &c.,

J. M. BOUNDS,
Lieutenant-Colonel, Commanding Eleventh Texas Cavalry.

Brigadier-General [M. D.] ECTOR.

No. 286.

Report of Col. J. L. Camp, Fourteenth Texas Cavalry (dismounted).

CAMP NEAR SHELBYVILLE, TENN.,
January 10, 1863.

In obedience to Special Orders, No. —, the following report of the battle of Murfreesborough is respectfully submitted:

On Tuesday, the 30th ultimo, our positions were assigned us in line of battle, subject to the fire of the enemy's batteries, the one directly in front at a distance of some 600 yards; the other on our right, but in range at a little greater distance. The batteries opened upon us in the evening and continued for some half hour a heavy fire, but without injury to my command.

On the morning of the 31st, orders were transmitted to me indicating a forward movement upon our part. Having hastily prepared to execute the order, the final order "forward" was given at about 6 a. m. The march was made in quick time, until the enemy's line appeared, and their batteries in full view, when the command "charge" was given, and faithfully, nobly, and gallantly executed upon the part of both men and officers, putting to flight the enemy and capturing the battery, horses, &c., immediately in front of my regiment. My command suffered greatly in this first charge, some of whom were killed, others wounded, among whom was my sergeant-major (Johnson), who fell among the foremost in the charge.

The enemy from thence retreated, and attempted to reform at a distance of some 200 or 300 yards, but the charge first ordered was not in the least checked, and they were again repulsed, with but little loss upon our part. Then ensued a running fight for some distance, until the enemy were driven out of sight before us. We continued our march in quick time in the direction indicated, and, coming in sight of the enemy in large force formed behind some woods, skirmishers were immediately thrown out. My regiment, by exhaustion, wounded, and killed, had been reduced to about 120 men. Soon the skirmishers began a brisk fire, and the order "charge" was given, and my regiment, in connection with the regiment on my left, advanced into the woods under the most fearful fire of infantry, which they repulsed, and continued the charge until they advanced in range of the cross-fires of three of the enemy's batteries, planted at a distance of some 300 or 400 yards from us. In this precarious condition we kept the enemy—so vastly superior in numbers, and aided, as they were, by artillery—in check, repulsing one charge upon us, and kept up a continued fire until ordered to fall back, which order was executed, and we reformed at a distance of half a mile. At this juncture men were never more exposed and suffered less. Each man acted well his part; each commanding officer of companies, as well as field, was at his post cheering his men, and each private conducting himself with such heroism as to inspire all around with courage.

Too much cannot be said in commendation of men who suffered with heroic patience the galling fire of the enemy in this last charge, when their only help visible was the small regiment on my left, reduced in like proportion to my own, in the face of an enemy ten times their number, supported, as they were, with the large batteries.

For a report* of the killed and wounded, I refer you to report previously made.

J. L. CAMP,
Colonel, Commanding Fourteenth Texas Cavalry Regiment.

General [M. D.] ECTOR,
Commanding First Brigade.

No. 287.

Report of Col. Julius A. Andrews, Fifteenth Texas Cavalry (dismounted).

NEAR SHELBYVILLE, TENN.,
January 10, 1863.

SIR: I claim your indulgence in submitting the following report of operations of the Fifteenth Texas Regiment (dismounted cavalry) during the recent engagement before Murfreesborough, Tenn., commencing on December 29, 1862, your brigade, in connection with the balance of Maj. Gen. J. P. McCown's division, having been moved from Readyville, Tenn., to the left wing of General Bragg's army on Monday, December 29, instant [ultimo]:

On my arrival on line of battle, I deployed my regiment, as directed by yourself, as skirmishers, covering the entire front of the brigade. My regiment numbered at the time 313 men, rank and file. The enemy failing to advance on our line of battle on Monday, the 29th instant [ultimo], the Fifteenth Regiment remained inactive during the day. My men were rallied after being relieved by a picket guard under command of Col. John C. Burks, of Eleventh Texas, at 8 p. m., at which time I resumed my position in line on the extreme left of the brigade, where I remained until ordered to advance with the brigade on Wednesday morning. However, a portion of the day on Tuesday, 30th instant [ultimo], we were under fire of artillery, which resulted in no damage to my command, as we were sheltered by a rail fence. The firing ceased about sundown; the night passed quietly; the weather rather inclement.

On Wednesday morning at 4 o'oclock my regiment was awakened and ordered to be in line of battle at 5 o'clock, which order was promptly obeyed. We remained in line until 6.30 o'clock, at which time we were ordered to move forward. The enemy, having advanced the evening before within 600 yards of our line, stationed their batteries opposite the right and center of the brigade. I advanced about 200 yards with my regiment in line of battle with the brigade, at which point the command "charge" was given. My regiment charged about 100 yards, which brought them in range of the enemy. We then opened fire on them, still continuing the charge, routing and driving the enemy before us for about 3 miles, killing and wounding and capturing numbers of them, after which time we were halted for rest and ammunition for about fifteen minutes. We were then ordered to advance, which we did (inclining to the right on the march), crossing the pike (the name of which I do not know), passing through woods and fields until we had advanced 1¼ miles

---

* Embodied in No. 191, p. 681.

farther. I was then ordered to deploy skirmishers covering the front of my regiment. I obeyed the order as promptly as possible. After advancing 300 yards farther, the skirmishers which had been deployed came in contact with the enemy. My regiment continued to advance, which soon brought us up to the position occupied by my skirmishers, at which time we found ourselves under a heavy fire of musketry. The enemy being ambuscaded in a hedge of cedars, rendered it impossible to open an effective fire on them. My regiment continued to advance until we arrived at a rail fence, which was 100 yards from the front of my regiment at the time the enemy opened fire on my skirmishers, and about 40 yards from the hedge of cedars. We soon arrived at the fence and passed over it, at which time I gave the command "charge." My regiment charged, driving the enemy promptly before them out of the hedge. We continued the charge for about 100 yards, which brought us some distance beyond the hedge in an open woods. The front of my regiment by this time was unmasked by the enemy's infantry, having driven them to our left. A heavy cannonading quickly ensued from masked batteries, stationed about 150 yards distant, and opposite the right of my regiment and the left of the Fourteenth Texas Regiment, commanded by Colonel [J. L.] Camp. The fire of shot, shell, and grape being so terrific, I ordered my regiment to stand, which they did. We were at this time under a heavy fire of musketry and artillery, my regiment, in conjunction with Colonel Camp's, having halted and held the enemy in check for about fifteen minutes. I at this time discovered that the two regiments composing the right of the brigade had been separated, from some unknown cause, from my regiment and Colonel Camp's. I cautioned my regiment to stand fast and continue the fire. I approached General M. D. Ector, who was stationed at the time in the rear of the center of my regiment, cheering my men on. I asked him where the balance of the brigade was. He replied he did not know. I then remarked to him it was impossible for my regiment and Colonel Camp's to contend against a brigade of infantry and the artillery, too, as our regiments were comparatively small. He then remarked, "We had better give back." I then returned to my command and ordered them to give back, the booming of cannon and musketry being so terrific at the time that it was impossible for my voice to be heard only by those who were near me. However, the men who heard the command obeyed it, which was discovered by the men up and down the line; also by the left of Colonel Camp's regiment, which caused both regiments to fall back in as good order as possible, under the circumstances. We retired the same route we advanced until we arrived in the woods, about 700 yards distant. We were then halted by General M. D. Ector in line and ordered to rest.

It was now about 2 p. m. We remained at this point about one hour, at the end of which time the Tenth and Eleventh Regiments joined us. We were then moved to the right and rear of this point, where we halted, the operations of the day in which my regiment was engaged having ceased. It was now New Year's night, and as we were fatigued from the toils of the day, we were permitted to rest undisturbed. The dawn of a new year soon hovered over us. We found ourselves stationed about 750 yards in front of the enemy's line of battle. The ground being covered with rock and fallen trees suitable for a breastwork, the men soon appropriated them for that purpose, anticipating an attack from the enemy. The breastwork being completed, every man was at his post awaiting the advance of the enemy. The enemy did not advance.

The day passed off quietly until 4.30 p. m.; the enemy at this time opened fire with artillery, endeavoring to shell us from our position, the woods in which we were stationed being so heavily timbered that the effects of their guns proved to be of no avail. The firing ceased about dark. Our pickets were stationed about 150 yards in front of the breastwork, frequently exchanging shots with the pickets of the enemy; with this exception, the night passed off quietly.

It was now January 2. We still held our position during the day, unmolested, until, about 7 p. m., the enemy renewed their fire, shelling the woods for about half an hour, but all to no effect. We still held our position until about 1 a. m., at which time we retired from our position, also the line of battle.

It was now January 3; the operations of my regiment in the battle before Murfreesborough ceased. It is with regret that I announce the casualties of my regiment to be as follows, viz: 5 killed, 32 wounded, and 5 missing.

With due deference to the Fifteenth Texas Regiment, I will take the liberty of stating that every officer, non-commissioned officer, and private behaved himself while in the recent engagement with honor to himself and country, as I never saw one of them falter. They were all at their post of duty, ready and willing to obey any command that might be given them, and never giving one inch of ground to the enemy until they were ordered. I therefore claim for them the name of being true and brave Confederate soldiers. I will here take pleasure in stating that Maj. W. [E.] Estes, of my regiment, was always at his post in the discharge of the duties of his position with honor and credit to himself and regiment, at the same time winning for himself the name of a true and brave soldier. Adjt. George M. Lindsay conducted himself during the engagement with much calmness, which has accomplished [commanded] the admiration of his brother officers and soldiers. Also Sergt. Maj. Luther A. Williams, who was always in the front rank sharing the fate of a battle. The action of the different officers of my command would not permit of any distinction, for I feel assured and am proud to say that all of them discharged their duties in a manner becoming them as officers.

I am, general, very respectfully, your obedient servant,
JULIUS A. ANDREWS,
Colonel, Comdg. Fifteenth Texas Regt. Dismounted Cav.*

Brig. Gen. M. D. ECTOR,
Comdg. First Brigade, Second Division, Army of Tennessee.

No. 288.

Report of Capt. James P. Douglas, Texas Battery.

ARTILLERY CAMP,
Near Shelbyville, Tenn., January 9, 1863.

SIR: In obedience to special orders from brigade headquarters, it becomes my duty to make a report of the operations of my battery in the recent battles before Murfreesborough. I therefore submit the following:

On the morning of December 31, [1862,] I received orders through Capt. George M. Mathes, chief of artillery of McCown's division, to move to a position in rear of the division, which I accordingly did. Subsequently, about sun-up, I was ordered to advance toward the enemy's lines, and as soon as practicable join my brigade. I ordered the battery forward immediately and rode rapidly in advance to ascertain the posi-

---

* This regiment appears subsequently on Texas register as the Thirty-second Texas Cavalry.

tion of the troops. After riding to the point where the enemy's first battery was captured, I found that the brigade had driven the enemy, and was advancing rapidly. I returned to the battery and put my horses to their best speed, to assist in holding the advanced position obtained. When I arrived within 150 yards of the captured battery (my battery being at its best speed), I discovered a large body of Federal infantry drawn up in line in front of the position occupied by the captured guns, and about 125 yards from my lead team. I immediately halted the battery and gave the command, "Front into line." While this was [being] executed, I discovered that the enemy did not know whether I was friend or foe. I therefore gave the command, "Left oblique and action front," thus bringing my guns into position not bearing exactly on the enemy. During this time the enemy had unfolded and waved conspicuously the Stars and Stripes. As no time was to be lost, I ordered the gunners to commence firing with canister. The enemy, doubtless hearing my command, opened a brisk fire, wounding 1 man and killing 3 horses and wounding 3. The cannoneers under the circumstances acted with great coolness, and in a moment threw a rapid and deadly fire into the enemy's ranks. They stood but a few discharges, when they retreated in considerable disorder.

In these rapid movements some of my horses had become entangled and broken their harness, and one of my caissons in running over a log had broken the pintle-pin. Some time was consumed in righting these things, during which time I was ordered to employ a portion of my horses in conveying the captured guns to the rear.

By this time General Hardee arrived and ordered me to take a position 600 yards in rear of where the infantry was engaged, which I accordingly did, remaining there until our lines had advanced considerably, when I moved forward in obedience to orders and took another position. While the battery remained in this position, I rode forward to the division and reported the position to General McCown. He ordered me to bring the battery forward to the Nolensville pike. I advanced to that point and took position on the extreme left, where I remained during the rest of the day. I remained bivouacked near this position during the night, and also on January 1 and 2, and until General McCown's division was ordered to the Lebanon pike.

During the protracted engagement every member of my command showed a willingness to do his duty. Lieutenants [J. H.] Bingham, [Benjamin] Hardin, and [M. L.] Fleishl, in command of their respective sections, were brave and efficient in the discharge of their duties.

Respectfully submitted.

JAMES P. DOUGLAS,
Captain, Commanding Battery.

Capt. C. B. KILGORE,
Assistant Adjutant-General.

No. 289.

Reports of Col. Robert B. Vance, Twenty-ninth North Carolina Infantry, commanding regiment and Second Brigade.

———— —, [1863.]

[The following is a] report [of the operations of the] Twenty-ninth North Carolina Regiment in [the] fight near Murfreesborough, December 31, 1862:

On the morning of December 31, the regiment, under my command, took its place in the line of battle on the left of the brigade (Rains'), which was the extreme left of General McCown's division. Ten minutes after forming, the order to advance was given, which was done in good order until a lane half a mile from the point of starting was reached, when the enemy's pickets were encountered, and a short but brisk firing commenced, without, however, retarding the progress of the command for one moment. The pickets fell back behind the cover of a field battery of one brass piece (12-pounder howitzer), which the men, sweeping on, took before it could be got into position to open fire. Four of the gunners were captured at their guns, besides some other of the enemy's vedettes, who were run down by our men in the chase, which had now extended to $2\frac{1}{2}$ miles. Not stopping at this gun longer than to send the prisoners to the rear, the regiment again pushed on (in its designated place in the brigade) for, perhaps, 2 miles farther, capturing meantime one six-mule team and wagon, loaded with ammunition, instruments of a brass band, kettle and bass drum, and one four-mule wagon, loaded with medical stores. Soon after, in passing through a dense oak wood, a battalion of the enemy's sharpshooters were discovered lying on the ground some 50 paces in advance. They fired one volley into us, which, being promptly returned, they retired rapidly across a corn-field and into a thicket of cedars, where the enemy were posted in strong force. This thicket of cedars was so dense that it formed in itself a natural breastwork and protection to the enemy posted therein. Halting the regiment but a moment for the stragglers to close up, the command was given to drive them out, and the men commenced promptly to advance. Here the struggle of the day took place. The enemy, sheltering themselves behind the trunks of the thickly standing trees and the large rocks, of which there were many, stubbornly contested the ground inch by inch. Our brave boys, cheered on and led by their field, staff, and company officers, advanced through a very tempest of leaden hail and drove them pell-mell from the thicket into an open field beyond. Here the enemy's batteries, on an eminence half mile beyond, began to play upon us. The men stood to their places amid this storm of shot and shell and grape and canister until it was ascertained that their ammunition was exhausted. Just at this moment, too, General Rains was seen to fall, and the news, running like wild-fire along the whole line, produced a temporary confusion, which induced the senior colonel of the brigade to order the command to fall back both to get ammunition and to shelter themselves from the enemy's batteries, against which they could do nothing.

During the engagement my horse was killed and Adjutant [John E.] Hoey's shot under him.

The regiment entered the fight with 300 men, but, from the long-continued chase, at least 50 fell out and were not in the fight in the cedars. We had 5 men killed, 46 wounded, and 5 missing, making a total of 56.

Some of the officers and men deserve especial mention for their daring, gallantry, and good conduct upon the field, while all engaged did their duty.

Respectfully submitted.

ROBT. B. VANCE,
Colonel, Commanding Twenty-ninth North Carolina Regiment.

Major [H. S.] BRADFORD,
  Assistant Adjutant-General.

HEADQUARTERS SECOND BRIGADE,
Shelbyville, Tenn., January 10, 1863.

SIR : I have the honor to submit my report of the part taken in the battle of Murfreesborough on the 31st ultimo by the Second Brigade, McCown's division.

On the morning of the 31st, the brigade was formed in line at day-break, the Twenty-ninth North Carolina Regiment having just arrived from McMinnville, Tenn. The command "forward" was soon given, and the whole command promptly sprang forward, soon taking the double-quick step, which was kept, under the direction of General Rains (who gallantly led his troops forward), until arriving at a lane, where we encountered the enemy's pickets, who fired upon us and fled. One man in the Twenty-ninth North Carolina was killed in the first fire. Crossing the fences, the double-quick was taken again, the enemy's skirmishers continuing to retreat rapidly before our shouting and triumphant troops. The charge was continued for about the distance of 3 miles, when the command was halted, the left flank resting on a creek. Here the stragglers were gathered up and the brigade reformed.

During the charge the Twenty-ninth North Carolina Regiment captured one 12-pounder howitzer, one six-horse wagon laden with ammunition, and one medical wagon, while the gunners were driven from a battery on the right of Colonel Stovall, Third Georgia, and the pieces sent to the rear. The charge was so rapid that time was not afforded to ascertain the number of pieces thus sent back, as the command was not halted for a moment.

After resting for a short time, the command was moved some distance by the right flank, then moved by the front through several fields into a grove of oaks.

At this point the brigade was changed somewhat. Colonel Stovall, Third Georgia [Battalion], was placed on right; Major [J. T.] Smith, Ninth Georgia, next; then Colonel Vance, Twenty-ninth North Carolina, leaving Colonel [G. W.] Gordon, Eleventh Tennessee, on left. In this manner we advanced, encountering the enemy in force in a few moments. He delivered one fire and fell back in confusion, our boys pushing on with enthusiasm, charging through the forest, and driving the enemy pell-mell before them. The enemy formed again on a slight elevation in our front, from which they were soon driven into a cedar thicket, and from thence finally into a large field under cover of their guns, a heavy battery of which opened on us at once with shell, grape, and canister, while the enemy's infantry rallied and opened fire from two or three heavy lines of battle. Here was the struggle for the day, and a hard one it was. Almost immediately after this hard contest began our gallant and noble brigadier-general (James E. Rains) was shot through the heart, falling dead from his horse. Still, the troops fought on, though the fall of so daring a leader necessarily produced considerable confusion. Owing to the dense cedar thicket through which we were charging, the Third and Ninth Georgia Battalions got separated from the Twenty-ninth North Carolina and Eleventh Tennessee, on the extreme right. From the reports of Colonel Stovall and Major Smith, I learn that these gallant commands were hotly engaged in front and on the right flank, being subjected to an enfilading fire. They drove the enemy from his position, and, finding the line falling back, joined it and reformed in the oak woods. They subsequently obtained position on the right of General Johnson's brigade, and continued there until placed in the new line of battle near the cedar swamp, and were kept in line until Friday night, January 2, having occasional skirmishes with the enemy in front.

In the mean time the Twenty-ninth North Carolina and Eleventh Tennessee, after continuing the engagement for some time, found their ammunition exhausted, and accordingly retired to get supplied and to recover the line fully.   Here again the Twenty-ninth [North Carolina] and Eleventh Tennessee became separated, as, through a mistake, the commands went to different points for ammunition.   From [Lieutenant]-Colonel [William] Thedford's report (Colonel Gordon having been wounded in the cedar thicket), I learn that after getting the cartridge-boxes filled they went in with General Liddell's brigade and sustained heavy loss in a severe action, capturing several pieces, which they were compelled to abandon for want of support.

The Twenty-ninth North Carolina also returned to the field, and were ordered to attack a brigade of the enemy which was trying to flank General McNair.   The command moved across the open field, being exposed to a raking fire from the enemy's battery near by; but meeting General McNair's brigade coming out, the command was ordered to join it, which it did in the woods to the rear, where they were also joined by the Eleventh Tennessee.

Receiving orders to obey the orders of Colonel Harper, I joined my two regiments to General McNair's brigade, and we were moved on the new line of battle, constituting General McCown's right, on General Cheatham's left.   Here we lay in line of battle until Friday night, January 2, occasionally skirmishing in front and constantly expecting the attack to be renewed.

From the report of First Lieut. W. A. McDuffie, Eufaula Light Artillery, I learn that his battery was engaged with the enemy for an hour on December 30, and that he was then ordered to take position in front of his own (Second) brigade (he having been supporting Robertson's battery), but could not do so for want of ammunition, which was supplied during the night.

On Wednesday (31st) he was ordered to the front, and took position near the Nolensville pike, but was not engaged; Second Lieutenant [W. J.] McKenzie was ordered to take position with two pieces on the extreme left, with General Buford.   Here he was engaged on the 31st for two hours, co-operating with General Wheeler's cavalry.   The report speaks highly of the conduct of the men.

From all that I saw, and have since heard, of the conduct of the troops on the field, I feel that I cannot speak too highly of them.   The ground charged over first and last was quite 5 miles, and the time occupied in the charge three and three-quarters hours.

The field and staff officers of the different commands, and the brigade staff officers, behaved nobly, and have surely merited high favors at the hands of their country.

It is perhaps unnecessary to speak further of General Rains.   His gallantry and daring exposure of himself was certainly not surpassed upon the field.   Peace to his ashes.

As coming under my own eye, I beg to mention Adjt. J. E. Hoey, of the Twenty-ninth North Carolina, who behaved with extraordinary courage upon the field, encouraging the men by word and deed.

Several officers had their horses killed.

For the casualties* of the command I refer you to report of killed, wounded, and missing.

Respectfully submitted.

ROBT. B. VANCE,
Colonel, Commanding Second Brigade, Army of Tennessee.
Major [H. S.] BRADFORD, *Assistant Adjutant-General.*

---

* Embodied in No. 191, p. 681.

No. 290.

Report of Lieut. Col. M. A. Stovall, Third Georgia Battalion.

—————— —, 1863.

[I have the honor to submit the following] report of the engagement of the Third Georgia Battalion with the enemy on December 31, 1862:

On the morning of December 31, [1862,] the troops of our brigade were called up and ordered to remove the fence which had concealed us the day before to avoid the enfilading fire of artillery to which we had been subjected. This was finished just as day began to dawn. The men lay under cover of the line of fence until objects became distinctly visible. The command "forward" was now given, and the Third Georgia Battalion moved rapidly about 300 yards, when "double-quick" ran along the line, and with a yell the whole sprang forward. We received the fire of the enemy's pickets, who fled. If there was any line of the enemy in front of the Third Georgia Battalion they fled without firing, and we swept entirely around that which was in front of Ector's and McNair's brigades. The whole force now opposed to our battalion fled in confusion, and we pursued them with a running fire for 3 miles, to their abandoned encampment. Here the line of battle, which had been broken, was reformed, and we moved rapidly by the right flank several hundred yards, then again by the left flank, our line of battle sweeping around to the pike. Crossing this, my battalion moved in advance of the remainder of the division, who had halted for ammunition. Soon after entering the wood we came upon a regiment and skirmishers, who had been engaged with the enemy. Passing the skirmishers, we found their line posted in a hollow. Though we had killed several in the pursuit, here our fighting began. We delivered our fire at a distance of 150 yards or less, killing many. At the word the battalion sprang forward down the hill, while the enemy scampered away up another and halted, and began a galling fire from under cover of a ledge of rocks and cedar thicket. The enemy in front of the Ninth and Eleventh finding no such cover, continued to give way, and while the Ninth and Eleventh swept forward my battalion was checked for a moment. We soon, however, forced our position directly in our front, and when we moved up to occupy it we were subjected to a galling enfilading fire on our right. The attention of our right wing being directed to this annoying force of the enemy, they were soon driven off. Our men were rallied and formed among the rocks, and we moved by the left flank toward the cedar swamp, where the fire was the hottest. Here we met our lines retiring in confusion before a destructive fire of artillery. We filed out of the woods, in order, to the top of the hill, where we first fired upon the enemy. Here we made a stand, until Polk's brigade was rallied, when we marched out into the field and allowed Cleburne's division to pass. Here we rested a few minutes to procure ammunition, and by order of General Cheatham marched again to the front. Finding myself entirely alone with 300 men, it was deemed imprudent to make an unsupported attack upon the enemy.

General Johnson's brigade came up about 2 p. m., and, having obtained his permission, we took position on his right and co-operated with him until 4 p. m., when we again learned McCown's division was near the place we fought first in the morning. We rejoined the division and remained until night in line of battle. For the casualties, I respectfully refer you to the list* already furnished.

M. A. STOVALL,
Lieutenant-Colonel, Commanding Third Georgia Battalion.

———
* Embodied in No. 191, p. 681.

No. 291.

Report of Maj. Joseph T. Smith, Ninth Georgia Battalion.

CAMP NEAR SHELBYVILLE, TENN.,
January 9, 1863.

SIR : 1 have the honor herewith to transmit a report of the part taken by my command in the late battle of Murfreesborough.

On the evening of December 30, 1862, we took up our position in line of battle on the left wing of the army, and soon after doing so the action commenced to our right. The position we had taken was such as to bring us directly within range of the enemy's artillery, and, though in open ground, no casualty occurred during the evening.

At a very early hour on Wednesday morning, December 31, we were under arms and informed by General Rains that we were to charge the enemy's line. At about 6 a m we commenced the advance, the men being so eager for the fray that it was in a manner impossible to restrain them in order. After advancing some 600 or 800 yards, we came upon the enemy's pickets, who were fleeing in all directions. We gave chase, and advanced so rapidly that we were at the enemy's batteries before he was able to fire upon us. We pushed forward without waiting even to examine the batteries, and, after thus advancing at a double-quick a mile or more, were halted by General Rains and reformed. We here swung round to the right, and, crossing the Franklin pike, passed into a dense woods. Upon proceeding a short distance we came upon the enemy occupying a strong position, and successfully resisting the advance of our right for a few moments, after which they fled. During the momentary check of our right wing, the left of my command, finding but little resistance, still advanced, and thus became separated from my right. A company or more of the left of my command by this means pushed forward with the Eleventh Tennessee Regiment, which occupied a position to my left, and did not join me again during the day. Upon routing the enemy from the clift of rocks where we first encountered them in the woods, we pushed forward in pursuit, but soon found ourselves confronted by the enemy's batteries, very heavily supported by infantry. My command, at this time not numbering over 130 men, and having no support, were reduced to the necessity of falling back, which was done in tolerable order. The men being utterly exhausted, I ordered a rest, and proceeded to gather together my stragglers, and in the mean time, ascertaining that we were to form a new line of battle near where we then were, in company with Lieutenant-Colonel Stovall's Third Georgia Battalion took our position in that line. At this place we remained until Friday night, January 2, having frequent skirmishes with the enemy's pickets, undergoing occasionally severe shelling from the enemy's batteries.

The conduct of my command, with some trifling exceptions, was worthy the highest praise.

The list of casualties * has heretofore been furnished.

The meagerness and incompleteness of this report must be accounted for by reason of my not having any facilities for writing with me at present.

All of which is very respectfully submitted.

JOSEPH T. SMITH,
Major, Commanding Ninth Georgia Battalion.

T. B. THOMPSON,
Acting Assistant Adjutant-General, Second Brigade.

---

* Embodied in No. 191, p. 681.

No. 292.

Report of Lieut. Col. William Thedford, Eleventh Tennessee Infantry.

————— —, 1863.

On Wednesday, at daylight, the Eleventh Tennessee Regiment, Col. G. W. Gordon commanding, was drawn up in line of battle on the left of General Rains' brigade and of McCown's division. We remained in this position with the Twenty-ninth North Carolina Regiment on the extreme left, when we were ordered to charge the enemy, stationed some 800 yards in advance. The charge was led by General Rains in person, and resulted in a complete rout of the enemy, who were pursued for some 3 miles. A halt was then ordered and the command reformed. After a short rest we were again ordered to advance in line until we encountered a large force of the enemy. A charge was immediately ordered, which was obeyed with alacrity, until the advance was checked by the enemy's battery, which rained shot and shell into our ranks. Here General Rains advanced to the front and was immediately killed. Colonel Gordon was severely wounded while gallantly leading his regiment, and the command devolved upon myself. The enemy opposed our advance with obstinacy, and being strongly re-enforced, and our ammunition failing, we retired to the rear. Collecting the scattered of the regiment and procuring ammunition, we again advanced to the front, and were a third time ordered to charge the enemy. As before, the men obeyed with a shout, and drove the enemy before them until they gained a strong natural position. Here the ground was hotly contested until we were ordered to retire. Though constantly in line, the regiment was not again actively engaged. A large number of the regiment were engaged only in the first charge, in consequence of guarding the prisoners taken.

The following is a list of the casualties.*

Respectfully,

WM. THEDFORD,
Lieutenant-Colonel, Comdg. Eleventh Regiment Tennessee Vols.

No. 293.

Report of Lieut. W. A. McDuffie, Eufaula Light Artillery.

————— —, 1863.

CAPTAIN: I have the honor to make the following report of my battery of the late engagement before Murfreesborough:

On [December] 30, [1862,] at 4 p. m., I engaged the enemy with four pieces, being ordered by General Rains to support Captain Robertson's battery. After an action of about an hour, I was ordered by General Rains to withdraw. I then received an order to go into position in the field occupied by the Second Brigade, but such ammunition as I could use having been expended, I was unable to comply. I was then ordered to retire beyond the range of the enemy's guns, there to await ammunition. It was supplied me during the night.

On the following morning I was ordered to the front, and took position near the Nolensville road and was not engaged.

_____

* Nominal list, omitted, reports 8 men killed, 11 officers and 51 men wounded, and 10 men missing; but see No. 191, p. 681.

Second Lieut. W. J. McKenzie, on the 29th, was ordered by the chief of artillery of General Bragg's staff to report with two pieces to General Buford, on the Salem road. He was engaged on the extreme left on the 31st at 3 p. m. He was in action about two hours and co-operated with General Wheeler's cavalry.

The men, during the engagement, acted well. I expended 213 rounds of ammunition.

My casualties are 1 corporal and 1 private wounded* and 1 horse killed.

I have the honor to be, very respectfully, your obedient servant,

W. A. McDUFFIE,
First Lieutenant Eufaula Light Artillery.

ACTING ASSISTANT ADJUTANT-GENERAL, SECOND BRIGADE.

No. 294.

Report of Brig. Gen. E. McNair, C. S. Army, commanding Third Brigade.

HEADQUARTERS THIRD BRIGADE,
In Camp near Shelbyville, Tenn., January 10, 1863.

SIR: Through you I have the honor to make the following report to the major-general commanding the division, of the action of my brigade in the late battle before Murfreesborough, on December 31, 1862:

In obedience to orders received from division headquarters at 7 p. m. on December 30, 1862, I formed my brigade in line of battle on the ground designated at that time.

At 6 a. m. on December 31, I moved forward about 150 yards, and joined Brigadier-General Ector's brigade on the right. We then moved forward together to meet the enemy, who was in force immediately in front of us. We had advanced but a short distance before the enemy's pickets and sharpshooters opened fire upon us. At this point I cautioned my brigade to reserve their fire and push forward. I had advanced but a short distance when the fire became general along the line, indicating that we were near the enemy in position; and at that moment he opened upon us with a six-gun battery a most terrific fire of shell and grape shot. I then ordered a charge, which was responded to with alacrity and good will. It was but a moment until his battery was ours, his long line of infantry routed and dispersed, and the strong position which he held in security but a moment before covered with his dead and wounded. My command continued to pursue the enemy for three-quarters of a mile, pouring a destructive fire into his broken and scattered ranks, strewing the ground with his killed and wounded. At this point, discovering that the support on my right had not come up as expected by me, and the enemy having thrown a heavy force partly in my rear, their sharpshooters having already commenced to fire upon my wounded men, I halted my brigade and moved them to the rear by the flank, for the purpose of protecting my wounded men. After having moved but a short distance, I discovered Brigadier-General Liddell advancing with his brigade on my right, thus obviating any further movement on my part in the direction in which I was then moving. I then

---

*Nominal list omitted.

immediately wheeled my brigade, thus changing my front and joining Brigadier-General Liddell on his left. Again I ordered a forward movement, pushing the enemy back upon his center in a direction due north from that point. Here a heavy skirmish commenced with fresh forces of the enemy, supposed to be about one division; they were driven from every position for the distance of half a mile. Here they took position, protecting themselves behind a rail fence to the right-oblique of my line of battle. The enemy had already engaged General Liddell's brigade, on my right, holding them in check and pouring a destructive fire into their ranks. Discovering his critical position, I immediately ordered a forward movement, and had to advance across an open field a distance of about 400 yards. Again I directed my brigade to reserve their fire, which was done, until we had advanced within about 300 yards. Though the enemy poured a heavy fire upon my line from behind their cover, yet not a man faltered, but pushed forward with the stern determination of veterans. Here I ordered a charge, and, as before, officers and men seemed to vie with each other in performing acts of gallantry, and one simultaneous shout rent the air. The enemy, made bold by his front being protected by the fences, held his position with more tenacity than usual; but the terrific fire poured upon his ranks, and the velocity with which my men charged, drove him from his position in confusion, thus relieving Brigadier-General Liddell's brigade, which was already faltering under the heavy fire of the enemy, thus for the second time driving the foe from his choice and strong position. This was perhaps the hardest contested engagement of the day. Here my loss in killed and wounded was heavy, though small compared with that of the enemy.

Without halting, I pursued the enemy through an open field, pouring a deadly fire into their disordered ranks for half or three-quarters of a mile, until I arrived at another fence in front of a dense forest. Fearing an ambuscade, and at the same time finding the men were out of ammunition, I ordered a halt and rested the men in rear of a fence, at the same time ordering up the ammunition train, which arrived in due time, and proceeded to replenish the cartridge-boxes.

At this place, general, as you are aware, having become exhausted (my health having been bad for several days previous), I was unable to remain longer upon the field, and placed Col. R. W. Harper, of the First Arkansas Mounted Riflemen (dismounted), in command of the brigade, and most respectfully refer you to his report for the further action of the brigade upon that day.

In regard to the casualties of the brigade—as already reported, killed 42, mortally wounded 6; killed, wounded, and missing 427—I am happy to report that a very large proportion of the wounds are slight, and most of the men will report for duty very soon.

And here, general, I beg leave to call your attention to the surgeons of my brigade. Surg. W. L. Gammage, with the limited means at his disposal, did all that could be done to relieve the sufferings of the wounded men. The regimental surgeons, with their assistants, proved themselves worthy of the high and responsible positions they occupy. By their united efforts, with the assistance of the infirmary corps, not one wounded man was left uncared for during the night.

As you are aware, general, we turned the right wing of the Federal army, driving them 4 miles or more, taking one brigadier-general (Willich) prisoner, a large number of officers of the line, and privates innumerable, capturing fourteen pieces of artillery, caissons, and ord nance stores, also a great quantity of small-arms and camp equipage; all of which, I presume, was collected by the proper persons.

For the action of Captain Humphreys' battery I beg leave to refer you to his own report, as he was detached from the brigade during the day, and consequently did not come under my observation; but I feel assured that the gallant Captain Humphreys and his company were not found wanting on this occasion.

I most respectfully ask leave to call your attention to the officers composing my staff: Capts. R. E. Foote (assistant adjutant-general) and W. C. Carrington (aide-de-camp), always at their posts, rendered me valuable assistance during the day.

Mr. James Stone, my volunteer aide, has placed me under lasting obligations for his active assistance.

To Major [S. H.] Mulherrin, acting commissary of subsistence, much credit is due for his continual attention to his department, which administered so much to the comfort of the men.

Maj. W. H. Eltsner, assistant quartermaster, was at his post as usual, keeping the train in proper order.

My little orderly (volunteer King) and his white pony were present, doing all that he could to complete the victory.

Though contrary to my usual custom, I beg leave to call your attention to the field officers of my brigade. It has been my fortune to be present at many a hard-fought battle, but never have I witnessed such deeds of moral courage and gallant daring as were displayed by the field and company officers of the line during the entire day. I forbear to mention names, for each seemed to vie with the other in deeds of gallantry, but one I must mention. That one is Maj. L. M. Ramsaur, First Arkansas Mounted Rifles. He was severely wounded in the last charge made upon the enemy's stronghold. To him much is due for the gallant charges of the day.

To officers and men I am indebted for the success of my command. Our country and the glorious cause we are engaged in can never suffer while defended by such gallant spirits.

To the friends of the dead it is enough for them to know that they baptized their country with their blood and gave their bodies a willing sacrifice upon the altar of liberty. Their gallant spirits have taken their flight to that land where the clash of arms and the shock of battle are unknown.

I am, major, most respectfully, your obedient servant,

E. McNAIR,
Brigadier-General, Comdg. Third Brigade, McCown's Division.

Maj. H. S. BRADFORD,
    Assistant Adjutant-General.

No. 295.

Reports of Col. Robert W. Harper, First Arkansas Mounted Rifles, commanding regiment and Third Brigade.

JANUARY 10, 1863.

SIR: Brig. Gen. E. McNair being compelled to leave the field on account of severe indisposition, the command devolved upon me, and, as soon as our cartridge-boxes were replenished, I moved forward in conjunction with Brigadier-General Ector, commanding Texas Brigade. I was ordered to swing around my left, making the right a pivot, which changed my front from a north to a northeasterly direction. This change of front threw the left of the division nearer to the enemy's line, which appeared afterward to run east and west, and, approaching a dense thicket of cedars, I ordered skirmishers to be thrown rapidly forward, to prevent anything like an ambuscade to our already jaded troops. Almost simultaneously that my skirmishers entered the thicket, Ector's brigade, on our left, became warmly engaged, and I received a message from him by Major [F. M.] Spencer, urging me to press forward as rapidly as possible. No time was now to be lost, as the enemy had evidently made this their last stand-point, and had opened upon us with artillery and musketry. Almost simultaneously with General Ector's request, I received an order from the major-general commanding to charge the batteries. The order was immediately repeated to the command, and, flushed with success and buoyant with hope, they rushed forward to accomplish more brilliant results. The growth through which the right was compelled to pass rendered it impossible to keep an unbroken line, but still they pushed forward. But the position proved too strong for the two gallant little brigades, the enemy having some five batteries in position, strongly supported by three long lines of infantry, and after one of the most brilliant charges that history records they were overwhelmed and compelled to fall back, not, however, until they had succeeded in driving a large portion of the infantry from their position and compelling the gunners of at least one battery to retire. I should have mentioned, however, when the firing became heaviest, and I found that one or more batteries on our extreme right were severely enfilading us, that I sent Captain [Mr. James] Stone, of General McNair's staff, and urged Major-General Cleburne or Brigadier-General Polk to move up rapidly on our right, so as to cover the enemy's front and remove the galling fire from our flank. This movement, however, was not made in time to assist us, and after ten or twelve minutes of the severest fighting it has ever been my lot to witness we were compelled to fall back with very heavy loss. After rallying and reforming the brigade, they were allowed to rest under the crest of a hill some 500 or 600 yards from the scene of the late fighting, having been under a continuous fire for nearly seven hours, and having driven the enemy with impetuosity for $4\frac{1}{2}$ to 5 miles.

The loss, which had been heavy in the three previous charges of the morning, was still greater at this point, our ranks being almost decimated before our troops could be forced to retire. Here fell, badly wounded, Maj. L. M. Ramsaur, commanding First Arkansas Rifles, while gallantly leading his regiment to the desperate charge. Major [James J.] Franklin, commanding Thirtieth Arkansas Volunteers, while cheering his soldiers to new deeds of daring, was severely wounded and fell into the hands of the enemy.

We were permitted to rest here for three-quarters of an hour, when I was ordered to move by the right flank, and took position, in obedience to instructions, in a cedar brake, where the brigade remained in line of battle, without any noticeable casualties, until we were withdrawn.

I cannot close without paying a tribute to the field officers and officers of the line, and the gallant spirits who compose their commands. Each seemed to vie with the other in deeds of daring, and where all exerted themselves so strenuously it is impossible to discriminate. The color-bearers along the whole line more than once elicited my admiration by the steadiness with which the Bonnie Blue Flag was constantly borne in the front line.

Capt. R. E. Foote, assistant adjutant-general, Third Brigade, has placed me under many obligations for the promptitude with which he delivered all orders, regardless of danger; and James Stone, volunteer aide to Brigadier-General McNair, who was ever with me, several times bearing his orders through the heaviest of the fight, is entitled to the thanks of the commander and his country.

I have the honor to be, major, your very obedient servant,

R. W. HARPER,
Colonel, Comdg. Third Brigade, McCown's Division.

Maj. H. S. BRADFORD,
Assistant Adjutant-General, McCown's Division.

———

JANUARY 10, 1863.

SIR: I have the honor to submit the following report of the part taken by the regiment under my command in the battle before Murfreesborough on December 31, 1862:

In obedience to the order received from the brigadier-general commanding, the regiment moved up 150 yards from the rear, where it had bivouacked for the night, and took its position on the right of the brigade, then in line. A few minutes before 6 a. m. we were ordered forward, and moved on a line parallel with the road leading by Cowan's house. About 6 o'clock our pickets became engaged, and soon after the firing opened along the whole line of the regiment. On account of a field fence my two right companies were formed in the rear, and at this point we were severely enfiladed by the enemy's sharpshooters, some 200 [yards] distant on our right. The order to charge was then given, and with impetuosity our men scaled the fence on our front, driving the enemy before them until we reached his encampment, which gave ample evidence of his want of preparation for a fight. Encamped as he was in a thick cedar brake, it would seem our progress must be impeded; but nothing could withstand the fury of the onset. The enemy's lines were broken, and the rout, so far as my observation reached, became general.

Turning to the right in the direction of the pursued, we moved constantly at a double-quick over field and brake, the dead and dying of the enemy but too plainly marking the track of the fleeing Abolitionists. It was at this point that young Clark D. Jenkins, a private of Company D, shot down a general officer, who was endeavoring to rally his scattered columns, supposed to be Major-General Sill, as his body was found soon afterward in a hospital near by. We had now driven the enemy about 1¼ miles, when, finding a line of Federal infantry endeavoring to gain our rear, we halted and formed our line with the intention of cutting through his ranks to our main army, but the opportune arrival of Liddell's brigade on our right relieved us. After a few moments' delay I was ordered to move forward, my right resting on the left of Liddell's brigade. We continued to move to the front, when, Liddell becoming warmly engaged with a heavy force, who had concealed themselves behind a fence, I was ordered to file right, move by the flank some 150 paces, then by the left flank, and then received the order to charge. Forward rushed our gallant men, with the wild yell of an infuriated soldiery, and for a few seconds the result seemed doubtful. The enemy, almost securely posted, stubbornly held their ground, and it seemed as if once during the war our lines would clash in close combat. But again the intrepidity of our troops prevailed, and, when distant only 50 or 75 yards, his lines gave way, and were soon thrown into utter confusion and terribly cut to pieces by our fire as they retreated across an open field some 700 or 800 [yards] wide. "Forward," again was the order, and forward moved our unwavering lines, and in the face of heavy volleys that were poured in upon us from the opposite fence, and the raking fire of grape and canister from two sections of a battery posted in the field, we charged and took two pieces of artillery. It was here that Capt. W. P. Campbell, acting major, was severely wounded in the leg, while gallantly urging his wing to the charge, and was compelled to leave the field. Here we were halted for a new supply of ammunition, having exhausted all but 3 or 4 rounds out of 40 to the man, which is the best evidence of the severity of the contest.

It was now 9.15 a. m. We had charged and driven the enemy with impetuosity for three and a quarter hours over not less than $3\frac{1}{2}$ miles of ground, captured and killed many field officers and officers of the line, and privates without number, taken several pieces of artillery, while vast amounts of camp equipage and small-arms, &c., were left in our rear, which our patriotic soldiery passed by unheeded.

A few moments served to replenish our ammunition, and we again moved forward 1 mile or more, when skirmishers were ordered to be thrown forward to a cedar brake from which we had been fired upon. Up to this time we had been advancing nearly due north, but, having made a half-wheel to the right, were moved nearly northeast. Here the extreme left of our division, being nearest the enemy's line, became first engaged; the order was given to charge the batteries strongly posted on an eminence beyond. Another thrill of excitement ran along the line, and another yell of stern defiance pealed forth as they moved rapidly to the new scene of slaughter. The enemy being strongly posted, his flank batteries *en échelon*, supported by three lines of infantry, the regiment after a most brilliant effort was compelled to fall back after being nearly decimated. Here fell, most severely wounded, and, I fear, mortally, Maj. L. M. Ramsaur, acting lieutenant-colonel. He was gallantly leading the regiment in the charge, and had well nigh succeeded in driving the enemy from one of his batteries. We had now been under heavy fire almost continuously six and three-quarters hours; had driven the enemy from his extreme left to his center, and our jaded troops were reformed and allowed to rest under the crest of a hill for an hour or so, when we were again moved by the right flank half a mile and took position in a cedar brake, where we remained, in line, without any serious casualties until we were withdrawn.

My loss, in addition to the two field officers already named, is severe; but I am happy to add that the wounds are, for the most part, slight and not likely to render them unfit for active duty hereafter. The whole loss in killed, wounded, and missing is 96, as already furnished in my official report, which I ask may be taken as a part of this.

Where all exerted themselves and gave such evidences of individual heroism, it is impossible for a commander to discriminate. I must, however, [mention] Color-bearer Cotten, who always moved with unfaltering step in the front rank.

Our surgeons are also entitled to be mentioned for the promptness with which our wounded were cared for; and I conclude by saying that, whatever fate betides the First Arkansas Rifles in future, their actions on this day have shed imperishable glory on them and their cause.

I have the honor to be, sir, your very obedient servant,

R. W. HARPER,
Colonel, Commanding First Arkansas Rifles.

Capt. R. E. Foote,
Asst. Adjt. Gen., Third Brigade, McCown's Division.

No. 296.

Report of Lieut. Col. James A. Williamson, Second Arkansas Mounted Rifles (dismounted).

CAMP NEAR SHELBYVILLE, TENN.,
January 10, 1863.

CAPTAIN : I have the honor to submit the following report of the part taken by the Second Regiment Arkansas Riflemen (dismounted) in the battles before Murfreesborough, Tenn., on the 30th and 31st ultimo :

On the evening of the 30th, from the position my regiment occupied in line, it was exposed to the fire of the enemy's batteries and sharpshooters, the casualties from which were 1 killed and 14 wounded.

About dark on the evening of the 30th, we were moved forward about 150 yards, stacked arms, and bivouacked for the night.

On the morning of the 31st, about 5.30 o'clock, I was ordered to form my regiment, and as soon as formed ordered to load. A few moments before 6 o'clock we were ordered forward, moving west. About half a mile from the starting point we attacked the enemy in a cedar thicket. As my command crossed the fence into the thicket, I observed the enemy's line give way. They were routed and pursued for a distance of about 1 mile. During this engagement a large number of the enemy were killed, wounded, and taken prisoners. I was ordered to halt my command and move back about 150 yards. We then changed direction to the right, and moved about half a mile to a lane fence and halted for a few moments. I was then ordered to move by the right flank, then by file right, and then by left flank, which brought my command against the right of the enemy that were engaging General Liddell's brigade. I was then ordered to charge the enemy, which order was promptly executed. As the enemy fell back from the fence, an enfilading fire from our rifles strewed the ground with their dead.

I regret to have to report that Capt. T. F. Spence, an officer and a gentleman, was instantly killed in this charge. The enemy left two pieces of artillery on this field. After pursuing the enemy for about 1 mile, I was ordered to halt my command to replenish their ammunition. I was here notified that Colonel Harper was in command of the brigade. We were then moved forward, and then right oblique for a distance of 1½ miles, when the enemy's artillery opened upon us. I was ordered to halt for a moment and then charge the battery. The ground over which I had to pass was covered with a dense growth of cedar, underbrush, and vines, rendering it impossible for my command to move with much rapidity or to keep a perfect line.

While passing through this thicket two other batteries turned their fire upon my command. The enemy's lines of infantry were seen to give way, but their artillerists seemed to renew their energies, and poured in a continuous fire of grape and canister shot, and when many of my command were in less than 100 yards of the enemy's guns were compelled to give back.

I feel it my duty to call attention to the gallant conduct of Ensign H. W. Hamblen, who bore the colors of the regiment gallantly through the day, and was shot down in this last charge within less than 100 yards of the enemy's guns; also to the conduct of Corpl. J. W. Piles, of the color-guard, who took up the colors when the ensign was shot down, and, when our troops were compelled to give way, brought them safely from the field.

I am indebted to Maj. J. T. Smith for his valuable assistance through the entire day.

I regret to report that Adjt. C. W. Woods was dangerously wounded in the first engagement in the morning, and I was thus deprived of his valuable services for the remainder of the day.

Our loss in killed, wounded, and missing is 119, as already exhibited in my official report, which I ask to be considered as a part of this report. I am happy to report that many of the wounds are slight.

I am indebted to my regimental surgeon for his untiring and efficient services in his attendance to the wounded.

Through the entire day the officers and men of my command deported themselves in a manner highly creditable to themselves and the noble cause they have espoused.

I have the honor to be, sir, your obedient servant,

J. A. WILLIAMSON,
Lieutenant-Colonel, Comdg. Second Regt. Arkansas Riflemen.

The ADJUTANT-GENERAL THIRD BRIG., SECOND DIV.,
SMITH'S CORPS, ARMY OF TENNESSEE.

No. 297.

Report of Col. H. G. Bunn, Fourth Arkansas Infantry.

CAMP NEAR SHELBYVILLE, TENN.,
January 15, 1863.

CAPTAIN: I have the honor to make the following report of the part taken by the Fourth Arkansas Regiment in the battle of the 31st ultimo, before Murfreesborough:

I have already submitted a report of the casualties* in my regiment, and deem it necessary only to refer to the general events of the day which came under my observation, and such as were connected with the movements of my regiment. In submitting my report, I beg leave to say that, connected as I am and have been with the brigade, this report must be considered as one of events altogether peculiar to the regiment under my command. Throughout the entire day I moved with the brigade, my regiment filling up an intermediate space in the same.

At 6 o'clock on the morning of December 31, [1862,] in connection with the brigade, I moved my regiment forward to attack the enemy, in position 600 or 800 yards in our front. The general aspect of the ground over which we advanced was level corn-fields, with rail fences running at right angles and parallel to our lines. The enemy was in position in a dense thicket of cedar, the entrance to which was obstructed by a parallel fence, rendering his position one of great advantage. His sharpshooters fired upon us at long range, and continued to do so as we advanced. Arriving within a short distance of his lines, and his artillery having opened upon us with grape and canister shot, we were ordered to charge the enemy, and did so with dispatch and good order, routing and driving him confusedly from the field, then covered with his dead and wounded. He left his artillery in his flight. We pursued him near half a mile, but finding that we were far in advance of our main line, I was ordered to march back, reform, and prolong on the line to the left of

---

* Embodied in No. 191, p. 681.

General Liddell, who was then advancing. The whole line moved forward, gently swinging to the right. We were engaged in a sharp running skirmish fight over the space of a fourth of a mile, but at length halted to give the troops rest, sheltered by a rail fence. General Liddell's brigade (Arkansas), on our right, and at this time 100 yards in our rear, were attacked by a large force directly in its front and behind a double row of fences. We were ordered to charge the enemy thus on our right and front, which we did with promptness, driving him from the field again, his right in great disorder. We moved forward across a field and then a wood, and were halted near a fence. The enemy was in some force on our right and front, but, giving him a scattering fire, he fled, and we crossed a field, and finally halted to wait until the ammunition could be brought up, the troops having already expended their 40 rounds. After supplying the troops with the requisite number of rounds of ammunition, we again advanced, and, uniting with General Ector's Texas brigade, on our left, continued to advance, swinging our left around so as to make an angle of 40 ° with our lines in the last engagement, and make an angle of nearly 60° with our first line in the morning. It was evident that we had turned the enemy's right flank so far that our advance would now bring us in contact with his center. It could plainly be seen that the center of our army had gained but little ground during the day. It was still more evident that our extreme right had participated but little in the battle. The left had driven the enemy 5 miles, and changed the front of both armies. We moved forward through a wood which, at first, was clear of undergrowth, then a dense thicket of cedar trees and undergrowth, having to encounter now and then a rail fence. Soon the enemy's artillery opened upon us a terrific fire of shell. Our orders were to take the battery. Owing to the obstacles we had to encounter, the lines were necessarily broken, but our advance was steady until we arrived in full view of the enemy's guns. At this juncture, a battery on our left, one to our front, one to the right of front, and one on the right, poured upon us a most murderous fire of grape and canister shot. The farthest could not have been more than 400 yards distant; the nearest not more than 100 yards. This last was supported by either three or four columns of infantry, which gave way as we advanced, although in rear of their artillery; but it was impossible to maintain our position under the cross-fire of artillery. To advance and take the battery in front would have placed us in a position to be raked without any means of defense, and being unsupported on our right. Our ranks had been thinned during the day, and the troops were fatigued and worn out. We were then compelled to relinquish our attempt, and fall back to the woods in our rear.

No one who knows the nature of the ground and the great odds against which they had to contend, can reproach the gallant troops for giving way at this period. They had won the day, if, indeed, the day was ours. Too much praise cannot be given them for their conduct. Their retreat was their misfortune, and not their fault.

We took little or no part in the battle after this, and I deem it unnecessary to continue a report further.

To the notice of my superior officers I commend the gallant soldiers whom I have the honor to command, having no individuals to commend above others. The gallant men who have won laurels wherever and whenever they have been called to battle do not expect me to notice particular individuals among them. Were I to mention one for gallant conduct, I should have to mention all.

My color-bearer (John B. Bryant) was wounded in the first engagement, and Lieut. John Armstrong, Company D, bore the colors through the other engagements, but fell, mortally wounded, in the last. Lieutenant [G. D.] Goodner then took the colors, and soon after was himself wounded. Captain [John W.] Lavender bore the colors during the remainder of the day. I mention these names, not wishing to commend them above others, but to show how determined officers and men seemed to maintain the honor and integrity of their regiment.

To my field officers, Lieutenant-Colonel [James H.] May and Major [J. B.] McCulloch, I am indebted for their efficient aid.

To my only staff officer present (Sergeant-Major Johnson) I am indebted for the promptness and dispatch with which every order was executed.

I cannot give the names of all whose gallantry deserves notice. The captains and other officers of the line seemed to vie with one another in courage and gallantry. The men seemed to imbibe the spirit of their officers.

I am, captain, your obedient servant,

H. G. BUNN,
Colonel, Commanding Fourth Arkansas Regiment.

Capt. R. E. FOOTE,
Asst. Adjt. Gen., Third Brigade, McCown's Division.

No. 298.

Report of Capt. William A. Cotter, Thirtieth Arkansas Infantry.

CAMP NEAR SHELBYVILLE, TENN.,
January 10, 1863.

SIR: In obedience to General Orders, No. 7, I have the honor to make the following report as being the part taken by this regiment in the engagement before Murfreesborough on December 31, 1862:

We were ordered into line about 6 o'clock on the morning of the 31st ultimo. Our strength was found to be 9 captains, 17 lieutenants, and 240 privates. As soon as the brigade was formed we were ordered to move forward in the direction of where the enemy's battery had been actively operating the afternoon before. After moving forward about 400 yards at quick time, we came up in full view of the enemy's line, and directly in front of one of their batteries. Here occasional firing along our [line] commenced and continued until we moved 50 yards farther, becoming more general as we advanced. This brought us within 100 yards of the battery, when the command "charge" was given, which command was enthusiastically responded to by the entire regiment, every one moving at a double-quick until our hands were upon the captured guns. These we reached in advance of the brigade, inasmuch as we had the advantage in ground. The battery taken, we were now able to do most effective service, as the enemy were driven from the thicket on our right. We had an open fire upon them at close range; but while we were thus employed the enemy did not neglect to retaliate, for here we had the commanders of seven companies cut down (3 killed and 4 wounded), besides several lieutenants, the color-bearer, and many gallant privates. After pursuing the enemy for several hundred yards, the men being very much scattered, a halt was ordered and the brigade reformed.

About this time the enemy were seen advancing to our right upon one of our batteries, and making some little demonstration, as if they had an idea of charging it. We were immediately moved by the right flank sufficiently far to protect the battery, and then by the left flank in the direction of the enemy, who lay concealed in the corners of a cross-fence. Here again was the opportunity offered us for doing valuable service. As the brigade moved by the front, we were forced to cross the fence to the side on which the enemy lay watching our right wing. Here we fired on them at a distance not exceeding 40 yards before they discovered we had crossed the fence. Now was heard the second command, "Charge their battery," which command was as readily responded to as the first, and equally as successful in execution. We were called to a halt, and after forming in regular line moved forward several hundred yards farther, when another halt was ordered, for the purpose of recruiting our supply of ammunition. We were engaged at this when General McNair was forced to retire from the field, to the deep regret of us all. This being attended to, we moved on near a mile in the direction the enemy had retreated, when it was discovered that they had rallied and stood in line of battle in rear of a most powerful battery, which was planted upon a hill commanding the country for some distance on three sides, and which was also supported by two small batteries, holding a cross-fire upon any advance by the front. When we arrived within 500 yards of this battery, the third command to "charge that battery" was given. This, too, was responded to with a joyous shout and a rapid onward. All were fatigued, but all were willing, all were sanguine. But here we were disappointed, for it was here that we met with our first repulse. But it was unavoidable on the part of our brigade, for by the time we had advanced to within 300 yards of the center battery the enemy began to pour in grape at such a murderous rate that it appeared little less than suicide to advance farther. Still, some few, nothing daunted, determined to go on, and some did go to within 100 yards of the enemy's stronghold. Among the rest was our gallant flag-bearer, whose hand was shot off and he was compelled to abandon his colors. It was under that battery that we sacrificed some of our noblest spirits—first of all our gallant major, J. J. Franklin. Knowing a second attempt upon this stronghold of the enemy to be altogether impracticable, we fell back near 1,200 yards, where we rallied our scattered men and moved forward again about 800 yards. Here we were ordered to remain until nightfall.

There were a number who acted most gallantly, reflecting more than ordinary credit upon the command to which they belong and their country, yet, lest I do some injustice by overlooking them, I forbear personating any.

We pursued the enemy during the day about 4 miles; the country over which we passed generally open and slightly undulating.

WM. A. COTTER,
Commanding Thirtieth Arkansas.

[Capt.] R. E. FOOTE,
Assistant Adjutant-General.

No. 299.

Report of Maj. J. A. Ross, Fourth Arkansas Battalion.

NEAR SHELBYVILLE, TENN., *January 10, 1863.*

I have the honor, through you, to make to the brigadier-general commanding Third Brigade the following report of the part taken by the

Fourth Arkansas Battalion in the battle of Murfreesborough, Tenn., fought on December 31, 1862:

Just at daybreak the battalion, in line of battle with the other regiments forming the brigade, moved upon the enemy.

After marching across the field for some half mile to the fence, a brisk fire opened between the skirmishers in the cedar brake immediately in our front.

At this time, observing a disposition among the men to fire at long range, I ordered them to hold their fire. The command moved briskly forward through the brush until within 100 yards of the enemy's line of battle, when a most destructive fire was poured into the enemy's ranks. After a short resistance, the enemy fled, leaving his dead and wounded and several pieces of artillery upon the field. I pushed forward the battalion in pursuit of the retreating foe, crossing a field and several fences. After crossing the last fence, our line of battle became disordered in getting through a very dense cedar thicket which intervened. Upon emerging from the thicket, I could only see a portion of the left wing of the battalion. With this I continued to push forward in the original direction of the line of battle, and, uniting with the Second Brigade, under command of Brigadier-General Ector, pursued the fleeing enemy for the distance of some 4 miles, until recalled by Capt. R. E. Foote. Upon returning to the brigade, I learned that the right wing of the battalion, under command of Lieutenants [E. D.] McLaughlin and [J. S.] Dougan, had assisted in a second brilliant and successful charge.

At this point the battalion was furnished with a fresh supply of ammunition, and again moved forward upon the enemy. The line swept forward through the forest for the distance of a mile, when it reached the foot of a ridge extending to the right and left as far as I could see, the side of which was covered with a dense undergrowth, in places almost impenetrable. Here the fires of three heavy batteries were opened upon us. Nothing daunted, the line moved steadily forward, halting and reforming twice in the midst of a shower of bursting shells, grape, and canister. When within 50 yards of the brow of the hill the command was given to charge. It was most gallantly executed. The men, with an infuriated yell, rushed to the top of the hill. A short, sharp contest ensued, when the enemy's line of infantry began to give way; but the enemy's batteries, being entirely protected by the nature of their position, continued to pour showers of grape and canister into our already more than decimated ranks. It was impossible for men to withstand such a fire from an unseen foe, and reluctantly the battalion with the rest of the brigade retired.

This was the last action in which the battalion was engaged. After falling back some distance, the battalion reformed, moved farther to the right, and lay upon the battle-field during the night.

It is with pride that I call attention to the fact that the men of my battalion took as deliberate aim as if engaged in target practice, each shot telling with fearful effect, as will be seen by an examination of the ground occupied by the battalion during the engagement. Never before have I seen such a reckless disregard of life exhibited. Where all fought so well comparison would be odious.

In the first charge the flag-staff was shot in two and the right arm of Color-Sergt. Joseph R. Perry so paralyzed that the flag fell from his hand. Sergt. J. C. Davis, of Company A, immediately snatched up the colors and bore them gallantly forward until Sergeant Perry recovered from the shock and resumed his position.

I herewith report the following list of casualties, to wit:

Command.	Killed.	Wounded.	Missing.
Company A	2	4	......
Company B	1	8	5
Company C	1	4	......
Company E	1	7	......
Total	5	23	5

I have the honor to be, captain, your obedient servant,

J. A. ROSS,

Major Fourth Arkansas Battalion.

Capt. R. E. FOOTE,

Assistant Adjutant-General, Third Brigade, McCown's Division.

No. 300.

Report of Capt. John T. Humphreys, Arkansas battery.

CAMP NEAR SHELBYVILLE, TENN.,

January 10, 1863.

SIR: In obedience to orders, at daylight on the morning of December 31, [1862,] my battery advanced to the position occupied the day previous by Robertson's battery. Your brigade, then advancing, engaged the enemy and was rapidly driving him back. I followed as closely as the nature of the ground would admit, but, turning to the right too suddenly, became separated from your brigade, and, having advanced in a northern direction about 1 mile, engaged a battery of the enemy, a part of which was soon after captured by our advancing lines. I then passed through an interval in our infantry lines caused by our left swinging too far in that direction, and, taking position near Mr. Cowan's house, some 3 miles from and northwest of our original lines, opened fire upon the enemy's batteries, some 500 yards distant, in position on an elevation equal to our own and partially concealed by a narrow skirt of timber intervening between our position and his. The enemy's guns (supposed to have been sixteen in number), then firing upon our infantry and other troops in his front, were immediately turned upon us with great precision and rapidity. We responded as fast as our guns could be served, and for more than half an hour drew the entire fire of all the guns on the opposite hill. Two of my guns were rendered useless by ammunition too large, and two others were, during the action, disabled by the enemy's shot, one having a wheel shot off and otherwise injured, and the cannoneers of the other being in the same way disabled. Five horses were killed by an exploding shell. With two pieces (a 3-inch rifle and 6-pounder gun) we maintained the fight until our advancing lines were charging the enemy's guns, when we were ordered to fall back, which we did, to a point some 300 yards in rear of that position. Eight men were disabled by wounds.

During the engagement there were many acts of individual gallantry displayed, some of which I beg leave to mention. Lieut. John W. Rivers, when the cannoneers at a piece were disabled, seized the sponge-staff, and, calling others to his aid, filled the post of No. 1 with energy and determination.

First Lieut. William H. Gore was acting as gunner when he was knocked down and wounded by a shell. He immediately rallied and called upon the men, wounded like himself, to rally to their work.

Lieut. Oliver P. Richardson, whose gallantry on the field of Richmond, Ky., attracted the attention of General Churchill, commanded his section with ability.

Lieut. Henry C. Riggin, after Lieutenant Gore was wounded, was intrusted with the command of that officer's section, and rendered efficient service through the day.

All the above-named officers in this engagement behaved with a gallantry and displayed a devotion to cause and country which should entitle them to the favorable consideration of the commanding general.

First Sergt. William Shea was fearless and efficient. Ensign Cameron, when a part of the flag-staff was shot down, observed coolly that they were "shooting a little close."

Private Samuel M. Tucker had a sponge-staff shot out of his hand, and by the same force he was knocked over, but immediately returned to duty. Private Joseph W. Adams was wounded in the foot and had his pantaloons torn off by an exploding shell. Dennis Corcoran was severely wounded in the neck by splinters from a shell, and reluctantly was compelled to leave the field.

Duty Sergeants Thompson, Casey, Greer, Long, Brewer, and Burkett are all deserving of favorable mention for high courage and efficiency. In fact, to do ample and full justice I should have to mention every name on the company rolls. All were in trying positions, and suffice it to say that no men could have behaved better while subjected to a terrific fire of shot and shell which tore down trees like the whirlwind and scattered them like the lightning.

Fortunately, while horses and guns were destroyed the men were protected by the "Giver of all victories." It is to that power and the officers and men mentioned and referred to that the success of this battery can be ascribed.

Very respectfully,

JOHN T. HUMPHREYS,
Captain Artillery.

General E. McNAIR,
Comdg. Third Brigade, McCown's Division, Army of Tennessee.

No. 301.

Reports of Maj. Gen. Joseph Wheeler, C. S. Army, Chief of Cavalry, including skirmishes at and near La Vergne, December 26 and 30, and January 1; at Stewart's Creek Bridge, December 27; at Stewart's Creek, December 28; at Wilkinson's Cross-Roads, December 29; at Cox's (or Blood's) Hill, January 3; at Murfreesborough, January 4; on Manchester pike, January 5; at Mill Creek Bridge, January 8; near Nashville, January 12; and capture of transports, January 13, 14, and 17, and of construction train at Antioch, January 25.

HEADQUARTERS CAVALRY,
Six miles from Murfreesborough, January 5, 1863—6 p. m.

GENERAL: I left Murfreesborough last night, about 9 o'clock p. m., having engaged the enemy between Murfreesborough and the river for about an hour before sunset. I left a picket in front of the town. We formed our first line this a. m., 4 miles from Murfreesborough. The cavalry we kept back with the greatest ease, but finally they brought up several regiments of infantry in line of battle, colors flying, with cavalry on the flanks and artillery placed in a favorable position. By this means they succeeded in driving us 2 miles. The last attack was 5 miles from Murfreesborough, the shock of which was sufficiently great to prevent them from making any farther advance to-night. We must have killed and wounded a great many of them. Our loss, 6 or 7 wounded, including my aide, Lieutenant Wailes. My adjutant, Lieutenant Burford, was slightly wounded yesterday by a shell. I shall have no difficulty in keeping back the enemy from Bellbuckle for several days, if General Wharton succeeds in keeping them back on the Shelbyville pike. Of course, it will take more time to reach Wartrace and Shelbyville.

Very respectfully, your obedient servant,

JOS. WHEELER,
Brigadier-General and Chief of Cavalry.

Lieutenant-General POLK.

—

HEADQUARTERS CAVALRY,
Near Fosterville, Tenn., January 26, 1863.

COLONEL: I have the honor to report that my command—consisting of the First Alabama Cavalry, Colonel [William W.] Allen; Third Alabama, Major [F. Y.] Gaines; Fifty-first Alabama, Colonel [John T.] Morgan; Eighth Confederate, Colonel [W. B.] Wade, and two Tennessee battalions, under Majors [D. W.] Holman and DeWitt C. Douglass, together with [Capt. J. H.] Wiggins' battery—was, on the 26th ultimo, stationed at Stewart's Creek, on the Murfreesborough and Nashville pike, and about 10 miles northwest of Murfreesborough. My line of vedettes, forming a continuous line, extended from a point east of Stone's River, on my right, crossing the Nashville and Murfreesborough pike about 10 miles from Nashville, and extending to a point about half way from said pike to Brentwood, the posts of the pickets and grand guards being at favorable positions on the avenues of approach and at points varying from 300 to 1,000 yards in rear of the line of vedettes. General Pegram's brigade was stationed on the right and General Wharton's brigade on the left of my line.

About 7 o'clock on the morning of December 26, [1862,] the enemy advanced in large force, driving in our vedettes. On arriving at the front and seeing the extent of the movement, I ordered up the entire command and deployed it in line of battle. We engaged the enemy during the entire day, falling back about 3 miles. We also engaged the enemy during the 28th and 29th ultimo, killing and wounding large numbers, meeting but very slight losses ourselves.

By the evening of the 29th we had reached the line of battle of our infantry and had placed my brigade on the extreme right of the line.

At midnight, pursuant to orders from General Bragg, I proceeded with my command, re-enforced by Colonel [James E.] Carter's regiment, to the enemy's rear.

By daylight on the 30th we had reached Jefferson, and soon after met a brigade train, with all the equipage of one brigade. We attacked vigorously, drove off the guards, and destroyed the train, baggage, equipage, &c., also capturing about 50 prisoners. We then proceeded toward La Vergne, and captured a party of Federals out stealing and gathering stock, and soon after overtook and captured a small foraging train.

About noon we arrived in the vicinity of La Vergne and found it filled with soldiers and large trains parked in the fields surrounding the place. We immediately charged in three columns, completely surprising the guards, who made but slight resistance. We immediately paroled the prisoners, amounting to about 700, and destroyed immense trains and stores, amounting to many hundred thousands of dollars. We then proceeded to Rock Spring, attacked, captured, and destroyed another large train. We then marched on Nolensville without opposition, capturing large trains, stores, and arms, and about 300 prisoners. We slept for a few hours 5 miles from Nolensville, and at 2 o'clock the next morning proceeded to the left flank of our army, having made a complete circuit of the enemy's rear. On arriving the line was engaged. We pressed on and attacked enemy on the Murfreesborough and Nashville pike, just north of Overall's Creek. After a brisk engagement we moved across the creek and made an attack on the enemy at that point, driving him for 2 miles and successfully engaging him until dark, when we fell back to the left of our line, where we remained during the night.

In this latter engagement Colonel Allen and Lieutenant-Colonel [James D.] Webb were wounded.

Early on the morning of January 1, I proceeded, pursuant to directions from General Bragg, with my own and General Wharton's brigade, to the rear of the enemy. We attacked a large train near La Vergne, dispersing its guards, and captured and destroyed a large number of wagons and stores. We also captured one piece of artillery. Toward evening we received orders to return, and we regained our positions on the flanks of the army by 2 o'clock on the morning of the 2d instant. We remained in position that night and next day, engaging the enemy at every opportunity.

At 9 o'clock that evening I proceeded again to the rear of the enemy, according to directions from General Bragg, and succeeded next morning in capturing a number of horses, wagons, and prisoners. About 2 p. m. we attacked a large ordnance train at Cox's Hill, heavily guarded by cavalry and infantry, and succeeded in driving off the cavalry guards and in breaking down and upsetting a large number of wagons. The enemy's infantry being in such force (quite treble our numbers), we were prevented from destroying the train, but succeeded in preventing its making any further progress that day. By this time we received orders to immediately return to the army, which order was obeyed, we reaching our former position on the left flank of our army about 4 o'clock next morning. We here learned that the army had fallen back, and about 9 o'clock that morning we crossed Stone's River and took position in front of Murfreesborough.

About 3 p. m. the enemy advanced to the river and commenced a brisk skirmish with artillery and infantry. After dark the enemy retired a short distance, and our pickets in front of Murfreesborough were unmolested during the night.

At daylight on Monday, the 4th [5th] instant, we fell back to a point on the Manchester pike about 3 miles from Murfreesborough. About 1 o'clock the enemy advanced, and after a short skirmish we fell back half a mile to a favorable position. Here we formed line of battle in conjunction with General Pegram's brigade, in a very favorable position, behind fences, entirely obscured from view. About 3 o'clock the enemy advanced with a brigade of infantry and artillery in line of battle, with heavy force of cavalry on their flanks. When they arrived within about 250 yards, we opened on them a heavy fire of small-arms and artillery with excellent effect, killing and wounding large numbers. After an engagement of about thirty minutes they turned off and left the field, and have not since advanced any farther from Murfreesborough on this road.

During the many engagements incident to the battle of Murfreesbor ough, I take pleasure in commending the gallantry and good soldierly conduct of Colonel Allen, Captain [V. M.] Elmore, and Lieutenant [Edward S.] Ledyard, of the First Alabama, and Major [C. J.] Prentice and Captain [Richard] McCann, who commanded detachments. Colonel Allen and Major Prentice were severely wounded while fighting gallantly.

Lieutenants [E. S.] Burford and [William E.] Wailes, of my staff, were at all times distinguished for gallantry, zeal, and efficiency, and were both wounded.

Very respectfully, colonel, your obedient servant,

JOS. WHEELER,
Major-General and Chief of Cavalry.

Col. George William Brent,
Assistant Adjutant-General.

—

HEADQUARTERS CAVALRY, DEPARTMENT No. 2,
January 29, 1863.

Colonel : I have the honor to state that the cavalry of Lieutenant-General Hardee's corps, under my command, engaged the enemy as they advanced upon the Nashville and Murfreesborough pike, and on the adjoining approaches, from the morning of the 26th ultimo to the evening of the 29th. At midnight on the night of the 29th ultimo I proceeded with the command across the West Fork of Stone's River, by way of the Lebanon road, hence by a circuitous route to Jefferson, where, at about 9 a. m. on the 30th, we attacked, captured, and destroyed an entire brigade train. We then proceeded toward La Vergne; capturing a party sent out after horses and mules, and also a foraging party. We attacked La Vergne about 1 p. m., capturing about 500 prisoners, 200 stand of arms, and the reserve wagon trains of the enemy; the wagons were destroyed. We then proceeded to Rock Spring, capturing a brigade train, which we destroyed, with its equipage. We then proceeded to Nolensville, capturing a train and about 200 prisoners and 200 stand of arms.

We then made a circuit around Triune, and the next morning attacked the enemy, stationed on the Nashville and Murfreesborough pike north of Overall's Creek. We then moved down toward Murfreesborough, and again attacked them south of Overall's Creek, driving the enemy for a distance of 2 miles from the Wilkinson pike to the Nashville pike, engaging their infantry and cavalry until dark. We then withdrew to our position on the left of our wing. At daylight we proceeded again to La Vergne, in the enemy's rear, attacked a large train, burned several wagons, and captured many prisoners. We then received orders to return to the army, where we arrived at about 2 o'clock the next morning, and placed our pickets out to the front. We remained in this position until dark, when we moved again to Antioch, capturing a few wagons, and at about 3 p. m. attacked a large train on Cox's Hill. After capturing the train, and injuring some of the wagons, four regiments of infantry attacked us, and we were obliged to retire. I then received orders to return, and arrived at my old stand, on the left of our wing, at about 4 o'clock on Sunday morning, January 3 [4]. As our army had retired, I moved over the river and remained in Murfreesborough that day. Toward evening I skirmished with the enemy and withdrew my pickets 3 miles at daylight the next morning.

At 3 p. m. Monday, the enemy advanced and engaged us warmly. The enemy did not advance any farther.

On January 8, I moved over to the Cumberland, and a detachment, under Captain [Richard] McCann, destroyed the railroad bridge over Mill Creek and a construction train.

On the 12th, we drove in a large foraging party to Nashville, and on the 13th and 14th we captured a gunboat and four transports. We also destroyed a large amount of stores at Ashland, which the enemy had left under guard, but the guard ran off as we approached. Many other transports threw off a great part of their cargo to avoid capture.

On the 25th, we captured a construction train near Antioch.

A detachment, under Major [D. W.] Holman, captured another transport on the 17th.

Respectfully, colonel, your obedient servant,

JOS. WHEELER,
Major-General.

Col. T. B. ROY, *Chief of Staff.*

No. 302.

Report of Capt. T. H. Mauldin, Third Alabama Cavalry, Wheeler's brigade, including skirmishes December 26–January 5.

FOSTERVILLE, TENN.,
February 19, 1863.

COLONEL: The Third Alabama Cavalry was engaged in skirmishing with the enemy on December 26, 27, 28, and 29, 1862, from La Vergne to Murfreesborough, Tenn.

On the 30th, was present at a skirmish near Jefferson, La Vergne, and Nolensville.

On the 31st, was in a charge made by the cavalry upon the right of the Federal army, where it was subjected to a heavy fire of small-arms from infantry and cavalry, losing, however, but 1 man killed and 2 lieutenants and 2 men wounded and left on the field.

On January 1 and 2, the regiment was in front of the enemy upon the extreme left of the Confederate army without any fighting.

On the night of the 2d, it marched to the rear of the Federal army, and on the 3d was engaged in an attack upon one of the enemy's wagon trains, upon the Nashville and Murfreesborough turnpike, and returned to the field of battle near Murfreesborough about an hour before day the morning of the 4th.

During the day of the 4th, this regiment moved through Murfreesborough, and bivouacked at night about 2 miles from town, on the Manchester turnpike.

On the 5th, was engaged in a fight with some of the Federal infantry 6 miles from Murfreesborough, on the Manchester pike.

This ended the series of battles and skirmishes from December 25, 1862, to January 5, 1863, in which the regiment was engaged.

During this time the regiment lost, in killed, wounded, and missing, 25, including 3 lieutenants wounded.

I would respectfully report that on the memorable field of Murfrees-borough, Sergt. Maj. H. M. Cooper and Sergt. J. W. Norwood, of Company A, are worthy of promotion for their gallantry in rallying the regiment and assisting in bringing it out in order from under a galling fire from the enemy's infantry and cavalry combined on December 31, 1862.

Very respectfully, your obedient servant,

T. H. MAULDIN,
Captain, Commanding Third Alabama Cavalry.

Col. W. B. WADE,
Commanding First Cavalry Brigade.

No. 303.

Report of Lieut. Col. J. D. Webb, Fifty-first Alabama Partisan Rangers including skirmishes December 26–January 5.

OLD FOSTERVILLE, TENN., *February* 23, 1863.

In obedience to General Orders, No. 6, in the absence of Col. John T. Morgan, Fifty-first Alabama Regiment, Partisan Rangers, who was in command on the occasion of which report is to be made, I beg leave to submit the following:

On Friday evening, December 26 [ultimo], the regiment left their camp on Stewart's Creek, on the Murfreesborough and Nashville turnpike, and promptly reported to the general commanding at La Vergne, which is a distance of 5 miles from the camp. They were ordered to the right of the railroad and to the front of La Vergne. The command was dismounted to fight, and soon became engaged along the line with the sharpshooters and skirmishers of the enemy's infantry, as also their advanced guard, on the left of their line. This was kept up steadily on both sides until the order was given to fall back, to take a position nearer the turnpike, and to be in supporting distance of the artillery. The order was executed in good order. They then formed a line of battle, the right resting on the turnpike and extending near to the railroad. The enemy did not pursue. Night came on, and the regiment remained in line of battle until 10 o'clock. They were ordered to return to camp.

In this skirmish we lost 1 private of Company C, supposed to be captured and not killed; 1 private from Company D, known to be captured.

At early dawn on Saturday, the 27th, was ordered to the front. They were again ordered to take position in advance of the ground on which they were formed the evening before. Soon after reaching the position we were again engaged with the enemy's left, advancing in line of battle under cover of his artillery, throwing grape and shell. We continued the engagement until our artillery was forced to retire on the pike, when we fell back slowly to the right of and along the Jefferson pike, in the direction of the town of Jefferson. Heavy rain commenced to fall and continued for several hours. When the command had reached the Jefferson pike, and near the residence of Mr. York, Captain [N. D.] Johnson, of Company F, with his company, was ordered to go in the direction of Buchanan's Mill on a scout; and Lieutenant [J. J.] Seawell, in command of Company I, with his company, was ordered, too, as a scouting party in the direction of La Vergne, neither of whom joined the regiment again that day. In a few minutes after each of these companies left, in obedience to orders, a large force of cavalry, accompanied by artillery and infantry, advanced on the Jefferson pike, and commenced a heavy and brisk firing upon us as we were crossing Stewart's [Creek], where the Jefferson pike crosses that stream. Their fire was returned with vigor, and their advance checked until their artillery and infantry came up. Being heavily pressed by greatly superior numbers, and opened upon by their artillery with grape, canister, and shell vigorously, we retired in good order on the pike in the direction of Jefferson.

While the enemy were pressing our rear, after crossing Stewart's Creek, in this engagement, the conduct of Capt. M. L. Kirkpatrick, Company H; Capt. L. W. Battle, Company B; Lieut. William [M.] Fitt, Company G, deserves especial mention in rallying their men and leading them in a charge on the enemy's cavalry.

Justice requires that the name of James W. Copiley, of Company I (who was then and is now acting ordnance sergeant for this regiment), should be mentioned for his gallantry and daring at the head of the column in this charge.

The gallant and brave Lieut. William [M.] Fitt, Company G, was killed; Private Holey, of Company G, and Private Urley, of Company K, were killed; Lieutenant [John O.] Zeigler, of Company B, and 2 privates of Company G, were wounded. Lieutenant [J. J.] Seawell, with 12 of his company, were captured. We are informed by those of his command who made their escape that they are almost certain that he with those of his men who were captured, were wounded. They saw several of their horses fall.

The coolness and bravery of Orderly Sergt. H. Clay Reynolds, of Company I, distinguished him while he brought off several of his company under a heavy fire in crossing Stewart's Creek, [and] rejoined his command. His conduct commends him for special mention. The regiment bivouacked that night on Stone's River without rations.

On the morning of the 28th, we formed line of battle to the right of the Nashville turnpike, 8 miles from Murfreesborough, and opposite to a church on the pike. We occupied the position until nightfall, and, with the exception of slight skirmishing with the enemy's pickets, were not engaged. We bivouacked for the night opposite to Miller's, near the pike.

On the morning of the 29th, we advanced on the pike and again formed line of battle on the ground of the day before, and remained until we were ordered to fall back to the left and along the turnpike in the direction of Murfreesborough, skirmishing with the enemy's advance forces from that point until we entered our infantry lines, drawn up in front of Murfreesborough in line of battle, which was late in the afternoon of that day, being the whole distance under the fire of the enemy, both artillery and small-arms.

After reaching our infantry lines we were ordered to form a line of battle, our left extending toward and within a short distance of the Lebanon turnpike, about 2 miles from Murfreesborough. We remained there until 12 o'clock that night. We then took up the march and proceeded down that pike, crossing Stone's River, until we reached the Jefferson pike, and proceeded on that pike in the direction of Jefferson until daylight; then, turning to the right, continued the march until we encountered the enemy on Tuesday morning. This regiment remained to support the artillery, and were not actively engaged with the enemy at this point.

At 2 o'clock on that day the regiment charged at La Vergne a train of wagons parked on the plains; captured 36 wagons laden with ammunition, commissary and quartermaster's stores, which were burned; the teams of mules and horses attached to them, 8 or 10 wagons, and 50 prisoners. After which they proceeded to Nolensville, and, with other commands of this brigade, captured 20 wagons, 50 prisoners, the teams of horses and mules, late in the afternoon of that day. From thence they proceeded in a westerly direction for 6 or 8 miles and bivouacked for the night.

Before daylight on Wednesday morning, the 31st, we were ordered to march, and at 2 o'clock on that day, on the Wilkinson pike, engaged in skirmishing with the infantry of the enemy's right in front of Murfreesborough. The engagement was kept up until nightfall.

In this engagement Lieutenant-Colonel Webb was struck on the forehead by a fragment of a shell; 1 private of Company A wounded; 4 privates of Company B wounded; Company D, 1 private wounded; Company H, 1 private; Company F, 3 privates; Company E, 1 private.

Again on January 1, 1863, we engaged the enemy at La Vergne, on the left of the pike, facing toward Murfreesborough, for nearly one hour. They were well posted on an eminence behind houses, a train of wagons parked, and fences. The contest for the time was very warm. We captured some 15 or 20 prisoners, 5 or 6 wagons, destroyed some 8 or 10 wagons laden with army stores, and carried off the teams of mules. We held our position until we were ordered to retire.

The casualties were—Company C, 1 sergeant wounded; Company D, 1 private; Company E, 2 privates; Company F, 1 private; Company G, 1 private; Company H, 2 privates; Company I, 1 private; Company K, 1 private killed and 2 wounded. We returned to a place on the Nashville and Shelbyville dirt road, and at 2 o'clock in the morning halted to rest.

Friday morning, the 2d, we were ordered to march, and proceeded to the point on the Wilkinson pike where we engaged the enemy on the afternoon of the 31st. We remained drawn up in line of battle until after sunset that evening, when we were ordered to proceed down the Wilkinson pike several miles, and, turning on a dirt road, marched until a late hour in the night. We were halted and ordered to rest.

At daylight the next morning (the 3d) we were ordered to remount, and proceeded to Antioch Church. At that point we were ordered to proceed to the Nashville and Murfreesborough pike, at or near Blood's, which is within 8 miles of Nashville. We reached the point designated about 2 o'clock in the afternoon, and soon became engaged in a skirmish with the enemy, which was kept up for half an hour, when orders were received from General Wheeler to withdraw and return by Antioch Church and join him. We did so, and after a toilsome march we halted at the place from which we moved on Friday evening, and bivouacked until morning.

On Monday morning, the 4th, about sunrise, we crossed Stone's River and proceeded on the Manchester pike 3 miles. We halted and remained there until the next morning, when we were again ordered to march. We advanced on that pike for 4 miles farther, where we halted until the afternoon, when we [were] ordered to return on the pike some 3 miles. We were ordered to dismount to fight, and formed on the right of the pike facing Murfreesborough, and soon became engaged with the enemy's cavalry, who advanced under cover of their artillery, firing grape and shell. We checked their advance and kept up a brisk engagement until artillery retired on the pike, before a greatly superior force, with the following casualties: Company B, 1 private wounded; Company C, 2 wounded; Company E, 1 wounded; Company G, 1, mortally; Company H, 1 wounded; Company K, 1 killed. That night we bivouacked on the Manchester pike, 8 miles from Murfreesborough.

On the morning of the 6th, we moved slowly down the pike to Beech Grove, where we remained, and bivouacked until Friday, the 9th, at which time we set out on the march for the Cumberland River.

On each of the occasions mentioned the officers and men behaved with such coolness and bravery as to show that they could be relied on in an hour of danger or peril—not to be dismayed by unequal numbers and superior equipments.

I regret the absence of Colonel Morgan in making this report, as I had not expected to be called on to do so, and kept no memorandum from which to prepare a more accurate account or detailed report. The surgeon of the regiment has provided the list of the casualties mentioned.

Respectfully submitted.

J. D. WEBB,
Lieut. Col., Comdg. Fifty-first Alabama Regt. Partisan Rangers.

No. 304.

Report of Capt. J. H. Wiggins, Arkansas battery, including skirmishes at La Vergne December 26–27.

FEBRUARY 19, 1863.

In compliance with General Orders, No. 6, I have the honor to submit the following report of the part borne by Wiggins' battery in the fights before Murfreesborough:

On the evening of December 26, [1862,] the enemy advanced upon La Vergne, and one section of the battery was advanced, under Lieutenant [J. W.] Calloway, to engage the enemy. During the engagement that evening we lost 3 horses and had 2 men wounded. That night the section under Lieutenant Calloway retired about a mile, and one section under Lieutenant [J. P.] Bryant was left in La Vergne on picket.

On the morning of the 27th, Lieutenant Calloway, with his section, was ordered to the front to engage the enemy again, while Lieutenant Bryant, with his section, was posted on a hill to the left of the pike and in rear of La Vergne, to relieve the retreat of Lieutenant Calloway. The battery retired to Stewart's Creek that evening, engaging the enemy by sections alternately. Loss that day, one horse. One section, under Lieutenant Bryant, was left on picket at Stewart's Creek until Monday morning, the rest of the battery retiring farther to the rear.

On Monday, the 29th, we retired to our lines in front of Murfreesborough, firing in the same manner as at Stewart's Creek, and moved with the command to the right and encamped until midnight, when, in compliance with orders from General Wheeler, took Lieutenant Calloway with a section of guns and moved with the command on the Lebanon pike and north of Old Jefferson, where a camp of the enemy was attacked, and the battery fired about a dozen rounds; then moved on with the command by way of La Vergne and Nolensville, but had no other engagement until Wednesday evening, when the enemy was attacked and the battery engaged two hours. Lost 1 man wounded, 1 horse killed, and several horses wounded.

On Wednesday (31st), one piece of the section which was left behind was taken out by Lieutenant Bryant, by order of General Bragg, with

General Breckinridge's division, and was engaged in the action that day. Total loss, 3 men wounded, 4 horses killed, and several more wounded. The stock was very much exhausted, not having been unharnessed in six days.

The officers and men all bore themselves well and with coolness. Sergt. A. A. Blake especially displayed much gallantry.

Respectfully submitted.

J. H. WIGGINS,
Captain.

Colonel [W. B.] WADE.

No. 305.

Report of Brig. Gen. John A. Wharton, C. S. Army, commanding Cavalry Brigade.

HEADQUARTERS WHARTON'S CAVALRY BRIGADE,
Shelbyville Pike, Tenn., January 22, 1863.

MAJOR : I have the honor to submit the following report of the operations of the brigade acting under my orders during the battles before Murfreesborough, commencing December 31, 1862, and ending Saturday, January 3, 1863:

The brigade was composed of the following commands.† * * *

I received my orders from Lieut. Gen. W. J. Hardee in person. They were as follows: I was informed that at daylight on the morning of the 31st [ultimo] our left wing would attack the enemy's right. Being drawn up on the extreme left, I was ordered to reach the enemy's rear as soon as possible, and to do them all the damage I could. My command was formed before daylight. I had divided my brigade into three commands in order that it might be better wielded : Texas Rangers, Third Confederate, and Second Georgia, under Colonel Harrison; the First Confederate, Davis Battalion, Malone's battalion, and Murray's regiment, under Colonel Cox, and the remainder of the command acting as a support to the battery and as a reserve. I moved the command promptly at daylight. So vigorous was the attack of our left upon the enemy's right, proceeding first at a trot and then at a gallop, I had to travel a distance of 2½ miles before I reached the enemy's rear. I succeeded in getting into position near the Wilkinson pike, with the enemy in my front; caused Colonel Cox to form his command for a charge; directed Captain White to open on the enemy with his battery. After a brisk fire from the artillery, I ordered Colonel Cox to charge, which he did in gallant style, as evidenced by his capturing the Seventy-fifth Regiment Illinois Infantry.

About this time Captain [S. P.] Christian [Company K, Eighth Texas Cavalry], with four companies of Texas Rangers, charged a four-gun battery and captured it, including horses, drivers, harness, and everything pertaining to it.

Up to this time we had taken about 1,500 prisoners, which, with the artillery and one piece found without horses about a mile in the enemy's rear, were sent to the proper officer in Murfreesborough.

The enemy's immense wagon trains, guarded by a heavy force of cavalry, could be seen moving near and in the rear of the enemy in the direction of the Nashville pike. I determined to move across the country, give the cavalry battle, and to attempt to capture the train. Our infantry

---

† See Organization of the Army of Tennessee, No. 189, p. 661.

by this time had succeeded in driving the enemy across the Wilkinson pike. In reaching a point about three-quarters of a mile distant from the Nashville pike, I discovered the wagon train of the enemy, together with some artillery, moving along the pike. A heavy body of cavalry was drawn up near and parallel to the pike, facing me, and a considerable body was drawn up nearer me to give battle. The battery was placed in position. Ashby's regiment and L. T. Hardy's company formed in front of the enemy. Harrison's command formed on his right flank. The battery opened with considerable effect. It was ordered to cease firing and Ashby and Hardy ordered to charge, which they promptly did. They were met by a counter-charge of the enemy, supposed to be the Fourth Regulars, with drawn sabers. At the same time Harrison's command was ordered to charge, which they did in the most gallant and handsome manner. The Rangers, in advance, met the enemy, and completely routed them, relieving Ashby's command, which was hard pressed. Availing myself of the confusion caused by the rout of the enemy's advanced cavalry, the entire brigade was ordered to charge the enemy's whole cavalry force, drawn up in line half a mile in rear of their main line of battle, protecting their wagon train. The order was responded to in the most chivalrous manner, and 2,000 horsemen were hurled on the foe. The ground was exceedingly favorable for cavalry operations, and after a short hand-to-hand conflict, in which the revolver was used with deadly effect, the enemy fled from the field in the wildest confusion and dismay, and were pursued to Overall's Creek, a distance of 2 miles. After they had crossed Overall's Creek, the enemy reformed out of range of our guns.

The wagon train—consisting of several hundred wagons—many pieces of artillery, and about 1,000 infantry, who were either guarding the wagons or were fugitives from the field, were ours. The trains were turned round, and started back on the pike toward Murfreesborough.

I had proceeded but a short distance in the charge when I was informed that a heavy cavalry force immediately in my rear was about to charge my battery, which, being unable to keep up with the cavalry in a charge, was some distance behind. Knowing that it would be impossible to withdraw my men from the pursuit, and having no disposition to do so, I immediately returned in person with two of my staff—Lieutenants [D. S.] Terry, jr., and [G. W.] McNeal—and found the battery with no support save Colonel Smith and 20 of his men, the balance, with too much zeal, having engaged in the pursuit of the fleeing enemy. My arrival was most opportune. About 300 of the enemy's cavalry, not over 400 yards distant, were bearing down upon the battery with a speed that evinced a determination to take it at all hazards. A few men, with Colonel Smith, were promptly formed, and the battery unlimbered and ordered to fire upon the approaching enemy. Several shells were exploded in their ranks and they retired in confusion. The command that had captured the wagons, thinking that they had driven the entire force of the enemy's cavalry across Overall's Creek, and apprehending danger alone from that quarter, were prepared to meet it only from that direction. Besides, many were scattered along the entire length of the wagon train, directing its movements and guarding the numerous prisoners taken. In this condition they were attacked by the same party of cavalry from the direction of Murfreesborough that I had repulsed with the artillery, the enemy's cavalry that we had driven across Overall's Creek being in condition likewise to attack them in the rear. Owing to this and to my being detained to defend the battery, we were able only to bring off a portion of the wagons, 5 or 6 pieces of artillery, about

400 prisoners, 327 beef cattle, and a goodly number of mules cut from the wagons.

In this engagement the enemy suffered severely, losing many officers and men, both killed and captured. Among the former was Col. Minor Milliken, who was killed by Private John Bowers, of Company K, Texas Rangers, in single combat.

My loss was about 150 killed, wounded, and missing.

Captain [R. J. C.] Gailbreath, of Murray's regiment; Lieutenant [William] Ellis, Company G, Texas Rangers, and Lieutenant [W. H.] Sharp, Company B, same regiment, were wounded and left upon the field. Adjt. N. D. Rothrock, of Third Confederate Regiment, was killed. My assistant inspector-general, Walker, was also wounded, and has since died of his wounds.

To Capt. Paul [F.] Anderson and his gallant company (my escort) I am indebted for the capture and safe delivery of 327 beeves and the guard accompanying them.

Having placed the booty within our lines, I again returned to the rear of the enemy and to the vicinity of the Nashville pike, and continued to engage the enemy until the middle of the afternoon. At dusk I stationed the command upon the left of our infantry and picketed for its protection. All soldiers in the command who were armed with shot or other indifferent guns exchanged them for those of a more approved character.

When it is borne in mind that the operations of this brigade were entirely in rear of the enemy, and not a mile from his line of battle; when it is likewise borne in mind that it successfully engaged all arms of the service—infantry, artillery, and cavalry—and captured and sent to the rear more prisoners than the command numbered, I think it will be cheerfully conceded that they performed meritorious and important services and are entitled to the commendation due from the commanding general to gallant soldiers.

On Thursday morning, the enemy being reputed to be in full retreat, I was directed by the commanding general to attack them at any point deemed practicable on the Nashville and Murfreesborough pike. I moved my command, in connection with Generals Wheeler and Buford, around to La Vergne, reaching that place about 4 p. m. A large train of wagons and some artillery were seen moving along the pike with a strong escort of cavalry in the direction of Nashville. General Wheeler moved across the country and attacked the train a mile below La Vergne. I attacked the enemy in front, in La Vergne, having dismounted a portion of my command. We captured about 100 wagons, 150 prisoners, 300 mules, and 1 piece of artillery. Ten of the wagons, the piece of artillery, and the mules were brought away and delivered to the proper officer. The remaining wagons, with the quartermaster's commissary, and ordnance stores contained in them, were burned. A regiment of infantry under Col. ——— Dennis was stationed in a cedar brake and fortifications near this point. I caused the battery under Lieutenant [Arthur] Pue [jr.], who acted with great gallantry, to open on it. The fire at a range of not more than 400 yards was kept up for more than an hour, and must have resulted in great damage to the enemy. I caused the enemy to be charged on three sides at the same time by Colonels Cox and Smith and Lieutenant-Colonel [James C.] Malone, and the charge was repeated four times, but the enemy was so strongly posted that it was found impossible to dislodge him.

Colonels Cox and Smith and Lieutenant-Colonel Malone and their commands behaved with the utmost gallantry. To Capt. Fergus Kyle, of the Texas Rangers, I am indebted for the capture and safe delivery of many of the mules taken. Major Bledsoe, of Murray's regiment, was prompt and efficient in burning the wagons which could not be removed. Lieut. G. W. McNeal, of my staff, and Private Copeland, of Third Confederate Regiment, burned several wagons under very heavy fire from the enemy. The wagons were riddled with bullets during the firing.

Night coming on, I started for Murfreesborough, which place I reached at 1 a. m. next morning, after a march of 40 miles and four hours' fighting. My loss in Murray's, Smith's, and Cox's regiments and Malone's battalion in officers and men was very considerable. The command encamped the remainder of the night on the left of our line of battle.

Upon Friday I was ordered by General Bragg to the right. When Breckinridge's division attacked the enemy's left on Friday afternoon, having received no intimation that such an attack was contemplated, I accompanied Pegram's battery to the front and right with Companies D and K, of the Texas Rangers, and my escort company. Capt. Paul [F.] Anderson not being able to induce General Pegram to open with his battery (he being fearful of firing into our own troops), I took charge of the battery, placing it upon a commanding hill, and opened fire upon a heavy column of the enemy advancing from their extreme left to turn Breckinridge's right. The fire was so effective (the range not being over 500 yards) as to shoot down their standard and throw them into confusion. The fire was continued until my horse was shot. I was thrown in his struggles, and when I succeeded in getting another horse the battery had been run off without any occasion whatever. Shortly after this, Breckinridge's division gave way. I sent an order back for my command to dismount and to advance to cover our retreating forces. I rode across the field and joined General Preston, whom I found at the head of the remnants of his brigade, going to where my men were formed on foot. The command remained in saddle all night in rear and as the support of a battery on our extreme right.

During Saturday nothing of importance occurred, the command being held upon the extreme right to prevent the enemy from turning that flank.

In obedience to orders from Lieutenant-General Polk, I moved the command before daylight Sunday morning into Murfreesborough. I left three regiments to burn a bridge, and fell back slowly before the enemy, and sent the remainder 6 miles on the Shelbyville pike to feed, since which time I have been at this point picketing and protecting the front of our army.

It is considered proper to state that on Monday, the 29th, we were engaged the entire day between the Franklin dirt road and the Wilkinson pike with a large force of the enemy's cavalry, and that the Texas Rangers acted with even more than their usual gallantry in a dashing charge, saving one regiment of the brigade from a complete rout by the enemy's forces.

I take pleasure in reporting the conduct of the entire command in the different engagements as characterized by intrepidity and a determination to conquer at all hazards. The Rangers, being armed with revolvers, are better prepared to meet the enemy's cavalry than other regiments in the brigade. The battle of Wednesday was fought at great disadvantage on our part, the enemy's cavalry being much more efficiently armed and equipped. The proper weapon for cavalry has proven to be the revolver.

It affords me great pleasure to commend in the highest terms both officers and soldiers. Colonels Cox, Harrison, and Smith, Lieutenant-

Colonels Malone and Estes, Captains [G.] Cook and [S. P.] Christian, of Texas Rangers, and Captain [L. T.] Hardy, of General McCown's escort, behaved with the utmost gallantry and judgment. Maj. F. M. Ison commanded the Second Georgia during Wednesday's fight. The members of my staff were prompt and efficient, and reckless of danger.

The loss of the brigade was 108 killed and wounded, and 107 captured; 150 horses killed. A detailed account of the casualties has been sent to General Bragg.

Captain [B. F.] White, jr., of my battery, whose gallantry upon this and every other field was most conspicuous, was taken so violently ill upon Wednesday night as to render it entirely impossible for him to be removed upon our evacuation of Murfreesborough.

Colonel Ashby was ordered to report early Thursday morning to General Pegram with his regiment, and was not in my brigade afterward. The entire strength of the brigade was about 2,000.

I have the honor to remain, your most obedient servant,

JNO. A. WHARTON,
Brigadier-General of Cavalry.

Maj. T. B. ROY,
Assistant Adjutant-General.

No. 306.

Report of Brig. Gen. Abraham Buford, C. S. Army, commanding Cavalry Brigade, including skirmishes December 31–January 3.

HEADQUARTERS BUFORD'S CAVALRY BRIGADE,
Camp near Beech Grove, Tenn., January 11, 1863.

GENERAL: I have the honor herewith to forward report of my brigade during the battle of Murfreesborough, [Tenn.]

My brigade, composed of Colonel Smith's regiment, assigned for duty with Colonel Grigsby, numbering 220 effective men, Colonel Grigsby's regiment, 230, and Colonel Butler, 180 men, in all 631 effective men, in accordance with orders from the general commanding, moved to Rover, 18 miles southwest of Murfreesborough, on the Shelbyville and Nashville pike, where I remained until Wednesday, 31st [ultimo].

Having received an order from General Bragg to move upon the enemy's flank and be ready for a vigorous pursuit, delivered at 12 m. Tuesday night (30th), I moved at daylight Wednesday morning (31st), and reached the battle-field at 12 m., taking position on the extreme left. I there joined General Wheeler, and, in concert with him, moved rapidly along the enemy's flank, my brigade being in advance, until we encountered a force of the enemy, consisting of artillery, cavalry, and infantry, escorting a large wagon train, the enemy occupying quite a strong position on a hill near Miller's. I immediately disposed my command for an attack, threw forward Captain [T. H.] Shanks' company, of Colonel Grigsby's regiment, as skirmishers, and formed the brigade in line of battle, Colonel Butler on the right, threatening the enemy's flank, and Colonel Grigsby on the left, in front of the enemy's lines. The attack was opened by our skirmishers, the enemy replying with artillery. After firing a few rounds, I received an order from General Wheeler to withdraw my brigade.

In this skirmish I lost 1 man (private of Colonel Butler's regiment) killed and 3 wounded; 2 horses killed and 2 disabled. We captured some 30 prisoners, who were paroled on the field.

Having withdrawn my force in good order, and acting in conjunction with General Wheeler, I moved back on the right toward and on the Wilkinson pike, on the left bank of Overall's Creek, near Mrs. Washington's. Here we found the enemy posted on the right bank of the creek, under cover of the woods. General Wheeler, on the right bank, attacked them, and I immediately drew up Colonel Grigsby's regiment (holding Colonel Butler's in reserve) on the right flank of the enemy, crossed the creek, charged the enemy, and drove him back with severe loss upon the lines of his heavy infantry.

My loss was here 2 commissioned officers (Major Chenoweth and Capt. William Campbell) and 6 privates wounded. We captured some 10 or 15 prisoners, who were paroled on the field.

Night coming on, my brigade was withdrawn from the field, receiving orders to move the next day (Thursday), in conjunction with Generals Wheeler and Wharton, to the rear of the enemy. Uniting my brigade with theirs, I marched to La Vergne, co-operating with them in capturing and destroying a large number of wagons laden with commissary and quartermaster's stores, taking a large number of prisoners. Ninety-five of the Twenty-second Indiana Infantry came out and voluntarily surrendered to Lieut. D. E. Myers, who was alone a short distance in front of his command.

I returned the next morning (Friday) to my original position on the left of our line of battle, near Mrs. Washington's, and remained there during the day, with no material results. At 9 p. m. I was ordered again to co-operate with General Wheeler in rear of the enemy, and moved at once. We encountered the enemy near Cox's Hill, about 8 miles from Nashville, on the Nashville and Murfreesborough pike. My brigade being in the rear, found on arriving that General Wheeler had already engaged the enemy, who was drawn up along the pike, his cavalry opposite the right wing of my brigade, which I had moved into a corn-field adjoining the pike. Receiving an order from General Wheeler to move back to the woodland skirting the field, I did so, to support the attack in which he was engaged. I drew up the brigade, dismounted them to act as skirmishers, preparatory to an attack on the enemy's left. Before engaging, I was ordered by General Wheeler to withdraw my command, as he had been ordered to return immediately to Murfreesborough.

I returned that (Saturday) night to my original position on the left of our line of battle, near Mrs. Washington's, and remained there until sunrise Sunday morning, when a dispatch from General Wheeler informed me that the army had commenced a retreat. I fell back to Murfreesborough, and retired on the Shelbyville pike in rear of the army.

I take pleasure in calling the attention of the commanding general to the good conduct and military bearing of most of the officers and men of my command, and particularly the gallant conduct of Maj. J. Q. Chenoweth, of Colonel Butler's regiment, who was on duty as a member of my staff, and Capt. G. M. Tilford and Lieut. D. E. Myers, of Colonel Smith's regiment, who were on duty with Col. J. Warren Grigsby's regiment during the engagement of Wednesday evening.

My thanks are due to the officers acting on my staff for the efficient aid rendered me during the engagement.

I have the honor to be, your obedient servant,

A. BUFORD,
Brigadier-General, Provisional Army.

GENERAL COMMANDING ARMY,
(*Through George William Brent, Assistant Adjutant-General.*)

No. 307.

The Confederate Roll of Honor.

GENERAL ORDERS, } ADJT. AND INSPECTOR GENERAL'S OFFICE,
No. 93.   }   Richmond, Va., November 22, 1862.

I. The following acts of Congress, having been approved by the President, are published for the information of the Army:

*   *   *   *   *   *   *

No. 27.—AN ACT to authorize the grant of medals and badges of distinction as a reward for courage and good conduct on the field of battle.

The Congress of the Confederate States of America do enact, That the President be, and he is hereby, authorized to bestow medals, with proper devices, upon such officers of the armies of the Confederate States as shall be conspicuous for courage and good conduct on the field of battle, and also to confer a badge of distinction upon one private or non-commissioned officer of each company after every signal victory it shall have assisted to achieve. The non-commissioned officers and privates of the company who may be present on the first dress-parade thereafter, may choose, by a majority of their votes, the soldier best entitled to receive such distinction, whose name shall be communicated to the President by commanding officers of the company; and if the award fall upon a deceased soldier, the badge thus awarded him shall be delivered to his widow, or, if there be no widow, to any relative the President may adjudge entitled to receive it.

Approved October 13, 1862.

*   *   *   *   *   *   *

By order:

S. COOPER,
Adjutant and Inspector General.

—

GENERAL ORDERS, } ADJT. AND INSPECTOR GENERAL'S OFFICE,
No. 131.   }   Richmond, Va., October 3, 1863.

Difficulties in procuring the medals and badges of distinction having delayed their presentation by the President, as authorized by the act of Congress approved October 13, 1862, to the officers, non-commissioned officers, and privates of the armies of the Confederate States conspicuous for courage and good conduct on the field of battle, to avoid postponing the grateful recognition of their valor until it can be made in the enduring form provided by that act, it is ordered—

I. That the names of all those who have been, or may hereafter be, reported as worthy of this distinction, be inscribed on a Roll of Honor, to be preserved in the office of the Adjutant and Inspector General for reference in all future time, for those who have deserved well of their country, as having best displayed their courage and devotion on the field of battle.

II. That the Roll of Honor, so far as now made up, be appended to this order and read at the head of every regiment in the service of the Confederate States at the first dress-parade after its receipt, and be published in at least one newspaper in each State.

III. The attention of the officers in charge is directed to General Orders, No. 93, section No. 27, of the series of 1862, Adjutant and Inspector General's Office, for the mode of selecting the non-commissioned officers and privates entitled to this distinction, and its execution is enjoined.

BATTLE OF MURFREESBOROUGH

Alabama.

Twenty-second Regiment of Infantry :

Sergt. W. D. Sumner, Co. A.
Private William Sellers, Co. B.
Corpl. J. L. Husbands, Co. C.
Sergt. B. T. Nelson, Co. D.
Sergt. P. A. Minton, Co. E.

Corpl. N. B. Walker, Co. F.
Private J. R. Black, Co. G.
Corpl. W. R. Larry, Co. H.
Private J. J. McVey, Co. I.
Private J. N. Eilands, Co. K.

Twenty-fourth Regiment of Infantry :

Capt. W. D. Smith,* Co. A.
Capt. W. P. Fowler, Co. F.
Capt. John B. Hazard, Co. I.
Capt. W. J. O'Brien, Co. B.
Lieut. J. A. Hall, Co. K.
Lieut. A. B. Nelson, Co. D.
Lieut. R. T. B. Parham, Co. H.
Lieut. A. Young, Co. A.
Sergt. Maj. William Mink.
First Sergt. J. M. J. Tally, Co. K.

Sergt. John Ives, Co. A.
Private Martin Duggan, Co. B.
Private Melbourn Deloach, Co. C.
Sergt. Samuel S. Wylie, Co. D.
Private Joseph Hall, Co. E.
Private Samuel M. Roberts,* Co. F.
Private A. W. Scott, Co. G.
Private James R. Green, Co. H.
Private N. Lankford,* Co. I.
Private A. Posey, Co. K.

Twenty-fifth Regiment of Infantry :

Sergt. Isaac N. Rhoades, Co. A.
Private Warren A. Jackson, Co. B.
Private Samuel Ellison, Co. C.
Private James A. Mote, Co. D.
Sergt. J. F. Coker,* Co. F.

Sergt. Patrick H. Smith, Co. G.
Private Marion F. Hazlewood, Co. H.
Private Charles W. Ropers,* Co. I.
Private J. B. Peacock,* Co. K.

Twenty-sixth Regiment of Infantry :

Private B. A. Thomason, Co. A.
Sergt. J. E. Gilbert, Co. B.
Private L. P. Roberts, Co. C.
Private Reedy Ward, Co. D.
Sergt. F. E. Mitchell, Co. E.

Private J. T. McClain, Co. G.
Private J. H. Cotrel, Co. H.
Private John A. Uselton, Co. I.
  Companies F and K made no selection.

Twenty-eighth Regiment of Infantry :

Private Topley Murphey, Co. B.
Sergt. Elias Wood, Co. G.
Sergt. W. B. Curry, Co. K.

Sergt. William E. Short, Co. L.
  The other companies made no selection.

Thirty-second Regiment of Infantry :

Private James Clemens,* Co. A.
Corpl. Vincent H. Joiner, Co. B.
Private Edmund Davis, Co. C.
Corpl. John C. Oliver,* Co. D.
Private Reuben Dumas, Co E.

Private Nathaniel F. Wheelis,* Co. F.
Corpl. James H. Dove, Co. G.
Private Alfred C. Hutto, Co. H.
Sergt. George W. Vansandt, Co. I.
Corpl. Elijah P. Gabel,* Co. K.

Thirty-fourth Regiment of Infantry :

Corpl. S. J. Numney, Co. A.
Private J. R. Browning, Co. C.
Private C. P. Greer, Co. D.
Private James Shehorn, Co. E.
Private S. W. Reynolds, Co. F.

Private J. G. Whaley, Co. G.
Private T. N. Cloud, Co. H.
Private B. R. Covington, Co. L.
Private J. G. Metts, Co. K.

Thirty-ninth Regiment of Infantry :

Adjt. J. M. Macon.
Second Lieut. E. Q. Thornton, Co. K.
Second Lieut. E. O. Petty, Co. B.
Sergt. C. K. Hall, Co. H.
Sergt. W. J. White, Co. H.
Sergt. E. Priest, Co. K.
Private W. C. Menefee, Co. A.
Sergt. A. J. Talbot, Co. A.
Private Samuel M. Martin, Co. B.
Private John Dansby, Co. C.

Private Evander Burkett, Co. D.
Private Frank Jones, Co. E.
Private William W. Meadows, Co. F.
Sergts. John H. Poyner and T. F. Espy,
  Co. G. (Company G was unable to de-
  cide between these two sergeants.)
Sergt. Abner Flowers, Co. I.
Sergt. James S. Wilson, Co. K.
  Company H made no selection.

* Killed in action.

Seventeenth Battalion Sharpshooters:

Private John H. Rutherford,* Co. A. | Private Walter S. White, Co. B.

Waters' battery:

Private John Hutchison.

Ketchum's battery:

Capt. James Garrity. | First Lieut. M. A. Hassell.
First Lieut. Philip Bond.

Arkansas.

First Regiment of Infantry:

Lieut. Col. D. McGregor.*   Private G. Bogy, Co. D.
Adjt. S. N. Greenwood.   Private W. W. Chaney, Co. E.
Capt. O. F. Parrish, Co. D.   Private H. J. Bullion, Co. F.
Lieut. J. E Letson, Co. D.   Private A. P. Green,* Co. G.
Capt. W. H. Scales, Co. C.   Private J. Beeson, Co. H.
Corpl. G. M. McKenzie,* Co. A.   Private J. H. Curd,* Co. I.
Private J. S. T. Hemphill, Co. B.   Private O. C. Choat,* Co. K.
Private G. W. Sallee,* Co. C.

Second Regiment of Arkansas Mounted Rifles:

Corpl. James W. Piles, Co. A.   Private William Till,* Co. F.
Private Tilman Peavy,* Co. B.   Sergt. Jessee Shepard, Co. G.
Private J. H. Eagle,* Co. C.   Private M. M. McGee, Co. H.
Private E. A. Ballew, Co. D.   Sergt. H. M. Graves, Co. I.
Private W. A. Thompson,* Co. E.   Sergt. F. C. Jett, Co. K.

Fourth Regiment of Infantry:

Sergt. S. H. Smith, Co. A.   Private J. M. Vinson,* Co. G.
Private James M. Pate,* Co. C.   Sergt. S. T. Ward,* Co. H.
Private Daniel Hudson, Co. D.   Private Simpson Jackson, Co. I.
Private Thomas Caldwell, Co. E.   Private T. P. Williams, Co. K.
Sergt. J. F. Garrett,* Co. F.

First Regiment of Mounted Rifles:

Private Patrick Callanan, Co. A.   Private W. W. Coe, Co. F.
Private W. T. Blakemore, Co. B.   First Sergt. W. S. Colburn, Co. G.
Private James Pearson, Co. C.   Corpl. Thomas Thomson, Co. H.
Corpl. C. D. Jenkins, Co. D.   Corpl. Isaac L. Caston, Co. I.
Private T. J. Underwood, Co. E.   Private G. B. House,* Co. K.

Twenty-fifth Regiment of Infantry:

Private J. Alphin, Co. A.   Private John A. Wright, Co. F.
Corpl. J. S. Ferguson, Co. B.   Private J. S. Gardner, Co. G.
Private W. G. Evans, Co. C.   Private J. W. McNabb, Co. H.
Private M. N. Jones, Co. D.   Corpl. A. M. Ragsdale, Co. I.
Private S. H. McBride, Co. E.   Corpl. H. D. Holdaway, Co. K.

Fourth Battalion of Infantry:

Private James Vines,* Co. A.   Private George W. Ayler, Co. C.
Corpl. L. Heggie,* Co. B.   Private C. G. Warren, Co. E.

Humphreys' artillery company:

Private John Campbell.

Georgia.

Fifth Regiment of Infantry:

Private Newton Rice,* Co. A.   Corpl. B. D. Bedell, Co. H.
Corpl. Michael McNamara,* Co. C.   Private George W. Horsley,* Co. K.
Private Thomas J. Brantley,* Co. E.   Companies D and G declined to select.
Sergt. Samuel P. Kiddoo,* Co. F.

---

* Killed in action.

Third Battalion of Infantry:

Private A. S. Kimrey,* Co. B.
Private W. D. Clark,* Co. C.
Private Mathew Hall, Co. D.
Private John Capps, Co. E.

Private Michael Kinney, Co. F.
Private Thomas Nolan, Co. G.
Private G. W. Sanders, Co. H.

Ninth Battalion of Infantry:

Private Obey McCurry, Co. A.
Private W. J. Wood, Co. B.
Private N. W. Rice, Co. C.

Corpl. William M. Gaines, Co. D.
Private C. M. R. Palmer, Co. E.

Kentucky.

Second Regiment of Infantry:

Color-Corpl. W. H. Robinson, Co. A.
Private R. H. Graves, Co. B.
Private Thomas Clark, Co. C.
Sergt. C. A. Haskell, Co. D.
Sergt. F. M. Chambers, Co. E.

Sergt. W. O. Coppage, Co. F.
Sergt. D. E. Turney, Co. G.
Corpl. E. S. Wright, Co. H.
Sergt. John H. Crane, Co. I.
Sergt. James A. Pearce, Co. K.

Fourth Regiment of Infantry:

Corpl. G. W. Rogers, Co. A.
Sergt. E. L. Johnson, Co. B.
Private John McGuire, Company C.
Color-Corpl. R. H. Lindsey, Co. D.
Sergt. J. S. Whittington, Co. E.

Private Joseph Nichols, Co. F.
Private H. D. Wallace, Co. G.
Sergt. A. M. Hathaway, Co. K.
  Companies H and I declined selecting

Sixth Regiment of Infantry:

First Sergt. J. B. Lewis, Co. C.
Corpl. E. S. Jones, Co. D.
Private Thomas W. Payne, Co. E.
Private James T. Prather, Co. G.

Second Sergt. William Harned, Co. H.
Private J. O. Cushenberry, Co. I.
  Companies A and B declined selecting.

Ninth Regiment of Infantry:

Capt. Joseph Desha, Co. I.
Capt. James T. Morehead, Co. G.
Private J. G. Wakefield, Co. A.
Private Jacob Blackshear, Co. B.
Private J. L. Collins, Co. C.

Private Nathan Board, Co. G.
Sergt. William K. Kinman, Co. H.
Sergt. Drakeford Gray, Co. I.
Private H. B. Roberts, Co. K.
  Company B declined to select.

Louisiana.

Thirteenth Regiment of Infantry:

Color-Sergt. Roger Tammure.
Sergt. Maj. John Farrel.
Private Daniel Dunn, Co. A.
Private George K. Higgins, Co. B.
Private Lewis Brown, Co. C.
Corpl. F. Druvot, Co. D.

Private J. M. Harris, Co. E.
Private Michael McAuliffe, Co. F.
Private James Kinsley, Co. G.
Private M. Branigan, Co. H.
Sergt. Patrick Johnson, Co. I.
Private Francis Mackin, Co. K.

Twentieth Regiment of Infantry:

Private Frank Monahan, Co. A.
Corpl. Charles Sneider, Co. B.
Corpl. John Bellejean, Co. C.
Private Walter Haynes, Co. D.
First Sergt. P. Mooney, Co. E.

Private Justus Heisser, Co. F.
Private Michael Sullivan, Co. G.
Private Michael Carey, Co. H.
Private John Gorman, Co. I.
First Sergt. G. G. Smith, Co. K.

Austin's battalion of sharpshooters:

Private J. A. Stovall,* Co. A.

Private Andrew Develbiss, Co. B.

Fifth Company Washington Artillery:

Private John W. Anthony

---

* Killed in action.

Mississippi.

Fifth Regiment of Infantry:

Sergt. William Dabbs, Co. A.
Private Jesse Glass, Co. B.
Corpl. J. J. Smith, Co. C.
Private S. G. F. Jayroe, Co. D.
Sergt. J. N. Richardson, Co. E.

Sergt. W. A. Snow, Co. F.
Private S. F. Fondren, Co. G.
Sergt. D. L. McCollum, Co. H.
Private W. R. Flanagan, Co. I.
Private H. H. McMichael, Co. K.

Seventh Regiment of Infantry:

Private John A. Higginbotham,* Co. A.
Private H. H. Price, Co. B.
Private Richard R. Chaddick, Co. C.
Private Jeptha Creel, Co. D.
Sergt. George Stewart, Co. E.

Private B. Drummond, Co. F.
Private M. B. Stringer, Co. G.
Private A. Z. Coker, Co. H.
Private P. W. Rogers, Co. I.
Sergt. A. E. Ford, Co. K.

Eighth Regiment of Infantry:

Private W. T. Robertson, Co. A.
Private J. H. Bonds, Co. B.
Private W. J. Pitman, Co. C.
Corpl. G. B. Risher, Co. D.
Private S. T. Massey, Co. E.

Private D. F. Hilbun, Co. F.
Corpl. A. W. Atwood, Co. G.
Private J. C. Lucy, Co. H.
Private Joel Foster, Co. I.
Private W. W. Watson, Co. K.

Ninth Regiment of Infantry:

Private T. E. Bowden,* Co. A.
Private Thomas Gill, Co. B.
Color-Sergt. H. A. McCrosky, Co. C.
Sergt. George F. Duffy, Co. D.
Private John McAfee,* Co. E.

Corpl. E. W. Dowty, Co. F.
Private W. T. Hollis, Co. G.
Private B. C. Lipscomb,* Co. H.
Sergt. D. R. Biles, Co. I.
Private W. H. Wheeler, Co. K.

Forty-first Regiment of Infantry:

Sergt. John A. Moore, Co. A.
Private A. W. Bell, Co. D.
Private A. F. Anderson, Co. E.
Private A. Sanders, Co. F.
Private Samuel N. Richey, Co. G.

Private G. D. Nelson, Co. H.
Private P. Ledbetter, Co. I.
Private F. L. Constantine, Co. K.
Corpl. W. M. Baker, Co. L.

Companies B and C declined making selections.

Ninth Battalion of Sharpshooters:

Fourth Sergt. M. Murphy, Co. A. | First Sergt. Joseph B. O'Brien, Co. A.

Sergeant Murphy was selected by Maj. W. C. Richards, commanding battalion.
Companies B and C declined making selections.

Stanford's Light Battery:
Private Richard H. Elliott.

Jefferson Artillery:
Capt. P. Darden.   Maj. R. B. Snowden, assistant adjutant-
                                         general.

North Carolina.

Twenty-ninth Regiment of Infantry:

Corpl. Abner B. Freeman, Co. A.
Private Thomas Elkin, Co. B.
Color-bearer James R. Lanning, Co. C.
First Sergt. Erwin F. Roberts, Co. D.
Corpl. Willburn S. Smith, Co. E.

Private Devania Millsaps,* Co. F.
Private Abraham Hedrick, Co. G.
Private James A. Gillespie, Co. H.
Private Thomas Willis, Co. I.
Private Robert King, Co. K.

Thirty-ninth Regiment of Infantry:

Col. David Coleman.
Lieut. Col. Hugh H. Davidson.
Actg. Adjt. Isaac S. Hyams.
First Lieut. Abram Booker, Co. A.
First Lieut. William T. Anderson, Co. B.
Sergt. John C. Rogers, Co. A.

Private William T. West, Co. B.
Private James W. Cobb, Co. C.
Private James B. A. Staten, Co. D.
Private Moses Fulbright, Co. E.
Sergt. John W. Wiggins, Co. H.
Sergt. John E. Moore, Co. I.

Companies G and H made no selection; Company K not in action.

---

* Killed in action.

South Carolina.

Tenth Regiment of Infantry:

First Lieut. C. C. White, Co. A.
Private A. J. McCants, Co. A.
Private J. S. Beaty, Co. B.
Private W. D. Hewitt, Co. C.
Private G. S Flowers, Co. D.
Sergt. C. W. Cockfield, * Co. E.
Private G. W. Curry, Co. F.

Private J. Cannon, Co. G.
Private N. Gray, Co. H.
Private W. H. Posten, Co. I.
Private J. W. H. Bunch, * Co. K.
Private J. A. Boatwright, Co. L.
Sergt. S. B. Rhuarck, Co. M.

Nineteenth Regiment of Infantry

Col. A. J. Lythgoe.
Maj. John A. Crowder.
Private Benjamin W. Boothe, Co. A.
Private Samuel S. Horn, Co. B.
Sergt. W. H. Burkhalter, Co. C.
Private W. A. Black, Co. D.

Private S. D. McCoy, Co. E.
Private Samuel Bloodsworth, Co. F.
Sergt. Seth A. Jordan, Co. G.
Private James McClain, Co. H.
Private James Jones, Co. I.
Sergt. Martin Yonce, Co. K.

Tennessee.

Second Regiment of Infantry:

Color-Sergt. John C. Ferris.

Fourth Regiment of Infantry:

Sergt. J. B. Wendall, Co. B.
Corpl. M. R. Brown, Co. C.
Private R. L. Matthews, Co. E.

Private G. M. Whitson, Co. G.
Sergt. J. F. Seay, Co. H.
Private R. W. Mullins, Co. I.

Fifth Regiment of Infantry:

Sergt. J. P. Hardcastle, Co. A.
Second Lieut. Z. B. Hamrick, Co. B.
Color-Sergt. W. Davis, Co. C.
First Lieut. W. T. Grissom, Co. C.
Capt. R. B. Roberts, Co. D.
Second Lieut. W. W. Masey, Co. E.
First Lieut. J. B. Blair, Co. G.
Sergt. J. Swan, Co. G.
Second Lieut. S. R. Richards, Co. H.
Second Lieut. W. H. Ballard, Co. L.

Corpl. W. F. Diggs, Co. A.
Second Sergt. J. A. Aguilar, Co. B.
Sergt. L. D. Holland, Co. C.
Private W. T. Ballard, Co. D.
Corpl. W. A. Thompson, Co. E.
Private J. J. Hagler, Co. F.
Private D. C. Baucum, Co. G.
Private W. C. Malin, * Co. H.
Private G. W. Costen, * Co. I.
Corpl. J. B. Johnson, Co. K.

Eighth Regiment of Infantry:

Private D. T. Perkins, * Co. A.
Private R. E. Coalson, * Co. B.
Sergt. J. M. Jones, Co. C.
Sergt. W. J. Armstrong, * Co. D.
Sergt. Willie Simmons, * Co. E.

First Sergt. E. B. Little, * Co. F.
Private R. H. Gaines, * Co. G.
Private T. G. Hall, Co. H.
Sergt. J. T. Luna, Co. I.
Sergt. Maj. W. H. Holmon, * Co. K.

Seventeenth Regiment of Infantry:

Col. A. S. Marks.
Lieut. Col. W. W. Floyd.
Adjt. James B. Fitzpatrick.
Capt. F. B. Terry, Co. A.
First Lieut. G. W. Corn, Co. D.
First Lieut. H. M. Kinsey, Co. B.
Second Lieut. M. W. Black, Co. E.
Corpl. John N. Lowry, * Co. A.

Sergt. P. L. Shaffner, Co. B.
Sergt. W. T. Jones, Co. C.
Sergt. Robert Rollins, Co. D.
Private J. D. Martin, Co. E.
Private John L. Conley, Co. F.
Private J. H. Gober, Co. G.
Private M. G. Liggett, * Co. H.
Private T. C. Mitchell, Co. K.

Company I declined making a selection.

Nineteenth Regiment of Infantry:

First Sergt. Joseph Thompson, Co. I.
First Sergt. Amos C. Smith, Co. B.

Sergt. George N. Richardson, Co. K.

The other companies declined making selections.

---

* Killed in action.

Twenty-third Regiment of Infantry:

Lieut. Col. R. H. Keeble.
Capt. W. H. Harder, Co. G.
Capt. N. R. Allen, Co. E.
Private W. M. Haynie, Co. A.
Private W. J. Pennington, Co. B.
First Sergt. J. N. Holt, Co. D.

Private H. C. Haynes,* Co. E.
Private S. M. Foster, Co. C.
Private Jasper M. Harris,* Co. F.
First Sergt. William K. Kelly, Co. G.
Corpl. L. W. Jernighan, Co. H.

Twenty-fourth Regiment of Infantry:

Private R. H. Jones, Co. A.
Private Willis P. Jones, Co. B.
Private J. M. Sullivan, Co. C.
Sergt. W. H. Lofton, Co. D.
Private William Jordon, Co. E.

Color-bearer Cuthbert Ferrell, Co. F.
Sergt. G. W. Anderson, Co. G.
Private Allen W. Williams, Co. H.
Private R. A. Dean, Co. I.
Private Andrew J. Powers, Co. K.

Twenty-fifth Regiment of Infantry:
This regiment declined making any selections.

Twenty-sixth Regiment of Infantry:

Private James Deatherage,* Co. A.
Private John H. Edwards, Co. B.
Private William T. Williams,* Co. C.
Private Wesley Collins, Co. D.
Private William L. Rice, Co. E.

Private William Wright, Co. F.
Private A. M. Bronson, Co. H.
Private Washington Fuller, Co. I.
Private John Alford, Co. K.

Twenty-eighth Regiment of Infantry:

Capt. Franklin Fowler, Co. I.
First Lieut. James M. Lowe, Co. B.
Private Elijah W. Greer, Co. A.
Private Thomas W. Patton, Co. B.
Private Lafayette Chilton, Co. C.
Private James A. Rash, Co. G.

Color-bearer Houston B. Graves, Co. F.
Corpl. John F. Moore, Co. G.
Private Pinkney Craighead, Co. H.
Sergt. Claiborne D. Griffith, Co. I.
First Sergt. J. R. Pirtle, Co. K.

Thirty-third Regiment of Infantry:

Corpl. J. W. Mosier, Co. A.
Private T. E. Mercer, Co. B.
Sergt. J. C. Stublefield, Co. C.
Private W. J. McDaniel, Co. D.
Private E. M. Arnold, Co. E.

Sergt. George T. Parham,* Co. F.
Private W. R. Gauntlett, Co. G.
Private J. L. Mizell,* Co. H.
Sergt. J. E. Hays,* Co. I.
Private J. D. Hill, Co. K.

Thirty-seventh Regiment of Infantry:
Maj. J. T. McReynolds.

Forty-fourth Regiment of Infantry:

Col. John S. Fulton.
Lieut. Col. J. L. McEwen, jr.
Maj. H. C. Ewin.
Capt. Samuel Jackson, Co. I.
Private James D. Stone, Co. B.

Private S. G. Heflin,* Co. C.
Corpl. John W. Gill,* Co. F.
Corpl. J. D. Crenshaw, Co. H.
Corpl. Isaac S. Berry, Co. I.
Private J. M. Sellers, Co. K.

Forty-fifth Regiment of Infantry:

Private A. W. Loftin, Co. A.
Private J. H. Henderson, Co. B.
Private J. E. Watkins,* Co. C.
Corpl. P. C. F. Miller, Co. D.
Private James Flowers,* Co. E.

First Sergt. L. P. Cawthon,* Co. F.
Private A. T. Lanom,* Co. G.
Corpl. B. A. Baird, Co. H.
Sergt. Hugh Hope, Co. I.
Private John N. Williams, Co. K.

Steuben Artillery:
Private James L. Gibbs.*

Texas.

Ninth Regiment of Infantry:

Lieut. Col. M. A. Dillard.
Private F. M. Sellman, Co. A.
Private John Bradshaw, Co. C.
Private T. J. Cox, Co. D.
Sergt. J. C. Hamilton, Co. E.

Private J. M. Byrd, Co. F.
Private D. F. Moore, Co. G.
Private M. H. Dixon, Co. H.
Sergt. G. W. Bodford, Co. K.

Companies B and I declined making selections.

---

* Killed in action.

Tenth Regiment of Cavalry (dismounted):

Private Alexander Cook, Co. A.
Private F. M. Rodgers, Co. B.
Sergt. J. T. McGee, Co. C.
Sergt. A. Sims, Co. D.
Private James Terry, Co. E.

Private W. W. Corley, Co. F.
Private Stokely Hutchins, Co. G.
Private J. O. Manning, Co. H.
Private Joel Reynolds, Co. I.
Private S. L. Birdwell, Co. K.

Fourteenth Regiment of Cavalry :

Private W. R. Strapp, Co. A.
Private Jordon Welcher, Co. B.
Private Thomas A. Latimer, Co. C.
Private William D. Melton,* Co. D.
Corpl. John H. Wyche, Co. E.

Private William Spencer, Co. F.
Private George P. Woodall, Co. G.
Private William Hull, Co. H.
Private Richard Stiles, Co. I.
Private J. V. Keil, Co. K.

Thirty-second Regiment of Cavalry (formerly Fifteenth) :

Corpl. James A. Rogers,* Co. G.
Private James W. Clark,* Co. G.

First Sergt. S. L. Easley, Co. I.
Private E. Watson, Co. I.

The other companies declined making selections.

Ninth [Fifth] Confederate Regiment:

Col. J. A. Smith, commanding.
Capt. Joseph H. Beard.
First Sergt. William Powers, Co. A.
First Sergt. John Price, Co. B.
Private Hugh McHugh, Co. C.

First Sergt. Walter Laracy, Co. D.
Private John Hogan, Co. E.
Private Curran Kenny, Co. F.
Private Luther Hessey, Co. G.
Sergt. A. P. Burns, Co. H.

Captain Douglas' battery:

Corpl. W. L. Waits.

*   •   •   •   •   •   •

By order:

S. COOPER,
Adjutant and Inspector General.

JANUARY 8–14, 1863.—Wheeler's raid, including affairs at Mill Creek, Harpeth Shoals, and Ashland, Tenn.

REPORTS.

No. 1.—Maj. Gen. William S. Rosecrans, U. S. Army.
No. 2.—Chaplain Maxwell P. Gaddis, Second Ohio Infantry.
No. 3.—Surg. Luther D. Waterman, Thirty-ninth Indiana Infantry.
No. 4.—Brig. Gen. Robert B. Mitchell, U. S. Army.
No. 5.—General Braxton Bragg, C. S. Army.

No. 1.

Report of Maj. Gen. William S. Rosecrans, U. S. Army.

HEADQUARTERS DEPARTMENT OF THE CUMBERLAND,
Murfreesborough, Tenn., February 15, 1863.

GENERAL : Supposing it well to furnish the Department evidence of the inhuman violations of the rules of civilized warfare by the rebel authorities, I inclose copies of the lists of our medical officers who were robbed of their private and personal property at the late battle, and statement of Chaplain Gaddis, who was on a hospital boat that was fired

---

* Killed in action.

on and robbed at Harpeth Shoals by Wheeler's cavalry. I can multiply documentary evidence on these outrages and many others, fully revealing the barbarism of these rebel leaders, and will do so, if you think desirable.

Very respectfully, your obedient servant,

W. S. ROSECRANS,
Major-General.

Brig. Gen. LORENZO THOMAS,
Adjutant-General U. S. Army, Washington, D. C.

No. 2.

Report of Chaplain Maxwell P. Gaddis, Second Ohio Infantry.

CAMP AT MURFREESBOROUGH, TENN.,
February 4, 1863.

SIR : In accordance with your request, I herewith transmit a condensed account of the capture and subsequent destruction of a portion of your transportation by fire on the Cumberland River, on January 13, at the head of Harpeth Shoals, 30 miles from Nashville and 35 miles from Clarksville. I was on the steamer Hastings at the time of her being ordered by the guerrillas to land, and, at the request of the captain of the Hastings the officers and men on board (near 260 wounded), assumed command. I answered their hail and order by saying that we were loaded with wounded and could not stop. They again ordered us " to come to," and backed their orders by three volleys of musketry, after which I ordered the pilot of the Hastings, " Round the steamer to the shore." This he immediately endeavored to do. The current being swift, the boat yielded slowly, and the enemy again fired two rounds of artillery, one of the balls taking effect on the steamer, seriously wounding one of the men. As soon as the boat struck the steamer that had been captured some two hours previously, a gang of drunken rebels, under command of Colonel Wade, took possession of the Hastings.

Then followed a scene of plunder and theft never before witnessed. They robbed soldiers and passengers indiscriminately ; took from your wounded soldiers their blankets, rations, medicines, and in many instances their clothing ; robbed the officers of their side-arms, overcoats, hats, &c.; the boat of all her freight, stores, and money, and her officers of their personal property. I demanded of Colonel Wade some explanation of this inhuman course. He, being so drunk, only made me an idiotic reply. I then looked around for some other officer, and discovered Captain Burford, General Wheeler's assistant adjutant-general, in whom I recognized an old acquaintance. I appealed to him. He was powerless, from the fact that the whole gang was drunk. He, however, reported the facts to General Wheeler, who authorized him to parole the Hastings, on condition that she carry no more supplies for the Federal Government. I accepted the parole. I then took on board the wounded off of the steamer Trio ; also from the steamer Parthenia, and had succeeded in obtaining permission to pass on, when they, for the first time, discovered that the deck of the Hastings was covered with bales of cotton, on which our wounded were lying. Wade instantly ordered me to put ashore all the wounded (over 400), that he might burn the cotton, it being theirs by capture, and, with them, a contraband of war.

To move the men again was almost impossible. They had been virtually stripped of everything—medicines, rations, and clothing; we 35 miles from any military post; night coming on; no place of shelter; no place to put our wounded and dying men save a muddy corn-field; a heavy snow had begun to fall, and in view of all this, and my sympathy for men who for eighteen months had done their duty as true soldiers, and who for days had fought under you, and only ceased when borne from the field, I demanded other terms. I told him I would not move a soul from the boat, &c.

All this was reported to Wheeler (at least they say so), and he ordered that I should be held personally responsible for the burning of their cotton on reaching Louisville, under penalty of my return to their lines as a prisoner of war. I deemed the terms mild, under the circumstances, and I immediately accepted them, in which I claim I did my duty.

The passengers and soldiers of the Trio and Parthenia were robbed in like manner.

After they had done us all the harm they could, barely escaping with our lives, they allowed us to cross the river during the burning of the steamers.

While they were preparing to burn, the gunboat Sidell hove in sight, and to all appearance made preparation to drive the enemy away, but, from some cause or other, Van Dorn made no fight, and surrendered the boat without firing a single shot. They then took possession of her, threw over her guns and arms, fired the three boats, and in a short time nothing remained but the charred hulls.

On reaching Clarksville, I reported by telegraph to Major Sidell, who ordered me to proceed on as rapidly as possible to Louisville and report to Generals Boyle or Wright. This I did, and the inclosed papers will explain the final result of the unfortunate affair.*

Thus hoping that in all this you will not condemn me, I remain, most respectfully, your obedient servant,

M. P. GADDIS,
Chaplain Second Regiment Ohio Volunteer Infantry.

Major-General ROSECRANS,
Commanding Department of the Cumberland.

No. 3.

Report of Surg. Luther D. Waterman, Thirty-ninth Indiana Infantry.

GENERAL HOSPITAL, NO. 17,
Nashville, Tenn., January 27, 1863.

SIR: I have the honor to report that on January 13, 1863, as surgeon in charge, I started with 212 wounded and sick soldiers of the United States Army on the steamer Hastings, on the Cumberland River, bound for Louisville, Ky. At Harpeth Shoals, on that same day, the boat was captured by the Confederate forces (after being fired upon by artillery and musketry, the hospital flag flying). The lists of about 212 soldiers and officers, from General Hospitals, No. 8, No. 15, and No. 6, Nashville, Tenn., were taken, and the boat and men permitted to proceed only on condition that I certified to the lists as captured and paroled. They

---

* See Series II.

dictated and I appended the following certificate to each of the hospital lists, no copy of which was left me:

ON CUMBERLAND RIVER, NEAR ASHLAND,
January 13, 1863.

I certify that the above lists of sick and wounded United States soldiers on board the steamer Hastings were captured by the Confederate forces (or forces of the Confederate States) on January 13, 1863, on the Cumberland River, and duly paroled by E. S. Burford, assistant adjutant-general of General Wheeler's cavalry corps.

L. D. WATERMAN,
Surgeon Thirty-ninth Indiana Volunteers, in Charge of Sick and Wounded.

There were also 8 or 9 wounded officers of the United States Army on board, whose names were taken and who were sworn not to take up arms, &c., but who, being passengers and not under my charge, and immediately mingled with 500 others from other steamboats, I am unable to name. The Confederate officers, being intoxicated and getting rapidly more so, took the lists, names, and plunder, and hurried off, in spite of my protest and demand for copies, only giving me in return the following statement, the original of which I have:

HEADQUARTERS CAVALRY,
On Board the Hastings, on the Cumberland River, Tenn., January 13, 1863.

The steamer Hastings having been captured by the Confederate forces on the 13th January, 1863, and having 212 United States soldiers, wounded in the late battles before Murfreesborough, [they] do swear that they will not aid or abet or in any wise do anything prejudicial to the interests of the Confederate States until they are duly exchanged according to the cartel.

Witness:

E. S. BURFORD, JR.,
Assistant Adjutant-General, General Wheeler's Cavalry Corps.

These wounded officers and soldiers were mingled with others unavoidably and scattered to different hospitals, with no evidence, some of them without an understanding, of the transaction. Such are very briefly the essential facts concerning this capture and attempt at parole, the report of which has been somewhat delayed by sickness.

I have the honor to be, very respectfully and obediently, yours,

L. D. WATERMAN,
Surgeon Thirty-ninth Indiana Volunteers,
In charge General Hospital, No. 17, Nashville, Tenn.

Maj. Gen. W. S. ROSECRANS,
Commanding Department of the Cumberland.

No. 4.

Reports of Brig. Gen. Robert B. Mitchell, U. S. Army.

HEADQUARTERS,
Nashville, January 13, 1863.

MAJOR: The steamer Charter was burned last night about 8 o'clock, with her cargo. But two regiments have arrived from Gallatin yet; two locomotives have given out. Stanley went on the Hillsborough pike, as you directed. I think our force should have been sent nearer the train. Damn the railroad, say I!

ROBT. B. MITCHELL,
Brigadier-General, Commanding.

Major GODDARD.

NASHVILLE, *January* 13, 1863.

GENERAL : Charter was loaded principally with commissary stores. She was 5 miles this side of the shoals, near Ashland. Ewing's brigade has not arrived. The last of Harlan's brigade has just arrived. There is "something rotten in Denmark" with the management of the railroad. Harlan's brigade is moving out on the Charlotte pike to-night. General Fry is here, and will go out in the morning. Stanley says the enemy have two full batteries and 4,500 men.

ROBT. B. MITCHELL,
Brigadier-General, Commanding.

General ROSECRANS.

—

NASHVILLE, *January* 13, 1863.

GENERAL : The rebels are burning everything on the river. There are at least four more freight boats destroyed, and the Sidell taken and burned.

ROBT. B. MITCHELL,
Brigadier-General.

General ROSECRANS.

—

NASHVILLE, *January* 14, 1863.

GENERAL : One of the gunners of the gunboat Sidell has arrived, and confirms the report of the burning of the boat. He says the pilot left the wheel, which was the cause of the disaster. He furthermore says that they knocked out the side of the boat next the enemy with their own guns, endeavoring to elevate their pieces to reach the enemy on the high bank. Van Dorn is a prisoner ; the balance were paroled by Wheeler.

ROBT. B. MITCHELL,
Brigadier-General.

General ROSECRANS.

—

No. 5.

Reports of General Braxton Bragg, C. S. Army.

TULLAHOMA, *January* 17, 1863.

General [Joseph] Wheeler, with a portion of his cavalry brigade, after burning the railroad bridges in the enemy's rear, pushed for the Cumberland River, where he intercepted and captured four large transports; destroyed three, with all the supplies, and bonded one to carry off the 400 paroled prisoners. He was hotly pursued by a gunboat, which he attacked and captured, and destroyed her with her whole armament. I ask his promotion as a just reward to distinguished merit.

BRAXTON BRAGG.

ADJUTANT-GENERAL.

—

TULLAHOMA, *January* 21, 1863.

After the capture of transports and gunboat, our cavalry made a dash for a large fleet of transports just below Harpeth Shoals. They threw overboard their cargoes of subsistence, ordnance, and quartermaster's stores in immense quantity and escaped by a hasty retreat. Our troops, in the midst of snow and ice, crossed to the north side of Cumberland by swimming their horses through the angry torrent, much swollen by recent rains; routed the guard, and captured and destroyed an immense collection of subsistence just loaded for transportation to Nashville by wagons.

BRAXTON BRAGG.

General S. COOPER.
Adjutant and Inspector General.

JANUARY 13-15, 1863.—Reconnaissance from Murfreesborough to Nolensville and Versailles, Tenn.

Report of Col. George D. Wagner, Fifteenth Indiana Infantry.

HDQRS. SECOND BRIG., FIRST DIV., LEFT WING,
ARMY OF THE CUMBERLAND,
In Camp near Murfreesborough, Tenn., January 16, 1863.

SIR: In accordance with orders from General Rosecrans, on the morning of the 13th, at 2 o'clock a. m., I marched from camp, in the direction of Triune. The force consisted of the Third Brigade, Colonel Streight commanding, my own, the Second Brigade, and Captain Otis' brigade of cavalry, about 700 strong.

The crossing of the river was difficult, detaining us some time. The route was by way of Lizzard and Lane's store, to the pike at Bole Jack. Here was [were] seen some 8 or 10 mounted men, who seemed to be posted as lookouts on the hill; only one was taken. I sent from here a cavalry force up the pike beyond Triune; saw nothing of importance. Learning that General Wheeler had passed down the road, in the direction of Nashville, we moved forward to Nolensville and camped for the night. Here I ascertained that Wheeler had been joined by Forrest with about 1,000 men, which made their force about 3,000 men and seven pieces of artillery.

On the morning of the 14th I was about starting in pursuit, by way of Brentwood, when an order was received from General Rosecrans, directing me to send two regiments to the Wilkinson pike, and with the remainder to move to Eagleville, 14 miles toward Shelbyville, then to Versailles, 7 miles east, join forces with the two brigades there and at Salem, and to move with the whole force to strike the enemy. This the rain prevented, as, on the morning of the 15th, it was impossible to move except by the pike, and that led only to camp, where I had started with the entire command, when an order was received from the general directing a return. On the 14th, learning there was a large mill, west 2 miles from Eagleville, that was grinding for the enemy, I directed Captain Otis to send a party of cavalry to destroy it, so they could not use it, but not to burn it unless it was the only way to prevent their using it. They found a large amount of meal stored in it and ready to send to the rebels, and burned it.

The advance, under command of Colonel ———, Tennessee cavalry, had a skirmish with the enemy at Eagleville, capturing 12 or 15 and their horses. The colonel had his horse shot under him. There was also a large lot of horses and mules taken by the different quartermasters. I estimate the entire number at 100 head. The quartermaster of my brigade reports 8 mules and 2 horses.   A valuable lot was taken by Captain Otis from the rebel Captain Lytle.

I am of the opinion, had it not been for the storm, we could have hit the enemy a hard blow on the 15th, at Fosterville.   There is, or was, but one company of cavalry at Unionville, and nothing but cavalry at Fosterville.   I do not think they have any infantry this side of Shelbyville and Wartrace.   Cheatham on the 14th was at the former place.

Owing to the rain and the cold, the men suffered much, and are entitled to as much consideration as if they had gained a victory in dry weather.   The officers, particularly the mounted ones, did not suffer so much, yet, I am sorry to say, some of them complained more than those who waded water knee-deep ; the men, when they came to a vast pond or creek, raised a shout or song and plunged in.   The stone of the pike, much of it recently made, cut the shoes up badly.   I need in my brigade 700 pairs before the men can march.   No doubt the other brigade needs as many.

To the commanders of brigades, Colonel Streight, Lieutenant-Colonel Wood, and Captain Otis, I am much indebted for the efficient manner in which they did their duty, as well as Captains Hume and Martin, of General Hascall's staff, who were of much service.

Which is respectfully submitted.

Your obedient servant,

G. D. WAGNER,
Colonel, Commanding.

[Brigadier-General HASCALL.]

[Indorsement.]

HEADQUARTERS FIRST DIVISION, LEFT WING,
January 15, 1863.

Respectfully forwarded for the information of the commanding general.   The men underwent great hardships, and are entitled to credit for the soldierly manner in which they endured the same.

MILO S. HASCALL,
Brigadier-General, Commanding.

JANUARY 19, 1863.—Skirmish near Woodbury, Tenn.

Report of Capt. Thomas D. McClelland, Third Ohio Cavalry.

HDQRS. SECOND BATTALION, THIRD OHIO CAVALRY,
Camp near Readyville, Tenn., January 20, 1863.

SIR: In accordance with instructions, the Second Battalion, consisting of Companies E, F, A, and D, reported to Col. W. B. Hazen, commanding Second Brigade (January 10, 1863), and were marched to this place, a distance of 12 miles.   Our time since has been fully occupied in patrolling and scouting, with an occasional skirmish with the enemy's pickets and scouting parties, until yesterday we had quite a brilliant little affair with a portion of Morgan's command, under Colonel Hutcheson.   About noon, picket firing was heard to the front.   The colonel commanding ordered me to send out and see what it meant.   I made a detail from Companies E, F, and A, consisting of 44 men, under command of Lieutenant Hansey, of Company F, and Lieutenant Clark, of

Company E. They found it to be our vedettes firing on some rebel cavalry, who had come within range, and upon receiving their fire retreated. Our party followed them, and, after proceeding within 2 miles of Woodbury, came upon the enemy's pickets, driving them in. At this time they discovered a party of the enemy charging on them in their rear. Lieutenant Clark, who was in command of the rear, immediately wheeled his men, and poured into them, from his carbines, a galling fire, and then drew sabers and charged them in fine style, scattering them in all directions, killing 2, wounding 1, and taking 10 prisoners, with no loss on our side except 2 horses wounded. The enemy was now in force in front and on the flanks. A retreat was ordered, the prisoners being sent forward under a guard; the party was divided equally, each lieutenant taking command of a party. One formed a line and held the enemy in check, while the other fell back, and *vice versa*, by which means they succeeded in bringing their prisoners in without loss. The enemy followed to the pickets, and quite a skirmish ensued, without loss on our side.

Permit me to offer a suggestion. Morgan's brigade is scattered from McMinnville to Woodbury, one and two regiments in a place. Now, in my opinion, with an adequate force of cavalry, and probably some artillery, his command could be taken in detail and routed completely.

I am, very respectfully, your obedient servant,

T. D. McCLELLAND,
Captain, Comdg. Second Battalion, Third Ohio Cavalry.

Lieut. Col. D. A. MURRAY,
Commanding Third Ohio Cavalry.

---

*ALTERNATE DESIGNATIONS OF ORGANIZATIONS MENTIONED IN THIS VOLUME.**

Adams' (Samuel) Infantry. See *Alabama Troops, 33d Regiment.*
Adrian's (T. W.) Cavalry. See *Tennessee Troops, Confederate, 12th Battalion.*
Aldrich's (Simeon C.) Infantry. See *Indiana Troops, 44th Regiment.*
Alexander's (John W. S.) Infantry. See *Illinois Troops, 21st Regiment.*
Allen's (Thomas G.) Infantry. See *Illinois Troops, 80th Regiment.*
Allen's (William W.) Cavalry. See *Alabama Troops, 1st Regiment.*
Allin's (P. T.) Sharpshooters. See *Tennessee Troops, Confederate.*
Altemire's Infantry. (Official designation unknown.) See *Colonel Altemire.*
Anderson Cavalry. See *Pennsylvania Troops, 15th Regiment.*
Anderson Troop Cavalry. See *Pennsylvania Troops.*
Anderson's (Charles) Infantry. See *Ohio Troops, 93d Regiment.*
Anderson's (John H.) Infantry. See *Tennessee Troops, Confederate, 8th Regiment.*
Anderson's (Nicholas L.) Infantry. See *Ohio Troops, 6th Regiment.*
Anderson's (Paul F.) Cavalry. See *Baxter Smith's Cavalry.*
Anderson's (R. W.) Artillery. See *S. A. Moses' Artillery.*
Andrews' (Julius A.) Cavalry. See *Texas Troops, 15th Regiment.*
Ashby's (H. M.) Cavalry. See *Tennessee Troops, Confederate.*
Austin's (J. E.) Sharpshooters. See *Louisiana Troops, 14th Battalion.*
Autry's (James L.) Infantry. See *Mississippi Troops, 27th Regiment.*
Bacot's (W. C.) Cavalry. See *N. B. Forrest's Cavalry.*
Baldwin's (William W.) Cavalry. See *Virginia Troops, Confederate.*
Barker's (J. D.) Cavalry. See *Ohio Troops, 1st Regiment.*

---

* References are to index following.

Barnes' (Milton) **Infantry.** See *Ohio Troops*, 97th *Regiment.*
Barnett's (Charles M.) **Artillery.** See *Illinois Troops*, 2d *Regiment, Battery I.*
Barret's (O. W.) **Artillery.** See *Missouri Troops, Confederate.*
Barrett's (Wallace W.) **Infantry.** See *Illinois Troops*, 44th *Regiment.*
Bartleson's (Frederick A.) **Infantry.** See *Illinois Troops*, 100th *Regiment.*
Bassford's (Stephen A.) **Infantry.** See *Ohio Troops*, 94th *Regiment.*
Baucum's (George F.) **Infantry.** See *Arkansas Troops*, 8th *Regiment.*
Baxter's (Ed.) **Artillery.** See *Tennessee Troops, Confederate.*
Beebe's (Yates V.) **Artillery.** See *Wisconsin Troops*, 10th *Battery.*
Belding's (Edmund B.) **Artillery.** See *Ohio Troops*, 1st *Regiment, Battery A.*
Bell's (A. W.) **Infantry.** See *North Carolina Troops*, 39th *Regiment.*
Benneson's (William H.) **Infantry.** See *Illinois Troops*, 78th *Regiment.*
Bennett's (James D.) **Cavalry.** See *Tennessee Troops, Confederate.*
Bennett's (John E.) **Infantry.** See *Illinois Troops*, 75th *Regiment.*
Benton's (S. J.) **Artillery.** See *F. H. Robertson's Artillery.*
Berry's (William W.) **Infantry.** See *Kentucky Troops, Union*, 5th *Regiment.*
Bingham's (George B.) **Infantry.** See *Wisconsin Troops*, 1st *Regiment.*
Black's (W. T.) **Infantry.** See *Georgia Troops*, 5th *Regiment.*
Blake's (John W.) **Infantry.** See *Indiana Troops*, 40th *Regiment.*
Blake's (William H.) **Infantry.** See *Indiana Troops*, 9th *Regiment.*
Bledsoe's (W. S.) **Cavalry.** See *J. P. Murray's Cavalry.*
Block's (David) **Infantry.** See *Kansas Troops*, 8th *Regiment.*
Blythe's Infantry. See *Mississippi Troops*, 44th *Regiment.*
Bounds' (J. M.) **Cavalry.** See *Texas Troops*, 11th *Regiment.*
Bowen's (William L. L.) **Infantry.** See *Florida Troops*, 4th *Regiment.*
Boyle's (John) **Cavalry.** See *Kentucky Troops, Union*, 9th *Regiment.*
Bradley's (Cullen) **Artillery.** See *Ohio Troops*, 6th *Battery.*
Bradley's (Luther P.) **Infantry.** See *Illinois Troops*, 51st *Regiment.*
Brantly's (W. F.) **Infantry.** See *Mississippi Troops*, 29th *Regiment.*
Bratton's (H. L. W.) **Infantry.** See *Tennessee Troops, Confederate*, 24th *Regiment.*
Breckinridge's (W. C. P.) **Cavalry.** See *Kentucky Troops, Confederate*, 9th *Regiment.*
Briant's (Cyrus E.) **Infantry.** See *Indiana Troops*, 88th *Regiment.*
Bridges' (Lyman) **Engineers.** See *Union Troops, Pioneer Brigade*, 1st *Battalion.*
Brigham's (Joseph H.) **Infantry.** See *Ohio Troops*, 69th *Regiment.*
Bristol's (Hiram W.) **Infantry.** See *Illinois Troops*, 34th *Regiment.*
Broaddus' (Green B.) **Infantry.** See *Kentucky Troops, Union*, 8th *Regiment.*
Brown's (John Mason) **Cavalry.** See *Kentucky Troops, Union*, 10th *Regiment.*
Buckner's (Allen) **Infantry.** See *Illinois Troops*, 79th *Regiment.*
Buell's (George P.) **Infantry.** See *Indiana Troops*, 58th *Regiment.*
Bunn's (H. G.) **Infantry.** See *Arkansas Troops*, 4th *Regiment.*
Burke's (Joseph W.) **Infantry.** See *Ohio Troops*, 10th *Regiment.*
Burks' (J. C.) **Cavalry.** See *Texas Troops*, 11th *Regiment.*
Bush's (Asahel K.) **Artillery.** See *Indiana Troops*, 4th *Battery.*
Butler's (J. R.) **Cavalry.** See *Kentucky Troops, Confederate*, 3d *Regiment.*
Butler's (W. R.) **Infantry.** See *Tennessee Troops, Confederate*, 18th *Regiment.*
Byrd's (Robert K.) **Infantry.** See *Tennessee Troops, Union*, 1st *Regiment.*
Byrne's (Edward P.) **Artillery.** See *Kentucky Troops, Confederate.*
Cahill's (James B.) **Infantry.** See *Illinois Troops*, 16th *Regiment.*
Caldwell's (James N.) **Infantry.** See *Union Troops, Regulars*, 18th *Regiment.*
Calvert's (J. H.) **Artillery.** See *Helena Artillery.*
Cameron's (F. J.) **Infantry.** See *Arkansas Troops*, 6th and 7th *Regiments.*
Cameron's (J. F.) **Infantry.** See *Confederate Troops, Regulars*, 3d *Regiment.*
Camp's (J. L.) **Cavalry.** See *Texas Troops*, 14th *Regiment.*
Campbell's (Archibald P.) **Cavalry.** See *Michigan Troops*, 2d *Regiment.*
Carnes' (W. W.) **Artillery.** See *Tennessee Troops, Confederate.*

Carpenter's (Stephen D.) **Infantry.** See *Union Troops, Regulars.* 19th Regiment, 1st Battalion.

Carpenter's (Stephen J.) **Artillery.** See *Wisconsin Troops,* 8th Battery.

Carr's (Henry M.) **Infantry.** See *Indiana Troops,* 72d Regiment.

Carroll's (William B.) **Infantry** See *Indiana Troops,* 10th Regiment.

Carter's (James E.) **Cavalry.** See *Tennessee Troops, Confederate.*

Carter's (John C.) **Infantry.** See *Tennessee Troops, Confederate,* 38th Regiment.

Casey's (Thomas S.) **Infantry.** See *Illinois Troops,* 110th Regiment.

Cassil's (Alexander) **Infantry.** See *Ohio Troops,* 65th Regiment.

Cassilly's (William B.) **Infantry.** See *Ohio Troops,* 69th Regiment.

Chalmers' Sharpshooters. See *Mississippi Troops,* 9th Battalion.

Chandler's (William P.) **Infantry.** See *Illinois Troops,* 35th Regiment.

Chapin's (Alfred R.) **Infantry.** See *Wisconsin Troops,* 10th Regiment.

Chapman's (Charles W.) **Infantry.** See *Indiana Troops,* 74th Regiment.

Charlton's (R.) **Infantry.** See *Mississippi Troops,* 45th Regiment.

Chenault's (D. W.) **Cavalry.** See *Kentucky Troops, Confederate,* 11th Regiment.

Chester's (John) **Infantry.** See *Tennessee Troops, Confederate,* 51st Regiment.

Chicago Board of Trade Artillery. See *Illinois Troops.*

Church's (Josiah W.) **Artillery.** See *Michigan Troops,* 4th Battery.

Clay's (E. F.) **Mounted Rifles.** See *Kentucky Troops, Confederate,* 3d Battalion.

Claybrooke's (F.) **Infantry.** See *Tennessee Troops, Confederate,* 20th Regiment.

Clements' (Robert) **Pioneers.** See *Union Troops, Pioneer Brigade,* 3d Battalion

Cluke's (R. S.) **Cavalry.** See *Kentucky Troops, Confederate,* 8th Regiment.

Cobb's (Robert) **Artillery.** See *Kentucky Troops, Confederate.*

Cockerill's (A. T. M.) **Infantry.** See *Ohio Troops,* 24th Regiment.

Cockerill's (Daniel T.) **Artillery.** See *Ohio Troops,* 1st Regiment, Battery F.

Coleman's (F. W.) **Artillery.** See *P. Darden's Artillery.*

Collier's (Daniel R.) **Infantry.** See *Kentucky Troops, Union,* 3d Regiment.

Collins' (Henry E.) **Cavalry.** See *Kentucky Troops, Union,* 2d Regiment.

Collins' (Joseph P.) **Infantry.** See *Indiana Troops,* 29th Regiment.

Colquitt's (John W.) **Infantry.** See *Arkansas Troops,* 1st Regiment.

Connell's (John M.) **Infantry.** See *Ohio Troops,* 17th Regiment.

Cook's (Ed. C.) **Infantry.** See *Tennessee Troops, Confederate,* 32d Regiment.

Cooper's (Joseph A.) **Infantry.** See *Tennessee Troops, Union,* 6th Regiment.

Cotter's (Charles) **Artillery.** See *Ohio Troops,* 1st Regiment, Battery A.

Cotter's (W. A.) **Infantry.** See *Arkansas Troops,* 30th Regiment.

Cowen's (D. D. T.) **Infantry.** See *Ohio Troops,* 52d Regiment.

Cox's (Jerome B.) **Artillery.** See *Indiana Troops,* 10th Battery.

Cox's (J. J.) **Sharpshooters.** See *Georgia Troops,* 2d Battalion.

Cox's (John T.) **Cavalry.** See *Confederate Troops, Regulars,* 1st Regiment.

Craddock's (Jesse J.) **Cavalry.** See *Kentucky Troops, Union,* 2d Regiment.

Cram's (George H.) **Infantry.** See *Kentucky Troops, Union,* 9th Regiment.

Creighton's (J. R. J.) **Sharpshooters.** See *P. T. Allin's Sharpshooters.*

Cribbs' (H. H.) **Artillery.** See *C. L. Lumsden's Artillery.*

Crofton's (Robert E. A.) **Infantry.** See *Union Troops, Regulars,* 16th Regiment.

Croxton's (John T.) **Infantry.** See *Kentucky Troops, Union,* 4th Regiment.

Cummins' (John E.) **Infantry.** See *Ohio Troops,* 99th Regiment.

Cunningham's (P. D.) **Infantry.** See *Tennessee Troops, Confederate,* 28th Regiment.

Cupp's (Valentine) **Cavalry.** See *Ohio Troops,* 1st Regiment.

Daniel's (Charles P.) **Infantry.** See *Georgia Troops,* 5th Regiment.

Darden's (P.) **Artillery.** See *Jefferson Artillery.*

Davidson's (George S.) **Artillery.** See *Virginia Troops, Confederate.*

Davis' (John R.) **Cavalry.** See *Tennessee Troops, Confederate.*

Davis' (Samuel) **Infantry.** See *Tennessee Troops, Confederate,* 25th Regiment.

Dawson's (Andrew R. Z.) **Infantry.** See *Ohio Troops,* 15th Regiment.

Dibrell's (G. G.) **Cavalry.** See *Tennessee Troops, Confederate.*
Dick's (George F.) **Infantry.** See *Indiana Troops, 86th Regiment.*
Dickerson's (C. J.) **Infantry.** See *Michigan Troops, 10th Regiment.*
Dickey's (Frank W.) **Cavalry.** See *Michigan Troops, 2d Regiment.*
Dickinson's (William H.) **Cavalry.** See *Michigan Troops, 4th Regiment.*
Dils' (John, jr.) **Infantry.** See *Kentucky Troops, Union, 39th Regiment.*
Dodge's (Joseph B.) **Infantry.** See *Indiana Troops, 30th Regiment.*
Douglas' (James P.) **Artillery.** See *Texas Troops.*
Douglass' (De Witt C.) **Cavalry.** See *Tennessee Troops, Confederate.*
Douglass' (W. F.) **Infantry.** See *Arkansas Troops, 6th and 7th Regiments.*
Drake's (Levi) **Infantry.** See *Ohio Troops, 49th Regiment.*
Drury's (Lucius H.) **Artillery.** See *Wisconsin Troops, 3d Battery.*
Duke's (Basil W.) **Cavalry.** See *Kentucky Troops, Confederate, 2d Regiment.*
Duncan's (H. H.) **Mounted Rifles.** See *Kentucky Troops, Confederate, 3d Battalion.*
Dunlop's (J. E.) **Cavalry.** See *Georgia Troops, 2d Regiment.*
Dunn's Regiment. See *Ambrose C. Dunn.*
Dunn's (David M.) **Infantry.** See *Indiana Troops, 29th Regiment.*
Dunwoody's (James A.) **Artillery.** See *Indiana Troops, 12th Battery.*
Dysart's (Alexander P.) **Infantry.** See *Illinois Troops, 34th Regiment.*
Edgarton's (Warren P.) **Artillery.** See *Ohio Troops, 1st Regiment, Battery E.*
Ehrler's (Francis) **Infantry.** See *Missouri Troops, Union, 2d Regiment.*
Eldridge's (L. B.) **Cavalry.** See *Michigan Troops, 4th Regiment.*
Elliott's (George F.) **Infantry.** See *Ohio Troops, 69th Regiment.*
Ellis' (Ephraim J.) **Infantry.** See *Ohio Troops, 33d Regiment.*
Ellsworth's (Alban A.) **Artillery.** See *Kentucky Troops, Union, Battery B.*
Ely's (John J.) **Artillery.** See *Michigan Troops, 5th Battery.*
Embree's (James T.) **Infantry.** See *Indiana Troops, 58th Regiment.*
Enyart's (David A.) **Infantry.** See *Kentucky Troops, Union, 1st Regiment.*
Erdelmeyer's (Frank) **Infantry.** See *Indiana Troops, 32d Regiment.*
Este's (George P.) **Infantry.** See *Ohio Troops, 14th Regiment.*
Estep's (George) **Artillery.** See *Indiana Troops, 8th Battery.*
Estes' (William N.) **Cavalry.** See *Confederate Troops, Regulars, 3d Regiment.*
Eufaula Artillery. See *Alabama Troops.*
Evans' (James C.) **Infantry.** See *Kentucky Troops, Union, 21st Regiment.*
Farrar's (F. H. jr.) **Infantry.** See *Louisiana Troops, 1st Regiment, Regulars.*
Faulkner's (John K.) **Cavalry.** See *Kentucky Troops, Union, 7th Regiment.*
Faulkner's (W. W.) **Cavalry.** See *Kentucky Troops, Confederate.*
Feild's (H. R.) **Infantry.** See *Tennessee Troops, Confederate, 1st and 27th Regiments.*
Fisk's (S. W.) **Infantry.** See *Louisiana Troops, 16th and 25th Regiments.*
Fitzpatrick's (E. J.) **Artillery.** See *H. C. Semple's Artillery.*
Flegle's (Jacob) **Sharpshooters.** See *Ohio Troops, 4th Company.*
Floyd's (W. W.) **Infantry.** See *Tennessee Troops, Confederate, 17th Regiment.*
Foley's (James L.) **Cavalry.** See *Kentucky Troops, Union, 10th Regiment.*
Forman's (James B.) **Infantry.** See *Kentucky Troops, Union, 15th Regiment.*
Forman's (Joseph T.) **Cavalry.** See *Kentucky Troops, Union, 2d Regiment.*
Forrest's (N. B.) **Cavalry.** See *Tennessee Troops, Confederate.*
Frizell's (Joseph W.) **Infantry.** See *Ohio Troops, 94th Regiment.*
Franklin's (James J.) **Infantry.** See *Arkansas Troops, 30th Regiment.*
Freeman's (S. L.) **Artillery.** See *Tennessee Troops, Confederate.*
Fulmer's (Jesse) **Infantry.** See *Union Troops, Regulars, 15th Regiment, 1st Battalion.*
Fulton's (John S.) **Infantry.** See *Tennessee Troops, Confederate, 44th Regiment.*
Funkhouser's (John J.) **Infantry.** See *Illinois Troops, 98th Regiment.*
Fyffe's (James P.) **Infantry.** See *Ohio Troops, 59th Regiment.*
Gaines' (F. Y.) **Cavalry.** See *Alabama Troops, 3d Regiment.*
Gano's (R. M.) **Cavalry.** See *Kentucky Troops, Confederate, 7th Regiment.*

Garrity's (James) **Artillery.** See *William H. Ketchum's Artillery.*
Garver's (William) **Infantry.** See *Indiana Troops,* 101st *Regiment.*
George's (James) **Infantry.** See *Minnesota Troops,* 2d *Regiment.*
German's (Obadiah) **Artillery.** See *Wisconsin Troops,* 8th *Battery.*
Gibson's (J. G.) **Artillery.** See *Georgia Troops,* 14th *Battalion, Battery F.*
Gibson's (Randall L.) **Infantry.** See *Louisiana Troops,* 13th *and* 20th *Regiments.*
Gibson's (William H.) **Infantry.** See *Ohio Troops,* 49th *Regiment.*
Gilchrist's (James G.) **Infantry.** See *Alabama Troops,* 45th *Regiment.*
Gillem's (Alvan C.) **Infantry.** See *Tennessee Troops, Union,* 10th *Regiment.*
Gilmer's (Daniel H.) **Infantry.** See *Illinois Troops,* 38th *Regiment.*
Giltner's (H. L.) **Cavalry.** See *Kentucky Troops, Confederate,* 4th *Regiment.*
Given's (Josiah) **Infantry.** See *Ohio Troops,* 18th *Regiment.*
Good's (Joseph) **Infantry.** See *Ohio Troops,* 108th *Regiment.*
Gooding's (Michael) **Infantry.** See *Indiana Troops,* 22d *Regiment.*
Goodspeed's (Wilber F.) **Artillery.** See *Ohio Troops, Union,* 1st *Regiment, Battery A.*
Gordon's (G. W.) **Infantry.** See *Tennessee Troops, Confederate,* 11th *Regiment.*
Govan's (D. C.) **Infantry.** See *Arkansas Troops,* 2d *Regiment.*
Gratz's (Louis A.) **Cavalry.** See *Kentucky Troops, Union,* 6th *Regiment.*
Gray's (Isaac P.) **Cavalry.** See *Indiana Troops,* 4th *Regiment.*
Gray's (Samuel F.) **Infantry.** See *Ohio Troops,* 49th *Regiment.*
Green's (Ezekiel) **Artillery.** See *Benjamin S. Nicklin's Artillery.*
Greusel's (Nicholas) **Infantry.** See *Illinois Troops,* 36th *Regiment.*
Grider's (Benjamin C.) **Infantry.** See *Kentucky Troops, Union,* 9th *Regiment.*
Griffin's (Daniel F.) **Infantry.** See *Indiana Troops,* 38th *Regiment.*
Grigsby's (J. W.) **Cavalry.** See *Kentucky Troops, Confederate,* 6th *Regiment.*
Guenther's (Francis L.) **Artillery.** See *Union Troops, Regulars,* 5th *Regiment, Battery H.*
Guillet's (Charles) **Infantry.** See *Louisiana Troops,* 13th *and* 20th *Regiments.*
Hagan's (James) **Cavalry.** See *Alabama Troops,* 3d *Regiment.*
Hale's (Luther F.) **Artillery.** See *Michigan Troops,* 6th *Battery.*
Halisy's (Dennis J.) **Cavalry.** See *Kentucky Troops, Union,* 6th *Regiment.*
Hall's (Michael T.) **Infantry.** See *Kentucky Troops, Union,* 33d *Regiment.*
Hall's (William S.) **Cavalry.** See *Tennessee Troops, Union,* 2d *Regiment.*
Hambright's (Henry A.) **Infantry.** See *Pennsylvania Troops,* 79th *Regiment.*
Hamilton's (O. P.) **Cavalry.** See *Tennessee Troops, Confederate.*
Hamrick's (Thomas H.) **Infantry.** See *Kentucky Troops, Union,* 23d *Regiment.*
Hapeman's (Douglas) **Infantry.** See *Illinois Troops,* 104th *Regiment.*
Hardy's (L. T.) **Cavalry.** See *Tennessee Troops, Confederate,* 12th *Battalion.*
Harman's (E. V.) **Cavalry.** See *Virginia Troops,* 34th *Battalion.*
Harmon's (Oscar F.) **Infantry.** See *Illinois Troops,* 125th *Regiment.*
Harper's (R. W.) **Mounted Rifles.** See *Arkansas Troops,* 1st *Regiment Rifles.*
Harrington's (Fazilo A.) **Infantry.** See *Illinois Troops,* 27th *Regiment.*
Harris' (John L.) **Infantry.** See *Tennessee Troops, Confederate,* 6th *and* 9th *Regiments.*
Harris' (Samuel J.) **Artillery.** See *Indiana Troops,* 19th *Battery.*
Harrison's (Benjamin) **Infantry.** See *Indiana Troops,* 70th *Regiment.*
Harrison's (Thomas) **Cavalry.** See *Texas Troops,* 8th *Regiment.*
Harvey's (Reuben F.) **Infantry.** See *Arkansas Troops,* 2d *Regiment.*
Hathaway's (Gilbert) **Infantry.** See *Indiana Troops,* 73d *Regiment.*
Hawkins' (A. T.) **Sharpshooters.** See *Mississippi Troops,* 15th *Battalion.*
Hawkins' (Hiram) **Infantry.** See *Kentucky Troops, Confederate,* 5th *Regiment.*
Hawkins' (Joseph G.) **Infantry.** See *Ohio Troops,* 13th *Regiment.*
Hays' (William H.) **Infantry.** See *Kentucky Troops, Union,* 10th *Regiment.*
Heg's (Hans C.) **Infantry.** See *Wisconsin Troops,* 15th *Regiment.*
Helena Artillery. See *Arkansas Troops.*
Hescock's (Henry) **Artillery.** See *Missouri Troops, Union,* 1st *Regiment, Battery G.*

Hewett's (John M.) **Artillery.** See *Kentucky Troops, Union, Battery B.*
Hewitt's (James W.) **Infantry.** See *Kentucky Troops, Confederate, 2d Regiment.*
Hibbard's (Elisha C.) **Infantry.** See *Wisconsin Troops, 24th Regiment.*
Hickcox's (Eli J.) **Infantry.** See *Ohio Troops, 69th Regiment.*
Hill's (B. J.) **Infantry.** See *Tennessee Troops, Confederate, 5th [35th] Regiment.*
Hill's (Samuel) **Cavalry.** See *Indiana Troops, 2d Regiment.*
Hill (Washington) **Artillery.** See *Wisconsin Troops, 5th Battery.*
Hines' (Cyrus C.) **Infantry.** See *Indiana Troops, 57th Regiment.*
Hobart's (Harrison C.) **Infantry.** See *Wisconsin Troops, 21st Regiment.*
Hobson's (William E.) **Infantry.** See *Kentucky Troops, Union, 13th Regiment.*
Holman's (D. W.) **Cavalry.** See *Tennessee Troops, Confederate.*
Hood's (Calvin) **Pioneers.** See *Union Troops, Pioneer Brigade, 2d Battalion.*
Hoskins' (William A.) **Infantry.** See *Kentucky Troops, Union, 12th Regiment.*
Hotchkiss' (Charles T.) **Infantry.** See *Illinois Troops, 89th Regiment.*
Hotchkiss' (William A.) **Artillery.** See *Minnesota Troops, 2d Battery.*
Houghtaling's (Charles) **Artillery.** See *Illinois Troops, 1st Regiment, Battery C.*
Houk's (Leonidas C.) **Infantry.** See *Tennessee Troops, Union, 3d Regiment.*
Housum's (Peter B.) **Infantry.** See *Pennsylvania Troops, 77th Regiment.*
Howard's (James R.) **Cavalry.** See *Confederate Troops, Regulars, 3d Regiment.*
Howard's (William) **Infantry.** See *Ohio Troops, 59th Regiment.*
Hughs' (John M.) **Infantry.** See *Tennessee Troops, Confederate, 25th Regiment.*
Hull's (James S.) **Infantry.** See *Indiana Troops, 37th Regiment.*
Humphrey's (Charles B.) **Artillery.** See *Wisconsin Troops, 5th Battery.*
Humphrey's (George) **Infantry.** See *Indiana Troops, 88th Regiment.*
Humphreys' (John T.) **Artillery.** See *Arkansas Troops.*
Hunter's (Morton C.) **Infantry.** See *Indiana Troops, 82d Regiment.*
Hunt's (Thomas H.) **Infantry.** See *Kentucky Troops, Confederate, 9th Regiment.*
Hurd's (Orrin D.) **Infantry.** See *Indiana Troops, 30th Regiment.*
Hurt's (C. S.) **Infantry.** See *Tennessee Troops, Confederate, 6th and 9th Regiments.*
Innes' (William P.) **Engineers.** See *Michigan Troops, 1st Regiment.*
Ison's (F. M.) **Cavalry.** See *Georgia Troops, 2d Regiment.*
Jarnagin's (C. G.) **Infantry.** See *Tennessee Troops, Confederate, 37th Regiment.*
Jarvis' (Dwight, jr.) **Infantry.** See *Ohio Troops, 13th Regiment.*
Jefferson Artillery. See *Mississippi Troops.*
Jeffress' (William C.) **Artillery.** See *Nottoway Artillery.*
Johnson's (A. R.) **Cavalry.** See *Kentucky Troops, Confederate, 10th Regiment.*
Johnson's (J. B.) **Infantry.** See *Tennessee Troops, Confederate, 29th Regiment.*
Johnson's (Ole C.) **Infantry.** See *Wisconsin Troops, 15th Regiment.*
Johnson's (Samuel) **Infantry.** See *Illinois Troops, 22d Regiment.*
Johnson's (Thomas) **Mounted Rifles.** See *Kentucky Troops, Confederate, 2d Battalion.*
Jones' (Fielder A.) **Infantry.** See *Indiana Troops, 39th Regiment.*
Jones' (Frederick C.) **Infantry.** See *Ohio Troops, 24th Regiment.*
Jones' (Griffith) **Cavalry.** See *Pennsylvania Troops, 9th Regiment.*
Jones' (T. M.) **Infantry.** See *Mississippi Troops, 27th Regiment.*
Kammerling's (Gustave) **Infantry.** See *Ohio Troops, 9th Regiment.*
Keeble's (R. H.) **Infantry.** See *Tennessee Troops, Confederate, 23d Regiment.*
Kell's (John) **Infantry.** See *Ohio Troops, 2d Regiment.*
Kelly's (John H.) **Infantry.** See *Arkansas Troops, 8th Regiment.*
Kennett's (Henry G.) **Infantry.** See *Ohio Troops, 79th Regiment.*
Kessler's (John G.) **Cavalry.** See *Indiana Troops, 2d Regiment.*
Ketchum's (William H.) **Artillery.** See *Alabama Troops.*
Key's (Thomas J.) **Artillery.** See *Helena Artillery.*
King's (John H.) **Infantry.** See *Union Troops, Regulars, 15th Regiment, 1st Battalion*
Kinley's (Isaac) **Infantry.** See *Indiana Troops, 36th Regiment.*
Kirby's (Isaac M.) **Infantry.** See *Ohio Troops, 101st Regiment.*

Klein's (Robert) **Cavalry.** See *Indiana Troops, 3d Regiment.*
Knefler's (Frederick) **Infantry.** See *Indiana Troops, 79th Regiment.*
Laiboldt's (Bernard) **Infantry.** See *Missouri Troops, Union, 2d Regiment.*
Lane's (John Q.) **Infantry.** See *Ohio Troops, 97th Regiment.*
Lanier's (R. F.) **Infantry.** See *Tennessee Troops, Confederate, 13th Regiment.*
Larmer's (S. P.) **Cavalry.** See *Trigg's Cavalry.*
Laughlin's (James) **Cavalry.** See *Ohio Troops, 1st Regiment.*
Lavender's (F. M.) **Infantry.** See *Tennessee Troops, Confederate, 20th Regiment.*
Lawson's (Orris A.) **Infantry.** See *Ohio Troops, 3d Regiment.*
Leaming's (Henry) **Infantry.** See *Indiana Troops, 40th Regiment.*
Lennard's (George W.) **Infantry.** See *Indiana Troops, 57th Regiment.*
Lesley's (John T.) **Infantry.** See *Florida Troops, 4th Regiment.*
Lewis' (Joseph H.) **Infantry.** See *Kentucky Troops, Confederate, 6th Regiment.*
Leyden's (A.) **Artillery.** See *Georgia Troops, 9th Battalion.*
Lillard's (John M.) **Infantry.** See *Tennessee Troops, Confederate, 26th Regiment.*
Lilly's (Eli) **Artillery.** See *Indiana Troops, 18th Battery.*
Lister's (Frederick W.) **Infantry.** See *Ohio Troops, 31st Regiment.*
Livingston's (Cortland) **Artillery.** See *Wisconsin Troops, 3d Battery.*
Locke's (M. F.) **Cavalry.** See *Texas Troops, 10th Regiment.*
Loomis' (C. O.) **Artillery.** See *Michigan Troops, 1st Regiment, Battery A.*
Louisville Legion, Infantry. See *Kentucky Troops, Union, 5th Regiment.*
Ludlow's (Israel) **Artillery.** See *Union Troops, Regulars, 5th Regiment, Battery H.*
Lumsden's (C. L.) **Artillery.** See *Alabama Troops.*
Lythgoe's (A. J.) **Infantry.** See *South Carolina Troops, 10th and 19th Regiments.*
McCann's (Richard) **Cavalry.** See *De Witt C. Douglass' Cavalry.*
McClain's (Richard W.) **Infantry.** See *Ohio Troops, 51st Regiment.*
McClelland's (James S.) **Infantry.** See *Illinois Troops, 25th Regiment.*
McClelland's (Thomas D.) **Cavalry.** See *Ohio Troops, 3d Regiment.*
McComas' (Hamilton C.) **Infantry.** See *Illinois Troops, 107th Regiment.*
McCook's (Anson G.) **Infantry.** See *Ohio Troops, 2d Regiment.*
McCown's Escort Cavalry. See *L. T. Hardy's Cavalry.*
McCreery's (William B.) **Infantry.** See *Michigan Troops, 21st Regiment.*
McCulloch's (Miller R.) **Cavalry.** See *Kentucky Troops, Union, 2d Regiment.*
McDonald's (Bedan B.) **Infantry.** See *Ohio Troops, 101st Regiment.*
McDowell's (B. G.) **Infantry.** See *North Carolina Troops, 62d Regiment.*
McDowell's (Joseph A.) **Infantry.** See *North Carolina Troops, 60th Regiment.*
McDuffie's (W. A.) **Artillery.** See *Eufaula Artillery.*
McFarlane's (John A.) **Cavalry.** See *Virginia Troops, Confederate.*
McGraw's (John S.) **Infantry.** See *Indiana Troops, 57th Regiment.*
McIlvain's (Alexander) **Infantry.** See *Ohio Troops, 64th Regiment.*
McKee's (David) **Infantry.** See *Wisconsin Troops, 15th Regiment.*
McKee's (Samuel) **Infantry.** See *Kentucky Troops, Union, 3d Regiment.*
McKelvaine's (R. P.) **Infantry.** See *Mississippi Troops, 24th Regiment.*
McKinstry's (Alexander) **Infantry.** See *Alabama Troops, 32d Regiment.*
McMackin's (Warren E.) **Infantry.** See *Illinois Troops, 21st Regiment.*
McMurry's (James A.) **Infantry.** See *Tennessee Troops, Confederate, 4th Regiment P. A.*
McNeill's (A.) **Infantry.** See *Mississippi Troops, 8th Regiment.*
McReynolds' (J. T.) **Infantry.** See *Tennessee Troops, Confederate, 37th Regiment.*
Magee's (David W.) **Infantry.** See *Illinois Troops, 86th Regiment.*
Magevney's (M., jr.) **Infantry.** See *Tennessee Troops, Confederate, 154th Regiment.*
Malone's (James C., jr.) **Cavalry.** See *Alabama Troops, 14th Battalion.*
Manderson's (Charles F.) **Infantry.** See *Ohio Troops, 19th Regiment.*
Maney's (Frank) **Sharpshooters.** See *Tennessee Troops, Confederate.*
Maple's (Thomas S.) **Cavalry.** See *Anderson Troop, Cavalry.*
Marks' Artillery. See *H. C. Semple's Artillery.*

Marks' (A. S.) **Infantry.**   See *Tennessee Troops, Confederate,* 17th *Regiment.*
Marsh's (Jason) **Infantry.**   See *Illinois Troops,* 74th *Regiment.*
Marshall's (Alexander) **Artillery.**   See *Ohio Troops,* 1st *Regiment, Battery* G.
Marshall's (John J.) **Cavalry.**   See *H. L. Giltner's Cavalry.*
Marshall's (L. G.) **Artillery.**   See *W. W. Carnes' Artillery.*
Martin's (John A.) **Infantry.**   See *Kansas Troops,* 8th *Regiment.*
Mauldin's (T. H.) **Cavalry.**   See *Alabama Troops,* 3d *Regiment.*
Maury's (Henry) **Infantry.**   See *Alabama Troops,* 32d *Regiment.*
May's (Reuben) **Infantry.**   See *Kentucky Troops, Union,* 8th *Regiment.*
Mebane's (John W.) **Artillery.**   See *E. E. Wright's Artillery.*
Melton's (James M.) **Infantry.**   See *Tennessee Troops, Union,* 2d *Regiment.*
Mendenhall's (John) **Artillery.**   See *Union Troops, Regulars,* 4th *Regiment, Batteries* H and M.
Mihalotzy's (Geza) **Infantry.**   See *Illinois Troops,* 24th *Regiment.*
Miller's (Silas) **Infantry.**   See *Illinois Troops,* 36th *Regiment.*
Miller's (William) **Infantry.**   See *Florida Troops,* 1st *and* 3d *Regiments.*
Milliken's (Minor) **Cavalry.**   See *Ohio Troops,* 1st *Regiment.*
Minty's (Robert H. G.) **Cavalry.**   See *Michigan Troops,* 4th *Regiment.*
Mitchell's (Joseph A. S.) **Cavalry.**   See *Indiana Troops,* 2d *Regiment.*
Mix's (Frank W.) **Cavalry.**   See *Michigan Troops,* 4th *Regiment.*
Monroe's (James) **Infantry.**   See *Illinois Troops,* 123d *Regiment.*
Moody's (Granville) **Infantry.**   See *Ohio Troops,* 74th *Regiment.*
Moore's (Orlando H.) **Infantry.**   See *Michigan Troops,* 25th *Regiment.*
Moore's (Robert S.) **Infantry.**   See *Illinois Troops,* 85th *Regiment.*
Moore's (W. L.) **Infantry.**   See *Tennessee Troops, Confederate,* 8th *Regiment.*
Morehead's (James T.) **Infantry.**   See *Kentucky Troops, Confederate,* 9th *Regiment.*
Morgan's (J. B.) **Infantry.**   See *Mississippi Troops,* 29th *Regiment.*
Morgan's (John T.) **Partisans.**   See *Alabama Troops,* 51st *Regiment.*
Morgan's (W. E.) **Infantry.**   See *Tennessee Troops, Confederate,* 13th *Regiment.*
Moses' (S. A.) **Artillery.**   See *Georgia Troops.*
Mottley's (Erasmus L.) **Infantry.**   See *Kentucky Troops, Union,* 11th *Regiment.*
Mullen's (Bernard F.) **Infantry.**   See *Indiana Troops,* 35th *Regiment.*
Mulligan's (James B.) **Infantry.**   See *Union Troops, Regulars,* 19th *Regiment,* 1st *Battalion.*
Munday's (Reuben) **Cavalry.**   See *Kentucky Troops, Union,* 6th *Regiment.*
Munger's (William A.) **Infantry.**   See *Illinois Troops,* 100th *Regiment.*
Murray's (Douglas A.) **Cavalry.**   See *Ohio Troops,* 3d *Regiment.*
Murray's (Eli H.) **Cavalry.**   See *Kentucky Troops, Union,* 3d *Regiment.*
Murray's (John E.) **Infantry.**   See *Arkansas Troops,* 5th *Regiment.*
Murray's (J. P.) **Cavalry.**   See *Tennessee Troops, Confederate.*
Neff's (Elias) **Infantry.**   See *Indiana Troops,* 40th *Regiment.*
Neibling's (James M) **Infantry.**   See *Ohio Troops,* 21st *Regiment.*
Neilson's (E. R.) **Infantry.**   See *Mississippi Troops,* 27th *Regiment.*
Nell's (G. W.) **Artillery.**   See *Kentucky Troops, Union, Battery* B.
Newell's (Nathaniel M.) **Artillery.**   See *Ohio Troops,* 1st *Regiment, Battery* D.
Nicholas' (Thomas P.) **Cavalry.**   See *Kentucky Troops, Union,* 2d *Regiment.*
Nicklin's (Benjamin S.) **Artillery.**   See *Indiana Troops,* 13th *Battery.*
Nodine's (Richard H.) **Infantry.**   See *Illinois Troops,* 25th *Regiment.*
Nottoway Artillery.   See *Virginia Troops.*
Olson's (Porter C.) **Infantry.**   See *Illinois Troops,* 36th *Regiment.*
Osborn's (John) **Infantry.**   See *Indiana Troops,* 31st *Regiment.*
Osburn's (Norval) **Artillery.**   See *Ohio Troops,* 1st *Regiment, Battery* F
Otis' (Elmer) **Cavalry.**   See *Union Troops, Regulars,* 4th *Regiment.*
Owsley's (John Q.) **Cavalry.**   See *Kentucky Troops, Union,* 5th *Regiment.*
Paine's (Hendrick E.) **Infantry.**   See *Illinois Troops,* 59th *Regiment.*

Palmer's (Baylor) **Artillery.**   See *Tennessee Troops, Confederate.*

Palmer's (Joseph B.) **Infantry.**   See *Tennessee Troops, Confederate,* 18th *Regiment.*

Paramore's (James W.) **Cavalry.**   See *Ohio Troops,* 3d *Regiment.*

Park's (Harvey S.) **Cavalry.**   See *Kentucky Troops, Union,* 2d *Regiment.*

Parkhurst's (John G.) **Infantry.**   See *Michigan Troops,* 9th *Regiment.*

Parsons' (Charles C.) **Artillery.**   See *Union Troops, Regulars,* 4th *Regiment, Batteries H and M.*

Pattison's (T. F.) **Sharpshooters.**   See *P. T. Allin's Sharpshooters.*

Phelps' (Edward H.) **Infantry.**   See *Ohio Troops,* 38th *Regiment.*

Pickens' (William C.) **Cavalry.**   See *Tennessee Troops, Union,* 3d *Regiment.*

Piepho's (Carlo) **Infantry.**   See *Ohio Troops,* 108th *Regiment.*

Pinney's (Oscar F.) **Artillery.**   See *Wisconsin Troops,* 5th *Battery.*

Pioneer **Brigade.**   See *Union Troops;* also *James St. C. Morton.*

Polk's (W. M.) **Artillery.**   See *W. L. Scott's Artillery.*

Powell's (Frank) **Cavalry.***   See *Frank Powell.*

Presson's (William A.) **Infantry.**   See *Illinois Troops,* 73d *Regiment.*

Pritchard's (E. E.) **Artillery.**   See *Georgia Troops.*

Pue's (Arthur, jr.) **Artillery.**   See *B. F. White's, jr., Artillery.*

Pugh's (John L.) **Cavalry.**   See *Ohio Troops,* 4th *Regiment.*

Putnam's (David) **Infantry.**   See *Ohio Troops,* 69th *Regiment.*

Quackenbush's (M. W.) **Infantry.**   See *Michigan Troops,* 14th *Regiment.*

Raffen's (Alexander W.) **Infantry.**   See *Illinois Troops,* 19th *Regiment.*

Ramsaur's (L. M.) **Mounted Rifles.**   See *Arkansas Troops,* 1st *Rifles.*

Ransom's (Albert G.) **Artillery.**   See *Ohio Troops,* 1st *Regiment, Battery E.*

Ray's (Daniel M.) **Cavalry.**   See *Tennessee Troops, Union,* 2d *Regiment.*

Read's (Sheridan P.) **Infantry.**   See *Illinois Troops,* 79th *Regiment.*

Reaney's (William) **Cavalry.**   See *Ohio Troops,* 7th *Regiment.*

Reynolds' (Francis E.) **Cavalry.**   See *Samuel B. Sherer's Cavalry.*

Riley's (William E.) **Cavalry.**   See *Kentucky Troops, Union,* 11th *Regiment.*

Roberts' (B. Emory) **Cavalry.**   See *Kentucky Troops, Confederate,* 6th *Regiment.*

Roberts' (Franklin) **Artillery.**   See *J. H. Wiggins' Battery.*

Robertson's (C. S.) **Cavalry.**   See *Confederate Troops, Regulars,* 1st *Regiment.*

Robertson's (F. H.) **Artillery.**   See *Florida Troops.*

Robinson's (Milton S.) **Infantry.**   See *Indiana Troops,* 75th *Regiment.*

Robison's (W. D.) **Infantry.**   See *Tennessee Troops, Confederate,* 2d *Regiment, P.* 1.

Rose's (Thomas E.) **Infantry.**   See *Pennsylvania Troops,* 77th *Regiment.*

Rosengarten's (Adolph G.) **Cavalry.**   See *Pennsylvania Troops,* 15th *Regiment.*

Ross' (Isaac N.) **Infantry.**   See *Ohio Troops,* 90th *Regiment.*

Ross' (J. A.) **Infantry.**   See *Arkansas Troops,* 4th *Battalion.*

Rue's (George W.) **Cavalry.**   See *Kentucky Troops, Union,* 9th *Regiment.*

Russell's (Roswell M.) **Cavalry.**   See *Pennsylvania Troops,* 9th *Regiment.*

Savage's (John H.) **Infantry.**   See *Tennessee Troops, Confederate,* 16th *Regiment.*

Scales' (Junius I.) **Infantry.**   See *Mississippi Troops,* 30th *Regiment.*

Schmitt's (William A.) **Infantry.**   See *Illinois Troops,* 27th *Regiment.*

Schultz's (Frederick) **Artillery.**   See *Ohio Troops,* 1st *Regiment, Battery M.*

Scott's (Joseph R.) **Infantry.**   See *Illinois Troops,* 19th *Regiment.*

Scott's (W. L.) **Artillery.**   See *Tennessee Troops, Confederate.*

Searcy's (A.) **Infantry.**   See *Tennessee Troops, Confederate,* 45th *Regiment.*

Sedgewick's (Thomas D.) **Infantry.**   See *Kentucky Troops, Union,* 2d *Regiment.*

Semple's (Henry C.) **Artillery.**   See *Alabama Troops.*

Shanklin's (James M.) **Infantry.**   See *Indiana Troops,* 42d *Regiment.*

Shanks' (Quintus C.) **Cavalry.**   See *Kentucky Troops, Union,* 12th *Regiment.*

Shannon's (H.) **Artillery.**   See *Warren Light Artillery.*

Shannon's (S. E.) **Infantry.**   See *Tennessee Troops, Confederate,* 24th *Regiment.*

---

* Improvised.

Shearon's (Thomas R.) **Infantry.** See *Tennessee Troops, Confederate, 47th Regiment.*
Shelley's (James T.) **Infantry.** See *Tennessee Troops, Union, 5th Regiment.*
Sherer's (Samuel B.) **Cavalry.** See *Illinois Troops.*
Sherman's (Francis T.) **Infantry.** See *Illinois Troops, 88th Regiment.*
Shoemaker's (Michael) **Infantry.** See *Michigan Troops, 13th Regiment.*
Shryock's (Kline G.) **Infantry.** See *Indiana Troops, 87th Regiment.*
Simonson's (Peter) **Artillery.** See *Indiana Troops, 5th Battery.*
Simpson's (Robert V.) **Infantry.** See *Illinois Troops, 104th Regiment.*
Sirwell's (William) **Infantry.** See *Pennsylvania Troops, 78th Regiment.*
Slemmer's (Adam J.) **Infantry.** See *Union Troops, Regulars, 16th Regiment.*
Slemp's (Campbell) **Infantry.** See *Virginia Troops, 64th Regiment.*
Slocomb's (C. H.) **Artillery.** See *Washington Artillery, 5th Battery.*
Smith's (Baxter) **Cavalry.** See *Tennessee Troops, Confederate.*
Smith's (D. H.) **Cavalry.** See *Kentucky Troops, Confederate, 5th Regiment.*
Smith's (Frank C.) **Infantry.** See *Illinois Troops, 102d Regiment.*
Smith's (Frank G.) **Artillery.** See *Union Troops, Regulars, 4th Regiment, Battery I.*
Smith's (J. A.) **Infantry.** See *Confederate Troops, Regulars, 5th Regiment.*
Smith's (Joseph T.) **Infantry.** See *Georgia Troops, 9th Battalion.*
Smith's (M.) **Artillery.** See *Mississippi Troops.*
Smith's (Robert F.) **Infantry.** See *Illinois Troops, 16th Regiment.*
Smith's (S. G.) **Infantry.** See *Arkansas Troops, 6th and 7th Regiments.*
Smith's (T. B.) **Infantry.** See *Tennessee Troops, Confederate, 20th Regiment.*
Snider's (Joseph R.) **Infantry.** See *Kentucky Troops, Union, 15th Regiment.*
Southwick's (Daniel K.) **Artillery.** See *Ohio Troops, 1st Regiment, Battery C.*
Squires' (William H.) **Infantry.** See *Ohio Troops, 26th Regiment.*
Stafford's (Joab A.) **Infantry.** See *Ohio Troops, 1st Regiment.*
Staley's (M.) **Cavalry.** See *Tennessee Troops, Confederate, 16th Battalion.*
Standart's (William E.) **Artillery.** See *Ohio Troops, 1st Regiment, Battery B.*
Stanford's (T. J.) **Artillery.** See *Mississippi Troops.*
Stansel's (M. L.) **Infantry.** See *Alabama Troops, 41st Regiment.*
Stanton's (S. S.) **Infantry.** See *Tennessee Troops, Confederate, 84th Regiment.*
Starnes' (James W.) **Cavalry.** See *Tennessee Troops, Confederate.*
Stem's (Leander) **Infantry.** See *Ohio Troops, 101st Regiment.*
Steuben Artillery. See *William W. Carnes' Artillery.*
Stevens' (Alanson J.) **Artillery.** See *Pennsylvania Troops, Battery B.*
Stewart's (Robert R.) **Cavalry.** See *Indiana Troops, 2d Regiment.*
Stiles' (Henry E.) **Artillery.** See *Wisconsin Troops, 8th Battery.*
Stivers' (Joseph W.) **Cavalry.** See *Kentucky Troops, Union, 14th Regiment.*
Stokes' (James H.) **Artillery.** See *Chicago Board of Trade Artillery.*
Stokes' (William B.) **Cavalry.** See *Tennessee Troops, Union, 5th Regiment.*
Stone's (David C.) **Artillery.** See *Kentucky Troops, Union, Battery A.*
Stoner's (R. G.) **Cavalry.** See *Kentucky Troops, Confederate.*
Stoner's (R. G.) **Cavalry.** See *Kentucky Troops, Confederate, 9th Regiment.*
Stoughton's (William L.) **Infantry.** See *Michigan Troops, 11th Regiment.*
Stout's (Ira H.) **Cavalry.** See *Kentucky Troops, Union, 12th Regiment.*
Stovall's (M. A.) **Infantry.** See *Georgia Troops, 3d Battalion.*
Strahl's (O. F.) **Infantry.** See *Tennessee Troops, Confederate, 4th and 5th Regiments*
Streight's (Abel D.) **Infantry.** See *Indiana Troops, 51st Regiment.*
Sutermeister's (Arnold) **Artillery.** See *Indiana Troops, 11th Battery.*
Swaine's (Peter T.) **Infantry.** See *Ohio Troops, 99th Regiment.*
Swallow's (George R.) **Artillery.** See *Indiana Troops, 7th Battery.*
Swanwick's (Francis) **Infantry.** See *Illinois Troops, 22d Regiment.*
Swett's (C.) **Artillery.** See *Warren Light Artillery.'*
Sykes' (W. L.) **Infantry.** See *Mississippi Troops, 5th Regiment.*
Tafel's (Gustavus) **Infantry.** See *Ohio Troops, 106th Regiment.*

Taggart's (Wesford) **Infantry.** See *Illinois Troops, 25th Regiment.*
Talbird's (H.) **Infantry.** See *Alabama Troops, 41st Regiment.*
Tansil's (E. E.) **Infantry.** See *Tennessee Troops, Confederate, 31st and 33d Regiments.*
Teetor's (Henry B.) **Cavalry.** See *Ohio Troops, 4th Regiment.*
Terrill's (William R.) **Artillery.** See *Union Troops, Regulars, 5th Regiment, Battery H.*
Terry's (B. F.) **Cavalry.** See *Texas Troops, 8th Regiment.*
Terry's (Henry) **Infantry.** See *Ohio Troops, 24th Regiment.*
Thedford's (William) **Infantry.** See *Tennessee Troops, Confederate, 11th Regiment.*
Thompson's (R.) **Cavalry.** See *Georgia Troops, 3d Regiment.*
Thompson's (T. W.) **Infantry.** See *Kentucky Troops, Confederate, 4th Regiment.*
Throckmorton's (C. B.) **Artillery.** See *Union Troops, Regulars, 4th Regiment, Co. H.*
Timberlake's (John) **Infantry.** See *Indiana Troops, 81st Regiment.*
Toler's (Silas C.) **Infantry.** See *Illinois Troops, 60th Regiment.*
Tolles' (William R.) **Infantry.** See *Ohio Troops, 105th Regiment.*
Townsend's (Frederick) **Infantry.** See *Union Troops, Regulars, 18th Regiment.*
Trabue's (R. P.) **Infantry.** See *Kentucky Troops, Confederate, 4th Regiment.*
Trigg's Cavalry. See *Virginia Troops, 27th Battalion.*
Tripp's (Hagerman) **Infantry.** See *Indiana Troops, 6th Regiment.*
Turner's (William B.) **Artillery.** See *M. Smith's Artillery.*
Twyman's (Henry G.) **Cavalry.** See *Kentucky Troops, Union.*
Vallette's (Henry F.) **Infantry.** See *Illinois Troops, 105th Regiment.*
Vance's (Robert B.) **Infantry.** See *North Carolina Troops, 29th Regiment.*
Van Derveer's (Ferdinand) **Infantry.** See *Ohio Troops, 35th Regiment.*
Van Pelt's (George W.) **Artillery.** See *Michigan Troops, 1st Battery.*
Vanosdol's (Argus D.) **Cavalry.** See *Indiana Troops, 3d Regiment.*
Vaughan's (A. J., jr.) **Infantry.** See *Tennessee Troops, Confederate, 13th Regiment.*
Vaught's (W. C. D.) **Artillery.** See *Washington Artillery, 5th Battery.*
Vezin's (Alfred) **Cavalry.** See *Pennsylvania Troops, 15th Regiment.*
Wade's (W. B.) **Cavalry.** See *Confederate Troops, Regulars, 8th Regiment.*
Wadleigh's (John) **Infantry.** See *Illinois Troops, 104th Regiment.*
Walker's (Francis M.) **Infantry.** See *Tennessee Troops, Confederate, 19th Regiment.*
Wallace's (William) **Infantry.** See *Ohio Troops, 15th Regiment.*
Walworth's (Nathan H.) **Infantry.** See *Illinois Troops, 42d Regiment.*
Ward's (Frank B.) **Cavalry.** See *Pennsylvania Troops, 15th Regiment.*
Ward's (John H.) **Infantry.** See *Kentucky Troops, Union, 27th Regiment.*
Ward's (William D.) **Infantry.** See *Indiana Troops, 37th Regiment.*
Warren Light Artillery. See *Mississippi Troops.*
Washington Artillery. See *Louisiana Troops.*
Waters' (D. D.) **Artillery.** See *Alabama Troops.*
Waters' (Louis H.) **Infantry.** See *Illinois Troops, 84th Regiment.*
Watkins' (W. M.) **Infantry.** See *Tennessee Troops, Confederate, 47th Regiment.*
Webb's (J. D.) **Partisans.** See *Alabama Troops, 51st Regiment.*
Weber's (John) **Infantry.** See *Missouri Troops, Union, 15th Regiment.*
Weller's (Enoch) **Infantry.** See *Ohio Troops, 24th Regiment.*
Wescott's (Henry F.) **Infantry.** See *Illinois Troops, 51st Regiment.*
West's (O. F.) **Sharpshooters.** See *Mississippi Troops, 9th Battalion.*
Wharton's Escort Cavalry. See *Baxter Smith's Cavalry.*
Whitaker's (Walter C.) **Infantry.** See *Kentucky Troops, Union, 6th Regiment.*
Whitbeck's (Horatio N.) **Infantry.** See *Ohio Troops, 65th Regiment.*
White's (B. F., jr.) **Artillery.** See *Tennessee Troops, Confederate.*
White's (Moses) **Infantry.** See *Tennessee Troops, Confederate, 37th Regiment.*
White's (T. W.) **Infantry.** See *Mississippi Troops, 9th Regiment.*
Wiggins' (J. H.) **Artillery.** See *Arkansas Troops.*
Wilder's (John T.) **Infantry.** See *Indiana Troops, 17th Regiment.*
Wiley's (Aquila) **Infantry.** See *Ohio Troops, 41st Regiment.*

Wilkinson's (J. C.) Infantry.   See *Mississippi Troops*, 8th *Regiment.*
Williams' (Thomas D.) Infantry.   See *Illinois Troops*, 25th *Regiment.*
Williams' (William C.) Infantry.   See *Indiana Troops*, 44th *Regiment.*
Williamson's (J. A.) Mounted Rifles.   See *Arkansas Troops*, 2d *Rifles.*
Witcher's (V. A.) Cavalry.   See *Virginia Troops*, 34th *Battalion.*
Wolford's (Frank) Cavalry.   See *Kentucky Troops, Union*, 1st *Regiment.*
Woods' (Gustavus A.) Infantry.   See *Indiana Troops*, 15th *Regiment.*
Woods' (McLain F.) Infantry.   See *Illinois Troops*, 10th *Regiment.*
Wood's (William B.) Infantry.   See *Alabama Troops*, 16th *Regiment.*
Wood's Sharpshooters.   See *Mississippi Troops*, 15th *Battalion.*
Woodbury's (Horatio) Infantry.   See *Indiana Troops*, 81st *Regiment.*
Woodward's (Pyrrhus) Infantry.   See *Indiana Troops*, 36th *Regiment.*
Woodward's (T. G.) Cavalry.   See *Kentucky Troops, Confederate*, 2d *Regiment.*
Wooster's (Moses F.) Infantry.   See *Ohio Troops*, 101st *Regiment.*
Wright's (E. E.) Artillery.   See *Tennessee Troops, Confederate.*
Wyatt's (J. N.) Infantry.   See *Tennessee Troops, Confederate*, 12th *Regiment.*
Wynkoop's (George C.) Cavalry.   See *Pennsylvania Troops*, 7th *Regiment.*
Wynkoop's (John E.) Cavalry.   See *Pennsylvania Troops*, 7th *Regiment.*
Yancey's (B. C.) Sharpshooters.   See *Alabama Troops*, 17th *Battalion.*
Young's (William H.) Infantry.   See *Texas Troops*, 9th *Regiment.*
Zacharie's (F. C.) Infantry.   See *Louisiana Troops*, 16th *and* 25th *Regiments.*

INDEX.

Brigades, Divisions, Corps, Armies, and improvised organizations are "Mentioned" under name of commanding officer; State and other organizations under their official designation. (See Alternate Designations, pp. 986–997.)

---

* Organizations, pp. 230–233, not included. See note, p. 233.

---

* Organizations, pp. 230–233, not included. See note, p. 233.
† Also called Roberts' Battery.

Page.

Page.

Page.

---

* Organizations, pp. 230–233, not included. See note, p. 233.
† Claimed also for Alabama.

Page.

* Organizations, pp. 230–233, not included. See note, p. 233.

---

* Organizations, pp. 230–233, not included. See note, p. 233.

† December 17, 1862, with Breckinridge's battalion formed 9th Kentucky Cavalry.

* Organizations, pp. 230–233, not included. See note, p. 233.

Page.

Page.

---

          * Of the Western Department.
       † Organizations, pp. 230–233, not included. See note, p. 233.

Page.

Mullen, Bernard F.

Mentioned.. 181,608

Report of battle of Stone's River, Tenn., Dec. 31, 1862–Jan. 31, 1863 609

Mulligan, James B.

Mentioned... 177, 204, 397

Report of battle of Stone's River, Tenn., Dec. 31, 1862–Jan. 3, 1863......... 405

Mullins, R. W. Mentioned.. 977

Munfordville, Ky. Skirmish near, Dec. 26, 1862. See *Bacon Creek, Ky.*

Mungen, Robert. Mentioned... 43_5

Munger, William A. Mentioned.. 222, 48_2

Munitions of War. Supplies of, etc. Communications from

Dils, John, jr 8

Paul, J. R 224

Semple, Charles.. 792

Simmons, Samuel 224

Taylor, John W... 225, 226

Murdoch, Lieutenant. Mentioned 296

Murdock, T. F. Mentioned.. 575, 578, 595

Murfreesborough, Tenn.

Battle of, Dec. 31, 1862–Jan. 3, 1863. See *Stone's River, Tenn. Battle of*
Occupied by Union forces, Jan. 5, 1863. See

Dec. 26, 1862–Jan. 5, 1863. *Stone's River Campaign. Reports of*

Negley, James S.   Rosecrans, W. S.   Thomas, George H.

Reconnaissance from, Jan. 13–15, 1863.

Communications from Milo S. Hascall 985

Report of George D. Wagner...................................... 984

Skirmishes at and near.

Dec. 29–30, 1862. Report of Braxton Bragg........................... 661

See also Dec. 26, 1862–Jan. 5, 1863. *Stone's River Campaign. Reports of*

Anderson, Charles.	Harker, Charles G.	Raffen, Alexander W.
Anderson, J. Patton.	Hathaway, Gilbert.	Ransom, Albert G.
Barret, Overton W.	Hescock, Henry.	Rose, Thomas E.
Bennett, John E.	Hewitt, James W.	Rosecrans, W. S.
Bradley, Cullen.	Hibbard, Elisha C.	Ross, Isaac N.
Bradley, Luther P.	Hunt, Thomas H.	Sedgewick, Thomas D.
Breckinridge, John C.	Johnson, J. B.	Semple, Henry C.
Bush, Asahel K.	Kirby, Isaac M.	Sheridan, Philip H.
Carlin, William P.	Lewis, Joseph H.	Sherman, Francis T.
Chandler, William P.	McCown, John P.	Shoemaker, Michael.
Cheatham, B. F.	McCreery, William B.	Standart, William E.
Cobb, Robert.	McDuffie, W. A.	Stanford, T. J.
Collins, Joseph P.	McIlvain, Alexander.	Stanley, Timothy R.
Crittenden, Thomas L.	Magevney, Michael, jr.	Stewart, Alexander P.
Cruft, Charles.	Maney, George.	Stiles, Henry E.
Davis, Jefferson C.	Marsh, Jason.	Streight, Abel D.
Dodge, Joseph B.	Marshall, Alexander.	Taggart, Wesford.
Dysart, Alexander P.	Mathes, George M.	Thomas, George H.
Edgarton, Warren P.	Mendenhall, John.	Trabue, Robert P.
Ehrler, Francis.	Miller, John F.	Vaughan, A. J., jr.
Ellsworth, Alban A.	Olson, Porter C.	Waters, David D.
Given, Josiah.	Osborn, John.	Webb, J. D.
Gooding, Michael.	Paine, Hendrick E.	Withers, Jones M.
Greusel, Nicholas.	Palmer, John M.	Whitbeck, Horatio N.
Grose, William.	Parsons, Charles C.	Wood, Thomas J.
Hamrick, Thomas H.	Polk, Leonidas.	Woodruff, William E.
Hardee, William J.	Post, P. Sidney.	Woodward, Pyrrhus.

Jan. 4, 1863. Report of Joseph Wheeler............................. 957

---

* Organizations, pp. 230–233, not included. See note, p. 233.

* Afterward Co. K, 79th Ohio Infantry.

Page.

Organization, strength, etc.

Overall's Creek, Tenn. Skirmish at, Dec. 31, 1862. See

Dec. 26, 1862–Jan. 5, 1863. *Stone's River Campaign.* *Reports of*

Buford, Abraham.	Otis, Elmer.	Webb, J. D.
Cupp, Valentine.	Paramore, James W.	Wharton, John A.
Hardee, William J.	Parkhurst, John G.	Wheeler, Joseph.
Klein, Robert.	Pugh, John L.	Wiggins, J. H.
McDuffie, W. A.	Rosecrans, W. S.	Wynkoop, John E.
Minty, Robert H. G.	Stanley, David S.	Zahm, Lewis.
Murray, Douglas A.		

Page.

Page.

*Organizations, pp. 230–233, not included. See note, p. 233,

Page.

Page.

Tennessee.

Tennessee, Army of. (Confederate.)

Tennessee Troops. Mentioned. * (Confederate.)

---

* Organizations, pp. 230–233, not included. See note, p. 233.
† Designation changed June 6, 1863.

---

*Also called 1st Middle Tennessee.

†Also called 1st Middle Tennessee Infantry.

‡Organizations, pp. 230–233, not included. See note, p. 233.

---

*1st Battalion and Co. B, 2d Battalion.   ‡ Also Cos. B, C, E, and F, 3d Battalion.
†Also Cos. A and D, 3d Battalion.   § Department of the Cumberland.

* Joseph E. Johnston's geographical command.

Page.

Page.